Luke

BAKER EXEGETICAL COMMENTARY
ON THE NEW TESTAMENT

ROBERT W. YARBROUGH
and JOSHUA W. JIPP, EDITORS

Volumes now available:

Matthew   *David L. Turner*
Mark   *Robert H. Stein*
Luke   *Darrell L. Bock*
Acts   *Darrell L. Bock*
Romans, 2nd ed.   *Thomas R. Schreiner*
1 Corinthians   *David E. Garland*
2 Corinthians   *George H. Guthrie*
Galatians   *Douglas J. Moo*
Ephesians   *Frank Thielman*
Philippians   *Moisés Silva*
Colossians and Philemon   *G. K. Beale*
1–2 Thessalonians   *Jeffrey A. D. Weima*
James   *Dan G. McCartney*
1 Peter   *Karen H. Jobes*
1–3 John   *Robert W. Yarbrough*
Jude and 2 Peter   *Gene L. Green*
Revelation   *Grant R. Osborne*

Darrell L. Bock (PhD, University of Aberdeen) is executive director for cultural engagement at the Hendricks Center at Dallas Theological Seminary in Dallas, Texas, where he also serves as senior research professor of New Testament studies. He is the author or editor of many books, including *Jesus the God-Man, Jesus according to Scripture, Studying the Historical Jesus,* and major commentaries on Luke and Acts.

Luke

VOLUME 2 | 9:51–24:53

Darrell L. Bock

BAKER EXEGETICAL COMMENTARY
ON THE NEW TESTAMENT

Baker Academic
a division of Baker Publishing Group
Grand Rapids, Michigan

© 1996 by Darrell L. Bock

Published by Baker Academic
a division of Baker Publishing Group
P.O. Box 6287, Grand Rapids, Michigan 49516-6287
www.bakeracademic.com

Printed in the United States of America

Library of Congress Cataloging-in-Publication Data

Bock, Darrell L.
    Luke / Darrell L. Bock.
        p. cm. — (Baker exegetical commentary on the New Testament ; 3B)
    Includes bibliographical references and indexes.
    ISBN 0-8010-1053-5 (v. 1)
    ISBN 0-8010-1052-7 (v. 2)
    ISBN 0-8010-1051-9 (set)
    1. Bible. N.T. Luke—Commentaries. I. Title. II. Series.
BS2595.3.B58 1994
226.4'077—dc20   94-33507

        21   22   23   24   25   21   20   19   18   17   16

Contents

Note to the Reader

This commentary is historical, exegetical, and (in the remarks summarizing each exegetical section) pastoral. The treatment of each pericope is structured consistently to help the reader find information quickly. Each unit begins with a quick overview (in gray shading) of how it fits in the movement of Luke. Then comes a discussion of sources and historicity, including summary observations about how Luke is like and unlike parallel passages (these discussions are set in smaller type to distinguish them from the exposition). Four items follow: questions of form, a detailed outline tracing the argument of the particular passage, a paragraph summarizing the unit's themes, and a translation of the unit. All this initial material concentrates on synthesis, thus orienting the reader to the verses under discussion and setting the stage for the exegesis. The exegesis proceeds one verse at a time and cites a full range of tools so that excellent discussions of an issue can be quickly located. More-detailed comparisons to parallel texts, where they occur, are also treated here. The last paragraph or two of this section (labeled "Summary" and shaded gray) seeks to answer one question: How did Luke want the reader to respond to this event or teaching? The additional notes cover mostly text-critical questions. In each exegetical unit, gray shading is used to assist the reader in locating salient sections of the treatment of each passage: the introductory comments, the discussion of structure, and the concluding summary.

Textual variants in the Greek text are signaled in the author's translation by means of half-brackets around the relevant English word or phrase (e.g., ⌜Gerasenes⌝), thereby alerting the reader to turn to the additional notes at the end of each exegetical unit for a discussion of the textual problem.

The documentation uses the author-date method, in which the basic reference consists of author's surname + year + page number(s): Fitzmyer 1981: 297. The only exceptions to this system are well-known reference works (e.g., BAGD, LSJ, *TDNT*). Full publication data are given in the bibliography at the end of volume two, as are the indexes for the entire commentary.

Abbreviations

Bibliographic and General

ABD   *The Anchor Bible Dictionary*, edited by D. N. Freedman et al. (6 vols.; New York: Doubleday, 1992)

BAA   *Griechisch-Deutsches Wörterbuch zu den Schriften des Neuen Testaments und der frühchristlichen Literatur*, by W. Bauer, K. Aland, and B. Aland (6th ed.; Berlin: de Gruyter, 1988)

BAGD   *A Greek-English Lexicon of the New Testament and Other Early Christian Literature*, by W. Bauer, W. F. Arndt, F. W. Gingrich, and F. W. Danker (2d ed.; Chicago: University of Chicago Press, 1979)

BDB   *A Hebrew and English Lexicon of the Old Testament*, by F. Brown, S. R. Driver, and C. A. Briggs (Oxford: Clarendon, 1907)

BDF   *A Greek Grammar of the New Testament and Other Early Christian Literature*, by F. Blass, A. Debrunner, and R. W. Funk (Chicago: University of Chicago Press, 1961)

BDR   *Grammatik des neutestamentlichen Griechisch*, by F. Blass, A. Debrunner, and F. Rehkopf (Göttingen: Vandenhoeck & Ruprecht, 1984)

DJD   Discoveries in the Judaean Desert of Jordan (Oxford: Clarendon, 1955–)

ISBE   *The International Standard Bible Encyclopedia*, edited by G. W. Bromiley et al. (4 vols.; Grand Rapids: Eerdmans, 1979–88)

KJV   King James Version

LSJ   *A Greek-English Lexicon*, by H. G. Liddell, R. Scott, and H. S. Jones (Oxford: Clarendon, 1968)

LXX   Septuagint

MM   *The Vocabulary of the Greek Testament: Illustrated from the Papyri and Other Non-literary Sources*, by J. H. Moulton and G. Milligan (repr. Grand Rapids: Eerdmans, 1980)

MT   Masoretic Text

NA   *Novum Testamentum Graece*, edited by [E. Nestle], K. Aland, and B. Aland (26th ed.; Stuttgart: Deutsche Bibelstiftung, 1979)

NASB   New American Standard Bible

NIDNTT *The New International Dictionary of New Testament Theology*, edited by L. Coenen, E. Beyreuther, and H. Bietenhard; English translation edited by C. Brown (4 vols.; Grand Rapids: Zondervan, 1975–86)

NIV   New International Version

NJB   New Jerusalem Bible

NJPSV   New Jewish Publication Society Version

NKJV   New King James Version

NRSV   New Revised Standard Version

NT   New Testament

OT   Old Testament

PG   *Patrologiae Cursus Completus, Series Graeca*, edited by J. P. Migne (161 vols.; Paris, 1857–66)

PL	*Patrologiae Cursus Completus, Series Latina*, edited by J. P. Migne (221 vols.; Paris, 1844–55)
RSV	Revised Standard Version
SB	*Kommentar zum Neuen Testament aus Talmud und Midrasch*, by H. L. Strack and P. Billerbeck (6 vols.; Munich: Beck, 1922–61)
TDNT	*Theological Dictionary of the New Testament*, edited by G. Kittel and G. Friedrich; translated and edited by G. W. Bromiley (10 vols.; Grand Rapids: Eerdmans, 1964–76)
UBS	*The Greek New Testament*, edited by B. Aland, K. Aland, J. Karavidopoulos, C. M. Martini, and B. M. Metzger (4th ed.; New York: United Bible Societies, 1993)

Hebrew Bible

Gen.	Genesis	2 Chron.	2 Chronicles	Dan.	Daniel
Exod.	Exodus	Ezra	Ezra	Hos.	Hosea
Lev.	Leviticus	Neh.	Nehemiah	Joel	Joel
Num.	Numbers	Esth.	Esther	Amos	Amos
Deut.	Deuteronomy	Job	Job	Obad.	Obadiah
Josh.	Joshua	Ps.	Psalms	Jon.	Jonah
Judg.	Judges	Prov.	Proverbs	Mic.	Micah
Ruth	Ruth	Eccles.	Ecclesiastes	Nah.	Nahum
1 Sam.	1 Samuel	Song	Song of Songs	Hab.	Habakkuk
2 Sam.	2 Samuel	Isa.	Isaiah	Zeph.	Zephaniah
1 Kings	1 Kings	Jer.	Jeremiah	Hag.	Haggai
2 Kings	2 Kings	Lam.	Lamentations	Zech.	Zechariah
1 Chron.	1 Chronicles	Ezek.	Ezekiel	Mal.	Malachi

Greek Testament

Matt.	Matthew	Eph.	Ephesians	Heb.	Hebrews
Mark	Mark	Phil.	Philippians	James	James
Luke	Luke	Col.	Colossians	1 Pet.	1 Peter
John	John	1 Thess.	1 Thessalonians	2 Pet.	2 Peter
Acts	Acts	2 Thess.	2 Thessalonians	1 John	1 John
Rom.	Romans	1 Tim.	1 Timothy	2 John	2 John
1 Cor.	1 Corinthians	2 Tim.	2 Timothy	3 John	3 John
2 Cor.	2 Corinthians	Titus	Titus	Jude	Jude
Gal.	Galatians	Philem.	Philemon	Rev.	Revelation

Other Jewish and Christian Writings

Bar.	Baruch	2 Esdr.	2 Esdras (4 Ezra)
2 Bar.	2 (Syriac) Baruch	Jub.	Jubilees
Barn.	Letter of Barnabas	Jdt.	Judith
1 Clem.	1 Clement	1 Macc.	1 Maccabees
2 Clem.	2 Clement	2 Macc.	2 Maccabees
1 Enoch	1 (Ethiopic) Enoch	3 Macc.	3 Maccabees
2 Enoch	2 (Slavonic) Enoch	4 Macc.	4 Maccabees
3 Enoch	3 (Hebrew) Enoch	Odes Sol.	Odes of Solomon
1 Esdr.	1 Esdras	Pr. Azar.	Prayer of Azariah

Ps. Sol.	Psalms of Solomon		T. Judah	Testament of Judah
Sir.	Sirach (Ecclesiasticus)		T. Levi	Testament of Levi
Sus.	Susanna		T. Moses	Testament of Moses
T. Abr.	Testament of Abraham (A)		T. Naph.	Testament of Naphtali
T. Asher	Testament of Asher		T. Reub.	Testament of Reuben
T. Ben.	Testament of Benjamin		T. Sim.	Testament of Simeon
T. Dan	Testament of Dan		T. Sol.	Testament of Solomon
T. Gad	Testament of Gad		T. Zeb.	Testament of Zebulun
T. Iss.	Testament of Issachar		Tob.	Tobit
T. Job	Testament of Job		Wis.	Wisdom of Solomon
T. Jos.	Testament of Joseph			

Rabbinic Tractates

The abbreviations below are used for the names of tractates in the Mishnah (indicated by a prefixed m.), Tosepta (t.), Babylonian Talmud (b.), and Jerusalem (Palestinian) Talmud (y.). The last column gives the numbers of the order and tractate in the Mishnah.

ᶜAbod. Zar.	ᶜAboda Zara	4.8	Nazir	Nazir	3.4
ʾAbot	ʾAbot	4.9	Ned.	Nedarim	3.3
ᶜArak.	ᶜArakin	5.5	Neg.	Negaᶜim	6.3
B. Bat.	Babaʾ Batraʾ	4.3	Nid.	Nidda	6.7
B. Meṣ.	Babaʾ Meṣiᶜaʾ	4.2	ʾOhol.	ʾOholot	6.2
B. Qam.	Babaʾ Qammaʾ	4.1	ᶜOr.	ᶜOrla	1.10
Bek.	Bekorot	5.4	Para	Para	6.4
Ber.	Berakot	1.1	Peʾa	Peʾa	1.2
Beṣa	Beṣa	2.7	Pesaḥ.	Pesahim	2.3
Bik.	Bikkurim	1.11	Qid.	Qiddušin	3.7
Dem.	Demaʾi	1.3	Qin.	Qinnim	5.11
ᶜEd.	ᶜEduyyot	4.7	Roʾš Haš.	Roʾš Haššana	2.8
ᶜErub.	ᶜErubin	2.2	Šab.	Šabbat	2.1
Giṭ.	Giṭṭin	3.6	Sanh.	Sanhedrin	4.4
Ḥag.	Ḥagiga	2.12	Šeb.	Šebiᶜit	1.5
Ḥal.	Ḥalla	1.9	Šebu.	Šebuᶜot	4.6
Hor.	Horayot	4.10	Šeqal.	Šeqalim	2.4
Ḥul.	Ḥullin	5.3	Soṭa	Soṭa	3.5
Kel.	Kelim	6.1	Suk.	Sukka	2.6
Ker.	Keritot	5.7	Ṭ. Yom	Ṭebul Yom	6.10
Ketub.	Ketubot	3.2	Taᶜan.	Taᶜanit	2.9
Kil.	Kilʾayim	1.4	Tamid	Tamid	5.9
Maᶜaś.	Maᶜaśerot	1.7	Tem.	Temura	5.6
Maᶜaś. Š.	Maᶜaśer Šeni	1.8	Ter.	Terumot	1.6
Mak.	Makkot	4.5	Ṭohar.	Ṭoharot	6.5
Makš.	Makširin	6.8	ᶜUq.	ᶜUqṣin	6.12
Meg.	Megilla	2.10	Yad.	Yadayim	6.11
Meᶜil.	Meᶜila	5.8	Yeb.	Yebamot	3.1
Menaḥ.	Menahot	5.2	Yomaʾ	Yomaʾ	2.5
Mid.	Middot	5.10	Zab.	Zabim	6.9
Miqw.	Miqwaʾot	6.6	Zebaḥ.	Zebahim	5.1
Moᶜed Qaṭ.	Moᶜed Qaṭan	2.11			

Targumim

Targumim on the Writings and Prophets are indicated by the abbreviation Tg. placed in front of the usual abbreviation for the biblical book. Targumim on the Pentateuch use one of the following abbreviations:

Frg. Tg.	Fragmentary Targum
Tg. Neof. 1	Targum Neofiti 1
Tg. Onq.	Targum Onqelos
Tg. Ps.-J.	Targum Pseudo-Jonathan

Midrashim

Midrash Rabbah is indicated by the abbreviation Rab. placed after the usual abbreviation for the biblical book (e.g., Gen. Rab.). Other midrashim are indicated by the abbreviation Midr. placed in front of the usual abbreviation for the biblical book (e.g., Midr. Ps.). Titles of other midrashim are spelled out.

Qumran / Dead Sea Scrolls

1Q14	*Pesher* on Micah (1QpMic)
1Q28a	Rule of the Congregation (1QSa or Rule Annex)
1Q28b	Benedictions; Book of Blessings; Collection of Blessings (1QSb)
1QapGen	Genesis Apocryphon
1QH	Thanksgiving Hymns/Psalms (*Hôdāyôt*)
1QM	War Scroll (*Milḥāmâ*)
1QpHab	*Pesher* on Habakkuk
1QS	Manual of Discipline (Rule/Order of the Community)
4Q161	Commentary on Isaiah (A) (4QpIsa^a)
4Q169	*Pesher* on Nahum (4QpNah)
4Q174	Florilegium (4QFlor)
4Q175	Testimonia (4QTestim)
4Q181	(unnamed)
4Q246	4QpsDan ar^a (formerly 4QpsDan A^a or 4Q243)
4Q372	(unnamed)
4Q504	*Dibre Hammĕʾôrôt* (= "Paroles des Luminaires") (4QDibHam^a)
4QEnGiants^a	Book of the Giants
4QMess ar	Aramaic messianic text
4QMMT	*Miqsāt Maʿăśê Tôrâ*
4QPBless	Patriarchal Blessings (formerly 4QpGen 49)
4QpPs^a	*Pesher* on Psalm 37
4QPrNab	Prayer of Nabonidus
11QMelch	Melchizedek text
11QPs^a	Psalms Scroll
11QTemple^a	Temple Scroll
11QtgJob	Targum to Job
CD	Damascus Document
Mur	scrolls from Murabbaʿat

Greek Manuscripts

Sigla for Greek manuscripts basically follow that laid out in UBS[4], pages 4*–52*. The original hand of a manuscript is indicated by an asterisk (ℵ*), successive correctors by superscript numbers (ℵ[1], ℵ[2], etc.). Nonbiblical papyri are abbreviated according to the following list (see BAGD xxxi–xxxii for bibliographic information):

P. Eger.	Papyrus Egerton
P. Fay.	Papyrus Fayûm
P. Lond.	Papyrus London
P. Oxy.	Papyrus Oxyrhynchus
P. Tebt.	Papyrus Tebtunis

Greek Transliteration

α	a	ζ	z	λ	l	π	p	φ	ph
β	b	η	ē	μ	m	ρ	r	χ	ch
γ	g (n)	θ	th	ν	n	σ ς	s	ψ	ps
δ	d	ι	i	ξ	x	τ	t	ω	ō
ε	e	κ	k	ο	o	υ	y (u)	ʽ	h

Notes on the transliteration of Greek

1. Accents, lenis (smooth breathing), and *iota* subscript are not shown in transliteration.
2. The transliteration of asper (rough breathing) precedes a vowel or diphthong (e.g., ἁ = *ha*; αἱ = *hai*) and follows ρ (i.e., ῥ = *rh*).
3. *Gamma* is transliterated *n* only when it precedes γ, κ, ξ, or χ.
4. *Upsilon* is transliterated *u* only when it is part of a diphthong (e.g., αυ, ευ, ου, υι).

Hebrew Transliteration

א	ʾ	בָ	ā	qāmeṣ
ב	b	בַ	a	pataḥ
ג	g	חַ	a	furtive pataḥ
ד	d	בֶ	e	sĕgôl
ה	h	בֵ	ē	ṣērê
ו	w	בִ	i	short ḥîreq
ז	z	בִ	ī	long ḥîreq written defectively
ח	ḥ	בָ	o	qāmeṣ ḥāṭûp
ט	ṭ	בוֹ	ô	ḥôlem written fully
י	y	בֹ	ō	ḥôlem written defectively
כ ך	k	בוּ	û	šûreq
ל	l	בֻ	u	short qibbûṣ
מ ם	m	בֻ	ū	long qibbûṣ written defectively
נ ן	n	בָה	â	final qāmeṣ hēʾ (בָה = āh)
ס	s	בֶי	ê	sĕgôl yôd (בֶי = êy)
ע	ʿ	בֵי	ê	ṣērê yôd (בֵי = êy)
פ ף	p	בִי	î	ḥîreq yôd (בִי = îy)
צ ץ	ṣ	בֲ	ă	ḥāṭēp pataḥ
ק	q	בֱ	ĕ	ḥāṭēp sĕgôl
ר	r	בֳ	ŏ	ḥāṭēp qāmeṣ
שׂ	ś	בְ	ĕ	vocal šĕwāʾ
שׁ	š	בְ	–	silent šĕwāʾ
ת	t			

Notes on the transliteration of Hebrew
1. Accents are not shown in transliteration.
2. Silent *šĕwāʾ* is not indicated in transliteration.
3. The unaspirated forms of בגד כפת are not specially indicated in transliteration.
4. *Dāgeš forte* is indicated by doubling the consonant. *Dāgeš* present for euphonious reasons is not indicated in transliteration.
5. *Maqqēp* is represented by a hyphen.

IV. Jerusalem Journey: Jewish Rejection and the New Way (9:51–19:44)

Jesus' visit to a Samaritan village in Luke 9:51–56 begins Luke's lengthiest section, comprising almost 37 percent of the Gospel (424 of 1,151 verses).[1] Most of this section is unique to Luke, containing many pericopes and parables that are found only in his Gospel. In addition, Luke emphasizes Jesus' journey in a way the other Gospels do not.

The section has been called "journey to Jerusalem" (Fitzmyer 1981: 823), "travel narrative" (Arndt 1956: 271; Huck and Lietzmann 1936: 112), and "central section" (Ellis 1974: 148).[2] It starts at 9:51, but its end point is debated:[3]

End of Central Section	Adherents
18:14	Luce 1933: 194; Hendriksen 1978: 531; Klostermann 1929: 110
18:30	Lagrange 1921: xxxviii; Feine 1922: 421
18:34	Blomberg 1983: 245; Nolland 1993a: 531
19:10	Marshall 1978: 400
19:27	Fitzmyer 1985: 1242; Schürmann 1994: 1; most commentators (cf. Miyoshi 1974: 1; Resseguie 1975: 3 n. 2)
19:40/41	Morganthaler 1948: 1.170; W. Robinson 1964: 22–23
19:44	Ellis 1974: 146
19:48	Egelkraut 1976: 10

The break should not be placed earlier than 19:41, which mentions that Jesus was drawing near the city. Against a break at 18:34 is the continuation of the journey toward Jerusalem, including the increasing specific notes of location after this verse (against Nolland 1993a: 529). Most treat 19:28 as noting the arrival, but it is really a

---

1. If one counts lines, as Egelkraut 1976: 2 n. 1 does (using the twenty-fifth edition of Nestle-Aland), then the figure is closer to 44 percent. Since both verse length and line length vary, such counts are only approximations.

2. "Central section" is the least descriptive and the least debatable title. The term *journey* is better, provided one does not think of a straight-line trip.

3. For the debate about its ending, see Egelkraut 1976: 3–11 and Resseguie 1975: 3 (a good survey of the history of interpretation).

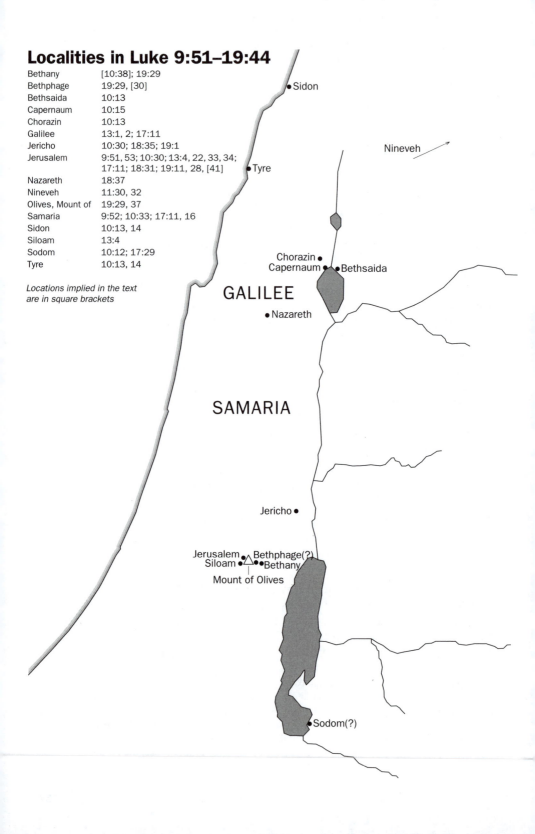

Localities in Luke 9:51–19:44

Bethany	[10:38]; 19:29
Bethphage	19:29, [30]
Bethsaida	10:13
Capernaum	10:15
Chorazin	10:13
Galilee	13:1, 2; 17:11
Jericho	10:30; 18:35; 19:1
Jerusalem	9:51, 53; 10:30; 13:4, 22, 33, 34; 17:11; 18:31; 19:11, 28, [41]
Nazareth	18:37
Nineveh	11:30, 32
Olives, Mount of	19:29, 37
Samaria	9:52; 10:33; 17:11, 16
Sidon	10:13, 14
Siloam	13:4
Sodom	10:12; 17:29
Tyre	10:13, 14

*Locations implied in the text
are in square brackets*

Sidon

Nineveh

Tyre

Chorazin
Capernaum Bethsaida

GALILEE

Nazareth

SAMARIA

Jericho

Jerusalem Bethphage(?)
Siloam Bethany
Mount of Olives

Sodom(?)

transition, given 19:41. In other words, at this point Jesus is not yet in Jerusalem. Against 19:48 is the temple milieu of 19:45–48, where Jesus is clearly in the city. Thus, 19:44 seems to the best candidate, especially since Jerusalem is clearly set as the goal of the journey (9:51, 53; 13:22; 17:11; 18:31–34; 19:28). Regardless of where between 19:27 and 19:44 the break is placed, 19:28–44 serves as a bridge into the final ministry events in Jerusalem. The journey prepares for this decisive moment in Jesus' career. All the tension of Luke 9–19 is resolved in the reality of the cross, and Jesus prepares his disciples for that approaching reality.

The material in 9:51–19:44 has several distinguishing characteristics:

1. It is uniquely Lucan, with much of the material found only in Luke. According to Egelkraut, more than one-third overlaps with Matthew, more than one-third is unique to Luke, and less than one-third of the material has Marcan parallels. But a careful look shows that the percentages are not quite so evenly divided.[4]
2. Much of the section does not parallel Mark. The Marcan sequence is not resumed until 18:15.
3. There are few chronological or topographical notes in the entire section (Egelkraut 1976: 16–24).
4. Miracles are scarce (13:10–17; 14:1–6; 17:11–19; 18:35–43; as well as a miracle summary in 11:14–23), in contrast to the thir-

---

4. The amount of material in these groups can be variously measured, depending on the division of the pericopes and one's judgment about the presence of parallels. Egelkraut 1976: 27 bases the percentages in Luke's central section (for him 9:51–19:48) on the pericope delineation in two common synopses:

	Lucan Parallels to to Matthew (i.e., Q)	Unique Lucan Material	Lucan Parallels to Mark
Aland 1985	26 of 75 pericopes (35%)	27 of 75 pericopes (36%)	22 of 75 pericopes (29%)
Huck and Lietzmann 1936	25 of 60 pericopes (42%)	24 of 60 pericopes (40%)	11 of 60 pericopes (18%)

Resseguie 1975: 4 calculates the same section this way: of 60 Lucan pericopes, 31 (52%) parallel Matthew/Q and 29 (48%) are uniquely Lucan. Resseguie argues that only one-tenth of the material in 9:51–18:14 has even a possible Marcan connection. Teaching material that is capable of being repeated might slightly alter the exact count. Nonetheless, the numbers of Huck-Lietzmann and Resseguie are closer to the real percentages, since Luke 9:51–18:14 lacks any significant Marcan parallels. In addition, most of the Q pericopes and unique Lucan material are long units. Conceptual overlap with Matthew and unique Lucan material abound (see the introduction in vol. 1, pp. 10–12). Goulder (1989: 455) notes that in 9:51–13:21 one of every three words comes from Q or L, while in 13:22–18:14 (where Goulder ends the unit) one in six words comes from this material.

teen miracles in the shorter Galilean section. Narratives focusing on individuals are more plentiful, but they also are relatively sparse.[5] Thus the section has a different flavor than Luke's Galilean section, which had more miracles and narratives.

5. Sayings and parables dominate the section. The presence of seventeen parables alone shows that teaching is a major concern.[6] In fact, up through the end of Luke 14 there is interplay between instruction of the disciples and rebuke of the Jewish leadership. Thus, the message of the section appears to be that Jesus gives a new way to follow God. One is to listen to him, for his way is not the way of the Jewish religious leadership (Ellis 1974: 146–47).

These features have led to great debate about the formation and historical character of 9:51–19:44. Egelkraut (1976: 11–59) lists the options and examines the entire question in detail:

1. Currently, the most popular view is that Luke arranged this section for theological purposes, so that a specific journey or set of journeys in some chronological sequence is not being presented.[7]
2. On the opposite end of the spectrum is Arndt (1956: 272), who from a conservative perspective argues for a tighter chronological sequence and relates the events of Jesus' departure from Galilee to John's chronology starting in John 7. Arndt argues for several journeys to Jerusalem, the last one starting in Luke 17:11. Others argue that the final journey starts in 18:15, where Luke's Gospel again parallels material from Mark (Mark 10:13–16). This debate about where a final journey might start shows how hard it is to link the various Lucan notes precisely (Fitzmyer 1981: 67, 824, although below I reject his more sym-

5. Twelve narratives (depending on how one counts) focus on individuals: 9:52–56; 9:57–62; 10:29–37; 10:38–42; 11:14–23; 11:27–28; 13:31–35; 18:15–17; 18:18–30; 19:1–10; 19:29–40; 19:41–44 (note the gap from 14:1 to 18:14). Egelkraut 1976: 28 has a slightly different list.

6. Blomberg 1982b concentrates on the fifteen uniquely Lucan parables: 10:25–37; 11:5–8; 12:13–21; 13:6–9; 14:7–14; 14:15–24; 14:28–33; 15:8–10; 15:11–32; 16:1–9; 16:19–31; 17:7–10; 18:1–8; 18:9–14; 19:11–27. Only 13:18–21 and 15:3–7 have parallels.

7. Resseguie 1975 puts five of fourteen possible interpretations in this category. C. F. Evans 1990: 433 points out the lack of chronological notes, especially at the end of the section. Vague indications of time and place are provided only in the beginning of the section: 9:52, 56–57; 10:1, 21, 38; 11:14, 27; 13:10, 31; 14:1, 25. Schürmann 1994: 1 speaks of a metaphorical journey account in which Jesus goes his way to Jerusalem as an itinerant prophetic teacher who divides Israel. On Luke's use of journey and way terminology, see Schneider 1977a: 227.

bolic reading of Luke). The view of a single, straight-line journey seems to be negated by Luke 10:38–42, which occurs in Bethany, and 17:11, which has Jesus once again in the north. Arndt is correct to speak of journeys, if one sees Luke ultimately indicating a complex travel schedule. Clearly the term *journey* is to be taken in a broad descriptive sense.

3. Hendriksen (1978: 542–43) speaks of one general journey not given in exact chronological sequence. He specifically rejects three sequential Jerusalem journeys, thereby also rejecting the connection between John's Gospel and Luke's journey. Hendriksen's discussion is quite full, though his efforts to argue that the travel allusions in Luke 13:22 and 17:11 are references to the journey's start seem forced. This interpretation is correct in its general view of the journey, but it lacks a clear explanation of why the journey motif is present.

Of these three approaches, the first, which sees a theological organization in the section, is best, since Luke's own text makes clear that a straight journey is not in view. However, the third view is not incorrect, just incomplete. The absence of clear chronological and geographical indicators is the major clue that Luke presents the journey as a summary of Jesus' final phase of ministry.

Many, however, overpress the portrait of theological motives in contrast to the section's historicity. For example, Fitzmyer (1981: 826) calls it an "artificial expansion of an inherited tradition" (which he sees as Mark 10:1–52) and argues the possibility that Jesus did not do or say all these things on the way to Jerusalem.[8] But this opposition of theological arrangement against historicity is not necessary. Luke can present a general movement toward Jerusalem as an accurate reflection of what Jesus did and taught as he came closer to that fateful city. There was no need for him to create the journey motif or the events associated with it. The journey is expressed in time, not direct geographic direction. Jesus is headed to Jerusalem and his fate there. One need not insist, however, on strict chronology when Luke himself avoids it.

In a careful study, Blomberg (1983: 245) plausibly argues against a chiasmus in Luke 9:51–19:44, but suggests that behind the section lies a parable source that was laid out chiastically (pp. 233–47).[9] Blomberg defends Luke's care and motives in arranging the section.

8. Fitzmyer 1981: 825–26 mentions the tension between matter and form in the travel account, citing K. Schmidt's remark that "though Jesus is always traveling to Jerusalem, he never makes any real progress on this journey."

9. Talbert 1982: 111–12 sees chiasmus in 9:51–19:44, but has to omit Luke 15 and place 14:1–6 out of its Lucan order! Goulder 1964: 196 argues for the following chiastic links:

The section's features show that Luke arranged a large summary unit about the latter portion of Jesus' ministry. The concern is not so much a straight-line journey but an accurate, representative portrayal of this decisive period. During this time Jesus began to complete his earthly mission, prepared his disciples for his death, challenged the Jewish leadership, and continued to move toward Jerusalem (Ellis 1974: 146–47; Marshall 1978: 401). It is in the movement of God's plan toward Jerusalem that Luke accurately presents a "journey," a description that is both theological and historical. Some sequencing may be present and traceable, and where it exists it is important; it is not, however, the major concern of the section. Arndt's view of three journeys, though possible because of John's chronology, is hard to confirm in Luke because of the lack of specific notes in Luke's material. Plummer (1896: 260–61) sees the same difficulties and says that Luke has left a certain "indistinctness" in the narrative that one should not try to make more specific. What Carson (1984: 197) said of Matt. 8–9 can also be said of Luke 9–19: the arrangement is not haphazard, but is governed by themes. As a result, one should pinpoint the place and time only when Luke makes the connection clear and otherwise be content to know that Luke is describing something in the final phase of Jesus' ministry.

The section shows what Jesus taught and did as his ministry faced its inevitable end in Jerusalem. Liefeld's conclusion (1984: 932) seems sound:

10:25	eternal life
11:1	prayer
11:14	healing
11:37	pharisaic hypocrisy
12:1	money
12:35	repentance
13:10	rejection of Israel and invitation to outcasts
14:1	rejection of Israel and invitation to outcasts
15:1	repentance
16:1	money
16:14	pharisaic hypocrisy
17:11	healing
17:5	prayer
18:18	eternal life

The most plausible case for chiasmus is made by Farrell 1986. Blomberg also deals with and rejects theories that make the central section a Christian Deuteronomy; see C. F. Evans 1955. My main criticism of Blomberg's article is that it regards the section's end as falling at 18:34, ignoring later literary clues that Jesus has not arrived in Jerusalem (19:28, 41). This may be the Achilles' heel against his theory that the section's parable source was laid out chiastically, especially if 19:11–27 is taken into consideration. Still, aspects of Blomberg's case and the general outline of a possible Lucan source may surface in my discussion; see also Nolland 1993a: 530–31.

If there is a travel motif in this section, it is not an artificial scheme but one that is (1) consistent with the nature of Jesus' ministry, which has been itinerant all along; (2) consistent with the emphasis on travel in both Luke and Acts, possibly to maintain the reader's interest; and (3) consistent with the fact that, while Jesus did not go directly from Galilee to Jerusalem, his mind was definitely set on the impending events he faced in that city. Even at times when he may have traveled north again, his ultimate goal was Jerusalem.

Fixing the section's subdivisions is difficult. Various approaches have been taken, with none winning consensus. A case could be built around the journey markers in 13:22; 17:11; 18:31 (Arndt 1956: 272; Tiede 1988: 194, 252, 295). But the rationale for such groupings is hard to delineate.[10] Schneider's names (1977a: 226) for these sections are too broad to be helpful: discipleship and mission (9:51–13:21), saving of the lost (13:22–17:10), and discipleship and end-time hope (17:11–19:27). Blomberg (1983: 245) outlines the section in fourteen divisions (starting at 9:51; 10:1; 10:25; 11:1; 11:14; 12:1; 13:10; 14:25; 15:1; 16:1; 17:1; 17:20; 18:9; 18:31), but he omits the section's final portion, and his rationale depends on his case for a unified source behind the parables. Marshall (1978: 9–10) has ten divisions (9:51; 10:25; 11:14; 12:1; 13:22; 15:1; 16:1; 17:1; 17:11; 18:9), but closes the section at 19:10. Ellis (1974: 149–50) speaks of six divisions (9:51; 11:1; 12:35; 13:22; 16:14; 18:15), but his reason for divisions such as 18:15 is not compelling. Does a return to the Marcan outline really indicate a literary transition?

I appeal to unity of content and largely follow suggestions made by Blomberg and Marshall in proposing the following twelve divisions:

9:51–10:24	blessing of decision: privilege, mission, and commitment
10:25–11:13	discipleship: looking to one's neighbor, Jesus, and God
11:14–54	controversies, corrections, and calls to trust
12:1–48	discipleship: trusting God
12:49–14:24	knowing the nature of the time: Israel turns away, but blessing still comes
14:25–35	discipleship in the face of rejection: basic elements
15:1–32	pursuit of sinners: heaven's examples
16:1–31	generosity: handling money and possessions
17:1–10	false teaching, forgiveness, and service

10. Fitzmyer 1981: 825 uses this division, but says it is one of "convenience, since the division at these points is otherwise insignificant and somewhat arbitrary." Plummer 1896: 261 also speaks of "convenience." Such markers do not really note a shift of themes, and so are less than adequate.

17:11–18:8	faithfulness in looking for the king, the kingdom, and the kingdom's consummation
18:9–30	humbly entrusting all to the Father
18:31–19:44	turning to Jerusalem: messianic power, personal transformation, warning of responsibility, and entry with mourning

This outline reflects the central section's emphases. In the first portion of the section, there is an interchange between debate with the Jewish leadership and instruction on discipleship. Jesus points to the Jewish leadership as an example of how *not* to walk with God; in 11:37–54 he offers his indictment of such leadership. The turning point comes in 13:31–14:35, where the nation's rejection of Messiah is made clear, resulting in Jesus' lament over Israel's desolate house. Jesus now begins to concentrate almost exclusively on discipleship, starting with basic commitment (14:25–35). Except for brief notes of criticism, the Pharisees and scribes are largely absent from the section after this (they return when Jesus enters Jerusalem). In Luke 15–18 there is a large concentration of teaching about how the disciple must walk in light of rejection. Luke's emphasis on discipleship, rejection, and suffering is similar to Mark's, without using much Marcan material. Luke's section complements Mark's portrayal. The Davidic character of Jesus reasserts itself near the end of the section in 18:35–43, a passage that looks much like the texts of the Galilean ministry. The king draws near to the city. The section ends with a sad note. Jesus enters Jerusalem and weeps for it, because he knows the short-term consequence of the nation's rejecting him. Blessing will come for humankind, but the nation will suffer greatly.

A. Blessing of Decision: Privilege, Mission, and Commitment (9:51–10:24)

The journey's first major section concentrates on disciples, first their failures and then their success. Luke 9:51–56 tells of rejection in Samaria, which causes the disciples to ask for instant judgment. Jesus refuses this request since now is the time to offer hope, not bring down the hammer. Then in 9:57–62 a few disciples suggest that other priorities are greater than following Jesus. Jesus quickly rebukes them, since discipleship requires one's full commitment. These two failures are followed by the successful mission of 10:1–24. Jesus notes that the key is not the power that the disciples wield, but that they know God. To know God is to be blessed; to reject him is to be condemned. Thus, the journey begins with instruction: knowing God is both a blessing and life's highest priority.

1. Rejection in Samaria (9:51–56)

The Jerusalem journey begins as it will end—with a note of failure (19:41–44). The disciples respond improperly to rejection. This uniquely Lucan unit shows Jesus rebuking the disciples for wanting to judge immediately a Samaritan village that refuses to respond to their message. The point is simple: though the Samaritan decision is a crucial one, the current period is not one of instant judgment. God gives time for people to respond to the kingdom, and he continues to pursue the mission of taking the gospel to all people (2 Pet. 3:9). Thus, Jesus and his disciples move on to another village. The time is one of offering God's grace. The time for judgment has not arrived, though decisions made now influence how people are treated later, as subsequent pericopes show (Luke 10:13–16). Also, just as Luke opened the Galilean ministry with an account about rejection, so the travel section opens with opposition (Fitzmyer 1981: 827). Jesus' ministry heads inexorably toward rejection and death.

Sources and Historicity

The event is unique to Luke, so it is part of the L material (though Schürmann 1994: 31 makes a case for Q). But is the event authentic? Because the journey is a Lucan emphasis, Bultmann (1963: 25–26) regards the material as grounded in the early church's missionary work. But there is no reason to place the event outside of Jesus' ministry (Schürmann 1994: 32). In fact, the negative portrait of the Samaritans is out of character with Luke's generally favorable view of the Samaritans (Luke 10:30–37; 17:11–19; Acts 8:4–25). Thus, a source is quite likely here. Evans (in Evans and Sanders 1993: 97) argues for a primitive source, though he does not choose between L and Q. He sees Luke stylizing 9:51, 53, 56. The event is authentic, especially given the negative portrayal of the disciples and Samaritans. Nolland (1993a: 533–34) sees the negative Elijah motif as unlike Luke, but is more circumspect about a historical mission to Samaria in light of Matt. 10:5. However, that text seems to describe an earlier missionary period of Jesus' ministry, which should not preclude later efforts to reach out to Samaria, as John 4 also suggests. The event shows Jesus' desire to include outsiders.

Form critics debate whether the unit is a pronouncement story or, correctly, a story about Jesus (Fitzmyer 1981: 827).[1] Berger (1984: 352) refines this latter term by speaking of "biographical episode" (also V. Taylor 1935: 153). The outline of Luke 9:51–56 is as follows:

a. Turning to Jerusalem (9:51)
b. Samaritan rejection of the messengers (9:52–55)
   i. Rejection (9:52–53)
   ii. The disciples' call for judgment (9:54)
   iii. Jesus' rebuke (9:55)
c. Continuation of the mission (9:56)

Turning his attention to Jerusalem, Jesus as an itinerant preacher takes his mission through Samaria. There is rejection in Samaria, because of destiny in Jerusalem. So Jesus is rejected beyond Israel's borders. And yet, Jesus rebukes his disciples' call for immediate judgment. The disciples are still learning about their mission, whereas Jesus' heart and mission are revealed through his response.

Exegesis and Exposition

[51]When the days drew near for him to be received up, he set his face to go to Jerusalem. [52]And he sent messengers ahead of him. And they went into a Samaritan village to make ready for him, [53]but they did not welcome him, for his face was set toward Jerusalem. [54]When his disciples James and John saw it, they said, "Lord, do you want us to bid fire come down from heaven and consume them?"⌐ ⌐ [55]But he turned and rebuked them.⌐ ⌐ [56]And they went on to another village.

a. Turning to Jerusalem (9:51)

Using his normal introductory style and recalling the LXX, Luke brings up Jesus' turning to Jerusalem. Luke frequently uses ἐγένετο (*egeneto*, it came to pass) to begin a new unit (1:5; 2:1; 3:21; 5:1, 12, 17; 6:1, 12; 7:11; 8:1, 22; 9:18, 28, 37). The mood is biblical and solemn. Key events in Jesus' career draw near.

9:51

Most crucial is the drawing near of Jesus' "being received up" (ἀναλήμψεως, *analēmpseōs*). Though some suggest that this term

---

1. Bultmann 1963: 25–26, 64, 68 opts for a pronouncement story, but also notes the absence of any pronouncement. Jesus' response comes in his simply turning away. This makes a pronouncement account unlikely and explains why the Jesus Seminar makes no comment on the text in *The Five Gospels* (Funk and Hoover 1993: 316).

refers only to Jesus' death, it can also refer to the resurrection-ascension.[2] Acts 1:2, 11, 22 clearly refers to the ascension with a related verb—a connection that makes likely the inclusion of the resurrection-ascension here.[3] This "reception" is part of what was earlier called Jesus' "exodus" (Luke 9:31).

The verb chosen for the approach of this period is also interesting: συμπληροῦσθαι (symplērousthai) means "to fulfill." Divine design is tied to these events (Liefeld 1984: 933; Delling, TDNT 6:308–9; Jer. 25:12). Nothing is happening by accident.

Jesus is determined to go to Jerusalem. The Hebrew idiom "to set one's face to go somewhere" indicates a determination to accomplish a task (Gen. 31:21; Isa. 50:7; Jer. 21:10; 44:12; Ezek. 6:2; 13:17; 14:8; 15:7; Dan. 11:17–18; Grundmann 1963: 201; Klostermann 1929: 111; Lohse, TDNT 6:776 n. 45).[4] In addition, Jesus heads to Jerusalem to face opposition, much as the prophets had done. Certainly the comparison with prophets of old fits both the idiom's mood and background as well as Luke's teaching (Luke 11:45–52; 20:9–18; Acts 7). Ellis (1974: 152) suggests an allusion to the "Jerusalem pilgrimage" concept found in the Psalms (cf. the superscriptions on Ps. 120–34), but perhaps a prophetic background is stronger. Jerusalem will be noted consistently as the goal, with references extending beyond mere travel notes (Luke 9:53; 13:22, 33–35; 17:11; 18:31; 19:11, 28, 41; note how they cluster at the journey's end).

b. Samaritan Rejection of the Messengers (9:52–55)
i. Rejection (9:52–53)

9:52 The statement about Jesus' mission to Jerusalem precedes his mission into an unnamed town of Samaria. This presents Jesus moving

2. Danker 1988: 207–8; Fitzmyer 1981: 828. BAGD 57 and BAA 112 note that ἀναλήμψεως, a NT hapax legomenon, alludes to the ascension. The LXX uses it of Elijah's departure (2 Kings 2:9, 11; 1 Macc. 2:58; Sir. 48:9; 49:14). For more discussion, see the additional note on 9:51.

3. In the NT, the verb is a technical term for resurrection: Mark 16:19 (longer version); 1 Tim. 3:16.

4. Marshall 1978: 405 notes that the Hebrew idiom may suggest a source behind Luke's remarks. Appealing to Ezek. 6:2; 13:17; 15:7; 20:46 [21:2 MT], C. A. Evans 1987a argues that the force is "to dispatch," a view possible for the term but awkward for this context. In a reworking of this article in Evans and Sanders 1993: 93–105, Evans makes less of the lexical argument and argues for an allusion to Ezek. 21:2–6 [21:7–11 MT], with the implication that with the journey comes not only destined suffering for Jesus but also judgment for Israel (he also adds Ezek. 25:2; 28:21; 29:2; and 38:2, while emphasizing the parallel in 20:46 [21:2 MT]; p. 100). If so, then Jesus' act is like that of the prophet and has a place in the divine drama of Israel's history. This view is possible, but not certain. For a denial of judgment here, see Giblin 1985: 31–32.

south from Galilee, at least for a time. Messengers are sent ahead to prepare (ἑτοιμάζω, *hetoimazō*) the townspeople for his arrival. This term could refer to preparing for mass preaching or lodging (Creed 1930: 141; Arndt 1956: 274; Fitzmyer 1981: 829).[5] Some believe that the messengers' role is much like that of John the Baptist for Jesus' ministry, except no specific preaching ministry is mentioned in connection with the disciples.[6] Others see an allusion to Elijah's ministry (Mal. 3:1; 4:5 [3:23 MT]; Fitzmyer 1981: 828). This is possible, but less than clear. Of course, entry into the town is not a guarantee of success, as the unnamed messengers soon discover.

This is the only negative pericope of three Lucan Gospel passages that allude to the Samaritans. Both 10:33 (the good Samaritan) and 17:16 (the one grateful Samaritan leper out of ten who are healed) are significant in positively contrasting Samaritans to others (Samaritan references in Acts are 1:8; 8:1–14, 25; 9:31; 15:3). Samaria was originally the name of the city that Omri founded as the capital of the northern kingdom of Israel (1 Kings 16:21–24). The Samaritans were a mixed race of Israelite and non-Israelite blood, who were despised by many pure-blooded Israelites because they believed that the Samaritans compromised the faith (2 Kings 17:30–31; Ezra 4:2; John 4:9; Luke 17:18; Josephus, *Antiquities* 11.4.9 §§114–19; 11.8.6 §341; 12.5.5 §257). They dwelt in northern Israel in a region between southern Israel (Judea) and Galilee. They worshiped at Mount Gerizim, rather than at Mount Zion (John 4:20–24), and recognized only the Pentateuch. Tension heightened when their temple on Gerizim was destroyed around 128 B.C. Even though it took three days to pass through the region, many Jews preferred to lengthen their journey and go around it.[7] Jesus, challenging this attitude, tried to reach these people.

9:53   The mission meets with failure: the Samaritans do not "receive" (ἐδέξαντο, *edexanto*) Jesus. The reason highlights the section's mood, since Jesus is destined for Jerusalem (ὅτι [*hoti*] is causal). All races

---

5. Ἑτοιμάσαι is an infinitive of purpose tied to εἰσῆλθον: "they came to prepare." On the use of ὡς (untranslated) with the infinitive to express purpose, see BAGD 898 §IV.3.b and BAA 1793 §IV.3.b. Some support the distinction between preaching and lodging because ἑτοιμάζω can mean "preparing a place"; BAGD 316 §1; BAA 640 §1; Matt. 22:4; John 14:2–3.

6. Three of the four previous uses of ἑτοιμάζω in Luke (1:17, 76; 3:4) refer to John the Baptist. Such Lucan usage and the lack of welcome in 9:53 suggest that "prepare" entails more than lodging. If the preaching mission of 9:1–6 is a precedent, then preaching could be implied as well.

7. Josephus, *Jewish War* 2.12.3 §232; Jeremias 1969: 352–58; Jeremias, *TDNT* 7:88–94. On Jewish attitudes, see Sir. 50:25–26; T. Levi 7.2; Gen. Rab. 81.3 on 35:2; Jub. 30.5–6, 23; C. A. Evans 1990: 164. On the relationship between Jews and Samaritans, see Brindle 1984.

reject his ministry (Acts 4:24–29). Most see the cause of Jesus' rejection as based on his failure to recognize Gerizim, so that the Samaritans avoided him just as they avoided other Jews. The two people shared little in common but a history of division (Josephus, *Antiquities* 20.6.1 §§118–23; *Jewish War* 2.12.3 §§232–33; Danker 1988: 209; Ernst 1977: 318). It is hard to reverse such traditional hostility. The note of rejection is important, because it shows that such rejection is not limited to Jews or to Israel or to its leadership. Rejection of Jesus is widespread. (A similar non-Israelite, Gentile rejection occurs in Luke 8:26–39 with the reaction to the Gerasene demoniac.) Thus, the pericope speaks against Jervell's view (1972: 113–32) that the Samaritans are seen positively as the lost sheep of Israel recaptured. Since some participate in the general rejection of Jesus and can even be called foreigners by him (17:18), it is hard to argue that Luke sees them explicitly as part of Israel. They seem rather to be viewed as a mixed people, for when the gospel goes to them, the apostles are brought in to confirm the expansion; apostolic presence is called for when the gospel reaches a new stage (Acts 8:14–24; 10:34–43). One such "new" stage was the movement to the Samaritans, who like all people can be included in the promise tied to Jesus. People of all sorts reject Jesus, just as later in Acts people of all sorts will accept him.

ii. The Disciples' Call for Judgment (9:54)

9:54   The Samaritan rejection produced a reaction. James and John suggested to the Lord that cataclysmic judgment be sent on the village. The phrase *fire from heaven* has verbal OT precedent, including a parallel incident in Elijah's ministry.[8] These two disciples wanted God to wipe out the village. Their question shows their zeal for Jesus' honor, but it is misguided; it might also reflect their attitude about Samaritans. They thought it was time to judge lack of faith powerfully and directly, as in the days of old. Some suggest that their nickname, "Sons of Thunder" (Mark 3:17), grew out of this request, but this is not likely.[9] What is clear is that the disciples took

---

8. 2 Chron. 7:1, 3 (concerning Solomon's offering at the temple's dedication); 2 Kings 1:10, 12, 14 (the fire sent by Elijah that consumed two companies of fifty men from Ahaziah in Samaria!); Miyoshi 1974: 13. 2 Kings 1:16–17 condemns some Samaritans' lack of faith in Yahweh and their turning to Baal-Zebub. The image of fire conceptually recalls the destruction of Sodom and Gomorrah (Gen. 19:24–28).

9. Plummer 1896: 264 notes that Luke makes nothing of this nickname. Marshall 1978: 406 rejects the suggestion of the nickname's connection with this incident, noting that the name is absent and that it is not likely that Jesus would give them a derogatory nickname. In addition, Mark 3:17 does not say that the name came from Jesus. Nolland 1993a: 536 notes that the concern of James and John in Mark 10:35–45 also revolves around power. But disciples are to serve. The nickname may allude to their character, which is undergoing reformation.

the Samaritans' rejection seriously. They also recognized that the authority granted to them was extensive, since they would request the consuming fire at Jesus' word. The account implies for the disciples a prophetlike authority derived from Jesus when ministry is done "in his name" (Luke 9:49; Ellis 1974: 152). The allusion to Elijah is striking in that the Elijah motif also appears in the key opening event of the Galilean ministry (4:25–27; Ellis 1974: 152). Still, the disciples are submissive and will not act without Jesus' approval (note θέλεις, *theleis*, do you wish?).

iii. Jesus' Rebuke (9:55)

Jesus' response is succinct and graphic. As he turns (he is at the front of the group), he refuses the request of James and John with a rebuke.[10] The request to judge immediately is out of character with Jesus' current ministry. There are warnings of judgment in Jesus' ministry, but the judgment itself will come later (10:13–16; 17:20–36). The decision made about him is all-important, but judgment is not for now. The Twelve realize from their earlier mission and the shaking of the dust from their feet that refusal has eschatological consequences (9:5), but God graciously gives people time to reflect on their decision.[11] Luke does not tell what Jesus says, only that he rebukes the disciples. They still need to learn about Jesus' ministry. They can preach and warn like Elijah, but the act of judging will be left to God for another time and place (19:24–27; Schürmann 1994: 29).

9:55

c. Continuation of the Mission (9:56)

In the face of rejection, the disciples move on with Jesus to another locale. Jesus had said in 4:43 that he must go to other cities, and so he does. The village in question is probably Samaritan as well, but it too remains unnamed. The entourage, refusing to retaliate, continues its journey.

9:56

The journey section of Luke's Gospel starts (9:51–56) as it will end (19:41–44): with rejection. Jesus is headed for Jerusalem to face the consequences of his being rejected. But rejection is not evinced only by those in Galilee or by the religious leadership. It is widespread. A variety of reasons prevent a hearing: the leadership has theological concerns; the Samaritans have a history of

Summary

---

10. The aorist participle στραφείς and the aorist verb ἐπετίμησεν suggest either a simultaneous action or a turning followed by the rebuke. Jesus responds similarly in Luke 22:47–51; Nolland 1993a: 537.

11. Acts 8 narrates a return to this region; 2 Pet. 3:9 speaks of God's patience with Israel.

racial and religious hostility that makes accepting a Jew difficult. But despite rejection, the disciples' desire for immediate cataclysmic judgment is wrong. God has a time and a place to evaluate what people do with Jesus. That will be his business, though the negative outcome for those who reject his messengers is clear, as is the validity of warning about such consequences (Luke 10:13–16; 12:5; Acts 10:42; 17:31). The disciples' call is to continue to offer the message; so they learn and move on. The message is an invitation of grace, but the decision does have ultimate consequences. It is a precious message, and one that requires a decision. In his rebuke, Jesus is not rejecting the disciples' conclusion, but their timing and spirit. Of course, what the village pictures is how people respond to Jesus. Significantly, the journey to Jerusalem begins with rejection and an allusion to Elijah, just as did the Galilean ministry (Luke 4:24–30). It is a sad time for Israel and its neighbor. Sitting on the edge of opportunity, they risk missing the call. Such rejection leads to Jesus' death and a "reception" that points beyond death to resurrection. Paradoxically, rejection paves the way for broader opportunity for forgiveness (Rom. 11). Rejection does not kill the promise; it resurrects it.

Additional Notes

9:51. The picture of Jesus' being taken up into heaven has a rich background: Ps. Sol. 4.18 (a figure of death); 2 Esdr. [= 4 Ezra] 6:26; 8:19; 14:49 (Syriac addition); and T. Moses 10.12 (Creed 1930: 141; Plummer 1896: 262). Grundmann (1963: 201) and Ellis (1974: 152) note that John's concept of Jesus' being "glorified" is parallel to this idea (John 13:31). Schweizer (1984: 169) argues for the nuance of death, citing Ps. Sol. 4.18 and Pseudo-Clement, *Homilies* 3.47 as lexical support. But Nolland (1993a: 534) notes that only Ps. Sol. 4.18 refers to death, despite claims by others for T. Moses 10.12, 2 Bar. 46.7, and the Pseudo-Clement text. Judaism emphasized the translation of Moses and Elijah (Pseudo-Philo, *Biblical Antiquities* 32.9; Josephus, *Antiquities* 4.8.48 §326; 9.2.2 §28; Philo, *Life of Moses* 2.51 §291; T. Abr. (A) 15–20; T. Job 39.12; *Sipre* 357 on Deut. 34:5 [= Neusner 1987: 2.453–62]; and an isolated manuscript of the very late *Midrash ha-Gadol* on Deuteronomy [noted by Jeremias, *TDNT* 4:855 n. 99]). Clement of Alexandria (*Stromata* 6.15.132) discusses Moses' ascension, and Jerome (*Homily on Amos* 9:6) notes this Enoch-Moses-Elijah theme (C. A. Evans 1990: 163–64).

9:54. A variant reading at the end of the verse (ὡς καὶ Ἠλίας ἐποίησεν, as Elijah also did) makes an explicit connection to Elijah but is probably not original. In support of the addition are A, C, D, W, Θ, and Byz, but against it are $\mathfrak{P}^{45}$, $\mathfrak{P}^{75}$, ℵ, B, and other major Alexandrian witnesses. If originally present, it is hard to explain why it would have been omitted (Plummer 1896: 264).

9:55. Several variant readings supply the rebuke's content, but they are given in diverse forms, which makes them look like later additions. The variants are in D, K, Γ, family 1, family 13, as well as in some Syriac manuscripts. One variant asks a question of the disciples: "Do you not know of what sort of spirit you are?" Another addition reads, "For the Son of Man came not to destroy souls, but to save them." This statement appears in different forms and appears to be influenced by 19:10. In fact, both variants are absent from the early manuscripts as well as from a variety of uncials. The UBS–NA text is supported by $\mathfrak{P}^{45}$, $\mathfrak{P}^{75}$, ℵ, A, B, C, L, W, Δ, Ξ, and Ψ (Liefeld 1984: 934; Fitzmyer 1981: 830; Marshall 1978: 407–8; Schürmann 1994: 29 n. 55).

2. Warnings about Discipleship (9:57–62)

A passage on the demands of discipleship appropriately follows a passage on Jesus' rejection in Samaria (Grundmann 1963: 203; Egelkraut 1976: 138). Association with the kingdom will not mean power, but sharing in Jesus' suffering and rejection (Danker 1988: 210). Any disciple who would follow Jesus needs to understand that this choice will require total commitment. In this passage, three would-be disciples clearly receive this message from Jesus. Since disciples will suffer rejection from the world, just as Jesus did, they need to place top priority on following Jesus. They cannot look back once they ally themselves to him, for the opportunity to look back will be frequent and the dangers of doing so are great. The individuals who converse with Jesus are not a focal point in the account, for there is no indication of their response. The point resides solely in Jesus' responses, which are given for the reader's reflection.

The account contains a triad of sayings prompted by statements from three would-be disciples. The first and third men volunteer, while the second is called (Liefeld 1984: 935). The demands of discipleship are the same no matter how one comes to Jesus.

Sources and Historicity

Luke 9:57–60 has a parallel in Matt. 8:18–22 (Aland 1985: §176), where the first two parts of the Lucan passage are found with only slight variations. What is interesting is that the Matthean event is placed in the Galilean portion of Jesus' ministry (though Matt. 8–9 itself is not strictly chronological). The amount of agreement in the first two events makes it clear that this is not a repeated incident. So in which context is the incident to be placed?

Arndt (1956: 276) notes the three options (besides the rejected possibilities of distinct events or a rejection of historicity): (1) Matthew has the right placement, (2) Luke has the right placement, or (3) neither intends a chronological placement. Under the first two options, only one of the Gospel authors makes a topical placement; this is possible, since neither of them gives a specific setting. A clear decision is difficult.

A topical placement by both (view 3) is most likely, as is a general Galilean setting (Arndt 1956: 276; Ellis 1974: 152 [apparently]). As noted, both authors place the account without detailed notes about the setting. In addition, the exchange appears in sections that have a topical character. Luke's note in 9:52 about the disciples going ahead to prepare for Jesus assumes that the disciples are already out in mission, which in turn assumes a period after events such as 9:1–6. A time after this initial thrust seems likely. Luke's placement as part of his introduction of the "mission" theme purposefully comes after Samaria's rejection of Jesus. He places the incident here because disciples need to understand the nature of the mission, especially in new areas. They need to be highly committed to Jesus, since the call will include rejection and, for many, itinerant ministry. The Lucan association with the Jerusalem journey is appropriate because Jesus is moving to face rejection. In fact, 10:1–24 will describe a larger mission of the disciples, while 9:51–56 showed that a new geographical setting does not change the fact that many refuse Jesus. Mission on behalf of Jesus is not easy.

Most see a common source behind Luke 9:57–60 and Matt. 8:18–22, especially given the extent of verbal agreement in the verses (Schürmann 1994: 47). For most, with Schürmann, this source is Q; for Matthean priorists it is Matthew. The radical nature of the statements speaks for their authenticity. The Jesus Seminar accepts these sayings as authentic, printing them in pink type (Funk and Hoover 1993: 316–17). The seminar sees a Cynic philosophical background for the sayings, but Hengel (1981: 5–6) challenges this. Luke 9:59–60 is one of the least doubted statements of Jesus (Hengel 1981: 6 n. 12), while 9:58 is also often accepted, though some question its use of "Son of Man" (Nolland 1993a: 540; Casey 1985). Crossan (1991: 255–56) notes a parallel for 9:57–58 in the Gospel of Thomas 86. In Crossan's view, Thomas uses "Son of Man" as a reference to humans, but Luke has it as a title for Jesus. Crossan sees the statement as doubly attested and thus authentic, but with "Son of Man" reinterpreted by Luke. Here Crossan prefers the early tradition in Thomas, which I reject. The saying makes more sense as a remark about a rejected Jesus than about a humanity whose existence is more transient than animals (see the exegesis of 9:58). In these sayings, Jesus is more than a rabbi, wandering teacher, or prophet (Schürmann 1994: 48), and his radical claims and call make him suspect to most. So his disciples had better be ready for a similar negative reaction.

But what is the origin of Luke 9:61–62, which appears only in Luke? The options are plentiful (Marshall 1978: 408–9):

1. Some see 9:61–62 as Luke's creation.[1] This seems unlikely, because this third saying is stylistically like the other two (Schneider

---

1. Dibelius 1934: 160–61, esp. 160 n. 1, says that the general nature of the remark shows that it comes from the evangelist, but how "general principles" can come from the evangelist is not clear. It is the unique attestation of this saying in Luke that ap-

1977a: 231; Crossan 1991: 256). The sayings seem to belong together. Those who argue for this option suggest that the saying is formed to parallel 1 Kings 19:19–20 (Fitzmyer 1981: 837 argues that it may be Lucan).

2. Others argue that Luke had access to this third man in his special source (Grundmann 1963: 204; Ernst 1977: 320 [Q or L]; Wiefel 1988: 192; Schneider 1977a: 231 [undecided between options 1 and 2]; Fitzmyer 1981: 833 [slightly prefers this over a Lucan creation]; Manson 1949: 72).

3. Still others argue that these verses were present in Q (the source shared by Matthew and Luke), which would mean that Matthew omitted the third portion (Hengel 1981: 4 n. 5, who also defends the authenticity of these remarks, appealing to the parallel style of the three sayings). Hengel sees Matthew omitting the third saying because it is negative and interrupts the flow from Matt. 8:18 to 8:23.

4. Finally, a remaining option is that a source like Q, but a distinct version of it not known to Matthew, is the source, since it is hard to explain why Matthew would omit the third element if he knew of it (Hahn 1969: 119 n. 99).

A clear decision is not possible, though it seems that Luke had access to additional sources (views 2 and 4). It is hard to understand why Matthew would omit the saying, if he knew it. The radical tone of the saying speaks for its authenticity and coheres with other texts in Luke (10:4 [don't greet others on the road]; 14:26 [hate your family and your own life]; Nolland 1993a: 540). It is not a Lucan creation.

This passage is significant, because it shows that discipleship is not a fly-by-night affair. Discipleship requires that Jesus and the kingdom be the priority of life. The disciple is aware that allying oneself to Jesus sets one apart from the world and involves tackling tasks in a way that is different from the world. Jesus' response—whether seen as strong and unusual or as hyperbolic—only reinforces the mood of urgency and commitment already present.

In terms of form, the account is a series of three pronouncements or apophthegms (Bultmann 1963: 28–29; V. Taylor 1935:

---

pears to be the only reason for this conclusion, along with its possible use of OT imagery from Gen. 19:26. The Jesus Seminar sees these verses as going back to Luke, claiming that the saying assumes too much self-identity for disciples (Funk and Hoover 1993: 316 prints it in black type). But the distinctive behavior and identity are already indicated in the first two sayings, which the seminar accepts. On the rejection of other attempts to argue that the early church is responsible for the sayings, see Marshall 1978: 409, in particular his evaluation of Schulz 1972: 435 n. 239, who relies on Dibelius. Glombitza 1971 also makes a case for Lucan creation.

72). Berger (1984: 81, 182–87) speaks of pronouncements that are also warnings. Jesus' sayings dominate the account. The outline of Luke 9:57–62 is as follows:

    a. Warning about alienation from the world (9:57–58)
    b. Warning that proclamation comes first (9:59–60)
    c. Warning that commitment is first and must be constant (9:61–62)

Discipleship and the nature of mission are the key ideas. It is assumed that all share in the mission. Discipleship must be seen in the context of Jesus' being rejected. The cost of discipleship needs attention as one turns to mission. Disciples must place Jesus and the kingdom first. Disciples must recognize that they will be distanced from the world by their discipleship, and that family matters may suffer inattention in comparison to their discipleship. Relative to each other, God comes before family. Disciples must not look back from their commitment to Jesus. It is a constant commitment.

Exegesis and Exposition

[57]And as they were going along the road, a man said to him, "I will follow you wherever you go." [58]And Jesus said to him, "The foxes have holes, and the birds of the air have nests; but the Son of Man has nowhere to lay his head." [59]And he said to another, "Follow me." But he said, "Lord, permit me to go first and bury my father." [60]But he said to him, "Leave the dead to bury their own dead; but as for you, go and proclaim the kingdom of God." [61]Another said, "I will follow you, Lord; but first let me say farewell to those in my house." [62]But Jesus said to him, "No one who ⌜puts his hand to the plow and looks back⌝ is fit for the kingdom of God."

a. Warning about Alienation from the World (9:57–58)

The first incident involves a volunteer who commits to follow Jesus wherever he may go. Nothing is told about this man or how he came to this decision. Since his declaration is so open-ended, Jesus responds with equal openness about what such a commitment means. In the parallel, Matt. 8:18–19, the man offers to be Jesus' student and follow him, since there the man calls Jesus "teacher" (διδάσκαλε, *didaskale*). But, of course, Jesus wants more than a student. Students of Judaism lived with their teachers in order to learn the Torah, but what Jesus offers is a more compelling and dangerous course (Plummer 1896: 265; Ellis 1974: 153; Luke 6:40). To follow Jesus means more than sitting at his feet and learning Torah. It is a reori-

9:57

entation of life, involving suffering and perhaps death. If one is to go wherever Jesus goes, one must be ready for the rejection that he experienced (9:51–56; Talbert 1982: 117–19). Jesus is no mere rabbi; his claims challenge commonly held views. Thus the offer to follow him means facing risk and rejection.

The setting of the man's remark is vague. Jesus and his disciples are on the road, engaging in itinerant ministry (9:56–58). Matthew 8:18–19 also contains a general introduction, but with more detail. There Jesus is journeying to the other side of Galilee because of the great crowds. Matthew specifically notes that a scribe comes up to Jesus and makes this statement. The promise to follow Jesus is verbally the same in both Gospels, except that Matthew has the scribe address Jesus as "teacher." Jesus warns the man about what his worthy goal entails. Luke lacks the note about the statement's coming from a scribe because what Jesus says is relevant to anyone. Nolland (1993a: 541) thinks it likely that the remark about the scribe and the address of Jesus as διδάσκαλε are Matthean additions. But Luke could just as easily have generalized the remarks as Matthew could have made them specific. What is clear is that Luke's lack of detail gives a less scholastic, rabbinic feel to the remarks.

9:58 Jesus describes what disciples can expect when he is their example. His situation is worse than that of beasts: foxes and birds have places to stay, but the Son of Man has no home. Bultmann (1963: 28 n. 3) argues that the Son-of-Man reference is generic and applies to people in general, but this contradicts the conception of Scripture that God loves and cares for people more than he does other creatures.[2] Most people have homes, so the reference must be to Jesus (Liefeld 1984: 935; Marshall 1978: 410). "Homelessness" has been Jesus' fate from his birth (Hengel, *TDNT* 9:55). A disciple of Jesus must realize that following him means living as a stranger in the world, because a choice for Jesus is a choice rejected by many in the world. Many will not follow Jesus and will reject his disciples. To be a disciple takes resolve (Talbert 1982: 118).

Danker (1988: 210) provides proverbial or conceptual parallels to Jesus' saying. Plutarch (*Lives of Tiberius and Gaius Gracchus* 9.5 [828]) mentions the hardship of being a soldier: "The wild beasts roam over Italy and each one has its own hole or lair, but those who fight and die for Italy have only the light and the air as their portion" (attributed to Tiberius Gracchus). Sirach 36:31 (NRSV numbering) refers to the hard position of a wanderer, a "street person," in a pe-

---

2. Colpe, *TDNT* 8:432–33, argues that the reference is to "a man such as Jesus." But in 12:22–34, Jesus teaches that God cares for the birds. Jesus also argues, however, that God cares for people, who are "greater" than the birds. The remark is not generic.

jorative manner: "For who will trust a nimble robber / that skips from city to city? / So who will trust a man that has no nest, / but lodges wherever night overtakes him?" These parallels show that Manson (1949: 72) is wrong to reject the proverbial character of Jesus' saying, but he is right to note that the saying does not apply proverbially to all people as generic "Son of Man." The proverb applies primarily to Jesus and then to those who follow in his steps. What is true of the suffering Son of Man is true of his disciples. To live "rejected" and "homeless" means to trust God and know that one's home is with him. There is a deep note of pathos in Jesus' remark. The disciple must realize that the choice to follow Jesus is not an easy one. Matthew 8:20 reproduces Jesus' saying word for word.[3]

b. Warning That Proclamation Comes First (9:59–60)

Jesus asks a second man to follow him.[4] Unlike Levi (Luke 5:28), **9:59** who when called immediately left all, this man comes up with a reason not to follow, at least initially: he wants to take time to bury his father. The request seems reasonable, as this responsibility was one of the most important a family member could perform (Tob. 4:3–4; 12:12). Jesus' teaching often has a surprising twist to portray emphatically what God desires. The twist in this passage causes the reader to reflect on Jesus' reply.

The man's reaction seems normal. Proper burial was a major concern in ancient culture.[5] That cultic purity was regarded as less important than burying the dead shows that burying the dead was a Jewish ethical priority (Ellis 1974: 153; Ernst 1977: 321; Talbert 1982: 118).[6] The language of the request follows 1 Kings 19:19–21,

---

3. The Gospel of Thomas 86 also has a parallel, but with Gnostic overtones, since it speaks of laying one's head down and of rest; Fitzmyer 1981: 835.

4. Plummer 1896: 266 argues correctly that efforts to identify this man as Philip or Thomas are speculative and cannot be confirmed, though the identification dates back to Clement of Alexandria, *Stromata* 3.4.522.

5. On Jewish "works of love" and for the key ancient texts, see Egelkraut 1976: 139 nn. 3, 5; SB 1:487–88; 4:578–92; Hengel 1981: 8–10 and n. 21. Quick burials are mentioned in Acts 5:5–6, 10; John 11:1, 14, 17. On Jewish burial customs, see the exegesis of Luke 7:12. The OT notes periods that might demand that burial not take place, e.g., the time of exile (Jer. 16:5–7; Ernst 1977: 321).

6. Lev. 21:1–3 shows that even the priests had such obligations if a close relative was involved, but the high priest was exempt in all cases (Lev. 21:11). As acts of mercy or works of love, such action was considered to have priority over normally important religious activity; see also Mic. 6:8; Tob. 1:17–18; 2:3–9; 4:3–4; 6:15; 12:12–14; 14:11–13; *m. Peʾa* 1.1; *m. Ber.* 3.1; *b. Ber.* 18a (some of these texts even prohibit study of the Torah during mourning!). Only Nazirites were excepted from this requirement (Num. 6:6–8). In the Mishnah, *m. Ber.* 3.1 reads, "He who is confronted by a dead relative is free from reciting the *Shemaʿ*, from the Eighteen Benedictions [*Shemoneh Esreh*, the prayer of Israel], and from all the commandments stated in Torah."

where Elisha asked Elijah for permission to kiss his parents good-bye (Schweizer 1984: 171; cf. Luke 9:61–62). Sirach 38:16 expresses the sentiment of this would-be disciple: "My child, let your tears fall for the dead. . . . / Lay out the body with due ceremony, / and do not neglect the burial." So in refusing this request, Jesus describes a demand that is greater than this important familial responsibility, that is seemingly rooted in the commandment to honor one's parents. In fact, the remark may point to Jesus seeing himself as bringing in the new era. The ability to set priorities that go beyond the Ten Commandments may suggest the presence of messianic authority (Witherington 1990: 139–40). The new Moses has come. Following Jesus is top priority.

Is the remark as harsh as it seems, or is the father already dead and awaiting burial? Arndt (1956: 277) argues that the man is asking to wait until his father has passed away—whenever that may be. If this is the request, then discipleship is delayed indefinitely and the rebuke seems more reasonable. Adherents of this view note that ἀκολούθει (akolouthei, follow) is a present imperative that means "be my follower." They also argue that it is unlikely that a man with a dead father awaiting burial would be out traveling about town. Those who prepared a body for a funeral were unclean for a week and therefore would not be out in public, except for the funeral (so Luke 7:12; Num. 19:11). If this view is correct, then the son wants to postpone devoting himself to Jesus until basic familial duties are behind him, putting commitment to family ahead of service to the kingdom. Jesus' response shows that his call has priority.

However, Liefeld (1984: 935) notes that the parallel Luke 14:25–27 makes a similar point with hyperbolic language. More important, the request is parallel to 9:61–62, where an immediate request is in view. Plummer (1896: 266) also seems to reject Arndt's explanation, though he allows that perhaps the father is very ill. Rejecting this "down the road" option regards the effort to press the present imperative as unlikely and argues more correctly that Jesus' reply about burial becomes unnecessary if a later burial were in view. The demand appears much too urgent for this view (correctly Hengel 1981: 6).

Matthew 8:21, leaving out that Jesus initiated the discussion, offers only the would-be disciple's request. The request is similarly phrased, except for word order, an infinitive in Matthew (ἀπελθεῖν, apelthein, to go out) that is rendered as a participle in Luke (ἀπελθόντι, apelthonti, going out), and Matthew's extra καί (kai, and).

9:60 Jesus' reply involves a pun that is not so much a logical answer as it is a rhetorical response. The reply is designed by its stark character to show the extent of commitment that discipleship requires (Tannehill 1975: 162–64). Instead of allowing the disciple to postpone following Jesus until he has fulfilled a sacred family duty, Jesus tells him to leave the dead to bury the dead. There is OT precedent for neglecting funeral customs, but only in the "antisocial" behavior of prophets who revealed the presence of God's judgment (Ezek. 24:15–24; Jer. 16:1–9; Hengel 1981: 11–12). The unusual call signals an important period of time in the divine calendar.

Some take this obviously impossible task as a literal command to abandon the parent, but this fails to develop the principle intended in the rhetoric (see Klemm 1969–70 for a history of the passage's interpretation). Fitzmyer (1981: 836) notes four options: (1) to deny that the remark goes back to Jesus; (2) to take it as a rhetorical overstatement; (3) to see the first use of νεκρούς (nekrous, dead) as a reference to pallbearers through appeal to (mistranslated) Aramaic;[7] or (4) to see here a reference to the spiritually dead.

The problem of literalism versus rhetoric is raised because the dead can bury no one. The contrast with reality reveals the saying's rhetorical character and argues against a strictly literal interpretation. The sense is either that the first use of νεκρούς has a special meaning (Plummer 1896: 267; Creed 1930: 142–43; Fitzmyer 1981: 836; Marshall 1978: 411; Ellis 1974: 153–54) or that the remark is purely rhetorical, meaning "let it take care of itself" or "do not be excessively preoccupied with less important concerns" (Nolland 1993a: 543, who rejects any reference to the "spiritually dead"). The first νεκρούς probably refers to those who do not have kingdom commitments and are therefore spiritually "dead" or, better, separated from God and so not involved in the mission (Eph. 2:1–3; for references in Judaism, see SB 1:489; 2:165; Hengel 1981: 7–8 notes an array of parallels; against this is Schneider 1977a: 232). The point is that those without kingdom priorities can take care of such matters. The saying is so harsh and out of character for a Jewish setting that it is widely accepted as authentic (Fitzmyer 1981: 835).

In essence, a "best" excuse—in fact a reasonable one—has been submitted for postponing discipleship. Nevertheless, Jesus rejects the excuse. As Tannehill (1975: 163) says, the words of the saying "show the kind of demand that Jesus makes and so indirectly illumine many other situations in which duties and desires may conflict with the demands of discipleship." Nothing is to block the pursuit of discipleship and nothing is to postpone its start. The kingdom's coming requires such priorities (Egelkraut 1976: 140). Old ways of doing things have passed and new priorities are required. As Danker

---

7. Fitzmyer notes that there is no evidence for this third view, which goes back to Perles 1919–20; see also Black 1967: 207–8. SB 1:489 rejects the suggestion.

(1988: 210) notes, "Many a would-be follower of Jesus has pleaded the requirements of social obligation or prior business demands as an excuse for not meeting the imperative of obedience." Jesus rejects such excuses.

In contrast to de-emphasizing familial responsibility comes the priority of doing the disciples' task: preaching the kingdom. The disciple is to explain what God is doing.[8] This part of the verse is unique to Luke; Matt. 8:22 concludes the unit after a call to follow Jesus and to let the dead bury the dead. The Matthean bury-the-dead unit verbally matches Luke. Luke has utilized some additional material here since the verb for "proclaim" (διαγγέλλω, diangellō) is not the usual one for Luke (he prefers εὐαγγελίζω, euangelizō [Luke 4:43; 8:1; 16:16; Acts 8:12, plus twenty-one more times in Luke–Acts], or κηρύσσω, kēryssō [Luke 9:2; Acts 28:31, plus fifteen more times in Luke–Acts]; for the options, see Schürmann 1994: 42 n. 69). The concept parallels Jesus' commission (Luke 4:43) and anticipates the Great Commission (24:44–47).

c. Warning That Commitment Is First and Must Be Constant (9:61–62)

9:61 The pericope closes with a third figure, who also volunteers to follow Jesus. He also wishes to introduce a proviso before starting. He asks for the right to tell his family that he is leaving and to bid them farewell (ἀποτάσσω, apotassō; BAGD 100 §1; BAA 202 §1; Luke 14:33; Acts 18:18, 21). Only Luke includes this third scene.

Again the request seems reasonable. It parallels Elisha's response to Elijah's call (1 Kings 19:19–21), a passage that also had some conceptual parallelism to the previous request to Jesus (Marshall 1978: 412). Elisha, an OT "disciple," asked to kiss his mother and father before joining the prophet, and Elijah granted that request. As in other Lucan texts, the story of Elijah supplies the background (1:15–17; 4:25–27; 7:27; 9:30–32, 54; Leaney 1958: 173–74; on Elijah in Jewish tradition, see Wiener 1978; in Luke, see R. Brown 1971 and Brodie 1987). It may well be that the nature of Jesus' response is purposefully contrastive to this OT text, suggesting a greater urgency in the present situation because this is a greater era in God's program (Danker 1988: 211; see the OT parallels noted in the exegesis of 9:60). As with the first man, this volunteer indicates that he will follow Jesus. And Jesus similarly replies in terms of what that

---

8. The term διάγγελλε is a present imperative. On its meaning "to proclaim far and wide," see BAGD 182; BAA 364; elsewhere only in Acts 21:26 and Rom. 9:17. Schniewind, TDNT 1:68, speaks of proclaiming God's eschatological lordship, that is, his sovereignty over humans in rule and in time.

volunteer's commitment really requires. One cannot follow after two things at once; following Jesus means making him the compass of one's life. It is easy to miss what discipleship demands. Jesus makes sure this commitment is clear (Rengstorf, *TDNT* 4:450).

To criticize these would-be disciples robs the story of its focus (but so Hendriksen 1978: 559–63, who risks overpsychologizing the text). Jesus' demands are new and radical, and these men could hardly have known that their requests would be countered so directly and emphatically. The point is not so much to rebuke the would-be disciple for having deficient desire as to warn about what association with Jesus involves and to point out with rhetorical clarity the newness of times that Jesus brings. C. A. Evans (in Evans and Sanders 1993: 80) suggests that the warning prepares the way for later rejections by Jesus (16:15; 18:9–14 [of the Pharisees]; 18:18–30 [of a rich ruler]).

Jesus' reply is really a warning, since he sees a danger in the request. **9:62** One may follow him initially, only to long for the old life later. Such looking back does not promote spiritual health. If one is going to follow Jesus, one needs to keep following him and not look back. Jesus' reply here is not so much a refusal as it is a warning (Arndt 1956: 278). The nation of Israel looked back after the exodus (Exod. 16:3). Lot's wife looked back after departing Sodom (Gen. 19:26). Once we commit to Jesus, we are to hold fast our confession. If one confesses Jesus, only to renounce permanently that confession later, then the apparent confession is false, and one's position is as perilous after the "departure" as before the profession (1 Cor. 15:2; Col. 1:21–23; Matt. 7:21–23; 22:11–13; Luke 13:25–27; cf. the warnings in Hebrews). Perhaps in the desire to bid farewell, the heart never leaves the attachment to old values and the old way of life. It is this lack of a clean break that Jesus warns against here. To follow Jesus means to not look back to the way life was before one came to follow him. Good service requires undivided loyalty (Ellis 1974: 154). Discipleship is not an emotional decision of one moment, but a walk of life (K. Schmidt, *TDNT* 1:588).

The metaphor is proverbial. It refers to plowing with the eyes ahead so that one plows a straight furrow. This is especially necessary in Palestine, where a backward look might easily knock one off course in the rocky soil. While one hand guides the plow and the other goads the oxen, the eyes should look ahead to where the farmer is directing the plow (Jeremias 1963a: 195). This idea has many parallels in ancient literature. In a picture of total dedication to a task, Hesiod (*Works and Days* 442–43) speaks of "one who will attend his work and drive a straight furrow and is past the age of gaping after his fellows, but will keep his mind on his work" (Marshall 1978: 412; Danker 1988: 211; SB 2:165; *m. ʾAbot* 3.8; Sir. 38:25; Phil. 3:13–14; Heb. 12:1–3; Klostermann 1929: 133 notes that the sometimes-cited reference in Pliny's *Natural History* 18.179 has a completely different meaning). A person who tries to follow Jesus but looks back during the journey is not suitable for the kingdom.

Εὔθετος (*euthetos*) refers to being "suitable" or "usable" (BAGD 320; BAA 648; Luke 14:35 [of unusable salt]; Heb. 6:7). Double-minded discipleship is worthless. Given this term, "getting saved" is not the only point. Rather, the issue is how one serves and follows Jesus effectively. These categories come after an initial commitment, though the two processes are closely related.

Schweizer (1984: 172) observes that Jesus restores one who fails later (Peter). The point is that, though the demand is present, absolute, and incumbent on those who desire to please him, God is gracious to those who fall and desire to repent. One who falls should turn and continue to rely on God's goodness (Luke 22:32). By contrast, one who turns back—renouncing one's commitment without reservation or regret, as Judas would—is unfit for the kingdom. This is probably the type of situation in view here. For Jesus, discipleship is serious business and an all-consuming priority in terms of the constancy of one's allegiance. As Karris (1977: 130) says, "Following him is not a task which is added to others like working a second job. . . . It is everything. It is a solemn commitment which forces the disciples-to-be to reorder all their other duties." Family and home are prioritized in relation to one's relationship to God (9:23–26; 14:26–27, 33; Tannehill 1986: 231). Jesus gives such a call to these three men. The new era he brings and what he represents demand total commitment.

Summary   Jesus is a realist. So in 9:57–62, when people express the desire to follow him, he wants to make it clear what following him will entail. Whether Jesus calls the person or the person volunteers, one must know that following him involves following one whom the world does not embrace. Prospective disciples must recognize that even sacred family duties are secondary to one's commitment to God. They must know that to ally oneself to Jesus means a break with one's past and its old ties. The highest priority is God's kingdom. Everything else pales in comparison. Such a commitment is what Jesus desires. Such commitment is suitable for the kingdom and renders one useful in its service. Though the road is not easy, the way down the road is clear. The disciple is to go forward and travel a straight path. One must look ahead with a singular dedication to the task and not look back. The task's greatness requires that those who follow Jesus have a greater standard of dedication than did the great OT disciples, like Elisha. A great call demands a total response. Luke wants the reader to see this commitment. Following Jesus is a hard walk, but it is worth it, because it is a walk with God.

Additional Note

9:62. A few texts ($\mathfrak{P}^{45}$, D, some Itala) reverse the order, so that the farmer first looks back and then plows, but such a reading does not make good sense. With slight variation, early Alexandrian manuscripts and Byzantine texts support the order printed in the UBS–NA text ($\mathfrak{P}^{75}$, B, ℵ, C, Byz, some Itala, Syriac; Metzger 1975: 149).

3. The Mission of the Seventy-two (10:1–24)

This large, significant unit describes the second mission of Jesus' disciples. Rather than sending out only the Twelve (Luke 9:1–6), Jesus sends out a larger group. The passage is composed of several subunits: instruction about the mission proper (10:1–12), woes on unresponsive cities (10:13–16), the report and return of the disciples (10:17–20), and Jesus' thanksgiving and blessing for them (10:21–24). The unit's size reveals its importance.

Jesus has journeyed through a Samaritan village and faced rejection. He has explained that discipleship entails some rejection and involves separation from old priorities and intimate ties. Now he will send out the disciples, not with a mood of gloom, but of excitement, authority, revelation, and opportunity (Tannehill 1986: 232). These representatives carry God's message of peace (Luke 10:6; 1:79; Eph. 2:11–22). They proclaim the kingdom's approach and carry the kingdom's authority, in that rejection of them is rejection of God's message for humankind (Luke 10:9, 16). Their ministry is like that of John the Baptist (3:4), the earlier mission (9:52), and the ministry of Acts (Tannehill 1986: 233–36).[1] These disciples return excited about the work God has done through them, yet Jesus reminds them that the greatest blessing is not their power but their position. They are securely related to God. For this blessing Christ offers thanksgiving to God. God's plan allows the disciples to know him as a part of his sovereign work through Jesus. Jesus also reminds the disciples that the prophets and kings who preceded them longed for this experience. Thus, the unit provides a positive note in contrast to the two previous somber accounts. The long-awaited time of initiated kingdom fulfillment has drawn near. The power of God to deliver is present in Jesus.

Sources and Historicity

The source discussion is complex and may be characterized as confused. Matthew 9:37–38 and 10:7–16 have many elements that parallel what is

---

1. The Acts parallels include the messengers shaking dust from their feet (13:51) and healings (3:6; 4:10).

found in Luke 10:1–12 (Aland 1985: §177). Many contend that Luke got much of his material from Q, the source he shared with Matthew (Marshall 1978: 413 [with influence from Mark 6:7–13]; Fitzmyer 1985: 842; Schneider 1977a: 235; Ernst 1977: 329; Egelkraut 1976: 142, esp. n. 4). Most who compare Matthew's and Luke's versions of Q argue that Luke's presentation is the more original in keeping Q's structure (Nolland 1993a: 547; Meier 1994: 485 n. 155; Schulz 1972: 404). Matthean prioritists simply appeal to Matthew as the source, but Matthew's mission involves the Twelve (Matt. 10:5), not the larger mission, which leads others to question whether there was a second, larger mission. In addition, some note the parallelism to Mark 6:7–13 for a mission for the Twelve. The options are that there were two missions, one mission (Matt. 10 + Mark 6:7–13) that Luke distinguished, or no mission at all.[2] A key factor in deciding this issue is that Jesus' words in Luke 22:35 (special Lucan material), when he is with the Twelve on the last night, allude to 10:4. This suggests that the Twelve served in addition to the larger group. At a minimum, there is one mission, but the detail of 22:35 may indicate that Luke knows about two missions. Nonetheless, many see the larger mission as Luke's creation (Creed 1930: 143–44, in light of sources; Luce 1933: 198).[3]

Plummer (1896: 269) and Arndt (1956: 279) argue for a second mission and place it sometime just after the events of John 7.[4] In addition, Plummer argues that the event reflects Luke's universalism since there is no restriction to go only to Israel. Whether this is a correct motive is hard to establish (see the first additional note on 10:1). In fact, Plummer (p. 270) notes that efforts to argue for either a Lucan creation or a doublet fail to honor Luke's clear distinction of the two commissions. Manson (1949: 74) suggests that there is no reason to doubt two missions and argues that Luke has used material from Q and from a special Lucan source (22:35). Marshall (1978: 413) opts for two missions and notes that Luke avoids doublets, while suggesting that the charge for this journey may have come from the source for the earlier journey. Since the missionary charges are summaries in both Luke 9:1–6 and 10:1–12, they do not need to match or overlap exactly in detail. Thus, the attempt to discredit the tradition of a mission on the basis of differences in the mission charges is misguided (but so Funk and Hoover

2. Egelkraut 1976: 142, esp. n. 3, mentions the options. Schweizer 1984: 174 argues that Luke likes to split accounts from Q and Mark into distinct events (e.g., the Olivet Discourse in 17:22–37 ≈ 21:6–36 and Jesus' condemnation of the religious leadership in 11:37–54 ≈ 20:45–47). Fitzmyer 1985: 843, citing 22:35, argues that Luke created the mission in the split. For detailed discussion of texts where Mark and Q overlap, see Laufen 1980.

3. Bultmann 1963: 145 sees much of this material as church formulated and as regulations for the church. Beare 1970 rejects the mission and the discourse's historicity, as does the Jesus Seminar (Funk and Hoover 1993: 317–23, esp. 320).

4. Morosco 1979 sees a discourse tradition but does not make clear whether it was tied to a formal commission or whether this material belongs to such a setting.

1993: 318). Nothing in these differences represents contradictions in the tone of the missions.

Such an extrareligious mission is not inherently problematic. That the instructions to both groups should be basically the same is not surprising, since efforts by the same person to organize different groups for a similar task often share similar elements. That Jesus often sends disciples ahead of him is suggested by 9:51–56. Luke 10:1–24 may be seen then as another confirmation of multiple missions. It is also likely that Luke used a distinct source about this mission, or that he knew that the instructions given to the larger group paralleled the smaller mission. Thus, he drew on the earlier instructions for this account since they could serve as instructions for this later mission also (Plummer 1896: 270; Liefeld 1984: 937). Either explanation is better than suggesting a Lucan creation or a pure doublet.

The Jesus Seminar (Funk and Hoover 1993: 317–20) rates the sayings of this first subunit as follows: 10:7a, 8 is probably like what Jesus said (in pink type); 10:4–6, 7c is probably not authentic (gray type); and 10:2–3, 7b, 9–12 is not authentic (black type). The seminar rejects 10:2–3 because it assumes a mission for Jesus and attributes judgment to him. But the precedent of John the Baptist, the rise of opposition to Jesus, and the multiple levels of attestation for a mission by disciples all speak for authenticity (Nolland 1993a: 548). Luke 10:4–6 is questioned, despite the background of Jewish practice (the peace greeting) and a parallel in the Gospel of Thomas 14.4, because the parallel is absent in Matthew. This shows the seminar's tendency to rely heavily on multiple attestation and give the singly attested tradition no benefit of the doubt. Luke 10:7b–c is rejected because it reflects "later missionary activity," a decision based on the belief that Jesus had no mission. The issue of laborers being worth their wages is one of the few sayings by Jesus to resurface in the NT Letters, a point that argues for its roots in Jesus (1 Cor. 9:14; 1 Tim. 5:18). Luke 10:9–12 is rejected because of its notes of judgment and its clear assertion about the kingdom— reasons similar to the seminar's rationale for rejecting 10:2–3. One of the best-attested aspects of Jesus' preaching is his kingdom proclamation (e.g., Mark 1:15; Luke 11:20). If Jesus sent a mission out with a message, the kingdom and the consequences of not responding would be a part of the calling (for roots in Jesus, see Nolland 1993a: 554, who argues for some Lucan reframing in 10:10–11).

The material in Luke 10:13–15 has parallels in Matt. 11:20–24. In fact, they are almost exact verbally (Aland 1985: §178). Both Matthew and Luke have general introductions to the unit, though Matthew associates it with the questions about John the Baptist, events that Luke has in 7:18–35. That association may exist because of the similarity in and linkage between John's and the disciples' missions. Since both Luke 7 and Matt. 11 may be thematically arranged, the event's exact locale is hard to place (see the introduction to Luke 7:18–35). Luke links the account directly to the disciples' second mission and appears to warn them that their mission will not be a popular success. Luke also indicates the extent of Jesus' concern for the cities' rejection. However, Jesus' woes are directed at Galilean cities, so it is clear that the remark is not a part of the previous mission to Samaria (9:51–56). Jesus recalls that nothing changes about how his ministry is received. Wherever it goes, even when it comes through the disciples, it meets with rejection (but see Fitzmyer 1985: 850–52, who sees a Lucan shift of the Matthean context). The unit is authentic, since Chorazin does not appear elsewhere in the Synoptic tradition as a location of miracles. Thus the argument that the unit is a creation of the early church has no basis (correctly Nolland 1993a: 548 and Mussner 1968: 18–22 ["if there is one pre-Easter logion, then it is this lament of Jesus over these three cities of his native Galilee"]; incorrectly the Jesus Seminar in Funk and Hoover 1993: 320).

An independent situation is possible, especially when one notes that 10:16 is almost a proverbial expression and is expressed uniquely.[5] The woes are like the response to rejection in 9:5, so a repetition of such a remark is not improbable. However, one cannot rule out the possibility that Luke arranged the material thematically, so that the second Galilean mission is placed after the first mission and near the Samaritan mission. The only temporal note, Luke 10:1, indicates that the event occurred after the discussion on discipleship, which Matthew had in Matt. 8:18–22.

Of course, as just noted, another—not improbable—way to take the Matt. 11 parallels is to see them as reflecting the mission's specific placement earlier in Jesus' ministry, as largely parallel to Luke's event here. The Galilean locale of the cities of the woes might suggest this conclusion. This is close to the position of Fitzmyer (1985: 850–52), but lacks his view that creative elements are present. If Luke did this, it was for topical reasons: to contrast the success of the mission with the previous somber accounts of failure. If one sees the connection this way, then Luke would have saved the mission's discussion until the period when he considers what Jesus did as he faced Jerusalem. The Lucan event would then belong to the early part of this "toward Jerusalem" period and would have followed the initial mission of the Twelve, a possible connection, since the Matthean version of their earlier mission came in Matt. 10:7–16 (= Luke 9:1–6). In this way, Luke 10:13–15 may match Matt. 11:20–24. Many recognize the possibility that Luke had additional source material.[6]

The group's return and their report in Luke 10:17–20 is, of course, unique since there is no Synoptic parallel to this commissioning of the sev-

---

5. Luke's wording is similar to Matt. 10:40 and John 13:20 conceptually, but not verbally; Aland 1985: §179.

6. Egelkraut 1976: 143 sees this as possible, especially for the unparalleled 10:17–20, as well as for 10:21–24.

enty-two (Aland 1985: §180).[7] The disciples' excitement about the power of Jesus' name and Jesus' response about the blessedness of being saved are natural in the setting, and there is no reason to reject their historicity (so also Nolland 1993a: 561, but with some uncertainty on 10:19). Even the Jesus Seminar prints 10:18 in pink type, affirming its basic roots in Jesus (Funk and Hoover 1993: 321). The reason that some dispute 10:19 is that it has apocalyptic overtones as well as a conceptual parallel in the late Mark 16:18. But the association of snakes and scorpions has OT and Jewish roots as a picture of divine protection in the exodus or in salvation (Deut. 8:15; Sir. 39:30; Ps. 91:13), so the metaphor is accessible to Jesus. As to whether 10:17–20 was originally a single unit in the tradition, many argue that Luke put together two pieces: 10:17, 20 with 10:18–19 (Nolland 1993a: 565; Schürmann 1994: 96). Three concepts (rejoicing, demon possession, and name) tie together 10:17 and 10:20, making this explanation possible. But word links need not appear in successive sentences, so an original unit of 10:17–20 is not precluded by this point.

Luke 10:21–24 is paralleled in Matt. 11:25–27 and 13:16–17 (Aland 1985: §181).[8] Such general remarks of encouragement need repeating in a mission under constant pressure. They are not truly doublets, despite what Fitzmyer (1985: 865–66) suggests. The remarks in Luke 10:21–22 sound like material from John 10:15 and 17:2. This Johannine tie suggests that some Gospel sayings are similar because they were repeated—an idea stubbornly out of vogue for many, but natural for an itinerant ministry![9] In addition, the imagery of Luke 10:21–22 points to concepts like the Abba tradition, whose historicity is not questioned (Nolland 1993a: 570). Jesus circumspectly expresses his authority as derived from the Father, another

---

7. Fitzmyer 1985: 859 sees the material as a Lucan creation, but coming from an authentic saying reflected in a variant form in 10:18. Such a distinction is not necessary. Marshall 1978: 427–28 notes the options: a Lucan creation, the Q source, or a special Lucan source. He opts for Q and notes that the subunit's historicity is tied to how one views the mission's historicity as a whole.

8. Fitzmyer 1985: 865 sees Luke joining this material together in a new context, as does Marshall 1978: 431–32, who notes the various options and argues that both sayings go back to Jesus.

9. This passage is the first of several in Luke 9–19 where sayings material that is split up in Matthew has a single location in Luke, a situation that has led to either/or thinking about these sayings. Most see Luke bringing such sayings together in one setting, while Matthew has the original, simpler form of Q. But such judgments are hasty for three reasons: (1) Q may well have existed in multiple forms (even holders of the Q hypothesis recognize this as a real possibility); (2) Luke had access to special source material with sayings in it, which increases the combinations; and (3) an itinerant ministry has repetition, which could lead to the use of similar material in distinct settings. These factors raise the probability that additional material is the reason for such differences. One need not choose between Luke and Matthew in such cases. In addition, the argument for this material being a unit is usually that Luke is closer to Q; if this is correct, it runs counter to the normal situation noted above, which is a possible argument against Lucan compilation.

common theme for him (for discussion of options, see Kloppenborg 1978: 135–39, who is undecided on historicity).

The Jesus Seminar (Funk and Hoover 1993: 322–23) sees 10:22 as inauthentic (black type) and 10:21, 23–24 as probably inauthentic (gray type). The Christology of 10:22 is too strong for the seminar (but see my comments above for refutation of this approach). The seminar rejects 10:23–24 on the premise that it assumes an arrogant sectarian position that Jesus would not have espoused. This fits the seminar's attempt to argue that Jesus did not preach judgment or call for decision. Such a Jesus is a phantom, not only lacking prophetic quality but giving no reason for opposition to form against him. Meier (1994: 435–39) gives four reasons for the authenticity of 10:23–24: (1) the style is like the Beatitudes (Luke 6:20–23 = Matt. 5:3–12) and Jesus' reply to the emissaries of John the Baptist (Matt. 11:2–6 = Luke 7:18–23); (2) the thrust of the beatitude that Jesus' ministry of miracles points to a special period coheres with his teaching; (3) Jesus' role is subtly stated; and (4) the stress on eyewitnesses is against a created saying from the church, since it would exclude most in the intended audience.

The nature and especially the placement of these subunits are difficult issues to resolve clearly, since many possible combinations exist. Nevertheless, the proclamation ministry extends beyond the Twelve and reflects roots in a real mission sent out by Jesus.[10]

> The form of each subunit should be considered individually (Fitzmyer 1985: 842, 852, 857, 859, 865): Luke 10:1–12 is a missionary charge composed of several instructions and sayings of Jesus;[11] 10:13–15 is a prophetic woe of warning;[12] 10:16 is an

10. Plummer 1896: 271 notes that early church historians attempted to name some of the seventy-two. Eusebius, *Ecclesiastical History* 1.12, mentions Barnabas, Sosthenes, Matthias, Joseph Barsabbas, and Thaddaeus. But the tradition is problematic, since it also includes the Cephas of Gal. 2:11—as distinct from the apostle Peter! Even though some later fathers (beginning with Clement of Alexandria) argue that a different Cephas was in view in Galatians, the Cephas of Galatians must be Peter, since he is called a "pillar." It may be that the fathers wanted to spare Peter the criticism that he received from Paul, since they found it hard to believe that he erred so publicly.

11. Berger 1984: 68, 167, sees both a speech and a mission. Bultmann 1963: 145 places it among legal sayings and church rules, arguing that it was a missionary tract for the church (see the discussion of sources and historicity for rejection of this view).

12. Bultmann 1963: 112 also rejects its historicity since it views Jesus' work as past and speaks of the possible exaltation of Capernaum to heaven. Neither of these reasons has merit. Mission failure certainly did occur in Jesus' ministry—why else did he meet with crucifixion? On the possibility of cities being exalted before God, one need think only of the imagery of the OT prophets, where Israel is exalted above its foes. Berger 1984: 200, 205, speaks of woes of warning. For the woe oracle form, see Amos 6:1–7; Mic. 2:1; Hab. 2:6–7; Zeph. 2:5. Witherington 1990: 166 defends their authenticity, along with Matthew's mention of Chorazin, which is not mentioned outside of these parallel passages.

"I-saying";[13] 10:17–20 is a collection of two "I-sayings" and an exhortation; and 10:21–24 is a note of praise, a revelatory utterance, and a beatitude (Berger 1984: 190 speaks of a saying of blessing). The last subunit has the flavor of wisdom sayings, where God's mind is revealed. The unit as a whole is a discourse, including participation and response.

The outline of Luke 10:1–24 is as follows:

a. The larger mission of the seventy-two (10:1–12)
   i. Setting (10:1)
   ii. Jesus' instructions (10:2–12)
       (1) Call to prayer (10:2)
       (2) Lambs in the midst of wolves (10:3–4)
       (3) Instructions about reception (10:5–9)
       (4) Instructions about rejection (10:10–12)
b. Jesus' woes on the unrepentant cities (10:13–15)
   i. Woe on Chorazin and Bethsaida (10:13–14)
   ii. Woe on Capernaum (10:15)
c. Jesus' messengers (10:16)
d. The messengers' report (10:17–20)
   i. The joy of the disciples at their authority (10:17)
   ii. Jesus' response about the greater honor (10:18–20)
e. Jesus' thanksgiving and blessing (10:21–24)
   i. Thanks to the Father (10:21–22)
   ii. Blessing on the disciples (10:23–24)

Mission is the basic topic of the entire pericope. In 10:1–12, the proclamation ministry includes more than the Twelve; it is not restricted to a special few. Careful preparation for the message's arrival stresses the mission's importance in the face of opportunity. The recognition that more laborers are needed moves ministry beyond even this larger group of disciples. Mission involves risk, rejection, and a humble lifestyle. Needs are supplied from those who respond favorably to the message. The kingdom message is a word of peace. With the disciples' coming, the kingdom comes near. The disciples' message requires a decision about the kingdom, judgment, and one's future before God.

The woes in 10:13–16 show the greatness of the time. The level of judgment is greater for current works. The authority of Jesus' commissioned messengers matches that of Jesus or God.

---

13. Bultmann 1963: 153 rejects the historicity of "I-sayings" because of their connection to the larger unit. This saying is authentic on the basis of the criterion of dissimilarity.

In 10:17–20, the mission's authority is clear. The disciples' work involves the subjection of demons and Satan's fall. Jesus' messengers have authority, but their greatest focus is to be on the security of being known by God.

In 10:21–24, the saved reflect God's sovereign will. The Son's authority comes from the Father. God's revelation is the work of both the Father and the Son. The Father knows the Son, and the Son knows the Father. There is great blessing in experiencing the effects of Jesus' ministry, since kings and prophets longed for these days. Promises of old are now being fulfilled.

Exegesis and Exposition

[1]After this, the Lord appointed ⌜seventy-two⌝ others and sent them ahead of him ⌜by twos⌝ into every city and place where he was about to go. [2]And he said to them, "The harvest is plentiful, but the laborers are few; pray therefore the Lord of the harvest to send out laborers into his harvest. [3]Go! Behold, I send you out as lambs in the midst of wolves. [4]Carry no purse, no bag, no sandals, and salute no one on the road. [5]Whatever house you should enter, first say, 'Peace on this house.' [6]And if there be a son of peace there, your greeting shall rest on him; but if not, it shall return to you. [7]And remain in the same house, eating and drinking what they provide; for a worker is worthy of his wages. Do not go from house to house. [8]And whenever you enter a town and they receive you, eat what is set before you, [9]and heal those who are sick in it, and say to them, 'The kingdom of God is come upon you.' [10]But whenever you enter a town and they do not receive you, go into its streets and say, [11]'Even the dust of your town that clings to our feet we wipe off against you; nevertheless know this, that the kingdom of God is come.' [12]I say to you, it shall be better for Sodom in that day than for this town.

[13]"Woe to you, Chorazin! Woe to you, Bethsaida! For if the mighty works done in you had been done in Tyre and Sidon, they would have repented long ago, sitting in sackcloth and ashes. [14]Nevertheless, it shall be better for Tyre and Sidon than for you in that day. [15]And you, Capernaum, will you be exalted into heaven? You shall be brought down into Hades.

[16]"He who hears you hears me, and he who rejects you rejects me, and he who rejects me rejects him who sent me."

[17]The ⌜seventy-two⌝ returned with joy, saying, "Lord, even the demons are subject to us in your name!" [18]And he said to them, "I saw Satan fall like lightning from heaven. [19]Behold, I ⌜have given⌝ you authority to tread upon serpents and scorpions, and over all the power of the enemy; and nothing shall hurt you. [20]Nevertheless, do not rejoice that the spirits are subject to you, but that your names stand written in the heavens."

[21]In that hour he rejoiced ⌜in the Holy Spirit⌝ and said, "I thank you, Father, Lord of heaven and earth, that you have hidden these things from the wise and the understanding and have revealed them to babies; yes, Father,

for such was pleasing to you. [22]All things have been delivered to me by my Father; and no one knows who the Son is except the Father, or who the Father is except the Son and any one to whom the Son chooses to reveal him." [23]And turning to the disciples he said privately, "Blessed are the eyes that see what you are seeing. [24]For I say to you, many prophets and kings wished to see what you are seeing and did not see, and to hear what you hear and did not hear."

a. The Larger Mission of the Seventy-two (10:1–12)
i. Setting (10:1)

10:1 The introduction is clear. Jesus appoints a number of disciples outside the Twelve to go and prepare different areas for his coming (ἑτέρους [heterous] refers to a group outside the apostolic band).[14] He tells them to travel in pairs, a typical way to travel in the ancient world (Rengstorf, *TDNT* 1:417, 427). This pairing may be to allow the messengers to function as "double witnesses" (cf. Deut. 19:15; Jeremias 1959). The mission follows Jesus' challenge to three would-be disciples (so μετὰ δὲ ταῦτα, *meta de tauta*, after these things). Other than this general temporal note, no other geographic or chronological information is given (Arndt 1956: 280). Much of the verse's wording uses typical Lucan terminology.[15] The disciples' going ahead of Jesus recalls the disciples in Luke 9:52 and John the Baptist in 1:17, 76; and 3:4 (Tannehill 1986: 234).

The major issue in the verse reflects one of the most difficult text-critical problems in Luke, that is, the number of disciples sent. I opt for the originality of the number *seventy-two* and argue that no symbolism is present in the number (see the additional note). What is significant is that Jesus expands the ministry beyond the Twelve. Ministry is not confined to a select few.

ii. Jesus' Instructions (10:2–12)
(1) Call to Prayer (10:2)

10:2 First, the mission is a time of opportunity, but currently there are too few to do the task. Second, the mission's growth will be determined not only by efforts in the field, but also by prayer and God's sovereign

---

14. On the use of ἕτερος (another), see the additional note on Luke 7:19. If 22:35 indicates a connection to this mission, then the seventy-two disciples appointed for this mission served alongside the Twelve, who had already been commissioned (also Nolland 1993a: 550).

15. Egelkraut 1976: 143, esp. n. 1; Miyoshi 1974: 59–61. For example, μετὰ ταῦτα occurs nine times in Luke–Acts, but not at all in Matthew and Mark (unless one counts the textually uncertain Mark 16:12). The use of ὁ κύριος (the Lord) in narrative introductions is Lucan; see the exegesis of Luke 2:11. The verb ἀναδείκνυμι (to appoint) appears only here and in Acts 1:24; Schlier, *TDNT* 2:30.

direction. The time of opportunity is depicted by the plentiful harvest, a figure commonly used of missionary labor. It refers to gathering God's people in the midst of the threat of God's judgment.[16] The reference to a plentiful harvest suggests that, although rejection will follow in Jesus' wake, there still will be much positive response.

The main problem is that there are few to help reap the harvest. Part of the mission's goal then is to expand the number of disciples, so that the number of those who can engage in the missionary task can grow. In other words, if people receive the message, they will help deliver it. Many commentators miss this point when they suggest that Matthew's Galilean setting is more appropriate for the passage. Luke is saying that one of the results of the mission is that more take responsibility for it. Such expansion can fit any time during Jesus' ministry in Palestine.

Jesus shows the disciples that they are to ask God for aid and to rely on his sovereign provision. Laborers are not to be coerced into the kingdom. The message is set out for people, and their response must be given freely (Luke 10:5–6). That is, behind the scenes and alongside the proclamation, the disciples are to beseech God for more laborers. The emphasis on God's sovereignty (which will reappear in 10:21–22) is seen in Jesus' use of the title *Lord of the harvest* (τοῦ κυρίου τοῦ θερισμοῦ, *tou kyriou tou therismou*). The message's expansion is in God's control. He is the one who will "thrust out" laborers.[17]

The passage has an exact verbal parallel in Matt. 9:37–38, a summary text about Jesus' Galilean ministry where he makes this appeal to the disciples.[18] Neither setting is any more appropriate than the other; it fits well in both. In fact, the Lucan setting adds a missionary flavor and context that Matthew's passage does not have. As Plummer (1896: 272) says, "The Twelve [Matthew] and the Seventy [Luke—Plummer sees seventy disciples present] were answers to

16. Note that Luke 10:10–16; John 4:31–38; Rom. 11:16–24; 1 Cor. 3:6–7 use the same image, although the last three texts lack judgment overtones. A similar usage is found at Qumran (1QS 8.5–6; CD 1.7; 1QH 8.4–11) and in Judaism (Odes Sol. 38.17–21; SB 1:720–21). Hauck, *TDNT* 3:133, and Wiefel 1988: 197 note Joel 3:13 [4:13 MT]; Hos. 6:11; Isa. 27:11–12, as OT texts where Israel is seen as wheat among Gentile chaff. For an eschatological use of the imagery that looks at consummation, see Matt. 13:36–43; Rev. 14:15. Nolland 1993a: 550–51 argues for a slightly distinct use from the OT, since the call is to enter the kingdom with less concern about judgment. But the options are clear in Luke 10:8–11.

17. On the term ἐκβάλλω (to thrust out), see BAGD 237 §2 and BAA 478 §2. Against Hendriksen 1978: 572, the term does not mean "force out" here. It is, however, a strong, graphic term that shows that God calls and equips; so Arndt 1956: 281.

18. The passages match except for the reversal of two words, ἐργάτας ἐκβάλῃ (thrust out workers), in Matthew. Gospel of Thomas 73 also has an exact parallel; in Judaism, see *m. ʾAbot* 2.15.

the prayer thus prescribed." But in the Lucan setting, even more workers are to be prayed for, since the task continues.

(2) Lambs in the Midst of Wolves (10:3–4)

10:3 This mission, however, does involve risk. While emphasizing the opportunity and the need to ask God to increase the number of laborers, Jesus explains that the Samaritan situation of Luke 9:51–56 and the discipleship call in 9:57–62 are no accident. Disciples will minister under duress. They will be as vulnerable as lambs before wolves. Examples in Judaism where the lamb represents God's people include "God was proven right in his condemnation of the nations of the earth, / and the devout of God are like innocent lambs among them" (Ps. Sol. 8.23); "Do not neglect us, our God, / lest the Gentiles devour us as if there were no redeemer" (Ps. Sol. 8.30); "Hadrian said to Rabbi Jehoshua: 'There is something great about the sheep [Israel] that can persist among the seventy wolves [the nations].' He replied, 'Great is the shepherd who delivers it and watches over it and destroys them before them' " (*Tanḥuma* [Vilnius-Grodno] *Toledot* 5; SB 1:574).[19] These Jewish texts show the nation of Israel before hostile nations. The image is rooted in Isa. 40:11 and developed in Ezek. 34:11–31. With the image comes the idea that protection comes from the Great Shepherd, God himself. This is why, though the risk is great, survival is possible. Jesus sends them out to dangerous territory, but they are not alone. They are to depend on him.

The NT image lacks the national flavor it had in Judaism, though it still describes God's people. John 10:1–18 develops the idea in full, and it reappears in Heb. 13:20 and 1 Pet. 5:4. Sirach 13:17 is closest to the usage found in Luke. The OT gives the ultimate hope that lamb and wolf can live together (Isa. 11:6; 65:25; Bornkamm, *TDNT* 4:309–11). The use of ἀποστέλλω (*apostellō*, to send out) adds a note of commission to the passage (Marshall 1978: 417). It is by Jesus' authority and as his representatives that they go; they represent heaven itself (Luke 10:16).

Matthew 10:16 is like this saying, with a synonymous term for lambs, πρόβατον (*probaton*; BAGD 703; BAA 1408), where Luke has ἀρήν (*arēn*; BAGD 106; BAA 213), a NT *hapax legomenon*. Matthew follows this saying with an exhortation to be wise as serpents and innocent as doves, but Luke simply has the image without an exhortation. Luke wants to focus on the note of trust.

---

19. Grundmann 1963: 209; Ernst 1977: 332; also 1 Enoch 89.14, 18–20, 55; 90.6–17; Sir. 13:17 ("how can wolf and lamb agree? / just so with sinner and devout" [NJB]); 2 Esdr. [= 4 Ezra] 5:18.

Jesus gives travel instructions. Given the danger and urgency, the **10:4** disciples are to travel light and press on to their goal. Provisions will be a concern, but purse, bag, and sandals are not to be taken, an exhortation that recalls 9:3 (Rengstorf, *TDNT* 1:526; Luke 12:33; 22:35–36). A πήρα (*pēra*) was a traveler's bag or knapsack that often was a part of the ancient itinerant preacher's equipment; it held supplies and indicated independence (Michaelis, *TDNT* 6:119–21). The Cynics were well known for carrying such a bag (BAGD 656; BAA 1321). Jesus' restriction shows that the disciples are to rely on God's aid. Mission must be marked by prayer (10:2) and dependence (10:3–4). The sandal was normal travel wear (Oepke, *TDNT* 5:310–12). People either went barefoot or wore sandals, especially on long journeys in Palestine (9:3). Jesus seems to here forbid taking a backup pair. To lack sandals was to be identified with the poor, if later Jewish attitudes are a guide—in fact, it was considered better to be dead and buried (*b. Šab.* 152a; Schürmann 1994: 64 n. 51). Ministry in Jesus' name should have no hint of ostentation.

The urgency of the task is illustrated in Jesus' command to salute no one on the way (2 Kings 4:29 [Elisha's instruction to Gehazi]; Danker 1988: 213–14; Schweizer 1984: 175).[20] Their task is important; they are not to be distracted. The spirit of the passage is similar to Luke 9:1–6, 61–62. Traveling Essenes also received help from other community members (Josephus, *Jewish War* 2.8.4 §§124–27).

Matthew 10:9–10 has a longer list, mentioning gold, silver, copper, bag, tunics, sandals, and staff. Matthew explains that the laborer is worthy of food, but does not mention a lack of greeting. The sayings are not truly parallel in setting, but such differences merely reflect distinct summaries about mission. Only the mention of the bag overlaps. Luke 22:35 does allude back to this instruction about provisions. At the Last Supper, Jesus changes the instruction in light of his rejection, so that from the time of the cross the disciples are to carry provisions.

(3) Instructions about Reception (10:5–9)

Jesus explains what the disciples are to do when they enter a town: **10:5** they are to seek out a place to stay and enter with a greeting of peace (Windisch, *TDNT* 1:499). The greeting is an offer of goodwill from God. The next verse makes clear that it can be received or rejected (von Rad and Foerster, *TDNT* 2:402, 406, 413). The greeting reflects the Hebrew concept of שָׁלוֹם (*šālôm*, peace, well-being).[21] It really

---

20. Windisch, *TDNT* 1:496–99, gives a description of how involved these greetings could be: hugs, kisses, and news were often exchanged.
21. Gen. 43:23; Judg. 6:23; 19:20; 1 Sam. 25:6; Isa. 52:7; Luke 2:14; 24:36; Acts 10:36; 16:36. Ellis 1974: 156 calls it a benediction more than a greeting.

says, "May God be with you." The disciple represents the presence of God's gracious offer. Such greetings were common in Judaism (*m. ʾAbot* 4.15). By metonymy of container for contents (Marshall 1978: 419), the blessing on the house results in blessing on those in it. Matthew 10:12 is less specific: when you enter a house, "salute" (ἀσπάσασθε, *aspasasthe*) it. If a standard greeting is in view, Matthew is not that different.

10:6 This benediction is no trivial matter. It is the beseeching of God's favor for someone. As such, its benefit depends on the person's response. If one is a "child of peace" (υἱὸς εἰρήνης, *huios eirēnēs*; lit., son of peace), that is, a child of the kingdom who responds to the disciples' offer of peace with reception and hospitality, then God fulfills the promise and resides there.[22] In contrast, Nabal was called a "son of folly" (1 Sam. 25:25) for attacking God's messengers. In Isa. 59:1–15, the prophet condemned Israel for not knowing the way to peace (Danker 1988: 214). Plummer (1896: 273–74) notes that negative phrases abound.[23] If the greeting is refused, then the benefit is lost.[24]

The disciples' mission is likewise no trivial matter. Blessing or lack of it lies in their message. The peace offered is so real that it can be said to rest on a house or return to the one who offers blessing (Schweizer 1984: 175)! The offer is not merely present for a moment; it resides with the person into the future (Marshall 1978: 420).[25]

Matthew 10:13 is conceptually similar: the disciple's peace comes on a worthy house; for an unworthy house, the peace returns to the disciple. Power and authority exist in Jesus' directly commissioned messengers, since they convey the message of God's peace.

10:7 Jesus next notes the disciples' conduct and provisions: they are to stay in one house and accept whatever is provided for them. The expression about workers being worthy of their wages is common in the NT (Matt. 10:10; 1 Tim. 5:18 [similar to Luke]; 1 Cor. 9:14;

---

22. See Matthew's synonymous phrase *child of the kingdom* (Matt. 13:38). *Child of peace* focuses on what one has, while *child of the kingdom* describes where one resides. Danker 1960–61; Klassen 1980–81. SB 2:166 notes parallel Semitic phrases like *child of power, child of knowledge, child of Haggadah*, and *child of the future world*.

23. So *child of Gehenna* (Matt. 23:15), *child of destruction* (John 17:12), *children of disobedience* (Eph. 5:6), *child of death* (2 Sam. 12:5 LXX), *children of wrath* (Eph. 2:3). Schweizer, *TDNT* 8:365, calls this use of υἱός a term "of relationship," noting positively *children of light* (Luke 16:8) and *children of resurrection* (20:36).

24. Γέ (indeed) is emphatic, stressing rejection's consequences; see the exegesis of 10:12 for details.

25. Windisch, *TDNT* 1:499 n. 23, argues that the Spirit is meant here, citing Num. 11:25–26; Isa. 11:2; and 1 Pet. 4:14. Although the Spirit is related to the provision of blessing, at this point in Luke–Acts it is too early to see a direct reference, since the abiding Spirit is not bestowed until Acts 2.

Didache 13.2). The spiritual benefit the worker brings with the kingdom message is worthy of support. In this Lucan context, the wage is the hospitality of food and shelter (1 Cor. 9:12 makes a similar point). Luke's saying states positively what the OT and Jewish tradition state negatively (Lev. 19:13; Deut. 24:14–15; Mal. 3:5; Sir. 34:26–27 [NRSV numbering]; Tob. 4:14).[26] In the OT the stress is on the crime of withholding a wage from one who has labored. Payment often was made daily in this cultural setting (Preisker, *TDNT* 4:698). The action contrasts with Cynic philosophers who begged for money (Danker 1988: 214; cf. the instructions of Luke 10:4). In contrast, the provisionless messengers are to have their needs met in homes of peace.

The parallel in Matt. 10:10b is placed in the midst of the mission by the Twelve. Matthew's version is shorter, agreeing verbally with Luke except for τῆς τροφῆς (*tēs trophēs*, food) where Luke has τοῦ μισθοῦ αὐτοῦ (*tou misthou autou*, his wages). The ideas are synonymous; Matthew speaks of provision of food and Luke uses a general term, μισθός, to describe the provision of food and shelter.[27]

Jesus tells the disciples how to respond to acceptance: when a town **10:8** is responsive, the disciples are to receive food graciously. The picture is of open table fellowship, not in the sense of moving from house to house, but simply responding to individual meals. They are to see such actions as God's provision through their hosts' kindness (Matt. 25:34–46). Some suggest that Jesus here frees the disciples to eat both clean and unclean food (Danker 1988: 214–15; Schweizer 1984: 175–76). However, given that they are in Jewish and Samaritan territory, this is less than clear (Liefeld 1984: 938). They simply are to eat what is set before them. Acts 10:9–16 and 1 Cor. 10:27 develop the concept so that unclean food is no longer an issue, but Matthew has no such statement.

Jesus summarizes the message and ministry of the disciples. As later **10:9** sections of the journey material will make clear, acts of healing are signs of the in-breaking of the kingdom (Luke 11:14–23). Given the power to heal, the disciples are to heal those who receive them, as a tangible example of God's blessing coming on those who respond

26. Through tracing the saying's later tradition history, Harvey 1982b: 211 n. 8 argues that its original context is not certain, but the Matthean and Lucan settings are a natural starting point. There is good cultural precedent in the Essene and other communities for such hospitable reception for traveling religious messengers. Rabbis were forbidden to receive direct wages for their teaching, though such provision was allowed; *m.* ʾ*Abot* 1.13; 4.5; Daube 1956: 395–96.

27. Creed 1930: 145 argues that Matt. 10:10 is different from Luke, since it mentions food. This view ignores Matt. 10:11, which speaks of finding a worthy house and staying there.

(10:5–6). Disciples heal and declare the kingdom's nearness (9:60). Such healing recalls Elijah's ministry (1 Kings 17:17–24; Danker 1988: 215).

This key passage in Luke's kingdom theology demonstrates the nearness of the kingdom via Jesus' commissioned followers.[28] John the Baptist had declared the approach of a decisive time, and now that time has come "upon" them (Luke 3:1–18). The perfect tense ἤγγικεν (ēngiken, is come) stresses the lingering effect of its coming. The demonstration of healing power shows that things have changed significantly. The healings signal the start of a new divine age.

Presenting a full lexical study of ἐγγίζω (engizō, to draw near), Perrin notes the difficulty of determining if the sense is "it approaches" or "it has come near so as to arrive."[29] Since Luke's use of ἐπί (epi, upon) is conceptually spatial, arrival seems to be more likely.[30] This meaning also fits the Lucan usage of the term and the verb-preposition combination φθάνω ἐπί (phthanō epi, to come upon) in Dan. 4:24, 28 [Theodotion].

This is not to say that everything associated with the kingdom has come. It has only begun. Luke 24:49 speaks of the coming of the Father's promise, Acts 2 declares the promised Spirit's arrival as a fresh fulfillment of promises made to David, and Acts 3:18–24 shows that some events are still expected in association with God's kingdom program. Jesus' point in Luke 10:9 is that the kingdom program has begun to demonstrate the initial phases of fulfillment. In a confirmation of this inauguration picture, in 10:17–18 Satan is seen falling from heaven as a result of the mission's healing ministry (Ladd 1974a: 256–57). A key characteristic of this phase of the kingdom is its function as "rule"—the exercise of God's saving power upon humans in the face of opposing forces. This is not to say that

28. For the variety of ways the kingdom is said to come, see K. Schmidt, *TDNT* 1:584.

29. Perrin 1963: 64–66; Acts 21:33; Luke 12:33; 22:47; 24:15, 28. Luke 15:1 and 18:40 show that Luke often uses ἐγγίζω to mean "arrive." Fitzmyer 1985: 848–49 argues that when the verb is tied to a time reference it speaks of the approach of an event in the near future.

30. Schweizer 1984: 176 notes that the force is spatial. Marshall 1978: 422 notes that in 11:20, which uses a different term, φθάνω, Luke clearly means "arrived." On the relationship between ἐγγίζω and φθάνω, see Fitzer, *TDNT* 9:89, esp. n. 10. Does 10:9 say the same thing as 11:20? It most likely does. Marshall does not think the spatial argument is as key as the argument of 11:20. For a full defense of the kingdom declared as arrived in this verse, see Bock 1992c. For the debate over the Aramaic behind the sayings and the difficulty of determining it, see Meier 1994: 432–34, 486–87. Luke's ἐφ' ὑμᾶς (upon you) is missing in the Matthean parallel and may represent his explanation of the sayings' force. The present effects of the kingdom are clearly in view (10:23–24; Nolland 1993a: 554). Schürmann 1994: 74 cites 7:28; 16:16; and 17:20–21 as conceptually parallel.

the idea of a realm, which is the OT emphasis, is now lost to the kingdom idea (*pace* Ladd). "Sons of peace" are being discovered in the mission. Again, Acts 3:18–24 looks to a day when Jesus will return and physically demonstrate that rule in accordance with all that the OT prophets promised. Thus, Luke's view of the kingdom is rich and complex, being laid out in clear stages.

The kingdom comes in distinct yet related stages. The central images of Satan's fall (Luke 10:18) and the disciples' healing show that the kingdom is near. Such healing recalls 4:16–18 and anticipates 11:14–23. The kingdom arrives with Jesus, and the reality of its arrival is reflected in these events of power. However, the kingdom's more lasting personal benefits are really inaugurated with the bestowal of the Spirit promised by the Father (Luke 24:49; Acts 2:16–36). Jesus calls this hope of God's rule and the presence of its blessing the "gospel of the kingdom" (4:16–30, 43). Nothing can stop the kingdom from coming. Jesus' ministry is the transition into its arrival. The king is here, and images of his power are present. It is time to respond and enter in.

Matthew 10:7–8 is similar except that the order of healing and kingdom declaration is reversed. Matthew also has more detail, since he speaks of dead people raised, lepers cleansed, and demons cast out—which sounds like parts of Luke 7:22 (Fitzmyer 1985: 848). In addition, Matthew lacks the phrase "upon you" (ἐφ᾽ ὑμᾶς, *eph' hymas*). Again, each is saying similar things, because similar things happened in the two missions.

(4) Instructions about Rejection (10:10–12)

How does rejection contrast with reception? What happens when **10:10** rejection occurs? These concerns develop the Samaritan episode as the disciples learn how to handle rejection (9:51–56). The disciples are to make a public warning, a key sign of which is the absence of any healing ministry (cf. Mark 6:1–6). Only a simple public, prophetic proclamation occurs. It is a sign of God's rejection, as is clear from Luke 10:11. The public character of the declaration is seen in the reference to πλατεῖα (*plateia*), a main, broad, well-traveled street (BAGD 666; BAA 1340; elsewhere in Luke's writings only at Luke 13:26; 14:21; Acts 5:15; Marshall 1978: 423). One could almost speak of the "marketplace" or the "city square." Matthew 10:14 speaks of a parallel action of shaking the dust, but omits reference to the kingdom's coming.

Jesus specifies what the disciples are to do if rejected: they are to an- **10:11** nounce rejection by shaking the dust from their feet and declaring their response to the people (Luke 9:5; Acts 13:51; 18:6; Danker 1988: 215), an action that declares their separation from the city (SB

1:571). They are also to declare the kingdom's nearness. The kingdom is said to come, but this time Luke does not include ἐφ' ὑμᾶς (*eph' hymas*, upon you), as in 10:9. The point is that the people are culpable for their decision in this crucial time, and thus judgment comes "against" them.[31] The kingdom comes regardless of their response. They have missed out because of their refusal. The declaration's seriousness is underlined by the solemn introduction: "Nevertheless know this" (πλὴν τοῦτο γινώσκετε, *plēn touto ginōskete*; Luke 21:31; Mark 13:28–29; Eph. 5:5; Rom. 6:6; Gal. 3:7).

The parallelism with Paul and Barnabas's actions in Acts 13:51 is significant and shows continuity between the precross message and the postcross message—a continuity that strongly equates the two messages. Though the message in Acts has more detail and focuses on Jesus, it is essentially the same: "God's reign is inaugurated in the promised Messiah's coming." For in that reign, God's deliverance comes and his full, future rule is guaranteed. Matthew 10:14 speaks only of the action, not its public declaration, while Mark 6:11 refers to the act as a testimony against the city.

10:12   Jesus closes his instruction with a solemn word of judgment for the city that rejects his disciples. On judgment day, Sodom, the most despicable of ancient Gentile cities and a symbol of unrighteousness, will fare better than the city that rejects the kingdom message (Marshall 1978: 424; SB 1:574; 4:1188; Hendriksen 1978: 576).[32] Besides the physical judgment that Sodom received in Gen. 19, there is God's eschatological judgment, which it must face with cities of all periods (2 Thess. 1:7–10; Rev. 20:12–15). Cities that reject these messengers will have a more severe judgment, because more and greater revelation has come to them, making their sin worse (Leaney 1958: 177; Arndt 1956: 282).[33] The passage assumes God's universal sovereign authority and the cruciality of the kingdom message for humankind. Jesus' direct declaration of judgment (λέγω

---

31. Here ὑμῖν is a good example of a dative of disadvantage: "against you." Marshall 1978: 423 and Grundmann 1963: 210 note that this is true—unless the town repents. The declaration is not decisive, but it indicates where the town is headed. The danger of refusal now is that there will be refusal later. For more on "shaking dust," see Cadbury 1933: 269–71.

32. Gen. 19; Deut. 29:23 [29:22 MT]; Isa. 1:9 (cited in Rom. 9:29); 3:9; 13:19; Lam. 4:6; Ezek. 16:48–50; Amos 4:11; and Zeph. 2:9 show that Sodom was a symbol of the worst possible judgment; the NT texts are 2 Pet. 2:6–7 and Jude 7. Conceptually this Lucan passage is like the Lam. 4 text. So severely were Sodom and Gomorrah viewed in Judaism that some thought they would not even be raised to face final judgment (*m. Sanh.* 10.3; *t. Sanh.* 13.8 [= Neusner 1977–86: 4.240]).

33. On degrees of judgment, see 12:47–48. "That day" is the day of judgment; Matt. 7:22; 2 Tim. 1:12, 18; 4:8; Zech. 12:3–4; Jer. 30:8; Isa. 10:20; Delling, *TDNT* 2:952. It looks to the fearful day-of-the-Lord judgment.

ὑμῖν, *legō hymin*, I say to you) shows his exalted authority in the midst of that message. Matthew 10:15 says virtually the same thing as this text, but in different words since it also mentions Gomorrah. These remarks also set up the specific woes of Luke 10:13–15.

b. Jesus' Woes on the Unrepentant Cities (10:13–15)
i. Woe on Chorazin and Bethsaida (10:13–14)

We now come to the second woe oracle in Luke's Gospel (see the exegesis of 6:24–26). These woes are directed against specific cities in the Galilean region where the response to Jesus' work has been poor. The cities are located near Capernaum, though Chorazin is otherwise unattested.[34]   **10:13**

These cities are compared unfavorably with two unrighteous OT cities, Tyre and Sidon (Isa. 23; Jer. 25:22; 47:4; Ezek. 26:1–28:24; Joel 3:4–8 [4:4–8 MT]; Amos 1:9–10). A form of prophetic reversal is present, for these wicked OT cities will be better off than cities that should have responded to God's kingdom offer (Tannehill 1975: 125, 193 n. 65). The current generation is less responsive than these notoriously wicked generations of past ages. To reject the kingdom of God is the most serious of sins.

These OT cities would have repented and worn sackcloth and ashes, a familiar act of contrition (Josh. 7:6; 1 Kings 20:31–32; 2 Kings 19:1; 1 Chron. 21:16; Neh. 9:1; Esth. 4:2–3; Job 42:6; Ps. 30:11 [30:12 MT]; 35:13; Isa. 58:5; Jer. 6:26; Ezek. 7:18; 27:30; Dan. 9:3; Joel 1:13; Amos 8:10; 1 Macc. 3:47; Stählin, *TDNT* 7:57–60). It denotes self-humiliation as well as grief (C. Schneider, *TDNT* 3:443). One rabbi says it pictures humankind reduced to an animal, because sackcloth had animal-like coarse hair (*b. Ta'an.* 16a; SB 4:84 n. 3, 103–4). Sackcloth was often made of animal hair, usually a goat, and served as a loincloth (Fitzmyer 1985: 854; Michaelis, *TDNT* 4:551). The penitent would sit in sackcloth and throw ashes and dust on themselves.

In effect, the utterance puts these current cities at the bottom of God's list, the objects of his wrath. The saying's force is heavily rhetorical and comparative; in fact, its most important element is its rhetorical mood of shame. It should be read in terms of what it says about the current cities, rather than reflecting on the ancient ones. Luke 7:28 made the same point in reverse: the lowest in the kingdom

---

34. BAGD 883, BAA 1762, and esp. Fitzmyer 1985: 853 discusses the uncertainty about Chorazin's exact location: either two to three miles north of Capernaum at Khirbet Karazeh (R. W. Smith in *ABD* 1:912) or a site on Lake Gennesaret. Wiefel 1988: 198–99 prefers the location near Capernaum, as does Manson 1949: 77. Manson also notes that Bethsaida is on the east side of the Jordan near its entry into the Sea of Galilee, about five miles from Capernaum.

are higher than the greatest prophets of old. Two stylistic elements underline this quality: (1) the sentence is laid out in a contrary-to-fact conditional clause (εἰ, *ei*, plus the past tenses means, "If these works had been done, but they were not"), and (2) the clause about repentance is emphasized by πάλαι (*palai*, long ago) at its head. If mighty works had been performed in these ancient cities, these sinners—unlike the current ones—would have repented long ago. These ancient cities exhibit more sense than the total lack of spiritual discernment of these current cities. What a stinging rebuke!

Matthew 11:21 also has this saying, but places it after the inquiry and discussion about John the Baptist (Luke 7:18–35). The wording is almost exact; the reference to "sitting" is lacking in Matthew and the verb form differs slightly.[35] The Matthean temporal connection to the saying is loose (τότε, *tote*, then). The saying is, however, of a prophetic, proverbial type that could be repeated. Luke's placement of the saying makes it clear that the disciples can expect rejection in their mission despite the power they will demonstrate. For Luke, sin's ability to blind people in the face of God's working is great.

10:14 Luke 10:14 repeats the argument of 10:12: the ancient cities will fare better in the final judgment than Chorazin and Bethsaida. The repetition emphasizes the point. Matthew 11:22 is close verbally to this text: Luke lacks Matthew's "I say to you," and Matthew makes clear that the day is "the day of judgment."

ii. Woe on Capernaum (10:15)

10:15 Jesus now turns to Capernaum. The fate of this Galilean city, which served as the center of Jesus' ministry, is no better than Chorazin and Bethsaida. This town had seen much of Jesus' power (Luke 4:23, 31–37; 7:1–10; John 2:12; 6:24–65; Hendriksen 1978: 578). The question about ascending to heaven expects a negative answer, as the interrogative particle μή (*mē*, shall not?) indicates. The question is rhetorical and thus can be translated as a statement.[36] Heaven is not Capernaum's destination; Hades is.

The judgment's eschatological character is made clear by the reference to Hades (ᾅδης) opposite the reference to heaven (οὐρανός, *ouranos*). The city's ultimate fate is in view, since ᾅδης is used in the LXX to translate the MT's שְׁאוֹל (*šĕʾôl*) (Jeremias, *TDNT* 1:146, 148; Isa. 14:15; Ps. 89:48 [89:49 MT; 88:49 LXX]; Marshall 1978: 425; C. A. Evans 1990: 174; cf. also Ezek. 26:20; 28:1–23; Ps. Sol. 1.5; Isa.

---

35. Matthew has ἐγένοντο, Luke ἐγενήθησαν. Stählin, *TDNT* 7:61–62, makes too much of this difference.

36. On the external evidence favoring reading a question here, see Metzger 1975: 30–31. The meaning is not affected by the choice.

66:24). After the exercise of judgment, Hades is the place where the unrighteous reside (Luke 16:23; Rev. 20:13–14). Thus, another Galilean city faces judgment for its rejection.

Matthew 11:23–24 has a longer version of this saying. The Lucan portion is almost verbally exact to Matthew, with only the definite article τοῦ (*tou*, the) lacking before the reference to Hades. Matthew goes on to say that the judgment will be more tolerable for Sodom, because if these works had been done there it would have repented. It is hard to know why Luke would leave this reference out if it was in his source, since Luke likes pairings of three. Is this an indication of dual tradition for this text? The shortened Lucan form breaks up the trio of referents. Regardless, the shorter, distinct reference to Capernaum makes the description of its demise stronger by isolating it.

c. Jesus' Messengers (10:16)

A final word to the disciples legitimates and underlines their authority. The remark looks back to 10:8–10: to receive the disciples is to listen to them, while refusing to receive them is to reject them. But more than messengers are present. The disciples represent Jesus: the one who listens to them listens to Jesus; the one who rejects them rejects Jesus. The stress of the passage is on rejection, since the second line emphasizes that to reject Jesus is to reject the one who sent him, an implicit reference to God (4:43). The disciples are important because they carry the message of God's kingdom (Rengstorf, *TDNT* 1:413–20; SB 2:167; Marshall 1978: 426).[37]

10:16

This saying has parallels in Matt. 10:40 and John 13:20 (Aland 1985: §179), both of which use different verbs meaning "to receive": Matthew uses δέχομαι (*dechomai*), and John has λαμβάνω (*lambanō*). Of course, the saying is proverbial and as such is repeatable (conceptually, John 5:23; 7:28; 12:44–45, 48; 13:20; 15:23; Acts 7:51; 1 Thess. 4:8; Danker 1988: 216). The occasions for the remarks are distinct, and so it is futile to reflect on which form is original. Matthew has it in a section on teaching the disciples, and John includes it at the Last Supper, where Jesus prepares the disciples to take out the message. The commissioned disciples' authority reflects God's authority. Jesus repeats the saying because the idea is important and gives assurance. John 5:45–47 adds that to reject Jesus is also to reject Moses (Liefeld 1984: 939). The point of John 5 is that Moses' teaching points to Jesus.

---

37. The "representative" concept is common, reflecting the Jewish institution of the שָׁלִיחַ (*šālîaḥ*, the sent one). *M. Ber.* 5.5 says, "The one sent by the man is as the man himself."

d. The Messengers' Report (10:17–20)
i. The Joy of the Disciples at Their Authority (10:17)

10:17 The report of the seventy-two finds them excited and rejoicing (on the number *seventy-two*, see the exegesis and additional note on 10:1; on joy, see the exegesis of 24:52). Their excitement focuses on their authority over the demons, an authority that parallels Jesus' (4:41). They address Jesus as Lord (see the exegesis of 5:8), showing their recognition of his position. They recognize that they do not exercise their authority, for they speak of demons being subject to them "in your name" (ἐν τῷ ὀνόματί σου, *en tō onomati sou*). The authority of Jesus' name will be a key in Acts (Bietenhard, *TDNT* 5:271, 277; Mark 9:38; 16:17; Acts 3:6; 4:7, 10; 16:18). These disciples represent Jesus and share his power, which is the focus of their joy. The name of Jesus and its power show that demonic forces are subject to the servant of God, a subjection that normally is the prerogative of God himself. This authority was not mentioned in the commission of the seventy-two, but it clearly was included as part of their kingdom task (Luke 9:1–6, 49). The interchangeability of elements from each mission shows their inherent relationship (Nolland 1993a: 562). The remark reflects the mission's success. The charge given to the disciples had been fulfilled, and the new ministers were impressed (Luce 1933: 201; Hendriksen 1978: 580). The report has no Synoptic parallels (Aland 1985: §180).

ii. Jesus' Response about the Greater Honor (10:18–20)

10:18 Jesus explains what the disciples' authority means by describing a fall from the heights (Oepke, *TDNT* 3:213; Luke 11:14–23). These exorcisms by the disciples show Satan's defeat. The allusion suggests the language of Isa. 14:12 (Ernst 1977: 337).[38] That the fall itself is the issue is seen in the isolation of the participle πεσόντα (*pesonta*, falling) at the end of the verse for emphasis (lit.: "I was seeing Satan as lightning from heaven falling"). There is no way to be certain if this was a vision (Manson 1949: 258; U. Müller 1977) or simply a remark, a prophetic declaration about the implications of these events. Nolland (1993a: 563–64) apparently argues for

---

38. Satan's access to heaven is assumed in Job 1:6–12; 2:1–7. Fitzmyer 1985: 862 and Nolland 1993a: 563 are against the Isaianic allusion, but Luke's language suggests that passage. As an allusion it does not identify Isaiah's referent, since Isaiah probably refers to an earthly king who arrogantly takes on the role of a god and is cast down by God. In later Jewish thinking, the king correctly becomes typological of what Satan also does. The phrase overlapping with Isa. 14:12 is ἐκ τοῦ οὐρανοῦ (from heaven). For Jewish handling of Isa. 14, see Miyoshi 1974: 100; see especially T. Sol. 20.16–17, which pictures demons falling like lightning to earth.

both, citing Amos 8:1–2; Jer. 1:13–19; Ezek. 2:9–10; and Isa. 6. He may well be right.

The point is clear: the disciples' ministry spells defeat for Satan. Satan in the OT is the "arch-accuser" (Job 1; Zech. 3:1–2; 1 Chron. 21:1; Fitzmyer 1985: 862).[39] The coming of Messiah was regarded as bringing Satan's end in rabbinic expectation as well as in the NT (Ellis 1974: 157; SB 2:167–68; Rev. 12:8–9).[40] Jesus says that he watched (Ellis 1974: 157 translates ἐθεώρουν, *etheōroun*, as "was observing") Satan fall, which suggests that God cast Satan out of heaven.[41] The defeat of Satan and the demons is more often associated with the cross or Christ's return (John 12:31–32; Col. 2:14–15; Rev. 12:10–12; 20:1–3). But Luke 11:20 speaks of a current defeat. Satan's defeat is part of a long series of events (Hendriksen 1978: 581). The disciples' work is no small affair and is part of an increasingly significant set of theological realities.

Jesus spells out the disciples' role and their wide-ranging authority **10:19** of his commission. The point of the perfect δέδωκα (*dedōka*, I have given) is that this authority was given in the past and extends throughout the mission. They have the right to overcome hostile creation as represented by serpents and scorpions, as well as to overcome the enemy's power, an allusion to Satan (Rev. 12:9; Foerster, *TDNT* 2:813–14; 5:579; also 2 Cor. 11:3; Rev. 12:14–15; 20:2).[42] Acts 28:3–6 will show Paul surviving a snake bite in Malta. The point is not so much that such beings can be handled safely, as much as that such forces and what they represent can be opposed and crushed.[43]

---

39. Foerster, *TDNT* 2:80, speaks of this as the end of Satan's right to accuse humans; but the fall means much more than this.

40. In Judaism, 1 Enoch 55.4; Jub. 23.29; T. Sim. 6.6; T. Judah 25.3; Sibylline Oracles 3.796–807; T. Moses 10.1–3. Leaney 1958: 179 notes that the specific picture of a fall from heaven (for the wicked angels, not Satan specifically) comes later in Judaism (e.g., the eighth-century *Pirqe de Rabbi Eliezer* 22 [= Friedlander 1916: 160]). In Tg. Ps.-J. on Gen. 6:4 (= Bowker 1969: 151), the angels that fell are named Shamhazi and Azael. In *Pirqe de Rabbi Eliezer* 14 [= Friedlander 1916: 99]), the angel Sammael is cast down from heaven for deceiving Eve. For Judaism, Sammael in all likelihood equals the devil (Wis. 2:24; Tg. Ps.-J. on Gen. 3:6 [= Bowker 1969: 121]).

41. Manson 1949: 258 notes that Jesus' passive role argues for authenticity, since God is still the major actor.

42. In the Apocrypha and Pseudepigrapha, Satan is commonly viewed as the defeated enemy or associated with serpents: T. Dan 6.3–4; T. Moses 10.1; and possibly Sir. 25:15, 24. Grundmann, *TDNT* 3:400, adds T. Levi 18.12; T. Zeb. 9.8; and Jub. 10.8. In later Judaism, see Midr. Ps. 91.8 on 91:13 (= Braude 1959: 2.107). Seesemann, *TDNT* 5:943, sees a figure of speech referring to protection, but it is better to speak of a miracle picturing victory and protection, since miraculous authority is present. Other Jewish texts on Satan include T. Asher 7.3 and T. Dan 5.10–11.

43. The latter idea is explicit in the textually uncertain Mark 16:18; Hendriksen 1978: 581.

The disciples are secure in God's hands. Nothing can really hurt them (οὐδέν, *ouden*, nothing, is emphatic).

The picture is drawn from OT figurative language, which describes God's protection in terms of trampling over created beings (Leaney 1958: 179): in Deut. 8:15, over wilderness, snakes, and scorpions; in Ps. 91:13, over the lion and cobra (see also Sir. 21:2; 39:30; Num. 21:6–9; 1 Kings 12:11, 14; Isa. 11:8; Rom. 16:20). The Deuteronomy allusion is more likely (Fitzmyer 1985: 863; Grundmann 1963: 212; SB 2:168–69).[44] In fact, the allusion may go back to Gen. 3:15, where it says that the offspring of the woman would crush the serpent's head (Liefeld 1984: 939). The picture is of crushing these creatures and thereby defeating the hostility they represent. The disciples are reasserting humanity's vice-regent role in creation. When it comes to evil, the disciples can overcome anything that opposes them, for Christ's authority overcomes the enemies' power (Foerster, *TDNT* 2:569).[45] In the war with Satan, Jesus' ministry is D-day.

10:20 This emphasis on power is not the one Jesus wants the disciples to have. He wants them to focus on their gracious and secure standing before God. There is a joy greater than their authority: their names are written in heaven.[46] Χαίρετε (*chairete*, rejoice) is a present imperative and speaks of continual rejoicing (Plummer 1896: 280). The statement is given weight by the use of the perfect ἐγγέγραπται (*engegraptai*, stand written). In everyday Greek ἐγγράφω referred to making a list in a public register or census (Schrenk, *TDNT* 1:769–70). The disciples' names stand written in heaven, the census of life. In Judaism, as in the NT, the book of life is a common image.[47] The book indicates that the disciples are personally known by God and that

44. Num. 21:6–9; Ps. 58:4 [58:5 MT]; 140:3 [140:4 MT]; 1 Kings 12:11, 14 = 2 Chron. 10:11, 14; Sir. 21:2; 39:30. Meanwhile, Midr. Ps. 91.8 on 91:13 (= Braude 1959: 2.107) gives such power to Noah; *Sipra* 227 on Lev. 22:29–33 (= Neusner 1988b: 3.231) attributes a power to judge to the "Omnipresent"; while T. Levi 18 gives such power to the messianic high priest. Miyoshi 1974: 102–5 has a full survey of the Jewish texts and regards Deut. 8:15 as key.

45. Plummer 1896: 279 notes two later traditions about John's being preserved from boiling oil and his failing to succumb to hemlock, but the origin of these accounts is uncertain. Tertullian, *Prescription against Heretics* 36, records the first incident.

46. Marshall 1978: 430 notes that the rhetorical remark is not a denial or a rebuke about their joy over their authority; it is a comparative idea. Knowing God, or better, being known by him, is a more important source of joy; Zerwick 1963: §445.

47. Exod. 32:32; Ps. 69:28 [69:29 MT]; Isa. 4:3; Dan. 7:10; 12:1; Mal. 3:16–17; 1 Enoch 47.3; 104.1; 108.7; Jub. 5.13–14; 23.32; 30.19–23; 1QM 12.2; Phil. 4:3; Heb. 12:23; Rev. 3:5; 20:12, 15; 21:27; Ellis 1974: 157; Fitzmyer 1985: 863–64; SB 2:173–76; Schrenk, *TDNT* 1:619–20; Traub, *TDNT* 5:532 n. 295. Manson 1949: 258–59 lists the various "books" mentioned in the Bible and Judaism: (1) book of life, (2) book of human deeds, (3) book of the earthly destiny of people, and (4) book of the divine plan. Only the first two are in the Bible.

their eternal presence before him is certain. As such, this final word is one of comfort and encouragement, for in this context it means that the evil one's power cannot remove their secure position before God. Disciples can rejoice in this important truth. While Satan is cast down from heaven, disciples are a part of the heavenly census.

e. Jesus' Thanksgiving and Blessing (10:21–24)
i. Thanks to the Father (10:21–22)

Jesus has one more response.[48] At this key time, Jesus' own rejoicing reflects his teaching.[49] He, too, is grateful to the Father for the disciples' salvation. This gratitude is noted by ἐξομολογοῦμαι (*exomologoumai*, I thank), which often opens psalms of praise and refers to confessing God's great acts (Fitzmyer 1985: 871–72; 2 Sam. 22:50; Ps. 6:5 [6:6 LXX]; 9:1 [9:2 LXX]; 35:18 [34:18 LXX]; 45:17 [44:18 LXX]; 1QH 2.20, 31; 3.19, 37). Jesus' rejoicing is described as Spirit directed, thus underscoring its solemnity (Leaney 1958: 179).[50]

10:21

Ἠγαλλιάσατο (*ēgalliasato*, he rejoiced) refers to eschatological rejoicing, that is, rejoicing tied to fulfillment (Luke 1:14–15, 44, 47; Acts 2:26, 46; 16:34; Schneider 1977a: 243). God's sovereign work is highlighted in this prayer of thanksgiving, just as it was in Luke 10:2. Even Jesus' address highlights God's sovereign yet intimate position by juxtaposing the reference to God as Father with the title *Lord of heaven and earth* (Schrenk, *TDNT* 2:747; 5:985 n. 251; Stauffer, *TDNT* 3:116; Acts 17:24; Matt. 11:25). It is ultimately from the Father, the Sovereign over all creation, that authority and protection comes to the disciples. The Lord of heaven and earth is responsible for Satan's fall, as well as the benefits the disciples receive (Plummer 1896: 281; SB 2:176; Fitzmyer 1985: 872; Acts 17:24; Gen. 14:19, 22; Jdt. 9:12; Tob. 7:16 [NRSV numbering]; 1QapGen 22.16, 21). The double use of πατήρ (*patēr*, Father) stresses the intimate relationship between Jesus and God (Luke 6:36; 9:26; 11:2).

Yet it is not just God's goodness that gives Jesus pleasure. It is also the way in which God has administered salvation. He has not chosen the wise and understanding to receive his benefits, but babies (νηπίοις, *nēpiois*; found in the Gospels only three times: here = Matt. 11:25; 21:16; Bertram, *TDNT* 4:920). Nolland (1993a: 572) notes that a νήπιος in the OT is one who receives God's care and provision (Ps. 19:7 [18:8 LXX]; 116:6 [114:6 LXX]; 119:130 [118:130

---

48. See Manson 1949: 79 for a defense of the authenticity of this saying.

49. Ellis 1974: 158 notes that ἐν αὐτῇ τῇ ὥρᾳ (in this hour) refers not so much to chronology as to "this key eschatological time"; cf. Luke 12:56; 19:44; 21:24; 22:53; 23:43; John 4:23; 5:25; 2 Cor. 6:2; Heb. 3:7–4:10.

50. A reference to the Spirit in 10:21 is clear, regardless of the passage's exact wording. For the difficult textual problem, see the additional note.

LXX]). In Judaism, the "simple" are the pious or those who in their weakness can be helped by God (1QpHab 12.4; 1QH 2.9; 4Q169 [= 4QpNah] fragments 3–4 3.5; 11QPs^a 18.2, 4). This emphasis represents a generalization about salvation and has many parallels (Luke 1:51–54; Rom. 1:22; 1 Cor. 1:26–31; 2 Cor. 4:3–4; James 2:5; 4:6; Dan. 2:26–30; Bar. 3:14; Ernst 1977: 340). The focus on babies challenges a common understanding in Judaism that salvation comes to the wise (2 Esdr. [= 4 Ezra] 12:35–38; Marshall 1978: 434). Emphasis is on the giving of revelation, as the verbal contrast of ἀπέκρυψας (*apekrypsas*, you hid) to ἀπεκάλυψας (*apekalypsas*, you revealed) shows (Grundmann 1963: 215). Schürmann (1994: 106) suggests correctly that the νήπιος here is the poor or *Anawim* of other Lucan texts (1:46–49; 2:4–7; 4:18; 6:20; 7:22). God's pleasure reaches down to those who seem to have nothing to offer but their need, yet he gives them everything in terms of spiritual blessing. The reference to the Father's pleasure highlights God's sovereignty in the process (Luke 2:14; 12:32).

Plummer (1896: 281) suggests plausibly that σοφῶν (*sophōn*, the wise) refers especially to the religious leadership of the Pharisees (so also Danker 1988: 217; Marshall 1978: 434; Job 34:34; Prov. 16:21; Eccles. 9:11; Hos. 14:9 [14:10 MT]; Sir. 3:29; 9:14–15; 1QH 1.35). A later verse notes that to come to God one must come like a child (Luke 18:17; Arndt 1956: 286). Conceptual parallels include Sir. 51:25–30 (which Matt. 11:25–26 also parallels); Ps. 111; Wis. 2:17–18; 4:10, 13–15; and 1QH 7.26–27 (Danker 1988: 218).

This verse parallels Matt. 11:25–26. In fact, except for the introduction, where Luke alone mentions joy and the Holy Spirit, and the form of a verb (Matthew has ἔκρυψας, *ekrypsas*, and Luke has the prefixed verb ἀπέκρυψας, *apekrypsas*, both meaning "you hid"), the two prayers are verbally exact to the end of the verse. Matthew's introduction is general ("at that time"), so it is possible that both writers are referring to the same situation. Luke places the situation in association with this mission, as it represents Jesus preparing the disciples to function without him. Matthew seems to have saved his reference for a section where Jesus is offering a series of short teachings. However, this material is so proverbial that Jesus may have repeated it here to reassure disciples who serve in a challenging context of acceptance/rejection and intense pressure. It is hard to know which option is most likely, although the unique combination of material in Luke 10:21–24 could favor repetition, since it seems unlikely that any shared sources would have these two sets of remarks together.[51]

---

51. Fitzmyer 1985: 865–68, though going a different way, recognizes that it is unlikely that the text was a unit in a source shared with Matthew because, had Luke

The verse is important at four levels (Liefeld 1984: 939). It shows (1) God's sovereignty in salvation, (2) the intimacy of the relationship between Jesus and God, (3) the privilege of the disciples' participation in this salvation, and (4) the praise to God that should result in gratitude for the position the disciples have.

Turning from the Father's sovereign authority, Luke goes on to record one of his strongest christological statements. This passage sounds so much like John's material that it has been called "a bolt out of the Johannine blue" (Fitzmyer 1985: 866; John 10:15; 17:2, as well as 3:35; 6:65; 7:29; 13:3; 14:7, 9–11; 17:25—all of which are more conceptual than verbal). Both the Father's total authority and revelation from him are said to reside in the Son. This type of activity is clearly divine in its character. In addition, the term υἱός (*huios*, son) is mentioned three times, as is πατήρ (*patēr*, father).[52] The close collaboration between the two, as well as their relationship, reflects the heights to which Luke's Christology extends. This "co-regency" emphasis will not reappear until the fateful last week of Jesus' ministry (Luke 20:41–44; 22:69; also Acts 2:29–38). Yet Jesus' utterance still expresses the point with reserve: the Son is subject to the Father's direction. The Son is a mediator of blessing. (For a defense of this unique emphasis on mutual knowledge and family imagery, see Nolland 1993a: 574; Hoffmann 1970: 175; Jeremias 1971a: 58.)

10:22

The passage starts with a reference to the Son's total authority, to his current rule with God.[53] Both the authority's extent and timing are important. The passage parallels Jesus' remark in the commission passage of Matt. 28:18. Some imply that all of Jesus' teaching is received from the Father (Ellis 1974: 158; Fitzmyer 1985: 874). However, when it is combined in this context with Satan's overthrow, the reference to revelatory authority skips over into the area of soteriological power. When one considers what the disciples received from Jesus, a more comprehensive reference for Luke is assured (Luke 10:17–20; Arndt 1956: 287; Schrenk, *TDNT* 5:992–93 and n. 289). Jesus' rule is presented as absolute and as the product of the Father's bestowal, an idea consistent with John's

---

possessed Matthew's version, he would have used it. Fitzmyer is against the position of E. Norden, who argues that the original form is in Q and is reflected in Matthew. Norden cites not only Sir. 51 but also the Hermetic text *Poimandres* 32. Fitzmyer notes problems of artificial addition in Norden's citation of the Hermetic text.

52. Υἱός as an absolute term in the Synoptics occurs only here and in Mark 13:32.

53. On the idea of total authority in παραδίδωμι (to give over), see Büchsel, *TDNT* 2:171; Matt. 11:27; 28:18 (δίδωμι); 1 Cor. 15:24; Exod. Rab. 15.30 on 12:2. Stauffer, *TDNT* 2:348, calls this passage the "cry of jubilation."

presentation of Jesus doing only what the Father shows him (John 5:19–30). Jesus describes his authority over salvation and revelation.

The second point is that knowledge of the Son is tied to the Father. This idea supports Luke 10:21 and renders unlikely all judgments that separate verses 21 and 22 in an original tradition.[54] The idea is not foreign to the context, but shows how parallel the work of the Father and the Son are. Jesus' point is that the Father holds the key to knowing the Son and revealing him.

But the third point is most crucial (Ernst 1977: 341). Knowledge of the Father is left in the hands of the Son and is given to whomever the Son wishes to reveal it. The Son and the Father have switched roles from the description of 10:21, so that the Son's significant position is clear. No one can really understand the Father or what God is about without listening to the Son and his revelation. The point is not that Jesus' message is incomprehensible, but that it will not be perceived and accepted as God's message without the Son's revelatory work. This indeed is a strong description of the Son's central, mediatorial role in salvation. He functions like the Father. Arndt (1956: 287) notes that the offer is made to the "simple," or to the "weary and heavy-laden" as Matt. 11:28 puts it. It now becomes clear why all must "listen to him" (Luke 9:35; Danker 1988: 219). Jesus' role parallels that of Wisdom in the OT and Jewish texts, except what is said here is stated more emphatically than anything said of Wisdom (Job 28:25–28; Prov. 8:22–30; Sir. 1:1–10; Bar. 3:27–28; Wis. 8:3–4; Marshall 1978: 437; esp. Nolland 1993a: 574). Wisdom is not said to know God or have anything handed to her. She just participates with God.

Matthew 11:27 closely parallels Luke's wording. Matthew's word order and his choice of verb differ slightly from Luke, since Matthew selects the compound form of "to know," ἐπιγινώσκει (epiginōskei), where Luke has γινώσκει (ginōskei). The passage openly declares Jesus' knowledge of the role he has in God's plan. Thus, the saying cannot be limited to Johannine christological enthusiasm, though attempts to deny its authenticity abound, because of its strong Christology (against authenticity is Luce 1933: 202–3; but see Schweizer, *TDNT* 8:372–73, esp. n. 282).

54. Such efforts, beginning with Harnack, regard this verse as too harsh a literary transition. This view appeals to the church fathers, who often cite the phrase and reverse the position of the Son and Father. Creed 1930: 147–48 rightly rejects such attempts because they are without strong external textual support; see also Schweizer, *TDNT* 8:372 n. 276. Marshall 1978: 435 notes that Marcion and codex N reverse the expression in Luke, while Justin Martyr and codex N reverse it in Matthew; for more reversal passages in the fathers, see Grundmann 1963: 218 n. 16.

ii. Blessing on the Disciples (10:23–24)

Jesus reinforces the special situation in which the disciples find **10:23**
themselves. They are blessed and experience God's favor, because of
what they see. Βλέπετε (*blepete*, you are seeing) notes that they are
eyewitnesses to great events. The passage corresponds to the disciples' feeling expressed in 10:17. This remark is made to them alone,
since those who do not appreciate or respond to the events before
them do not share in the blessing. The sentiment of eschatological
hope is paralleled in Ps. Sol. 17.44; 18.6 (Plummer 1896: 283; Manson 1949: 80).

A parallel exists in Matt. 13:16–17 in the midst of the Matthean
parables. Again, the remark is general and proverbial enough to fit
both settings, though most see two distinct sets of sayings brought
together here by Luke (Marshall 1978: 431). Matthew 13:16 is verbally distinct from the Lucan passage by speaking of being blessed
"for seeing what your eyes see and hearing what your ears hear."[55]
The Matthean remark is made directly to the disciples, while Luke's
blessing is generalized to anyone who understands Jesus (Marshall
1978: 438). This difference allows application to people outside the
seventy-two, including Luke's readers. It is hard to explain Luke's
change if he knows the Matthean form of the saying, since Luke
mentions hearing in 10:24. A distinct saying is therefore a real probability (Arndt 1956: 287; for a defense of authenticity, see Meier
1994: 434–39).

Jesus gives the reason for the honored and blessed situation in which **10:24**
the disciples find themselves. Many past greats, both prophets and
kings, longed to experience the Jesus events. However great the
former era was, it pales when compared to the present. Other texts
speak of people or angels looking ahead to this time (John 8:56; Acts
2:30–32; Heb. 11:13; 1 Pet. 1:10–12). The beginning of fulfillment is a
special time above all other past events (Horst, *TDNT* 5:553).

Matthew 13:17 is similar except for minor differences of word order. Matthew speaks of the prophets and the righteous, which is significant because if Luke had a version with this wording it is hard to
see why he would make a change.[56] Matthew also uses a more emotive verb to express the desire of the greats to see these events
(ἐπεθύμησαν, *epethymēsan*, they longed, instead of Luke's ἠθέλησαν,

---

55. Klostermann 1929: 118 notes six differences between Matt. 13:16–17 and
Luke 10:23–24, but this one is the most crucial.

56. For the options, see Meier 1994: 489–90, who opts for a Matthean change to
"righteous" because of Matt. 10:41 and 23:29 and because "kings and prophets" is a
more natural combination. If a change is made from one tradition, this direction
makes more sense than Luke's making the change.

ēthelēsan, they wished). The point in each text is that this is a special time of fulfillment of promise, a unique time when the kingdom is coming.

Summary Luke 10:1–24 stresses mission. As Jesus draws near to his time of suffering and rejection, he sends out disciples to declare the kingdom's coming. Those sent out have made the commitment to follow him. They face a mission in which they carry little because they depend on God to provide. They are to go and pray that others will join them. They go with great authority: they can bless or remove blessing; they can heal sicknesses and cast out demons. They must also be aware that the pattern of Jesus' ministry shows rejection is coming, which means judgment for those who reject his message. Such rejection is worse than that of the most wicked OT cities. There is no greater sin than rejection of God's long-promised kingdom. The disciples' message is "dead serious," for everything is at stake in the response.

There is an excitement about what happens on this mission. The disciples are thrilled that demons are subject to them. In fact, such power pictures Satan's fall and the presence of initial fulfillment of the kingdom. But power is not the most important thing in God's plan. A greater cause of joy is the disciples' secure position before God. In fact, even Jesus rejoices that God chooses the simple. The sovereign bestowal of benefits rests in the hands of the Father and the Son. Despite rejection of their message by many, these disciples should realize that many saints of old longed to see this unique time of fulfillment. Mission involves trust, responsibility, authority, rejection, but above all privilege. To see the blessing of mission is why Luke narrates the story of the seventy-two. This sense of privilege is to inspire disciples to continue the task. Whatever their success, they need to understand that God is behind their cause. In that knowledge is real joy.

Additional Notes

10:1. One of the most difficult Lucan textual issues appears in 10:1 and 10:17 (see Metzger 1958–59 and Metzger 1975: 150–51, which includes not only his remarks but also a note from K. Aland). Were there seventy or seventy-two disciples? The external evidence is almost evenly divided: *seventy* is found in ℵ, A, C, L, W, Δ, Θ, Ψ, family 1, family 13, Byz, some Itala, Coptic, some Syriac; *seventy-two* is found in $\mathfrak{P}^{75}$, B, D, some Itala, Vulgate, and some Syriac. $\mathfrak{P}^{45}$ is fragmentary at 10:1, although Metzger (1958–59: 299) holds that it reads *seventy* here. At 10:17, UBS4 cites $\mathfrak{P}^{45}$ with "vid"—"apparently."

Intrinsic factors include the possibility of a symbolic meaning in the number. The OT use of *seventy* might have influenced its presence here:[57]

1. Moses' seventy elders (Exod. 24:1, 9; Num. 11:16–17, 24–25)
2. the seventy nations of the earth (Gen. 10–11; but the LXX lists seventy-two)
3. a rabbinic tradition about Moses' commandments being heard in seventy languages (*b. Šab.* 88b, though this is late; even later is *The Alphabet of Rabbi Akiva* [see Strack and Stemberger 1991: 381])
4. the Sanhedrin's seventy members (when the high priest is not counted; *m. Sanh.* 1.5–6)

The use of the number *seventy-two* in various Jewish sources could also have influenced the reading in Luke:

1. the local counsels of seventy-two (*m. Zebaḥ.* 1.3; *m. Yad.* 3.5; 4.2)
2. the seventy-two translators of the LXX (*Letter of Aristeas* 46–50)
3. the LXX tradition of the seventy-two nations in Gen. 10–11
4. the seventy-two princes and kings in the world (3 Enoch 17.8; 18.2–3; 30.2)[58]

These listings show that the number *seventy* is of greater significant than *seventy-two* (also Rengstorf, *TDNT* 2:634). Thus, a copyist looking for significance in the number would be more likely to change *seventy-two* to *seventy* than vice versa.[59] However, if Luke was making an OT allusion, then *seventy* is the stronger candidate.

But does Luke intend the number to be interpreted symbolically? Two OT events have been suggested as conceptual background for a symbolic meaning for the number: the LXX numbering of seventy-two nations (Marshall 1978: 415;[60] Ernst 1977: 331) and Moses' selection of seventy elders. Against the first suggestion is the absence of a clear universal context in this mission. It is true that the restriction to Israel is missing (unlike the Matthean mission with the Twelve), but it also is clear in Luke's writings that an active Gentile mission develops only in the Book of Acts (Schmid 1960: 184; Fitzmyer 1985: 846).[61] The second suggestion for a symbol fails also,

---

57. Metzger 1958–59: 303–4 notes other examples from the Targums and Pseudepigrapha that develop the number *seventy*.

58. Tannehill 1986: 233 prefers *seventy-two*, but does not know which symbolic idea is present, other than a stress on universal mission; so also Talbert 1982: 115.

59. This is why K. Aland (in Metzger 1975: 151) is certain that *seventy-two* was original. Wiefel 1988: 195 asks if *seventy* is not an attempt to get a round number.

60. Marshall sees an allusion to the nations in the wolves of 10:3, but if so the allusion is negative, which does not reinforce the universal element alleged as present here; Jellicoe 1959–60.

61. Egelkraut 1976: 145–48 emphatically and correctly shows that Israel is in view in this mission, since the woes of 10:13–15 are only to Israelite cities. At most, the inclusion of Samaria could be implied by 9:51–56, but it looks as if the failure of that effort led to a return to Galilee.

since Moses' selection of seventy is not picked up and developed anywhere in Acts. It is hard to establish a clear rationale for an intended OT allusion, and thus it is unlikely that the number is symbolic.

Although Metzger finds it impossible to establish a clear choice between the textual variants, given the absence of a symbolic reference, the more difficult reading seems to be *seventy-two*. For this reason, it is slightly more likely to be original.[62]

10:1. Were the disciples sent out "by twos" (ἀνὰ δύο) or "two by two" (ἀνὰ δύο δύο) as in Mark 6:7? The meaning is the same in either case. The combination of א, A, C, D, and Byz suggests ἀνὰ δύο. Seventy-two disciples are sent out in thirty-six pairs, though it is also likely that the Twelve went out in a similar manner, probably separately from this group, as Luke 22:35 suggests.

10:17. See the first additional note on 10:1. The evidence is virtually the same except for $\mathfrak{P}^{45}$.

10:19. The perfect δέδωκα (I have given) is better supported in the manuscripts ($\mathfrak{P}^{75}$, א, B, C*, L, W) than the present tense δίδωμι (I give) ($\mathfrak{P}^{45}$, A, D, Θ, Byz). The point of the perfect is that the authority, given in the past, still resides with these disciples. If the tense were present, the point would simply be the authority's current bestowal.

10:21. Metzger (1975: 152) lists the four textual options, of which the best two mention the Holy Spirit. The debate centers on whether the preposition ἐν (in) precedes the reference to the Spirit. The weight of the manuscripts between including and excluding the preposition is very close: $\mathfrak{P}^{75}$, B, C, Θ, and family 1 exclude the preposition; א, D, L, Ξ, 33, and 1241 include it. Other options leave out the adjective τῷ ἁγίῳ (holy) or both τῷ ἁγίῳ and the preposition ἐν. The choice does not alter the passage's basic idea that Jesus speaks in the Spirit.

---

62. The RSV and NRSV read *seventy*; see also Schweizer 1984: 174; Danker 1988: 212 (who attributes the number *seventy-two* to Moses' addition of two elders when he appointed his seventy [Num. 11:26] and sees Gentile symbolism in the choice); Tiede 1988: 200–201; Ellis 1974: 155–56; C. F. Evans 1990: 444–45; Schürmann 1994: 54. The NIV reads *seventy-two*; also Manson 1949: 74; Liefeld 1984: 940; Hendriksen 1978: 570–71 ("leans" this way); Creed 1930: 144; Arndt 1956: 280; Ernst 1977: 331; Marshall 1978: 414–15 (who has a good summary of the issue); Fitzmyer 1985: 845–46; Wiefel 1988: 195; C. A. Evans 1990: 172; Nolland 1993a: 546. Those who are undecided include Luce 1933: 198–99; Plummer 1896: 272; and Schneider 1977a: 235 (who argues that a decision is less than certain).

B. Discipleship: Looking to One's Neighbor, Jesus, and God (10:25–11:13)

After defining the nature of mission and the importance of commitment, Luke turns to the disciple's relationships. In three steps, he works from one's fellow human inward to the more fundamental relationship with God (10:25–11:13). First, 10:25–37 relates an exhortation about loving one's neighbor. Launched by a lawyer's question, the dialogue leads into the parable of the good Samaritan. Second, 10:38–42 places the disciple's focus on looking to Jesus, as Mary makes the better choice over Martha. Third, 11:1–13 calls on the disciple to look to and trust God through prayer. With this three-part sequence, Luke stresses the inherent interrelationship between how one reacts to people and how one relates to God.

1. Looking to One's Neighbor: Parable of the Good Samaritan (10:25–37)

Luke 10:25–37 consists of two parts linked by shared vocabulary: ποιέω (*poieō*, to do) in 10:25, 28, 37 (twice) and πλησίον (*plēsion*, neighbor) in 10:27, 29, 36 (Egelkraut 1976: 84, esp. n. 4). The lawyer inquires about eternal life, which is answered in terms of the commandments (10:25–28). Then follows an explanatory parable about the exemplary Samaritan (10:29–37), which shows that one's obligation includes all, not just certain people.[1] This racial leveling is a key part of Jesus' ethic. Basic mercy and love is to extend to all.

The parable turns around the question by the lawyer, who asked who his neighbor is in hopes of having the strong ethical demand of the law qualified. Jesus answers with an exhortation to "do" as the Samaritan has done. The real issue is not whom we should serve, but that we serve. The concern moves from how we see others to how we are to act. The shift internalizes the demands and radicalizes them. We are not to ask who our neighbor is; we are to be a neighbor.

Jesus' choice of a Samaritan is significant, since Jews disliked Samaritans and would not have seen them as neighbors. In effect Jesus says, "Neighbors can come from surprising places." There is an ethnic point, then, in the racial choice of this character.

Sources and Historicity

The source of Luke 10:25–37 is debated since the parable is unique to Luke, though the initial exchange in 10:25–28 has a clear conceptual parallel in Matt. 22:34–40 = Mark 12:28–34 (Aland 1985: §182). The placement in Matthew and Mark is virtually identical: it is part of the controversies early in the Passion week. All three accounts involve a scribe, and all three cite Deut. 6:5 and Lev. 19:18 as a summary of the law. Mark has a longer account, with the lawyer responding to Jesus fully and favorably.

The Lucan account differs from the other Synoptic accounts (Stein 1992: 314–15 n. 39). The questions differ: Matthew and Mark ask about the greatest commandment, while Luke is interested in the issue of inheriting eternal life. In Luke, it is the lawyer who cites the OT passages, while in Matthew and

---

1. Tannehill 1986: 179 argues that the first subunit shows where Jesus and the lawyer are similar, while the parable shows where Jesus' emphasis is unique.

Mark, Jesus quotes these texts. Luke's placement is clearly before Jesus' last week of ministry, in contrast to the other Synoptics. Jesus' response in Luke ("do this and you shall live") differs from that in the other accounts with their statements that this is the greatest commandment. In Luke, the lawyer tests Jesus and is portrayed in a strictly skeptical light (in fact, Talbert 1982: 120 speaks of a "controversy dialogue"; see also Bultmann 1963: 51); in Mark 12:34, the lawyer is praised at the end. Only Luke has the parable, which clearly relates to the preceding exchange. The combination of controversy and parable produces a unique set of Lucan emphases.

Many believe that these emphases show Luke's rearranging of the material and argue that the two parts of the account do not fit (so the Jesus Seminar; Funk and Hoover 1993: 323–24). Creed (1930: 151) holds that the parable ignores the lawyer's question. This objection misses the literary and pedagogical beauty of Jesus' reply. Jesus answers the question by turning the onus back on the lawyer, saying in effect, "Do not worry about the other guy, but rather be a neighbor yourself."[2] Jesus answers the question, but redirects its thrust.[3] In fact, except for the OT citations, there is little verbal overlap between Luke and the other accounts, which, by contrast, are very similar to each other.

Although many see Luke reworking a Synoptic tradition in 10:25–28 (usually seen as the Marcan version), it is possible, given all the differences just noted, that an independent event is present.[4] Manson (1949: 260) is cor-

2. Creed misses the point when he says that Jesus' goal is to say that anyone is your neighbor. The answer includes this and more. Klostermann 1929: 118–19 makes the same error in seeing the point as only that the compassionate Samaritan is closer to the kingdom than is the representative of Judaism.

3. Many explain the difference in the Lucan form of the question (eternal life) versus that in the other Synoptics (greatest commandment) as a Lucan reworking that highlighted the real issue; Marshall 1978: 440–41.

4. Klostermann 1929: 118 and Egelkraut 1976: 85–90 favor a Lucan reworking of Mark. Schneider 1977a: 247 and Wiefel 1988: 207 see an independent source for the parable and Luke 10:25–28 using Mark. Bultmann 1963: 51; Luce 1933: 204 (citing Q); and Daube 1956: 247–50 see a version like that in Matthew. Zahn 1920: 427; Manson 1949: 259–61; and Jeremias 1963a: 202 see independent incidents or sources. Plummer 1896: 283 calls the possibility of one incident precarious, but not impossible. Fitzmyer 1985: 877–78 clearly ascribes the material to a special Lucan source, but sees only one incident, a distinction that seems hard to insist upon. Marshall 1978: 441 also leans toward two incidents, as do Hendriksen 1978: 591; Liefeld 1984: 942; and Blomberg 1990: 230–31, who speaks of "proem midrash" here. Ellis 1974: 159, though noting that two incidents are probable, regards the exchange as set in Jerusalem, which is possible, since the next account is in Bethany. Grundmann 1963: 221–22 speaks only of an independent source with the parable coming from L, while Ernst 1977: 344–46 leans this way, clearly noting that the parable is from special Lucan material. Nolland 1993a: 580 argues for an original link of neighbor and the parable, but that Luke is responsible for placing the great-commandment discussion here, drawing on Mark 12:28–34. Schürmann 1994: 136–40, 149–50 sees the parable emerging from L material and rooted in Jesus' intention, but 10:25–28 is probably rooted in Mark's account and does not testify to a separate event.

rect in observing that this question is so basic that it would likely be discussed on multiple occasions:

> The chief connecting link, the conjunction of the great commandments, is precisely the sort of thing that could appear over and over again. If a modern teacher of religion thought of such a thing as that, he would print it and it would make its way into the minds of millions. But in the first century A.D. in Palestine the only way of publishing great thoughts was to go on repeating them in talks or sermons.

Given the likelihood that two events are present and that significant differences exist in Luke's version, in 10:25–28 I shall not make a comparison of Luke with the other accounts, especially since the major differences have already been noted.

The Jesus Seminar rates all the dialogue in 10:25–29 and 10:36–37 as not coming from Jesus, printing it in black type. The seminar argues that the connection to and differences from Mark and Matthew reveal Luke's hand (Funk and Hoover 1993: 323–24). The seminar also notes the shift in meaning of πλησίον (neighbor) between 10:25–29 and 10:30–37. In reply, one could make a case, because of the differences, for a multiply attested theme in both Mark-Matthew on one side and L on the other. The teaching in 10:27 also fits a Jewish milieu, but with Jesus' characteristic twist. The linkage of commandment, neighbor, and neighbor parable fits the kind of linkage made in Jewish texts (reminiscent of Blomberg's "proem homily"). The style of question or introduction, answer in a parable, and comment is like other texts in diverse traditions (L in Luke 7:40–47 and M in Matt. 21:28–32). The linkage of these events and the dialogues that surround the parables make for a credible unit of teaching. Interestingly, the Jesus Seminar ties the parable in 10:30–35 to Jesus (it is printed in red type). Its parabolic theme and "subversion" through the appeal to the Samaritan is seen to speak for its authenticity.

Nolland (1993a: 588–90) notes attempts to doubt its authenticity by Sellin (1974–75) and Goulder (1989: 487–92). Goulder argues that Luke built the parables from 2 Chron. 28:1–15 and reflects elements of Lucan style (illustration story, response at the end of the parable, use of an outsider, emotional and colorful detail). He notes that 2 Chronicles alone cannot explain the parable and argues that Matt. 11:28–12:14 also supplied material. But how do we get from the prophets and Oded in Samaria to a Samaritan or from a war scene to thieves? The elements of Lucan parabolic style are really elements of the unique parabolic material that Luke uses and are a product of Luke's drawing on more parabolic material than the other Synoptics. Thus, Goulder's appeal to style is lame, for the emphases he notes may simply reflect Lucan sources. Nolland rightly critiques these efforts, correctly concluding (p. 590) that the parable's "imaginative core goes back to the historical Jesus." It coheres with Jesus' identification with the outsider and his ethic that translates devotion to God into service for others.

The account is a pronouncement story that contains a parable (Fitzmyer 1985: 878). Berger (1984: 30, 81–82) speaks of a moral example in the parable and calls both parts of the texts apophthegms, since each unit concludes with a saying. Nolland (1993a: 580) points out a structural parallel between 10:25–28 and 10:29–35: (1) reason for lawyer's question, (2) lawyer's question, (3) Jesus' counterquestion, (4) lawyer's answer, and (5) Jesus' concluding challenge. The parable is best called an example story, since the Samaritan's response is held up as exemplary. It is told from the perspective of the wounded man, in terms of who helps him "out of the ditch" (contra Nolland 1993a: 591). Trudinger (1976) makes the helpful observation that the lawyer is not to see the call to service as extending his "superior" favor to another. This solid observation should not be used to argue that the parable only focuses on the man who fell among thieves. Rather, the point is an exemplary reaction to this tragic situation.

The outline of Luke 10:25–37 is as follows:

a. Legal questions about inheriting eternal life (10:25–28)
  i. The lawyer's question (10:25)
  ii. Jesus' question (10:26)
  iii. The lawyer's reply: the great commandment—love God and neighbor (10:27)
  iv. Jesus' commendation (10:28)
b. Call to be a neighbor: the exemplary Samaritan (10:29–37)
  i. The lawyer's question about neighbors (10:29)
  ii. The parable of the priest, Levite, and compassionate Samaritan (10:30–35)
  iii. Jesus' question about the neighbor (10:36)
  iv. The lawyer's recognition of the Samaritan (10:37a)
  v. Jesus' command to do like the Samaritan (10:37b)

The passage's themes are ethical and practical. At the heart of believing in God is loving him and one's neighbor. In fact, life is found in loving God and one's neighbor. One should be a neighbor by showing compassion to anyone in need. Being a neighbor does not make distinctions in offering care. Compassion may involve time and sacrifice. The issue is not to define who the neighbor is or to seek to do the minimum one can do. This is a simply a call to be a neighbor.

Exegesis and Exposition

[25]And, behold, a certain lawyer stood up to put him to the test, saying, "Teacher, what shall I do to inherit eternal life?" [26]And he said to him, "In the law, what stands written? How do you read?" [27r]And he replied, "You shall love⌐ the Lord your God with all your heart and with all your soul and with all your strength and with all your mind; and your neighbor as yourself." [28]And he said to him, "You have answered well; do this and you will live."

[29]But he, wishing to justify himself, said to Jesus, "And who is my neighbor?" [30]Jesus replied, "A certain man was going down from Jerusalem to Jericho, and he fell among robbers, who stripped him and beat him and departed, leaving him half-dead. [31]And by chance a certain priest came down that road; and when he saw him he passed by on the other side. [32]Likewise also the Levite, ⌐when he came⌐ to the place and saw him, passed by on the other side. [33]But a certain one, that is, a Samaritan, as he journeyed, came to where he was; and when he saw him, he had compassion [34]and went to him and bound up his wounds by pouring oil and wine and, setting him on his own beast, brought him to an inn and took care of him. [35]And the next day he took out two denarii and gave them to the innkeeper, saying, 'Take care of him; and whatever more you spend, I will repay you when I return.' [36]Which of these three, do you think, became a neighbor to the man who fell among the robbers?" [37]And he said, "The one who showed mercy on him." And Jesus said to him, "Go and do likewise."

a. Legal Questions about Inheriting Eternal Life (10:25–28)
i. The Lawyer's Question (10:25)

10:25 Luke gives no setting for this event. The introductory καὶ ἰδού (*kai idou*, and behold) is frequent in Luke (twenty-six times, including 2:25; 5:12; 7:12; 13:11; 14:2; 24:13; Zahn 1920: 427 n. 1). There is no way to know if this incident followed immediately after 10:21–24 or if some time elapsed. Luke's normal usage of καὶ ἰδού suggests a relationship between this event and what preceded. Ellis (1974: 159) proposes that a Jerusalem setting is required. Two factors have lead to this suggestion: the mention of the Jericho–Jerusalem road in 10:30 and the location of the next event in Martha's house in Bethany (Luke 10:38–42; John 12:1–2). The detail may, however, only give a particularly notorious route without saying where Jesus is when he tells the story. Given the loose arrangement of this material, the location is unclear.

The passage begins as a broad soteriological discussion, initiated by a lawyer. Νομικός (*nomikos*) is Luke's term for a scribe (Luke 7:30; 11:45, 46, 52; 14:3; Ellis 1974: 160; Wiefel 1988: 208; in the Gospels, the term is only used by Luke, except for Matt. 22:35). The lawyer challenges Jesus, to test him (ἐκπειράζων [*ekpeirazōn*] a participle of purpose). Luke as narrator reveals the question's motive. Plummer (1896: 284) denies any malicious force in the remark, but this view seems unlikely given the less than flattering portrait of the religious leadership in this section. A visual image of confrontation may exist, since it seems that the speaker rose to question Jesus in what had possibly been an informal discussion (Seesemann, *TDNT* 6:28, notes that the πειράζω word group often involves the leaders' challenge of Jesus; Luke 11:16; Mark 8:11; 10:2; 12:15; Matt. 22:35). The question appears simple, but in fact is theologically complex. The lawyer wants to know what he must do to inherit eternal life (Matt. 19:29; Mark 10:17; Titus 3:7; 1 Pet. 3:7; Bultmann, *TDNT* 2:864 n. 274).

Is the lawyer asking only about "getting saved" or is he asking a broader question about pleasing God and receiving all that God has to offer him? The historical setting is key as is the phrase's background. Some see here a discussion between two Jews and argue that the assumption behind the remark is that they share in God's blessing. They are part of the "in" crowd, so the issue becomes what the lawyer can do to guarantee or maintain his position (Talbert 1982: 121). Others cite the parallel between this question and the one asked by the rich young ruler in Luke 18:18, where the language is clearly parallel to remarks about entering the kingdom and thus looks eschatologically at "being saved" (Luce 1933: 204). "To inherit" (κληρονομέω, klēronomeō) is to receive something (Ps. Sol. 14.9 [negatively]; 12.6). This request involves the reception of eternal life, which is part of the future world that God brings—and the lawyer wants to be sure to earn it (Dan 12:2; 2 Macc. 7:9; Ps. Sol. 3.12; Ellis 1974: 160; Liefeld 1984: 942; Lev. Rab. 16.2 on 14:2; Bultmann, *TDNT* 2:856–57; Braun, *TDNT* 6:479). The lawyer's question is really this: "What must I do to share in the resurrection of the righteous at the end?" SB (1:808–9, 829) shows this to be a fundamental question among later rabbis and that the final eschatological blessing among the righteous is the issue at hand (Grundmann 1963: 222; *b. Ber.* 28b; *m. ʾAbot* 2.7; 4.16; 5.19; *b. Soṭa* 7b).

"Eternal life" (ζωὴν αἰώνιον, zōēn aiōnion) is a technical expression for the eschatological blessing of the righteous as opposed to the rejection of the unrighteous (the allusion to eternal life probably goes back to the image of resurrection in Dan. 12:2). The test was to see if Jesus could correctly answer the fundamental question: "How can I be sure I'll be saved in the final resurrection?"

ii. Jesus' Question (10:26)

Jesus responds with a question about the law (νόμος, nomos), which **10:26** is the expression of God's revealed will for that time. By responding this way, Jesus identifies himself not as a radical who wishes to deny the teaching of Jewish tradition but as one who wishes to reflect on what God requires. He sends the lawyer to their shared source of authority: the law, God's instruction to his people. The deflection of the original question also avoids the lawyer's test, since now the lawyer will take advantage of the opportunity to give the answer to his own question! There is a note of irony in this reversal: he will expound what stands written (γέγραπται, gegraptai) by God, because Jesus has asked him for scriptural support.

The second question, "How do you read?" might be an allusion to reciting the *Shema*ᶜ (Deut. 6:4; Klostermann 1929: 119; Ellis 1974: 160; Marshall 1978: 443; Grundmann 1963: 222).[5] If an allusion is present, Jesus gave the man a clue to the proper answer. At a minimum, the phrase asks for specific biblical support and not an appeal to oral tradition (Plummer 1896: 284).[6] This latter, general explanation still seems more likely than a specific allusion to Deut. 6:4. Marshall notes that the phrasing makes it unlikely that Luke is responsible for its wording.[7]

iii. The Lawyer's Reply: The Great Commandment—Love God and Neighbor (10:27)

10:27 The lawyer answers in terms of what has been called the "great commandment," a combination of Deut. 6:5 (recited twice a day as part of the *Shema*ᶜ) and Lev. 19:18 (Schrenk, *TDNT* 2:549–50).[8] One could call this text the "law of love," since one's relationships to God and humans are both covered in the command. The essence of pleasing God in Deuteronomy is being devoted to him. The text in Leviticus expresses a parallel devotion in terms of how one treats others (Marshall 1978: 443–44; Fitzmyer 1985: 878 [though he stresses that Deuteronomy and Leviticus are distinct contexts in the OT]; Moran 1963; Deut. 11:13, 22; 19:9; 30:16; Josh. 22:5; 23:11). The lawyer answers the question about receiving life in the future in concrete terms of love and devotion, not in an abstract sense. Both God and humans

---

5. Jeremias 1971a: 187 argues that the verb ἀναγινώσκω renders Semitic קרא (qrʾ) and means "to recite," so that Jesus is calling for a specific text. Derrett 1970: 224 n. 1 notes that this view goes back to J. B. Lightfoot.

6. Daube 1956: 433 believes that the verse asks simply for a biblical exposition of how the scribe sees the issue; so also Derrett 1970: 224. Daube cites as support *m. ʿAbod. Zar.* 2.5, where the question "how do you read (קרא)?" seeks a specific scriptural response (though in fact what is asked for in the mishnaic example is a defense of a certain vocalization of the text).

7. Luke cites the Jewish form of the question and the phrase ἐν τῷ νόμῳ (in the law), which is paralleled in Matt. 22:36, though Matthew places it on the lawyer's lips.

8. There can be no rabbinic-style distinction between legal duty and voluntary acts of love after Jesus expounds these texts; correctly, Gutbrod, *TDNT* 4:1064.

are to receive love. Such love is not marked by the presence of great feeling but is objectively manifested in considerate responsiveness. This answer does not defend righteousness by works. Jesus' approval of the answer in the next verse comes because at its heart the answer is an expression of total allegiance and devotion that in other contexts could be called faith. At the heart of entering the future life is a relationship of devotion, a devotion that places God at the center of one's spiritual life and responds to others in love. The depth of one's devotion is emphatically underlined by the repeated reference to the various parts of the person that contribute energy to this love. Heart, soul, strength, and mind—the whole person—contribute to this response. Mark and Luke are distinct in having four terms where Deut. 6:5 and Matthew have three.[9]

The elements of a person described by the four terms depict the emotion (καρδία), consciousness (ψυχή), drive (ἰσχύς), and intelligence or cognitive abilities (διάνοια) (Fitzmyer 1985: 880). But there is no compartmentalization of response; the entire person responds. In addition, devotion to God is expressed by devotion to others, so that there is no distinction between devotion to God and treatment of people. They go together. Jesus encourages total love for God and humankind.[10] Luke develops this theme in the next two pericopes by showing how one places attention on Jesus (Luke 10:38–42) and how one is to trust the Father in dependent prayer (11:1–13).

The NT elsewhere connects displaying love for one's neighbor to devotion to God. Paul's greetings often link faith toward God and love for the saints (Col. 1:3–5; Philem. 6; 1 Thess. 1:3). Many passages cite the language of Lev. 19:18 (Matt. 5:43; 19:19; Rom. 13:9; Gal. 5:14; James 2:8). Other texts closely relate love for God or Jesus and love for one another (John 13:34–35; 15:9–12; 1 Pet. 2:17; 1 John 4:11; Leaney 1958: 182). To "do" the law means, in essence, to love. To live by the Spirit means to love and do righteousness (Rom. 8:1–11).

The lawyer's answer has parallels in Judaism (Manson 1949: 260–61):[11]

9. Five Greek terms are found in Deut. 6:5 LXX and its quotation in the Synoptics: καρδία (heart), ψυχή (soul), δύναμις (power), διάνοια (mind), and ἰσχύς (strength). Deut. 6:5 has καρδία–ψυχή–δύναμις; Matt. 22:37 has καρδία–ψυχή–διάνοια; Mark 12:30 has καρδία–ψυχή–διάνοια–ἰσχύς; and Luke 10:27 has καρδία–ψυχή–ἰσχύς–διάνοια. See Egelkraut 1976: 86, esp. n. 1. In addition, Luke uses both ἐκ (ek, from, with) and ἐν (en, with), while Deut. 6:5 and Mark 12:30 use only ἐκ and Matt. 22:37 only ἐν.

10. The lawyer provides this answer in Luke. In contrast, Jesus replies in these terms in Mark 12:29–31 = Matt. 22:37–39, which reflect a different, later setting.

11. There is debate about the age of these sections of the Testaments of the Twelve Patriarchs and, as a result, whether they reflect the Judaism of Jesus' period. Fitz-

> Keep, therefore, my children, the law of God,
> and get singleness, and walk in guilelessness,
> not playing the busybody with the business of your neighbor.
> But love the Lord and your neighbor,
> have compassion on the poor and weak.   (T. Iss. 5.1–2)

> Love the Lord through all your life,
> and one another with a true heart.   (T. Dan 5.3)

Love for one's neighbor is often seen as a summary of the law (SB 1:907–8; cf. "fear God" and "love your neighbor" in T. Ben. 3.3; Jub. 36.4–8; Philo, *Special Laws* 2.15 §63). Judaism also recognized that if humans were created in God's image to love God, one must love humans (Derrett 1970: 223–24). There were, however, ways to circumvent the command. One was through an "isolationist" approach that says "I want to be left alone, so I will not involve myself with others." The other is the one the lawyer will raise by trying to define and thus restrict who one's neighbor is (10:29; Danker 1988: 221; Marshall 1978: 444; Wiefel 1988: 209–10).

iv. Jesus' Commendation (10:28)

10:28 Jesus commends the lawyer's reply as a recognition of the relationship and devotion to God that is the essence of proper response (similar approval is found in Luke 7:43). Jesus encourages the lawyer for seeking to love God and to serve his fellow humans; he is headed in the way of life. Jesus' answer assumes that the person who loves God will respond to what he requires and be attentive to his teaching. The answer is conceptually similar to other passages where the emphasis is on a call to faith or on salvation (7:36–50; 19:1–10). As such, it should not be placed in contrast to such texts. Jesus not only accepts the answer but also emphasizes that the lawyer needs to carry it out. Jesus gives a command and a promise: "Do so and you will live." The present imperative ποίει (*poiei*, do) speaks of an abiding love and action (Plummer 1896: 285; Luce 1933: 205 suggests a possible allusion to Lev. 18:5). The reply has a definite OT ring to it (see also Deut. 4:1; 6:24; 8:1; Ezek. 20:11; Schürmann 1994:

---

myer 1985: 879 questions their value, while Derrett 1970: 225 n. 5 holds that this uncertainty is insufficient to reject the presence of these ideas in this time. Nolland 1993a: 580–82 argues that the theme has Jewish roots, but that Jesus gives more focus to these two laws being the center of godliness. In Luke, the lawyer has such insight as well. Would the early church put such a reply in the lips of a Jewish lawyer? Nolland rightly rejects insistence on a Hellenistic background (against Schürmann 1994: 135, who speaks of piety toward God and righteousness toward others), but it must be noted that nowhere in Judaism do Deut. 6 and Lev. 19 appear explicitly side by side. See also the additional note.

136). Knowledge of what God requires is not enough. Such knowledge needs to be put into practice. Love that comes from the heart responds with the hands. In the NT, the Spirit enables the believer to respond (Rom. 8:1–11).

What does such love require of humans in terms of how they see themselves in relation to Jesus and God? This is what the NT message is all about, for as Luke has just said, one cannot know the Father except by way of the Son (Luke 10:22). How can one love someone whom one does not know? In the connection of the Father to the Son, one can see that response to Jesus is a part of love for God. In the connection of the Father to the Son, one can see the Son respond faithfully to the Father. The disciple is to follow in Jesus' footsteps. If Jesus or his messengers bring God's gospel, then love calls for a response to that message and alliance with Jesus (10:1–24). The word to the lawyer is not really preevangelistic. Jesus' point is not just that the lawyer needed Jesus because he could not keep the law. The issue of love is key to evangelism. To love God is to be devoted to the teaching and person of Jesus. One may see God's love in Jesus. Anyone who loves God will respond to his message and, as a result, to fellow humans. Luke achieves this association by having this account next to 10:21–24 (see also 1 Cor. 2:9; James 1:12; 2:5, where "those who love God" is a summary description of believers).

b. Call to Be a Neighbor: The Exemplary Samaritan (10:29–37)
i. The Lawyer's Question about Neighbors (10:29)

This transitional verse gives the lawyer's response to Jesus' command and sets up the parable. The question looks innocent enough. It seems to be an effort to clarify how extensive the demand is that one love one's neighbor. Given the Jewish restrictions that apply such love only to people of the covenant, the question is a natural one (see the additional note on Luke 10:27; Greeven, *TDNT* 6:311–18).

10:29

But the narrator's comment clarifies how one should judge the lawyer's question. The lawyer "wished to justify himself" (δικαιόω, *dikaioō*, here means "to vindicate"; see Schrenk, *TDNT* 2:215 §C3; Luke 7:29; 16:15; 18:9, 14). To what does this qualification refer (Luce 1933: 205): (1) Did he ask it to justify his past conduct (so Bailey 1980: 39)? (2) Was he anxious to correct his past neglect (so most)? or (3) Was he seeking a clarification that would allow him to feel confident about where he stood? The implication is clear that he wished to soften the demand and not feel a sense of obligation to respond. If the demand were expressed softly enough, he could rest in his interpretation. But if challenged, the lawyer would need to examine how he responded in love to God and to people. He would be exposed through Jesus' demand. In fact, the parable's layout, with its negative use of the priest and Levite, suggests what the danger is for someone of traditional Jewish religious orientation. It is here that Jesus turns the discussion into a confrontation with broader application than just this religious leader or his circle (so the negative portrayal of Pharisees in 11:37–52; 16:15; 18:9–14; Grundmann 1963: 223). Jesus rejects all attempts to shrink the scope of responsibility. The lawyer is looking for the *minimum* obedience required, but Jesus requires *total* obedience. That the lawyer seeks the minimum shows that something is wrong in approaching God on human terms and not on God's. Jesus refuses to allow this limitation.

The third view, that the lawyer was seeking to be confident of his position, is the most likely. The parable leaves no doubt that the man is challenged by God's demand. The question becomes whether he loves God enough to respond to his demand. Does he love others by being a neighbor to them regardless of their origin? Talbert (1982: 122) paraphrases the lawyer's question this way: "How can I spot others who belong to God's people so that I can love them?"[12] Jesus rejects this limitation. As Derrett (1970: 225 and n. 5) says, the lawyer's question about identifying his neighbor is really an attempt to say there is such a person as a "non-neighbor." Jesus refuses to turn people into a subspecies or into things that can be ignored. Derrett defends the idea that the parable answers directly and midrashically the lawyer's question in a very Jewish fashion.[13] Marshall (1978: 446) defends the parable's authenticity, showing that it fits this setting.

Jesus' answer to the lawyer's real question is, "Do not worry about spotting God's people first, just be a neighbor to all, as this Samaritan was." The scope of the demand is greater than the lawyer might have anticipated. It suggests the need for his fresh response, especially given the apparent limits of Lev. 19:18 with its appeal to aiding fellow citizens (Deut. 10:19). Such "focused" and specific texts may have motivated the lawyer's question. Jesus' reply is formulated more in terms of Lev. 19:33–34. All people, even "sojourners," are to

12. But Talbert's imposition (1982: 122–25) of an exclusive post-Easter transformation of the story from a challenge to an exemplary account misses the force of the pre-Easter legal arguments. What is true for pleasing God is always true—whether one is entering into relationship with him or responding to being in relationship with him. In addition, there is no limitation to such love. The parable does not speak about how God's people are treated in an ecclesiastical or religious setting. When it comes to fundamental human needs and rights, all people deserve such consideration and basic care (Gal. 6:10). There is no more open, public context than the highway that this parable (and moral) travels.

13. Whether it is a midrash on Hos. 6:6, as Derrett suggests, rather than Deut. 6 and Lev. 19, is less clear. The passage speaks against a view like Sir. 12:1–4: one does good to a person one knows, and definitely not to sinners.

be loved and treated fairly. By choosing the Samaritan as the model, Jesus shows that neighbors may be found anywhere, among any racial group, even in those groups despised by the Jewish leadership. C. A. Evans (1990: 178) plausibly argues that the parable has conceptual roots in 2 Chron. 28:8–15, where Samaritans show mercy on some captives. If this is so, Jesus' exposition develops Deut. 6, Lev. 19, and Hos. 6.

ii. The Parable of the Priest, Levite, and Compassionate Samaritan (10:30–35)

Jesus begins to tell a story about a man who falls prey to robbers. The **10:30** reference to a "certain man" (ἄνθρωπός τις, *anthrōpos tis*) is a common way that Luke begins one of Jesus' parables (12:16; 14:16; 15:11; 16:1, 19; 19:12; Nolland 1993a: 592 notes that the phrase may not originate with Luke). The victim is only minimally described since he is not the focus, those who react to him are. Traveling the road from Jerusalem to Jericho (another journey going the other direction is found in 2 Chron. 28:15), he would have gone through the Pass of Adummim (Josh. 18:17), a name that is related to the Hebrew word for blood. This journey had a reputation for being dangerous long before Jesus' time (Fitzmyer 1985: 886). The journey went from almost 2,600 feet above sea level to 825 feet below sea level (Fitzmyer 1985: 886; Luce 1933: 206; Hendriksen 1978: 593; Kistemaker 1980: 167; Bishop 1963; Bishop 1970; and Beauvery 1957) and was about seventeen miles in length. It was a rocky thoroughfare winding through the desert and surrounded by caves, which made good hideouts for robbers who laid in wait. Even centuries after Christ's time, robbers continued to exploit travelers on this road.[14]

To meet such robbers was the fate of this man (on περιπίπτω, *peripiptō*, to fall into, meet, see Michaelis, *TDNT* 6:173). Λῃστής (*lēstēs*) means highwaymen or bandits, but can also refer to political zealots or what we might call terrorists today.[15] The man is outnumbered, since λῃσταῖς is plural. Such robberies were often group affairs (Rengstorf, *TDNT* 4:257–59, 261). The robbery left the man in a serious state, for not only was he robbed, stripped, and beaten, he was also "left for dead" (ἡμιθανής, *hēmithanēs*, half-dead, is a NT *ha-*

---

14. Manson 1949: 262 notes both Josephus, *Jewish War* 4.8.3 §474, who describes the region's barren character, and Jerome, who observes that Arab robbers were frequent on this route in his day some four centuries after Jesus. Nolland 1993a: 593 adds to the list Strabo 16.2.40–41 (c763), who mentions Pompey's problem with robbers and then describes the city.

15. BAGD 473; BAA 960; Josephus, *Jewish War* 2.8.4 §125 (which speaks about how Essene travelers took arms to protect themselves from such robbers) and 2.12.2 §228 (where robbers caused major social unrest). Luke refers to a robber, not a terrorist.

pax legomenon; BAGD 348; BAA 705; MM 280; LSJ 772; 4 Macc. 4:11). The man is fighting for his life.

10:31 What is the reaction to this tragic scene? Who will respond to this man in dire need? The first man with an opportunity to help is a priest. The mention of the cleric opens optimistically by noting that the priest was coming down the road "by chance" (κατὰ συγκυρίαν, *kata synkyrian*; a *hapax legomenon*). This appears to be fortunate; help is around the corner. Having a priest on the road would not be entirely surprising, since many priests lived in this region (Grundmann 1963: 223; SB 2:66, 180; Marshall 1978: 448). Here is God's servant who ministers in his temple and represents the height of piety (on priests, see the exegesis of 1:5). What will he do?

When the priest sees the man, he passes on the other side of the road. There may be a small wordplay here in the choice of the verb, for ἀντιπαρῆλθεν (*antiparēlthen*, he passed by on the other side; in the NT only here and 10:32) contains the prefix ἀντί (*anti*), whose basic meaning is "against" or "opposite." There will be no help from the priest.

Many motives have been suggested for the priest's refusal: fear of becoming unclean from touching a corpse, hesitation to help someone who may be a sinner, fear of being robbed while giving aid.[16] However, the text gives no motive, nor is it concerned with the reason (Ellis 1974: 161; Ernst 1977: 348). Derrett (1970: 212–17) shows that, although Lev. 19:16b might encourage the priest to offer aid, later Judaism exhibited efforts to get around the text (*b. Sanh.* 57a). Derrett makes much of the fear of defilement (also Grundmann 1963: 223–24, citing Lev. 21:1–3). Jeremias (1963a: 203–4) refutes any attempt to excuse the priest on grounds of potential defilement: that the priest is traveling alone rather than in a group indicates that he is headed away from the temple not to it. In fact, an exception in contracting uncleanness existed when the body was a "neglected corpse" (*m. Nazir* 6.5 [an exception even for a Nazirite!]; 7.1; *b. Nazir* 43b; 48b; B. Scott 1989: 195–96; on uncleanness and corpses, see *m. ʿEd.* 8.4). This lessens the likelihood of concern that defilement would prevent service in the temple. Marshall (1978: 448) notes that the text is clear that the man is alone, so uncleanness is not the key issue. In short, no motive is given. The point is that he gave no help. Danker (1988: 223) cites A. H. Clough's poem "The Latest Decalogue" as a good summary of this attitude: "Thou shalt not kill; but need'st not strive / Officiously to keep [others] alive."

---

16. On priestly uncleanness, see Lev. 21:1; on priests' being excused from helping sinners, see Sir. 12:4–6 and Midr. Sam. 5 §9 (31a). Nolland 1993a: 593 adds Num. 5:2; 19:2–13; Ezek. 44:25–27 to the list of texts on uncleanness, but rightly refuses to name these as a motive in the parable.

A second Jewish religious leader also comes down the road. He too **10:32** passes on the other side and offers no help. A Levite (Λευίτης, *leuitēs*) was a member of the tribe of Levi but not of Aaron's family. He was responsible for the less important tasks at the temple and could be thought of as a priest's assistant (BAGD 472; BAA 958; other NT uses are John 1:19 and Acts 4:36; Fitzmyer 1985: 887; Ezra 2:40; Neh. 10:37–38 [10:38–39 MT]). His action is grouped with that of the priest by two terms: ὁμοίως (*homoiōs*, likewise) and the reuse of the verb ἀντιπαρῆλθεν (*antiparēlthen*, passed by). The possible addition of γενόμενος (*genomenos*, happened by) with ἐλθών (*elthōn*, coming) suggests that he took a closer look (ἰδών, *idōn*, seeing) at the man and the place where he lay, and then he walked away. If so, then the disappointment with the lack of help is heightened. (But see the additional note for the textual issue.)

A second refusal by a supposedly exemplary person is a literary way to speak of a generalized condemnation of official Judaism. The lawyer, as a part of this group, would recognize this (Ellis 1974: 161; Ernst 1977: 348 [who argues for the possibility of a two-witness motif]; Deut. 19:15). At a minimum, it shows that the priest's response in Luke 10:31 was not unique. Official, pious Judaism had two tries to respond and did not. The drama remains, "Who will love this dying man?"

Everything changes as a new man arrives on the scene. The empha- **10:33** sis is on the Samaritan, for Σαμαρίτης (*Samaritēs*) is thrown forward (unlike the relative position of the previous terms for priest and Levite) and should be translated something like "a certain one, that is, a Samaritan" (Schweizer 1984: 186; Marshall 1978: 449). For a Jew, a Samaritan was among the least respected of people (see the exegesis of 9:52; Jeremias, *TDNT* 7:88–92). Eating with Samaritans was equated with eating pork (*m. Šeb.* 8.10; *b. Sanh.* 57a). Such people were unclean and to be avoided. The Samaritan would be the last type of person the lawyer would expect to be the climactic figure who resolves the story. What he likely expected was a reference to an Israelite layperson, thus yielding a story that was anticlerical in focus (Jeremias 1963a: 204; Marshall 1978: 449). Again the parable's twist in the story is key.[17] It is such a despicable person, a "despised schismatic," who helps the man, outshining the "exemplary" Jews

---

17. B. Scott's treatment (1989: 190–202) underplays the twist and argues that the Jewish hearer could not identify with the Samaritan because of cultural prejudice. But this is exactly what Jesus challenges the lawyer (and the hearer of the parable) to do and see: be a neighbor and do so without prejudice. Scott's effort to see 10:37 as Lucan on the basis of parallels and because of a shift of meaning for "neighbor" ignores Jesus' penchant for redirecting thinking and playing with meaning (e.g., 5:24; 20:41–44; see the discussion of sources and historicity above).

with his sensitive response (Plummer 1896: 287; Luce 1933: 206). It is he who "showed compassion" (ἐσπλαγχνίσθη, *esplanchnisthē*) to the half-dead man (Luke 7:13; 15:20; Köster, *TDNT* 7:554). Here is the essence of being a neighbor: having the sensitivity to see a need and act to meet it. Contextually, it also is a way to define love (10:27; Nolland 1993a: 594), called "showing mercy" in 10:37a and 6:35–36. By choosing this example, Jesus may not only be instructing the lawyer but also his disciples about how they had responded to the Samaritans (Luke 9:51–56; Plummer 1896: 287). Such racial outcasts may respond to God correctly. Enemies can be loved.

A simple word count of the NA text demonstrates where the focus of the account lies: 10:30–33 has fifty-six words (omitting Luke's introductory setting); 10:34–35 has fifty words just to describe all that the Samaritan does; and 10:36 has thirteen words.[18] The account focuses on the Samaritan's activity as a neighbor, not on his entering the kingdom.[19] While the others scurried past, this man lingered over the one who needed aid.

Some question the parable's authenticity by saying that it is unlikely a Samaritan would be on the Jericho road.[20] Three factors show the weakness of this objection: (1) an illustrative story is present, not history; (2) in Jesus' parables, the surprises often contain the central element, and such is the case here; and (3) if the Samaritan is a business man, which seems likely, he might well be traveling through the region (Marshall 1978: 449). His presence in the story suggests that he should be seen as a traveling merchant (Zahn 1920: 433 n. 12), though this is not explicitly stated.

10:34   Jesus describes six concrete compassionate actions that the Samaritan undertakes for this man. He (1) comes up to him and (2) binds his wounds. This might have involved the Samaritan's ripping up some of his own clothes for bandages (his head cloth and linen undergarment would be likely candidates; Jeremias 1963a: 204).

---

18. Crossan 1971–72: 293 argues that Jesus' original parable was altered into an example story in the tradition and redaction, a theory that makes too much of a distinction between the actions that set up the story and the point made from it. For Crossan, the original parable by Jesus was only about seeing the possibility that a Samaritan could be good. According to Crossan, the lesson that others could enter the kingdom was the key parabolic insight. The point is correct, though overstated, but Crossan's tradition history is not on target.

19. This distinction shows the problem with Crossan's view (see previous note), as he minimizes the presence of this focus by saying that the element of goodness in the story is obvious and taken for granted. But two ideas are present: (1) an enemy like a Samaritan can be good and (2) a note about what good neighborliness is.

20. Manson 1949: 262 notes this objection and rejects it, as does Luce 1933: 206–7. Luce notes that those who take the position see the original third man as an Israelite layman, a view mentioned earlier.

As he engages in the process of bandaging the wounds he (3) anoints the cuts with oil and wine. Oil soothed the wound, while wine disinfected it (Isa. 1:6; *m. Šab.* 14.4; 19.2; SB 1:428; Jeremias 1963a: 204; Manson 1949: 262; Schlier, *TDNT* 1:230 and *TDNT* 2:472; Hesse, *TDNT* 9:496 n. 3). He may have deprived himself of refreshment in the midst of his journey to care for the man. In some Jewish circles, to receive oil or wine from a Samaritan was not allowed.[21]

He (4) loads the man on his own mule, which probably meant that the Samaritan walked from here on. And then he (5) takes him to an inn, where he (6) can provide care and comfort to this man he has just met. He does not dump and run (10:35), but stays the night to care for him. Πανδοχεῖον (*pandocheion*, inn; a *hapax legomenon*) is probably a better place to stay the night than the κατάλυμα (*katalyma*, inn) of 2:7 (Plummer 1896: 288; Fitzmyer 1985: 888; see the exegesis of 2:7; BAGD 607; BAA 1229; LSJ 1296–97; Stählin, *TDNT* 5:20 n. 143; Hengel, *TDNT* 9:54 n. 46). Danker (1988: 223) notes that such innkeepers were not noted for their care, and so the man's choosing to stay and offering his money "up front" insures that the man will be treated until he recovers.[22] As a neighbor, the Samaritan did everything he could.

The Samaritan insures the continued care of the man by laying out two days' wages and offering to pay additional expenses. The innkeeper is to look after the man until the Samaritan returns. The money was enough to take care of the man's room and board for twenty-four days, since the daily rate for a poor man was about one-twelfth of a denarius (SB 1:291).[23] As was noted in the exegesis of 10:34, the deal is a rather formal one between the innkeeper and the Samaritan. That the Samaritan plans to foot the entire bill is made clear by ἐγώ (*egō*, I) plus με (*me*, me), which has an emphatic force. The sense is, "I will repay, not the man." Of course, the man has been robbed, so it is unlikely that he could pay. The Samaritan has taken care of this problem, as well as helping with the man's physical wounds. This compassionate act, as many compassionate acts do, involved a concrete price that the Samaritan was willing to pay.

10:35

Some attempt to spiritualize the story, with the Samaritan being Jesus and the return his second coming. Egelkraut (1976: 89–90,

---

21. Derrett 1970: 220–21; *b. Šab.* 13b; 17b; *m. ʿAbod. Zar.* 2.3. Derrett overinterprets the imagery here when he makes allusions to the temple setting.

22. Derrett 1970: 217–18 gives details of the transaction that show how the innkeeper was bound to offer aid. The exchange of money is part of a deal noted in *b. B. Bat.* 174a.

23. Jeremias 1969: 122–23 argues for twenty-four days, while Heutger 1983: 98 prefers fourteen. But Heutger does not consider the "poor man's" rate, speaking rather of a pensioner's rate of a denarius a week.

esp. 90 n. 2) applies the story to Jesus, though he does not include the return motif. He defends this approach by noting that elsewhere in parabolic settings σπλαγχνίζομαι (*splanchnizomai*, to show compassion) is applied to Jesus.[24] Fitzmyer (1985: 885) details more elaborate symbolic readings of the parable from the time of the fathers: the Samaritan is Jesus, the inn is the church, and the oil and wine allude to the sacraments (see also Schürmann 1994: 146). C. A. Evans (1990: 178) is right that efforts to allegorize other aspects of the parable fail. The man leaving Jerusalem does not equal the Adamic fall nor are the robbers Satan. The priest does not represent the Law nor the Levite the Prophets. The parable focuses on basic morals and compassion, not salvation history. The text gives no basis for reading the parable symbolically. Jesus' exhortation to go and do likewise shows that the point is not christological. Jesus is not telling the lawyer to look for him in the parable, but to be this kind of caring person.

iii. Jesus' Question about the Neighbor (10:36)

10:36 Jesus asks the lawyer's opinion about which character acted as a neighbor. The expression he chooses to ask the question is significant: which of the men "became" (γεγονέναι, *gegonenai*) an example of a neighbor (Plummer 1896: 289)? Compassion, response, and love make a neighbor, not locale or race (Manson 1949: 263). Jesus' question shows what a neighbor is. One should not seek to narrowly define who is a neighbor so as to limit one's responsibility. The obligation is not to see what can be avoided, but to render aid when it can be readily supplied.

iv. The Lawyer's Recognition of the Samaritan (10:37a)

10:37a The lawyer gives the obvious answer to Jesus' question, though he cannot bring himself to say "Samaritan" (Plummer 1896: 289; Jeremias 1963a: 205). He focuses instead on the showing of mercy, which was the key to the Samaritan's exemplary action.[25] The lawyer has seen the point, but has yet to break through his prejudice. So Jesus calls him to respond.

v. Jesus' Command to Do like the Samaritan (10:37b)

10:37b Jesus' response to the reply is simple: the lawyer is to emulate the Samaritan. Ποίει (*poiei*, do) recalls Jesus' earlier instruction in 10:28

---

24. The term occurs in Luke at 7:13; 10:33; and 15:20. The exceptions to Egelkraut's claim, Matt. 18:27 and Luke 15:20, undercut his argument.

25. Fitzmyer 1985: 888 sees a possible allusion to Mic. 6:8. The expression recalls God's action in Luke 1:72.

when he said "do (ποίει) this and you will live." The present tense of the command in this context looks at continuous response (Plummer 1896: 289). The lawyer should be a neighbor—like the Samaritan was. Love for God expresses itself in a life that is sensitive to others. This combination is how life is to be pursued and found.

Summary

Luke 10:25–37 is a significant passage about a disciple's ethics. What kind of action does God require of his people? Disciples are to love God fully and to manifest that love toward others. This is the thrust of Jesus' reply to the lawyer's question about participating in the resurrection of the righteous. If the lawyer loves God, he will respond obediently to what God asks of him and will recognize his need to respond to what God teaches, since the Father is seen through the Son, as 10:21–24 just indicated.

The outgrowth of that love for God is a response to our fellow humans. We are to love and be a neighbor to those who are part of our lives. Neighborliness is not found in a racial bond, nationality, color, gender, proximity, or by living in a certain neighborhood. We become a neighbor by responding sensitively to the needs of others. Such was the example of the Samaritan, who not only soothed the beaten man's wounds, but also took him to a place of shelter, cared for him, and made sure his needs were met. The Samaritan cared for a person he had never seen before. Without asking questions, he served a cup of mercy to a person half-dead. By reviving life, he showed life. If we seek to restrict those we serve, we need to hear the lesson Jesus taught the lawyer. The issue is not who we may or may not serve, but serving where need exists. We are not to seek to limit who our neighbors might be. Rather, we are to be a neighbor to those whose needs we can meet.

Additional Notes

10:27. The textual issues associated with this verse mostly center around minor details: the presence of καί or of qualifying pronouns and the case of certain nouns (Marshall 1978: 443). With the possible exception of including τῆς (the) before καρδίας, UBS–NA is the harder reading and has good manuscript support: 𝔓[75], ℵ, B, C, L, W, Θ, and Byz (except for τῆς). However, the wide variety of variants in the citation make determining the exact text difficult.

10:27. At Qumran and among the Pharisees, certain groups were excluded from the "love" command (1QS 1.10; 9.21–22). Later Judaism excluded Samaritans, foreigners, and resident aliens who did not convert within a year (Fichtner and Greeven, *TDNT* 6:315–16, esp. nn. 30, 38; *Mekilta de Rabbi*

Ishmael, tractate *Nezikin* 11 on Exod. 21:35 [= Lauterbach 1933–35: 3.95]). Judaism did, however, exhibit concern for one's neighbor: " 'You shall love your neighbor as yourself.' Rabbi Akiva said, 'This is a great and comprehensive principle in the Torah' " (*Sipra* 200 on Lev. 19:18 [= Neusner 1988b: 3.109]; Akiva died around A.D. 135). And Hillel, one of the great rabbis of the late first century B.C., said: "What is hateful to you, do not do to your neighbor; that is the whole Torah, while the rest is commentary. Go and learn" (*b. Šab.* 31a). See also T. Naph. (Hebrew version) 1.6; T. Zeb. 5.1; T. Iss. 7.6; and Philo, *Special Laws* 2.15 §63 (on this theme, see Burchard 1970 [who argues for a Hellenistic background, a view I rejected above]; Nissen 1974; and J. Stern 1966).

10:32. A textual problem concerns whether one or two descriptive references to the Levite's approach are present. $\mathfrak{P}^{75}$, $\aleph^2$, B, L, Ξ, family 1, 33, and 1241 exclude the participle γενόμενος. $\mathfrak{P}^{45}$, A, C, D, E, G, H, W, Γ, Δ, Θ, and most minuscules (i.e., Byz) include it (Metzger 1975: 152). Some manuscripts that include γενόμενος do not have the participle ἐλθών (coming): $\mathfrak{P}^{45}$, D, and some minuscules. If a reading is adopted that has only one of these terms, any intensification in the scene is lost. It is hard to be certain, however, that both terms were present in the text and which is original if one is omitted. Plummer (1896: 287) argues that both terms cannot be genuine. Fitzmyer (1985: 887) omits γενόμενος. UBS–NA includes it in brackets, which expresses doubt about its presence in the original. Marshall (1978: 448) accepts it. It is not at all clear that both terms for the approach are original.

2. Looking to Jesus: Martha and Mary (10:38–42)

Jesus' visit with Mary and Martha is an object lesson on the priority of responding to Jesus over worldly concerns. The visit is built around a contrast. Martha and Jesus are the focus of the action, though Mary is the point of the example—despite her saying nothing. The literary style of the "silent testimony" recalls the woman of Luke 7:36–50, as does the presence of an exemplary action (Schweizer 1984: 188). First, we see Martha, busy and harried, engaged in getting everything right for Jesus' visit, and disturbed over Mary's lack of help. The presence of sibling tension adds a touch of real life to the dispute. We find Mary seated at the feet of Jesus, the position of a disciple, listening to his every word (Talbert 1982: 125). Jesus notes that it is Mary who has chosen well. Time with Jesus is more important than preparing an elaborate meal for him. Sometimes the activity associated with ministry can prevent us from more important endeavors—such as hearing God's word so that he can touch us (8:15, 21). The image recalls Deut. 8:3.[1] Service of the hand cannot supersede service with the ear, since the ear guides the heart and the hand. In addition, the picture of a woman in the disciple's position, at the feet of Jesus, would be startling in a culture where women did not receive formal teaching from a rabbi (Fitzmyer 1985: 892; Oepke, *TDNT* 1:781–82).[2]

This pericope is part of a three-unit section that deals with a disciple's responsibilities before God. The previous passage (10:25–37) gave the first point: disciples are to love their neighbor, which involves service to one in need. Loving one's neighbor means being a neighbor (on links to 10:25–37, see Nolland 1993a:

---

1. Wall 1989 argues that this story is a call to hear the word similar to Deut. 8:3. He also argues that Luke 10:25–37 is an example story expounding Deut. 7:12. This connection with Deuteronomy is stronger in Luke 10:38–42 than in 10:25–37.

2. M. Soṭa 3.4 shows that some rabbis were against any instruction for women, while others thought it advisable. Josephus expresses a negative attitude toward women when he argues that the law says they are inferior to men in all things (*Against Apion* 2.24 §201). The connection of this text to Josephus is debated, since he does occasionally praise women, such as Alexandra (*Antiquities* 13.16.6 §§430–31). However, that she is regarded as an exception shows Josephus's general attitude.

600). This account shows that attention to Jesus is a key element in the disciple's life. In fact, this account also develops the lawyer's response about wholehearted devotion to God. While love of neighbor is illustrated by the Samaritan, Mary pictures devotion to God and his teaching through faithful attention to Jesus (Marshall 1978: 450; Klostermann 1929: 122; Grundmann 1963: 225).[3] The next passage, 11:1–13, will stress being dependent on a good and gracious God through an active prayer life. To serve others, like the Samaritan, does not mean that we should be so distracted by service that we ignore God. Our service to others is best set in the context of being in contact with God.

Sources and Historicity

This event is present only in Luke, though Martha and Mary appear in John 11:1–12:8. This is an account from special Lucan material (Fitzmyer 1985: 891; Ernst 1977: 354; Wiefel 1988: 212). John makes it clear that their home is in Bethany, about two miles (three kilometers) from Jerusalem (Zahn 1920: 435). Luke does not note the location of this event, probably because he is not yet stressing in the journey sequence being near to Jerusalem. The Jesus Seminar treats the teaching as inauthentic, printing 10:41–42 in black type. The episode is "entirely crafted by Luke," and the words are "fabricated for the occasion" by him (Funk and Hoover 1993: 325). The only reason the seminar gives is that the saying does "not have the character of aphorisms that would have been remembered as independent sayings."

However, there is no reason to question the event's authenticity (for other defenses of authenticity, see Marshall 1978: 451 and Nolland 1993a: 601). The Jesus Seminar's claim about memorable aphorisms seems to suggest that only short, pithy sayings can be recorded or authentic. This sounds more like a presupposition than something demonstrated. In all likelihood, it is the lack of parallels that is the real issue. But the passage has conceptual parallels: (1) Jesus elsewhere hesitates to enter disputes (Luke 12:13–15; Mark 10:13–16); (2) Jesus attributes value to his teaching and call (Luke 6:47–49; 8:19–21; 9:57–62; 11:27–28); and (3) the saying fits Jesus' style of strong contrasts (4:3; 8:14; Brutscheck 1986: 159). Brutscheck (1986: 65–95, 133–43) also argues for a pre-Lucan form of the story, against the claims of Lucan creation (see also Schürmann 1994: 164; Ernst 1977: 354). Jesus' emphasis on the word (the second item above) is multiply attested. Following Brutscheck, Nolland (1993a: 602

---

3. Fitzmyer 1985: 891 sees no connection between the accounts, regarding such an association as stretching the point (so also Ernst 1977: 354). But literary sequence and theme make it seem likely; see esp. Talbert 1982: 125.

[10:38], 603 [10:39–40], 604 [10:41–42]) lists evidence of Lucan stylistic touches in the account. Most stylistic touches occur early in the account and are almost totally absent in Jesus' remarks. The early church saw the lesson as the superiority of the contemplative life over the active life (Grundmann 1963: 226 notes the view of Gregory the Great, *Homily on Ezekiel* 2.2.9), reflecting its monastic emphasis. The point of the text's contrast is probably not that strong (see the exegesis of 10:42).

The account is a pronouncement story, since Jesus' final remark is central (Fitzmyer 1985: 891–92; Bultmann 1963: 33). Berger (1984: 81–82) speaks of apophthegm. One can also speak of a commendation account and an example story (the silent character is the example; Nolland 1993a: 601). Schürmann (1994: 163) prefers to speak of a "meeting" narrative, such as 19:1–10. However, it is clear that the key to the passage is the pronouncement that also commends behavior like Mary's (Tannehill 1981a and 1981b speaks of an objection-commendation story).

The outline of Luke 10:38–42 is as follows:

a. Setting (10:38–39)
b. Martha's complaint about Mary (10:40)
c. Jesus' comment about Mary's good choice (10:41–42)

The key image is of the disciple at Jesus' feet listening to his word. Labor at the expense of Jesus' word is not a good choice. The disciple is to make sitting at Jesus' feet a priority. Jesus' rebuke is not of Martha's action per se, but of action taken at the expense of sitting and listening to God's word and of her attitude toward another serving in a different way. It is better to be a listening disciple than an immaculate host.

Exegesis and Exposition

[38]Now as they went on their way, he entered a certain village; and a woman named Martha received ⌜him⌝. [39]And she also had a sister named Mary, ⌜who⌝ sat at the Lord's feet and listened to his teaching. [40]But Martha was distracted with much service; and she went to him and said, "Lord, do you not care that my sister has left me alone to serve? Speak to her then so she might help me." [41]⌜The Lord⌝ replied to her, "Martha, Martha, you are anxious and ⌜troubled⌝ about many things. [42]⌜One thing is needful.⌝ Mary has chosen the good portion, which shall not be taken away from her."

a. Setting (10:38–39)

Luke briefly lays out the setting. As they journey, Jesus and the disciples enter a certain village. The picture of Jesus on the move con- **10:38** tinues the journey account but no locale is named, because the event is more important than the place (9:51; 10:1; Ernst 1977: 355; Nolland 1993a: 603). If Bethany was the only home of these women (John 11:1, 18; 12:1) and if these two are the same ladies that are present in John, then Luke's arrangement of the journey section is more thematic and topical, since Jesus is now near Jerusalem, whereas in 17:11 he is well north of Jerusalem (on Bethany, see the exegesis of Luke 19:29).

Jesus receives a meal at Martha's home, one of several Lucan events at a meal (5:29; 7:36; 14:1; 24:30, 43). Since Martha alone is mentioned, it seems likely that she is the hostess and that the home is her own, possibly as the older sister (the assumption is that no husband is present, but she could be unmarried).

Though Luke makes nothing of it, the Aramaic form of the name *Martha* (Μάρθα) does not mean "hostess" (so SB 2:184–85; Marshall 1978: 451) but is the feminine form of "lord, master," thus "mistress" (Fitzmyer 1985: 893). This is the first specific mention of women since 8:1–3. A simple lesson will follow the simple setting.

10:39 Luke introduces the key silent figure.[4] Martha's sister, Mary, is sitting at Jesus' feet listening to his teaching like a disciple (Luke 8:35; Acts 16:14 [conceptually]; 22:3; Ernst 1977: 355). *M. ʾAbot* 1.4 says, "Let your house be a meetinghouse for the sages and sit amid the dust of their feet and drink in their words with thirst." That a woman has this position is somewhat unusual, paralleling the Samaritan's surprising response in the previous account (Ernst 1977: 355; Ellis 1974: 162; Goppelt, *TDNT* 8:328 n. 95; Leipoldt 1955: 69–114; Jeremias 1969: 363; Witherington 1984: 101). In fact, Mary took the initiative, as the reflexive παρακαθεσθεῖσα (*parakathestheisa*, she sat herself beside) indicates (Fitzmyer 1985: 893). Jesus' ministry breaks molds. Those who are sensitive to him recognize that he invites them to come to him. They sense that he will receive them, that he is ready to teach all types of people. In the early church, women are noted for their service (Wiefel 1988:212): Phoebe (Rom. 16:1–2), Priscilla (Rom. 16:3), Lydia (Acts 16:14–15), and the four daughters of Philip (Acts 21:9). Creed (1930: 154) compares Mary to the pious woman of 1 Cor. 7:35, while Martha depicts the woman who is too worried about the cares of this world (Marshall 1978: 452 notes that an adverb meaning "without distraction" [ἀπερισπάστως, *aperispastōs*] occurs in 1 Cor. 7:35). In addition, Mary continually listens to Jesus. It is significant that Jesus is described here as ὁ κύριος (*ho kyrios*, the Lord), so it is the "Lord's teaching" that Mary is hearing.

---

4. The initial καί probably means "also" and introduces the second figure in the house, Mary. On the use of ὅδε (this person), here τῇδε, see BDF §289, §290.1.

b. Martha's Complaint about Mary (10:40)

In a vivid scene, we see only Martha slaving away. She alone is pre- **10:40**
paring the meal for Jesus and the others. Mary is relaxing at the
Master's feet, doing nothing—at least according Martha, who turns
to enlist the teacher's aid in getting help for her "ministry" (on δια-
κονίαν, diakonian, as a reference to food preparation, see Beyer,
TDNT 2:87). Also significant is μόνην (monēn, alone), which points
out Martha's solitary service. Ἐπιστᾶσα (epistasa) pictures her leaving her work and stepping up to Jesus to address him (from
ἐφίστημι, ephistēmi, to come up to; BAGD 330 §1a; BAA 668 §1a).

The strong and direct request includes three elements. (1) The
Lord is placed in the position of being potentially insensitive. The
rhetorical question raises the issue of whether he cares about what
is taking place. A "yes" answer is anticipated by the use of οὐ (ou,
not), so that the question is asked with the expectation that the Lord
does care and will react. But that Martha has to raise the issue
shows her irritation. (2) Martha is concerned that she is left alone.
The aorist κατέλιπεν (katelipen) says that Mary "has left" Martha to
serve alone. In Martha's point of view Mary has deserted her (BAGD
413 §1d; BAA 840 §1d).[5] (3) As a result, what follows is really a demand that Jesus speak to Mary so that she might help. The use of
ἵνα (hina) seems to indicate purpose here, since Martha wants help.
In sum, Martha is miffed at Mary!

All of this is couched in the narrator's contrasting description of
Martha's attitude as "distracted" by her service. Περισπάω (peri-
spaō), a NT *hapax legomenon* (BAGD 650 §2; BAA 1311 §2), indicates
"being pulled away" by something, and can refer not only to distraction but also to being overburdened with an affair. This remark
characterizes both Martha's response and her failure. Her activity
has influenced and skewed her perspective. Perhaps she tried to listen to Jesus, but could not because of her work. She is confident that
if Jesus speaks to Mary he can convince her delinquent sister to help
(συναντιλάβηται, synantilabētai, means "to take up and help, to bear
a burden"; Delling, *TDNT* 1:376; Exod. 18:22; Num. 11:17). The narrator indicates that her agitation is misguided and her perspective is
improper. She is too busy for him, even though she is doing a good
thing.

Jesus' response fits a pattern: whenever anyone asks him to step
in and help in a dispute, he is slow to take the side of the one asking
for help (Luke 12:13; John 8:4).

---

5. Διακονεῖν (to serve) is an infinitive of result: Martha is left with the result that
she serves alone; BDF §392.1f.

c. Jesus' Comment about Mary's Good Choice (10:41–42)

10:41 Jesus offers a tender response signaled by the use of a double vocative, which is a sign of emotion (Luke 6:46; 8:24; 13:34; 22:31).[6] Jesus paints a picture of a woman overwhelmed, using descriptive words that confirm what the reader was told in 10:40 about Martha's being distracted. She is anxious and troubled by many things.[7] In her focus on these things she is forgetting the most important person, and the circumstances are overwhelming her. The result was that she risked running over others with her poor attitude. Jesus intends to correct her misperception.

10:42 The rest of the reply commends Mary's decision. She has chosen the one thing that counts: to sit and reflect on Jesus' teaching and the kingdom of God (Manson 1949: 264). She has chosen the "good portion" (τὴν ἀγαθὴν μερίδα, *tēn agathēn merida*), a figurative reference to "the right meal," the word of God (Luke 4:4; Deut. 8:3). A figurative reference is indicated by Jesus' saying that what she has chosen will not be taken away, a reference that cannot be about literal food (John 6:35; Ps. 16:5; 73:26–28 [of God as the portion]; 119:57 [of God, whose word will be obeyed]; Fitzmyer 1985: 894; Schürmann 1994: 159). In fact, the reply is very much like Ps. 119:57–64: to be close to God and have him as one's portion is to be ready to be taught. Response to God's word is most important for a disciple (Luke 8:18; 11:27–28; 12:19–21, 33; Schneider 1977a: 252; Arndt 1956: 293–94; *m. ʾAbot* 2.8; 3.2). Mary has done right. Martha should slow down and relax. The disciple should never be too busy to sit at Jesus' feet.

Summary Luke 10:38–42 highlights a major feature of discipleship: choosing to order one's affairs properly. One of the facts of life is that its demands are often all consuming. In fact, much of life is spent fulfilling these demands. Such was Martha's situation when Jesus visited her. She was diligent in preparing an appropriate meal for the teacher. In contrast, Mary simply sat down. She was not lifting a finger to help, and Martha was disturbed. But Mary had made the right choice, according to Jesus. The disciple who reflects on Jesus' teaching receives a meal that is never removed. To sit at Jesus' feet is the disciple's priority. The worries of life should never prevent one from consuming God's word. This is Luke's

---

6. This emphatic figure of repetition is called "epanadiplosis"; BDF §493.1.

7. The verb θορυβέω (to be troubled), is related to the verb used here (θορυβάζω, a *hapax legomenon*). Both verbs look at a situation of disorder, not in terms of illness but stress; BAGD 362–63; BAA 737; Acts 17:5; 20:10; Matt. 9:23 = Mark 5:39; 13:7 (variant reading in Codex D).

message to disciples: sit at Jesus' feet and devour his teaching, since there is no more important meal.

Additional Notes

10:38. The details about the setting are related to a textual problem: did the original text read (1) αὐτὸν εἰς τὸν οἶκον αὐτῆς (him in her house; A, D, W, Δ, Ψ, family 1, family 13, Byz, Lect, most Itala, Syriac); (2) αὐτὸν εἰς τὴν οἰκίαν (him in her house; 𝔓³, ℵ, C, L, Ξ); or (3) αὐτόν (him; 𝔓⁴⁵, 𝔓⁷⁵, B, some Coptic)? The first option has a feminine possessive pronoun, while the second has a feminine reference to house (and translates just like the first). The third option, found in UBS–NA, omits reference to the home, but implies that Jesus is in Martha's home, since only she is said to receive him.[8] That many manuscripts include the longer phrase in different forms speaks against either of the first two options being original. The reading chosen does not affect the general meaning, only its specificity (Fitzmyer 1985: 893). I prefer the third reading as the shorter reading.

10:39. The presence of ἥ (who) is textually uncertain: omitted by 𝔓⁴⁵, 𝔓⁷⁵, ℵ, and L, it is found in A, B, C, D, W, Θ, Ψ, family 1, family 13, and Byz. This geographic distribution speaks for its originality. Its presence indicates that the first use of καί should be translated "also."

10:41. Some manuscripts read Ἰησοῦς (Jesus; A, B, C, D, W, Θ, Byz, Itala, most Syriac, some Bohairic). But ὁ κύριος (the Lord) occurs in several early texts (𝔓³, 𝔓⁴⁵, 𝔓⁷⁵, ℵ, L, Vulgate, Sahidic, some Bohairic) and is original because of its distribution and Luke's tendency to use κύριος in narrative remarks.

10:41. The verb θορυβάζῃ (you are troubled; 𝔓⁴⁵, 𝔓⁷⁵, C*, W, Θ, Vulgate, some Syriac, Sahidic, Bohairic) is probably original over τυρβάζῃ (you are troubled; A, family 13, Byz, Lect). The rare first verb is a slightly harder reading (Fitzmyer 1985: 894; Marshall 1978: 453). If original, τυρβάζω would be a NT *hapax legomenon* (BAGD 830; BAA 1655). A clear decision is difficult.

10:42. What is needed: one thing or one out of many? 𝔓⁴⁵, 𝔓⁷⁵, A, C, Δ, Ψ, Byz, Lect, and most versions have ἑνὸς δέ ἐστιν χρεία (but one thing is necessary). 𝔓³, ℵ (lacks χρεία), B, L, family 1, 33, and some versions read ὀλίγων δέ ἐστιν χρεία ἢ ἑνός (few things are needed, or one). This difficult problem is a close call. Many favor the reading cited in the UBS–NA text, but the longer reading also has support. Marshall (1978: 454) is undecided and leans to the longer reading (with Danker 1988: 225 and Wiefel 1988: 211–12). Fee (1981) has a full discussion and also opts for the longer reading.

8. On ὑποδέχομαι as "receiving into a home," see Luke 19:6; Acts 17:7; James 2:25; BAGD 844; BAA 1682.

The UBS–NA text does seem more likely, based on geographical distribution and the reading's shorter form, not to mention the variation found in the wording of the longer variant. The shorter text cannot, however, explain the presence of the variants. Though the wording of the text is unusual, the point is clear, regardless of the reading. Mary is right to sit at Jesus' feet and will be blessed for her choice. Martha should learn from her example, slow down, and not complain.

3. Looking to God: Call to Prayer (11:1–13)

An exhortation to prayer follows Jesus' teachings on being a neighbor and on giving attention to him. The disciple is to look to God. This point comes in three steps. In Luke 11:1–4, Jesus' model prayer expresses the disciple's dependence on God and their desire that God's will and glory be revealed. In 11:5–8, a brief parable exhorts disciples to be bold and aggressive in prayer. And in 11:9–13, there appears a two-part exhortation to prayer. Disciples are to come to God as a child comes to a parent, knowing that God meets their basic needs. Jesus promises that those who ask will receive spiritual blessing, pointing out that the Father's kindness is greater than a human's compassion. God expresses his compassion by sending the Holy Spirit to those who ask. The disciple's requests are for God's presence and insight, and the initial fulfillment of this promise is the coming of the "promise of the Father" (Luke 24:49; Acts 2:1–39). Jesus promises direction from God's Spirit (Talbert 1982: 133; Tannehill 1986: 239; Smalley 1973). Such insight is essential to the disciple and should be eagerly sought, because the one who seeks God can know that he is gracious. The theme of seeking God reappears in Luke 12:30–32 (Tannehill 1986: 238).

Sources and Historicity

Luke 11:1–4 parallels the well-known version of the Lord's Prayer found in Matt. 6:9–13 (Aland 1985: §185). In fact, many hold that what is present here reflects the prayer's shorter original version (e.g., Schneider 1977a: 256). So Creed (1930: 155) argues by suggesting that the unusual term ἐπιούσιος (daily), shared by both versions, looks back to an original, single version.[1] Others see an original version in Matthew that Luke shortened (Ott

---

1. Ellis 1974: 163–64 attributes the original context to Luke, a view that is possible only if the Sermon on the Mount is a Matthean topical sermon (which, though possible, is not likely). In favor of one occasion or point of origin are Manson 1949: 265; Godet 1875: 2.47; Zahn 1920: 448–49 (favoring a view like Ellis's); Schneider 1977a: 256; and Wiefel 1988: 215. A good summary of recent discussion may be found in Meier 1994: 291–93, 353–57. Meier sees Luke as reflecting the original size and structure of the prayer, with Matthew expanding the petitions and Luke altering some wording. But unlike many, he sees two versions in circulation. The Jesus Seminar (Funk and Hoover 1993: 325–27) sees Q as the source, with Matthew making ad-

1965: 112–23). Many thus identify the two passages as having the same origin (Schweizer 1984: 190; Fitzmyer 1985: 897 [with Matthew lengthening the prayer]).[2] Nolland's view (1993a: 610) is complex: where Matthew and Luke overlap, Matthew is usually more original. The additional petitions in Matthew predate him and indicate that the prayer existed in more than one form, but Luke's version reflects the prayer's original purpose.

But the one-source approach is not so clear, since the setting and form of the two prayers differ. The Matthean prayer occurs in the Sermon on the Mount, a public setting in which Jesus simply prays the prayer. If Luke had wanted to present the prayer as Matthew or his source did, why did he not place it in the Sermon on the Plain? Either Luke's focus on love made prayer irrelevant or Matthew created the sermon setting for the prayer. More important, in Luke the disciples ask for instruction and Jesus responds with this shorter form. Luke's setting is a private one, though his placement of the event is general and vague enough to allow one to argue for a topical arrangement. However, Luke's form of the prayer, though almost verbally the same as Matthew's prayer, lacks two lines of Matthew's version: the reference to God's will being done and the request to be delivered from evil. These omissions are hard to explain if Luke knew Matthew's version.[3] It seems more likely that these are distinct prayers in distinct settings or, at the least, distinct versions of the prayer (Liefeld 1984: 946; Arndt 1956: 294; Hendriksen 1978: 608–9 [unclear]).[4] Others argue that two distinct versions existed in the tradition, but are less specific on whether two scenes are in view.[5] If two events are present, Jesus takes a public prayer and

---

ditions and Luke introducing some changes in vocabulary. The seminar's view of these details parallels many critics.

2. Fitzmyer 1985: 897–98 is skeptical about the Lucan setting, though he does regard it as likely that the prayer goes back to Jesus. See also Egelkraut 1976: 153, esp. n. 1.

3. Other variations will be noted in the verses. In fact, everything about Luke's version is difficult—if the premise is that Luke had Matthew and that the two events are one.

4. Plummer 1896: 293 argues that if the prayer was delivered only once, then Luke has the original setting, which came earlier in Jesus' ministry. I agree that this is the next best option, given the possibility that the Sermon on the Mount is an anthology or a preaching summary.

5. Marshall 1978: 455 sees either two versions or Matthew's adding to an original short edition like that in Luke. These reflect distinct recensions of Q; but he does not discuss the number of events. Jeremias 1971a: 193–96 argues for the originality of the Lucan form and posits an Aramaic form behind it. He regards its structure as memorable in an oral context, carrying rhyme and a two-four rhythm (so also Meier 1994: 293). Beasley-Murray 1986: 147 argues that Luke's version is original in extent, but that Matthew's is closer to the original wording, a view close to Nolland's (noted above). For him Luke's prayer circulated in Gentile Christian circles, while Matthew's was the Jewish-Christian version. Nevertheless, for him the prayer's roots go back to Jesus. Wiefel 1988: 215 is less certain of this attempt to distinguish communities.

makes it a model for the disciples to follow. He offered the prayer to the disciples in the Sermon on the Mount and now makes it a model, though it is not the prayer's exact wording that concerns him, as much as the prayer's focus on the Father.[6] Dependence on God and submission to his desires are the key lessons of the prayer.

The Jesus Seminar rates the portions of the prayer differently (Funk and Hoover 1993: 325–27; their view of sources and editing was summarized in n. 1 above). The seminar does not believe that Jesus taught his disciples this prayer, so 11:2a is printed in black type. The seminar accepts πάτερ (Father) as going back to Jesus (red type) and regards the first two petitions on holiness and kingdom as likely for Jesus (pink type). The three remaining requests (bread, forgiveness, and temptation) are seen as revisions of what Jesus said (gray type). The seminar's reason for rejecting the idea that Jesus taught the prayer is that it is unlikely that each petition would be recalled as individual prayers under oral-discourse transmission. This reasoning is weak in the light of Jewish precedent for memorizing prayers or confessions, starting with the *Shemaᶜ* of Deut. 6:4–5 and extending to national prayers like the "Eighteen Benedictions" (*Shemoneh Esreh* or *Amidah* [see Schürer 1973–87: 2.456–61]).[7] Qumran also had lengthy community prayers. These texts show that oral tradition did pass on such prayer. Defending the prayer's early date, Meier (1994: 293–94) notes that (1) the relationship of "debt" to "sin" is an Aramaic concept (also Fitzmyer 1985: 906; 4QMess ar 2.17); (2) the linking of "kingdom" and "come" in a prayer does not fit Judaism or later Christianity; and (3) this is the only prayer that Jesus taught, despite numerous NT prayers. The prayer goes back to Jesus (Schürmann 1994: 206).

Luke 11:5–8 has no Synoptic parallel and belongs to Luke's special material (Aland 1985: §186; Fitzmyer 1985: 910). The parable is one of many graphic pictures that Jesus uses to urge people to pray (18:1–8, 9–14). The Jesus Seminar (Funk and Hoover 1993: 327) regards it as authentic (pink type), though it thinks that Luke relocated it here to make it apply to prayer, not hospitality—a claim that is unprovable. The parable coheres nicely as it is (Nolland 1993a: 623).

Luke 11:9–13 also has a parallel in Matthew's Sermon on the Mount: Matt. 7:7–11 (Aland 1985: §187). Again, the setting is somewhat different in Luke with its private instruction. And the Lucan form, with its focus on the Holy Spirit rather than on "good things" in general, may suggest a different setting. It is possible that Luke has taken a saying related to his theme and brought it in at this point, since he has no introduction to this section (so Fitzmyer 1985: 913–14; Grundmann 1963: 234; and Wiefel 1988: 217 [cit-

6. To regard such a repetition as unbelievable underestimates the role of "liturgical-style" community prayers in the ancient world. Such repetition is not unusual.

7. Also, the Jewish prayer *Kaddish* is often cited as relevant, but it is uncertain that its roots go back this far (for discussion, see Petuchowski and Brocke 1978).

ing Q]). The more likely explanation is that the exhortation's repetition with its graphic illustration was slightly altered to fit the more narrow setting.[8]

The Jesus Seminar sees 11:9–13 as rooted in Jesus to varying degrees (Funk and Hoover 1993: 328–29). Luke 11:9–10 is seen as authentic (pink type) because of multiple attestation in Matt. 7:7–8 (Q) and the Gospel of Thomas 94, 92, and 2. The use of gray type for 11:11–13 reflects differences between Luke and Matthew (the seminar prints the Matthean version in pink type; Funk and Hoover 1993: 155). Nolland (1993a: 628) suggests that the difference may be rooted in Luke's using his parable source rather than a source shared with Matthew. The theme of asking God and the family analogy fit well with Jesus (John 15:7, 16; 16:24; Mark 11:24; James 1:5–6; 4:2–3 [James's teaching is often rooted in Jesus]). This material reflects Jesus' teaching.

This unit contains teaching (11:1–4), elaborated by a parable (11:5–8), exhortation (11:9–10), and illustration (11:11–13). As such, it shows the graphic variety of Jesus' teaching through illustrations drawn from everyday life. Such illustrations make their point through a twist introduced into the normal state of affairs (such as the meal of serpents and scorpions in 11:11–12!).

The form of the unit is a discourse on prayer that contains prayer, parable, and sayings.[9] The outline of Luke 11:1–13 is as follows:

    a. Example prayer to the Father (11:1–4)
      i. The disciple's request (11:1)
      ii. Example prayer (11:2–4)
        (1) Address: Father (11:2a)
        (2) First declaration: holy be your name (11:2b)
        (3) Second declaration: your kingdom come (11:2c)
        (4) First request: give us our daily bread (11:3)
        (5) Second request: forgive us our debts (11:4a)
        (6) Basis: we have forgiven all others (11:4b)
        (7) Third request: do not lead us into temptation (11:4c)
    b. Parable about boldness in prayer (11:5–8)
      i. Parable (11:5–7)
      ii. Point: shameless boldness in prayer (11:8)
    c. Exhortations to trust a gracious Father (11:9–13)
      i. Exhortation to ask (11:9–10)
      ii. God's compassion: the comparison (11:11–13)

---

8. Without discussing the settings, Marshall 1978: 466 speaks only of different versions of the teaching having reached Matthew and Luke.

9. Bultmann 1963: 324 is similar. Berger 1984: 46, 239–40 argues that two parables conclude the passage, but it is hard to know if 11:11–13 is a parable or a wisdom saying that makes a simple comparison.

The topic clearly is prayer. The dependent disciple communicates with the Father. The model starts with Jesus at prayer. Certain suppositions characterize the moral attitude: the holiness of God, kingdom expectation with the desire that it come in fullness, dependence on God for daily provision and forgiveness, a recognized need to forgive others based upon the divine example, and a request for spiritual protection. The disciple should be bold in prayer and should ask for spiritual insight from a willing Father. Jesus promises the Spirit's insight to those who ask. The passage is an exhortation to disciples to pray constantly, because prayer reflects an intimate relationship with the Father.

Exegesis and Exposition

¹And he was praying in a certain place, and when he ceased, one of the disciples said to him, "Lord teach us to pray, as John taught his disciples." ²And he said to them, "When ⌜you pray⌝ say,

⌜'Father'⌝,
let your name be sanctified;
⌜let your kingdom come⌝;
3   give us each day our daily bread;
4   and forgive us our sins, for we ourselves also forgive everyone who is indebted to us;
⌜and do not lead us into temptation⌝.'"

⁵And he said to them, "Which of you who has a friend will go to him at midnight and say to him, 'Friend, lend me three loaves, ⁶for a friend of mine has arrived on a journey and there is nothing to set before him,' ⁷and he will answer from within, 'Do not bother me; the door is closed, and my children are with me in bed; I cannot get up and give you anything.'? ⁸I say to you, if he does not get up and give to him because he is his friend, indeed because of his bold shamelessness he will rise up and give him what he needs."

⁹And I say to you, "Ask and it will be given to you. Seek and you will find. Knock and it will be opened to you. ¹⁰For the one who asks receives, and the one who seeks finds, and to the one who knocks ⌜it will be opened⌝. ¹¹What father among you, if his son asks for a ⌜fish⌝ will give him a serpent instead of a fish? ¹²Or of he asks for an egg, will give him a scorpion? ¹³If you then, who are evil, know how to give good gifts to your children, how much more will the heavenly Father give the Holy Spirit to those who ask him!"

a. Example Prayer to the Father (11:1–4)
i. The Disciple's Request (11:1)

Luke introduces the teaching in general terms. Jesus is praying again **11:1** (as in Luke 3:21; 5:16; 6:12; 9:18, 28). The disciples wait for him to finish and when he does, one of them asks for instruction about prayer. There may be a slight note of urgency in the request, since διδαξον (didaxon) is an aorist imperative ("teach us now to pray"; Arndt 1956: 294). As is common in the journey section, no locale or time is given. The disciples want a prayer like the one John the Baptist taught his disciples (5:33 shows a similar concern about the practice of John's disciples). The request for teaching from a religious leader is common, but this is the only place in the Gospels where such a direct request appears (Marshall 1978: 456; SB 2:186).[10] Danker (1988: 226) notes that Judaism possessed fixed prayers for its liturgy, such as the *Shemoneh Esreh* [Eighteen Benedictions] (= Schürer 1973–87: 2.456–61).[11] To share a common prayer would add a sense of community and give the disciples some identity (Manson 1949: 265; Egelkraut 1976: 154; Jeremias 1971a: 170).

A debate exists whether Luke created the wording in the introduction, since certain terms in the verse are frequently used in his Gospel and its style is Lucan.[12] The significance of this debate is minimal, for whether Luke introduced the account in his own words or reflected a source, he relates an incident that shows the disciples' desire to learn from Jesus. It is likely, however, that Luke introduced the scene in his own words (Plummer 1896: 293–94).

ii. Example Prayer (11:2–4)

Jesus responds to the request by giving a prayer that the community can share (Greeven, *TDNT* 2:804). Jesus' response is important for the life of today's church, since some reject the use of liturgical prayer. In saying "when you pray say . . . ," Jesus endorses the communal and liturgical function of the prayer (the ὅταν [whenever] temporal clause anticipates the prayer's repetition). That we have two versions of the prayer makes another point: the issue is not the

10. Egelkraut 1976: 154 n. 5 notes that none of SB's examples are about prayer. Although 17:5 is similar, it is not a direct request for teaching but encouragement.

11. Fitzmyer 1985: 902 mentions the Qumran community prayers, such as the *Hôdāyôt* or Thanksgiving Psalms. On comparison with the *Shemoneh Esreh*, see Beasley-Murray 1986: 148–57; K. Kuhn 1950: 30–33, 40–46.

12. So καὶ ἐγένετο (and it came to pass), ὡς (when), παύω (to cease), and καθώς (even as). Schweizer 1984: 190–91 sees the verse as Lucan, because Luke typically poses a question or notes an attitude at the beginning of a teaching of Jesus: 11:27, 45; 12:13, 41; 13:1–2, 23, 31; 14:15; 15:2; 16:14; 17:5, 20; 18:9; 19:11, 39; 22:24, 49; 23:27. Of these, only 17:5 is not uniquely Lucan, though the request to increase faith is unique. Luke 15:2 and 16:14 reflect complaints, while 11:27, 45; 12:13; 13:31; 14:15; 15:2; 16:14; 17:20; 18:9; 19:11, 39; 22:24; and 23:27 reflect statements, attitudes, or actions. Only four other verses are questions (12:41; 13:1–2, 23; 22:49). Nowhere is Jesus asked to instruct, only to explain or call to act. So the type of request is unusual. In addition, the presence of other features are less likely to be Lucan. For example, the reference to John is not necessary to set the scene. These unique features reduce the chance that Luke created the setting.

prayer's exact wording, but its themes. Thus, more important than liturgy is the prayer's emphasis, both in its teaching and in its corporate thrust as a community prayer: the stress is not on personal items, but on a shared concern for the relationship with God and approach to him.

The structure of the Lucan prayer could be viewed in either of two ways. One division splits the prayer into three parts: (1) two second-person singular addresses to God, (2) two first-person plural requests of God, and (3) a final closing request that is singled out structurally, because it has no parallel member as the other sets in the prayer do (Jeremias 1971a: 197). The first-person plural requests show the prayer's community focus. Jesus wants the disciples to see the prayer as *their* prayer. Religion among disciples is not a personal affair, but one in which they are placed into relationship with one another, interceding for one another. What one member requests, all should request with regard to God's general spiritual activity for his people.

A second way to divide the prayer is to regard it as having two parts. The first portion gives a set of second-person singular declarations to God, followed by first-person plural requests. This division seems slightly better, for the second request in the second portion is not laid out in pure parallelism, since it has an explanation with it. The prayer is simple, having an address, two statements, and three requests (Talbert 1982: 128). The simple structure makes the prayer easy to recall. Schweizer (1984: 191) makes the interesting suggestion that the order of the first three petitions reverses the order of Jesus' temptations. However, the comparison of the test of God's goodness in the third temptation and God's holiness in the first request seems stretched.

(1) Address: Father (11:2a)

This community recognizes its intimate relationship to God, since it will address him as πατήρ (*patēr*, Father). The expression goes back to the Aramaic אַבָּא (*'abbā'*, father), which in turn has roots in the liturgy of Judaism (Kittel, *TDNT* 1:5; Schrenk, *TDNT* 5:981). Πατήρ points to respect for the Father's authoritative rule, though it also suggests intimacy.[13] The title's isolated use without a qualifier is un-

11:2a

13. In Sir. 23:1, 4; 51:10 πατήρ often occurs alongside κύριος (Lord) or δεσπότης (master) (Schrenk, *TDNT* 5:979 n. 209, 981, 984–85). Elsewhere in Judaism at *Shemoneh Esreh* [Eighteen Benedictions] nos. 4–6 (= Schürer 1973–87: 2.456–57, 460); Wis. 14:3; 3 Macc. 6:3, 8. In the OT at Deut. 32:6; Isa. 63:16; 64:8 [64:7 MT]; Jer. 3:4; Ps. 68:5 [68:6 MT]; 89:26 [89:27 MT] (of God's relationship to the king, as also 2 Sam. 7:14); Mal. 1:6; 2:10; 1 Chron. 29:10. As a NT term of intimacy, see Rom. 8:14–16; Gal. 4:6; Mark 14:36.

usual, as is its personal use in a prayer.[14] As such, the address presupposes a close, intimate relationship between the disciple and God (Danker 1988: 227).[15] It is to a caring, kind Father that Jesus' disciples can make their requests (Marshall 1978: 456). Such intimacy is the opening note in the prayer that Jesus gives to his disciples.

(2) First Declaration: Holy Be Your Name (11:2b)

11:2b Addressing God in intimate terms need not nullify respect. Thus the prayer's first declaration is that God sanctify or hallow his name. The God addressed is holy and is to be approached with that recognition (Ps. 111:9; Isa. 5:16; 29:23; Ezek. 20:41; 28:22, 25; 38:23; 1 Pet. 3:15; Plummer 1896: 295; Schneider 1977a: 257; SB 1:406–8). The petition is made to the Great One, whose position is unassailable (Godet 1875: 2.49 notes the parallel mood of the scene in Isa. 6:1–7). Letting the name be sanctified asks that God establish and show his uniqueness, since to refer to his name is to refer to his person (Isa. 52:5–6; Ezek. 36:20; Rom. 2:24; Danker 1988: 227–28; Procksch, *TDNT* 1:111). The *Kaddish*, an eschatological Jewish prayer that ended ancient synagogue services, is similar in force: "Exalted and hallowed be his great name / in the world which he created according to his will. / May he let his kingdom rule / in your lifetime and in your days and in the lifetime / of the whole house of Israel, speedily and soon."[16] The picture is of the creator God, enthroned and manifesting his rule. His glory is made evident to all. The disciple opens the prayer with recognition of the one being addressed, trusting and hoping that God in his greatness will manifest himself (note that the passive verb looks to God to act).

14. Jeremias 1971a: 63–68 notes no example of "my Father" in the literature. In fact, in Judaism such intimacy was avoided. Jeremias 1967b: 16–29 lists the potential Jewish parallels. Dunn 1975: 21–26 notes that Jeremias overstates the case in allowing no exceptions, but suggests that Jeremias's general portrait is correct. Plummer 1896: 296 remarks that God as the Father of Israel is an OT image; the concept of God as Father to individual people begins to appear only in intertestamental Judaism (see the texts in the previous note). Jesus' reference to "my Father" is highly unusual, though not unprecedented: 4Q372; 3 Macc. 6:3; Wis. 14:3; and Sir. 23:1 use "my Father" or "Father." In the NT, see Luke 2:49; 10:22 = Matt. 11:27; Luke 22:29; 24:49; Matt. 7:21; 10:32–33; 12:50; 15:13; 16:17; 18:10, 35; 20:23; 25:34; 26:29, 39, 53. The contrast is striking and significant.

15. This view has been qualified recently by Barr 1988; see Witherington 1990: 217–18 for an evaluation of Barr's critique. On relating to God as a child does to a parent, see Luke 18:15–17; Dunn 1975: 23. R. Brown 1994: 172–75 has a full discussion of ʾabbāʾ.

16. Translation from Jeremias 1971a: 198. See also *Shemoneh Esreh* [Eighteen Benedictions] no. 3 (= Schürer 1973–87: 2.456, 460). However, Jesus' prayer is more like Jewish "short" prayers than this long Jewish liturgical prayer; C. A. Evans 1990: 182. As such, the prayer's form and function come as no surprise in a Jewish context.

(3) Second Declaration: Your Kingdom Come (11:2c)

The second declaration is for the kingdom to come (on terms for the **11:2c** kingdom's coming, see K. Schmidt, *TDNT* 1:584). The hope is in the full realization and culmination of God's promised rule. God is holy, set apart from all others, and the kingdom's coming will show this to be true in a way that nothing else can. It is this desire for God to visibly manifest himself that is at the heart of this second affirmation. The kingdom program may be in progress as a result of Jesus' presence, but it is its culmination that will show to all the greatness of God's love, justice, and righteousness (11:17–20; 10:13–20). The disciple shares in that program and is to eagerly expect its completion (Talbert 1982: 129 speaks of disciples called to look expectantly for its coming). Ultimately, it is the eradication of evil and the manifestation of righteousness that is anticipated (Plummer 1896: 295). God is honored by such a total revelation of his person and power. To speak of the meaning as "where God is reverenced, His Kingdom comes" (Luce 1933: 210) misses the petition's eschatological thrust (Arndt 1956: 295 and Hendriksen 1978: 609–10 soften this eschatological thrust). Both requests are made in the aorist tense, which summarizes the request by looking at its arrival and not stressing the process leading to completion (Arndt). The prayer reflects Jewish roots, for the later rabbis held that a benediction that omitted the Name or the kingdom was not a benediction (Ellis 1974: 164; Grundmann 1963: 231; *Shemoneh Esreh* [Eighteen Benedictions] nos. 7 and 11 [= Schürer 1973–87: 2.457]; *b. Ber.* 40b). As Jesus' model prayer begins, God's greatness and the desire that he manifest himself through his kingdom program set a tone of worship and awe. Having established God's character and authority, Jesus will turn to requests. Once we reflect on who God is, we can better approach him.

(4) First Request: Give Us Our Daily Bread (11:3)

The first personal request is for daily provision of food.[17] Such a re- **11:3** quest suggests the disciple's recognition that God is the provider, while expressing gratitude to the heavenly Father for his provision. But this rather straightforward reading of the text is not the only one. Some argue that Jesus is teaching the disciples to pray for daily provision of the bread of life, which is also how the early church read the verse (Talbert 1982: 129; Schneider 1977a: 257).[18] The debate turns on the meaning of a single term. Does ἐπιούσιον (*epiousion*) refer to (1) "necessary" or "daily" bread, (2) basic provision, or (3) "future" or

---

17. A similar metonymic meaning for ἄρτος as food, not just bread, is found in Luke 7:33; John 13:18; 2 Thess. 3:8, 12; Marshall 1978: 458; Behm, *TDNT* 1:477–78.

18. Jeremias 1971a: 199–201 cites Jerome's *Commentary on Matthew* on Matt. 6:11 and Marcion. On ancient interpretation, see Fitzmyer 1985: 900, 904–5.

"continual" bread (which, in light of the previous request, can be read as the eschatological provision of salvation)? The Greek term seems to be coined for the translation of Jesus' Aramaic remarks, which is why it is difficult to evaluate; clear parallel uses do not exist.[19]

Jeremias (1971a: 200) appeals to Jerome's understanding of ἐπιούσιον as "future" bread and argues for this understanding, since Jerome gave both the Latin and Aramaic forms of the term.[20] The major problem with this eschatological view is that the phrase τὸ καθ' ἡμέραν (to kath' hēmeran) is a clear reference to what is provided "each day." As such, it is unlikely that the reference is eschatological, since the kingdom's coming is only one act in the previous request. Foerster's exhaustive discussion (TDNT 2:592–95, esp. 592) gives the basic meaning accepted by most today: "for the following day" (so Creed 1930: 157; Ellis 1974: 165; Jeremias 1971a: 200). However, Foerster is not certain of that sense and opts for either "for today" or "necessary," meanings that would suggest the rendering "daily" when tied to the reference to "each day" at the end of the verse (Fitzmyer 1985: 905 and Arndt 1956: 296 opt for "essential," which equals "necessary"). In fact, even the popular meaning "for the following day," when made part of a daily request, results in a sense of asking daily for God's provision. Thus, the most likely sense is that each day the disciple is to ask for provision, though the more precise force, whether "today" or "for the following day," is uncertain.

Most see in the image an allusion to the picture of God's constant provision of manna, not because of the miraculous provision but because of its regularity (Exod. 16:18; Prov. 30:8; Ellis 1974: 165). Luke's present imperative with καθ' ἡμέραν (kath' hēmeran, daily) looks to continual daily provision, while Matthew's aorist imperative with σήμερον (sēmeron, today) looks at provision as one comprehensive act (Plummer 1896: 296). The request stands in contrast to Shemoneh Esreh [Eighteen Benedictions] nos. 9 and 18 (= Schürer 1973–87: 2.457–58), which ask for an annual supply of provision (Grundmann 1963: 233).[21]

---

19. BAGD 296–97 and BAA 601–2. Creed 1930: 157 notes objections to saying that the evangelists coined the term, citing a disputed papyrus reading of a fragmentary text (Preisigke #5224). Fitzmyer 1985: 905–6 lists three possible etymologies: ἐπί + οὐσία = "necessary"; ἐπί + οὖσα = "for today" (supplying ἡμέρα [day] to make a complete idea); ἐπί + present participle of εἰμι (to come) = "for the coming day" (with ἡμέρα again supplied to complete the thought). Determining the etymology is not crucial, since a word's meaning is not determined by etymology.

20. Seeberg 1914: 11–12. In an exhaustive study of the problem, Carmignac 1969: 122–28 notes that "necessary" and "for the future day" were the most popular ancient options.

21. Danker 1988: 229 suggests that Luke 12:16–21 and 21:1–4 elaborate on the petition. Since disciples recognize that God gives, they are generous with what they receive.

(5) Second Request: Forgive Us Our Debts (11:4a)
(6) Basis: We Have Forgiven All Others (11:4b)

The next petition seeks God's forgiveness for sin. The petitioner is to **11:4a–b** ask for forgiveness, not because it is deserved, but because the petitioner is forgiving to others. Such an idea is common in Judaism and the NT. For example, Sir. 28:2 (NRSV) reads, "Forgive your neighbor the wrong he has done, / and then your sins will be pardoned when you pray" (SB 1:424–26; Hauck, *TDNT* 5:560–63; Manson 1949: 170; Luke 6:36–38; Matt. 5:23–24; 6:14–15; 1 Pet. 3:7). Luke interchanges terms for sin (ἁμαρτία, *hamartia*) and debt (ὀφείλω, *opheilō*) in giving the request and its basis, while Matt. 6:12 uses only ὀφείλω. Ὀφείλω commonly occurs in the parables for sin and the debts owed for it (Matt. 18:23–35; Luke 7:41–43; 13:4 [uses ὀφειλέτης]).[22] The connection between the request and the willingness to forgive shows an inherent recognition that what the disciple asks of God one should be ready to do as well (cf. 6:37). In addition, the disciple is to be ready to forgive everyone, since παντί (*panti*, all) is made emphatic by its preceding the participle (Danker 1988: 229). The participle ὀφείλοντι suggests in this context a wrong that is willingly forgiven (ἀφίομεν, *aphiomen*) (cf. 17:3–4). As such, the lessons learned from God should influence how one treats others (Eph. 4:32; Col. 3:13). The request's explanation shows that forgiveness is not presumed but comes with awareness: a forgiven person is to be a forgiving person. In fact, the right to ask assumes a willingness to respond similarly.[23] The request (ἄφες, *aphes*, forgive) makes a particular appeal for granting forgiveness. God is quick to forgive the humble who do not demand their rights, but see their failings instead (Luke 18:9–14). When the community asks for "our" sins to be forgiven, it shows itself to be a community of compassion and forgiveness touched by an awareness of God's forgiveness.

(7) Third Request: Do Not Lead Us into Temptation (11:4c)

The final petition in Luke's version is a request for spiritual protec- **11:4c** tion. The key term πειρασμόν (*peirasmon*) may refer to trial and the character to not succumb to it (Manson 1949: 170; Luce 1933: 211 [who cites Gethsemane as an illustration]), or it may refer to temp-

---

22. Fitzmyer 1985: 906 notes similar usage at Qumran and suggests that Luke refers to sins to prevent confusion for his Greek audience. The use of ἁμαρτίας looks like the LXX, esp. Ps. 24:18 [25:18 Eng.]; also Gen. 50:17; Exod. 32:32; Num. 14:19; Plummer 1896: 297.

23. Marshall 1978: 461 notes that the asking of forgiveness is conditional, meaning that the request for forgiveness assumes that the disciple is ready to be forgiving, while God's granting of forgiveness is a work of his grace (cf. Matt. 18:21–35).

tation and thus seduction into sin (Creed 1930: 157; Arndt 1956: 296). The former sense is quite possible, alluding to religious persecution with its threat of apostasy.[24] Given this meaning (8:13; Schneider 1977a: 258) and the context of religious rejection that Jesus and his disciples faced, the request is to avoid the intense persecution that might lead to denial of their relationship to God.

It is possible, however, that it is a general remark about not being given over into the power of sin. In the Babylonian Talmud, *b. Ber.* 60b expresses a similar sentiment: "Bring me not into the power of sin, nor into the power of guilt, nor into the power of temptation" (translation from Creed 1930: 157). This latter view is better contextually. The previous request to forgive sin is general and suggests a general reference to sin following it. There is a desire to avoid falling into the situation where one needs forgiveness (Plummer 1896: 297; Marshall 1978: 461–62). The request implores divine aid to prevent succumbing to sin's power, not because God desires the disciple to fall into sin, but because he can prevent it from overwhelming the believer.[25] This latter meaning would include the threat of succumbing to apostasy through persecution, but is broader in scope. In short, the wise disciple knows that the only way to avoid falling into sin is to follow where God leads and to be dependent upon him and his protection.[26] This request reflects a spirit of dependence on God, as does the whole prayer. The disciple praying a prayer like this expresses both the community's and one's submission to God and the desire for his glory to manifest itself. Disciples want God to be honored, and they want to honor God.

b. Parable about Boldness in Prayer (11:5–8)
i. Parable (11:5–7)

11:5 Jesus' model prayer does not address the attitude that one is to have in approaching prayer. Since God is so holy, perhaps one should keep requests to a minimum and be careful about bothering the sovereign God. As a result Jesus turns from what one should pray to

---

24. 1 Macc. 2:49–64. Sir. 2:1–2 (NRSV) says: "My child, when you come to serve the Lord, / prepare yourself for testing. / Set your heart right and be steadfast, / and do not be impetuous in time of calamity."

25. Marshall argues for a causative force here ("cause us not to succumb to temptation") citing 4Q174 [= 4QFlor] 1.8 as reflecting the Hebrew idiom. So also Talbert 1982: 130, citing Luke 4:13; 22:28; Acts 14:22; 20:19 as illustrations of this kind of request.

26. James 1:14–15 looks at the issue from the perspective of our response to such temptation and with the awareness that we are responsible for our own sin. Fitzmyer 1985: 906 notes OT parallels to the thought: Exod. 16:4; 20:20; Deut. 8:2, 16; 13:3 [13:4 MT]; 33:8; Judg. 2:22.

how one should undertake such intercession. A brief parable found only in Luke makes his point: God is approachable and should be approached often and with confidence. The parable is presented as a question that runs through 11:7, with the answer—and the point—given in 11:8. The question is almost lost in the story.[27]

The picture introduces a problem that reflects the ancient culture (Kistemaker 1980: 176–77). In first-century Palestine, food was not as readily available as it is today. There were no evening shops, and bread was baked each day to meet the day's needs (Jeremias 1963a: 157). Another cultural requirement was being a good host to a visitor. In fact, the community was also responsible to help (Liefeld 1984: 948). The host in this parable has a real problem: he has a late-night visitor and no food to offer.[28]

The man with the visitor has a choice: go to a neighbor who might have the bread but is probably asleep, or not be so bold with the neighbor and thus not be a good host. If the host called on the neighbor, then culturally the neighbor would be under obligation to respond (Stählin, *TDNT* 5:20; 9:161). One other item should be noted: the ancient house was basically a one-room affair, so waking the master of the house was likely to wake everyone else. In effect, Jesus begins the account by saying, "Which of you has the nerve to wake up the neighbor—and his family—at midnight to ask for bread?"

Three loaves was enough to meet the need and satisfy what custom required (Danker 1988: 230; Blomberg 1990: 275). The nature of the request is also clear in that the host asks to be loaned the bread. Χρῆσον (*chrēson*) means lending without interest, while δαν(ε)ίζω (*dan[e]izō*) is the usual term for the interest-bearing loan that is part of a more formal business deal (on the latter term, see the exegesis of 6:34). The host plans to pay back his groggy neighbor. The picture is vivid and somewhat humorous, but the tension is real.

Noting the personal introduction, some take the original parable's meaning differently.[29] Jeremias (1963a: 158–59) argues that the original parable is eschatological in focus and is like 18:1–8 in meaning. The point is that just as the host at midnight responds to the request, so God will grant the appropriate requests of his chil-

27. Plummer 1896: 298 notes the shift from the awkward future indicative to a deliberative subjunctive in reporting the call to the friend. See also n. 30.

28. The φίλος (friend) in 11:5 is the neighbor, while the traveling friend (also φίλος) is not introduced until 11:6. The parable is told from the perspective of the midnight petitioner. The NEB/REB reverses the syntax with the "friend" being the petitioner.

29. On this style of introduction to a parable, compare Luke 11:11; 12:25; 14:28; 15:4; 17:7. In the OT, see Isa. 42:23; 50:10; Hag. 2:3; Fitzmyer 1985: 911.

dren speedily (Ernst 1977: 366). For Jeremias it is God, not the petitioner, who is the parable's original subject. But this surely misreads the introduction, which draws the disciple into the story's twist. The effect of the introduction is simply to point out how committed the host was to meeting the traveler's need and thus his boldness and shamelessness. God is not to be compared to the neighbor and his irritation, but contrasted to him, since 11:9–13 shows God to be gracious in granting requests for aid and provision (Marshall 1978: 462). The point of the parable is that if an irritated person responds to boldness, so you can be bold with the Gracious One. Thus, continually pray (Stählin, *TDNT* 9:164).

11:6–7 The dilemma becomes clear. A traveler has arrived from a journey (Matt. 2:9 shows the possibility of such night travel in the ancient world). When he arrives, there is nothing to eat. The only way to meet the cultural demands for hospitality is for the host to seek help from a neighbor.

The neighbor's thinking is encased in the reflective question of the one who needs the bread. The host in need has nerve, since it is clear that the neighbor will be irritated at the timing of the request. In fact, the presence of this hypothetical situation may indicate why a shift in tense from the (future) indicative to the subjunctive is present in Luke 11:5.[30] It may well be that the explanation of the need presents the petitioner's internal thought as he anticipates how the neighbor will respond to this late request. The petitioner knows that no matter how delicately he makes the request by addressing his neighbor as "friend" or how severely he paints his dilemma, the neighbor will still be bothered by the request.

The response is clear; there is no polite direct address in the reply. The host is not to bother the neighbor (κόπους πάρεχε, *kopous pareche*, do not cause trouble). The present tense in this circumstance could picture the annoyance ("stop being a bother"; BAGD 626 §1c; BAA 1266 §1c; Hauck, *TDNT* 3:829; Matt. 26:10 = Mark 14:6; Luke 18:5; Sir. 29:4). The neighbor notes that the door stands closed; the family has retired for the evening (κέκλεισται, *kekleistai*). The door would have had a wooden or iron bar placed through rings in the door panels, and removing it would be noisy (Jeremias 1963a: 157; Song 5:4–5). In addition, the children (τὰ παιδία, *ta paidia*, is plural) are asleep with him in bed, a reply that reflects the likelihood that all the family was sleeping on one mat, as was the custom. Getting up will wake the children—a major inconvenience! The hesita-

---

30. On the syntactical debate of 11:5–7, see Hendriksen 1978: 610. The basic issue is this: does Jesus' question end with 11:6 or 11:7? That Jesus' answer starts with 11:8 speaks in favor of the question extending through 11:7.

tion that the neighbor expresses is not so much a lack of ability to provide the food but an unwillingness to do so because of the chaos it would cause.[31] Elements of tension and humor abound in the reply. Any adult, especially those with children, can identify with the tension.

ii. Point: Shameless Boldness in Prayer (11:8)

Jesus applies the picture, but leaves unstated the implication that the disciple is to emulate in prayer the petitioner's boldness.[32] Aid will not come because of friendship, but because of shameless boldness.[33] To some, the picture is of a petitioner who keeps asking despite an initial rejection (Manson 1949: 268). But the idea of a repeated request is not clear. The shameless boldness would consist of having the nerve to ask even once at midnight. Danker (1988: 230) argues that the image may well be that, if the neighbor does not get up, then the whole town will soon be up (but this in not implied in the context). Ἀναίδειαν (anaideian), a NT *hapax legomenon*, with the particle γέ (ge, indeed) is key here. The term introduces the clause and as such is emphatic (Arndt 1956: 297). It is a hard word to translate into English, for it refers to a combination of boldness and shamelessness.[34] Thus, the stress is not on persistence or repetition of the request, as much as it is on the boldness or nerve of the request (see 18:1–8 for the parable that stresses persistent prayer). This petitioner has gall. He is willing to go to great lengths and to suffer great rebuke to get the bread so that he could be a good host. It takes nerve to wake up a neighbor (and possibly his whole family) in the middle of the night. The host drives his neighbor to a desperate response. The argument here is a lesser-to-greater argument (Ernst 1977: 366; Grundmann 1963: 234). If a person responds this

11:8

---

31. Manson 1949: 267 accurately uses the descriptive and emotive term *nuisance* to describe how the neighbor saw the request.

32. Λέγω ὑμῖν (I say to you) elsewhere introduces applications in Luke: 14:24; 15:7, 10; 16:9; 18:8, 14; 19:26; Fitzmyer 1985: 912.

33. The viewpoint is that of the neighbor concerning the friend who makes the request. It is their mutual friendship that is in view; Marshall 1978: 465.

34. BAGD 54; BAA 107; Sir. 40:30. Luke 18:4 is a conceptual parallel. For the lexical and interpretive debate on the term, see Blomberg 1990: 276, esp. nn. 51–53. For a careful study of ἀναίδεια, see A. Johnson 1979. He argues, however, citing Bailey 1976: 124–33 in support, that the line is about the neighbor, not the host, and that the antecedent of the second αὐτοῦ (his) in 11:8 is the neighbor because the neighbor is the constant subject in the verse. But this ignores αὐτῷ (to him) earlier in the verse, which refers to the host. Johnson sees the point as God's responding because his honor is at stake. But this meaning dishonors the gracious God that Jesus seeks to describe. Johnson is aware of this issue (p. 131 n. 39) and argues that Westerners do not appreciate Eastern cultural values. I hold that it contradicts the tone of 11:11–13.

way, surely a gracious God will respond to those who have the nerve to make their requests.

The point of comparison is not between the neighbor and God but between the petitioner and the disciple. God's response stands in contrast to the neighbor's begrudging help, as 11:9–13 will make clear in contrasting humans and God (Luce 1933: 212). Answer to prayer is not wrung out of the Father with much effort like water from a towel. He gives willingly (11:9–13). Disciples are to make their requests boldly to God. They have access to God and are to make use of it. One view of God says that God knows what the disciple needs and is sovereign, so disciples should not bother him, rather just let him do his will. But Jesus' parable stresses the need to approach God boldly with requests. This communication with God is part of the right disciples have because of their relationship with God. Manson (1949: 268) notes that when God does clearly answer, disciples will accept that too (Phil. 4:11–13).

Another interpretation of the parable compares the neighbor and God (Liefeld 1984: 948–49; Jeremias 1963a: 158–59; Marshall 1978: 465; Bailey 1976: 125–33): just as the neighbor avoids shame and responds to the request, so will God. This view of the parable has four problems. First, it breaks the focus of the parable on the petitioner, since the parable is told from his perspective. Second, it ignores the contrastive lesser-to-greater argument of the following verses. Third, the reference in 11:8 to "his" friend and "his" boldness refers to the same figure, the petitioner (Fitzmyer 1985: 912). Fourth, it underplays the stylistic shift in 11:6 to the subjunctive, a point that suggests where the major lesson is. As such, attaching shamelessness to God's mood is not the way to read the parable. The disciple is the point of comparison throughout, while God's response contrasts with the neighbor's attitude.

c. Exhortations to Trust a Gracious Father (11:9–13)
i. Exhortation to Ask (11:9–10)

11:9 Three pictures tell the disciples to bring their requests to God. The introduction to the verse, κἀγὼ ὑμῖν λέγω (ka'gō hymin legō, and I say to you), indicates that Jesus is now applying the parable and developing the response that should emerge from it (the first-person reference to Jesus is in the emphatic position). In this context, where a principle is being asserted, the three present imperatives indicate that disciples are to ask, seek, and knock continually (Plummer 1896: 299; Marshall 1978: 466–67 has an excellent discussion of these three verbs). In asking (αἰτέω, aiteō), there is an invitation to pray (Luke 11:10, 13; Matt. 18:19; Mark 11:24; John 11:22; Eph. 3:20). In seeking (ζητέω, zēteō), there is an invitation to pursue God and his will (Deut. 4:29; 2 Sam. 21:1; Ps. 105:4 [104:4 LXX]; Isa.

65:1; Luke 13:24; Acts 17:27; esp. Jer. 29:12–14 [36:12–14 LXX]). The seeking of kingdom goals is especially to be first in the disciple's heart (Luke 12:22–34; Manson 1949: 81). The disciple is to seek the things that bring righteousness and advance God's plan. In knocking (κρούω, krouō), there is the picture of coming into God's presence and blessing (Bertram, *TDNT* 3:955).

To each action, there is a corresponding response: it will be given, the disciple will find, and the door will be opened. The verbs in the response are artistically balanced. Two passive verbs indicate that God is the supplier, while one active verb shows the disciple's active involvement. God supplies as the disciple seeks, and the disciple discovers what God supplies in his response. The point is not that one gets exactly and always what one asks for, but that God supplies graciously in terms of the request (Arndt 1956: 298 [in discussion of 11:13]). God is ready to give, so ask (Luce 1933: 212). The disciple, aware of personal need, asks earnestly, seeks the answer, and brings the request directly to God. The verse, starting with the first imperative, verbally matches Matt. 7:7, which appears in a different setting (Creed 1930: 158; on the Jewish parallel, see SB 1:458).

The threefold image is reinforced by the assurance of a response to **11:10** all who ask, seek, and knock. These prayerful disciples receive, find, and have the door opened for them. The terms of this verse parallel the previous verse. The first two verbs look to the promise that God will respond (Ernst 1977: 367).[35] The explanation offers reassurance to the command. One is to ask with the expectation that God will respond. To put it another way, one is to ask with faith in God's desire to respond appropriately.

The passage matches Matt. 7:8 verbally if one reads the last verb as future tense. A contrast to this image appears in the closed door of Luke 13:25–30, where the picture is simply a soteriological one of being unable to enter the eschaton (Danker 1988: 231).

ii. God's Compassion: The Comparison (11:11–13)

Jesus now illustrates his point about God's willingness to answer **11:11** prayer. The picture is of a father who gets a request for food, specifically fish. What father would serve his child a snake?[36] No one! Indeed, to do so would be unthinkable. Human parents are willing to give essential things to their children. Jesus has intensified the image by moving from an illustration of friendship to that of parent

---

35. The last verb is probably future tense but as a passive adds the note that God will open the door; see the additional note. The present tense suggests immediacy, since the reply is not put in the future.

36. A water snake is probably referred to by ὄφις, since this snake was used as bait for fishing; see Grundmann 1963: 235; Fitzmyer 1985: 915; Foerster, *TDNT* 5:566–68.

and child (Creed 1930: 158). In 11:13, Jesus makes the minor-to-major argument clear. Surely God will respond graciously, since sinful people do.

The picture differs slightly from Matt. 7:9–10. In Luke, the sequence is fish-snake and egg-scorpion, while Matthew has bread-stone and fish-snake (Creed 1930: 158; see the additional note for the textual issue).[37] Another difference is Matthew's reference to a man, while Luke refers to the more intimate image of a father. These differences are sufficient to suggest that Luke is not referring to the same incident as Matthew, but to similar teaching. Plummer (1896: 299) also notes a shift in the saying's perspective: Jesus has gone from speaking initially about the father to making the son the subject of the illustration. This change of orientation makes the point more emphatic, as it shifts attention on the recipient.

11:12 Jesus gives a second image to make the same point. The child who requests an egg will not receive a scorpion. Again the question is rhetorical and expects the answer, "Not one of us would do this." It has been suggested that a rolled-up scorpion might be mistaken for an egg (Fitzmyer 1985: 915; Pegg 1926–27), but the issue is not confusion (Luce 1933: 213). Neither is the point the possible similarity of the items. Rather, Jesus' point is ironic. In asking for essential items, no one would supply dangerous ones. To do so not only denies the request, it reverses it. People are not so cruel and neither is God. Plummer (1896: 300) combines the images of Matthew and Luke: "God gives neither what is useless (a stone) nor what is harmful (a serpent or scorpion)."

11:13 Jesus now makes the point and also reveals the subject of his teaching. This "how much more" argument is frequent in rabbinic literature (Isa. 49:15; Klostermann 1929: 126; Danker 1988: 231). It accents the point that if something is true in this little instance, how much more so in the larger case. In this case, if evil people can give good gifts to their children, how much more can the heavenly Father make provision for his children. The title *Father* applied to God is no accident. The point is that intimacy extends to the disciple as the object of God's tender care.

The specific good gift Luke has in mind is the Holy Spirit.[38] Since the prayer comes from a disciple, the request is for God's presence,

---

37. Marshall 1978: 496 notes five explanations offered for the Matthean-Lucan difference and opts for each Gospel representing different strands of oral tradition; see also Foerster, *TDNT* 5:579–80.

38. Matt. 7:11 refers more broadly in another setting to good things, so there is no need to discuss which wording is original; but see Marshall 1978: 470 for options. James 1:5–8, 17 is conceptually parallel. For δόμα (gift), see Eph. 4:8 (where the Spirit is referred to as gift) and Phil. 4:17; Büchsel, *TDNT* 2:166.

guidance, and intimacy.[39] God will provide a specific good thing for his disciple. The one who walks with God should be bold and diligent in asking for such benefits. As such, the passage is not simply a blank-check request, but a blank-check request for the necessities of the spiritual life, such as those mentioned in the Lord's Prayer and those related to spiritual well-being. The reference to the Spirit need not be seen as early church vocabulary introduced into a Jesus saying (so Fitzmyer 1985: 916), though it is possible that Luke is explaining a specific "good thing" that God gives. It seems clear that Jesus taught that the Spirit was a guide, at least the promise of the Spirit's coming is attributed to him (Luke 24:49; John 14–16). Such teaching by Jesus explains the disciples' emphasis on the Spirit's presence (Acts 2). The illustration is designed to encourage the disciples to ask boldly. In short, ask—and expect God to answer.

Summary

Luke 11:1–13 speaks of the importance of looking to God and of approaching him. Sometimes God's greatness causes one to think that he is unapproachable. If he is busy with the universe, surely he is not concerned with one person's request. Or maybe he knows all, so there is no point in burdening him with what he already knows. In teaching the model prayer and in addressing God as a heavenly Father, Jesus shows that God has a tender concern for his children. He is not so great or so distant as to be unavailable. The disciples should be bold in their requests for blessing. Be assured that God is more gracious than human parents who give good things to their children.

In the Lord's Prayer, Jesus teaches about the disciple's fundamental attitudes in prayer: a concern for God's character and honor and the desire to see him overcome evil in his kingdom. Disciples should pray for these things, being jealous of God's honor and asking that his glory be displayed to all. In addition, there are requests for basic material provision, forgiveness, and spiritual protection. Disciples recognize that in asking for forgiveness they too are required to forgive others. This attitude toward prayer should also translate into life. Disciples who are concerned about honoring God will show it in the way they live—in dependence upon him.

Perhaps the most ignored feature of the prayer is that it is a community prayer, not an individual one. Provision, forgiveness, and protection are asked for the community. The lesson of the Lord's Prayer is that we pray not just for the individual, but also for the community, for the spiritual benefit of all who know God.

39. The prayer's broad setting makes a baptismal reference unlikely, contra Ernst 1977: 367. This is basic exhortation about the life of faith.

That lesson may be as important as the content of the prayer it-self. Referring to this prayer as the "Lord's Prayer" is thus a mis-nomer; it is the "Disciples' Prayer."

Additional Notes

11:2. There are three reasons for reading the subjunctive προσεύχησθε (you pray) and not the indicative προσεύχεσθε (you pray): (1) support from the major uncials of all families, (2) the normal grammatical style with a temporal clause using ὅταν (whenever), and (3) the absence of parallelism with Matt. 6:9, which has the indicative. This difference with Matthew makes the subjunctive the harder reading, and thus makes it more likely to be the original one (Fitzmyer 1985: 902; Zerwick 1963: §325).

11:2. Two major additions bring the Lucan text into conformity with Matthew, which makes them unlikely to be original here. It is hard to explain how a shorter prayer emerged if Luke's original version was virtually identical to Matthew. It is more likely that copyists would bring the two prayers into agreement. The two additions are (1) the phrase ἡμῶν ὁ ἐν τοῖς οὐρανοῖς after πάτερ (Father), yielding an address to "our Father in heaven," and (2) the phrase γενηθήτω τὸ θέλημά σου ὡς ἐν οὐρανῷ καὶ ἐπὶ τῆς γῆς after the request about the kingdom, so that an additional request appears: "Your will be done as in heaven, also on earth." This second addition comes in a variety of forms, adding to the likelihood it came from copyists.[40]

11:2. Less well attested is the addition "let your Holy Spirit come upon us and cleanse us," noted by Gregory of Nyssa (*Homily on Our Father*) and conceptually noted by Tertullian in debate with Marcion (Tertullian, *Against Marcion* 4.26; Grundmann 1963: 232; Wiefel 1988: 214). Some in the early part of this century accepted this text as original, because of its difficulty and because of the mention of the Holy Spirit in 11:13, but it is too weakly attested to be considered original (Marshall 1978: 458).[41]

11:4. A popular variant that agrees with Matthew is the presence of the request that God deliver the petitioner from the evil one. As with Luke 11:2, it is likely that this longer text is an effort to harmonize the two versions. Otherwise it is hard to explain the omission if this longer phrase had been original.

---

40. For example, some manuscripts (ℵ², A, C, D, P, W, Δ, Θ) omit the feminine article before γῆς and some manuscripts of the Itala, Vulgate, and Coptic lack reference to heaven and earth.

41. Manson 1949: 265–66 is uncertain about its originality in Luke. Streeter 1924: 277 thinks it original. Ernst 1977: 362 and Fitzmyer 1985: 904 believe it was added later as a baptism formula to be prayed over the individual being baptized. On the use of the prayer in the history of the church, see Manson 1955–56. Besides Marcion and Gregory of Nyssa, the text is found only in manuscripts 162 and 700 and in a shorter form in Maximus the Confessor.

Many of the manuscripts agreeing with Matthew in Luke 11:2 also show the addition here (A, C, D, W, Θ, Ψ, family 13, Byz). Nonetheless, besides being the harder reading, early manuscripts support the shorter text ($\mathfrak{P}^{75}$, ℵ*, B, L, Marcion, Tertullian, Origen).

11:10. Many manuscripts ($\mathfrak{P}^{45}$, ℵ, C, L, Θ, Ψ, family 1, family 13) have the second future passive ἀνοιγήσεται (shall be opened); others have the first future passive ἀνοιχθήσεται (A, W, Γ, Δ); and still others have the present passive ἀνοίγεται ($\mathfrak{P}^{75}$, B, D).[42] A present tense makes the three verbs of Luke 11:10 agree, while the future tense fits Matt. 7:8. External evidence slightly favors the future tense. The meaning is little altered by the choice (Fitzmyer 1985: 915).

11:11. The difference between Luke and Matthew probably causes the textual variations found in this verse. Many Lucan manuscripts refer initially to bread and stone (ℵ, A, C, D [with different word order], L, W, Θ, Ψ, family 1, family 13, and Byz). But the earliest manuscripts omit bread, and the slight difference in word order in D suggests that the longer reference is an addition to make Luke more like Matthew. Texts that omit the reference to stone are $\mathfrak{P}^{45}$, $\mathfrak{P}^{75}$, B, 1241, and many Itala manuscripts (Fitzmyer 1985: 915).

---

42. On the first and second future, see BAGD 71; BAA 140.

IV. Jerusalem Journey: Jewish Rejection and the New Way (9:51–19:44)
  B. Discipleship: Looking to One's Neighbor, Jesus, and God (10:25–11:13)
➤ C. Controversies, Corrections, and Calls to Trust (11:14–54)
  D. Discipleship: Trusting God (12:1–48)

C. Controversies, Corrections, and Calls to Trust (11:14–54)

Controversy introduces the third portion of Luke's journey section, which describes Jesus' conflict with the Jewish leadership. The debate in Luke 11:14–23 is about the source of Jesus' power to heal. Something unusual is clearly happening through Jesus, so he is working by the power of either God or the devil. In 11:24–36, Jesus warns about how one should respond to him. Jesus compares himself to Jonah and to light. Last, in 11:37–54, Jesus denounces the Pharisees and scribes, condemning them for their hypocrisy. Events take a dire turn here, for after this meal the leadership decides that something must be done about Jesus. The section is held together by the mixture of amazement and skepticism that greets the first and last events (11:14, 38).

Most events in 11:14–54 involve controversy, correction, or a call to trust God. As such, the material reviews elements from Luke 4–9, but the approach is slightly different. For example, in the miracle accounts of the earlier section, the telling of the miracle dominated, while the comment on it was minimal. In 11:14–23, it is the exact reverse: the miracle is told briefly, and the discussion about the miracle's importance is dominant. This section helps explain how events led to Jesus' death. After these events, an inevitability sets in about where things are headed, an inevitability that becomes even clearer after 12:49–14:24.

1. Controversy: What Do Healings Mean? (11:14–23)

At issue in Luke 11:14–23 is the source of Jesus' authority. Is it from Satan or God? If it is from God, what are the implications for the nature of the times? Watching Jesus work requires a decision about who he is. Jesus clearly performs unusual works, and they must be explained. What does his work mean? The passage has two main parts: the dispute over what Jesus' healing means (11:14–20) and the short parable of the overrun house (11:21–23).

Luke locates the event after the Martha-Mary incident and the Lord's Prayer discussion. Why should one sit at Jesus' feet? Why should one adopt the attitude reflected in Jesus' distinctive prayer, even to the extent of encouraging a community prayer? What gives Jesus the right to form his own band of followers? This event gives the answer. The only logical deduction from Jesus' miracles is that God is working through Jesus, who in turn is bringing the kingdom, victory, and judgment. Thus, Jesus' miraculous work signals the in-breaking of the kingdom in authority and power. In short, Jesus' work forces a choice about who he is. His work is too unusual to be ignored. The Marcan version of this passage raises the "lunatic, liar, Lord" options that C. S. Lewis develops in *Mere Christianity*. Adding one other category to Lewis's options, Jesus is either wrong, crazy, lying, or sent from God—there are no other options. His works suggest that the only real options are related to the supernatural. Luke explores those two alternatives.

Sources and Historicity

One of the more interesting issues tied to this pericope is that of sources and the event's placement in Jesus' ministry. The potential parallels to the passage are found in Matt. 12:22–30 and Mark 3:22–27 (Aland 1985: §188). Six explanations of their relationship are possible:

1. Three similar events are in view, each taking place at a distinct time in Jesus' ministry: Mark's event is early, Matthew's is in the middle, and Luke's is last. This approach is unlikely, given the extent of the agreement between the three versions.

2. Two events are in view, with Matthew and Luke looking at one event and Mark, with his distinct presentation and his failure to mention the kingdom, looking at another.

3. Two events are in view, with Mark and Matthew looking at one event and Luke's account being distinct (so Thomas and Gundry 1978: 77, 139). Some argue that Luke's event is distinct from Matthew because (a) Luke is in Judea, not Galilee; (b) Luke's man is only mute, while in Matt. 12:22 he is blind and mute; and (c) the following episodes in each account differ. This approach will be evaluated shortly.

4. One event is in view and at least two accounts have a topical placement. However, Mark and Luke most likely arranged this material to focus on opposition at distinct points in their presentation. Mark 2:1–3:6 is a series of five controversies, while the material in Luke's journey section has parallels in a variety of positions in the other Synoptics (Liefeld 1984: 950; Hendriksen 1978: 617 [treats the accounts as one event that occurred in the Galilean phase of Jesus' ministry]).

5. The accounts go back to the same event or represent a compilation of Jesus' teaching, but tracing where the event(s) fall is not possible (Creed 1930: 159; Manson 1949: 83; Luce 1933: 213; Ernst 1977: 372; Tiede 1988: 216; Wiefel 1988: 219–20).[1]

6. The event's distinct placement reveals the lack of historicity. It is a polemical account by the early church.[2] It is hard to deny historicity, however, as Jesus was clearly regarded as a miracle worker of some sort.[3] A controversy like this one is thus quite natural. People were

---

1. In this view, a tighter connection is seen between Matthew and Luke than between Luke and Mark, and proponents tend to speak of Q tradition. If Q is the source, this is the only exorcism in Q, a point that, by its uniqueness, argues for authenticity. Marshall 1978: 471–72 sees the account reflecting several controversies and that reconstructing the tradition history must be speculative. Fitzmyer 1985: 918 discusses only 11:19 as possibly reflecting an early church setting. Detailed evidence for Matthew's and Luke's being closer to each other than to Mark comes from Easton 1913.

2. Bultmann 1963: 13–14 argues that Matthew and Luke have the story's original core (Luke 11:14–15, 17–18), to which various sayings have been added.

3. Twelftree 1993 gives a detailed survey of the texts involving Jesus as exorcist. After a careful study, he concludes: "The first result we can record from our study is that we are able unhesitatingly to support the view that Jesus was an exorcist" (p. 225). This theme is too widely attested in the sources to be denied. Meier 1994: 646–77 is more circumspect in his approach to the seven NT exorcisms, rating some as having historical roots: the possessed boy (Mark 9:14–29 = Matt. 17:14–21 = Luke 9:37–43a), Mary Magdalene (Luke 8:2), and the Gerasene demoniac (Mark 5:1–20 = Matt. 8:28–34 = Luke 8:26–39). Luke 4:33–37 = Mark 1:21–28 (man in the synagogue) probably reflects "the sort of thing" that Jesus did in ministry. Meier is uncertain about the account of the mute/blind demoniac (in part, because of its brevity), though leaning toward historicity (Luke 11:14–15 = Matt. 12:22–23). Meier doubts Matt. 9:32–33 (mute demoniac) and Mark 7:24–30 = Matt. 15:21–28 (Syrophoenician woman). With typical circumspection, Meier concludes: "A decision that in any of these exorcisms a true miracle has taken place—in other words, that God has directly

wrestling with who Jesus was. Surely he had to justify his activity before his doubting opponents. That the miracle is uniquely found in Q also speaks for historicity, since Q, by its nature, deals with Jesus' sayings, not his acts. It shows that the point is the teaching.

Given that each Synoptic writer rearranges material throughout his Gospel, different positioning here is not a reason to challenge historicity. Taking the event as historical means that options 2–5 have the most possibility of being correct. Which is it?

Certain items are clear in looking at the parallels. First, no version has a clear setting. The strongest temporal tie is Matt. 12:22, which uses τότε (then) to tie the account to Jesus' withdrawal and a summary account. Mark 3:22 and Luke 11:14 use καί (and), which simply introduces another event. In Mark, the account follows the controversy section of Mark 2:1–3:6, Jesus' withdrawal, and a summary account of the choosing of the Twelve—events that are earlier in Luke (e.g., the choosing in Luke 6:12–16).

Second, the Lucan account has strong verbal ties to both Mark and Matthew—but in different places in the narrative: (1) Luke 11:15b is like Mark 3:22b; (2) the unusual phrase about a kingdom being divided "against itself" appears in Luke 11:17b and Mark 3:24a; and (3) the reference to Satan rising up against himself in Mark 3:26 is very similar to Luke 11:18.[4] The Matthean connections are even more extensive: (1) some verbal elements in Matt. 12:25 and Luke 11:17 overlap ("every kingdom"; "is laid waste"); (2) much of Luke 11:18 matches Matt. 12:26; (3) Luke 11:19–20 is almost verbally exact to Matt. 12:27–28; and (4) Luke 11:23 matches Matt. 12:30. These connections suggest that attempts to separate the Matthean and Lucan versions are not likely, so view 3 is unlikely.

In fact, other objections exist against separating the traditions. First, many regions are covered in the journey section, so the assumption that Judea must be in view here (as Thomas and Gundry 1978: 139 n. *o* argue) is not established by the passage. The failure of Luke 11:14 to allude to blindness (unlike Matt. 12:22) is not decisive, since he is not interested in telling all the healing details. Luke is concerned only with the healing itself and so abbreviates the story, since the point of the unit is the debate about the healing. The likelihood of topical arrangement cannot be excluded. The parables of Matt. 13, which according to Thomas and Gundry parallel Mark

---

acted beyond all human potentiality to heal a particular individual—goes beyond what any scholar can say on purely historical grounds" (p. 661). Ironically enough, to decide for miracle is the very conclusion that Jesus' remarks desire.

4. Egelkraut 1976: 91–92, esp. 91 n. 2, argues for six Marcan connections in Luke, but only three are clear. The phrase *that you say* in Luke 11:18 and Mark 3:30 and the use of ἐπί (against) in Luke 11:17 are a part of these connections, so that separate points about them are really the same point. It is doubtful that Luke 11:21–23 is just Mark 3:27 expanded, since Luke is not any closer to Mark than to Matt. 12:29–30.

4 and thus link Mark and Matthew, actually come eighteen verses later in Matthew. In these extra eighteen verses, one event is shared among all three accounts: the family's attempt to speak with Jesus. This shared event, however, has different placements: Mark 3:31–35 = Matt. 12:46–50 = Luke 8:19–21. Thus, Mark and Matthew do not agree against Luke's timing (see Thomas and Gundry 1978: 139 n. *o* for another view). At the least, someone has engaged in rearranging, and the rearranging might extend to more than one writer.

At this point one might suggest that Luke equals Matthew but not Mark (view 2), especially since in Mark there is no introductory exorcism. Against this are the linkages that exist between Matthew and Mark and seem to identify them. For example, Mark 3:26 and Matt. 12:26 start out similarly. More impressive is the significant match of Matt. 12:29 and Mark 3:27. The picture of binding the strong man is expressed with the same balanced line in both passages. So this attempt to separate Mark from the other accounts also fails.

Thus, all three accounts discuss one incident, since they are linked together by various details at different points (views 4 or 5). But can one be more specific than view 5, which simply speaks of tradition and does not try to place the event? I suggest, with view 4, that Mark and Luke are handling the event on a topical basis, while Matthew has its relative position in Jesus' ministry. Both Mark and Luke have as a theme the rejection that Jesus faced in sections that elsewhere look topical. Mark chooses to introduce it early in his account, while Luke presents it later. As already noted, Matthew has a tighter note about the setting (Matt. 12:22). Against the event's fabrication is the amount of agreement and significance attached to the event, mixed with unique elements in each account. The event is deeply embedded in the tradition, so that view 6, which rejects historicity, is not possible. Exorcisms are multiply attested in the sources and also use the same form, so such a controversy is likely (Meier 1994: 406; see n. 3 above). As Dunn (1988: 31–33) notes: "Jesus' reputation as a highly successful exorcist must surely be regarded as part of the base-rock historical data concerning Jesus. . . . Jesus' reputation as a successful exorcist is as firmly established a historical datum as we could hope for."

View 4, arguing for one event that Mark and Luke have located topically, is thus the most satisfactory. It is also likely that Matthew and Luke used a similar source (Luce 1933: 213; Marshall 1978: 471).[5]

---

5. Creed 1930: 159 speaks of Q here, as does Manson 1949: 83. The amount of Matthean-Lucan agreement makes this source connection likely, though whether it is Q or another shared tradition is debatable (Matthean prioritists see Matthew as the likely source). Grundmann 1963: 236–37 correctly notes that Matthew is closer to Luke than to Mark (see also Easton 1913, as discussed in n. 1 above). Fitzmyer 1985: 918 argues for Lucan additions in 11:16, but is uncertain about it in 11:14, 21–22. Additional source material cannot be ruled out. Tiede 1988: 216 notes that Matt. 12:23

The Jesus Seminar, departing from its usual approach of rejecting dialogue tied to miracles, sees 11:17–22 as largely attributable to Jesus, since these verses are printed in pink type (Funk and Hoover 1993: 329–30). The seminar is less certain about 11:23 (in gray type) because of its "exclusivism." For the seminar, the earlier verses fit Jesus' subtle style in dealing with opposition, and the parallel in the Gospel of Thomas 35 adds weight to the sayings. The seminar questions the original unity of this material, but the kingdom-Satan contrast fits Jesus' ministry in light of the prominence of exorcism (see also Luke 4:33–37). In addition, there is no reason to doubt that healings and exorcisms like the one Matthew and Luke use to introduce this event sparked the reflection noted here (Dunn 1988: 37), though whether the juxtaposition of Luke 11:14–20 with 11:21–23 reflects literary summarization is not certain. What is clear is that a unit like 11:14–16 demands a response like that found in 11:17–20 to be circulating in the tradition. Nolland (1993a: 635–36) favors units originally transmitted separately, breaking up 11:20, 11:21–22, and 11:23 as possibly distinct units. I prefer to see the three "if" clauses of 11:18–20 as pointing to a unit transmitted in a form that would be easy to recall, though the other elements may be gathered together topically here. All the material goes back to Jesus, even the "exclusive" saying of 11:23.[6] It is a multiply attested theme since this saying reflects Q (Matt. 12:30), while Mark 9:40 (= Luke 9:50) points to the theme in Marcan source material. Dunn (1988) makes a strong case for the authenticity of the key verse, Luke 11:20.

The account is an extended pronouncement story that combines Jesus' sayings with a comparative picture (Bultmann 1963: 13). Berger (1984: 81) calls it an apophthegm and sees it as special Lucan material. It is a controversy account, which Schulz (1972: 206, 208) compares to rabbinic debate (Wiefel 1988: 220 notes that 13:10–17 and 14:1–6 are similar in tone). The outline of Luke 11:14–23 is as follows:

---

and Mark 3:11 stress Christology, while Luke emphasizes controversy with the leadership; but Luke also has strong Christology in light of the parable in 11:21–23. Of the three accounts, Mark has less confrontation than the other two.

6. For detailed defense of authenticity, see Meier 1994: 408–9 (on 11:17–18), 409–10 (11:19), 414–17 (11:20), 417 (11:21–22). Meier prefers to separate 11:20 from 11:17–18 in the earlier tradition, as well as from 11:21–22. He does think it likely that 11:20 was tied to 11:19. For agnosticism about this entire process of sorting out the relationship of 11:20 to 11:19, see Dunn 1988: 40–41 and n. 31. As noted above, I too am agnostic, if not outright skeptical, of sorting out clearly the question of the original unity of this tradition. However, I see no compelling reason to reject its unity, especially in light of the connection between 11:19 and 11:21–22 that I shall argue for below (see the exegesis of these verses).

a. Discussion about healing (11:14–20)
   i. Healing of a mute man (11:14)
   ii. Skepticism concerning the healing (11:15–16)
   iii. Jesus' reply: two choices—Satan or God? (11:17–20)
      (1) What if by Satan? (11:17–19)
      (2) What if by God? (11:20)
b. Picture about the significance of the healings (11:21–23)
   i. Parable of the victorious plunderer (11:21–22)
   ii. Point of the parable (11:23)

This account is crucial, since in it Jesus comments on his own work. Popular debate and skepticism rage over Jesus. Some acknowledge what has happened but attribute his work to Satan. Jesus raises an objection: how can Satan work against himself and have his kingdom abide? If Jesus' works are rejected, what about the miraculous works of others? Others will judge those who reject Jesus. But if Jesus' work is by God, then the kingdom has come. Jesus as the Strong One overtakes the enemy and divides the spoils. He divides people. Not to be with him is to be against him. To join him is to aid him in bringing others to God. Not to join him is to hinder others from coming to God. One cannot be neutral about Jesus. One must decide where Jesus' authority comes from. Luke presses for a decision here; sitting on the fence about Jesus is an option. One cannot be agnostic about him, for agnosticism is a decision against Jesus.

Exegesis and Exposition

[14]And he was casting out a demon that was mute. When the demon had gone out, the mute man spoke, and the people marveled. [15]But some of them said, "In Beelzebul, the ruler of the demons, he casts out demons." [16]While others who were testing him were seeking a sign from heaven. [17]But he, knowing their thoughts, said to them, "Every kingdom divided against itself is laid waste, and a divided house falls. [18]And if Satan also is divided against himself, how will his kingdom stand? For you say I cast out demons by Beelzebul. [19]But if I by the power of Beelzebul cast out demons, by whom do your sons cast them out? Therefore they shall be your judges. [20]But if by the finger of God I cast out demons, then the kingdom of God has come upon you.

[21]"When a strong man, fully armed, guards his own house, his possessions are secure; [22]but when one stronger than he comes and overwhelms him, he takes away the armor in which he trusted and divides his spoils. [23]He who is not with me is against me, and he who does not gather with me scatters."

a. Discussion about Healing (11:14–20)
i. Healing of a Mute Man (11:14)

The account begins with a summary note about the healing of a **11:14**
mute man who had a demon. No specific setting is given. The miracle has three simple steps: the work, the result, and the reaction.
Jesus exorcises a demon from a man who cannot speak. The result
is that the man speaks. In reaction, the crowd marvels.

The interesting note is that this marveling cannot be seen as entirely positive, since the following verses record the crowd's skepticism. The amazement is at the reality of the unusual work and not
necessarily that it represents something good. A parallel use of θαυμάζω (thaumazō, to be amazed) is found in 4:22. The term can be
positive or negative, depending on its context. People can be amazed
and still not like what they see. In fact, despite the amazement,
Jesus' work splits the crowd. Luke 11:15 mentions the skepticism of
some, while 11:16 mentions the uncertainty of others. Jesus' work
demands a response, but the judgment made about his work is not
guaranteed. Something is going on that is accepted by all. But how
to read what is happening is debated. For Luke, the significance of
Jesus' act is already clear. The healing of the mute is a sign that Jesus
is the Coming One (Luke 7:22; Isa. 35:6; Liefeld 1984: 951; Danker
1988: 231; Tiede 1988: 216). Luke typically describes the crowds
(ὄχλος, ochlos) and the people (λαός, laos) as rather fickle, though
mostly open (crowds in 3:10; 4:42; 5:1; 6:19; but 11:29; 23:4, 48; people in 6:17; 7:29; 18:43; 22:2; but 23:13–18, 35).

Matthew 12:22–23 notes some additional details: the man was
blind and mute, so after the healing he both spoke and saw. Some
of the crowd asked if Jesus could be the Son of David, a question
that suggests they were trying to come to grips with who Jesus was.
The Matthean concern for Christology surfaces with more emphasis
than is found in Mark or Luke. The Davidic emphasis is seen in the
juxtaposition of healing and regal office. Luke does not note the
mixed reaction found in Matthew or the possibility of Jesus' ties to
David (Schneider 1977a: 265). Luke focuses only on the rejecters,
since Jesus' response is prompted by their skepticism. Mark 3:22
simply launches into Jesus' response with no miracle preceding it,
though the response in Mark 3:23 clearly presupposes that Jesus'
miraculous work is the grounds for his response.

In this account, unlike some other instances of healing, Luke attributes the impediment to demonic activity (Ellis 1974: 167; Klostermann 1929: 127).[7] Exorcism was not uncommon in Judaism, as
Acts 19:11–16 shows.

---

7. In Luke 1:20 the impediment is said to be from God; in Mark 7:32 no cause is
stated, but Mark 9:17 links demonic activity with the lack of speech. On Jewish think-

ii. Skepticism concerning the Healing (11:15–16)

11:15 The miracle causes a reaction. The opinion of some in the crowd shows a note of skepticism. How are the healing and exorcism of the mute man to be explained? Some emphatically attribute the exorcism to the power of Beelzebul, the prince of demons, that is, Satan (a similar charge was raised against John the Baptist; Luke 7:33).[8] Given the OT warnings about testing those who bring signs, the reaction is not surprising (Deut. 13:1–3 [13:2–4 MT]; Nolland 1993a: 637). If one is not going to see such power as coming from God, then this is about the only alternative to those who see supernatural activity in the world.

The origin of the title *Beelzebul* goes back to a description of the old Canaanite god, Baal. The name in its original form may derive from expressions that mean "Exalted One" (Fitzmyer 1985: 920). The English form of the name comes from Latin and may refer to Baal-Zebub, the Philistine god of Ekron (1 Kings 1:2–3, 6, 16),[9] a derisive term that meant "Lord of the flies." Disagreement about the word's form has led to the proposal of other origins for the name.[10] Liefeld (1984: 952) notes a suggestion that would read something like "Lord of the dwelling or temple," which might explain the illustration that follows in Luke 11:21–23 (also discussed in Aitken 1912; Zahn 1920: 458; Schneider 1977a: 265 [perhaps]; Plummer 1896: 301; Arndt 1956: 299; Foerster, *TDNT* 1:605–6; SB 1:631–35; Gaston 1962; MacLaurin 1978). Despite the attractiveness of the last suggestion, Luke is interested only in the title, not in the term's origin or a wordplay built around it.[11] Satan is clearly referred to by this name, because the alleged source of Jesus' power is also described in the verse as the "prince of the demons." According to the charge, the power behind Jesus is not divine; it is demonic. In fact, it is the chief of demons who is said to empower him.

---

ing about the association of disease or disability and demons, see SB 4:501–35; Van Der Loos 1965: 351–53; Ernst 1977: 373.

  8. The phrase ἐν Βεελζεβούλ (by Beelzebul) is in the emphatic position and is to be read as expressing the agent by whom Jesus supposedly heals: "by means of Beelzebub." This title appears in Luke only here and 11:18–19.

  9. Though in this case the normal Greek form would be Βεελζεβούβ (Beelzebub); Marshall 1978: 473; BAGD 139; BAA 277–78.

  10. Other unlikely options are "Master of the complaint," "Lord of dung," or "Baal, the Flame"; Fitzmyer 1985: 920; Godet 1875: 2.60; Marshall 1978: 473; and Ernst 1977: 374.

  11. Fitzmyer 1985: 921 notes other names used for Satan in Judaism: Belial (2 Cor. 6:15; 1QS 1.18, 24), Mastemah (1QS 3.23; 1QM 13.4; Jub. 10.8), and Asmodeus (Tob. 3:8, 17).

It is interesting that in Matt. 12:24 = Mark 3:22, the Pharisees (Matthew) and the scribes (Mark) make the charge. Luke keeps the criticism more general, perhaps to focus on perceptions about Jesus and not draw undue attention to the complaint's source, since the view may have extended beyond the original complainers. It is not unusual for Luke not to specify the source of a remark. Nolland (1993a: 637) notes that Luke is fond of the expression τις (*tis*, a certain one), so the difference may reflect Lucan style.

Yet another reaction exists. Other people are not quite so skeptical **11:16** but want more proof. They want to test Jesus and have him give a sign from heaven (on "tests," see Luke 10:25 = Matt. 22:35; Mark 8:12; 10:2; 12:15; Seesemann, *TDNT* 6:34). It is hard to know what exactly would suffice, given the healings he had already performed. Grundmann (1963: 238), citing Mark 8:11–12, suggests that an eschatological sign, such as causing the heavenly bodies to stand still, may be behind the request.[12] It is also unclear what was to be proved: his messiahship, his authority, or his prophetic office?[13] The Pharisees rejected all of these possibilities. But for some, the jury was still out on who Jesus was, despite his earlier activity.

Luke alone mentions the request for a sign, although Matt. 12:23 has some in the crowd ask if Jesus could be the Son of David, which is an eschatological question about the promised Davidic ruler. Jesus' answer is along eschatological lines; whatever they were asking for, Jesus' reply places the discussion in a fulfillment mode. A comment similar to Luke's reference to signs appears in Mark 8:11 (Marshall 1978: 473). Signs will come up again in Luke 11:29–32. At the third temptation, Jesus had rejected a "signs on demand" approach to revealing himself (4:9–12; Plummer 1896: 301; see also Mark 8:12). The imperfect verb ἐζήτουν (*ezētoun*, were seeking) perhaps reflects ongoing requests for such a sign.[14] The crowd had enough evidence to decide who Jesus was, so Jesus poses the basic question that his healings raise. He notes the only two options from which they may choose to explain his unusual power.

---

12. Nolland 1993a: 637 adds other signs like turning back the sun (2 Kings 20:8–11) or providing manna like Moses (cf. Luke 9:12–17). SB 1:726–27 discusses this category in later rabbinic writings.

13. Manson 1949: 83–84. Friedrich, *TDNT* 6:847, argues that the office of eschatological prophet was the issue. Matthew's discussion of David seems to envision something more; for a discussion of the test, Rengstorf, *TDNT* 7:234.

14. So Arndt 1956: 300, though Luke's usual use of this tense makes this conclusion less than certain.

iii. Jesus' Reply: Two Choices—Satan or God? (11:17–20)
(1) What If by Satan? (11:17–19)

11:17 Jesus is again portrayed as knowing the thoughts of his audience (5:22; 6:8; 7:39–47; Wiefel 1988: 221). Whenever Jesus is reading someone's thoughts, there is controversy coming. In addition, there is irony here: the crowd seeks a sign and Jesus' knowledge reveals one! How did he know what they were thinking? Somehow he knows that the crowd's thoughts (διανοήματα, *dianoēmata*; a NT *hapax legomenon*; Behm, *TDNT* 4:968) are hostile!

Jesus appeals to what was in all likelihood a common illustration: the divided house. His point is that if Satan is in the business of casting out his own demons, then the demonic world is a divided house—a sure formula for defeat. The unasked question is whether Satan would do this to himself. The implied answer is, "of course not," at least not by design. So the satanic proposal is excluded by logic. Behind the remark is the assumption that Satan is out to destroy humankind. His influence is seen in disease and death. So, when disease and death are reversed, this cannot be the work of the arch-demon because then Satan is working against himself.

The picture may well allude to Israel's history. The nation's greatest period was when it was united in rule. When it divided, chaos entered, followed by destruction (Michel, *TDNT* 5:132).[15] The house of the nation collapsed under the strain. The phrase οἶκος ἐπὶ οἶκον πίπτει (*oikos epi oikon piptei*) literally means "house falls upon house" and graphically depicts the destructive internal conflict that has a domino effect on the divided community. The imagery would be clear to those questioning Jesus.

Luke's form of the saying is condensed in comparison to Mark 3:24–25 (Plummer 1896: 301–2). Mark's two sentences use two images: a fallen kingdom and a fallen house. Matthew 12:25 is even more condensed than Mark but has three pictures: a divided kingdom, a divided house, and a divided city. The point in the accounts is the same: division leads to destruction. Civil war at any level, even among spiritual beings, is counterproductive and devastating (Fitzmyer 1985: 921).

11:18 Jesus drives home the lack of logic in the suggestion, using three conditional sentences (εἰ, *ei*, if) in 11:18–20 to express the alternatives. These three conditions suggest the inherent unity of 11:17–20. First, how can Satan have a standing kingdom, if he is working against himself? The question assumes that Satan is active and that

---

15. SB 1:635 cites *Derek ʾereṣ Zuṭṭa* 5 (see Strack and Stemberger 1991: 251): "A house in which there is disunity will assuredly be destroyed at the last."

he has a potent rule. Βασιλεία (*basileia*, kingdom) is referred to in a dynamic sense: the act of ruling and the evidence of its presence. Jesus' point is that the charge does not make sense. His accusers cannot acknowledge the strong satanic presence in the world *and* claim that Satan is fighting himself. Both cannot be true. Since Satan's power is a given, the conclusion about Jesus must be wrong.[16]

Matthew is close in wording to the first portion of Luke 11:18. Luke has an abbreviated form of the saying, since Matt. 12:26a speaks first of Satan casting out Satan before mentioning division. Luke alone repeats the charge against Jesus, and his version heightens the contradiction in the position (Βεελζεβούλ is in the emphatic position and parallels σατανᾶς, *satanas*, Satan). Mark has no parallel to Luke 11:18b–20 = Matt. 12:27–28.

Jesus moves from the lack of logic in their response to its implications in his second conditional statement. If what Jesus does is by Satan's power, then what does that say about the same things their "sons" do?[17] Many see Jesus' arguments this way: if Jesus exorcises by satanic power, what about Jewish exorcists?[18] However, the argument may look not so much at Jewish exorcists, as at the work of Jesus' own disciples.[19] In this view, υἱοί would refer to disciples as sharers in Israelite heritage. The point is that what the opponents say about Jesus, they must accept for anyone else who does the same thing. If Jesus exorcises by Satan, then so do other exorcists. But if others—whether Jewish exorcists or the disciples—exorcise by God's power, then so does Jesus. It is one or the other. Their works

11:19

---

16. Fitzmyer 1981: 186–87 rightly notes that this verse destroys Conzelmann's claim (1960: 156–57) that the period of Jesus' ministry is "Satan free." Jesus is engaged in victorious battle against Satan here, as 11:21–22 also stresses.

17. The phrase οἱ υἱοὶ ὑμῶν refers to "your own people" (Arndt 1956: 300), although most see it as referring to the "sons of the Pharisees" (Rengstorf, *TDNT* 4:443) or more broadly to "countrymen" (Godet 1875: 2.64) (see BAGD 833 §1cα; BAA 1663 §1cα; Heb. 12:5; 1 Pet. 5:13). Nolland 1993a: 639 states the question this way: "What will other Jewish exorcists, in light of their own exorcizing activity, make of such a view?" For a different (and I think more preferable) view, see n. 19 below.

18. Josephus ties the origin of Jewish exorcism to the days of Solomon; *Antiquities* 8.2.5 §§45–49; 2.13.3 §286; Tob. 6:1–7; 8:1–3; 1QapGen 20.29; SB 4:533–35; Grundmann 1963: 238; Talbert 1982: 137.

19. Godet 1875: 2.64 notes that W. M. L. de Wette and H. A. W. Meyer held this view in the nineteenth century. Shirock 1992 now ably defends this view, noting that it was the view of Chrysostom, *Homilies on Matthew* 41 (on Matt. 12:25–26). He gives six reasons for the view, the most compelling of which I note on p. 1078. If this view is correct, a major reason for separating 11:19 from 11:20 in the original tradition—namely, the difference in meaning of "you" in each verse—disappears. Evidence of the presence God's kingdom is seen in Jesus and his followers. If this is the argument, Jesus is noting evidence of God's grace in Israel!

go together. If the opponents' judgment about Jesus is wrong, they can know that these exorcists will judge them for their refusal to accept God's work.

This remark about judging is what suggests that the disciples are the referents of υἱοί, for they will have a role in the judgment, while Jewish exorcists will not. This point about the exorcists' authority to judge is so difficult that some interpreters see an insertion of an early church remark here. In their view, a reference to judgment by disciples must allude to an early church setting, or else a reference by Jesus to Jewish exorcism makes no historical sense (Creed 1930: 161). But another view—one that does not see Jewish exorcism in general as in view—provides a better understanding of Jesus' point: given the disciples' missions, in which they have already performed exorcisms, there is no need to posit either a church setting or a general Jewish reference (9:1–6; 10:1–12).

In fact, Jesus' point is complex, for in effect he says that the Jewish observers are not only dealing with him in this matter, but also with others, with their "own sons." To reject them is to set them up to be their judges. Jesus' argument about consistency is really a transition into his decisive point: the authority he displays and shares with others. It also points to a now "divided" Israel (2:34).

However, if the disciples are not being referred to, then the argument, though *ad hominem*, is purely rhetorical. It can still make sense, despite Bultmann's objections, though this sense is more difficult. If Jewish exorcists are described, Jesus is not saying that every Jewish exorcist will be in the eschaton, but that Jewish exorcists will condemn them for rejecting exorcism that is from God's hand. To fail to appreciate Jesus' exorcism is to fail to appreciate exorcism in general. The issue is, how can one reject God's work as God's and ever hope to recognize him when he comes! This is the most widely held view, but it is less directly relevant to the setting than a reference to the disciples.

The passage has virtually identical wording to Matt. 12:27, while it is absent in Mark.[20] It contains an interesting grammatical point: the first-class condition is presented as if it were currently so (εἰ plus the present tense). But it is clear that the presentation does not match reality, for Jesus is not saying that he exorcises by Satan's power. First-class conditions are not automatically true; they are just a means of presentation. For the sake of argument, Jesus assumes his opponents' position and takes it to its logical dead end.

---

20. Matthew introduces the verse with καὶ εἰ (and if), while Luke has εἰ δέ (but if). In addition, Matthew's word order on the judgment passage differs slightly from Luke, but uses the same terms.

(2) What If by God? (11:20)

Jesus presents what the miracles really show in the third conditional **11:20**
statement: the arrival of God's kingdom in Jesus' activity. It would
not be an exaggeration to see this passage as a crucial text for estab-
lishing Luke's view of the kingdom (see also 9:27; 10:9, 18; 17:20–
21). The meaning of the passage is disputed.

Clearly the conditional clause alludes to God's work, as seen in
the mention of his finger. Interestingly, Matt. 12:28 agrees verbally
with Luke except at this point, where he refers to God's Spirit. Luke,
who normally emphasizes the Spirit, does not refer to him here.[21]
Their point is the same: God is the source of power for the exorcism.
Most see in the reference to God's finger an allusion to Exod. 8:19
[8:15 MT], where pagan magicians recognize divine work in their
opponent Moses. The image is often used for God's activity and intervention, whether in creation, miracles, or the giving of the law
(Deut. 9:10; Ps. 8:3 [8:4 MT]; Schlier, *TDNT* 2:20–21; C. A. Evans
1990: 186).[22] Jesus is suggesting here that if Satan is not behind his
work, God is.

The main dispute involves the term ἔφθασεν (*ephthasen*). Does it
mean "come near" or "arrive"? The difference is crucial (although
Fitzer, *TDNT* 9:91–92, minimizes it). Jesus is either teaching that
the kingdom draws close in the present activity or that it arrives. At
stake is whether an inaugural kingdom is present in Jesus' first
coming or whether *kingdom* functions as it did in the OT and intertestamental Judaism, as an eschatological term referring exclusively to the consummation of God's rule on earth through Israel.[23]

21. The difference may suggest a distinct form of the tradition for Luke, since
the Spirit's work is a Lucan emphasis. Schulz 1972: 205 and Manson 1949: 86 argue
that Matthew probably changed the reference to the Spirit, possibly in light of
Matt. 12:18. But the reason for such a change is not entirely compelling, since Matthew also loves OT allusions. However, if there is a change here, Matthew is more
likely to have made it, since it is hard to see Luke's removing a reference to the
Spirit for explanatory reasons (but so argue Wall 1987 and Goulder 1989: 504, noting that Luke does not use the phrase *Spirit of God*). For a Lucan change are
Hamerton-Kelly 1964–65; Yates 1964; and Nolland 1993a: 639–40. Nolland notes
that Luke alone uses anthropomorphisms like "hand of God" (1:66) and "arm of
God" (1:51).

22. Wall 1987 sees an allusion to Deut. 9:10 and not to the Exodus text. He argues
that, just as Moses reminded the rebellious people that God's finger had written the
law, so Jesus reveals his messianic mission and covenant connection, since Satan is
cast out. Though possible, this approach seems overly subtle and understates the
force of the war imagery in 11:21–22, which explains this remark through parable.

23. For the debate, see Ladd 1974a; Ladd 1974b: 57–69; Kümmel 1957 (a full presentation of the NT kingdom passages, dividing them into present and/or future aspects); Lundström 1963; Chilton 1984; and Beasley-Murray 1986. For the term in Judaism, see Lattke 1984.

Ladd (1974b: 61) notes that the idiom "kingdom of God" itself was not used in the OT, though the concept is found in the prophets. It was found later among the rabbis. But the concept of God's physical rule in a great age of fulfillment was expected both in the OT and in Judaism. This expectation took two forms: the prophetic hope that God would bring this promised age to pass on earth through sociopolitical rule, and the apocalyptic hope that he would usher it in with heavenly signs (G. von Rad, K. Kuhn, and K. Schmidt, *TDNT* 1:566–76, 580–89).

Those who argue for the kingdom being "near" suggest that behind the reference is the same Aramaic term translated by ἐγγίζω (*engizō*, to be near) in Mark 1:15.[24] Ἐγγίζω can carry such a sense (Luke 15:1; Matt. 26:45). In Judaism, *kingdom* is an apocalyptic, eschatological term, so the idea of its arrival without apocalyptic and political elements is not possible if traditional usage applies. However, against this understanding and in favor of the idea that the kingdom "arrives" is the normal meaning of φθάνω when linked to ἐπί.[25] Also for the idea of arrival is a passage such as Luke 10:18, which clearly ties Satan's fall to the disciples' miraculous activity. In addition, there is the immediacy of the image that follows in 11:21–22. Above all considerations, however, stands the prepositional reference to "upon you" (ἐφ' ὑμᾶς, *eph' hymas*), which because of its personal object cannot look at approach, but must refer to arrival.[26] The point is that Jesus' activity gives evidence of the arrival of God's kingdom (Schrenk, *TDNT* 1:610). That arrival is vividly evident in his power, which his followers also exhibit. Jesus' work and demonstration of saving authority in their midst must be dealt with. It calls for decision. Twelftree (1993) brings out how Jesus' exorcisms and claims were unique, though he seems to underplay the messianic dimension of the actions, given their delivery and end-time character.

If the kingdom has come in an initial but not consummative form,

24. So E. Scott 1911; J. Campbell 1936–37; Clark 1940. Ἐγγίζω means "arrives soon" in Mark 14:42.

25. See BAGD 856 §2 and BAA 1708 §2. With ἐπί, φθάνω means "to overtake." Appeals to the ability of ἐπί to mean "near" (as in John 21:1) are not good enough to refute the force of the verb-preposition combination. In the LXX, φθάνω normally means "to reach, arrive, happen to." When combined with ἐπί in the LXX, it means for something to reach someone; Dan. 4:24, 28 [Theodotion]. Caragounis's appeal (1989: 20–23) to the proleptic aorist here fails (even though he sees a fulfillment with resurrection); see also Nolland 1993a: 640.

26. On the meaning of φθάνω, see above and Kümmel 1957: 107 n. 8; Ladd 1974b: 65–68; Dodd 1936–37; Marshall 1978: 476. On the verb in NT as "arrival," see Rom. 9:31; Phil. 3:16; and esp. 1 Thess. 2:16, which has a similar present-future tension with its reference to the wrath of God having arrived and residing until the end.

what does its current form involve?[27] The portrait of Luke–Acts provides a good answer (see also the exegesis of 4:43). Jesus is perceived as ruling over God's many salvation benefits. He has authority to distribute them to anyone who responds to his message (Luke 3:15–17 [where the Stronger One brings the Spirit, showing that he is the Messiah]; Acts 2:16–39). In addition, he provides the Spirit as a sign of the arrival of the promised age and as a source of guidance over those he rules (Luke 24:44–49; Acts 2). The emphasis of the kingdom picture in the present phase is not on realm, but rule.[28]

Nonetheless, a realm is envisioned. Jesus' realm is the world as it is manifested in his scattered followers and contained in his total authority over salvific blessing, an authority that is present over everyone. The presence of his rule in believers anticipates his coming to earth to rule physically, when he will exercise dominion and judgment over the earth. This theme of reign and authority is expressed in various ways in Luke–Acts. (1) Acts associates the concept of Jesus' universal lordship and rule with the fulfillment of Davidic promise (Acts 2:30–39; 13:32–39; see also Luke 1:68–79). (2) Acts 3:19–24 makes clear that the program is not yet consummated or completed but will come to pass as the OT prophets taught. (3) Acts 10:42–43 and 17:31 show Jesus' authoritative rule over salvation and his ultimate function as judge. (4) The parables of Jesus speak of the Son's going away soon to receive a kingdom and so look at his present authority.

The rule expressed in Luke 11 is the first phase of this kingdom program, what we might call the "invisible kingdom." The kingdom in Acts is expressed in the ministry of the Spirit during the time of Jesus' physical absence (thus the term *invisible*) from the earth. It is this rule that Jesus says is arriving now and that is pictured in his work of exorcism. The result of his presence is powerfully evident in the transformed people over whom he rules in the church, even though he is not physically visible. The first phase of his rule is really put in place with the resurrection-ascension and the distribution of

27. There is a sense in which God is always said to rule over his kingdom in the OT. But in the NT, God's kingdom is a technical eschatological term that refers only to the fulfilled manifestation of God's rule as promised in the OT. This kingdom is the "promise" of the OT, so it does not equal the providential kingdom rule of God expressed as present in the OT. Rather, kingdom expectation is tied specifically to his promise and future program. God's providential kingdom applies to him as Creator, but the promised kingdom represents his work as Redeemer and Restorer of creation.

28. Ladd 1962 notes four kinds of kingdom sayings: (1) kingdom strictly as rule (Luke 19:12, 15; 23:42; and John 18:36, to which one could add 1 Cor. 15:25); (2) the future apocalyptic order that the righteous will enter at the end of the age (Mark 10:23–30); (3) the kingdom as something present among humans (Matt. 12:28 = Luke 11:20; 17:20); and (4) kingdom as a present realm in which people enter (Col. 1:13, to which could be added 1 Cor. 4:20 and Rom. 14:17).

salvation's benefits (Acts 2:30–39), the roots of which are in the promise of the new covenant (Luke 22:19–20; 24:49; Acts 1:7–8). From that time on, Jesus rules from God's right hand. He is not present on earth for all to see, but rules through the benefits he bestows on those who come to him, especially forgiveness of sins, the Spirit, and the life he brings. The Spirit reflects God's presence in people, as well as God's work of power and his promise. Humans are now able to live as God would desire because they respond to his Spirit, so that his rule becomes evident in their lives. This group of disciples, which becomes the church, is not all there is to the kingdom nor is it all there is to God's plan and promise, but it is a microcosm of what the kingdom will be when OT promises are completely fulfilled at Jesus' return. The Spirit is the down payment of the redemption to come (Eph. 1:13–14).

At his return, Jesus' rule will be made visible by his physical presence on earth during the millennium and beyond. This is the second phase of the kingdom program and can be referred to as the "visible" kingdom, since Jesus' presence in rule is manifest (Acts 3:18–20; Rev. 20:1–6). In this latter sense, the idea of the kingdom as physical rule fits traditional Jewish usage and Israelite hope.[29]

b. Picture about the Significance of the Healings (11:21–23)
i. Parable of the Victorious Plunderer (11:21–22)

11:21 Jesus illustrates his point with a picture of war. His battle with Satan is a cosmic struggle, so the image fits. A man, strong and fully armed, made preparations to defend his home. As such, his possessions may be characterized as "at peace" (ἐν εἰρήνῃ, en eirēnē; Foerster, *TDNT* 2:411). In this context, Satan is the strong man whose home is secure, and Jesus is the stronger man who overruns him (Grundmann, *TDNT* 3:399–400). Such eschatological imagery is not unprecedented in Judaism: "Beliar shall be bound by him [an eschatological priest], / and he shall give power to his children to tread upon evil spirits" (T. Levi 18.12; Ellis 1974: 167).[30]

---

29. For a full presentation of this theme in Luke–Acts and a critique of aspects of Ladd's description of the kingdom, see Bock 1992c. As a result, the NT does not redefine or resignify OT promise; it expands it with complementary revelation. Promises to Israel remain, even as blessing and promise come now in and through the church.

30. Battle imagery with evil angels in the OT includes Isa. 24:22–23; in Judaism, T. Sim. 6.6 and T. Zeb. 9.8. Plummer 1896: 303; Danker 1988: 233; and Schürmann 1994: 243 see an allusion to Isa. 49:25–26. The battle imagery is similar, but the application to spiritual forces does not fit Isaiah's language in 49:26a, which clearly pictures humans. At best, Isaiah shows the principle involved. Such a move with imagery, however, is not surprising; see Luke 1:67–79 and Bock 1993. The point in the language for Luke is how Jesus, as God's representative, is God's victorious warrior.

Only Luke introduces Jesus' illustration. In fact, the Lucan form of the illustration goes its own way throughout and looks like an abbreviated summary of other things Jesus taught, given that Matt. 12:31–32 = Mark 3:28–30 agree by each mentioning the blasphemy of the Spirit, a teaching that Luke has later in 12:10. In addition, Matthew and Mark speak of an οἰκία (*oikia*, house) where Luke uses αὐλή (*aulē*), often translated "castle, palace, fortress, or court."[31] A secure abode is in view.

11:22 Jesus notes that miracles mean a fall. From the initial image of security, Jesus moves to the portrait of defeat. Above all, exorcism means that Satan is overrun (νικάω, *nikaō*; Bauernfeind, *TDNT* 4:944). Defeat comes when the stronger one arrives, lays siege, and gains victory.[32] Victory is graphically portrayed as Satan's entire armor is stripped away.[33] Satan's armor pictures his power, while the seizing and defeat pictures what Jesus accomplishes through his ministry as the Stronger One (3:15–18). It is important to remember that though the Stronger One is Jesus, it is a Jesus who works by God's power (11:20). The alliance is the point of the claim and is what the actions evidence. To the victor goes the spoils, which in turn are divided among those who fight with him. The dividing of spoils recalls the wording of Isa. 53:12, but the presence of a definite allusion is uncertain, since other texts share this imagery. An image, not a specific OT text, is in view (Creed 1930: 161; Isa. 49:25–26; Grundmann 1963: 239; Jeremias, *TDNT* 5:713 n. 460; Gospel of Thomas 35). Jesus' work means that Satan is no longer in control. Victory belongs to Jesus, who casts out demons by the finger of God (Paul later uses other victory images with reference to the cross: Col. 2:14–15; Eph. 4:7–10; Plummer 1896: 303). The spoil is the whole of salvation benefits: forgiveness, the Spirit, his gifts, and living eternally with the king.

Luke's description is unique. Matt. 12:29 = Mark 3:27 mentions binding and plundering the strong man and his home, and all three picture Satan being overcome by Jesus, but Luke is most emphatic in stating the victory, since he alone mentions the distribution of the spoils.[34]

---

31. "House" is probably the meaning of αὐλή here (BAGD 121 §2, §4 and BAA 243 §2, §4), but the different term suggests once again the possibility of a distinct source. Nolland 1993a: 641 argues against a distinct source for Luke because of the presence of Lucan vocabulary (Luke's version has more intense imagery for a battle scene). Αὐλή has the meaning "palace" in 1 Macc. 11:46; 3 Macc. 2:27; 5:46; Matt. 26:3; Mark 15:16.

32. Ἐπάν (when) is a temporal conjunction used with the subjunctive; BAGD 282; BAA 572. Matt. 2:8 and Luke 11:34 are the only other NT uses.

33. The word πανοπλία refers to "full armor"; BAGD 607–8; BAA 1229. The image is one of victory; 2 Sam. 2:21. The term is also found in Eph. 6:11.

34. Marshall 1978: 478 notes that the Lucan image is one of messianic war; Isa. 59:16–18; O. Betz 1957–58.

ii. Point of the Parable (11:23)

11:23 Jesus' exorcisms make him the issue. To not consciously join Jesus
is to be against him. When it comes to deciding about Jesus, there
is no neutral ground. The images of 11:21–22 are strong. A war is going on, and one must choose sides (Manson 1949: 87). There are no
Switzerlands in this war. The one who does not gather with Jesus,
who does not participate in his ministry and mission, ends up being
the cause of division. Such a holdout scatters in contrast to joining
those who gather.[35] Rather than helping to bring in the harvest, the
harvest is lost in their hands (Ps. Sol. 17.18 says, "They were scattered over the whole earth by these lawless ones"). To reject Jesus—
or even to fail to decide about him—influences not only the individual, but others as well.

Some speak of the image as picturing a shepherd gathering
sheep, but this seems less likely, since then the figure would be more
about the leadership of Jesus' community than about humans.[36] In
the NT, the figure of the Great Shepherd applies to Jesus, and the
image of shepherding the flock is strictly a leadership figure (John
10; 21:17; 1 Pet. 5:2). Thus, a harvest image, which is more mission
focused and applies universally, is more likely, though Jesus' ability
to mix the images makes certainty about the figure impossible.[37]
The point of the figure is clear: people either follow Jesus and join
with him in bringing others into the kingdom or they stand against
him and influence other people not to come in. In a variation of Nolland's observation (1993a: 636), the question is, in the battle, will
they help to gather or scatter the harvest?

Summary Luke 11:14–23 shows that Jesus' miraculous work is not an enter-
taining diversion from his ministry. His work forces people to decide who he is and contains a visual picture of what his ministry
represents: either Satan's power or God's power. Jesus rules out
the first option logically by showing that to accuse him of working by satanic influence is to declare that Satan is working to destroy himself. In addition, if one is consistent, this means that exorcisms by others are done by Satan's power. Is this how

---

35. On gathering as a figure of bringing together God's people, see Michel, *TDNT*
7:419–20, who also interprets the imagery as picturing a harvest. *Shemoneh Esreh*
[Eighteen Benedictions] no. 10 (= Schürer 1973–87: 2.457) reads: "Blessed are you,
Lord, who gathers the dispersed of your people Israel."

36. Plummer 1896: 303 and Hendriksen 1978: 622 cite Matt. 9:36; Isa. 40:11; and
John 10:16 in support of a figure about sheep. To these could be added Ezek. 34
(where God is the Great Shepherd) and Zech. 13:7–9 (with its image of scattered
sheep).

37. See the intermingled metaphors in Matt. 9:35–38. On the image in general,
see Michel, *TDNT* 7:418–20.

exorcism is to be explained? Is this how to explain the works of Jesus' disciples? That leaves the other option: Jesus works by God's power and so do those who are with him. If he heals those ravaged by the effects of decay, it means that satanic forces are overcome by him. God's kingdom has come with him, not in its totality and consummation, but in inauguration. Satan is overrun by Jesus, his house is plundered, and the spoils are divided with others who join him. That is the message of Jesus' work.

The reality of Jesus' work forces a choice; no neutral ground can be taken. The one who is not joined to Jesus is against him. The one who does not share with him in gathering people for the kingdom is working against him by preventing their entry. There is no fence to sit on. To decide against Jesus is to argue that his work is satanic, which Jesus shows to be impossible. To decide for him is to share in the spiritual benefits that emerge from the victory of Jesus, the one who is stronger than Satan. Luke's readers are to make a choice or, having already made the choice, be reassured that their decision for Jesus is the correct one. In Jesus is found the presence of God's kingdom promise. In him resides the authority to overcome the destructive forces that stand opposed to humankind, whatever they might be. The miracles of Jesus testify visibly to this authority—an authority etched by God's finger.

2. Warnings about Response (11:24–36)

The issues of conflict and trust continue in this five-part unit. The elements largely alternate between warnings and calls to respond. A parable (11:24–26) about the return of the unclean spirit warns of the danger of experiencing God's work, only to leave one's spiritual condition unfilled with anything from God. As such, the threat of renewed satanic attack is real, with a worse condition emerging afterward. This is followed by a beatitude unique to Luke about keeping the word (11:27–28). Then Jesus offers a new rebuke and warning (11:29–32). This generation will not be given a sign other than that given by Jonah. Old Testament figures will rise up in judgment against them for their lack of faith. The unit concludes with two calls to respond to the light (11:33–36). First, light in a lamp is not to be hidden but displayed so it can provide guidance (11:33). The idea is to make use of the light. Second, disciples are called to be such a light (11:34–36). The quality of that light is determined by what goes in the eye. If we take in light and are possessed by light, we will be bright. We will be able to provide the light that helps others. We are always faced with a choice: we can reject God or remain neutral. Either option makes one's spiritual condition worse. Light ignored leaves darkness. Alternatively, we can choose to respond to God and grow spiritually.

Sources and Historicity

The discussion of sources in this unit varies considerably, as each subunit has its own distinct character.

Luke 11:24–26 has a parallel in Matt. 12:43–45 (Aland 1985: §189). Except for a few minor differences of vocabulary and word order, Luke and Matthew match one another (see the exegesis for details). This is a genuine parallel, though the presence of Luke 11:27–28 suggests that Luke also used a supplemental source. It may be that material such as 11:24–26 was in both sources. The material in 11:24–26 is so distinctive and dissimilar to anything else in Judaism or the early church that the Jesus Seminar rates it as substantially authentic (Funk and Hoover 1993: 330–31). Nolland (1993a: 645) says that "it is surely a parable of Jesus." Given texts such as 11:4c with the threat of temptation, the utterance here coheres with the historical Jesus (Schürmann 1994: 253).

Luke 11:27–28, the only unparalleled subunit, is special Lucan material (so most commentators, including Marshall 1978: 481 and Aland 1985: §190). But it is directly associated with the previous remark about the wandering spirit. In fact, 11:27–28 provides the contrast to the warning of 11:24–26 and, as such, the context fits nicely, even though it has no parallels. Both texts stress responding to God. The Jesus Seminar rates the saying as unlikely to go back to Jesus, but is the kind of thing he might have said (in gray type; Funk and Hoover 1993: 331). The seminar rejects this setting for the saying and sees the variation it has in other settings as a problem. The seminar sees the self-effacement of this text as like Jesus, but the text is too similar to 6:47 and 8:21 to be authentic. Yet these parallels reflect multiple attestation of this concept: Luke 6:47 is found in Q (Matt. 7:24) and Luke 8:21 is part of a triple tradition (= Mark 3:33–35 = Matt. 12:48–50)—not to mention the Gospel of Thomas 99. Nolland (1993a: 648) argues that, though the wording here may be Lucan in places, the sentiment is in accord with Jesus (so also Schürmann 1994: 260 speaks of the voice of Jesus). The incident is a summary of a simple exchange between Jesus and this woman.

Luke 11:29–32 looks like a parallel to Matt. 12:38–42 = Mark 8:11–12, though the Lucan form is closer to Matthew's version with its longer discussion about a sign of Jonah (Aland 1985: §191).[1] In contrast, Mark's abbreviated version says that no sign will be given. The Lucan Jonah passage looks at the same event as Matthew and Mark, especially since Matthew's and Mark's accounts have the same relative position and since Matthew and Luke make reference to the "return of the many spirits" in the same general setting. Luke's placement seems to be later in order to set the remarks in the context of rejection. Luke stresses that rejection is a part of the journey theme and that it is a key, consistent part of Jesus' ministry (Mark and Matthew place this remark before Peter's confession at Caesarea Philippi; Luke places it after). In his ministry, Jesus gives the call to obey in the same context where he warns of the consequences of rejection. Luke's placement fits this juxtaposition of obedience and warning, which is so basic to Jesus' ministry.

What is more difficult is that, in Luke, the saying about the return of the spirits comes before the sign-of-Jonah passage, while in Matthew the Jonah passage comes first. While all agree that Matthew and Luke are using sim-

---

1. This is one of the few units in the journey narrative with material that might be parallel with Mark. That the first three subunits in this pericope have a variety of traditional contacts (Q, L, triple tradition) shows that this material's tradition as a whole existed in some variety. Tiede 1988: 218 speaks of Q material for all of 11:29–36. Luke may be pulling material together here to stress the importance of response as rejection grows.

ilar sources, the issue of the original order of that material is divided (Fitz-myer 1985: 931–32 and Marshall 1978: 482 note the options). Some re-gard Luke's order as original because the Matthean conclusion to the unclean spirit passage is viewed as an added element (Manson 1949: 87). Others argue that Matthew has the original order, with Luke doing some the-matic rearranging. There is no way to make a clear decision. But the already noted probability of a Lucan relocation of the Jonah pericope makes the orig-inality of the Matthean order slightly more likely. Also in favor of this conclu-sion is the proximity in Luke's return-of-the-spirits passage to the Beelzebul dispute (in fact, one could argue that Luke omitted the Matthean ending ["thus also shall be this evil generation"] because it would have been redun-dant when followed by the evil generation–sign of Jonah discussion).

The Jesus Seminar rejects a connection to Jesus here, printing 11:29–32 in black type (Funk and Hoover 1993: 331–32), because (1) there is vari-ation as to whether no sign (Mark 8:12) or one sign (Luke) would be given; (2) the phrase *evil generation* is too strong for Jesus; and (3) the reference to the end-time judgment is too apocalyptic for Jesus. This rejection fits the seminar's view of a nonjudging Jesus, who is a sage, not a prophet. But the tradition of Jesus as prophet is too deeply embedded for us to reject the el-ement of challenge and judgment in his teaching. As to the view that more than a prophet is present, making the rationale for challenge even stronger, one can appeal to 11:20 or 10:24 to show that this fits Jesus' intention (Schürmann 1994: 290; Nolland 1993a: 651). As to the variation on the is-sue of a sign, Mark may have in mind the working of miracles, since he stresses miracles in his Gospel.

The final two sayings also have parallels: Luke 11:33 is similar to Matt. 5:15 = Mark 4:21 (Aland 1985: §192), while Luke 11:34–36 is similar to Matt. 6:22–23 (Aland 1985: §193). Thus, these sayings have parallels in the Sermon on the Mount and in the Marcan parable discourse, making the concepts of 11:33 multiply attested. The Jesus Seminar therefore prints them in pink type (Funk and Hoover 1993: 332 commend the images' vivid-ness). The seminar prints 11:34–36 in gray type to indicate that these verses might be similar to something Jesus would have said, but have been recast, that is, the saying is too proverbial to be certain that it goes back to Jesus. The seminar prefers to see this as an example of sayings that are attracted to the sage "like a magnet." But this is a mere assertion, espe-cially given the distribution of the light theme. As Schürmann (1994: 300) argues, 11:34–35 belongs to the "oldest Jesus tradition" (so also Wiefel 1988: 223). Schürmann also notes that 11:36 lacks Lucan expression, so it is not a Lucan creation (against Nolland 1993a: 656, 658). It represents a summary of the theme, which Matthew lacks because of potential redun-dancy with Luke 11:34 (= Matt. 6:22). These sayings are proverbial enough to have been repeated. In fact, repetition seems likely, given the distinct dis-course setting of the parallels. If so, this material is special Lucan material.

Another option would be that these sayings are placed here because of their thematic relevance, but this account looks too much like a coherent discourse of warning, especially Luke 11:29–36. In fact, the unit is closely tied to 11:14–23, where Jesus makes the point that his power is evidence of God's presence and victory.[2] That passage forms the supposition for this unit. If Jesus works by God's power, then what should be done? Jesus' answer is simple: respond in faith, for the risks of refusal are great and because the benefits of acceptance mean illumination of the soul and life.

The passage, as a discourse, has a variety of forms, mainly pronouncements and sayings:

11:24–26 is a short saying (Fitzmyer 1985: 924; Bultmann 1963: 14)
11:27–28 is a pronouncement and a beatitude (Fitzmyer 1985: 927; Bultmann 1963: 30–31 [though he incorrectly calls the setting imaginary]; Berger 1984: 81–82)
11:29–32 is a saying (Fitzmyer 1985: 932; Berger 1984: 198 [a word of disgrace with a saying of judgment])
11:33–36 is a collection of wisdom sayings, since it is a call to receive revelation (Fitzmyer 1985: 939; Bultmann 1963: 92, 96; Berger 1984: 37 [speaks of metaphor])

All the remarks are unsolicited, except Jesus' response to the woman's beatitude in 11:27–28. The outline of Luke 11:24–36 is as follows:

a. Parable of the returning spirits (11:24–26)
    i. The restless spirit (11:24a)
    ii. The effort to return (11:24b–25)
    iii. The worse condition: return with seven other spirits (11:26)
b. Blessing for keeping God's word (11:27–28)
    i. The woman's blessing (11:27)
    ii. Jesus' response: obedience not just praise (11:28)
c. No sign except Jonah (11:29–32)
    i. No sign from the Son of Man but Jonah (11:29–30)
    ii. First judge: Queen of Sheba (11:31a)
    iii. Something greater than Solomon is here (11:31b)
    iv. Second judge: Ninevites (11:32a)
    v. Something greater than Jonah is here (11:32b)

2. One could easily divide the units into 11:14–28 and 11:29–36, since a break comes after 11:29. To do so, however, prioritizes form over conceptual unity in 11:24–36. If Luke pulled in material for thematic reasons, 11:24–28 is the best candidate.

d. Two sayings about light (11:33–36)
  i. Purpose of a lamp: to guide with light (11:33)
  ii. The light in a person (11:34–36)
     (1) The eye is the center of perception (11:34)
     (2) Take care that light is in you (11:35)
     (3) Light inside equals shining outside (11:36)

The unit deals with response. Neutrality in the face of God's act is not advisable. If an act of God like exorcism is not followed by response, a disaster of a worse condition may follow. It is dangerous to ignore revelation; blessedness is related to keeping God's word. The evil generation of Jesus' time will receive only the sign of Jonah: a call to repent. Condemnation at the judgment follows those who do not respond in faith to Jesus. Revelation is light and is designed to guide. It is tied to Jesus' message. Being light is possible only for those who take care about what they focus on. Take in the light, for what one is will be determined by what one takes in. To be light, one must draw on the word of Jesus.

Exegesis and Exposition

24"And when an unclean spirit comes out from a man, it goes through waterless places seeking rest; and finding none, ⌜then⌝ he says, 'I will return to my house from which I came.' 25And when he comes he finds it ⌜swept and put in order⌝. 26Then he goes and brings seven other spirits more evil than himself, and they enter and dwell there; and the last state of that man becomes worse than the first."

27And as he said this, a woman in the crowd raised her voice and said to him, "Blessed is the womb that bore you and the breasts that you sucked!" 28But he said, "Blessed rather are those who hear the word of God and keep it."

29When the crowds were increasing he began to say, "This generation is an evil generation; it seeks a sign, but no sign shall be given it except the sign of Jonah. 30For even as Jonah became a sign for the Ninevites, so also the Son of Man shall be for this generation. 31The Queen of the South will arise at the judgment with the men of this generation and condemn them; for she came from the ends of the earth to hear the wisdom of Solomon, and behold, greater than Solomon is here. 32The men of Nineveh shall rise up at the judgment with this generation and judge it. For they repented at the preaching of Jonah, and behold, greater than Jonah is here.

33"No one after lighting a lamp puts it in a cellar or under a ⌜bushel⌝, but on a stand, that those who enter may see the light.

34"Your eye is the lamp of your body; when your eye is healthy, your whole body is full of light; but when it is not healthy, your body is darkness. 35Take care, therefore, whether the light in you is darkness. 36If then your whole body is lit, having no portion that is dark, it will be wholly bright, as when a lamp by shining gives you light."

a. Parable of the Returning Spirits (11:24–26)
i. The Restless Spirit (11:24a)

Emphasizing the need for response, this parable warns of the dev- **11:24a** astating consequences of experiencing God's work only to fail to follow it up. The image of a spirit seeking a dwelling place is common in Judaism (Tob. 8:3; Bar. 4:35) and is also reflected in Luke 8:29–31 (Plummer 1896: 304; Fitzmyer 1985: 925; Ernst 1977: 376; SB 4:516; Böcher 1972: 9–11). This earlier Lucan passage suggests that a "waterless place" is necessary for them to inhabit a being.[3] The picture is of a spirit restless to return and indwell. That indwelling, as the next few verses suggest, is only possible in certain conditions.

Except for the particle δέ (*de*, but [or untranslated]) and a shift in word order, the Lucan passage virtually matches Matt. 12:43–44a. In addition, Luke has ὑποστρέψω (*hypostrepsō*, I will return) where Matthew has ἐπιστρέψω (*epistrepsō*, I will return). The difference probably reflects Lucan style, since he uses ὑποστρέφω twenty-one times in his Gospel, while Matthew never does. Matthew's verb is used four times by him and seven times by Luke. In the NT, this concept is more common in reference to the Holy Spirit's indwelling or working in a believer or in the community of believers (1 Cor. 3:16; 2 Cor. 6:6; Eph. 2:22). The idea here is parallel, but refers to the opposite, evil force (Michel, *TDNT* 5:154; Wiefel 1988: 222).[4]

To what does the imagery of the restless spirit refer?

1. It is a figurative reference to people who do not respond to Jesus. Such a person is symbolically pictured as someone who has received exorcism but has put nothing positive in its place (Plummer 1896: 304; Ellis 1974: 166 [citing Heb. 6:4–6 as parallel]; Ernst 1977: 377).
2. It is the result of a general exorcism, like that which Jesus and the disciples perform. Jesus is referring to the danger of experiencing an exorcism and then not following it up with faith. There is no symbol in this view (Schweizer 1984: 195; Creed 1930: 162; Fitzmyer 1985: 924–25 [apparently]; Talbert 1982: 138; Manson 1949: 88).

3. Some see the starting point as Isa. 13:21 and 34:14, with the suggestion that the wilderness or deserted cities are the abode of demons.

4. In *b. Giṭ.* 52a, Satan says of Rabbi Meir's work of reconciling two men, "Woe is me; he has driven me out of my house"; cited in SB 1:217. See *b. Ḥul.* 105b on the "demon of the poor."

3. More specifically, Jesus is warning those who expose themselves to the work of Jewish exorcists and do not respond in faith that they leave themselves vulnerable to a worse condition (Grundmann 1963: 239–40).[5] Jesus here reverses the Beelzebub charge (11:15). In a variation, Marshall (1978: 479) argues that the point is to warn Jewish exorcists that to exorcise without offering a positive alternative is a fruitless, even dangerous exercise.

4. Looking to the Matthean reference about the wicked generation, the reference is directed against Israel as a nation. Israel is in danger of coming under demonic control and entering a worse condition (Danker 1988: 234; Arndt 1956: 301).

Which view is more likely? View 4 is unlikely, at least in its Lucan form, because there is no corporate reference in Luke. This does not mean that Matthew's reading is different than Luke's, as much as it suggests that Luke is not as comprehensive as Matthew. The corporate remark only reflects more broadly what is true of any individual. Luke focuses on the individual, while Matthew treats what will be true of many in the current generation. That exorcisms were not regarded only symbolically in ancient times but as real events, speaks against a figurative reference (view 1). However, the point about the danger of leaving one's soul a vacuum is true.

The choice between the other two views is more difficult. In favor of Jesus' here referring to exorcism in general (view 2) rather than Jewish exorcism (view 3) is that he has just made a point about the significance of his own exorcism in the previous verses. His point is not the act of exorcism, but what it portrays. His exorcisms reveal the nature of the times, but exorcism also requires faith to make the action's benefit "stick." Thus, it is more contextually satisfying to see the reference to exorcism in general (both potential Jewish exorcisms and his own), with the point being that exorcism alone is not sufficient. Exorcism only benefits when one then responds to God. This point may help to evaluate a later miracle in 17:11–19, where only one of the ten healed lepers is commended for having faith.

ii. The Effort to Return (11:24b–25)

11:24b–25 When the demon returns it finds the house clean but ready to be reoccupied. Nothing has been done to prevent reentry of the evil

---

5. Liefeld 1984: 952 and Plummer 1896: 304 argue that spiritual renewal is the issue, not exorcism. For Liefeld, exorcism would lead to Spirit indwelling. But demons formerly at home now looking for a home suggests exorcism, and there is no guarantee that exorcism automatically produces Spirit indwelling.

one. The perfect participles indicate the state of the home's condition.[6] The house in turn pictures the man's condition. The man is
living, but is spiritually empty. He is ready to host some kind of
spiritual guest (Fitzmyer 1985: 925). The passage does not teach
the inevitability of the spirit's return, but the result of what happens if it returns. There is great risk in not being already occupied
by the protecting presence of God that comes with faith (Marshall
1978: 480 notes the conditional force of 11:24b–25).

iii. The Worse Condition: Return with Seven Other Spirits (11:26)

The man's house does not remain empty. The original spirit and **11:26**
seven other spirits more evil than the first come to the house. Their
entry pictures their control of the man. The presence of additional
spirits suggests a greater demonic effort to resist exorcism a second time (Fitzmyer 1985: 925). This idea is also suggested by κατ-
οικέω (*katoikeō*), which looks at a more permanent stay, in contrast to παροικέω (*paroikeō*), which refers to a sojourn (Luce 1933:
216; Plummer 1896: 305). It is not clear why seven spirits are mentioned, though some suggest that the total number portrays com-
pleteness of possession (similar imagery in T. Reub. 2–3; T. Judah
20; 1QS 3.16–4.26; Grundmann 1963: 240). The number of spirits
present is eight, not seven. The number does, however, match
T. Reub. 3.1–8, where the spirits present at creation seek to destroy
those who do not turn to God. Jesus remarks that this latter situation is "worse than the first" (2 Pet. 2:20; John 5:14; Matt. 27:64;
Heb. 10:29; Plummer 1896: 305). A demonic host is hard to overcome.

The picture is of a person who has experienced a great act of God,
but has not responded to it, since the occupied house is left empty.
The person has learned nothing and is still subject to the same demonic influence. The tragedy is that, by not responding, the opportunity for a permanent reversal is lost. Failure to have God enter in
has left the person in peril (contrast 1 Cor. 6:19).

The Lucan form of the verse is almost verbally exact to Matt.
12:45a: Matthew adds a phrase μεθ' ἑαυτοῦ (*meth' heautou*) to note
that the spirits came "with him," and the number *seven* has a different placement.

---

6. Matthew's description of the house's condition is "empty, swept, and put in order," rather than just "swept and put in order." Otherwise, Luke and Matt. 12:44
match verbally. See the additional note.

b. Blessing for Keeping God's Word (11:27–28)
i. The Woman's Blessing (11:27)

11:27 Perhaps to break the tension of confrontation or to offer a note that some were receptive to him, a woman offers a blessing for Jesus' mother. Ταῦτα (*tauta*, these things) most logically refers back to the previous discussion to make the point that the frightening things in Jesus' parable brought a response. Whatever the motive for her action (it is not given), the woman responds with a beatitude for the womb that bore Jesus and the breasts that fed him. The statement would have been a brave one in a mixed audience, where women were generally expected to be silent (Arndt 1956: 302). The remark is an expression of gratitude for or acceptance of his ministry, since a mother was valued in the accomplishments of her son.[7] Jesus will make clear by his reply that praise is not his concern; responsive action is. The comment is not a rebuke of the woman's remark, for Luke expresses his agreement with it in the infancy section (Luke 1:42, 48; Plummer 1896: 305; Schneider 1977a: 269). The point is simply that Jesus is concerned with a favorable response to his ministry. Luke is alone in noting this incident (also Gospel of Thomas 79), though some of the events of Matt. 12 include the seeking out of Jesus by his family. It may be that Matt. 12 gives the background to this remark, which Luke has topically saved for a later setting on rejection and response.

ii. Jesus' Response: Obedience Not Just Praise (11:28)

11:28 Jesus offers his own beatitude. It is a familiar theme: blessing comes to those who give attention to and follow God's word. The saying recalls Luke 8:21, where blessing comes on those who hear and do the word of God (also Luke 6:47; 8:15; James 1:22; Deut. 4:6; 28:13, 15). The crucial issue is not heaping praise on Jesus, but responding with action to his teaching.

The only issue in the verse is how it relates to what was said in Luke 11:27. The connective μενοῦν (*menoun*) has three possible senses (Fitzmyer 1985: 928): (1) an adversative meaning "on the contrary," thus rejecting the previous remark (Manson 1949: 88; Marshall 1978: 482); (2) an affirmation meaning "indeed" (as in Phil. 3:8); or (3) a correction meaning "yes, but rather" (Luce 1933: 216; Arndt 1956: 302; Plummer 1896: 306; Danker 1988: 235; Schneider 1977a: 269). The first meaning is not likely, since Luke

---

7. Gen. 49:25; Prov. 23:24–25; Fitzmyer 1985: 928; Grundmann 1963: 222 (who notes the contrast to Gospel of Thomas 79); Hauck, *TDNT* 4:369; SB 2:187–88; *m. ʾAbot* 2.8; 2 Bar. 54.10; and later targumim on Gen. 49:25 (i.e., Ps.-J., Neof. 1, and Frg. Tg.). Manson 1949: 88 notes that *Pesikta Rabbati* 37.2 (= Braude 1968: 2.689) says this of Messiah's mother (cited as §149a by Manson according to an older numbering scheme; see SB 1:161).

has already affirmed such a blessing (Luke 1:42, 48) and elsewhere uses οὐχί, λέγω ὑμῖν (*ouchi, legō hymin*, no, I say to you) to express rejection of an idea (12:51; 13:3, 5; Fitzmyer 1985: 928). The sense is not complete affirmation either. Rather, the woman's remark is correct, but not exhaustive. The recent examples provided by Jesus' teaching about the Samaritan, Mary, and prayer are but three illustrations of what is expected of disciples (Schneider 1977a: 269). Blessing resides in obedient response, whether in care for others, in attention to Jesus, or in discourse with God.

c. No Sign except Jonah (11:29–32)
i. No Sign from the Son of Man but Jonah (11:29–30)

From a call to respond, Jesus turns to a rebuke of this generation for   **11:29** seeking signs (the crowd in 11:16 also sought a sign). They sought a sign despite having been given many already. The word of God goes unheeded in the midst of all this activity. Luke introduces the remark by noting that the crowds were increasing at this point. It is almost as if Luke wants to make clear that the current attention that Jesus is getting is not going to last. Those who know the subsequent story already know this.

The evil character of this generation is demonstrated by its current desire for a sign (so the present tense ζητεῖ, *zētei*, are seeking). Jesus will offer them none, except the sign of Jonah. In Matt. 12:40 the reference to three days in the belly of the whale clearly alludes to the resurrection. Matthew goes on to mention Ninevite repentance, thus creating a complex image involving resurrection and repentance. Matthew's condemnation is stated more fully by referring to "an evil and adulterous generation," while Luke speaks only of an evil generation.

Luke's abbreviated version focuses on the response of repentance and shortens the rebuke (Schweizer 1984: 196; Talbert 1982: 138; Fitzmyer 1985: 933; against Schürmann 1994: 278–79). Fitzmyer speaks of Jonah's preaching and the following reform as the sign, a point that makes the sign visible and concrete beyond the proclamation of the word. This detail counters the claims of those favoring resurrection as the sign, since the mere giving of the word itself is not a sign, a minstry is. Luke may have removed the reference to the "adulterous" generation for the sake of his Gentile audience who might not have understood it (Danker 1988: 235). The resurrection is not alluded to in Luke.[8] It is Lucan to draw attention to the need

---

8. Plummer 1896: 306 argues that resurrection is implied at the end of the verse by the giving of a sign, but the Lucan context alone does not make such a reference clear. Hendriksen 1978: 627 and Arndt 1956: 302 make resurrection the only point, though Arndt admits that only Matthew makes this connection clear.

for a concrete response of repentance. In effect, Jonah's message and the reaction to it are the sign, just as Jesus and his new community are the sign for this generation (Rengstorf, *TDNT* 7:233–34).[9] A prophetic ministry becomes a sign (Luke 2:34–35; Isa. 8:18; 20:3; Ezek. 12:6). Seen in this way, Luke places the event here to show that God's word and Jesus' message are to be identified with one another (Fitzmyer 1985: 934). One cannot accept Jesus and reject his call to repent. Mark says that no sign will be offered, by which he means no *additional* miraculous sign, since Jesus had already done miracles.

The reference to Jonah might also be related to the parousia and resurrection (Ellis 1974: 169; Schneider 1977a: 271; esp. Jeremias, *TDNT* 3:408–10, stressing the idea of authority). In this view, the sign is not so much the resurrection itself as what it brings with it: judgment. The view has much to commend it, including the context of Luke 11:31–32. It is unlikely, however, that the original audience could clearly relate to its application, since "this generation" did not see the parousia or judgment—unless A.D. 70 is meant (Marshall 1978: 482–83). Against an allusion to A.D. 70 is the condemnation of 11:31–32, a picture of final judgment. It also runs counter to Luke's emphasis on present eschatological fulfillment and on Jesus' current authority. Jesus as the Son of Man appears to "this generation" now (11:29–30), but their response has consequences for "this generation" when the righteous acknowledge their just condemnation by the unrighteous in future judgment (11:31–32). These factors make this view unlikely, though its point is an implication of Jesus' teaching.

Nolland (1993a: 652–53) argues that the sign is the preaching of judgment, not repentance (Jon. 3:4, 10; 4:1). In one sense, this idea works, but the parallel of the Queen of Sheba and the Ninevites is against it. These OT characters share a response to God's word—a comparison that favors seeing repentance as the sign, because transformation is what allows the Ninevites to share in condemning this generation's failure to respond with faith.

What is the origin of this statement? It has been regarded as too difficult for Jesus to be its source, at least in its Matthean "resurrection" form (Edwards 1971). Luce (1933: 217) cites the following reasons: (1) Jesus did not know of his resurrection nor did he foretell it; (2) calling an event that occurs after a rejection a sign is absurd; (3) the Ninevites did not know about Jonah's stay in the whale, so it could not have been a sign for them; and (4) Jesus must have spoken

---

9. Grundmann 1963: 242 argues that Jonah was seen as a sign in Judaism because of his miraculous deliverance from the whale; see SB 1:642–49. But these Jewish references are late, as Fitzmyer 1985: 935–36 notes, adding that Josephus's account of Jonah (*Antiquities* 9.10.2 §§208–14) makes nothing of the fish episode.

of no sign. Luce suggests that Luke's form of the statement is possible for Jesus, so he rejects only Matthew's version.

However, Jesus could well anticipate a vindication and resurrection, as 9:21–22 suggests. A sign can occur after rejection if opportunity to respond still remains, as it did. Also, it is not certain that the Ninevites did not know about Jonah's stay in the whale; it is not mentioned in Jonah's preaching in the book, but his message is given only in brief form. It is likely that, in addressing the Ninevites, Jonah would have mentioned his hesitation in coming to preach to them and how he was coerced into coming. In fact, his mere presence among such Gentiles as a prophet from Israel would have been a sign. Finally, that Jesus did not speak of a sign is a deduction from Luce's other three points, not a refutation. Jesus might be making a rhetorical case for Jonah as a sign, in that even if the Ninevites do not know about Jonah's travail in the whale, readers familiar with the whole story know the saga. In a sense, mere knowledge of the whole story is the sign.

Solutions that deny that Jesus made the statement are highly problematic, if not impossible to defend, despite the confidence of some scholars. A better approach is to see Luke's version as a focused summary about one theme: responding in faith to Jesus' remarks (Liefeld 1984: 953).[10] In short, the saying goes back to Jesus, whose message and hope of vindication was strong enough to suggest the connection to Jonah.

11:30 Jesus elaborates on the sign of Jonah. The point of comparison (note καθώς [kathōs, even as] and οὕτως [houtōs, so]) is between Jonah and the Son of Man, as well as between the Ninevites and the current audience. This suggests that Jonah's preaching and ministry is the point of comparison for 11:29. The only thing that Jesus' audience and the Ninevites share is the hearing of God's message. The following verses confirm this view, since Solomon and Jonah share only one quality: they display a message. Solomon shared God's wisdom, while Jonah brought his word. Response to God's truth is in view here. The reference to Jesus as the Son of Man alludes to his present ministry with its call to repentance (7:34–35; Fitzmyer 1985: 936). The Son of Man, as God's prophet, brings God's message, and failure to respond to him in faith will bring consequences. The future verb ἔσται (estai, will be) does not look at a future event, such as the parousia, but is a vivid reference to a ministry in progress whose efforts extend into the future. Ἔσται in this verse matches δοθήσεται

---

10. An older solution regards the reference to Jonah as a textual corruption that originally referred to John the Baptist, but there is no manuscript evidence for this understanding. Creed 1930: 163 seems attracted to this view. Fitzmyer 1985: 931–39 presents the various options on source and tradition history.

(*dothēsetai*, shall be given) in 11:29, a verb that describes the current giving of the sign in preaching. In fact, the reference to the Son of Man may suggest Jesus' authority, since Jesus will later connect the title to his right to rule at God's right hand (22:69). Jesus is greater because he brings a greater message and he bears a greater authority.

ii. First Judge: Queen of Sheba (11:31a)
iii. Something Greater Than Solomon Is Here (11:31b)

11:31 The contrast between the wisdom of the Gentiles in responding to saints of old and the people's current refusal now shows the "culpability" of this generation.[11] The picture of Gentiles judging Jews is the opposite of OT expectation and is a severe rebuke to Jesus' audience (Talbert 1982: 138–39). The Queen of the South, also known as the Queen of Sheba (in southern Arabia), appears in 1 Kings 10:1–13 = 2 Chron. 9:1–12 (also Josephus, *Antiquities* 8.6.5–6 §§165–75). She came to verify Solomon's reputation and found that he was more than she expected. In a rhetorical remark, Jesus comments that this woman will execute judgment on this generation because she responded to Solomon, while this generation failed to receive Jesus, who is greater than Solomon (Lohse, *TDNT* 7:465).

The neuter term πλεῖον (*pleion*, greater thing) looks not so much at the person of Jesus, as the message he brings and the time he represents.[12] The exact christological role referred to in this final remark is not clear (Messiah or Exalted One or both?), but it is clear that Jesus sees himself as greater than one of the major regal figures of Israel's history. If the queen responded to Solomon, they should respond to him. He is the bearer of greater wisdom from God.[13] Plummer (1896: 307) notes three contrasts in the verse: between the pagan queen and the Jews, between the travel from the ends of the earth and the presence of Jesus, and between Solomon and the one greater than Solomon.

The wording of the verse matches Matt. 12:42 except for a few minor differences. In Luke, the additional term τῶν ἀνδρῶν (*tōn andrōn*, of men) appears after μετά (*meta*, with): "with the men of this generation" (Matthew speaks of "with this generation"). The pronouns also differ, although the meaning is the same: αὐτήν (*autēn*,

---

11. Outside of this pericope and its parallels, τῆς γενεᾶς ταύτης occurs in Luke 7:31 = Matt. 11:16; Luke 11:50–51 = Matt. 23:36; Luke 17:25; 21:32 = Mark 13:30 = Matt. 23:34; Büchsel, *TDNT* 1:663. Note that the concept is multiply attested in Q and Mark.

12. Arndt 1956: 303 equates person and time. In contrast, Ellis 1974: 168 and Talbert 1982: 139 suggest that the Spirit is referred to, but this is too specific, since there is no clear contextual indication to him. He is only an implication of what Jesus brings.

13. On Jesus as bearer of God's wisdom, see Luke 7:35; 10:21–22; 1 Cor. 1:24, 30. On the Son of Man as bringer of wisdom, see 1 Enoch 49.1–3; Grundmann 1963: 242.

it) in Matthew refers to generation and αὐτούς (*autous*, them) in Luke refers to men. Some think that the Lucan reference to men may add a note of shame to the remark by contrasting them to the woman, but this is probably a generic reference to humankind and not to be read as a male-female contrast (Fitzmyer 1985: 936; note that a woman is in the audience in 11:27, so she is included in Jesus' remarks). There is shame, but it is not tied to gender. Response is the issue and is the "honorable" thing. Matthew's order is Jonah and then the Queen of the South, while Luke has the reverse. Either Luke made a change to put the references in their chronological order (which might enhance the wisdom motif; Fitzmyer 1985: 931–32) or Matthew placed the Jonah references together (Godet 1875: 2.72) or both writers used different sources for the same event. No clear choice exists.

iv. Second Judge: Ninevites (11:32a)
v. Something Greater Than Jonah Is Here (11:32b)

After the queen comes a second example: the Ninevites (the wording **11:32** exactly matches Matt. 12:41). A Gentile response contrasts with Jewish rejection. The shame is great because again the expected pattern is reversed. The remarks parallel the previous example, except the point of comparison here is repentance at a preached message (Jon. 3:6–10; on κήρυγμα, *kērygma*, as "preaching with exhortation," see Friedrich, *TDNT* 3:715–16 §B). Jesus is greater than Jonah or, more precisely, given the repetition of the neuter πλεῖον (*pleion*), his message is greater. Two groups of Gentiles have been wiser than this Israelite generation. History does not speak kindly of rejecting God's messengers. Neither will the final judgment. Here is a warning to heed Jesus' message and respond to him. Jesus again uses Israel's history to rebuke its potential rejection (Luke 4:24–27).

d. Two Sayings about Light (11:33–36)
i. Purpose of a Lamp: To Guide with Light (11:33)

Jesus now turns to the image of light as a picture of his revelation. **11:33** Luke 11:33 points to the purpose of light as a source of guidance. It is almost an exact doublet to 8:16, but its proverbial character makes it likely that it was repeated.[14] The picture is a simple one: no

---

14. Note also the Gospel of Thomas 33. This repetition shows that Luke is not averse to repeating sayings and also suggests that he is aware that certain sayings were said by Jesus in different settings with slightly differing force. The possibility of the tradition having several such duplications cannot be excluded. Not every parallel is a genuine overlap, but might be what has been called "alibi analogies," where the saying looks like a parallel, but really is not (see Reicke 1968: 26–30 for a detailed discussion).

one goes to the trouble of lighting an oil lamp only to put it in a place where it will not illumine the room. The term κρύπτη (*kryptē*) is a *hapax legomenon* and refers to a dark, hidden place. Since a house is in view, a cellar is the likely hidden place (BAGD 454; BAA 921). A μόδιος (*modios*, bushel) is a vessel usually used to carry or measure corn (Matt. 5:15 = Mark 4:21; BAGD 525; BAA 1064; Luke 6:38 describes the act of measuring). The reference to the vault need not presuppose a non-Palestinian setting and home. Fitzmyer (1985: 940) notes that the term's various meanings makes this conclusion uncertain. Light should guide people through a room (on ancient lamps, see the exegesis of 8:16).

The intended association is between Jesus' teaching and light (Luke 1:78–79; 2:32; John 1:4; 3:19–21; 9:39–41; Acts 26:18; Liefeld 1984: 954). It may be that the disciples are also seen as light (as are believers in 2 Cor. 6:14–15 and Eph. 5:14–15) and so the idea is to let their light shine (cf. the believer's walk in 1 John 1:6–10). But this idea is at best an implication in Luke, while it is clearly present in Matt. 5:14–16 (Manson 1949: 93). Luke's main point is that Jesus' teaching is not secretly disseminated, it is openly proclaimed. Indeed, it is to function openly; it is to be put to use. The response called for is unlike the crowd's action. If one does not receive guidance, it is not because the lamp has been hidden, but because there has been no response to the light (Talbert 1982: 139). No further sign is necessary. Danker (1988: 237) sees the light imagery setting up the picture and application of 11:34–36. An ambiguity runs through the image, since in 11:33 the light is Jesus' message, while 11:34–35 speaks of our eyes as lamps, provided that they take in light. So one must receive light to be light (11:36).

The parallels to the passage are found in the Marcan section of parables (Mark 4:21) and in the Sermon on the Mount (Matt. 5:15). However, the saying's proverbial character and the different wording of each version suggests that this is a teaching that was used on a variety of occasions, in a variety of ways (Plummer 1896: 308). Luke 11:33 may reflect special Lucan material.

ii. The Light in a Person (11:34–36)
(1) The Eye Is the Center of Perception (11:34)

11:34 Jesus makes clear how response is related to perception. The eye is the vehicle of perception, the source of reception. What determines the body's health is the content of one's perception. If the eye brings in light, the whole person glows.[15] But this happens only if the eye is

---

15. At Qumran, the Spirit of truth is the light that illumines human hearts; 1QS 4.2; Grundmann 1963: 243. The OT image is found in Job 29:3; Ps. 112:4; Isa. 42:6–

healthy (ἁπλοῦς, *haplous*), if it takes in spiritual truth.[16] Ἁπλοῦς contrasts with πονηρός (*ponēros*, evil, diseased) and thus has an ethical thrust.[17] But if the eye is not sound, if its judgments are poor, then darkness results and spiritual light is nonexistent. There is no automatic "inner light" as far as Jesus is concerned. What we are is related to what we take in and accept as true. We are responsible for our spiritual condition by how we respond to our environment. Not to take in God's light is to risk darkness. Light cannot be found elsewhere. The implication is that if one has good eyes one will see the light Jesus offers, but if one's vision is clouded by evil one will miss the light.

(2) Take Care That Light Is in You (11:35)

Jesus issues a warning that is negative in thrust. He sees many moving toward rejection and notes that this is dangerous and has devastating consequences (11:31–32). Those who would hear Jesus are to be constantly on the watch that what they take in is light, not darkness.[18] The great danger is taking in the wrong thing (Grundmann 1963: 243; Prov. 20:27; T. Naph. (Hebrew version) 10.9 [= Charles 1913: 2.363];[19] 1QS 3.19–25; Philo, *On the Creation* 17 §53). Jesus' application calls for a check of the person and not a check of the eye, showing that he is talking about the inner, spiritual person (Fuchs, *TDNT* 7:416).

11:35

(3) Light Inside Equals Shining Outside (11:36)

The teaching ends with a positive thrust. If the body possesses light and has no share in darkness, then it is totally lit. Here is a spiritually healthy person, walking in the light and reflecting light. This person is able to receive instruction and is guided by God's teaching.

11:36

7; 45:7; 59:9–10; Mic. 7:8; Fitzmyer 1985: 940. The body is a metonymy of container for contents and refers to the person.

16. On ἁπλοῦς as "clear, pure, healthy," see BAGD 86 and BAA 171. When the eye is clear, it is healthy and takes in light. The eye is a figure for spiritual condition in Matt. 6:22; Prov. 4:18–19; 11:25 (ἁπλοῦς with a different sense); T. Iss. 3.4; 4.6; Bauernfeind, *TDNT* 1:386; Michaelis, *TDNT* 5:377; Harder, *TDNT* 6:556; SB 1:302, 431–32, 722, 833.

17. Πονηρός is used in 11:29 to describe the evil generation; Danker 1988: 237. The term's repeated use and the internal contrast make the meaning "generous" for ἁπλοῦς impossible; against Fitzmyer 1985: 940. The point is not the eye's "generosity" but its reception of good or evil.

18. Σκόπει (take care) is a present imperative and stresses the constancy of the care. The singular ἐν σοί (in you) makes clear the individual character of the examination.

19. The nature and age of the so-called Hebrew version of the Testament of Naphtali is disputed; see H. Kee in J. Charlesworth 1983–85: 1.775–76.

The light functions just as the lamp of 11:33 is designed to function: it illumines a dark room and allows one to make one's way. The verse has two emphatic, repeated terms: ὅλον (*holon*, whole) and φωτεινόν (*phōteinon*, brightly lit, illuminated). Jesus' teaching, like the rays of a lamp, entirely illumines the person and brings spiritual health (ἀστραπή [*astrapē*, gleaming, brightness] occurs in Matt. 24:27 = Luke 17:24; Matt. 28:3; Luke 10:18; Rev. 4:5; 8:5; 11:19; 16:18; Foerster, *TDNT* 1:505).

With the emphasis on light and spiritual health, 11:33–36 contains an *inclusio*. Jesus provides the light publicly, so all who receive it can see. If they are receptive, then they are given the guidance needed to negotiate a dark world. In fact, they themselves become light. What started out with Jesus may be shared by others who receive him. Schweizer (1984: 196) and Creed (1930: 164) complain that the verse appears tautologous by virtually saying, "If you are light, you are light." But this ignores the *inclusio* (correctly Arndt 1956: 304). Four major options deal with the supposed problem of the sense (Marshall 1978: 490):

1. The phrase is a mistranslation of the Aramaic, so a picture of lighting up the surroundings is the point (Manson 1949: 94; Torrey 1933: 145, 309–10). As a result, a view like Matt. 5:14 emerges. But this meaning is too speculative and alters the Lucan sense. It lacks any textual support and assumes that the saying is a parallel to Matthew.
2. The saying is applied to those who have yet to hear Jesus and yet have a good inner light (J. Weiss with some uncertainty, as cited by Marshall). The sense is, "If you are light, and have no portion that is dark, when you respond to Jesus, you will be wholly bright." This view is impossible, since Luke 11:13, 29 shows that, to Jesus, people are not so neutral. According to Jesus' preaching, the basic need of humankind is to repent; humans cannot start out being light.
3. The saying means, "If your heart is light, it will receive light from the true Light, Christ" (Zahn 1920: 474–75; Schlatter 1960: 517; Creed 1930: 164; Klostermann 1929: 129; Ernst 1977: 382; Grundmann 1963: 244). The difference between this view and the previous one is that this view deals with those who have already heard Jesus and are open to him, while view 2 looks only to those who have not yet heard him.
4. The reference to being fully lit is a picture of how one is received at the judgment (Wiefel 1988: 225; Hahn 1973: 129–31). This view is possible, but the context seems too focused on the present situation to make it likely.

It is best to see an *inclusio* in 11:33–36, yielding a progression in the sayings. The passage is a promise to those who will receive the light Jesus offers. He is light and has been placed for all to see. It shows where response can lead (so correctly view 3). The people's response to the light, through their perception, determines their spiritual health. If they take in Jesus' light, they will be healthy. And if they are spiritually healthy, they themselves will shine brightly and give off light. They will be lights, reflecting the rays of God's truth by the way they live. This positive ending contrasts with Matthew's ending in the Sermon on the Mount, where the point is, if darkness is present, that darkness is very great. Matthew has a more tragic conclusion: rejection produces darkness and death.

Summary

Luke 11:24–36 shows that the dangers of rejecting Jesus are great, just as the benefits of responding to him are numerous. An exorcised man who fails to respond to Jesus runs the risk of even greater possession by evil forces later. One cannot be spiritually neutral. Even though the verse refers to those who have received the specific benefit of exorcism, it applies to anyone who has benefited from the presence of God's work. The point is that people should respond to God.

In contrast, blessedness comes not from being grateful for or interested in Jesus' coming but by responding to the word of God that he brings. Such response means action, doing God's word. Unfortunately, many in Israel's present generation seek a sign, but the only one offered is the prophetic call to repent. Gentiles of old were more responsive to God's message than is the present generation of Israel. Those who reject Jesus will be the objects of judgment later, since he brings a greater time and message. He is greater than the wise King Solomon or the famous prophet Jonah. The exact nature of Jesus' greatness as Son of Man is not specified here, but in the larger context of Luke's Gospel it is Jesus' messianic authority and his message that makes him greater.

One's spiritual perception is central to one's spiritual fate. Care must be taken to respond to the light that leads to truth. Jesus' teaching is given openly, but it must be received. One will either possess darkness because of what one believes, or one will respond to Jesus and have light. With his light one is able to discern the choices of life with spiritual perception. In fact, one can become light to others. As far as Luke is concerned, that choice is the one the reader needs to make or be reassured about, since the way of darkness leads to certain destruction. The way of light offers blessing from God and security before him. Given these stark alternatives, the question for the reader is, "What kind of light is in you?"

Additional Notes

11:24. The presence of τότε (then) is disputed. $\mathfrak{P}^{45}$, ℵ*, A, C, D, family 1, family 13, and Byz do not include it, which yields a smoother style. $\mathfrak{P}^{75}$, ℵ², B, L, Θ, and Ξ include it, which is the harder reading. It is hard to explain its addition, so it is likely to be original.

11:25. Most manuscripts speak of the house as "swept and in order" ($\mathfrak{P}^{75}$, ℵ*, A, D, W, Δ, Θ, Byz, most Itala), but a few begin the description by noting that the house is also "empty" (B, C, L, Ξ, Ψ, family 1, family 13). The presence of two elements is favored by the manuscript evidence, plus it is the harder reading, in that the reading that includes three elements harmonizes with Matt. 12:44.

11:33. The reference to the bushel should be included in the text since ℵ, A, B, C, D, W, Θ, and Byz have μόδιον.

3. Rebuke of Pharisees and Scribes (11:37–54)

Luke follows the warnings about rejecting Jesus' message (11:24–36) with one of Jesus' strongest condemnation discourses. Luke 11:37–54 describes a dinner in a Pharisee's house. Jesus rebukes a confrontational attitude about his failure to wash hands and engage in ritual cleansing. His response involves seven denunciations, though they are structured in six woes: three woes are linked to the Pharisees and three to the scribes. The account summarizes the religious leadership's failings (Tannehill 1986: 180–82). Jesus castigates the leaders for being hypocritical, ignoring God's justice, burdening the people with demands that they themselves do not keep, following their murderous ancestors, and blocking the entrance to heaven. The condemnation could hardly be stronger: among the most wicked of those in this wicked generation are the religious leaders themselves. A chasm exists between Jesus and official Judaism. (This condemnation is immediately reaffirmed in a warning to the disciples in 12:1.)

Sources and Historicity

The setting and sources for this pericope are complex. Something of a consensus exists, though the reason for it seems not to be well founded. Most regard Luke as essentially deriving from Q and sharing traditional material with Matt. 23 (Aland 1985: §194). The list of those favoring this connection is impressive: Fitzmyer (1985: 942–44), Schneider (1977a: 274), Schweizer (1984: 199), Creed (1930: 164), Klostermann (1929: 129), Luce (1933: 220), Tiede (1988: 221), Grundmann (1963: 245–46), and Egelkraut (1976: 93 n. 1).[1] Most argue that Luke formed the meal setting either because it was a favorite setting for him (5:29; 7:36; 10:38; 14:1) or on the basis of suggestions provided by 11:39.[2] Others argue that pas-

---

1. Marshall 1978: 491–93 sees different recensions of Q. Manson 1949: 96 sees most of Matt. 23 coming from a special Matthean source. Ellis 1974: 170 and Schlatter 1960: 303–5 see a combination of Q and special Lucan material. But Wiefel 1988: 227 objects to this because of the material's similarity to Matt. 23.

2. Egelkraut 1976: 93 n. 1 argues that the question of 11:38 does not match the answer of 11:39 and thus Luke created the introduction (but see the exegesis of 11:38). Taking 11:39 as indicating the original setting, Marshall 1978: 492 argues that it is Matthew who shifted to a Mark 12 setting. He argues that Luke does not conflate sources, while Matthew has many topical rearrangements; so also Godet 1875: 2.87.

sages such as Mark 7:1–9 or Matt. 15:1–20 may have suggested the meal setting, so that Luke conflates several events (Ernst 1977: 383–84; Egelkraut 1976: 93 n. 1). Others suggest that Matthew's positioning of these remarks is influenced by Mark 12:38–40 (Marshall 1978: 492; Godet 1875: 2.87).[3]

But a shared tradition with Matt. 23 is problematic.[4] It seems more likely that Luke is dealing with special material that conceptually fits Matt. 23 but is distinct from it. In addition, it seems that this event is unique and is not a combination of other settings such as Mark 7, Mark 12, or Matt. 15.

Against associating this passage with Mark 7 and Matt. 15 are the following considerations:

1. In Luke the setting is a meal, while in Mark and Matthew the setting is a discussion about meal habits. If Luke were conflating, he did not need to create a meal setting to bring the events together. Such topics do not need meal settings for Luke (cf. 5:33–39).
2. The complaint in Matthew and Mark is against the disciples, while in Luke it is against Jesus. One could argue for literary heightening, but Jesus can defend himself while answering a complaint against the disciples. So a rationale for turning the charge into one against Jesus is unclear (in 5:33–39 and 6:1–5 the charges are against the disciples).
3. In Luke there is no rebuke of the Pharisees' failure to keep God's commandments, as in the other Synoptics. The omission is difficult to explain, since it fits the theme so well.
4. In Luke there is no citation of Isa. 29:13 as part of the rebuke, an allusion found in both supposed parallels. Once again, the omission is difficult to explain, since it also is well suited to the theme. Schweizer's claim (1984: 199) that there are striking connections between Luke 11 and Mark 7:4 is a vast overstatement. What is striking are the glaring differences.

Nonetheless, if one insists that Luke took his tradition and placed it into an

---

3. Godet does not note the Marcan connection, but does cite Luke 20:45–47 as showing awareness of a critique at the temple. The situation is little different for Matthean prioritists, since the question is why does Luke have here what Matthew and Mark have much later in Jesus' ministry? Any attempt to argue that Luke reflects the original tradition suffers from the Matthean and Marcan agreement in timing, if all are working with the same source material. Why would both Matthew and Mark diverge from an alleged earlier placement? Distinct traditions are more likely, since it is also hard to explain Luke's placement if all he had was Mark or Matthew. Even if Luke supplied the meal setting, the question remains, why did the event occur so early outside of Jerusalem?

4. Zahn 1920: 477–78 n. 73 sees an independent tradition from Matthew, but Zahn is less clear if the material of the various passages is essentially the same discourse.

existing Synoptic setting, the influence of Mark 7 and Matt. 15 is a better choice than Matt. 23. Against a tie to Matt. 23 are the following points:

1. The setting is different: in Matt. 23 Jesus is in public discourse in Jerusalem; in Luke he is at a meal. It is claimed that Matt. 23 itself may also be a conflation of sayings, but if he did not use Matthew as a source all this does is complicate how Luke got the speech and virtually reproduced it. If Matthew brought the material together, which is not certain, then the possibility of various recensions must be accepted and the rationale for a simple appeal to Q material is weakened. A Matthean anthology only increases the options.

2. Virtually none of the wording of Matt. 23 matches Luke 11. Of the six woes, only one produces any overlapping phrases (Luke 11:42 with Matt. 23:23). The agreement is conceptual, not verbal. Marshall (1978: 493) argues that a distinct recension of Q is used. But why not then appeal to a distinct event and source? Is it so difficult to believe that a leader in an ideological and religious struggle would repeat himself in various settings as he talked about his opponents and what they represented? The setting in Luke is a private discourse with the Pharisees, while Matt. 23 is a more public declaration. Repetition makes sense, given the different audiences.

3. The order of the woes is not at all similar, which makes a united tradition even more problematic. Manson (1949: 95) has two charts showing the disagreement in order (also Fitzmyer 1985: 944; Marshall 1978: 491–92). Following Luke's order, Matthew's woes appear in this order: woe 4, remark 2, woe 6, remark 1, woe 7, woe 1.[5] Reversing the comparison and following Matthew's order, Luke goes like this: woe 6, no parallel, no parallel, woe 1, remark, woe 3, woe 5 (in terms of Matt. 23 the order is 23–24, 6–7 [non-woe], 27–28, 4 [non-woe], 29–32, 13). The disagreement could not be greater. What we have is a jumble of sayings. How could this come from one basic source or even recensions of the same fundamental tradition? Where else do we have such a scramble? Efforts to explain the divergences appeal to Lucan redaction or to a combination of sources, but the argument's multiple levels of assumption seem forced. For example, Schürmann (1994: 330–35) sees three levels involved: a challenge to rabbis, words against the Pharisees, and the warning of judgment. His assumption appears to be one audi-

---

5. In this list, "remark" means a conceptual parallel not laid out as a woe. Fitzmyer notes the order in terms of Lucan verses as follows: 43, 46, 52, 42, [39], 44, 47. Manson has a similar listing (with a dash representing unparalleled material): 46, 52, 42, -, 44, 47–48, -. Interestingly, these two lists do not agree, suggesting that it is hard to know where the matches lie! Apparently Fitzmyer sees a parallel in 11:43 that Manson rejects.

ence or topic per tradition unit, along with a denial of the possibility of multiple events.

A simple solution is that Matt. 15 and Mark 7 belong together earlier in Jesus' ministry. Luke 11 is a unique event. Matthew 23 belongs in Jesus' final week, summarizing a ministry rejected by the leaders every step of the way. No conflations exist, just distinct events. Marshall (1978: 491) is right to see a distinct source for Luke; it is probably not Q however, but Luke's special source. The possibility of multiple confrontations with the leadership is not unlikely for a ministry of such significance to the Jewish hope, especially a ministry of prophetic character. Much was at stake. Emotions clearly ran high. The strong remarks fit Jesus' ministry, unless one wishes to argue for a particularly emotionless portrait of Jesus in the midst of a culture that was used to direct confrontation.

The Jesus Seminar rates the sayings of this discourse variously (Funk and Hoover 1993: 333–35):[6]

pink type	11:43 (prominent seats)
gray type	11: 39–41 (cups and dishes)
	11:44 (unmarked graves)
	11:52 (key of knowledge)
black type	11:42 (tithes)
	11:46–51 (burdens and monuments to prophets)

Thus the bulk of the discourse in the view of the Jesus Seminar has little direct tie to Jesus. The seminar sees Luke being responsible for the setting and for reordering the Q tradition (Nolland 1993a: 662 is similar, speaking of Luke's reordering a source shared with Matthew).[7] The seminar rejects the sayings because the images are of a mixed character (e.g., cups) or because the tone is too invective or vitriolic (e.g., tithing, graves, burdens). Only the initial critique of the scribes is seen as possible, given their "bureaucratic" approach. Nolland notes that what Jesus said to a specific, hypocritical group of people may have been turned into a generalization about all people in these groups (so also Stein 1992: 340). Nolland argues that the prophetic character of Jesus' remarks, including the use of rhetorical hyperbole, also influenced what is present here. There is little doubt that Jesus had ideological-theological differences with the Pharisees and scribes

6. Interestingly, Schürmann 1994: 334 divides the sayings into two categories: the voice of Jesus (11:39, 42a–b, 46a) and the voice of the early church (11:39b–41, 42c, 43, 44, 47–48, 49–51, 52). What the Jesus Seminar accepts (11:43), Schürmann rejects; while two of the verses that Schürmann accepts (11:42a, 46), the seminar rejects. The differences reflect just how much judgment and speculation goes into these assessments.

7. Stein 1992: 339 n. 83 notes five cases of likely Lucan omission.

about issues like the Sabbath and ritual cleansing. Some heated debate would be a part of the response to these differences, where views of God's will were at stake. In fact, in later Judaism the rabbis harshly criticized hypocrites in their midst (*b. Soṭa* 22b speaks of seven types of Pharisees and five are hypocrites; Stein 1992: 340).

First-century Palestine was not a religiously tolerant environment, and yet Jesus pressed for religious reform, believing that he had been sent by God. These themes fit the historical Jesus (see other critiques in 16:14; 20:47) and is not unlike the deuteronomistic critique found elsewhere in the Gospel of many in the nation (see the warnings of 13:6–9, 31–33; 19:41–44). It was confrontations like these that understandably caused the leadership to deal with Jesus.

From what has been said, it is clear that the pericope is a collection of sayings laid out in woes. This is a discourse of Jesus (Fitzmyer 1985: 944).[8] The outline of Luke 11:37–54 is as follows:

a. Setting (11:37–38)
b. Jesus' fourfold rebuke of the Pharisees (11:39–44)
　　i. Outside clean, inside not (11:39–41)
　　ii. Woe: neglecting God's justice and love (11:42)
　　iii. Woe: loving the best seats (11:43)
　　iv. Woe: leading people to death (11:44)
c. A scribe's complaint (11:45)
d. Jesus' threefold rebuke of the scribes (11:46–52)
　　i. Woe: giving burdens to others, but not to self (11:46)
　　ii. Woe: building the tombs of the prophets (11:47–48)
　　iii. Prediction of persecution and judgment (11:49–51)
　　iv. Woe: taking away the key of knowledge (11:52)
e. The Pharisees try to trap Jesus (11:53–54)

The unit's major theme is Jesus' opposition to hypocrisy within the leadership and his condemnation of them. The Pharisees' excessive concern with ritual matters is contrasted to Jesus' concern for the heart of such things. The dispute sparks Jesus' presentation of the dangers in the leaders' approach:

8. Bultmann 1963: 131–32 and esp. 113–14 speaks of a combination of legal (11:39, 41–42) and minatory (i.e., warning) sayings (11:43–44, 46–51). He sees Matthew taking Q material and adding it to the scene in Mark 12, along with other available material. Luke created his setting, and Bultmann doubts that the woes fit Jesus' teaching. Why Jesus would not have engaged in prophetic condemnation is not clear. Without it, it is hard to explain why the leadership ever sought to remove him. If he was just a pleasant messianic pretender or a mere sage, they could have waited him out. Berger 1984: 81 speaks of an apophthegm and a woe speech and sees special Lucan material.

hypocrisy	the danger of being clean outside and dirty inside
heartless legalism	the danger of closely observing laws that relate to insignificant practices, but ignoring God's justice and love
pride	the danger of wanting the best seats
false teaching	the danger of leading others to death
hypocrisy	the danger of setting standards for others, but not helping to meet them
false guidance	the danger of sharing in the rejection of God's messengers
false teaching	the danger of blocking the way of others to God

Unless the leaders change direction the results will be catastrophic. Judgment awaits those who reject God's messenger. But rather than turning, the Pharisees' rejection is intensified. They do not reform, but commit themselves to silencing Jesus.

Exegesis and Exposition

[37]After he was speaking, a Pharisee asked him to dine with him. So going in, he reclined. [38]And the Pharisee, as he watched, was amazed that he did not first wash before the meal.

[39]And the Lord said to him, "Now you Pharisees cleanse the outside of the cup and dish, but your inside is full of extortion and wickedness. [40]Fools, did not he who made the outside make the inside also? [41]Nevertheless, give alms for those things that are within, and behold, all things are clean.

[42]"But woe to you Pharisees, because you tithe the mint, rue, and every edible herb, but disregard justice and the love of God. These were rather the things one should practice, without neglecting the others.

[43]"Woe to you Pharisees, for you love the front seats in the synagogues and greetings in the marketplaces.

[44]"Woe to you, for you are like unmarked graves, over which men walk not knowing."

[45]And one of the scribes said to him, "Teacher, when you say these things, you are insulting us also."

[46]But he said, "Woe to you scribes also, for you weigh down the people with burdens they can scarcely carry and you will not lift a finger for these burdens.

[47]"Woe to you, for you build the tombs of the prophets, and your fathers murdered them. [48]Therefore you are witnesses and agree with the works of your fathers, for they murdered them and you build.

[49]"Therefore the wisdom of God said, 'I will send to them prophets and apostles and they will murder and persecute them,' [50]in order that the blood of all the prophets that ⌜was shed⌝ from the beginning of the world might be required from this generation, [51]from the blood of Abel to the blood of Zech-

ariah, the one who perished between the altar and the sanctuary. Yes, I tell you, it shall be required of this generation.

⁵²"Woe to you scribes, for you have taken away the key of knowledge; you did not enter yourselves, and you hindered those who were entering."

^{53r}And as he was going away from there, the scribes and Pharisees began to press him and to provoke him to speak of many things, ⁵⁴lying in wait for him, to catch something he might say.⌐

a. Setting (11:37–38)

As Jesus completes his remarks about the need to be responsive to God's teaching, a Pharisee invites him for a meal.[9] Jesus accepts. The meal is probably the early morning or midday meal, as seen in the presence of the verb ἀριστήσῃ (aristēsē, he might dine; Plummer 1896: 309; Ernst 1977: 384; Fitzmyer 1985: 947; SB 2:204–5).[10] Other meal scenes in Luke have no such detailed information about the type of meal (cf. 5:29; 7:36; 10:38; 14:1).

11:37

There is no indication of hostility at the start. The question that is raised may well be an attempt to understand how Jesus' behavior fits into the nation's traditions. Nonetheless, the note about Jesus' practice expresses criticism about his piety. It is clear from the subsequent remarks that the meal is not a private one, but that others, especially other leaders, have been invited as well (11:45). Luce (1933: 220) regards it as impossible that Jesus would have responded to his host this way. However, having already given a stinging public rebuke of this generation (11:29–32), a private elaboration may have been appropriate, particularly because the Pharisees and scribes would have seen themselves as immune to such rebuke. No one is spared the need to respond to Jesus.

Jesus is being watched (ἰδών, idōn). What brings Jesus' reaction is his host's amazement that he fails to wash before the meal. The host's surprise implies criticism. Jewish tradition made a point of such a practice (Gen. 18:4; Judg. 19:21; Josephus, *Jewish War* 2.8.5 §129; *m. Yad.* 1; Mark 7:1–5; Hendriksen 1978: 637; Fitzmyer 1985: 947; SB 1:695–704). Such washing, though described in the OT, was not prescribed. Jesus chooses not to follow it here, even though he

11:38

9. It is unclear whether the introductory phrase means "as he was speaking" or "after he had spoken." Lucan use of ἐν τῷ with the aorist infinitive favors "after" (2:27; 3:21; Fitzmyer 1985: 946). Regardless, this event and the previous discourse on responding to God are closely linked by Luke.

10. Marshall 1978: 493–94 notes the custom to eat two meals daily: a mid-morning meal called ἄριστον (BAGD 106; BAA 214) and a mid-afternoon meal called δεῖπνον (BAGD 173; BAA 346; *m. Šab.* 16.2). On the Sabbath, three meals were served, but a Sabbath meal is not indicated here. John 21:12, 15 refers to an early meal with a verb related to ἄριστον, so it is clear that this is not an evening setting. Josephus, *Life* 54 §279, notes a Sabbath meal at the sixth hour, or midday.

is in a Pharisee's house (Marshall 1978: 494; Rengstorf, *TDNT* 1:328; R. Meyer, *TDNT* 3:421; *m. ʿEd.* 5.6; Matt. 15:2 = Mark 7:5).[11] This is no neutral matter for the Pharisee or for Jesus, given what it signifies for both. For the Pharisees, the issue is ritual purity before God; for Jesus, it is additional burdens to God's revelation. It is significant that the host says nothing about what he is thinking and yet Jesus responds to his thoughts. Jesus knows what his opposition is thinking. In 11:29–36 Jesus is a light-bearing messenger greater than Jonah and Solomon. He now calls for repentance.

b. Jesus' Fourfold Rebuke of the Pharisees (11:39–44)
i. Outside Clean, Inside Not (11:39–41)

11:39 The question about hand washing brings a rebuke in terms of washing cups and plates. Jesus' authority is underlined by the title κύριος (*kyrios*, Lord), a Lucan feature in introductions to passages. Jesus' reply, which goes beyond hand washing to that of ritual cleansing as a whole, has been seen as so unnatural that it is regarded as decisive evidence that Luke created the setting (Schneider 1977a: 274). But is this conclusion necessary?

Goppelt (*TDNT* 6:149) shows how much care was taken to keep cups and plates spotless and ritually clean. Leviticus 11:33 and 15:12 formed the ground for this practice, which had been expanded to an art by Pharisees.[12] In dealing with cups and plates rather than with washing hands, Jesus' reply broadens the rebuke to cover not just what is asked about, but all such rules. An answer in terms of hand washing only misses the bigger question. The shift is logical, expanding the debate to the real issue—true purity. It is the principle, not the detailed example, that matters.

The complaint is clear. The cleanliness of things outside the person are a great concern to the Pharisees, while the uncleanness in-

---

11. Washings took place before and after the meal. According to later tradition in the Talmud, only the washing after the meal was commanded by the Torah, the other was commanded by the rabbis; *b. Ḥul.* 105a. What is unclear is whether such rules applied to all meals or just to Sabbath and festival meals (*y. Ber.* 12a [8.2–3] [= Neusner et al. 1982–93: 1.284–91]); the real issue here is meals on the eve of Sabbath or at festival. E. Sanders 1990: 31 argues that there is no evidence of washing before every meal. Evidently the Pharisees' concern for contracting impurity from a dead swarming thing in liquid (Lev. 11:31–38) caused them to expand the biblical injunctions. But such a danger was not limited to the Sabbath or festal meals. As such, it is likely that such care was present at every meal. Booth 1986: 119–50, 194–203 cites *t. Dem.* 2.11–12 (= Neusner 1977–86: 1.84) as key evidence.

12. The issue for some Jews was to avoid "fly-impurity," contact with a dead swarming thing from water, which if present, made the hands unclean. Just to be sure, the cup's outside and inside was washed; E. Sanders 1990: 29–42; *t. Ber.* 5.26 (= Neusner 1977–86: 1.31). On Jewish cup tradition, see Maccoby 1982.

side the person is ignored.[13] Such incomplete, personal cleansing is as worthless as cleaning the outside of a dish or plate and ignoring the inside. The image differs slightly in Matt. 23:25–26, where the uncleanness is tied to the food in the dish and how it was obtained (Creed 1930: 165 unnecessarily criticizes Matthew's distinct image). The indictment is one of current, habitual practice, as καθαρίζετε (*katharizete*, you clean) and γέμει (*gemei*, is full) with νῦν (*nyn*, now) show. The charge is hypocrisy: the Pharisees are full of extortion and wickedness. Ἁρπαγή (*harpagē*) refers to robbery and greed, which questions the integrity of some of the Pharisees' actions (BAGD 108 §3; BAA 218 §3). In other contexts, Jesus speaks of robbing widows or taking oaths so as to avoid paying vows (Matt. 23:16–22; Luke 20:45–47). Πονηρία (*ponēria*) is a broad term for wickedness—the one thing with which Pharisees did not want to be associated (BAGD 690; BAA 1384). Jesus' charge stings; it broadens the scope of the crime and serves as a summary of what follows (Luke 16:14; Mark 12:40; Ernst 1977: 385).

The rebuke's tone is like the OT (Isa. 1:10–17; 58:4–8; Amos 5:21–24; Mic. 6:6–8; Hendriksen 1978: 638). Its prophetic background is what keeps Jesus' remark from being rude culturally, for there is precedent for addressing the nation in this manner. Judaism was also aware of this problem. In the Jewish work T. Moses 7.7–9, this description was applied to the sinner, not the leaders, so a reversal of sorts is present (Danker 1988: 239; Grundmann 1963: 247). It is what is in the heart that counts. One can write rules to appear clean, but they do not necessarily reveal what really counts—the heart. Jesus argues that such rules should not be a major concern.

Jesus follows with a rhetorical question that appeals to the unity of creation. The rhetorical question is really a rebuke, as seen in the vocative ἄφρονες (*aphrones*, fools). The OT fool is one who is blind to God, who fails to respond well to God's will or his way.[14] The question introduced by οὐχ (*ouch*, not) expects a positive answer: the one who made the outside also made the inside. A person can-   **11:40**

---

13. Given its position ὑμῶν (your) modifies ἔσωθεν (inside) and refers to the inside of the person, moving from figure to application: "your inside." It does not refer to the later reference to extortion and wickedness as some suggest. In addition, there is no need to regard this wording as secondary and insist that Jesus kept to the figure throughout; against Manson 1949: 269. Such a view emerges when one ties the account in Luke 11 too closely to Matt. 23 and then tries to decide which wording is original.

14. Ps. 14:1; 53:1 [53:2 MT]; 92:6 [92:7 MT]; 94:8; Prov. 6:12; Luke 12:20; Rom. 2:20; 1 Cor. 15:36; 2 Cor. 11:16, 19; 12:6, 11; SB 1:280; 2:102 (discusses Jewish warnings about having an arrogant heart, with Deut. 8:11–14 being the key text); Schweizer 1984: 199; Plummer 1896: 310; Bertram, *TDNT* 9:230–31; Fitzmyer 1985: 947. On the OT background, see Donald 1963.

not divide life into inner and outer selves, appearance and substance, public and private. This is hypocrisy and an affront to the God who created both. As Schweizer (1984: 199) paraphrases, "If cups are subject to the sovereignty of God, how much more so are hearts!"

Some argue that the verse is lexically parallel to 2 Sam. 19:24 [19:25 MT] and does not refer to God, but rather to the person (Klostermann 1929: 130; Manson 1949: 269). According to this sense, the person creates or "makes up" the outside and inside. Codex D reads the verse this way by transposing "outside" and "inside" and by understanding ποιέω (*poieō*) as "to make right," not "to create": "Fools, he who has set right what is inside, has he not as a result also set right what is outside!" The exhortation is to be pure inside and out. Against this view stands the manuscript evidence and the passage's logic, which works from outside things to inside things, and reads like a rebuke, not a commendation. In addition, the position of the particle οὐχ, which signals a question, is against this reading (Marshall 1978: 495). Responsibility to be consistent before God is the issue here. The contrastive exhortation of what should be done in 11:41 also speaks for this view. There is no equivalent to this verse in Matt. 15, Matt. 23, or Mark 7.

11:41 Jesus uses a figure to describe a correct response. In Judaism, the giving of alms reflects sensitive religious concern and takes conscious intention and sacrifice (Bultmann, *TDNT* 2:485–87; Sir. 7:10; Tob. 12:8–9). Giving alms is the showing of mercy (Luke 12:33; Isa. 1:10–31 [cleansing imagery and justice]; Hos. 6:6; Danker 1988: 240). Alms was the act of giving money or food to the poor to relieve their destitute condition. It was an act of great kindness and love for fellow humans (Acts 10:2, 4, 31; 24:17). The attention given to this great act of piety is also to be applied to one's personal character.

The force of the allusion is difficult to specify, so there is dispute as to the phrase's exact meaning.[15] Basically, the options focus on the reference of τὰ ἐνόντα (*ta enonta*, things inside): is this an accusative of respect ("give alms with respect to inside things") or an adverbial accusative ("give alms inwardly," i.e., from the heart)? The

---

15. The NIV reads "give what is inside ˌthe dishˌ to the poor," perhaps by analogy to the parallel rebuke of 11:39: you need to fix what is wrong in terms of greed by giving alms to the poor (so also Schürmann 1994: 312). This reading is probably wrong, since 11:39 looks at the need to clean the inside, not to give things from it. The main issue is not giving alms, which the Pharisees did, but how alms reflect spirituality. At best, the NIV sense is an implication of how greed is put aside. Alms should come from a pure heart. Regardless, the point is a commitment to a pure heart. In a sense, the Pharisees' complaint against Jesus reflects a failure to give such alms from the heart. They are quick to react against him.

context is so largely pictorial that a figure is present and the first sense is best. If one gives sacrificial attention to inside things—those things tied to character, caring, and spirituality—then cleanliness will be present and complete (πάντα, *panta*, all, is in the emphatic position). The aorist imperative δότε (*dote*, give) urges that this change take place. Repentance, such as that alluded to in Luke 11:29–32, is urged.

The conceptual linkage to repentance and to 11:29–32 shows what Jesus is doing at this meal. He is explaining that the Pharisees are included in the evil generation he just condemned. Certainly the Pharisees would have agreed with Jesus that the current generation of Jews was evil, but they would have excluded themselves from that group. Jesus is saying that the Pharisees belong among the condemned. And if the pious Pharisees stand condemned, who is excluded from the call to repent? Clearly the answer is no one. All stand in need of God and the message that Jesus brings, whether they realize it or not.[16]

One more competing view remains. Wellhausen (1911: 27) suggests that Luke mistranslated the Aramaic term for "cleanse" (דכו, *dakkû*) as "alms" (זכו, *zakkû*) so that the reference was directly to cleansing the inside (as in Matt. 23:26), rather than through the metaphorical appeal to alms.[17] Such a view alters the passage's meaning. Even though the resulting translation makes good contextual sense, we must reject this view for two compelling reasons. First, Fitzmyer (1985: 941) argues that 11:40, not 11:41, is paralleled by Matt. 23:26. Going even further, Marshall (1978: 496) challenges the lack of a parallel because of the differences in wording, arguing that the saying is not mistranslated but misinterpreted, in effect, paraphrased. More telling still is a third objection: the verse is entirely independent of Matt. 23 (as argued in the introduction to this pericope). There is no need to appeal to mistranslation here since, if any of these points are correct, then the view fails to have a rationale. The verse as it stands makes good sense.

ii. Woe: Neglecting God's Justice and Love (11:42)

11:42

The first woe warns the Pharisees not to major on minor religious issues and ignore more important concerns (on "woes," see the exegesis of 6:24). Much care went into getting tithes right, and the Pharisees tithed precisely. The tithe was the donation of a tenth of one's

---

16. Jesus' message is like Rom. 2–3, where Judaism (and anyone else) stands in need of the gospel. The gospel is not discriminatory; all need it (also Eph. 2:1–3).

17. Manson 1949: 269 favors the suggestion. Grundmann 1963: 248 n. 8 argues the possibility for the original saying, but notes that it cannot be Luke's meaning. Fitzmyer 1985: 947 rejects the option.

material possessions for the nation, temple, or clergy.[18] Appeal is made to Lev. 27:30 for the practice of tithing mint, rue, and herbs (Bornkamm, *TDNT* 4:66; Manson 1949: 98; SB 1:923–24; 2:189),[19] but since the rabbinic regulations of this practice are later than the OT texts, we are dealing with a tradition in this pericope. The Mishnah discusses such tithes in several places: *m. Šeb.* 9.1; *m. Maʿaś.* 4.5; *m. Dem.* 2.1; and the entire tractate *m. Maʿaśer Šeni.* (The differences with Matt. 23:23 reflect distinct settings, because Matthew lacks a general reference to herbs and speaks of mint, dill, and cummin.)

Meanwhile, two central ethical imperatives—justice and love for God—are neglected. This is a serious omission, for these things are part of a basic response to God's demands (Mic. 6:8; Zech. 7:8–10; Col. 3:12–13; Büchsel, *TDNT* 3:941–42). The following verses specify Jesus' charge, as does Luke 18:9–14. In contrast, the Samaritan reflects justice and love (10:25–37). The Pharisees handle externals well, but lack internal responses. This woe specifies the earlier charge and sets the ethical standard.

A corrective concludes the woe. The virtues of love and justice should be practical *while* observing the tithing of herbs. Jesus condemns the Pharisees' selectivity in choosing to follow only certain minor rules while consistently ignoring the important matters. What they practice does not rile him, but what they fail to practice and what they emphasize does. They omit the important matters while scoring well on more trivial pursuits. They should tithe, but they should also be kind to their neighbor and honor God.

iii. Woe: Loving the Best Seats (11:43)

11:43 The second woe rebukes the Pharisees for seeking attention; it alludes to the pride that comes from receiving such honor. There is a

---

18. Three main OT texts deal with the tithe (E. Sanders 1990: 43–45). (1) According to Deut. 14:22–27, ten percent of farm produce, oil, and wine was to be tithed, except in the seventh year (Lev. 25:2–7). It was to be spent and enjoyed in Jerusalem or another appropriate locale. Every third year, this tithe was given to the Levites and the needy (Deut. 14:28–29). Whether "third year" meant only the third of the seven-year cycle or years three and six was debated, but the latter view was more popular. (2) Lev. 27:30–33 required that ten percent of crops and animals be tithed to the priesthood (Josephus, *Antiquities* 4.4.4 §§69–75). (3) Num. 18:21–32 declared that food be set aside for the Levites and their families. Other OT passages that give the background of tithes are Deut. 12:6–9; 26:12–15; Num. 18:12; Neh. 10:37–38 [10:38–39 MT]; 12:44; 13:5, 12; 2 Chron. 31:5–12; Fitzmyer 1985: 948.

19. *M. Šeb.* 9.1 is important, since it says that rue is not tithed; the presence of this statement in the Mishnah may suggest dispute. The Lucan reference may be to wild rue, not all varieties of rue; Liefeld 1984: 957. The terms are ἡδύοσμον (mint) (BAGD 344; BAA 698; elsewhere only at Matt. 23:23), the *hapax legomenon* πήγανον (rue) (BAGD 655; BAA 1320), and λάχανον (herb) (BAGD 467; BAA 950; elsewhere only at Matt. 13:32 = Mark 4:32; Rom. 14:2).

constant desire for such attention. Jesus' later teaching about not wanting the first seat is a reflection of the same problem (cf. 14:7–11; 16:14–15). These leaders enjoy the seats of honor at the synagogue and the attention in the public square. Some think that this is an allusion to the "seat of Moses," where the most distinguished elder would sit (Matt. 23:2; SB 1:915; Michaelis, *TDNT* 6:870–71). But the reference to plural *seats* suggests that more than this one seat is in view. It probably refers to a row of seats near the ark. The greeting in the public place is not so much a quick hello as an involved salutation of respect. In the Talmud, such elaborate greetings were compulsory for teachers of the law (Luke 20:46; *y. Ber.* 4b [2.1] [= Neusner et al. 1982–93: 1.66]; SB 1:382; Windisch, *TDNT* 1:498; Manson 1949: 99; Marshall 1978: 498–99). That Jews were aware of the problem is seen in the similar accusation of T. Moses 7.4.

iv. Woe: Leading People to Death (11:44)

The last rebuke is the most direct. The vocative naming the Pharisees is dropped, but the audience has not changed. The Pharisees are like unmarked graves, death traps that convey impurity. The picture is of an unmarked grave that might cause someone to come unknowingly into contact with a body. Such contact would make a Jew unclean and was to be avoided (Fitzmyer 1985: 949).[20] People who follow the Pharisees are compared to those who fall unknowingly into such a grave—a stark, tragic, and deadly image. The Pharisees, who saw themselves as the paragon of purity, are in fact leaders of spiritual uncleanness whose teaching leads people to death. The Pharisees think that they are leading their followers into life, but Jesus says the opposite is true (Ellis 1974: 171). The woes taken together not only condemn what the Pharisees themselves practice but also their destructive influence on others. Rather than leading people to heaven, the Pharisees' pseudo-spirituality leads them to the grave.[21]

11:44

Another factor adds to the image's negative picture. The law taught that contact with the dead caused uncleanness for a week, so Jesus' image has multiple negative associations (Num. 19:16; Lev. 21:1–4, 11; Plummer 1896: 312; Liefeld 1984: 956). The Pharisees' unclean hearts spread to others as they influenced them with their teaching. The unclean dish contains poisonous food.

20. In fact, in many traditions "overshadowing" such a corpse rendered one unclean; E. Sanders 1990: 33–35. Pharisees were particularly sensitive to this issue (Num. 19:11–22; Lev. 21:1–3; *m. Dem.* 2.3), as were the Essenes at Qumran (CD 12.15–18). This was a common Jewish concept; Josephus, *Antiquities* 18.2.3 §§36–38.

21. The association with death imagery has a variation in Eph. 2:1–3, although there no one holds the blame except the person who walks in the death of trespasses and sins. In Ephesians the person is led by evil spiritual forces and their own passions.

The image differs from Matt. 23:27, where these graves are called clean on the outside but foul on the inside (Creed 1930: 166). There is no need to decide which image is original. Manson (1949: 99) argues that it is not the practices themselves that are being condemned, but the attitudes and distinctions made around them. When work is done without looking at the spiritual consequences and the acts of concern serve only to draw attention to oneself, then the rebukes apply.

c. A Scribe's Complaint (11:45)

11:45 Someone, a scribe, finally reacts to Jesus and speaks. He notes that Jesus' attack is not a narrow one. If Jesus attacks the Pharisees, then the scribes are also in his line of fire, since scribes interpret the law and aid the Pharisees in their study of tradition. Ὑβρίζεις (*hybrizeis*, you are insulting) could not be stronger (elsewhere at Matt. 22:6; Luke 18:32; Acts 14:5; 1 Thess. 2:2; Plummer 1896: 312; Bertram, *TDNT* 8:305–6). If Jesus insults the scribes as well, he is taking on most of the traditional establishment. To this scribe's credit, his comment reveals how Jesus' remarks are perceived and argues the Pharisees' cause. He had the nerve to speak up publicly, but his assumption that the scribes and Pharisees are righteous is the problem. They too need to respond to God.

Jesus in effect calls on the religious leadership to repent. They, however, perceive themselves as insulted, for surely (as they see it) the charges are false. So repentance is not a possibility, only reaction. As a result, Jesus will address the scribes with words that are as strong as those to the Pharisees.

d. Jesus' Threefold Rebuke of the Scribes (11:46–52)
i. Woe: Giving Burdens to Others, but Not to Self (11:46)

11:46 Jesus responds directly: scribes are guilty too. The nature of the charge is disputed. One view argues that the charge is hypocrisy. The hypocrisy does not, however, involve their failure to perform these rules, for all the evangelists make clear the scribes' and Pharisees' meticulous concern for such matters. Rather, the hypocrisy concerns placing burdens on people without helping to perform them (K. Weiss, *TDNT* 9:85; Manson 1949: 101). The repeated term φορτίον (*phortion*) literally refers to a ship's cargo (e.g., Acts 27:10), but here it is a figure for the heavy weight of religious duties added to the law, which burden the people and actually direct them away from God (elsewhere in the NT, this concept is found in Mark 7:11–13; Acts 15:10; Danker 1988: 241). It is the spirituality of rules and ritualistic obligation in place of justice and mercy that is castigated here. Jesus' remarks run parallel to the prophets' complaints, who said that God desires mercy not sacrifice (Hos. 6:6).

The burden is just part of the problem, for the scribes are not only unwilling to help carry the burden, by they make the rules even heavier for the people. The people must take on the obligations alone and thus are devastated by their failure to keep them. They are spiritually crushed. Manson (1949: 101) puts it well: "There is something wrong with scribal labours which multiply the number of ways in which a man may offend God, but cannot help him to please God." Jesus is not condemning the goal of the scribes as much as their methodology. People need instruction and guidance, but it should not crush them. Rather, it should build them up and teach them to put their failures in the past. One can keep a rule and still be cold and unconcerned about others. This is the type of hypocrisy that Jesus condemns, for a genuine understanding of the law would not leave one so callous to others. Jesus' willingness to associate with sinners shows a different approach. Matthew 23:4 is similar to this text, though it has no woe.

A second approach argues that this could be a direct charge of hypocrisy. Marshall (1978: 500) argues that the point is about subtle interpretations that allow the Pharisees and scribes to make distinctions in the law. These distinctions let them off scot-free, while the less discerning are left to bear the burden (potential examples are given in SB 1:913–14). The remark about when oaths are or are not binding reminds one of such distinctions and makes this interpretation likely (Matt. 5:33–37). Seen in this light, the charge is double-edged: they don't aid the people by their example, and they hypocritically require rules of others but ignore them themselves.

It is hard to be sure which view is meant, but they may not be mutually exclusive. If this is a type of sophisticated interpretation that occasionally frees the Pharisees and scribes from obligations, it does not automatically rule out that they would still be hardened against aiding uninformed people who take on the burdens and fail. They provide no example and no compassion. The absence of either is wrong. If one must decide, the Pharisees are known more for their distance from the people than they are for their desire to shortcut the law. The first view that the Pharisees add burdens without offering aid is inherently more likely, especially with the reference to refusing to lift a finger. But other texts suggest both a callousness and an exegetical subtlety. Jesus condemns all such evasions of responsibility.

ii. Woe: Building the Tombs of the Prophets (11:47–48)

Jesus now strongly condemns the scribes (and by implication the **11:47** Pharisees), charging them with collusion in the murder of God's prophets (there is no vocative, so the rebuke's audience is probably broad). Of course, the remark is rhetorical, for they did not really kill the prophets like their ancestors did, but instead built tombs for them.[22] The point is that the spirit that caused their ancestors to slay the prophets still lives with them, as their rejection of Jesus shows. Jesus is essentially saying that the current generation is finishing the job the previous ones started.

What makes the imagery difficult is that the building of tombs for the prophets does not necessarily reflect an endorsement of their execution. But Jesus' point seems more complex: You say you honor the prophets, yet you reject those who inherited their message. The tombs you build then are memorials of rejection that reflect your agreement with what your fathers did (Michel, *TDNT* 4:681; Luce 1933: 223; Creed 1930: 167).[23] Their supposed act of honor in fact symbolizes the exact reverse, for by their larger acts they reject the prophets. By ignoring the prophets' message in its contemporary form, they are hypocritical, like their murderous fathers (Danker 1988: 242; Fitzmyer 1985: 949–50; Acts 7:52). To say it another way, "The only prophet you honor is a dead prophet" (Manson 1949: 101) or "They killed the prophets; you make sure they stay dead."

11:48 The picture of the endorsement of their ancestors' murder of the prophets continues. Jesus says they agree with their ancestors' work. In effect, they finish the burial in their similar rejection of God's messengers. The harsh irony continues in this elaboration (ἄρα [*ara*, therefore] connects this remark to the charge in 11:47). The verb οἰκοδομεῖτε (*oikodomeite*, you build) has no object in the original text, but in 11:47 it clearly alludes to "their tombs."[24]

iii. Prediction of Persecution and Judgment (11:49–51)

11:49 Jesus predicts where such hypocritical and unrighteous behavior leads: the "wisdom of God" is going to send them prophets and apostles. Since the remark appears to be a citation of something already said, some look for a paraphrase of an OT allusion (perhaps 1 Kings 19:10, 14 or Jer. 7:25–26), while others suggest that Jesus is quoting a contemporary apocalyptic work (for options, see Liefeld 1984: 957; Luce 1933: 223; R. Meyer, *TDNT* 3:981; Oepke, *TDNT* 3:992;

22. On the expression *the fathers* in Judaism, see Schrenk, *TDNT* 5:976–77; 1 Esdr. 1:11 [1:12 LXX]; 4:60; 1 Macc. 2:19; 2 Enoch 33.12; 35.2. On the theme of holy graves, see Jeremias 1958a and 1961.

23. Matt. 23:29–32 is a more comprehensive statement of this theme. Marshall 1978: 501 notes that the vast differences in wording look at two distinct recensions of Q, a statement I take to refer to two events.

24. The various terms supplied in the manuscripts as objects betray scribal efforts to fill out the idea of the phrase. Contextually, it is clear that "their tombs" is meant.

Bultmann 1963: 114). If the OT is alluded to, the "prophets and apostles" allude to past OT figures.

Both suggestions have problems: the OT suggestion lacks any clear prophetic allusion, and the apocalyptic suggestion has no concrete evidence (Plummer 1896: 313). Danker (1988: 242) suggests that the closest allusion is 2 Chron. 24:19–22, but at best this is a conceptual connection, not a clear allusion. Instead, Jesus has probably picked a graphic way to portray God's plan by expressing it as a saying in the past. Their response to God's current representatives will be like that of their ancestors: murder and persecution. The Book of Acts will detail a Jewish response to Peter, John, Stephen, James, the church at large, and finally the mission of Paul. God's plan marches forward despite this type of reaction.

A similar idea is expressed in Matt. 23:34–36 and is illustrated in the parable of Luke 20:9–19 (Luce 1933: 223). In Matthew, Jesus utters these words himself and speaks of sending wise men and scribes. Many take this difference to show that Luke sees Jesus as Wisdom and has "contemporized" the reference: Jesus as Wisdom sends prophets and apostles. The point about wisdom is debatable (see next paragraph), but if the occasions are distinct, other conclusions do not follow. Efforts to determine which form of the saying is original become irrelevant, as does Ellis's suggestion (1974: 173) that Matthew's form has been "peshered" by Luke.

The other question in the passage is who or what is the "wisdom of God"? Is this a self-designation for Jesus (Christ 1970: 134–35; Fitzmyer 1985: 950; so 1 Cor. 1:24; Col. 2:3)? Or does "wisdom of God" describe God by use of the first-person ἀποστέλλω (apostellō, to send), much as one of God's prophets might in delivering his message?[25] The wisdom-of-God theme has rich roots. Many OT and other Jewish texts allude to the image (Job 28; Prov. 1; 8; Sir. 1; 24; 11QPs^a 18; Bar. 3–4; 1 Enoch 41–44; 2 Esdr. [= 4 Ezra] 5; Christ 1970: 13–60). In the OT texts, wisdom is a figure for God himself or an expression of his will. Judaism used similar terms: "the Holy Spirit says" or "the Righteousness of God says" (Grundmann 1963: 249; Ernst 1977: 388; SB 2:189; Tg. Lam. 2:20; Tg. Eccles. 10:7–8). For Jesus to refer to himself in this way is unprecedented, though possible. More likely, however, Jesus refers to God's will, though this need not include the idea that the saying comes before the world's creation (so correctly Marshall 1978: 503–4 against Suggs 1970: 14). At the least, normal usage of the term favors a reference

---

25. Plummer 1896: 313 speaks of divine providence. Marshall 1978: 502–4 distinguishes between the view that sees God speaking in his wisdom and one that sees "divine wisdom" like that found in Prov. 8. But the views are very close, since Prov. 8 is a figurative reference.

to God. This is the way Jesus' audience most likely understood the term (Arndt 1956: 309; Manson 1949: 102; thus, the NIV's "God in his wisdom said").

11:50   The consequences of this rejection is judgment. This generation completes a long line of rejection extending back to the earliest prophets, and justice will be exacted from them (Luke 11:29–31).[26] The perfect ἐκκεχυμένον (*ekkechymenon*) looks to the injustice of the prophets' blood being shed (see the additional note). This idea has roots in the OT (Gen. 4:10; 9:5; 42:22; 2 Sam. 4:11; 2 Kings 9:26; Job 16:18; Ps. 9:12 [9:13 MT]; Isa. 26:21; Ezek. 3:18, 20; 24:7–8; 33:6, 8; SB 1:940–43; Greeven, *TDNT* 2:895; Manson 1949: 103; Ernst 1977: 388–89) and in Judaism (T. Moses 9.6–7; 1 Enoch 47; *m. Sanh.* 6.5; Garland 1979: 181–82 n. 68).

The remark assumes that the current rejection is particularly significant because of the nature of the time and its connection to the past. Since the prophets pointed to this time, the rejection of God's current messengers is in fact a rejection of the whole line of prophets (Jer. 7:25 is conceptually parallel).[27] Such a view fits Luke's picture of Jesus as the focal point of God's promise, the promise toward which his plan has been headed all along (Luke 24:44–47).

There is some debate about what judgment is meant here. Is it the temporal judgment of Jerusalem's destruction in A.D. 70 (Schweizer 1984: 201; Plummer 1896: 314; Luke 21:32)? Or is it the ultimate judgment when God will evaluate people's responses to Jesus and his message? One could suggest that the focus on "this generation" looks at a special judgment for it, Jerusalem, while the ultimate judgment does not have such a limitation. But the remark's eschatological, salvation-historical character suggests something more enduring than Jerusalem's overthrow. It is the audience at the judgment, not its timing, that is referred to by "this generation." Since Luke sees Jerusalem as a picture of the ultimate judgment, the combination is likely in view, but the eschatological judgment is the major point.

11:51   Jesus elaborates about the line of prophets and shows that he is using the term προφήτης (*prophētēs*, prophet) broadly, since his list starts with Abel. Here a prophet refers to anyone who testifies to God's way of righteousness. The presence of Abel on this list ex-

---

26. For a comparison of conceptual parallels between 11:14–54 and 7:18–50, see Moessner 1989: 102–10, 115, who notes that Jesus' critique reflects teaching with roots in Deuteronomy.

27. Jesus' allusion to the beginning of the world (Foerster, *TDNT* 3:1029; Hauck, *TDNT* 3:620; Matt. 13:35; Heb. 4:3; 9:26) makes the expression a merism: "the whole line of prophets."

plains why 11:50 spoke of prophets "from the foundation of the world." The mention of Zechariah is obscure because several men by this name are found in the literature.

1. One solution is that Zechariah refers to a man killed in the temple precincts in A.D. 68, since Matt. 23:35 refers to Zechariah son of Berekiah, a reference that is taken to be contemporary to the writing of Matthew or his source (Josephus, *Jewish War* 4.5.3 §§334–44). The problem with this view is that it does not fit the setting of Jesus' ministry. Matthew would be unlikely to engage in such an anachronism (Liefeld 1984: 957; Garland 1979: 182–83 n. 69: Gundry 1967: 87 n. 1 [who argues that Matthew's source was written too early to have such a reference]). In addition, in Josephus the man is portrayed neither as a prophet nor as a martyr (he was murdered by Zealots). Since the man is unrelated to the church, an allusion to him is unlikely.
2. Neither is this a Christian gloss, since better known Christian martyrs could have been chosen for mention here (Marshall 1978: 506).
3. More likely is the suggestion that Zechariah is the figure of 2 Chron. 24:20–25 who was murdered in the temple precincts (Nolland 1993a: 668–69; Schürmann 1994: 325). Although this Zechariah seems to be a righteous one who is rejected like Abel, this suggestion does have its problems. In 2 Chronicles, the father's name is given as Jehoiada (Carson 1984: 485–86 argues that Jehoiada is the grandfather). Also, the location is simply stated as the court (for attempts to deal with these problems, see J. Payne 1967). This view has several advantages: this Zechariah is a prophet, he is murdered, his position in Chronicles makes him the last OT prophet murdered according to the canonical order of the Hebrew Bible, and his story was told often in Judaism (SB 1:940–43; Beckwith 1985: 215–16).
4. Some associate the remark with the writing prophet Zechariah, described in Zech. 1:1 as the son of Berekiah, although some texts call him the son of Iddo (Ezra 5:1; 6:14; Neh. 12:16). Is this a case of a double name? The textual reading in Zechariah is well attested (the LXX reads Iddo as a grandfather, but the Hebrew reference to Berekiah is textually secure in the manuscript tradition). The problems with this suggestion are that we have no clear record of this Zechariah having been slain, nor is it clear why he would be the last on the list.
5. Others bring up the possibility that Zechariah the father of John the Baptist is meant. This should be rejected on the

grounds that, if Jesus had intended to name a recent figure, John the Baptist would have been the obvious choice, not his father (Beckwith 1985: 212–13).

6. Many argue for a confusion between the Zechariah of 2 Chronicles and the prophet whose book bears his name (Plummer 1896: 314; Luce 1933: 224; Garland 1979: 183 n. 69). Such a confusion seems unlikely. The difference between a priest and a prophet was clear in the OT, though it must be acknowledged that other texts show evidence of a similar confusion.[28]

7. Gundry (1982: 471) argues for a theological-literary conflation to bring together the prophet Zechariah's predictions with the priest-martyr Zechariah's death. While initially this might strike a modern reader as too subtle, Beckwith gives evidence for the possibility of such combinations in the homiletics of ancient Judaism. If so, the remarks bring both figures together.[29]

A clear decision about the Matthean referent is difficult. Luke's reference must be to the martyr of 2 Chronicles or the writing prophet (or perhaps both). More likely it is the martyr, but it is hard to be sure. Regardless, the point is that the entire row of prophets—from Abel to Zechariah—testify against this generation's rejection of current prophets and apostles. The prophets' shed blood demands justice, so justice will be given.[30]

iv. Woe: Taking Away the Key of Knowledge (11:52)

11:52 The final charge is found in the last woe to the scribes: they are obstacles to others knowing God. Rather than supplying the key to knowledge, they take it away (H. Weiss, *TDNT* 9:48).[31] The key refers

---

28. Tg. Lam. 2:20 reads, "Zechariah son of Iddo, the high priest"; Gundry 1967: 86 n. 1. The Chronicles priest likely functioned as a prophet in 2 Chron. 24:19–22, but his priestly function was paramount in his identification as the son of a great priest. It should be noted that within three verses we have two potential points of contact with Tg. Lam. 2:20, though this second contact is not certain (see the exegesis of 11:49).

29. Beckwith 1985: 217–21 argues that the Targum on Lamentations (cited above as an example of confusion) is in fact an illustration of this very conscious technique.

30. Note that ἐκζητηθήσεται (shall be required) repeats the verb of 11:50. A key article discussing the options is Chapman 1911–12, with a summary in Manson 1949: 103–5.

31. Grundmann 1963: 250 suggests that γνώσεως (knowledge) is an objective genitive, thus "the key for knowledge." Another option, a genitive of apposition ("the key that is knowledge," by which is meant "obedient knowledge") is less likely. This latter reading would be an odd way to say "you have taken away knowledge," but so Jeremias, *TDNT* 3:747–48, who acknowledges that this image, though different from the other option, is similar.

to possessing access to God through heavenly blessing and relationship (Arndt 1956: 310).[32] The scribes have failed to enter into true knowledge, and they have become a hindrance to others trying to attain knowledge (the force of the participle εἰσερχομένους is conative: "those who were trying to enter"). The image of entering is similar to the picture of coming into the kingdom. For those who see themselves as instructors and protectors of the truth, this is a particularly devastating accusation. No one enters the house of the knowledge of God through them (J. Schneider, *TDNT* 2:677). What the "unmasked grave" charge said of the Pharisees (11:44) this charge says of the scribes.

e. The Pharisees Try to Trap Jesus (11:53–54)

11:53 The temperature in the room rose as a result of Jesus' accusations. The scribes and Pharisees who shared in the meal and the rebuke left the house with him. They crowded around him and engaged him in further rancorous discussion.[33] The tone of the dialogue is indicated by the *hapax legomenon* ἀποστοματίζειν (*apostomatizein*, to interrogate; BAGD 100; BAA 200). Here it means to examine closely, perhaps even to catch someone in something (the picture is of a prosecutor examining a criminal). These questions are not asked innocently, but with the idea of gaining an advantage and causing embarrassment (11:54). It is probable that since Jesus has charged them with lacking knowledge, they in turn are trying to dishonor his reputation by their questions (Liefeld 1984: 957; perhaps similar to the various controversies discussed after Jesus entered Jerusalem).

11:54 Luke makes clear the motive for the questions. The picture is of a trap ready to spring. Ἐνεδρεύω (*enedreuō*) means "to lie in wait" and suggests the picture of pending attack (BAGD 264; BAA 533; elsewhere at Acts 23:21). The other verb θηρεύω (*thēreuō*) appears only here in the NT and means "to hunt" or "to catch" (BAGD 360; BAA 733). Since speech is in view, the latter idea fits here; but the term's association with a hunt gives the mood. The scribes and Pharisees could not wait for Jesus to make a major blunder. They wanted to

---

32. Matt. 16:19 speaks of the kingdom's keys; Matt. 23:13 speaks of shutting up the kingdom of heaven. Manson 1949: 103 notes that the spirit of Jesus' charge against their lists of requirements might be found in the question, "Where is God the King, the Father, the one who rules with love and mercy in these rules?"

33. Ἐνέχω is a difficult term to translate (BAGD 265; BAA 536; Mark 6:19): "to press against someone," "to hold a grudge," or "to have it in for someone." With δεινῶς (terribly), the idea is "to be very hostile" to someone (BAGD 173; BAA 346; Matt. 8:6). Hanse, *TDNT* 2:828, argues for "to press against him," where the idea is that of being surrounded by hostile opponents.

get him now. They had rejected his criticism and identified him as an enemy. One way or another, they would stop him.

Summary Luke 11:37–54 reveals what Jesus thinks of the current religious leadership. A question about hand washing leads Jesus into a stinging rebuke of the Pharisees and scribes. A variety of charges can be raised against them: hypocrisy, majoring on minors, being a source of death, burdening those they are to serve while not aiding them. They are like their ancestors who murdered the prophets, and, worst of all, they have become an obstacle to those who seek God.

Why is this unit present? It seems to serve a variety of functions. It details how the hostility to Jesus arose and why the division between the old leadership and the new way exists. The passage also serves as an argument against finding the way to God through the route supplied by the Pharisees. The way that Jesus offers is not the way of the traditional Jewish religious establishment. What may appear to be pietistic is in fact a road full of obstacles to reaching God. The leaders block the way to God by refusing to accept Jesus' teaching and to humbly serve God. Indeed, as the condemnations show, the product and perspective of their lives leads to judgment. The section has historical (this is how hostility to Jesus arose) and theological (this is the lifestyle to avoid) motivations. The reader should see that hostility to God's way, even a subtle form of hostility, is often the product of rejecting his messengers. Sometimes a lifestyle of piety is a lifestyle of death, when it is self-commending. The reader should see that a life of insensitive, legalistic hypocrisy—like that which Jesus condemns in some of the Jewish leadership here—ends in the grave. The key to the knowledge of God is not found there.

Additional Notes

11:50. Is it blood that "was shed" (perfect tense ἐκκεχυμένον) or "is shed" (present tense ἐκχυν[ν]όμενον)? The perfect tense (read by $\mathfrak{P}^{45vid}$, B, and family 13) is the harder reading since the present tense (read by $\mathfrak{P}^{75}$, ℵ, A, C, D, L, Θ, and Byz) matches Matt. 23:35. Both readings have in view a whole line of prophets and saints from the past.

11:53–54. Codex D has a significantly different text (Fitzmyer 1985: 952) (differences are indicated by underlining): "While he was saying these things to them, the Pharisees and the lawyers began to react violently and to fight with him in the presence of all the people about many things, seeking some pretext to catch him in order that they might be able to accuse him." The differences are largely confined to D and a few allies, except for the last addition at the end of 11:54, which has slightly broader manuscript support (so A, C, D, W, Θ, Ψ, Byz) and might be original. However, this final addition looks like 6:7, and as such is suspect as an assimilation (Kilpatrick 1943: 33).

D. Discipleship: Trusting God (12:1–48)

Disciples are the major concern of Luke's next section. Luke 12:1–12 contains various warnings about fearing God: disciples should avoid pharisaic hypocrisy and should know that all that one does will be revealed. They are to fear God, stand up for him, and know that when persecution comes, his help will be present. Luke 12:13–21, the parable of the rich fool, warns against excessive dependence on material things. Luke 12:22–34 is a call to trust God and not be anxious. Disciples are to pursue the kingdom and know that God will be with them. Luke 12:35–48 closes the section with a parable about responsibility before God. Each one will give an account, so disciples should carry out their stewardship before God by showing concern for others. Disciples should live in a way that acknowledges the reality of God's return.

1. The Need to Avoid Hypocrisy, Fear God, and Confess Jesus (12:1–12)

Following the strong denunciation of the scribes and Pharisees, Jesus turns his attention to his followers. He both exhorts and warns them. His call is to trust and fear God, for he is the one with authority over the soul. One is also to avoid the Pharisees' hypocrisy. The tension seems to be that if one is concerned with pleasing people, the danger of hypocrisy is very real, especially in the midst of rejection. The disciples need to fear God and confess Jesus before people, so that Jesus will confess them before the angels. The great danger is blaspheming the Spirit, but if one trusts God, the Spirit will aid in speaking before authorities.

This passage is part of a larger section (12:1–48) dealing with the community of disciples in the world (Grundmann 1963: 251). This larger section's major theme is that one should seek God's priorities and agenda, realizing all the while that God is aware of and concerned about the fate of those who entrust themselves to him.

Sources and Historicity

Determining the placement of 12:1–12 is complex. Most argue that Luke brought together a diverse group of teachings based on thematic considerations.[1] The major reason for this approach is that much of the material found in this unit has parallels in various places throughout the other Synoptics:

> Luke 12:1 = Matt. 16:5–6 = Mark 8:14–15 (Aland 1985: §195)
> Luke 12:2–9 = Matt. 10:26–33 (Aland 1985: §196)
> Luke 12:10 = Matt. 12:31–32 = Mark 3:28–30 (Aland 1985: §197)
> Luke 12:11–12 = Matt. 10:19–20 = Mark 13:11 (Aland 1985: §198)

1. Most argue for Q: Fitzmyer 1985: 953 (12:1 from L), 956 (12:2–9 from Q), 962–63 (12:10 from Q or Mark; 12:11–12 from Q); Ernst 1977: 392 (for 12:2–9); and Schneider 1977a: 277. Grundmann 1963: 252 says it is "probably" Q. Marshall 1978: 510 speaks of Q material conflated with Marcan elements and also argues that Q has various recensions and that Luke's version is slightly different from that of Matthew. Nolland 1993a: 675–76 sees Q for 12:2–9 and a mixture of Q and Mark for 12:10–12.

In addition, Luke 12:11–12 is also paralleled in 21:14–15 as part of Jesus' final eschatological discourse (also Mark 13:9 and Gospel of Thomas 5.2; 6.4; 44–45). Luke's only note about the setting concerns the crowd's growth in 12:1. It is possible that Luke has a thematic arrangement (Nolland 1993a: 675–76), but the repetition of material in 21:14–15 makes this uncertain and may indicate another option that has not received enough consideration: that Jesus said many of these kind of things on different occasions, and therefore a distinct setting is in view.

In support of a distinct occasion is the sparsity of shared terminology between Luke 12:1 and Mark 8:14–15 = Matt. 16:5–6.[2] A warning about the threat of the Pharisees is likely to have been repeated. It may be that the middle section (12:2–9) is parallel to Matt. 10, since so much of this material is verbally parallel. If so, Luke has given it a placement opposite Jesus' denunciation of the Pharisees at a meal, an event Matthew did not discuss but likely occurred in the midst of a popular phase of Jesus' ministry (such as that in Matt. 10). This is even more likely when one considers that in Matthew these remarks come after the mission of the Twelve, a time when Jesus was drawing attention such as the crowd mentioned in Luke 12:1. Thus, Luke may have chosen to summarize an event from Jesus' ministry, whose actual location was slightly earlier, while including more elements that were part of the time when Jesus was receiving popular response. Luke also notes that, despite this apparent popularity, Jesus prepares his disciples for the reality of coming hostile rejection.

Of course, a final possibility is that Jesus repeated all of these sayings in various combinations and settings. This is quite possible, since the imagery of 12:2–3, for example, is used in a completely different way than it is in Matt. 10:26–27. The setting is appropriate (Godet 1875: 2.89–90 speaks of the possibility of Jesus' repeating these sayings). Regardless of which connection is correct, Jesus exhorted his followers to make a commitment to entrust themselves to a sovereign God who would care for them. They also were to entrust themselves to Jesus as God's delegated agent. Such trust included being prepared to confess Jesus before people who were rejecting them. In showing such trust and in speaking boldly about Jesus they would avoid the dangers that come from fearing people more than God—dangers that would manifest themselves in hypocrisy and ultimately, perhaps, in reckless rejection of God.

The Jesus Seminar (Funk and Hoover 1993: 335–37) gives mixed ratings to the sayings in this unit, arguing that 12:2, 6–7 is a good summary of Jesus' teaching (in pink type), while 12:1, 3–5, 8–12 does not go back to Jesus (in black type). Luke 12:2 is accepted because of its multiple attestation (Mark 4:22 = Luke 8:17; Gospel of Thomas 5.2; 6.5), while 12:6–7

---

2. Only five words from Luke's twenty-seven are shared in all three texts (Matthew and Luke share an additional term): ἀπὸ τῆς ζύμης (of the leaven) and τῶν Φαρισαίων (of the Pharisees). These are basic elements where an overlap is not surprising.

is seen as a vivid image like those used by Jesus. The seminar rejects the other sayings because it presupposes a level of persecution that fits the era of the early church, not Jesus' time. The seminar also rejects that Jesus singled out the Pharisees for criticism (12:1).

Two suppositions are key here: (1) that sayings on similar themes are not repeated by Jesus but are reformulated by the evangelists, and (2) that Jesus did not prepare his disciples for potential rejection despite rising opposition to him. The first premise, which looks more like an a priori argument, is especially weak, given the acknowledged itinerant nature of Jesus' ministry and the existence of independent oral-tradition streams. What would prevent sayings on similar themes but different settings from getting into distinct tradition streams? Against the second premise is the precedent of hostile reaction against John the Baptist, the nation's reaction to the prophets, the high emotion of religious differences in the region, and the rising anticipation by Jesus of his own rejection—something he could well expect to spill over to his followers (see also Nolland 1993a: 676). The works of Josephus testify to the volatile nature of the region when it comes to religion; other texts that indicate awareness of such tension include Luke 6:22; 9:21–27; 14:27; 17:33; and John 12:24–25. This teaching reflects an accurate summary of Jesus' concern to prepare for persecution, including his critique of the Pharisees, especially if Luke 11:37–54 is authentic (as I argue in that unit). On the textual rationale for distinct sayings, see the exegesis of 12:4, 6, 8. In favor of the authenticity of 12:10 is the sheer difficulty of arguing that the early church would create a saying that allows the Son of Man to be blasphemed, especially since the early church did not use this title on its own (Marshall 1978: 518).

This unit is a collection of various sayings of Jesus (Tiede 1988: 226). Considered as a whole, they yield a discourse on trust. The sayings can be subclassified as minatory sayings (12:1), warning or wisdom sayings (12:2–7), a Son-of-Man saying (12:8–9), a legal saying that also is a warning (12:10), and a final exhortation (12:11–12).[3] The outline of Luke 12:1–12 is as follows:

a. Call: avoid the hypocrisy of the Pharisees (12:1)
b. Promise: all that is done in secret will be exposed (12:2–3)
c. Call: fear God not humans (12:4–7)
    i. Fear the one who can cast souls into Gehenna (12:4–5)
    ii. Realize that God cares for you and knows you intimately (12:6–7)
d. Call: confess Jesus and avoid blaspheming the Spirit (12:8–12)

3. Fitzmyer 1985: 954, 957, 958, 963; Bultmann 1963: 83, 131–32; Berger 1984: 81, 144.

i. Confession and denial of the Son of Man (12:8–9)
ii. Blasphemy of the Spirit is not forgiven (12:10)
iii. Promise of the Spirit's aid in time of testimony
    (12:11–12)

This pericope discusses disciples and their uneasy relationship to the world. Jesus' first call is to avoid hypocrisy: disciples are to watch the way they live, for all will be revealed. Jesus' second call is to fear the God who has authority over the soul, not people who have limited authority only over the physical life. Disciples are to know that God cares for them more than he cares for birds. Therefore, confess Jesus. Confession of Christ leads to Jesus' confession of the confessor, but denial of Christ leads to Jesus' denial of the denier. A final warning concerns blasphemy of the Spirit. Rejection of the Spirit's presence and message about Jesus is not forgiven. The Spirit is given to aid disciples so that when they testify before the synagogues and rulers they will not be anxious.

Exegesis and Exposition

[1]In the meantime, when so many thousands of the crowd had gathered that they trampled on one another, he began to say to his disciples first, "Beware of the leaven of the Pharisees, which is hypocrisy.

[2]"Nothing has been covered over that shall not be revealed and is hidden that shall not be made known. [3]Therefore, whatsoever things you said in the dark shall be heard in the light, and whatsoever you whispered in private rooms shall be preached on the housetops.

[4]"I tell you, my friends, do not fear those who can kill the body and after this can do nothing more. [5]But I will show you who to fear. Fear the one who after the killing has authority to cast into Gehenna. Yes, I say to you, fear this one. [6]Are not five sparrows sold for two assarion? And not one of them is forgotten by God. [7]But even the hairs on your head are numbered. Do not fear; you are of more value than many sparrows.

[8]"But I say to you, everyone who confesses me before men, the Son of Man will confess him before the angels of God. [9]But the one who denies me before men will be denied before the angels of God. [10]And every one who speaks a word against the Son of Man will be forgiven; but he who blasphemes the Holy Spirit will not be forgiven. [11]But when they bring you before the synagogues, rulers, and authorities, do not be anxious how or what you will reply or say, [12]for the Holy Spirit will teach you in that hour what is necessary to say."

a. Call: Avoid the Hypocrisy of the Pharisees (12:1)

12:1   A contrast emerges between Jesus' current popularity and his warning to the disciples. Luke indicates that what happens here follows soon after the rebuke of the Pharisees (ἐν οἷς [*en hois*, during which time] may be smoothed out as "meanwhile"; but see Nolland 1993a: 677). Thousands are coming to hear Jesus (Acts 21:20 also has a crowd this size). Perhaps his rebuke of the wicked generation is bearing fruit. Perhaps Jesus will be received. The crowd is so large that people are pressing over one another to see and hear him (κατα-πατέω, *katapateō*, to walk over one another; BAGD 415 §1b; BAA 845 §1b; elsewhere in the NT at Matt. 5:13; 7:6; Luke 8:5; Heb. 10:29). Jesus knows that his popularity is temporary.

Instead of optimism, Jesus responds with realism. The popular crush of curiosity will not change the destiny of his movement, and so a warning is required. Jesus calls the disciples to constant vigilance (προσέχετε, *prosechete*, is a present imperative) against hypocrisy, the spiritual leaven that corrupts (1 Cor. 5:6 also uses this figure). This hypocrisy is like that of the Pharisees described and condemned in Luke 11:39–41. The OT background is the instruction not to allow leaven in the Passover bread (Exod. 12:14–20; Danker 1988: 244).[4] As the context suggests, the desire to impress people may lead to a double life. But a double life is a destructive, empty lifestyle that ignores what God always sees (Fitzmyer 1985: 955 notes a similar Qumranian critique of the Pharisees: 1QH 2.15, 32, 34; CD 1.18).

Πρῶτον (*prōton*, first) may highlight the priority that Jesus placed on the warning (Klostermann 1929: 133) or it simply may define his initial audience as disciples, with 12:13 later bringing in the crowds (Plummer 1896: 317; Marshall 1978: 511; Fitzmyer 1985: 954; Wiefel 1988: 232; Arndt 1956: 311). Against the first option, it may be noted that watching out for hypocrisy can hardly be called the first spiritual priority. But equally telling against the second option, it is not clear why identifying the audience is worth special mention. It may not be necessary to take the priority in absolute terms, that is, it may not say that the absolute first spiritual priority is to avoid hypocrisy (i.e., "primarily"; so Nolland 1993a: 677). It may mean rhetorically that such a concern is a main priority. Nonetheless, Luke's grammatical style favors the second option, a simple reference to the audience as disciples (Marshall 1978: 511; Acts 3:26; 7:12; 13:46).[5] The disciples should see that the way of the Pharisees is not the true way. If Luke employs a topical arrangement here, the wording makes sense in light of Luke 11:37–54. Of course, if the setting is not topical, the allusion to the Pharisees also makes sense.

4. On leaven as an evil disposition in Judaism, see SB 1:728–29; Windisch, *TDNT* 2:905–6; Manson 1949: 270.
5. Luke often uses πρῶτον as a temporal marker. Most of his thirty-six uses of πρῶτος in Luke–Acts fall in this category.

b. Promise: All That Is Done in Secret Will Be Exposed (12:2–3)

12:2 Jesus uses a proverbial saying to make clear that hypocrisy cannot work, because all is revealed in time. There is some debate whether the remark promises that the Pharisees' hypocrisy will be exposed (Manson 1949: 106; Friedrich, *TDNT* 3:705 [who includes 12:3]) or is a general remark. As a general remark, it would serve as a warning to all, though Pharisees would clearly be included. Given that the warning is addressed to the disciples, a general remark seems likely. There comes a time when the secrets of people's hearts will be revealed (1 Cor. 4:5; Rom. 2:16). The picture of God's omniscience and omnipresence informs the passage. Nothing that is done escapes his eye and mind. All are subject to him. In fact, this is why he must be feared most of all (Luke 12:4–5). The remark is emphatic, as the double use of the negative shows (Marshall 1978: 512). All becomes clear with God's judgment.

There is debate whether the passage is negative (warning that hypocrisy will be exposed) or positive (noting that proclamation in the midst of trial will be shown as bold; Liefeld 1984: 959; Creed 1930: 170; Ellis 1974: 175). This choice, however, seems to be a false one. The point is that God knows what one does, good or bad, whether with integrity or hypocritically. All is exposed for what it is (Fitzmyer 1985: 957 [though he highlights the saying as a warning]; Danker 1988: 244 [who notes that both hypocrites and disciples are addressed]). Eschatology is a key area in Jesus' teaching, for it is there that the scales of justice are brought into balance and behavior is brought to account.

12:3 Not only action but also speech will be evaluated. It is hard to know if ἀνθ' ὧν (*anth' hōn*) means "because" or "therefore" (Fitzmyer 1985: 958). The phrase is probably Lucan since only he uses it (Luke 1:20; 19:44; Acts 12:23; Nolland 1993a: 677). If it means "because," then the reason for revealing all is being given. But the logic of this connection is harsh, since 12:3 basically repeats the idea of 12:2 and under this view simply gives the cause: the reason that all is brought to light is because what is brought to light is preached on the housetops. More likely the consequence of judgment's reality is in view. The verse reinforces 12:2: all will be revealed in the light, "therefore" recognize that what is whispered will be preached on the housetops. The disciples should recognize that whatever is said in the dark, behind closed doors, in private, will be preached on housetops; it will become public knowledge. Ταμεῖον (*tameion*) is a home's innermost apartment, the most private location (Godet 1875: 2.90; BAGD 803; BAA 1603; elsewhere in the NT at Luke 12:24 [a storeroom]; Matt.

6:6; 24:26; in the OT at Gen. 43:30; Exod. 7:28 [8:3 MT]; Judg. 16:9; 1 Kings 22:25 [in the last two texts it is a place to hide]). This figure of speech describes our most private practices. This is a classic reversal theme: the most private of acts and utterances become the most public. It is this exposure that makes hypocrisy useless in the long run and the heroic deed done in private an object of admiration eventually. The contrasts are strong: darkness versus light and private whispering versus public preaching.

As in 12:2, commentators again want to make a choice about whether the remarks are negative or positive in thrust. Is it the exposure of hypocrisy, such as that in 12:1, that is in view? Or is it an exhortation to be bold in proclaiming Christ, as 12:4–7 suggests? Once again, the choice is a false one. The point of the passage throughout is that God is omniscient. He perceives and will reveal all. All the passive verbs in 12:2–3 point to God's activity (Tiede 1988: 228). If a person has things to hide, it is a warning. But if a person acts admirably, the passage is a motivation. The Pharisees have much to fear. True disciples, by their contrastive behavior, have little.

The image used in Matt. 10:26–27 has a different application, since there the disciples are to take their message to the public. The different application suggests a distinct setting for the remarks (see the introduction to this unit; but note Nolland 1993a: 677, who argues that Matthew has recast the saying).

c. Call: Fear God Not Humans (12:4–7)
i. Fear the One Who Can Cast Souls into Gehenna (12:4–5)

12:4   Jesus continues to instruct the disciples by warning them about who to fear. The address to φίλοις (*philois*) shows that his "friends," the disciples, are still in view (John 15:14–15; Ellis 1974: 175; Creed 1930: 171; Stählin, *TDNT* 9:163). Their concern is not for those who can kill only the physical body and nothing more. Obviously, the warning has to do with not fearing martyrdom and not bowing to pressure. The warning may also allude to the hypocrisy involved in attempting to protect one's physical life. Humankind's power over life is indeed limited. Fourth Maccabees 13:14–15 (NRSV) reads, "Let us not fear him who thinks he is killing us, for great is the struggle of the soul and the danger of eternal torment lying before those who transgress the commandment of God" (Manson 1949: 107). Jesus does not guarantee that he will protect one's physical life; this is not prosperity theology. God may require martyrdom of his disciples. The premise of this remark is that God has sovereign care of life after earthly life. Without such a view of care and justice, Jesus' remarks make no sense. Jesus' thrust is positive. God notes what disciples will face and that they are standing with him (Tiede 1988: 228–29). Jesus is aware of the opposition rising against him and of what it will mean for him and may mean for his followers. The history of the treatment of God's representatives—from the prophets to John the Baptist—has much to teach followers of God: if these did not escape rejection, then neither will the Son of Man and his followers.

Matthew 10:28 is similar, although there the contrast is between those who can kill the body but not the soul. Luke has an aorist subjunctive φοβηθῆτε (phobēthēte, fear) where Matthew has a present imperative φοβεῖσθε (phobeisthe, constantly fear). Luke commands the attitude, while Matthew emphasizes its continual character. Again, it is difficult to explain why any change to the wording was made, especially to the body/soul contrast, if one source were present. Multiple settings are more likely.

12:5 The emphatic contrast to not fearing people is noted in the threefold repetition of the call to fear God. Following the initial command not to fear (12:4), Jesus now says to fear God because he has authority to cast someone into Gehenna. This is the only time that Luke uses γέεννα (Gehenna, hell). It refers to the place of the dead, the place where the punished are put in the last judgment. It is named after a location in the Valley of the Sons of Hinnom, a ravine south and west of Jerusalem that served as a trash heap where material and dead criminals were discarded and burned. It also was the place that wicked kings had used earlier in Israel's history for the worship of Baal-Molech, which included offering children in a flaming sacrifice (2 Kings 16:3; 23:10; 2 Chron. 28:3; 33:6; Isa. 66:24; Jer. 7:31–32; 19:4–6; 32:34–35). The term could not have a more grisly or more dishonorable association (Arndt 1956: 312; Danker 1988: 245; Jeremias, *TDNT* 1:657–58; SB 4:1022–1118; Matt. 5:22; 10:28; 18:9; 23:33; Mark 9:45, 47; BAGD 153; BAA 306). It is better to fear the Judge than those with no real authority (Foerster, *TDNT* 2:566–67 §C1). God stands in contrast to the people, who can do nothing.[6] In fact, God will judge a person after death. Several NT texts warn of responding now, lest one meet judgment from God and be cast into fire (Mark 9:45, 47; James 4:12; Rev. 19:20; 20:11–15; Marshall 1978: 513), and many OT texts picture God's judgment as fire (Deut. 32:22; Isa. 31:9; 66:24; Nolland 1993a: 678).

Contrary to idealized conceptions of Jesus, he accepted the teaching of judgment in the afterlife, for this saying makes no sense without a real end-time judgment. An interesting text reflects a later Jew-

---

6. Fitzmyer 1985: 959 correctly notes that the contrast is to humans, not to Satan, evil, or the Son of Man.

ish view about the afterlife (*t. Sanh.* 13.3–4 [= Neusner 1977–86: 4.239]; Manson 1949: 107):[7]

> The wicked of Israel in their bodies, and the wicked of the nations of the world in their bodies go down to hell and are punished in it for twelve months. After twelve months their souls become extinct, and their bodies are burned up, and they turn to ashes, and the wind scatters them and strews them beneath the soles of the feet of the righteous.

The clearest NT passage on people's fate in the afterlife is Rev. 20:11–15. If 20:10 is a situation parallel to 20:11–15, then the NT teaches that torment is eternal (Preisker, *TDNT* 4:714 §B.4.1). Matthew 10:28 contains a similar idea, only there Jesus speaks of fearing the one who can destroy both body and soul in Gehenna.

ii. Realize That God Cares for You and Knows You Intimately (12:6–7)

Jesus turns now to the Father's care over his creation. Reminding the disciples of God's care for those general parts of creation that humans do not highly value, Jesus is going to compare that care to the value of people. He uses the example of five little sparrows, which sell in the marketplace for two assarion, a small Roman coin worth one-sixteenth of a denarius or a few cents.[8] The sparrow was the cheapest thing sold in the market (Manson 1949: 108) and may have been part of the diet of the poor (Ellis 1974: 175). Despite the cheapness of these insignificant birds, not even one of them escapes God's attention (Plummer 1896: 319 notes the "smallest of the small" argument in the passage). In the illustration, Jesus implies that God will care for the disciple even more than for the birds—even if death is a part of discipleship.

12:6

---

7. Earlier Jewish texts on the theme include Jdt. 16:17; 1 Enoch 10.13; 18.11–16; 27.1–3; 90.26; Jub. 9.15; 2 Esdr. [= 4 Ezra] 7:36; Fitzmyer 1985: 959–60. Apparently a debate in Judaism discussed whether hell involved eternal torment or limited suffering with extinction, a view called "annihilationism" today. The Tosepta text noted argues that there are three groups of people: one destined for eternal life, another destined for shame and everlasting contempt, and a third group that visits Gehenna but is healed as through a refiner's fire, citing Zech. 13:9 and 1 Sam. 2:6. As the portion of *t. Sanh.* 3 quoted above shows, some Jews believed that Gehenna burns the body and the soul perishes after twelve months of judgment.

8. On the coin, see BAGD 117; BAA 235; Matt. 10:29 (the only other NT use). Wiefel 1988: 233 puts its worth at five pfennigs, one of the smallest German coins. A denarius was a day's wage, so this is very little money. The most basic worker would earn this in roughly a half hour. The term for sparrow (στρουθίον) may also indicate simply a "little bird"; Plummer 1896: 319–20; Ps. 11:1 [10:1 LXX]; 84:3 [83:4 LXX]; MM 594; Bauernfeind, *TDNT* 7:730, 732 n. 19; Fitzmyer 1985: 960.

The remark has OT roots (Isa. 49:15). The text stresses that God does not forget his own. Marshall (1978: 514) recognizes this point and cites a Jewish parallel (rendered here is a form more like Neusner's translation): "No bird perishes without heaven—all the more so a man" (*y. Šeb.* 38d [9.1] [= Neusner et al. 1982–93: 5.303]; SB 1:582–83).

Matthew 10:29 uses the same illustration, except there the sparrow does not fall to the ground without God willing it. The Matthean picture is somewhat distinct from Luke's and is a more explicit reference to physical harm, but the illustrations are essentially the same. A detail of Matthew's illustration differs: "two sparrows for one assarion." Why would Luke alter this if he had the same tradition? Again, the difference suggests a distinct saying. One should not make much of the price difference, however, which may reflect the concept that the more one buys, the better the deal.[9]

12:7   God's concern for his creatures applies especially to people. For the third time, Jesus tells the disciples not to fear, this time amplifying the teaching. The exhortation not to fear involves a basic attitude, since the rendering of Jesus' remark uses a present imperative (φοβεῖσθε, *phobeisthe*). Earlier they were told to fear God, since he alone controls their destiny after death. Here they are told not to fear; that is, they need not worry about how God will care for them. God knows their needs and is aware of their situation as they face rejection for their stand for Christ. Jesus notes that God is aware even of the number of hairs on a person's head, and he reminds them that they are more important than sparrows. The argument is a minor-to-major argument typical of Judaism: if God cares for the sparrows, how much more will he care for you, since you are of more value than they are. Matthew 10:30–31 has a virtually identical concept in almost the same wording.[10]

d. Call: Confess Jesus and Avoid Blaspheming the Spirit (12:8–12)

i. Confession and Denial of the Son of Man (12:8–9)

12:8   The real issue is the disciple's ability to express commitment to Jesus before other people. The one who confesses the Son of Man

---

9. There is no need to suggest that Luke corrected Matthew's pricing, as Nolland 1993a: 678 intimates.

10. Only the verbal forms differ: Matthew has ἠριθμημέναι εἰσίν and Luke ἠρίθμηνται (both meaning "are numbered"). 1 Sam. 14:45; 2 Sam. 14:11; 1 Kings 1:52; and Dan. 3:27 use the idiom for the total protection indicated by not one hair being lost; Plummer 1896: 320; Fitzmyer 1985: 960; Luke 21:18; Acts 27:34. Luke's idiom is a variation on the OT idiom and means "God knows exactly where you stand."

will likewise receive acknowledgment before the angels. The phrase ὁμολογήσῃ ἐν ἐμοί (*homologēsē en emoi*, confesses me) is a Semitism (Michel, *TDNT* 5:208 n. 27; Fitzmyer 1985: 960). Up to this point in Luke, the term *Son of Man* has been an indirect way for Jesus to refer to himself in his authority to forgive sin (5:24), his table fellowship with sinners (7:34), or his approaching suffering (9:22). Here it alludes to a role in the judgment, a role that Luke reports in the apostolic preaching as well (Acts 10:42–43; 17:31). The force suggests a role for him at God's side before the angels. The Son of Man's authority is something that Jesus will allude to later (Luke 22:69, where the authority begins from the time of the passion). Some argue that the Son of Man and Jesus are distinct figures in this passage, but such usage would make this an exception to Jesus' pattern of using the term in reference to himself.[11] Jesus has a strong sense that he is God's appointed eschatological agent, since he has a role in divine judgment.

Matthew 10:32 has a similar concept, except there Jesus says he will offer the confession before his Father in heaven. The Lucan reference to angels alludes to their role as witnesses of the confession at the heavenly court (Marshall 1978: 515). Most resolve the difference between Matthew and Luke by regarding the reference to angels as a Jewish paraphrase for the Father (Luce 1933: 217). Interestingly, Matthew, who would be more likely to have such a paraphrase, has the direct statement.[12] A distinct saying is more likely.[13] Stephen's vision illustrates the Son of Man's response to one who confesses him (Acts 7:55–56; also Matt. 19:28; Mark 8:38; Luke 22:27–28; 2 Tim. 2:12; Schweizer 1984: 205).

In contrast to the idea in the previous verse, the one who denies **12:9** Jesus before other people will be denied in heaven. The passive mood does not specifically indicate who does the heavenly denying, but it is clear that rejection from heaven is in view. People have two options: to accept Jesus or reject him; there is no neutral position (Manson 1949: 108). But is Jesus referring to a single incident or a pattern in one's life? Peter's failure to confess Jesus suggests that

---

11. Many distinguish the saying's earliest form about a Son of Man other than Jesus from the later linkage of the Son of Man to Jesus, which appears throughout the NT. The original advocate of this distinction was Bultmann 1951–55: 1.29. The Son-of-Man sayings elsewhere refer exclusively to Jesus, making it unlikely that there are any "other than Jesus" Son-of-Man sayings. For more on the Son of Man, see Bock 1991c and excursus 6 in vol. 1.

12. Fitzmyer 1985: 960 notes that elsewhere Luke does not avoid the expression *before God* in 1:19; 12:6; 16:15.

13. On the debate (among those who regard both sayings as reflecting a single tradition) as to which saying is original, see Marshall 1978: 514–16, who opts for two forms of Q.

one incident is not in view (contra Nolland 1993a: 679). In contrasting Peter with Judas, it might be better to speak of denial of nerve versus denial of the heart. Peter did deny Jesus publicly three times, but he regretted his act and responded later with numerous public declarations of Jesus. Judas denied Jesus through betrayal and was tormented by his decision. Nevertheless, Judas's response was inadequate; rather than declaring Jesus, he committed suicide. Peter's denial was one of nerve, which was later dramatically reversed. Judas's denial was one of the heart. Thus, Judas—not Peter—better illustrates this verse. Other candidates might include those who depart the assembly in 1 John 2:19, which may be the same group referred to by the phrase *sin unto death* in 1 John 5:16. Those who deny or end up denying Jesus are in view here. As such, the aorist participle ὁ ἀρνησάμενος (*ho arnēsamenos*, the one who denies) functions as a summary description of a life of denial.

Matthew 10:33 is similar to Luke, but there Jesus makes clear that he will be the one giving the heavenly denial before his Father in heaven. Thus, the Matthean version is more explicit.

ii. Blasphemy of the Spirit Is Not Forgiven (12:10)

12:10   Jesus closes with one of the more enigmatic and debated sayings of his ministry. He distinguishes between blaspheming or acting dishonorably against the Son of Man and doing so against the Spirit. Blasphemy of the Son of Man is forgivable, but blasphemy of the Spirit is not. Marshall (1978: 517) notes that this forgiveness is not automatic but needs to be requested. Jesus has just said that failure to confess him before people will result in judgment (for OT background see Num. 11:17; 15:30–31; 27:18; Deut. 34:9; Isa. 63:7–14; Ps. 106:32–33; Lev. 24:11–23; Fitzmyer 1985: 966; Beyer, *TDNT* 1:624–25; SB 1:1009–10; see Lövestam 1968 for the Jewish background). What does it mean to blaspheme the Holy Spirit? At least five views have been put forward (Fitzmyer 1985: 964):

> 1. Some regard it as the Beelzebub charge raised in Mark 3:22 = Luke 11:15. Ellis (1974: 176) argues that in Mark 3:28–30 = Matt. 12:32, blasphemy against the Spirit is seeing Jesus' work as coming from Satan, while in Luke it is regarding the work of Jesus' servants as being tied to Satan. Ellis reasons that in both Matthew and Mark the remark is tied to the Beelzebub controversy, while in Luke the Beelzebub controversy is absent. However, Ellis's position can be qualified, though his Beelzebub observation is correct. Even in Matthew, the remark follows a comment about being allied to Jesus (Matt. 12:30), and so it does not relate exclusively to the Beelzebub is-

sue. The distinction that Ellis seeks between Matthew-Mark and Luke does not exist, at least in Matthew. This view, though having merit, is probably stated too narrowly to reflect the diversity of the Gospels.

2. Patristic interpretation often regarded the passage as referring to the believer's apostasy (Origen, *Commentary on John* 2.10 on John 1:3; Arndt 1956: 313 [a modern exponent]). This certainly fits the Lucan context of warning about not fearing people but fearing God in the midst of persecution. It is less clear in its relationship to the Matthean and Marcan forms of the saying.

3. A more nuanced position argues that speaking against the Son of Man consists of rejecting him during his ministry, while blasphemy of the Spirit consists of rejecting him after hearing the preaching of the apostles, who preach by authority of the Spirit (Ernst 1977: 395; Schneider 1977a: 280; Danker 1988: 246; Tiede 1988: 231). This view has much to be said for it, since it is historically sensitive to the progress of Jesus' ministry and places the blasphemy in terms of allegiance to Jesus. However, many who hold it also regard the statement as a product of the church (Procksch, *TDNT* 1:104), which is problematic.

4. A view that focuses on the Lucan form of the saying relates it to 12:11–12: blasphemy of the Spirit is failure to utter the message that the Spirit supplies when one is brought before the rulers and synagogues (Creed 1930: 172). The main problem with this view is its lack of connection to the concept in Matthew and Mark.

5. The last view is like view 3, but is more intense: blasphemy of the Spirit is not so much an act of rejection as it is a persistent and decisive rejection of the Spirit's message and work concerning Jesus. When a person obstinately rejects and fixedly refuses that message or evidence, that person is not forgiven (Plummer 1896: 321; Godet 1875: 2.93–94; Manson 1949: 110). Marshall (1978: 518–19) sees it as a warning to opponents not to deny the Spirit's work and argues that 12:8–9 deals with apostasy, while 12:10–12 deals with outsiders. Nolland (1993a: 679–80) says it well: blasphemy against the Spirit is "the denial or rejection of the manifest saving intervention of God on behalf of his People. . . . The one who hardens himself or herself against what God is doing as he acts to save places himself or herself beyond the reach of God's present disposition of eschatological forgiveness."

The advantage of view 5 is that it looks at the totality of a person's response to the Spirit, not just a moment in it. If single moments were in view, then Peter and Paul would fall into this category, and this is unlikely. Also, the concept should be broad enough to make sense of all the parallels. A view that fits all three settings is more likely than a view that fits only one or two of them or argues that Luke's form is original and the Matthean and Marcan forms are later (Luce 1933: 228 favors distinguishing Luke from Matthew and Mark). The probability that the remark is the same in all accounts effectively rules out views 1, 2, and 4.

Luce argues against view 5 on three grounds: (1) Would Jesus distinguish between himself and the Spirit? (2) Would Jesus think of any sin as unforgivable and of any soul as eternally lost? (3) Is mere speaking to be seen as such a terrible act? Good answers may be found for these objections. First, Jesus often distinguished between himself and the testimony given to him. This is especially clear in John 5:19–24, where he speaks of not working by his own authority but by that of the Father, a distinction that in one sense separates him from the Father. He also makes a distinction when he tells others not to believe only in the works he does, but also in the testimony of Moses (John 5:44–47). He does something similar when he ties the evaluation of his work to that of John the Baptist's work (Luke 7:31–35; 20:1–8). This type of "displacement" is common with Jesus. Granted, it is a type of rhetorical displacement, but its point is important: others testify to the importance of Jesus. Rejection of those witnesses is serious. Self-claim is one thing, but to ignore corroborating witnesses is another. Second, whether Jesus believed in unforgivable sin or eternal punishment depends on whether one regards all such statements attributed to Jesus as coming from the church. Numerous such statements and suggestions may be found in his teaching and parables, some even in this context (12:8–9). That Jesus made statements for eternal judgment seems clear and undeniable. They are multiply attested (see the discussion of sources and historicity for 11:37–54). Finally, to characterize the position as simply reacting against speaking is to misrepresent the teaching, since the utterance ultimately reflects the heart's condition. Speech is singled out because it reflects an attitude, a confession of the heart. Interestingly, Rom. 10:9–13 does the same thing with verbal confession for salvation. It is not the utterance that is key but what the utterance reveals. The "obstinate rejection" view has much to commend it.

As was noted, Matthew and Mark have similar sayings (as does the Gospel of Thomas 44–45), both involving the same event: the discussion following the Beelzebub incident. Blasphemy of the Spirit is mentioned in Matthew after a declaration that whoever is not for Jesus is against him. In Mark the reference includes the explanation of the charge that Jesus works by Satan's power. And Luke ties the issue to a hesitation to ally oneself to Jesus and confess him because of fear. The concept that unites the three passages is the rejection of allegiance to Jesus, whether because one fears people's response or one attributes Jesus' work to Satan. The blasphemy of the Spirit might be regarded as the by-product of rejecting the Son of Man.[14] The difference between blaspheming the Son of Man and blaspheming the Spirit is that blasphemy of the Son of Man is an instant rejection, while blasphemy of the Spirit is a permanent decision of rejection. Luke 22:65 and 23:39 look at instances of rejection, while speeches such as Acts 7:51, 13:40–49, and 28:23–28 show the implications once that rejection is solidified into an attitude. Once the Spirit's testimony about God's work through Jesus is permanently refused, then nothing can be forgiven, since God's plan has been rejected.

iii. Promise of the Spirit's Aid in Time of Testimony (12:11–12)

The attention shifts slightly. In the midst of discussing rejection of **12:11** the Son of Man, Jesus adds a word of assurance for his disciples. The prospect of being hauled in before political or religious authorities is real.[15] When this happens, the disciples are not to worry about what they will say; they will be given spiritual provision (12:12). The early accounts of Peter (Acts 3–5 [esp. 4:8]), Stephen (Acts 7:51–56), and Paul (Acts 21–28) are reflections of this promise coming to pass (Hendriksen 1978: 657; Arndt 1956: 314). The trust that Jesus calls for reminds one of the psalmist's trust as he faced the unrighteous and turned to God (Ps. 18, 40).

This passage has parallels in Mark 13:11 = Matt. 10:19–20. The Matthean passage is tied to the mission of the Twelve, while the Marcan text is part of the eschatological discourse. The remark is an important one about relying on God during persecution and is the type of statement that would have been repeated. In fact, Luke 21:14–15 has a similar saying in his version of the eschatological discourse. An occasion that is distinct from Matthew and Mark seems likely.

14. Manson 1949: 109–10 solves the problem by arguing that "Son of Man" refers to someone other than Jesus, which is linguistically possible but very difficult in Luke, since the title clearly refers to Jesus in 12:8–9. Arguments about what an "original form" of the saying said are purely speculative and do not show why the current sense is really problematic.

15. The synagogue is seen negatively in Matt. 23:34; 10:17 = Mark 13:9 = Luke 21:12; Schrage, *TDNT* 7:834. The political leaders in view are largely Gentile: Luke 20:20; 21:12; Acts 4:26–30.

12:12   Disciples can face persecution because of a promise. At such inqui-
sitions, God's spiritual provision will support them. There will be
guidance on how to reply to questioners. This provision is the reason that the disciples need not worry (γάρ, *gar*, for, connects the
thought to 12:11). Such an examination would be extemporaneous,
since questions would center around beliefs and activities. The
Spirit will instruct them with specific content in that hour. Rather
than speaking against the Spirit, they will be ready to speak through
him (Liefeld 1984: 960). As such, anxiety need not be a problem,
since the Spirit will meet their need. This is the only Lucan text that
explicitly mentions the Spirit as teaching.[16] It is interesting that
Matt. 10:20 = Mark 13:11 explicitly mentions the Spirit, while Luke
21:15 does not. The Luke 21 passage stresses that the reply will be
so adequate that opponents will have no response (examples are
found in Acts 4:13–22; 26:28–32). A similar teaching is found in the
angel's instruction to Balaam in Philo, *Life of Moses* 1.49 §274 (commenting on Num. 22:32–35): "Pursue your journey. Your hurrying
will not avail you. I shall prompt the words you need without your
mind's consent and direct the organs of your speech as justice and
convenience may require. I shall guide the reins of your speech and,
though you understand it not, use your tongue for each prophetic
utterance" (Fitzmyer 1985: 966).

God's care for disciples was mentioned in Luke 12:6–7. Here
Jesus specifies an aspect of that care: God will provide the Spirit to
help them answer their accusers. The answer will come immediately, as the phrase ἐν αὐτῇ τῇ ὥρᾳ (*en autē tē hōra*, at that hour)
makes clear. Disciples will not find they have nothing to say or that
God has abandoned them. Only loss of nerve will produce faithlessness. To those who depend on God in the hour of testing the Spirit
offers aid so that they can confess their faith. Paul makes a similar
request for boldness (Eph. 6:18–20; Col. 4:3–4), as does the early
church (Acts 4:24–30).

Summary   Luke 12:1–12 speaks about the disciple before a hostile world.
The disciple has a tough road to travel. Jesus warns against the
pressure to conform to surrounding attitudes and thus become a
hypocrite in one's religious activity. Pressure comes from raw
secular power that causes one to fear people, not God. Here a vi-
brant eschatology is the answer. The disciple should realize that
people can kill the body, but it is God who decides ones eternal
fate. Jesus says to fear the one with control of life after physical

---

16. Fitzmyer 1985: 966. 1 Cor. 2:7 has a different verb (λαλέω, to speak), while
John 14:26 and 1 John 2:27 use διδάσκω (to teach). Marshall 1978: 520–21 defends
the authenticity of the concept, citing Beasley-Murray 1970: 473–74.

death. But God is not only judge, he is also one who is aware of and cares for his creatures, especially humans. One can stand in the face of persecution because God is there. All of this should comfort and reassure the disciple (cf. 1:4).

A far greater warning also emerges. One can speak on occasion against the Son of Man and be forgiven, but the decision to deny him publicly and reject him obstinately is the sin that cannot be forgiven. The one who permanently denies the Son is judged. To blaspheme the Spirit is to deny decisively the testimony he offers about the Son.

In contrast, there are benefits to confession and trust. The one who confesses the Son of Man will be received by him before the angels. The one who relies on God in the midst of persecution will be given words by the Spirit to answer accusers. The entire unit calls the believer to trust the caring Father and not give in to human pressure, since it is he who has the authority that counts and it is he who supplies what is needed to endure. The disciple's commitment to stand with Jesus reflects the depth of trust in the Father, both as Judge and Provider. In other words, if one is to survive the ultimate heat of judgment, one must trust God. God enables one to withstand the heat of the world's kitchen. A decision for Jesus will produce reaction. The disciple must be ready. A decision to defer to the pressure that people exert may lead one to deny permanently the Son of Man and the Spirit that testifies to him, but a decision for the Son of Man will lead him to embrace the faithful one before God. If one understands who controls the soul and gives blessing to it, one will know whom to draw near to in faith. As with many passages in Luke, the choice belongs to the reader.

2. Parable of the Rich Fool
(12:13–21)

Jesus turns from the disciples' need to trust God in the midst of persecution to the obstacle that money can be to total devotion to God. It is hard to be sure why this topic surfaces here, but it may be that, since persecution often involves social ostracism and loss of livelihood, material security is an attractive alternative to rejection. Jesus is asked to resolve a family dispute over an inheritance, but he refuses to be put in the middle of the dispute. The request leads him into a brief saying on the danger of focusing on possessions. Perhaps the perception was that Jesus would be a fair and authoritative arbiter. Jews often took such disputes to the rabbi, so the request is natural and shows respect for Jesus and his judgment (Creed 1930: 172; Ellis 1974: 177; Liefeld 1984: 961). Though refusing to enter into the dispute, Jesus notes the kind of problems that greed can cause. This is the second time that Jesus has refused to intercede for someone complaining about a family member's activity (10:38–42).

After his refusal and brief maxim, Jesus tells a parable that shows the danger of placing one's trust in possessions. Part of the power of this parable is that much in the man's response seems so natural. However, his response is flawed in its perspective. The unit fits into the section's general thrust that many obstacles lie in front of disciples. The previous passage warned about fearing humans over God. Now another major danger is raised: excessive attachment to wealth.[1] The warnings given in Luke 12 parallel the warnings offered in the parable of the soils, for the obstacles there included trials and riches (8:4–15; also 16:19–31; 18:18–30). As a result of issues raised here, Jesus will go on to address the need to trust God (12:22–34), something true both in the midst of persecution and as one seeks life's provision.

---

1. Blomberg 1990: 267 states the points of the unit: (1) purely selfish accumulation of possessions is incompatible with true discipleship, and (2) this incompatibility stems from the transience of earthly riches and the coming reckoning that all will face before God. B. Scott 1989: 128 notes the parallelism between Luke 12 and 16, with their common themes of threats from hell, riches, and the issue of stewardship.

Sources and Historicity

The unit is unique to Luke and proceeds in two parts (Aland 1985: §§199–200). Luke 12:13–15 contains the dispute and Jesus' response about greed. The graphic parable follows in 12:16–21. Many regard the parable as having been inserted into the narrative at this point. Although the account is unique to Luke, there is no need to doubt that it reflects an incident in Jesus' life, even if its placement here by Luke is topical, since no temporal markers introduce the unit.[2] There is nothing unnatural within the account's general setting or movement (Luce 1933: 230 questions the historicity, but is not certain that the account is nonhistorical). Like 10:25–30, a question has spawned a parable (Plummer 1896: 322).[3] It is not likely that the question and parable were originally separate, given how often a question prompts Jesus to teach (see the exegesis of 12:13).

The Jesus Seminar (Funk and Hoover 1993: 338–39) rejects 12:15 (see n. 3 above) and 12:21, printing it in black type, since the Gospel of Thomas lacks it. It rates the opening remark in 12:14, where Jesus refuses to help, in gray type because it is proverbial and sounds like Exod. 2:14. But Jesus' refusal to enter into such controversy is similar to his response to Martha's request that he reprove Mary (Luke 10:38–42). The warnings about the danger of wealth and a wrong perspective toward it are fundamental themes of Jesus, fitting both his teaching (Matt./Q 6:19–21) and the character of his ministry, which focused on the poor (Matt./Q 11:5). Both of these ideas fit numerous passages in L and Q, while Jesus' parables often use possessions or money (Luke 19:11–27 = Matt./Q 25:14–30; Luke 12:22–32 =[?] Matt./Q 6:25–34; Luke 14:15–24 = Matt./Q 22:1–14; Luke/L 16:1–13; Luke/L 16:19–31). So the theme of the parable and of 12:15 coheres with Jesus' teaching, and 12:21 is similar to Matt. 6:19–21. Also speaking for these verses is the general recognition that the rest of the parable comes from Jesus; even the Jesus Seminar rates Luke 12:16–20 as typical of Jesus' words, printing these verses in pink type. It is the lack of additional attestation for 12:15 and 12:21 that calls these verses into question. Luke may simply be aware of additional sources (Marshall 1978: 523). Nolland

---

2. Manson 1949: 270 (who argues that the connection to 12:1–12 is literary and that 12:13–21 is a self-contained unit inserted between two Q passages) and Schweizer 1984: 207. There is little evidence that Matthew knew of the parable and omitted it, despite what Marshall 1978: 522 suggests, citing Matt. 6:19–20, 25. Fitzmyer 1985: 968 correctly notes that Luke alone gives evidence of this account.

3. The Gospel of Thomas 63, 72 has parallel material, but §63 is not primary, as B. Scott 1989: 130–31 correctly argues. However, Scott wrongly asserts that the separation of the question and the parable in the Gospel of Thomas shows that Luke put these two elements together (with Scott, Funk and Hoover 1993: 338 argue that 12:15 was written by Luke, printing it in black type). The Gospel of Thomas lacks any warning, and so is only conceptually parallel. In addition, the general nature of the Gospel of Thomas is to work with only one short saying at a time.

(1993a: 684) argues that 12:15 lacks Lucan language and syntax, though he questions (p. 687) the original connection of 12:21, as does Fitzmyer (1985: 971). Manson (1949: 272) expresses doubt on 12:21 (but see Marshall 1978: 524).[4] Luke 12:21 also lacks any evidence of Lucan style (Seng 1978: 137 and n. 5).

The account is a pronouncement story (12:13–15) and a parable (12:16–21) that serves as a negative example.[5] The outline of Luke 12:13–21 is as follows:

a. Jesus refuses to arbitrate a family dispute (12:13–15)
    i. The request (12:13)
    ii. Jesus' refusal (12:14)
    iii. Jesus' warning about greed (12:15)
b. Parable of the rich fool (12:16–21)
    i. The parable proper (12:16–20)
      (1) Plentiful crop (12:16)
      (2) Dilemma (12:17)
      (3) Decision to store and rest (12:18–19)
      (4) God's reaction: fool! (12:20)
    ii. The application (12:21)

The major idea is that focusing on material wealth is dangerous. Jesus warns against greed and stresses that life does not consist of possessions. A person who trusts in possessions and ignores God will be disappointed when God calls for an account. By negative example, Jesus calls people to be rich toward God.

Exegesis and Exposition

[13]And a certain one from the crowd said to him, "Teacher, tell my brother to divide the inheritance with me." [14]But he said, "Man, who appointed me judge or arbitrator between you?" [15]And he said to them, "Watch out and be on the guard against all forms of greed, for one's life is not from the abundance of his possessions."

[16]And he said a parable to them, "The land of a certain rich man was very productive. [17]And he was considering the matter to himself and said, 'What shall I do, since I do not have a place where I can store my yield.' [18]And he

---

4. For potential wisdom tradition in the parable's background and how the parable fits Jesus' teaching, see Seng 1978: 154–55, who is more circumspect on proving authenticity. The term in 12:15 for greed, πλεονεξία, is rare in the Gospels (only here and Mark 7:22), so it is unlikely to be an early church term put into Jesus' mouth. In fact, the word group is basically Pauline (fifteen of nineteen uses).

5. Bultmann 1963: 54–55. Berger 1984: 81, 207 speaks of an apophthegm and a warning. Fitzmyer 1985: 971 prefers to call the parable an example (on the genre of example story or *exemplum*, see excursus 8 in vol. 1 of this commentary).

said, 'I will do this; I will pull down my barns and build larger ones; and there I will store ⌜my produce and my goods⌝. [19]And I will say to my soul, "Soul, you have ample goods laid up for many years; take your ease; eat, drink, and be merry." ' [20]But God said to him, 'Fool, this night your soul is ⌜required⌝ of you; the things you have prepared, whose will they be?' [21]So it is for the one who accumulates treasure for himself and is not rich toward God."

a. Jesus Refuses to Arbitrate a Family Dispute (12:13–15)
i. The Request (12:13)

A brief introduction sets up the situation. There is no indication of **12:13** time or place for this event. An indefinite "certain one" (τις, *tis*) starts the account, as is often the case in Luke (9:57; 10:25; 11:27, 45; 13:23; Fitzmyer 1985: 969; Marshall 1978: 522). A question often launches Jesus' teaching. The request comes from someone in the crowd. Jesus is addressed as teacher (διδάσκαλε, *didaskale*), a title that shows people view him as a respected rabbi. A rabbi would often settle such disputes about inheritance because the regulations on them appear in the Pentateuch and the rabbi interpreted Torah (Deut. 21:15–17; Num. 27:1–11; 36:7–9; *m. B. Bat.* 8–9; Fitzmyer 1985: 969; Wiefel 1988: 236; SB 3:545). The dispute centers on the estate. A brother has refused to divide the inheritance, and this other brother hopes that Jesus will prevail upon him to be more generous. Possessions were often held jointly as undivided shares. But it is not clear whether the complainant was getting nothing or whether he wanted his own piece of the pie, independent of the family. No more details are given concerning the problem. Is the one making the request the younger brother? Is the fault simply that of the other brother (Ps. 133:1 raises another perspective on the dispute)? As Plummer (1896: 322) notes, the man is not really asking Jesus to arbitrate, but to decide against the other brother. Jesus will not honor such a partisan request.

ii. Jesus' Refusal (12:14)

Jesus refuses to get involved in the dispute. The vocative ἄνθρωπε **12:14** (*anthrōpe*, man) can be harsh (Luke 22:58, 60; Rom. 2:1, 3; 9:20; James 2:20) or gentle (Luke 5:20; 1 Tim. 6:11 [with the genitive θεοῦ, *theou*, of God]), depending on the context (BAGD 68 §1aγ; BAA 135 §1aγ). Here it is a rebuke. No one has appointed (καθίστημι, *kathistēmi*; BAGD 390 §2b; BAA 792 §2b; elsewhere in Luke at 12:42, 44) Jesus to be judge or arbiter (μεριστής, *meristēs*; BAGD 505; BAA 1024; a *hapax legomenon*) in a personal dispute. Arndt (1956: 315) suggests that a separation of church and state is intended here; but this conclusion is inappropriate, since personal concerns are present, not ecclesiastical. Jesus' refusal is not intended to establish any universal principles. He simply is choosing not to act in this dispute, for his current mission is not to settle personal disputes.[6] The wording of the refusal recalls the Israelite's rebuke of Moses in Exod. 2:14 (Manson 1949: 271; Acts 7:27, 35), but it is not a direct allusion, since the situations are vastly different.

iii. Jesus' Warning about Greed (12:15)

12:15 Jesus adds a warning about excessive focus on possessions. The warning is given to all, not just to the man (so πρὸς αὐτούς, *pros autous*, to them). Disciples are broadly warned to "be on their guard" (φυλάσσω, *phylassō*; Bertram, *TDNT* 9:240 §C1), not just against money but all forms of greed, of "the desire to have more," which is what πλεονεξία (*pleonexia*; BAGD 667; BAA 1342–43) means. Greed receives mention because it can fuel disagreement and disharmony. The danger of the pursuit of possessions is that it can make one insensitive to people. Greed can create a distortion about what life is, because the definition of life is not found in objects, but relationships, especially to God and his will.[7] To define life in terms of things is the ultimate reversal of the creature serving the creation and ignoring the Creator (Rom. 1:18–32). In Col. 3:5 and Eph. 5:5, greed is called idolatry because it tends to become a god that drives one to do things that are not good (Liefeld 1984: 961). (How often are modern disputes over estates motivated by the same idolatry?) Jesus will tell a parable to illustrate just how foolish this position is. Real life, he argues, possesses a far different focus. Real life is tied to God, his offer of forgiveness of sins, his values, and his reward (T. Schmidt 1987: 146, noting Derrett 1977b). It is being faithful in response to God's goodness. Real life, which is truly rich, is rich toward God, not things (Luke 12:21; Marshall 1978: 523).

b. Parable of the Rich Fool (12:16–21)
i. The Parable Proper (12:16–20)
(1) Plentiful Crop (12:16)

12:16 Jesus reinforces his remark with a parable. This is one of four passages in the journey narrative that treat possessions (12:22–34; 14:12–33; 16:1–13; 16:19–31; Pilgrim 1981: 109). It is also one of four

---

6. Paul responds similarly when he allows the Corinthian church to appoint a believer to arbitrate a lawsuit (1 Cor. 6:4–6; Danker 1988: 247). In fact, he regards the church to have failed if the matter goes to an outside arbitrator. Note also that, in Acts 6:1–4, a church's social problem is solved internally.

7. Tiede 1988: 233; Ernst 1977: 398; Fitzmyer 1985: 970; Lev. 19:18. Manson 1949: 271 notes the similar OT perspective: Job 31:24–25; Ps. 49; Eccles. 2:1–11. Note also T. Judah 18–19; Sir. 11:18–19; 1 Enoch 97.8–10; Mark 7:22; Rom. 1:29; 2 Cor. 9:5; 1 Tim. 6:10; 2 Pet. 2:3, 14; B. Scott 1989: 131–32.

unique Lucan parables with a negative illustration (10:29–37; 16:19–31; 18:9–14; Schneider 1977a: 281). Luke calls this story a παραβολή (*parabolē*, parable). It is one of the many instances where he uses this term to describe Jesus' teaching (4:23 [of a proverb]; 5:36 and 6:39 [of a metaphor]; 8:4, 9, 10, 11; 12:41; 13:6; 14:7; 15:3; 18:1, 9; 19:11; 20:9, 19; 21:29).

The story centers around one character, a man with very productive land (the *hapax legomenon* εὐφορέω, *euphoreō*, means "to yield a good crop"; BAGD 327; BAA 662). Χώρα (*chōra*) refers to extensive holdings, even a region (BAGD 889 §4; BAA 1773 §4). Jesus gives no other details about him. He is nameless and representative. Such a man would be envied in an agrarian context and might even be regarded as specially blessed by God, but he represents anyone in any profession who becomes greedy (Fitzmyer 1985: 972). Apparently, the harvest for the year was exceptional, leaving him in a favorable situation. It is important to note that the parable is initially neutral concerning the man's attitude. There is no hint of avarice, cheating, or immorality,[8] contra the claim of Schottroff and Stegemann (1986: 97) that this man was hoarding his crop to charge a higher price in case of famine. Jesus' parables always involve the element of surprise. The surprise here is that the man has a perfectly natural dilemma. Jesus' story is intriguing in that this man's additional wealth fell into his lap, he came by his wealth honestly because God's provision and kindness blessed him—and yet such blessing still can present a problem of stewardship. Jesus will develop these seemingly favorable circumstances in a disturbing direction.

(2) Dilemma (12:17)

This fortunate man has a dilemma: a large crop but no place to store **12:17** it. So the prudent man reflects on his situation in a type of vivid monologue that adds color to the parable as the main character defines his problem for all.[9] Luke often includes such soliloquies (12:45; 15:17–19; 16:3–4; 18:4–5; 20:13; Marshall 1978: 523). He quite naturally wants to preserve his crops, but there is a hint of a problem in his perspective, for throughout these verses the major

8. This stands in contrast to Prov. 11:26; Jer. 17:11; 1 Enoch 97.8–10. Sir. 11:18–19 is especially close to Jesus' picture, except that wealth comes through self-denial and diligence (lit., "from afflicting himself"), not simply fortune as in Luke. The LXX renders the key phrase "by his wariness and pinching," referring to frugality; Schweizer 1984: 207. Note also Ps. 49:16–20 [49:17–21 MT]; Plummer 1896: 323; Fitzmyer 1985: 972 (noting 1 Enoch 97.8–10, which rebukes unrighteous wealth); Nickelsburg 1978–79: 334–37. See n. 11 below for the Sirach and 1 Enoch texts.

9. B. Scott 1989: 135 notes that the rich man takes over the narration from the narrator, showing the theme of autonomy.

stylistic feature is the presence of the pronoun μου (*mou*, my), not to mention the numerous first-person singular verbs (Plummer 1896: 324). The fruit of the land and other elements of the parable are repeatedly described with μου: *my* fruit, *my* barn, *my* goods, *my* soul. Such language suggests exclusive self-interest, a focus that is often the natural product of "earned" wealth.

(3) Decision to Store and Rest (12:18–19)

12:18 The man moves to solve his problem. Given that he does not have sufficient storage space in his present barns, he develops a plan to expand his storage capability so that he will not lose what he now has. He will replace his barns with larger ones. The word for these storehouses (ἀποθήκας, *apothēkas*) is plural, showing the great success of his crop (Jeremias 1963a: 165; BAGD 91; BAA 182). Many new buildings are needed to cover the yield. After this expansion, he would have the capability to care not only for grain but for other goods as well. The parable pictures a man making prudent, efficient plans.

12:19 Having made plans to resolve his problems, the man concludes that he can now live in total leisure and self-indulgence.[10] Ψυχή (*psychē*, soul) is here used in self-address (as in Ps. 41:6 LXX [42:5 Engl.]; 42:5 LXX [43:5 Engl.]; Ps. Sol. 3.1; cf. Luke 12:17, 22; Fitzmyer 1985: 973; Marshall 1978: 523; Schweizer, *TDNT* 9:640–41 §D.I.3b). Jesus criticizes the man (12:21) for adopting the common philosophy of taking one's ease, eating, drinking, and being merry.[11] His future perspective is entirely self-centered and self-indulgent. As 12:21 will make clear, he has laid up treasure for himself alone. He has morally mismanaged his wealth, giving no thought to the needs of others or

---

10. B. Scott 1989: 135–36, esp. n. 26, compares this attitude to the Epicurean philosophy reflected in the inscription on Sardanapalus's tomb (recorded by Plutarch, *Moralia* 336c ["On the Fortune of Alexander" 2.3]): "Eat, drink, and sport with love; all else is nothing."

11. Fitzmyer 1985: 973; Marshall 1978: 524; Klostermann 1929: 136; Wiefel 1988: 237. Parallels for this concept are common; see 1 Cor. 15:32; Eccles. 8:15; Isa. 22:13; Tob. 7:10. Two other Jewish texts are especially relevant: Sir. 11:18–19 (NRSV) reads: "One becomes rich through diligence and self-denial, / and the reward allotted to him is this: / when he says, 'I have found rest, / and now I shall feast on my goods!' he does not know how long it will be/ until he leaves them to others and dies." 1 Enoch 97.8–10 reads: "Woe unto you who gain silver and gold by unjust means; / you will then say, 'We have grown rich and accumulated goods, / we have acquired everything that we have desired. / So now let us do whatever we like; / for we have gathered silver, / we have filled our treasuries [with money] like water. / And many are the laborers in our houses.' / Your lies flow like water. / For your wealth shall not endure / but it shall take off from you quickly / for you have acquired it all unjustly, / and you shall be given over to a great curse" (translation by E. Isaac in J. Charlesworth 1983–85: 1.78). For Hellenistic parallels, see Euripides, *Alcestis* 788–89; Menander, *Fragment* 301.

thanking God. As Nolland (1993a: 687) notes, with such a wealth of resources "his responsibilities had only just begun." The man mistakenly thinks he is only responsible for himself. The comfort that allows the man to focus on himself is the product of greed (12:15). As Marshall (1978: 524) notes, 16:19–31 gives a similar portrayal of a rich man who did not offer a crumb to a poor beggar outside his house (Bultmann, *TDNT* 2:774; James 4:13–14; 5:1–6).

(4) God's Reaction: Fool! (12:20)

Ironically, the years of ease this man eagerly anticipates are unexpectedly cut short by the one who has authority over his life (Danker 1988: 248; on drinking as reflecting selfish prosperity, see Goppelt, *TDNT* 6:139–40). He did not fulfill his moral responsibility before God to care for the needs of others. Now God issues a rebuke and takes action: he calls the man a fool and requires his soul. God rejects his covetousness (Pilgrim 1981: 110). The soul that had hoped for ease (12:19) is now ordered to attention. Ἄφρων (*aphrōn*, fool) is an important term, for in the OT a fool is one who either acts without God or without wisdom about potential destruction (Job 31:24–28; Ps. 14:1; 53:1 [53:2 MT]; Eccles. 2:1–11; Sir. 11:18–19). All the benefit of self-directed planning and labor comes crashing down by God's command. God demands an account of the man's mortal soul (ἀπαιτοῦσιν, *apaitousin*; Fitzmyer 1985: 974; Wis. 15:8 [of the short, "borrowed" time our souls live before returning to dust]; BAGD 80; BAA 159), and his grain and wealth cannot pay his debt.

12:20

The oddity of the verse is the third-person plural: "they demand your soul from you." This has been understood in one of two ways: either as the angelic execution of the task (Grundmann 1963: 258 [the angel of death, Satan; Heb. 2:14]; Marshall 1978: 524) or as a Semitic idiom for God (Job 4:19c; 6:2b; Prov. 9:11b; Creed 1930: 173; Fitzmyer 1985: 974). It is hard to be certain, since both possibilities make good sense. The point is that a heavenly call for death has been made and will be executed. It is perhaps more natural to see God referred to here, since the context discusses him and not angels. Either way, death is his sovereign call.

Regardless of the specific referent, the time for the man to report to his Creator comes just at the point when he is set to enjoy all his possessions. His life (ψυχή, *psychē*; Schweizer, *TDNT* 9:647) is over. As L. Johnson (1977: 153) notes, "The loss of the ψυχή is the loss of everything."[12]

---

12. Johnson notes that the desire for possessions may cloud one's willingness to suffer rejection on account of Christ, which is certainly part of Luke's point in having the parable in this setting (see 12:24–34).

One lingering question—one of deep irony and tragedy—remains for the man. Who will possess the things he has prepared for himself? The point of the question is that the one person who will not enjoy the ownership is the man (Arndt 1956: 316). The man has new, more eternal concerns! The pursuit of possessions has left him empty in terms of his ultimate priorities before God (the OT has similar thoughts: Job 27:16–22; Ps. 39:6 [39:7 MT]; 49:6 [49:7 MT]; 90:10; 103:15–16; Eccles. 2:18–23; Plummer 1896: 325). In this "you can't take it with you" parable, Jesus shows that to focus on possessions and not be concerned with spiritual things is a grave, long-term error. Though riches may be enjoyable in the short term, they do not exist in the long term. Their mere possession does not bring accreditation before God (James 1:9–11; 5:1–6).

ii. The Application (12:21)

12:21 Jesus applies the parable by noting that this is the fate of all who store up treasure for themselves but are not rich toward God. Οὕτως (houtōs, so it is) indicates a comparison. The basic contrast is between ἑαυτῷ (heautō, to himself) and εἰς θεόν (eis theon, toward God). The parable does not condemn planning or wealth per se. Rather, Jesus' complaint is against the person who takes wealth and directs it totally toward the self. Zacchaeus (Luke 19:1–10) will be a counterexample of a penitent rich man. Storing up treasure for oneself and not for God is the problem. "Laying up treasure" is a concept with Jewish roots (Sir. 29:8–17; Tob. 4:9; Ps. Sol. 9.5; Nolland 1993a: 687; see also the exegesis of Luke 12:33). The main element of the comparison is that wealth is ultimately a wasted accumulation, for the person cannot present it to God for admission to heaven. As Fitzmyer (1985: 974) says, "Divine scrutiny of the life given will not be concerned with barns bursting at their seams." Life does not consist of one's possessions, and to regard life as such is to be gripped by greed (Luke 12:15; Plummer 1896: 325). It is important to note that the issue in the parable is not wealth, but how wealth is directed. The sin is accumulating riches for oneself. Pilgrim (1981: 112) sees three errors: (1) hoarding one's possessions, (2) assuming that life can be secured and measured by possessions, and (3) regarding property as one's own.

Matthew 6:19 is close in concept to this passage. Paul also teaches that the love of money—not money per se—is the root of all evil (1 Tim. 6:10). It is how money can cause us to focus inwardly that is the danger. God's care is made available to those who have right priorities, as the next passage and other texts show (Luke 12:22–34 [esp. 12:33]; Ps. 37:4; Matt. 6:33; Hendriksen 1978: 664). The one who relies on God has the true wealth of life. James 4:13–17 is similar in tone, for James is not complaining about the making of plans or business arrangements, but that one does it without considering God and his will.

Summary

In Luke 12:13–21, Jesus uses a dispute over inheritance to teach about the danger of attraction to possessions. Treasure laid up only for oneself is short lived. One cannot present a suitcase full of riches to God for admission into heaven. God desires other priorities. Jesus tells all to be rich toward God. When thinking about the most beneficial way to live, long-term thinking is crucial. The disciple should realize that the pursuit of wealth is a dangerous distraction and a form of greed when it is self-directed. Wealth toward self is poverty before God. The comfort that comes from wealth and the power derived from materialism provide only a fleeting and false security, a vain effort at control. Jesus stresses that wealth is potentially a subtle, but devastating, obstacle to God. Where idols and selfish inwardness are present, God's judgment waits. Wealth's only legacy is its fleeting nature (Luke 6:24–25). Only wealth handled with generosity meets with God's approval (1 Tim. 6:17–19).

Additional Notes

12:18. It is difficult to be sure of the exact reading of the text: in various forms ℵ*, D, Itala, and Syriac read πάντα τὰ γενήματά μου (all my produce); manuscripts A, W, and Θ read πάντα τὰ γενήματά μου καὶ τὰ ἀγαθά μου (all my produce and my goods) (Marshall 1978: 523); while the UBS–NA reading, πάντα τὸν σῖτον καὶ τὰ ἀγαθά μου (all my grain and goods), is found in $\mathfrak{P}^{75}$, B, L, family 1, and family 13 (Fitzmyer 1985: 973). The meaning is not significantly altered by the options, though a broader reference of the last two options suggests a wider source of income. Either of those readings could be original, since it is hard to explain from the parable why a reference to goods (τὰ ἀγαθά) would have been added by a scribe. However, πάντα τὰ γενήματά μου καὶ τὰ ἀγαθά μου looks like a conflated reading of the other options, thus favoring the UBS–NA text.

12:20. The verb is disputed, but most manuscripts from all families attest the more difficult and less common ἀπαιτέω (to ask from), rather than the simpler αἰτέω (to ask). The former verb appears elsewhere in the NT only in 6:30, making it the harder reading.

3. Call to Avoid Anxiety (12:22–34)

Jesus continues to discuss trust with his disciples, trust for daily provision. He has warned the people with him of the dangers of putting their trust in possessions. Now he turns to his disciples and instructs them on where their trust should be placed (Luke 12:22–32; Plummer 1896: 325). As such, this unit extends the argument of the previous unit. In fact, 12:21 is virtually restated in 12:33–34 in a more concrete application. A series of illustrations from nature makes his point that they need not worry, for they can rely on God's gracious care. As God provides for the ravens, lilies, and grass, so will he provide for them. In fact, the disciples need to realize that as recipients of God's kingdom they need not be anxious, since God cares for them. A kingdom focus prevents excessive anxiety about one's earthly possessions.

In 12:33–34, Jesus encourages the disciples to use their possessions generously when he calls on them to give alms. Treasure is stored where the heart resides. This note concludes Jesus' discussion about materialism, which started with the negative example in 12:13–21. In contrast stands 12:22–34, with its positive exhortations to disciples to trust God, to be generous to others, and to seek God's kingdom.

Sources and Historicity

This section is very close in sense to two sections of Matthew's Sermon on the Mount: Luke 12:22–32 = Matt. 6:25–34 (Aland 1985: §201), and Luke 12:33–34 = Matt. 6:19–21 (Aland 1985: §202). Most attribute the material to Q (Manson 1949: 111; Grundmann 1963: 259 [12:22–32, while 12:33–34 are L tradition parallel to Matt. 6:19–21]; Tiede 1988: 234; Fitzmyer 1985: 976; Nolland 1993a: 690 [12:22–31, 33–34]). There is a high degree of verbal agreement between the passages. But there is also enough difference in wording and setting to suggest a distinct discourse, with Jesus repeating material he often used (Arndt 1956: 317). For example, Luke 12:24, 26, 29 are different from their Matthean counterparts, while 12:32–33 reflects the passage's distinct character and lacks any Matthean parallel. Marshall (1978: 525) is sufficiently impressed by the differences to speak of two versions of Q. But if this is possible, then two settings are also possible. Some see 12:25 as a logion inserted into the original tradition (Fitzmyer 1985: 976), but such a conclusion is speculative. This verse summarizes the futility of anxiety. Even though it intrudes on the three illustrations from nature, it fits the context and in fact heightens Jesus' point.

The Jesus Seminar (Funk and Hoover 1993: 339–41) agrees that the material in these verses comes from Q. A substantial portion of the unit is seen as a summary of Jesus' teaching (pink type for 12:22–25, 27–28). This material is multiply attested in Q and the Gospel of Thomas 36 and is vivid, like much of Jesus' teaching. Other portions are possibly rooted in Jesus but reformulated by the evangelist (gray type for 12:26, 29, 33–34). This material is seen either as Luke's expansion on the tradition or as being too proverbial to have a certain connection to Jesus. While recognizing that these themes fit Jesus, the seminar argues that famous sages had such material attributed to them "like iron filings are attracted to a magnet" (Funk and Hoover 1993: 341), the second time this figure is used (see p. 332). These verses are, however, multiply attested (Matt. 6:19–21; Thomas 76.3), so the material coheres nicely with Jesus' teaching and should be accepted as authentic. The seminar rejects some material as not tied to Jesus (black type for 12:30–32). The major reasons for this rejection are the theme of persecution (but see the discussion of sources and historicity for 12:1–12) and the reference to the "little flock," which, in the seminar's view, presupposes a church community. This figure has OT roots (Jer. 13:17; Ezek. 34; Zech. 10:3), however, and is thus a metaphor that Jesus could draw on. The NT verses assume a remnant perspective for Jesus, which is not surprising in a context calling for faithfulness and trust in the midst of rejection similar to that experienced by the prophets (Nolland 1993a: 694, who questions only 12:30a [p. 691]). In fact, Jesus' knowledge of John the Baptist's thrust, the reality of rejection for Jesus, and the analogy of the prophets' call for faithfulness in the face of judgment and exile speak for these verses (B. Meyer 1965). In addition, a summary application such as 12:31 is like 12:21 in form, while the passage's emphasis fits Jesus' themes of trusting the Father (the Lord's Prayer) and being generous with possessions (16:9–13, 19–31; 18:18–30; 19:1–10; see the discussion of sources and historicity for 12:13–21). The material's roots go back to Jesus, including the contrast in 12:30a with how the world does things. Such contrasts also fit Jesus (Mark 10:41–45 = Matt. 20:24–28; Luke 22:24–27).

Most of the teaching has an exhortatory and illustrative flavor. The passage has a mood of calm observation about it. Jesus appeals to a pastoral setting and gets his audience to focus on the gentle and constant care that God gives to birds and flowers. The illustrations (12:22–23; 12:29–30; 12:31–32; 12:33–34) share the similar structure: an exhortation followed by an explanation introduced by γάρ (*gar*, for) (12:31–32 omits γάρ). In fact, the flow of the passage moves from exhortation to illustration, repeats the basic exhortation, and then concludes with two more exhortations (Gospel of Thomas 36 has a variation of the theme present here).

The form of the account includes minatory sayings and prophetic counsel (Fitzmyer 1985: 976). Berger (1984: 194) speaks of an exhortation and admonition speech. The outline of Luke 12:22–34 is as follows:

a. Call not to be anxious (12:22–32)
   i. Exhortation: do not be anxious (12:22)
   ii. Reason: life is more than food and clothing (12:23)
   iii. Illustration: birds (12:24a)
   iv. Principle: you are more valuable than birds (12:24b)
   v. Reason: can you add to life by worrying? (12:25)
   vi. Reason: since worry does not help, why worry? (12:26)
   vii. Illustration: lilies (12:27)
   viii. Illustration: grass (12:28a)
   ix. Principle and call to faith: you are more important than lilies and grass (12:28b)
   x. Exhortation: do not be anxious (12:29)
   xi. Reason: your Father knows your needs (12:30)
   xii. Exhortation: seek God's kingdom (12:31)
   xiii. Assurance: God will give the kingdom to his children (12:32)
b. Call to sell possessions and give alms (12:33–34)
   i. Exhortation: sell possessions and give alms (12:33)
   ii. Reason: where your treasure is, your heart is (12:34)

The passage is a call not to be anxious about daily needs. Life is more than concern about food and clothes, as seen in the lessons from God's care of creation. Jesus' exhortation is based on the value of people in creation. Anxiety is useless; in fact, it reveals lack of faith. God knows one's needs. So seek his kingdom and one's daily needs will be met. God gives the kingdom to his children. Seeking his kingdom includes caring for others, so there is a call to sell possessions and be generous. In short, look at priorities: Where one's treasure is, there is one's heart.

Exegesis and Exposition

[22]But he said to his disciples, "Therefore I tell you, do not be anxious for yourself, about what you will eat or with what you will clothe the body. [23]For life is more than food, and the body more than clothing. [24]Consider the ravens: they neither sow nor reap; they have neither storehouse nor barn; and God feeds them. How much more value you are than the birds. [25]And

which of you by worrying can add an hour to his span of life? [26]If therefore you are unable to do such a trivial thing, why do you worry about the rest? [27]Consider the lilies: how they grow; they neither labor nor ⌜spin⌝; yet I say to you, Solomon in all of his glory was not clothed like one of these. [28]But if God so clothes the grass that today is alive in the field and tomorrow is cast into the oven, how much more will he clothe you, O you of little faith! [29]And do not seek what you are to eat and drink, and do not be of anxious mind. [30]For such things all the nations of the world seek; but your Father knows you need these things. [31]Nevertheless, seek ⌜God's⌝ kingdom and all these things will be added to you. [32]Do not fear, little flock, for your Father is pleased to give you the kingdom.

[33]"Sell your possessions, and give alms; provide yourselves with purses that do not grow old, with a treasure in the heavens that does not fail, where no thief approaches and no moth destroys. [34]For where your treasure is, there your heart will be also."

a. Call Not to Be Anxious (12:22–32)
i. Exhortation: Do Not Be Anxious (12:22)

After warning all about valuing possessions too highly, Jesus turns to address his disciples about trusting God (the contrastive δέ, *de*, but, signals the transition of audience). The connection between the two sets of exhortations suggest that the security that many look for in possessions is to be found only in God. Jesus says in effect that danger is found in storing up treasure for oneself and not for God. One should not deal with anxiety by pursuing possessions; rather one should trust God to meet needs (this is the force of διὰ τοῦτο, *dia touto*, because of this). Jesus tells them not to be anxious about what they will eat or wear.

12:22

The present imperative μεριμνᾶτε (*merimnate*, do not worry) looks at a constant attitude. A lack of anxiety about basic daily needs is to characterize the disciple (Marshall 1978: 526; Bultmann, *TDNT* 4:589–93). People are subject to God, whether they accept it or not; so it is best to look to him. In fact, the absence of anxiety involves trusting one's care to him, as the allusion to the soul (τῇ ψυχῇ, *tē psychē*) makes clear (Ellis 1974: 178).[1] The reasons for having an absence of anxiety follow in 12:23–28. The point is not asceticism, but a life lived with an eye to God, as he meets one's needs (Manson 1949: 111).

The Matthean statement is similar: Matt. 6:25a makes the same exhortation, except it adds a reference to "what you should drink" and has the possessive pronoun *your* connected to soul and body.

---

1. The dative is to be read as "for yourself" not "in yourself," as the repetition of ψυχή in 12:23 shows; Plummer 1896: 326.

ii. Reason: Life Is More Than Food and Clothing (12:23)

12:23   Jesus gives a reason (γάρ, *gar*) for his call not to worry. He offers a two-part assertion that sounds like a proverb: life is more than food, and the body is more than clothing. The point seems to be that, since there is more to life than food and clothing, to be overly concerned with them is to miss life's important concern—a relationship with God (1 Tim. 6:6–19). The illustrations of nature in 12:24, 27, 28 operate on the level of food (ravens) and clothing (lilies and grass). God will care for these basics. Food and clothing only sustain and shield us. As Danker (1988: 249) says, "Living is more than having." The Lord's Prayer shows the proper relationship (11:3–4). Daily needs are to be placed in God's hands and seen in relationship to him (Ernst 1977: 402), which is similar to the statement of 4:4 that people do not live by bread alone, but by every word that comes from God (1 Pet. 5:7; Marshall 1978: 526).

In Matt. 6:25 Jesus' statement is a question, introduced with the interrogative οὐχί (*ouchi*, is not?). That passage confirms how this explanation should be read. The question in Matthew expects a positive reply, conveying the idea that life is indeed more than food and clothing.

iii. Illustration: Birds (12:24a)
iv. Principle: You Are More Valuable Than Birds (12:24b)

12:24   The first example from nature is the ravens, the only NT reference to them (Job 38:41; Ps. 147:9 [146:9 LXX]; Plummer 1896: 326). Κόρακας (*korakas*, ravens) refers to a whole variety of crows residing in Palestine. Ernst (1977: 402) notes that they are unclean creatures (Lev. 11:15; Deut. 14:14). In antiquity, they were among the least respected of birds (Fitzmyer 1985: 978). But God even cares for them. The point is not to be as careless as ravens, but to show how comprehensive God's care is (Nolland 1993a: 692). Such illustrations from nature are common in the OT and Judaism (SB 2:191; Grundmann 1963: 260; Manson 1949: 112–13; Job 8:12; 14:2; 38:41; Ps. 37:2; 90:5–6; 103:15; Isa. 37:27; 1 Enoch 2.1–5.4; *Sipre* 306.1 on Deut. 32:1 [= Neusner 1987: 2.297–99]). The theme of the OT passages is that these created things come and go, but Jesus notes God's general care in that they do not labor to produce their food. In fact, they do not have a place to store food in vast quantities, yet God manages to feed them. Jesus then reminds the disciples that they are more important to God than the birds. The force of the "how much more" argument is clear. God will surely care for them, so they need not be anxious (Marshall 1978: 526–27). Speaking of the Matthean passage, McNeile (1915: 87) says, "The birds are an example not of idleness but of freedom from anxiety." Luce (1933: 231) adds, "They are not always worrying that the supply of worms may run out; yet they do not expect the worms to crawl down their beaks."

Matthew 6:26 refers to birds in general, while using a distinct verb in asking the disciples to examine the birds' habit: ἐμβλέψατε (emblepsate, observe) where Luke has κατανοήσατε (katanoēsate, consider).[2] Matthew refers to the heavenly Father feeding the birds and lacks a reference to a storehouse. Matthew closes with a question, as he did earlier in this unit, rather than with a statement. None of these changes alters the force, but the reasons for the changes, if Luke and Matthew used the same source, are less than clear. Distinct situations are possible.

v. Reason: Can You Add to Life by Worrying? (12:25)

Continuing his appeal not to worry, Jesus offers a practical objection: worrying is useless. This is the third reason that Jesus offers (Marshall 1978: 527).[3] The meaning is disputed: does the rhetorical question ask whether worrying can add any time to one's life or any height to one's stature? Ἡλικίαν (hēlikian) is ambiguous and may refer to the span of life or to the height of a person (BAGD 345; BAA 699). As a unit of measure πῆχυς (pēchys, cubit; BAGD 656–57; BAA 1322) refers to about eighteen inches (Fitzmyer 1985: 978); as a measure of time it can refer to an hour. Creed (1930: 174) points out the metaphorical use of a measure of length for a period of time in Ps. 39:4 [39:5 MT] (a small amount of time in Diogenes Laertius 3.11; Nolland 1993a: 692). Ἡλικία is used with reference to age in John 9:21, 23; Heb. 11:11. The figure about adding height through worry also communicates the uselessness of worrying (Danker 1988: 250; Manson 1949: 113; Talbert 1982: 142). Length of life is a more important item of worry for people than height. In addition, the thought of adding eighteen inches to one's height is a grotesque image, and it certainly does not qualify for the "little thing" mentioned in Luke 12:26 (Plummer 1896: 326; Fitzmyer 1985: 979; Marshall 1978: 528; J. Schneider, TDNT 2:941–43). It is hard to be certain which picture is intended, but time is more likely. In either case, the expected answer is that worrying does no good. Nothing is gained by it.

12:25

Except for word order and the presence of ἕνα (hena, one), Matt. 6:27 is similar to Luke (although the Matthean question centers spe-

---

2. Marshall 1978: 527 notes that no clear reason for the difference can be given. But Fitzmyer 1985: 978 observes that Luke often uses the verb κατανοέω: Luke 6:41; 12:24, 27; 20:23; Acts 7:31–32; 11:6; 27:39.

3. The first reason was that life consists of more than food and clothing. The second was that God cares for people in his creation.

cifically on adding one cubit to the span of life). Some regard the verse as an intrusion on the sequence of illustrations from nature, and it is. But such a break, a rhetorical aside, need not be understood as an extraneous insertion. Such asides are common in speech and in fact can have rhetorical value by breaking up a series of similar points.

vi. Reason: Since Worry Does Not Help, Why Worry? (12:26)

12:26 Jesus develops his rationale about the pointlessness of worrying: if a person cannot do a little thing like adding a little time to one's life span, then why worry about other matters that may well be beyond one's control and will not add to one's life (Marshall 1978: 528). The condition is stated as a current given, since it is a first-class condition (εἰ, *ei*, if, with the indicative). As such, the condition says that one is not able to do the "least" thing (Plummer 1896: 327). The disciples cannot add to their life by worry, so energy is wasted when it is directed toward things over which one has no control. The Matthean parallel lacks this remark.

vii. Illustration: Lilies (12:27)

12:27 Lilies are the second example from nature. Jesus tells the disciples to consider (κατανοήσατε, *katanoēsate*; the same verb as in 12:24) the lilies. Manson (1949: 112) suggests that the specific flower may be the purple anemone, which would compare to a king's purple royal garb (Grundmann 1963: 261; for other options, see Fitzmyer 1985: 979). Jesus notes that these flowers neither labor nor spin (an Aramaic wordplay may lie behind the phrase; Manson 1949: 112). Yet the lilies are more beautifully clothed than Solomon, the wealthiest of Israel's kings (1 Kings 10:4–23; esp. 2 Chron. 9:13–21).

Matthew 6:28–29 is worded much like Luke. Matthew speaks of the lilies "of the field." In addition, the verbs are plural rather than Luke's singular. The major point is similar to Luke: if God cares for the flowers, he will certainly care for you.

viii. Illustration: Grass (12:28a)

12:28a The third natural illustration, the grass, is laid out in a "how much more" argument like 12:24. The conditional clause is a first-class condition, so the presentation stresses that God does cloth the grass. The description of grass as being "here today but burned tomorrow" shows its insignificance. Nonetheless, God still attends to this part of creation. In the OT, grass is often a figure for transitoriness (Job 8:12; Ps. 37:2; 90:5–6; 102:11 [102:12 MT]; 103:15; Isa. 37:27; 40:6–8) and the NT (1 Pet. 1:24; Fitzmyer 1985: 979; Marshall 1978: 529; Tiede 1988: 236). The reference to burning describes the use of dry grass to fuel an oven (Luce 1933: 232; Creed 1930: 174).

ix. Principle and Call to Faith: You Are More Important Than Lilies and Grass (12:28b)

Jesus closes with a reminder and a rebuke. He reminds the disciples **12:28b** that they are more important than grass and rebukes their little faith, which suggests that they are susceptible to forgetting this truth. The reminder is also a rebuke, for anxiety shows that one believes that God is not in control; it reflects weak faith. Some things are out of one's control, and this reality should be accepted. However, disciples can trust that God is aware of their plight and cares about it. This is the only place that Luke uses the term ὀλιγόπιστος (*oligopistos*, little faith; elsewhere in the NT at Matt. 6:30; 8:26; 14:31; 16:8; Fitzmyer 1985: 979; in Judaism, SB 1:438–39).

Matthew 6:30 is close to Luke. Except for word order, there are two main differences: Matthew, as is common in this unit, has the plural ἀμφιέννυσιν (*amphiennysin*, they are clothed), not Luke's singular (ἀμφιέζει, *amphiezei*, it is clothed). Also, Matthew ends the remark, as is his custom in this pericope, with a question (οὐ πολλῷ μᾶλλον ὑμᾶς, *ou pollō mallon hymas*, are you not much more?), whereas Luke has a statement (πόσῳ μᾶλλον ὑμᾶς, *posō mallon hymas*, how much more you). Matthew's rhetorical question, which expects a positive reply, equals Luke's statement. These parallel the Matthean differences with Luke 12:23–24, 27.

x. Exhortation: Do Not Be Anxious (12:29)

Having illustrated his point, Jesus returns to his basic exhortation **12:29** of 12:22: disciples are not to be anxious about basic needs like food and drink. The *hapax legomenon* μετεωρίζεσθε (*meteōrizesthe*) normally means "to be lifted up, be puffed up" and can mean "to be overbearing."[4] It is a graphic picture of hovering between hope and fear, between heaven and earth (Danker 1988: 251). The picture is of anxious, emotional insecurity and instability as it races between various emotions. An idiomatic equivalent might be "to get worked up" over something. One who recognizes that God cares can be spared such anxious mood swings.

Matthew has no real parallel to this remark; the closest expression is Matt. 6:31, where Jesus reverses the order and uses different terms to say do not worry about what you eat, drink, or wear.[5] The exhortation is similar to a later remark attributed to Rabbi Eleazar,

---

4. Ps. 130:1 LXX [131:1 Engl.]; Josephus, *Antiquities* 16.4.6 §135; Marshall 1978: 529; Deissner, *TDNT* 4:630–31; Fitzmyer 1985: 980; BAGD 514; BAA 1041; P. Oxy. vol. 14 #1679 line 16 (where it is a term for "wrong").

5. Thus, it is useless to speak of the "original form" of this saying, which many regard as Matthew; Manson 1949: 113.

"Whoever has bread in his basket and asks, 'What shall I eat tomorrow?' is none other than those of little faith" (b. Soṭa 48b).[6]

xi. Reason: Your Father Knows Your Needs (12:30)

12:30 Jesus provides an explanation (γάρ, *gar*) to reassure the disciples. Unbelievers, Jesus argues, habitually seek such things. That is, they worry about the things of life. In contrast, the Father knows his children need such things. The point is clear. Since you are different from other people because of your relationship to the Father, do not worry, for he will care for you (Danker 1988: 251). The picture of God as Father is common to Luke (2:49; 6:36; 9:26; 11:2, 13; 22:29; 24:49; Fitzmyer 1985: 980). It adds a note of intimacy to the reminder. The phrase *nations of the world* is common in rabbinic expression (Grundmann 1963: 261; SB 2:191; *t. Soṭa* 13.8 [= Neusner 1977–86: 3.203]; *t. Ber.* 1.12 [= Neusner 1977–86: 1.5]). Luke is saying that disciples should not act like the rest of the world when it comes to being anxious, because disciples know the Father who cares for them. Security comes from the realization that God actively cares for his children.

Matthew 6:32 is similar in tone. Luke has "all the nations of the world," while Matthew speaks of the nations seeking "all" these things. Matthew also says that the Father "in heaven" knows you need "all" these things. Arguing for a different Lucan sense, Marshall (1978: 529) says that Luke, as is his custom (16:14; 18:21; 21:12, 36; 24:9), connects ταῦτα (*tauta*, these things) with πάντα (*panta*, all), a connection that would put Matthew and Luke in agreement, since the resulting reference would be to "all of these things." However, word order suggests that πάντα be connected to the nations, which is reflected in the translation "all the nations." The difference is not significant, especially if separate settings are present.

xii. Exhortation: Seek God's Kingdom (12:31)

12:31 Now comes the positive exhortation. What is to be the disciple's priority? Jesus puts it simply: seek God's kingdom. The present tense ζητεῖτε (*zēteite*, seek) indicates that this is to be the disciple's habit; that is, "keep seeking his kingdom." Disciples are to be engaged in the pursuit of representing God on earth. They are to seek God's rule (K. Schmidt, *TDNT* 1:588). God's followers are to respond to his call to walk as he desires. Followers also share in the spiritual benefits that come from such a walk (11:2). God's commitment to

---

6. Manson 1949: 113 notes that many pagan religions had rituals to coerce the gods to provide material provision.

disciples is to offer care, to provide fundamental things such as food and shelter. The reference to "the things added" alludes to life's basics, not vast material gain. This limitation is indicated by Luke 12 as a whole. But to use guilt as a tactic against those who have material holdings is not the point of such a verse either (though concern for how such holdings are used is indicated by 12:32). The point is simply that God promises to provide basic needs for his disciples. Matthew 6:33 has a longer form of this saying. He speaks of seeking "first" God's kingdom "and his righteousness," and "all" these things shall be added to you. These are not different ideas, since to seek his kingdom is to seek to live in a way that honors God's presence and rule.

xiii. Assurance: God Will Give the Kingdom to His Children (12:32)

Assurance follows. Disciples are to seek the kingdom; and yet they **12:32** are assured that the Father is committed, willing, even pleased to give them the kingdom. To speak of God's pleasure is to speak of his will (Mark 1:11; Luke 2:14; 10:21; Grundmann 1963: 262). Because the Father is pleased there is no reason (ὅτι, *hoti*) to fear (1:13, 30; 5:10; Marshall 1978: 530). Fear is probably a result of anticipating the pressure or persecution that the disciples will experience for responding to Jesus (12:1–12; Ellis 1974: 178). Such pressure brings terrific uncertainty about the future, so that anxiety is a natural response.

The tenderness of the reassurance is expressed in the address to the disciples as "little flock," an OT figure for God's fragile yet cared for people (Ps. 23:1; 28:9; 74:1; 77:20 [77:21 MT]; Isa. 40:11; Jer. 13:17; Zech. 11:11; 13:7; Matt. 9:36 = Mark 6:34; 14:27; John 10:12; Acts 20:28–29; Ellis 1974: 179; Ernst 1977: 404; Klostermann 1929: 137). The image adds to the picture of risk (suggested by the call not to fear), since it assumes that people are fragile.

With the call to trust, a promise is given that the Father is pleased to give his children the kingdom. The promise of the kingdom is not specified or described in detail. What seems to be in view are kingdom blessings that are the product of pursuing the kingdom. In other words, pursuit of the kingdom is a goal that can be realized. Above all, secure relationship with God is alluded to in the promise, one that can bring stability and absence of anxiety.

This verse has no Matthean parallel. Some suggest that it is a Lucan addition, while others suggest uncertainty about its origin (Fitzmyer 1985: 976 notes the options, but is undecided; Bultmann 1963: 111 rejects its authenticity). There is no reason to reject its tie to Jesus. Official Judaism clearly was reacting to his ministry, so that pressure on him and his followers was inevitable (see the discussion of sources and historicity above). Of course, Luke's readers would understand this reassurance to the disciples as applying to them as well.

b. Call to Sell Possessions and Give Alms (12:33–34)
i. Exhortation: Sell Possessions and Give Alms (12:33)

12:33 Jesus points the disciples to permanent treasure. He exhorts them to sell their possessions and offer alms, that is, give charitably to the poor. Pursuing the kingdom means caring for others, rather than for self. The security that one has in God frees one to be generous with possessions and to be generous with others (L. Johnson 1977: 155).[7] Alms were often regarded as an act of piety, both in the NT and in Judaism.[8] To show concern for others rather than for oneself is at the heart of Jesus' teaching, where love for others has a high place. To give up possessions to aid the poor shows the highest degree of such commitments.

The value of such action is that its significance can never be taken away or destroyed. The figurative reference to purses that do not grow old alludes to the money bag (βαλλάντιον, *ballantion*) used by business owners (Rengstorf, *TDNT* 1:525–26; BAGD 130; BAA 263; only in Luke's Gospel: 10:4; here; 22:35, 36). The picture of the thief and the moth suggests that nothing can affect the quality of such work. Moths are a common figure for riches that are naturally spoiled, since the little creatures can ruin expensive clothes. They depict decay (Marshall 1978: 532; Bauernfeind, *TDNT* 7:275–77). Heavenly treasure will not fail or spoil, unlike its earthly counterpart, which can disappear in a fleeting moment because it stays bolted to earth upon death. The picture is of heavenly treasure laid in nonperishable (ἀνέκλειπτον, *anekleipton*; BAGD 64; BAA 127; a NT *hapax legomenon*) receptacles. Such treasure is laid up in heaven for the one who cares for those in need. The treasure refers to the

---

7. With reference to seeking the kingdom, Tiede 1988: 238 says, "This reign may well seem foolish and vulnerable by the standards of those who have wealth and power, but it is the very strength of God for living in uncertain times with the security of God's reign."

8. Tob. 2:14; 4:7–11; 12:9; 14:8–11; Sir. 3:30; 29:12; 2 Enoch 50.5; Ps. Sol. 9.5; *m. Pe'a* 1.1; *t. Pe'a* 4.17–21 (= Neusner 1977–86: 1.45, 72–75); SB 1:430; Grundmann 1963: 262–63; Talbert 1982: 142; Wiefel 1988: 241; Matt. 19:21 = Mark 10:21 = Luke 18:22; 12:21. On the custom of alms, see BAGD 249–50; BAA 504. Ἐλεημοσύνη refers literally to "acts of mercy"; Bultmann, *TDNT* 2:486; Dan. 4:27 [4:24 MT]. Interestingly, the refrain of *t. Pe'a* 4.18 is, "My ancestors stored up treasures of money, but I have stored up treasures." The object of the last clause is not clear ("for heaven," "of benefits," "of souls," or "for myself in the world to come"), but the point about the value of alms is clear.

benefits of being faithful to God, so that one stores up God's plea-sure by having done his will. This faithfulness reaps rich, everlasting reward as a result (1 Cor. 3:10–15; 2 Cor. 5:10). God notices where people place their accounts, and death does not close them. Lack of attachment to possessions is a constant NT theme (1 Cor. 7:30; 1 Tim. 6:7–19; Luke 14:33 [an exposition of 12:33]; Plummer 1896: 329). The stress is not on literally selling all, but on making use of one's resources in a way that benefits others.[9] Zacchaeus is the pos-itive example of how resources are to be used (19:1–10).

This exhortation is given here because of the persecution a disci-ple will face. This opposition might lead to martyrdom or the de-struction of one's possessions. To be tied to possessions might cause a disciple to be divided in allegiance. Others attribute the re-marks to an eschatological expectation of the kingdom's nearness, but this is not clear (Luce 1933: 233). Acts 2 and 4 show that this exhortation was put into practice in Jerusalem, but it was not in-sisted upon. Rather, it was undertaken voluntarily, as seen in Pe-ter's recognition of Ananias and Sapphira's right to keep some pro-ceeds (Acts 5). This response to Jesus' teaching shows that the expression probably addressed an attitude of readiness to give over all into God's service.

Matthew 6:19–21 is similar in concept, though in Luke this verse has very distinct wording. Where Matthew speaks of laying up trea-sure as the main exhortation, Luke has a direct, nonfigurative com-mand to sell possessions and give alms. The Lucan command is summarized by the aorist tense and calls for decisive action (T. Schmidt 1987: 148). Both accounts, however, share the next verse's proverbial expression: where your treasure is, there your heart is also. Distinct sayings are more than likely.[10]

ii. Reason: Where Your Treasure Is, Your Heart Is (12:34)

Jesus explains the rationale for his exhortation with a proverbial **12:34** saying about loyalty. One is loyal to the things one values most. The references to the heart and to treasure are figurative for "priorities"

9. Pilgrim 1981: 94 says that it is selling all "in the service of the kingdom and the discipleship of Jesus" and that the remark is for all disciples.

10. Manson 1949: 114 regards the material as coming from distinct sources, as does Grundmann 1963: 262, though they differ as to which sources and give no rea-sons. Marshall 1978: 531 argues for the same source, but the distinct wording is a dif-ficulty for that view. Fitzmyer 1985: 981 argues that 12:33a is Lucan and cites 11:41 for support, but that verse is figurative for one's life and is not similar enough to argue that Luke created this saying. In addition, Fitzmyer argues that Luke abridged Mat-thew's saying, but this cannot explain entirely the distinct terminology. Wiefel 1988: 241 sees Q and special L material here that Luke combined to answer the point made in 12:21.

and "that which is valued." If one values people, then one will work to meet their needs. If one values self, then one will collect possessions that perish. As Danker (1972: 152) says, "If one's bank deposit is made in Heaven First National, then the real choices of a man's life will be governed by that perspective." If so, one will invest in others.

The parallel in Matt. 6:21 is similar (see also the Gospel of Thomas 76). Differences are limited to word order, since the verb in the last line comes earlier in Matthew. In addition, Matthew uses the singular in contrast to Luke's plural, an interesting reversal of verb number from 12:23–24, 27. Hellenistic parallels also exist (Epictetus 2.22.19; Sextus Empiricus, *Sentences* 1.136; Fitzmyer 1985: 983; Marshall 1978: 532; Nolland 1993a: 695).[11]

Summary   Luke 12:22–34 takes a look at the disciple's basic approach to life. Jesus reminds his disciples that worry is not to be characteristic of the believer, because it is the result of a faulty view of God. A proper view of creation and God's providence illustrates the correct view. God cares for the things of nature, and yet people are more important to him than are created things. God knows what his children need and he will provide the basics of life for those who know him. Anxiety is fruitless and ultimately reflects an absence of faith. It also reflects a self-focus that inhibits one from doing God's will. Rather the disciple is to seek God's kingdom, the realization of his promises, and his will. God will bless the seeker and promises to care for him or her. The disciple is not to hoard possessions, but to use them to meet the needs of those less fortunate. Real heavenly treasure is concerned to receive God's approval, which can never pass away. When one seeks such treasure, attention will be directed not at oneself and at things that fade away, but at those who stand in need, because God has called the disciple to love others. Attachment to the God of heaven manifests itself in an absence of attachment to the things of earth. God calls the disciple not to care for things, but to care for him and the people he created. Anxiety is self-focus, but treasure—and life—is found in God and in service to others.

Additional Notes

12:27. The vast majority of witnesses from various families read νήθει (spin; BAGD 537; BAA 1087) instead of ὑφαίνει (weave; BAGD 849; BAA

---

11. Grundmann 1963: 263 notes the contrast of Jesus' position to the Stoics, who tried to live without possessions and who tried to have no need of other people, so they could be "like the gods"; Diogenes Laertius 6.104. Danker 1988: 253 notes that monastic withdrawal is not the answer either, since Jesus assumes compassionate engagement with people.

1693). The manuscript evidence for the first reading is superior to any claims to a possible assimilation to Matt. 6:28, which is attested only in the Western text (Marshall 1978: 528).

12:31. Most manuscripts read τοῦ θεοῦ (of God; $\mathfrak{P}^{45}$, A, W, Δ, Θ, Byz, many Itala) rather than αὐτοῦ (his; ℵ, B, D, L, Ψ, some Itala, Coptic), so the reference is to "the kingdom of God," not "his kingdom." The difference in meaning is minimal. Given the external evidence, τοῦ θεοῦ may well be original.

4. Call to Be Ready and Faithful Stewards: Parable of the Faithful and Unfaithful Servants (12:35–48)

Treasure in heaven is to be the focus of a disciple's life. The disciples have just been instructed to trust God by not worrying, and now Jesus turns to how they are to live before God. How does trust express itself? Disciples are to live in light of the end-time. Jesus deals with their life in light of the things that await fulfillment. Recounting one of the most eschatologically oriented of Jesus' parables, this pericope concerns how disciples are to live in the face of Jesus' absence and return (Tannehill 1986: 249–51).[1] How should the disciples' conduct relate to the decisive return of God through his agent of judgment, the Son of Man? Jesus' discussion about seeking the kingdom (Luke 12:31) leads naturally into a discussion about the culmination of the kingdom (Danker 1988: 253). Though much material in Luke stresses the present kingdom, this pericope looks to its decisive coming through a demonstration of Jesus' authority in judgment. How are the disciples to respond to the reality of Jesus' return to judge in authority?

In the parable, the emphasis is on being faithful and ready at all times. One does not know the time of the master's return, so in the face of his absence, one should treat people decently. One should always be prepared for the master's return, when he will evaluate his servants' faithfulness. Those servants who are faithful in his absence will sit at the blessed banquet table and feast with the master. But those who ignore the fact of his return, act corruptly, and abuse those around them will receive rebuke. The nature of the judgment is not entirely clear and is one of the difficulties of the passage that must await further examination. The basic theme is evident: be faithful and attentive to the return of the master. Such faithfulness will be reflected in how one treats others.

---

1. This exhortation is similar to other Lucan texts: Acts 20:18–35, dealing with the responsibility of church leaders, and Luke 19:12–27.

Sources and Historicity

The Lucan setting for the parable and its explanation is unique. A similar version of the parable proper is found in Matt. 24:42–51 (Aland 1985: §203; Gospel of Thomas 21).[2] What Luke relates in the midst of Jesus' ministry to his disciples, Matthew records in the Olivet Discourse as part of Jesus' last week on earth. Much of Luke's unit (12:35–38, 47–48) has no parallel in Matthew, which may show that Jesus taught the parable on multiple occasions. Distinct traditions could be in view, though most regard the texts as being drawn from the same source.[3]

The clear reference to Jesus' return leads many scholars to regard the verses as reflective of the early church and not Jesus, at least in their current form (Marshall 1978: 533–34 cites Jeremias 1963a: 48–51; Grässer 1960: 84–95; and Schulz 1972: 268–77). So also the Jesus Seminar (Funk and Hoover 1993: 341–42) gives this as the major reason for rejecting the authenticity of 12:40, 42–48 (printed in black type). The seminar reads 12:35–39 (printed in gray type) as having roots in Jesus' teaching but heavily restyled. The key assumption behind this view is that Jesus did not teach about his own return or the Son of Man's return. The problem with this assumption is that without such teaching it is hard to understand how such a view emerged in the early church. Nolland (1993a: 699) argues that the boldness of the thief comparison indicates the tie to Jesus. The thief image left a deep impression on the early church, which suggests roots to Jesus (1 Thess. 5:2–4; 2 Pet. 3:10; Rev. 3:3; 16:15). In fact, of all the types of Son-of-Man sayings, the most widely distributed are the apocalyptic Son-of-Man texts:

2. Mark 13:32–37 is at best a conceptual parallel to this Lucan unit.

3. Luce 1933: 233; Manson 1949: 117–18; and Schneider 1977a: 288 say that the basic source is Q, while 12:47–48 is L. Tiede 1988: 238–42 and Marshall 1978: 533 see all but 12:41, 47–48 as coming from Q. Ellis 1974: 180 is undecided. Godet 1875: 2.106, 110–11 sees Luke and Matthew using different portions of the same tradition. Grundmann 1963: 264; Fitzmyer 1985: 984–85; and Wiefel 1988: 242, 244 regard the unique material as coming from Luke's special source, while the parable is a mix of Q (12:39–40, 42b–46) and L (12:35–38 for Grundmann and Fitzmyer; 12:36, 37a, 38 for Wiefel). These three treat 12:41–42a and 12:47–48 as Lucan additions. Grundmann defends the remark's authenticity as involving an original warning that included the Pharisees. A Matthean prioritist sees Matthew where others have Q, though the issue of Luke's placement of this pericope is more of a problem for the Two-Gospel hypothesis, than for a sayings source such as Q. Why did Luke change the location if he had Matthew? The possibility of other sources cannot be ruled out. The views on sources for this pericope are complex, but most see Luke bringing two sets of images together (12:35–38 and 12:42–46). For full discussions, see Weiser 1971: 161–225; Schneider 1975: 20–27; and D. Wenham 1984: 15–100. Wenham's work is part of a larger hypothesis on a pre-Synoptic form of Jesus' eschatological teaching, a view that traces substantial portions of this material back to Jesus, including 12:41, 44, 47–48, which others deny have such roots.

Marcan	Mark 8:38 = Matt. 16:27 = Luke 9:26
	Mark 13:26 = Matt. 24:30 = Luke 21:27
	Mark 14:62 = Matt. 26:64 = Luke 22:69
Q	Matt. 24:27 (like Luke 17:24)
	Matt. 24:37 (like Luke 17:26)
	Matt. 24:39 (like Luke 17:30)
	Luke 12:8 (Matt. 10:32 lacks the title)
M	Matt. 10:23
	Matt. 13:41
	Matt. 19:28 (Luke 22:30 lacks the title)
	Matt. 24:44
	Matt. 25:31
L	Luke 17:22

The critical principle of multiple attestation argues for the authenticity of these sayings. Marshall (1978: 534; 1973a: 16–25) rightly notes that Jesus clearly taught an "in-between" phase in his career and prepared the disciples for it. There is no incompatibility between not knowing the time of the return and calling for readiness since the return might come soon (Luke 12:35–38; 17:26–30; 21:34; Nolland 1993a: 700; Marshall 1978: 539). There is no need then to doubt the passage's essential authenticity.[4]

Fitzmyer (1985: 985) and Bultmann (1963: 118, 171) see a mixture of exhortation (12:35–38), similitude (12:39–40), and parable (12:42b–46). Berger (1984: 57, 129) speaks of a parenesis about the return and a parable discourse. Others speak simply and accurately of three parables here: 12:35–38; 12:39–40; 12:41–46 (Schneider 1975: 16). A question in 12:41 links the parts together and 12:47–48 is an extended application.

The outline of Luke 12:35–48 is as follows:

a. Parable on being prepared for the Master's return (12:35–36)
b. Blessing for those found waiting (12:37–38)
c. Parable on being ready for the return of the Son of Man (12:39–40)

4. Fitzmyer 1985: 987 speaks of elements going back to Jesus that focus on God's final vindicating judgment. This approach may be too broad in ignoring the Son of Man–Jesus linkage, about whose secondary character Fitzmyer is uncertain. Nolland 1993a: 700 accepts all the material as authentic except 12:42, 46c, 47–48. Though some Lucan summary touches exist (e.g., 12:41–42a), all of the material, including Peter's question, coheres with Jesus' teaching. For a defense of the traditional roots of 12:41, see D. Wenham 1984: 57–62.

d. Parable of the stewards (12:41–48)
    i. Peter's question (12:41)
    ii. Faithful steward (12:42–44)
    iii. Unfaithful steward (12:45–46)
    iv. Additional judgments according to knowledge
      (12:47–48)

The major focus of the pericope is being ready for Jesus' return. Blessings exist for the servant who awaits the Lord's return, namely, a seat at the banquet table. One must be ready because of the uncertainty about when the Lord will return. Jesus offers a promise that the faithful steward will receive much responsibility upon the Lord's return. In contrast stand various levels of unfaithfulness, which is expressed in a careless, unkind lifestyle or in disobedience. All who do not respond will be punished to varying degrees, depending on the amount of unfaithfulness and knowledge. The more one knows, the greater one's responsibility. Such people will be subject to more rigorous standards at the judgment.

Exegesis and Exposition

35"Let your loins be girded and your lamps burning, 36and be as men who are waiting for their master to return from the wedding feast, so that they may open to him at once when he comes and knocks.

37"Blessed are those servants whom the master finds waiting when he comes; truly I say to you that he will gird himself and recline at the table with them and, coming, he will serve them. 38If he comes in the second watch or in the third and he finds them so, blessed are those servants.

39"But know this, if the homeowner knew what hour the thief comes, ⌐he would not have left⌐ his house to be broken into. 40And you be ready, for the Son of Man comes at an hour when you do not think."

41And Peter said, "Do you tell this parable for us or for all?" 42And the Lord said, "Who then is the faithful steward, the wise one, whom the master shall set over all his household, to give them at the proper time their measure of food? 43Blessed is that servant whom when the master comes he finds doing so. 44Truly I say to you, he will set him over all his possessions. 45But if that servant says in his heart, 'My master is gone for a long time,' and he begins to beat the menservants and maidservants and to eat, drink, and get drunk, 46the master of that servant will come on a day when he does not expect him and at an hour he does not know, and will dismember him, and put his portion with the unfaithful. 47But that slave who knows the will of the master and does not make ready or act according to his will, he will receive a severe beating. 48But the one who does not know and does that which is worthy of a beating shall receive few blows. Everyone to whom much is given, much is required; and of him to whom they commit much, more they will ask of him."

a. Parable on Being Prepared for the Master's Return (12:35–36)

12:35　The unit begins with two images of preparedness. The first image, the girding up of the loins, pictures readiness.[5] Long garments in the ancient world were drawn up around the loins whenever anyone wanted to move quickly. The perfect imperative ἔστωσαν (*estōsan*) with the participle περιεζωσμέναι (*periezōsmenai*) alludes to a state of constant readiness to act (Talbert 1982: 143). The second image of burning lamps shows someone's readiness to move about during darkness (Exod. 27:20; Lev. 24:2; Matt. 25:1–13; Fitzmyer 1985: 988; Michaelis, *TDNT* 4:326).[6] The combined images point to an attitude of expectant watchfulness. Jesus calls his disciples to look for his return at any time of the day or night.

12:36　A third picture, which is a brief parable, completes the call to be prepared. Jesus compares his disciples to servants who await their master's return from a wedding feast (Plummer 1896: 330; Fitzmyer 1985: 988; Marshall 1978: 536).[7] Such feasts in the ancient world could last for days, often as long as a week (Tob. 11:18; Stauffer, *TDNT* 1:648). The servants are immediately ready to open the door and serve their master upon his return, an allusion to Jesus' second coming.

Luke's use of this image is unique to him, though picturing God's people as slaves is common throughout the Bible (Paul's greetings; Isa. 65:8, 13–15; Ezek. 20:40; Mal. 3:18; Danker 1988: 253). The wedding in this setting is merely a descriptive detail and carries no eschatological significance, since the messianic banquet in NT teaching follows the return and is not a part of it (Marshall 1978: 536). The image of Jesus knocking at the door appears in Rev. 3:20 (in Matt. 25:10–11 and Luke 13:25, Christ is the one who waits to open the door or the one who has already shut it; Creed 1930: 176; cf. *Didache* 16.1). The three pictures of Luke 12:35–36 call the disciple to labor with one eye toward heaven, looking for Jesus' return. The disciple eagerly anticipates the coming of God's kingdom with an

---

5. See Exod. 12:11 (of Israelites eating Passover); 1 Kings 18:46; 2 Kings 4:29; 9:1; Isa. 59:17; Eph. 6:14; 1 Pet. 1:13; Danker 1988: 253. Plummer 1896: 330 notes the emphatic position of ὑμῶν (your) to indicate a condition: "*your* loins are to *be* girded."

6. The distinct terminology of Matt. 25 and Luke 12 allows no connection in terms of source.

7. Ἀναλύσῃ is unusual since in Classical Greek ἀναλύω normally means "to loose." This is the only NT occurrence with the meaning "return," although it has this meaning in the LXX: Tob. 2:9; 2 Macc. 8:25; 12:7; 15:28; Wis. 2:1 (BAGD 57 §2; BAA 113 §2). The subjunctive mood with the adverb πότε (when) refers to the unspecified hour of his return: "whenever he 'might break loose' from the wedding"; BAGD 695; BAA 1393.

awareness that the master will evaluate the servant's faithful response and issue a call to additional service.

b. Blessing for Those Found Waiting (12:37–38)

Jesus offers a beatitude for those who heed his advice (on μακάριος, **12:37** *makarios*, blessed, see the exegesis of 6:20). Those who are the objects of God's pleasure are those who are found waiting when the Lord returns. Their expectation will meet with favor. Jesus promises to share a meal with them, recline at the table with them, and serve them at the meal (on "girding" as a figure for service, see Oepke, *TDNT* 5:306). One is reminded of when Jesus washed the disciples' feet (John 13:5), though what is in view here is an even more significant time. Jesus will be so pleased with those who wait for him that he will serve them at the great banquet table, which pictures final eschatological blessing (Luke 13:29; 22:30; Rev. 3:20; 19:9; Klostermann 1929: 139; Grundmann 1963: 265).[8] Efforts to compare this banquet feast to the Roman festival of Saturnalia are misguided (Plummer 1896: 330–31; Grundmann 1963: 265). Marshall (1978: 536–37) defends the statement's authenticity.

Jesus emphasizes the unknown timing of his coming by noting that **12:38** the "watch" (φυλακή, *phylakē*) on which he will come is uncertain. The Roman schedule for guard duty divided the time between 6:00 P.M. and 6:00 A.M. into four equal units; if φυλακή refers to this Roman custom, then the second and third watches would be between 9:00 P.M. and 3:00 A.M. (Zahn 1920: 505). However, other methods of time-keeping had three watches during the night, which would yield between 10:00 P.M. and 6:00 A.M. The most common Jewish custom is the three-watch pattern (SB 1:688–91; Judg. 7:19), and so most commentators adopt this view (Plummer 1896: 331; Marshall 1978: 537; Manson 1949: 116; Creed 1930: 176; Nolland 1993a: 702).[9] However, Luke elsewhere uses a four-watch pattern (Acts 12:4; also Mark 13:35). Regardless of which schedule Jesus refers to, the image points to the deep-night watch, the time when one would not normally be ready. Only a "perpetual watch" will get the job done (Talbert 1982: 143). The stress is on those who are ready, even when the hour is unknown. Those whom Jesus finds ready will be blessed. With the positive emphasis on blessing, Jesus in effect makes the exhortation again.

---

8. On watchfulness, see Mark 13:33–36; 1 Cor. 16:13; Col. 4:2; 1 Thess. 5:6, 10; 1 Pet. 5:8; Rev. 3:2–3; 16:15; Marshall 1978: 536.

9. For options, see BAGD 868 §4; BAA 1730; Fitzmyer 1895: 988; and Plummer 1896: 331. Josephus uses both approaches: three watches in *Jewish War* 5.12.2 §510 and four in *Antiquities* 18.9.6 §356.

c. Parable on Being Ready for the Return of the Son of Man (12:39–40)

12:39 Jesus reinforces the call to be ready with another illustration: a protected or unprotected home. If a householder (οἰκοδεσπότης, *oiko-despotēs*; BAGD 558; BAA 1131) knew when a thief was coming, he would be prepared and not leave his house unprotected. Exposure comes from lack of readiness. Jesus compares his coming to that of a thief breaking into a house. Thieves often entered by digging through a mud-brick wall (Manson 1949: 116–17).[10] The use of this negative figure adds vividness as well as emotive force to the illustration. Jesus frequently used this technique of surprise (e.g., the dishonest steward in Luke 16:8 and the inflexible judge in 18:1–6; Danker 1988: 254). The exact time of Jesus' coming is unknown, and the only way to be secure is to be ready for it. This image contrasts with those of earlier verses. Here Jesus warns about being prepared for his return, whereas in 12:35–38 he encouraged them to be ready by noting the reward and blessing that the return will bring (Marshall 1978: 538).

Matthew 24:43 is similar, but it has a few peculiarities of wording. Matthew introduces the verse with ἐκεῖνο (*ekeino*, this), not Luke's τοῦτο (*touto*, this). Matthew refers to any time at night, rather than to a specific watch, though the use of ὥρα (*hōra*, hour) in Luke 12:40 might be responsible for the difference in specificity (Klostermann 1929: 139; Marshall 1978: 538; Fitzmyer 1985: 989 [citing 12:46]). The illustration should not be understood to mean that Jesus' return can happen only at night. If the UBS–NA Lucan text is correct, Matthew has an additional phrase that the master "would have watched" (ἐγρηγόρησεν, *egrēgorēsen*) rather than leaving the house unprotected (see the additional note). The images, though similar, are expressed with enough distinct vocabulary to suggest two distinct versions of a teaching that Jesus used perhaps on more than one occasion (Marshall 1978: 538 prefers to speak of two different versions of Q).

12:40 Jesus commands the disciples to be ready because (ὅτι, *hoti*) they do not know (δοκέω, *dokeō*; BAGD 202 §1f; BAA 406 §1f) the time of his return. The risk of being unprepared for his coming is great, unless they are diligently looking for him. Given the benefits of being ready and the risks of not being ready, the disciples would do well to be

---

10. Διορύσσω is used elsewhere at Matt. 6:19, 20; 24:43; BAGD 199; BAA 400; cf. Exod. 22:2 [22:1 MT]; Job 24:16; Jer. 2:34. The image of Jesus returning as a thief is common in the NT: 1 Thess. 5:2, 4; 2 Pet. 3:10; Rev. 3:3; 16:15; Grundmann 1963: 265; Plummer 1896: 331.

looking for him.[11] Of course, the term *Son of Man* refers to Jesus as it has throughout Luke (see the exegesis of 5:24). The Son of Man's coming means blessing for those who know and respond to Jesus, but judgment for the rest (Manson 1949: 117 notes that Dan. 7 imagery lies behind the declaration of coming in judgment). The saying's authenticity is defended in the discussion of sources and historicity above (see also Marshall 1978: 538–39).

A major question is why disciples would need to be included in such a warning. The following parable gives the answer. Except for minor differences of word order and a different introductory term, the wording matches Matt. 24:44 (Matthew has διὰ τοῦτο καί [*dia touto kai*, because of this also] where Luke has καί [*kai*, and]).

d. Parable of the Stewards (12:41–48)
i. Peter's Question (12:41)

Peter now steps forward and tries to specify the audience (cf. Luke 5:8; 8:45). He inquires whether the parable is told for the sake of "us" (ἡμᾶς, *hēmas*) or for "all" (πάντας, *pantas*). The context determines the question's scope. Does Peter mean "us" as leaders among Jesus' followers and "all" as all disciples? Or does he mean "us" as disciples and "all" as all people? Or does "all" mean all who think they are related to the kingdom? Luke 12:46 provides a clue when one of the groups is called "the unfaithful." Thus, anyone who has a connection to Jesus is included in the scope of the parable, even if the relationship consists of not being faithful to him. This would suggest a broader meaning for πάντας (Nolland 1993a: 702 holds that "all" is the disciples; Fitzmyer 1985: 989 holds that "us" is the disciples and "all" is the crowd, citing the contextual contrast of these groups in 12:1, 22 and 12:1, 13, 54).

12:41

Most commentators note that in 12:22 the audience was designated as disciples and that nothing since then has indicated a change (e.g., Fitzmyer 1985: 989; Luce 1933: 234 [12:41 addresses Christian leaders]). In addition, the parable is about stewards and as such appears to look to leaders (Ellis 1974: 181). If this observation is correct, then Peter is asking whether the call to be alert is directed only at the "leadership," that is, at the Twelve or the seventy-two, and not to disciples at large (Marshall 1978: 540; Manson 1949: 117; Wiefel 1988: 245). If applied to leaders, the point is that they especially must be careful of the stewardship they have. They are to be

---

11. Grundmann, *TDNT* 2:706, says that the Bible uses ἕτοιμος to speak of three kinds of readiness: (1) ready to do good works (Titus 3:1); (2) ready to preach the gospel (1 Pet. 3:15); and (3) ready for the Lord's return (here and Matt. 24:44).

faithful to the Lord, to whom they will give an account (1 Cor. 3:10–15; 4:1–5; 1 Tim. 4:12–16; 2 Pet. 2:1–2, 13; Talbert 1982: 143).

What complicates the picture is that the master in the parable represents Jesus in terms of his sovereignty over all humans, which he will display to all upon his return. Second, the fundamental contrast in the passage, as noted above, is between disciples and the crowds (Luke 12:1, 13, 22, 54; Fitzmyer 1985: 989). Disciples are to be different than the multitudes. The ambiguity that Peter reads in the imagery is a real one that needs clarification.

Jesus will supply the answer indirectly by elaborating on the image. The key emphasis is seemingly related to stewardship and thus to religious leadership, as 12:48 suggests. In addition, the higher the position the greater the need to heed the admonition. Putting these points alongside the setting, we see that all are responsible to respond properly to the knowledge they have about God. Jesus is admonishing anyone who is expecting the kingdom and who is believing that they are related to it to recognize that he will return with authority.[12] Then he will deal with all people, but those who have knowledge of Christ will be subject to a more careful examination. The passage applies to all, but most especially to leaders within the community, since all are evaluated by the master on his return.[13]

Peter's question has no parallel in Matt. 24, which has produced speculation as to whether Luke created the saying or Matthew omitted it.[14] If the saying is part of a setting distinct from Matt. 24, as was argued earlier, then the choice is not necessary.

ii. Faithful Steward (12:42–44)

12:42 Jesus begins the elaboration with a question that may well introduce an idea that is completed in 12:43. His question focuses on the faithful and wise steward, whom 12:43 shows to be blessed.[15] The steward's faithfulness is described not in terms of his power, but in

12. The thought that someone is associated with the kingdom is key in light of the whole parable. Some who think they are in, in fact, are not, as 12:46 will make clear. Jesus' authority over the kingdom is comprehensive, and he will evaluate all who claim to be related to the kingdom, most especially those who have a leadership role in it.

13. Tiede 1988: 241 sees "all" people in the parable, for some are placed with the unfaithful, while others suffer some punishment without being banished.

14. Marshall 1978: 539–40 lists the options. He holds to Matthean omission, as does Manson 1949: 117–18. Klostermann 1929: 139 and Ellis 1974: 181 regard it as Lucan. On the assumption that one tradition is present, the influence of additional source material for Luke cannot be ruled out since there is additional material elsewhere in the unit. For defense of its authenticity, see the discussion of sources and historicity above.

15. On the syntax, see Marshall 1978: 540 and Black 1967: 118–19, who argue that the Greek structure reflects a Semitic idiom: "If there is a steward, . . . he will be blessed when. . . ."

relation to his service (Manson 1949: 118). The picture is of those given spiritual responsibility over God's community. The reality of the master's return and an evaluation of the steward's stewardship make it prudent that the servant be faithful.

In this culture, the steward (οἰκονόμος, *oikonomos*; BAGD 560; BAA 1135) was a slave left in charge of the master's household and estate when the master was away (Luke 16:1; 1 Cor. 4:1–5; Plummer 1896: 332; Michel, *TDNT* 5:149–51; SB 2:192).[16] His major responsibility was the welfare of the other servants (the infinitive of purpose, τοῦ διδόναι, *tou didonai*, describes the steward's job to give them bread using the present tense). Σιτομέτριον (*sitometrion*, portion of food), which appears only here in the NT, describes the distribution of rations like corn, which might by given out daily, weekly, or monthly (BAGD 752; BAA 1503; Gen. 47:12, 14). Why does Luke have this rare term?

The wording is similar to Matt. 24:45 and yet there are some differences. Matthew refers to a slave (δοῦλος, *doulos*), not to a steward. Matthew uses the aorist κατέστησεν (*katestēsen*, has set), instead of Luke's future tense, a rendering that draws out more clearly the future-looking perspective of the parable. Matthew calls the house an οἰκετείας (*oiketeias*) and speaks of giving τροφήν (*trophēn*, food) to the servants. Luke uses this term for food eight times in Luke–Acts, so the difference is hard to explain. Also, the infinitive in Matthew is the aorist δοῦναι (*dounai*, to give). The differences have little influence on the sense and are hard to explain as redactional. Some, however, suggest that Luke's focus on church leaders is responsible for the difference, or that they are caused by the different tense perspective that Luke used to describe the scene.[17]

Jesus now offers a beatitude to match those of 12:37–38. The blessings mentioned earlier are for the disciple who is watching for Jesus. Here the beatitude is for carrying out one's duties faithfully because the disciple knows the master will return. The steward who carries out the responsibilities the Lord gives will be blessed. This is the "faithful and wise" steward (12:42). Luke 12:44 specifies the nature of the blessing in terms of greater responsibility and service upon Jesus' return (Manson 1949: 118; Luke 19:11–27). Matthew 24:46 is

12:43

---

16. Θεραπεία refers to a body of servants only here in the NT; cf. Esth. 5:2b [= 15:16 NRSV]; BAGD 359 §2; BAA 729 §2; Creed 1930: 177.

17. So Schweizer 1984: 213 explains the reference to a steward and the use of the future tense in Luke. But a steward was a slave, as 12:43 makes clear, and the tense difference is not necessary to the point. If a stylistic preference exists, which is possible for the verb's tense, it has come in along with other differences that are more difficult to explain. For example, of the uses of καθίστημι (to appoint, put in charge) in Matt. 24:45, 47; 25:21, 23, only the first is aorist, and all are in an eschatological setting.

verbally exact with Luke, except that the order of the last two terms is reversed.

The scope of ἐκεῖνος (*ekeinos*, that) is important to the parable's meaning. Does this term refer to only one servant who is successful or to a single servant who could fall into any of the various categories mentioned in the parable? It would seem that the parable has four categories in two classes: one faithful steward (12:42–44) and three types of unfaithful stewards (12:45–48).[18] Type one in Luke 12:45–46 looks at the blatantly disobedient, where what is done is the opposite of what is commanded; while type two in 12:47 looks at conscious disobedience, but disobedience that is not as severe as in 12:45–46; type three in 12:48a looks at disobedience in ignorance. The steward of the parable faces a future life of responsibility and can fall into any of the four categories. In effect, the parable refers to anyone who enters into relationship with God and has responsibility before him.

12:44   Jesus describes the faithful steward's blessing. Continued management of the household is the reward as the master appoints the steward over all his possessions. This reward for faithfulness is a more permanent form of service to manage the house and the entire estate. With confidence won by faithfulness, the steward has his responsibilities increased upon the master's return. It is hard to be certain what this represents, but it appears that the reward involves continued stewardship in the period after Jesus' return, probably in aiding the kingdom's administration (Luke 19:17; 1 Cor. 6:2–3). Life after Jesus' return will not be passive, but will involve active service (Manson 1949: 118). Fitzmyer (1985: 990) paraphrases the thought this way: "He will give him a share in all of his own power and wealth." Schweizer (1984: 213–14) argues that the time after Easter is in view, but this is not the time of the return of the Son of Man. The time frame is after the second coming, not current "realized eschatology."

Matthew matches this Lucan passage verbally except for the introductory term: Matt. 24:47 has ἀμήν (*amēn*, truly), while Luke has ἀληθῶς (*alēthōs*, truly), a term that he uses elsewhere in 9:27 and 21:3 (the Synoptic parallels have ἀμήν in both cases). The rendering here looks Lucan, but since Luke also uses ἀμήν (4:24; 12:37; 18:17, 29; 21:32; 23:43), we cannot rule out the possibility of a distinct tradition here.

iii. Unfaithful Steward (12:45–46)

12:45   Jesus introduces another possibility: the unfaithful steward. The unfaithful steward's activity is described by a third-class condition

---

18. This three-to-one ratio is also found in the parable of the soils (8:4–15).

(ἐὰν δέ, *ean de*, but if). What if the servant is not concerned with the master's return? Instead he reckons (lit., "to say in his heart," meaning "to think"; Ps. 14:1; 53:1; Manson 1949: 118) that his master is gone for a while and will not be returning soon. As a result the servant does not carry out his responsibilities properly, but takes advantage of his position to treat the other servants poorly by beating (τύπτω, *typtō*) them.[19] He also ceases to live responsibly, eating and drinking until he is drunk.[20] Rather than doing his job, he abuses his position and acts self-indulgently. He does the opposite of caring for the servants. His abusive treatment is interrupted, however, as the next verse makes clear that his plans are exposed by the master's return. Plummer (1896: 332) speculates that the servant used some of the wages intended for the servants to pay for his binge, but this point is not explicitly present. Danker (1988: 255) suggests that the real-life situation is the threat of false teachers (alluded to in Acts 20:26–35) and attitudes reflected in OT texts such as Isa. 5:11–12 and Amos 2:6–16 (also 1 Tim. 3:3), where others are treated poorly, even among the people of God. Marshall (1978: 542) raises the possibility that the reference is to an immoral and irreverent lifestyle as well as to the treatment of others that surfaced later in the church (1 Cor. 11:21; 2 Pet. 2:13; Jude 12; for the Jewish background of this image, see Weiser 1971: 194–95).

Jesus' remarks in the next verse assume a delay in his return, but this does not indicate that the delay was a problem, as some scholars suggest. They argue that Jesus led his disciples to expect an immediate return without a long interval between his ascension and parousia. In view of this delay in the expected coming, only later did the church emphasize faithfulness.[21] However, the parable deals more with absence than delay, and the point is that some will ignore the fact of the master's return, which might be at any time (Liefeld 1984: 965; Marshall 1978: 542; Aune 1975). Watchfulness in relation to the day of the Lord was a common OT theme (Fitzmyer 1985: 987; Isa. 13:6; Ezek. 30:3; Joel 1:15; 2:1; Amos 5:18; Obad. 15; Zeph. 1:14–18). What Israel had looked to for years, because of the prophets, was that for which the disciples were to keep watch.

Matthew is similar, except that Matt. 24:48 explicitly calls the servant evil (κακός, *kakos*), the word order of the last two Matthean words is reversed (μου ὁ κύριος, *mou ho kyrios*, my master), and

19. See Stählin, *TDNT* 8:263 and n. 26, for ancient examples of the poor treatment of servants. Stählin calls the beating a "base abuse of power," but it was common.

20. On drunkenness as a negative picture of irresponsibility, see Isa. 28:1–4; Joel 1:5; Matt. 24:38; Luke 21:34; 1 Cor. 11:21; 1 Thess. 5:7; 1 Pet. 1:13; 5:8.

21. Grässer 1960 contains a full treatment of this issue from this perspective. For a different, better approach to the same issue, see A. Moore 1966.

Luke uses the infinitive ἔρχεσθαι (*erchesthai*, coming), which Matthew lacks. Matthew 24:49 expresses the servant's actions in rather distinct terminology with more detail. Only the first three terms in this verse match Luke. The rest of the Matthean passage speaks of beating fellow servants and of eating and drinking with drunkards. These differences suggest different versions of the same parable as well as a unique setting.

12:46 The action of the unfaithful servant is severely judged upon the master's return. Ἄπιστος (*apistos*) usually means "faithless," but in contrast to the faithful steward in 12:42, and in light of the severe nature of the punishment, it should be understood to mean "unbelieving." The servant is totally unconcerned about the master's return. The master reappears at an unexpected hour. The return's surprise is highlighted by the repeated reference to the unknown day and hour of his return.[22] The reference to the "day" of the return recalls OT day-of-the-Lord imagery (Joel 2:31 [3:4 MT]; Fitzmyer 1985: 990). It is judgment day.

The master's reaction to the slave's behavior is swift and strong. Some translations do not properly render the key term διχοτομήσει (*dichotomēsei*). The RSV says that the master will "punish" the slave, but the term is stronger and much more emotive than this: "to dismember, to cut in two" (BAGD 200; BAA 403; Marshall 1978: 543; Stählin, *TDNT* 3:852–53; Plummer 1896: 332–33; Schlier, *TDNT* 2:225–26).[23] Beating the servants now produces judgment in kind, only it is more severe. The steward receives a "mortal blow," a "declaration of judgment or prediction of cursing" (Stählin, TDNT 8:267–68). God's smiting the servant depicts punishment of the most severe type, but it is figurative, despite the opinion of some that it is literal (Plummer 1896: 332; Creed 1930: 177). A figurative sense emerges from the next line, which shows that the servant is still able to be placed among another group of people.[24]

22. The stereotyped pairing *day and hour* is common: Job 38:23; Dan. 12:13; Mark 13:32 = Matt. 24:36; 25:13; Rev. 9:15; Marshall 1978: 543. The NT references allude to the parousia.

23. This and Matt. 24:51 are the only two NT uses; in the LXX the word is used in Exod. 29:17. Similar imagery is found in 1 Sam. 15:33; Amos 1:3; and Sus. 55, 59. In the ancient world, see Homer, *Odyssey* 18.339; Herodotus 2.139. Kistemaker 1980: 125 notes that the contemporary expression "to skin alive" is parallel. 2 Sam. 12:31 and 1 Chron. 20:3 show other ways that slaves were made to labor as a result of being captured in war. This treatment is as severe as it gets.

24. Manson's suggestion (1949: 118) of an Aramaic mistranslation is unlikely, even though it is a common position (see Jeremias 1963a: 57 nn. 30–31). One can argue for a purposely emotive figure without having to resort to mistranslation. Marshall 1978: 543 lays out a full set of options: figurative, mistranslation, literal, and overliteral translation of the Aramaic. The last is Marshall's choice, following O. Betz

The reprimand and punishment are total, since the servant is placed with the unfaithful (ἀπίστων, *apistōn*) because of his complete lack of faithfulness. This is a picture of rejection. In fact, dismemberment is the most graphic way possible to express rejection. This is not a matter of dismissal or demotion, but departure. A high calling does not protect from the consequences of total unfaithfulness (Arndt 1956: 322), for with the call must come obedience. Such a warning is necessary, because Judas is among the disciples. The passage is addressed to anyone associated with Jesus who has undertaken responsibility in the church. Such a profession may be taken at face value, but Jesus will evaluate the genuineness of it on the day of judgment. (A similar evaluation is found in 1 Cor. 3:10–17; see n. 27 below.)

Matthew 24:51 is parallel, except that the slave is placed among the hypocrites (ὑποκριτῶν, *hypokritōn*) rather than among the unfaithful (ἀπίστων). To be placed with the hypocrites is to receive their punishment (Matt. 6:2, 5, 16; 23:13–19; on the terror of divine judgment, see Job 23:13–17 and Isa. 17:14). In addition, Matthew notes that there will be weeping and gnashing of teeth in the place where the slave goes (Matt. 8:12; 13:42, 50; 22:13; 25:30; Luke 13:28). The Matthean figure also indicates total rejection, since it is often associated with being cast into outer darkness. Outer darkness does not mean being on the edge of the kingdom or on the edge of light, excluded only from participating in kingdom administration. It means totally outside. The kingdom is light, so one cannot be in darkness and in the kingdom at the same time, much less in outer darkness! The point for both writers is the same: the totally unfaithful slave is rejected by the master for being an utterly irresponsible steward. Given the setting, it would seem that false teaching and a double life are the points of the allusion, since the essence of a leader's stewardship is found in the teaching and guiding role.[25]

1964–66, who notes a parallel idiom at Qumran. In 1QS 2.16, the term means "to cut off from the midst of" and refers to those who were accursed eternally (so 1QS 1.10–11; 6.24–25; 7.1–2, 16; 8.21–23). The idiom refers to those who suffer eschatological judgment, not excommunication. See also Weiser 1971: 199–200 and Ellingworth 1980. Those rejected like this often have treated others poorly or have taken advantage of them (Ps. 37:12, 14, 16, 32). The idiomatic background denotes complete separation.

25. Note the possible views mentioned in the exegesis of 12:41. The Matthean parallel of the hypocrite is enlightening, since a "play-actor" is addressed by ὑποκριτής; BAGD 845; BAA 1684. The term may well be Matthew's rendering, since he uses it seven times uniquely (Schneider 1975: 26 n. 14; Nolland 1993a: 704). Marshall 1978: 544 notes that Aramaic הנפא (*hnpʾ*) can be translated with the sense that appears in each version of the account. On false teachers, see esp. 2 Pet. 2:1–2, 13–14, 17–22.

Grundmann (1963: 268) notes that this unfaithful servant is treated and addressed as the scribes and Pharisees were (Wilckens, *TDNT* 8:568; Matt. 23:13, 15, 23, 25, 27, 29). Efforts to argue that this person is "saved, but disciplined" ignore the force of ὑποκριτής in Matthew's parallel, which, though distinct from Luke, is related to his account. It also ignores the picture of dismemberment. Both accounts picture total rejection.

iv. Additional Judgments according to Knowledge (12:47–48)

12:47 Jesus elaborates on the punishment for unfaithfulness and notes a second type of unfaithfulness. The unfaithfulness here is not as severe as that in 12:46, and so the punishment is less severe. This is a lesser category of unfaithfulness: ignoring Jesus' instruction. The slave who knows what the master wants but does not act accordingly will receive a "severe beating." Δαρήσεται (*darēsetai*) is key here and has been linked to one of two roots: δέρω (*derō*, to beat; BAGD 175; BAA 351) or δαίρω (*dairō*, to hit; BAGD 169; BAA 338). Since the term appears with πολλάς (*pollas*, many), one should supply πληγάς (*plēgas*, blows) as 12:48 suggests (Arndt 1956: 322; BDF §154, §241.6). Regardless of which root is behind the expression, it refers to harsh discipline. The punishment is more harsh for the one who knows what the master wants and does not do it than for one who does not know it, as 12:48 shows. This concluding section is unique to Luke, since Matthew lacks parallels to 12:47–48. It also seems to be focused on the leadership, with its emphasis on knowledge and levels of responsibility (Marshall 1978: 544).

The relationship between this verse and the punishment in 12:46 is debated. Jesus may be referring to the same unfaithful slave who receives both types of punishment (i.e., dismemberment equals "many blows"; Luce 1933: 234; Liefeld 1984: 967 [apparently]) or he may be referring to different slaves, the one here being less unfaithful than the one in 12:46 and so subject to a lesser punishment. A point that suggests the latter view is that the criticism here is of "that" slave who fails to respond to the master's will, rather than flaunting that will by acting entirely contrary to it, as the use of "that" slave of 12:45–46 did (Plummer 1896: 333; Creed 1930: 177–78; Ellis 1974: 182 [apparently]; cf. the imagery of Amos 3:2; on "that" see the exegesis of Luke 12:43). If this view is correct, then the less disobedient slave is disciplined but does not lack a relationship to the master (i.e., is grouped with the unbelievers)—unlike the previous servant (see as well the exegesis of 12:43).

Regardless of the view adopted, 12:47–48 shows that knowledge influences the severity of the punishment, which in turn is meted out with various intensities. Such distinctions based on knowledge were common in Judaism (Wis. 6:6–8; 1QS 5.12; CD 8.8; 10.3) as well as in the NT (Luke 10:12, 14; 23:34; James 3:1).[26] The distinction between sin with knowledge and sin without knowledge has OT roots (Num. 15:22–26; Deut. 17:12; Danker 1988: 255).[27]

Jesus continues to explain how punishment will come to those who **12:48** do not obey the master. The ignorant slave's situation is less severe than the one who fails to act with knowledge. What this servant did is worthy of a beating, but the servant acted out of ignorance. Such a servant will receive "few" blows compared to the "many" that the slave of 12:47 will receive. The reference is a general principle, so that a specific referent should not be sought for the remark.[28] The verse merely notes that servants will be evaluated according to their knowledge.

The parable and explanation conclude with the principle that is the basis for evaluation: the more one knows, the more responsible one becomes, so that more will be asked of one when evaluated. Contextually, this remark is directed at the disciples, since they know more about Jesus than anyone else. They bear the most responsibility of anyone that Jesus addresses, and they need to be faithful as a result.[29] The teaching closes with a warning and a rec-

26. For the various degrees of breaking Sabbath, see *m. Šab.* 7.1; *b. B. Bat.* 60b; Manson 1949: 119; Schweizer 1984: 214; Talbert 1982: 144; Fitzmyer 1985: 992; SB 2:192.

27. Paul elaborates on this image in 1 Cor. 3:10–4:5, which also has a three-part grouping in three conditional clauses: the faithful are rewarded (3:14), those who build inadequately on the house lose their reward (3:15), and those who desecrate the house are destroyed (3:16–17). The first two groups are in, the latter is out, because the argument is built literarily around a descending success rate, with the middle group barely making it.

28. On the general nature of the remarks, see Seesemann, *TDNT* 5:173. Others have suggested specific groups: (1) church leaders and laity, (2) scribes and Jewish people, (3) Jews and Gentiles, and (4) believers and unbelievers. See Marshall 1978: 544 for a discussion of the first three options and Kistemaker 1980: 127 for the final option. It is too early for a direct reference to the church; so view 1 is unlikely (though the church is the audience to whom Luke applies the parable). There are no Gentiles in the audience, so view 3 is unlikely. A reference to scribes and Jewish people leaves out the most obvious group to be alluded to, that is, the disciples, so view 2 is not adequate either. Against a simple division into believers and unbelievers is the difference in tone between 12:46 and 12:47–48. Probably in view in 12:46 are those like Judas and those like the Jewish leadership who wait for the kingdom but ignore the master and beat his servants. The parable is relevant to Israelites because they perceive themselves as heirs of the kingdom. In addition, though they reject the idea, Jesus came as their king. His remarks show that they defaulted on their role by failing to serve.

29. On αἰτέω meaning much is "asked" ethically of someone, see Stählin, *TDNT* 1:191. In the financial realm, the term can indicate the "payment asked" by someone (on the similar use of ζητέω [to seek], see Greeven, *TDNT* 2:892 §1). A similar commercial term is παρατίθημι (to commit or deposit) (Maurer, *TDNT* 8:163). The verse emphasizes ethical responsibility and uses imagery that compares such responsibility to fiscal responsibility.

ognition that there are degrees of faithfulness as well as degrees of responsibility.

The third-person plural ("they will demand") in the final statement is an "impersonal plural" and alludes to the master's judgment (Ellis 1974: 182; Luce 1933: 234; third-person plurals occurred earlier in 5:20; 6:38; 12:20). Some reject the saying as originating with Jesus because of its "casuistic" legal character (Weiser 1971: 224). But the remarks fit with the deeply imbedded Synoptic emphasis on the disciples' need to be ready for the Lord's return (see the discussion of sources and historicity). If there is nothing at stake in looking for the return, then why warn them to be alert? The statement belongs to Jesus.

Summary In the context of the entire parable, one is looking at four groups. First, those who are blatantly unfaithful to Jesus' call are seen as the Jewish leaders, potentially unfaithful disciples like Judas, and false teachers operating within the community. Second, those who are unfaithful and yet know what they ought to do will suffer discipline from the Lord. Third, those who act out of ignorance will be disciplined, but less severely so than those who knew the master's will. Finally, the faithful will receive honor from the Lord in terms of serving him on a more permanent basis. They receive his unqualified praise as they share fully in the Lord's banquet. The last three groups are made up of disciples and leaders of what became the church. In short, Jesus calls disciples to be faithful, because unfaithfulness is costly.

Luke 12:35–48 shows that Jesus' authority implies responsibility to him. Those who serve him are to await his return when he will evaluate all that everyone has done. The servant who works for God's people is to look for Messiah. Those who know he is returning but uncaringly flaunt his will are subject to rejection. Those who know but do not do his will are subject to discipline. Those who act out of ignorance are subject to less discipline. Jesus notes that the blessed servant is the one who looks expectantly for him and serves him faithfully. Jesus will serve that steward on his return, appoint the steward to more service, and reward the steward with a place at the blessed banquet table. Given the choice, Luke's reader is to see that faithfulness pleases the Lord and results in long-term benefits to the faithful follower. One is to serve, knowing that God's eye is on each one. The disciple serves with one eye looking for Jesus' return and the other knowing that the disciple will give an account of service. Faithfulness means walking with God and responsibly serving his children.

Additional Note

12:39. If ἐγρηγόρησεν (he would have watched) is original, then the wording of Luke and Matthew match. But most regard this as a variant because it looks like assimilation to Matthew. Ἐγρηγόρησεν is, however, widely attested, while the UBS–NA reading is supported only by $\mathfrak{P}^{75}$, ℵ*, D, and some Syriac.

E. Knowing the Nature of the Time: Israel Turns Away, but Blessing Still Comes (12:49–14:24)

The largest section in Luke's journey narrative contains warnings, Sabbath miracles, and laments, all of which produces a face-off with Israel. After these events, the cross is inevitable. Jesus brings division, warns about reading the signs of the time, and issues a call to settle accounts with the accuser (Luke 12:49–59). Then, in a response to tragedy, Jesus notes that death is the inevitable consequence of sin (13:1–5). Jesus' next parable makes it clear that the nation is an unfruitful fig tree that is being given a little more time to repent (13:6–9). A Sabbath healing follows, but the people complain, showing that they have learned nothing from Jesus' warnings (13:10–17). Two kingdom parables tell the story of the mysterious growth of God's kingdom from something small to something great (13:18–21). Nothing can stop God's plan.

Still more warnings follow, as Jesus urges the crowd to enter through the narrow door that will soon be shut tight (13:22–30). Jesus then laments for Jerusalem, since the nation is refusing to respond (13:31–35). Another Sabbath healing yields yet another negative reaction (14:1–6). No matter how often God works through Jesus, the reaction is the same. So Jesus warns about the dangers of pride and issues a call for humility (14:7–14). The section closes with the parable of the great supper, where the point is that those originally invited to the feast make excuses not to come, while others flock in to celebrate (14:15–24). This somber note closes the section as Jesus again turns to instruct his disciples. The nature of the time is clear: Jesus brings the kingdom, and many in the nation refuse the opportunity to enter in. But rejection will not stop the kingdom from coming. God's plan is grand enough to overcome the nation's current reaction and substantial rejection.

1. Knowing the Time (12:49–59)

After warning the disciples about preparing for his return, Jesus describes his present ministry in three short paragraphs, each of which focuses on a unique theme. Luke 12:49–53 expresses Jesus' desire to complete the ministry he was sent to perform. He also says that his coming will divide families (an allusion to Mic. 7:6) rather than bring peace, a remark that clearly recognizes that people respond differently to the hope he offers. Luke 12:54–56 addresses the crowds again and warns them to read the signs of the time. All the indications are that God is at work through Jesus, which the crowds would do well to recognize. Luke 12:57–59 is an exhortation to settle with one's accuser. Is Jesus speaking of personal relationships (as the somewhat similar Matt. 5:25–26 suggests), or is this passage an allusion to *the* accuser? If the latter view is meant, then the call is to settle accounts with God before he requires payment. The context supports a reference to God, since both the preceding and succeeding verses relate to responding to him. In fact, all of Luke 12 deals with responding either to God or the Son of Man (Talbert 1982: 140–45).

Sources and Historicity

The source of material in this pericope is unclear. Many see Luke drawing on Q or variations of Q in each subunit. Many also suggest that Luke adds some special material (Marshall 1978: 546; Schweizer 1984: 215; Schneider 1977a: 292 [12:49–50]; Manson 1949: 120–22).[1] The closest parallels for Luke 12:49–53 are Matt. 10:34–36 and Mark 10:38 (Aland 1985: §204).[2] For Luke 12:54–56, the closest connecting passage is Matt. 16:2–3 (Aland 1985: §205). Matthew 5:25–26 is the closest passage conceptually to Luke 12:57–59 (Aland 1985: §206). But in each of the three sections, there is little verbal overlap at any given point, so that if Q was used, it has been radically altered. For example, 12:57–59 makes a very different point than its alleged parallel in Matt. 5:25–26. Failure to note this

---

1. Fitzmyer 1985: 994, 999, 1001 holds that 12:49–50 is from L; 12:51, 53 is from Q; while 12:52 is a Lucan modification of Q material. In addition, 12:54–56 also comes from L and 12:57 is transitional, with 12:58–59 being from Q.

2. Luke 12:49 also has a parallel in the Gospel of Thomas 10, and Luke 12:51–53 in the Gospel of Thomas 16.

and read it as parallel clouds the discussion of the source issue at this point. Luke 12:51 is likewise different from its adduced parallels. These passages give evidence of multiple attestation of the concept, but they are not exact parallels. It is more natural, given the lack of extensive verbal agreement, to see Luke as having had access to independent sources. The exegesis will show the reasonableness of this position. Regardless of the source issue, these remarks fit Jesus' ministry and are authentic.[3]

The Jesus Seminar's analysis parallels the source discussion (Funk and Hoover 1993: 342–44). The seminar accepts the essential authenticity of 12:58–59 (in pink type), since it is attested in Q and speaks to human relationships. Though I question whether these passages are parallel, the vivid imagery and warning about accountability before God fit several sayings of Jesus that look like prophetic warnings (see my defense of the historicity of 11:29–32). The seminar prints 12:49, 51–53, 54–56 in gray type because these sayings have a "sage" quality and all are multiply attested, pointing to their roots in Jesus. But the seminar rejects the idea that Jesus spoke about himself and his mission in the first person, an odd claim for a visionary, prophetic, itinerant figure such as Jesus (see n. 3 above for 12:49–53; for 12:49, see Patterson 1989). The seminar rejects 12:50, 57 (in black type) as having any tie to Jesus. Luke 12:50 is rejected because of its first-person tone and the alleged Lucan theme of Jesus as martyr in the divine plan. Since the concept fits Mark 10:38–39, neither it nor the description of Jesus' emotion is decidedly Lucan in thrust. As already noted, the baptismal imagery does not fit the early church. Luke 12:57 is unparalleled. Nolland (1993a: 714) sees it as Lucan because of δὲ καί (but also) and the "clearly redactional" ἀφ᾽ ἑαυτῶν (for yourselves), but the former term merely links units and so is irrelevant to the verse as a whole, while the latter phrase occurs only twice in all the Synoptics, too rarely to establish a redactional tendency (21:30 is the other occurrence). Of the eighteen uses of this form of the pronoun in the Synoptics, nine are in Matthew, three in Mark, and six in Luke. Thus, one cannot say that Luke uniquely prefers this form. This kind of call to reflect is not out of character for Jesus (e.g., "Let the one who has ears . . ."). The unit's roots are all authentic.

In terms of form, the passage is a collection of sayings: "I-sayings" (12:49–53) and minatory sayings (12:54–59), though 12:57–59 might be considered a brief parable (Fitzmyer 1985: 1001; Bultmann 1963: 153–54, 116, 172).[4] The outline of Luke 12:49–59 is as follows:

3. Witherington 1990: 121 gives two reasons why 12:49–53 is unlikely to be a church creation: the baptism mentioned here is not water baptism and the saying suggests a historical limitation on Jesus.

4. Berger 1984: 264, 57 agrees with the "I-sayings" classification, but argues that 12:57–59 is a parable.

    a. Jesus as the cause of division (12:49–53)
        i. The longing to complete the baptism (12:49–50)
        ii. Jesus brings familial division (12:51–53)
    b. Reading the times like the weather (12:54–56)
        i. Example of weather forecasting (12:54–55)
        ii. Rebuke of hypocrites for not discerning the times
          (12:56)
    c. Settling accounts with the accuser (12:57–59)
        i. Call to make good judgment (12:57)
        ii. Call to settle with the accuser (12:58–59)

In this account we see Jesus' desire to accomplish his mission and his understanding of where things are headed. Jesus knows that he will be the source of division among family members. He rebukes those who are slow to discern the nature of the time and issues a call to interpret wisely the signs of the present time, for it is better to settle accounts with the divine accuser than to owe him.

Exegesis and Exposition

⁴⁹"I came to cast fire on the earth, and would that it were already kindled! ⁵⁰I have a baptism to be baptized with, and how I am distressed until it is finished. ⁵¹Do you think that I came to bring peace on the earth? No, I say to you, but rather division, ⁵²for it shall be from now on that five in one house are divided, three against two and two against three. ⁵³Father will be divided against son and son against father, mother against daughter and daughter against mother, mother-in-law against daughter-in-law and daughter-in-law against mother."

⁵⁴And he was saying to the crowds, "When you see a cloud rising in the west, immediately you say, 'A shower is coming'; and so it happens. ⁵⁵And when there is wind from the south, you say, 'There will be scorching heat'; and it happens. ⁵⁶Hypocrites, the situation of the ⌜earth and heavens⌝ you know to discern, but ⌜how do you not know to discern the present time?⌝

⁵⁷"Why do you not judge for yourselves what is right? ⁵⁸As you go with your accuser before the magistrate, make an effort to settle with him on the way, lest he ruin you before the judge, and the judge gives you to the officer, and the officer throws you in prison. ⁵⁹I say to you, you shall not come out of there until you have paid the last lepton."

a. Jesus as the Cause of Division (12:49–53)
i. The Longing to Complete the Baptism (12:49–50)

Jesus turns his attention to a new topic in speaking about fire. **12:49** Ἦλθον (*ēlthon*, I came) indicates that Jesus is giving the mission statement of his ministry (Fitzmyer 1985: 993, 996; Luke 5:32; 7:34; 9:58; John 3:2; 5:43; 7:28; 12:27, 47; 16:28; 18:37).[5] Πῦρ (*pyr*, fire) can have various meanings, since Luke uses it as a figure for judgment (3:9, 17; 9:54; 17:29) and for the Holy Spirit's coming (3:16).[6] Fire is also associated with God's word or his message through the prophets (Jer. 5:14; 23:29; Sir. 48:1; Schneider 1977a: 293). A similar usage tied to judgment and the Spirit's evaluative work is present here. Jesus came to judge and divide people, a division tied to one's decision about him and his message.

Division is clearly the point, as Luke 12:51–53 highlights the familial division that Jesus brings. The judgment that will decisively separate has not yet come, though Jesus expresses a desire to bring it to pass in his wish that the fire be kindled (Tiede 1988: 243). The Spirit will judge people's hearts to determine who will enter the kingdom and who will face the fire (Talbert 1982: 144; Ellis 1974: 182). Plummer (1896: 334) speaks of the fire of holiness, but this misses the point that this is a refiner's fire not in the sense of purifying, but in the sense of judging (Mal. 3–4 [3 MT]).[7] The tying together of the Spirit and fire is indicated by the linking of the images of baptism and fire. Such a linkage was present in Luke 3:16–17 (Marshall 1978: 547).

Jesus is ready to fulfill the program tied to his coming.[8] But other things must happen before he exercises such authority. To put it another way, with Jesus' arrival comes a period of decision and crisis for people and between people (John 9:39; Ellis 1974: 182–83).[9] Reconciliation to God can mean separation from people.

---

5. This form of mission statement appears at Qumran; Marshall 1978: 546. 1QH has numerous claims by the Teacher of Righteousness about what God is doing through him. Jeremias 1971a: 293 and n. 6 defends the age of the key tradition in Mark 10:45, another example where multiple traditions are possible with Luke 22:27. As a controversial figure, such statements of purpose from Jesus were inevitable (see Grundmann 1963: 269 for a critique of Bultmann).

6. The judging or separating function of the Holy Spirit is in view in 3:16. On πῦρ, see BAGD 730 §2; BAA 1461 §2, and the exegesis of 3:16. In the OT, fire is a common way to refer to judgment of both Israel and its enemies: Jer. 43:12; Ezek. 15:7; Hos. 8:14; Amos 1:4, 7, 10, 12, 14; 2:2, 5; Nah. 3:13; Zech. 13:9; Mal. 3:2–3. It is also a major judgment image in Jewish apocalyptic literature: 1 Enoch 18.15; 102.1; 2 Bar. 37.1; 48.39; 2 Esdr. [= 4 Ezra] 13:10–11; Ps. Sol. 15.4–5; Jub. 9.15; 36.10; 1QH 8.20; Wiefel 1988: 247; Lang, *TDNT* 6:936–37; Nolland 1993a: 708.

7. So Danker 1988: 256 argues, though he minimizes the fire as an image of judgment and emphasizes purification. This point can work only if the purification is seen as coming in judgment.

8. The grammar of the last phrase is difficult, but the idea is clear. For the options, see BDF §299.4, §360.4; BDR §299.4, §360.4; Moule 1959: 137, 187; Moulton and Howard 1929: 472. It is either a wish or an interjection that has Semitic roots.

9. A similar image is found in sayings in the Gospel of Thomas 10, 16, 82. In Thomas 10 and 82 fire alludes to the kingdom's closeness and focuses on purification,

Jesus notes that his program operates under constraint until certain **12:50**
events take place, namely, his baptism, which is a reference to his
approaching death (Mark 10:38–39 = Matt. 20:22–23 [variant read-
ing]). Jesus anticipates that the opposition he now faces will produce his death. Until his death occurs, aspects of what he can accomplish are held up. Συνέχω (*synechō*) refers to emotional distress
and expresses Jesus' desire to do more than he is able to do before
his death (BAGD 789 §5; BAA 1574 §5).[10] That Jesus could make
such an association and have such an expectation is not to be rejected, though some try to do so (Oepke, *TDNT* 1:538).[11] Interestingly, the term for "finished," τελεσθῇ (*telesthē*), has a link in church
tradition with Jesus' death, since when Jesus dies he declares that
"it is finished" (τετέλεσται, *tetelestai*; John 19:30).[12] In both texts,
Jesus' death is seen as a major demarcation in Jesus' career. After
his death, Jesus will be able to do many more things, some of which
Luke enumerates in Acts.

What is the specific referent of βάπτισμα (*baptisma*, baptism)?

1. One option is that it refers to Christian martyrdom or a baptism of blood (BAGD 132 §3c; BAA 266 §3c; such a view is
   present from the time of Irenaeus according to Oepke, *TDNT*
   1:538 n. 44). But a general reference to martyrdom is too broad
   for this context (Bayer 1986: 79). In addition, the conceptual
   parallel in Mark 10 says that only Jesus can experience this
   baptism.
2. It may be an allusion either to John's baptism or to Christian
   baptism, which is the normal meaning of the term. However,
   this context refers to an act of humiliation, which is not the
   picture given by either of these baptisms. Both John's baptism
   and Christian baptism are rites that one partakes in, but this
   baptism is something thrust upon Jesus (βαπτισθῆναι, *bapti-
   sthēnai*, is passive). In addition, the disciple's inability to experience this baptism in the parallel Mark 10:38–39 makes no
   sense if the rite is the focus (Bayer 1986: 79). John's baptism

---

a meaning that is also possible from the OT (Lev. 13:52; Num. 31:23); but that is too
positive for the division imagery here.

10. Köster, *TDNT* 7:884–85, argues that Luke formulated this remark because this
usage of συνέχω is unattested; but see Neh. 6:10. Only Köster's improper insistence
that a Greek base be present limits the options. It is also unlike Luke to note Jesus'
emotions, since he lacks such remarks, unlike the Marcan parallels.

11. Fitzmyer 1985: 995–96 notes that awareness of rejection by a religious leader
is not unparalleled and cites 1QH 2.11–14, 32–33 as examples. Jesus was capable of
anticipating his vindication in death; so correctly Bayer 1986: 77–85.

12. Τελέω suggests the completion of a destined course; Luke 2:39; 13:32; 22:37;
Marshall 1978: 547.

cannot be meant, since Jesus already had it (Fitzmyer 1985: 997). That this baptism is not in view argues against the church's creating this saying.

3. The best view argues for a figure depicting the "inundation of the waters of divine judgment" (Creed 1930: 178; Plummer 1896: 334; Oepke, *TDNT* 1:535–36; Job 9:31 [uses βάπτω, *baptō*, to dip]; cf. 9:28, 32, 35). The imagery of floods for persecution or judgment is common in the OT (Ps. 18:4, 16 [18:5, 17 MT]; 42:7 [42:8 MT]; 69:1–2 [69:2–3 MT]; Isa. 8:7–8; 30:27–28; Jon. 2:3–6 [2:4–7 MT]; Bayer 1986: 81).

Thus, the point of the metaphor is that Jesus faces a period of being uniquely inundated with God's judgment, an allusion to rejection and persecution. Luke will later describe Jesus' dying as "accursed," not as an act from God against Jesus but by God through Jesus against sin (Luke 24:44–47; Acts 5:30–31; 10:39–43). And here lies the judgment's uniqueness: God's plan and the coming of the Spirit's judging work of fire cannot occur until Jesus undergoes rejection and bears God's judgment. Only then can Jesus begin to do much of what he came to do. This is why Jesus longs for the baptism to occur. He wishes to suffer and save humankind at the same time. Though Mark 10:38 is conceptually parallel, it has a distinct point, since it relates to the disciples, rather than just to Jesus as Luke 12:49–50 does (Marshall 1978: 547).

ii. Jesus Brings Familial Division (12:51–53)

12:51 Jesus elaborates on the images of fire and baptism by noting that his work is not without pain. He reminds the disciples that one of the results of his coming is that he will divide people, even families (παρε-γενόμην [*paregenomēn*, I have come] is another mission statement). The key term is the *hapax legomenon* διαμερισμόν (*diamerismon*), which stands in opposition to the concept of peace (BAGD 186; BAA 374; Ezek. 48:29; Mic. 7:12; Plummer 1896: 335). The term pictures dissension and hostile division, something that the official rejection of Jesus is producing. Jesus leaves no doubt that he brings such division, for he answers his own question.

In noting this division, Jesus denies that he is bringing peace. Δοῦναι (*dounai*) may be a Semitism (Black 1967: 133 n. 1) meaning to "place" peace on earth as a part of Jesus' mission (Fitzmyer 1985: 997; cf. the use of δίδωμι in Mic. 3:5 and Frg. Tg. Gen. 27:40). This passage stands in contrast to other Lucan declarations about Jesus' offering peace to humans (Luke 2:14; 7:50; 8:48; 10:5–6; Acts 10:36). But in these texts, peace comes to those who have responded (cf. Eph. 2:13–17, being tied to the offer of the message and thus contingent on a favorable response). Without such response, division occurs. The peace that Jesus brings in his coming to earth is not universal, because some do not respond favorably to his offer. Jesus' offer contains the choice between aligning with the kingdom and standing against it.[13] One must take sides. The reference to familial division recalls Mic. 7:6, an idea expressed in similar ways in Judaism and the NT (Jub. 23.16, 19; *m. Soṭa* 9.15; 2 Esdr. [= 4 Ezra] 6:24; Manson 1949: 121; Mark 3:21; Luke 8:19–21; Ernst 1977: 414).[14]

The parallel to Luke 12:51 is Matt. 10:34. However, except for the references to peace and earth, not a single word is shared between the passages. Matthew contrasts the sword to peace. These differences are not simply editorial, especially when the divisional groupings in the following verses also differ. It seems unlikely that these passages have a single source in Q.[15]

Jesus details the type of division he brings: familial division.[16] The **12:52** groupings "three against two" and "two against three" show that this division penetrates the most intimate level, the family. Jesus also indicates that such division will surely surface. The phrase ἀπὸ τοῦ νῦν (*apo tou nyn*, from now on) is a popular Lucan expression to describe how things change with Jesus' coming (Luke 1:48; 5:10; 22:18, 69; Plummer 1896: 335; Stählin, *TDNT* 4:1113). In effect, Jesus is telling the disciples to expect division and rejection. Manson (1949: 121) observes that such division stands in contrast to the note of reconciliation found in many OT hope texts (Mal. 4:5–6 [3:23–24 MT]). In other words, Jesus offers an opportunity that results either in benefits from God or further distancing from him.

Luke alone mentions the numerical elements five, three, and two. Matthew 10:35–36 is similar to Luke, but the specific mention of division in a house is unique to Luke.

Jesus uses an image from Mic. 7:6 to detail the nature of the familial **12:53** division, though the Matthean form of the allusion with its younger-to-older order and the reference to opponents is closer to Micah (Matt. 10:35–36; Klostermann 1929: 141; Danker 1988: 257). Luke

---

13. Liefeld 1984: 968 notes that even in Isa. 11:1–9, where peace is associated with the coming of Messiah, the theme of judgment is present.

14. Acts 14:22 may be written with the realization of such divisions in mind; Arndt 1956: 324.

15. Marshall 1978: 548, though favorably disposed toward Q, admits the possibility of distinct sources. Matthew may well be speaking about an initial arrival of messianic woe; Isa. 34:5; 66:16; Ezek. 21; 1 Enoch 63.11; 91.12; 100.1–2; 2 Bar. 70.6; Ps. Sol. 17; Witherington 1990: 122–23.

16. The verbal complex ἔσονται . . . διαμεμερισμένοι (it shall be . . . divided) recalls the noun of 12:51; Fitzmyer 1985: 997; Marshall 1978: 548; N. Turner 1963: 89. This periphrastic construction is a future perfect that focuses on a state of division.

uses three pairs of comparisons: father and son, mother and daughter, and mother-in-law and daughter-in-law.[17] In each case the comparisons are given the first time to show that the division runs deep within the family, and then the image is reversed to make clear that the animosity goes both ways. Thus, this image is stronger than Micah's (Ernst 1977: 414–15; Grundmann 1963: 271; Wiefel 1988: 248; Marshall 1978: 549).[18] The syntactic position of διαμερισθή-σονται (diameristhēsontai, will be divided) is disputed: does it complete the idea of 12:52 or begin the comparisons of 12:53 (Marshall 1978: 549)? The sense is altered little by the difference, but the verb belongs to 12:53 since the term is present in 12:52 and would be redundant. The image of such division is hard for some, but Tiede (1988: 244) summarizes well what this means: "Those who would reduce Jesus to a sentimental savior of a doting God have not come to terms with the depth of divine passion, of the wrath and love of God which is revealed in Jesus' word, will, and obedience even unto death."

Some argue that the presence of six people here versus five in the previous verse shows that Luke altered the imagery from Matt. 10:35–36. However, the mother-in-law is the same person as the mother, so the objection has no force because five people are still in view: father, son, mother/mother-in-law, daughter, and daughter-in-law (Klostermann 1929: 141; Luce 1933: 235). Matthew has four comparisons with no reversals: man and father, daughter and mother, daughter-in-law and mother-in-law, and foes in the house. On the other hand, Luke's ἐπί (epi), not Matthew's κατά (kata), matches Micah (against the direction of Luke's other differences from Micah). These details suggest distinct versions.

b. Reading the Times like the Weather (12:54–56)
i. Example of Weather Forecasting (12:54–55)

12:54 Having raised the issue of division, Jesus now turns to the larger crowd and addresses it with an illustration that contains a rebuke (his remarks to the crowd extend through 13:9). His illustration is a simple one about weather. In Palestine, a cloud from the west meant moisture riding in from the Mediterranean Sea (1 Kings 18:44; Fitz-

17. Νύμφη (lit., bride; BAGD 545 §2; BAA 1103 §2) in this context means "bride" to the mother-in-law (πενθερά; BAGD 642; BAA 1295), thus, daughter-in-law (Marshall 1978: 549; Jeremias, TDNT 4:1099).

18. Ellis 1974: 183 notes that the image from Micah was applied to messianic times in Judaism: 1 Enoch 99.5; 100.1–2; Jub. 23.19; 2 Bar. 70.6; 1Q14 [= 1QpMic.] 20–21. M. Soṭa 9.9 applied the remark to the martyrdom of a rabbi, so the text was used as a common description of opposition. Division is also found in Luke 14:26; 17:34–35; Mark 10:29–30.

myer 1985: 1000; Manson 1949: 121).[19] Everyone who lived there knew that this combination signaled rain (ὄμβρος, *ombros*; BAGD 565; BAA 1146; only here in the NT; Deut. 32:2; Wis. 16:16; Plummer 1896: 335). A person can easily assess the environment and make judgments about what is taking place. In theory, it also should be easy to read the significance of Jesus' ministry.

Matthew 16:2–3 has a different weather illustration. In addition, Matthew's material is textually uncertain and may not be an original part of Matthew.[20] Nonetheless, Matthew speaks of the redness of the sky in the morning and evening, and what that difference means. Little in Luke 12:54–56 overlaps with Matthew (only six of forty-seven or forty-eight words; Fitzmyer 1985: 999). We are dealing with distinct traditions of what surely was a common set of weather illustrations (the Gospel of Thomas 91 has a similar saying expressed in even more general terms).

Jesus describes a second weather phenomena: southwesterly breezes (νότος, *notos*; BAGD 544; BAA 1100) that come from the desert and bring heat. This heat is so scorching (καύσων, *kausōn*; BAGD 425; BAA 865; Matt. 20:12; James; 1:11; Isa. 49:10) that it wilts plants. All in Palestine would know the weather that these conditions produce. **12:55**

ii. Rebuke of Hypocrites for Not Discerning the Times (12:56)

After citing the crowd's expertise about weather, Jesus rebukes them for not also being able to determine the nature of events before them. The force of the rebuke is indicated by the use of ὑποκριτής (*hypokritēs*, hypocrite; BAGD 845; BAA 1684), a common biblical address that indicates severe displeasure for certain actions.[21] How is it that they can discern the weather but not recognize what God is doing in their midst? Jesus has provided much evidence of God's activity. The people have not responded well and as a result have left themselves in jeopardy. **12:56**

The textually disputed Matt. 16:3b is close in sense to Luke, but contains entirely distinct wording. Matthew lacks the rebuke to hypocrites (which is interesting given his preference for ὑποκριτής) and

19. Δυσμή (only here and 13:29 in Luke) refers to the sun's setting, thus to the west; BAGD 209; BAA 422. These western rains were crucial for the well-being of Palestinian farmers.

20. The Matthean reading has Western and Byzantine support, including strong versional presence in the Itala, but lacks major Alexandrian witnesses.

21. Wilckens, *TDNT* 8:566–67, notes that ὑποκριτής is always a negative address in the NT: in Matthew fourteen times (seven of which are in Matt. 23); elsewhere only four times (Luke 6:42; here; 13:15; Mark 7:6).

speaks of discerning the face of the heavens (in comparison to Luke's "earth and heaven") and of not knowing the signs of the times (in contrast to Luke's singular "time"). The distinct wording shows that distinct traditions are present (Marshall 1978: 550). For Luke, καιρός (*kairos*) is the current period of God's significant activity in Christ, in contrast to χρόνος (*chronos*), which marks the consummative period of his action (Luke 1:20; 19:44; 21:24; Acts 1:6–7; 3:19–20; Bock 1992c; Delling, *TDNT* 3:459–60). The crowd has "missed the moment" of God's great salvific activity. Despite all the skill they have at anticipating weather, they are inept at reading what God is doing right before them. With respect to God's plan, they were either blind or unwilling (Arndt 1956: 325; Fitzmyer 1985: 1000). Ὑποκριτής suggests more of a problem with the will than anything else.

c. Settling Accounts with the Accuser (12:57–59)
i. Call to Make Good Judgment (12:57)

12:57 The time for personal reflection has come (ἀφ᾽ ἑαυτῶν [*aph' heautōn*, for yourselves] is slightly emphatic by its early position), and so Jesus calls the crowd to consider the correct judgment, the wise course of action. In the next verse Jesus uses an illustration to picture the danger for anyone who fails to evaluate the times correctly: a debtor who must pay every last cent unless things are made right. In context, the point is that one should consider the nature of the time and respond appropriately to one's spiritual indebtedness (Schneider 1977a: 295; Grundmann 1963: 273; Danker 1988: 258).[22]

Luke 12:57 has no Synoptic parallel, which leads some to see it as Lucan transitional material (Bultmann 1963: 91). But this assumes that the rest of the passage comes from Q, which can be challenged. The claim is also made without showing how the wording is distinctively Lucan (for details, see the discussion of sources and historicity). It is just as possible that a distinct tradition with a unique introduction is present.

ii. Call to Settle with the Accuser (12:58–59)

12:58 Jesus illustrates the point of reflection: a legal, civil dispute. Γάρ (*gar*, for) indicates that 12:58 explains 12:57. One needs to make a

---

22. Fitzmyer 1985: 1002 rejects the spiritual interpretation of 12:57–59, calling it allegorizing. Such a description says more about his seeing the material as derived from Q and reading it accordingly than it does about his literary sensitivity. There is no reason to regard this as a displaced saying about brotherly reconciliation (so Bultmann 1963: 172), since the contextual force is clear. Klostermann 1929: 141 errs in calling the accuser Satan (correctly refuted by Marshall 1978: 551).

judgment because of the legal situation in which a person might fall. That this is a civil, financial dispute is indicated by the double use of πράκτωρ (*praktōr*), an official who is a tax collector or holds some other financial office. This person functions like a bailiff and is in charge of debtor's prison (Marshall 1978: 551; Rengstorf, *TDNT* 8:539; Maurer, *TDNT* 6:642; BAGD 697; BAA 1398).[23] Jesus says that it is better to settle with the accuser than to go to court, have your guilt exposed, and be forced to serve time in jail. The infinitive ἀπηλλάχθαι (*apēllachthai*, to be released; BAGD 80; BAA 159) refers to effort (ἐργασία, *ergasia*) directed toward being freed from debt, which the example assumes is present. Since it is perfect tense, the contextual idea is that one works to settle the matter for good.[24] The verb κατασύρῃ (*katasyrē*) refers to being "dragged away by force" and may add an emotive note of shame, since in the LXX it can mean to ruin or demolish (Jer. 49:10 [30:4 LXX]; Plummer 1896: 336).[25] It is better to confess one's guilt and rectify the situation than to pay for it fully. The one who ignores God's call to repent will be dragged away into debtor's prison.

Matthew 5:25 is somewhat parallel, yet the wording is distinct and has a completely different word order. Some terms are shared ("accuser," "judge," "along the way," "prison"), but Matthew's term for the jailer (ὑπηρέτῃ, *hypēretē*) is different, as is the wording of the basic exhortation (ἴσθι εὐνοῶν [*isthi eunoōn*, make friends] versus Luke's δὸς ἐργασίαν ἀπηλλάχθαι [*dos ergasian apēllachthai*, give an effort to be settled]).

Jesus concludes the illustration by noting that the full debt must be **12:59** paid from prison. He also emphasizes the individual focus by saying, "I say to you [singular]." The picture is tragic. There will be absolutely no release (note the emphatic οὐ μή, *ou mē*) until the last lepton is paid. A lepton (λεπτόν) was the smallest coin available (BAGD 472; BAA 958; elsewhere only Mark 12:42; Luke 21:2), today worth about one-eighth of a penny (Fitzmyer 1985: 1003) or less than a half-pfennig (Wiefel 1988: 250 [a pfennig is the smallest German unit of currency]). The ancient value was half a quadrans or one-twenty-eighth of a denarius (Nolland 1993a: 714). As the denar-

---

23. Πράκτωρ does not imply a Hellenistic setting, since such prisons were widespread. Those who see a Roman figure in view and thus a Hellenistic setting distinguish this term from ὑπηρέτης (servant) in Matt. 5:25. Nolland 1993a: 714 speaks of Luke's careful choice of terms here.

24. Ἐργασία is largely a Lucan term in the NT: Acts 16:16, 19; 19:24, 25; Eph. 4:19; Fitzmyer 1985: 1002. Δίδωμι (to give) with ἐργασία is a Latinism; BDF §5.3b.

25. LSJ 915 notes a basic definition of "to pull down" for κατασύρω, a NT *hapax legomenon* (the simple σύρω occurs in John 21:8; Acts 8:3; 14:19; 17:6; Rev. 12:4); Fitzmyer 1985: 1003; BAGD 419; BAA 852–53.

ius was a day's basic wage, this represented the wage for about twenty-five minutes of work! Every last cent will be extracted from the debtor, although how this could be done from prison is never directly addressed. In ancient life, the debtor was beaten in prison as incentive to his family and friends to pay the debt (see Wolff 1974: 554–55 on private law and torts). In fact, generally there was little possibility that one would get out of debtor's prison.

Contextually, the allusion is to the debt one owes God. One must settle accounts with him. Such an interpretation is suggested by the previous rebuke concerning not interpreting the sign of the time and by the following passage concerning repentance. Unless the slate is wiped clean, the debtor will have to pay every cent of debt to God. Better to settle before one reaches prison than to have to pay the price from it (Plummer 1896: 337).[26]

Matthew is close in imagery to Luke: Matt. 5:26 speaks of a quadrans (κοδράντης, *kodrantēs*; BAGD 437; BAA 889), which is two lepta, and his word order is slightly different. Also, Matthew refers to personal relationships, rather than to a relationship with God. This significant difference suggests a distinct use of common imagery and probably implies a separate source.

Summary   Luke 12:49–59 shows that Jesus' coming brings pressure and forces choices. Among the pressures are divisions within families caused by the choice of some for Jesus. The disciple needs to recognize that divisions are possible and that one needs to be emotionally prepared. Commitments to God may mean separation from loved ones.

Jesus then turns to the crowd. He rebukes them for not spotting the obvious. They can read the weather, but they are blind to what God is doing. Jesus clearly reveals the nature of the time; yet they do not respond. So he issues a warning: settle accounts with the accuser, God, or else pay every last penny. The nature of the time makes the decision about Jesus crucial. A decision for Jesus may mean familial pain, but to decide against him will require even more. Luke reminds disciples about the cost of their decision, while warning those who do not respond about the cost of rejecting God. Which ledger is worse?

26. On sin as debt, see Matt. 18:23–25; Luke 7:41–43; 11:2–3; Manson 1949: 122. The image is rhetorical, so there is no need to argue that God cannot be meant, since final judgment is referred to and since no one can "pay" their way out of such a judgment. The rhetoric that "someone will pay" means that "the person will be judged and held accountable for all the sin."

Additional Notes

12:56. Some manuscripts ($\mathfrak{P}^{45}$, $\mathfrak{P}^{75}$, $\aleph^2$, D, L, some Vulgate, Syriac) have τοῦ οὐρανοῦ καὶ τῆς γῆς (heaven and earth). All other manuscripts read τῆς γῆς καὶ τοῦ οὐρανοῦ (earth and heaven), except Δ* and 1424, which have only τοῦ οὐρανοῦ (heaven). Neither paired phrase is frequent in the NT (heaven and earth in Matt. 11:25 = Luke 10:21; earth and heaven only here). So it is hard to suggest stylistic criteria. I prefer τῆς γῆς καὶ τοῦ οὐρανοῦ because of external evidence.

12:56. Did Jesus ask a rhetorical question ("how is it you do not know to discern?") or make a statement ("you do not know how to discern"). Either way the sense is the same. The evidence is fairly evenly balanced: the better Alexandrian witnesses favor the rhetorical question ($\mathfrak{P}^{75}$, $\aleph$, B, L, Θ, 33, 1241, some Syriac), while the statement has Alexandrian, Western, and Byzantine support ($\mathfrak{P}^{45}$, A, W, Ψ, family 1, family 13, Byz, Itala, some Syriac). Codex D lacks πῶς (how). It is perhaps easier to see πῶς being dropped than added. Whether οἴδατε (you know) is more likely to have been added for stylistic conformity or omitted to achieve more force is debatable. Nevertheless, with the presence of the term πῶς, a question is slightly more likely.

2. Lessons for Israel (13:1–9)

Only Luke records this event, which concludes the long discourse sequence that began in Luke 12:1. Once again the remarks are addressed to the crowds. When Jesus is asked to assess the theological reasons for two recent tragedies, he uses the occasion to warn about the need to repent (13:1–5). The historical incidents mentioned here are not recorded elsewhere, though similar events are known.[1] The warning is that those who do not repent will perish. Thus, the remarks appropriately come after the warning to settle accounts with God. Talbert (1982: 145) suggests that the issue was raised because some in the audience took the absence of tragedy in their life as a sign of God's approval and blessing. In the view of the questioners, others tragically met their death because of sin in their lives. Jesus replies that their sense of security is wrong and that the issue of perishing is only a matter of time. A person's life ultimately depends on responding in faith to God. In every death, there is the reminder that "the funeral bell tolls for thee" (Ellis 1974: 185; Luke 12:20). Manson (1949: 273) mentions that a subtle attempt to get Jesus to say something against Pilate may be present; perhaps Jesus would make a political statement that would let Rome deal with him.

The discussion about the two tragic incidents precedes a parable that might be entitled "God's patience with the fig tree" (13:6–9). The parable pictures a tree that is given one more brief chance to bear fruit or else face destruction. The final chance is allowed, despite a history of fruitlessness that already led the owner to call for its removal. The parable depicts the nation on the edge of judgment and God as a patient God, allowing the nation one final chance to respond to him in faith. In Luke 12, Jesus noted that the time was crucial. Luke 13 now shows that the time for the nation is very short. It had better decide for Jesus. When one puts the two sections together, the basic message is that all people must repent if they are to avoid truly perishing. The warning is especially urgent because the people's time is about to run out. Jesus describes the nation as a fig tree later in his ministry (the cursing of the fig tree in Matt. 21:18–19 = Mark 11:12–14).[2]

1. Ellis 1974: 184; Danker 1988: 259; Tiede 1988: 247; Creed 1930: 180. In addition to the Josephean references in the list in the exegesis of 13:1, see also *Life* 17 §92.

2. Marcion, who normally likes Luke's material, omits this section for reasons that are unknown; Klostermann 1929: 141. Luke may lack a parallel at this later point because of the parable here.

Sources and Historicity

The account is unique to Luke and so involves L material (Aland 1985: §207). The discussion is probably set in Galilee and is historical (Marshall 1978: 552; Blinzler 1957–58). The Jesus Seminar sees 13:2–5 as inauthentic (in black type; Funk and Hoover 1993: 344–45). The seminar argues that the passage is unique to Luke, that the imagery is common to the prophets and the early church, and that the sayings introduce Pilate and add to the Lucan theme of the destruction of Jerusalem. However, a case can be made for the pre-Lucan nature of the material. Farmer (1961–62) argues for unique stylistic structural parallels between this text and Luke 15. The themes fit Jesus' style of not addressing a question directly based on its premises, but answering is such a way that the question is seen in a new light. The Jesus Seminar treats 13:6–9 as substantially authentic (in pink type; Funk and Hoover 1993: 345). Interestingly, the seminar accepts the parable even though the vineyard imagery is standard in Judaism. Its style, in the seminar's view, is paratactic and fits an orally transmitted account, while its end is surprising and lacks a specific application. Such criteria is present in the previous account, so why the different assessment? Farmer's analysis may be applied to these verses as well.

The passage is a mixture of pronouncement (13:1–5) and parable (13:6–9) (Fitzmyer 1985: 1004).[3] The outline of Luke 13:1–9 is as follows:

a. Tragedy and the need to repent (13:1–5)
    i. Massacre by Pilate and the call to repent (13:1–3)
    ii. Tower of Siloam and the call to repent (13:4–5)
b. Parable of the spared fig tree (13:6–9)
    i. Instruction to destroy the tree (13:6–7)
    ii. Delay and warning (13:8–9)

Jesus challenges the crowd to turn to God. This necessity is made clear by the warning that all are at risk of perishing unless they repent. Tragedy is not necessarily related to a worse level of sin. Rather, tragedy shows life's fragile character and the importance of knowing God. The remark is not given only to individuals. The nation is without fruit and faces imminent judgment. God graciously delays cutting off the nation, though its time to yet repent is short.

3. Bultmann 1963: 23, 54–55 is undecided whether the pronouncement is controversy or scholastic dialogue, but there is no controversy raised for Jesus, so a scholastic dialogue is present. The people are asking his religious opinion.

Exegesis and Exposition

[1]And some arrived at that very time who told him about the Galileans whose blood Pilate had mixed with their sacrifices. [2]And he replied to them, "Do you think that these Galileans were worse sinners than all other Galileans, because they suffered these things? [3]No, I say to you; but if you do not repent all will perish likewise. [4]Or those eighteen upon whom the tower of Siloam fell and killed them; do you think that they were worse debtors than all the other people who live in Jerusalem? [5]No, I say to you; but if you do not ʳrepentˈ all will perish ʳin a similar mannerˈ."

[6]And he told them this parable, "A certain man had a fig tree planted in his vineyard, and he came seeking fruit in it, but he did not find any. [7]And he said to the vineyard keeper, 'Behold, three years I have come seeking fruit from this fig tree and I do not find any. Cut it down; why should it use up the ground?' [8]But he replied, 'Master, let it remain this year, until I dig around it and put down manure; [9]and if it should bear fruit ʳin the coming year, . . . but if notˈ, you can cut it down.'"

a. Tragedy and the Need to Repent (13:1–5)
i. Massacre by Pilate and the Call to Repent (13:1–3)

13:1 Perhaps Jesus' previous remarks about the signs of the time caused the next topic to be raised by some in the crowd (Arndt 1956: 327).[4] Is this a time of special judgment? Some people mention a recent incident in which some Galileans were put to death as they offered (or prepared to offer) their sacrifice.[5] Neither the exact location of the attack nor the number who lost their lives is given. It need not have been in the temple proper, but more likely took place near the temple, as people approached with their sacrifices in hand. Pilate, the Roman administrator, used force, and death resulted. It is unlikely that the Galileans were Zealots, at least no such point is raised. An attack like this in an area of sacred significance was bound to raise

---

4. Παρῆσαν (arrived), from πάρειμι (to arrive; BAGD 624 §1a; BAA 1261 §1), refers to the crowd's arrival, not only its presence as many translations suggest; so correctly Plummer 1896: 337; Acts 10:21; 12:20; 17:6; 24:19, Marshall 1978: 553. In addition, ἀπαγγέλλω (to announce) usually refers to recent news; Marshall 1978: 553; Matt. 2:8; 28:8, 11; Mark 5:14 = Luke 8:34; Mark 16:10, 13; Luke 7:18; BAGD 79; BAA 157.

5. Ἔμιξεν (he mixed) comes from either μείγνυμι (BAGD 499) or μίγνυμι (BAA 1055), both meaning "to mix." The expression is an idiom for two events occurring together; so Ellis 1974: 185, who cites Exod. Rab. 19.5 on 12:43–44, SB 2:193, and Blinzler 1957–58: 28–29. The midrash refers to a mixture of circumcision blood and Paschal blood to indicate the need of a person who eats Passover to be circumcised. Philo, *Special Laws* 3.16 §91, discusses the inappropriateness of mixing the blood of murderers and sacrifices at the temple (Nolland 1993a: 717–18). Wiefel 1988: 252 n. 11 calls the expression "Palestinian."

passions and create a stir. Perhaps the crowd is curious to know if Jesus plans to do anything in defense of his compatriots. Jesus does not enter into the social, racial, or national issues, but instead turns the incident into an opportunity to issue a warning.

The massacre may well have been associated with Passover, which is the only time that the laity slaughtered their own animals. Galileans most likely would be engaged in sacrifices during the feast (Marshall 1978: 553; Jeremias 1966: 207 n. 4). Five events recorded by Josephus have been proposed for the specific incident referred to here:

1. After effigies of Roman rulers were displayed in Jerusalem, some Jews marched to Caesarea to beg Pilate to remove the ensigns (Josephus, *Jewish War* 2.9.2–3 §§169–74; *Antiquities* 18.3.1 §§55–59). This event is too late (A.D. 26) and is in the wrong place.
2. Some Jews were massacred in connection with the building of an aqueduct in Jerusalem (Josephus, *Jewish War* 2.9.4 §§175–77; *Antiquities* 18.3.2 §§60–62; Olmstead 1942: 142–47). This event is not at the temple, and it involves Judeans.
3. Some Samaritans were attacked at Mount Gerizim in A.D. 36 (Josephus, *Antiquities* 18.4.1 §§85–87; mentioned by Rengstorf 1968: 169). The location and the victims are not correct, and the time of the incident is too late.
4. Archelaus slew three thousand Jews in 4 B.C. (Josephus, *Jewish War* 2.1.3 §§8–13; *Antiquities* 17.9.3 §§213–18; S. Johnson 1935). The time is too early, and it involves a different ruler.
5. Six thousand Jews were murdered by Alexander Janneus, who had been pelted with citrons during the Feast of Tabernacles (Josephus, *Antiquities* 13.13.5 §372; noted by Zahn 1920: 521). The incident is entirely too early, having occurred in the early part of the first century B.C.

No suggestion commends itself, but these events show that the region often experienced such violence (Marshall 1978: 553; Fitzmyer 1985: 1006–7). We also know that Josephus's list of such events is not exhaustive (Nolland 1993a: 717; Blinzler 1957–58: 39–40); note, for example, the incident in Philo, *Embassy to Gaius* 38 §§299–305. Our inability to identify the event in Josephus is not a corroboration problem. Whatever the incident, it made a great impression, and Jesus is asked to comment on it. But the opportunity for political commentary becomes an occasion for spiritual reflection. Talbert (1982: 145) makes the perceptive note that this incident was tragedy by human hands, while the following Siloam incident is tragedy by natural causes. The origin of tragedy does not alter Jesus' remarks or the spiritual realities.

13:2   Jesus responds with a question. As he begins to comment, Jesus raises the question of theodicy, rather than focusing on politics. Did these events occur because of God's judgment? Did these people suffer (πεπόνθασιν, *peponthasin*; BAGD 634 §3b; BAA 1280 §3b) because they were worse sinners than other Galileans?[6] Had they received "measure for measure" for what they had given? Some seem to have reached this conclusion, which was a common Jewish reaction to such tragedy (SB 2:193–97).[7] Jesus raises what would be the typical conclusion, only to reject it in his response.[8]

13:3   Jesus rejects the common answer with a simple negative: this did not happen because the Galileans were more horrible sinners. Even more, Jesus does not pick up the question; rather he uses the occasion to give an additional warning about a more fundamental issue: the threat of a tragic end is present for all (the third-class condition with ἐάν leaves open whether repentance will come). The issue is not when death will happen or why, but avoiding a terminal fate with even greater consequences. Only repentance will prevent the death that lasts (3:8; 6:24–26; 10:13; 12:58–59; 15:7; Danker 1988: 259; Grundmann 1963: 276). The comparison (ὁμοίως, *homoiōs*, likewise) is between dying tragically in this life and perishing ultimately before God. Without a change of view about Jesus, a black cloud of death hovers over all. This tragedy makes evident the fragile character of life. Jesus issues a call to repent, for disaster looms for the unresponsive.

Arndt (1956: 327) asks whether Jesus is referring to the national disaster of A.D. 70 (19:41–44; also Creed 1930: 181). But if so, then Jesus is making the point in an obscure fashion. It is more likely that he is referring to one's general spiritual risk before God. Three reasons support this option: the presence of 12:57–59 about settling spiritual accounts, the consistent nature of Jesus' message about repentance, and the general Jewish expectation that repentance is a part of the eschaton. Those who do not repent are wicked

---

6. Comparative παρά may be a Semitism; Jeremias 1963a: 141; Luke 13:4; 18:14; BDF §236.3; BAGD 611 §III.3; BAA 1236 §III.3. The term πάντας must mean all other Galileans; Marshall 1978: 553; Fitzmyer 1985: 1007.

7. For example, Job's friends wrongly but naturally assumed that his initial travail was the consequence of some past sin: Job 4:7; 8:4, 20; 22:5; also Exod. 20:5; Prov. 10:24–25; John 9:1–3; Plummer 1896: 338; Danker 1988: 259; Manson 1949: 273.

8. Indirect discourse (marked by ὅτι, that) follows δοκεῖτε (you think) and gives the crowd's possible thoughts. Ὅτι at the end of the verse is causal and thus translates as "because."

and will perish (Ernst 1977: 419 [though he argues that Luke may have read A.D. 70 into it, a view that requires a late date for Luke, which is uncertain]; Marshall 1978: 554; 1 Enoch 98.3, 16; 99.9; 103; Luke 9:24–25; 17:33). All sinners face the same fate before God, so that the natural end to their life, or its timing, is in a sense irrelevant (Ps. 7:10–17 [7:11–18 MT]; Jer. 12:17; Fitzmyer 1985: 1008).

ii. Tower of Siloam and the Call to Repent (13:4–5)

In a second example, Jesus mentions an otherwise unknown inci- **13:4** dent involving the collapse of a tower at Siloam (also known as Shiloah). Siloam, a reservoir for Jerusalem, was located near the intersection of the south and east walls of the city (Isa. 8:6).[9] The structural failure of what may have been nothing more than scaffolding killed eighteen people. Were those who perished worse sinners than others who lived in Jerusalem? The word that refers to sinners, ὀφειλέται (opheiletai), suggests the idea of debt (BAGD 599 §2cβ; BAA 1210 §2cβ). This is the only one of seven NT uses where this noun has such a precise force, but the usage has precedence in Judaism, and similar concepts appear in the NT, often with the verb ὀφείλω (Hauck, *TDNT* 5:561–63; 11QtgJob 21.5; 34.4; Matt. 6:12 = Luke 11:4; Matt. 18:24–34; Luke 7:41; Plummer 1896: 339; Fitzmyer 1985: 1008).[10] Does the standard explanation apply in this second case, where an "act of God" and the sacred city are involved? Again, Jesus' answer is surprising.

Jesus' response to this second situation matches the first one. He re- **13:5** jects the assertion that worse sin was the cause of the tragedy and again issues the warning to repent. The reply matches 13:3 except that the comparative term here is probably (see the additional note) ὡσαύτως (hōsautōs, in a similar manner), which is slightly stronger in force and suggests by the repetition a more emphatic call to respond (BAGD 899; BAA 1794). Failure to repent definitely leaves one exposed to death. Thus, it is imperative that everyone repent. Jesus will close with a parable to stress the immediate danger in which the audience stands. There is need for a quick response. The threat, as in 13:3, is not Jerusalem's fall, but not being able to stand before God. The parable confirms that an eschatological issue is present and that the nation is also at risk.

9. On the building of aqueducts to improve the city's water supply, see Josephus, *Antiquities* 18.3.2 §60; *Jewish War* 2.9.4 §175; SB 2:197; Klostermann 1929: 143.

10. Marshall 1978: 554 argues that this detail shows the Semitic conceptual origins of the story.

b. Parable of the Spared Fig Tree (13:6–9)
i. Instruction to Destroy the Tree (13:6–7)

13:6 The parable underscores not only the danger the crowd is in, but also the need to respond quickly.[11] Jeremias (1963a: 169–71) discusses the parable in a section he entitles "It May Be Too Late," though a better title might be "It Is Almost Too Late." Jesus compares the crowd to a fruitless fig tree, a comparison he frequently made (Matt. 21:19–21 = Mark 11:13–14, 20–21; Matt. 24:32 = Mark 13:28 = Luke 21:29). Fig trees bore fruit annually and grew from fifteen to twenty-five feet in height; the fig itself grew to the size of a cherry (Harrison, *ISBE* 2:301–2). The fig tree is a picture of the nation and is a variation on another common figure that pictures the nation as a vine or as caring for a vine (Kistemaker 1980: 186; B. Scott 1989: 332–34; SB 4:474; Hunzinger, *TDNT* 7:755–56).[12] The parable starts out simply enough: a man checks on the fig tree in his vineyard only to find that it continues to bear no fruit. (A reference to vineyards is common and might be best pictured as a fruit garden.)[13] His dilemma is what to do with this unproductive tree, especially since it takes nutrients from other trees in the vineyard.

It may well be that the parable alludes to Mic. 7:1, given that Mic. 7:6 is alluded to in Luke 12:53 (Danker 1988: 260). If so, the point is about the danger to the nation and to individuals within it. To press the details by taking the vineyard as Israel and the fig tree as Jerusalem is not advisable. The passage lacks contextual indicators that the fig tree should be taken so narrowly, or that the audience is from Jerusalem. Also, Luke does not single out Jerusalem as a city separate from the nation, but as representing it (13:31–35; 19:41–44), so the distinction is not appropriate.

13:7 The vineyard owner registers his complaint to the vinedresser. For three years the owner has come to get fruit from the fig, and nothing has been produced. Vines normally took three years to start produc-

---

11. Luke lacks the withering of the fig tree incident that Matthew and Mark have in the last week of Jesus' life. Many see this parable as replacing that one in Luke's mind.

12. In the OT, see 1 Kings 4:25 [5:5 MT]; Ps. 80:8–19 [80:9–20 MT]; Isa. 5:1–7; 34:4; Jer. 5:17; 8:13; 24:1–8; Hos. 2:12 [2:14 MT]; 9:10; Joel 1:7; Mic. 4:4; 7:1; Hab. 3:17; Matt. 20:1–8; 21:28, 33–41 = Mark 12:1–9 = Luke 20:9–16. In Judaism, see Syriac *Ahiqar* 8.35 (Charles 1913: 2.775). The picture of caring for the vine makes the figure refer to God's blessings. Manson 1949: 274 notes that in rabbinic literature the fig-tree image often alluded to the law, but that is not its referent in this parable.

13. Deut. 22:9; Judg. 9:7–15; 1 Kings 4:25 [5:5 MT]; 2 Kings 18:31; SB 1:872–73 §g; Marshall 1978: 555. On fig trees and vineyards, see Pliny, *Natural History* 17.35 §200 and Nolland 1993a: 718. Theophrastus, *De Causis Plantarum* 3.10.6, advises against mixing figs and vines.

ing fruit (Lev. 19:23; Jeremias 1963a: 170). This fig tree should have borne fruit annually, so the hope for fruit is not good (Hunzinger, *TDNT* 7:755–56). The act being considered does not reflect impatience. The owner's disgust is indicated by the remark that the fig takes up space in the vineyard and robs the ground of nutrients. Thus the other vines and fruit trees suffer. His judgment is that the vineyard would be better off without the fig, especially since it steals nutrients from the soil to sustain its growth (Stählin, *TDNT* 3:859).[14]

The fig tree pictures the nation and portrays Israel as not having borne any spiritual produce for some time. The owner's disgust pictures God's evaluation of Israel's current status. It is possible that the vinedresser represents the merciful element in God's character pleading for patience. Such imagery is vivid and descriptive, but it is not designed to indicate an argument within the Godhead. Rather, it is a graphic way to portray God's displeasure alongside his patience.

Another image that should not be pressed is the three-year image (correctly Arndt 1956: 327). It does not refer to the length of Jesus' ministry. The number merely provides background for the parable and indicates that an adequate time to be fruitful has been provided. Given such a lack of fruit, God could justly execute judgment, but he chooses not to, at least not yet. Marshall (1978: 555) asks an intriguing question: Does the threat to remove the tree suggest making way for a replacement?[15] Others will come into the vineyard (20:9–18).

ii. Delay and Warning (13:8–9)

The vinedresser asks to give the tree another chance to produce fruit **13:8** within one more year.[16] He will carefully care for it and fertilize it. Κόπριον (*koprion*, dung) alludes to fertilizing the plant to help it get the nutrients it needs to be fruitful (BAGD 444; BAA 902). Additional digging is designed to loosen the soil so moisture can get to the roots more easily. Perhaps additional care will yield fruit, even though the tree has done nothing to deserve such special attention or offer such hope (Jeremias 1963a: 170). The image suggests God's patience and

---

14. A cut tree is a common image for judgment: Matt. 7:19; Luke 3:9. Manson 1949: 274–75 portrays the fruitless tree as nothing more than a "glorified weed."

15. The image here is not used in the same way as the vine image in Rom. 11, since there the national groupings are pictured as the branches, not as the entire vine. In addition, Romans indicates a hope of future engrafting for Israel (esp. Rom. 11:12, 15, 25–26). In Rom. 11:26, to "turn godlessness away from Jacob" is to graft in the natural branches again—a clear reference to Israel. Rom. 11 surveys the whole future, while Luke is looking at the short term. On Rom. 11, see Burns 1992.

16. The conversation is shared in vivid terms through the use of the historical present, λέγει (he says).

alludes to the short time left for response. The tree faces removal if its response does not change.

In Jewish accounts where such imagery appears, either the request was denied or the yield of fruit was small (SB 4:474; Kistemaker 1980: 186 n. 3).[17] The vinedresser's successful intercession is a distinct element in this kind of account. The note of God's patience occurs elsewhere in the NT (2 Pet. 3:9).

13:9   The delay involves high stakes. If the fig tree yields fruit, then all is well. The apodosis is omitted, but the conclusion in the face of fruit-bearing is clear: the tree will remain.[18] Arguing for a slightly different interpretation of the grammar, but with similar results, Arndt (1956: 327) suggests, "If it will bring fruit, then let it stand in the time to come," in which case the apodosis is not omitted. This view still sees a partial ellipse, but is less likely because of the context. The time limit of a year (13:8) is here simply called εἰς τὸ μέλλον (*eis to mellon*, in the coming [time]; BAGD 501 §2; BAA 1016 §2). But if the tree fails a fourth year, it will fail no more; it will be cut down by the owner.

The verse has a subtle grammatical element. The if clause that mentions the bearing of fruit is a third-class condition (κἄν, *ka'n*, and if), while the if clause about the absence of fruit is a first-class condition (εἰ, *ei*, if). This difference suggests that the absence of fruit is more immediate—and thus more likely—than fruit being present, a detail suggested also by the broken construction for fruit-bearing versus the completed construction for absence of fruit.

The point is that the time left to repent is short and the prospect of their doing so is not good. The image is much like John the Baptist's warning that the ax lies at the root of the tree (3:9; Plummer 1896: 341). A quick response is needed, for once the time is up, it will be too late. When this time passes, nothing more can be done for this generation of the nation. Literarily, the parable's ending is open-ended, awaiting an appropriate response by those it represents.

Summary   Luke 13:1–9 focuses on repentance and Israel. The crowd is to repent while there is still time. The starting point for forgiveness and life is recognizing the need to repent. Getting reoriented with God and acknowledging the need for him creates the dependent spirit that one needs to walk with God. The decision is a crucial one, for if time passes without repentance, only rejection re-

17. Marshall 1978: 555 cites the refusal in Syriac *Ahiqar* 8.35 and the small yield in *ʾAbot de Rabbi Nathan* A.16 (= Goldin 1955: 86).

18. The omission of the apodosis is common in Semitic style; BDF §454.4; Acts 23:9; Rom. 9:22–24; Plummer 1896: 340. The apodosis in this case reads "well and good"; Manson 1949: 275.

mains. Luke concludes the speech on this basic note, which in Jesus' context had national overtones, though this encompasses individual applications. God is patient, but the clock will tick only so long before the nation will lose its current opportunity to respond. The Book of Acts shows that the nation failed to respond, an act that brought the Gentiles into the picture in a more significant way (Rom. 10:14–11:32). Tragedy is hard and life is short. But life is more tragic if one does not turn to God.

Additional Notes

13:5. The aorist μετανοήσητε (you repent) calls for immediate repentance (so Arndt 1956: 327), but the reading does not have enough external support to be likely (ℵ*, A, D, L, Θ; correctly Plummer 1896: 339). The present tense μετανοῆτε (read by $\mathfrak{P}^{75}$, ℵ¹, B, W, Ψ, and Byz) merely makes a call for repentance.

13:5. Some manuscripts ($\mathfrak{P}^{75}$, A, D, W, Δ, Θ, Byz) read ὁμοίως (likewise) with 13:3, but the harder and better attested reading is ὡσαύτως (in a similar manner).

13:9. Some texts ($\mathfrak{P}^{45}$ [apparently], A, D, W, Θ, Ψ, Byz, most Itala) transpose the approaching time to follow the failure to bear fruit: εἰ δὲ μή γε, εἰς τὸ μέλλον. Supporting the UBS–NA reading are $\mathfrak{P}^{75}$, ℵ, B, L, and some Coptic, which makes better contextual sense (Marshall 1978: 556; Metzger 1975: 162).

3. Sabbath Healing of the Bent-Over Woman (13:10–17)

The account of the healing of a bent-over woman is the first healing since Luke 11:14–23. It is also the first miracle account told in detail since 9:37–43. Its placement is crucial to Luke's argument. Jesus has spent much time telling his audience to note the nature of the time (11:37–54; 12:54–13:9). He has noted their failure to do so until now, and so Jesus also calls them to repent, for there is great danger in not responding. Miracles picture the time and the need for decision. Examples of the "weather" (12:54–56) that the crowd needs to recognize are miraculous healings.

The miracle is a "mirror miracle," in that it replays the Sabbath healings of 4:31–41 and 6:6–11 and will be reinforced by another Sabbath account in 14:1–6. Here is new opportunity and another chance. Will the fig tree bear fruit (13:6–9)? Have Jesus' previous warnings been heeded when miracles are again displayed on the Sabbath?

This miracle examines whether the crowds and leadership have responded to Jesus' strong and explicit warnings. The rebuke of 13:15 shows that they have not. In fact, those who fail to heed Jesus' warning treat animals better than people. The Pharisees, in their concern about Sabbath law and tradition, miss God's compassion. The decision against Jesus fails to discern the time. All that is left for those who refuse to respond is peril. Thus, more warnings will follow this passage (13:22–35), along with yet another failure to accept what God is doing on the Sabbath (14:1–6).

The account also underlines a second major theme: Jesus' struggle with Satan (Ellis 1974: 186). Jesus explicitly alludes to this struggle in 13:16 (also Luke 4:18–19 and Acts 10:38; Tannehill 1986: 65). The issue is stated in terms of supporting God's program or standing with Satan against it. Just as Luke 10:18 and 11:14–23 linked Jesus' actions with the kingdom's in-breaking, so 13:10–17 links Jesus' healing with Satan's collapsing hold on people. The teaching about the battle between Satan and God leads naturally into the kingdom parables that follow (Busse 1979: 290). God's rule is manifest.

A third theme is God's compassion. He is ready to exercise his power on behalf of those in need. The miracle vividly shows that any time is appropriate to come to God for healing and restoration.

Sources and Historicity

The miracle is unique to Luke (Aland 1985: §208), which has led to speculation about its origin and meaning. Bultmann (1963: 12) argues that it is
constructed around the saying now found in 13:15 (also Lohse, *TDNT* 7:25–
26). But many, though they see Luke's style in some of the wording, also
recognize that the account has roots in Jesus' ministry (Grundmann 1963:
279; Schweizer 1984: 221; Fitzmyer 1985: 1011; Marshall 1978: 556–57;
Hengel, *TDNT* 9:53). The Jesus Seminar rejects the authenticity of dialogue
here, arguing that the miracle is attested only in Luke and that the sayings
of 13:12, 15–16 were created for this account (Funk and Hoover 1993:
345–46).[1] Roloff (1970: 67–68) defends the integrity of this traditional unit,
questioning only 13:14b–15. But to argue that 13:15 is secondary erroneously assumes that the tradition records certain themes only once. The synagogue leader's choice to rebuke the crowd is an attempt to avoid direct
confrontation with Jesus, not an "inexact fit" in the story's movement. Two
details in the account have no redactional motive and show its traditional
roots (Meier 1994: 684): (1) the mention of the synagogue ruler runs
counter to Luke's tendency to make Pharisees the opposition; and (2) the
number *eighteen* has no symbolic force. Meier cautiously argues that these
details do not prove the case for historicity, but neither is there anything
compelling against it.

With regard to meaning, Loisy (1924: 364) argues that the healing is
symbolic: the woman represents the church and the fig tree (13:6–9) the
synagogue. The woman gets God's help, but the tree does not. One problem
with this view is that the tree is offered help in the text, so even if the symbolism were present, it is still not interpreted properly. But such an image
is not even suggested by the text (correctly Fitzmyer 1985: 1010 and Creed
1930: 182). The events themselves portray the reality. An appeal to added
symbolic correspondence is not necessary.

The story has elements of a miracle story and a pronouncement account mixed together.[2] The outline of Luke 13:10–17 is as
follows:

  a. Setting (13:10–11)
  b. Healing (13:12–13)

1. This skeptical approach to Jesus' discourse on miracles was analyzed and rejected in the discussion of sources and historicity for 5:17–26 and 6:6–11 (see also
p. 427 n. 10 in vol. 1 of this commentary).

2. Fitzmyer 1985: 1010–11 speaks of a miracle story, while Bultmann 1963: 12
speaks of a pronouncement. Elements of both are present, with the key being the pronouncement in 13:15 and the miracle itself being the dominating element. Berger
1984: 312 calls it epideixis, which is his term for a miracle. Such accounts are designed to show who Jesus is and to elicit a response of respect.

c. Reactions (13:14–17)
    i. The synagogue leader's reaction (13:14)
   ii. Jesus' rebuke (13:15–16)
  iii. Division (13:17)

Jesus renews his work in the nation. Will the reaction be different? His Sabbath healings meet with official rejection based on concerns about Sabbath law. The woman's illness pictures God's struggle with Satan, and so Jesus' compassion leads him to heal. The popular response is positive. God's compassion is always available, but sometimes people are more concerned with other things than with helping others. In fact, sometimes they treat the rest of creation better than they do those made in God's image. The danger and result of valuing tradition over compassion is callousness and hypocrisy. Jesus' ministry continues to cause division.

Exegesis and Exposition

[10]And he was teaching in one of the synagogues on the Sabbath. [11]And behold there was a woman who had a spirit that caused weakness for eighteen years, who was bent over and was not able to straighten herself.

[12]And when he saw her, Jesus called and said to her, "Woman, you are freed from your infirmity." [13]And he laid hands upon her; and immediately she was made straight, and she praised God.

[14]And the synagogue leader, while indignant that Jesus healed on the Sabbath, said to the crowd, "There are six days on which it is necessary to work; come during those days and be healed and not on the Sabbath." [15]But the Lord replied to him, "Hypocrites, does not each of you loose his ox on the Sabbath or take his donkey from the manger and lead it to the trough so it drinks? [16]But this woman, a daughter of Abraham whom Satan bound for eighteen years, is it not necessary for her to be freed from this bond on the Sabbath?" [17]And as he said these things, all his opponents were put to shame, and all the people rejoiced at all the glorious things that were done by him.

a. Setting (13:10–11)

13:10 For the last time in Luke's Gospel, Jesus is in the synagogue on a Sabbath. Jesus is teaching, but his instruction is about to be put into action.[3] Because of its public nature, such synagogue instruction reaches a wide audience.

---

3. Note the periphrastic imperfect (as in 4:31). The term for Sabbath is plural, as in 4:16. In both cases a single Sabbath is meant. For Sabbath synagogue customs, see the exegesis of 4:16; for the meaning of the Greek term, see the exegesis of 4:31 and Fitzmyer 1985: 1012.

Luke describes the spiritual and physical condition of a woman in   **13:11**
the synagogue.[4] She has been possessed, or at least influenced by, a
spirit that has left her in a weakened condition for eighteen years.[5]
Thus, the note of spiritual conflict is immediately introduced into
the account (also Luke 13:16; Foerster, *TDNT* 2:18 §C3).

The length of her condition indicates its severity and adds a note
of pathos, since she has suffered a long time. Among the suggestions
for the disease referred to are *spondylitis ankylopoietica* (a fusion of
the spinal bones; Marshall 1978: 557) and *skoliasis hysterica* (a type
of hysterical or muscular paralysis; Grundmann 1963: 279). Although it is hard to be sure, a condition similar to *spondylitis ankylopoietica* is perhaps more likely given the duration of the condition
(Wilkinson 1977).

The result of the evil spirit's presence is that the woman is bent
over or "bent double" (συγκύπτουσα, *sygkyptousa*; BAGD 775; BAA
1546; only here in the NT; Sir. 12:11; 19:26). She is not able to stand
erect (ἀνακύψαι, *anakypsai*; BAGD 56; BAA 111; John 8:7, 10). Παν-
τελές (*panteles*) goes with either the infinitive ἀνακύψαι to mean
"completely" (Oepke, *TDNT* 2:427 n. 30) or the participle δυναμένη
(*dynamenē*, being able) to mean "at all" (Delling, *TDNT* 8:66–67).
Most favor the first option so that the phrase refers to the woman's
not being able to straighten herself completely (Creed 1930: 183;
Van Der Loos 1965: 520 n. 3; Arndt 1956: 329).[6] It is hard to know
which sense is meant, though the apparent severity of her case
might suggest the second option and a translation of "at all" (Marshall 1978: 557–58). In either case, the woman is severely bent over.

b. Healing (13:12–13)

Jesus initiates the healing upon seeing the woman's sad condition.   **13:12**
His effort to help a woman is significant in a culture where men

4. On women and the synagogue, see Safrai 1976c: 919–20; *m. Ber.* 3.3. *Midr. ha-
Gadol* on Deut. 29:10 [29:11 MT] pictures women and children receiving teaching by
hearing the readings of the Targums. Safrai notes that these late rabbinic texts are
confirmed by Acts 16:13 and 17:4. Schweizer 1984: 222 is thus wrong to suggest that
the woman is outside the synagogue.

5. Luke 5:15; 8:2; 11:14; 13:12; Matt. 8:17. Demonic influence may be a better description than demonic possession, because it is not behavior but a diseased condition
that is the point; Luke 4:33, 38–39; 2 Cor. 12:7. Weakness is produced by the evil spirit;
1QapGen 20.17, 21–29; Stählin, *TDNT* 1:493; Marshall 1978: 557. Fitzmyer 1985: 1012
calls the genitival ἀσθενείας (weakness) an Aramaism; see Creed 1930: 183. Nolland
1993a: 724 suggests that the number *eighteen* may be conventional (2 x 9 = "a long
time"); Judg. 3:13–14; 10:8; 20:25, 44; 2 Sam. 8:13. This is possible, but not certain.

6. BAGD 608 and BAA 1230–31 list the options. Klostermann 1929: 144–45 cites
Heb. 7:25 as a grammatical parallel. Plummer 1896: 342 notes that παντελής always
appears next to the term it modifies in Josephus: *Antiquities* 1.18.5 §267; 3.11.3 §264;
3.12.1 §274; 6.2.3 §30; 7.13.3 §325.

publicly shunned women. It shows the extent to which Jesus responds to those in need (Grundmann 1963: 279; Oepke, *TDNT* 1:784 §B1).[7] Jesus acts by calling to her and declaring that she is free from her ailment. No mention is made of the woman's faith, for the only point here is Jesus' authority and what the healing represents. The declaration that she is "freed from her infirmity" will shortly become a declaration that she is freed from Satan's power (13:16).[8] This is a "rule miracle." Jesus' word has the authority to reverse her condition, and it does. She is no longer in bondage.

13:13   Jesus backs up his words with action. He lays hands on the woman, an action that Luke mentions in these terms only one other time (4:40).[9] The action demonstrates Jesus' identification with the woman's problem and verifies that his power heals, an important point in the midst of a potentially skeptical crowd. "Immediately" (παραχρῆμα, *parachrēma*) there are results: she straightens up. God's actions are stressed in the passive verb (ἀνωρθώθη, *anōrthō-thē*, she was made straight; BAGD 72; BAA 143).[10] Luke often mentions how quickly healing occurs.[11] The woman responds by offering praise to God, another common Lucan note (2:20; 4:15; 5:25–26; 7:16; 17:15; 18:43). Her long ordeal is over. The woman, by her praise, recognizes the connection between Jesus and the exercise of God's power, an association that will lead to indignation and confrontation in 13:14 (Schweizer 1984: 222). Acts 2:22–24 speaks of such acts as "attestation of Jesus by God."

c. Reactions (13:14–17)
i. The Synagogue Leader's Reaction (13:14)

13:14   At least one reaction to Jesus is highly negative, but rather than address the respected teacher directly, the synagogue leader chooses

---

7. Danker 1988: 261 notes that the woman might be unclean, in which case Jesus' action would be bold on two counts: one cultural, the other cultic. But the text is not clear on this point.

8. On the rare use of ἀπολύω as a description of being freed from the effects of disease, see BAGD 96; BAA 193; Josephus, *Antiquities* 3.11.3 §264. The term is generally used of freeing prisoners or releasing from debt. This common usage may inform the use of the term here. Contextually, the perfect tense announces entry into a state of healing; Arndt 1956: 329.

9. Elsewhere in the Synoptics at Matt. 9:18 = Mark 5:23; 6:5; 8:23, 25. The same action in different terms is found in Luke 5:13; 8:44, 54; 14:4; 22:51; Busse 1979: 295.

10. Ἀνορθόω is limited to OT quotations in its other NT uses: Acts 15:16; Heb. 12:12; Creed 1930: 183; Klostermann 1929: 145. It was used commonly in medical situations; LSJ 147.

11. Luke uses παραχρῆμα in 1:64; 4:39; 5:25; 8:44, 47, 55; 18:43; 19:11; 22:60. Fitzmyer 1985: 1013 remarks, "The instantaneous cure on the Sabbath stands in contrast to the eighteen years of infirmity."

to address those who have observed the Sabbath healing.[12] Nonetheless, it is Jesus who performed the labor and who stands rebuked (Fitzmyer 1985: 1013 suggests that the motive is to warn the people about Jesus). Luke clearly portrays the leader as angry. The leader speaks while "indignant" (ἀγανακτῶν, *aganaktōn* [BAGD 4 and BAA 7 refer to "intense displeasure"]) because Jesus has healed on the Sabbath.[13]

The leader's rebuke is direct and depends on a traditional reading of Deut. 5:12–15 and Exod. 20:8–11 (Danker 1988: 261; Tiede 1988: 250; Schneider 1977a: 300). Healing can be done on any day other than the Sabbath. In the leader's view, healing is labor. But consider the "effort" that went into the healing: Jesus spoke and laid hands on the woman, but the actual power to heal comes from God. Nonetheless, the complaint is that the Sabbath has been violated by Jesus' "labor." The leader refers to the necessity of labor on the other six days. Labor and healing are tied together in his remarks, a point that Jesus will note in his reply.

Rabbinic rules governed work on the Sabbath: thirty-nine forms of labor were forbidden (*m. Šab.* 7.2), while others were tolerated, for example, leading cattle to drink, a point similar to the one Jesus raises (Luke 6:2; Manson 1949: 189–90, 275; SB 2:199–200; Schweizer 1984: 222).[14] The complaint mirrors the reaction to the disciples' activity in 6:1–11. The leader is portrayed as having learned nothing from Jesus' earlier warnings. Despite all of Jesus' work and teaching, nothing has changed about how some perceive him.

ii. Jesus' Rebuke (13:15–16)

13:15 Jesus returns the synagogue leader's rebuke with a rebuke. The tone of Jesus' reply surfaces in the plural ὑποκριταί (*hypokritai*, hypocrites), which indicates that the leader is not alone in his thinking

12. On the synagogue leader (ἀρχισυνάγωγος), see Schrage, *TDNT* 7:847. This person was responsible for the order and progress of worship, so he is the right one to speak. The most learned member presents the official view on Jesus' act. There is no need to argue for a redactional seam at the shift of address to the audience. The leader is responsible for the assembly's worship (Nolland 1993a: 724). Nolland argues that "the directive fits only imperfectly in the flow of the story." I disagree: practice and custom is the issue here. The issue cannot arise until Jesus heals.

13. Ὅτι is either causal, giving the reason for the anger, or an indicator of indirect discourse, giving the leader's thinking about Jesus: that he "healed on the Sabbath," an act that in turn makes him angry.

14. Ellis 1974: 186 notes that the Qumranians in general were even stricter than the Pharisees; K. Schubert 1957: 127–28. CD 11.13–14 reads, "No one shall help an animal in its delivery on the Sabbath day. And if it falls into a pit or a ditch, one shall not raise it on the Sabbath." For details of Jewish practice, see the exegesis of the next verse.

(BAGD 845; BAA 1684; Luke 6:42; 12:1, 56). Many in the crowd or in the leader's circles must have shared his view, and so Jesus responds not just to the leader but to all who think like him. Luke notes Jesus' authority by calling him Lord (κύριος, *kyrios*).

Jesus contrasts the leader's indignation at the woman's being healed on the Sabbath with a Jew's readiness to untie cattle, feed them at the manger, and lead them to water on the Sabbath.[15] All are overt acts of labor and compassion. The Mishnah allows cattle to be lead on the Sabbath as long as they do not carry a load (*m. Šab.* 5) and tied up on the Sabbath lest they wander (*m. Šab.* 15.2). The Mishnah also describes the wells at which cattle can drink without violating the Sabbath (*m. ʿErub.* 2.1–4). At Qumran, CD 11.5–6 allowed travel up to two thousand cubits (three thousand feet) for pasturing (Marshall 1978: 558–59; Manson 1949: 275). Jesus' question is rhetorical, a statement that the Jews often labor for their cattle's sake. They cannot dispute that this is common practice (indicated by ἕκαστος, *hekastos*, each), which raises the issue of how an animal can fare better than a human on the Sabbath. Thus the leaders are condemned by their own practice. They show compassion to animals, but not to humans. It is this issue of inconsistency and priority in creation that Jesus raises. Some interpreters miss Jesus' point by arguing that his retort is not relevant, since he could have waited a day to heal (C. G. Montefiore, cited in Creed 1930: 183; also Schweizer 1984: 222). Jesus' point, however, is relevant: how can an animal be treated with more concern on the sacred day than a person? Such an attitude is a reversal of the created order (Luke 12:6–7; 1 Cor. 9:9; Danker 1988: 262).

13:16 Jesus explains why he acts: just as some feel free to aid animals on the Sabbath, one should feel the same moral necessity (ἔδει, *edei*) to aid this ailing daughter of Abraham on the Sabbath (cf. Luke 16:22; 19:9). Most see a minor-to-major argument here: what is true of animals is more true of people. Satan had bound the woman for eighteen years, and she should be loosed from this bond, even more than the ox should be loosed on the Sabbath to eat.[16] Jesus is arguing that the woman's relationship to Abraham, the man of God's promise, makes her healing on the Lord's day not wrong but appropriate, even necessary. What better day to reflect on God's activity than the Sabbath?

15. A wordplay around the idea of "loosing" or "untying" reappears in 13:16.

16. On the figurative use of "bound" and "loosed," see Fitzmyer 1985: 1013; MM 142, 144. The length of the woman's condition is underlined by the use of the interjection ἰδού (behold). On Satan's activity, see Job 2:1–7; Acts 10:38; 1 Cor. 5:5; 2 Cor. 12:7; 1 Tim. 1:20; Plummer 1896: 343. Fitzmyer notes that the verse argues against Conzelmann's view (1960: 27–28, 80) of a "Satan-free" period during Jesus' ministry.

The passive infinitive λυθῆναι (*lythēnai*, to be loosed) suggests that someone frees the woman. Since only God can exercise such power, the healing is another evidence of God working through Jesus and a token of the struggle in which God is engaged to reclaim and restore people. Such activity is ideal for the day when people are to rest and offer worship to God, the good Creator (Grundmann 1963: 280; Marshall 1978: 559). In effect, Jesus argues that his act does not violate the Sabbath, but fits the very spirit of the day. What better way to celebrate the Sabbath! The difference in the views of Jesus and the synagogue leader could not be greater.

iii. Division (13:17)

13:17

A great division is present, similar to the one described in 12:51–53, except that here the nation, not the family, is in view (Danker 1988: 262). Luke depicts the opponents as put to shame (κατῃσχύνοντο, *kateschynonto*; BAGD 410 §2; BAA 834 §2) by Jesus' remarks (Bultmann, *TDNT* 1:190; Creed 1930: 183; Isa. 45:16). Luke has in mind the leaders condemned in Luke 11:37–54 and warned as part of the crowd in 12:54–13:9. Nonetheless, some of the people rejoiced at the variety of wonderful things (τοῖς ἐνδόξοις, *tois endoxois*) that Jesus did.[17] Τοῖς ἐνδόξοις is plural, so that more than the woman's healing is in view. Many opportunities have been given to respond to Jesus, and some in the crowd have sensed that God is at work. Two large groups are forming with no one left in the middle. The healing leaves no room to sit on the fence. Note how various forms of πᾶς (*pas*) are used to refer to "all" the opponents and "all" the crowd and "all" the wonderful things. It is not possible to remain neutral about these events. Jesus' action forces a choice.

Summary

Earlier Jesus had warned the crowd to respond to him while there was still time (13:1–9). Many such opportunities have been given to the nation to respond. Similar events gave testimony to what Jesus was doing, as well as occasion to respond. In 13:10–17, the Sabbath healing of the handicapped woman is another such event. It follows a warning of the need to respond while there is still opportunity to do so. Jesus' Sabbath work had earlier met with rejection. And yet again the "mirror" miracle produces the same response. Less time is spent in this account on the healing, and more time is given to the reaction. Jesus produces indignation in some, who continually refuse to respond to the message of repentance. Rejection is stubborn and blind to the evidence. But

17. Exod. 34:10; Deut. 10:21; Job 5:9; 9:10; Luke 7:16; 19:37 are conceptually similar.

for others there is rejoicing. No one can sit on the fence and watch Jesus work without forming an opinion. He is too great a figure to be left to neutrality. To those sensitive to what God is doing, there is a picture of the woman now able to leave the scene and stand up straight. Through her posture, she points to God's work touching people from heaven. For Luke's readers, there is reassurance that Jesus is the one through whom God works. A special time in God's plan has come in him. Yet the question remains: with which part of the crowd does the reader identify—the complainers or those who praise God?

4. Kingdom Parables: Mustard Seed and Leaven (13:18–21)

Luke's concern since 12:49 has been that Jesus' ministry reflects a special time in God's plan. Yet with the coming of promise is the threat of judgment. The signs of the kingdom's approach are present, so now is the time to settle with one's accuser and repent. In fact, Satan's defeat is seen in Jesus' miracles, miracles that include God's working through Jesus on the Sabbath. The season for blessing also contains the threat of judgment for failing to respond.

Luke 12–13 alternates between notes of judgment and hope. Jesus provides the way to God, but that way is not found in the path offered by the nation's professional spiritual leaders. The crowds and leaders need to understand what God is doing and respond to the presence of his power.

When one speaks of the special time in God's program, one thinks of the promise of God's rule, the kingdom hope. Jesus tells some fundamental parables about the kingdom: the parable of the mustard seed (13:18–19) and the parable of the leaven (13:20–21). Luke gives less time to such parables than Matthew or Mark (Matt. 13 has seven parables, while Mark 4 has three parables and one similitude).

What is the kingdom's character; what does it look like? These parables contain a surprising answer to this question by picturing a gradual process of growth. Jewish expectation was of the quick establishment of a powerful, comprehensively present kingdom or of the kingdom's decisive in-breaking from outside of history. However, Jesus teaches that the kingdom comes gradually, with growth that will culminate in a total presence.[1] It is the image of

---

1. On the Jewish expectations of either a political kingdom or a kingdom coming directly and apocalyptically from God, see Goppelt 1981–82: 1.45–51 and Ladd 1974b: 60–63. Matt. 13:11 calls this gradual growth part of the "mystery" of the kingdom. Matt. 13:52 shows that the kingdom promise contains both new and old things side by side, indicating that NT kingdom revelation supplements and complements OT revelation. Beasley-Murray 1986: 194–201 lists the parables of growth in the Synoptics: mustard seed and leaven (Luke 13:18–21 = Matt. 13:31–33 = Mark 4:30–32), seed growing secretly (Mark 4:26–29), sower (Luke 8:4–8 = Matt. 13:1–9 = Mark 4:1–9), wheat and tares (Matt. 13:24–30), and the dragnet (Matt. 13:47–50).

transformation into total sovereignty that Jesus describes, though whether that kingdom, especially in its initial form, is linked to a current kingdom that will grow and seize power on earth is another matter.[2] The kingdom is best characterized in the current era not as an institution but as the presence of God's power in a special group of people. God's presence is expressed through those who are allied to the bestower of salvific gifts (Acts 2:32–36). The kingdom is not so much represented by any one location or institution as much as it is expressed through people of the believing community—at least until it becomes more visibly expressed upon Jesus' return. God's rule has a current realm where he is especially active—the community of believers. These parables argue that after its humble start under Jesus the kingdom will some day spread across all the earth.

The reason that Jesus mentions the parables here is that an exemplary exercise of that power has just occurred in the woman's healing, showing the initial presence of kingdom power. Its presence can only come to have greater extension and influence (Marshall 1978: 560; Fitzmyer 1985: 1016; Ezek. 17:22–24; 31:2–9).

Sources and Historicity

The Lucan material has parallels in Matt. 13:31–33 = Mark 4:30–32 (Aland 1985: §§209–10). There is not much verbal overlap in the accounts, though the wording of Luke's parable of the leaven is close to Matthew's. Most see a use of Q material here, and it is possible that Matt. 13 and Luke 13 belong to the same setting as part of a similar tradition.[3] Such parables about a major theme in Jesus' teaching might have been spoken on several occa-

2. Note Ellis 1974: 187. In its initial phase, the kingdom as manifested in the church is a community of people who all look to the same hope in Christ. Thus, the kingdom's presence primarily is manifested in believers who all serve and are accountable to the sovereign head, Jesus Christ (Eph. 1:19–22; Col. 1:12–14). The church universal is related to the kingdom, being its present expression, but the church is not all there is to the kingdom, since there is a kingdom to come. In addition, the church is not an institution seeking to seize power on earth or exercise coercive sovereignty, but is to serve and love humankind, reflecting the love of God, his standards of righteousness, and the message of his forgiveness and love in Jesus Christ (Rom. 12:9–13:7). These elements make up the mission of the church as light in the world (Matt. 5:14–16).

3. So Kistemaker 1980: 45 speaks of the same occasion. On Q, see Grundmann 1963: 281; Egelkraut 1976: 108; Marshall 1978: 559–60; Wiefel 1988: 257; Fitzmyer 1985: 1015. The same linkage of parables occurs in Matthew and, as noted above, the wording in the leaven parable is very similar. The Gospel of Thomas 96–97 links the leaven parable to a different parable, the jar full of meal, which has no canonical parallel. A parable of the mustard seed is found in the Gospel of Thomas 20; Hunzinger, *TDNT* 7:290 n. 32.

sions, so it is hard to be certain that a single setting is in view for Matthew and Luke, though it seems most likely that a single tradition is employed.

Mark 4 places these parables earlier in Jesus' ministry. Since the Lucan language of the parable of the mustard seed has no direct verbal overlap with Mark, it is unlikely that Luke shares a point of contact with Mark.[4] Nonetheless, Mark 4 may represent the same cluster of teaching, for it is possible that this chapter is arranged topically and placed early in Mark (much like the five controversies of Mark 2:1–3:6 are grouped together early in his account). If so, then all three parable clusters are part of the same fundamental tradition.

But there remains an interesting question: Why would Luke break apart what Matthew and Mark have together? This question is relevant regardless of what theory of Synoptic origins one holds. If Mark is first, then Luke has broken up and significantly delayed a tradition that he shows evidence of in Luke 8:4–15. If Matthew is first, then Luke has broken up and delayed part of a tradition that appears in Matthew before the Caesarea Philippi confession (some of Luke's material appears after the confession). Only three options are possible:

1. The traditions are independent. The verbal agreements, especially in the leaven account are somewhat against this option, not to mention the strain this puts on other parallels to the parabolic kingdom discourse.
2. Luke is not at all interested in a broad chronology in the journey material. If this is so, what is one to make of the general force of his journey motif and of the geographical markers found near the end of the journey narrative?
3. Luke broke up what was together because he knew that Jesus' ministry was characterized throughout by parables. Rather than concentrating the parables in a few discourses as do the other Synoptics, he distributes the parables throughout Jesus' ministry in a way that reflects that ministry. Luke's point is that Jesus regularly taught in parables and maintained similar themes throughout his ministry. The amount of fresh parabolic material in Luke serves to reinforce the likelihood that this is what he has done. In which case an additional point is valid: if Luke assumes that his readers knew about the "other accounts" (1:1–3), maybe he consciously complemented their presentation at this point. He breaks up what the other traditions had together to suggest that Jesus taught this theme on various occasions.

It should be noted that these points are merely suggestive, since it is difficult to unravel the tradition history of both this text and 8:4–15.

---

4. Since none of the four terms shared by Mark and Luke have the same position, a connection is unlikely.

Luke has less emphasis than the other Synoptic writers on the kingdom parables, perhaps because he wishes to stress the kingdom's activity and the key personality of the kingdom a little more, rather than focusing on pictures of what the kingdom is like. The authenticity of Jesus' teaching cannot be denied by schematizing Jesus' view as teaching instant imminency, while arguing that the image of gradual growth is a "later" concept.[5] The parables go back to Jesus.

> The passage is parabolic in terms of form (Berger 1984: 48). The outline of Luke 13:18–21 is as follows:
>
> a. The kingdom parable of the mustard seed (13:18–19)
> b. The kingdom parable of the leaven (13:20–21)
>
> The parables picture the kingdom's inevitable growth: it starts small but will become large, reaching everywhere. The imagery is like that promise made to the nation of a Davidic rule that would grow until the shade of its branches produced rest for many (Ezek. 17:22–24). The kingdom does not instantly appear as a colossus. Nevertheless, it will eventually become a residing place for many. Reassurance may be found in the way the kingdom will grow.

Exegesis and Exposition

[18]Therefore he was saying, "What is the kingdom of God like? And to what shall I compare it? [19]It is like a grain of mustard seed, which a man took and sowed in his garden, and it grew and became a tree, and the birds of heaven made nests in its branches."

[20]And again he said, "To what shall I compare the kingdom of God? [21]It is like leaven, which a woman took and hid in three measures of flour until it was all leavened."

a. The Kingdom Parable of the Mustard Seed (13:18–19)

13:18 Jesus raises the kingdom question because the woman's release from Satan raises the issue of authority and rule. To argue that "the context in Luke is poor" (Luce 1933: 240) misses the point of the connection between the previous event and the parable. Οὖν (*oun*,

---

5. But so Schulz 1972: 301–9; rightly refuted by Marshall 1978: 559–60. Multiple levels of the parable tradition (see n. 1 above) teach the kingdom's gradual growth and contrastive transformation. In addition, even the parables of this section appear in various wings of the tradition (Mark and Q [or Matthew]), so that multiple attestation speaks for authenticity. Jeremias 1963a: 146 n. 68 notes the Palestinian coloring in the parables, a point in favor of authenticity. Even the Jesus Seminar accepts the essential authenticity of these parables, printing 13:18–19 in pink type and 13:20–21 in red (Funk and Hoover 1993: 346–47).

therefore) is no accident, as Jesus develops the healing's implications and desires to draw pictures portraying the kingdom's character. By this comparison, Jesus reveals some kingdom qualities and the nature of God's program (Fitzmyer 1985: 1016; Jesus elsewhere uses comparative language in 6:47–49; 7:31–32; 12:36; 13:21).

Matthew 13:31 introduces the parable as part of a parabolic series. He begins the sequence by saying that Jesus put before them another parable. Like Luke, Mark 4:30 asks a pair of questions. However, the second question is slightly different and the first appears in different wording: "With what can we compare the kingdom of God? Or what parable shall we use for it?"[6] The singular-plural difference is merely a stylistic difference, since "we" and "I" are conceptually the same. Mark's question about the parable is more directly presented in Luke ("To what shall I compare it?").

Jesus' parable is simple: a small seed grows into a tree large enough **13:19** for birds to nest.[7] There are two elements in the image. First is the growth from a small entity to a large entity, from seed into tree. The fundamental image involves transformation from something small to something large enough to provide shelter for animals. The parable contrasts the start of the kingdom with its eventual character.

The type of tree is debated (Plummer 1896: 344–45; Hendriksen 1978: 703). It is either the *Salvadora Persica*, which can grow to twenty-five feet, or the *Sinapis Nigra*, a member of the mustard family that can grow up to ten feet, though as low as four feet is not unusual (Hunzinger, *TDNT* 7:288–89; B. Scott 1989: 374–78, esp. 380).[8] The specific tree alluded to is not important, since the point is the contrast between the seed and the tree. Nonetheless, it is likely that the smaller of the candidates is referred to here, given its association with the mustard family. Whatever tree is meant, Jesus is

---

6. Jesus' introduction of the parable compares with rabbinic introductions of similar material; SB 2:7–9; note also Isa. 40:18; Marshall 1978: 561; Hauck, *TDNT* 5:753–54.

7. On the mustard seed as proverbial for a small quantity in Judaism, see *m. Nid.* 5.2; *b. Ber.* 31a; Manson 1949: 123; Michel, *TDNT* 3:810–12, esp. 810 n. 1; SB 1:669. Citing Lev. Rab. 31 on 24:2, Lachs 1987: 225 notes that the mustard seed is proverbial in Judaism for the smallest size, a stark contrast to the strong image of the cedar. Lachs's citation of Lev. Rab. 31, which deals with the production of olive oil, is not clear. Is the mustard seed implied in the oil excluded as worthy in Lev. Rab. 31.10?

8. Scott makes much of the issue that a mustard tree is a shrub and yet yields cedar tree–like qualities in the parable. This "twist" may add a miraculous note to the image, though Scott believes (based on *m. Kil.* 3.2) its resultant force is an allusion to uncleanness (reflected in the sowing of mustard seed in a garden). If this idea is present, it is subtle. Only Luke's form, with its garden reference, could sustain the point. The point more likely addresses only the unusual nature of the growth, not ritual uncleanness, a theme that Jesus tended not to address in reference to the kingdom.

saying that the kingdom will start out small but end up big. The connection between the kingdom's starting out small and becoming large makes Nolland's claim (1993a: 728) of a distinction between church and kingdom unclear. Does he mean that the kingdom is more than the church? This is correct, but the small-to-large image suggests that the current era is the start, the church period is part of the period of growth, and the great culmination matches the end of the parable's promise.

Besides the contrast in the start and finish of the seed, the image's second point is the product: a place of shade and shelter. In fact, this is the major point of the parable. Not only is a tree present, but birds are able to nest there. The image of birds in the tree is a significant one. Κατεσκήνωσεν (*kateskēnōsen*, made nests) can reflect an eschatological image for the incorporation of Gentiles into the people of God.[9] The image of birds in the tree occurs several times in the OT. In Ps. 104:12, birds find shelter in the trees and sing in praise of God's creation. In Dan. 4:10–15 [4:7–12 MT], the image depicts Nebuchadnezzar's power protecting the nations. Daniel uses the image differently in that what starts out as a positive image ends up negatively, for the tree is reduced to a stump. Nebuchadnezzar represents a once-powerful earthly kingdom that falls to nothing (the picture of Assyria in Ezek. 31:6 is similar, but its image of shade is positive). Finally, Ezek. 17:22–24 provides the closest OT parallel to Luke. Here God promises to plant in Israel a cedar tree from a sprig, probably an allusion to the restoration of Davidic rule. This rule will grow into a sturdy cedar that will become a comfortable place to dwell. In the OT the picture of birds in a tree is consistently an image of calm and shelter (note also Judg. 9:15 and Isa. 51:16).

In Luke, the image starts and ends positively. In fact, as in the OT, the picture of shade is also positive. Interpretations that argue that the image of birds in the branches is negative, referring to the mixed character of the kingdom, cannot be right. The birds do not represent false believers in the branches (so Gaebelein 1910: 281–86; correctly V. Taylor 1966: 270). The kingdom is a pleasant place to dwell and protects those who live under its shade.

It is difficult, given the setting in Jesus' ministry, to know if a Gentile emphasis like that in Daniel is explicit here or whether it simply means that humans in general will find shelter in the kingdom (for the latter, Fitzmyer 1985: 1017). Given the passage's setting of min-

---

9. Paul's image of the olive tree in Rom. 11 is a variation on Jesus' picture. There the key point is not growth, but one's presence in the plant; Egelkraut 1976: 109; Jeremias 1963a: 147–49; *Joseph and Asenath* 15. On the verb κατασκηνόω (to live or nest), see BAGD 418 §2; BAA 851. Elsewhere in the NT at Matt. 13:32 = Mark 4:32; Acts 2:26.

istry among Israel, the reference is not likely a direct allusion to Gentiles. The implication, however, in light of God's subsequent plan, is hard to avoid (13:29–30). Nolland (1993a: 728–29) states the point with more caution for the parable, but argues that Luke does read it this way. The point is that the kingdom will end up with significant stature and will be a place where people of all races can reside comfortably.

Yet another point may be relevant. If the picture of the cedar tree was common in Judaism to describe the kingdom, and the image is a consistent one in the OT, then the use of a mustard seed to describe the kingdom is a surprise, a twist in the story. The twist functions like the Samaritan in an earlier parable. The Samaritan is not the character voted "most likely to help" by current cultural standards. So also the mustard tree is not the normal image of the kingdom and shelter. As such, Jesus makes the point that the kingdom comes in a surprising form, not the one anticipated. That is why Matt. 13 has this parable in his "mystery" section. But the surprising humble form of the kingdom's coming should not deceive anyone. The kingdom will still end up being a place of comfort and shelter under the protective shade of the Almighty. In fact, the shrub shall transform itself into a tree. This point is important: Jewish expectation had been of the magnificent arrival of a grand kingdom all at once (this is why the disciples wondered what role they would have in ruling). Jesus says that the kingdom comes now, but it starts out small and will gradually assume the grand scale they expected. That is why the parallels speak of the mystery of the kingdom in such texts. It is still kingdom truth, but it is a fresh element added alongside the OT picture.

The parable in Luke is expressed similarly in Matt. 13:31b–32 = Mark 4:31–32 (Luke is the briefest). Mark contains much detail with regard to the small size of the seed, the size of the shrub and branches, and the shade of the branches (Matthew also notes the smallness of the seed and refers to the shrub). This final Marcan image of the shade from the branches specifies the branches' role, as they protect those who dwell in the tree. Each writer uses a different term for where the seed is sown: Matthew has "in the field," Mark has "on the earth," and Luke has "in the garden." There is some tense variation as well: Mark uses his normal, vivid present tenses, while Luke uses past tense and Matthew mixes the two. These are merely stylistic variations.

b. The Kingdom Parable of the Leaven (13:20–21)

13:20 Jesus returns to his question in order to give a second illustration of the kingdom. Again he makes clear that he presents a comparison between life and the kingdom. Πάλιν (*palin*, again) is rare in Luke (only here, 6:43, and 23:20, in comparison to Matthew's seventeen uses and Mark's twenty-eight), so the introduction probably belongs to Luke's source (Marshall 1978: 561). In contrast to Luke 13:18, only one question is asked, but the same general topic is present. Matthew 13:33, which is the only parallel to the parable, speaks of Jesus' telling them "another parable" and presents the introduction as a statement without a preceding question.

13:21 The second picture of the kingdom involves another common phenomenon: leaven that is added to the ingredients for making bread and permeates it through and through. A "measure" (σάτον, *saton*) was equal to the Hebrew סְאָה (*sĕ'â*, seah), which is 13.13 liters or 4.75 gallons (Plummer 1896: 345; Kistemaker 1980: 48; Marshall 1978: 561).[10] Three seahs would total about 39.4 liters or 50 pounds of flour.[11] There is some question whether the image of leaven is negative, as it usually is (Mark 8:15 = Luke 12:1; 1 Cor. 5:6; Gal. 5:9), or positive. This use is positive since Jesus generally portrays the kingdom as positive and since this parable follows a positive one (Windisch, *TDNT* 2:905). The point is that the kingdom will eventually permeate the world. It may appear small and insignificant now, but it will eventually grow and be present everywhere. The emphasis is not so much on the process of growth as it is on the contrast between its start and finish, though the leaven image suggests a note of unseen or invisible growth (Danker 1988: 263; Kistemaker 1980: 49). In the contrast of start and finish, this parable matches that of the mustard seed. One other note may also be suggested by the image: permeation is inevitable once leaven is introduced (Manson 1949: 123). Jesus may well be answering complaints that such an insignificant-looking effort cannot reflect the kingdom's arrival, since the kingdom is great.

There is no need to find specific referents for the number *three*: the three elements of a human (body, soul, spirit); the three institutions of earth, church, and state; or the three races of Jews, Samaritans, and Greeks. The human interpretation individualizes the parable too much and the institutional and racial interpretations fail to see that the flour is not three kinds of material, but only one. Kiste-

10. Σάτον occurs elsewhere in the NT only at Matt. 13:33; BAGD 745; BAA 1490; also in Josephus, *Antiquities* 9.4.4 §71; 9.4.5 §85; Gen. 18:6; Judg. 6:19; 1 Sam. 1:24. Nolland 1993a: 730 questions this connection, since the LXX does not connect σάτον to סְאָה. If he is right, the amount is unclear. But a Semitic context for the parable makes a specific connection likely.

11. Jeremias 1963a: 147, who cites *m. Pe'a* 8.7. One is tempted to say that this woman was baking for an army, since this amount could feed over one hundred people.

maker (1980: 50–51) oversimplifies the parable by equating kingdom and church.[12]

Matthew 13:33 gives the parable as a statement and speaks, as is Matthew's custom, of the kingdom of heaven. From that point on, however, Matthew and Luke are in verbal agreement.

Luke 13:18–21 pictures the kingdom's character. Jesus' ministry does not look like the coming of God's mighty power and deliverance. Jesus therefore tells two parables to explain the meaning of healings like that of the bent-over woman. The point in both parables is similar: what starts out small will eventually come to the point where many may dwell securely (mustard seed) and where the penetration will be total (leaven). The kingdom looks deceptively weak and impotent now, but the exercise of its inherent power allows it to transform and spread its scope. An understanding of how the kingdom grows will provide the proper understanding of Jesus' ministry. The parables represent a call to trust in the way God is developing the kingdom. They are also designed to assure followers that the kingdom's current small size is not where the program will end. The kingdom will start small, but eventually God will cause it to penetrate the whole earth. He will reign in his kingdom.

The parables brought hope to those early disciples who participated in the kingdom while it was still in its early, small phase. Even now the parables have a note of hope and involve a call to trust, for God has not yet completed his kingdom program. Disciples need to be aware that the kingdom will eventually become a place of shelter over the whole earth. Jesus' current opponents are in powerful places, but that will not stop the kingdom from becoming a place of safety. Such opposition will not stop it from covering the world. Trees built with earthly hands, like that of Nebuchadnezzar, will become stumps, but the branches of God's kingdom will bring shade forever.

Summary

12. Ladd 1974b: 105–19 shows that the church is not identical to the kingdom, though his view is too abstract in minimizing the reference to a realm. On this latter issue, see Bock 1992c.

5. The Narrow and Soon-Shut Door (13:22–30)

The kingdom's coming has implications for the Jewish nation. The time to join God's eschatological program has come, so one had better respond quickly before the door closes. Jesus stresses the nation's situation in the picture of the narrow and soon-shut door. After this passage, Jesus will issue a lament, because the nation does not respond (13:31–35). What Luke has been showing since 11:37 is that the Pharisees and many others in the nation have not responded. Though they see themselves joined to the patriarchs and prophets, they are rapidly placing themselves in a position where they will be isolated from them. Jesus warns that the time is short and, once the door closes, it will be too late. In addition, he notes that many others from all around the world will be at the table with these great OT saints, while those racially related to them will be missing. The passage has a strong note of warning and pathos. It is no accident that it begins by noting that Jesus is heading for Jerusalem. The nation's very resistance to accept Jesus will drive him to his fate in the nation's religious center.

Sources and Historicity

Despite conceptual parallels to Matt. 7:13–14; 25:10–12; 7:22–23; 25:41; 8:11–12; 19:30; 20:16; and Mark 10:31, this passage is an independent tradition that Luke alone has or that represents the combining of various materials from Jesus' ministry (Aland 1985: §211). Egelkraut (1976: 169–70) prefers the latter view and cites many who agree with him, while arguing that Mark, Q, and special Lucan material have all been used at one point or another. In Egelkraut's view, Luke has drawn up an "artificial parable" to express his concerns. Jeremias (1963a: 95–96, 110) speaks of a "new parable" emerging through the fusion of the conclusion of one parable with other similes. Creed (1930: 184) argues that Luke arranged this material, while Tiede (1988: 253) and Schneider (1977a: 304–5) speak of Q. But why must Luke be the source of such a synthesis? Could not Jesus be working with his own imagery in a creative way like any expressive teacher (Godet 1875: 2.126)? If an anthology of national images from Jesus' ministry is present, then Luke has briefly summarized Jesus' teaching in one place. The possibility of some in Israel missing blessing is a natural part of Jesus' prophetical call to the nation to repent (Nolland 1993a: 732–33). In addition, the differences in the imagery actually suggest that independence of sources is most likely.[1] The order in which the Matthean conceptual parallels appear (see above) suggests that different material is in view. This differing order also shows that the imagery of these passages is different. For example, Matt. 7:13–14 compares the narrow door with destruction's wide door, an image that is totally absent in Luke. What is shared between the passages are basic conceptual pictures that Jesus used on various occasions.[2]

The Jesus Seminar prints 13:24 in pink type, 13:25–29 in black, and 13:30 in gray (Funk and Hoover 1993: 347–48). The seminar argues that Jesus' comparison in 13:24 appears in a simple, unembellished form. The rejection of 13:25–29 is built mostly around its theme of judgment, which is "inimical" to Jesus and reflects "the invective of the young sectarian movement." But the theme fits prophetic criticism and warning to Israel (3:8–9; 11:31–32) and is attested throughout the Q tradition: Luke 7:31–35 = Matt. 11:16–19; Luke 10:13–15 = Matt. 11:20–24; Luke 11:31–32 = Matt. 12:41–42; Luke 11:49–51 (like Matt. 23:34–36); Luke 14:15–24 (like Matt. 22:1–10) (Beasley-Murray 1986: 172–73). Are all of these creations of the church or do they reflect a prophetic challenge to Israel? Jesus seems quite capable of the latter. Meier (1994: 316) gives four reasons for seeing 13:28–29 as historical: (1) the presence of Gentiles at a future banquet would not be a church creation; (2) not all of Israel is rejected, only some; (3) the combination of eschatological pilgrimage of Gentiles, banquet, and kingdom is unique; and (4) Jesus is absent as the key figure at the meal. What Meier (1994: 317) says about Jesus' future kingdom hope could also be applied to the idea that Jesus did not preach judgment:

> The historical Jesus did expect a future coming of God's kingdom, and that king-dom was in some way a transcendent one, surmounting this world's barriers of time, space, hostility between Jews and Gentiles, and finally death itself. A

1. Schweizer 1984: 225–26, though noting links to Matthew, suggests that the tradition may have come together before Luke, because of non-Lucan language in 13:25–27. Luce 1933: 240 sees too little correspondence to attribute the material to Q, as does Grundmann 1963: 284, who speaks of a special Lucan source. Michaelis, *TDNT* 5:71, argues for distinct traditions of the image of the open door.

2. Marshall 1978: 563 also leans toward independence for the door imagery, though he sees elements of connection with the tradition in the rest of the passage and sees Luke bringing some elements of this material together. Fitzmyer 1985: 1021–22 sees a Lucan hand in most of the material and sees only 13:24–29 as Q material, though he acknowledges that the case is not certain. Nolland 1993a: 732 attributes 13:22–23 to Luke and the rest mainly to traditional roots, most shared with Matthew. Most argue that the theme of presence or entry of blessing brought the texts together (Meier 1994: 310) and that Luke rearranged 13:28–29 by placing what was at the end at the start of the saying. Meier 1994: 311 lists the Lucan order of Matthean elements as 9, 10, 4, 5, 6, 7, 2, 3, 5, with four Lucan redactional stichs. It is more credible, however, to see a fresh tradition, given all the restructuring required of the alternative.

completely un-eschatological Jesus, a Jesus totally shorn of all apocalyptic traits [and, one could add, themes of judgment], is simply not the historical Jesus, however compatible he might be to modern tastes, at least in middle-class American academia.

This material has authentic roots in Jesus' teaching in terms of judgment themes, warning to Israel, and hope of surprising elements at the banquet table.[3] The statement of eschatological reversal in 13:30 is so widely attested that it too has roots in Jesus' teaching (Matt. 20:16; Mark 10:31 = Matt. 19:30; Gospel of Thomas 4).

The passage is a fusion of similitude and pronouncement.[4] The outline of Luke 13:22–30 is as follows:

a. Setting (13:22)
b. Picture of the narrow but soon-shut door (13:23–30)
   i. Question about the number of the saved (13:23)
   ii. The picture proper (13:24–27)
   iii. Three sayings on the significance of the image (13:28–30)
      (1) Some will be cast out (13:28)
      (2) Many will sit at the table (13:29)
      (3) Reversal of the first and the last (13:30)

The journey to Jerusalem continues and so does the note of religious division. Jesus makes clear several things: the way to salvation is narrow, the door to enter is small, entering comes on God's terms, the time remaining before the door closes is short, and contact with or racial connection to Jesus is not good enough. Many in the nation who think they are in the kingdom will not sit at the banquet table with Jesus, the patriarchs, and the prophets. In contrast, many from all corners of the world who

---

3. I disagree with Meier 1994: 315 that Jesus' teaching did not suggest a Gentile mission soon, but solely held out for an eschatological inclusion in the distant future. The previous parable in 13:18–19 suggests such an inclusion. The eschatological hope implies the possibility of current mission.

4. Berger 1984: 57–59, 81. Fitzmyer 1985: 1022 prefers to speak of a collection of minatory sayings, while Bultmann 1963: 93, 117 speaks of wisdom sayings in 13:23–24, 26–27. The passage is a warning and a wisdom background is not clear, except in 13:24. Bultmann also regards 13:26–27 as a church reflection that presents Jesus as judge of the world, but this saying is like OT prophetic utterances that warn about salvation and judgment. The parable portrays Jesus as the judge, with an identity between his message and the authority it carries. The crowd must respond to him. However, it was this very emphasis on response that caused the leadership to do away with him. It is not a post-Easter development. Jesus' view of himself was dangerous to the leadership. Luke 22:69 makes the same point conceptually.

would not be expected to experience God's blessing will sit at the table. The eschaton reverses the position of many but not all. The warning is a call that needs to be heeded.

Exegesis and Exposition

[22]And he went on his way through towns and villages, teaching and journeying, making his way to Jerusalem.

[23]And someone said to him, "Lord, will those who are saved be few?" And he said to them, [24]"Work to enter through the narrow door, for many, I say to you, will seek to come in and will not be able. [25]From which time the householder has risen and shut the door, you will begin to stand outside and knock on the door saying, 'Lord open to us.' And he will reply to you, 'I do not know where you are from.' [26]And then you will begin to say, 'We ate with you and drank with you, and in our streets you taught.' [27r]And he will reply, 'I say¹ to you, I do not know where ⌐you¬ are from; depart from me, all you workers of unrighteousness.' [28]And there shall be weeping and gnashing of teeth when you see Abraham, Isaac, Jacob, and all the prophets in the kingdom of God, but you are cast out. [29]And men will come from east and west and from north and south and sit at the table in the kingdom of God. [30]And behold the last shall become first, and the first shall become last."

a. Setting (13:22)

This verse marks the first "travel note" in the journey section since 9:51 (13:31–34 [conceptually]; 17:11; 18:31; 19:28, 41). Jesus is on the move through the nation, heading steadily and inexorably toward Jerusalem. The imperfect διεπορεύετο (*dieporeueto*, was going on his way) also suggests progressive movement (Grundmann 1963: 285; Luke 9:56). The ministry involves teaching in all the nation's inhabited regions (8:1; 9:6). The use of the substantive πορείαν (*poreian*) is idiomatic and expresses the idea of Jesus' "taking a journey himself."[5]

13:22

b. Picture of the Narrow but Soon-Shut Door (13:23–30)
i. Question about the Number of the Saved (13:23)

Jesus' many warnings finally make an impression on at least one person. The question is raised whether the number of those saved will be small.[6] The inquiry arises naturally, for Jesus has warned

13:23

---

5. BDF §310.1 and BDR §310.1.2 note that even the noun has the force of a verbal term in the middle voice, thus: "He went on his way through towns and villages, teaching, and taking a journey *himself*, making his way to Jerusalem."

6. The present participle οἱ σῳζόμενοι refers to those who are being delivered, but it looks to the future; Marshall 1978: 564; Isa. 37:32; 1 Enoch 102.7 [variant reading]; 2 Esdr. [= 4 Ezra] 7:66; Mark 10:26; 1 Cor. 1:18; 2 Cor. 2:15.

about the nature of the time, said that he comes to divide, and declared that judgment is near. Luke often introduces teaching in response to a question or comment such as this (Danker 1988: 264; Tiede 1988: 253; Luke 1:18, 34; 4:22; 10:29; 11:45; 12:13, 41; 13:1).[7]

In Judaism, views varied about the fate of the saved in terms of experiencing blessing, though all agreed that the nation of Israel would share in the blessing after the resurrection (Grundmann 1963: 285; Danker 1988: 264; SB 1:883; 2 Esdr. [= 4 Ezra] 7:47; 9:15).[8] In addition, Isa. 60:21 is cited in *m. Sanh.* 10.1 to argue for Israel's salvation, a common Jewish view that allowed only a few exceptions: those who denied the resurrection; those who denied that the law came from heaven; Epicureans; and those who read heretical books, uttered charms, or pronounced the holy name. Jesus' teaching makes it clear that there will be distinctions within Israel and that heritage and genetic origin are not enough for election.

ii. The Picture Proper (13:24–27)

13:24 Jesus answers the question indirectly with what is in effect a warning. He does not describe the number of saved as few, but he shows that people come into blessing from everywhere (13:29), and he suggests that many who thought they were inside will find themselves outside. His remarks suggest that many such people reside in Israel (13:28).

Jesus exhorts his audience to labor hard to enter through the narrow door (Marshall 1978: 565; Stauffer, *TDNT* 1:137).[9] The idea is not to work one's way to God, but to labor hard at listening and responding to his message. The concept is very much like passages in Proverbs that exhort one to incline the ear to wisdom and pursue it like riches (e.g., Prov. 2:1–5).

The narrow-door imagery suggests that fewer may enter than expected. There is no automatic entry. The narrow (στενός, *stenos;*

---

7. On the use of εἰ to introduce questions, see N. Turner 1963: 333; BDF §440.3; BDR §440.3.5; Gen. 17:17; Matt. 12:10; 19:3; Luke 22:49; Acts 1:6; 22:25. Luke uses this construction for an "indirect question" nineteen times.

8. Some Jews believed that only a few of the truly righteous would experience immediate blessing, while the rest would wait in Gehenna for resurrection. Two verses in 2 Esdr. [= 4 Ezra] (NRSV) are close to the tone of this question: "Many have been created, but only a few shall be saved" (8:3) and "The Most High made this world for the sake of many, but the world to come for the sake of only a few" (8:1). See also 2 Bar. 21.11; 44.15; 48.23, 45–50; 51.1–6.

9. Ἀγωνίζομαι suggests intense effort or straining labor; BAGD 15; BAA 27. With the present tense it contextually denotes continual striving. This is the only use of the word in the Synoptics; elsewhere at John 18:36; 1 Cor. 9:25; Col. 1:29; 4:12; 1 Tim. 4:10; 6:12; 2 Tim. 4:7. It is a term of Hellenistic, Jewish, and early Christian exhortation; Nolland 1993a: 733; Hoffmann 1967: 196.

BAGD 766; BAA 1530; elsewhere in the NT only at Matt. 7:13, 14) door, like the narrow way, pictures the way of righteousness or entry into God's presence and blessing (Danker 1988: 264; Bertram, *TDNT* 7:605–6; Jer. 21:8; 2 Esdr. [= 4 Ezra] 7:3–7, 12–14; John 10:7). Getting through the door presupposes favorable response to Jesus' message (Luke 13:3, 5; Fitzmyer 1985: 1024–25). A door is often an image of entry into the banquet of eschatological blessing at God's palace or is related to the image of the great wedding (Matt. 7:7–8, 13; 22:12; 25:10, 21, 23; Luke 14:23; Jeremias, *TDNT* 3:174, 178).[10] The Lucan stress is not only that the door is narrow so that people must come in the right way, but also that it is only open for a short time (13:25).

The reason Jesus gives for such diligent effort is that many will seek entry and will not be able to enter. The reason for their inability follows, but the basic idea is that the Lord will not recognize who they are because they did not respond to his call in time. Many will discover the truth after the door is closed, but it will be too late to share in blessing (Plummer 1896: 346; Liefeld 1984: 973). Esau is an example (Heb. 12:17). After that time, nothing can be done. Manson (1949: 125) summarizes nicely:

> The reply of Jesus begins by asserting that the way of salvation is a door which God opens and man enters. The entry cannot be made without God. The gate of heaven opens only from the inside. But also man has to make his own way in, once the door is opened. And this is not easy. The entrance is narrow, and it is a case of struggling through rather than strolling in. If men fail to enter, it is not that God is unwilling to admit them, but that they will not enter on the only terms on which entrance is possible.

One must enter on God's terms, which are set forth in Luke 5:30–32: one must recognize one's need and come to Jesus for aid.

Matthew 7:13–14 uses the contrasting image of the narrow door and the broad way. Many miss the door because of the width of the way they travel. The Matthean image is distinct and complementary (on the differences, see Jeremias, *TDNT* 6:923; contra Nolland 1993a: 733, who argues that Luke is responsible for the gate-door difference in order to set up 13:25; see n. 2 above and the exegesis of 13:25).

13:25 Jesus develops the idea that some will not be able to come in. Access after a certain point becomes impossible. In fact, most of the imagery deals with this explanation, since it extends through 13:28. The

---

10. Jeremias notes that the closed door means the irrevocable loss of opportunity; Isa. 22:22; Matt. 25:10; Rev. 3:7.

fundamental point is that there comes a time when response is too late. The door into the banquet will be forever shut. The owner of the house will close it once and for all. Those left outside will try to get in, they will knock to enter, but the owner will refuse to let them in because he does not recognize who they are (Hendriksen 1978: 706; Luce 1933: 241; Fitzmyer 1985: 1025; Manson 1949: 125; SB 1:469; 4:293 [cites exclusions from the synagogue in later texts]).[11] The warning is graphic and straightforward: without response now or soon, there will be no access later. They must listen now to sit at the table.

There is much discussion about how the image of the shut door fits with the picture of the narrow door (e.g., Nolland 1993a: 733–34 argues for Lucan redaction of 13:24; see the exegesis above). The most natural connection is that not only is the way narrow, but also that the access will soon be closed. The focus in 13:25 is on the activity of the householder who rises, shuts the door, and denies entry to those seeking to have the door reopened (on the grammatical issues here, see the additional note).

Many regard this shut-door image as an early church development of Matthew's narrow door/wide way image (Schulz 1972: 309–11). Others argue that Matthew developed Luke's shut door (J. Wellhausen, cited by Creed 1930: 185). Those who see church development argue that the two images do not belong together. But the teaching that the time is short is a frequent theme in Jesus' ministry and has been an especially repeated point in the journey section, though not always in unparalleled material (12:54–59; 13:1–9, esp. 13:6–9). Surely warnings like these, which are similar in tone to John the Baptist's warnings (Matt. 3:7–12 = Luke 3:7–18), are something that Jesus said as a prophet of warning. They are one of the sources of the leadership's extreme irritation, which lead them to deal with Jesus.[12] Jesus' point is not an "either/or" choice. The door is narrow *and* it will be shut soon. One must come God's way, and the decision needs to be made while there still is time.

13:26   The initial rejection by the doorkeeper meets with shock and protest, so that those at the door try again. Their appeal is that they were present with Jesus during his ministry. It is significant that Jesus' identity as the householder is made clear by their appeal

---

11. Matt. 25:10–13 is conceptually parallel. The image of not knowing "where one is from" comes from the OT: Ps. 138:6; Isa. 63:16; Jer. 1:5; Hos. 5:3; 13:5; Amos 3:2; cf. 2 Tim. 2:19. Seesemann, *TDNT* 5:117, notes that in later Judaism the expression meant excommunication or total rejection.

12. Marshall 1978: 566 is right to suggest independence of Matthew and Luke at this point.

(Grundmann 1963: 286, noting Mark 2:5, 15–17; 3:31–35; 5:34). Though we are still in parabolic material, the reference is very clear: before the door to the banquet was shut they had sat at other tables with the householder and had listened to him speak. They claim knowledge and intimate familiarity with Jesus' ministry, especially since table fellowship was a sign of relationship in this culture. Jesus did have meals with many in the nation. The problem is that it is not familiarity with Jesus, but response to him that he desired. Such response was not present, as 13:27 makes clear. Outward contact with the message and person of Jesus counts for nothing; inward reception is everything (Arndt 1956: 333; Mark 2:18–19; 3:35; Luke 6:46–49).

In Matt. 7:22–23, the connection to Jesus' ministry is stronger: some claim to prophesy, cast out demons, and do other mighty works in Jesus' name. Whether this connection is real or merely a claim to be associated with such activity is not entirely clear. The protesters in Luke and Matthew argue that they shared in the community's activity, but neither work nor involvement is the point, only real relationship to Jesus. Because Jesus never knew them he tells them to depart (13:27). Jesus' rejection is underlined in that they are addressed as evildoers. The Matthean basis of rejection is similar, but the more intense imagery and distinct setting suggest an independent tradition.

Jesus replies in the same essential terms of his initial response. He **13:27** rejects this second appeal in most emphatic terms. The point is that these people may have seen Jesus and been physically close to him, but they never responded to him in such a way so that he could now recognize them as his own. In fact, after saying he does not know them, Jesus commands them to depart and calls them workers of unrighteousness. Their appeal, rather than meeting with an open door, meets with severe rebuke. They are counted among the enemies of righteousness (Ellis 1974: 189; Marshall 1978: 567; Ernst 1977: 428–29; SB 1:469; cf. Matt. 25:31–32).[13] The rejection shows Jesus' ultimate authority to judge and an awareness that not all will enter in. Among those rejected are some who were physically close to Jesus but who never responded to his message with repentance, never entered into a relationship of faith.

13. Ps. 6:9 LXX [6:8 Engl.] supplies much of the wording for the rejection, from which Luke differs slightly in the final phrase with his πάντες ἐργάται ἀδικίας (all you workers of unrighteousness) rather than the psalm's πάντες οἱ ἐργαζόμενοι τὴν ἀνομίαν (all those who work unrighteousness). Luke's rebuke is more direct. Matt. 7:23 virtually matches the LXX. Some suggest the presence of something similar to the rabbinic ban formula, which pictured excommunication or exclusion from the community. For the texts, see the exegesis of 13:25 and n. 11.

iii. Three Sayings on the Significance of the Image (13:28–30)
(1) Some Will Be Cast Out (13:28)

13:28   Jesus now describes the exclusion of some who had expected to be in the kingdom simply because they observed his ministry. The image is clear, graphic, and painful: weeping and gnashing of teeth will accompany the awareness that the patriarchs and prophets are in the kingdom, while the present audience is excluded. The combination ὁ κλαυθμὸς καὶ ὁ βρυγμὸς τῶν ὀδόντων (*ho klauthmos kai ho brygmos tōn odontōn*, the weeping and gnashing of teeth) is common in Matthew and depicts the emotional and physical reaction to traumatic news, in this case exclusion from God's promise (Matt. 8:12; 13:42, 50; 22:13; 24:51; 25:30).[14] The figure depicts remorse for rejection. In rabbinic Judaism, the picture of weeping was applied to the ungodly (*Sipre* 103 on Num. 12:8 [= Neusner 1986: 2.125]). The reference to being cast out of the kingdom develops the image.[15] Although their birth made them ideal candidates for inclusion in the kingdom, their close proximity to promise has worked against them as they failed to respond. Thus they have removed themselves from experiencing the promise proclaimed by their ancestors and the prophets. Without a response to Jesus, these members of the nation become outsiders. Jesus adds to the pain when he not only describes their exclusion but also notes that many others will enter the kingdom (13:29). The inclusion of others contrasts with the opportunity lost. The warning Jesus gives here is real—and quite tragic.

Matthew 8:11–12 has similar, more emphatic imagery: the "sons of the kingdom will be thrown into the outer darkness and there men will weep and gnash their teeth." All this occurs while many from east and west sit with the patriarchs and prophets.[16] Luke's order moves from negative image to positive, while Matthew's is the

---

14. On βρυγμός (gnashing), see BAGD 147–48; BAA 294–95; Rengstorf, *TDNT* 1:642; Prov. 19:12; Sir. 51:3; Plummer 1896: 347. On κλαυθμός (weeping), see BAGD 433; BAA 882; Rengstorf, *TDNT* 3:726; Job 30:31; Jer. 3:21. The verb βρύχω (to gnash) is used as an expression of anger in Job 16:9; Ps. 35:16 [34:16 LXX]; 37:12 [36:12 LXX]; 112:10 [111:10 LXX]; Marshall 1978: 567. On darkness and judgment in Judaism, see 1 Enoch 103.7–8; 108.5–14; Ps. Sol. 14.9; 15.10; Lev. Rab. 27.1 on 22:27; and Exod. Rab. 14.2 on 10:22. Leviticus Rabbah cites Ps. 35:6; Gen. 1:2; Isa. 29:15; and Eccles. 6:4 in describing Gehenna's darkness. Exodus Rabbah cites Job 10:22; Ezek. 31:15; Isa. 29:15; and Gen. 1:2. The partial overlap of OT texts is interesting.

15. Ἐκβάλλω is a term for judgment in Matt. 8:12; 22:13; 25:30; John 12:31; Bertram, *TDNT* 4:839 n. 56.

16. The combination of Abraham, Isaac, and Jacob occurs frequently in the OT: Deut. 1:8; 6:10; 9:5, 27; 1 Kings 18:36; 2 Kings 13:23; Acts 3:13; 7:32; Matt. 8:11; Fitzmyer 1985: 1026. Luke, on the other hand, likes to mention all the prophets; Luke 1:70; 24:44.

---

reverse. Luke will speak in the next verse of people coming from around the world to sit at table in the kingdom (including a unique reference to north and south; Luke 13:29), while the reference to past people of God is tied to the exclusion image in this verse. Creed (1930: 186) attributes the Lucan usage to rearrangement of the Matthean material. But a distinct figure from a similar image is more likely, given the extent of rearrangement with little real alteration of meaning (for the rearrangement, see n. 2 above). A rationale for such rearranging is not clear.

(2) Many Will Sit at the Table (13:29)

In contrast to those who are absent from the kingdom are those who are present. They will come from everywhere: east, west, north, south (Schlier, *TDNT* 1:352).[17] Such imagery for the gathering of God's elect is common in the OT, where it usually referred to the dispersed, defeated Gentiles who come to worship God in Zion, as Israel also reclaims its authority in ultimate victory.[18] In Luke the direct beneficiaries are from a broader spectrum of races. In addition, there is no emphasis on Israelite sovereignty. These Gentiles, in contrast to the crowd, will sit down at the blessed banquet table with Abraham, Isaac, Jacob, and the prophets.[19] As Acts 10–11 makes clear, God's active work is required to actualize the universal implications in the passage. A pattern in God's salvific activity is alluded to here; but the pattern has a surprising feature, a feature that would shock Jesus' Jewish audience. The gathering of people from every nation and race for the banquet has not been anticipated. Even the disciples are slow to realize this part of the program. Jesus suggests it here, but God must direct its implementation in anticipation of the final celebration Jesus discusses here.

13:29

(3) Reversal of the First and the Last (13:30)

Jesus closes with a saying that marks the eschatological reversal he has just described. Such remarks are common in the Synoptics (Ellis

13:30

---

17. The compass dimensions provide a merism referring to the whole world. People will come from everywhere.

18. Beasley-Murray 1986: 171–72; 1 Chron. 9:24; Ps. 96:3; 107:3 (the gathered are dispersed Jews); Isa. 2:2; 25:6–9; 40:5; 43:5–6; 45:6, 14; 49:12; 51:4; 52:10; 55:5; 56:7; 59:19; 66:19–20; Mic. 4:1–2; Zech. 2:13 [2:17 MT]; Mal. 1:11; Luke 14:15; 22:16, 29–30; Rev. 19:9; Plummer 1896: 348.

19. Ellis 1974: 189 notes that Qumran had a similar banquet expectation, but with a very different and exclusive audience, namely Messiah, the high priest, the priests, the chief of the tribes, and the congregation of Israel's righteous; 1Q28a [= 1QSa = Rule Annex] 2.11–22. Fitzmyer 1985: 1026 and Marshall 1978: 568 add other Jewish references: 1 Enoch 62.14; 2 Enoch 42.5; 2 Bar. 29.4; *m. ʾAbot* 3.17; SB 4:1148, 1154–59.

1974: 189; Fitzmyer 1985: 1027).[20] The saying has a proverbial air to it and was probably repeated on numerous occasions (Plummer 1896: 348). This remark applies to the end-time when the fullness of the kingdom comes. Luke 13:30 and Matt. 20:16 mention the last becoming first before mentioning the first becoming last, while Matt. 19:30 = Mark 10:31 has the reverse order. The Lucan emphasis fits Luke 13:29 with its description of those who come from the four corners of the earth to sit at the table. The absence of definite articles on the grammatical subjects of the verse shows that not all the last are elevated nor are all the first demoted, only some of them.[21] Those who appear to be close may in fact end up far off. Some Gentiles who are distant will end up near, while many Jews will miss the promised kingdom (Creed 1930: 186).[22]

Summary Luke 13:22–30 emphasizes that entrance into the kingdom requires careful attention. The passage puts all people on the same footing (Michaelis, *TDNT* 6:868 n. 14; Marshall 1978: 568). As Manson (1949: 126) notes, "The only passports to the Kingdom are repentance and submission to God." Repentance and submission to God simply mean coming to Jesus for forgiveness of sins (24:44–47). Many in Israel thought that they were in and had no need—but they were dead wrong. Jesus' answer to the question about whether few will be saved is essentially, "Whatever their number, respond to me and be sure that you are among them, because racial or spatial proximity to me is no guarantee" (Plummer 1896: 348). Jesus says that the door of opportunity is currently open, but it will not remain so forever. Once it is shut, it will be bolted. So respond and do not miss the opportunity. Do not assume that because you are exposed to the truth, you have it. As

20. Matt. 19:30 = Mark 10:31 applies the phrase to the powerful and wealthy, while Matt. 20:16 deals with the taking of the kingdom from the vineyard keepers in order to give it to another, a point similar to Luke's. Similar conceptual references are found in Barn. 6.13 and the Gospel of Thomas 4.

21. Fitzmyer 1985: 1020 translates: "Some of those who are now last will be first, and some of those first will be last"; see also p. 1027. The line literally reads, "And behold are last ones, they shall be first, and are first ones, they shall be last."

22. Manson 1949: 125–26 notes that this saying rules out the idea of automatic blessing as a result of Abrahamic ancestry. The opposite idea is expressed in Ps. Sol. 9.9–10. Paul's attitude, as expressed in Rom. 9:4–6, is similar to Jesus' remark. Marshall 1978: 568 adds Mark 9:35; Luke 14:9–10; and 1 Cor. 4:9 as being similar in concept, as well as the remarks in Luke 1:51–53 and 3:8. One could also add Eph. 2:14–18, though here the idea of Jews being excluded is not prevalent. Rather Gentiles and Jews form a new community, where those who were far off and those who were near are equal. Paul, however, appears to believe that at some point in the future, Israelites will believe again en masse (Rom. 11:11–27, esp. 11:12, 15, 25–27), which may explain why only "some" are mentioned here as moving from first to last.

Jesus will make clear in a later parable (14:15–24), one must come when the invitation to the banquet is given, or one's seat will go to another. Jesus' words thus warn his Jewish audience of the peril of not joining him. This warning is true for all, since all are called to approach God on the same basis. One need not worry about full attendance at the table, for many others, coming from everywhere, will find a seat. In effect, Jesus turns the question from "Will the saved be few?" to "Will you be among the saved?"

Additional Notes

13:25. The punctuation is disputed: does 13:24 end with a full stop (so UBS–NA) or with a comma, which makes the connection between 13:24–25 closer? If the connection is present, then it is clear that the shut-door image explains the narrow door. The lack of a clear connective makes it unlikely that 13:25 is tied syntactically to 13:24. Creed (1930: 185) regards the sentences as independent, but notes that this leaves the syntax of 13:25 unclear. If 13:25 starts an independent sentence, there are three options for where the apodosis of the ἀφ' οὗ ἄν (when the householder rises . . .) clause begins (Plummer 1896: 347): (1) καὶ ἄρξησθε (and he began to say) in 13:25b, (2) καὶ ἀποκριθείς (and he will answer) in 13:25c, or (3) τότε ἄρξεσθε (then you began to say) in 13:26a. The most natural way to take 13:25 is as an independent sentence with the focus on the response of the householder, the main figure. This connection prevents any hanging participles and puts the focus on the householder, whose reaction is the point. His rising and shutting the door and the request of others to enter serve as background to explain his reply. All these things have happened when the refusal to open the door comes. The RSV solves this dilemma nicely by creating two sentences, which communicates the concept well, though it obscures the syntactical issue. The NRSV adopts option 1. The NIV splits the construction into three sentences, leaving the connection unclear. The UBS–NA text takes option 2, even though this leaves καί with the unusual sense of "then." Option 3, however, makes for a long wait for the apodosis, though τότε is a normal introduction to the apodosis. Either option 2 or 3 is possible. The sense of the whole unit is not altered by the choice.

13:27. With $\mathfrak{P}^{75c}$, B, and a few minuscules, the UBS–NA text reads καὶ ἐρεῖ λέγων ὑμῖν (and he will reply, saying to you), a common redundancy that represents the Semitic infinitive absolute. This reading is seen as the reading that explains the other variants (Metzger 1975: 163). But καὶ ἐρεῖ λέγω ὑμῖν (and he will reply, "I say to you") has strong external evidence ($\mathfrak{P}^{75*}$, A, D, L, W, Δ, Θ, Ψ, Byz, Lect) and could be favored by the internal evidence, since the UBS–NA reading could be due to dittography (the *upsilon* of ὑμῖν being read twice, the first time as *nu*). On the other hand, if the *nu* on λέγων is original, its omission through haplography would account for the variant.

Of course, if a copyist missed an original *nu*, then the variant would result. Codex ℵ omits any form of λέγω, reading ἐρεῖ ὑμῖν (he will reply to you). This looks like a copyist's attempt to avoid the problem. The issue is a close call, but I prefer, by a slight margin, the reading of 𝔓⁷⁵* et al. The sense is little altered by the choice.

13:27. The UBS–NA text takes the householder's reply in the same terms as in 13:25, which is likely to be the original wording. The reading οὐκ οἶδα πόθεν ἐστέ (I do not know from where you are) is found in 𝔓⁷⁵, B, L, a few minuscules, and Itala. External evidence favors the inclusion of ὑμᾶς (you): ℵ, A, W, Δ, Θ, Ψ, family 1, family 13, many minuscules, Byz, Lect, many Itala, and Syriac.

6. Lament for the Nation as Jerusalem Nears (13:31–35)

Jesus has warned the nation repeatedly of the consequences of rejection. Now, sounding very much like an OT prophet, he laments the nation's lack of response and issues another severe warning to them of God's impending abandonment. The sand in the hourglass is running out. They repeat the pattern of Israel's historic rejection of God's messengers, a point that Acts will make as well (Acts 7:51).

The warning is triggered by concern for Jesus' safety, as some try to get him to change his course and avoid Jerusalem. Some Pharisees suggest that Herod Antipas awaits his arrival and plans to kill him.[1] Jesus expresses God's affection for the nation in a picture: he has desired to care for them as a hen cares for her brood. The nation rejects Jesus and is declared fit only for exile unless it acknowledges that Jesus is sent from God. This event is a turning point in the journey narrative. Most see it as the center of the unit. It certainly represents a major transition. Much of the journey up to this point has been consumed with warning the nation. From this point on, much of the section is concerned with teaching the disciples. The open door that Jesus mentioned in the previous parable is closing for this generation of Israel. The fig tree is about to be uprooted (13:6–9).

Sources and Historicity

Luke 13:31–33 has no Synoptic parallel (Aland 1985: §212), but 13:34–35 reads almost verbatim with the lament in Matt. 23:37–39 (Aland 1985: §213). For 13:34–35, most see Luke using material from Q and relocating the text. Luce (1933: 243) notes that earlier in this century many saw the most natural setting as Jesus speaking in anticipation of coming to Jerusalem (so apparently Godet 1875: 2.129–30). Under this view, Matthew made a more topical arrangement in order to focus on Jesus' denunciation of the leadership. The current consensus is that, if the tradition has been rearranged, Luke is responsible for it (Marshall 1978: 569–70, 573–74 ties

---

1. If this report is true, Herod has moved from anxious curiosity (9:7–9) to full-fledged fear about Jesus. The event as it relates to Herod is seen as historical; Fitzmyer 1985: 1028.

13:31–33 to L and 13:34–35 to Q, as does Fitzmyer 1985: 1028, 1034, who also believes that Luke relocates the passage). Egelkraut (1976: 176–79) argues for a Lucan relocation for a variety of reasons:

1. The most important reason is the presence of the uniquely Lucan introductory phrase ἐν αὐτῇ τῇ ὥρᾳ (in that hour), which no other Synoptic author uses (Luke 2:38; 10:21; 12:12; 20:19; 24:33; Acts 16:18; 22:13). This note is irrelevant to the discussion, however, since a chronological specification need not demonstrate evidence of relocation. Narrative editorial introductions need not mean that the entire passage is by the writer or has been moved by him.

2. Jesus mentions healings here but there are not many healings in the journey section. It is not clear, however, why the healings alluded to must be part of recent journey events. Certainly enough activity about Jesus' ministry is given in the earlier sections to serve as a basis for the point. In addition, healings do not occur with any greater frequency later in Jesus' life, so Matt. 23 is no more appropriate as a setting for the passage on the basis of this reasoning than is Luke 13. There is also the recent "mirror miracle" of 13:10–17, which replays the Sabbath healings of 4:31–41 and 6:6–11.

3. Herod would be located in Galilee not Jerusalem. Although Herod spent much time in Galilee and ruled over it, Jerusalem was not a foreign city to him, as the passion narrative makes clear. It is also possible that Jesus is in Galilee or Perea during these remarks, given that the Lucan journey narrative is not a "straight-line" journey (Arndt 1956: 333; see the exegesis of 13:31 and the introduction to §IV).

4. The more natural setting for the remarks is Jerusalem, as Matt. 23 indicates. While it might initially seem likely that Jerusalem is more appropriate, Jesus merely uses a figure of speech known as synecdoche, whereby a part stands for the whole (in the OT, Jerusalem or Zion frequently stands for Israel; Ps. 99:2; 102:13 [102:14 MT]; 137:1–3; 149:2 [parallel to Israel]; Isa. 1:27; 4:3–4; 28:16; 59:20 [parallel to Jacob]; Amos 6:1; Zech. 9:9). This remark could be made from anywhere in the nation, in the same way that a modern protester can denounce Washington without being in Washington to do it.

The major reason for arguing that Luke relocated the passage is simply the extensive verbal agreement between Matt. 23 and Luke 13. If there is a relocation, it would be like Luke's move with the synagogue speech in Luke 4; but it seems more likely that independent material is present or that such a speech was given on multiple occasions. Psalm 118, which is alluded to here, is used in a variety of other places, which may suggest that it was a popular passage for Jesus and that images associated with it were used on a variety of occasions (so Arndt 1956: 334; Luke 19:38).

The Jesus Seminar doubts the authenticity of most of this pericope (Funk and Hoover 1993: 348–49). In its view, Jesus may have said something about Herod, and so 13:32 is printed in gray type. Luke 13:33–35 is regarded as inauthentic and so is printed in black type. The emphases on Jerusalem and exorcism are seen as Lucan. In the seminar's view, the unique attestation of 13:33 is not authentic, and 13:34–35 is rejected because it parallels OT prophetic woe laments. The seminar argues that Jesus' remarks assume that he visited Jerusalem several times, but this view ignores the possibility that Jesus speaks as a prophet for God's repeated attempts to call Israel to faithfulness. The seminar's overliteral reading of this text causes it to ignore the very real possibility that Jesus, as a prophet of reform, speaks in OT terms to warn Israel about the risk of rejecting God's message through his agent.[2] Regardless of how one views this discussion about the setting of this material, the remarks fit the tone of Jesus' prophetic ministry to Israel and explain in part why the leadership felt threatened by him.[3] Some question 13:35b as secondary (Nolland 1993a: 739), claiming a parallel in Mark 11:9 or appealing to an established Ps. 118 tradition. But these settings are quite different and should not be equated: Luke 13 is judgment, while Mark 11 is praise. All this material has a solid claim to authenticity, since Jesus' challenge to the nation is multiply attested.

The passage is a prophetic speech of judgment that involves a double pronouncement (Wiefel 1988: 263; Fitzmyer 1985: 1028; Bultmann 1963: 35; Berger 1984: 81 speaks of apophthegm). The outline of Luke 13:31–35 is as follows:

a. The necessity of Jerusalem and the refusal to run (13:31–33)
   i. Herod's intent: he wants to kill Jesus (13:31)
   ii. Jesus' response: he must go to Jerusalem (13:32–33)
b. Lament over Jerusalem (13:34–35)

The passage suggests that the national officials are reacting to Jesus, as the opposition of Herod Antipas shows. Jesus does not fear this opposition, since he must fulfill his task in Jerusalem. Jesus is pictured as a prophet lamenting Israelite rejection. Israel stands alone until it responds and recognizes God's sent one.

2. See Borg 1987: 162–63, 170, who notes Jer. 12:7 and Ezek. 11:22–23. So also Horsley 1987: 300–302, who calls Luke 13:32–33 part of a "fairly solid tradition" (p. 190). For the debate on 13:31–33, see Nolland 1993a: 738–39, who accepts 13:31–32, but regards 13:33 as a Lucan redaction that makes the transition from 13:32 to 13:34. However, the use of δεῖ is too widespread in the Gospel tradition to make this conclusion solid (see the exegesis of 13:33). In addition, as Marshall 1978: 570 suggests, 13:33 is an integral link to 13:32.

3. Interestingly, Nolland 1993a: 739 argues that both Matthew and Luke selected the location for this tradition in their respective Gospels.

Exegesis and Exposition

[31]In that hour some Pharisees came to him and said, "Get up and go from here, for Herod wishes to kill you." [32]And he said to them, "Go and tell that fox, 'Behold I cast out demons and perform cures today and tomorrow, and on the third day I complete my task. [33]Moreover I must go my way today, tomorrow, and the following day, for it cannot be that a prophet should perish outside of Jerusalem.'

[34]"Jerusalem, Jerusalem, the one who killed the prophets and stoned those sent to you, how many times I longed to gather your children together as a hen gathers her brood under her wings, and you did not wish it. [35]Behold, I declare your house is left to you. And I say to you, you shall not see me until you say, 'Blessed is the one who comes in the name of the Lord.'"

a. The Necessity of Jerusalem and the Refusal to Run (13:31–33)
i. Herod's Intent: He Wants to Kill Jesus (13:31)

13:31 Luke connects this event to 13:22–30. At about the time Jesus is warning the nation about missing the banquet, he receives a warning from some Pharisees: Herod Antipas seeks to kill him (θέλω, *thelō*, here depicts a "fixed desire"; Schrenk, *TDNT* 3:46 n. 18). Josephus pictures Herod as a man who liked his region to be as peaceful as possible (*Antiquities* 18.7.2 §245; Grundmann 1963: 288; Ellis 1974: 190); Herod undoubtedly wishes to remove any source of agitation. While this looks like a friendly attempt to help Jesus (Fitzmyer 1985: 1030), it might be an expedient way to get Jesus out of the region without resorting to violence (Marshall 1978: 570–71). There is not enough detail to decide this issue. Luke does not, however, note any malice on the part of the Pharisees (Manson 1949: 276).[4] Nonetheless the effort will fail. The event occurs in either Perea or Galilee. Most favor the latter (Marshall 1978: 570; Hoehner 1972: 217).

ii. Jesus' Response: He Must Go to Jerusalem (13:32–33)

13:32 Jesus refuses to cower at the prospect of death. He knows that his mission is to go to Jerusalem and face the response that awaits him, so he gives a message to those who warn him about Herod Antipas: he will continue to minister by casting out demons and healing the sick. He will finish his task.[5] The remarks to Herod, expressed in the

---

4. Tyson 1960: 245 supports the account's historicity because of the positive or at least neutral portrayal of the Pharisees here.

5. Τελειόω (to complete) is a key NT term for the completion of God's plan: Luke 12:50; 22:37; John 19:30; and Heb. 2:10; 5:8–9; 7:28 (though in Hebrews it has the additional nuance of perfecting).

personal first person, extend through 13:33. Then Jesus makes a prophet-like address to the nation in 13:34–35.

Jesus views Herod with something less than respect. He calls the king a fox. The signification of ἀλώπηξ (*alōpēx*) is debated (Ellis 1974: 190): it can refer to (1) a person of no significance (SB 2:201; Neh. 4:3 [2 Esdr. 13:35 LXX]); (2) a deceiver, a person of cunning (which was the rabbinic force of the term; Daube 1956: 191; Song Rab. 2.15.1 on 2:15); or (3) a destroyer (Ezek. 13:4; Lam. 5:18; 1 Enoch 89.10, 42–49, 55; Leaney 1958: 209). The normal Greek sense is the second meaning (Fitzmyer 1985: 1031; Epictetus 1.3.7–8; Plutarch, *Life of Solon* 30.2 [95]), although either of the first two senses or a combination of them is possible, depending on how the context fills out the metaphor (Manson 1949: 276 and Marshall 1978: 571 mention the first two, while Darr 1992: 140–46 sees the third as primary and the second as possible). Considering how the Synoptics portray the way Herod removed the Baptist, the meaning of deceiver or destroyer is possible. Luke's emphasis seems to be destructiveness, since Herod murdered "the greatest born of woman" (Luke 7:28) and later stands opposed to Jesus (Acts 4:26–28). In Luke 13 the issue is his willingness to kill Jesus. That the leaders can pass on Jesus' reply to Antipas suggests that the Pharisees had a cordial relationship with Herod—at least when it comes to Jesus.

There is debate concerning the reference to three days. Is Jesus speaking literally of coming to Jerusalem in three days? Is this a figurative way to speak of a quick succession of events? Or is it a figure for a day-by-day sequence of events (Black 1967: 206)? The most likely meaning is the second: a quick succession of events. Jesus will continue his ministry and on the "third day," at the end of the sequence, he will enter Jerusalem and complete the task of his ministry through his death. Interestingly, a healing follows this exchange, so that the short-term reference to healing sees immediate fulfillment (14:1–6). It is clear that more than three days separates Jesus from Jerusalem. Many things have yet to happen, so a figurative sense is obvious.

This language is also a possible allusion to Jesus' resurrection on the third day. Such an allusion is possible, given the significance of the third day in the early church. This allusion, however, would be one that only Luke's readers (and not Jesus' audience) would sense, since only the readers know about Jesus' death and resurrection.[6]

---

6. Tannehill 1986: 153–56 objects, stressing that the goal in this context is only Jerusalem, not death. The point, however, is what Jerusalem represents and what it will do to this prophet. To separate Jerusalem from a reference to Jesus' death is artificial.

13:33 Jesus defines his mission in terms of Jerusalem.[7] He must continue to fulfill his mission,[8] and then depart from where he is to head for Jerusalem. Manson (1949: 277) argues that there is no contradiction with lack of departure in Luke 13:32, because there the point was fleeing the region to avoid death, while here it is going to Jerusalem to complete his call in death.

Jesus must go to Jerusalem. In fact, it cannot be otherwise, for a prophet is to perish in Jerusalem (Ernst 1977: 432; Fitzmyer 1985: 1032).[9] Several things are significant about Jesus' remark. He sees himself functioning as a prophet (a major Lucan theme: Luke 7:16, 39; 24:19; Acts 3:22–23; 7:37; Ernst 1977: 432). He is ready to assume the role of a suffering sent one, a righteous messenger rejected and wronged (also a common theme in Luke: 4:24; 11:50–53; Ellis 1974: 191; Lohse, *TDNT* 7:329).[10] Jesus knows that his destiny is tied to Jerusalem by divine necessity (so τελειοῦμαι [*teleioumai*, I finish my course] in 13:32 and δεῖ [*dei*, it is necessary] here).[11] Jesus is determined to carry out what God has sent him to do—and that includes suffering. This is the second time he has predicted his death in the journey section (12:50) and the fourth prediction overall (9:21–22, 44). Plummer (1896: 351) notes the irony in Jesus' reply: "I have nothing to fear from Herod; I am safe here, for death comes in Jerusalem." Not only is he safe, God's will is done.

b. Lament over Jerusalem (13:34–35)

13:34 Jesus speaks about Jerusalem, since the city represents the nation. He has long had a desire to care for it and protect it. The tone is sorrowful as well as prophetic, as the double vocative shows (cf. David's mourning over Absalom in 2 Sam. 18:33 [19:1 MT]; Jeremiah calling to the nation in Jer. 22:29; Jesus' calling to Martha in Luke 10:41 and

---

7. Marshall 1978: 572 and Thrall 1962: 20–21 interpret πλήν as "moreover." BAGD 669 §1b and BAA 1346 §1b see it as contrastive, but in this context it is more of an emphatic explanation (§1c in the lexicons).

8. Although more complex and rhetorical, the Greek expression σήμερον καὶ αὔριον καὶ τῇ ἐχομένῃ resembles Semitic references to three days as a short period of time; Marshall 1978: 572; Ezra 8:32; Jdt. 12:7.

9. For OT prophetic suffering, see 1 Kings 18:4, 13; 19:10, 14; 2 Chron. 24:21; Jer. 2:30; 26:20–23; 38:4–6; Amos 7:10–17; Josephus, *Antiquities* 10.3.1 §38; *Martyrdom and Ascension of Isaiah* 5.1–14; Acts 7:52.

10. Jeremias, *TDNT* 5:714, notes that a false prophet ran the risk of being killed (*m. Sanh.* 11.1). Friedrich, *TDNT* 6:834–35, points to Matt. 23:37. See also Fischel 1946.

11. Δεῖ is not necessarily a Lucan term, though he prefers it more than the other Synoptic writers. Matthew uses it eight times, Mark six times, and Luke eighteen times (plus an additional twenty-two times in Acts). Such data raise the question of whether this verse is purely redactional.

to Saul in Acts 9:4; Hendriksen 1978: 710; Gen. 22:11; Exod. 3:4; Luke 6:46). Jesus' use of the first person reflects a prophetic tone and parallels the OT prophets who spoke God's message in the first person. Some suggest that Jesus speaks as a suprahistorical figure here, as hidden wisdom, but this seems unnecessary given Jesus' remarks in 13:32–33 about himself as a prophet. Also, Luke is capable of making clear when wisdom speaks.[12]

Jerusalem is described in graphic terms as the city where the prophets are slain and God's messengers are stoned, a point that explains why Jesus must suffer in Jerusalem. Marshall (1978: 575) notes that the mention of killing and stoning, but not crucifying, shows that this is not a postresurrection saying of the church or a prophecy after the fact (against Ellis 1974: 191). Jerusalem, as the nation's religious center, reflects the nation's response, which historically has not responded well to God, even though he longed to care for it.

Jesus, as prophet, speaks of repeatedly longing to gather the nation as a hen would gather her brood under her wing. In fact, the image of God as a bird is common in the OT and in Judaism (Deut. 32:11; Ruth 2:12; Ps. 17:8; 36:7 [36:8 MT]; 57:1 [57:2 MT]; 61:4 [61:5 MT]; 63:7 [63:8 MT]; 91:4; Isa. 31:5; 2 Bar. 41.3–4; 2 Esdr. [= 4 Ezra] 1:30; Plummer 1896: 352; Grundmann 1963: 289; Marshall 1978: 575). Gentile converts to Judaism were said to come under the wings of the Shekinah (SB 1:927, 943; Marshall 1978: 575). In this image, Jesus reveals God's heart. God's constant desire is to intimately care for, nurture, and protect his people.[13] The allusion to repeated attempts to gather the nation may allude to the prophets' work in the past, as well as to the work of this messenger now. There is a pattern to the people's behavior, which the parables also pick up (Luke 20:10–13; Lohse, *TDNT* 7:328–29). Only one thing stopped God from exercising such care: the people did not wish him to do so. As a result, the gathering, with its accompanying offer of protection, could not take place.

Jesus' address to Jerusalem shows that this was a painful reality and a tragic situation. In fact, the situation becomes even more

---

12. Bultmann 1963: 114 sees wisdom here. Leaney 1958: 210 cites Matt. 23:34; Luke 2:40, 52; 7:35; 11:31, 49 as parallels. See also 1 Enoch 42. Luke 11:49–51 uses the wisdom motif openly. For more reasons not to see wisdom here, see Bock 1987: 120. Marshall 1978: 573–74 and Fitzmyer 1985: 1034 opt for wisdom terminology, but without Jesus alluding to himself as wisdom, since Jesus sees himself as wisdom's messenger. Sir. 24:7–12 provides a plausible background. If wisdom is in the background, this is the best way to argue for it. Nolland 1993a: 739 questions the presence of wisdom here, as do I.

13. The inhabitants of Jerusalem are often called τέκνα (children): Joel 2:23; Zech. 9:13; Bar. 4:19, 21, 25; 1 Macc. 1:38; Matt. 23:37; Luke 19:44; Oepke, *TDNT* 5:639.

tragic, since the city is about to manifest its tendency to kill yet another divine messenger. Jerusalem will miss an opportunity for blessing (19:41–44).

Matthew 23:37 is almost verbally exact to this verse. Matthew twice uses the verb meaning "to gather," once as an infinitive (ἐπισυναγαγεῖν, episynagagein) and once as a verb (ἐπισυνάγει, episynagei), while Luke uses only an infinitive ἐπισυνάξαι (episynaxai). The writers handle the collective reference to "brood" with different styles: Matthew has neuter plural τὰ νοσσία (ta nossia), and Luke has feminine singular τὴν νοσσιάν (tēn nossian). Also, Luke uses ἑαυτῆς (heautēs, her) where Matthew has αὐτῆς (autēs, her).

13:35 The upcoming rejection requires that the prophet Jesus declare that Israel is in peril. The language of the empty, desolate house recalls Jer. 12:7 and 22:5 (cf. Ps. 69:25 [69:26 MT]; Ezek. 8:6; 11:23; Ernst 1977: 434). The parallel in Matt. 23:39 mentions specifically that the house is desolate (ἔρημος, erēmos), but Luke lacks this term. The OT declared the possibility of exile for the nation if it did not respond to God's call about exercising justice (Jer. 22:5–6; Tiede 1988: 259). As such, Jesus' use of οἶκος (oikos) does not allude to the temple.[14] Jesus is more emphatic than Jeremiah's statement of the potential rejection of the nation. He states that a time of abandonment has come. Rather than being gathered under God's wings, their house is left empty and exposed. The now-empty house is the nation. The tree is being cut down (Luke 13:6–9).

Jesus adds a note about the duration of this judgment: they will not see God's messenger until they recognize "the one who comes in the name of the Lord" (ὁ ἐρχόμενος ἐν ὀνόματι κυρίου, ho erchomenos en onomati kyriou), a citation of Ps. 117:26 LXX [118:26 Engl.]. The original psalm alluded to the priests' blessing of those who came to worship in the temple, in all likelihood pilgrims led in procession by the king.[15] Jesus says that until the nation acknowledges him as blessed by God it will be judged.

The question arises as to what office Jesus possesses according to this allusion: prophet, Messiah, or both? The pericope itself and Jesus' actions in the passage (esp. Luke 13:32–33) suggest that he is acting only as a prophet. However, Luke's earlier use of certain terminology and the general use of Ps. 118 by Jesus suggest a messianic

---

14. For this reason Manson 1949: 127 rejects this view, which Ellis 1974: 191 accepts, citing Luke 11:51; 19:46; Acts 7:47. Marshall 1978: 576 notes that when a pronoun is attached to "house" in the sense of "temple," the pronoun refers to God, which is not the case here, since the desolate house is Israel.

15. In ancient Judaism, Ps. 118 was seen as messianic; SB 1:849–50, 876; m. Suk. 3.9; Midr. Ps. 118.19–20 on 118:21–22 (= Braude 1959: 2.243–44); Jeremias 1966: 256–57.

force (Bock 1987: 118–21).[16] The key ὁ ἐρχόμενος has already been given a technical force in Luke: in 3:15–16 and 7:19 this phrase alludes to the coming messianic figure who brings God's deliverance. So the use of the phrase here has a clear messianic flavor. Luke 19:38 also has a messianic force in its use of Ps. 118: the nation is depicted as missing another opportunity to respond to the king's coming; a lament follows in 19:41–44. Israel is to accept Jesus as its deliverer. Until it accepts him—like the priests of the psalm received the leader of the worshiper's entourage—it stands alone, exposed to the world's dangers.

It is debated whether Luke by this remark holds out hope for Israel's future.[17] Luke 21:24 and the speech of Acts 3 show that Jesus and the church continued to extend hope to Israel. They believed that God would restore the nation in the end. In fact, the NT suggests that such a response will precede Christ's return, thus Luke's later reference to the current period as "the time of the Gentiles" (Luke 21:24; see also Rom. 11:11–32 [esp. 11:12, 14, 25–27, 31–32] and probably Rev. 7:1–8). The triumphal entry of Luke 19 cannot be the fulfillment of this remark, since a note of rejection is present in 19:41–44. Neither is Jewish conversion throughout the age a fulfillment (Plummer 1896: 353; Arndt 1956: 336), since this can hardly explain the NT and Lucan phrase *the time/fullness of the Gentiles*, which appears in other passages. Still another faulty explanation is that Jews will be forced to recognize him at the second coming (but so Hendriksen 1978: 711, citing Isa. 45:23; Rom. 14:11; Phil. 2:10–11). The quotation from Ps. 118 is positive and anticipates a positive recognition, not a forced one.

Matthew 23:39 agrees with the Lucan wording, except that Matthew adds the qualifier "from now on" (ἀπ᾽ ἄρτι, *ap' arti*) to the phrase "you will not see me until." The Lucan absence of the qualifier is interesting, since Luke likes the equivalent ἀπὸ τοῦ νῦν (*apo tou nyn*, from now on; Luke 1:48; 5:10; 12:52; 22:18, 69; interestingly the phrase is absent from Acts). The difference may suggest a distinct tradition.

Luke 13:31–35 shows that nothing will deter Jesus from his call **Summary** and that Israel's situation grows worse. Jesus was sent by God on a mission: he is headed to Jerusalem to die, and the threat of an

16. I have already rejected the idea that Jesus sees himself as hidden wisdom here; see the exegesis of 13:34.

17. Tannehill 1986: 155–56 argues that Luke holds out hope for Israel's future, citing Allison 1983: 75 as support. Allison argues that Jesus uses the standard Jewish form for giving a conditional prophecy; see also Allison 1985: 157. Marshall 1978: 577 leans this way.

earthly ruler like Herod will not stop him. However, Israel is responsible to God for its rejection. Its track record has not been good in this regard, since historically it has murdered and stoned God's messengers, the prophets. God often wished to gather in, love, and protect his people, but they were not willing. Here again they are not willing. The result is clear: God abandons them until they recognize Jesus. The necessity to choose Jesus is again brought forward, along with a clear sense of the result of national rejection. These consequences also apply to individuals who reject Jesus. But Israel's rejection cannot stop God's plan.

Jesus' coming is either a warning or an opportunity. Peter's speech in Acts 3:11–26 makes a similar plea with a similar choice between blessing or cursing. The Book of Acts issues a call to hear the prophet like Moses who has come. The options are reminiscent of Deut. 28–32; but something greater than the law is here, since "the one who is to come" has come. Israel's house is empty; the Messiah is here.

7. Another Sabbath Healing and Silence (14:1–6)

Luke relates another Sabbath miracle after Jesus' prophetic warning to the nation. Have Jesus' repeated warnings and appeals done anything to change the official view of him? This event quickly provides the answer to such a question: nothing has changed. Jesus' opponents watch for an opportunity to trap him, but Jesus is not fazed. He heals a man with dropsy and justifies it by appealing to the Sabbath practice of the leadership. They are left in silence to ponder his statement. Jesus exposes the inconsistency of the leadership's Sabbath practice and continues his ministry of extending compassion to those in need. The practice of pulling up the ox recalls Deut. 22:4; *m. Šab.* 18.3; and *b. Šab.* 128b (Fitzmyer 1985: 1040).

This is the first of three events that are tied to the image of table or banquet fellowship in Luke 14:1–24. Meal settings are common in Luke (5:29; 7:36; 9:16; 10:38; 11:37; 22:14; 24:30). Schweizer (1984: 233) credits this setting to Luke's creativity, an unnecessary conclusion (Marshall 1978: 578). Ellis (1974: 192) opts for the likelihood that Luke has put together a representative sample of what Jesus taught on such occasions and placed it here. However, the motive behind framing this kind of collection in the same table setting is unclear, since in Luke's Gospel, Jesus utters teachings in a variety of settings. Why put the material in one place and yet have a variety of such scenes? Despite such legitimate questions concerning the presence here of simple event or accurate, summarizing anthology, what is presented is an eventful meal. Luke is no doubt conveying the kind of exchanges Jesus had with the religious leadership (Schürmann 1957: 96 n. 325 argues for the unity of the material predating Luke). Ernst (1977: 434) has a fitting title for 14:1–24: "Guest Meal Discussion." Grundmann (1963: 290) speaks of a "symposium," a literary form that suggests Jesus is sharing his wisdom with others (also Ellis 1974: 192; Wiefel 1988: 266). The major topic of 14:1–24 is criticism of the Pharisees. The theme is not new, since the journey has many pericopes where the leadership or the nation has been criticized (11:37–54; 12:1; 13:1–9; 13:22–30; 13:31–35). The nation still has not read the signs of the time correctly (12:54–56). Jesus brings a new era of restoration that the Pharisees refuse to acknowledge.

Sources and Historicity

This passage is the last of several Sabbath incidents recounted by Luke (4:16–30; 4:31–37; 6:1–5; 6:6–11; 13:10–17).[1] It is special Lucan material (Aland 1985: §214).[2] Luke's repeated Sabbath incidents show that nothing Jesus says changes matters. Neither side backs down in their approach to this issue. The two groups are headed for confrontation. In Luke's view, the religious leadership is hard-hearted and unwilling to respond to repeated evidences that God is working through Jesus. Confrontation is clear from the start of the passage, since the leadership is eyeing Jesus as he enters the house (14:1). Such repeated Sabbath healings should imply something about Jesus' authority, but the Pharisees' skeptical frame of mind makes such a conclusion impossible for them.

The above remarks depend, of course, on authenticity, which the Jesus Seminar (Funk and Hoover 1993: 349–50) questions by rating 14:3 as inauthentic (black type) and 14:5 as possibly having roots in Jesus (gray type). The seminar regards the account as a Lucan creation. But the mention of dropsy is unprecedented in either the OT or the NT (so Nolland 1993a: 745, who sees this as evidence of a pre-Lucan account that Luke presented in his own style as a controversy dialogue). And the argument that Jesus might have said something like 14:5 but not something like 14:3 seems to be an inconsistent way to see Jesus' teaching about the law, an area of clear dispute in his ministry. Jesus' reputation about how he handled the Sabbath is multiply attested. In addition, the healing uniquely takes place at a Pharisee's home, not at a synagogue, and in a meal context (so Meier 1994: 711, who is undecided about historicity). The event is too atypical to claim that it is created by Luke. I prefer to see it as yet another authentic piece of evidence about Jesus' Sabbath disputes where his actions cause offense in a fresh context (with Marshall 1978: 578).

In terms of form, Theissen (1983: 113) calls this a "rule miracle," while Schneider (1977a: 312) speaks of a controversy saying. Both are correct, since the pericope has both elements (Fitzmyer 1985:

---

1. Plummer 1896: 353 notes that Luke has five of the seven Sabbath healings in Scripture: 4:31–37, 4:38–39, and 6:6–11 have Synoptics parallels, while 13:10–17 and 14:1–6 are unique to Luke (the other two are John 5:10 and 9:14).

2. Fitzmyer 1985: 1039 remarks that, even though Matt. 12:11 has a similar saying, the rest of the detail is too different to be attributed to Q. In fact, it is too difficult for any other shared tradition. Fitzmyer also correctly denies that Luke 6:9 is a doublet to this verse. Marshall 1978: 578 sees a Q connection as possible. Bultmann 1963: 12 and Lohse, *TDNT* 7:26, argue that the text was a variant tradition created from Mark 3:1–6, but Ernst 1977: 435 correctly notes that the distinct terminology and motives suggest too much distance for this connection; so also Meier 1994: 710.

1039).[3] The account stresses what Jesus says more than what he does. The emphasis is on the significance of the miracle and the reaction it creates, along with the silence that Jesus' teaching brings. Jesus rules, but the Pharisees will not accept his authority.

The outline of Luke 14:1–6 is as follows:

a. Sabbath authority: discussion about a miracle (14:1–4)
   i. Setting (14:1–2)
   ii. Jesus questions the lawyers and Pharisees (14:3–4a)
   iii. Jesus heals the man (14:4b)
b. Reaction: Jesus' comment produces silence (14:5–6)

The passage contains yet another confrontation between Jesus and the Pharisees. Jesus' criticism of the Pharisees concerns Sabbath hypocrisy: they treat animals better than people. Jesus' authority emerges in the healing, as God works again through him on the Sabbath. Jesus' act demonstrates his ability to restore with God's power and approval, an ability that the Pharisees reject. Yet they make no reply to Jesus' work. What answer or explanation can they give? The passage closes in reflective silence.

Exegesis and Exposition

[1]And it came to pass that he entered into the house of one of the leaders of the Pharisees on the Sabbath to eat bread, and they were watching him. [2]And, behold, a certain man who had dropsy was before him. [3]And Jesus said to the lawyers and Pharisees, "Is it right on the Sabbath to heal or not?" [4]But they were silent. And taking the man, he healed him and let him go.

[5]And he said to them, "Which of you who has a ⌜son⌝ or an ox fall into a well, also does not immediately pull him out on the Sabbath?" [6]And they were not able to reply to these things.

a. Sabbath Authority: Discussion about a Miracle (14:1–4)
i. Setting (14:1–2)

The miracle's setting is described simply: a leader of the Pharisees **14:1** has Jesus over for a meal. Luke's general terminology makes it impossible to be specific as to the leader's exact position: he might have been a synagogue official, a synagogue head (8:41), or a higher official, a "chief priest."[4] The host is a prominent official, but a setting

---

3. Bultmann 1963: 12 opts for pronouncement; Berger 1984: 81 speaks of apophthegm. These are the same classification, since controversy accounts are a specific kind of pronouncement. On such classifications, see Bock 1991b.

4. Josephus, *Life* 5 §21, mentions the position of chief priests. Marshall 1978: 578 notes this reference, but is undecided on what it means.

in Jerusalem is not required (with Fitzmyer 1985: 1040; against Ellis 1974: 192). The meal is probably the midday meal, since bread is the main course (Schweizer 1985: 234; Van Der Loos 1965: 504; SB 1:589–90, 611–15; 2:202–3; Josephus, *Life* 54 §279). A Sabbath meal was prepared the day before to avoid breaking the Sabbath (*m. Šab.* 4.1–2; Klostermann 1929: 149). This type of meal is important to Luke because it shows that Jesus had table fellowship with the Pharisees and that he had their attention (Luke 7:36–50; 11:37–54; H. Weiss, *TDNT* 9:41–42).

The mood is clear from the start: they were watching him carefully (11:53–54; 20:20), as seen in the periphrastic construction ἦσαν παρατηρούμενοι (*ēsan paratēroumenoi*). The term means to "watch lurkingly" (Riesenfeld, *TDNT* 8:147). Their question seems to be, "What will he do this time?"

14:2 Luke explains why the Pharisees are curious. Sitting with them at the meal is a man with dropsy (ὑδρωπικός, *hydrōpikos*; a *hapax legomenon*), also called hydrops after its Greek name (Van Der Loos 1965: 507). Its symptoms are swollen limbs and tissue resulting from excess body fluids.[5] Technically, dropsy is not a disease, but indicates that another medical problem is present. Dropsy was discussed in ancient Jewish material as well as in the OT (Lev. 15:1–12; SB 2:203).[6] Some rabbis argued that dropsy resulted from sexual offenses (*b. Šab.* 33a) or from intentionally failing to have bowel movements (*b. Ber.* 25a) (for Greek examples, see Van Der Loos 1965: 506). The tradition is late, but it does show that dropsy was often viewed as God's judgment, either for sin or uncleanness.

Was this man invited to the meal in order to trap Jesus or did he simply come in (uninvited guests were a part of this culture; Luke 7:37; Van Der Loos 1965: 504–5)? The use of ἰδού (*idou*, behold) to indicate surprise might suggest the possibility that he has walked in. The account, however, gives no other indication that he was not already there. In this view the surprise of ἰδού is that such a person is at the meal. Combined with the presence of the "watching eyes" of the leadership (14:1), this verse probably suggests a trap, especially since 11:54 indicates that after the last meal the leadership deter-

---

5. Herod the Great was said to have suffered from dropsy; Josephus, *Antiquities* 17.6.5 §§168–70. In the apocryphal Acts of Paul 4, Paul heals a man of this condition; Schneemelcher 1991–92: 2.247.

6. Lev. Rab. 15.2 on 13:2 comments on Job 28:25: "Man is evenly balanced, half of him is water, and the other half is blood. When he is deserving, the water does not exceed the blood, nor does the blood exceed the water; but when he sins, it sometimes happens that the water gains over the blood and then he becomes a sufferer from dropsy; at other times the blood gains over the water and he then becomes leprous"; Van Der Loos 1965: 505.

mined to catch Jesus. A set-up is likely.[7] Regardless, the man now sits before Jesus, so that a response is possible. Jesus will take the initiative. Trap or no, Sabbath or no, he will help the man.

ii. Jesus Questions the Lawyers and Pharisees (14:3–4a)

14:3 Jesus sets the stage before acting. His question suggests that he knows what the Pharisees are thinking. In fact, Luke says that Jesus "replied" (ἀποκριθείς, apokritheis), indicating that he is in dialogue with their suspicion (Creed 1930: 189). Jesus asks a simple "legal" question about healing on the Sabbath: is it permitted (on ἔξεστιν, exestin, see the exegesis of 6:2)? No doubt the scribes and Pharisees have an opinion on the topic, but no one speaks.

Jesus' question leaves them in an unenviable position. If they say that healing is permitted, it raises problems about their tradition and their view of the law. If they say that it is not permitted, they will be seen as standing against doing good and showing compassion on the Sabbath. In addition, if they have invited the man and now desire to prevent Jesus from acting, it will raise questions about their motive in inviting the man to the meal. Jesus' question recalls the Sabbath healing in 6:9, where Jesus asked if it was permitted to do good on the Sabbath. Jesus' previous ministry shows what his answer would be (13:14–16). Have the Pharisees learned anything from Jesus' ministry or from God's activity on the Sabbath? Even if these particular leaders were not at these earlier events, surely they would have been aware of the debate surrounding Jesus. More important, Luke's readers know the history and are called to reflect on it through this question.

14:4a The "enlightened luminaries" and theologians remain silent, making it clear that they have learned nothing from Jesus' previous Sabbath healings. The reason why they are silent is not clear. Leaney (1958: 213) suggests division among them, while Arndt (1956: 337) suggests discomfort at not showing compassion for the man and his condition, as well as guilt over their tradition. The group is so fixed in their tradition, however, that it is unlikely that they feel guilty about their beliefs. It may be that they are embarrassed at their inability to respond to Jesus' question. In any case, the text does not say. The narrative leaves these reflections to the reader, adding to the mood and mystery. One is not to assume approval by the silence.

---

7. If this is the case, then the man being healed probably would not have been in on the trap. He would have been invited on the pretext of having an opportunity to meet Jesus. Though one cannot be sure that it was an intended trap, such a conclusion fits Luke's literary characterization of the Pharisees up to this point, indicating the mounting tension between Jesus and these officials.

Neither does it mean ambivalence, though technically silence is tacit approval in an ancient legal setting, since it allows events to continue (Fitzmyer 1985: 1041).[8]

iii. Jesus Heals the Man (14:4b)

14:4b Jesus acts, heals the man, and lets him go, doing a good work on the Sabbath. The text says that Jesus took (ἐπιλαβόμενος, *epilabomenos*) the man as he healed him, perhaps an embrace or some other form of physical contact that places the man in Jesus' compassionate care. This verb is often used of arresting or seizing somebody (Luke 9:47; 23:26; Acts 16:19; 17:19; 18:17; 21:30; 23:19). The action makes clear that the healing came through Jesus.

b. Reaction: Jesus' Comment Produces Silence (14:5–6)

14:5 Jesus takes the offensive, defending his action, despite the Pharisees' silence. He knows what they are thinking. Jesus points to the scribes' and Pharisees' own Sabbath practice to justify his actions: what would they do if a son (see the additional note) or an ox was in danger on the Sabbath? The remark is significant, for the appeal is to a basic act of compassion and rescue. These concerns should govern human relationships, even on God's day of rest. If people do this for possessions, how much more readily ought they do so for other people?

This reply is similar to 13:15, though that passage speaks only of cattle. The Mishnah mentions Sabbath exceptions for cattle (*m. Šab.* 5; 15.2; *m. ʿErub.* 2.1–4). Cattle could be led or fed as long as they did not carry a load. At Qumran, such aid would not be given to an animal, but it could be given to a person (CD 11.13–17; Marshall 1978: 580; SB 1:629).[9] The leadership has learned nothing from Jesus' teaching, his work, or even their own practice! Jesus' rhetorical question expects a positive reply (so οὐκ, *ouk*, not): of course, they would assist a son or ox in danger. With their inconsistency exposed, no reply is possible. The miracle becomes a rebuke and a call to repentance.

14:6 The leaders' silence replays their reaction to Jesus' first question. Ταῦτα (*tauta*, these things) is plural and refers to more than Jesus'

8. On silence, see Luke 6:9 = Mark 3:4, but contrast Luke 13:14–16. Objectors could stop the proceedings, similar to the opportunity given at modern weddings for anyone to object to a couple's getting married. If no one speaks, the ceremony proceeds.

9. *M. B. Qam.* 5.6 is not parallel, since that passage deals with legal damages, not the Sabbath; so correctly Creed 1930: 189. *B. Šab.* 128b gives both rulings: one that allows and one that forbids help (also *m. Šab.* 18.2). This was a debated point among Jews, even in the fifth century.

remark in 14:5. In other words, there was no response to Jesus throughout the entire episode. Ἀνταποκρίνομαι (*antapokrinomai*, to dispute) means that they were not able to refute him (Büchsel, *TDNT* 3:945). None of "these things" produced a reply, just as in 13:17 (other Lucan notes of silence are found in Luke 20:26; Acts 11:18; 12:17; 15:12; 22:2; Fitzmyer 1985: 1042). For Luke, silence speaks louder than words, for it suggests that no response is possible and that the leadership stands condemned. Luke wants his readers to contrast Jesus' style of response with that of his opponents and reflect on the difference.

Summary

Luke 14:1–6 is another Sabbath confrontation where Jesus acts with compassion. The opponents are watching him closely, but they no longer say anything in reply. They have given up complaining to him. Jesus acts and heals, while raising questions about the Sabbath practice of the Jewish leadership. There are two sides in the dispute: Jesus' work and the opposition's silence. Luke wishes his readers to note the difference and recall that numerous Sabbath healings have produced no change in the leadership. Where is God working? Where is the evidence of his authority? Where is his power and presence displayed? It resides in Jesus, not in the leadership. In addition, what does God desire of his people, as indicated by the one he has sent? He desires mercy and compassion that reaches out to meet needs. Even on the day of rest there is no cessation of compassion.

Additional Note

14:5. A textual problem influences the nature of the argument: is the first term of the pair υἱός (son; $\mathfrak{P}^{45}$, $\mathfrak{P}^{75}$, A, B, W, Δ, Byz, Lect, a few Itala, Syriac) or ὄνος (ass; ℵ, L, Ψ, family 1, family 13, minuscule 33, most Itala, Vulgate)? The evidence is divided, but the combination of papyri, B, and Byz suggests that υἱός is original. It is easy to explain a change to ὄνος: since 13:15 discusses only animals, a copyist probably made the two texts similar (Klostermann 1929: 149; Plummer 1896: 355–56; Schweizer, *TDNT* 8:364 n. 209; Marshall 1978: 579–80). In addition, the combination *ass and ox* would be familiar from the OT: Deut. 22:4; Isa. 32:20. The suggestion by Luce (1933: 245) that ὄις (sheep) or ὗς (pig) was the original reading lacks manuscript support. The reading πρόβατον (lamb) in Codex D is influenced by Matt. 12:11. There is no mistranslation from Aramaic (Fitzmyer 1985: 1042, citing Connally 1948: 31).

8. Lessons on Humility and Generosity (14:7–14)

For much of Luke's journey narrative, Jesus engages in polemic with the Jewish leadership. Now he begins to turn his attention more directly to instruction about what following him means. Yet polemic remains, since the Pharisees are still the negative example (as in 15:1–32 and 16:14–31; Tannehill 1986: 183). But the major concern is how God's people should live. Placed side by side, the two themes make sense. Many might have thought that the way to God was to follow the religious leaders, and so Luke must show that their rejection of Jesus does not reflect God's opinion of Jesus. Rather, the leadership's approach involves a stubborn refusal to hear God's representative. In fact, their way of following God is not what God desires. But if that is the case, how is one to follow God? What is Jesus' way? Luke now turns to this question in this pericope.

Humility is to mark the disciple. Do not seek the front seats of honor, but the less conspicuous seats. This way others will be the ones to call you to the front. In fact, do not only be humble, but give to the humble without hope of repayment. In other words, be generous without expecting to be paid back. Humility expresses itself in ignoring issues of class or rank.[1] God honors the one who befriends the poor, the lame, and the blind. The note struck here is the opposite of that found later in the church of Corinth or in the church that James wrote to, where social division existed within the community (1 Cor. 11:17–22; James 2:1–5; 4:6; 5:1–6; Phil. 2:1–11).

Luke 14:7 marks this pericope as a parable that pictures the attitude with which one approaches God and the kingdom: "I am not worthy, I will accept the invitation on the host's terms, knowing that he lifts up the one with such an attitude."[2] To see a parable here is better than seeing another setting that Luke redacted

---

1. Tannehill 1986: 183 sees two points of concern for Jesus: (1) humility and (2) no attitude of social exclusion or pride in wealth. Tiede 1988: 263 has a revealing title for this unit: "Seating Charts and Guest Lists in the Kingdom."

2. As Marshall 1978: 584 notes, the reference to resurrection at the end adds an eschatological umbrella to the passage alluding to the resurrection of the just (cf. 2 Macc. 7:9; Luke 20:35; John 5:29).

out of the story or rejecting its authenticity (Bultmann 1963: 104–5 rejects its authenticity because it is not different enough from the Jewish parallels; see n. 3 below). Other passages clearly linked to Jesus condemn the taking of the first seats (Luke 11:43; 20:45–47; Marshall 1978: 581). Humility is a key theme of Jesus' teaching (cf. Luke 22:24–27 = Mark 10:35–45).

Sources and Historicity

This section is unique to Luke and belongs to his special material, though its theme is not unique to him (Aland 1985: §215), for Jesus often called his disciples to humility (Matt. 18:4; 23:12; Luke 18:14; cf. 1 Pet. 5:6). The passage is a comment on the OT teaching of Prov. 25:6–7 (Ellis 1974: 193). Such illustrations were common among the rabbis and fits the teaching of Jesus (Sir. 3:17–18; SB 2:204; Ernst 1977: 437; for Greek examples, see Klostermann 1929: 150). The church fathers also adapted the saying (1 Clem. 30.2; Ignatius, *Ephesians* 5.3; Schweizer 1984: 235). The theme reflects Jesus' basic ethical stance.

The Jesus Seminar rejects the authenticity of most of this unit, printing 14:8–10, 12–14 in black type and 14:11 in gray (Funk and Hoover 1993: 350–51). The seminar argues that the passage is in the Greco-Roman symposium tradition (see the introduction to 14:1–6), and that Lucan themes of humility and concern for the poor as well as Jewish wisdom themes (Prov. 11:2; 25:6–7; Ps. 18:27 [18:28 MT]; Sir. 32:1–2) stand behind the text. But the theme of humility versus pride is common to Jesus' teaching (Mark 10:35–45; Luke 11:43; 18:14; 20:45–47; 22:24–27; Matt. 18:4; 23:12). Such a portrait of Jesus' egalitarianism is basic to his ministry (Crossan 1991: 261–62; Horsley 1987: 240). It is not unlikely that such topics would have been part of Jesus' public discussion, especially as they fit the Jewish milieu.

The form of the account is a collection of sayings that contains admonition and proverbial counsel (Fitzmyer 1985: 1044 [with a wisdom saying in 14:11]; Bultmann 1963: 103–4; Berger 1984: 165 [admonition]; Tiede 1988: 264 [proverbial counsel]). The outline of Luke 14:7–14 is as follows:

a. Exhortation to take the back seat (14:7–11)
  i. A parable in response to seating customs (14:7)
  ii. First illustration: what not to do (14:8–9)
  iii. Second illustration: what to do (14:10–11)
b. Exhortation to invite those who cannot repay (14:12–14)
  i. Who not to invite (14:12)
  ii. Who to invite (14:13)
  iii. The promised heavenly reward (14:14)

This unit focuses on humility, a fundamental attribute of faith. To make the point, it pictures the shame of being asked to step down to the next seat at the table. If one is exalted, it should come from others. In addition, humility expresses itself in how one views and treats others. There is a call to invite the needy, with a note that this is an act honored by God. Humility and generosity illustrate how one draws near to God and to others.

Exegesis and Exposition

[7]And he told a parable to those who were invited, while noting how they chose seats of honor, saying to them, [8]"When you are invited to a wedding feast, do not sit in the seat of honor, lest a more eminent man than you is invited by him. [9]When the one who invited you and him comes and says to you, 'Give this place to this one,' you begin with shame to head to the last seat. [10]But when you are invited, go sit in the last spot, in order that when the one who invited you comes, he will say to you, 'Friend, move up to a better seat.' Then you will be honored before all those who sit with you. [11]For everyone who exalts himself will be humbled, and the one humbling himself will be exalted."

[12]And he was saying to the one who invited him, "When you give a dinner or a supper, do not invite your friends or your brothers or your relatives or your rich neighbors, lest they also invite you in turn and you are repaid. [13]But when you give a reception, invite the poor, crippled, lame, and blind, [14]and you will be blessed, for they cannot pay you back. For you will be paid back in the resurrection of the righteous."

a. Exhortation to Take the Back Seat (14:7–11)
i. A Parable in Response to Seating Customs (14:7)

14:7 After instructing the Pharisees about the obligation to be compassionate on the Sabbath, Jesus turns to another problem: pride. His teaching results from watching the guests head for the seats of honor. The tables are reversed from 14:1, since Jesus is doing the watching here. The πρωτοκλισία (*prōtoklisia*, seat of honor) was located next to the host or master of the house (Matt. 23:6 = Mark 12:39 = Luke 20:46; Michaelis, *TDNT* 6:870–71; BAGD 725; BAA 1451). The middle voice ἐξελέγοντο (*exelegonto*, they elected) shows that the guests chose seats for themselves.[3] Seating often followed the washing of hands (Mark 7:3; *m. Ber.* 6–8, esp. 8.2; Safrai 1976b: 801–4). Seating custom varied from culture to culture and even

---

3. Manson 1949: 278 notes a passage in Theophrastus, *Characters* 21.2, where the sign of a proud man is that he seeks the seat beside the host. Lev. Rab. 1.5 on 1:1 (commenting on Prov. 25:7) has a similar exhortation for people to stay two or three seats down; see also Josephus, *Antiquities* 15.2.4 §21.

within cultures. For example, later Judaism spoke of a U-shaped table with a three-person couch located on each prong of the table. The host sat at the bottom of the U, in the middle between the two wings of the U; the most honored seat would be to the left and the next honored seat would be to the right.[4] In any culture, the seats by the host were the seats of honor. As to whether honor was given to rank or age, the configuration used in the first century is not entirely clear (Ernst 1977: 438; Manson 1949: 278). Marshall (1978: 581) notes that rank determined seating, although by A.D. 300 it was age that determined seating. He also points out that the honored guest tended to arrive after most of the other guests. Evidently, rank ("the more eminent" in 14:8) is the issue at this meal. As Jesus watches the guests rush to claim the honored seats, he notes what such behavior reveals about them.

Jesus uses a παραβολή (parabolē), the significance of which is debated. Is this a teaching on humility (Fitzmyer 1985: 1046), on relating to God (Creed 1930: 190), or on both (Marshall 1978: 581)? Some even question Luke's description that a parable is present (so A. Jülicher, cited in Creed). However, a broad point about humility before people and God is certain, since one's attitude to God is often seen in how one treats others (1 John 2:3–11 is the clearest example of this linkage). If one takes παραβολή seriously, then the passage pictures how one approaches God, as well as the call to humility. The result is that Jesus calls on his hearers to relate to all types of people, which in turn pictures a basic approach to God. This relationship of humility to divine response comes in the conclusion of Luke 14:11 (Grundmann 1963: 293).

ii. First Illustration: What Not to Do (14:8–9)

14:8 Jesus' exhortation is clear: at a wedding feast or major meal, do not go to the seat of honor—just in case a more eminent person has been invited.[5] Evidently, it was easy to recognize an invited guest's stature, and the ranking protocol in ancient society required giving this person the best seat. The guest would then have to take one of the last seats, since all the others would have been filled in the meantime (Manson 1949: 278). Prudence and wisdom suggest that one not be anxious to take the honored seat (μήποτε [mēpote, lest] gives

---

4. Plummer 1896: 356 notes that two to four people could recline on a couch. SB 4:617–20 cites the variety of customs and notes another configuration with the host at the head of the table.

5. Fitzmyer 1985: 1046 suggests that γάμος is broad enough to describe any feast, not just a wedding; cf. Esth. 2:18; 9:22. It can simply be a celebration. The difference in sense is not significant, since a representative picture is present.

the qualifying reason for not taking the first seat; Zerwick 1963: §452; BDF §370.2; BDR §370.2.4).

14:9 Jesus describes the embarrassing reversal: a self-appointed place at the front produces shame (αἰσχύνη, *aischynē*; BAGD 25 §2; BAA 48 §2; the noun only here in Luke, the verb only in 16:3), as the host intercedes for the more eminent guest and asks the presumptuous person to move to the "least honorable" seat (ἔσχατος, *eschatos*, is figurative; Kittel, *TDNT* 2:698 §3).[6] In front of everyone, the guest must get up and move to the remaining seat at the end of the table. The Greek is graphic, ἄρξῃ . . . κατέχειν (*arxē . . . katechein*, you begin . . . to head for the last seat), depicting the shame felt with each very public step away from the center of action (Plummer 1896: 357). In effect, Jesus tells them that it is better not to overestimate one's importance, which can put one at risk of public disgrace.

iii. Second Illustration: What to Do (14:10–11)

14:10 Jesus advises the opposite course of action: take the last seat, not the first. The contrast is seen in ἔσχατον (*eschaton*, last) versus the use of πρωτοκλισία (*prōtoklisia*, first seat) in 14:8. By taking the last station, the host's reaction may be entirely different: he may ask the person to take a better seat, and in doing so, rather than being shamed, that person will be honored before all who sit at the table. Luke makes two further contrasts to 14:8–9: προσανάβηθι ἀνώτερον (*prosanabēthi anōteron*, move up) contrasts with δὸς τούτῳ τόπον (*dos toutō topon*, give this place), and δόξα (*doxa*, honor) is opposite αἰσχύνης (*aischynēs*, shame).[7]

Some commentators dislike this teaching, suggesting that the motive for sitting in the last place seems to be the desire for honor (Luce 1933: 246; Leaney 1958: 213).[8] This looks like practical, and perhaps self-focused, wisdom speaking. But this is much ado about nothing. The main point is that it is better for others to recognize who you are than to suggest to them your "proper" (or improper!) place. Humility is the best course in all affairs. Station should be suggested by others, not seized by oneself (Grundmann, *TDNT* 8:16; Arndt 1956: 339; Marshall 1978: 582). Luke 14:11 shows this to be the point. The remark works in two spheres at once: personal relationships and one's relationship with God. An explanation is not found by relegating the point to God's requiring humility. Jesus'

---

6. On shame in ancient culture, see Malina and Neyrey 1991; on seating priority, see Neyrey 1991: 366.

7. Δόξα sometimes means "honor"; see Kittel, *TDNT* 2:237; 1 Cor. 11:15; Eph. 3:13; 1 Thess. 2:6.

8. Whether ἵνα denotes purpose or result is debatable.

concern is comprehensive: God's view and that of others. Manson (1949: 279) notes that the influence of this passage is found in the variant reading after Matt. 20:28.[9] Schneider (1977a: 315) remarks that Luke 18:9–14 pictures a similar contrast of attitude.

For Jesus, the real issue is humility, which God honors with exalta- **14:11** tion. The theme of eschatological reversal is common in Luke (1:52–53; 6:21, 25; 10:15; 18:14; also Matt. 18:4; 23:12; Rom. 12:16; Phil. 2:5–11; 1 Tim. 6:17; James 4:6, 10; 1 Pet. 5:5; Marshall 1978: 583). The proud will be brought down and the humble exalted (on exalted, see Bertram, *TDNT* 8:608). The passage has OT roots and Jewish parallels (Ezek. 21:26 [21:31 MT]; 17:24; Sir. 3:19–23; Fitzmyer 1985: 1047; Ernst 1977: 439).[10] Jesus tells how God will treat both the proud and the humble. Such wisdom is not merely practical but has spiritual, eschatological overtones. A couplet by George Herbert applies to this text: "Humble we must be, if to heaven we go; / High is the roof there, but the gate is low."

b. Exhortation to Invite Those Who Cannot Repay (14:12–14)
i. Who Not to Invite (14:12)

Jesus turns to another image of graciousness as he addresses his **14:12** host: hospitality to those who are not able to return the favor. Jesus advises not inviting friends, family, relatives, and wealthy neighbors to dinner. Rather, invite those who are not able to pay you back. Μὴ φώνει (*mē phōnei*, do not invite) depicts a habitual invitation and has the force of a command not to do this exclusively (Plummer 1896: 358; Marshall 1978: 583).[11] All kinds of meals are in view since ἄριστον (*ariston*) indicates a late morning meal, while δεῖπνον (*deipnon*) is the main late afternoon meal (Arndt 1956: 340; Fitzmyer 1985: 1047; SB 2:204–6; Luke 11:38; Behm, *TDNT* 2:34). The invitation of friends is limited to repayment in an invitation to eat at their home. But the more gracious action that Jesus suggests has a bigger, more permanent, reward from God.

9. Prov. 25:6–7 (NRSV) says, "Do not put yourself forward in the king's presence / or stand in the place of the great; / for it is better to be told, 'Come up here,' / than to be put lower in the presence of a noble." For Jewish parallels, see Sir. 3:17–20; 4:8; 12:11; 29:5; Lev. Rab. 1.5 on 1:1 (fifth century); *'Abot de Rabbi Nathan* A.25 (= Goldin 1955: 110); Bultmann 1963: 104; Fitzmyer 1985: 1047; SB 1:916.

10. Lev. Rab. 1.5 on 1:1 attributes a noneschatological statement to Hillel: "My humiliation is my exaltation and my exaltation is my humiliation." For more on this midrash, see n. 3 above.

11. The Semitic rhetorical idiom "not x . . . but y" means "not so much x . . . but y" (also 10:20). On this use of φωνέω (to call), see O. Betz, *TDNT* 9:303. On ἀντικαλέω (to invite back), a NT *hapax legomenon*, see K. Schmidt, *TDNT* 3:496.

The major point is that customary "pay back" hospitality is of no great merit to God. Fellowship should not have social limits. The best hospitality is that which is given, not exchanged (Manson 1949: 279; Luke 6:33–35 [love without repayment]; Klostermann 1929: 151). Some challenge the appropriateness of Jesus' remarks to this host. But if the teaching exalts an attitude like that of the host of 14:9–14, it is a friendly rebuke to broaden one's associations. After all, a Pharisee is supposed to represent God, so he should do it in a way that pleases him.

ii. Who to Invite (14:13)

14:13 Jesus exhorts the Pharisees to invite not their friends but the poor, crippled, lame, and blind (these four groups also occur in 14:21).[12] The focus is on those who have need and cannot repay the invitation. Such hospitality is given without concern for reciprocity and so it pleases God. Δοχή (*dochē*) is a reception or banquet, a major meal (BAGD 206; BAA 414; Gen. 21:8; 26:30; Esth. 1:3; Dan. 5:title; 1 Esdr. 3:1; elsewhere in the NT only at Luke 5:29 [of Levi's dinner for Jesus]). The spirit of this passage, in terms of its openness to the downcast, is also found in 6:20 (Ernst 1977: 441). Such people were excluded from the temple (Lev. 21:17–23; 2 Sam. 5:8). Qumran also excluded such people from their community (1Q28a [= 1QSa = Rule Annex] 2.3–10; 1QM 7.4; Nolland 1993a: 751; Schneider 1977a: 315; Fitzmyer 1985: 1047). But even the somewhat parallel Jewish teaching reflects a totally different spirit. For example, *m. ʾAbot* 1.5 speaks of having the doors of the house opened wide and having the needy in the household, but these needy are probably not at the banquet table, but serve it (as *m. ʾAbot* 1.3 suggests). So the mood is not one of inclusion. The OT does teach such concern for the poor and powerless (Deut. 14:28–29; 16:11–14; 26:11–13; also Tob. 2:2; SB 2:206–7). Unlike much of ancient culture, Jesus urges that reciprocity not be a factor in deciding whom to invite (Marshall 1978: 584).[13] Hospitality is generosity when no motive exists besides giving.

iii. The Promised Heavenly Reward (14:14)

14:14 God honors such selfless graciousness. Jesus promises that blessing will come. For, although those in need cannot reciprocate, God can

---

12. Ἀνάπειρος probably describes the severely maimed or mutilated (BAGD 59; BAA 117; LSJ 116; elsewhere in the NT only at Luke 14:21), as opposed to χωλός, which refers to all the lame (BAGD 889; BAA 1772; Plummer 1896: 359).

13. Stählin, *TDNT* 9:160, also n. 117, exaggerates the ancient debate: some ancients (Plato, *Phaerdus* 233D–34A) said to invite only family and friends, while *m. ʾAbot* 1.5 said to leave the door wide open (but for reasons of exclusion noted above). B. Scott 1989: 164 calls Jesus' instruction the "law of no return."

and will. At the resurrection, when the stewardship of one's actions is weighed, such kindness will be paid back by the Father. The passive voice ἀνταποδοθήσεται (*antapodothēsetai*, it will be paid back) suggests that God is the source of the reward. This verb is strong (having two prefixes) and emphatic (appearing twice in the verse) (Büchsel, *TDNT* 2:169). It refers to the inability of the invited to pay back, while also noting that God will. The contrast is significant. The picture of the resurrection of the righteous has Jewish roots (2 Macc. 7:9; Josephus, *Antiquities* 18.1.3 §14; SB 4:1182–83; Luke 20:34–36; Schweizer 1984: 235).[14]

Summary

Luke 14:7–14 contrasts Jesus' ministry with that of the Jewish leadership. Two characteristics in particular stand out: humility and openness to all. As Jesus sits at the table with these leaders, he notes their attempts to seize the seats of honor. In contrast, he advises taking the lowest seat. The one who takes a higher seat may end up losing that seat in shame. It is better to be humble and let others honor you.

In addition, the tendency is to be hospitable only to one's own friends and relatives. But Jesus exhorts the leaders to open their table fellowship to all, especially those in need who cannot pay back the favor. Jesus opens up the community of relationship so that no boundaries of class or rank exist. To invite those who cannot repay is not the cultural norm. Though a return invitation from them is not possible, there awaits a different, better reward: God will repay with blessing in the resurrection.

Jesus wishes to direct a person's attention outward. One should not bring honor to oneself, but let others judge one's importance. The question is not "What can one do to receive something equivalent back?" but "What can one give to meet the needs of others?" Humility and openness to all are two major facets of Jesus' ethics. For the disciple, service and meeting the needs of others is not an option. It is the appropriate response to Jesus' call to follow him. In short, the church is not to worry about the chair of honor. Rather, it is to make chairs available to those who are looking for a place to sit—even for those who think there are no chairs for them.

14. On general resurrection and judgment of all, see Luke 10:12; 11:31–32; John 5:29; Acts 17:30–31; 23:6; 24:15; Rom. 2:5–11; 2 Cor. 5:10; 2 Tim. 4:1; Rev. 20:12; Ellis 1974: 194.

9. Parable of the Great Supper
(14:15–24)

The third unit that revolves around the meal with the Pharisees is the parable of the great supper. It concludes a section that has been loaded with confrontation and warning to the leadership: the Sabbath healing of the man with dropsy (14:1–6) and the parable about taking the lowest seat (14:7–14). Both events confront misdirected leadership attitudes, a motif continued in this parable. Jesus makes the point that many in the nation will miss the opportunity to sit at the banquet table because they have priorities higher than responding to the host's current offer. Rejection means that the invitation goes to others, who will flock in. The parable closes by noting that the original invitees miss the meal because they do not respond. Ironically, those who seek the best seats will lack any seats at the most important occasion. They will not be honored; in fact, they will be excluded entirely. Those whom the leadership shunned will be at the most important meal in seats that the leaders thought were reserved for them.

Three points dominate the passage, similar to themes in 11:37–54, 13:6–9, and 13:31–35. First, the leadership is missing its last opportunity and risks missing God's blessing entirely. This is the last time in Luke that Jesus dines with the Pharisees (Egelkraut 1976: 182). The meal is filled with hostility, as 14:1–14 indicates. Jesus boldly challenges the leadership's thinking on their secure position before God. The summons to repent in response to the opportunity for blessing is going unheeded. If they miss the banquet, it will not be for lack of invitation (Fitzmyer 1985: 1053).

Second, the kingdom will not miss the original invitees. The kingdom still comes and a new invitation is extended to others. Although those who seemed most likely to sit at the table miss the celebration, others sit in their seats. The allusion in the first set of new invitations is to the poor and other needy people for whom the gospel call is especially intended (1:50–53; 4:16–30; 6:20–23). But the parable also has a second set of new invitees. They may picture an additional group that is invited and may suggest for Luke a preview of Gentile mission (20:9–19; 4:25–30).

A third point remains: if those who followed Jesus are not those one would have expected, it is not because Jesus excluded some, but because some excluded themselves. Others took advantage of the opportunity that Jesus offered, and they are at God's table.

A fourth point should also be noted: the celebration comes regardless of the invitees' response. The party is not delayed. This detail stresses that now is the time to respond.

Sources and Historicity

The source issue for this parable is complex. It is commonly regarded as parallel to Matt. 22:1–14, with a fairly parallel version in the Gospel of Thomas 64–65 (Aland 1985: §216; Wiefel 1988: 274). Egelkraut (1976: 180) notes the different efforts to reconstruct the original version, while remarking that most see Luke as the more primitive version (also B. Scott 1989: 163, 167). Glombitza (1962) prefers Matthean originality, with Luke shortening the account. Jeremias (1963a: 63–69, esp. 176) speaks of a double tradition, but regards the Lucan version as shorter and more original, though both have expanded on the original. Manson (1949: 129) regards Luke as Q material that Matthew reworked, so that the original sense is clouded.[1]

I question a one-tradition approach, since almost none of the vocabulary overlaps and numerous differences make the presence of one tradition in various redactions unlikely. The following table enumerates these differences (cf. Ernst 1977: 442):

Element	Matthew	Luke
giver of the banquet	king	master of the house
banquet	wedding feast	dinner banquet
structure of the first invitation	two invitations by many servants	one invitation by one servant
reaction to the invitation	invitees return to field and business with laughter, while others beat the servants	three excuses given, no beatings
host's response	king sends troops to destroy invitees and invites new guests	host invites new guests

1. Also Schulz 1972: 391–98; Crossan 1973: 72; Fitzmyer 1985: 1052. Jeremias 1963a: 63–64, 176 argues that the Gospel of Thomas may be more original than Matthew, except for its expansion of excuses. The Thomas parable is closer to Luke than to Matthew and so is often discussed with Luke's version, but it introduces a fourth figure who cannot come to the banquet. Thomas gives no setting, since the document is just a list of teachings. But the excuses in Thomas use more urban imagery; Luke's use of agrarian imagery fits Jesus' tendency to use agrarian illustrations. Horsley 1987: 180 sees Luke as the more original of the versions, noting that the economically prosperous are the excluded; so also the Jesus Seminar (Funk and Hoover 1993: 352), though it regards the symposium-table setting as Lucan.

second set of invitees	many	poor, lame, blind, and crippled
response to second set of invitations	one gathering comes	one gathering does not fill the house, so another set of invitations is given
ending	uninvited visitor without a wedding garment is removed	a saying about original invitees not being at the meal

Some of these differences could be explained as specification of certain points or as deletion, but the sheer number of differences and the absence of corresponding vocabulary seem to indicate distinct traditions and parables, though their theme is much the same.[2] In my judgment, one theme is addressed and the same basic idea is taught, but the variations reflect Jesus' development of the idea in his ministry on distinct occasions. Church recasting and redaction do not explain the differences.

This is one of the few parables regarded as largely authentic by the Jesus Seminar (Funk and Hoover 1993: 351–53): 14:16–23 is related to Jesus' teaching (in pink type), with only 14:24, which excludes the Pharisees from the banquet, being rejected (in black type) as a "Lucan addition" (so also Nolland 1993a: 754). But such an exclusion is inherent to the imagery and should be seen as a part of the genuineness of the parable's basic thrust. Even the Gospel of Thomas 64 has such a conclusion, making it multiply attested. In favor of the parable's authenticity is its structure of "threes" (showing its oral roots) and its challenge to social expectations. The account is like 13:22–30 in tone and has the basic qualities of an authentic parable of Jesus. Jesus teaches that the "apparently elect" will not make it without response.

> The form of the text is a kingdom parable that functions as a pronouncement (Fitzmyer 1985: 1049, 1053 [a parable of warning as a call to respond]; Bultmann 1963: 175; Berger 1984: 51, 81 [speaks of parable and pronouncement]). The outline of Luke 14:15–24 is as follows:
>
> a. A remark about blessing and the kingdom (14:15)
> b. Inclusion and rejection: parable of the great supper (14:16–23)
>   i. Invitations go out (14:16–17)
>   ii. Excuses come in (14:18–20)

2. So Blomberg 1990: 237–39; Kistemaker 1980: 193–201; Plummer 1896: 359–60; Liefeld 1984: 979. Those accepting one parable but distinct sources are Luce 1933: 248; Grundmann 1963: 296 (L); Ernst 1977: 442 (L); Marshall 1978: 584; Tiede 1988: 266 (apparently). Ellis 1974: 194 is uncertain. Blomberg 1990: 233–36 has a good discussion of this parable.

      iii. The master's new invitation to the outcast (14:21)
      iv. Invitations given with room to spare (14:22)
      v. Third set of invitations given to even more (14:23)
    c. Jesus' application: the originally invited group will be
      absent (14:24)

This unit warns of the danger of missing the opportunity to enter the kingdom, especially the Jewish leadership's failure to enter. God offers the invitation to all, but some miss the banquet. The misperception about priorities or expectations may prevent entry. Such excuses are lame, considering what is offered. In contrast stands the gospel invitation to the poor and needy. Many will come in who were not originally expected to enter, and many will not enter who were expected to be there. Failure to enter is not because of lack of opportunity. Nonetheless, the banquet will be filled with people of all types, since God is generous and his banquet comes despite the original invitees' refusals. The time for celebration has come; response now is crucial.

Exegesis and Exposition

[15]And when one of them reclining with him heard these things, he said to him, "Blessed is the one who eats bread in the kingdom of God."
[16]And he said to him, "A certain man had a great supper and invited many. [17]And he sent his servant at the dinner hour to say to the invited, 'Come, for now ⌐it is ready⌐.' [18]And they all with one consent began to make excuses. The first one said to him, 'I have bought a field and it is necessary that I go see it; I beg of you, have me be excused.' [19]And another said, 'I have bought five yoke of oxen, and I am on my way to try them out; I beg of you, have me be excused.' [20]And another said, 'I have married a wife, and because of this I cannot come.' [21]And the servant came and reported to the master these things. Then the householder became angry and said to his servant, 'Go quickly into the streets and lanes of the city and bring in the poor, maimed, blind, and lame.' [22]And the servant said, 'Master, what you have commanded has been done, and there is still room.' [23]And the master said to the servant, 'Go to the highways and hedges and urge them to come in, in order that my house might be filled.'
[24]"For I say to you, none of those men who were invited shall taste my meal."

a. A Remark about Blessing and the Kingdom (14:15)

The banquet imagery and the mention of the resurrection of the **14:15** righteous in Luke 14:14 causes one of the guests to reflect on the greatest banquet of all: the eschatological fellowship that comes in God's future glorious kingdom (Isa. 25:6; also Ps. 22:26 [22:27 MT];

23:5 [in a noneschatological sense]; 1 Enoch 62.14; Luke 22:16; Rev. 19:9; Ellis 1974: 194; Plummer 1896: 360; Fitzmyer 1985: 1054; SB 4:1154–56).[3] This guest declares the blessedness of anyone who is permitted to eat at that table (Fitzmyer 1985: 1054; on eating bread, see Gen. 37:25; 2 Sam. 9:7, 10; 12:20; 2 Kings 4:8; Eccles. 9:7). In fact, the underlying assumption of this remark is that the Pharisees will be the blessed at that table. Such hope is a significant one, for at that time God's people will be fully vindicated and blessing will come to all whom he receives in his kingdom. The remark will cause Jesus to expound on who will be at the table. In the following parable he will challenge their assumption on the basis of their current response.[4] In fact, the kingdom promise and hope of entry into participation is closer than they think!

Fitzmyer (1985: 1052) argues that Luke supplied this verse, but the setting makes good sense (so Manson 1949: 129 [who calls the dinner guest's utterance "a characteristic piece of apocalyptic piety"] and Marshall 1978: 587).

b. Inclusion and Rejection: Parable of the Great Supper (14:16–23)
i. Invitations Go Out (14:16–17)

14:16   Jesus replies with a parable of a man who gave a great supper (δεῖπνον, *deipnon*; see the exegesis of 14:12) at his house (in Matt. 22:2, it is a king who gives a wedding feast). He invites many to come to this major occasion, this grand time. The invitees evidently accepted the invitation and then awaited the servant's word to announce the celebration's start. Their initial response is like responding affirmatively to an R.S.V.P. request. The imagery pictures Israel's and the leadership's invitation to the table.

14:17   When the meal is ready, the master sends out a servant to tell the invitees to come. It was common in such upper-class meals to send servants to call guests to come to the table (Jeremias 1963a: 176; Marshall 1978: 587–88; Esth. 6:14; Lam. Rab. 4.2 on 4:2; Philo, *On the Creation* 25 §78; SB 1:880–81).[5] To refuse an invitation at this

---

3. Similar settings are found in Luke 10:25–30; 12:13–15; 15:1–3. The idea is to share in eternal reward or eternal life. On the eschatological banquet in Judaism, see Exod. Rab. 25.7 on 16:4; 2 Bar. 29.8; 1 Enoch 25.5; Behm, *TDNT* 2:691.

4. Such introductions to teaching are common in Luke: 11:27, 45; 12:13, 41; 13:1, 23; 15:2; 16:14; 17:5, 20; 18:9; 19:11, 39; 22:24, 49; 23:27; Schweizer 1984: 191. Almost all of the examples are in the journey-to-Jerusalem section, so that the style is not uniform throughout the Gospel.

5. See C. Kim 1975 for an ancient invitation. Fitzmyer 1985: 1055 correctly notes that Jeremias's appeal to this as a custom of Jerusalem has only a fifth-century text as support, but Esther and Philo suggest that the custom is possibly older. Nolland

stage shows an absence of courtesy, much like being a no-show after already responding positively to an R.S.V.P. (Creed 1930: 191). Regardless of the custom of meal invitations, in the parable's narrative framework, failure to come is rude. The opportunity to be at the meal is no surprise. The meal at the table pictures entry into salvation's ultimate benefits.

Luke's version stands in contrast to Matt. 22, where many servants are sent. Discussion centers on who altered the image, but the prospect is that different stories on the same theme are present.[6] It is common to see the Lucan servant as Christ and the Matthean servants as including the prophets (Luce 1933: 249). The first detail is possible, while the second may not be if Jesus' disciples are meant. The issue centers on who is the host: if the host is God, then the servants are Christ and the apostles; if the host is Christ, then the servants are the disciples. It is likely that God hosts the banquet, since he is responsible for the plan and the blessing.

ii. Excuses Come In (14:18–20)

Those invited to the great supper ask to be excused, one at a time. **14:18** They act separately, yet they act as if they were one. The idiomatic phrase ἀπὸ μιᾶς (apo mias), which perhaps means "with one consent" or "with one mind," might reflect an Aramaic idiom meaning "all at once" (Jeremias 1963a: 176; Black 1967: 113). But Marshall (1978: 588) and BDF §241.6 argue that it is a Greek expression meaning "unanimously" (because of the feminine gender, BAGD 88 §VI and BAA 176 §VI see an idiom that means either "at once" or "unanimously"). Whatever the sense, the excuses vary, but the basic reason is similar, dealing with either financial or familial concerns. Something else is ultimately more important than attending the celebration.[7] Since the eschatological banquet is the object of the allusion, Jesus is making the point that other concerns get in the way of deciding for Jesus and sharing the hope of the eschaton. Such excuses are lame, even insulting, in light of the occasion and their previous willingness to come.

The first man's priority is a field. He says that it is necessary for him to see it, although why this is so, when he already owns it, is not

---

1993a: 755 adds Terence, *Self-Tormentor* 169–70, and Apuleius, *Metamorphoses* (*Golden Ass*) 3.12, which may suggest that more than Jewish custom is in view here.

6. See the introduction to this unit. Klostermann 1929: 151 sees Luke reducing the servants to one, while Marshall 1978: 588 prefers to see Matthew expanding the image.

7. Jewish excuses in other contexts include Deut. 20:5–7; 24:5; *m. Soṭa* 8.1–6. Marshall 1978: 588–89 correctly argues that Luke's concern about excessive attachment to possessions or family is present. Unfortunately, material concerns are dominant.

clear. The key term ἀνάγκην (*anankēn*, necessity) suggests a priority judgment. Plummer (1896: 361) calls the reply a "manifest exaggeration," but in some later deals, purchase depended on postpurchase inspection (Marshall 1978: 589; SB 2:208; *b. ʿAbod. Zar.* 15a). The man asks to be excused to go view his property (on the idiom ἔχε με παρῃτημένον, *eche me parētēmenon*, see BDF §471.1; BDR §471.1; MM 484; Josephus, *Antiquities* 7.8.2 §175; 12.4.7 §197). In fact, it is the judgment that other things are more valuable than Jesus' ministry that will create the tragedy of missing the celebration.

In Matthew, the excuses are handled all at once, with one going to the field, the other to his business, while the others kill the servant. Luke, however, excludes the excuses as well as the reference to the king sending troops to slay those who refused. This last omission is obvious, since Luke does not have a king.

14:19 The second excuse is like the first: a recent purchase—this time livestock—needs to be inspected. That this man owned five yoke of oxen suggests that he owned more land than the average farmer, who would have owned one or two yoke of oxen (Jeremias 1963a: 177). The size of landholdings in the ancient world is variously estimated. The *Letter of Aristeas* 116 puts it around 70 acres, but this is probably an exaggeration.[8] Jeremias speaks of 10 to 20 hectares, or 24 to 50 acres (a hectare equals 2.471 acres). According to Eusebius, *Ecclesiastical History* 3.20 §§1–2, two kinsman related to Jesus shared a tract of 3.9 hectares. And holdings during the Second Temple period averaged 2.5 hectares, with some purchases being as small as one-tenth hectare (*m. B. Bat.* 1.6). By any ancient standard, this man is quite wealthy, perhaps owning up to 250 acres.[9]

This man could go see the land at any time, but his business and social priority is to do it immediately. The initial invitation gave him an opportunity to refuse, but here he is refusing at the last minute after having already said yes. The language of decline matches that of the first man as he asks to be excused of his commitment. Marshall (1978: 589) notes that in the Gospel of Thomas 64 the excuses are urban-oriented: one invitee needs to collect a debt, another just bought a home, one had to prepare a banquet for a friend getting married, and another one just bought a farm and so needed to collect rent (Funk 1985: 2.153).

---

8. R. J. H. Shutt's translation of *Aristeas* (in J. Charlesworth 1983–85: 2.20) says that each settler had 100 acres, based on 600,000 settlers on 60,000,000 acres or *arourae*. But this figure is too high, since one *aroura* is 0.275 hectare or about two-thirds of an acre. One hundred *arourae* is thus around 70 acres.

9. Lesser figures for the average size of land ownership are presented by Applebaum 1976: 656–58, who argues that seven hectares may be optimistic. Even on these numbers, five yoke of oxen points to a large landowner.

The third excuse is short and rather curt: the invitee has just married **14:20**
and so cannot attend. The marriage is recent, given the aorist ἔγημα
(*egēma*, I have married) and the nature of his response (Marshall
1978: 589; BDF §101; BDR §101.16). The OT did free a newly married man from certain obligations like war (Deut. 20:7; 24:5), but it
is hard to see how marriage would disqualify one from attending a
social meal, even though only men came to such a banquet in the
first century (Jeremias 1963a: 177; Herodotus 1.36; Palmer 1976).[10]
Thus, this third concern is also not a substantial reason to miss the
occasion. In fact, the man makes no effort to ask to be excused. He
simply declares that he will not attend, period.

iii. The Master's New Invitation to the Outcast (14:21)

The servant returns and tells his master about the excuses he has **14:21**
heard from those originally invited to attend. Ταῦτα (*tauta*, these
things) is a summary expression for the three responses. The host is
angered by their response. A change in plans is required, and it is to
be acted on quickly (ταχέως, *tacheōs*) since the meal is ready. This
suggests that the table is already open for visitors. Jesus' current
kingdom offer is in view here, an offer that culminates in the meal
of God's blessing (14:24). Jesus does not postpone the banquet or
withdraw the meal; he gets a new audience. The time of blessing is
now and continues into the future. The "already" and the "not yet"
merge in the decision about Jesus. One can accept or reject the invitation, but in either case, the party is coming and it will not be re-
scheduled or postponed.

The host sends the servant out again, this time into the city's
streets and back alleys (Klostermann 1929: 152; Marshall 1978:
590).[11] He is to invite the poor, maimed, blind, and lame. To find
these outcasts and afflicted takes effort, and so the servant searches
the city.[12] This list recalls 14:13 and is similar to 1:51–53; 6:20–23;
and 7:22. The OT background is Isa. 61:1–2; 35:5–6; and 29:18–19.
The order here differs from Luke 14:13 in reversing the blind and
lame (on these terms, see the exegesis of 14:13). The blind and lame
are subclasses of the maimed (Manson 1949: 130; Plato, *Crito* 53A).

10. Hendriksen's remark (1978: 730) about taking the wife along is unlikely for
the first century. An insult is likely, because the man had accepted the original invitation without mentioning his marriage and now he refuses to attend.

11. Ῥύμη is a side street (BAGD 737; BAA 1476; Isa. 15:3; Tob. 13:17–18; elsewhere
in the NT at Matt. 6:2; Acts 9:11; 12:10) versus πλατεῖα, a wide street (BAGD 666; BAA
1340; in the Gospels and Acts at Matt. 6:5; 12:19; Luke 10:10; 13:26; Acts 5:15).

12. Jeremias 1963a: 177 calls them "the *ipso facto* beggars in the East." On this
theme, see the later Jewish story of Bar Maʿjan; *y. Sanh.* 23c (6.6) (= Neusner et al.
1982–93: 31.181–82).

The inclusion of the maimed is significant in that they were banned from full participation in Jewish worship (Lev. 21:17–23; 1Q28a [= 1QSa = Rule Annex] 2.3–10; CD 13.4–7; Ellis 1974: 194). The move pictures Jesus' offer of the gospel to the nation's common and needy people, after the leadership's hesitation to respond to him. It also suggests a note of initiative in the effort to find guests for the feast. This type of association with the "classless" causes reaction from Jesus' opponents. Some in the nation will respond, but they will come from surprising places.

The transition here stands in contrast to Matt. 22, where the king sends out soldiers to slay those who refused to come to the wedding before sending out more invitations. Matthew 22:8–9 has a saying at this point about the wedding being ready, but that those who were invited are not worthy to attend. Then there follows an order to invite as many as can be found. Matthew 22:10 speaks of the good and the bad. One could make a case that Luke has given expanded specificity to Matthew's general remarks here (Luce 1933: 249–50), but the other differences in detail still suggest a distinct tradition, so addition is not an issue.[13]

iv. Invitations Given with Room to Spare (14:22)

14:22 The second set of invitations has been issued and those who have responded are now present. The servant reports that there is still room. The host is anxious that the banquet be given to a full house. He is generous in his desire to have others share in the occasion. This represents God's generosity in seeking people for salvation. Nolland (1993a: 757) argues that these remarks, in the original setting, indicated the open-ended, roving nature of Jesus' ministry.

v. Third Set of Invitations Given to Even More (14:23)

14:23 The master sends the servant out yet a third time, this time onto the highways outside of the city and the hedges around highways, roads, or houses where a traveler might stop during a journey. The hedges (φραγμός, *phragmos*) are probably those outside of the town located around vineyards (Matt. 21:33 = Mark 12:1; Michaelis, *TDNT* 5:68), where beggars are often found (BAGD 865; BAA 1725). The master will take in anyone who will respond. The appeal is not so much to compel people to come in as it is to urge them to attend (ἀναγκάζω, *anankazō*; BAGD 52; BAA 101; Gen. 19:3 [conceptually parallel]). Urging is necessary because the people do not know the

---

13. But so Schweizer 1984: 238, who regards this as Jew-Gentile distinction; but that distinction is not in this group. The Gentiles may be in the set of invitations in 14:23.

host and so need encouragement to attend (Fitzmyer 1985: 1057; Grundmann 1963: 300). He is not going to force anyone to come, as his response to the original invitees shows. He is, however, going to try to persuade them to participate.[14] The goal is to have a full house at the meal. The third invitation to outsiders is lacking in Matt. 22 and is perhaps another evidence of independence (Marshall 1978: 590 argues that Matthew may have shortened his account). Luke's twofold division suggests as well a constant expansion of the mission effort.

These invitations picture the expansion of Jesus' ministry outside the bounds of the needy in Israel and probably allude to Gentile mission.[15] One should avoid the idea that the first new invitations (the second batch overall) go only to Jews and the second new invitations (the third overall) only to Gentiles. The picture is of reaching out to people in all directions, Diaspora Jews and Gentiles alike. Jews and Gentiles are both in view. The tone is much like Rom. 15:7–16.

The whole point is that the invitation to the banquet comes through Jesus. The blessings he offers are beginning to arrive. If the original invitees do not come, the supper will still be given and the blessings still will come. They will just go to others, and many others will respond.

c. Jesus' Application: The Originally Invited Group Will Be Absent (14:24)

Jesus summarizes the parable for his audience. That Jesus is now **14:24** speaking and has ended the parable is indicated by plural ὑμῖν (*hymin*, you), while the parable mentioned only a single servant. Also, the host's address in the parable used the third person, not first person as here.[16] Jesus commonly ends his parables and teaching with a personal note (Luke 11:8; 15:7, 10; 16:9; 18:8, 14; 19:26).[17]

---

14. Many commentators note that Augustine's interpretation (*Contra Gaudentium Donatistarum Episcopum Libri II* 1.25 §28 [Corpus Scriptorum Ecclesiasticorum Latinorum 53.226–27]), which sought to compel pagans to enter the faith, badly misreads the imagery. Fitzmyer 1985: 1057 notes that this interpretation made Augustine the spiritual father of the Inquisition.

15. Manson 1949: 130 suggests that Isa. 49:6 is alluded to in the parable. Blomberg 1990: 235–36 says that the second invitation merely reflects Middle Eastern custom, but with all the representation present in the parable, surely the arrival of "outsiders" suggests a correspondence in real terms. See R. Martin 1976.

16. For the view that this is still a part of the parable, see Plummer 1896: 363, who incorrectly argues that the final remark here is not like others where Jesus is clearly marked out as speaking. Marshall 1978: 590–91 argues that the host is speaking but is pictured as the Lord. Another "hidden" parabolic application appears in 16:8b–13.

17. So Jeremias 1963a: 177, who nonetheless argues that the saying originally ended the parable and was the host's remark. This view, though possible, is not nec-

Those originally invited to the feast will not be present. If the host is speaking, the allusion is the refusal to send food from the banquet to them. Even this favor will not be performed (Marshall 1978: 591; Derrett 1970: 126–55, esp. 141; Neh. 8:10–12).[18] If Jesus is speaking, then the point is simply that the leadership missed an opportunity to sit at the table of God's blessing, even though it appeared that they were at the head of the line. They rejected their opportunity, so appearances are deceiving. Under either view, the point is that those who seemed to be in line will miss out, and others who do not seem even close at the time of initial promise will end up at the meal.

Summary
Luke 14:15–24 is a graphic description of opportunity lost and of God's grace shown. The Jewish leadership, though invited and in line for God's blessings, opted out of the invitation. Jesus made an offer, and they refused. They will not be at the table with many others who are poor, needy, or racially distinct. The parable makes clear that such exclusion is not God's desire. Absence at the table will be because the invitation was rejected and the invitees refused to attend. The opportunity to attend was given in advance and then made again—but the offer was still refused. The allusion is to the leadership who refused to respond to Jesus' invitation. A note of rejection appears as it did in 13:28–29, 31–35. As Manson (1949: 130) says, "The two essential points in His teaching are that no man can enter the Kingdom without the invitation of God, and that no man can remain outside it but by his own deliberate choice. Man cannot save himself; but he can damn himself. And it is this latter fact that makes the preaching of Jesus so urgent." In rejecting Jesus, the leaders reject God's greatest gift: the opportunity to sit at the table of eternal fellowship with God. They also missed the chance to share in the blessings he gives. But the kingdom's bounty is not lost because of their rejection, for many others will be invited and will attend. The opportunity for rich blessing and fellowship from God's hand remains available to others. In fact, many who attend will be among those who were least expected to attend. God makes himself available—even to those whom many reject. Often it is the rejected who respond favorably to God. Disciples should seek such people. In warning the Pharisees, Jesus also instructs his own. God's people must be sought and found in surprising places.

---

essary. The application that Jesus makes comes more powerfully and directly by looking back to the parabolic imagery. The shift to the first person indicates the shift of perspective.

18. Blomberg 1990: 235 compares this custom to the British custom of sending wedding cake to the invited who could not attend.

Additional Note

14:17. Although the evidence is not overwhelming, ἐστίν is well attested in several variants. The UBS–NA reading, ἕτοιμά ἐστιν, is supported by B and most Itala. Assimilation to Matt. 22:4 (πάντα ἕτοιμα, everything is ready) is probably behind the use of πάντα in two Lucan variants that differ only in word order (Metzger 1975: 164): πάντα ἕτοιμά ἐστιν (everything is ready; D) and ἕτοιμά ἐστιν πάντα (everything is ready; A, W, Δ, Ψ, Byz, Lect, some Itala). Another option, ἕτοιμά εἰσιν (they are ready; 𝔓[75], ℵ, L, Θ), creates numerical agreement between the verb and adjective. Such grammatical smoothing likely reflects a later "improvement." Two canons of textual criticism (the shorter reading and assimilation) argue in favor of seeing the UBS–NA reading as original.

F. Discipleship in the Face of Rejection: Basic Elements (14:25–35)

A shift of emphasis occurs with this section. In many of the pericopes up to this point, Jesus has been embroiled in controversy with the Jewish leadership, most often the Pharisees (esp. 11:37–54; 13:31–14:24; Carroll 1988). Most of the passages from Luke 11:14 on have had the leadership as the major audience, with only 12:1–12 and 12:22–53 giving respite from this concern. But now in 14:25, Jesus returns to address the crowds. In doing so, he begins to describe in detail what discipleship requires. In effect, through this arrangement Luke is asking, "If the Jewish leadership does not teach the way to follow God, then what *is* required to follow God?" His answer is simple: you must count the cost and make Jesus the number one priority of life if you are going to follow him. This section highlights that emphasis by noting two absolute statements of discipleship, using the family and bearing the cross as illustrations (14:26–27). Then come two illustrations of counting the cost, using the builder and the king as examples (14:28–32). This is followed by a briefly stated application, which addresses a third topic, possessions (14:33). Finally, Jesus' warns about the lack of value that tasteless salt has. Do not be a useless disciple (14:34–35).

The unit as a whole says that Jesus must have first place if one wishes to follow him. If Jesus does not have this position, then one is not good for anything of value in terms of usefulness for God. What Jesus tells the multitudes he has already told the apostles and disciples (9:18–27, 57–62; Ellis 1974: 195). Tannehill (1986: 149) notes that the three areas addressed—(1) putting God above family, (2) bearing one's cross, and (3) leaving all—are issues that threaten discipleship. Tiede (1988: 269–70) notes that these three "cases" are what discipleship may entail for a believer, but they are not entrance requirements that one must do in order to enter the kingdom. Nonetheless, real discipleship entails these commitments. Jesus' disciples "grew" into some of these commitments as time passed; for example, Peter did not "bear his own cross" during his denials, but he did later.

This material stands as a unit because it represents a turning point in the journey. From now on, Jesus deals almost exclusively with discipleship (the exceptions are 15:1–32; 16:19–31; 18:9–14, where Pharisees are the main audience). This unit is conceptually related to 14:15–24, where excuses for discipleship lead to a rebuke and warning by Jesus. Some, in fact, see this passage as an epilogue to those remarks (Ernst 1977: 446). This is true both literarily and conceptually, but the distinct audience and setting, along with the shift of emphasis from this point on, make it more appropriate to separate this account from what proceeds and what follows. This passage is a key hinge in the Gospel.

Sources and Historicity

Most of the material in this unit is unparalleled; it is mostly special Lucan material. The double statement of discipleship involving the family and the cross in Luke 14:26–27 is like Matt. 10:37–38 (Aland 1985: §217). So some claim that these verses come from Q (Luce 1933: 250; Schneider 1977a: 320; Leaney 1958: 214; Fitzmyer 1985: 1060).[1] However, there is almost no overlap in vocabulary between these two pericopes and the contrast is distinct: (1) Matthew speaks of loving mother and father more than Jesus, while Luke speaks of hating mother and father; (2) Matthew speaks of being worthy of being a disciple, while Luke speaks of not being able to be a disciple; and (3) Matthew speaks of taking one's cross, while Luke speaks of bearing it (Manson 1949: 131). Since the sense of these sayings is so similar and the wording is so different, it seems better to see two variations on a similar teaching than to see one teaching from one tradition.

The only other potential parallel is Matt. 5:13 = Mark 9:49–50 with Luke 14:34–35 (Aland 1985: §218).[2] The Marcan form of this saying is close in setting and wording to the Lucan version, while the Matthean form appears to be a distinct version of the same kind of teaching. But even the Lucan connection with Mark is uncertain. Mark's image is different (his picture of salt stresses being "salty" by being at peace with one another), and Mark lacks mention of throwing away the salt, a note that is the key to the Lucan warning. In this form, the Lucan version stands closer to Matthew, although the wording is very different. Again, it seems best to see a standard theme

1. Marshall 1978: 591 sees the presence of other sources. Wiefel 1988: 277 mentions Q, but also suggests that the passage may be independent (he sees 14:28–33 coming from special Lucan material). Grundmann 1963: 301 says that it is uncertain whether the material is from Q or from a source in Luke's special material. Ernst 1977: 447 is also uncertain. The double tradition in the Gospel of Thomas 55 (family and cross) and 101 (family) raises the possibility of the existence of multiple traditions in the church and, thus, whether they were said on multiple occasions. (The Gospel of Thomas 98 has a third picture of an assassin who practices by thrusting his sword into a wall.)

2. Manson 1949: 132 sees the Matthean and Lucan sayings as related. Luce 1933: 251, along with most, calls this a Q passage.

that Jesus used in a variety of settings. There is no need to appeal to Q here (cf. Ernst 1977: 447).

The Jesus Seminar treats most of this unit as inauthentic, printing 14:27–33 in black type (Funk and Hoover 1993: 353–54). The seminar is hesitant to attribute 14:35b to Jesus because it is too sagelike (hence the gray type). Luke 14:26, however, is a hard enough saying and 14:34–35a is striking enough imagery to warrant a link to Jesus (pink type). The rejected sayings are seen as too full of proverbial wisdom or "late" cross imagery to be authentic, while 14:33 is questioned as a typical Lucan conclusion (like 12:21; 15:7, 10; 17:10). But the theme of 14:33 fits Jesus' teaching (Mark 4:19; Matt. 8:20–22; 6:19–21), as do the warnings about the cost of following Jesus (Luke 12:49–53 = Matt. 10:34–38). Precedents like John the Baptist could make such warnings necessary. Though the two parabolic pictures are unique to Luke, there is nothing here that falls outside Jesus' directness about the conflict that his ministry raises. The call to hear fits Jesus' exhortation that he brings God's word (Mark 3:31–35 = Matt. 12:46–50). Since the salt image is used with such variation in Matt. 5:13 and Mark 9:50, only the assumption that it could appear just once in the Jesus tradition stands behind the insistence that only one tradition is present here. In sum, the call to take discipleship seriously coheres with the themes of Jesus' teaching.

> The passage is a combination of sayings and parables.[3] The outline of Luke 14:25–35 is as follows:
>
> 1. Two costs of discipleship: family and suffering (14:25–32)
>   a. Setting (14:25)
>   b. Two statements and two pictures on discipleship (14:26–27)
>   i. "Hating" the family (14:26)
>   ii. Bearing one's cross (14:27)
>   c. Two illustrations on assessing the cost (14:28–32)
>   i. Building the tower (14:28–30)
>   ii. The king and his army (14:31–32)
> 2. A third cost of discipleship: possessions (14:33)
> 3. Warning about saltiness (14:34–35)

3. Fitzmyer 1985: 1061 speaks of "prophetic words" as well. Bultmann 1963: 328 speaks of a discourse on discipleship composed by Luke; but how one can argue that Luke is responsible for the discourse is not clear. Berger 1984: 51, 97 speaks of parables and a warning. The text is a combination of "I-sayings" (14:26–27) and parabolic comparisons (14:28–35). Blomberg 1990: 281 calls the comparisons "which one of you?" parables, showing Jesus' desire to cause the audience to reflect: "If people must carefully calculate their chances of success in major human endeavors, how much more so must they take seriously the results of spiritual commitments."

The basic theme is simple: discipleship requires that Jesus be the first love. This means that he is a priority over one's desire to please family. One should be prepared to suffer shame for and count the cost of alliance to Jesus. In fact, discipleship requires renunciation of anything that comes before Jesus. The disciple who loses saltiness becomes useless and is tossed out. The disciple has a purpose in the world, but uselessness makes the disciple's role expendable and results in God's displeasure.

Exegesis and Exposition

[25]Now a great multitude accompanied him; and he turned and said to them, [26]"If anyone wishes to come to me and does not hate his own father and mother and wife and children and brothers and sisters and even his own soul, he cannot be my disciple. [27]Whoever is not bearing his own cross and coming after me cannot be my disciple. [28]For which of you who wishes to build a tower does not first sit down and count the expense whether he has enough to complete it? [29]Lest laying the foundation and not being able to finish, all who see it mock him, [30]saying, 'This man began to build but was not able to finish.' [31]Or what king, going to engage another king in war, will not first sit down and take counsel whether he is able with ten thousand men to meet him who comes against him with twenty thousand? [32]And if not, while the other is still a long way off, he sends an emissary and asks terms of ⌐peace⌐.

[33]"So also whoever of you does not renounce all that he has cannot be my disciple.

[34]"Now salt is good, but if the salt has lost its taste, how shall its saltiness be restored? [35]It is suitable neither for the soil nor for the dunghill; they cast it out. The one who has ears, let him hear."

1. Two Costs of Discipleship: Family and Suffering (14:25–32)
a. Setting (14:25)

Luke briefly notes the setting. Great crowds (ὄχλοι πολλοί, *ochloi* **14:25** *polloi*) still follow Jesus as he continues to draw nearer to his time in Jerusalem (Creed 1930: 193–94). Luke is probably responsible for the language of the setting (Fitzmyer 1985: 1060, 1063; Jeremias 1980: 241).[4] The reference to the multitudes broadens the audience of Luke 14 and recalls other passages where large crowds follow Jesus (4:42; 5:15; 6:17; 7:9; 8:4, 42; 9:37; 12:1). This teaching is directed to all, not just the converted. Jesus wants those who are contemplating a relationship with him to know what it means. Jesus' re-

---

4. Συμπορεύομαι (to accompany) is Lucan, since he has three of its four NT occurrences: Luke 7:11; 14:25; 24:15; Mark 10:1; Gen. 13:5; 14:24; 18:16; Plummer 1896: 364; BAGD 780 §1; BAA 1556 §1.

marks recall the excuses of 14:15–24 (Creed 1930: 193 notes that it complements the previous text [14:24] by noting that the coming involves a shift in priorities). If excuses about priorities will not do, what will? Jesus wants commitment, not just numbers.

b. Two Statements and Two Pictures on Discipleship (14:26–27)
i. "Hating" the Family (14:26)

14:26 Jesus spares no one who claims to have a disciple's commitment. The desire to come to Jesus is a good one, but it is not to be considered casually (Matt. 10:38; Mark 8:34 = Luke 9:23). The remark recalls Jesus' invitation in 14:17 (Tannehill 1986: 157 n. 28; Egelkraut 1976: 181). This verse can also be compared to the next one. The preposition πρός (*pros*) suggests coming "to" Jesus; but this is no different than coming "after" (ὀπίσω, *opisō*) him, as 14:27 expresses it. The conclusion of the two sayings is definitely the same, as the use of "cannot be my disciple" at the end of both makes clear. If there is a slight difference in force, to come "to" Jesus stresses entering into relationship, while coming "after" Jesus refers to the pursuit of that relationship. But discipleship involves both a start and a journey, so the two ideas are intertwined. Faith, since it is trust in another, is essentially an entry into relational discipleship. Faith does not stop with decision; it commences. As with any relationship, faith is an ongoing affair. Beyond the decision comes the expression in action. This dynamic of faith, fundamental to its essence, is a key idea of NT theology, which is why, for example, Rom. 4 leads to Rom. 5–8 or why Col. 2:6–8 is worded as it is. Faith is entry into relationship.

Discipleship is fundamentally a call to allegiance. Jesus is to have first place over all, including family. Luke's list is more comprehensive than that in Matt. 10:37. Matthew refers to father, mother, son, and daughter; while Luke mentions father, mother, wife, children, brothers, sisters, and one's own soul. Nothing else is to be first.

The call to "hate" is not literal but rhetorical (Denney 1909–10).[5] Otherwise, Jesus' command to love one's neighbor as oneself as a summation of what God desires makes no sense (Luke 10:25–37). The call to hate simply means to "love less" (Gen. 29:30–31; Deut. 21:15–17; Judg. 14:16).[6] The image is strong, but it is not a call to be

5. Epictetus 3.3.5 speaks of choosing good over one's father and, as a result, having nothing to do with the father. Jesus' image is similar. If what God requires is greater than what the family desires, God comes first.

6. Ernst 1977: 448 is hesitant about this connection. Manson 1949: 131 shows the idiom by citing a late Jewish text, *b. Ta'an.* 7b, where it is said of certain rabbis, "If they hated their beauty, they would be more learned." The opposite attitude where other things are loved more is found in Luke 14:20 and 18:20–24.

insensitive or to leave all feeling behind. Marshall (1978: 592) suggests "renounce," which is possible depending on how it is defined (Grundmann 1963: 302; Michel, *TDNT* 4:690–91).[7] Following Jesus is to be the disciple's "first love." This pursuit is to have priority over any family member and one's own life, which means that other concerns are to take second place to following Jesus (Luke 8:19–21; 9:59–62; 12:4, 49–53; 16:13). Matthew 10:37–39, Luke 9:24, and John 12:25 make a similar point, though Matthew speaks of loving family more, rather than hating, thereby softening the remark's emotive force.

This saying needs to be set in the context of its first-century setting. At that time a Jewish person who made a choice for Jesus would alienate his or her family. If someone desired acceptance by family more than a relationship with God, one might never come to Jesus, given the rejection that would inevitably follow. In other words, there could be no casual devotion to Jesus in the first century. A decision for Christ marked a person and automatically came with a cost. (Contemporary comparisons may be seen in certain formerly Communist Eastern European settings, in Moslem countries, or in tight-knit Asian families.) The modern Western phenomenon where a decision for Christ is popular in the larger social community was not true of Jesus' setting, which complicates our understanding of the significance of a decision to associate with Christ. Today one might associate with Christ simply because it is culturally appropriate, rather than for true spiritual reasons. Such a "decision" was impossible in the first century. If one chose to be associated with Jesus, one received a negative reaction, often from within the home.

The language of the apodosis is absolute: if one does not make Jesus the first priority, one cannot be his disciple. The point is that only when one forsakes all others is one totally following Jesus, otherwise something else will have a greater pull on one's allegiances than Jesus does. This statement is not so much soteriological in force (for no one is this faithful all the time), as much as it is pragmatic and rhetorical. The parallel in Matt. 10:37, which speaks of not being worthy to be Jesus' disciple, says the same thing in less rhetorical terms and makes the force clear: the person is not living up to the standard of discipleship. One cannot "follow" Jesus and learn from him if other realities have a stronger pull.

A disciple (μαθητής, *mathētēs*) is a "learner," a pupil. In ancient culture, a disciple sat at the feet of great teachers like Socrates or Plato, served as an initiate in a mystery religion, or sat at the feet of a great rabbi. In the pagan world, the disciple had a master who

---

7. Marshall notes that Levi's devotion to Torah is expressed in terms of a similar commitment in Deut. 33:9 and 4Q175 [= 4QTestim] 15–16. Schrenk, *TDNT* 5:983, defines μισέω as "to set aside for."

taught about the gods and the cult into which one was entering. In the Jewish world, one learned about the law and God (Rengstorf, *TDNT* 4:419–21). The LXX does not use μαθητής, but the equivalent תַּלְמִיד (*talmîd*, scholar) was often used in rabbinic literature. Those seeking to become scribes or rabbis were called disciples (Rengstorf, *TDNT* 4:432–35; Fitzmyer 1985: 1064).[8] The Jewish disciple sat under a rabbi who taught Torah and the proper way to interpret it. It is no accident that the other evangelists often call Jesus rabbi (ῥαββί, *rhabbi*), while Luke addresses him with the more Hellenistic "teacher" (διδάσκαλος, *didaskalos*).[9] The difference between Jesus and these other models of discipleship is that Jesus' call requires more, even everything, in terms of priority from the disciple. One who follows Jesus is led and instructed by him in the way to God. Such instruction and relationship is to have the first priority.

ii. Bearing One's Cross (14:27)

14:27 As he declares what real discipleship means, Jesus has a second area of concern: one must be able to bear one's own cross. The process of discipleship is stressed here, not the decision to enter into it, since βαστάζει (*bastazei*, bears) and ἔρχεται (*erchetai*, comes) are both present tense: "whoever is not bearing and is not coming after me. . . ." Βαστάζω (*bastazō*) means "to carry an object" or "to bear a burden" (Büchsel, *TDNT* 1:596; Black 1967: 195–96 [with possible Aramaic roots]; Luke 7:14; 10:4; 11:27; 22:10; Acts 3:2; 9:15; 15:10; 21:35; BAGD 137 §2bα; BAA 274 §2bα).

Matthew 10:38 has the less intense figure of "taking up the cross." If there is a difference in the two pictures, it is this: Matthew looks at the willingness to endure suffering and Luke looks at the willingness to go through the process of suffering. Jesus bore a cross as he marched to his death (John 19:17, using the same verb: βαστάζω). To follow Jesus means to follow in suffering, for the world rejects the disciple.

The figure of cross-bearing denotes a willingness to bear the pain of persecution as a result of following Jesus. It is another way to express willingness to "hate one's soul" in self-sacrifice. The picture is similar to Luke 9:23–24, with its portrait of daily cross-bearing (Plummer 1896: 364), as well as Matt. 16:24 = Mark 8:34; Acts 14:22; and Heb. 13:13 (Creed 1930: 194 sees it as a community saying, but

---

8. Josephus refers to Joshua as Moses' disciple and to Elisha as Elijah's disciple; *Antiquities* 6.5.4 §84; 8.13.7 §354.

9. Ῥαββί is used in Matt. 26:25; Mark 9:5; 11:21; Matt. 26:49 = Mark 14:45; John 1:38 (plus seven more times in John's Gospel); διδάσκαλος in Luke 7:40; 8:49; 9:38; 10:25; 11:45; 12:13; 18:18; 19:39; 20:21, 28, 39; 21:7; 22:11 (Matthew and Mark use this term twelve times each). See Goppelt 1981–82: 1.163–64, esp. n. 2.

there is no reason to reject the metaphor's availability to Jesus since such events were common; see the exegesis of 9:23). In the constant willingness to suffer reproach, the disciple follows the path that Jesus took and honors the desire to "come after me." This phrase means to follow in someone's path; in the OT, it referred to following after Yahweh or false gods (J. Schneider, *TDNT* 2:669; Seesemann, *TDNT* 5:291–92; Marshall 1978: 593; Deut. 6:14; 13:4 [13:5 MT]; 1 Kings 11:2; 14:8; 18:21; Jer. 11:10; 13:10; 16:11; Hos. 2:5, 13 [2:7, 15 MT]). As such, it is an allusion to allegiance and obedience. The disciple is ready to share Jesus' fate of rejection by the world (1 John 3:13; John 15:18–19; 17:14).

c. Two Illustrations on Assessing the Cost (14:28–32)
i. Building the Tower (14:28–30)

Using a rhetorical question, Jesus presents the first of two pictures to illustrate what discipleship should involve: assessing the cost of building a tower before beginning construction.[10] Πύργος (*pyrgos*) refers to a watchtower built to guard a vineyard or to protect a house or city (BAGD 730; BAA 1461; MM 560; elsewhere in the NT only at Matt. 21:33 = Mark 12:1; Luke 13:4). Michaelis (*TDNT* 6:955) correctly notes that ἐξ ὑμῶν (*ex hymōn*, of you) shows that a private tower for a house is in view, not a public tower for a city. Such towers could become quite elaborate and might encompass a barn where produce and tools were located (Jeremias 1963a: 196 n. 19). The reference to the foundation (14:29) suggests a substantial structure. The building would increase security on one's property.

14:28

Before building, the wise person assesses the expense.[11] One does not build the tower, despite its benefits, until one knows it is affordable and that can be brought to completion (ἀπαρτισμός, *apartismos*; BAGD 81; BAA 162; a *hapax legomenon*). The wise decision involves reflection, not reaction. Sitting and calculating the cost means a reasoned assessment (Plummer 1896: 365). So, Jesus suggests, should it be with discipleship: one should assess whether one is ready to take on the personal commitment and sacrifice required to follow Jesus.[12] As Danker (1972: 167) says, "Following Jesus is no

10. Derrett 1977a and Jarvis 1965–66 argue that the subject of the parable is Jesus, who has counted the cost. However, the previous remarks make an exhortation to the multitudes about discipleship far more likely.

11. Jesus uses two monetary terms: the *hapax legomenon* δαπάνη (BAGD 171; BAA 341; MM 137), which refers to the expenses of a given enterprise, and ψηφίζω (to count) (BAGD 892; BAA 1780; elsewhere in the NT only at Rev. 13:18). This last term often means to count with pebbles and can also mean to vote or make a calculated choice; MM 698.

12. In Prov. 24:3–6, wisdom builds a house and wages war; Schweizer 1984: 241; Tiede 1988: 270–71.

invitation to an ice-cream social." Danker also cites a similar teaching from Epictetus 3.15.10–13, a portion of which says, "Look these drawbacks over carefully, and then, if you think best, approach philosophy, that is, if you are willing at the price of these things to secure tranquillity, freedom, and repose." The object for Epictetus is different, but the attitude is similar (Danker 1988: 273). Jesus' teaching is in common with the moral exhortations of the day. A decision to pledge allegiance to Jesus is one of great moment and is to be entered into with sober reflection.[13]

14:29 A graphic picture of the result (ἵνα, *hina*) of not counting the cost is that the project will not be completed. Such an error means the building will stand unfinished, as a monument to one's foolishness. People will see the unfinished edifice and snicker. Ἐμπαίζειν (*empaizein*) has the nuance of ridiculing and making fun of someone (Bertram, *TDNT* 5:634; BAGD 255; BAA 516; Luke 22:63; 23:11, 36 [of the soldiers' treatment of Jesus]). What an embarrassment to start a project and not be able to complete it. Such is the danger for a disciple who does not assess what it means to follow Jesus. The failure is not God's, but the disciple's—because of lack of commitment, resolve, and reflection.

14:30 Public mocking underlines the failure to count the cost. The derogatory tone of the remark is indicated by οὗτος ὁ ἄνθρωπος (*houtos ho anthrōpos*, this man).[14] One can almost hear the snickering. People mutter that the builder was not able to complete what was started.[15] The effort is fruitless, because the structure will not be completed. How foolish to start something, only to leave a shell.

ii. The King and His Army (14:31–32)

14:31 Jesus supplies a second example about the importance of examining a situation and reflecting before acting. Moving from personal projects to political intrigue, he tells about a king deciding whether to go to war. Πόλεμος (*polemos*; BAGD 685; BAA 1373) may mean a war or a single engagement; in either case armed conflict is in view.[16] The king has fewer troops than the enemy. In fact, he has half the troops. Before pressing into battle, the king determines

---

13. One might compare the picture to the phrase used at modern weddings: "It is not to be entered into lightly or unadvisedly."

14. So οὗτος in Luke 5:21; 7:39; 13:32 and especially in the numerous remarks about Jesus in the passion account: 23:4, 14, 22, 35.

15. Ἐκτελέω (to finish) basically means to perform a task completely; BAGD 245; BAA 495; MM 198. It appears only here and in Luke 14:29 in the NT.

16. Συμβάλλω means "to meet," thus "to meet in battle"; BAGD 777 §1b; BAA 1551 §1b; 1 Macc. 4:34; 2 Macc. 8:23; 14:17. Μάχη (battle) is usually the object of this verb.

whether he can win with the smaller number. He assesses the cost of war before entering the battle (Manson 1949: 281 sees a possible allusion to 2 Sam. 8:9–12).[17]

The example is in the form of a rhetorical question, "What king will not consider the cost?" If the king has any competence at all, he will investigate the situation. So also the disciple should assess discipleship in preparing to follow Jesus. It is foolish not to consider what it will take to be a disciple (Plummer 1896: 365: "It is folly to begin without much consideration").

The wisdom of such assessment is seen in the king's response to being outnumbered.[18] Rather than going to war, he asks for terms of peace. Πρεσβείαν (*presbeian*) literally means "embassy" and clearly refers to representatives sent to negotiate terms of peace or surrender (Creed 1930: 195; BAGD 699; BAA 1401; MM 534).[19] The ambassador is to secure an agreement that will stop the possibility of war. To have launched into battle without reflection would have been disastrous. Jesus pictures the value of reflecting on becoming a disciple. To avoid an embarrassing and deadly outcome, one is to count the cost (Arndt 1956: 345).

14:32

The second parable differs slightly from the first: in the first, the option rests with the builder whether to start a project; in the second, a decision is forced upon the king. Both pictures are important and may well show the slight difference between the parables of 14:28–30 and 14:31–32. The first pictures coming to Jesus; the second deals with following after him. First, consider what discipleship will cost. Second, consider what refusing the "more powerful one" will mean. Can you enter battle against him? In short, consider the cost of entry and the benefits of allying with the one who carries the power.

2. A Third Cost of Discipleship: Possessions (14:33)

Jesus has applied his illustrations so now he introduces another cost of discipleship. Discipleship is more than "hating" family or bearing a cross: one must also distance oneself from materialistic attachment to the world. The use of οὕτως (*houtōs*, in the same way) makes

14:33

---

17. Philo, *On Abraham* 21 §105: "Virtue's nature is most peaceable; she is careful, so they say, to test her own strength before the conflict, so if she is able to contend to the end she will take the field; but if she finds her strength too weak, she may shrink from entering the contest at all."

18. So εἰ δὲ μή γε (otherwise) gives the alternative to battle. The phrase always occurs without a verb; Luke 5:36; 10:6.

19. Thackeray 1912–13 discusses an idiom ("surrender unconditionally") possibly found in the greetings in Judg. 18:15; 1 Sam. 10:4; 17:22; 25:5; 30:21; T. Judah 9.7. But this force is less clearly documented; see Nolland 1993a: 764.

the comparison. The disciple is to renounce possessions (ἀποτάσσω, *apotassō*; Delling, *TDNT* 8:33; Marshall 1978: 594; BAGD 100 §2; BAA 202 §2; elsewhere in Luke at 9:61).[20] A disciple's attachments are potentially the most destructive thing for discipleship. This verse expresses positively what is required, in contrast to the negatively formed statements of 14:26. Hating family and self equals renouncing all possessions, that is, all earthly attachments. The will to renounce all possessions and to ally oneself totally to Jesus is the essence of discipleship. Jesus is first. He is the one object of focus. Persevering with Jesus means being attached to him, not to possessions. The force of this radical call is "all are called to be prepared for it although it will not be a reality for all" (Schweizer 1984: 241).[21] If Jesus offers what he says he offers, then there can be no greater possession than following him. Jesus seeks to lead people in doing the Father's will, offering to the disciple the treasures of heaven. Luke–Acts notes specific fulfillments of this promise and attitude (Schneider 1977a: 321–22; Luke 5:11, 28; 12:3; 14:26; 18:22; Acts 2:44–45; 4:32). One is not really an effective, worthy disciple without this attitude (Luke 14:26–27).[22] The one who comes to Jesus is to realize this standard. Jesus is not a minimalist when it comes to commitment. It is not how little one can give that is the question, but how much God deserves.

3. Warning about Saltiness (14:34–35)

14:34 Jesus raises a new question through the picture of salt. Salt (ἅλας, *halas*) functions as seasoning, fertilizer, or preservative (Job 6:6; Luke 14:35; BAGD 35; BAA 67). While it is salty, it is good because it has a valuable function. But once salt has shown itself to be of no value, it is worthless. How does such a situation arise? In the ancient world, a couple of settings are possible. Bakers covered the floor of their ovens with salt to give a catalytic effect on the burning fuel, which was usually cattle dung. After a time, the effect wore off and the salt was thrown away (Marshall 1978: 596; Creed 1930: 195).[23] Also, most salt in the region came from the evaporated pools around

---

20. Tannehill 1986: 157 n. 27 suggests that, in light of the journey imagery, the force is "say farewell." Disciples know that life is not in possessions, so they can part with them and avoid pursuing them as the world does.

21. Schweizer's point is that not everyone is forced to give away their possessions or be rejected by family as a result of coming to Jesus, but they need to be prepared to do so.

22. The force of these remarks is that the claim of discipleship and the reality of discipleship do not match in such cases. One is not being a true disciple.

23. Jeremias 1963a: 168–69 mentions the option and rightly rejects it, since the issue in Matt. 5:13 = Mark 9:50 and here is taste, not cooking.

the Dead Sea and was mixed with gypsum and other impurities. When moisture hit the salt, it evaporated and left behind these impurities, which were mixed with it in the soil. The salt loses its saltiness and is thrown away (Jeremias 1963a: 168–69; Deatrick 1962; Kistemaker 1980: 3–4; Hauck, *TDNT* 1:229; Nolland 1993a: 765).[24] It can no longer season anything (ἀρτύω, *artyō*; BAGD 111; BAA 222; elsewhere in the NT only at Mark 9:50 and Col. 4:6). The modern idiom would be "running out of gas." "Running out of gas" as a disciple is always the result of not having Jesus be primary.

The question arises as to the force of the figure, which is clearly a warning. Is it national in scope, warning the nation that judgment is coming for its failure to be "seasoning" for the world (Jeremias 1963a: 168; SB 1:236; Manson 1949: 132)?[25] If so, the warning is much like the parable of the vineyard. The point then is that the nation does not assess the cost of allying to Jesus and refuses to go God's way. To reject Jesus is to cease being salt and results in being cast out by God. But though the national image fits, an individual application is more natural contextually and fits other uses of the image. To fail to ally oneself totally to Jesus or to only hear him from a distance is a tragic waste of what could be a valuable opportunity. It is to take something potentially useful and make it useless.

The parallel Matt. 5:13 is more explicit in applying the image directly to the crowds of potential disciples gathered around Jesus (on the distinct use of the image in Mark 9:50, see the introduction to this unit). This use of the salt imagery is distinct and should be evaluated accordingly. Response to Jesus and the resulting difference in life is the point. To be of use to God, one must respond to him. Useless "discipleship" is of no value to God, while useful discipleship pays the price to serve God. The basic image is similar, but the vocabulary and application are quite different. Distinct settings seem likely.[26]

24. The verb μωρανθῇ literally means for salt "to become foolish," a personification that shows its total lack of value because it is no longer salty; BAGD 531 §2; BAA 1075 §2. There may be a wordplay on the Semitic תָּפֵל (*tpl*), which can mean "to be foolish" or "to be unsavory"; Job 1:22; Jer. 23:13; Marshall 1978: 595; Black 1967: 166; Schwarz 1978. Nolland 1993a: 765 notes that the figure is based on the result of salt losing its saltiness, regardless of whether it actually happens.

25. In later Judaism, the picture of salt was applied nationally in a passage that is seen as a polemic against Jesus' teaching: *b. Bek.* 8b, which argues that salt cannot lose its saltiness.

26. Plummer 1896: 366 notes that three distinct settings of the salt image "may be right" in terms of its historical background. He includes Mark 9:50 in his remark. This warns us not to assume that multiple sayings on a topic must have one point of origin.

14:35   The conclusion pictures the removal of salt that is of no value. It is not suitable (εὔθετος, *euthetos*) for anything (BAGD 320; BAA 648; elsewhere in the NT at Luke 9:62 and Heb. 6:7). It cannot even be used for secondary functions such as fertilizer or as a preservative with manure to slow fermentation (Marshall 1978: 596–97).[27] Salt used for fertilizer wilted weeds and improved the soil at a deeper level, but useless salt was discarded. So, too, the "saltless" disciple is no longer used by God. This remark could allude to final judgment like the "odd man out" in certain parables (Luke 12:46; 19:21–26 with Matt. 25:30) or it could refer to the judgment of physical death that befalls some in the community (1 Cor. 11:30). The ambiguity may well be intentional. Failure to pursue discipleship can indicate that faith is not really present, even though it was thought to be, or spiritual rebellion. In either case, the situation displeases God. It is better to obey and not be subject to this threat. The warning is clearly marked by the call to hear, which appears in many texts (Matt. 11:15; 13:43; Mark 4:23; Matt. 13:9 = Mark 4:9 = Luke 8:8; Horst, *TDNT* 5:552 §B1b). It is tragic that one would lose the opportunity to be used by God. In fact, combined with the picture of mocking in 14:29, it is not only tragic to be a useless disciple, but one becomes the object of scorn as well (Matt. 5:13 speaks of salt being trampled under foot). The text suggests as a possibility that some disciples do not produce as they should, something the Corinthian letters also reveal.

Summary   Luke 14:25–35 makes clear that discipleship is demanding. Jesus asks both the disciple and the potential disciple to consider the cost of following him. It is better to assess the risk, complete the task, and remain useful to God. Associating with Jesus is not an easy affair. Commitments come with the territory. In fact, Jesus is to come ahead of all one's possessions, family, and soul. It is embarrassing and fatal to enter into discipleship and not complete the task. Higher commitments to other things make completing the task impossible and render the disciple useless to God. The uncommitted disciple is like a builder who cannot complete a planned project or a foolish king who enters a war he cannot win. Those around him mock his failure. What an embarrassment to fail to be all that God would have one be because the price was not assessed ahead of time. To be useful, salt must stay salty.

27. Gressmann 1911 notes the nature of the customs. Perles's attempt (1919–20) to suggest an Aramaic element תבל (*tbl*) behind the tradition that should be translated "seasoning" instead of "soil" fails on lexical grounds. The תבל/γῆ interchange is found in Isa. 14:21; 26:9, 18; 1 Chron. 16:30; cf. 11QtgJob 24.8; 29.3 with Job 34:13; 37:12. Correctly Fitzmyer 1985: 1069–70 and Black 1967: 166–67.

How horrible to be thrown away by God when one could have been used by him. So consider the cost and have the resolve of a disciple who fully pursues God. Luke's call is to hear the warning and respond with faithfulness.

Additional Note

14:32. Codexes ℵ and B lack the definite article τά (the) before πρὸς εἰρήνην (for peace) (B also has εἰς for πρός). Failure to read double TA in ΕΡΩΤΑΤΑΠΡΟΣΕΙΡΗΝΗΝ may explain the variant. A Semitic idiom may be present: ἐρωτᾷ τὰ πρὸς εἰρήνην (ask for peace) (2 Sam. 8:10; 11:7; T. Judah 9.7). If so, the force is to ask for peace in the context of surrendering. The king is outnumbered, and so he gives in rather than subjecting his people to destruction (Marshall 1978: 594; Foerster, *TDNT* 2:412; Ernst 1977: 449; Wiefel 1988: 279).

G. Pursuit of Sinners: Heaven's Examples (15:1–32)

The previous description of the cost of discipleship contrasts with Jesus' word of comfort to tax collectors and sinners in Luke 15:1–32. Three parallel parables portray God's desire to find the lost sinner. The first two parables, the lost sheep (15:2–7) and the lost coin (15:8–10), are treated together. Concluding the trilogy, a longer parable emphasizes the father's welcome and reception of his returning and formerly lost son (15:11–32). The picture of the father exhorting others to receive the lost one back also shows heaven's view of the sinner regained.

1. Parable of the Lost Sheep (15:1–7)
2. Parable of the Lost Coin (15:8–10)

The parables of the lost sheep and the lost coin are so similar that they are best treated together. In both cases the basic motif is the search, and the basic emotion expressed is joy. They represent Jesus' explanation of why he relates to tax collectors and sinners (15:1–2). God will go to great effort and rejoice with great joy to find and restore a sinner to himself. Jesus wishes to emphasize that God is not a God of the few, a God of the wise, or a God only of those who think they pursue God. He is a God who searches, finds, and cares for the sinner. In a culture where tax collectors were hated and sinners were mocked, Jesus gives a word that encourages the rejected to come to him. The way to God is through repentance. God's arms are open to the person who will seek him on his terms. God's arms close around the child ready to run to him and receive what he offers. It is not mere humanitarianism that Jesus offers, but a chance to acknowledge who one is before God and to respond to the opportunity for transformation that God offers (Manson 1949: 282).

The theme offered here expands the picture of 5:32 and is later developed in 19:10 (Tannehill 1986: 106). The passage also serves to explain why God is so quick to invite others to the banquet table depicted in 14:15–24 (Marshall 1978: 597–98). These two parables are preceded by an introduction (15:1–3) and followed by the full exposition of the theme in the parable of the forgiving father (15:11–32). In fact, the passage is part of a sequence of passages concerned mainly with forgiveness and discipleship. Fitzmyer (1985: 1072) argues that the emphasis starts here, but it actually reaches back to 14:15, with a change in audience at 15:1. In this passage tax collectors and sinners hear Jesus speak in comforting words. In addition, the presentation of the rationale for a broad offer of the gospel is more focused here.[1]

---

1. Fitzmyer is right to reject other attempts to understand the unit as only a polemic against the Pharisees, though allusions to them are present. Neither is the passage an exposition of Jer. 31:10–20 (so Kossen 1956), a view also rejected by Ellis 1974: 196.

Sources and Historicity

The first two parables in Luke 15 are unique to Luke. The only possible exception is Matt. 18:12–13, which uses imagery similar to the parable of the lost sheep in Luke 15:4–7 (Aland 1985: §§219–20).[2] But their differences are sufficient to regard these two passages as not from the same source and setting (Manson 1949: 283; Luce 1933: 253; Nolland 1993a: 770).[3] It is futile to try to decide which setting is original (Creed 1930: 196 and Jeremias 1963a: 39–40 take Matthew as secondary; but Fitzmyer 1985: 1074 argues that Luke is secondary, reflecting Lucan redaction; for more discussion, see Marshall 1978: 600–601). The parables of Luke 15 are part of the many parables that Luke alone gives, many of which appear in the journey narrative.[4] A few focus on the role of sinners to God or contrast the sinner and the righteous (10:25–37; 14:7–14; 14:15–24; 15:1–32; 16:19–31; 18:9–14). The non-Lucan language of Luke 15 may indicate that Luke received the parables from a source (Marshall 1978: 598, citing Jeremias 1971b, a view that Fitzmyer 1985: 1074 challenges, citing Petersen 1981, who argues that the Thomas version is more primitive than the Synoptics). Examples of traditional wording are "which of you?" and "man" in 15:4 (Nolland 1993a: 770; Luke 11:5, 11; 14:28; 17:7). The literary pattern of three occurs often in Luke (9:57–62; 11:42–52; 13:1–9; 14:18–20; 20:10–12; Schweizer 1984: 243).

The Jesus Seminar (Funk and Hoover 1993: 354–56) distinguishes the authenticity of the parables proper (15:4–6, 8–9 in pink type) from that of the conclusions (15:7, 10 in black type). The parable of the lost sheep is multiply attested (Matt. 18:12–14; Gospel of Thomas 107) and also has the kind of rural and hyperbolic style that fits Jesus. The parable of the lost coin has no parallels, but neither is it a clear example of something gone astray on its own. This "lack of fit" as well as the exaggeration of searching for a coin of little value makes it look original to Jesus versus being a Lucan creation. The conclusion is debated because the theme of repentance in 15:7, 10 looks Lucan and fits other parables that have conclusions (12:21; 14:33; 17:10). But the call to repentance is not found only in the Lucan tradition (Luke 10:13–15 = Matt. 11:20–24). The theme of joy in Luke 15:7, 10 fits 15:22–33, thereby linking to the fundamental theme holding the unit

2. So Fitzmyer 1985: 1073 argues that 15:4–6 is from Q and that originally the two parables were not told together. He sees Matthew's setting as more original. But why Jesus could not tell back-to-back parables that make the same point is not clear. Nor is it clear that 15:4–6 is from Q. Tiede 1988: 273 sees independent oral tradition here.

3. For the presence of these verses in Q are Schneider 1977a: 324–25 and Wiefel 1988: 282. Fitzmyer 1985: 1073 sees 15:4–6 in Q and 15:8–9 in L. Other parallels are found in the Gospel of Thomas 107 and the Gnostic *Gospel of Truth* 31.35–32.9.

4. Luke's indisputably unique parables are 10:25–37; 11:5–8; 12:13–21; 13:3–9; 14:7–14; 16:1–9; 16:19–31; 17:7–10; 18:1–8; 18:9–14. Synoptic parallels to other parables in the journey narrative are debated: 14:15–24; 14:25–33; 19:11–27.

together. The term even makes for paronomasia in Aramaic (Marshall 1978: 602; Black 1967: 184). As such, the whole unit reaches back to Jesus.

The form consists simply of two parables (Fitzmyer 1985: 1074, 1080; Berger 1984: 44–48, 69).[5] The question of structure is carefully examined by Bailey (1976: 144–45, 156), who argues persuasively for the following conceptual links in the first parable: "you" (15:4, 7), "one" (15:4, 7), "ninety-nine" (15:4, 7), "lost" (15:4, 6), "found" (15:4, 5, 6), "rejoice" (15:5, 6, 7), with arriving home as the center (15:6). The second parable is simpler: "loss" (15:8, 9), "find" (15:8, 9 [twice]), with the center being joy in the community over restoration as friends are gathered (15:9). The outline of Luke 15:1–10 is as follows:

a. Setting (15:1–3)
   i. Approach of sinners and tax collectors (15:1)
   ii. Grumbling of Pharisees and scribes (15:2)
   iii. Jesus tells a parable (15:3)
b. Parable of the lost sheep (15:4–7)
   i. Parable (15:4–6)
   ii. Application: heavenly joy over the lost repenting (15:7)
c. Parable of the lost coin (15:8–10)
   i. Parable (15:8–9)
   ii. Application: angelic joy over the lost repenting (15:10)

The major themes are God's desire to pursue sinners and God's joy at sinners' repentance, since heaven's rejoicing is in view. As such, the passage also shows the value of repentance. Love undertakes the search for the sinner and is active in both the search and the restoration. Though God's desire is pictured, the parable is also about those who follow Jesus and God. They should identify with the efforts of the shepherd and the woman. They should always seek the lost.

Exegesis and Exposition

[1]And all the tax collectors and sinners were drawing near to him to listen to him. [2]And both the Pharisees and the scribes were grumbling, saying, "This one receives sinners and eats with them." [3]And he told them this parable:

5. Bultmann 1963: 171, 334 sees the discourse composed by Luke. But it is not clear why it cannot go back to Jesus. If he pursued sinners and was criticized for it, surely he produced an explanation for his actions. Bultmann calls the two parables similitudes, his name for detailed comparisons where a common event is described (see excursus 8).

[4]"What man among you who has a hundred sheep and, losing one of them, does not leave the ninety-nine in the wilderness and go after the one that is lost until he finds it? [5]And when he finds it, he places it on his shoulder, rejoicing. [6]And coming back to his house, he calls together his friends and neighbors, saying to them, 'Rejoice with me, for my lost sheep is found.' [7]Thus I say to you that there will be more joy in heaven when one sinner repents than over ninety-nine righteous who have no need of repentance.

[8]"Or what woman who has ten drachmas, if she loses one drachma, does not light a lamp and sweep the house and seek diligently until she finds it? [9]And finding it, she calls together her friends and neighbors, saying, 'Rejoice with me, for I have found the coin that was lost.' [10]Thus I say to you, there is more joy before the angels of God over one sinner who repents."

a. Setting (15:1–3)
i. Approach of Sinners and Tax Collectors (15:1)

15:1 The setting involves a crowd, which is significant since the previous scene also included a crowd. The tax collectors and sinners here receive special attention in one of three Lucan texts where these two groups are paired (Luke 5:30 [= Matt. 9:10–11 = Mark 2:15–16]; Luke 7:34). Sinners were perceived as forfeiting their relationship to God because of a lifestyle unfaithful to God's law.[6] The tax collector also was not respected (see the exegesis of Luke 3:12; Michel, *TDNT* 8:101–4). It was these "reprobates" who were drawing near to Jesus. Jesus' popularity is highlighted by the exaggerated note that "all" (πάντες, *pantes*) the tax collectors and sinners are drawing near to him. Marshall (1978: 599) notes irony in the reference to whom is drawing near to hear, given Jesus' call to hear in 14:35. Those responding are, surprisingly, the tax collectors and sinners (Plummer 1896: 367; Luke 7:29, 37; 11:29). They sense that Jesus cares for them and has something to say to them.

ii. Grumbling of Pharisees and Scribes (15:2)

15:2 The Jewish leadership still complains about Jesus' associations.[7] The complaint is similar to remarks in 5:30 and 7:39. Eating with sinners and tax collectors is particularly galling, for table fellowship with such people suggests a level of acceptance that is distasteful to the leaders (Plummer 1896: 368; Acts 10:28; Luke 7:34; 14:22–24;

---

6. Rengstorf, *TDNT* 1:327, speaks of ἁμαρτωλοί as murderers, robbers, deceivers, and those of dishonorable vocation, which would include tax collectors; also Herrenbrück 1981.

7. Διαγογγύζω (to grumble) appears in the NT only here and in 19:7. This idea is a significant one in the OT and is often negative in force: Num. 11:1; 14:27, 29 (using the simple γογγύζω); Danker 1988: 274. The word order, with Pharisees first, is unusual; so 5:30, but not 5:21; 6:7; 11:53.

Grundmann 1963: 305). Nolland (1993a: 770) notes that προσδέχε-ται (*prosdechetai*) here means "to have good will toward" (Mic. 6:7; Zeph. 3:10 variant reading). This change in meaning from other Lucan uses of the verb could indicate the influence of a source. Rather than referring directly to Jesus, they use the derogatory οὗτος (*houtos*, this one). Their reaction to Jesus' associations reflects OT injunctions about associating with the godless (Deut. 21:20–21; Ps. 1; Prov. 1:15; 2:11–15; 4:14–17; 23:20–21; Isa. 52:11; Talbert 1982: 148; Marshall 1978: 599). A later saying in *Mekilta de Rabbi Ishmael*, tractate *Amalek* 3.55–57 on Exod. 18:1 (= Lauterbach 1933–35: 2.166) reads, "Let not a man associate with the wicked, even to bring him near to the law" (for other texts, see SB 2:208; 1:498–99; e.g., *m. Dem.* 2.3 [speaks of not eating with the *Am-haaretz*, the uninstructed people of the land, for fear of contracting uncleanness]; *m. Ḥag.* 2.7). Jesus does not share the separatist mentality of the scribes and Pharisees (Mark 2:15 = Luke 5:32; 19:10). He is interested in befriending such undesirables, regardless of what others may think. His rationale is simple: he wishes to draw them to God.

iii. Jesus Tells a Parable (15:3)

Jesus responds to the criticism with a multifaceted picture told in three parallel parables.[8] An inherent unity exists in what Jesus will say in these parables. The parable is told to "them" (αὐτούς, *autous*), clearly a reference to the grumbling Pharisees and scribes. Jesus is responding primarily to their complaint, but also to the crowds, who are potential beneficiaries of God's grace. Some argue that Luke constructed the setting, since the addressed Pharisees were not shepherds, as the parable implies in 15:4–6 (Nolland 1993a: 771; Jeremias 1963a: 132). Others appeal to Ezek. 34:11–16 to argue that the shepherd image is intended to shock the Pharisees. Another option is that Jesus addressed the crowd of rural folks so that the Pharisees can hear his complaint. The point of Luke's introduction is that the parables are an apologetic for Jesus' unusual relationship, a context that hardly looks artificial, given the parables and Jesus' well-attested reputation (Luke 5:27–32 = Mark 2:13–17 = Matt. 9:9–13).

15:3

b. Parable of the Lost Sheep (15:4–7)
i. Parable (15:4–6)

The picture is of a shepherd who is trying to account for all his sheep and finds that one is missing. Jesus introduces the parable as a rhetorical question and notes that any shepherd would do what he is

15:4

---

8. Παραβολήν (parable) is singular, as in 5:36, where it also referred to more than one parable. Marshall 1978: 600 suggests that it means "a parabolic discourse."

about to describe.[9] The parable pictures a shepherd of modest means, since a flock might have up to two hundred sheep (Jeremias 1963a: 133 cites Gen. 32:14 [32:15 MT]). In Jewish tradition, three hundred sheep was considered a large herd (*t. B. Qam.* 6.20 [= Neusner 1977–86: 4.32]). The occupation of tending sheep was common in the region (Preisker and Schulz, *TDNT* 6:689; Jeremias, *TDNT* 6:486).[10] It appears that the owner looks after the flock himself, since he does not have a guard, another sign of modest means. A shepherd usually counted his flock before putting them up for the night (Bishop 1962: 50).[11] In the story, he comes up one short. In all likelihood, if this was a typical search, he left the ninety-nine with someone to protect them and went out to look for the missing animal.[12] The shepherd would look until he failed to find the sheep, found its tattered remains, or located the animal. The point is that the lost sheep receives special attention over those that are safe and sound.

A comparison of Luke's image with Matt. 18:12–14 is instructive (Talbert 1982: 148). In Matthew, the parable illustrates pastoral care among believers and the issue is the sheep of the community that go astray, since it is in a set of passages that deal with the behavior of believers (Matt. 18:6–11, 15–18). Almost none of the vocabulary of the two passages overlaps, though the images are similar.[13] Much debate exists as to which version is original.[14] The arguments are

9. This style of rhetorical opening is frequent in Luke: 11:5, 11; 14:28, 31; 17:7; Ernst 1977: 453. The answer to the "which of you?" question is that all would, if they react with their heart, given the risk to the animal.

10. Wool, mutton, and cloaks were the three basic products from sheep. Bailey 1976: 148 suggests that the number of sheep indicates that the shepherd is not the owner but represents a larger group. As Bailey appeals to contemporary custom to make this point, which is not clearly linked to ancient practice, the observation is possible, but not demonstrable.

11. It is disputable whether everyday shepherds were seen as negative in the culture, so that Jesus' choice of a shepherd would be shocking; but so Bailey 1976: 147. See the exegesis of 2:8.

12. Some see a problem in the shepherd's leaving behind the ninety-nine, but this is probably a detail omitted in the abbreviated telling of the story. Ἔρημος is an open field, a heath, where the animals grazed; Manson 1949: 283; 1 Sam. 17:28. On the use of the numbers *ninety-nine* and *one*, see SB 1:784–85; *m. Pe'a* 4.1–2; Fitzmyer 1985: 1076.

13. Only the reference to the ninety-nine appears in the same place; a few other terms appear in a different order. The conscious difference between the use of "lost sinners" in Luke and "wayward believers" in Matthew is significant.

14. Marshall 1978: 600–601 has details and notes the views. Bultmann 1963: 171 and Linnemann 1966: 67–70 opt for Matthean originality, while Jeremias 1963a: 40 and Ellis 1974: 197 are convinced that Luke has the original form. Marshall is undecided, as is Nolland 1993a: 769. All of this assumes that only one tradition of the story originally existed, which may not be true, as Marshall notes. Bultmann 1963: 202

complex, but the whole debate is unnecessary. Jesus may make distinct applications of a basic image in two settings. Such a view is natural, especially given the lack of parallels for the other parables in Luke 15. Luke uses special material here (Kistemaker 1980: 207; Grundmann 1963: 306 says this is possible).

The search proves fruitful. The shepherd finds the animal, places it **15:5**
on his shoulder, and takes it home (Isa. 40:11; 49:22; SB 2:209; Marshall 1978: 601).[15] The imagery clearly alludes to God's tender and protective care (Preisker and Schulz, *TDNT* 6:690). Given the possibility that the sheep could have been permanently lost, stolen, or destroyed by wild animals, the shepherd rejoices that the lost sheep has been found.[16] This note of joy is the focus in the rest of the story: χαίρων (*chairōn*, rejoicing; 15:5), συγχάρητε (*syncharēte*, rejoice with; 15:6), and χαρά (*chara*, joy; 15:7). The point of comparison is that God rejoices at a sinner who is led back to him by Jesus' ministry (or by his disciples' ministry). Even though the shepherd pictures God's desire, disciples are to share this attitude. In addition, the joy that accompanies such a return should match the joy of heaven and should be present in all who see it happen. Even the discovery of one such person is a cause for joy. Such is God's heart for the lost. This attitude stands in contrast to the leadership's complaint. God's people should always seek to find more of the lost.

The shepherd does not rejoice privately. He calls his friends and **15:6**
neighbors.[17] They are to share in the joy of the rediscovered sheep. The picture is a simple one: a great celebration at the recovery of a lost sinner. This point reappears in 15:9 and 15:23–24 and links the three parables together. The use of συγκαλέω (*synkaleō*, to call together) may suggest a formal celebration (Jeremias 1963a: 134; 1 Kings 1:9–10).[18] If so, the image of celebration is enhanced, and the joy of heaven is compared to a great party—all over one creature! Here is God's heart for sinners as he works through Jesus. So also seeking the lost should be at the heart of the disciple's activity. Those who claim to serve God should be aware that this is part of

---

also notes a similar parable in the later Gen. Rab. 86.4 on 39:2, where one of twelve cows is lost; also SB 1:785.

15. On the regal image of the shepherd, see Jer. 31:10–14; Ezek. 34:11–16; Mic. 5:2–5 [5:1–4 MT]; John 10:11–12. On people as sheep, see Ps. 23; 119:176; Oepke, *TDNT* 1:395.

16. The image of the sheep on the shoulder is common in the ancient world; Fitzmyer 1985: 1077; G. Wright 1939; V. Muller 1944.

17. Only Luke has the detail about the γείτων (neighbor); see BAGD 153; BAA 307; elsewhere in the NT only at Luke 14:12; 15:9; John 9:8.

18. Συγκαλέω is frequently used by Luke: Luke 9:1; 23:13; Acts 5:21; 10:24; 28:17; Fitzmyer 1985: 1077.

their mandate. The total separation of the Pharisees and their grumbling about associating with sinners stand in stark contrast to Jesus' approach.

ii. Application: Heavenly Joy over the Lost Repenting (15:7)

15:7 Jesus' application of the parable emphasizes the shared joy and heaven's perspective: the repentance of one sinner is a cause for joy in heaven.[19] Heaven is compared to the shepherd and his neighbors who rejoice at the recovery of the lost sheep.[20] In fact, the discovery of the lost sinner is the cause of even greater joy than the "righteousness" of the ninety-nine. The comparative remark is rhetorical and recalls the picture of 5:31–32, where some are said not to need a physician. The leadership also needs a physician and needs to repent, but its failure to recognize that makes it unreachable (also Mark 2:17). But Jesus does not make a direct reference here to the needs of the leadership. Rather, his remark stays within the framework of the parable: there is more joy when something is found than when there is in no change in status (Ezek. 18:23 is conceptually parallel). The rescue has removed the danger. Those who recognize where they stand before God and respond accordingly are the cause of great joy in heaven. The possibility for such a reversal is why Jesus reaches out to tax collectors and sinners. Interestingly, in Judaism a true penitent was held in high esteem (Manson 1949: 284; G. Moore 1927–30: 1.530–34; *b. Yoma* 86a; *Pesikta Rabbati* 44.9 [= Braude 1968: 2.779–80]).[21] Some rabbinic material, however, shows God's joy at the fall of the godless: "But just as it is a delight before the Omnipresent to see the strengthening of the righteous, so it is a joy before the Omnipresent to see the downfall of the wicked, as it is said, 'When the wicked perish, there is rejoicing' (Prov. 11:10)" (*t. Sanh.* 14.10 [= Neusner 1977–86: 4.245]; cf. Marshall 1978: 602; SB 2:209; *Sipre* 117 [37a] on Num. 18:8; *m. Sanh.* 10; Nolland 1993a: 773).

---

19. The future tense may have eschatological overtones or it may be a customary future alluding to God's habitual response. The wording may have Aramaic roots and betray a pre-Lucan form; Fitzmyer 1985: 1077–78; Black 1967: 184; Jeremias 1980: 247.

20. The phrase *in heaven* parallels the idiom *before the angels* in 15:10 (SB 2:209). Both expressions are used to avoid direct mention of God.

21. This *Pesikta Rabbati* text treats Hos. 14:1 [14:2 MT] and says that repentance raises a heart to the seventh firmament (i.e., into God's presence) before the throne of glory itself. Other portions of this text read: "'Come back as far as you can according to your strength, and I will go the rest of the way to meet you.' So the Holy One, blessed be he, says to Israel: 'Return unto me, and I will return unto you' (Mal. 3:7). . . . For the Holy One, blessed be he, is merciful and gracious and desires a turning to him before he sits as your judge on the dais whence he must release the full force of his judgment upon you" (Braude 1968: 2.779).

The point of Matt. 18:12–14 is different (Creed 1930: 198). There a believer is like a child, and God's will is that not one of his "children" be lost, an allusion to pastoral care of the flock.

c. Parable of the Lost Coin (15:8–10)
i. Parable (15:8–9)

Jesus introduces a second picture, which parallels the first, except **15:8** that a woman is involved and the search is presented in slightly more detail. Nonetheless, the image is the same. A silver coin has been lost. The drachma (δραχμή) was equivalent to a denarius or a quarter of a shekel, a day's wage for an average worker (Fitzmyer 1985: 1081; Josephus, *Antiquities* 3.8.2 §195).[22] Thus, the lost coin represents a very modest sum of money. Such coins were not circular and so would not roll very far away (Nolland 1993a: 775; Derrett 1979–80: 41). Jeremias (1963a: 134) refers to the custom of coins hung on a headdress as part of a dowry, but it is not certain that the custom is this old.[23] Still, the woman proceeds on a deliberate search. She lights a lamp to help her see in what was probably a windowless house. She sweeps the house, probably with a broom of palm twigs, to see if the coin rolled into some corner or became mixed with some debris, or in the hope that she will hear it roll on the floor. She seeks diligently until she finds it. The use of εὕρῃ (*heurē*, she finds) recalls the language of 15:4. She goes to great lengths to try to recover the coin.[24]

Plummer (1896: 370) attempts to heighten the difference between the two parables in that the man is moved by pity to find a sheep that strays, while the woman is moved by self-interest to find a coin that she lost. In this view, the second parable pictures the church while the first looks to divine wisdom and the mind of God. But such distinctions are not present, given the extensive parallelism between the two parables. If there is any difference in the two passages, it is in the detailed description of the woman's effort, which focuses the picture on the effort given to finding the lost coin (Ernst 1977: 454).

---

22. This parable contains the only uses of δραχμή in the NT, though the double drachma is found in Matt. 17:24. In LXX, see Gen. 24:22; Exod. 39:3 [38:26 Engl.]; Josh. 7:21; Jeremias 1969: 111.

23. Kistemaker 1980: 212 assumes this background and argues that the equivalent today would be losing a diamond from a wedding ring. If the woman has a dowry, it is not a significant amount. Against this understanding, which must remain only an implication of the text, are Klostermann 1929: 157 and Fitzmyer 1985: 1051.

24. SB 2:212 narrates a similar Jewish parable from a later period in Song Rab. 1.1.9 on 1:1, where the subject is seeking wisdom like silver, a reference to the Torah.

15:9 The woman's joy parallels the shepherd's: she calls together her lady friends and neighbors (φίλας [*philas*] and γείτονας [*geitonas*] are both feminine). She tells them to rejoice because she found the coin that was lost. Many of the terms of 15:6 are also here: συγκαλεῖ (calls together), φίλας καὶ γείτονας (friends and neighbors—with a gender difference), συγχάρητέ μοι (rejoice with me), and ὅτι εὗρον (for I have found). The emphasis is on the joy and celebration that comes from finding what was lost.

ii. Application: Angelic Joy over the Lost Repenting (15:10)

15:10 The point of this parable matches 15:7: there is much joy in heaven over a single repentant sinner (note the repetition of οὕτως [thus], χαρά [joy], and ἐπὶ ἑνὶ ἁμαρτωλῷ μετανοοῦντι [over one sinner who repents]). Rather than speaking of a joy focused on the sinner's future deliverance, as 15:7 did, the joy here is the joy of the present—an indication that the sinner's repentance brings present as well as future joy. Unlike 15:7, this parable does not speak of joy in heaven but angelic response. The expression is probably a circumlocution, especially in light of its parallelism to 15:7, and is to be read not just as the response of angels but of God as well (Luke 12:8; Jeremias 1963a: 135; Walls 1959; SB 2:212; Marshall 1978: 604). The courts of heaven are full of celebration at the coming of a sinner to God. Heaven's joy and the angels' desire for sinners to come to God is to be matched by the efforts of those who seek to serve God.

Summary Luke 15:1–10 explains why Jesus associates with sinners. Jesus' associations and his lack of separation from the unrighteous were a constant irritation to the Jewish leadership. Jesus did not share in the sinners' activity, but he did befriend them, encourage them to come to know God, and challenge them to repent. The kingdom is meant for people who recognize their need for God, and Jesus pointed the way. Jesus showed the way to heaven in a way that sinners knew he could be approached. The parables of the lost sheep and the lost coin picture God's heart for sinners and his initiative toward them. He has not abandoned them, but wishes for them to be drawn to him. Here is a God in search of people who will turn to him. He is like the shepherd and the woman.

The passage is not just about God. There is a contrast between Jesus' approach to humans and that of the grumbling leadership. Jesus is the model for the disciple, just as his activity reflects the heart of God himself. Jesus reflects the way to God and the way of God. People are to hear his message of repentance, and disciples are to reflect his concern. The danger of seeking righteousness is that one can withdraw from the world in pursuit of heaven's blessings and the fellowship with those of like mind. The disciple is not to withdraw into a cocoon, inoculated from people of the world. Rather, part of the mission is to love people and draw them to God. God searches for sinners who need to find their way to him, just as the shepherd left the ninety-nine to find the one that was lost. Among the tools he uses is the caring concern of a disciple. The primary expression of God's concern for the sinner is found in Jesus himself (Rom. 5:8; Kistemaker 1980: 213).[25] And God's work in Jesus continues as disciples show God's concern for people. Luke's readers are to learn from Jesus' example that they are to seek out sinners and point the way to God. Disciples are to look for lost sheep and missing coins and to celebrate finding what was lost. Evangelism is grounded in the joy of recovery.

25. Geldenhuys 1951: 403: "Because the Saviour has paid with His precious blood for the redemption of man, every soul has an infinite value in God's sight and the way to the throne of grace lies open to everyone who desires to enter."

3. Parable of the Forgiving Father (15:11–32)

The third parable in Luke 15 is designed to illustrate heaven's receptivity toward a sinner's repentance, as well as to condemn the protest of those who react against such divine generosity. This passage and the two previous parables show that nothing has changed since the complaint of 5:29–30. In contrast to the officials' complaint stands the heavenly Father's reaction: unconditional acceptance and joy.

This unit is popularly called "The Prodigal Son," a title whose roots go back to the Vulgate (Fitzmyer 1985: 1083). Some call it "The Gracious Father," a good alternative. Nonetheless, a title like "A Father and His Two Different Sons" may be even better.[1] The parable is close in genre to an allegory, because there are many levels of application, though not all the details should be pressed. Basically, there are three points of contact: the prodigal pictures the sinner, the older son is the self-righteous leadership (or anyone who claims to serve God), and the father pictures God (Kistemaker 1980: 216). Sinners are to come to God, and the righteous are to accept the sinner's decision to turn to him. It is the father's reaction to the sons that is at the center of the parable. His response, in turn, instructs people on how they should respond. The picture of table fellowship in 15:25–32 is a "parabolic mirroring" of the real situation, since that is part of the Pharisees' complaint (Tannehill 1986: 171). The parable shows that God is pleased to have the penitent at his table.

Sources and Historicity

The parable is unique to Luke, a part of his special material (Schneider 1977a: 327; Fitzmyer 1985: 1084). The picture is from everyday life, as a poignant ancient letter shows.[2] Some doubt is expressed about the para-

---

1. Manson 1949: 284 calls it "The Two Sons," but the father is too crucial to the picture to be left out. Jeremias 1963a: 128 calls it "The Parable of the Father's Love," a title that Fitzmyer 1985: 1084 likes. Jesus likes to use the two-son imagery (Matt. 21:28–31).

2. Danker 1988: 275 cites F. Preisigke's edition of an ancient letter in which an impecunious son pleads with his mother to be received back into the family: "I am writing to tell you I am naked. I plead with you, forgive me. I know well enough what I have done to myself. I have learned my lesson."

ble's originality with Jesus, especially the elder son's protest in 15:25–32 (Wellhausen 1904: 81–85, esp. 83–84; J. T. Sanders 1968–69).[3] But the issue of how others should respond to the sinner's return is an integral part of the chapter (15:2, 7, 10; Schneider 1977a: 327–28; Manson 1949: 285).[4] The authenticity of the parable is accepted by most, including the Jesus Seminar, which prints the whole of it in pink type (Funk and Hoover 1993: 356–57). The seminar accepts the parable because of the "sinners" theme (Luke 7:33–34 = Matt. 11:18–19), the evidence of non-Lucan vocabulary in the account, and the gentle treatment of the elder brother, who, representing the Jewish leadership, is not rejected in the story.

The parable neatly fits a precross setting. The only issues are repentance and God's willingness to forgive, with no mention of the cross (Creed 1930: 197).[5] The absence of an allusion to Christ's death troubles some, but the omission is appropriate to the precross setting. Thus, the parable's focus is on theology proper—and rightly so, since it is God's love for and commitment to sinners that causes him not only to accept those who return to him but also caused him to send the Messiah to die for them (Arndt 1956: 350). The parable defends God's grace and compassion. People find an open door when they turn to God for forgiveness. As Jeremias (1963a: 131–32) suggests, the parable vindicates the offer of good news to sinners in the face of severe criticism (Jeremias defends its historicity). The parable also shows that in Jesus' actions toward sinners God's love is made visible by the one who represents him and reveals his ways.

The account is clearly a parable (Fitzmyer 1985: 1084; Bultmann 1963: 196; Berger 1984: 51–56).[6] The outline of Luke 15:11–32 is as follows:

3. For effective refutation, see O'Rourke 1971–72 and Jeremias 1971b. Marshall 1978: 605 rejects attempts to posit a Lucan origin for the parable, such as Schottroff 1971 defends. Goulder 1989: 614–16 argues for Lucan authorship of the parable, attempting to refute the various cases made for authenticity on linguistic grounds by Jeremias, O'Rourke, or Hofius 1977–78. Goulder (pp. 611–12) argues that Luke is relying consciously or unconsciously on the story of Joseph in Genesis, but the cause of the "lostness" of the son in the Joseph cycle of Gen. 39–50 and of the prodigal could not be more different. Nolland 1993a: 780–81 correctly rejects attempts to split the parable in two.

4. Bultmann 1963: 196 accepts the parable's historicity. Other contrastive parables involving two figures or groups are Matt. 21:28–31; 25:1–13; Luke 7:41–42; 18:9–14.

5. Efforts to argue that Lucan repentance concerns only changing one's mind about Jesus are too narrow. This picture and that of the Great Physician (5:32) show that sin is an issue, since that is why Jesus is necessary. One comes to Jesus for healing and righteousness, which he graciously offers and supplies.

6. For the structure, see Bailey 1976: 159–61; Blomberg 1990: 173–74; and Tolbert 1979: 98–100. Blomberg argues for a plausible threefold division: younger son's departure (15:11–20a), father's welcome (15:20b–24), and older son's reaction (15:25–32).

The basic theme centers on God's character, and the parable offers vindication of criticism for associating with sinners. God's forgiveness is always available. No history of sin is too great to be forgiven. Our need is to turn to God and take what he offers on his terms. We need also to accept those who seek forgiveness, for there is joy in heaven over those who repent. One should not compare how God blesses, but be grateful that he does bless. In turning to God, one gains total acceptance and joyful reception into God's family.

Exegesis and Exposition

[11]And he said, "A certain man had two sons. [12]And the younger one said to his father, 'Father, give me the portion of property that is coming to me.' So he divided his estate between them. [13]And after a few days the young man gathered together all that he had, turned it into cash, and left home for a distant land, and there he squandered his possessions, living a dissolute life. [14]When he had spent everything, a great famine came in the land, and he began to be in need. [15]So he went and hired himself out to one of the citizens of that region, and he sent him to his farm to feed his pigs. [16]He deeply desired ⌜to have his fill⌝ of carob pods on which the pigs fed, but nobody would give him anything. [17]He came to his senses and said, 'How many hired hands of my father abound in food, and I am here being destroyed by hunger. [18]I shall rise up and go to my father and say to him, "Father, I have sinned against heaven and before you. [19]I am no longer worthy to be called your son. Make me one of your servants."' [20]And rising up, he came to his father. While he was still some distance away, his father saw him, had pity on him, and, running, embraced him about the neck and kissed him tenderly. [21]And his son said to him, 'Father, I have sinned against heaven and before you, I am no longer worthy to be called your son.⌝' [22]The father said to his servants, 'Immediately bring the best robe and put it on him, and give him a ring for his finger and sandals for his feet, [23]and bring a fattened calf,

kill it, and, eating, let us rejoice, [24]for my son was dead and now he lives, was lost but now is found.' And they began to rejoice.

[25]"Now his elder son was in the field; and as he came and drew near to the house, he heard music and dancing. [26]And calling one of the servants, he inquired what these things meant. [27]He said to him, 'Your brother has come and your father killed a fattened calf, because he received him safe and sound.' [28]And he was angered and did not wish to go in. His father came out and entreated him. [29]And replying, he said to his father, 'Behold, I have served you these many years and I have never transgressed your command, and you never gave me a ⌜kid⌝ so I could rejoice with my friends, [30]but when your son came, this one who devoured your livelihood with harlots, you killed for him the fattened calf.' [31]And he said to him, 'My child, you are always with me, and all my things are yours. [32]But it was fitting to celebrate and be glad, for your brother was dead and is alive, and was lost and is found.'"

a. The Prodigal's Sojourn (15:11–24)
i. Introduction (15:11)

A brief introduction simply names the three characters: a father and two sons. The two sons control the literary action, but it is the father's response to the sons that provides the parable's lessons by showing how the father views each son's reaction. The opening "a certain man" is like 15:4 and 15:8, the latter of which has a woman at the parable's center. The focus of this parable is on the father.   **15:11**

ii. The Son's Separation (15:12)

The story begins with the younger son requesting to receive the assets that will eventually be his so he can go his own way.[7] The boy is probably in his late teens, since he is still single (Marshall 1978: 607). Interestingly, the reference to the estate is graphically called τὸν βίον (ton bion), which literally means "the life." The son requests his portion of what his father's life will leave him.   **15:12**

The request's historical and legal background is much discussed, since estates usually were not divided until the father's death. If Jewish law prevails, the son would receive half of what the elder son receives, or one-third of the estate (Deut. 21:17). Some Jewish texts suggest the right of a father to break up his holdings before his death, because they exhort him not to do it too early (Plummer 1896: 372; Tiede 1988: 277; Sir. 33:19–23).[8] Creed (1930: 199) notes

---

7. Τὸ ἐπιβάλλον means "that which falls to me"; Tob. 3:17; 6:12; P. Oxy. vol. 4 #715 lines 13–15; Creed 1930: 198; Hauck, *TDNT* 1:529; MM 235; Fitzmyer 1985: 1087. As a noun, οὐσίας refers to property; Tob. 14:13; 3 Macc. 3:28; Josephus, *Antiquities* 7.5.5 §114. On διεῖλεν (he divided), see Schlier, *TDNT* 1:184.

8. Sir. 33:20 (NRSV) reads: "To son or wife, to brother or friend, / do not give power over yourself, as long as you live; / and do not give your property to another, / in case

that SB 3:545–49 refers to the right of a father to dispose of his property by gift and thus ignore the rules of inheritance (Num. 27:8–9; *m. B. Bat.* 8–9, esp. 8.7; *b. B. Meṣ.* 75b). But Creed also notes that actual distribution does not occur until death, so that this custom is not alluded to here.[9] Others argue that the son's request treats the father as if he were already dead (Bailey 1976: 165). This is not certain, but the son clearly looks to sever his relationship to his father and go away.

Nonetheless, the key element is that the son's request is graciously granted. Once the son receives his portion, all other claims to the estate are abrogated (see the exegesis of 15:19).[10] Each son receives his due and the young son is free to go. Apparently, the elder son chose not to go his own way, but to keep his holdings at home.[11] Schrenk (*TDNT* 5:983–84) perceptively suggests that this image pictures the heavenly Father letting the sinner go his own way.

iii. Life of Sin (15:13–15)

15:13 The young son's life collapses soon after his departure. He takes his inheritance and after some time leaves his father.[12] He is obviously anxious to gain his freedom. He converts all his inheritance into cash (συνάγω, *synagō*; BAGD 782; BAA 1561; MM 600; Plutarch, *Life of Cato Minor* 6.4 [742]), goes to a distant land, and squanders his possessions. Διασκορπίζω (*diaskorpizō*) normally means "to scatter or disperse," but with property, it means "to waste or squander." The picture is of tossing one's possessions into the wind (Michel, *TDNT* 7:422; BAGD 188; BAA 378; elsewhere used by Luke in Luke 1:51; 16:1; Acts 5:37). The son throws away his wealth through an undis-

---

you change your mind and must ask for it." A more positive attitude and example appears in Tob. 8:21 (Nolland 1993a: 782).

9. Though exceptions do exist; see Jeremias 1963a: 129 and Daube 1955: 334, though his explanation that the father gave property to the younger son but not to the older is not correct, given the end of this verse. On this custom, see Horowitz 1953: 402–21 and Pöhlmann 1979.

10. Rengstorf 1967 suggests as allusion to the Jewish custom of *qĕṣāṣâ* (קְצָצָה), which cut off from society a member who sold a family heirloom to an outsider or who married beneath their social rank (Jastrow 1903: 1407–8). There is no indication that such a custom applies here, though Rengstorf's study does show the parable's social context and background in terms of the familial symbolism of the ring and robe in 15:22. For refutation, see Marshall 1978: 606 and Bailey 1976: 167–68.

11. So Manson 1949: 287, who argues that there is no need to see inconsistency in the parable because the older son is still subject to the father; 15:22–23, 29–30 show that the father is still in control.

12. The phrase οὐ πολλὰς ἡμέρας (not many days) is a figure of speech called litotes, an understatement that affirms something by using the negative. This figure is frequent in Luke: Luke 21:9; Acts 1:5; 12:18; 14:28; 15:2; plus twelve more times; Fitzmyer 1985: 1087.

ciplined, wild life.[13] The next verse pictures a young man on a spending spree for things of no value. His approach to life will lead to his downfall. He will quickly come into dire straits.

Some of the boy's hard time is not his own doing. True, he has spent **15:14** all and has nothing to show for it, but now comes another blow— famine (λιμός, *limos*). It is a severe famine, since the adjective used to describe it is ἰσχυρά (*ischyra*, strong). Nature makes his bad situation worse. His world is collapsing. With no money, no family, and suffering in a distant land, the boy is in trouble. The parable understates the problem with its literal ἤρξατο ὑστερεῖσθαι (*ērxato hystereisthai*, he began to lack). He enters into poverty and has nowhere to turn.

The son responds prudently. Desperate for food and funds, he seeks **15:15** employment (κολλάω, *kollaō*, normally means "to associate with someone," but in this context it means "to hire out to someone"; BAGD 441 §2bα; BAA 897 §2bα; K. Schmidt, *TDNT* 3:822). He works for a Gentile, as the nature of his work shows, and is sent to an animal farm to supervise the pigs. This was the most dishonorable work for a Jew, since pigs were unclean animals (Lev. 11:7; Deut. 14:8; Isa. 65:4; 66:17; 1 Macc. 1:47; Jeremias 1963a: 129; Manson 1949: 288; Creed 1930: 199).[14] In effect, the son has taken the lowest job possible—one that no Jew would even want. He is clearly taking whatever he can get.

iv. Consequences of Sin (15:16)

The job is unable to meet the prodigal's needs. He still suffers from **15:16** hunger. In fact, the pigs are better off than he is. He intensely desires (ἐπιθυμέω, *epithymeō*, an idiom for hunger; 16:21) to have as much to eat as the pigs (Büchsel, *TDNT* 3:170; BAGD 293; BAA 594). Their food (κεράτιον, *keration*) may have been a sweet bean from a carob or locust tree (Klostermann 1929: 159; Plummer 1896: 373–74; SB 2:215) or a bitter, thorny berry (Bailey 1976: 172–73).[15] The son

13. The *hapax legomenon* ἀσώτως speaks of a debauched, profligate life (BAGD 119; BAA 239; Prov. 7:11; 28:7), and so Luke 15:30 speaks of the son's time with prostitutes. Conceptual parallels are found in Eph. 5:18; Titus 1:6; 1 Pet. 4:4; Creed 1930: 199; Foerster, *TDNT* 1:507, esp. n. 4.

14. Ἀγρός refers to fields associated with a farm where animals graze; BAGD 14 §3; BAA 24 §3. Βόσκω means "to tend animals"; Matt. 8:33 = Mark 5:14 = Luke 8:34; BAGD 145; BAA 289. SB 1:492–93 cites several Jewish texts that condemn or forbid Jews to raise swine, including *b. B. Qam.* 82b: "Cursed is the man who raises swine, and cursed is the man who teaches his son Greek philosophy."

15. Κεράτιον (little horn) was eaten only by the poorest humans; BAGD 429; BAA 873; a NT *hapax legomenon*. Marshall 1978: 609 cites a saying from Lev. Rab. 35.6 on 26:3: "When the Israelites are reduced to carob pods, then they repent." This food was nicknamed "John the Baptist's bread," on the erroneous idea that John ate

wants the meal of unclean animals and cannot have it. How much lower can he go? Worse, there is no one in this distant land to offer him comfort or give him food. Οὐδείς (*oudeis*) is emphatic: "nobody" will help him; he is all alone (cf. Sir. 12:4–7; Grundmann 1963: 312; Marshall 1978: 609).[16] Is the son meeting his just fate?

v. Conversion and Return (15:17–21)

15:17 The son's plight finally hits him as he realizes how far he has plunged. The phrase εἰς ἑαυτὸν δὲ ἐλθών (*eis heauton de elthōn*) literally means "and coming to himself" and is equivalent to our idiom "coming to one's senses" (J. Schneider, *TDNT* 2:668; T. Jos. 3.9; Fitzmyer 1985: 1088–89; BAGD 311 §I.2.c; BAA 631 §I.2.c). There is deep irony in his situation: his father's hired hands are in better shape than he is. Μίσθιος (*misthios*) appears in the NT only here and in 15:19 and refers to a day laborer who worked for minimal pay on a day-to-day basis (Lev. 25:50; Job 7:1; Tob. 5:15; Fitzmyer 1985: 1089; Preisker, *TDNT* 4:701; BAGD 523; BAA 1059). These workers, as a matter of course, have "plenty of bread" (περισσεύονται ἄρτων, *perisseuontai artōn*). In contrast, the son is perishing from hunger. Whatever the merits of his current employment, his father is a better master (Klostermann 1929: 159; Manson 1949: 288; SB 1:568).[17]

15:18 The son develops a plan of action. The shift to soliloquy in 15:17–19 changes the perspective of the story from external narration to internal motive, revealing a key turning point in the account. Many parables contain such a shift (12:17–19; 16:3–4; 18:4–5). The struggling son decides to acknowledge his folly before God and to his father.[18] This combination is a merism to indicate that he sinned against God and his father (Traub, *TDNT* 5:519; Hofius 1977–78: 241).[19] The combination ἀναστὰς πορεύσομαι (*anastas poreusomai*)

---

carobs. John's carob was sweet, while this carob was bitter; Nolland 1993a: 783; Bailey 1976: 171–73.

16. Sir. 12:6–7 (NRSV) reads: "For the Most High also hates sinners / and will inflict punishment on the ungodly. / Give to the one who is good, but do not help the sinner." Though this attitude is harsh, the prevalent Jewish view would be that the boy got what he deserved—something the boy himself comes to realize.

17. Lam. Rab. 1.34 on 1:7 reads, "When a son abroad goes barefoot [through poverty], then he remembers the comfort of his father's house."

18. To speak of sinning before heaven is to acknowledge that one has sinned against God; SB 2:217. OT conceptual or idiomatic parallels are found in Exod. 10:16; 1 Sam. 7:6; 20:1; Tob. 3:3; Jdt. 5:17; Sus. 23; Plummer 1896: 374; Manson 1949: 288; Lohfink 1975. Jer. 31:18–20 shows the proper attitude of repentance. In Hos. 2:7 [2:9 MT], Israel returns to her first husband.

19. Danker 1988: 276 notes a similar appeal to Caesar for clemency in Cicero, *On Behalf of Quintus Ligarius* 30.

refers to "going at once."[20] The son will act quickly and humbly. He knows he has forfeited all rights to sonship and inheritance, but it is better to cast himself on his father's mercy than remain in a distant land, living a life lower than the unclean beasts and suffering hunger. The confession pictures his repentance, coming to the father bearing nothing but his need. He plans to turn and come home, openly confessing his failure. His attempt to live carelessly and independent of any constraints is a failure. It has resulted in something less than a human existence.

The son decides what he will tell his father: he will place himself at his father's discretion, assert no rights, and recognize that he has no claims. He is unworthy of being received as a family member. His request is simply for daily care and sustenance as a day laborer (μίσθιος, *misthios*; BAGD 523; BAA 1059), the lowest of three classes of laborers. A slave (δοῦλος, *doulos*; Luke 17:7–9) was like part of the family, although part of the lower class. The day laborer was hired only on special occasions for one day at a time, and so was less cared for. The son's request shows that he wants to be a minimal burden. He is prepared to be the lowest of the low. As one of these laborers, he still will be better off than he now is on his own. He accepts the consequences of his choices. There are no excuses, only confession and a humble request. The picture shows what repentance looks like: no claims, just reliance on God's mercy and provision. **15:19**

The son departs and carries out his resolution to return and confess. Little can he anticipate the response that awaits him. The father spots him while he is still far way and reacts immediately with compassion and acceptance.[21] As the one who initiates, the father now becomes the center of the story. Surely the son must have wondered how his father would respond to his confession. He does not have to wonder long: the father runs to him and gives him a giant hug, breaking all protocol (Jeremias 1964a: 130).[22] Compassion reigns (Luke 7:13; 10:33; Nolland 1993a: 784–85; esp. Ps. 103:13). The expression ἐπέπεσεν ἐπὶ τὸν τράχηλον αὐτοῦ (*epepesen epi ton trachēlon autou*) literally means "he fell upon his neck" (Gen. 33:4; 45:14–15; 3 Macc. 5:49; Acts 20:37; Fitzmyer 1985: 1089). The father expresses **15:20**

20. Jeremias 1963a: 130 calls the phrase an Aramaism and cites Tg. 2 Sam. 3:21 (cf. Acts 5:17; 9:6, 18). Fitzmyer 1985: 1089 calls it a Septuagintalism and cites Gen. 22:3, 19; 24:10; 43:8; Tob. 8:10 [8:9 NRSV]. All that this really shows is that the idiom is cross-cultural.

21. Holding the emphatic position in the clause is the reference to the son being distant when spotted. Danker 1988: 277 sees a picture of Jer. 31:18–20 here. Tobit 11:5–6 has a similar observation from a distance.

22. Blomberg 1990: 176 makes clear that this action is the "twist" in the story. No Middle Eastern father would greet or respond to his wayward son this way.

his joy by greeting the son with a kiss (καταφιλέω, *kataphileō*, refers to the tender kiss of affection; Plummer 1896: 375; BAGD 420; BAA 855; elsewhere in Luke at 7:38, 45). It pictures acceptance of the son before the son says a word (2 Sam. 14:33). A relationship is being restored (Marshall 1978: 610). With repentance comes reconciliation. All of these details are designed to picture the basic emotion expressed. The scene reminds one of the common picture of soldiers returning from a long separation from their families. The emotion is basic to the love that exists within a family and powerfully portrays the love of God.

15:21 Despite the warm welcome, the son offers his confession, just as he had resolved to do. It is stated in exactly the terms he used in 15:18b–19a, omitting only the request to be made a slave (see the additional note). The confession of humility leaves the son in the hands of his father. Many see the father interrupting the son's remarks (Luce 1933: 256; Danker 1988: 277; Marshall 1978: 610; Fitzmyer 1985: 1089). Nolland (1993a: 785) may have the best solution: the father's greeting of compassion would have made the "daily laborer" request an insult.[23] Bailey (1976: 183) disagrees.[24] The account has a "literary gap" that is not answered directly. It is clear, however, that the father will not debase his son. There is no indication that the text regards the prodigal's return as negative or contrived. Those who come humbly to God can know that he will receive them (John 1:12). A picture of genuine repentance is also in view. Such a parallel fits the picture of the sinner who turns to the Father.

vi. The Father's Acceptance (15:22–24)

15:22 The father receives the son back with full privileges: the servants are told to clothe the son immediately and put a ring on his finger and sandals on his feet. The robe is a long, flowing garment, στολή (*stolē*), a term used of angels in Mark 16:5 and of glorified believers in Rev. 6:11 (Wilckens, *TDNT* 7:690; BAGD 769; BAA 1535), and pictures formal attire (Luke 20:46 uses it of scribal robes). The son is given the best clothes to wear (cf. the use of πρῶτος [*prōtos*, first] in Song 4:14; Ezek. 27:22; Amos 6:6; Klostermann 1929: 159). The re-

---

23. So also Plummer 1896: 375 argues that the father's warm reception prevents the son from finishing, since it is clear that he is accepted.

24. Bailey argues that this omission of his resolve to be a worker is key: the son backs off from his confession and is disappointed that his effort to earn back his relationship, a picture of his "rabbinic-like repentance," has failed. Bailey is right that the son understands that the father "gifted" him with a new relationship, but his characterization of the son is too negative, as Nolland 1993a: 784 correctly notes. The parable describes a returned prodigal, a sinner found, which for Jesus is a positive, not a conniving, category.

ceiving of a ring (δακτύλιος, *daktylios*; a *hapax legomenon*) adds to the image of being ornately dressed. The ring may contain a seal and thus represent the son's membership in the family (BAGD 170; BAA 339; Grundmann 1963: 313; Plummer 1896: 376), but it stops short of being a transfer of authority. Jeremias (1963a: 130) suggests an allusion to Joseph's being clothed by Pharaoh with a ring, fine clothes, and a gold chain (Gen. 41:42), while Nolland (1993a: 785) prefers a picture like that in Esth. 6:6–11 of the king knowing Mordecai (cf. Esth. 3:10; 8:2; Ezek. 16:10; 1 Macc. 6:15). Certainly it matches the picture of acceptance present in these texts, but the son is not assuming an office above his brother. They have equal access to the father. The sandals are also a symbol of wealth; contextually the suggestion is that the son had been barefoot and destitute (Linnemann 1966: 77). The son goes from destitution to restoration.

The picture of joy and triumph continues: the father calls for a cele- **15:23**
bration in honor of his son's return. They will sacrifice the fattened calf (ὁ μόσχος ὁ σιτευτός, *ho moschos ho siteutos*) eaten on major religious holidays like the day of atonement (Michel, *TDNT* 4:760–61; Fitzmyer 1985: 1090; Judg. 6:25; 1 Sam. 28:24 [conceptually]; Jer. 26:21 LXX [46:21 Engl./MT]; Heb. 9:12, 19; 1 Clem. 52.2; BAGD 528; BAA 1070). Such an animal was specially fed and prepared for these occasions (Marshall 1978: 611). Meat was rarely consumed at meals in first-century Palestine, so this is a special time (Jeremias 1963a: 130). It would take hours to fulfill this request. But the son has been reinstated, and so it is time to eat lavishly and rejoice (Bultmann, *TDNT* 2:774).[25] Some argue that the death of the fattened calf may symbolize Christ's death (Bailey 1976: 189–90), but this is not at all certain, since here death is for a celebration, not the somber sacrifice that Christ gave.

In synonymous images laid out in parallelism, the father gives the **15:24**
reason (ὅτι, *hoti*) for the celebration. The son has been "resurrected." The father has regained a "lost" son; the son he expected never to see again has returned. Regaining the lost and the subsequent joy are images that recall the first two parables of this chapter (joy in 15:6–7, 9–10, 32; lost in 15:4, 8, 27). Nolland (1993a: 786) correctly argues that the verse is not a later addition to the parable. New life and recovery of the lost are what results from repentance. The father explains the significance of what has happened, and the celebration begins.

---

25. So the passive εὐφραίνω (to rejoice); BAGD 327 §2; BAA 663 §2; Luke 12:19; 16:19; Acts 2:26; 7:41; Rom. 15:10; Gal. 4:27. Used in other passages for eschatological joy, here its meaning is more mundane. The participle φαγόντες (eating) functions like a second verb (BDF §420.3; Marshall 1978: 611): "Let us eat and rejoice."

b. The Elder Son's Protest (15:25–32)
i. The Elder Son's Anger (15:25–28a)

15:25 Attention now turns to the elder brother's response, who from this point on dominates the story with the father. Apparently a son who always did his duty, he had been laboring in the field during his brother's return. The party was going on when he returned. As the elder brother approaches the house he hears the revelry of music and dancing (Klostermann 1929: 160 and Plummer 1896: 377 note Latin parallels to this combination). The *hapax legomenon* συμφωνία (*symphōnia*) refers to band music and perhaps singing (BAGD 781; BAA 1559; Dan. 3:5 [LXX/Theodotion]; 3:7, 10, 15 [Theodotion]). Flute players probably supply the music, but the term does not refer to a single instrument (G. Moore 1905). The *hapax legomenon* χορός (*choros*) refers to dancing (BAGD 883; BAA 1762; Exod. 15:20; 32:19; Judg. 11:34). Something is happening, but the elder brother does not know the cause of the celebration.

15:26 The brother certainly would be curious about a celebration that he does not know about. He has no idea what has brought the party about. So he calls one of the servants to inquire about the cause of the festive atmosphere. It is possible that this is a young servant (Grundmann 1963: 314 and Fitzmyer 1985: 1090) or a special servant (BAGD 604 §1aγ and BAA 1224 §1aγ), since παῖς (*pais*) is used, not δοῦλος (*doulos*, slave). The imperfect ἐπυνθάνετο (*epynthaneto*, he was inquiring) suggests a process of inquiry (BAGD 729; BAA 1459; contrast the aorists in 15:25). The brother is intently interested in what is happening, a natural response given the surprising situation.[26]

15:27 The servant explains the reason for the party: the father has killed the calf because the younger brother has returned healthy.[27] The verse provides a second explanation for the father's joy, reinforcing the reason given in 15:24. The safe return of a healthy son was a time for celebration, and the father has taken him back with joy. The matter of factness of the request suggests how natural the response is.

15:28a The elder brother is not pleased with the festivities. In fact, he is angered. As the next verse makes clear, he regards his father's action as a sign of favoritism, especially in light of his own faithfulness to his father. Perhaps this son fears a further paring away of

---

26. The optative εἴη introduces an indirect question; BDF §299.1, §386.1. In effect, he is asking, "What is going on?"

27. Ὅτι is used twice, first in indirect discourse ("that") and then causal ("because"); Plummer 1896: 377. Ὑγιαίνω refers to physical well-being: the younger son returned "safe and sound"; BAGD 832; BAA 1660.

his estate. The parable's literary use of space is interesting and ironic: the brother stays outside the house and cannot bring himself to go in and celebrate his brother's return. The apparent insider is an outsider.

ii. The Elder Son's Protest (15:28b–30)

15:28b The father again takes the initiative, coming out and pleading with the son to join the celebration. Reconciliation with the father should extend across the whole family. Παρεκάλει (*parekalei*, was entreating) indicates a repeated effort to persuade the elder son, not a single request (Jeremias 1963a: 130). Perhaps the brother did not realize that the son had returned in humility. Quite a discussion ensues, as the following verses show. The elder son is unmoved by his brother's safe return. He focuses on himself in opposition to his brother. He demands justice, making comparisons with his father's treatment of him. The father's joy contrasts with the elder brother's anger. It is all a matter of perspective.

15:29 The elder brother explains his position, reflecting the parable's deep irony, which works at two levels and allows the parable to be called a "parable of reversal" (Crossan 1973: 73–75). First, as already noted, the son who was lost and outside is now inside, while the "inside" elder brother complains from outside. In addition, the son who was faithful and obedient—even to the point of working like a slave (δουλεύω, *douleuō*)!—has no reward or celebration, while the son who wandered and squandered is given a huge celebration. What the younger son felt fortunate to become (a mere servant) the older brother resents. The complaint is like Matt. 20:11 (Nolland 1993a: 787). In effect, the older son demands, "Where is justice?"

Numerous efforts criticize the son's complaint and draw comparisons to the historical situation that Jesus addressed. Some see evidence of the Pharisee's attitude in the idea of keeping all the law, which is seen as proof that the Pharisees are pictured in the elder son (Plummer 1896: 378; Fitzmyer 1985: 1091; cf. Luke 18:11–12, 21; Phil. 3:6). But it is hardly clear that such a detailed claim is intended, given the absence of any rebuke from the father (so correctly, Klostermann 1929: 160 and Linnemann 1966: 79; but see Merkel 1967–68). Nevertheless, the self-righteous, inward focus displayed here is probably intended as a rebuke. The reference is to anyone who disdains repentance, including especially the Pharisees and scribes (Luke 15:2). The brother is seen only in relationship to the father's treatment of him. However, it does not seem that all the details should be pressed. The father does not condemn or reject the elder son. This son has the same access to the father as his brother does. The imagery does not suggest a necessary estrangement with the leadership or others who do not include sinners (correctly C. A. Evans 1990: 235, who notes that there is no anti-Semitism here).

The elder brother's concern for justice is natural. But the point is that God's action is gracious, not deserved. Repentance yields God's kindness, which wipes the slate clean and is a reason to rejoice. A proper response is not to compare how you are treated in relationship to the penitent, but to remember that repentance yields the same gracious fruit for all, so it is just. Repentance also represents a new direction in life, and one might share in the joy of a changed direction. The brother is so consumed by the issue of fairness that he cannot rejoice at the beneficial transformation that has come to his brother.

The brother's anger emerges clearly as he complains directly and publicly to the father. He contrasts his own faithfulness with the supposed lack of generosity of his father. He does not formally address his father, thus indicating his anger, but immediately launches his attack by declaring his faithfulness in terms that portray himself as a slave: he "served" and obeyed "every command." But the elder's refusal to serve as host and welcome his brother is an insult to the father in this patriarchal culture. Irony abounds: the "obedient" son is disobedient here, and the gracious father is made to look unfaithful and unfair.

The son's rebuke is expressed in strong terms, for not only does he complain about the lack of generosity toward him but he also notes that not even a goat (ἔριφος, *eriphos*; BAGD 309; BAA 627)—an animal worth very little—was made available, much less a special fattened calf (in our culture, it would be the difference between a fast-food hamburger and a four-course meal). The "faithful" son's feelings are hurt, and the father's integrity and evenhandedness are called into question. He separates himself from his sibling entirely and faults his father for being so kind to the reprobate family member (Talbert 1982: 151 notes that the attitude of the elder son indicates that he has become a covert sinner).

15:30 The complaint continues. The elder son now turns from the father's lack of support for him to his gracious treatment of his brother. His anger is clearly apparent, as he will not even acknowledge his relationship to his brother: he calls him "your son" and "this one."[28] He contrasts the son's activity and the father's response in an unfavorable light. Describing the lifestyle of the brother in most unflattering terms, he charges him with devouring the father's earnings with im-

---

28. Οὗτος (this one) represents contempt in Matt. 20:12; Luke 18:11; Acts 17:18; Jeremias 1963a: 131; BDF §290.6. It will reappear in Luke 23 as the characters discuss and rebuke Jesus (23:2, 35).

morality, namely harlots, a change echoing Prov. 29:3. Plummer (1896: 378) suggests the elder is contrasting the brother's illicit company with the elder's more suitable friends mentioned in 15:29. Given the younger brother's move to a distant land, how did the older know what his brother did when he was away? Had they heard about his behavior and subsequent plight through some grapevine? Is the elder brother engaging in purely hostile speculation? Does he simply know his brother so well that he can guess what had happened to him? None of these questions are directly answered in the narrative, but the elder's attitude is clear: his brother is the rebellious son of Deut. 21:18–21 who should be disowned, not honored. How can his father give such a celebration, including a precious fattened calf, for such a despicable character? In effect, the brother is complaining that immorality holds more merit with the father than faithfulness. Where is justice? If ever a complaint should put one on the defensive, it is this one.

iii. The Father's Explanation: Rejoice at Repentance (15:31–32)

The father has a ready reply. He speaks to the son's concerns first **15:31** and then to the issue of the brother in 15:32. The father's reply is as gentle as the son's complaint was harsh. He addresses his son tenderly with τέκνον (*teknon*, child), a vocative that could easily be rendered "my child" in our idiom (Jeremias 1963a: 131; Matt. 21:28; Mark 10:24; Luke 2:48; 16:25).[29] He affirms the faithfulness of the elder brother and his special place in his heart. He accepts that this son has always been at his side. He reminds the son that all he owns belongs to him; neither the father's activity nor the brother's return in any way diminishes the elder's status. The double use of πᾶς-related terms emphasizes that just as the elder son is "always" with the father, so too he has "all." In fact, πάντοτε (*pantote*, always) here stands in contrast to the elder's οὐδέποτε (*oudepote*, never) in 15:29 and corrects the charge that the father is unfair (Marshall 1978: 612). The elder should not lose sight of the benefits he has always had because of his access to the father (Gutbrod, *TDNT* 4:1060). In a sense, he has always had access to the celebration. The animals are his!

The second issue is the brother. The father will not allow the son's **15:32** complaint to stand nor will he allow the elder to separate himself from his brother. So the father speaks of the younger brother as ὁ ἀδελφός σου οὗτος (*ho adelphos sou houtos*, this brother of yours). In other words, "He is not just my son—he is your brother!" The father

---

29. Fitzmyer 1985: 1091 notes this idiom in wider Greek usage as well.

affirms the necessity of celebration, not just its appropriateness, by the use of ἔδει (*edei*). It was morally right to rejoice, given the circumstances of the return. A resurrection of sorts has occurred. A dead brother is now alive. That which was lost has been found. Such circumstances should result in joy, not questions about fairness. The father's reply matches his remark in 15:24. Justice means that acceptance should greet such a turnaround. Jesus' listeners are left with an implied question: what will the elder son do now?

Summary   Jesus teaches two major truths in this parable. First, an absolute reversal results from repentance, in that not only is the repentant one restored, but also welcomed by the heavenly Father with joy and total acceptance. The Father receives such a one with open arms and offers his home. Great celebration erupts when a sinner comes to the Father to enter into his care (5:32). Second, there is a call to respond to the repentant one, not with comparison or jealousy, but with joy that reflects the Father's response. If God can be gracious and forgiving, so can people.

The story leaves us hanging, for we are not told what the elder son does (Marshall 1978: 613; Talbert 1982: 151). The parable is left so that Luke's readers may reflect on the proper response. Would they, if they were in the brother's shoes, go inside? Will they share in the joy? Will they join in the opportunity to help the lost find God? Will they join the Father or stay outside? Will they learn from and imitate the father? Grumblers and readers are now faced with a moral choice, and mere spectating is no longer possible. One must choose how to respond to Jesus' challenge to seek out sinners.

The parable of the forgiving father and his two sons is one of the most illustrative of Jesus' stories. It truly is a "parable of reversal," which pictures the beautiful transformation that comes with humble repentance before God. The picture of the Father is particularly instructive. He is running to the one with arms outstretched, ready to hug the returning child, and rejoice in the return. He dispenses gifts richly to those who turn, welcoming them into the family. No matter how destitute the circumstances under which one turns, the Father is there to receive the child back. Such is the joy in heaven over one who repents.

This detailed parable complements the two earlier parables of Luke 15 and adds one additional lesson: the response of those who see the Father's gracious generosity is also to be joy. They are not to act like the elder brother. They are to share in the mission and the joy. It is the hope of restoring the lost and leading people back to the joy of the Father that causes Jesus to receive sinners and dine with tax collectors (15:2). What is lost must be pursued until it is found. People should not grumble about Jesus' or his followers' associations. They should realize that God calls on disciples to encourage the "rejected" to be accepted by God. Part of that call means associating with sinners, not by sharing in unrighteous activities, but by having a relationship with them that is available and approachable. The gospel is not to be hoarded by the righteous, but is to involve them in reclaiming the lost for God. After all, how did those who share the benefits of the gospel come to share in it, except by receiving the same generosity they should now offer to others? God's love for his community requires that his love for people be displayed by those who claim to know him (Jeremias 1963a: 132). Those who grumble should be criticized, for they refuse to display God's concern. The prodigal reminds disciples that God calls them to seek the lost (19:10) and to rejoice when the search is successful. As the Father is gracious, so it should be with his offspring.

Additional Notes

15:16. The variant γεμίσαι τὴν κοιλίαν αὐτοῦ, an idiom meaning "to fill the stomach" (Behm, *TDNT* 3:787), is accepted as original by some, since the syntax is awkward (Grundmann 1963: 312; Marshall 1978: 609). Supported by A, Θ, Ψ, Byz, Lect, and most Itala, it may be original. The UBS–NA text is supported by $\mathfrak{P}^{75}$, ℵ, B, D, L, family 1, and family 13—an impressive alliance of Alexandrian and Western texts. Apparently, the food was saved only for the animals, or the son was too disgusted to eat it (Fitzmyer 1985: 1088 prefers the latter).

15:21. A longer reading completes the son's remark with a request to be made a slave (ℵ, B, D, 33). In favor of the shorter text is that it does not look like harmonization with 15:19 and it has wide manuscript distribution: $\mathfrak{P}^{75}$, A, L, W, Δ, Θ, Ψ, family 1, family 13, Byz, Lect, most Itala, most Syriac, and Vulgate.

15:29. Some manuscripts ($\mathfrak{P}^{75}$, B) read ἐρίφιον (baby goat), but the evidence is not sufficient for it to be the original reading.

H. Generosity: Handling Money and Possessions (16:1–31)

From the sinner, Luke turns to another issue of discipleship: possessions. The section contains three units. It starts with the parable of the unjust steward and the subsequent exhortations about handling money generously and faithfully (16:1–13). Then a short unit rebukes the Pharisees, sets forth the values of the new era, and declares the entrance of a new time (16:14–18). Finally, the parable of the rich man and Lazarus shows that God cares not only about how resources are used but also about how the poor are treated (16:19–31). In sum, one is to handle possessions generously and faithfully, expressing concern through the use of one's resources.

　　Though other issues receive mention, the chapter is dominated by the two parables. Luke 16:1–13 is a positive exhortation to be generous with money and possessions, while 16:19–31 is a negative example, seen in the rich man's lack of response. The latter passage also warns about what such treatment yields. The short unit between the parables is also important, for it rebukes the Pharisees as "lovers of money" and declares God's coming judgment of the heart, a judgment that 16:19–31 illustrates. Included in this middle unit is a declaration of the current period as a time of fulfillment. Association with the eschaton has ethical, worldview, and lifestyle implications—even down to the use of personal resources.

1. Parable of the Crafty Steward (16:1–13)

The parable of the "unjust steward" is one of the most difficult of Jesus' parables to understand.[1] The story centers on a steward who is fired but has the temerity to forgive at least some of the debt owed his master. This is followed by an exhortation grounded in the steward's use of money, contrasting the children of this age and the children of light—the reason and point of which are not immediately clear. Particularly troubling to interpreters has been the master's praise of his steward in 16:8a. It seems as if the master has lost money and yet praises the steward's crooked action. The details of the thrust of the parable and how its argument works are much debated (see the additional note).

Regardless of the view taken, the chapter is not intended merely as an explicit criticism of the Pharisees, since the parable is addressed to disciples (Luke 16:1; Manson 1949: 291; Austin 1985). It is also an exhortation to the disciples not to be like the Pharisees in the way they handle money (Luke 16:14). Do not use money for self, but use it generously for others. The Pharisees are frequently a negative example in Luke's central section (12:1; 14:7–14; 18:9–14). The criticism links nicely to the critique of the Pharisees' attitude toward sinners and tax collectors in Luke 15. The parable that closes Luke 16 also elaborates on this passage with its negative picture of the rich man's handling of his wealth (on this connection, see Ireland 1992: 196). So Luke 15–16 together shows that the righteousness that Jesus calls for is altogether different than the values that the Pharisees tend to display about sinners and money. An absence of concern about social status is implied in all of this teaching (on the links between Luke 15 and Luke 16, see Bailey 1976: 109). Luke seems responsible for bringing these parables so closely together (Nolland 1993a: 796).

Finally, several additional exhortations conclude the parable, each making a slightly different point: (1) be generous (16:9);

---

1. Marshall 1978: 614–17 has an excellent overview of the difficult issues in this parable. For a historical survey of the parable's interpretation, see Krämer 1972; Ireland 1992: 5–47; and Ireland 1989.

(2) be faithful even in small things, whether small things tied to money or any area where one is a steward for another (16:10–12); and (3) serve God first, for one cannot serve God and mammon (16:13). Were all of these points tied to the original parable or did Luke topically arrange 16:10–13? Regardless, they work together to make the point that one serves a master no matter what, so make sure that it is God. Serving God means that the disciple will be filled with generosity and faithfulness.

Sources and Historicity

The parable and its application are part of Luke's special material (Aland 1985: §§222–23). It is difficult to reach a conclusion about the source and setting of the concluding exhortations because only Luke 16:13 has any verbal parallel (Aland 1985: §224).[2] Luke 16:10–12 has thematic parallels in the parables of Matt. 25:21–30 = Luke 19:17–27, but the ideas expressed here are unique. Only if we assume that a parable can have only one point can we conclude that Luke 16:9–13 must necessarily be merely a compilation of thematically related sayings and not part of the parable's original application. The main reason some see a later addition is because the master's praise for his apparently dishonest steward seems to conflict with the exhortations to faithful stewardship that follow in 16:9–13 (Creed 1930: 201–3). But if Derrett's view is correct (see below), the problem disappears, since then the master would not have lost any of his own money.

That the subsequent sayings seem to offer conceptually divergent applications linked only loosely by common vocabulary (ἀδικία in 16:8–9 and ἄδικος in 16:10–11; μαμωνᾶς in 16:9, 11, 13; πιστός in 16:10 and πιστεύω in 16:11; δέχομαι in 16:4, 9; and φρονίμως in 16:8a and φρόνιμος in 16:8b) is another reason that many see a compilation here.[3] But the technique of word linkage is so common in Jewish exposition that anyone familiar with it could use it, including Jesus. The use of a variety of applications is also likely for a speaker of Jesus' depth. The ethical thrust of the sayings fits Jesus' emphases nicely, as does his playing down of wealth and his warnings about excessive attachment to it. Usually suspected of indicating a compilation is 16:9, which is argued to have a different point from the par-

---

2. Luke 16:13 is exactly parallel to Matt. 6:24, except Luke has an additional word: οἰκέτης (servant). A different version is found in the Gospel of Thomas 47.

3. So, e.g., Jeremias 1963a: 45–48. Marshall 1978: 622–23 notes that even if, as he believes, this is a compilation, the teaching still comes from traditional material. Since he defends the authenticity of 16:13, this seems to imply the authenticity of the whole of 16:9–13. Pilgrim 1981: 127, however, alludes to the work of a Christian preacher or teacher. Talbert 1982: 153 is probably incorrect to call 16:8b an initial interpretation of the parable, since it is really an observation that produces an application only by implication. The phrase *but I say to you* in 16:9 is the start of the parable's formal application and is not a Lucan expression (Jeremias 1980: 106).

able, conflicting especially with 16:8b. But 16:9 is not a different application, only a more specific one related to the disciple and money. Once this topic comes forward, the additional remarks fit in well (see the exegesis of 16:9). The case for a topical compilation is circumstantial. Though possible, it is not necessary.[4] It is just as possible that Jesus spoke all these sayings in this original setting.

The parable is usually regarded as originating from Jesus (Nolland 1993a: 796), even by the more skeptical critics, since the early church is not likely to have created such a difficult parable, and the linkage between the parable and what follows in 16:9–13 is on the surface conceptually indirect. On the basis of the parable's internal difficulty, the Jesus Seminar (Funk and Hoover 1993: 357–59) gives 16:1–8a one of its few authentic ratings, attributing the wording directly to Jesus (red type). Some question the parable's authenticity; for example, Goulder (1989: 618–21) implausibly argues for a Lucan rewriting of two vineyard parables from Matt. 21:28–32 and 20:1–16. The surprising twist in the account is actually very much like Jesus and speaks for authenticity.

More debated are the comments after the parable. The Jesus Seminar rates the rest of the unit much more skeptically: 16:8b–12 is printed in black type and 16:13 in pink type. The seminar views 16:8b–12 as a later attempt to soften the parable, but is uncertain whether these verses originate in the tradition or with Luke. The seminar accepts 16:13 as rooted in Jesus because the two-masters theme is multiply attested (Matt. 6:24; Gospel of Thomas 47) and is put in an orally memorable form. Nolland (1993a: 805) argues that 16:9 is a Lucan link and that the roots of 16:10–12 are uncertain. The prospect of a wordplay with Semitic מָמוֹן (*māmôn*) (Nolland 1993a: 805–6) speaks for a possible early origin of 16:10–12. The enigmatic character of 16:9 is similar to the argument for the parable's authenticity in 16:1–8 and so might suggest its originality as well. The twist of juxtaposing "making friends" with "unrighteous mammon" sounds like the provocative and prophetic Jesus. The comment of 16:8b is simply an explanatory remark necessary to make the original point of the parable clear. Without it the parable would be unintelligible. The thematic unity of these sayings makes their circulation possible and memorable (Bailey 1976: 110–18). Whether Luke placed 16:9–13 here or whether it was originally associated with the parable is not certain, but since the teaching coheres well with Jesus' its authenticity is defensible. Blomberg (1990: 245) makes a good case for linkage between the applicational points and the parable's characters, increasing the possibility of an original linkage here.

In form, the passage is a parable with an extended application composed of a series of wisdom sayings (Fitzmyer 1985: 1095,

---

4. On the debate in older commentaries, see Creed 1930: 202–3, who holds that 16:9–13 was added later. Blomberg 1990: 245–47 builds a case for unity.

1106; Bultmann 1963: 75–77; Berger 1984: 51–56, 64–65 [speaks of parables and sentences). The outline of Luke 16:1–13 is as follows:

a. The parable proper (16:1–8)
  i. Setting (16:1)
  ii. The steward's firing (16:2)
  iii. The steward's response: lessening others' debts (16:3–7)
  iv. The master's commendation and Jesus' observation (16:8)
b. Three additional implications of the parable (16:9–13)
  i. Be generous with money (16:9)
  ii. Be faithful with money and in stewardship (16:10–12)
  iii. Serve God, not mammon (16:13)

The major theme of the pericope is stewardship. In light of the end and one's status as a child of God, look to the future with foresight. Use money generously and for the benefit of others. It is better to be generous with money and enter heaven than to hoard it selfishly and fail to enter. Faithfulness starts in little things. One cannot serve both God and money, so let primary devotion go to God. He is the one we must serve, and he will evaluate and reward our stewardship.

Exegesis and Exposition

[1]And he was speaking to his disciples, "There was a certain rich man who had a steward, and a report was brought to him, how the steward was wasting his goods. [2]And he called him and said to him, 'What is this I hear about you? Turn in the account of your stewardship, for you are no longer able to be a steward.' [3]The steward said to himself, 'What shall I do? My master is taking my stewardship from me. I am not able to dig; I am ashamed to beg. [4]I know what I will do, so that when I am removed from my stewardship people will receive me into their homes.' [5]And summoning each one of his master's debtors, one by one, he said to the first, 'How much do you owe?' [6]He said, 'One hundred measures of oil.' And he [the steward] said to him, 'Take your bill and sit down quickly and write fifty.' [7]Then to another he [the steward] said, 'What do you owe?' And he said, 'One hundred measures of wheat.' He [the steward] said to him, 'Take your bill and write eighty.' [8]The master commended the unrighteous steward because he had acted shrewdly; ⌜for⌝ the sons of this age are more shrewd in dealing with their own generation than are the sons of light.

[9]"I say to you, make friends for yourselves by means of unrighteous mammon, so that when it fails they may receive you into the eternal dwellings. [10]The one who is faithful in little is also faithful in much, and the one who is unfaithful in little is also unfaithful in much. [11]If then you are not faithful with

unrighteous mammon, who will entrust to you true riches? [12]And if you have not been faithful in that which is another's, who will give you that which is your own? [13]No servant is able to serve two masters; for either he will hate one and love the other, or he will be devoted to one and despise the other. You are not able to serve God and mammon."

a. The Parable Proper (16:1–8)
i. Setting (16:1)

There is a shift of audience in this pericope, though whether the oc- **16:1**
casion shifts as well is not clear. Ἔλεγεν δὲ καί (*elegen de kai*, and he
was saying) does not give a clear indication as to when Jesus taught
this parable. This phrase can suggest a conceptual relationship to
what precedes (5:36; 9:23; 10:2; 14:12), but not necessarily a temporal connection (12:54; 13:6; 14:7; 18:1). Jesus is now teaching his
disciples by telling them another parable. There are two main figures: a wealthy man and his steward (οἰκονόμος, *oikonomos*) who is
responsible for the administration of the estate (BAGD 560 §1a; BAA
1135 §1a; Michel, *TDNT* 5:149–50).[5] The steward may have been a
slave who grew up in the house and was trained for this role (Gen.
15:3; 14:14; Fitzmyer 1985: 1099). Luce (1933: 259) regards him as
a slave or freeman having a higher station than the figure of Luke
12:42, who is a short-term appointee, since this estate manager (a)
is "let go," (b) finds himself on his own, and (c) is unable to work
manually (so also Manson 1949: 291). Regardless, the wealthy man
may not live at the estate the administrator manages (Jeremias
1963a: 181; Matt. 25:14). That the steward kept careful records
(16:2) suggests this higher appointed station. Reports are coming in
to the owner about the steward, and they are not positive. In this
passage, διαβάλλω (*diaballō*) means "to bring charges with hostile
intent" (BAGD 181; BAA 363).[6] According to these reports, the steward is incompetent. He is wasting the owner's possessions. Διασκορπίζω (*diaskorpizō*) here means "to disperse resources" (BAGD 188;
BAA 378; Michel, *TDNT* 7:422; cf. Luke 1:51; Acts 5:37; esp. Luke
15:13). Clearly, it is in the owner's best interest to act.

ii. The Steward's Firing (16:2)

The master asks about the complaints in a way that suggests that he **16:2**
believes the charges: "What is this I hear?" (τί τοῦτο ἀκούω, *ti touto*

---

5. The second parable of this chapter also centers around a rich man (16:19). In
Rome, the steward was called a *dispensator, vilicus*, or *procurator*, though the latter
title usually was reserved for a more comprehensive role; Derrett 1970: 52–55.

6. Such charges tied to this verb can be false (e.g., 4 Macc. 4:1) or true (2 Macc.
3:11; Dan. 3:8), but the point in raising them is to discredit the one described. Ὡς
(how or that) introduces the content of the complaint.

akouō, suggests that the charge is believed; Gen. 12:18; 20:9; 42:28; esp. Acts 14:15; BDF §299.1; Fitzmyer 1985: 1100; Marshall 1978: 617). He also asks for an inventory (λόγος, *logos*; BAGD 478 §2a; BAA 971 §2a; Matt. 12:36; Acts 19:40; Heb. 13:17; 1 Pet. 4:5) of the servant's stewardship so he can verify the charges. The master does not seem to anticipate that the records will exonerate but confirm the charges, since he dismisses the steward. Interestingly, the request for the prepared inventory implies that the steward kept good records of his activity. Thus the problem may involve monetary mismanagement more than outright immorality. He is no longer to function as a steward (οὐ δύνῃ [*ou dynē*] is equivalent to οὐ δύνασαι [*ou dynasai*, you are not able]; BDF §93). The steward has only to wrap up his affairs and those of the estate. After that, he is on the streets. Once he is dismissed, he can only hope to find somewhere else to work. The steward's failure to reply may indicate that he knew he was guilty.

iii. The Steward's Response: Lessening Others' Debts (16:3–7)

16:3 The parable uses soliloquy, introduced by content ὅτι (*hoti*, that), to portray the steward's dilemma (Mark 12:6 = Luke 20:13; 12:17; 15:17–19; Klostermann 1929: 162). The steward knows that his job is gone and that his options are not appealing. He is unwilling to do any digging, the toughest form of manual labor (the expression *I am not able* is idiomatic of people who do not like their prospects). Digging (σκάπτω, *skaptō*) is the labor of the uneducated (BAGD 753; BAA 1505; elsewhere in the NT only at 6:48; 13:8; Aristophanes, *Birds* 1432). He had a white-collar job and does not feel capable of returning to menial labor (in Judaism such labor was less honorable; Sir. 38:24–32; Plummer 1896: 383; Schweizer 1984: 254). But the remaining option is to beg (ἐπαιτέω, *epaiteō*), which would be even more shameful for one who was used to doing the bidding of a wealthy person (Sir. 29:24; 40:28; BAGD 282; BAA 571; elsewhere in the NT only at Luke 18:35). The steward needs to devise a solution that will leave him with the possibility of finding work from sympathetic business associates. He must act to clean up the situation as much as possible, or else his future will be full of pain (Marshall 1978: 618).

16:4 The steward devises a plan in light of his impending unemployment,[7] designed to create a favorable response from those who owe money, so that (ἵνα, *hina*) when he is let go they will take him in. Μεθίστημι

---

7. Ἔγνων is a dramatic use of the aorist: "I have determined what I will do," which might be idiomatically rendered, "I've got it!" (Kistemaker 1980: 230–31; Burton 1900: §45; Zerwick 1963: §258). The asyndeton in the verse suggests that the idea came to him suddenly; Plummer 1896: 383.

(*methistēmi*) can have the force of "being deposed" (BAGD 499 §1; BAA 1011 §2; Acts 13:22 uses the term of God's removal of King Saul; also 1 Clem. 44.5). In this context, it means to be summarily fired. The steward's fate with the master is sealed, so he seeks to improve his status with others. The third-person plural δέξωνται (*dexōntai*, they will receive) looks ahead to the debtors mentioned in 16:5. The steward hopes that they will take him into their care or employment.[8] The steward's plan recognizes what his future entails, so he prepares himself for the difficulties of unemployment. He acts in a way appropriate to a steward wrapping up his affairs. He recognizes that his long-term interests lie outside his current home and job.

The steward systematically goes through the inventory of bills, one **16:5** debtor at a time. Each debtor is asked to declare his debt, and the steward determines how much to lessen the debt. By having the debtors declare how much they owe, they will better appreciate the reduction they receive. In fact, the question is unnecessary except for psychological value, since stewards would normally have a record of what was owed.[9] As 16:6–7 shows, the debt was agricultural, indicating that the master either sold food or lent money in exchange for commodities or rented out land and was paid in produce.[10] There are three explanations for the steward's alteration of the debt.

1. The steward wielded his authority as steward and simply lowered the price, an act that either undercut his boss or finally rectified the financial situation.[11] If so, this act might have been a strike at the owner, since it would make him look like

8. A wordplay is set up with 16:9 by the mention of reception into homes here, since the same form (δέξωνται) there refers to reception into heavenly habitations.

9. Fitzmyer 1985: 1100 says that the question serves to advance the story, but it does more than that because of the question's psychological value. Marshall 1978: 618 notes that the typical procedure was for the debtor to write a promissory note that the steward would keep until the debt was paid; cf. Philem. 18.

10. Luce 1933: 260 suggests that rent is unlikely since that would be a fixed rate; but if a fraction of anticipated yield was the payment, this figure could also vary. Jeremias 1963a: 181 notes that either situation is possible.

11. This was the most popular position until recently, though it is making something of a comeback (e.g., Blomberg 1990: 244–45; Blomberg 1994; Ireland 1992: 73–82). Plummer 1896: 383 holds a quite plausible variation of this view, arguing that the steward simply lessened the excess cut he took from the debtors, a view close to the "righteous" cut option (no. 3 below), except it suggests that the steward did take something additional. The inflationary trend may suggest that the debtors knew that not all of the money was getting to the owner. Jeremias 1963a: 181 speaks of the steward covering up his previous embezzlements by the new accounting, a view that requires that the master does not have proof for his firing the steward in 16:1–2. Such an internal inconsistency in the parable is unlikely.

the "bad guy" in the pricing, which the steward was cleverly fixing before his firing.

2. He removed the interest charge from the debt in accordance with the Mosaic law (Exod. 22:25 [22:24 MT]; Lev. 25:35–37; Deut. 15:7–8; 23:19–20 [23:20–21 MT]; Derrett 1970: 56–63, esp. 56–57). This would benefit not only himself in his future job search but also bring his master in line with the law. The differing rate of reduction (the first bill is halved, the second is reduced by 20 percent) is a problem for this view, unless different materials drew different interest rates, a point that Derrett (1970: 66, 69) acknowledges, arguing that oil was charged at 80 percent.

3. The steward removed his own commission, sacrificing his own money, not that of his master.[12] The differing rate or reduction is less of a problem for this view, since the commission, instead of being fixed, might fluctuate depending on the material.

It is not entirely clear which view is correct, though Derrett (1970: 65–72) collects much evidence in the Jewish setting for the view that the steward removed interest from the bills. The clear motive was to create broad appreciation for the steward so that he would be treated with sympathy upon his release. Either of the final two approaches is slightly more likely than seeing a strictly dishonest steward, though a decision for view 3 and full discussion await the additional note on 16:8. However, it must be noted that Plummer's variation (see n. 11) on the traditional view—that the steward takes a commission plus an excess cut—is quite possible. Regardless of which view is taken, the point of the steward's action is to lessen the debtor's burden and to create future goodwill toward him upon his release into the labor market.

16:6 The time to discount has come. It is debated whether the debtors are tenant farmers on the master's land or outside business people. They are probably outsiders, since the amounts owed show that the debtors are wealthier than tenant farmers would be, and they would have to be wealthy enough to hire the steward after his dismissal. But the decision makes no difference to the parable's point. In fact, it may be that the master's books included both types of debtors.

The first of two representative debtors owes 100 measures of oil, a significant debt. The standard liquid measure, a bath (ὁ βάτος, *ho batos*), was equal to 8.75 gallons or 33.1 liters (BAGD 137; BAA 275). One hundred baths would therefore be about 875 gallons, the yield

---

12. Fitzmyer 1985: 1101 argues that no debt cancellation occurred, only a rewriting of the old debt that removed the steward's commission—something he had the right to do.

of nearly 150 olive trees (Klostermann 1929: 163; Plummer 1896: 383; SB 2:218).[13] (The measuring standard is Jewish, and Luke does not convert the measures for his audience, a detail that reveals the parable's Jewish origins and suggests its authenticity.) This much oil would be priced at around one thousand denarii. At the rate of one denarius per one day's work for the average day laborer (see the exegesis of 7:41), this debt is the equivalent of over three years' salary. This debtor was clearly not the average laborer, since he was allowed to run up such a large debt. The steward tells the debtor to act quickly and reduce the payment on his note by half—to fifty measures.[14] The note is written with the debtor's hand, so that the transaction will look original. One can only imagine the relief and appreciation that this sudden deflationary trend produced.

The discount program continues. The second debtor owed 100 measures of wheat. One cor (κόρος, *koros*; BAGD 444–45; BAA 903) was equal to 10 ephahs or 30 seahs, or in modern terms about 10–12 bushels or nearly 400 liters.[15] On Josephus's larger standard, 100 cors was around 1,100 bushels or 39,000 liters and represented the yield of about 100 acres of grain (Jeremias 1963a: 181; Manson 1949: 292). A cor cost about 25–30 denarii (*m. B. Meṣ.* 5.1; Manson 1949: 292). So the debt was between 2,500 denarii and 3,000 denarii—or about 8–10 years' salary for the average laborer. (On Josephus's smaller standard, the debt is equivalent to around one year's salary; either way, a large amount of grain is in view.) The steward reduces this bill by 20 percent, reflecting an interest rate of 25 percent (Fitzmyer 1985: 1101).[16] (Assuming a large scale for a cor, the reduction is about 500–

16:7

13. Jeremias 1963a: 181 notes that the average olive tree yields 120 kilos of olives or 25 liters of oil. Kistemaker 1980: 231 and Manson 1949: 291–92 put the number more precisely at 868 gallons or 3,946 liters, using the scale provided by Josephus, *Antiquities* 8.2.9 §57. Marshall 1978: 618–19 notes that ancient measuring jars found in archeological digs vary from 5 gallons to 10 gallons. Given this variation, precise numbers are difficult to determine, but the number is not as important as recognizing that this is a large debt.

14. Similarly high interest for items is found in ancient Egyptian documents; Derrett 1972b. The term τὰ γράμματα describes the promissory note; BAGD 165 §2a; BAA 330 §2b; Schrenk, *TDNT* 1:764–65; Fitzmyer 1985: 1100.

15. Measures in the ancient world varied somewhat, so an exact figure is uncertain; see Plummer 1896: 383 and Marshall 1978: 619. BAGD 445 places the measure of a cor at 393 liters or 10–12 bushels. Fitzmyer 1985: 1101 points out that Josephus defines κόρος variously: *Antiquities* 15.9.2 §314 says that it equals 10 *medimnoi*, while *Antiquities* 3.15.3 §321 says four-sevenths of a *medimnos*—a significant difference (a *medimnos* was an Attic measure that equaled about 1.5 bushels, a figure that seems very high and is thus questioned). Fitzmyer figures the amount on Josephus's smaller standard, which produces a debt of slightly more than 100 bushels, but he notes that the variation makes certainty difficult.

16. Twenty-five percent fits the ancient rate for grain; Derrett 1970: 66–68.

600 denarii.) The difference in the rate of reduction between oil and grain may reflect that oil was more precious than grain and thus received a higher commission.[17] We can assume that the steward instituted an array of other reductions like the ones illustrated by oil and grain, in anticipation that they would return the favor.

iv. The Master's Commendation and Jesus' Observation (16:8)

16:8 The complex and intertwined issues of 16:8a are discussed in the additional note, the conclusions of which are summarized here. Luke 16:8a closes the parable, while 16:8b gives a necessary explanation revealing the story's point. Thus, in 16:8a the parabolic master commends his recently shrewd, but formerly unrighteous, steward, while 16:8b gives Jesus' explanation of the point (note the shift from "his shrewdness" to "the sons . . . are more shrewd in dealing with their own generation"). The reference to the "dishonest" steward alludes back to the charges of 16:1. What 16:8 commends is the steward's acting "shrewdly" (φρονίμως, phronimōs), a term that appears only here in Luke–Acts (the noun occurs in Luke 12:42; 16:8). This is not a Lucan term, so it speaks against Luke's having created this verse or its comment (in contrast, Matthew uses the noun seven times: Matt. 7:24; 10:16; 24:45; 25:2, 4, 8, 9). Irony or sarcasm in this verse is excluded by the use of ἐπαινέω (epaineō, to praise), which is uniformly positive in the NT (Rom. 15:11; 1 Cor. 11:2, 17, 22 [twice]; so also the eleven uses of the noun [in 1 Cor. 11:17, 22b ἐπαινέω has to be negated with οὐκ for it to show a negative force]).

"Ὅτι (hoti, for) introduces Jesus' rationale for noting the master's reaction, thus pointing to the parable's lesson. Jesus is saying that the master's remark is right "because" of the principle of 16:8b. In the parable, a normally unrighteous man acts to his benefit. He has been shrewd. Jesus' remark is that those of the world ("the sons of this age") give more foresight to their future, they are more shrewd in their dealings with people than are God's children ("the sons of light").[18] God's children should be shrewd with possessions by being generous. Such acts show charity and foresight. The description of God's children as children of light is common in Judaism (1 Enoch 108.11; 1QS 1.9; 2.16; Klostermann 1929: 163; Marshall 1978: 621) and the church (John 12:36; Eph. 5:8; 1 Thess. 5:5). The Jewish id-

---

17. Ernst 1977: 464; Klostermann 1929: 163; and Creed 1930: 204 argue that the variation is only for literary value; but ancient parables were based on daily life, so the point may not be an either/or proposition. Derrett 1970: 66, 69 also defends a much higher charge for oil.

18. Εἰς (toward) looks to the treatment of the people of this generation; Plummer 1896: 384. The phrase οἱ υἱοὶ τοῦ αἰῶνος is found in the NT only here and in 20:34.

iom as evidenced in 1 Enoch and at Qumran is evidence for the parable's authenticity, since it indicates that such an expression was available to Jesus in a Palestinian context. In pointing to the children of this age, there is an inherent comparison with God's children as the children of "the age to come." Jesus is saying that God's children, who have a heavenly future, should be as diligent in assessing the long-term effect of their actions as those who do not know God are in protecting their earthly well-being (1 Cor. 15:58 is similar in tone, as are the other parables of the "prudent"). Christians should apply themselves to honor and serve God in their actions as much as secular people apply themselves to obtain protection and prosperity from money and the world. The point is not so much the means chosen to do this, though that is important, as it is the wisdom of having such a concern. In making this remark, the parable shifts from story to application. Additional applications follow.

b. Three Additional Implications of the Parable (16:9–13)
i. Be Generous with Money (16:9)

16:9 The applications get specific. Prudence is not the parable's only lesson. Jesus exhorts the disciples to be generous. That the connection between this verse and the parable is original finds support in the parallelism with 16:4 (ἵνα ὅταν [in order that when], δέξωνται [they may receive], and εἰς [into] with the accusative). In addition, most parables have an explicit application, which 16:9 supplies. Luke introduces the verse with the solemn καὶ ἐγὼ ὑμῖν λέγω (kai egō hymin legō, and I say to you) to stress the application's importance (15:7, 10; 18:8, 14; esp. 11:9). Μαμωνᾶς (mamōnas, mammon), an Aramaic term for wealth or possessions, is not to be hoarded and used selfishly but to make friends (BAGD 490; BAA 994; Hauck, TDNT 4:389–90; in the NT only three times in this pericope and Matt. 6:24 [= Luke 16:13]; 1QS 6.2; CD 14.20).[19] It is not just alms to the poor that is in view here, but the general use of one's money. The way to make friends from money is to be generous. Jesus parallels the disciple's situation with the parable. One should use money in such a way that one is received into eternal dwellings.[20]

---

19. The preposition ἐκ here means "by means of"; Fitzmyer 1985: 1109; Rüger 1973.

20. Σκηνή is the OT term used for "booths" and alludes to the picture of blessing that was tied to celebrating the exodus; Lev. 23:34. See also Mark 9:5; Rev. 7:15; 21:3; 1 Enoch 39.4; 2 Esdr. [= 4 Ezra] 2:11. On the eschatological use of σκηνή (booths or habitations), see Michaelis, TDNT 7:378–79. T. Schmidt 1987: 154–55 argues that the passage refers neither to alms nor to the generous use of money, but to a prudent person acting in a "critical impermanent situation with that which has been entrusted to him in order to gain lasting benefits." This may be the broad application if one had

Why is mammon called τῆς ἀδικίας (of unrighteousness)? Probably because the pursuit of it can make people selfish, cause them to take advantage of others, and cause them to be unfaithful to God (Manson 1949: 293; 1 Enoch 63.10; Sir. 27:2; SB 2:220; Marshall 1978: 621; Fitzmyer 1985: 1109).[21] Wealth, being so attached to the world, tends to produce "worldly" responses by keeping one's focus on this age and on self, not on the age to come and God.

The reference to "they may receive you" is (1) a reference to friends who receive the benefit and welcome the generous one into heaven, (2) a reference to angels who represent God, or (3) a circumlocution for God himself (6:38, 44; 12:20, 48; 14:35). God responds to disciples who love their neighbors with concrete action, even down to the use of money. Such disciples evidence an active walk with God that is a product of a faith commitment to him. The disciple is aware of heavenly reward and will respond appropriately. This yields a better way to take the remark than seeing the friends as the subject (so Arndt 1956: 357), since they could not provide eternal habitations. God will reward the person who is generous with money.[22]

Money ultimately fails, a point also made in OT wisdom literature and NT teaching elsewhere (Danker 1988: 281; Prov. 23:4–5; Luke 12:21).[23] Money can and does run out, so one had best be prepared for when it does.[24] Whether this refers to money becoming useless at death, as in 12:20, or to the exchange of temporal treasures for eternal heavenly treasure at Jesus' return cannot be decided and is ultimately irrelevant. The end, in either case, is the same. The idea is that money does not last. Rather than rely on it, one should put it to beneficial use. Use money in a way that pleases God and serves him.[25]

Zacchaeus (Luke 19:1–10) is a positive example of the application; the rich man (16:19–31) is the negative example (so also 18:18–

---

just this one verse, but the Lucan context suggests that using money generously is a central concern.

21. The exact phrase is unattested elsewhere, but at Qumran the phrases *wealth of evil* (CD 6.15) and *wealth of violence* (1QS 10.19) occur.

22. Leaney 1958: 223 prefers to see the verse as ironic and addressed to the Pharisees, but nothing in the context indicates irony or suggests that Pharisees are the most direct audience (though they are the negative, contrastive example). Leaney's view accepts the ironic interpretation of the parable discussed in the additional note on 16:1–13 (view 5).

23. Other texts on money are Matt. 6:19–21 = Luke 12:33–34; Mark 10:21; Luke 11:41; 19:8; and James 1:9–11. Another key text on the transience of wealth and the importance of generosity is 1 Tim. 6:6–10, 17–19. On the improper use of wealth, see James 5:1–6.

24. Ἐκλείπω (to fail) speaks of money failing in the sense of becoming useless; BAGD 242; BAA 488.

25. For a defense of the verse's appropriateness to this setting, see Marshall 1978: 622.

24). Jesus probably intended this remark for the wealthy among the disciples. A concern to be received by God into one's eternal habitation will influence how one looks at and uses money. To know God and to be generous is better than to know the greenback and risk spiritual bankruptcy. If we know that God watches our stewardship, we will be sensitive to use the resources God provides in ways that are pleasing to him.

ii. Be Faithful with Money and in Stewardship (16:10–12)

16:10 The attention shifts to a second application. Character is character whether one is dealing with little things or larger issues. If one is unfaithful in small things, one will handle large things in the same way.[26] If, however, one is faithful in small things, one will also handle large things in a similar way (cf. Luke 19:17 = Matt. 25:21, 23).[27] What one is, one is. The association of faithfulness and stewardship is natural (1 Cor. 4:2; Marshall 1978: 623). All of one's activities matter, for they reveal the nature of one's character. Whether the area of responsibility is big or little has no bearing from a moral standpoint. Selfishness in little things reveals one's character and can indicate how big areas will be handled. A specific illustration follows in 16:11.[28]

16:11 A specific example of faithfulness is the handling of money, unrighteous mammon (16:9; Marshall 1978: 623).[29] There are things greater than money, but if one cannot handle money, who is willing to let that one administer greater riches? The point here is that being faithful in a small thing like money demonstrates that one is ready to handle more important items, "the true things," which most see as the spiritual blessings of future service in the kingdom (Paul makes a similar comparison between earthly and spiritual resources in 1 Cor. 9:11). The one who commits such true future riches to people is God, and the reference pictures future reward for faithful ser-

26. Ἄδικος normally means "unjust" (BAGD 18; BAA 33); when opposite the term πιστός (faithful), it means "unfaithful." Ἐλάχιστος indicates faithfulness in the "smallest" thing. But the comparison is general; so the sense is "small," since the term is in parallelism to πολύς (much).

27. In Exod. Rab. 2.2 on 3:1, David and Moses are faithful in tending sheep, so God lets them rule the people. *Mekilta de Rabbi Ishmael*, tractate *Baḥodesh* 5.1–11 on Exod. 20:2 [= Lauterbach 1933–35: 2.229–30] makes a comparison between overt and secret acts. See also *m. ʾAbot* 3.7; Manson 1949: 293.

28. Luke 16:10–11 makes clear that dishonesty is not the only point, but also faithfulness at every level of stewardship (see also 16:12). Creed 1930: 205 may unduly limit the application to wealth only, a point that is explicit only in 16:11.

29. Either ἀδίκῳ μαμωνᾷ means "worldly wealth" or it is an exhortation to be a good steward of money gained dishonestly—an impossible sense. There is a pattern in these applications: stewardship (16:8b), money (16:9), stewardship (16:10), money (16:11), and stewardship and money (16:12–13).

vice (Luke 6:20–21, 38; 19:17; Plummer 1896: 386; Marshall 1978: 623). This is a better way to read the verse than to see a reference to wealth gained dishonestly, for surely Jesus would not be praising the use of money gained dishonestly. This is what would result if the phrase ἀδίκῳ μαμωνᾷ (16:11a) were taken to mean "wealth obtained dishonestly or unrighteously."[30]

16:12   Jesus' next example broadens the scope beyond money to caring for another's affairs (compare the structure of 16:12 to 16:11). If you cannot be faithful in caring for someone else's things, who will give you responsibility for your own things? If one cannot care for things when there is no risk to them, why give them things to care for that put them directly at risk? Most see a spiritual allusion in this verse. If one cannot care in this life for what God has given, how can one expect anything from God in the life to come (Plummer 1896: 386; Marshall 1978: 624; Matt. 25:34)? This earthly life is a God-given stewardship for which one is responsible. It is a preparation for life to come and in fact helps determine how much the person will possess in the age to come (1 Cor. 6:2; 2 Cor. 5:10). Given, the spiritual-physical contrast in the context, such a reading of the verse makes sense. The exhortation is be faithful now, so that one may be given greater responsibility in the life to come.

iii. Serve God, Not Mammon (16:13)

16:13   The last illustration is the most distant of the implications. Money is not and cannot be the ultimate priority. A steward cannot be faithful to two masters at once. There comes the moment when one must choose a priority: loving and being devoted to one, while hating and despising the other. Mammon here is personified and treated as if it could be an idolatrous threat to God (L. Johnson 1977: 158). The parallel structure equates the paired verbs *love* and *hate* with each other and produces a rhetorical contrast. The thing loved has priority over the thing hated. It is impossible to serve both God and mammon, for there are times when the pursuit of money will necessarily mean that God is slighted (Fitzmyer 1985: 1111; see 16:19–31 for an illustration). Or there will come a time when a choice for God will mean that the pursuit of money is slighted. There might even be a time when a choice for God is a choice not to have money or not quite so much money. In this context, money is a litmus test about greater issues and responsibilities, and it is clear that one should choose to serve God. Indeed, to be generous with money—as the basic parable advises—is a way to choose God over

---

30. Fitzmyer 1985: 1110 correctly notes that "true" (ἀληθινός) wealth has the force "what is really good"; BAGD 37 §3; BAA 72 §3b.

money. One can serve God by putting one's resources to use for others. The attitude of giving, sharing, and meeting of needs as exemplified in the Book of Acts (e.g., 2:44–45; 4:32–37) pictures such service through money (Talbert 1982: 155). It may well be that the relationship between money and service is why this final remark is present. One always serves something; it had better be God, not the things of the creation.

The saying is matched by Matt. 6:24, except that Luke speaks specifically of a steward, while Matthew speaks more generally of no one (οὐδείς, oudeis) being able to serve both God and money (see also the Gospel of Thomas 47). Of course, if life is a test of stewardship as 16:11–12 suggests, then there is no real difference in the two biblical forms of this saying, since all disciples are regarded as servants or stewards.

Summary

Luke 16:1–13 argues that life is a stewardship from God. This parable pictures the example of a man in dire straits who assesses what the future holds. By thinking ahead, he acts prudently to maximize his future interests. Jesus exhorts disciples to be prudent and use money generously, so that God will richly reward them in the life to come. He notes that people of this world are often wiser in preparing for future realities than are God's children. Jesus also notes that character is established in little things. What one does with little things is what one will do with larger concerns, so that if one is a poor steward of money or of other affairs in this life, how can one expect great things from God in the life to come? One needs to make a choice to serve God or money, for one cannot serve both. A choice to serve God is a choice to be generous with money. Divided loyalties are prohibited. A generous stewardship now will yield a rich reward later. The disciple, just like the dishonest steward, should look ahead. The disciple should consider what God can do and what he has done. The follower should use money not selfishly, but generously and faithfully, so that one may possess all the future riches God has for the disciple. Once again, Luke makes the options crystal clear.

Additional Notes

16:1–13. The original point of the parable is much discussed, as is the structure of its argumentation. Part of the debate turns on points of historical background:

1. The parable is about using money wisely in the face of imminent crisis and thus pictures God's coming in judgment (Jeremias 1963a: 47–48 sees this as a "crisis" parable).

2. The parable is about being prepared for the coming crisis, but without reference to money (Dodd 1961: 17). In this view, only 16:1–8 is relevant to the parable's meaning.

3. The parable is strictly a moral parable about making good use of the present with foresight to a pleasant future and therefore lacks any eschatological reference to judgment or crisis (Jülicher 1899: 2.511 [discussing only 16:1–7 as an original part of the parable]).

4. The parable straightforwardly teaches what not to do through the negative example of the steward (Milligan 1892: 126). The issue here is that the unfaithfulness of the steward is not to be followed. The roots of this view go back to J. F. Bahnmaier in 1827 (according to Ireland 1992: 25).

5. The parable ironically teaches what not to do through the negative example of the steward. The difference between view 4 and this view is the emphasis on irony: the sarcasm states the opposite of what Jesus really means in 16:8–9. Bretscher (1951: 757–59) argues that the point of 16:8–9 is that worldly sinners avoid repentance through wisdom and so condemn themselves. However, the best-known expression of this view (Fletcher 1963) argues that the point involves reading 16:9 ironically: we should not be drawn to money as the unjust steward was. Money as "worldly wealth" will fail, but the kingdom of God with its eternal dwellings will not. Security should not be bought with money, but by faithfulness to God. Fletcher and Bretscher see other examples of such irony in Matt. 23:32; 26:45; Luke 13:33; 15:7. The premise for irony in these verses is that the statement taken straightforwardly is too works-oriented or too worldly to be supported by Jesus. The reasons for rejecting this view and the previous one appear in the exegesis of 16:8.[31]

6. The parable is an exhortation to use money wisely and generously so as to enter heaven fully blessed, lacking any note of approaching crisis (Plummer 1896: 380–81). This is my preferred view of the parable's point, though many subpoints are debated.

Part of the decision about the parable's detailed meaning turns on whether the parable proper ends with 16:7 or 16:8a, and whether the subsequent verses are part of the original setting or joined by Luke because of a common theme (Fitzmyer 1985: 1096–99 has a detailed treatment). If the parable proper ends with 16:7, then the κύριος of 16:8 is not the master of the story, but Jesus (Bultmann 1963: 175–76, 199–200). The exact details of the parable's force are faced and defended in the exegesis. However, it seems likely that 16:8 is part of the parable, since Jesus' parables usually

---

31. Recent affirmation of this approach is found in Porter 1990 and noted by Blomberg 1994: 90 n. 81.

end with a moral. This would make 16:8 the end of the parable proper (with 16:8b giving a short application) and 16:9 the beginning of its expanded application. Fitzmyer (1985: 1096) says that the majority view sees 16:8 as part of the parable, although he ends the parable at 16:8a and starts the application at 16:8b (so also Nolland 1993a: 796). Luke is clearly concerned about possessions, since 16:9–13 comments on wealth, but whether possessions were a concern in the parable's original setting depends on the material's original unity, a matter treated above in the discussion of sources and historicity (see also the exegesis of 16:8–10 and the additional note on 16:8).

As the various interpretations show, it is not clear whether the steward is praised for acting righteously, or he acted craftily—though unrighteously—with regard to the future, or he is an illustration of how one should *not* use money, a kind of "reverse" or "negative" illustration occasionally appearing in Jesus' parables where the "bad guy" is used to illustrate the point (e.g., the thief of 11:21–23).[32] Manson (1949: 292–93) sees a lesser-to-greater argument: if a "bad guy" works to gain friends dishonestly, how much more should a righteous person seek good goals by good means. Believers should have the same foresight and show genuine charity. Manson's comment on the parable's lesser-to-greater thrust is correct, though Jesus seems to make the point without arguing that the man gained friends dishonestly.

One point of background helps to decide this question. Is the steward's canceling of the debt an act of brazen dishonesty whereby he ingratiates himself to others so that he can win their compassion upon his release (Arndt 1956: 355; Danker 1988: 279–80)? Or did the steward cancel only the interest owed, which was illegal according to God's law?[33] This latter view renders his act meritorious as well as personally beneficial, and, if correct, makes the steward a hero rather than a villain. In addition, if this interpretation is correct, whether in Derrett's or in Fitzmyer's form, then a better title for the unit might be the "Parable of the Shrewd Steward."

Only a detailed treatment and the discovery of more information can totally resolve the issue, though Derrett's suggestion appears to have merit (so Marshall 1978: 614–15; Kistemaker 1980: 228–30; in Fitzmyer's form, see Ellis 1974: 199 and Pilgrim 1981: 125–26; against it are Ireland 1992: 79–82; Blomberg 1990: 245; Blomberg 1994: 90–91). If this Jewish legal background is assumed, then the master's praise becomes more comprehensible. He would not then have lost all, and the steward's actions could be seen

32. Blomberg 1990: 244–45 opts for this, seeing him as a "son of this world." Bailey 1976: 86–110 sees the servant enhancing the master's reputation by forcing him to absorb the loss graciously in order to save face.

33. Ireland 1992: 36, 41 reports that this view goes back to D. Schulz in 1821 and was tied to ancient practice by J. J. Van Oosterzee in 1859. It has recently been defended through appeal to Jewish practice by Derrett 1970: 48–77. Fitzmyer 1964 adds an additional twist to this view: this interest was the steward's commission, making his action of canceling the interest only a clever pretense of personal sacrifice.

as motivated by obedience to God's law against charging usury (Exod. 22:25 [22:24 MT]; Lev. 25:36–37; Deut. 15:7–8; 23:19–20 [23:20–21 MT]).

16:8. Luke 16:8 is perhaps the most difficult verse in the entire Gospel. Two basic questions are involved: (1) Where does the parable end—at verse 7, 8a, 8b, or 9?[34] and (2) Why is the steward called "unrighteous"—because of his actions in 16:1 or in 16:5–7? I hold that the parable ends at 16:8a, that only the unethical acts in 16:1 are in view, and that the commission view of debt relief (discussed in the exegesis of 16:5) is more likely correct. Options on the first issue are as follows:

1. The parable consists of 16:1–7, with the rest of the passage being secondary additions to the original parable by Luke or his source.[35] Against this understanding is the absence of any reaction to these events by the characters, which would be most unusual for a parable. In addition, καὶ ἐγὼ ὑμῖν λέγω (and I say to you) in 16:9 looks like the start of the formal application.

2. The parable consists of 16:1–8a, ὁ κύριος is the parabolic master (Fitzmyer 1985: 1101), and 16:8b is indirect speech (in contrast to 16:8a) and shows a shift of perspective and speaker.[36] The argument against ending the parable at 16:7 is also valid here: parables usually close with a reaction by the participants, with Jesus' application following. This means that the parable must go at least to 16:8a if it is to conform to normal parabolic style. When one adds to this the previous references to the master in 16:1, 3–5, then the natural view is that the master is the speaker in 16:8a (cf. the use of κύριος in 14:23–24). If so, the question becomes: how could he praise his steward? If either Derrett's (1970: 56–72) or Fitzmyer's (1985: 1096–1101) explanation is correct (views 2 and 3 discussed in the exegesis of 16:5), then the praise is for the steward's foresight, which is the parable's focus. The steward ingratiates himself to many, while not hurting his master significantly. Either the law had been followed in not charging interest or the steward has sacrificed some of his own money by dropping his commission in the hope that he will find suitable employment later. Either way, the steward behaved in a way that reaps significant long-term benefits. Porter (1990: 132–34) challenges this "honest" approach to 16:5–7, using Bailey

---

34. Codex D makes clear the break midway through 16:8, reading διὸ λέγω ὑμῖν (therefore I say to you) instead of ὅτι (for). This reading is too poorly attested to be original, but does provide a fifth-century example of how the text was understood (i.e., that 16:8b begins Jesus' explanation and application of the parable).

35. Bultmann 1963: 175–76, 199–200; so also Grundmann 1963: 318–20, esp. 320, who also argues that Luke changes an original parabolic reference to the master to refer to Jesus. Luce 1933: 260 regards ὅτι (for) in 16:8b as difficult for any other view.

36. Talbert 1982: 153 calls 16:8b the first interpretation of the parable, though this is true only by implication; also Marshall 1978: 619–20 (opting for an end at 16:8a).

(1976: 86–94) to argue that this reading assumes too much and that hostile charges by the master and his steward would not be tolerated for long. But Porter's objections have less force if (1) the master was previously unaware of the steward's actions as 16:1–2 suggests and (2) the steward's actions in 16:5–7 are seen to reflect his heart, given his release by the master. In this light, the "sometimes dishonest but now honest steward" has gotten wise. Thus the parable especially works in Fitzmyer's form. A little sacrifice now yields huge rewards later, when things really count. This latter view, the commission approach, seems most likely, since "prudence" (φρονίμως) rather than obedience to the law is the specific point of 16:8a.[37] However, Fitzmyer's view (1985: 1105) that 16:8b–13 was appended later to the originally distinct parable is not convincing (see the discussion of sources and historicity above). To argue that distinct points means later material is to argue that a parable is only capable of making one point. But a mixture of parable and related implications is something that any speaker can do. Luke 16:9 seems especially well suited as a provocative transition into the implications, since stewardship and possession is the point. Money is nothing but a special area of stewardship. Though a topical compilation is possible, it is not necessary to view it this way. If the more traditional view if taken, such as Plummer's, where the steward dishonestly reduces the price and his cut, then the parable can still be seen to end at 16:8a and only then is the owner hurt by the action. This view is also possible.

3. The parable consists of 16:1–8b, and ὁ κύριος in 16:8a is either the parabolic master (Plummer 1896: 384; Danker 1988: 280) or Jesus (Klostermann 1929: 163; Schneider 1977a: 331; Ellis 1974: 199).[38] The force of this division is that the steward is praised by the master for being an exceedingly clever fellow. Most who hold this view regard the steward as not only clever but also dishonest (see below and the unit introduction). It is tempting to view the steward's actions in 16:5–7 as dishonest, especially given the use of ἀδικία (unrighteous) to describe him. Does this not show that he acted unrighteously? The one factor against it is that it means that Jesus praised unethical actions, whether he is speaking directly or through the parabolic master. The praise is for the "cleverness" of the steward, but that cleverness, in this case, entails an unethical act. Char-

---

37. Matt. 24:45 = Luke 12:42 uses φρόνιμος to describe a steward in another parable who thought ahead and lived in light of his master's return; so also Matt. 7:24; 25:2, 4, 8, 9; BAGD 866; BAA 1728.

38. Jeremias 1963a: 182 and Fitzmyer 1985: 1096–99, 1105 regard 16:9–13 as later additions and 16:8 as originally describing Jesus. Fitzmyer includes 16:8b in the applicational expansions and ties it to 16:9, which is problematic given the introductory "and I say to you" in 16:9. I agree that 16:8b is an application of the parable, but it must be seen as the original end to Jesus' remarks, given the break in 16:9a.

acter and action cannot be separated since the action is included in the comment (a point clearly argued by Porter 1990: 130–32). This approach is possible, given (a) Jesus' penchant for the unusual in his parables and (b) that the point is merely illustrative. Nonetheless, this approach seems too difficult, since it clouds the parable's exemplary force and makes Jesus' or the master's commendation difficult to accept as sincere. (The master's commendation is especially difficult, since he would have been robbed of significant income. It is this difficulty that leads many to the "irony" and "sarcasm" views.)

Ellis (1974: 199) holds that Jesus is the speaker, citing (a) 18:6 as illustrative of Luke's absolute use of κύριος to refer almost always to Jesus, (b) the need for a word from Jesus in 16:8, and (c) the problem of the remark in 16:8b clearly being tied to Jesus.[39] None of these reasons is compelling. The reference to κύριος is contextually tied to 16:3–5, the word from Jesus is in 16:8b, and the relationship of 16:8a to 16:8b can be treated consistently, while honoring contextual and stylistic concerns. In fact, absolute κύριος can clearly mean "master" and refer to a parabolic figure in Luke (12:37, 42b; 14:23). In two parabolic contexts (12:42a; 18:6) it refers to Jesus; however, in these cases it is clear that Jesus is continuing to speak, unlike 16:8, where the speaker is ambiguous. A more natural guide to the antecedent of κύριος in 16:8 is the parabolic context of Luke 16, not Luke 18. The introductory first person in 16:9 may also point to a clarifying speaker distinct from the one in 16:8a. What appears to be the case is that the parable's close comes in the master's reaction in 16:8a, while the explanation for his reaction is applied in Jesus' comment in 16:8b. The explicit twist to Jesus' message surfaces in 16:9.

4. The parable consists of 16:1–9, and ὁ κύριος is Jesus. The parable proper consists of 16:1–7, and 16:8–9 is Jesus' application of the parable.[40] The main reason for this view is that 16:8b looks like Jesus' comment, and since 16:8b gives the reason for 16:8a, so one might expect 16:8a also to be Jesus' comment. Against this view is that, if Jesus is the speaker in 16:8a, then there is no reaction to these events by the characters, which is unusual for Jesus' parables. In fact, the point made by this division is still valid, even if ὁ κύριος is not Jesus. By noting in 16:8b the owner's commendation (16:8a), Jesus still makes the point with approval. (This is why the explanatory 16:8b is irrelevant in deciding the issue, since it can be explained easily in any approach.)

---

39. Jeremias 1963a: 45 gives the details on the absolute use of κύριος to refer to Jesus, which occurs seventeen other times in Luke.

40. Fitzmyer 1985: 1096 places Manson 1949: 292 here, though Manson really regards 16:9 as a separate application and so belongs to the 16:8b view. Luke 18:6 is regarded as a parallel example for the use of κύριος.

One question still remains for the view presented in the exegesis: why is the steward called dishonest or unrighteous (ἀδικία; 16:8)?[41] The simplest way to read this phrase is to recognize it as an allusion to the charges of 16:1–2 (Fitzmyer 1985: 1101). Arguments that the description be applied to the steward's activities in 16:5–7 are not compelling in light of other factors surrounding the parable's interpretation. If the description refers back to 16:1–2, it is not superfluous here, as Stein (1981: 109) argues. Jesus' point is that the steward has acted prudently in 16:5–7. It is precisely the contrast to the steward's general reputation that is the point. If the description applies to 16:5–7, then the master's (and thus Jesus') praise is based on an immoral action. In holding that the steward acted unethically, many seek to distinguish between the shrewdness of the steward and the ethical character of his actions. But nowhere else does Jesus make an unethical act the point of a parable's teaching. Luke 11:5–8 and 18:1–8 are not parallel: 11:5–8 uses a culturally bold, but not immoral, act, and in 18:1–8 it is not the "unjust" judge's actions that are unethical, but his character. He does not act improperly, but agrees to do right out of weariness. Thus, these texts do not establish a precedent for arguing that Jesus praises an unethical action here. The closest possible example is the eschatological "thief in the night," who overcomes the person in the house, but that is a metaphor.

In addition, with the master speaking, there is no irony present within the parable. When the master offers praise, it is a direct result of the steward's action. There is no hint of sarcasm or irony. Could the master say this to him if his latest actions showed that he was a thief? The point is that the steward is unrighteous, not because of what he just did (16:5–7), but because of his general stewardship previously (16:1–2). Those earlier charges are regarded as true in the parable's movement and so are alluded to here.[42] Of course, such an unrighteous, unscrupulous, but selfishly clever man is tied to the world, which is why he is called a "son of this world" in 16:8b.

41. This key term links 16:9 and 16:11. In this context, ἀδικία is a Hebraistic "genitive of quality," describing the steward's character; Zerwick 1963: §40; Büchsel, *TDNT* 3:943 n. 2 (for κριτής). Schrenk, *TDNT* 1:157, calls it a "genitive of definition."

42. Schwarz 1974 sees these commendatory remarks as ironic; they are really condemnatory. This interpretation is forced and is not a possible rendering of ἐπαινέω (to praise); BAGD 281; BAA 569 (elsewhere in the NT at Rom. 15:11; 1 Cor. 11:2, 17, 22 [twice]). Also failing is Bailey's attempt (1976: 107) to argue that ἐπαινέω has eschatological force in picturing approval at the judgment. Other than the use of praise in Matt. 25:21, 34, the Gospels do not have this eschatological force, and in this Matthean context the eschatological force is clear, not inferred as it would have to be here. Porter 1990: 146–47 recognizes that the term must be positive, for the steward is commended for choosing to associate with the sons of this age, a comment dripping with bitter irony from the master. If one is to argue the irony position, this is the best way to do it. Against it, however, is the comparison in 16:8–9, which makes the steward look like a positive example through the commendation, not a negative one.

2. Responses to the Pharisees' Scoffing (16:14–18)

This short unit forms a bridge between the parable of the unrighteous steward (Luke 16:1–13) and the parable of the rich man and Lazarus (16:19–31). The logic of the thought is difficult and has been the object of much discussion. Talbert (1982: 156–58) argues that the parable in 16:19–31 elaborates the themes in 16:14–18 in the same order: God's looking at the heart, the inclusiveness of the kingdom, and the continued validity of the law. But the last point is not clear and should be restated, since the emphasis in 16:16–17 is not on the law's continued validity, but on its ability to offer continued guidance, despite its existence only "until John." The point, however, about the law and the prophets in the parable of 16:19–31 is that, if one really understood what the law (Moses) and the prophets declared, then one would understand that resurrection is promised and that each person is responsible to God for his or her treatment of people. The point is not the role of the law as law, but the pictures of law as promise and as a guide to caring for others. It is law as promise, anticipating the arrival of a new era, which is also the point in 16:16–17. Those who understand the law know that the new era is coming (16:16). In addition, the law was not designed to show how little one can do for God, but to show how responsible one is to God and people. This latter point is why 16:18 is present: it illustrates that the change in era does not mean a change in moral standards in terms of commitments made to God and others. Jesus mentions divorce to picture how the new era still calls for righteous living. The law's permanence resides in its ability to prepare one for the arrival of promise and to call one to be faithful before God and others.

The unit has three distinct parts: condemnation of the Pharisees for their self-justification (16:14–15), declaration of the kingdom's coming and the law's completion (16:16–17), and a statement on divorce (16:18). A common way to link 16:18 to the rest of the unit is to treat it as an example of the law, but Fitzmyer (1985: 1119) rightly notes that the statement, at least in its current form, looks stricter than the law (see the exegesis of 16:18).

A better approach is to tie the section together by the theme of values and Jesus' authority. Tiede (1988: 284) shows that the authority of God's kingdom should influence one's values: the kingdom causes one to (1) renounce divided loyalties (16:10–13), (2) have idolatries revealed (16:14–15), and (3) raise standards of obedience (16:18).[1] The issue of how 16:16–17 fits into the picture is not clear from this perspective. Perhaps the point is that promise and authority have come in the kingdom and in Jesus' teaching. Yet the kingdom's coming fulfills the law's promise and still calls for ethical living. The kingdom picture is crucial here, and the issue of Jesus' authority and the values it leads to unifies the passage.

The Pharisees have scoffed at Jesus' teaching, but their derision does not stop Jesus from warning them that God is not pleased with them, since God hates their pride (on the split motives of their hearts, see 21:1–4). The issue here is authority pure and simple. Who enlightens people about the way to find God—Jesus or the leadership? That is where the statement on the epochs of God comes in. The time until John the Baptist was characterized by law; but now is the time for the kingdom, which fulfills the promise contained in the law. The exact meaning of the disputed 16:16b awaits discussion in the exegesis. But it is clear that the law and the prophets look ahead to the current era that Jesus brings. The new epoch, however, does not reduce the law to nothing. All that it desired to accomplish is fulfilled in this new time.[2] God's standards at the level of the heart still remain. And so follows Jesus' word about divorce, not as an illustration of law, but as an illustration of his authority to proclaim God's standards, which relate to the heart and reflect the law's goal. As Ernst (1977: 469) suggests, the unit says in effect that the pharisaic way of looking at the law is insufficient. Jesus shows that the law is promise and that the heart's transformation into genuine righteousness is its goal. The power to achieve that transformation is not in the law, but is present through entry into the kingdom to which the law pointed.

Sources and Historicity

Luke 16:14–15 is a unique piece of material with no parallel elsewhere (Aland 1985: §225). It is a part of Luke's special material and highlights one

1. Tiede sees this unit starting in 16:10. But the theme of money is tied to the parable of the crafty steward and thus 16:8–13 needs to be kept with 16:1–7. Luke 16:14–15 is a bridge moving from money to the morality of the new era.

2. Given what Jesus does and says in relationship to the law in other texts and given the context of epochs here, this is the best way to tie the law and the kingdom together.

of his major themes: Jesus' condemnation of the Pharisees' scoffing and rejection of his teaching. The Jesus Seminar (Funk and Hoover 1993: 358–59) rejects the saying's authenticity (black type) because it is unattested elsewhere and sounds proverbial. But surely this critique of the Pharisees fits Jesus. Bultmann (1963: 105) argues that the saying, though proverbial, reaches beyond popular wisdom and is characteristic of the preaching of Jesus. The saying fits the polemical relationship emerging between Jesus and the Jewish leaders. Schürmann (1960) shows that the saying's roots may have a parallel in Matt. 5:20.

Luke 16:16–17 has parallels in Matthew (Aland 1985: §226). The epoch saying is like Matt. 11:12–13; but Matthew lays out the saying in reverse order, with the law and prophets reference coming last. The heaven-and-earth saying occurs in Matt. 5:18. Most attribute these sayings to Q because of the Matthean parallels, but it is hard to be sure that they had the same source because of the word-order reversal in Luke 16:16 and the different vocabulary in Luke 16:17 and Matt. 5:18 (only the conjunction ἤ is the same in the two sayings; four other terms have some overlap, while distinct terms abound). Although a similar source is possible, it is more likely that distinct sayings are present.[3]

The Jesus Seminar (Funk and Hoover 1993: 359–60) rates this saying as heavily worked over by Luke, but possibly rooted in Jesus (gray type). Assuming that a saying can belong to only one level of the tradition, the seminar holds that the variations between Matt. 11:12–13 and Luke 16:16 argue for editorial work (so also Meier 1994: 158–61 and Nolland 1993a: 814–15). Nolland, despite seeing redactional work, argues for roots in the historical Jesus, seeing that the kingdom of God and conflict imagery cohere with Jesus' teaching. Even though the seminar struggles to make sense out of the mention of violence in Luke 16:16, the enigmatic character of this saying is an argument against Lucan creation. Wink (1968: 20–21) argues that Luke or the early church would not create a saying that gives John the Baptist such a prominent role. Meier (1994: 163) argues that the teaching coheres with much traditional material (Matt. 11:2–19), and thus he leans in favor of acceptance. The Jesus Seminar also prints Luke 16:17 in gray type because the saying reflects the early church's discussion about whether the law was still binding. The seminar regards this saying about continuity with the law as standing against "Jesus' relaxed attitude towards the Law." But the saying better fits Jesus' understanding

---

3. For Luke having Q's original order and not Matthew, see Manson 1949: 134; Fitzmyer 1985: 1114; Schneider 1977a: 337 (perhaps); Meier 1994: 157; and Marshall 1978: 627. Ernst 1977: 469 speaks of Q material, special Lucan material, and Lucan redaction. Wiefel 1988: 294 speaks of Q in 16:16–17 and of Mark in 16:18. Godet 1875: 2.173 prefers Luke's positioning of material to Matthew's. However, the warnings are so general that parallel traditions may exist, reflecting a variety of settings.

that he brings fulfillment to the law in the new era (Marshall 1978: 627; Banks 1975: 218). Jesus' practice did not so much reject the law as argue for a redefinition of its role (see the exegesis of 16:17). Only such a reading of Jesus can make sense of his claims of continuity between the law and his actions.

Luke 16:18 has parallels in Matt. 5:32 and Matt. 19:9 = Mark 10:11–12 (Aland 1985: §227), and Paul appears to be aware of this teaching in 1 Cor. 7:10–11. Here is multiple attestation of the earliest kind, a point that argues against the Jesus Seminar's rating this verse as only loosely rooted in Jesus (gray type; Funk and Hoover 1993: 360). Most see a Q saying here because of the link to Matt. 5:32 (Fitzmyer 1985: 1119; Marshall 1978: 630). The form of Luke's saying is closer to Matt. 5:32 than to Matt. 19:9 = Mark 10:11–12, though Matthew has an exception that Luke does not note.[4] But again there is much distinct wording.[5] It is hard to know whether one source recorded this saying or whether this teaching was remembered in various forms and taught on various occasions. Even excluding the Lucan material, the tradition has this remark in various settings. Thus, the core of this saying is multiply attested. Various settings again seem more likely, given the differences, at least in the case of Luke 16:18 and Matt. 5:32. It is unlikely that Jesus discussed divorce on only one occasion. Matthew 5:32 and Luke 16:18 both tie this teaching to the issue of the law, whereas Mark 10:11–12 and Matt. 19:9 address a specific question about divorce. Thus, for the extent of the Jesus tradition on divorce, it is clear that we are dealing with at least two distinct settings, and it is possible that three settings are addressed in the four pericopes.

Because the latter two units (16:16–18) are attributed to Q, it is often argued that Luke arranged the bridge here. Though possible, the sayings' distinctness as well as their differences suggest that the appeal to Q is misleading and that, in fact, Luke has an independent source that may have placed these elements in this setting. This conclusion fits nicely with Luke's use of sources in chapter 16 as a whole, since almost all the other elements in the chapter appear to be of independent origin. Luke may be responsible for a "bridge" here, but it is also possible that his special material already linked these remarks with the two parables of chapter 16. Jesus' shift from speaking to his disciples to the Pharisees in 16:14–15 is sudden, but the relationship of these remarks to each parable is clear. It may be that the condemnation of the Pharisees' approach to money led to the linkage in the

4. Mark also lacks the exception; Wiefel 1988: 294 therefore speaks of Mark as Luke's source. The variation in the tradition is what causes the Jesus Seminar's uncertainty about the saying. But only the exception should be a topic for such a discussion. Against a Matthean redaction is the probable Semitic background to the exception as stated in Matt. 5:32 (noted in Nolland 1993a: 816, although curiously he sees the detail as a redactional addition).

5. However, it does look like Mark 10:11–12 and Matt. 19:9 go together, since almost every word of Mark is paralleled in Matthew.

previous parable with the call for generosity, while the issues of law, values, stewardship, and money led to the tie to 16:19–31. In short, the seam here fits both ways and may be original. If Luke is responsible for the seam, then he has topically juxtaposed the discussions to show how Jesus saw clear differences between himself and the Pharisees.

The form of the passage is a combination of various types of sayings.[6] The outline of Luke 16:14–18 is as follows:

a. Jesus' warning to the Pharisees about their scoffing (16:14–15)
   i. The Pharisees' scoffing (16:14)
   ii. Jesus' warning: God searches hearts and hates pride (16:15)
b. The law and the kingdom (16:16–17)
   i. The coming of the kingdom since John (16:16)
   ii. The law's permanence and promise (16:17)
c. The standard of the heart and divorce (16:18)

The passage is really an abbreviated controversy account. The Pharisees deride Jesus' teaching about stewardship because of their love for money. Jesus warns that God judges the heart and that self-justification and pride are condemned by God. A new time has come. John is the last representative of the law and the prophets, bridging the two eras. Jesus brings the good news of the kingdom, a new message announcing a new era (4:16–18, 43–44). The message of the kingdom must be preached with the urgency it deserves. The law has a lasting role, however, despite the kingdom's coming: it serves as a reminder of the promise and a call to righteousness. Righteousness means the condemnation of divorce, which breaks a vow made before God. In fact, some remarriages are adulterous. The example of maintaining the covenant of marriage shows a desire not to get out of doing righteousness, but to keep one's commitments. Being faithful is only a problem for those who desire to break their commitment to others. Breaking such commitments is sin. The new era is a call to integrity in one's promises to God and others.

6. Fitzmyer sees polemical sayings in 16:14–15 (1985: 1112), a saying in 16:16–17 (p. 1115), and a legal saying in 16:18 (p. 1120). Bultmann sees a wisdom saying in 16:15b (1963: 73), an "I-saying" in 16:16 (p. 164), and a legal saying in 16:18 (p. 132). Berger agrees that 16:18 is a legal saying (1984: 199) and argues that the passage is a warning made up of pronouncements, since he has the remarks in the apophthegm category (pp. 81, 89, 186).

Exegesis and Exposition

[14]The ⌜Pharisees⌝, who were lovers of money, heard all of these things and scoffed at him. [15]But he said to them, "You are those who justify yourselves before men, but God knows your hearts; for that which is exalted among men is an abomination before God.

[16]"The law and the prophets were until John; since then the good news of the kingdom of God is preached, and everyone is urged insistently into it. [17]But it is easier for heaven and earth to pass away than for one jot of the law to fall.

[18]"Everyone who divorces his wife and marries another commits adultery, and he who marries a woman divorced from her husband commits adultery."

a. Jesus' Warning to the Pharisees about Their Scoffing (16:14–15)
i. The Pharisees' Scoffing (16:14)

Though Jesus is teaching his disciples (16:1), the Pharisees keep an **16:14** eye on him and hear his parable and its exhortation to be generous with money. Luke notes that the Pharisees are "lovers of silver" (φιλάργυροι, *philargyroi*), a reference to avarice, and so they do not like Jesus' teaching (Plummer 1896: 387; BAGD 859; BAA 1713; elsewhere in the NT only at 2 Tim. 3:2). Manson (1949: 295–96) thinks that the rebuke was more appropriate for the Sadducees, since they were known for being wealthy and proud (Josephus, *Antiquities* 13.10.6 §298).[7] But Marshall (1978: 625) notes that the Pharisees, especially the scribes, had this reputation.[8] There is no need to see the Sadducees as the real audience, though they may have shared the Pharisees' view.

Given the Pharisees' philosophy, they wish to downplay Jesus' teaching and so they scoff at it. The graphic term ἐκμυκτηρίζω (*ekmyktērizō*) literally means "to turn one's nose up" at someone; it indicates strong contempt (Bertram, *TDNT* 4:796–99; BAGD 243; BAA 490; elsewhere in the NT only at Luke 23:35; in the LXX see Ps. 2:4; Prov. 1:30; Jer. 20:7). The opposition of Luke 15:2 has intensified. The Pharisees thoroughly reject Jesus' teaching and clearly wish to

---

7. 1 Enoch 102.9–10 shows the Jewish contempt for the selfish rich. T. Moses 7.3 may apply to the Sadducees or Pharisees. Lachs 1987: 311–12 revives Manson's thesis and rejects the idea that this is a description of the Pharisees. On the Pharisees' relatively modest means (not every lover of money succeeds in being rich), see Jeremias 1969: 259; Bammel, *TDNT* 6:901–2.

8. In *t. Menaḥ.* 13.22 (= Neusner 1977–86: 5.162), the leadership's love of money and hatred of one another is why the temple came to be destroyed; also SB 1:937; 2:222; 4:336–39; Jeremias 1969: 49, 114. Luce 1933: 264 objects to this description, but fails to interact with the ancient sources. C. A. Evans 1990: 245 is right that a story about the afterlife would hardly be a meaningful rebuke to the Sadducees.

challenge it. Given this term, the rejection might reflect more than contempt for Jesus' material values; perhaps it is a reflection of conflict based on social or geographical issues as well.

ii. Jesus' Warning: God Searches Hearts and Hates Pride (16:15)

16:15 The authorities' assessment does not impress Jesus. The issue is not self-praise, but the heart's attitude. What God thinks and sees counts for more than what people think (*before men* is in contrastive parallelism to *your hearts*). The idea to be supplied contextually may be that the Pharisees give alms, but they do so to impress others (Creed 1930: 206).[9] It is the heart that God knows, and exaltation of the self does not please him (Plummer 1896: 388; Danker 1988: 282; Tiede 1988: 286; Stauffer, *TDNT* 3:111; Behm, *TDNT* 3:612 §D2d).[10] Jesus' remark is given in the spirit of the prophetic tradition, where it is not sacrifices that count, but caring for other people (Hos. 6:6; Mic. 6:6–8). Similar complaints against the Pharisees are made in Luke 10:29; 11:39–41; and 18:9–14.

Jesus goes on to say that he can make this complaint because (ὅτι, *hoti*) the things that people exalt are an abomination before God. Βδέλυγμα (*bdelygma*, detestable) is a strong term of rejection (Foerster, *TDNT* 1:600; BAGD 137; BAA 275). Idiomatically, it indicates something that stinks (Luce 1933: 244). God rejects such self-adoration (Prov. 16:5; Isa. 2:9–11).[11] He considers those who exalt themselves detestable. Contextually, the "exalted one" may well picture the rich man of Luke 16:19.

b. The Law and the Kingdom (16:16–17)
i. The Coming of the Kingdom since John (16:16)

16:16 Luke 16:16 brings in the additional dimension of the eschaton. This verse has been an exegetical minefield in Lucan studies for two reasons. First, the Lucan framework for dividing God's plan into dis-

---

9. Klostermann 1929: 166 argues that the Pharisees claimed that their wealth showed God's blessing, but this approach fits the wealthy Sadducees more than the Pharisees.

10. God knows the heart: 1 Sam. 16:7; 1 Chron. 28:9; Ps. 7:9 [7:10 MT]; Prov. 17:3; 21:2; 24:12; Jer. 11:20; Acts 1:24; 15:8; Rom. 8:27; 2 Cor. 11:11. Jesus will also examine the heart and exercise judgment: Luke 2:35; Acts 17:30–31.

11. *Mekilta de Rabbi Ishmael*, tractate *Baḥodesh* 9 on Exod. 20:21 [= 20:18 in NJPSV] (= Lauterbach 1933–35: 2.274): "All who are lofty of heart are called an abomination, as it is said, 'Everyone who is lofty of heart is an abomination to the Lord.'" Manson 1949: 295–96 notes that the OT describes idolatry in similar terms (e.g., 1 Kings 11:5). Because it is the ultimate worship of the creature over the Creator, pride may be the most common form of idolatry.

tinct periods is present in the verse. Second, the meaning of βιάζεται (*biazetai*) is notoriously difficult to determine. The teaching of the passage is subsumed under these two questions.

As elsewhere in Luke and Acts, Luke here sees two parts in God's plan: promise and fulfillment (Luke 1–2; 3:1–6, 15–20; 7:18–35; Acts 10:37; 13:34–35).[12] John the Baptist is consistently portrayed as the transition figure and belongs to the era of promise as a forerunner to the era of fulfillment (Luke 1–2; 3:1–18; 7:22–28). Luke reasserts this basic division here. Jesus speaks of the law and the prophets existing until or through John the Baptist.[13] Is John in the era of fulfillment? Luke 7:18–35 and 3:1–6 (where John only prepares the way) suggest not; but Luke 3:18 and Acts 1:22 make the issue debatable (see Luke 7:27–28; Marshall 1978: 628 sees John in the new era). In a sense, as a transition figure John has one foot in each era. But as the pointer of the way, he really belongs to the old era in terms of his function. He is its end. Perhaps the key is that John announces the arrival of Jesus, who is the only one who preaches the kingdom. This observation separates John from the message of the new era. Since his time, however, the kingdom is preached, which suggests that the new era has come and that the law and the prophets, as the era of promise, now cease to exist.[14] The period before Jesus was regulated through the law and the prophets. They operated in a context of promise as Luke 24:44–49 and Acts 3:11–26 show, where the law and the prophets proclaim the promise and program of Christ. The frequent temporal markers ἀπὸ τοῦ νῦν (*apo tou nyn*, from now on) and ἀπὸ τότε (*apo tote*, henceforth) are key phrases used by Luke to denote significant turning points in the sequence of events (Luke 1:48; 5:10; 12:52; 22:18, 69). God's plan has turned over a new leaf with Jesus' coming. The preaching of the kingdom's message is no longer a matter of declaring a distant promise, but can be preached in terms of nearness and arrival. A new era has come—with new realities and new authority.

Luke 16:16b has been handled variously. Two issues are essential to determining the meaning. First, is βιάζεται middle or passive voice (i.e., do all act for themselves ["enter forcibly themselves"] or is something done to all ["are forced to enter"])?

---

12. Conzelmann 1960: 16 presents a threefold division: Israel, Jesus, the church. Fitzmyer 1981: 182–87 and 1985: 1115 defends a modified threefold division: the law and the prophets, Jesus, and the early church. But the Lucan passages cited know of only a law-and-prophets period (promise) and a kingdom-Jesus-church period (fulfillment).

13. Friedrich, *TDNT* 6:840, argues that the meaning is that they prophesied about John, but the passage's temporal markers are against this view.

14. On "the law and the prophets," see Luke 16:29, 31; Acts 13:15; 28:23; Schrenk, *TDNT* 1:756 n. 28; Friedrich, *TDNT* 6:832.

Second, what is the meaning of βιάζω: to enter, insist, or violently come? In discussing the options, it is hard to separate these two questions.

A third issue greatly clouds the discussion: the influence of Matt. 11:12–13 in interpreting Luke 16:16. Each passage must be addressed on its own terms, since it is likely that they address distinct situations (see the discussion of sources and historicity). Matthew's wording is different ("prophets and law" instead of "law and prophets"). He also says that the kingdom of heaven comes violently or suffers violence (βιάζεται, *biazetai*) and that men of violence take it by force (βιασταί, *biastai*). While "kingdom of heaven" and the "kingdom of God" present the same idea, the rest of the verse's imagery is very different. What Matthew attributes to violent men must—if Luke equals Matthew—be attributed here to all people. And if Luke rewrote the saying, then he changed the sense entirely.[15] This third issue is not really of value in dealing with the passage's teaching. Luke should be handled on his own terms.

We turn, then, to the meaning of βιάζω, the basic sense of which is "to apply force." Several interpretations have been proposed for this term (Leaney 1958: 223–24; Cortés and Gatti 1987 [on options 1, 3, and 4]; BAGD 140–41; BAA 280–81):

1. The term is negative and in the middle voice: "all act violently against it"; that is, the kingdom is subject to universal opposition (Ellis 1974: 203 mentions demonic forces). This view reflects a linkage to Matthew, since in the Matthean passage the force is clearly negative.[16] In this negative light, the world—and everything in it—stands opposed to the kingdom. But such a pessimistic view is not likely for Luke, since Jesus has gathered some disciples, and in 2:34–35 he divides people, rather than being opposed by them all. Arndt (1956: 361) qualifies this view by suggesting that the entry is not necessarily violent, but neither is it always pursued on God's terms. This refinement is possible, but if rejection were the dominant image, one would still expect a contrastive particle countering the earlier

---

15. So Schrenk, *TDNT* 1:612, argues, while opting for Matthew's version as the more original form in Q. But Chilton 1979: 205–23 argues that Luke's saying is from Lucan Q, a version distinct from but parallel to Matthew's Q. Chilton also defends the originality of Luke's form of the saying. Given all the other anomalies in the text, it is more satisfactory to argue for distinct sources and settings.

16. On Matthew, see Hill 1972: 200–201. Perrin 1963: 172–74 does not discuss Luke 16:16b because, in his view, it is a later addition to the tradition, a view that grows out of his identifying the two texts as the same tradition. Marshall 1978: 630 argues almost single-handedly for a positive sense in Matthew: "Men of violence seize at the opportunity of entering the kingdom." This is not likely.

positive reference to preaching. However, only καί (*kai*, and) appears.

2. The term is negative and should be translated: "everyone forces his way into it"; that is, people try to violently bring the kingdom to earth. Such a remark by Jesus is seen as a criticism of the Zealot movements (Luce 1933: 266 calls this view "attractive"). Against this view is the supposed juxtaposition of kingdom preaching and political criticism without any use of a contrastive conjunction, not to mention the almost complete absence of explicit political critique in every portrayal of Jesus.[17] If Jesus ever took on Zealots or people like them, this is the only place he did so.

3. The term is positive and in the middle voice: "everyone tries to force his way into it [the kingdom]" (Hendriksen 1978: 774; Manson 1949: 134–35; Schrenk, *TDNT* 1:612; Klostermann 1929: 167; Marshall 1978: 630 [apparently]). The problem with this approach is that it is entirely too positive. Jesus has faced severe opposition in every period of his ministry. And only in this context does Jesus rebuke the Pharisees' scoffing. In Jesus' view, they are hardly pressing to enter the kingdom.

4. The verb has a softened force and is in the passive voice: "all are urged insistently to come in" (Schweizer 1984: 258; Fitzmyer 1985: 1117).[18] This view fits remarkably well in the current context. Why is Jesus warning and exhorting his opponents so constantly? Because he is attempting to persuade them to respond morally. In a sense, his mission is bound up in his proclamation to and effort toward those most opposed to him, those on the road to rejection. The opportunity is always placed before them. The risk is always expressed to them. Indeed, the special nature of the time creates the urgency. People may think that they can take or leave the kingdom message, but the warnings are necessary because the message will take or leave them, depending on how they respond. Thus the need to urge insistently. Jesus presents the message to all, and all are given the chance to enter and share in the kingdom's benefits (14:15–24 is similar in thrust). The time of fulfillment has come and all are invited to share in the good news. The king-

17. I distinguish political critique from social or ethical critique that have political and social ramifications.

18. So also Godet in the third French edition of his commentary, but not in the English translations of his earlier French editions (see Cortés and Gatti 1987: 255 n. 27). Lexical support for this sense comes from the LXX (Gen. 33:11; Judg. 13:15–16; 19:7; 2 Sam. 13:25, 27; 2 Kings 5:23 [variant reading]), the related verb παραβιά-ζομαι (to urge insistently; Luke 24:29; Acts 16:15), and Koine sources (MM 109–10 and Spicq 1995: 1.290–91).

dom comes, regardless of whether one responds. But if one is to share in the kingdom message, one must respond to Jesus' authority—not scoff at it (16:14).

ii. The Law's Permanence and Promise (16:17)

16:17 Jesus puts his remark in the larger context of revelation: if the kingdom has come and if the period of the law and the prophets has passed, has the law of God ceased to function? No, Jesus declares; the law does not fail (πεσεῖν, *pesein*) in even its smallest point (κεραίαν, *keraian*). Κεραία literally means "little horn" and here refers to a small writing stroke that enables one to distinguish, for example, Hebrew ד (*d*) from ר (*r*) or ח (*h*) from ה (*ḥ*). It may even refer to the decorative apexes or crowns surrounding letters in a Torah scroll (Luce 1933: 266; SB 1:248–49; BAGD 428; BAA 871–72).[19] In fact, Jesus says, creation is more likely to pass into oblivion than the law is likely to fail.[20]

But what does this saying mean? How can the law exist only until John, and yet not fail? Various answers have been given.

1. Jervell (1972: 140–41) argues that for Luke the law is "eternally valid."[21] This is part of Luke's conservative view of the law that shows Christians are to be faithful to it. For Jervell, whatever 16:16 means, it does not mean the passing away of the period or epoch of the law. This view has problems. Seen in isolation, 16:17 might be able to sustain such a meaning, but given the previous verse where delineations of epochs are present, Jervell's meaning cannot be right. Texts like 6:1–5 raise questions about this reading. Some contextual qualification of what the law means is necessary for the passage to make sense.

2. Manson (1949: 135–36) takes the verse by itself and argues that Luke uses it as bitter irony. The scribes view the law in such a way that it is easier for creation to pass than for the law to fail at any single point. But to isolate the verse like this is

19. Fitzmyer 1985: 1118 is against a decorative reference because such usage is found only in later rabbinic materials, not early Jewish documents. He also rejects the suggestion of Schwarz 1975 that κεραία refers to the Hebrew letter waw (ו). Regardless, the emphasis is on the whole of the law down to its smallest point. The law as a synthetic whole is in view here.

20. On the idiom of heaven and earth passing away, see Matt. 5:18; 24:35 = Mark 13:31 = Luke 21:33; J. Schneider, *TDNT* 2:682.

21. Creed 1930: 207 adopts this meaning, but regards it as unlikely that Jesus said it. On the endurance of the law in Judaism, see Bar. 4:1; 2 Esdr. [= 4 Ezra] 9.37; 2 Bar. 77.15.

unwise. Neither Matthew's nor Luke's usage requires such an alteration.

3. Blomberg (1984a: 60–61) distinguishes between the law being valid in this age and the Mosaic law, which has lost its validity and become superfluous. The law that is still valid accomplishes everything it intends. This reminds one of Conzelmann's distinction (1960: 160–61) between law as epic (Mosaic law) and law as principle, which is always valid (Ernst 1977: 470–71).[22] This explanation goes in the right direction in seeing law used with a special force, but it places the emphasis in the wrong category, that of moral law. The sense is broader than this.

4. Banks (1975: 214–15) and Luce (1933: 267 ["absolutely and completely fulfilled in . . . Jesus"]) argue that the law points to the kingdom and so does not fail. It is transformed and fulfilled in Jesus. It does not fail because its goal is Jesus and its authority is expressed through him. Wilson (1983: 50) objects to this view, arguing that it really means that the law has been set aside.

5. Wilson (1983: 50–51) offers his own explanation in terms of Jesus' authority: the law's demands are valid and have been intensified and extended in Jesus' teaching, as 16:18 illustrates. But he also argues that there is ambiguity in Luke's position, since the full extension of the law is not being followed. Is this explanation precise enough? How can all the demands of the law be valid, when Jesus appears to challenge some laws (6:1–5)? The resolution through Jesus' authority appears helpful, but in what sense is law appealed to, if not in its demands?

What makes determining the best view difficult is that 16:17 is the only verse in the Lucan corpus that directly concerns the law. When one looks at the whole of Luke's writings, then both views 4 and 5 have merit. But Wilson's view fails to distinguish clearly how the law is seen by Luke, though his note on Jesus' authority is helpful. There is no doubt that Luke holds that the law functions as part of the period of promise and that it points to Christ and his activity (Luke 16:19–31; 24:44–47; Acts 3:11–26). This is the emphasis of the Lucan introduction in Luke 1–2 and, less directly, the circumcision debate in Acts 15. The law and the prophets point to God's final activity in

22. Berger 1972: 209–26 argues that the law refers to the "will of God." Schweizer 1984: 258 says the law is newly interpreted by Jesus' kingdom preaching and is valid as a moral norm (at least in some of its elements). Plummer 1896: 389 and Arndt 1956: 361 see a distinction between moral law and defunct ceremonial law.

Christ. View 4 as articulated by Banks is most satisfactory: the law does not fall only in this salvation-historical sense (also Fitzmyer 1985: 1116 [law is vindicated in the demands of the kingdom] and Marshall 1978: 627). The limits of the remark mean that Wilson's objection to this view does not hold.

In this Lucan context, the point is a powerful one to the Pharisees, who are lovers of the law. If they are to keep the law, they must embrace Jesus' kingdom message to which it points. Responding to Jesus represents fulfilling the law and so receiving him brings its intention to pass (Rom. 9:31–10:13). They must respond and adhere to the teaching of the one sent to present the message of God's rule. The statement underlines Jesus' authority.

The similar statement in Matt. 5:18 is in a greatly different context: it is part of Jesus' exposition of the law's real force and meaning. The Matthean remark is followed by six illustrations, one of which is marriage and divorce. Jesus also says there that the law does not pass away and that he comes to fulfill it, a meaning similar to Luke, though Luke presents the nature of the law's ethical application less comprehensively than does Matthew.

c. The Standard of the Heart and Divorce (16:18)

16:18 Jesus' remark on divorce (ἀπολύω, apolyō; BAGD 96 §2a; BAA 193 §2a) represents an example of his authoritative teaching. Two points are implied here: (1) an example from everyday life shows how the desire for righteousness produces a high standard of ethics, especially in the commitments that one makes before God; and (2) such righteousness does not need law. Jesus lays out the standard, in effect saying that if you make a vow to marry and be faithful to your spouse before God, then breaking that vow and entering into another marital union can be called adultery because the original vow was not kept. Divorce is a violation of a three-way covenant between God, the husband, and the wife. If you are faithful, you will keep your vows and not get into this situation. The essence of righteousness is integrity; the essence of sin is violating one's promises made to God. Living in the kingdom means keeping one's commitments to God and others.

The rabbinic schools of Hillel and Shammai had a well-known debate about the proper grounds for divorce. Shammai held that immorality was the only allowable ground for divorce, while Hillel allowed divorce for a variety of reasons, including something as trivial as meal preparation (m. Giṭ. 9.10; b. Giṭ. 90a). Jesus could have cited Deut. 24:1–4, as he does in other passages. Instead he notes the condition of those who divorce and remarry: they are committing adultery, an offense punishable by death under Mosaic law (Exod.

20:14 [20:13 in NJPSV]; Lev. 20:10; Deut. 5:18 [5:17 MT]; 22:22).[23] Jesus' remark is strong in a culture that had a variety of views on divorce. (Qumran shared Shammai's absolute position; 11QTemple[a] 57.11–19; CD 4.20–5.1; Fitzmyer 1985: 1121.)

Jesus' words are put in absolute terms: divorce leads to adultery because the presupposition is that a person seeks a divorce in order to remarry, in which case the remarriage itself represents an act of unfaithfulness to the original vows (Marshall 1978: 631). Jesus' statement covers both possibilities: the one who divorces and remarries commits adultery, and the one who remarries a divorced person commits adultery, regardless of whether this third person was divorced.[24]

It is important to note that Luke's citation has a wider concern than just divorce: it illustrates that moral authority resides in and comes through Jesus' teaching. He is the ethicist for God's kingdom. Nonetheless, the unqualified form of this statement leads many to regard divorce for any reason as prohibited by Scripture.[25] Jesus sets forth, however, only the basic principle here, not every possible scenario.

The larger question of divorce and remarriage is complicated by the Synoptic parallels. In Mark 10:11–12, which is similarly unqualified, both the man and the woman are mentioned as divorcing their spouses, and it is their remarrying that causes adultery.[26] Matthew 5:32 mentions that divorcing a woman on unbiblical grounds makes her commit adultery. The assumption, as in Luke 16:18, is that divorce will lead inevitably to remarriage. Matthew 5:32 and 19:9 further complicate the issue by noting an exception called πορνεία (*porneia*), which is variously explained as unfaithfulness in the betrothal period or some form of interfamily marriage that automatically makes the first marriage null and void (on the latter, see Lev.

23. The penalty was apparently never carried out in Jesus' time since Jews did not have the right to execute capital punishment under Roman rule; Creed 1930: 208. The idea of such punishment still remains, as Jub. 30.8–9 shows. The standard was to pursue holiness. Such an act of adultery rendered a woman defiled (Jub. 33.9; *m. Soṭa* 2.6; 5.1). In fact, these Mishnah texts almost require divorce for the adulterous wife since she becomes unclean to the husband. Thus, adultery was seen as extremely serious in Judaism (on the Greco-Roman view of adultery tied to shame, see Nolland 1993a: 818).

24. Marshall notes that Jesus' reference to not marrying a divorced person goes beyond what Judaism allowed; SB 1:320–21.

25. For an excellent discussion of the history of interpretation of these passages, see Heth and Wenham 1984. For the debate, see House 1990.

26. In ancient Judaism, a woman could not divorce her husband, although (as Manson 1949: 136–37 notes) if a man were immoral she could compel him to divorce her. Manson also notes the exceptional practice of the Jewish community at Elephantine in the fifth century B.C., where women could initiate divorce.

18:6–19; 20:11–21; Deut. 27:20; Ezek. 22:10; CD 4.20–5.10; Ellis 1974: 203 notes the options and observes that polygamy is ruled out). The most natural use of πορνεία, however, is as a broad reference to any kind of sexual immorality (BAGD 693; BAA 1389).

Matthew appears to give the most comprehensive form of Jesus' remarks on divorce and remarriage. The question becomes, then, why mention an exception at all, unless it in some way qualifies the rest of the remarks. It is here that Heth and Wenham (1984: 50–52, 69–71) overplay the grammar of Matthew, arguing that the exception applies only to the right to divorce and not to remarriage. Against this view is the purpose of divorce in the ancient world: to put one in a position to remarry. It would appear that to qualify the right to divorce is to qualify the right to remarry by implication. Otherwise, why else divorce, since one could just be permanently separated? Luke's presentation of Jesus' teaching on divorce is not as full as Matthew's because he is using this teaching as an illustration of Jesus' authority; it is a presentation of the basic principle, not the full teaching (Arndt 1956: 362). Matthew, however, addresses Jesus' teaching in detail and seems to allow divorce on the grounds of sexual unfaithfulness, though the ideal, as passages such as 1 Cor. 7:10–11 show, is that the marriage should be maintained if at all possible. The implication of Matthew's teaching seems to be that, if divorce is given because of unfaithfulness, the partner who was not unfaithful has the right to remarry.[27] Jesus' point here is that marriage is permanent, since it involves a vow. One should not try to figure out how to get out of marriage, for if one gets out of it, one suffers a moral fall.

Summary Luke 16:14–18 speaks about authority and values. Who shows the way to God? Jesus is in the midst of a challenge about authority with the Pharisees, who scoff at his teaching. Their two different approaches to God are battling over destinies. Jesus does not back off from the confrontation, but accuses the Pharisees of pride, which God abhors. He notes that the time of kingdom fulfillment has come with him. All that the law intended to accomplish in terms of God's plan will come to pass. He is the source of authority in terms of revealing the way to God, a major theme

27. For a defense of this position, see Murray 1953 and Hoehner 1987. For a defense of these grounds for divorce, but with no right to remarry, see Heth and Wenham 1984. Against a no-divorce-no-remarriage position stands Paul's reading of Jesus' command in 1 Cor. 7:12–16, which allows for divorce in the case of an unbeliever's desertion. Surely if Jesus' remarks were to be taken in the most strict sense, Paul would not have allowed this possibility, since an absolute view of a text such as Luke 16:18 apparently would have prohibited this option.

throughout Luke's journey section. Jesus' authoritative pronouncement prohibiting divorce is an illustration of that authority. It goes beyond the exception of Moses in its description of the perils of remarriage. It shows that righteousness hates divorce. Luke wishes the reader to see Jesus' identity as the authoritative messenger of God's kingdom. God's values mean that we do not serve money (16:10–13) or worship self (16:14–15). We are urged to enter the kingdom (16:16–17) and have values that honor commitments to others and to God (16:18). It is to him that we must respond, and it is through him that the will of God is revealed, even in such difficult areas as divorce and remarriage. One is not to serve the creation or its creatures, one is to serve and honor God by responding to Jesus with integrity.

Additional Note

16:14. Who is the audience for this unit? Only the Pharisees ($\mathfrak{P}^{75}$, ℵ, B, L, Ψ, most Itala, Syriac, Coptic) or also (καί) the disciples (A, P, W, Δ, Θ, family 1, family 13, and Byz [though some in diverse word order])? A reference to the Pharisees alone is more likely, given the versional distribution and the focus of Jesus' criticism on this group. In addition, the presence of καί in this verse would be redundant in light of 16:1. Regardless, the audience is broad, including disciples and Pharisees, since the Pharisees were an addition to the audience. However, the attention is now on the leadership.

3. Parable of Lazarus and the Rich Man (16:19–31)

The parable of Lazarus and the rich man (or Dives, from the Latin rendering of πλούσιος, *plousios*, rich) is the second major teaching unit on wealth in Luke 16 (the other is the parable of the crafty steward in 16:1–13). The account contrasts the fate of the dependent poor and the callous rich through a graphic picture of eschatological reversal (cf. 1:50–53; 16:13–15). All the benefits that the rich man possesses in this life are lost in the next, while all that the poor man lacks on earth is provided for him in the afterlife. The account is a warning that the possession of wealth now does not necessarily mean one will possess wealth later. It also calls on the wealthy to be generous with what they have to meet the needs of those who have nothing (Tannehill 1986: 131–32). Callous indulgence in this life will be met with an absence of blessing from God in the next. One reaps what one sows. The story's focus is the negative example, since the rich man has much painful dialogue in his attempt to alter his irreversible and tragic fate, as well as his attempt to rescue his family from the same potential destiny (16:24–31). In Luke's contrasting literary touch, Lazarus does not say a word.[1] In the end, he needs no defending.

One additional point concludes the account (16:27–31). Revelation has already made clear what God desires. If Moses and the prophets have not been believed, neither will a return from the dead convince people to change how they live before God. The Scriptures are true, and they promise a resurrection when all will face God. One should live in that light. The OT also shows how to care for the poor, another case where the law continues to have moral value.[2] Deuteronomy 24:10–22 appears to be the basis for this remark.

---

1. This silence recalls the woman who anointed Jesus' feet in 7:36–50. Her actions spoke for her, as did those of Mary in 10:38–42.

2. L. Johnson 1977: 141–43 notes the link between this text and 16:14–18 concerning the dispute over generosity and the law's value. So also T. Schmidt 1987: 155–57 speaks of 16:14–31 as a unit to make the point about this connection. He calls this warning to the godless rich a "polemical blow to opponents [and an] ethical sting to" Luke's readers. The parable is eventually a parable of rejection, and thus a parable of warning.

The account divides neatly into three parts: the situation of the characters in this life (16:19–21), the situation of the characters in the afterlife (16:22–23), and the rich man's painful pleading with Abraham during the afterlife, when it is too late (16:24–31). It has two settings: this life (16:19–21) and the afterlife (16:22–31). This is a parable of reversal, since the situation in the two settings reverses.

Sources and Historicity

The account is unique to Luke, so it is L material (Aland 1985: §228). Its uniqueness causes some to ask whether the account goes back to Jesus. But Jesus' critique of wealth for its own sake exists in many levels of the tradition, even if Luke emphasizes it more than others (Matt. 19:16–24 = Mark 10:17–25; Luke 6:20, 24). He also teaches about callous treatment of others (Matt. 18:23–35). It is important to note that the parable is not against the rich per se, but against the callous rich, which makes the theme a variation on Luke's treatment of the wealthy. The reversal theme is unlike other afterlife texts, which typically have a judgment scene. Reversal is also a key theme for Jesus (Matt. 20:1–16; 22:2–13 = Luke 14:16–24 = Gospel of Thomas 64). The parable has four points: (1) the treatment of people in this life, (2) the consequences of being callous to the needs of the poor, (3) the permanence of judgment, and (4) the inability of a person not hearing the Scripture to respond to God's action in the world—even miraculous action. A major point is that once one dies, one's fate is sealed. This account allows no room for those in Hades to eventually win their way into heaven. Another idea is also present: many who seem poor now will experience the riches of heaven later. It is not necessarily the case that the rich are blessed and the poor are not.

The story comes in two steps, since the issue of resurrection in 16:27–31 follows the issue of the treatment of others in 16:19–26. Such two-step stories are rhetorically common for Jesus (Matt. 20:1–16; 22:1–14; Luke 15:11–32). The parable was originally unified.[3] There is no need to challenge its historicity because of its appeal to the resurrection. Such hope was widespread in ancient Judaism (Dan. 12:2; 1 Enoch 108). Divine retribution in the afterlife is a fundamental Jewish concept. Nolland (1993a: 826–27) argues that 16:30–31 was added later because of (a) its explicit reference

---

3. For unity are Marshall 1978: 633–34 and Grobel 1963–64. Bultmann 1963: 178 denies unity (although he says that Luke received a unified story), wrongly assuming that a parable can only have one point. Crossan 1973: 66–67 and B. Scott 1989: 142–46 argue that 16:19–26 go back to Jesus and 16:27–31 to the early church, citing conceptual ties to Luke 24. The Jesus Seminar (Funk and Hoover 1993: 360–62) makes a similar break, printing 16:19–26 in gray type (arguing that its roots may go back to Jesus) and 16:27–31 in black type (arguing that these verses were added later and are inauthentic). For refutation, see Pilgrim 1981: 114–15 and Hock 1987: 454–55.

to resurrection, (b) the common Lucan appeal to Moses and the prophets, and (c) the mention of repentance (Meier 1994: 829–30 argues only against 16:31). But 16:30 parallels the appeal to father Abraham in 16:24, and its mention of "going from the dead" does not equal resurrection but refers to a visit from the dead. The appeal to resurrection in Luke 16:31 serves as literary heightening of the appeal in the parable and makes sense in the tone of the account. The remark also has an enigmatic edge, since it asserts that the resurrection is not convincing. In light of the resurrection's central role in preaching, would the early church create such a statement? The entire remark makes more sense as a defense of Moses and the prophets, thus fitting a precross setting.

The basic story line has parallels in the larger culture. Egypt had a story about a finely clothed man in royal linen and a poor man on a mat (Creed 1930: 209–10; Kistemaker 1980: 236 n. 1; B. Scott 1989: 156–57).[4] Judaism had a story about a rich tax collector named Bar Ma'jan and a poor teacher of the law (*y. Ḥag.* 77d [2.2] [= Neusner et al. 1982–93: 20.57]).[5] In both stories, the roles of the two men are reversed in the afterlife.

Several interesting questions surround this story. Is it technically a parable? How much can one infer about the afterlife from the account's details?

Some say that the account lacks the signs of a parable, since a parable is a comparison of everyday life drawing on repeated phenomena.[6] Several issues support this distinction. First, it is neither called a parable (e.g., 8:4; 12:16, 41; 13:6; 15:3; 18:9) nor introduced with a comparative that suggests a parable (e.g., 13:18, 20). However, this consideration is not decisive, since some parables lack such introduction (e.g., Mark 12:1; Luke 15:1 [a series of stories, only the first of which is called a parable]; 19:12; Linnemann 1966: 16).

Second, its characters have names, unlike every other parable,

4. The Egyptian account is dated before 331 B.C. by Jeremias 1963a: 183 n. 47 (the earliest manuscript is from A.D. 100), but Hock 1987: 452 shows that the Egyptian folk tale is not the likely background, since Luke lacks key elements of it. Hock's appeal, however, to Micyllus in Lucian of Samosata's *Gallus* and *Cataplus* likewise errs. These parallels merely show that the theme is a general one in the ancient culture. Hock calls the parable's criterion of judgment unique, but it is not. The standards of care for the needy come from the Torah and should be followed, a common theme for Jesus.

5. On the parallelism between Luke 16 and 1 Enoch, see Nickelsburg 1978–79. These conceptual contacts show how Jesus' remarks fit a Jewish milieu.

6. Blomberg 1990: 205 argues for a parable since the phrase *a certain man* is often used in Jesus' parables as well as rabbinic parables. Blomberg also notes that the story shares the three-point structure of other parables (e.g., 14:16). Against a parable is Gooding 1987: 277, who argues that parables deal with actual things and activities in the world, not things such as the afterlife directly.

where the figures are nameless or belong to generic categories, showing their everyday quality.[7] The passage is also unique in portraying the afterlife, not just judgment or the banquet table. So, technically speaking, the account is not a simple parable.

Linnemann (1966: 4–5) calls it an illustration, along with the stories of the good Samaritan (10:25–37), the rich fool (12:13–21), and the Pharisee and the tax collector (18:9–14). Of these, the good Samaritan lacks an introductory note that a formal parable is present. But saying that the account is not exactly like most parables does not mean that it is not illustrative or comparative. The account should be called an example story (Fitzmyer 1985: 1126). Blomberg (1990: 73) calls example stories a subclass of parables, making it a special category. Thus, to call this account parabolic is not entirely incorrect. It teaches a lesson through comparison of a graphic hypothetical situation with true life. It depicts, not a single real event, but a representative one. It contains instructive detail about behavior that is not to be followed. It does not present a historical event, much like the good Samaritan does not. The example story simply pictures possible behavior.[8] Some in the early church read the account as a parable, as seen in Codex D's opening: "And he said another parable" (εἶπεν δὲ καὶ ἑτέραν παραβολήν).

Calling the account an example story implies that its details about the afterlife are graphic portrayals, not necessarily actual descriptions of the afterlife. This does not mean that there is no afterlife or no place like Hades. It means that the conversations are simply part of the story's literary means to depict the great chasm in the afterlife between the righteous in paradise and those in Hades. Such a separation is permanent.

The outline of Luke 16:19–31 is as follows:

a. The rich man and Lazarus in this life (16:19–21)
   i. The rich man (16:19)
   ii. Lazarus (16:20–21)
b. The rich man and Lazarus in the next life (16:22–23)
   i. Lazarus at Abraham's bosom (16:22a)
   ii. The rich man tormented in Hades (16:22b–23)

---

7. Parallel literary phenomena to Lazarus and Abraham are the Levite and the Samaritan in the story of the good Samaritan, which is also an example story.

8. Bultmann 1963: 178 calls the account a similitude, which is where he puts parables and such. Berger 1984: 51 sees it as a parable. Ernst 1977: 472 rightly compares it to 15:11–32 and 16:1–8. Hauck, *TDNT* 5:752, calls it an illustrative story and compares it to 10:30–37; 12:16–21; and 18:9–14. For the structure, see B. Scott 1989: 146–48.

c. The rich man's pleas to Abraham (16:24–31)
　　i. The appeal for water (16:24–26)
　　　　(1) Request (16:24)
　　　　(2) Reversal (16:25)
　　　　(3) The unbridgeable chasm in the afterlife (16:26)
　　ii. The appeal for Lazarus to be sent to the family
　　　　(16:27–29)
　　　　(1) Request (16:27–28)
　　　　(2) Reply: Scripture is enough (16:29)
　　iii. The appeal for a message from the dead (16:30–31)
　　　　(1) Request (16:30)
　　　　(2) Reply: to refuse Scripture is to refuse the sign
　　　　　　(16:31)

Through appeal to a negative example, the unit gives a warning to live generously. Jesus challenges the wealthy to use their money generously because they are accountable before God (a common NT theme: Luke 1:52–53; 1 Tim. 6:7–18; James 1:9–11; 5:1–6; Wiefel 1988: 298 compares it to the blessings and woes of Luke 6:20–26). The rich man's callousness is critiqued through the picture of eschatological reversal for the rich and poor. Absence of mercy for those in torment is part of a judgment on the callous rich. The chasm between the righteous and the condemned can never be crossed. The ethic that calls for righteousness is already given in Moses and the prophets. If Moses and the prophets are not believed, neither will a sign like resurrection be convincing. To see God's work as divine, one must hear the Scripture.

Exegesis and Exposition

[19]"There was a ⌐rich man⌐ who was clothed in purple and fine linen and who ate sumptuously every day. [20]A certain poor man, Lazarus, lay at his gate full of sores, [21]who desired to be fed from ⌐what⌐ fell from the rich man's table; moreover the dogs came and licked his sores.

[22]"And it came to pass that the poor man died and he was taken up by the angels into Abraham's bosom. And the rich man also died and was buried. [23]And while he was in Hades, he lifted up his eyes, being in torment, and he sees Abraham from afar and Lazarus at his bosom.

[24]"And he called out, 'Father Abraham, have mercy on me, and send Lazarus to dip the end of his finger in water and cool my tongue, for I am in anguish in this flame.' [25]But Abraham said, 'Son, remember that you in your lifetime received your good things, and Lazarus in like manner bad things. But now he is comforted ⌐here⌐, and you are in anguish. [26]And besides all this, a great chasm has been fixed between us and you, in order that those

who would wish to pass from here to you are not able, and neither can they pass from there to us.' [27]Then he said, 'I beg you, father, to send him to my father's house, [28]for I have five brothers, so that he may warn them, lest they come into this place of torment.' [29]But Abraham said, 'They have Moses and the prophets; let them listen to them.' [30]But he said, 'No, father Abraham, but if someone goes to them from the dead, they will repent.' [31]But he said, 'If they do not listen to Moses and the prophets, neither will they believe if someone should rise from the dead.'"

a. The Rich Man and Lazarus in This Life (16:19–21)
i. The Rich Man (16:19)

The rich man—the focus of the story—is introduced in terms of his **16:19** wealth. This story begins in the same way as the parable of the crafty steward in 16:1: ἄνθρωπός (δέ) τις ἦν πλούσιος (*anthrōpos* [*de*] *tis ēn plousios*, a certain man was rich). This type of introduction signals a parable. The rich man, who is fancily clothed and eats well, is anonymous, unlike the poor man, because the story's generic focus on the wealthy would be compromised by a specific name. Jesus has no particular person in mind.

Purple clothes came from dye derived from snails and were extremely expensive (Kistemaker 1980: 236–37; SB 2:222). Πορφύρα (*porphyra*, lit., purple) probably refers to outer garments, while βύσσος (*byssos*, fine linen) refers to undergarments (Manson 1949: 298; Luce 1933: 268; Fitzmyer 1985: 1130–31; Ernst 1977: 473).[9] Some people have nothing, while others can afford expensive underwear. This man celebrated life daily with great feasts (Bultmann, *TDNT* 2:774).[10] Such was the daily life of comfort that the rich man experienced.

ii. Lazarus (16:20–21)

In contrast to the rich man stands, or rather lies, Lazarus (Manson **16:20** 1949: 298 calls this a "violent" contrast). The Hebrew name לְעָזָר (Lazar) is a contraction of אֶלְעָזָר (Eleazar) and means "God helps." The name is significant, for it indicates someone dependent on God.[11] In addition, one suspects the significance of this name from

---

9. For πορφύρα, see BAGD 694; BAA 1391; 1 Macc. 8:14; 10:62; Esth. 8:15; Mark 15:17, 20. For βύσσος, see BAGD 148; BAA 296–97; Ezek. 16:10; 27:7. The terms occur together in Rev. 18:12; Prov. 31:22; 1QapGen 20.31. On the use of purple to indicate power and regal dress, the late Exod. Rab. 38.8 on 29:1 is illustrative.

10. Εὐφραίνω in the passive means "to make merry, to cheer oneself"; BAGD 327; BAA 663 §2; elsewhere in Luke's Gospel at 12:19; 15:23, 24, 29, 32. MM 267 notes a papyri that describes such a feast.

11. For discussion of the name *Lazarus*, see Dunkerley 1958–59; Derrett 1970: 78–99; Cave 1968–69; B. Scott 1989: 149 n. 28; SB 2:223; Meier 1994: 825, 868 n. 158.

Lazarus's being the only figure in any of Jesus' stories who receives a specific name (Jeremias 1963a: 185). That he is named may also suggest that, though unrecognized by people, the person and fate of Lazarus is known by God (Ernst 1977: 473–74). The name also sets up a poignant detail in 16:24: the rich man shows he knows who Lazarus is (on the reasons posited for its presence, see Nolland 1993a: 828). The name had numerous religious associations for the Jews. Among those who had the name were Aaron's son and successor as high priest (Exod. 6:23), a priest who dedicated the rebuilt wall of Jerusalem (Neh. 12:42), a brother of the Jewish patriot Judas Maccabeus (1 Macc. 2:5), a respected martyr of the same period (2 Macc. 6:18–23), and Abraham's chief trusted servant (Gen. 15:2). Many suggest that the latter figure is the source of the name because of Abraham's presence in the story, while others suggest an allusion to Mary and Martha's brother (Leaney 1958: 225; Luce 1933: 268; Creed 1930: 211; Dunkerley 1958–59: 323–25).[12] The connection with Abraham's servant is hard to establish, and the connection to the contemporary NT figure is to be rejected, since the Lazarus of John 11 had a family of some means that could have cared for him (Meier 1994: 822–31).

Lazarus is very poor (πτωχός, *ptōchos*), since he is lying at the rich man's gate in hopes of receiving food. He is probably crippled and has been placed at the gate; the passive ἐβέβλητο (*ebeblēto*, was lying) suggests someone too ill to move (Matt. 8:6; 9:2; Josephus, *Jewish War* 1.32.3 §629; BAGD 131 §1b; BAA 264 §1b). The term here suggests that Lazarus is a cripple or at least so hungry that he is immobilized (this is affirmed by the next verse, where Lazarus cannot avoid the dogs who lick his sores and thus render him unclean). He is not, however, a leper for then he would not be begging in public (Fitzmyer 1985: 1131; Marshall 1978: 635).

Lazarus lies before the home's high ornate gate. Πυλών (*pylōn*) is usually used of entrances to cities, temples, or palaces (cf. the synonymous πύλη, *pylē*, in Luke 7:12; Acts 3:10; 9:24; Heb. 13:12; Jeremias, *TDNT* 6:921; BAGD 729; BAA 1459). The rich man is portrayed as living in a mansion. The imagery is graphic: the rich man feasts inside, while the crippled poor man lies outside in hopes of receiving a few crumbs.

Lazarus is not only crippled, he is suffering, since his body is full of sores (ἑλκόω, *helkoō*), likely surface ulcers or abscesses (BAGD 251; BAA 507). This condition sharply contrasts the rich man's fine ap-

---

12. This view sees the name as introduced into the story later, but it is hard to substantiate such interpolations. SB 2:223 traces the name's usage and popularity. Fitzmyer 1985: 1131 notes that the name exists on numerous ossuaries, so it is clearly very common.

parel. Later rabbis would have described Lazarus's condition as no life at all. They had a saying that three situations resulted in no life: one who depended on food from another's table, one ruled by his wife, and one whose body was full of sores (*b. Beṣa* 32b; Manson 1949: 299). Fulfilling two of these three conditions, Lazarus's situation is as desperate and tragic as the rich man's is full and sumptuous.

Lazarus has a basic desire: to eat—even scraps if necessary **16:21** (ἐπιθυμέω, *epithymeō*, refers to strong desire, often involving food; Luke 15:16; Fitzmyer 1985: 1131). All he wants is the man's leftovers. This might be something as simple as the bread used as a "finger towel" to mop up any gravy from the dish and then tossed under the table for the dogs after the meal (Jeremias 1963a: 184 n. 53, although Marshall 1978: 636 is skeptical of this detail). This is hardly an extravagant request, since such food would have been thrown out anyway. Some suggest that he is fed (Luce 1933: 269; Plummer 1896: 392; Danker 1988: 283), but the parallelism to the scene in Hades where the rich man does not receive even a single drop of water makes it unlikely that the rich man responded (Arndt 1956: 364). Schweizer (1984: 260) notes that the rich man is like the priest and Levite of the earlier parable of the good Samaritan: he does not really see the suffering, he simply moves on (10:31–32).

To add insult, Lazarus has to endure wild dogs licking his sores, which both infect him and leave him ceremonially unclean.[13] There is no more pathetic scene. There is no suggestion that the dogs picture mercy extended to Lazarus, since such dogs were not viewed positively (1 Kings 14:11; 16:4; 21:19, 23–24; 22:38).[14] Lazarus desires food and gets only the embarrassing attention of unclean animals. By all observable criteria, one would conclude that the rich man is blessed and Lazarus is not. Lazarus never speaks in the parable; he suffers alone and in silence.

b. The Rich Man and Lazarus in the Next Life (16:22–23)
i. Lazarus at Abraham's Bosom (16:22a)

The story switches settings. Time passes and Lazarus dies. His death **16:22a** is stated matter of factly in typical Lucan style (ἐγένετο δέ [*egeneto de*, and it came to pass] and the infinitive occurs twenty-two times in Luke–Acts, only once in Mark, and not at all in Matthew; Fitzmyer 1981: 118). But death is not the end, and so the story continues. Laz-

---

13. A κύων is a wild, undomesticated dog; BAGD 461; BAA 936; Phil. 3:2; Rev. 22:15; Klostermann 1929: 168.

14. On the negative portrayal of dogs in Judaism, see 1 Enoch 89.42–43, 47, 49; B. Scott 1989: 151; Michel, *TDNT* 3:1103. For the view that this is a positive act, see Zahn 1920: 585.

arus is borne up immediately to Abraham's bosom by the angels (other direct-presence texts are Luke 23:43; Acts 7:55; Schweizer, *TDNT* 9:647 n. 182). An angelic escort is a common Jewish image.[15] In the Christian apocrypha, such imagery took on great detail, with pictures of angels doing battle over the souls of people who had passed away (*Apocalypse of Paul* 14 [Schneemelcher 1991–92: 2.720–21]), imagery that recalls Jude 9.

Abraham's bosom was a place of blessing and represents the patriarch's reception of the faithful into heaven.[16] Its origin may parallel the "bosom of Mother Earth" as a Greek reference for the abode of the dead (MM 353). It may also be a more graphic way to speak of someone's "being gathered to the fathers" (Gen. 15:15; 47:30; Deut. 31:16; Judg. 2:10; 1 Kings 1:21; Plummer 1896: 393; Leaney 1958: 226; Ernst 1977: 474). Lazarus goes from being a lonely sufferer at the rich man's gate to an accepted, blessed saint at the side of Judaism's patriarch. Some speculate that Lazarus is at a banquet table, a total reversal of his earthly experience, but there is no explicit reference to banquet imagery anywhere in the parable (but so Jeremias 1963a: 184, citing John 13:23; Klostermann 1929: 168 adds Matt. 8:11). Lazarus is at Abraham's side in intimate fellowship (Manson 1949: 299; Marshall 1978: 636).[17] This fits Luke's concern to show God's compassion for the poor (Luke 4:18; 6:20; 7:22; 14:13, 21; J. Green 1994: 67–68).

ii. The Rich Man Tormented in Hades (16:22b–23)

16:22b The rich man also passes away. His death and burial are mentioned in the same simple fashion as that of Lazarus. His burial is perhaps mentioned specifically to avoid any suggestion that the rich man is condemned to torment for failing to receive a proper burial.[18] Death

---

15. T. Job 47.11; 52.2, 5; T. Abr. (A) 20.11–12. For the reprobate, a satanic escort to hell is also a possibility; T. Asher 6.4–6 (Marshall 1978: 636 notes that this text is textually disputed); SB 2:223–27; Tg. Song 4.12.

16. Because it is a first-century work, 4 Macc. 13:17 provides key evidence: a martyr for the law is welcomed and praised by Abraham, Isaac, and Jacob. See also b. Qid. 72a; b. Giṭ. 57b; *Pesikta Rabbati* 43.4 (= Braude 1968: 2.761); R. Meyer, TDNT 3:825–26. In *Pesikta Rabbati*, if a person bows down to an idol, he or she will have a place at Esau's bosom, not Abraham's.

17. Plummer 1896: 393 notes correctly that Abraham's bosom is not a synonym for paradise, but that Abraham is there shows that Lazarus is among the righteous. The image indicates the story's Jewish flavor; so also Jeremias, *TDNT* 5:769 n. 37, citing T. Abr. (A) 20.13–14.

18. 1 Enoch 22.10–11 speaks of a place for the dead who have sinned and yet have received a proper interment; SB 2:227. Not unlike Jesus' warning, 1 Enoch 103.5–8 delivers a stinging indictment of wealthy Sadducees who live extravagantly only to descend to Sheol.

reduces the rich man's stature. His wealth no longer counts for anything. His extravagance becomes indigence (B. Scott 1989: 154).

Death permanently changes everything. A reversal occurs as the rich **16:23** man looks up and sees Lazarus at Abraham's side, a situation vividly displayed with the present tense ὁρᾷ (hora, he sees). The reference to Abraham's bosom is plural, κόλποις (kolpois), but the meaning is the same as the previous verse (this is a classical plural; Robertson 1923: 408; BDF §141.5; BDR §141.5.9). An image of looking up to the heavens is not necessarily present, especially if the chasm described in 16:26 depicts a canyon. In addition, 16:31 speaks of one rising from the dead, which perhaps suggests that Lazarus comes from below. While the spatial imagery is graphic and figurative, the image creates a mood of distance. The passage depicts the dead being conscious of their fate quickly, though it should be recalled that the picture is symbolic, so that no conclusions can be drawn about the timing of God's judgment in contrast to other texts that put such judgment later.[19]

The rich man's situation stands in stark contrast to Lazarus's new position. Again, one should not press the details of the graphic imagery, though the image has some NT parallel, since the blessed and rejected in 13:28 can see each other as well. This detail pictures the conscious awareness of where one resides after death. We might speak of "Peter at the pearly gates" in the same way that Jesus uses this imagery. It is graphic and pictorial and reflects a reality, rather than describing it literally.[20] The image is Jewish, for in their eschatology the unrighteous and righteous can see each other (2 Esdr. [= 4 Ezra] 7:85, 93; 2 Bar. 51.5–6; Fitzmyer 1985: 1132). The point is that both Lazarus and the rich man know where each other are.

The rich man is in torment in Hades, the place in the OT (שְׁאוֹל, šĕʾôl, Sheol) and in Judaism where the dead were gathered (Ps. 16:10; 86:13). The righteous (2 Macc. 6:23; 1 Enoch 102.4–5) and unrighteous (Ps. Sol. 14:6, 9–10; 15:10) both reside there, though they are separated from one other (1 Enoch 22). However, 1 Enoch 39 seems to place the righteous in a separate locale called heaven (Creed 1930: 212). Thus, within Judaism there is some dispute

---

19. See the unit introduction for a discussion about afterlife symbolism. Klostermann 1929: 168–69 notes the tension and cites 23:43 as another example of instant awareness of blessing after death. Arndt 1956: 365 notes that Acts 7:59; 2 Cor. 5:8; and Phil. 1:23 express a similar hope of instant awareness by the righteous. It may be that instant consciousness occurs in what has been called the "intermediate state," with confirming judgment and glorified resurrection coming later.

20. Maddox 1982: 103 notes that the modern pearly-gate picture is not intended to be a conflation of Rev. 21:10–15 and Matt. 16:19 (which is designed to picture reality in detail). The absence of Jesus or God in such eschatology shows it to be only graphic.

about who inhabits Hades (SB 4:1017–19; 2:228; Josephus, *Antiquities* 18.1.3 §14; *Jewish War* 2.8.14 §163; 3.8.5 §375).

The NT shares this ambiguity, for Acts 2:27, 31 (cf. Matt. 12:40) states that Jesus was not abandoned or left in Hades after his resurrection, which implies that he went there. But Hades generally has negative connotations in the NT, since other parts of Jesus' teaching suggest that only the power of death and judgment is associated with Hades (Matt. 16:18; 11:23 = Luke 10:15). If so, Hades comes close to equaling Gehenna, although technically Gehenna is the place where the final judgment of the unrighteous occurs (Creed 1930: 212).[21] In the NT, Hades is where the dead are, while Gehenna is where they experience final judgment (Jeremias, *TDNT* 1:148–49, 658; Jeremias 1963a: 185). It is clear that the righteous do not end up in Gehenna. Wherever the rich man is, Lazarus is not there (16:26). As a righteous man, Lazarus does not seem to be in Hades in its negative sense, but it is not clear that he is not in a compartment of Hades (so Plummer 1896: 394; Arndt 1956: 365). Marshall (1978: 637) suggests that the distinction between the rich man's locale and Lazarus's is real but states it with some reservation (so also Fitzmyer 1985: 1132 and Grensted 1914–15). The point is that the rich man is suffering from judgment, while Lazarus is enjoying blessing at Abraham's side. Their roles have reversed as a result of their journey into the afterlife.

Βάσανος (*basanos*) means torture or torment and often described the punishment one inflicted on a slave to elicit a confession (Wis. 3:1–10; 4 Macc. 13:15; MM 104; J. Schneider, *TDNT* 1:563; BAGD 134; BAA 270).[22] Luke 16:25 shows the rich man wilting from the heat of Hades. This suffering, however, is probably more mental than physical, since otherwise the fire could be expected to consume him. There is great anguish in discovering that one's ultimate abode is not with the righteous and that this position is eternal (on judgment as eternal, see Matt. 25:46; 2 Thess. 1:9; Jude 7).

c. The Rich Man's Pleas to Abraham (16:24–31)
i. The Appeal for Water (16:24–26)
(1) Request (16:24)

16:24 The rich man tries to change his circumstance by appealing to Abraham. This may suggest that he was relying on his heritage to pull

---

21. For an attempt to distinguish Hades, Gehenna, and paradise, see Jeremias, *TDNT* 5:769 n. 37.

22. Torment in both the intermediate state and the resurrection is found in Jewish (1 Enoch 22) and early Christian texts (2 Clem. 10.4; 17.7). In the 2 Clement texts the torture of hell is presented quite vividly as physical suffering.

him through, but John the Baptist had already warned against this in 3:8 (Schweizer 1984: 261; Danker 1988: 284; Ernst 1977: 475; Fitzmyer 1985: 1133).[23] Such an appeal to Abraham, protector of the Jews, was natural since he was the bearer of the great covenant (Gen. 12:1–3; Marshall 1978: 637; Jeremias, *TDNT* 1:8; SB 1:116–21).

The situation is ironic. The rich man seemed not to notice Lazarus on earth, but now he appeals through Abraham for the poor man's aid. The use of Lazarus's name in his appeal suggests that the rich man knew about Lazarus all along, making his neglect of the poor man that much worse. Perhaps even now he sees Lazarus as a servant (Plummer 1896: 394), or perhaps he concludes that if someone like Lazarus can be at Abraham's side, surely he can get relief from the patriarch's intercession. The rich man acts as if nothing has changed despite his present locale. He is sadly mistaken, for his fate was determined by his lack of response during his earthly life. As he had measured, so now it is measured to him (Luke 6:38). His lack of aid to those in need then means no aid for him now. The rich man's former wealth does him no good in the afterlife.

Jewish discussions of the afterlife commonly included physical torment (16:23) and the ability of the dead to see and converse with others (2 Esdr. [= 4 Ezra] 7:79–85, 91–93; Eccles. Rab. 1.15.1 on 1:15; *y. Ḥag.* 77d [2.2] [= Neusner et al. 1982–93: 20.57–58]; Creed 1930: 213). Fire in the underworld is a common image in the OT (Isa. 66:24), Judaism (Sir. 21:9–10; 1 Enoch 10.13–14; 63.10), and the NT (Mark 9:48; Rev. 19:12). The OT uses the idea of quenching thirst as a general image for desiring God's presence (Ps. 42:1–2 [42:2–3 MT]; 143:6; Rev. 21:6; Grundmann 1963: 329), while being thirsty is an image of divine judgment (Isa. 5:13; 50:2; 65:13; Hos. 2:3 [2:5 MT]; 2 Esdr. [= 4 Ezra] 8:59; 1 Enoch 22.9; Bertram, *TDNT* 2:228–29; Klostermann 1929: 169; Manson 1949: 300). The rich man requests that Lazarus put just a drop of water on his parched tongue to relieve his anguish from the heat. The request is a small one, but it recalls Lazarus's similar small request for scraps of food. Just as there were no crumbs for Lazarus, there will be no water for the rich man. The difference is that now the rich man has no hope of reversing his fortune. He sealed his own fate by his actions.

(2) Reversal (16:25)

Jesus summarizes the eschatological reversal that has come to both **16:25** of the story's main figures (Grundmann 1963: 329; cf. 1:53). Abraham's words are tender but firm in addressing the rich man as τέκνον

23. On Abraham as father and the Jews as his children, see Luke 1:73; 13:16; 19:9. Josephus called Abraham "the father of all Hebrews"; *Antiquities* 14.10.22 §255.

(*teknon*, son). Some "sons" will not be in heaven. The rich man has gone from self-indulgence to anguish. Luke here uses a different term for suffering than that used in 16:23: ὀδυνάομαι (*odynaomai*) refers to continual pain and grief, especially mental pain, which is why "anguish" is a good way to render the term (Hauck, *TDNT* 5:115; BAGD 555; BAA 1125).[24] Lazarus has gone from suffering to comfort. Παρακαλέω (*parakaleō*) is a difficult word to define precisely; it can mean to encourage or comfort (BAGD 617 §4; BAA 1248 §4). In this setting, it clearly refers to the mental comfort that Lazarus receives from his new situation. The fate of the two men in the afterlife stands opposite what each experienced in his earthly life. The rich man has already received in full what life can give him.[25] In the afterlife, he is destitute and tormented. In contrast, Lazarus receives life forever.

This contrast is part of Abraham's reason for not calling Lazarus to the rich man's aid. The point is stated rather briefly and cryptically. In essence, Abraham says, your roles are reversed. What Lazarus was in the old life, you have become. What Lazarus lacked, you now lack. What you did not provide him then, he cannot provide you now. You are reaping what you sowed. The lesson is in the reply, for in effect Abraham says that the rich man's extravagant wealth and lack of compassion on earth has resulted in spiritual poverty and absence of mercy eternally. There is no mercy in the afterlife for those who fail to show compassion in this life (Jeremias 1963a: 185). The teaching pictures what Jesus declared in 6:20, 24.

It is important to recognize that the parable illustrates Jesus' teaching in 16:9 about using wealth generously. The rich man is not condemned because he is rich, but because he slipped into the coma of callousness that wealth often produces. He became consumed with his own joy, leisure, and celebration and failed to respond to the suffering and need of others around him. His callousness made his earthly riches all that he would receive from life. Realizing the relationship of the parable to other teachings of Jesus is important, for some regard this parable as so overstated in its condemnation of the wealthy that it could not be Jesus' point.[26] Some understand the

24. Luke 2:48 and Acts 20:38 show that it is mental pain that is often described by ὀδυνάομαι.

25. So ἀπέλαβες means "you have received." BAGD 94 and BAA 189 note that ἀπολαμβάνω has a commercial sense here: the rich man is "paid up." The sense equals that of ἀπέχω (to receive) in 6:24.

26. So E. Scott 1924: 91 (cf. Luce 1933: 272): "[Luke] was plainly a man of tender and generous sentiment, who in his warm sympathy for the poor had come to idealize poverty. It need not be doubted that the sayings which he attributes to Jesus are genuine; but he is at pains to put this side of the teaching into the forefront. . . . The original meaning of the parable may have been little more than that earthly positions will be reversed in the coming age. But the rich man's fate is so presented that he

verse to teach that there is a fixed quota of wealth and poverty to experience in life and the wealthy who run up their quota in this life end up with nothing later. Such a reading disregards not only the teaching of a passage like 16:9, it also ignores the poignant picture that Luke will deliver later in 19:8–9, where Zacchaeus becomes a model for how to handle wealth. Luke 14:12–13 also illustrates the call to generosity, with a promise that such generosity will be paid back at the resurrection (Schneider 1977a: 342). More radically stated forms of the same emphasis are found in 12:33–34 and 18:22. (On Luke's view of the rich and poor, see Heard 1988.)

(3) The Unbridgeable Chasm in the Afterlife (16:26)

The book closes for the rich man. In a decisive remark, Abraham **16:26** portrays himself as helpless to act because of sovereignly established boundaries between the rich man on one side and Lazarus and himself on the other. There is what he calls a great gulf between them. The *hapax legomenon* χάσμα (*chasma*, chasm) describes an "unbridgeable space between Abraham and the place of torture" (so BAGD 879; BAA 1754).[27] No one can pass from one area to the other in either direction. Διαβαίνω (*diabainō*) was often used to describe crossing a river or a trip from one region of land to another (BAGD 181; BAA 363; elsewhere in the NT only at Acts 16:9; Heb. 11:29). The theological passive that such a place "has been fixed" asserts that God has set up the afterlife in such a way that the righteous and unrighteous do not mix (Fitzmyer 1985: 1133–34; 2 Esdr. [= 4 Ezra] 7:102–5; 1 Enoch 18.11–12; 22.8–10). As Danker (1988: 285) says, there is no bridge over the chasm. The image is strong and suggests that how we respond in this life is decisive for where we reside in the next, a key point that some find hard to accept.[28] If righteous and unrighteous do not mix in the afterlife, then the possibility of being saved after death is excluded.[29]

---

seems to be punished simply because he is rich, while Lazarus is rewarded for his poverty. This false and puerile lesson cannot be that which Jesus intended." Scott reads the parable too much in isolation from Jesus' other teachings and fails to see that material possessions are not the point; the use of them is.

27. Bishop 1973 suggests that the chasm pictures the deep wadis of the Judean desert, which are high and deep but not so wide that one is prevented from seeing what is on the other side.

28. So, e.g., Luce 1933: 270 objects to the teaching of an eternal punishment where one cannot be forgiven in the afterlife. This objection, however, is philosophical, not biblical.

29. Jeremias 1963a: 186 argues that purgatory is excluded, but technically this is not correct, since the doctrine of purgatory teaches that the elect go to Hades to be purified. Purgatory must be evaluated on grounds other than this passage. Purgatory is not in view here, but the permanent rejection of the unrighteous is.

ii. The Appeal for Lazarus to Be Sent to the Family (16:27–29)
(1) Request (16:27–28)

16:27   The rich man changes his approach since he realizes that his own situation is hopeless: he appeals on behalf of his family members who are still alive and have a chance. The rich man does have compassion; it was just limited (contrast Luke 6:31–35). Now that he realizes the reality of his situation, he wishes to spare his family the same mistake he has made. He knows his brothers need to repent. Literarily, the rich man becomes an advocate of the very position that Jesus is taking. In addition, he speaks as one who made a fatal, eternal mistake in his life and he wishes to help others avoid doing the same. In effect, the rich man is saying, "Do not let them make the same mistake I made. Warn them that the way I lived ends in disaster." The rich man wants no descendants when it comes to his deadly lifestyle. Significantly, the rich man's current conversion of perspective does not change his fate, which was already irreversibly determined by his earthly life. The parable teaches that some realizations, even though they are right, come too late to be of any good to anyone. This point lends a note of tragedy to the story.

There is also irony, for the rich man asks for Lazarus to go from the dead to communicate to his brothers. The request is refused, but in the parabolic world, the rich man actually gives the message that he wants communicated to his brothers. He warns Luke's readers to avoid his error.

What form this requested visit would take is not clear; perhaps a vision or dream. Saul's vision of Samuel may be an example of what the rich man proposes (1 Sam. 28:7–20; Jeremias 1963a: 186).[30] This seems better than to see a request for a resurrection, for the remark of Luke 16:30–31 is best seen as heightening the request and foreshadowing what will happen with Jesus. These later verses make the point that even a resurrection would not be good enough.

16:28   The rich man explains his concern for his five brothers, who apparently share the same philosophy of life that he had on earth.[31] These brothers need to be warned, for if they continue with their lifestyle they also will end up in torment. The rich man believes that only a

---

30. Fitzmyer 1985: 1134 notes Greek parallels of the dead returning to speak to those on earth: Lucian, *Demonax* 43; Plato, *Republic* 614D (10.13).

31. Some see in the reference to five brothers a possible allusion to Herod's brothers, but this connection is unlikely (Leaney 1958: 226 notes the view). It is a rich man, not a ruler, who is addressed. Others suggest that five plus one makes six and as such represents the nation's unbelieving half (Jülicher 1899: 2.639). This suggestion also seems unlikely, since "half" the nation did not come to Jesus. Such a detail would suggest allegory, which is not the story's genre.

warning from someone who has died and now knows better can save them. Διαμαρτύρομαι (*diamartyromai*) means "to warn" or "to give solemn testimony about something" (Strathmann, *TDNT* 4:512; Exod. 19:10; Acts 2:40; 20:21, 24; 1 Tim. 5:21; 2 Tim. 2:14; 4:1; BAGD 186; BAA 373). The warning would obviously call them to repent and be more generous, lest they share their brother's fate (Manson 1949: 301). Their heritage and wealth are no guarantee of eternal blessing. The rich man wishes to spare them eternal pain through the testimony of a sign from the netherworld.

(2) Reply: Scripture Is Enough (16:29)

Abraham responds that a warning from one who has died is not necessary.[32] Since God had already spoken on the matter in the OT, Abraham tells the rich man that his brothers can hear (i.e., obey) the warning from Moses and the prophets.[33] Many OT passages teach how to treat fellow humans, especially the poor: Deut. 14:28–29; 15:1–3, 7–12; 22:1–2; 23:19 [23:20 MT]; 24:7–15, 19–21; 25:13–14; Isa. 3:14–15; 5:7–8; 10:1–3; 32:6–7; 58:3, 6–7, 10; Jer. 5:26–28; 7:5–6; Ezek. 18:12–18; 33:15; Amos 2:6–8; 5:11–12; 8:4–6; Mic. 2:1–2; 3:1–3; 6:10–11; Zech. 7:9–10; Mal. 3:5. If these brothers heard the Scriptures and responded, they would be in good shape. Any message that someone from the dead could bring them would be no clearer than what they already had. Plummer (1896: 396) says, "Wonders may impress a worldly mind for the moment; but only a will freely submitting itself to moral control can avail to change the heart." God is only impressed with a heartfelt change, a change of conviction that the Word is capable of generating in a receptive heart. The spirit of the passage is summarized by Luke 11:28 (Arndt 1956: 366). To respond to Jesus means to become more sensitive to others, and the ability to respond this way will be supplied by the Spirit, as seen in the responses by believers in the Book of Acts.

16:29

iii. The Appeal for a Message from the Dead (16:30–31)
(1) Request (16:30)

The rich man does not give up. He disagrees that Moses and the prophets are enough, since he himself failed to heed them (Plummer

16:30

---

32. The present tense λέγει (he says) is a historical present: "he [Abraham] said." This is one of five historical presents in Luke's parables (13:8; 16:7, 23; 19:22). Since Luke normally avoids this tense, it probably indicates pre-Lucan material; Jeremias 1963a: 182–83.

33. On the phrase "Moses and the prophets," see Luke 16:16, 31; 24:27, 44; 1QS 1.3; 8.15–16; CD 5.21–6.1. The combination is not found in formal Judaism; SB 4:415–17; Marshall 1978: 639. On the theme that God has so revealed himself in the OT that neglect makes one culpable, see Lorenzen 1975–76.

1896: 396)! The rich man's false premise—that there is something greater than God's message through his servants—is significant. He is convinced that some type of sign from the afterlife will be more effective.[34] The premise could not be more incorrect. This focus on a specific type of sign is something that Jesus has already warned against (11:16, 29–32). The only sign that people need is the preached call to repent. God's revelation of his will and his call to love others should be enough. That sign is present in Moses, the prophets, and Jesus' teaching. Ultimately, this message must be heeded. A supernatural wonder alone is not good enough. There were many other indicators and signs of this type in Jesus' ministry, but they went unheeded as people pursued a specific sign or tried to make Jesus fit their expectations. Why add another sign, when many had already been made available? As Abraham makes clear in 16:31, even when such a sign is given graciously, response will still be lacking.

(2) Reply: To Refuse Scripture Is to Refuse the Sign (16:31)

16:31 Abraham again disagrees, revealing God's mind in this clash of worldviews. Abraham does not share the rich man's optimism. God has often worked mightily, only to see people lack belief.[35] Since the OT message of hope is tied to the power of God's work, Abraham argues that even a resurrection from the dead will not lead to belief, because failure to believe Moses and the prophets shows where one's heart really is. The remark suggests that a lack of empirical evidence does not stop people from believing; their will does. What is needed is a heart that responds to God and does not seek heavenly signs. To see God's work and hear his call the heart must be open and the eyes must be looking for him. Only faith yields understanding.

The first condition in this verse is a first-class condition that means the premise about not believing Moses and the prophets is presented as the current live option: "If they do not listen to Moses and the prophets—and they do not—neither will they believe if someone is raised from the dead." The promise that response to resurrection parallels the response to the revelators of old underlies the theme of continuity that Luke's theology emphasizes. Jesus' message is not a surprise to anyone who really understands what the promise concerns. How one responds to the previous revelation will

---

34. Grammatically this is a third-class condition that means the premise is presented as possible but not yet occurring: "If someone should go to them from the dead, then. . . ."

35. For example, many psalms testify to the great work of the exodus and the accompanying unbelief (e.g., Ps. 78). Schweizer 1984: 261 notes that the raising of Lazarus in John 11:43–53 failed to stop opposition to Jesus.

determine how one responds to Jesus. One is to take revelation as a whole. The two—Jesus and ancient Scriptures—are linked. To reject the ancient message is to reject Jesus, and to reject his teaching is to reject the ancient message. If God's Word is believed, a resurrection is not necessary to engender faith; it only bolsters it.[36] If they cannot hear God's voice, they will not see his hands at work.

The second condition is a third-class condition presenting the possibility of resurrection without comment: "If a resurrection should come." Abraham has raised the stakes a little. The rich man asked for a message from someone in the afterlife, a mere visit from the afterlife. Abraham says even if a person were to do more than just visit, if one were to rise from the dead, such a sign would not change the way the man's brothers respond if they are not inclined to believe God. Such resurrections were rare in the OT and are better called resuscitations since all the figures died again (1 Kings 17:17–24; 2 Kings 4:18–37; 13:20–21). Abraham's comment clearly alludes to Jesus' approaching resurrection. Literarily, this makes Abraham testify to Jesus' approaching work, though that would only become clear after the fact.[37] Luke often refers to Jesus' resurrection using a form of ἀνίστημι (anistēmi, to rise).[38]

There is great irony in the parable. Jesus' listeners (and Luke's readers) hear the testimony of one from the dead, which the brothers in the story are denied. Thus, the parable ends with the listeners facing a choice. Will they become generous in response to God's demands to love others? Or will they live in a self-indulgent way, unconcerned about those in need? In the movement of the narrative, the Pharisees may be the audience in view (16:14–15), but the warning also calls for Luke's audience to consider the kind of values that God desires of his people. The message of the afterlife issues a call to repent and a warning about the importance of the decision.

Summary

Luke 16:19–31 is one of the most complex of Jesus' stories and makes four fundamental points. It is mainly a call to the rich to examine how they use their wealth. They should know that God is not pleased with a self-indulgent lifestyle that has little care and compassion for those in need. As such, the parable is a call to the

36. Danker 1988: 285–86 notes that Jesus appears only to his disciples after his resurrection, a point that confirms this emphasis. Even in the Book of Acts, the resurrection is not preached as a bare fact, but as a fulfillment of Scripture, so that the call is always to believe God's promise.

37. The issue of authenticity raised by this allusion is discussed in the sources and historicity section above.

38. Luke 18:33; 24:7, 46; Acts 10:41; 17:3; BAGD 70; BAA 138–39. The related noun ἀνάστασις (resurrection) is used of Jesus in Acts 1:22; 2:31; 4:2, 33; 17:18, 32; 26:23; BAGD 60; BAA 119–20.

rich to repent of their inappropriate use of wealth and is a reply to the Pharisees' grumbling of 16:14. The life of the rich man is a counterexample to 16:9. The parable's sympathetic portrait of the faithful poor gives a word of comfort to them that God will judge the uncaring rich in the afterlife. But the passage's main message is to the rich, since the rich man is the major figure.

The unit also teaches that nothing can change one's fate in the afterlife beyond the factors present in this life. Whatever the force of the images of torment for the rich man and blessing for Lazarus, one message rings clear: once God has rendered judgment, it is permanent. The ethical choices of this life last for eternity. The encounter with Jesus and his teaching has long-term implications, bringing either comfort or torment. As such, a proper ethical reading of one's heart before Jesus is crucial to one's welfare.

Third, Jesus' parable closely links his teaching and the OT's ethical message. As such it illustrates a passage like 16:16–17. Jesus' ethic, though not respected by those who see themselves as custodians of the Torah and the prophets, is in line with what God's ancient servants taught. Because this is so, one's response to Jesus is an indicator of how one has responded to Moses and the prophets (John 5:39–47). In the area of wealth and generosity to the poor, this point is especially true. Jesus does not stray from the OT, but proclaims its message. The foundational ethical demands found in this parable apply to any who would follow him, since he came to fulfill the righteousness and love that the OT calls for, especially love for one's fellow humans.

Finally, the parable shows that signs in themselves are of no value if the heart is not right. Only a responsive heart will listen to God's message and respond to his great works. No amount of wonder-working can change a heart that is unwilling to be challenged by God's demand for righteousness. A lack of signs is not why people reject Jesus. Rather, people willfully reject him. The heart cannot see what it is not looking for. Jesus' message is a call to recognize the need to repent. Those with ripe hearts recognize that need and come to him for the forgiveness he makes available to them. They also receive the righteousness and relationship he supplies. Compassion for those in need is the result. Those whose hearts are hardened will never accept the call to recognize their need to let God change them. They will not respond to the evidence that God leaves in Jerusalem's empty tomb. Even the great patriarch Abraham testifies to this fundamental truth about sin. In effect, the parable ends by calling the listener not only to believe Jesus but also that great patriarch and custodian of promise, the father of the nation of Israel. To disagree is to reject the testimony of God's servants, stretching back to the patriarch Abraham. To disagree is to challenge divine history.

Additional Notes

16:19. In some texts the rich man is named. For example, $\mathfrak{P}^{75}$ gives his name as Νευης (Neves), but this reading does not have enough support to be original. A more poorly attested name, Finaeus, appears in some Latin sources (Fitzmyer 1985: 1130; Marshall 1976: 634; Metzger 1975: 165–66; Cadbury 1962; Cadbury 1965; Grobel 1963–64).

16:21. The variant τῶν ψιχίων τῶν πιπτόντων (the scraps that fell) is found in $\aleph^2$, A, D (with the alternate spelling ψιχῶν), W, Δ, Θ, Ψ, family 13, Byz, Lect, and most versions. While it could be original, it looks like assimilation to Matt. 15:27. Nevertheless, it captures the sense of the original reading, even though the UBS–NA text (read by $\mathfrak{P}^{75}$, $\aleph^*$, B, L, some Itala, Syriac, Coptic) lacks specific mention of food or scraps.

16:25. The term ὧδε (here), with vast external support, is the original reading, not ὅδε (this one). The force is that Lazarus is comforted "here" but you (the rich man) are comforted there. Only family 1, a few minuscules, and Marcion have ὅδε.

IV. Jerusalem Journey: Jewish Rejection and the New Way (9:51–19:44)
    H. Generosity: Handling Money and Possessions (16:1–31)
➤ I. False Teaching, Forgiveness, and Service (17:1–10)
    J. Faithfulness in Looking for the King, the Kingdom, and the Kingdom's Consummation (17:11–18:8)

I. False Teaching, Forgiveness, and Service (17:1–10)

Jesus turns from wealth in Luke 16 to a brief discussion of four discipleship characteristics in 17:1–10. The audience addressed also changes. In Luke 16, the audience was broad, including Pharisees. In 17:1, Luke makes the point that Jesus is teaching the disciples. The passage is difficult to summarize because its unity is hard to determine. In fact, most hold that these are four unrelated teachings that Luke has brought together (Klostermann 1929: 170; Marshall 1978: 639–40; Fitzmyer 1985: 1136), an observation that seems likely. The topics covered are guarding against false teaching (17:1–3a), forgiving the repentant believer (17:3b–4), exercising faith (17:5–6), and having a servant's attitude (17:7–10). Seen in this light, the unit functions much like a collection of proverbs, each addressing its own topic without a direct relationship to the other sayings. The common thread is that every point deals with the disciple's walk.

There is some dissent to viewing this unit as unconnected proverbs. Arndt (1956: 367) and Hendriksen (1978: 794), for example, argue for a link between the subunits.[1] The warning about sin leads naturally into the issue of forgiving the one who has done wrong. Jesus' insistence that forgiveness be granted continually is a hard teaching, so hard in fact that the disciples ask for an increase in faith. Jesus responds that such faith, even though small in size, can accomplish great things. But these great works can lead to another danger: attributing our great works before God to personal achievement. In fact, some might think that what the disciple does for God obligates him to honor the disciple. Jesus warns the disciple to regard service as strictly that—service. What the disciple does for God is simply fulfilling a duty. While this un-

---

1. Hendriksen argues that seeing the passage as disconnected goes against the declaration of an orderly account in 1:3. This view interprets Luke's remark too narrowly. For Hendriksen, the connection is that disciples are not to commit the sin of harming others, which Jesus warned against in Luke 16. However, this connection ties only the first part to the previous unit and does not relate the pieces of this unit to each other.

derstanding of the passage is possible, especially at the beginning and end, the transitions between forgiveness and faith and between faith and duty seem harsh and inferred, not obvious. Arndt may be right in putting the passage together like this, but given the lack of connectives between the subunits and the harsh transitions, a more proverbial reading in terms of four distinct themes seems likely. If so, then Luke's theme is simply various aspects related to discipleship.

Sources and Historicity

The issue of sources is obviously complex. What Manson (1949: 138) says of 17:1–2 could be said of the entire unit: to disentangle this tradition, given its confusion (i.e., its variety of expressions in the Gospels), makes any conclusion mere conjecture and renders tentative results at best. Luke 17:7–10 is clear, since it has no parallels and belongs to Luke's special material (Aland 1985: §232; on the parable's unity, see Blomberg 1990: 261–62). The other three subunits are more complex. Most see Luke using Q, though there are some overlaps with Mark (Aland 1985: §§229–31):

Luke 17:1–3a	Matt. 18:6–7; Mark 9:42
Luke 17:3b–4	Matt. 18:15
Luke 17:5–6	Matt. 17:19–21; Mark 9:28–29

Most see Q present throughout, while Mark is seen as influencing 17:1–3a and either Mark or special Lucan material is seen as significant in 17:5–6. Great variation exists, however, among interpreters on the particulars.[2]

Yet another possibility combines the lack of verbal correspondence and the differences in the illustrations with the general makeup of 15:1–17:10 to conclude that Luke likely drew all this material from his special source.

---

2. Fitzmyer 1985: 1136–37 argues that all of the material is from Q, but that 17:2 has been influenced by Mark 9:42. Marshall 1978: 640 agrees that Q and Mark overlap in 17:1–2 and also sees (pp. 642, 643–44) the rest of 17:3–6 as coming from Q, though he entertains the possibility that Q has various forms from which Matthew and Luke drew. Creed 1930: 215 sees Q and Mark 11:23 exercising influence in 17:5–6. Ernst 1977: 477–80 sees 17:1–3a as coming from either Q or a form of oral tradition that circulated in a variety of forms, 17:3b–4 as rooted in Jesus' teaching, and triple tradition (i.e., Mark and Q) influencing 17:5–6. Ellis 1974: 207 speaks of Mark and Q in 17:1–4 and regards Luke's special source as responsible for 17:5–10. Egelkraut 1976: 120–21 speaks of Q/Mark overlap in 17:1–2 and multiple tradition in 17:5–6. Grundmann 1963: 331 suggests that it is hard to know if Q or Luke's special material is responsible for the unit, except for 17:7–10, which is L. Grundmann sees its roots in material earlier than the versions of Matthew and Mark. All of this assumes that only one form of these sayings existed in the tradition and that it emerged from a single saying. If this was a theme repeated by Jesus, multiple renderings could well exist.

This source may have had points of contact with elements in Matthew.[3] As the exegesis will make clear, there is little verbal overlap in any of the passages. In addition, while making similar points, the sayings have significant differences in how they illustrate the point. It is hard to explain these differences in terms of a fixed source.

For example, Matt. 18:6–7 discusses the elements in Luke 17:1–3a in reverse order. The material in 17:3–4 is located in two distinct sections: Matt. 18:15 and 18:21–22. In addition, Matthew's discussion of forgiving a brother seventy times seven comes as a response to Peter's question, while Luke uses it as a direct teaching.[4] In Matt. 17:20, a mountain is moved by faith, while in Luke 17:6 a sycamine tree is told to be uprooted and planted in the sea. These botanical illustrations are radically different and the problematic one in terms of imagery is Luke's, so that one is unlikely to argue that Luke's change is a logical one if he had used a version like Matthew's. Since virtually all of 15:1–17:10 is special Lucan material, it is easier to suggest that this material is distinct from Matthew, coming from L, and indicating a distinct setting. Regardless, Jesus is seen to instruct his disciples on a variety of matters related to discipleship.

The Jesus Seminar (Funk and Hoover 1993: 362–63) questions the authenticity of most of this material, rendering 17:1b–4, 7–10 in black type (not Jesus' sayings) and 17:6 in gray type (probably not Jesus' words, but possibly has contact with him). While acknowledging that the theme of faith is multiply attested, the seminar argues that the saying's variation in the Gospels speaks against its authenticity. The seminar argues that the themes of apostasy, backsliding, and heresy (17:1b–4) are community issues, not those of Jesus' ministry, and that the "protocol" for forgiveness resembles church instruction. But these observations formalize the remarks too much. The only protocol on forgiveness is to forgive repeatedly, hardly a detailed discussion of procedure (as Bultmann 1963: 141 admits). The rise of opposition and pressure on the disciples could easily lead Jesus to address the possibility of defection. One suspects that the note of judgment from Jesus is the real point of the seminar's objection, since it mentions

---

3. If one sees multiple versions of Q and recognizes how much teaching and parabolic material is in special Luke, then the possibility of overlaps with Matthean teaching (or Q) becomes very likely. The presence of a teaching in one strand of tradition does not mean it is banned elsewhere. Proverbial statements may exist in this tradition outside of Q because the Lucan tradition also would have preserved different settings. Of course, Matthean prioritists see Matthew's influence instead of Q, but the issues of the shift in setting and variation of wording are problems for all approaches that see Luke using Gospel material or sources. Any theory of alternate Q can just as well be evidence of special Lucan material. The possibility of "alibi parallels" is real, but this means that we have conceptual parallels, rather than source parallels. For the view that Luke uses Matthew, see Goulder 1989: 639–43.

4. Although Luke loves to introduce teaching through questions (e.g., 10:29, 40; 18:18), this is an example where he apparently ignores this approach.

that note elsewhere (e.g., on 11:37–54). Against the seminar's view of 17:7–10 is the likelihood that the theme parallels Jewish wisdom (*m. ʾAbot* 1.3; 2.8) and Greco-Roman symposium teaching, as well as the Lucan theme of service and meal teaching (Luke 12:35–38; 14:1–24; 22:27). The theme of service is well attested for Jesus (e.g., Mark 10:35–45). Marshall (1978: 646) notes evidence for its authenticity in the "which of you?" formula (see the exegesis of 17:7). Nolland (1993a: 836) argues that the roots of Luke 17:1–6 go back to Jesus and that claims of the secondary nature of 17:8, 10 cannot be sustained. Manson (1949: 301–3) assumes that the material is original to Jesus (see Blomberg 1990: 261).

In terms of form, the passage is a collection of sayings: warning (17:1–3a), instruction (17:3b–4), exhortation (17:5–6), and parable (17:7–10).[5] The outline of Luke 17:1–10 is as follows:

1. Warning about false teaching (17:1–3a)
   a. Woe to the one who entices others to sin (17:1)
   b. Terrible fate of the tempter (17:2)
   c. Call to watch (17:3a)
2. Instruction about confronting the sinner and forgiving the penitent (17:3b–4)
   a. Rebuke the sinner (17:3b)
   b. Forgive the penitent (17:3c)
   c. Forgive again and again (17:4)
3. Exhortation to exercise even a little genuine faith (17:5–6)
   a. Request for faith (17:5)
   b. The power of a little genuine faith (17:6)
4. Parable of the dutiful servant (17:7–10)
   a. The parable proper (17:7–9)
   b. Application: we have only done our duty (17:10)

The themes are all related to discipleship and how disciples are to be treated. Do not cause a disciple's defection, for the consequences are severe. Rebuke sinning believers, but forgive them as often as they repent. In fact, disciples are obligated to forgive repenting believers. A little genuine faith can accomplish marvelous things. Disciples are to do their duty before God and to view service as duty. Service does not put God in their debt; rather, service is part of what God requires of his servants.

5. Fitzmyer 1985: 1137 and Bultmann 1963: 144 call 17:1–3a a legal saying, while Berger 1984: 65 calls it a "sentence." Luke 17:3b–4 is like a wisdom saying according to Ernst 1977: 479 and a warning according to Berger 1984: 119, 165. Fitzmyer 1985: 1142 calls 17:5–6 a wisdom saying, while Berger 1984: 81 calls it a pronouncement ("apophthegm"). All agree that 17:7–10 is a parable.

Exegesis and Exposition

[1]And he said to his disciples, "It is impossible for enticement not to come, but woe to the one through whom it comes. [2]It would be better for him if a millstone were hung around his neck and he were cast into the sea than that he should cause one of these little ones to stumble. [3]Take heed to yourselves.

"If your brother sins, rebuke him; and if he repents, forgive him. [4]And if he sins against you seven times during the day, and seven times he turns to you and says, 'I repent,' you shall forgive him."

[5]And the apostles said to the Lord, "Increase our faith." [6]But the Lord said, "If you ⌐have⌐ faith like a mustard seed, you can say to this sycamine tree, 'Be uprooted and be planted in the sea'; and it will obey you.

[7]"Which of you, who has a servant who plows or shepherds, says to him when he comes in from the field, 'Come immediately and sit at the table?' [8]But will he not say, 'Prepare what I shall eat for dinner, and girding yourself serve me until I eat and drink, and after these things you shall eat and drink'? [9]Does he thank the servant because he did what was commanded? ⌐⌐[10]So also you, when you do all that is commanded you, say, 'We are worthless servants, what we were obligated to do we have done.'"

1. Warning about False Teaching (17:1–3a)
a. Woe to the One Who Entices Others to Sin (17:1)

17:1   Jesus instructs his disciples directly about some elements of following him. First, it is impossible (ἀνένδεκτος, *anendektos*; BAGD 65; BAA 128) to avoid stumbling or sinning.[6] Σκάνδαλον (*skandalon*) is an enticement to sin, especially to false faith or apostasy (BAGD 753; BAA 1505 §2). In the LXX, this word group usually translated words related to יָקַשׁ (*yāqaš*, to bait or lure; Judg. 8:27) and כָּשַׁל (*kāšal*, to stumble; Lev. 19:14; 1 Sam. 25:31; Ps. 119:165 [118:165 LXX]; Fitzmyer 1985: 1138) and pictures entrapment in sin (Creed 1930: 214; Danker 1988: 286; Stählin, *TDNT* 7:344–47).[7] Apostasy or something as serious is in view, as the severe rhetorical picture of

---

6. The grammatical construction τοῦ μή plus the infinitive here means the inability to do something or to hinder something from happening; BDF §400.4; BDR §400.4.6; Plummer 1896: 398. Conceptually similar expressions are found in Luke 4:42; 24:16; Acts 10:47; 14:18; 20:20, 27.

7. Σκάνδαλον is used of the wicked in Josh. 23:13; Judg. 2:3; 1 Sam. 18:21; Ps. 68:23 LXX [69:22 Engl.]; of idols in Ps. 105:36 LXX [106:36 Engl.]; of the arrogant in Ps. 139:6 LXX [140:5 Engl.]; and of evildoers in Ps. 140:9 LXX [141:9 Engl.]. See also Wis. 14:11; Ps. Sol. 16.7. In the NT, σκάνδαλον is used of false teaching (Rom. 16:17) and of action that causes others to sin (Rom. 14:13). Stählin, *TDNT* 7:351, sees the σκάνδαλον causing the loss of faith; that is, it is a serious sin that leads to defection. Matt. 11:6 declares the blessing of the one who is not "scandalized," who is able to confess Jesus. The term refers to placing an obstacle in someone's way and thus, in this context, of enticing them to proceed in a wrong direction.

the next verse shows: the crime is so serious that death is to be considered a better fate. Jesus' point is that the presence of decisive temptation to defect is unavoidable, and in addressing the disciples he suggests that temptation can come from inside the community of faith (i.e., 17:3a looks back). Judas represents a disciple who, in the end, revealed his heart, showed his lack of commitment to Jesus, and became an object of divine wrath (Stählin, *TDNT* 5:440; cf. Luke 17:23; 21:8; Acts 20:29–30).

Matthew 18:6–7 is conceptually parallel to Luke. In Matthew, however, the world is described as the source for such temptation. Thus, Matthew's version is less focused on the disciple. In a reversal of Luke 17:1–2, Matthew begins with the illustration about the millstone and ends with the note about sin's inevitability and the woe. This is a familiar teaching, probably repeated with some variation; it does not come to Luke from the same source as Matthew's version. Regardless of the relationship of the sayings, we have a comment about the relationship between the world and false teachers (Phil. 3:18–20; Col. 3:2; 2 Tim. 3:1–5; 2 Pet. 2:1–3; 1 John 4:4–6).

b. Terrible Fate of the Tempter (17:2)

Jesus warns that the individual who leads his "little ones" into sin is **17:2** subject to God's wrath. The warning is real, as the graphic image of the punishment shows. The "woe" is a sign of condemnation to the false teacher (on woes, see the exegesis of 6:24–26). The fate of the false teacher is severe: death would be better than the consequences of leading Jesus' beloved little ones astray (Tiede 1988: 292–93). The *hapax legomenon* λυσιτελέω (*lysiteleō*, to be advantageous) was often a commercial or political term (Plummer 1896: 399; Klostermann 1929: 171; BAGD 482; BAA 978; MM 382; Tob. 3:6; Josephus, *Antiquities* 15.5.1 §110). A harsh death would be a "better deal" than what this one will get from God. The hard and heavy millstone (μυλικός, *mylikos*) was used as the upper stone in a grinding mill (Judg. 9:53; BAGD 529; BAA 1071; LSJ 1152). Needless to say, when hung around the neck, it would make drowning certain (the perfect tense ἔρριπται [*erriptai*, be cast] makes the sea's presence enduring). Jesus says that it is better to drown than to cause one of his little ones to go astray (σκανδαλίσῃ [*skandalisē*, he should cause to stumble] is the verbal cognate of σκάνδαλον [*skandalon*] in 17:1). The seriousness of teaching other disciples and guiding them properly is implied in this warning. The reference to "little ones" (μικρῶν, *mikrōn*) may allude to new disciples who need instruction. Grundmann (1963: 332) plausibly suggests that the term alludes to the poor who hear the gospel, an especially appropriate connection, given 16:19–31, though the verse should not be seen as a commentary on the parable of Lazarus and the rich man (Marshall 1978: 641; Michel, *TDNT* 4:651–52). It may well be that new disciples are the primary focus, though the remark's proverbial character would make it applicable to any disciple being led astray. As such, it could apply to anyone outside the community who leads disciples astray. The Jewish leadership could be included by application. In sum, disciples are to watch themselves (17:3a), for the warning is to anyone through whom (δι' οὗ, *di' hou*; 17:1) such enticement comes.

The millstone illustration appears in Matt. 18:6 = Mark 9:42, though the only terms parallel in all three accounts are περὶ τὸν τράχηλον αὐτοῦ (*peri ton trachēlon autou*, around his neck) and εἰς τὴν θάλασσαν (*eis tēn thalassan*, into the sea; Matthew has ἐν τῷ πελάγει τῆς θαλάσσης, *en tō pelagei tēs thalassēs*, in the depth of the sea). Mark and Luke share an additional term: περίκειται (*perikeitai*, is hung around). Matthew and Mark speak earlier about those who "cause the little ones who believe in me to sin," using μικρῶν and σκανδαλίσῃ to make the point. Luke has the same terminology in a slightly different syntactical presentation. In any case, the image is the same in all three texts.

The reference to "little ones" need not be seen as a reference to children (Manson 1949: 138–39). The image is a tender way of saying that disciples need care and protection like a parent gives a child. There is no indication of children in the Lucan context, which Manson regards as the shortest, most primitive form of the saying. Even Matthew's context, which has children in it, is ambiguous on the force of the phrase. All three writers are summarizing Jesus' teaching, but Matthew and Mark seem closer to one another than to Luke (e.g., they both describe the stone as μύλος ὀνικός [*mylos onikos*, donkey stone], while Luke has λίθος μυλικός [*lithos mylikos*, millstone]). As this difference is not merely a difference in translation (BAGD 570; BAA 1156), it seems likely that more than one occasion is in view, with Luke providing a setting distinct from Matthew and Mark.

c. Call to Watch (17:3a)

17:3a Jesus tells the disciples to be careful to watch themselves.[8] The present imperative προσέχετε (*prosechete*) speaks of a constant watch. They are to be careful about what they teach others. Some question whether this exhortation should go with 17:3b–4, but its warning tone fits more naturally with 17:1–2.[9]

8. Elsewhere in Luke, Jesus instructs about obedience (8:18), hypocrisy (12:1), covetousness (12:15), false piety (20:46), and readiness (21:8, 34).

9. Marshall 1978: 642 ties it to 17:3b–4 by arguing that it is anticlimactic if it looks back. In fact, the reminder can be seen as emphatic.

2. Instruction about Confronting the Sinner and Forgiving the Penitent (17:3b–4)
a. Rebuke the Sinner (17:3b)
b. Forgive the Penitent (17:3c)

The disciples' relationships with another is a key concern of Jesus. **17:3b–c**
They have the responsibility to rebuke one another about sin and to
forgive one another upon repentance. Both exhortations are third-
class conditions: "If a brother sins, and I'm not currently saying he
will or will not"; "If a brother repents, and I am not currently saying
he will or will not."[10] The point is that when one disciple does certain things, other disciples have certain responsibilities. It is likely
that the sin is something the person has witnessed or is the object
of, since 17:4 speaks of sin "against you" that is to be forgiven (so
also Matt. 18:15 speaks of having a private discussion over sin done
"against you").

Two fundamental relational commitments are expressed in the
exhortations to rebuke and forgive. First, disciples are to share in
each other's commitment to pursue righteousness. Thus, Jesus exhorts them to rebuke a believer who sins, not because he wishes disciples to meddle in the affairs of others, but because he wishes the
community to desire righteousness that results in accountability to
one another for the way they walk. Such exhortations are common
in the NT (Matt. 18:15–18; Luke 6:37; Gal. 6:1 [a key text that warns
against spiritual smugness as this process is carried out]; 1 Thess.
5:14–15; 2 Thess. 3:14–15; Titus 3:10). Second, disciples are not to
pursue their spirituality in isolation from one another. For Jesus,
faith is not merely a private affair, but something the community
pursues together. The community of believers is a family in the
sense that the best interests of each member is a concern of each
other member. Thus, the call to rebuke is the exercise of a familial
responsibility (Lev. 19:17 is similar; Plummer 1896: 400). The assumption in all of this is that disciples have a certain quality in their
relationships that allows this type of positive, honest, loving, confronting behavior to occur without destroying their relationships
(Manson 1949: 139).

How does one prevent a watchdog approach? The first preventa-
tive is to recognize that one is dealing with known actions. In other
words, one is to confront when the action is done directly against
one, in front of one, or because one has formal responsibility to confront. This is not the judging of another that Jesus prohibits and

10. This type of conditional clause uses ἐάν (if). The aorist imperatives probably
denote something generally done; Arndt 1956: 368. For ἐπιτιμάω (to rebuke), see the
exegesis of 4:35a.

qualifies elsewhere (Matt. 7:1–5 = Luke 6:37–38). The exhortation's second half also lends balance to the teaching: disciples are not only to rebuke, but also to be quick to forgive when repentance is present. Sin is not to be held against someone. If a disciple recognizes that sin is present and acknowledges error ("turn" and "repent" in 17:4), then forgiveness should be readily extended (Judaism recognized this process as well and tied it to the responsibility to love one another; T. Gad 6.3–4; Fitzmyer 1985: 1140; Schweizer 1984: 263). The community is not a legalistic association but one committed to righteousness and to building up members into restored relationships. A central element in that restoration is the ability to forgive, which allows people to move past their failures. Jesus will emphasize in 17:4 that such forgiveness is to be available on a repeated basis.

Matthew 18:15 has a similar exhortation to rebuke, but it is worded very differently. Matthew speaks of confronting a believer who has sinned against you. The rebuke should initially occur in private with the goal of "gaining" the believer. If there is no response, then the church may be brought into the process (Matt. 18:16–17). Thus, Matthew has a much fuller treatment of the topic than does Luke, and he emphasizes the larger ecclesiastical responsibility, while Luke stays focused on individual responsibility. Luke gives the principle, while Matthew relates the process so it has integrity and does not disintegrate into a personal battle. The contrastive teaching on forgiveness comes a few verses later in Matt. 18:21–22. So Matthew also has many exhortations about disciples' relationships, though his arrangement differs from Luke's briefer treatment.

c. Forgive Again and Again (17:4)

17:4   What is the response to a rebuke that is heeded? Jesus says that forgiveness is imperative. A question might arise with his command to forgive: "How often should I forgive?" In fact, the parallel Matt. 18:21 introduces a teaching similar to this one with a question by Peter. In Luke, Jesus simply anticipates the question and teaches his disciples. The picture is graphic and clear. The disciple is always to forgive the repentant disciple, no matter how often forgiveness is requested. The passage assumes that the sin is directed personally at a disciple (ἁμαρτήσῃ εἰς σέ, hamartēsē eis se, sins against you) and thus directly affects their relationship.

The point about frequency of forgiveness is made in the telling illustration of seven requests in one day. Surely, one would question the genuineness of the repentance if every couple of hours forgiveness was requested. But Jesus notes that each time the request is

made it should be granted (11:4; 6:37–38; cf. Peter's restoration).[11]
The picture of repentance uses two ideas together: turning and repenting. The sinner takes the initiative in admitting error and requesting pardon for the action. The combination may be significant, since a "forced" request might not be genuine. There is no
special meaning in the number *seven* other than to communicate
the frequency of the sin and the forgiveness (Schneider 1977a: 346–
47).[12] Judaism had a parallel: Gad, after alluding to his hatred of
Joseph and what he learned through the experience, says (T. Gad
6.3–4, 7):

> Love one another from the heart, therefore, and if anyone sins against
> you, speak to him in peace. Expel the venom of hatred, and do not
> harbor deceit in your heart. If anyone confesses and repents, forgive
> him. If anyone denies his guilt, do not be contentious with him, oth-
> erwise he may start cursing, and you would be sinning doubly. . . . But
> even if he is devoid of shame and persists in his wickedness, forgive
> him from the heart and leave vengeance to God.

This Jewish text is similar to Rom. 12:16–21 (for other Jewish parallels, see SB 1:798–99).

Matthew 18:21–22 is the closest parallel to this passage, but it is
set out in a different way. It is introduced with a question by Peter,
and the accompanying illustration says that one should forgive seventy times seven. The two passages are thus parallel in concept, but
distinct in form.

3. Exhortation to Exercise Even a Little Genuine Faith (17:5–6)
a. Request for Faith (17:5)

The disciples ask the Lord to help them develop their faith. The be-   **17:5**
ginning of the verse is expressed in Lucan terms, since Luke alone
uses ἀπόστολος (*apostolos*, apostle) to describe the disciples (see the
exegesis of 6:13), and he alone uses κύριος (*kyrios*, Lord) in such introductions (5:17; 7:13, 19). The disciples request that Jesus "add" to
their faith, not give a gift of faith.[13] Some say that this request means
"provide us faith" and argue that the verse speaks of asking for a gift

---

11. The command to forgive appears in the future tense and is somewhat more
emphatic than using an imperative; Fitzmyer 1985: 1141.

12. Ps. 119:164 uses the number *seven* as a figure to mean "frequently" or "constantly."

13. Προστίθημι (to add) is also Lucan, appearing thirteen times in Luke–Acts and
only three times in the other Gospels; Schneider 1977a: 347; Isa. 26:15. As Fitzmyer
1985: 1143 notes, the apostles would already have had some faith, so the idea is to
add faith (against BAGD 719 §2; BAA 1440 §2).

of faith to do great wonders. Such a view appeals to the example of 17:6 for support and argues that the idea of "adding faith" is not logical (Klostermann 1929: 171; Creed 1930: 215). But if Jesus can speak of possessing a little bit of faith, then a metaphor about the size and presence of faith is likely. Jesus alters the request for more faith, speaking of "having" faith. Faith's presence is more crucial than its quantity. Jesus is essentially saying that God can do a lot with a little trust.

The issue of faith and trust has come up previously in Luke's Gospel. Jesus mentioned faith as a catalyst for healing and forgiveness (7:50; 8:25, 48, 50), and he called the disciples to fear God in order to stand up to the pressure of confessing Jesus (12:4–12, 24–34). The leaders among the disciples discerned that faith was important, not only initially but as a consistent part of life. It is this daily faith that they want increased, so that they can faithfully serve their God. They know that faith is not a moment, but a journey. Jesus' authority is highlighted by Luke's description of him as the Lord to whom the request is made. The apostles' willingness to be taught is also implied, as they are dependent on the Lord for guidance about their growth.

The Synoptic passages that are conceptually parallel to this Lucan text have different settings; none have an introduction like Luke's. Matthew 17:20 speaks of faith like a mustard seed being able to move mountains, but it comes after the disciples ask why they were not able to perform a particular exorcism. Confusion of Matthew's and Luke's contexts is the only way to read this Lucan reply as a request of faith for wonders. Matthew 21:21 = Mark 11:22 is Jesus' reply in the face of the withered fig tree. Matthew speaks of telling mountains to go into the sea as well as being able to wither fig trees, while Mark mentions only the mountain (1 Cor. 13:2 also has this idiom). The repetition of this saying within Matthew shows its proverbial and repeatable character. This Lucan passage has all the signs of special Lucan material, given the distinct character of its imagery, though many regard it as Q material (Marshall 1978: 643–44; Fitzmyer 1985: 1141; Luce 1933: 273; Manson 1949: 141; Ellis 1974: 208 is for L).

b. The Power of a Little Genuine Faith (17:6)

17:6   Jesus' answer shifts the focus: faith is not a matter of quantity but presence. A little bit of genuine faith can accomplish a great deal. Faith like a mustard seed pictures a small bit of faith, since the mustard seed was popularly referred to as the smallest of all seeds (σίναπι, sinapi; BAGD 751; BAA 1502; Michel, *TDNT* 3:810–11; Matt. 13:31–32). Jesus' point is that even a little trust responds and follows, leading to great things. It is the total absence of faith that prevents results. Uprooting and replanting a tree in the sea pictures faith's ability to accomplish incredible things. This tree, the *hapax legomenon* συκάμινος (*sykaminos*), is probably the black mulberry, with a vast root system that enabled it to live up to six hundred years (BAGD 776; BAA 1548; Hunzinger, *TDNT* 7:758; Michel, *TDNT* 3:811 n. 2). It is not the sycomore/sycamore tree.[14] A sycomore tree is a full fig-mulberry tree (Luke 19:4; συκομορέα, *sykomorea*, BAGD 776; BAA 1549), which also has a deep root system, while the Western sycamore tree is like a maple tree.

The idea of planting (φυτεύω, *phyteuō*; BAGD 870; BAA 1735) a mulberry tree in the sea is a paradoxical image similar to that of a camel going through the eye of a needle (Mark 10:25 = Matt. 19:24 = Luke 18:25). It is designed to graphically and hyperbolically illustrate that faith can do the amazing (Ernst 1977: 480) and is by no means intended to be taken literally.[15] The metaphor of a tree and the sea fits Jesus' style of using surprising images. This image is designed to delight and provoke thought and wonder about faith. As Danker (1972: 179) says, "It scarcely needs to be said that Jesus does not encourage the disciples to spend their time watching sycamine trees leap into the sea." What he desires is a little trust that can produce surprising results.

Jesus says that the way to increase faith is simply to have it and watch it produce significant results.[16] The results are expressed in Greek as so certain that a translation reflecting this stylistic touch is difficult to produce. The term ὑπήκουσεν (*hypēkousen*, it obeyed) is aorist, even though the action is a condition expressed in the future, thus portraying the obedience as preceding the command. The tree was ready to obey before the command was given! Faith is certain to accomplish its goal. This is another touch of rhetorical heightening in the saying (Marshall 1978: 644).

14. Grundmann 1963: 333 and Luce 1933: 273, 292 are clear on the sycomore/sycamore distinction. Plummer 1896: 400–401 is uncertain about the difference and argues that the hyperbole is more natural for a sycamore tree. Manson 1949: 141 sees an original sycamore tree, appealing to an Aramaic mistranslation and to the use of the term in the LXX as a rendering of Hebrew שִׁקְמָה (*šiqmâ*) for the sycamore, not to mention rabbinic discussions like *m. B. Bat.* 2.11. Schneider 1977a: 347 agrees with Manson and cites SB 2:234 for rabbinic images. Nonetheless, many use sycamore when they mean sycomore (Fitzmyer 1985: 1143–44 is uncertain).

15. The image is neither strange nor derived; but so Fitzmyer 1985: 1144 (apparently) and C. A. Evans 1990: 256.

16. The use of εἰ (if) plus ἄν (untranslated particle) yields a mixed condition; Arndt 1956: 369; BDF §372.1a. On the idiom πίστιν ἔχειν (to have faith), see 4 Macc. 16:22; Matt. 17:20; 21:21 = Mark 11:22; Acts 14:9; Rom. 14:2 (conceptually); 1 Cor. 13:2; 1 Tim. 1:19; 3:9; Philem. 5; James 2:1, 14, 18; Hanse, *TDNT* 2:826 n. 58.

Conceptual parallels exist in Matt. 17:20; 21:21; and Mark 11:22. Matthew 17:20 mentions faith like a mustard seed that is able to move mountains, not a tree as in Luke. Such faith can do impossible things. Matthew 21:21 = Mark 11:22, while not mentioning a mustard seed, speaks of faith that can cause a mountain to be cast into the sea. Matthew 21 also mentions not doubting and alludes to the withered fig tree as well as to the mountain. Mark 11 speaks of faith from God. Jesus evidently used this image on many occasions and with a variety of illustrations, but the fundamental point is that faith can accomplish marvelous things.[17]

4. Parable of the Dutiful Servant (17:7–10)
a. The Parable Proper (17:7–9)

17:7 Using a first-century institution to illustrate a point, Jesus compares the disciple to the δοῦλος (*doulos*, slave), a term that Paul often applied to himself (Rom. 1:1; Phil. 1:1; Titus 1:1). This little parable, found only in Luke, illustrates the ideal attitude that a disciple should have in serving God. The story begins simply enough with a phrase that often introduces parables: "Which of you?" (Luke 11:5, 11; 12:25; 14:28, 31 [which king]; 15:4, 8 [which woman]; Matt. 6:27; 7:9; 12:11; Klostermann 1929: 172; Ernst 1977: 481). The illustration may suggest that some of Jesus' followers had been slaves, but it is told from the master's point of view ("which of you if you had a slave?"). Regardless, common practice is present. The scene starts near the end of daytime chores. A servant who plows the field or watches the sheep returns from a full day's work. Jesus raises the question whether this slave will get to rest and eat upon returning to the house: will the master prepare a meal for the slave to sit down and enjoy?[18] Of course, as 17:8 makes clear, the master does not. So the answer is, "None of you would do this!" The slave will prepare the master's meal immediately after completing the chores. The house that serves as the basis of the illustration is not a wealthy one, since one servant does all the chores. However, the point is not the economic level, but the sense of duty a slave is to have.

17. Against Creed 1930: 215, who argues that Luke's saying is like Matt. 21:21 and that Luke has turned the fig tree into a sycamine tree. This saying does come with some variety, but this is only a problem if we assume that the saying had only one original form. If the tradition has complex roots, then we may only be seeing a rich conceptual field for the imagery.

18. Danker 1972: 179 notes that the disciples would have considered the reversal in the question humorous. The image is similar to the president of a company opening the door to the presidential office for the janitor and giving the janitor the presidential chair.

The slave must serve the master before taking care of himself. Jesus **17:8**
asks a rhetorical question that expects a positive reply, as the use of
οὐχί (*ouchi*, not) makes clear. The slave must prepare a meal, serve
it, and then wait until the master has finished eating.[19] Only then
can he feed himself. The force of the aorist ἑτοίμασον (*hetoimason*,
prepare) and the present διακόνει (*diakonei*, serve) is interesting
(Plummer 1896: 401): "Go at once and prepare the meal and then
gird yourself so you can continue to serve the meal at the table."[20]
As always with a servant, the master's wishes come first.

Jesus concludes his parable with the question that is the center of **17:9**
the comparison: does the master thank the slave for doing what he
is commanded to do? Again, the question is rhetorical and the expected negative answer is indicated by the particle μή (*mē*, not). No
"thank you" accompanies the activity, for the slave has only performed what he is supposed to do. Other NT uses of διατάσσω (*di-
atassō*, to order or direct; BAGD 189; BAA 380) show God instructing the angels what to accomplish (Gal. 3:19), the apostles directing
churches what to do (1 Cor. 7:17), and the state commanding soldiers what to perform (Luke 3:13). The servant does his duty.

b. Application: We Have Only Done Our Duty (17:10)

Jesus now applies the parable, comparing its picture to the disciple's **17:10**
service to God.[21] Obedience is not to be accepted as a cause for merit
but as a fulfillment of duty, for we serve another who is over us
(Marshall 1978: 648; contrast the Pharisee of 18:12). The disciple
has done what is required. In putting the parable in these terms, the
stress is on the disciple's humble self-esteem. The disciple is God's
servant, laboring faithfully and dutifully in all areas (1 Cor. 4:1–3).
It is significant that Jesus speaks of doing all that is commanded.
The servant cannot pick and choose what to obey. The servant
serves dutifully, and God offers thanks for faithful service (1 Cor.
4:5). God in his grace notices and commends.

The self-description of slaves as "useless" (ἀχρεῖος, *achreios*;
BAGD 128; BAA 258; Arndt 1956: 369) troubles some, and so the

---

19. The verb διακονέω (to serve) has religious significance later in the NT: Matt.
20:28 (twice) = Mark 10:45 (twice); 2 Cor. 8:19; 1 Pet. 4:10; esp. 1 Tim. 3:10, 13 (of the
diaconate office). Here we have an everyday meaning: "to wait on tables"; Luke 12:37;
22:26–27 (three times); Acts 6:2; BAGD 184; BAA 368.

20. On δεῖπνον, a full, formal meal in the evening, see Luke 14:12; John 13:4, 21;
BAGD 173; BAA 346 (cf. δειπνέω, to dine, in Luke 22:20; 1 Cor. 11:25; Rev. 3:20). For
Jesus' reversal of the image, see Luke 12:37 and John 13:4.

21. Οὕτως (so) is the link between parable and application in Matt. 5:16; 13:49;
18:14; 20:16; Luke 12:21; 14:33; 15:7, 10 and between parable and teaching in Matt.
12:45; Luke 21:31; and John 3:8; BAGD 597 §1b; BAA 1209 §1b.

suggestion is made that ἀχρεῖος might mean "unworthy" as it does in 2 Sam. 6:22 (Creed 1930: 216; Jeremias 1963a: 193 n. 98; Marshall 1978: 647).[22] Whatever the exact force of the term here, the remark must be read contextually. The servants are unworthy in the sense of not having the authority to command themselves. Disciples respond to God just as slaves respond to their master. Worth or usefulness is defined by the believer's relationship to God. This idea perhaps means that "unworthy" is a better translation of ἀχρεῖος than is "useless." The text is not describing inherent worth, but function. Slaves bring nothing "worthy" to their tasks as servants, especially with regard to where they stand before God. The remark reflects a sense of total humility before God. Contextually, the instruction applies the themes of 17:1–7: disciples are to avoid misleading believers into unfaithfulness, to be forgiving, and to have faith (Fitzmyer 1985: 1147).

Jewish tradition applied a similar expression to the law. The following comment is attributed to Rabbi Johanan ben Zakkai: "If you have studied much Torah, do not claim merit for yourself, because for this you were created" (*m. ʾAbot* 2.8; SB 2:235; Ellis 1974: 208; Grundmann 1963: 333–34). Antignos of Soko is reported to have said: "Be not like the slaves who minister to their master for the sake of receiving reward, but be like slaves who minister to the master not for the sake of the bounty; and let the fear of heaven be upon you" (*m. ʾAbot* 1.3). Respect for God leads to dutiful service. In fact, one could argue that such duty should apply much more to serving God (Fitzmyer 1985: 1147). Paul shared this attitude of dutiful service (1 Cor. 9:16; Manson 1949: 302).[23]

Summary In Luke 17:1–10, Jesus speaks to his disciples about four areas crucial to their spiritual walk. He warns that some will tempt believers and that some of these tempters may come from within the community of faith. He exhorts the disciples to watch themselves and notes that the fate of the one who causes someone to defect from the faith is worse than a grotesque death.

Next, Jesus calls on the community to be mutually accountable. If a believer sins against another, the offended person should rebuke the sinner. But there is a corollary to rebuke: upon repentance, forgiveness should be offered just as readily. Not only

22. Wellhausen 1904: 550 notes that the Syriac version omitted the term. Fitzmyer 1985: 1147 notes the etymological suggestion of Kilgallen 1982 that the term means "those to whom something is not owed." Usage is against this sense, though Blomberg 1990: 262 takes it as possible.

23. "Going on strike" before God is not an option for a believer; Schweizer 1984: 264.

should repentance be offered, but it should be made available repeatedly. The disciple's graciousness and willingness to promote restoration should have no limit.

When it comes to faith, the issue is not quantity. The need is not to have more faith, but genuine faith, to rely truly on God. Jesus says here that even a tiny seed's worth of faith can produce marvelous fruit. The picture of a tree being uprooted and planted in the sea indicates that unexpected and surprising things are the product of genuine trust.

Finally, there is service. A disciple should never forget one's position before God. Obedience does not obligate God to the disciple. God does not owe the disciple anything for faithfulness. The disciple is to humbly serve God and respond as part of duty. God is gracious, but the disciple is not to presume on God's grace. Rather, one is to experience God's grace by faithfully submitting to the Master (Mark 9:41; Luke 6:20–23). To do what God asks is to do one's duty. Stay true, guard against sin, be forgiving, have faith, and serve dutifully—these are the traits of a growing disciple.

Additional Notes

17:6. Because of the mixture of tenses in the condition, the Western family (D, E, G, some Itala) reads εἴχετε (were having) instead of UBS–NA's ἔχετε (have). This grammatical smoothing of the mixed condition is unlikely to be original (Marshall 1978: 644; Fitzmyer 1985: 1143).

17:9. Some manuscripts end the question with αὐτῷ (to him?; some Syriac, Coptic, one Itala manuscript) or add οὐ δοκῶ (I think not; A, W, Δ, Θ, Ψ, Byz, Lect, some Itala, one Syriac manuscript) or both phrases (D, family 13, most Itala, Vulgate, one Syriac manuscript). These additions are superfluous, since the object of the question is obvious. The expected reply is clear from the use of the particle μή. The other questions in the parable lack a reply and are merely stated rhetorically. The UBS–NA reading (supported by 𝔓75, ℵ, B, L, family 1, one Itala manuscript, and one Syriac manuscript) is likely to be original (Metzger 1975: 166).

IV. Jerusalem Journey: Jewish Rejection and the New Way (9:51–19:44)
   I. False Teaching, Forgiveness, and Service (17:1–10)
➤ J. Faithfulness in Looking for the King, the Kingdom, and the Kingdom's Consummation (17:11–18:8)
   K. Humbly Entrusting All to the Father (18:9–30)

J. Faithfulness in Looking for the King, the Kingdom, and the Kingdom's Consummation (17:11–18:8)

The next division in the journey section turns to eschatology. It begins with a miracle that reemphasizes faith (17:11–19). After the miracle, a question about the arrival of the end-time leads Jesus to note that, with him, the kingdom is in their midst (17:20–21). Because miracles evidence who Jesus is (11:14–23) and the nature of the times (7:22–23), this miracle naturally leads to questions about the kingdom. This kingdom remark is followed by an overview of events that precede his final coming (17:22–37). This final period is a fearful time of judgment, but the disciples should not expect the end too soon, since Jesus must suffer first. Then a parable calls on the disciples to pray for consummation and to expect a quick vindication (18:1–8). Thus, at the center of this division stands trust in God and his sovereign plan. The disciple is to walk in faith and to look for Jesus' return when he will vindicate the saints. The disciple can do this because God's kingdom program is intimately bound together with Jesus.

1. Healing of Ten Lepers and a Samaritan's Faith (17:11–19)

As Jesus nears Jerusalem and his fate there, he continues to act with mercy and call for faith (Fitzmyer 1985: 1150–51). The travel note in 17:11 begins the final movement to Jerusalem, since such notes are more frequent after this (9:51–53; 10:38; 13:22, 33; 14:25; 17:11; 18:35; 19:1, 11, 28, 41). The cleansing of the ten lepers is Luke's first miracle since 14:1–6 and is the fourth of five miracles in the journey section (11:14; 13:12; 14:4; 18:35). Significantly, each miracle emphasizes not the healing but the teaching that follows. This account is really about one man, the Samaritan leper, and may be better named "The Thankful Samaritan Leper."

The miracle contains two levels of tension: Samaritans were disliked by Jews, and lepers were shunned by society in general (on lepers, see the exegesis of 5:12b). The miracle is told in two stages: the miracle itself (17:11–14) and the Samaritan's effort to thank and praise Jesus, who responds with commendation (17:15–19). Healing and pronouncement are combined into one story (Fitzmyer 1985: 1150).[1] This complex miracle story recalls the healing of Naaman in 2 Kings 5:1–19.[2]

The miracle highlights several ideas. Jesus is still actively showing his mercy to those who take the initiative to ask for it. The miracle's conclusion shows faith's value, for faith is what causes Jesus to commend the Samaritan. It links back to the idea of "little faith" in 17:5 and gives an example of the benefits of faith. The account also stresses the appreciation that Jesus receives from a "foreigner" and "outcast." In fact, the foreigner is

---

1. Bultmann 1963: 33 calls it a "biographical apophthegm" and sees the account as a variant of Mark 1:40–45 (on the Marcan connection, see the discussion of sources and historicity). Berger 1984: 314, 317 speaks of "deesis" or "petitio" because of the appeal for help. Tannehill 1986: 118–20 calls it a "quest story."

2. So Wiefel 1988: 305 and Bruners 1977. Bruners also argues that the account is Lucan. Fitzmyer 1985: 1150–51 and H. Betz 1981 question the connection. At most, it is a form parallel. Betz's main thesis (1971) that the account is a polemic against healing miracles is incorrect; see Marshall 1978: 649. Meier 1994: 750–51 shows how an appeal to Lucan creation from 2 Kings cannot explain four differences in the account: (1) no mention of Elijah, (2) no mention of Jesus as prophet, (3) no delay in the miracle's occurrence, and (4) the different kind of miracle in the account (punitive versus healing).

contrasted to Israel in a picture of gratitude that indicates how one should respond to God's mercy (Talbert 1982: 165–66).[3] In addition, Luke's placement of the account before the discussion about Jesus' return demonstrates Jesus' current power before he speaks of the power he will ultimately have at his return. Jesus saves the leper and then explains how such salvation has come, along with what follows it (Meier 1994: 427).

It is disputed whether the account contrasts the nine men who were healed and the Samaritan in terms of salvation. In other words, is there a contrast being made between the short-term benefit of being exposed to Jesus and the long-term value of responding to him in faith? H. Betz (1971) turns this thrust into a reason for Lucan composition, seeing the point as a critique of healing miracles. Fitzmyer (1985: 1152) is rightly skeptical of this polemical point, seeing it as too subtle. The text, however, does highlight the contrast between being exposed to Jesus and trusting him in two ways: (1) Jesus distinguishes the Samaritan's response from the other nine and issues a word about faith and salvation only to him, and (2) the earlier picture of 11:24–26 made the point that someone who experiences an exorcism and yet does not then respond with faith runs the risk of sinking into a worse state. This passage illustrates that teaching.

Sources and Historicity

The source issue has been made complex in modern discussion. The miracle is unique to Luke, which would seem to make clear that it is special Lucan material (Aland 1985: §233; Wiefel 1988: 304; Marshall 1978: 649 [leans in this direction]; Fitzmyer 1985: 1149 [a pre-Lucan source that Luke heavily edited]). But some argue that this account is an expanded and rewritten form of Mark 1:40–45 (Creed 1930: 216; Luce 1933: 274–75; Bultmann 1963: 33; Theissen 1983: 187). It is hard to see the reasoning for this conclusion as the stories are very different and there is virtually no overlap in vocabulary. More important, Luke has another account (5:12–16) that parallels Mark 1:40–45. The Jesus Seminar (Funk and Hoover 1993: 363–64) questions the account on the grounds of the connection to Mark and argues that the Samaritan theme is Lucan (17:14, 17–19 are in black type). But the text's respect for a foreigner's faith is like Luke 7:1–10 (= Matt. 8:5–

---

3. The parable of the good Samaritan (10:25–37) also portrays these so-called half-breeds in a good light, a Lucan theme repeated in Luke 4:25–27; Acts 10–11; 26:16–18; 28:26–27. It is too much to see Samaritans as part of Israel; so Jervell 1972: 113–32. That the Samaritans are the target of the church's expansion in Acts 8 also shows that they are not part of Israel.

13), making such a theme multiply attested. There is nothing in the account that does not fit Jesus (note Fitzmyer 1985: 1156 [on the authenticity of the key verse, 17:19], 1149 [on the debate over whether the tradition is Lucan or pre-Lucan]). Ernst (1977: 482) rightly calls the attempt to associate this story with Mark 1 "fantastic speculation" (Van Der Loos 1965: 495 agrees). Nolland (1993a: 845) notes that the parallels with Mark exist simply because leprosy is in view (Meier 1994: 701–5 also questions the connection). Luke, as in many units in his Jerusalem section, uses unique material. The roots of this event reach back to Jesus. Nolland (1993a: 844, citing Glöckner 1983: 125–60) notes that evidence of Lucan language is unevenly distributed in the passage, which argues for roots in a source.

As noted already, the form is a combination of miracle and pronouncement. The outline of Luke 17:11–19 is as follows:

a. Healing of the ten lepers (17:11–14)
   i. Setting (17:11)
   ii. Ten lepers call for mercy (17:12–13)
   iii. Healing (17:14)
b. The Samaritan's response and Jesus' commendation (17:15–19)
   i. The Samaritan's gratitude and praise (17:15–16)
   ii. Jesus' comment and commendation (17:17–19)
      (1) Question (17:17)
      (2) Observation (17:18)
      (3) Commendation of faith unto salvation (17:19)

As Jesus continues his journey to Jerusalem, he responds to a cry for mercy. Jesus' power is again displayed. The Samaritan's praise and gratitude in response to God's mercy receives commendation, because exposure to God's grace is not good enough, one must receive it. The response of faith to God's grace leads to salvation.

Exegesis and Exposition

[11]And it came to pass while he was going to Jerusalem, he was passing along ⌜between⌝ Samaria and Galilee. [12]And as he entered a village, he was met by ten lepers, who stood at a distance. [13]And they called out, "Jesus, Master, have mercy on us." [14]And looking, he said to them, "⌜Go and show yourselves to the priests⌝." And it came to pass in their going that they were cleansed.

[15]And one of them, upon seeing that he was healed, returned and with a loud voice began praising God. [16]And he fell on his face before his feet, giv-

ing thanks to him. And he was a Samaritan. ¹⁷And Jesus replied, "⸢Were not ten cleansed?⸣ Where are the other nine? ¹⁸Was no one found who would return and give thanks to God except for this foreigner?" ¹⁹And he said to him, "Rise up and go. Your faith has saved you."

a. Healing of the Ten Lepers (17:11–14)
i. Setting (17:11)

17:11 This Lucan travel note is one of several that dot his journey section. Such notes intensify from this point in the Gospel, heightening the sense of expectation about what awaits Jesus in Jerusalem (9:51–53; 10:38; 13:22, 33; 14:25; 18:35; 19:1, 11, 28, 41). It has caused no lack of comment, for it is both revealing and somewhat unclear. The note makes clear that Luke is not describing a straight-line journey. In 10:38–42, he narrates a story that is clearly located near Jerusalem, in Martha's house at Bethany (John 11:18; Arndt 1956: 370). But previously, Luke had noted that Jesus had already traveled through Samaria (Luke 9:51–56), and now he portrays Jesus as back in the Samaritan and Galilean region. Clearly the "journey" to Jerusalem takes Jesus in and out of regions near the city. The journey motif becomes more rhetorical-theological as Jesus moves closer to his appointment with destiny in the holy city (see the introduction to §IV). As time moves on and opposition mounts, Jesus moves closer and closer to the confrontation in Jerusalem.

Many see in the comment about Jesus' traveling through the midst of Samaria and Galilee an example of Luke's imprecise, even errant, knowledge of Palestinian geography (Conzelmann 1960: 68–73; Leaney 1958: 228; Fitzmyer 1985: 1152–53). The problem is that Samaria and Galilee are not situated in such a way that one can journey to Jerusalem in Judea and pass between them; a journey on their borders takes you east and west, while to get to Jerusalem you must go south (this language would seem more realistic if one were moving away from Jerusalem; Plummer 1896: 403). Without giving any examples of usage, in his commentary Marshall (1978: 650) suggests another possibility: Luke is speaking of Perea as a part of Galilee. But Marshall notes elsewhere (1970: 70–71) that Judea, when under one ruler, would have included Perea and Galilee (Pliny, *Natural History* 5.15 §70; also Tacitus, *Annals* 12.54; Strabo 16.2.21 [c756]; Dio Cassius 37.16.5). This assumes that Luke is using broad geographical descriptions that fit his time. The problem was not unknown to ancient readers of Luke, since a textual problem shows early attempts to clarify the language (see the additional note). They simply missed the "broad" sense. A historical geographical reference is not, however, the best way to examine the verse, though it does help explain Luke 4:44.

The problem is somewhat artificial in that, as already noted, the journey idea in the section is not a straight-line proposition, but should be seen as more temporal or literary. In this sense, we can say that Jesus is "nearing" Jerusalem without getting physically closer to it. Luke is noting that, while the time is drawing near for Jesus to go to Jerusalem, he ministers on the Galilean-Samaritan border (the mention of Samaria prepares for the reference to the Samaritan in 17:16).

ii. Ten Lepers Call for Mercy (17:12–13)

Luke begins the miracle account by noting that in the midst of his **17:12** travels Jesus enters an unnamed village in the region (Luke commonly fails to mention specific places: 5:12; 9:52; 11:1; 13:10; 14:1; Van Der Loos 1965: 496 n. 2). Ten lepers intend to speak with him, but they cannot approach him because of their despised disease (Lev. 13:45–46; Num. 5:2–3), so they call to him from a distance. Perhaps the closest cultural equivalent to first-century attitudes about leprosy would be current attitudes about AIDS. The number *ten* has no hidden significance (2 Kings 7:3 mentions a group of four lepers).

The lepers obviously have heard about Jesus' ministry and desire his **17:13** help. They have a simple request and couch it in recognition of Jesus' authority. They address the master (ἐπιστάτης, *epistatēs*) by name and ask for mercy. The NT use of ἐπιστάτης is limited to Luke (5:5; 8:24 [twice], 45; 9:33, 49; 17:13), who uses it in passages where the Synoptic parallels use διδάσκαλος (*didaskalos*, teacher), ῥαββί (*rhabbi*, rabbi), or κύριος (*kyrios*, Lord).[4] This is the only use of the title by nondisciples (Marshall 1978: 651). These lepers obviously knew about the name *Jesus* through his reported reputation (Fitzmyer 1985: 1154; also Luke 18:38–39 = Mark 10:47–48).

The call for mercy is a request to someone of superior position to show compassion. Such cries for mercy (ἐλεέω, *eleeō*) were frequent during Jesus' ministry (Matt. 9:27; 15:22; 17:15; 20:30–31 = Mark 10:47–48 = Luke 18:38–39; 16:24; BAGD 249; BAA 503). It is really an entreaty to be healed immediately. The form of the verb ἐλεέω reflects an urgent request. In raising their voices, they get Jesus' attention.[5] Will Jesus show such compassion after all the conflict and warning that has attended his ministry?

4. Greek tutors also held this title: Aristaeus (tutor of Dionysus), Olympus (tutor of Zeus), and Pherecydes (tutor of Pythagoras); BAGD 300; BAA 608.

5. On the use of φωνή (voice), see Luke 11:27; Acts 4:24; Gen. 39:15, 18; Judg. 21:2; 1 Sam. 11:4; Van Der Loos 1965: 496 n. 4; Klostermann 1929: 173. The call for mercy is also used in the Psalter (e.g., 109:21; Glöckner 1983: 139–40), but not much can be made of this general expression, as Nolland 1993a: 846 indicates.

iii. Healing (17:14)

17:14 Any doubts about Jesus' compassion are removed immediately. He tells the lepers to go show themselves to the priests, which is what the law enjoined a leper to do after being cleansed (Lev. 13:19; 14:1–11; Mark 1:44 = Luke 5:14; Ernst 1977: 484). Of course, one does not go to the priest until after being healed, but here Jesus tells them to go before the healing is accomplished. The command itself shows that Jesus will act as they turn to present themselves to these officials. They probably were responsible to go to the local priest, who would certify that they were healed and allow them to return to society. If sacrifices were offered, then Jerusalem would come into view. For the Samaritan, this might mean a trip to Mount Gerizim. If they believed that Jesus could heal or that God might work through him, they would turn and go. Second Kings 5:10–15 has a similar test for Naaman when he is told to wash in the Jordan seven times; but Luke's account is not formed after that one since the details are so different, especially Naaman's indignant reaction to the instruction (Nolland 1993a: 845; Ellis 1974: 209; Klostermann 1929: 173; against Bruners 1977: 118). The lepers depart as a group and are healed as they journey.[6] Once again Jesus heals from a distance (7:1–10 is the other distance healing), as opposed to the healing in Luke 5:13 where he touched the man. Such miracles demonstrate the presence of messianic times (7:22; Arndt 1956: 371). As a result of this healing, these men could resume a normal life—no small cause for thanksgiving and continued faith (Fitzmyer 1985: 1155).

b. The Samaritan's Response and Jesus' Commendation (17:15–19)
i. The Samaritan's Gratitude and Praise (17:15–16)

17:15 Only one of the lepers expresses gratitude to Jesus for his healing. When he sees that the healing has occurred on his way to the priests, he returns to offer thanks and praise. Ἰάθη (*iathē*, he was healed) in this verse defines precisely what ἐκαθαρίσθησαν (*ekatharisthēsan*, they were cleansed) meant in 17:14. The healing is the cleansing (Marshall 1978: 651). In addition, the theological passive makes clear that God did the healing. The terms ὑποστρέφω (*hypostrephō*, to turn back) and δοξάζω (*doxazō*, to glorify) are favorites of Luke.[7]

---

6. Καθαρίζω (to cleanse) is often used of leprosy: Matt. 8:2 = Mark 1:40 = Luke 5:12; Matt. 10:8; Luke 4:27; 7:22 = Matt. 11:2; Luke 17:17; Lev. 14:7; 2 Kings 5:13; BAGD 387; BAA 785.

7. Thirty-two of thirty-five NT uses of ὑποστρέφω occur in Luke–Acts (none occur in the other Synoptics), including Luke 1:56; 2:45; 4:1, 14; 8:39; 17:18; 24:9; Acts 8:25; 12:25; 13:13; BAGD 847; BAA 1688–89. Δοξάζω occurs in Luke 2:20; 4:15; 5:25, 26;

Luke notes the response of praise because, in his judgment, it is a particularly appropriate way to respond to God's mercy.

Only one man comes back, not only joyful because he is physically restored but also confident because he is socially restored as well (17:16 shows him coming right up to Jesus, where before he could only stand at a distance). That he praises God in a loud voice also shows his understandable excitement at what has happened.

Some call this element of the story illogical (Luce 1933: 276), arguing that God can be glorified anywhere and that Jesus would have shunned the public attention of the ten had they all returned to offer him praise. Even Nolland (1993a: 847) suggests that this detail is a secondary expansion of the original narrative. In fact, the view argues that Jesus does not tolerate such public doting. This objection misses the point: the man's unique, bold, and spontaneous reaction of faith. Jesus does not demand this praise; it is offered freely. The man has correctly connected Jesus with God's work. His actions simply reveal the depth of his perception. His reaction is worthy of the commendation it receives in 17:19. It is not anti-Jewish, since the man is noted to be a Samaritan; it is pro-faith, challenging all to be like this most surprising foreigner.

Several literary touches show the returning man not only praising **17:16** God but also showing respect to Jesus and giving him thanks for his role in the healing (Marshall 1978: 651; K. Weiss, *TDNT* 6:628).[8] The man's respect shows his awareness that God is working through Jesus, though how the man sees Jesus specifically is not made clear by the action, since his thanksgiving is directed to God (17:15). That he approaches Jesus shows a contrast between the distance he had observed when asking Jesus to heal him and the closeness he has now after being healed. This is a wonderful example of the literary use of space.

Another literary touch comes at the end of the verse when this man is identified as a Samaritan. The assumption might well be that this leper was a Jew. But the one who shows such spirituality is called an "outsider," a despised Samaritan (αὐτός is emphatic: "And *he* was a Samaritan"; Plummer 1896: 404). A "schismatic" or, at the least, someone distant from covenant promise was the only one to

---

7:16; 13:13; 18:43; 23:47; Acts 3:13; 4:21; 11:18; 13:48; 21:20; BAGD 204; BAA 411 (in the other Synoptics it is limited to Matt. 5:16; 6:2; 15:31; Mark 2:12 = Matt. 9:8). Other words for praise occur in Luke 1:64; 2:13, 20; 9:43; 19:37; 24:53; Acts 2:47; 3:8, 9. This verse reflects Lucan description of the reaction.

8. The woman who anointed Jesus' feet demonstrated a similar sign of respect and recognition that Jesus is sent from God (7:38). Other such acts are found in 5:12 and 8:41.

show gratitude (other exemplary Samaritans are described in Luke 10:25–37 and Acts 8:5–8; another foreigner is described in Luke 7:1–10). Luke saves this detail for the end of the decription, which draws attention to it. Jesus will comment on this detail because it raises the issue of who is responding favorably to him. The answer is, "Not those we would have expected." It is not stated, but it may be implied that the other nine are Jewish. Though Jesus will ask about the nine, he focuses attention on the appropriate response of this one foreigner, a key point regardless of the identity of the other beneficiaries. How Jesus knows that this man is Samaritan is not made clear by the narrative.

ii. Jesus' Comment and Commendation (17:17–19)
(1) Question (17:17)

17:17   Jesus responds to the Samaritan's action with the first of three rhetorical questions designed to cause reflection: "Were not ten cleansed?" The first question expects a positive answer, as the particle οὐχί (*ouchi*, not) makes clear. Jesus had reached out to all the lepers, and all had experienced God's mercy. But where is the response that the OT suggests is appropriate (Ps. 30:10–12 [30:11–13 MT]; Danker 1988: 290)?

Jesus' second rhetorical question is, "Where are the other nine?" The interrogative ποῦ (*pou*, where?) trails at the end of the question and is emphatic: "The nine, . . . where?" (Plummer 1896: 404; Marshall 1978: 652; Grundmann 1963: 337).[9] Why don't they praise God? Where is their gratitude? Where is their recognition of Jesus' role in healing them? Surely they also are capable of expressing appreciation to God. The question is really an expression of Jesus' negative evaluation of their ingratitude (Van Der Loos 1965: 499). This rhetorical rebuke is an indictment for not responding to God's gracious act (Tiede 1988: 297). Jesus is not asking for an answer; he is making a stinging observation. They have "missed the moment."

(2) Observation (17:18)

17:18   Jesus' final question is also rhetorical: "Was not one found . . . , except this foreigner?" The particle οὐχ (*ouch*, not) expects a positive answer: the foreigner alone responded in gratitude. In the LXX, the term ἀλλογενής (*allogenēs*) often means "pagan" or "heathen" (Exod. 12:43; 29:33; 30:33; Lev. 22:10; Plummer 1896: 405; Van Der Loos 1965: 500). There may be an emotive edge in the choice of this NT *hapax legomenon*, since, as Marshall (1978: 652) notes, this term

---

9. The two questions are laid out chiastically: the first has the particle in the initial position, while the second has the particle at the end.

appeared on the signs prohibiting foreigners from passing the inner barrier of the temple (Josephus, *Antiquities* 15.11.5 §417; *Jewish War* 5.5.2. §194; 6.2.4 §§124–26). The question is a rebuke and parallels Jesus' remark about the centurion in Luke 7:9. It also strongly suggests that the other lepers may have been Jewish. Jesus expected some concrete response from those who were missing. This Samaritan receives the commendation that the others will miss because he, a foreigner, had more spiritual sensitivity than they did.

(3) Commendation of Faith unto Salvation (17:19)

The commendation comes at the conclusion. Jesus' remarks are **17:19** short: he tells the Samaritan to depart and that his faith has delivered him. Luke has noted before that faith saves (7:50; 8:48), and he will note it again (18:42). The allusion must be to the full saving faith of the Samaritan, since the deliverance related to the healing had already occurred and that healing was something he shared with the other nine. What the man receives here the others do not.

This view, however, is less than unanimous. Plummer (1896: 405) sees a reference only to the healing. Even more radical is Luce's suggestion (1933: 276) that this point is Luke's addition and that it spoils the story, since each leper would have had faith in order to get healed. This understanding misses a key point of this account: God's gracious acts extend to all people, but some do not respond, and as a result they miss out on blessing. The accounts about Jesus need not be as one dimensional as some suggest.

Fitzmyer (1985: 1156) also sees a Lucan addition here, but does not make the same point as Luce. He argues that the remark goes back to Jesus, even though he did not say it in this setting. I am not so confident that we can discern when an occasion is inappropriate for an authentic remark by Jesus. Marshall (1978: 652) rightly calls the verse essential to the story, since the issue is the man's relationship to Jesus, not just that he gave thanks. Marshall also regards it as unclear that the others lacked faith; they may have been rebuked for lack of gratitude and incomplete faith, a view that is possible but may soften the implications of what Jesus says uniquely to this man. Van Der Loos (1965: 500), who sees this man as fully saved, notes that without this verse the account ends with rhetorical remarks, an ending that would be unique for Jesus' miracles. What Jesus says to the man reflects the Samaritan's unique position among the ten.

If full salvation is in view, it means that the Samaritan alone benefited fully from Jesus' act of mercy and gained a relationship with God (Arndt 1956: 372). When his house was swept clean he did not leave it empty (11:24–26), but gratefully turned to God. One can experience God's grace in terms of general mercy and still not benefit fully from it, because the response never moves beyond reception of kindness to the exercise of faith. Faith responds to God's goodness and publicly acknowledges God and Jesus, a response that the Samaritan illustrates (Rom. 10:9–13). Once again, Luke notes the link between faith and ultimate salvation (Danker 1988: 291; Oepke, *TDNT* 3:211).[10]

Summary Luke 17:11–19 shows that Jesus still acts with mercy and commends faith. Jesus is under great pressure, but in the midst of it he stills responds to all who call upon him. The ten lepers as a group picture Jesus' continued general compassion.

Another point of this unit is who might respond to that compassion. It is here that the Samaritan reflects a surprise. Such reaction often comes from a person that we might not expect to respond sensitively. Here a foreigner is the model. His acknowledgment and thanks to God for his gracious acts brings Jesus' commendation, in part because it is in the face of popular opposition to the agent of grace. An outsider provides the lesson. Grace works in surprising places.

There is also a third significant point: the manner in which one responds to God's kindness is important. Anyone is a candidate for God's general acts of grace, but that does not mean one has received grace's ultimate benefit. God's grace extends to all, but only some receive the gift of salvation. That greater gift is received by faith, faith like that of the Samaritan who comes to Jesus. Only he among the ten walks away with a commendation that explains why he is so blessed. It is only to him that Jesus says, "Your faith has saved you." Luke desires the reader to identify with the Samaritan's exemplary faith, since it yields God's mercy.

Additional Notes

17:11. Some manuscripts (A, W, Θ, Byz) have διὰ μέσου (through the midst). Others (family 1, family 13) have ἀνὰ μέσον (between). Still another (D) has only μέσον (in the midst of). The best reading ($\mathfrak{P}^{75\text{vid}}$, ℵ, B, L, 1424) has διὰ μέσον (through the midst of, between), which is the harder, more ambiguous reading that the variants attempt to clarify.

17:14. Jesus' simple remark to go to the priests was evidently too cryptic for some copyists. The scribe who handled $\mathfrak{P}^{75}$ added a marginal note that

---

10. Luke uses σῴζω (to save) thirty times, including 7:50; 8:12, 48, 50; 9:24 (twice); 13:23; 19:10. Ironic uses occur in Luke 23:35 (twice), 37, 39. The term also occurs in Acts 2:21; 4:9, 12; 14:9; 15:11.

translates, "I will [it], be cleansed, and they were immediately cleansed." Codex D has simply, "Be healed."

17:17. Arndt (1956: 372) suggests that the reading of D, Itala, and Syriac is original: "These ten have been healed." But this reading lacks sufficient external evidence to be original. The reading of the UBS–NA has overwhelming support: ℵ, Θ, Ψ, family 1, family 13, and Byz.

2. Question about the Consummation (17:20–37)

This section has two parts, both of which are crucial to Luke's view of the kingdom and eschatology. The first unit is a short remark about not hunting for the kingdom's presence (17:20–21). Jesus represents its presence. The exact force of this comment is debated, but it is clear that Jesus intends to bind himself tightly to the kingdom program. The second unit details the signs of the kingdom's full arrival and consummation, in which authority and judgment are fully exercised (17:22–37). Many things happen as the kingdom comes. Most important, Jesus must first suffer. However, in the end, all authority will be manifest in him.

a. Basic Reply (17:20–21)

This short unit serves as a key transition passage and is theologically significant. The Pharisees are warned not to miss the kingdom by looking for it in certain kinds of coming apocalyptic signs. The link to 17:11–19 is that they must not miss what is happening before their eyes in signs like the lepers' healing. Such an error recalls the nine lepers' lack of appreciation for Jesus' work (Danker 1988: 291; Marshall 1978: 652). The link forward to 17:22–37 is found in the theme of Jesus' authority and kingdom consummation. He will show his total authority then, but such authority is related to what is happening now.

Nonetheless, differences between this passage and 17:22–37 suggest why these verses should be treated as distinct units. First, Jesus' remarks here are to the Pharisees, while the following text is addressed to the disciples. Second, the temporal perspective here is the present, or at least the near future, while the next passage looks at the still-delayed coming of the Son of Man; that is, 17:20–21 focuses on the kingdom "in the midst," while 17:22–37 discusses the coming Son of Man. This present/future mix tied to the message of Jesus is common in Luke (3:16–17; 9:26b–27; 11:2–3, 13, 20, 31–32; 12:37–46, 49, 52; 16:16, 19–31; Ellis 1974: 210). The near and far perspectives are held in tension by the juxtaposition of these two passages in Luke 17. In fact, the longer exposition seems to depict what is left of God's plan, a plan that Jesus is initiating now.

This unit contains a crucial pronouncement by Jesus about the kingdom. In fact, one's view of this passage may well determine one's view of Jesus' and Luke's kingdom theology. Before addressing the details in the exegesis, a few initial comments may be helpful. Jesus' goal is to correct the Pharisees' perception that the kingdom is tied to specific signs (Marshall 1978: 652; so also 11:29–32; 13:10–17 with 13:18–21). In looking for certain future signs, they fail to read the current "weather" signs properly (12:54–56). In fact, given Jesus' healing of the ten lepers, their question shows a certain insensitivity, since healing was a sign of the eschaton (7:22–23; Geiger 1976: 29). Another point Jesus makes is that the kingdom is not to be hunted for; it is associated with the one who stands before them.

The debate centers on whether Jesus views the kingdom as present now or coming in the future. If the kingdom is present, in what sense is it here, given the future hope expressed in 17:22–37? The most likely conclusion is that Jesus is telling them the kingdom has come, at least in some sense, in him. The Pharisees are to see in Jesus the kingdom's arrival. At the least, they must deal with him as the one who holds the key to the kingdom. They should not worry about the time and place of the kingdom's arrival. Since Jesus is present, they must deal with him to deal with God's plan, as seen in Jesus' kingdom preaching (Fitzmyer 1985: 1159).

Sources and Historicity

The passage's source is a vexing question (Aland 1985: §234). Many commentators attribute the unit to Q even though these verses have no parallel in Matthew (Schneider 1977a: 354; Schürmann 1968: 237; Schnackenburg 1970: 214–16). This argument is linked to the view that Q is the source of 17:22–37, since it has Matthean parallels (see the introduction to the next unit). This view suggests that Matthew omitted Luke 17:20–21 for a variety of reasons. Goulder (1989: 648–49) argues that Luke uses Matthew in the larger section.

More natural, however, is the view that Luke drew on a special source here (Creed 1930: 217–18 sees Luke editing the source). On this view, there is no need to explain the absence of the verses in Matthew, and the approach fits with the many pericopes in this Lucan section that come to us only through him. Strobel (1961a: 26–27) sees the saying as Luke's creative work, but Perrin (1967: 69–72) and Zmijewski (1972: 379–80) rightly reject this view. Jeremias argues that at least 17:20b–21 is traditional in origin.[1] Even Bultmann (1963: 25) attributes the saying to Jesus. Later parallels (Gospel of Thomas 3; 113; P. Oxy. vol. 4 #654 lines 9–16) are distinct from, yet related to the passage (Fitzmyer 1985: 1157; Wiefel 1988: 308; Meier 1994: 476–77 [who argues that the Thomas passages are Gnostic, later, and dependent on Luke]).

The Jesus Seminar sees the roots of this teaching going back to Jesus and therefore prints 17:20b–21 in pink type (Funk and Hoover 1993: 364–65). This stance is based mainly on parallels to the Gospel of Thomas, but the seminar also notes that Jesus' nonapocalyptic emphasis differs from that of the early church (a point somewhat exaggerated in light of a text such as Rom. 14:17). What is interesting about the seminar's analysis is

---

1. Jeremias 1980: 266 argues that ἐντὸς ὑμῶν (in your midst) in 17:21 is not Lucan. Whether Luke worded the introduction is an open question. After a detailed presentation of the options, Zmijewski 1972: 387–90 decides for a special Lucan source.

that in accepting this saying it misses the point, namely, that the kingdom's presence is tied to Jesus and his activity, especially when linked to Luke 11:20, as the seminar notes. If the seminar had followed through on this observation, it might not have been so skeptical about so many of Jesus' other sayings that emphasize his authority and the time he brings. Meier (1994: 429–30) makes a strong but carefully stated case for the authenticity of 17:21b, citing the theme of the coming kingdom, coherence with other teaching, and a balanced Semitic line in 17:20b and 17:21b. Meier does question the setting of 17:20a and 17:21a under the assumption that Luke 17 material matches the setting of Mark 13 = Matt. 24–25. If L material is present, then it may record a distinct tradition and setting. Those who favor one tradition base for all of this material argue that Luke separated Q and L and placed L in Luke 17:22–37, while leaving the Mark 13 material for Luke 21:5–36 (Meier 1994: 424). But the possibility of additional source material and background complicates the simplicity of this approach (for details see the discussion of sources and historicity for 17:22–37).

The form of the account is a pronouncement by Jesus (Fitzmyer 1985: 1159; Bultmann 1963: 25; Berger 1984: 81). The outline of Luke 17:20–21 is as follows:

    i. The Pharisees question when the kingdom comes (17:20a)
    ii. How the kingdom does not come (17:20b–21a)
    iii. Where the kingdom is (17:21b)

The Pharisees question Jesus about the kingdom. Jesus says the kingdom is not coming with signs. One need not hunt here and there for it. The kingdom is related to Jesus' presence before them.

Exegesis and Exposition

[20]When Jesus was asked by the Pharisees when the kingdom of God comes, he answered them, "The kingdom of God is not coming with signs to be observed, [21]nor will they say, 'Look, here or there,' for behold the kingdom of God is in your midst."

i. The Pharisees Question When the Kingdom Comes (17:20a)

Despite the healings, the Pharisees still have not seen enough, so **17:20a** they ask Jesus when the kingdom comes. Such pharisaic questioning of Jesus is a common Lucan note (5:21, 30; 6:2, 7; 18:18; plus seven other times that have no Synoptic parallels: 7:39; 11:38, 45;

13:31; 14:15; 15:2; 16:14; Geiger 1976: 32).[2] The very raising of such questions in most pericopes is a sign of impending controversy. The view that there is no hint here of contempt or testing in the question understates the situation (but so Plummer 1896: 405; Fitzmyer 1985: 1160). At the narrative level, controversy is suggested by this pattern of questioning.

The present tense ἔρχεται (*erchetai*, come) is translated by some as a futuristic present, since the question's assumption is that the kingdom is not yet here. But the question is merely a temporal query: "When is it coming?" The use of the present tense in both the report and the reply suggests this simple force.[3] The probability is that certain specific eschatological signs are being asked about, since Jesus warns in 17:21 about not needing to go to certain locales to see the coming. Jesus' humble style of ministry and way of revealing the mystery of the kingdom did not match the glorious picture of the kingdom's coming in some Jewish settings (Ps. Sol. 17; Marshall 1978: 654; W. Davies 1962: 19–30; Neusner, Green, and Frerichs 1987). With much of Judaism, the Pharisees believed that the coming of the glorious kingdom would be so clear and powerful that great heavenly signs would signal its arrival. The question is not surprising, given the nature of Jesus' ministry. Jesus' reply will challenge this assumption, noting that the signs indicate not arrival but the move toward consummation.

ii. How the Kingdom Does Not Come (17:20b–21a)

17:20b Jesus begins by noting that the kingdom is not coming (ἔρχεται, *erchetai*, has the same ambiguity as in 17:20a) "with observation." The phrase μετὰ παρατηρήσεως (*meta paratērēseōs*) is variously interpreted (Dalman 1909: 143–47; Marshall 1978: 654; Mattill 1979: 191–92; Beasley-Murray 1986: 97–100; Meier 1994: 424–26; BAGD 622; BAA 1258):[4]

> 1. Some take παρατήρησις to mean "legal observation," looking to its use in Gal. 4:10 and Josephus, *Antiquities* 8.3.9 §96

---

2. I do not follow Aland 1985: §114 and §194 in positing Synoptic parallels for 7:39 and 11:38. See the discussions of sources and historicity for 7:36–50 and 11:37–54.

3. On the possibility of the futuristic present and the likelihood that it is not in force, see the discussion below on whether the kingdom's coming is present or future. Semantically, there is little difference in the choice at this point of the verse, since the process of the kingdom's approach is the point; but the difference is crucial for the passage's theological point, since the contrast of the present tense here and the future tense in 17:22–37 is important.

4. The noun is a *hapax legomenon*, while the verb occurs in a few, mostly Lucan, texts: Mark 3:2; Luke 6:7; 14:1; 20:20; Acts 9:24. In Gal. 4:10, it has the meaning "legal, ritual observation"; Geiger 1976: 38.

(Leaney 1958: 230; Sneed 1962).[5] The point is that one must prepare for the kingdom with a certain level of righteousness. Dalman (1909: 143–47) notes more subtly the Jewish view that such speculation or observation should not detract from study of Torah (all late texts: *b. Sanh.* 97a, 99b; *b. B. Bat.* 10a). Dalman therefore retains the apocalyptic sense of observation, but adds to it the idea that the end could be hastened by righteousness. Proponents of this view relate the concept to Rom. 14:17. The two major problems with this view are that there is no hint of legal controversy in Luke's context and the rabbinic texts are late (Meier 1994: 425).

2. Others see παρατήρησις referring to the kingdom's "hidden" quality, which comes not visibly but mysteriously.[6] The context is decidedly against this view, as is the word's meaning. The following verses (beginning with 17:23's parallel allusion to the concept of 17:21) mention signs related to the glorious coming of the Son of Man (Mattill 1979: 191), so observation is not ultimately ruled out by what Jesus says. The issue becomes its timing.

3. In a more specific development of the next option, some refer παρατήρησις to the kingdom's coming on the night of Passover, "the eschatological night of Passover" (Grundmann 1963: 339; Ellis 1974: 211 [possibly]; Strobel 1958b: 164–74 [who develops this view from A. Merk; see BAGD 622 and BAA 1258]). Appeal is made to the rabbinic interpretation of Exod. 12:42.[7] The major problem with this view is the lack of connection with Christian tradition, as well as the larger question about whether this view existed in the first century (Fitzmyer 1985: 1160; Meier 1994: 425).

4. Most likely παρατήρησις alludes to general apocalyptic signs, so prevalent in early Jewish eschatological speculation, including the desire to calculate the kingdom's arrival by what is

---

5. Though not accepting this view, Schweizer 1984: 272 notes a rabbinic tradition that if two Sabbaths were perfectly observed the kingdom would come, citing Isa. 56:4–7; *b. Šab.* 118b; SB 1:600 §B. Against this view is the late tractate *Derek 'ereṣ Rabbah* 11.13 (= A. Cohen 1965: 2.565), which cites Rabbi Jose as saying, "Whoever calculates the end has no portion in the future world." This fits the later rabbis' tendency to discourage apocalyptic speculation.

6. Dalman 1909: 143–44 notes this suggestion by A. Meyer, who appeals to Aramaic נְטִיר (*nĕṭîr*, observation) and בִּנְטִיר (*binṭîr*, secretly) in Tg. Job 4:12.

7. While Frg. Tg. Exod. 12:42 provides an example of the rabbis' eschatological reading of this event, appeal is made to Aquila's translation of this verse, which uses παρατήρησις (see also *Mekilta de Rabbi Ishmael*, tractate *Pisha* 14 on Exod. 12:42 [= Lauterbach 1933–35: 1.115–16]). The variety in the ancient tradition shows the age of this association.

seen (1 Enoch 91, 93; 2 Bar. 53–74). Such anticipation was grounded in OT prophetic imagery, which the NT reflects in passages such as Luke 17:22–37. This is the most natural reference (Riesenfeld, *TDNT* 8:150; Klostermann 1929: 175 ["signs from heaven"]; SB 2:236; Marshall 1978: 654; Fitzmyer 1985: 1160; Plummer 1896: 406; Schweizer 1984: 272; Meier 1994: 425–26; Sir. 8:8; Matt. 24:36; Mark 13:32; 1 Thess. 5:1).[8] The Pharisees ignore what is happening before their eyes and instead look for signs, thus missing what God is doing through Jesus (Luke 11:29; 12:54–56; 16:27). Jesus is not objecting to calendar-reckoning so much as their failure to see the present "sign of the time."[9]

17:21a This verse is a crux on Luke's view of the kingdom. The first half clearly sets up Jesus' remark that the kingdom does not need to be hunted for by looking here and there. This remark is made in a variety of ways in the NT (Matt. 24:26–27; Mark 13:21; Luke 17:23; 21:8; Marshall 1978: 655; Geiger 1976: 43).

iii. Where the Kingdom Is (17:21b)

17:21b Jesus now explains (γάρ, *gar*) why one need not hunt for the kingdom. The structure contrasts with the previous verse: in 17:20b the verb οὐκ ἔρχεται (*ouk erchetai*, does not come) is first and the reference to signs trails at the end, while in 17:21b ἡ βασιλεία (*hē basileia*, the kingdom) is first and ἐντὸς ὑμῶν ἐστιν (*entos hymōn estin*, is in your midst) is held off until the end. In this way Jesus' reply puts a double emphasis on kingdom and the time of its coming: "For behold, the kingdom of God in the midst of you is." By delaying the verb, the verbal idea is emphasized slightly. In short, the sign is Jesus.

---

8. In everyday Greek, παρατήρησις was used of the symptoms or signs of disease. To make such calculations, Judaism played off chronological imagery in Ps. 90:4 (seven thousand years); Jer. 25:11; 29:10 (seventy exile weeks); Dan. 9:2 (seventy yearweeks), although Ernst 1977: 486 notes that not all rabbinic Jews accepted such speculation (for which, see SB 4:977–1015 and n. 5 above).

9. Most, like Talbert 1982: 166, see Jesus attacking apocalyptic calendar-setting, but this needs careful definition in view of NT exhortations to watch carefully for the Son of Man's return. Granted, a specific date cannot and should not be sought, but sensitivity to general eschatological sequence or to watchfulness is never condemned (Matt. 24–25 = Mark 13; Luke 21:5–36; Acts 3:11–26). The view is right to deny datesetting, but is wrong to see the only sign as "Spirit-empowered ministry." New Testament eschatological hope is more specific and futurist than this denial suggests. In a more balanced approach, Beasley-Murray 1986: 100 notes that there are "signs" to see—if one has the eyes to see them. Meier 1994: 425 mentions texts where Jesus urges the community of faith to be prepared for a long ministry (Luke 21:7–24; 19:11; Acts 1:6–7; Mark 13:10). But disciples are still to keep looking for Jesus (Matt. 24–25 = Mark 13 = Luke 21:5–36).

The structure of 17:21b has contact with 17:20b at three points (Meier 1994: 426): (1) the kingdom of God is the subject in both passages; (2) in 20b the kingdom is "coming," while in 21b it "is"; and (3) in 20b it approaches "with observation," while in 21b it is "among you." The speculation of how it comes (20b) is contrasted with what is now becoming evident (21b). Meier (1994: 428–30) argues that the balance of these two texts is no accident and reflects an origin in L. He also defends the authenticity of these two portions of the declaration, noting that the idea of the coming kingdom and the Semitic dialectic are evidence of their roots in Jesus and that they cohere with other texts (Matt. 11:2–6 = Luke 7:18–23; Matt. 11:11 = Luke 7:28; Matt. 11:12–13 = Luke 16:16; Matt. 12:27–28 = Luke 11:19–20 [he also suggests (p. 483) what the Aramaic might have looked like]).

The meaning of this verse turns on two issues: (a) Is the kingdom said to be future or present? (b) What does ἐντὸς ὑμῶν mean?[10] Taking the last question first, three major options exist for ἐντὸς ὑμῶν (Beasley-Murray 1986: 100–103; Noack 1948 [for the history of interpretation]):

1. Many, including numerous ancient interpreters, take the phrase to mean that the kingdom is "inside you" (Ps. 39:4 [38:4 LXX]; 103:1 [102:1 LXX]; 109:22 [108:22 LXX]; Isa. 16:11).[11] This view has two major problems. Contextually, Jesus is addressing the Pharisees, who are the last group of people that Jesus would say has the kingdom in them (Luke 11:37–52, esp. 11:52). Meier (1994: 426) argues that it would be strange if Jesus said this to the Pharisees and never to his disciples! Second, nowhere else in the NT is the kingdom spoken of in internal terms (Manson 1949: 304; Fitzmyer 1985: 1161; Meier 1994: 480; against Sneed 1962). Granted, the Spirit is sent as a token of God's promise and does relate people to the kingdom (Creed 1930: 219). Marshall (1978: 655), however, is right when he says that in the NT people enter the kingdom, but the kingdom does not enter people. The Spirit is a sign that one has come into the kingdom, but his presence does not equal the kingdom. The kingdom is a community of residence, blessing, and enablement, while it is the Spirit who marks one for membership.

10. The only other NT use of ἐντός is Matt. 23:26, where it refers to the inside of a cup.

11. Creed 1930: 218–19; Sneed 1962; Dalman 1909: 145–47; Dodd 1961: 62–63 (who later switched to view 2). See Mattill 1979: 193 and Beasley-Murray 1986: 101 for details on the Gospel of Thomas, Origen, Chrysostom, Athanasius, Ambrose, Jerome, and Luther.

2. Others argue on the basis of its usage in the papyri that the phrase means "in your grasp or power."[12] This means that the kingdom's coming is related to one's power to repent; that is, whether it comes depends on one's response. This view is possible, but the case made for it from the papyri is challenged by Riesenfeld (1949) and Wikgren (1950), who argue that the phrase could mean "in your presence or domain." Also against this view is that it could be regarded as a non-answer. On this view, Jesus has said it is not by signs that the kingdom comes, but it is within your grasp. The essential question still remains, "Where is it so that I can obtain it?" Thus, this option does not really supply a sufficient answer to deal with the question. A clearer way to state that the kingdom comes through one's choice is to mention directly the need to repent, which Jesus often says to the Pharisees (5:31–32; 11:29–32). Meier (1994: 427) rejects the reading, arguing that it puts the stress on human control and calculation when the context argues for God's manifesting his presence in his sovereign way. In addition, to say that the kingdom is within one's grasp in the present is to say in effect that it is present, since one can reach for it now. It is this force that Beasley-Murray fails to develop in his study. Conceptually, the view ends up being very similar to view 3.

3. A final option argues that the phrase means "in your presence" or "before you" (Isa. 45:14 ["God is among you"]; Danker 1988: 292; Marshall 1978: 655; Ellis 1974: 211; Arndt 1956: 373–74; Plummer 1896: 406 [undecided]). The emphasis here would be that the Pharisees confront the kingdom in Jesus. They do not need to look all around for it because its central figure is in front of their eyes. Mattill (1979: 196–97) objects that Luke has a more common phrase for this idea (ἐν μέσῳ [en mesō, in the midst] in Luke 2:46; 8:7; 10:3; 21:21; 22:27, 55; 24:36; Acts 1:15; 2:22; 17:22; 27:21). But Mattill understates the synonymity of the phrases.[13] Since Jesus and his

---

12. So Leaney 1958: 230; Fitzmyer 1985: 1161–62; Mattill 1979: 201; Roberts 1948; Rüstow 1960; Cadbury 1950; Tertullian, *Against Marcion* 4.35.12. Beasley-Murray 1986: 102–3 takes this view, though he fails to evaluate this option when it is taken with a present force. Riesenfeld 1949 does not mention the evidence from Aquila noted in n. 13 below—a grave omission—in arguing that "in your midst" is not possible. Schlosser 1980: 1.202–4 argues that "in one's power" is a possible first-century meaning, but he opts for "in the midst of." His discussion is the latest careful examination of the evidence.

13. Jeremias 1980: 266 attributes this digression from Luke's common expression to the presence of a traditional source. Also, Mattill 1979: 197 notes that, since the Greek versions variously translate Exod. 34:9 with ἐν μέσῳ (Theodotion, Symma-

authority are the major obstacles in the Pharisees' way, this view fits the context nicely. To see the kingdom, look to Jesus and what he offers.

Does the passage refer to the present or the future? Those who argue for the future point to three major contextual factors: (1) the two uses of ἔρχεται in 17:20 are futuristic presents according to this view, so that is how ἐστίν (*estin*) in 17:21 should be read; (2) the signs discussed in 17:22–37 are future (Ridderbos 1962: 475); and (3) the reference to looking for signs "here and there" is future.[14] Other proponents of a future sense opt for the idea that "the kingdom or Son of Man will come suddenly" (J. Weiss 1971: 91; Klostermann 1929: 175; Luce 1933: 277; Manson 1949: 304; Bultmann 1963: 121–22; Luke 21:34).

There are strong reasons to reject this future option. First, ἔρχομαι is far more common as a futuristic present than is εἰμί (BDF §323.1; Geiger 1976: 45). As such, the shift of verbs should be seen as significant, even decisive. If Luke had wanted to keep the emphasis on the future, Jesus did not need to change verbs within his reply (eloquently stated by Meier 1994: 426). Second, ἐστίν is placed in an emphatic position, so that the stress falls even more on the verb. Third, though this is a small point, when Jesus elaborates about the return of the Son of Man in 17:22–37, he never uses the word *kingdom* to describe the period. It could be argued that Luke is making a distinction between Jesus' reply about the kingdom's coming now (17:20–21) and the period that will represent its glorious completion (17:22–37). In other words, the Son of Man's day is not the kingdom's coming, but its movement toward consummation, since then his authority will be revealed in its totality (17:24, 30). Fourth, if one argues that the point about the future coming is its suddenness, then the saying's key idea is the very point that must be supplied, which is unlikely.

If Jesus refers to a present coming of the kingdom, then he is saying that his presence represents the kingdom's arrival. He is the answer to the Pharisees' question (17:20a). Such is the consistent declaration of Luke (4:16–30; 7:22–28; 9:1–6; 10:17–20; 11:20; 16:16;

---

chus) and ἐντός (Aquila), the phrases can be synonymous (Field 1875: 1.144). Beasley-Murray 1986: 101–2 adds a similar example from Exod. 17:7 (Field 1875: 1.111). Note also Symmachus in Lam. 1:3 and Ps. 87:6 LXX [88:6 Engl.] (Field 1875: 747, 239). Meier 1994: 479 notes that this translation appears in the literal Aquila and the more idiomatic Symmachus, making the meaning of ἐντός clear. These ancient texts show that "in the midst" is a well-attested sense for the term.

14. Mattill 1979: 198–201 lays out the reasoning and opts for a sense of "the kingdom will be among you and be in your power to grasp"—an example of the semantic error of totality transfer, since he gives two meanings to one term.

Tiede 1988: 300).[15] They do not need to search for the kingdom, be-cause the one who brings the kingdom and its program is before them. They need only to respond to him to find its presence and ben-efits (Marshall 1978: 656; Ellis 1974: 211; Schweizer 1984: 273; Ernst 1977: 487; Kümmel 1957: 32–35, esp. 35 n. 54).[16] They need to learn the lesson of the Samaritan leper who was healed: the way to God's kingdom is through Jesus. He controls the kingdom's benefits and represents its power and presence.

What does this mean for Luke's view of the kingdom? It comes in stages: one present and the rest in the future (see 10:18 and 11:20). This is the kingdom's "already–not yet" character, as the kingdom mystery parables suggest (13:18–20). In his ministry, Jesus offers forgiveness and the Spirit, which is central to kingdom promise (3:15–18; 24:44–49). The kingdom invitation continued to be offered and was not withdrawn with Israel's rejection (14:15–24). Jesus heals to show Satan's demise (11:20–22). He promises to bestow the Spirit as a token of the kingdom's presence and the promise's com-ing (Acts 2:30–39; 13:32–39). Thus, the kingdom currently manifests itself in the church, which is where God is active through Christ, manifesting his transforming power (Rom. 1:16–17; 14:17–18; 16:25–27) and distributing salvific blessing to his people. In fact, one can argue that the kingdom really arrives in terms of benefiting Jesus' disciples after the new covenant is cut with his death (Luke 22:19–20) and after "the promise of the Father," the Spirit, is distrib-uted (Luke 24:49; Acts 2). In the church one is to see God overcom-ing the forces of evil and the enemy. The church reflects Jesus' mes-sage in its life (Luke 1:79; 4:18–19; 11:20; Acts 13:47 [of his messengers]; 26:23 [of his message as a result of resurrection]).

In the elaboration to the disciples in Luke 17:22–37, Jesus will make clear that there is coming a day when all the world will see the rule of the Son of Man, a rule that completes God's plan of redemp-tion (Acts 3:18–26). As such, it is clear that the kingdom is not merely the church, for the church is a but a part of the total kingdom program. The church shares in aspects of what the kingdom is, but the kingdom program is larger than that of the church. The church

15. On the various expressions used to say that the kingdom is near or present, see K. Schmidt, *TDNT* 1:584. Fitzer, *TDNT* 9:89 n. 10, sees the expression here as syn-onymous to that of 10:9. Note especially how the preaching of the kingdom and the gospel are linked in 9:1–6, while the kingdom and Jesus' activity are associated in 11:20. Luke 7:18–23 (esp. 7:22); 7:28; 11:20; and 16:16 seem to place the initial phase of fulfillment in the present.

16. To speak of the kingdom's plan in two stages (arrival and consummation) means that in consummation God will complete promises made to Israel (Acts 3:18–21). Fulfillment of OT kingdom hope is now–not yet, so some applies to the current era and some to the future; Bock 1992a.

is in the kingdom, but it is not the kingdom. Given the need for personal response in order to enter the kingdom, it is also clear that the kingdom is not equal to society at large. Rather, the kingdom is made up of those people who have responded to Jesus and share in the benefits he has to offer. Kingdom citizens are those who turn and come to him. They form a new community and are to reflect God's love and care by the way they live: loving God and fellow humans. One need not search high and low for the kingdom or look for a sign in the sky about it, for its presence is here now. It is present in the person of Jesus and his offer of forgiveness and in the community of faith that he spawns and rules.

Summary

Luke 17:20–21 represents a fundamental description of the kingdom. Jesus' coming and activity naturally raise questions about the kingdom's coming. The Pharisees ask how one can see when it will come. They assume, as most Jews did, that cosmic signs will announce its impending arrival. So they ask, "What are these great cosmic introductory signs?"

But Jesus surprises them. They do not need to hunt for the kingdom. They do not need to look into the distant future for it. It is right before them. If they would read "the sign of the present time" correctly (12:54–56), they would recognize the King and God's kingdom program. Jesus' coming inaugurates the kingdom; the process of kingdom growth has begun (13:18–20). Much of Luke's Gospel is consumed with this point. Whether Jesus teaches or heals, Luke is showing that in him God's promise is fulfilled according to OT hope (7:22). Luke wants his readers to realize the same fundamental truth. To deal with God, one must go through Jesus. To enter the courts and blessings of heaven and to share in relationship with God, one must come to the King and enter his kingdom court with praise.

b. Its Quick Coming and Accompanying Judgment (17:22–37)

The kingdom may be in the midst, but its presence does not mean that the day of the Son of Man's glorious coming has occurred. So Jesus now turns to the theme of his return, which will bring about the kingdom's consummation. The Son of Man's arrival will be sudden and visible, so do not be deceived by those who point to its presence in a certain locale. It will come after the Son of Man suffers, in the midst of a godless period similar to the days of Noah and Lot. It will be a day of judgment, where vultures gather over the dead. In sum, the kingdom may be revealed in Jesus now, but it will show itself in judgment and power one day.

The unit's major concern is to warn the disciples of the nature of the time and to encourage them to endure the interval. They are not to fall away before the end, the negative example of which is Lot's wife. Loyalty to Jesus means loyalty to the end, despite the severe trials that God's people may face in the meantime. This unit leads nicely into the parable of the nagging widow and the judge (18:1–8), where part of the point is that God's people are to pray for swift vindication.

Sources and Historicity

The issue of sources is complex and difficult to unravel (Aland 1985: §235).[1] Several elements, most involving the presence of Synoptic parallels, create the difficulties in assessing this material:

1. Both Matthew and Mark seem to know of only one eschatological discourse (Matt. 24–25 = Mark 13). Yet Luke divides in two (17:20–37 and 21:5–36) what these writers keep together. Luke 21 parallels the Matthean and Marcan setting in Jerusalem during the final week of Jesus' ministry. The picture is complicated in that certain themes from the Jerusalem discourse in Matt. 24–25 = Mark 13 are not

---

1. I confine my discussion here to 17:22–37. The larger issue of Jesus' apocalyptic discourse teaching is discussed in detail in the sources and historicity section of 21:5–38. For an overview of the larger discussion, Beasley-Murray's survey (1993) has a full discussion of points that I can only touch on here and in 21:5–38.

found in Luke 21 where one would expect them, but in Luke 17—
which is given before Jesus gets to Jerusalem:

Luke	Matthew	Mark
17:21	24:23	13:21
17:23	24:23	13:21
17:24	24:27	—
17:27	24:38–39	—
17:31	24:17–18	13:15–16
17:35	24:41	—
17:37b	24:28	—

These similarities and differences—including the different sequencing of these themes—raise the question whether more than one discourse existed in the tradition.

2. Many elements in the Luke 17 speech have conceptual, if not also
   verbal, parallels in the later Matt. 24–25 (beyond the above, Luke
   17:26a with Matt. 24:37a, and Luke 17:30 with Matt. 24:39b).
3. The Luke 17 discourse has a few ties with Mark 13 alone.[2]
4. Luke has a few verses unique to him (17:22, 28–29, 32, 34, 37a).
5. Luke has no overlap between Luke 17 and 21. In other words, what
   Matthew and Mark record Jesus speaking inside Jerusalem and Luke
   records him speaking outside of Jerusalem does not overlap with
   what Luke records him speaking in Jerusalem. Another complication
   is that Luke 12:35–48 also has close, even verbal parallels to the
   eschatological discourse in Matt. 24–25 = Mark 13, making yet a
   third place where Luke has material that Matthew and Mark have in
   a single location (Luke 12:39–40 with Matt. 24:43–44; Luke 12:42–
   46 with Matt. 24:45–51; Luke 12:39 with Mark 13:35–36). Finally,
   similar data show Luke to be much closer to Matt. 24 than to Mark
   13 throughout the Luke 17 material.

These data raise several questions: (1) Why does Luke split up what Matthew and Mark have in a single place? (2) From where does Luke's unique
material come? (3) Given that the evangelists made choices in the presentation of their material, who chose what? The options are (a) Luke had access to more information, (b) Luke chose to supply more information on this
theme (and split it up) in contrast to the other Synoptics, or (c) Matthew and
Mark kept their eschatological discourse to a single unit. There are a variety
of approaches to this problem:

2. Luke 17:23 with Mark 13:21, and Luke 17:31 with Mark 13:15–16. In addition,
Marshall 1978: 656 notes that Luke 17:25 is often tied to Marcan passion predictions
and Luke 17:33 to Mark 8:35.

1. Some attribute all the material to Q and argue that the Lucan peculiarities are the result of Matthew's choosing not to reproduce all that he had (Manson 1949: 141–48; Grundmann 1963: 342 [apparently]). One source supplies all the details for Luke's material, which he consciously divided so that he could discuss the coming's suddenness in Luke 17, while saving other eschatological concerns for Luke 21.[3]

2. A variation on this "single source" approach is D. Wenham's view (1984) that the origin is a single pre-Synoptic, pre-Pauline source that is not Q, but a circulating eschatological discourse of Jesus. Wenham provides fine, detailed analysis of the differences between Luke and the other Synoptics, as well as intriguing notes of contact with Paul. He also argues that Luke split up this material for thematic reasons.

3. Another view attributes the unique portions to Lucan redaction and the rest of the material to Q (Schneider 1977a: 354). The major problem with this straightforward approach is that it cannot explain those additions that do not contribute to the theme (17:25) or that use different wording but do not really alter the point of other material available to Luke (17:34, 37a).

4. Most see a combination of Lucan and Q material and argue for Luke's splitting up the setting for thematic reasons. The uniquely Lucan material comes from Luke's special source, an eminently reasonable proposal, since so much of Luke 9–19 involves Luke's special material (Ellis 1974: 209–10; Marshall 1978: 656–57; Schlatter 1960: 394–96, 553–56; Fitzmyer 1985: 1164–65 [limits L to 17:28–32]; Zmijewski 1972: 352). This solution handles the source issue plausibly, but still has difficulty sorting out why Luke placed this discourse here, while leaving no doublets from the discourse in Luke 21. In other words, Luke could have just as reasonably gone with the setting Matthew and Mark gave him and put all this material in one place. What caused him to go a different way?

5. I suggest that Luke had at least three eschatological discourse sources. It is clear that he shared a source with Matthew, since so much of the material here and in Luke 21 overlaps with Matt. 24–25. The few points of contact with Mark also suggest that he had access to a Marcan form of the speech, though he chose not to rely on it greatly, as seen in the few unique parallels with Mark (noted above). It is possible that either of these sources could equal much of Wenham's posited source, but the differences between Matthew and Mark make it unlikely that Wenham's source explains everything. The key to Luke's division of material is that his special Lucan

---

3. Since Q is a list of sayings, the settings would be the responsibility of the evangelists. Even if Q exists, I am less certain of this assumption about settings than most, since the roots of the tradition reach back to participants (Luke 1:2).

source placed a discourse outside Jerusalem, with the majority of other events it contained.[4] This gave Luke a choice: go for one discourse along with the other Synoptic sources or follow his additional source and split the material into at least two parts.[5] Luke opts to go with his special source, which recorded a discourse outside of Jerusalem, and he also chose not to duplicate in Luke 21 those elements that he had already outlined in Luke 17. This explanation seems to be the only one sufficient to explain Luke's peculiar twofold (or threefold) arrangement of this material. It is a straightforward explanation that need not engage in complex discussion as to why certain authors omitted certain things in certain places from one source alone. This approach questions the premise that the best explanation is the one that posits the simplest source hypothesis. Thus it seems likely, though one cannot be dogmatic about this point, that Luke's two eschatological discourses reflect his sources' indication that there were at least two such speeches.

The uniquely Lucan features provide great difficulty for these first two options. Explanations as to why Matthew omitted material or why Luke rearranged it presuppose the view under discussion, and the evidence is forced into the model to make it plausible. Manson has great difficulty with 17:28–30, 31–32, while Wenham struggles to explain 17:25, 29–30.[6] Wenham's suggestion does raise another possibility: the eschatological material existed in two forms with the possibility that Luke knew both. If Wenham's discourse source exists at all, then one might posit at least two traditions (Mark–Matthew and this second source) that contained eschatological remarks from which Luke could choose.

The Jesus Seminar is skeptical of this discourse's connection to Jesus (Funk and Hoover 1993: 365–68). Only 17:33 is regarded as having a strong link to Jesus (pink type) because this saying (losing one's life) is multiply attested (Luke 9:24 = Mark 8:35 = Matt. 16:25; 10:39; John 12:25). Other sayings in the discourse (Luke 17:22–24, 34–35, 37) are printed in gray type in the belief that they may have had contact with Jesus but have been

---

4. This may also explain the thematic tie to 18:1–8, since the Lucan special material majors in parabolic material. This distinct discourse and this parable were in this source.

5. I suggest that 12:35–48 may reflect this distinct tradition, which might also explain its placement. The same choices that apply in Luke 17 apply also in Luke 12 and 21. If this was really all one source, why divide material that already had thematic unity into three units?

6. Manson 1949: 144 never really explains how the Lot material in Luke 17 entered Q or why Matthew left it out. To his credit, Wenham notes his three major problems (1984: 149, 157–65), but seems hard-pressed to defend the form of 17:25, 29–30, 31–32. His discussion posits many reasons for the presence of some items. The argument is plausible, even possible, but is it the most likely?

significantly reshaped by Luke. Rejected as unconnected to Jesus, 17:25–32 is viewed as too apocalyptic and judgmental for Jesus (black type).

Such an approach raises a larger question about Jesus as teacher of apocalyptic. This tradition—especially its apocalyptic features—left a strong impression on the early church that it was the Lord's teaching. Beasley-Murray (1993: 355–56, 361 n. 24) notes several points of contact between Jesus and Paul, of which the following seem most relevant:

Mark 13:5	2 Thess. 2:3a
Mark 13:6	2 Thess. 2:2, 9
Mark 13:7	2 Thess. 2:2
Mark 13:14	2 Thess. 2:3–4
Mark 13:22	2 Thess. 2:9
Mark 13:24–27	1 Thess. 4:15–17; 2 Thess. 2:1
Luke 21:34–36	1 Thess. 5:3, 6

Arguing for catechetical roots for this teaching, Beasley-Murray notes four key themes: (1) false Christs and prophets, (2) persecution and suffering, (3) judgment for Jerusalem, and (4) watchfulness. What is evident, even if every correlation in Beasley-Murray's list is not correct, is a strong conceptual influence on the church that must have reached back to Jesus. If Jesus were not apocalyptic in his expression, where did this strand of church teaching come from? Who besides Jesus could have created the intense expectation found in this generation of the early church?

Once the reality of an apocalyptic Jesus is affirmed, then we are in a better position to assess the details of this discourse. Nothing in the remarks of Luke 17:25–32 is beyond an apocalyptic-prophetic warning by Jesus about an event with conceptual roots in the judgment of the day of the Lord. Even the suffering prediction in 17:25 is possible, given that Jesus predicted the Son of Man's suffering (see excursus 10). And a separating judgment at the end-time is not beyond Jesus' grasp. The imagery is graphic but similar to that of John the Baptist's (Luke 3:17 = Matt. 3:12) and Jesus' kingdom parables of Matt. 13 (see the exegesis of Luke 13:35). The day of the Son of Man has connections to the Jewish day of the Messiah. In sum, all of this material has roots in the OT end-time expectation and is capable of reaching back to Jesus—provided that he taught apocalyptically, which seems certain (Beasley-Murray 1993: 361–62, 376). I lay out the case for authenticity of key verses within the exegesis since the two issues are so tightly bound together (see the exegesis of 17:22, 24, 25, 26, 28, 29, 32, 33, 35, 37). The themes of this discourse—the longing for the day, the warning about not pursuing false claims of the arrival, the obviousness of the day, the suffering that precedes it, its coming in an era that is unprepared, the call to flee the day, the separating of the judgment, and its devastating character—all have roots in Jesus' teaching.

Since the passage is from an eschatological discourse, it is a combination of prophetic and apocalyptic pronouncements (Fitzmyer 1985: 1166 [prophetic and minatory sayings]; Bultmann 1963: 122–23; Berger 1984: 296, 305 ["apocalyptic speech"]). The outline of Luke 17:22–37 is as follows:

i. The timing of the coming of the kingdom (17:22–25)
   (1) The disciples' desire to see the days of the Son of Man (17:22)
   (2) Jesus' warning not to go when some call (17:23)
   (3) The day's quick coming (17:24)
   (4) The Son of Man's suffering (17:25)
ii. The nature of the coming of the kingdom (17:26–30)
   (1) Like Noah's day (17:26–27)
   (2) Like Lot's day (17:28–30)
iii. The response to the coming of the kingdom (17:31–35)
   (1) Move quickly, do not turn back (17:31)
   (2) Remember Lot's wife (17:32)
   (3) Lose life to gain it (17:33)
   (4) Judgment will be quick (17:34–35)
iv. The judgment accompanying the coming of the kingdom (17:37)
   (1) The disciples' question (17:37a)
   (2) Jesus' picture of vultures and corpses (17:37b)

The major focus of this unit is on the consummation of the kingdom with the vivid display of Jesus' rule. Disciples will desire the coming of this day, but it is not here yet. They are not to heed cries of its presence. The coming will be sudden and visible. The Son of Man must first suffer and be rejected. The coming will be in the midst of godless days and will bring judgment. When it comes, flee and do not look back, for to lose one's life is to gain it. Judgment will come and vultures will surround the corpses, for this will be a period of judgment and death.

Exegesis and Exposition

22And he said to the disciples, "There will come days when you desire to see one of the days of the Son of Man and you will not see it. 23And they will say to you, ⌜'Behold there!' or 'Behold here!'⌝ ⌜Do not go out or pursue them.⌝ 24For just as lightning that flashes from one side of the heavens to the other lights up the sky, ⌜so will be the Son of Man in his day.⌝ 25But first it is necessary for him to suffer many things and be rejected by this generation.

²⁶"And even as it was in the days of Noah, so it will be in the days of the Son of Man. ²⁷They ate, drank, married, they were given in marriage, until the day that Noah went into the boat and the flood came and destroyed them ⌜all⌝. ²⁸Likewise as it was in the days of Lot: they were eating, drinking, buying, selling, planting, building, ²⁹but on the day that Lot went out from Sodom, he rained down ⌜fire and sulfur⌝ ⌜from heaven⌝ and destroyed them all. ³⁰So the day of the Son of Man will be revealed ⌜like these things⌝.

³¹"On that day, let whoever is on the housetop, with his goods in the house, not come down to take them away; and likewise let him who is in the field not turn back. ³²Remember the wife of Lot. ³³Whoever seeks to ⌜gain⌝ his life will lose it, but whoever loses his life will preserve it. ³⁴I say to you, in that night there will be two in one bed: one will be taken and the other left. ³⁵There will be two women grinding together: one will be taken, the other left." ⌜36⌝

³⁷They asked him, "Where, Lord?" He said to them, "Where the body is, there the vultures will be gathered."

i. The Timing of the Coming of the Kingdom (17:22–25)
(1) The Disciples' Desire to See the Days of the Son of Man (17:22)

17:22 Jesus begins this discourse to his disciples with a note about an unrealized desire. The shift of audience from 17:20–21 is significant, since the remarks about the kingdom's presence were directed at the Pharisees. The concern, however, is not just for the beginning of what God is doing, but also with its expected consummation. Jesus tells his followers that they will desire (ἐπιθυμέω, *epithymeō*; cf. Matt. 13:17; 1 Pet. 1:12) the coming of the Son of Man, but they will not see it (Büchsel, *TDNT* 3:170). The phrase τοῦ υἱοῦ τοῦ ἀνθρώπου (*tou huiou tou anthrōpou*, the Son of Man) refers to Jesus, as the note in 17:25 about his suffering makes clear. In this context, the title refers to Jesus' authority, since when he comes he will act in judgment. In the OT the phrase ἐλεύσονται ἡμέραι (*eleusontai hēmerai*, days will come) was frequently an allusion to approaching judgment (Isa. 39:6; Jer. 7:32; 16:14; Ezek. 7:10–12; Amos 4:2; Zech. 14:1; Marshall 1978: 657; Fitzmyer 1985: 1168; Wiefel 1988: 310). Uses in the NT are Luke 5:35 (not a judgment text); 21:6; 23:29.[7]

The remark about the day of the Son of Man is unique in Synoptic eschatological material, which leads many to attribute the remark to Luke and his concern to deal with the "delay of the parousia."[8] There

---

7. Note the similar ἡμέραις ἐκείναις (those days) in Joel 3:2 LXX [2:29 Engl.] and Acts 2:18 to refer to the last days.

8. Conzelmann 1960: 105 n. 3, 123 suggests that this speech is the "insider" explanation for Jesus' remarks. So also Zmijewski 1972: 417–19, although he acknowledges the possibility of a special Lucan source. Against a Lucan redaction are Kümmel

is no doubt that the text warns disciples not to be impatient if the kingdom does not come as soon as they wish it. It is also clear that disciples will have those desires. But the function of the discourse is to reassure the disciples that the Son of Man will eventually come and wield authority in justice for them. All of Jesus' teaching about trial and patience suggests the attitude found here, so that this teaching is something that goes back to him (Matt. 10:21–22 = Mark 13:12 = Luke 21:16; Matt. 24:6 = Mark 13:7 = Luke 21:9; 12:11–12).

The expression τῶν ἡμερῶν τοῦ υἱοῦ τοῦ ἀνθρώπου (tōn hēmerōn tou huiou tou anthrōpou, the days of the Son of Man) is unique to this verse and 17:26. The usual reference is to the singular *day* of the Son of Man, a period of his concentrated activity (17:24, 30). The term is formed in parallelism to the "days" of Noah and Lot in 17:26, 28, so that its presence is not surprising when placed in context. The meaning of the phrase is disputed (Marshall 1978: 658; Fitzmyer 1985: 1168–69):

1. The phrase is equivalent to "the days of Messiah" and refers to the return of the Son of Man (*m. Ber.* 1.5; SB 2:237; 4:826–27, 857–72; Klostermann 1929: 175; Creed 1930: 220; Arndt 1956: 374; Ellis 1974: 211; Schweizer 1984: 273–74; Luce 1933: 277; Fitzmyer 1985: 1169; Wiefel 1988: 311; 2 Esdr. [= 4 Ezra] 13:52).
2. The phrase refers to a period that ends with the return, as 17:26 suggests (noted by Manson 1949: 142). This view stresses the period just before the return of the Son of Man.
3. The phrase refers to the entire period from Easter to parousia (Zmijewski 1972: 400–403). If this is the case, however, the remark makes no sense, for all the disciples did see this period. If this sense exists, it can only refer to the end of this period, not to its entirety.
4. If we are dealing with a totally realized eschatology, the phrase refers primarily to the Son of Man's earthly days. In this case what is desired is a return to the "golden days" of Jesus' ministry, as they look to the future in the midst of suffering (Dodd 1961: 81 n. 31; Nolland 1993a: 858 [apparently]). This suggestion also is problematic, since nowhere does the church long to return to the "old days" of Jesus. What they always seek is his glorious return to judge.
5. The phrase alludes to Jesus' glorious manifestations to Stephen or Paul, as well as to the restoration of Israel at the fi-

---

1957: 29; Colpe, TDNT 8:450–51; and Marshall 1978: 659, who notes that Luke does not create Son-of-Man sayings and that the text has a good claim to authenticity. In addition, the criterion of multiple attestation favors authenticity.

nal consummation (Leaney 1958: 68–72, 231). Again, this broad type of reference seems unlikely, since consummation is the issue, as the link to 17:26 shows. A consummative reference seems more appropriate.

6. The phrase is Luke's way of showing that a period, not an instant, is in view (Conzelmann 1960: 124). The major problem with this suggestion is that the singular *day* of the Son of Man is also used by Luke in 17:24, 30, and that expression, which also clearly focuses on the return, appears to refer to the same event (so correctly Marshall 1978: 659).

The distinction is significant, for what is it that the disciples desire to see? Options three through six are excluded for the reasons stated above, so which of the first two options is best? The best option seems to be the first: the phrase is equivalent to "the days of Messiah." The return brings the saints' vindication and the Messiah's total rule. It cannot refer to the period before, which is full of ungodliness that would be offensive to the disciples (17:26–30). This sense also explains the presence of the singular μίαν (*mian*, one): μίαν focuses on the initiation of a broad period, which is a key turning point of the expectation.[9] When that day comes (17:31, 34–35), things will happen decisively and quickly. In short, the period of fulfillment is made up of inauguration (17:20–21) and consummation (17:22–37). Jesus refers to the beginning of consummation here. Fitzmyer (1985: 1168) regards the phrase as equal to the angelic references to Jesus' return in Acts 1:11. The disciples will long for the Son of Man's glorious reign, but desire alone will not bring it, for there is an appropriate time for its coming, as Luke 17:26–30 shows. In fact, something must precede its coming (17:25).

(2) Jesus' Warning Not to Go When Some Call (17:23)

17:23 Jesus warns the disciples not to let their desire mislead them. They are not to listen to others' claims to have found the Son of Man (R. Meyer, *TDNT* 6:826–27; M. De Jonge, *TDNT* 9:520–21).[10] Matthew 24:23, 26 and Mark 13:21 are conceptually parallel, except that they speak of not believing the claim, instead of, with Luke, not following them. The disciples are not to pursue claims that the Son of Man is present. When they hear calls to go see the Son of Man, they

9. Fitzmyer 1985: 1168–69 defends the ordinal μίαν as meaning "one," not "first" (against Plummer 1896: 407) or "very much" (against Torrey 1933: 312; Manson 1949: 142) or "just one" (against Rigaux 1970: 410).

10. Fitzmyer 1985: 1169 notes how Jewish historian Josephus reacted to eschatological claims; *Jewish War* 6.5.4 §§310–15 (also Tacitus, *Histories* 5.13).

are not to go. The Son of Man is not where others claim him to be. (See the additional notes for two textual issues in this verse.)

Luke is closer to Mark 13:21 in this verse (except for reversing ἐκεῖ [ekei, there] and ὧδε [hōde, here]) than to Matt. 24:23 (which has ὧδε twice). Mark also has the remark in the singular ("if anyone says to you"), while Luke uses the plural ("and they will say to you") (Geiger 1976: 60). Although Lührmann (1969: 72) sees Matthew's influence in the plural, Matt. 24:23 is singular, with third-person plurals not emerging until Matt. 24:24–26—a mixture that makes a claim of Matthean influence hard. Zmijewski (1972: 403–4) prefers Q (i.e., Matthew) along with the Lucan use of ἀπέρχομαι (apercho-mai, to go away) and διώκω (diōkō, to pursue), while noting how the construction differs from 17:21 in five ways (e.g., the ἐκεῖ-ὧδε order), even though it is somewhat parallel. But this form of ἀπέρχομαι is not particularly Lucan, being common in all the Synoptics; neither is διώκω, being more common in Matthew than in Luke (Zmijewski also argues that διώκω has discipleship overtones, but this is less than certain). Given so little data to work with, it is virtually impossible to establish the source of this single verse, especially given the possibility of multiple sources.

(3) The Day's Quick Coming (17:24)

The basic reason (γάρ, gar) that the disciples do not need to hunt for **17:24** the Son of Man's coming is that, when he comes, it will be obvious: it will be like (οὕτως ἔσται, houtōs estai) lightning flashing across the sky. This lack of emphasis on signs of the coming is unlike Judaism and speaks for its authenticity (Marshall 1978: 661; Jeremias 1971a: 276). The image of lightning or meteorological phenomena in the OT (Exod. 24:15, 18; Ps. 97:2–4; Ezek. 1:4, 13) and Judaism (2 Bar. 53.8–9 [cf. 54–74 for the full sequence of events]) is tied to theophany (Geiger 1976: 67), so that the figure suggests that the coming involves God acting on behalf of his people (Foerster, *TDNT* 1:505; Marshall 1978: 661). In Luke 10:18, lightning pictures Satan's sudden fall, but the stress in Luke 17 falls on the visibility of the coming (Colpe, *TDNT* 8:433 n. 251; Oepke, *TDNT* 4:25; Marshall 1978: 661; Plummer 1896: 407), not its suddenness (Danker 1988: 292; Grässer 1960: 170) or brightness (Leaney 1958: 231, appealing to the brightness of the transfigured Christ in 9:29). Visibility is the point, given the contextual emphasis on not needing to go and find the day when it comes.

Both ἐκ τῆς (ek tēs, from the) and εἰς τήν (eis tēn, to the) lack objects indicating where the lightning goes (cf. Exod. 17:14; T. Levi 18.4). The possibilities are γῆ (gē, earth), μέρος (meros, portion), or χώρα (chōra, region) (Traub, *TDNT* 5:534 n. 312; Marshall 1978:

660; Fitzmyer 1985: 1169–70; Plummer 1896: 408 [χώρα, on the basis of Deut. 25:19; Job 1:7; 2:2; 18:4; 34:13; 38:18; 42:15]). Whichever noun is chosen to fill the ellipses, the point is that lightning covers the sky and is seen by all (Fitzmyer). Conceptually, "region under the heaven" works well.

The visibility of the Son of Man's return is compared to lightning. The "day of the Son of Man" (also 17:26, 30), probably a variation of the expression "day of the Lord," is the decisive time of judgment that starts with Jesus' return (Zmijewski 1972: 414 n. 65).[11] The start of the day of the Lord will be obvious to all.

The parallel Matt. 24:27 speaks of the lightning going from east to west (instead of Luke's "across the heaven") and uses φαίνω (*phainō*, to shine) to describe the lightning (instead of Luke's λάμπω, *lampō*, to light).[12] The discussion about which version is more original is pointless if there are two sources and two settings. These may be nothing more than variant renderings of the same remark. Most who pursue this issue regard Matthew as more original than Luke 17:24a and Luke 17:24b as more original than Matthew (Zmijewski 1972: 412–14; Geiger 1976: 65; see Marshall 1978: 660 and Klostermann 1929: 175 for the options). I am less confident of such conclusions, given the option of multiple sources.

(4) The Son of Man's Suffering (17:25)

17:25 Yet another factor will figure in the return: the necessity of the Son of Man's suffering and rejection. Luke again uses δεῖ (*dei*, it is necessary) to stress the point that God designed events to proceed in this way (4:43; 24:7, 26, 44). This is the fifth passion prediction in Luke (explicit in Luke 9:22 [= Matt. 16:21 = Mark 8:31]; Luke 9:44 [= Matt. 17:22–23 = Mark 9:31]; Luke 18:32–33 [= Matt. 20:18–19 = Mark 10:33–34]; implicit in Luke 12:50; 13:32–33; Tiede 1988: 302). This is the second shortest of the six Lucan predictions, since it is limited to suffering and rejection (Luke 9:44 is the shortest, speaking only of the Son of Man being given over). The two elements mentioned here match the first two of four elements in Luke 9:22 = Mark 8:31 = Matt. 16:21, but this saying has no verbal matches with Luke 18:32–33 (Jeremias 1980: 267). By mentioning the rejection of

---

11. Matt. 24:36, 44, 50; 25:13; Mark 13:24–32 (ties to these events Isa. 13:10 and 34:4, passages that allude to the day of the Lord); Luke 12:40, 46; Rom. 13:11; Rev. 3:3; 4:5; 8:5; 11:19; 16:18. Most of the passages in Revelation also refer to lightning and describe a variety of events associated with the return.

12. This is the only Lucan use of λάμπω in his Gospel (Matthew uses it three times); Matthew likes φαίνω (thirteen of seventeen Synoptic uses are his). This variation may simply reflect synonyms, like the similar Theodotion-LXX variation in Dan. 12:3.

this generation (cf. 7:31; 11:29–32, 50–51; 21:32), the people as a whole are viewed as responsible for Jesus' suffering, not just the Jewish leadership as in 9:22 (Büchsel, *TDNT* 1:663). Some see the Son of Man's suffering as corporate, including that of the disciples (so Schneider 1977a: 356), but nothing contextually suggests this broad reference.[13] In addition, the parallel passion sayings are against it. Luke 17:25 is the only passion prediction given in an eschatological discourse. Consummation cannot come until the Son of Man suffers.

Most regard the saying as a Lucan insertion into Q material, with ties to 9:22 (Leaney 1958: 231; Klostermann 1929: 175; Zmijewski 1972: 406–10; Geiger 1976: 76 n. 68). The major question for this view is why Luke would create a saying and not mention the resurrection (as does 9:22), especially since resurrection is necessary before Jesus can return as the Son of Man (Marshall 1978: 661–62; Manson 1949: 142).[14] It is more likely that Luke is substantially following a source here, and a special Lucan source is the most natural possibility (Kümmel 1957: 70–71; Jeremias 1980: 267–68 [a mixture of Lucan and traditional elements]).

ii. The Nature of the Coming of the Kingdom (17:26–30)
(1) Like Noah's Day (17:26–27)

Jesus compares the end-time with the cataclysmic flood of Noah **17:26** (Gen. 6–8) and in the next verse details the point of comparison. Like that time, people will be conducting life with little attention to God when judgment comes (Manson 1949: 143–44). In 17:26–30, Jesus picks two periods that preceded significant judgment against Gentiles. The juxtaposition of Noah and Lot was common in Judaism.[15] Luke's reference to the "days" of the Son of Man refers to the period immediately preceding his return (Marshall 1978: 663). This time will be a day of judgment against those not related to God. In this Lucan context, where there has been so much opposition to Jesus, the point is that failure to embrace Jesus leaves one exposed to this judgment when it comes. Rejection will eventually yield light-

---

13. While Acts 14:22 uses δεῖ to say that the disciples' suffering is also inevitable (Fitzmyer 1985: 1170), it does not speak of Jesus' suffering. For the view that the disciples' suffering in Luke–Acts mirrors Jesus', see Moessner 1990.

14. The saying here is broader than the Marcan parallels on which it is supposed to be based. Q, which Manson thinks is the source of Luke 17:25, contains the idea of an inevitable period of suffering before the final vindication (Luke 11:47–51; 12:4–12, 49–53; 13:34–35). See excursus 10.

15. T. Naph. 3.4–5; 3 Macc. 2:4–5; Wis. 10:4–6; Philo, *Life of Moses* 2.10–12 §§52–65; Gen. Rab. 27 on 6:5–6; *m. Sanh.* 10.3; SB 1:574; Marshall 1978: 662; Lührmann 1969: 75–83. In the NT see 1 Pet. 3:20; 2 Pet. 2:5–7; at Qumran see 1QapGen 6.6.

ning, rain, and cataclysmic flood. Failure to decide for Jesus leaves one defenseless before God. Jesus speaks of the end because those in the present era face a choice about how the end will impact them.

The parallel Matt. 24:37 almost exactly matches Luke. Matthew speaks of the parousia and Luke of the days of the Son of Man. Luke likes καθώς (twice in this unit, plus fifteen more times, versus three Matthean uses: Matt. 21:6; 26:24; 28:6), whereas Matthew likes ὥσπερ (ten times, versus twice in Luke: 17:24 and 18:11). In Matthew the saying follows remarks that the time of the return is unknown, whereas in Luke it follows remarks about the necessity of suffering. The difference is probably due to different sources and settings. The saying is authentic (Colpe, *TDNT* 8:434; Marshall 1978: 663; Jeremias 1971a: 263).

17:27 Jesus makes the comparison clear. What were the days of Noah like? There was eating, drinking, marrying (asyndeton with a series of verbs is not Lucan; Jeremias 1980: 268–69). The imperfect tenses probably reflect the repetitive nature of these activities during this time (Plummer 1896: 408). Life and celebration were the order of the day. The verbs may seem neutral, but anyone familiar with the flood story would know that they connote moral corruption (Fitzmyer 1985: 1170; 2 Pet. 2:5). People were unconcerned about God and unprepared for him (Klostermann 1929: 175). And then life ended. Noah went into the boat, and the subsequent flood (κατακλυσμός, *kataklysmos*; BAGD 411; BAA 836) destroyed everyone left behind (Gen. 7:7, 10, 21; 1 Pet. 3:20; 2 Pet. 2:5). The judgment came suddenly.

Matthew 24:38–39 is more conceptually parallel than verbally so (only the wording about Noah going into the boat matches). Matthew uses participles for the verbal ideas and speaks of the flood sweeping the judged all away. Both accounts show that the endtime, like the day of the flood, will come upon people who are unprepared for the disaster, but in Matthew the flood sweeps away the judged (i.e., Noah stays on earth and the judged are removed), whereas in Luke, the saved are removed and the judged are left as corpses for the birds.[16] This suggests independent imagery. What is interesting is that the bird-and-corpse imagery in Matt. 24:28 is similar to Luke's usage, though it comes long before the allusions to those in the field and those at the mill. The different positioning and imagery probably reflect different settings.

16. One could argue that Noah is taken, but Matthew's swept-away image must look at the judged, not Noah, since the flood did not touch the patriarch. The force of the two distinct images is the same, however, since the people in Matthew are taken away in judgment, while in Luke they are left to be judged.

(2) Like Lot's Day (17:28–30)

Jesus refers to another OT figure, Lot, in wording parallel to 17:26– **17:28**
27a. Both passages use καθώς (*kathōs*) to state the comparison with
the days of the OT figure, and they share references to eating and
drinking, but 17:28 also refers to buying, selling, planting, and
building, also in asyndetic imperfect-tense verbs (the new activities
are laid out in two pairs; Zmijewski 1972: 437–39). This portrayal of
life's activity matches Gen. 19:15–23 (Fitzmyer 1985: 1171; cf. 2 Pet.
2:6–7; 1QapGen 20.11–22.11). The reference to Sodom alludes to the
activity of an immoral people, though this idea is not emphasized in
Luke's description (cf. Deut. 32:32–33; Isa. 1:10; Jer. 23:14; Lam. 4:6;
Ezek. 16:46–52 [esp. 16:49]; Jude 7; Luke 10:12; Ernst 1977: 489).
The basic picture is concentrated human activity that results in a
lack of preparation for God's concerns (Manson 1949: 144). Some of
the activities mentioned here are criticized elsewhere in Luke ("buy
and sell" in 14:18–19 and 19:45; "plant and build" in 12:18–19;
Schneider 1977a: 356–57).

Neither Matthew nor Mark allude to Lot, an omission that leads
to speculation about this material's origin. Some speak of Luke
constructing it on analogy with 17:26–27a, but why then the differences in the activities described (see Marshall 1978: 662–63 for options)? Fitzmyer (1985: 1165) and Leaney (1958: 231) argue that
Luke is responsible. Some opt for Q (Geiger 1976: 91–94; Marshall
1978: 662; Manson 1949: 143 [Matthew drops it "for brevity"]); but
why would Matthew omit it when his eschatological material is so
full, covering two chapters? Others are undecided (Zmijewski 1972:
452–57). Still others argue that it was a separate saying unknown
to Matthew (Colpe, *TDNT* 8:434 n. 257). A more likely suggestion is
the presence of additional source material. The authenticity of this
material is linked to that of the comparison to Noah (see the exegesis of 17:26).

Like the days of Noah, the days of Lot were ones of judgment. When **17:29**
Lot departed Sodom (in all probability located on the southern edge
of the Dead Sea), death resulted (Gen. 19:16–17). The conclusion of
Luke 17:29, καὶ ἀπώλεσεν πάντας (*kai apōlesen pantas*, and de-
stroyed them all), matches 17:27. The allusion to fire and sulfur de-
scribes the judgment that God brought on Sodom in Gen. 19:24.[17]
In the OT, this judgment image pictures volcano-style destruction
(Deut. 29:23 [29:22 MT]; Job 18:15; Ps. 11:6; Isa. 30:33; Ezek. 38:22;

---

17. The phrase πῦρ καὶ θεῖον (fire and sulfur) occurs elsewhere in the NT only in
Rev. 9:17, 18; 14:10; 19:20; 20:10; 21:8; BAGD 353; BAA 718; Philo, *Life of Moses* 2.10
§56. It is apocalyptic-judgment language whose concepts reflect the apocalyptic-prophetic teaching of Jesus.

3 Macc. 2:5; Zmijewski 1972: 441).[18] Ἔβρεξεν (*ebrexen*) has God as the subject (BAGD 147 §2a; BAA 294 §2a). As with the previous illustration, the days of Lot picture the destruction that will come when the Son of Man returns.

17:30   The Son of Man's day will follow this same pattern.[19] Just as Lot's generation was busy with life and unprepared for God's activity, so also people will not be ready for the Son of Man's return. Ἀποκαλύπτω (*apokalyptō*) suggests a major revelation of God's sovereign presence (Marshall 1978: 664; Klostermann 1929: 176; Plummer 1896: 408–9; Rom. 8:18; 1 Cor. 3:13; 2 Thess. 2:3–8).[20]

iii. The Response to the Coming of the Kingdom (17:31–35)
(1) Move Quickly, Do Not Turn Back (17:31)

17:31   When the day of the Son of Man comes, one will have to escape quickly (Nolland 1993a: 861).[21] Departure is clearly in view, since disciples are instructed not to turn back. Two separate getaways are described. Someone on the roof of a house is not to go back into the house to retrieve possessions.[22] Rather, one is to scurry down the outside stairs and leave quickly. Imminent danger must be avoided by fleeing. The second picture is similar. Someone in a field should flee as quickly as possible in order to miss the dire consequences of that day. One should not turn back, as Lot's wife did (17:32). If one is not already prepared for the day, there will be no time to prepare. There will be time only to flee.

Luke's language is close to Matt. 24:17–18 = Mark 13:15–16 (Jeremias 1980: 269). Matthew and Mark connect the remark to the pres-

---

18. Fire alone is used of judgment in Jer. 4:4; 5:14; 43:12; Ezek. 21:31 [21:36 MT]; Amos 1:4, 7, 10, 12, 14; 2:2, 5; 2 Thess. 1:7–8; 2 Pet. 3:7; Jude 7; BAGD 730 §1b; BAA 1460 §1b.

19. Κατὰ τὰ αὐτά (according to the same things) has the same force as καθώς; 6:23, 26; Geiger 1976: 91. Singular ἡμέρᾳ (day) matches 17:22 (but plural) and 17:24 and may be influenced by the comparison with the "day" of Lot. In all three cases, the reference is to the return and its accompanying judgment-vindication. See the additional note for the textual issue.

20. Some regard ἀποκαλύπτω as conceptually equal to Matthew's παρουσία (parousia). The noun ἀποκάλυψις (revelation) does have an eschatological force; 1 Cor. 1:7; 2 Thess. 1:7–8; 1 Pet. 1:7, 13; 4:13; Zmijewski 1972: 442 n. 50.

21. Marshall 1978: 664 and Plummer 1896: 409 deny the idea of escape, arguing that the point is a prohibition against coming down to collect possessions; but are the two points mutually exclusive? The comparison with Lot's wife in 17:32 suggests an escape. Nolland 1993a: 861 argues that part of the point is a willingness to flee and leave one's possessions behind, which reinforces earlier teaching about how riches can ensnare their possessor.

22. For δῶμα, see BAGD 210; BAA 423; Luke 5:19; 12:3; Josh. 2:6, 8; 2 Sam. 16:22; Isa. 22:1. The flat roof was probably used as living space (Acts 10:9; Nolland 1993a: 861).

ence of desolation and mention that those in Judea should flee to the mountains, a remark that Luke has in 21:21. In the view of many (e.g., Danker 1988: 293; Arndt 1956: 375), the Marcan language looks at the events of A.D. 66–70; yet since that event is used in the NT to picture what the return is like, the Lucan association with the end is not surprising. But the Marcan connection to Jerusalem's fall in A.D. 70 is not clear, since the days are described in Mark 13:19 as unequal in terror, which cannot be a reference to Jerusalem's fall in A.D. 70, since the end-time is the only event that could meet that description. In addition, Matt. 24:14 refers to the gospel's going out into all the nations of the earth, an action that was not likely completed in A.D. 70. Luke has a more condensed form of the saying, but the picture is similar: when the day comes, it will be time to flee without hesitation. Attachment to possessions might lead to disaster, since one might not wish to flee (Creed 1930: 221; Marshall 1978: 664). Luke alone mentions possessions in the home and makes an explicit comparison between the two pictures by using ὁμοίως (*homoiōs*, likewise).

(2) Remember Lot's Wife (17:32)

Jesus invokes the memory of Lot's wife (Gen. 19:26), who in Judaism was seen as an illustration of an unbeliever (Wis. 10:7; Fitzmyer 1985: 1172). Her death resulted from turning to look back at Sodom and Gomorrah. She is a negative illustration of the consequences of holding on to life's possessions. The call to remember is a call to pay heed to that lesson (Marshall 1978: 665; Michel, *TDNT* 4:682–83; SB 2:237). Jesus has already warned about not looking back (Luke 9:62; Danker 1988: 293). The theme is well attested and fits nicely with Jesus' emphases.

17:32

The reference has no Synoptic parallel, leading some to question whether it existed in a source or Luke supplied the reference (Marshall 1978: 665 leans toward a Lucan addition). This verse may well reflect a source, since the previous reference to Lot also suggests a source (17:28–29). Luce (1933: 278) sees a popular proverbial image in use here.

(3) Lose Life to Gain It (17:33)

Jesus now explains that disciples need to be prepared to suffer for their relationship to God. The one who seeks to gain life will lose it, while the one who loses life will keep it.[23] Ψυχή (*psyche*) refers to

17:33

---

23. On περιποιέω (to gain), see BAGD 650; BAA 1310; Gen. 12:12; Exod. 1:16; elsewhere in the NT only at Acts 20:28; 1 Tim. 3:13. On ζῳογονέω (to preserve alive), see BAGD 341; BAA 690; Exod. 1:17; Judg. 8:19; 1 Sam. 2:6; elsewhere in the NT only at Acts 7:19; 1 Tim. 6:13; Bultmann, *TDNT* 2:873–74.

both the physical and religious entities of a person's life. The first half of the verse emphasizes physical preservation, the second half spiritual preservation. The two halves are laid out in contrastive parallelism so that the second clearly says that a relationship with God defines life. In the end, the one who identifies with God will suffer for it. Seeking to avoid persecution will lead to a lack of commitment ultimately to God (Arndt 1956: 376). It is a costly choice either way. God does not promise immunity from death and suffering, but he does promise abiding life with him to the one who survives this judgment by the Son of Man. As 9:25 says, it profits little to gain the world but lose one's soul.

The passage is conceptually similar to Luke 9:24 = Matt. 16:25 = Mark 8:35 and Matt. 10:39 and John 12:25 (Marshall 1978: 666). Its presence, however, in the midst of an eschatological discourse is unique. Most tie the saying's source to Q and Matt. 10:39 (Creed 1930: 221; Fitzmyer 1985: 1172; Geiger 1976: 120–21), while others argue that it is derived ultimately from Mark (Klostermann 1929: 176; Leaney 1958: 232; Grundmann 1963: 344; Zmijewski 1972: 479–82 [who lists the options]). Key to the source issue is Luke's use of ζω-ογονέω (to preserve alive). This Gospel *hapax legomenon* is synonymous to other terms used in the parallels, so why would Luke change to this term if he had these sources before him?[24] Why would he so radically alter the remark's context, especially when he shunned doublets? It is more likely that an independent source is responsible for this unusual term.[25] Luke's use of περιποιέω (to gain) is also unusual.

(4) Judgment Will Be Quick (17:34–35)

17:34   It is disputed whether the two people in bed are husband and wife or two men. The double use of the masculine article is not decisive, since it could refer back to "two people" using the masculine to

---

24. Cf. εὑρίσκω (to find) in Matt. 10:39 and 16:25 and σῴζω (to save) in Luke 9:24 = Mark 8:35. Geiger 1972: 121 speaks of the influence of Ezek. 13:18–19 (which uses περιποιέω), and Zmijewski 1976: 479 n. 56 sees a connection to Exod. 1:17 (which uses ζωογονέω). Neither LXX reference satisfies, however, since each has only one element of Luke 17:33, and one can hardly argue for a double LXX allusion. In addition, if the LXX alteration is based on an earlier, existing traditional saying, what does it add? Περιποιέω appears only three times in the NT (Acts 20:28; 1 Tim. 3:13) and the noun περιποίησις is never used in the Gospels (five times elsewhere). Since the conscious shift of terminology appears to have no point, the rare terminology is probably from a source.

25. Marshall 1978: 666 speaks of the possibility of different recensions of Q. Manson 1949: 145 argues that the Lucan saying reflects Q and that Matthew moved it. But is this any better, given the double use of this saying in Matt. 10:39 and 16:25, with neither being in an eschatological context? Plummer 1896: 409 suggests that the idea was often repeated. If he is right, a special Lucan source is just as likely. The theme gives evidence of going back to Jesus through such a source.

cover both. If a balancing parallelism is present, however, the use of feminine articles in 17:35 suggests a contrast and implies that men are intended here (Fitzmyer 1985: 1172). The reference to the night is not an indication that the Lord's return will be at night or on Passover night (so Strobel 1961a).[26] The evening imagery is a metaphor for the end of the period in which the Son of Man's coming represents a new day's dawning (1 Thess. 5:2; Manson 1949: 146). According to the eschatological tradition the exact time of the return is uncertain (Mark 13:32).

When the time comes, one will be taken and the other left. It is debated (see Marshall 1978: 668 for options) whether one is taken for judgment (Strobel 1961a: 20 n. 1) or salvation (Delling, *TDNT* 4:13). In either case, the two have opposite fates and picture the absolute separation of people into two classes upon the return. The most natural reading, based on the previous examples of Noah and Lot, is that one is taken for salvation (Ellis 1974: 212; Plummer 1896: 410; Fitzmyer 1985: 1172; Marshall 1978: 668; Tiede 1988: 303). In addition, the final "where" question of 17:37 appears to look back to the image of death and judgment in the comparison with the gathered birds. If so, then those who are "left to the birds" experience judgment. Finally, this understanding matches Luke's use of ἀφίημι (*aphiēmi*, to leave) for judgment in 13:35 and of παραλαμβάνω (*paralambanō*) for "close association" or "taking along" in 9:10, 28 and 18:31 (cf. Matt. 24:31 = Mark 13:27; John 14:3; 1 Thess. 4:17; BAGD 619; BAA 1252). The picture is of the separation that will take place at the Son of Man's return and not to anything preceding that return. As such, the Marcan and Matthean passages are the true conceptual parallels, though they lack this particular comparison.

This illustration is unique to Luke, and, as in other passages where Luke is unique, there is debate about the origin of the material. It is suggested that Q material is present, but there is no consensus whether Matthew (Marshall 1978: 667; Bultmann 1963: 123) or Luke (Zmijewski 1972: 497–501) changed the tradition. Another possibility is that each chose from three illustrations (Manson 1949: 146 argues that Matthew used two and Luke used all three [including the textually suspect 17:36; see the additional note]). Still others speak of two independent traditions. This latter option seems likely, if the case for special Lucan material made up to this point is correct.[27]

26. Fitzmyer 1985: 1172 doubts that the idea of an eschatological Passover existed this early in Judaism.

27. The source question here is answered by how one sees sources before getting to this point in the text, though a case could be made that Matthew shortened his tradition.

17:35   A second illustration also pictures the division that will come with the return: two women (indicated by the feminine articles) grinding (ἀλήθω, *alēthō*; BAGD 37; BAA 72; elsewhere in the NT only at Matt. 24:41). It is disputed whether such grinding occurred at night or early in the morning, but the timing only provides background imagery (Marshall 1978: 668). The picture of one being taken and the other left matches the verbs of Luke 17:34 and carries the same force. When the Son of Man returns, a separation will occur, one to judgment and another to deliverance. The imagery of separation at judgment is similar to that in Luke 3:17 and parables such as Mark 4:26–29 and Matt. 13:24–30, 37–43, 47–49. The teaching fits the apocalyptic-prophetic Jesus.

   The picture of two women at the mill is paralleled in Matt. 24:41. Matthew explicitly mentions that they are grinding "at the mill" (ἐν τῷ μύλῳ, *en tō mylō*), while Luke says they are grinding "together" (ἐπὶ τὸ αὐτό, *epi to auto*), a favorite phrase used elsewhere by Luke in Acts 1:15; 2:1, 44, 47; 4:26 (Marshall 1978: 668).[28] Matthew uses μία ... μία (one ... one) rather than Luke's μία ... ἑτέρα (one ... the other). The illustration functions the same in both passages: Jesus returns as life's activity proceeds.

[17:36]   See the additional note regarding the unlikely possibility that Luke included a third illustration.

iv. The Judgment Accompanying the Coming of the Kingdom (17:37)
(1) The Disciples' Question (17:37a)

17:37a   It is difficult to tie 17:37 into Luke's argument. Jesus has just said that his return will be visible to all, as lightning lights the whole sky (17:24). Why, then, do the disciples ask "where"? Fitzmyer (1985: 1173) regards the question as a reflection of the disciples' lack of comprehension. Nevertheless, the question is appropriate. When the Son of Man returns, he will return somewhere. Even though the judgment will be visible to all, it would still be interesting to know exactly where it will be rendered. But the short question (ποῦ, κύριε; *pou, kyrie*; where, Lord?) is unclear in itself. What exactly are the disciples asking: where one will be judged or where one will be taken? Jesus' answer about vultures gathering makes it clear that they are concerned about the location of judgment. The gruesome image shows that judgment occurs where death reigns. For the unprepared, the day of the Son of Man will be a day of judgment.

---

28. For description of the millstone, see the exegesis of 17:2 (cf. Exod. 11:5; Isa. 47:2; Zmijewski 1972: 496).

(2) Jesus' Picture of Vultures and Corpses (17:37b)

Jesus responds by recalling the image of vultures circling over dead **17:37b** bodies, which has engendered a variety of interpretations:[29]

1. The location will be as plain as birds hovering over dead bodies (Fitzmyer 1985: 1173). In this sense, the reply is little different from the picture of lightning in 17:24. The return will be as obvious as the signs of death. It seems unlikely, however, that this is merely a repetition of the idea in 17:24. The image is too gloomy to just point to visibility; so this view is unlikely, even though such a view is parallel to the sense in Matt. 24:28. In fact, this approach appears to be guilty of reading Luke in light of Matthew.

2. Just as vultures cannot miss a dead body, so people cannot miss the judgment of the Son of Man on his return (Klostermann 1929: 177). This view is similar to view 1, but it argues that people are taken in judgment. It is not clear, however, that a comparison is present, as much as an emotive description of the mood and nature of the event.

3. Death will accompany the return. When the time is right for judgment, deadly clouds will gather (Geldenhuys 1951: 445; Arndt 1956: 376; Plummer 1896: 410). This view suffers from a contextual problem: in 17:26–30, the idea is that people will be living rather normally when the return suddenly comes upon them. If so, the gathering of dark clouds seems an excessive description of the time preceding the return, though it should be noted that this immoral time is subject to judgment. This view may be the second best option.

4. Judgment will appear where it is needed (Creed 1930: 221; Luce 1933: 279). It will be neither "here" nor "there," as 17:21 suggests. This view says very little. Of course, judgment comes where it is needed. Nonetheless, the idea that the specific locale is not important is a correct way to read the force of Jesus' answer.

5. People should not be like the dead. Danker (1988: 294) applies Jesus' remark to the fall of Jerusalem and says that the point is that people should not wait around to be devoured; they

---

29. On ἀετός, see Lev. 11:13; Deut. 14:12; Job 39:27; Matt. 24:28; BAGD 19; BAA 36; Marshall 1978: 669. Ἀετός can refer to an eagle, but not here, since eagles do not seek out dead meat; Rev. 12:14; 4:7; 8:13; Arndt 1956: 376. Attempts to interpret ἀετός as eagle, recalling the Roman emblem that accompanied the invasion of Jerusalem, assume a post–A.D. 70 date for Luke, as well as suggest an image contextually distant from the metaphor here; but so Danker 1988: 294; Leaney 1958: 232; and Fitzmyer 1985: 1173 (with less certainty).

should not act in such a way that death is inevitable. The equation of people acting like the dead, however, infers a connection not made in the text.

6. The return will be swift. Manson (1949: 147) argues that the image is positive in the OT (Exod. 19:4; Deut. 32:11; Job 9:26; Isa. 40:31; Hab. 1:8). This view, however, is a contextually dislocated reply in which Jesus responds to a "where" question with a "how" answer about the quickness of the coming.

7. Judgment will be visible, universal, and permanent. Once separation occurs, there is no turning back. Vultures gather to feed off the dead bodies (Zmijewski 1972: 518). This point that once judgment is rendered it is final seems the most likely sense. In effect, Jesus is saying, do not worry about where the judgment will occur, for once it comes, it will be too late and all will see it. As such, the point is not the correctness of judgment (view 4), but its finality when it becomes visible. All will see the judgment's horrific finality. As such, this view uses points made by view 1, but says much more. The graphic and emotive image of vultures is a warning that the return will be a grim affair. The return of the Son of Man saves some but permanently condemns others. The return will be what was longed for in 17:22, but when it comes it will mean ultimate judgment for those who are not prepared. This is a classic day-of-the-Lord warning to the unprepared.

The similar image in Matt. 24:28 follows Matthew's reference to the coming's being like lightning. The image depicts more clearly the visibility of the Son of Man's return: it will be as visible as vultures pointing out dead bodies (cf. view 1 above). When judgment comes, it will be obvious. The accounts exhibit some minor differences in terminology: Matthew has πτῶμα (*ptōma*, corpse) where Luke has σῶμα (*sōma*, corpse);[30] Matthew has the conditional particle ἐάν (*ean*, if), which Luke lacks; and Matthew has the simple verb where Luke has the compound ἐπισυναχθήσονται (*episynachthēsontai*, will be gathered). In terms of sources shared with Matthew, it is hard to explain Luke's placement at the end of the discourse, especially given the lack of a question from the disciples in Matt. 24 and the saying's placement in the middle of Matthew's discourse. Again, a special Lucan source seems to have influenced this presentation, whose roots could well fit the apocalyptic-prophetic Jesus.

---

30. Σῶμα (normally "body") means "corpse" in Luke 23:52, 55; 24:3, 23; Acts 9:40; BAGD 799 §1a; BAA 1593 §1a.

As Luke 17:20–21 suggests, the kingdom has come. Luke 17:22– **Summary**
37 makes clear that there is more to be expected. Consummation
will not come as soon as the disciples desire, nor will they need
to look for the kingdom's coming. When it appears, it will come
quickly and will be as visible as lightning. But the Son of Man
first must suffer. When the end does come, destruction will inter-
rupt life's normal flow, just as it did in the days of Noah and Lot.
When it comes, be ready to flee and do not be committed to possessions, for to try to preserve the things of life will result in
death. Only the willingness to lose life will preserve it. The separation of judgment will be quick and permanent. Do not ask
where the judgment will be, for it will be visible, and once it
comes it will be too late. The time will be gruesome, like vultures
gathered over dead bodies.

This Lucan note on eschatology is a grim image. With salvation
comes separation from and judgment on those who have not followed after God. The Son of Man's authority is total, but believers
who look for the return had better be prepared for rough times. It
will not come as soon as some would like; but neither will one
have to hunt for it. When it comes, all will know it, and its results
will be final.

The focus is on the seriousness of the return for all. The implication, in light of the previous passage, is also clear. In Jesus, the
kingdom is in their midst. One must respond to him. If one fore-
goes the opportunity, his return will mean judgment. The period
in between will be filled with pressure for believers, which they
must endure. The return, however, will bring pressure on all, especially those who fall into irreversible judgment. The vulture
image closing the discourse is purposely black. The reader
should realize that the Son of Man returns to execute judgment
on those who refuse to respond to him in faith. The day of the Son
of Man will be a time when one wants to be sure that one is already on his side.

Additional Notes

17:23. Of no less than seven variants, the UBS–NA reading is the only one
where ἐκεῖ (there) comes first in the ἐκεῖ-ὧδε pairing: ἰδοὺ ἐκεῖ, ἤ, ἰδοὺ ὧδε
(behold there or behold here). Supported by $\mathfrak{P}^{75}$, ℵ (καί for ἤ), B, L (omits
ἤ), and some Syriac (following ℵ), this reading is regarded as original because of its support by the Alexandrian witnesses and because it is the
harder reading. It reverses the order of a similar phrase in Luke 17:21 and
Mark 13:21. The UBS–NA wording of Luke is closer to Matt. 24:23 than to
Mark 13:21 (Luke differs from Mark in the reversal of ἐκεῖ and ὧδε; Matthew

has ὧδε twice). Most see this reversed order as an attempt to harmonize Luke 17:21 and 17:23 or as an attempt to match Mark 13:21 (Metzger 1975: 167; Marshall 1978: 659). The second best reading is ἰδοὺ ὧδε, ἤ, ἰδοὺ ἐκεῖ (behold here or behold there). Read by A, Δ, Θ, Ψ, several minuscules, Byz, Itala, and Ethiopic, this reading has a claim to originality because it explains so many of the other variants. Codex D and Lect have a third, similar variant, lacking only the correlative conjunction ἤ. Still another variant speaks of ὁ Χριστός (the Christ), but this reference is clearly secondary and is influenced by Mark 13:21 = Matt. 24:23, especially since nowhere else in this Lucan speech does Jesus speak of the Messiah.

17:23. Of five variants, the UBS–NA reading, μὴ ἀπέλθητε μηδὲ διώξητε (do not go out or pursue), has overwhelming external support: ℵ, A, D, W, Θ, Ψ, several minuscules, Byz, Lect, most Itala, Vulgate, and some Syriac. The second best option (supported by L, Δ, and a few minuscules) has the indicative διώξετε for subjunctive διώξητε: "Do not go out nor are you to follow them." Both readings say that the disciples are not to pursue such claims.

17:24. Some manuscripts refer to the παρουσία (parousia) instead of ἡμέρα (day), but Luke never uses the former term, so it is not a likely reading, being too difficult, especially since the variant became a popular technical term. A shorter reading translated "so shall be the Son of Man" has strong attestation ($\mathfrak{P}^{75}$, B, D, many Itala). Nonetheless, it is harsh and may simply be the result of an error of sight called homoeoteleuton, since both ἀνθρώπου (man) and αὐτοῦ (his) end with the same two letters, and a copyist's eye could easily skip over the intervening words (Metzger 1975: 167; Fitzmyer 1985: 1170). The UBS–NA reading has exceptionally broad attestation: ℵ, A, L, W, Δ, Θ, Ψ, family 1, family 13, Byz, Lect, some Itala, Vulgate, Syriac, and Coptic.

17:27. Zmijewski (1972: 429 n. 3) and apparently Marshall (1978: 664) support reading ἅπαντας (all) in place of πάντας (all) since ἅπαντας is so frequent in Luke–Acts (twenty-three of thirty-four NT uses). The external evidence (πάντας is read by $\mathfrak{P}^{75}$, B, D, Θ; ἅπαντας by ℵ and Byz) and the harder reading support πάντας, though there is no difference in sense.

17:29. Θεῖον καὶ πῦρ (sulfur and fire) occurs in some manuscripts (A, D, W, Θ, family 13), but this reflects the influence of Gen. 19:24 (Marshall 1978: 664; Lang, *TDNT* 6:942 §D.III.2). The UBS–NA reading, πῦρ καὶ θεῖον (fire and sulfur), is supported by $\mathfrak{P}^{75}$, ℵ, B, L, Ψ, family 1, Byz. Luke also differs from the LXX by using ἀπ᾽ οὐρανοῦ (from heaven), not ἐκ τοῦ οὐρανοῦ (out of heaven) (Zmijewski 1972: 440 n. 43).

17:30. Κατὰ ταῦτα (according to these things), read by $\mathfrak{P}^{75vid}$, ℵ*, A, W, Θ, family 1, family 13, and Byz, has a force similar to κατὰ τὰ αὐτά (according to the same things) and may be original, though the UBS–NA reading has slightly better attestation (ℵ², B, D, Ψ). An error of sight may be involved here, since one of the two consecutive alphas could have dropped out of ΚΑΤΑΤΑΑΥΤΑ to create ΚΑΤΑΤΑΥΤΑ.

17:33. Many manuscripts read σῶσαι (to save) instead of περιποιήσασθαι (to gain). Σῴζω is the more common verb and looks like assimilation to 9:24, though its manuscript support is impressive: ℵ, A, W, Δ, Θ, Ψ, family 1, family 13, Byz, Lect, many Itala (περιποιήσασθαι is supported by 𝔓⁷⁵, B, L, a few Itala). Codex D and a few Syriac manuscripts read ζωογονῆσαι (to preserve) to keep the parallelism with 17:33b, but this reading is too poorly attested to be original. If περιποιήσασθαι is not original, it is hard to explain its presence in the text (Metzger 1975: 167).

17:36. In what is traditionally numbered verse 36, some manuscripts have a third illustration about two men in a field: D, most Itala, some Syriac, some Lect, several minuscules, and family 13. Since Matthew starts with this illustration, this looks like assimilation to Matt. 24:40. An impressive agreement of Alexandrian and Byzantine witnesses do not include this illustration (𝔓⁷⁵, ℵ, A, B, L, Δ, Θ, Ψ, family 1, Byz, Coptic), and it should not be considered part of Luke's original text (Metzger 1975: 168).

3. Expectant Prayer and Promised Vindication: Parable of the Nagging Widow (18:1–8)

The parable of the nagging widow and the consenting judge is linked to the previous eschatological discourse by the reference in Luke 18:8 to the Son of Man's return. Its plea that believers ask God for justice looks back to the vindication of the saints described in 17:22–37. The intercession described is related to the persecution that saints undergo for their decision to ally with Jesus. As such, it reflects the description in 17:22, 33 of the social pressure placed on disciples. With Christ comes rejection by some (Phil. 1:29).

The application of the parable is complex. The believer is to identify with the widow's persistence in praying for the decisive coming of God's justice in the kingdom's full expression (18:1, 8). She pictures someone vulnerable and in dire need—like the believer in a hostile world. The judge's response provides a contrastive message: if a dishonest judge responds to a persistent woman, how much more will God respond to his children! Putting these two ideas together, an additional point is made: if a widow's nagging causes a response in the unrighteous, how much more will the disciple's request be honored by a righteous God (Fitzmyer 1985: 1177; Colpe, *TDNT* 8:435 n. 265; Blomberg 1990: 273). The final verses make two additional points: God will respond quickly to requests, and faith is needed in the face of delay. Jesus' musing about finding anyone faithful on his return implies that steadfastness is desired—even necessary. This remark also implies that unrighteousness will be widespread on earth until the return and that opportunity for unfaithfulness will be great (so the comparisons to Noah and Lot in 17:26–30, 32). This is almost a backhanded way to say to the disciples, "Be faithful and be ready for me." Steadfastness will be hard to achieve unless one is faithful. The account presupposes an interval before the consummation that disciples must be prepared to deal with (Marshall 1978: 669; Talbert 1982: 169).[1] The account also looks ahead

---

1. The delay of the return is mentioned in Luke 12:45–46; 2 Pet. 3:4–9; 1 Clem. 23.3; 24.1; 2 Clem. 11. Jews also had this problem in longing for Messiah's coming; Blomberg 1990: 272.

to the picture of dependent prayer in 18:9–14 (Jeremias 1963a: 156). Taken as a whole, 18:1–14 argues that the disciple should pray persistently and humbly for the coming of God's justice in the kingdom.[2] One survives in the world through prayer that recognizes that justice will ultimately come when the Lord returns.

Sources and Historicity

The parable is unique to Luke (although Goulder 1989: 658 sees a theme from Matt. 24:44–49 and teaching drawn from Sir. 35:12–26) and has its source in the special Lucan material, which has a large amount of parabolic material (Aland 1985: §236). Although Sirach does reveal conceptual parallelism to Luke's theme of God's quick vindication and a mention of widows in Sir. 35:18–19, Luke has not formulated the material. It has roots in the parables source of L, and Luke 18:6b–7 contains non-Lucan language (Marshall 1978: 670–71; Nolland 1993a: 865, 869–70; Fitzmyer 1985: 1177). Some see 18:6–8a as a later addition to the parable, developing its force in a direction different than the original parable (Bultmann 1963: 175; Ernst 1977: 492; Ellis 1974: 212 [maybe]; the Jesus Seminar [Funk and Hoover 1993: 368] prints 18:2–5 in pink type and 18:6–8 in black).[3] Others speak of 18:8b as a later addition because of its unrelated remark about the Son of Man finding anyone faithful when he comes (Bultmann 1963: 175; Schneider 1977a: 360 [by Luke]; Grundmann 1963: 346 [a double conclusion, with 18:8b perhaps linked to Luke's source and originally tied to 17:22–37]; Ernst 1977: 492 [like Grundmann, appealing to a tie also to 17:19]).[4] Nonetheless, some see unity in the account (Marshall 1978: 670–71; Jeremias 1963a: 153–57; Jeremias 1980: 271–72). Marshall notes that 18:6b–7 lacks Lucan terminology. The double ending on parables is characteristic of some Lucan parables from his special material (11:8 and 11:9–13; 12:46 and 12:47–48; 16:8 and 16:9–13; Ellis 1974: 212). Luke 18:8b allows for a tighter conceptual link with 17:22–37 (note also 17:19, with its mention of faith), yet nothing in 18:8b is uniquely Lucan in emphasis, but fits Jesus' teaching (Luke 7:9 = Matt. 8:10; Colpe, *TDNT* 8:435).

2. Tiede 1988: 304 adds three other themes: (1) being faithful in prayer (18:1), (2) knowing that the delay does not mean that God is indifferent (18:2–7), and (3) keeping the faith (18:8).

3. Grundmann 1963: 345 sees a saying about persistence in prayer appended to a parable like 11:5–13; esp. B. Scott 1989: 177–78. The Jesus Seminar argues that the themes of prayer and the returning Son of Man are Lucan. But a connection to the parable sources shows that prayer has traditional roots and the concept of the "elect" is only in Luke here. It is not a Lucan expression.

4. For a detailed argument against authenticity, see Linnemann 1966: 187 n. 14, who argues that the application in 18:8 is too stylistically distinct and that the term ἐκλεκτός (elect) 18:7 is not appropriate in the ministry of Jesus. Linnemann has since renounced this view.

The teaching of the whole unit goes back to Jesus, with a narrative introduction provided by Luke in 18:1.

The form of the text is a parable, with sayings of application tied to it (Fitzmyer 1985: 1176; Bultmann 1963: 175; Berger 1984: 51). The outline of Luke 18:1–8 is as follows:

a. Setting (18:1)
b. Parable of the judge and the widow (18:2–5)
   i. The judge (18:2)
   ii. The widow's request (18:3)
   iii. The judge's responses (18:4–5)
c. Jesus' comments (18:6–8)
   i. Comparison of the judge to God (18:6–8a)
   ii. Contrast to the Son of Man finding faithful people
      (18:8b)

A disciple's attention is to remain on God's kingdom. The passage calls for maintaining a hopeful perspective about God's plan. The disciple is to persistently pray for the kingdom's full coming, trusting that God will respond to this request, though there is delay. Jesus expresses the hope that the Son of Man will find faithful people on his return, a remark that serves as a call to stay faithful.

Exegesis and Exposition

[1]And he told them a parable, to the effect that they ought always to pray and not grow tired, [2]saying, "There was a judge in a certain city who did not fear God or regard men. [3]And there was a widow in that city, and she was coming to him again and again, saying, 'Vindicate me against my adversary.' [4]And he refused for a time; but after a while he said to himself, 'Although I fear neither God nor men, [5]yet because this widow bothers me, I will vindicate her, in order that she may not wear me out by her continual coming.'"
[6]And the Lord said, "Hear what the unrighteous judge says. [7]And will not God make vindication for his elect, who cry out to him day and night? And will he delay over them? [8]I say to you, he will make their vindication speedily. Nevertheless, will the Son of Man, when he comes, find faith on earth?"

a. Setting (18:1)

18:1   The introduction is probably a Lucan editorial note giving the parable's context in terminology similar to other texts (1:13; 4:23; 12:16; Jeremias 1980: 271). Jesus is telling the parable "to them," αὐτοῖς (autois), which must look back to 17:22, where the disciples are the audience. The use of this pronoun to introduce a parable is common

(6:39; 21:29; Fitzmyer 1985: 1178). The call is to continued prayer, not in the sense of praying at all times, but in praying again and again (Marshall 1978: 671).[5] The use of δεῖ (*dei*, it is necessary) makes such prayer a moral imperative (Grundmann, *TDNT* 2:22; cf. Luke 15:32; Acts 5:29; 20:35). The context of Luke 18:8 makes clear that the ultimate request is for God's justice and the Son of Man's return (see similar prayers for the kingdom program in Luke 11:2; 22:42; Acts 4:25–30; 12:5 [for God's justice in releasing Peter]). The disciples are not to grow weary in making this request. Since an activity is in view, "growing tired or weary" is a more natural translation of ἐγκακέω (*enkakeō*) than is "losing heart."[6] The point is that in the midst of persecution and possible delay, the disciple should not stop praying for justice and for the return that will bring justice.

b. Parable of the Judge and the Widow (18:2–5)
i. The Judge (18:2)

The story begins with a judge whose reputation is clearly stated. **18:2** Luke frequently uses the indefinite τις (*tis*, a certain) in the parables (10:25, 30; 15:11; 16:1, 19–20). The judge is probably a Jew and may have been a powerful man, since the Romans allowed the Jews to manage many of their own legal affairs (M. Stern 1974: 336–40).[7] The Romans stayed out of most matters, except those involving capital punishment (Schürer 1973–87: 2.223–25). Many concerns were left to religious authorities (e.g., the Sanhedrin and synagogue elders), but because this man is described as one who does not fear God it is unlikely that he is a religious leader (on the custom, see SB 1:289; *m. Sanh.* 1.1; 3.1; *b. Sanh.* 4b allows rabbis such judging functions). He is possibly a political type of "police" judge (Derrett 1971–72: 181–85, although Fitzmyer 1985: 1178 questions this background). The dispute is probably financial (Jeremias 1963a: 153; Stählin, *TDNT* 9:449–50; 1 Cor. 6:1–11). Perhaps the widow was not being cared for by her husband's estate (B. Scott 1989: 180), although her reference to an adversary suggests a problem with someone alive.

The judge is not known for his compassion: he does not fear God or respect people, a description common in extrabiblical materials

---

5. This is Luke's only use of πρὸς τό with a purpose infinitive in his Gospel; BDF §402.5; BDR §402.4.5; cf. Acts 3:19.

6. Ἐγκακέω almost has the force "do not give up faith." The term can mean "to become weary" (2 Thess. 3:13; Gal. 6:9) or the more eschatological "to lose heart" (2 Cor. 4:1, 16; Eph. 3:13); BAGD 215; BAA 434; Grundmann, *TDNT* 3:486. Symmachus uses the verb in Gen. 27:46; Num. 21:5; Prov. 3:11; Isa. 7:16 (Delling 1962: 6 n. 23).

7. This point makes it unlikely that the judge was a Gentile, but so Plummer 1896: 411 and C. A. Evans 1990: 269. On the historical background, see B. Scott 1989: 184, citing Chajes 1892, who notes that most cases were heard by one judge (though he uses late texts).

of people with fiercely independent wills (Klostermann 1929: 177; Fitzmyer 1985: 1178).[8] This type of person was often an authority with enough power not to worry about how others responded to him. Ideally, judges should defend the poor and widowed (Exod. 22:22–24 [22:21–23 MT]; Deut. 24:17–18; Ps. 68:5 [68:6 MT]; 82:2–7; 146:9; B. Scott 1989: 181 [like God: Sir. 35:14–26]). This judge, however, did not care what people thought. This judge was not the type to be moved out of compassion. As Manson (1949: 306) says, "Neither the laws of God nor public opinion can stir his conscience." Appeal to this character would be difficult.

ii. The Widow's Request (18:3)

18:3 The story's second character is the helpless widow. She need not have been very old, since in this culture women married at age thirteen or fourteen and widows were frequently quite young (Jeremias 1963a: 153). The OT is clear that widows should be helped; the theme permeates the entire corpus (Kistemaker 1980: 250; Plummer 1896: 412; Grundmann 1963: 347; Tiede 1988: 305).[9] Luke shares this concern for the fate of widows (Luke 2:37; 4:25–26; 7:12; 20:47; 21:2–4; Acts 6:1; 9:39, 41; Fitzmyer 1985: 1179).

The widow is probably facing some financial difficulty and so appeals to the judge again and again to give her justice (ἐκδικέω, ekdikeō; BAGD 238 §1; BAA 480 §1; T. Levi 2.2; Josephus, Antiquities 6.13.7 §303; Schrenk, TDNT 2:442–43; Delling 1962: 9–11). The imperfect ἤρχετο (ercheto, was coming) in this context is iterative and suggests repeated appeals for aid. She seeks relief from the opponent (ἀντίδικος, antidikos; BAGD 74; BAA 147) who wronged her.[10] The helpless, powerless woman appeals over and over to someone with the authority and power to vindicate her.

iii. The Judge's Responses (18:4–5)

18:4 The judge did not respond to the widow's pleas for some time (ἐπὶ χρόνον [epi chronon, for a time] is indefinite; BAGD 289 §III.2b;

8. Josephus, Antiquities 10.5.2 §83 (of Jehoiakim); Dionysius of Halicarnassus, Roman Antiquities 10.10.7; Livy 22.3.4. Ἐντρέπω is used in Luke 20:13 = Matt. 21:37 = Mark 12:6 to describe the respect that the master's son should get; elsewhere in the NT at 1 Cor. 4:14; 2 Thess. 3:14; Titus 2:8; Heb. 12:9; BAGD 269 §2b; BAA 544 §2b. On not fearing God, see Deut. 25:18 (of the Amalekites).

9. Besides the texts noted in the exegesis of 18:2, see Deut. 27:19 (God curses those who withhold judgment from widows); Ruth 1:20–21; Job 32:9; Isa. 1:17, 23; 54:4; Jer. 7:6; 22:3; Lam. 1:1; Ezek. 22:7; Mal. 3:5; James 1:27; Luke 20:47.

10. In 1 Pet. 5:8 Satan is described as an ἀντίδικος in a context that clearly has adversarial, legal overtones. Elsewhere in the NT, ἀντίδικος is found only at Luke 12:58 and twice in Matt. 5:25.

BAA 586 §III.2b). Actually, he did not wish to act initially (so probably the imperfect οὐκ ἤθελεν [*ouk ēthelen*] in this context). As often as the widow came, he refused. But as 18:5 shows, she just kept coming because her case had to be heard (Stählin, *TDNT* 9:450 n. 86; Marshall 1978: 672). No specific reason for the refusal is given, but the judge's character is a clue that he is not sensitive to people's needs. He is here living up to his reputation as a nonrespecter of people.

The appeals continue, so after a while the judge begins to engage in some internal reflection. Εἶπεν ἐν ἑαυτῷ (*eipen en heautō*, he said to himself) points to a revealing soliloquy giving the judge's state of mind (Fitzmyer 1985: 973, 1179; Grundmann 1963: 347; Creed 1930: 223; Ernst 1977: 493; cf. Luke 12:17; 15:17–19; 16:3–4). Knowing his reputation and perhaps even taking pride in it, the judge repeats the description of him given in 18:2. Introducing a first-class condition to present the judge's perception of current reality, εἰ (*ei*) is translated with a concessive force, in light of the prefatory remark: "Although I do not fear God . . ." (BAGD 220 §VI.4; BAA 443 §VI.5).[11] This judge knows that others think that he will stand up to anyone and disregard their needs. He does not care what people think of him. But as the next verse makes clear, the woman is "getting on the judge's nerves" (Jeremias 1963a: 153; Kistemaker 1980: 251).

The widow's persistence wears down the judge. Παρέχειν . . . κόπον   **18:5** (*parechein . . . kopon*) refers to the trouble or bother that the woman causes by her continual appeals (BAGD 626 §1c, 443; BAA 1266 §1c, 901; the phrase is found elsewhere at Matt. 26:10 = Mark 14:6; Luke 11:7; Gal. 6:17; Sir. 29:4). An additional description gives the judge's frame of mind: he fears being "beaten down," ὑπωπιάζῃ (*hypōpiazē*), a term that literally means "to give someone a black eye." Used figuratively, it means to wear down emotionally or to beat down someone's reputation (Stählin, *TDNT* 9:450 n. 88; K. Weiss, *TDNT* 8:590–91; BAGD 848; BAA 1691).[12] Since this judge is not concerned with loss of reputation (18:2, 4), the term here refers to the woman wearing him down emotionally (against Derrett 1971–72: 189–91 and Marshall 1978: 673).[13] She is a nuisance (Fitzmyer 1985: 1179)! Go-

---

11. Another Lucan parable (11:8) with this construction and theme also uses διά γε (yet because) in the second portion of the statement; Creed 1930: 223.

12. 1 Cor. 9:27 uses ὑπωπιάζω positively to refer to spiritual discipline, but here the judge intends it negatively.

13. Marshall discusses the options for the syntax of εἰς τέλος, which can be translated "finally," "completely," or "unceasingly." This term can describe either when the coming occurs or how it occurs. Does the woman *finally* come? Does she *completely* wear out the judge? Does she *unceasingly* come? The middle option is more likely.

det (1875: 2.201) sees the woman coming in frustration and literally beating on the judge, but such action would guarantee that she would never get justice (correctly Manson 1949: 306–7). The judge foresees that the woman's constant requests will eventually wear him out, and so he purposes (ἵνα, hina) to take up her cause. He wants to avoid the hassle of her coming (ἐρχομένη, erchomenē) on a regular basis. Διά γε (dia ge, yet because) states the cause of his action rather emphatically (cf. 11:8; Arndt 1956: 377). If he continues to refuse, she will continue to come. He decides to vindicate her (ἐκδικέω, ekdikeō) in order to stop her from bothering him any longer. The woman's constant intercession has brought success. Here is the example that the disciples' prayer should emulate.

c. Jesus' Comments (18:6–8)
i. Comparison of the Judge to God (18:6–8a)

18:6   Jesus now turns his attention to application. Fitzmyer (1985: 1180) links this verse to the parable proper as its concluding comment about the judge, arguing that 18:6 places the focus properly on the judge, who is contrasted with God, rather than on the widow. But for Jesus to talk about the judge draws attention to the widow as well. Fitzmyer wrongly assumes that the parable can only develop one character (Blomberg 1990: 274). Though the verse does form a transition with clear linkage to the parable, it is the beginning of Jesus' reflections on his story. Jesus tells the disciples to reflect on the judge's response.[14] The judge is called ἀδικία (adikia, unrighteous) because of his lack of compassion toward the woman, a description that recalls the judge's characterization in 18:2, 4. He is a judge of "this age" (Marshall 1978: 673; Schrenk, *TDNT* 1:155 §A5, 157 §B5; Grundmann 1963: 347 [an unrighteous judge]; Delling 1962: 13–14, esp. nn. 52, 56).[15] The point of application plays off this portrait in a lesser-to-greater argument (*qal wahomer*): if such an insensitive character responds to repeated pleas from someone he does not know or care about, how much more will a righteous God respond to his children (Fitzmyer 1985: 1180; Kistemaker 1980: 252; Wiefel 1988: 315). Later Judaism shared this belief in the value of persistent prayer (Lachs 1987: 323; *y. Ber.* 13b [9.1] [= Neusner et al. 1982–93: 1.315]; Midr. Ps. 4.3 on 4:1 [4:2 MT] and Midr. Ps. 55.2 on 55:17 [55:18 MT] [= Braude 1959: 1.61–67, 492–93]).

---

14. Ἀκούσατε is an aorist imperative: "listen now" to what the judge says. Linnemann 1966: 121 n. *a* says that it is equivalent to "he who has ears, let him hear" in 8:8 and 14:35.

15. Luke 18:3 shows how widows ought to be treated. The steward in 16:8 was called ἀδικία for acting in a way that undermined his master.

God's response is laid out in two closely connected rhetorical ques- **18:7**
tions introduced by οὐ μή (*ou mē*, not) and linked by καί (*kai*, and)
(Jeremias 1963a: 154–55;[16] Plummer 1896: 413; John 18:11; BDF
§365.4; BDR §365.4–5). Ἐκδίκησιν (*ekdikēsin*, vindication) links
Jesus' application to the parable, since ἐκδικέω was also used in
18:3, 5. God will bring justice in the face of trouble. He will judge
those who persecute the righteous (Acts 7:24; T. Sol. 22.4; Jeremias
1963a: 154 n. 8; Marshall 1978: 673–74).[17] The promise imbedded in
this question is that God will vindicate his elect (ἐκλεκτῶν, *eklektōn*).
The term ἐκλεκτός is a collective (the only such time in Luke–Acts,
though the singular is applied to Jesus in Luke 23:35; elsewhere in
the Synoptics at Matt. 22:14; 24:22, 24, 31 = Mark 13:20, 22, 27). The
term has a traditional flavor, since so many other authors use it
(Rom. 8:33; 16:13; Col. 3:12; 1 Tim. 5:21; 2 Tim. 2:10; Titus 1:1; 1 Pet.
1:1; 2:4, 6, 9; 2 John 1, 13; Rev. 17:14; Fitzmyer 1985: 1180; Manson
1949: 307).[18] The uses in 1 Peter, Colossians, and Romans share the
collective overtones of this text, with Peter using OT imagery. God
will come to the defense of his chosen people (Sir. 35:14–22 is similar in tone).

The need for their rescue is expressed by their constantly entreating God.[19] Luke elsewhere uses βοάω (*boaō*) to describe the cry of
those in need of mercy (9:38; 18:38), and the sense is the same here.
Believers are under pressure, so they are to pray as the passage exhorts them to do. God is listening.

The exact force of the second question—"and will he delay over
them?"—is much disputed (Marshall 1978: 674–75). The question is
made difficult because Luke does not use either the verb μακρο-
θυμέω (*makrothymeō*, to be patient) or the noun μακροθυμία (*ma-
krothymia*, patience) elsewhere (he uses the adverb μακροθύμως
[*makrothymōs*, patiently] in Acts 26:3). There are at least twelve interpretations of this question:

16. Jeremias discusses the syntax of the questions by noting that the change of
mood—from subjunctive to indicative—points to two questions, but one should be
careful not to separate them too greatly, given the nature of the reply in 18:8.

17. Delling 1962: 16 n. 68 cites numerous LXX uses of ἐκδικέω: Ps. 149:7 (of the
punishment of the wicked); 1 Macc. 3:15; 7:9, 24, 38; Exod. 12:12 and Num. 33:4 (of
what God did to the Egyptians in the plagues); Mic. 5:14 [5:15 Engl.] (of judgment on
the nations); Ezek. 16:41 and 23:10 (of what the nations did to Israel).

18. Delling 1962: 15 gives Qumranian usage and OT background (n. 63) for ἐκλεκτός: 1 Chron. 16:13; Isa. 42:1; 43:20; 65:9; Ps. 105:6, 43 [104:6, 43 LXX]; Sir. 47:22. He
also covers NT usage (n. 64).

19. For βοάω (to cry out), see BAGD 144; BAA 288 §1d; Stauffer, *TDNT* 1:625–26;
elsewhere in the NT at Matt. 3:3 = Mark 1:3 = Luke 3:4 = John 1:23; Mark 15:34
(= Matt. 27:46 [ἀναβοάω]); Luke 9:38; 18:7, 38; Acts 8:7; 17:6; 25:24; Gal. 4:27. In the
LXX at Gen. 4:10; Judg. 10:10 (B); Num. 20:16 (ἀναβοάω). Rev. 6:9–11 is conceptually
similar.

1. God is patient about their prayer requests. This view softens the point too much, especially since eschatological concern is the topic (Marshall does not cite any proponents of this view). This is a popular reading of the text, but it ignores the passage's context, which focuses on God's vindication.
2. Horst (*TDNT* 4:381 n. 56) holds that it is a parenthetical rhetorical question. This view detaches the question too much from its context.
3. Manson (1949: 307–8) holds that it represents a mistranslated Aramaic phrase that originally meant "postpones wrath because of the elect." This view is too speculative when other possibilities are more straightforward.
4. Sahlin (1945b: 9–20) appeals to a rare use of καί (*kai*) and reads the clause as conditional: "Shall not God vindicate his elect, those whom, if (καί) they cry out to him day and night, he patiently hears?" This sense of καί is unusual.
5. Ott (1965: 44–59) holds that καί is a relative and that μακροθυμεῖ means "hear graciously": "Will not God make vindication for his elect who cry to him day and night and whom (καί) he hears patiently?" This view asks double duty of καί.
6. Ljungvik (1963–64: 291) holds that καί is adversative: "But (καί) does not God remain unmoved toward them?" Adversative καί is harsh because the two questions are so closely bound together. The reply in 18:8 treats the answer with more unity than this approach suggests.
7. Creed (1930: 223), Wellhausen (1904: 556), and Grundmann (1963: 348) hold that the objects of hesitation to act are the enemies of the elect: God is patient with the nonelect, a thought that has NT precedent (2 Pet. 3:9–10). This approach appeals to a sense that reverses the force of Sir. 35:22, with its expectation of crushing the unrighteous, a judgment now said to be delayed through compassion. The major problem with this harsh reading is that there is no contextual reference to the nonelect.[20]

None of these seven proposals is tenable. The remaining options provide the likely meaning of the question.

8. Jeremias (1963a: 154–55) argues for concessive καί and appeals to an Aramaic stative verbal idea (BDF §468.3; Plummer 1896: 414): "God will vindicate, even if (καί) he is patient about responding."

---

20. Cranfield 1963 has a variation of this view that sees concessive καί: "God will vindicate even though (καί) he suffers long with the wicked."

9. Beyer (1968: 268 n. 1), also appealing to Semitic, takes καί with causal force: "God will vindicate them, because (καί) he is patient with them."

10. Ellis (1974: 213), Danker (1988: 295–96), and Rengstorf (1968: 206) read the verse with the sense that "God is patient about the complaint of the elect in their call for justice" (cf. James 5:7–8; see Luke 11:8).

Any one of meanings 8–10 is possible, but they must read 18:8 as reassurance that, however long God tarries, it will not be forever. Such a reading could be defended, but it seems harsh.

11. With better contextual support, many commentators hold that the idea of patience has to do with God's response: God will not delay (Arndt 1956: 378; Fitzmyer 1985: 1180; Linnemann 1966: 186–87; Schneider 1977a: 362; Schweizer 1984: 279; BAGD 488; BAA 990 §§2–3; Tiede 1988: 306; Wifstrand 1964–65). A parallel in Sir. 35:19 speaks for this view, as does Luke 18:8. In fact, this view might make the most sense because of the Sirach association.

The problem with this view comes when we look at Lucan theology as a whole. Luke's perspective seems to include a concern about the return's delay (better discussed as the "interim" before the delay; e.g., he both emphasizes the present blessings and calls for patience in the intervening period). However one evaluates Conzelmann's thesis (1960: 96–97) about the centrality of this theme in Luke's purpose, Conzelmann shows that it is a concern of Luke's. Why, therefore, would Luke include a remark about immediacy? The answer seems to be that he never loses hope that the return might be soon. It is among the next items in God's plan, and so this remark, which emphasizes immediacy, is retained. Other texts show the church explaining the delay in terms of God's mercy, since such a delay gives people additional opportunity to respond (2 Pet. 3:8–9). Nonetheless Jesus here asks the disciples to be ready, knowing that, once his work is accomplished, the return will be one of the key events left to occur.

It is legitimate to ask how this view can be sustained in the face of what is clearly now a lengthy delay. The answer is not addressed in these verses but in the larger concerns of Lucan and NT theology. The NT views the entire time between Jesus' departure and his return as a period of fulfillment in which God acts on behalf of his people (thus the "last days" of Acts 2:17; Heb. 1:2; 1 Pet. 1:20; Jude 17–19). God's vindication is both now and not yet. Acts 2–3 seems to stress the presence of blessing now, even though full vindication (i.e., the removal of enemies through judgment) is not yet. This vindication involves blessing and spiritual provision now, as well as physical deliverance upon the return. Luke 18 focuses on the ultimate vindication, though God is currently hearing the prayers of his people. In other words, vindication may be broader than the fact of the return, since the initial form of eschatological vindication comes with the Spirit's provision and entry into the fulfillment of promise (this seems to be the tone of the offer in Acts 2:38–39 and Acts 3:24–26). Such a reading fits Luke's effort to stress that salvation has both present benefits and future rewards, culminating in the future earthly display.[21]

12. A final view also treats the reference to patience as God's response, but sees it in terms of his restricting the enemies' power to persecute until the vindication (Catchpole 1977). Catchpole cites numerous LXX passages where the μακρο-θυμέω word group indicates God's patience with the Israelites (Exod. 34:6; Num. 14:18; Ps. 86:15 [85:15 LXX]; 103:8 [102:8 LXX]; Joel 2:13; Nah. 1:3; Wis. 15:1; Sir. 5:4; cf. Rom. 2:4; 9:22) and Gentiles (Jon. 4:2; Sir. 18:11; 32:22 [= Rahlfs's 35:19]; 2 Macc. 6:14; cf. Matt. 18:26, 29). God is patient with his elect in lightening the intensity of their suffering until he comes. He does not spare them, but he does protect them. This option has lexical merit and speaks of God's providential care that comes quickly in the interim. If this sense is correct, accounts like Acts 4:23–32 and 12:6–17 may picture the attitude called for here.

It is hard to be sure which of the last two options is more likely. It is clear that God vindicates his people. Whether his patience is reflected in a current care that culminates in ultimate deliverance or in keeping persecution from being too great is not certain. Luke 18:8 and the association of the Son of Man probably favors view 11 over 12. If so, God's current and ultimate care is in view, though the focus is on where that care ends—with vindication.

18:8a   Luke 18:8 makes two additional points. First, Jesus answers his rhetorical question about God's delay by noting that God will speedily (ἐν τάχει, *en tachei*) bring vindication for his elect. Two possible translations are proposed for this phrase:

---

21. 1 Thess. 1:5–10 also seems to have this twofold sense: salvation and faith now are tied to what happens later. 1 Thess. 1:10 marks the faithful out as those who are spared this vengeance.

1. On the basis of Josh. 8:18–19; Ps. 2:12; Ezek. 29:5; and Sir. 27:3, ἐν τάχει means "suddenly." The point is that, when the return comes, it will happen quickly (Jeremias 1963a: 155; Horst, *TDNT* 4:381; Colpe, *TDNT* 8:435 [the point as whether the Son of Man will find faith at the return]; Grundmann 1963: 348 [citing Luke 16:6]; Ellis 1974: 213; Delling 1962: 19–20 n. 83).[22]

2. Ἐν τάχει means "soon," indicating that vindication is near (Fitzmyer 1985: 1181; Marshall 1978: 676; Klostermann 1929: 179; Danker 1988: 295; Cranfield and Linnemann as cited in n. 21). Lexical evidence favors this view (BAGD 807; BAA 1609): in six (Acts 12:7; 22:18; 1 Tim. 3:14) of the other seven NT uses, including three eschatological contexts (Rom. 16:20; Rev. 1:1; 22:6) and one noneschatological context (Acts 25:4), ἐν τάχει means "soon." The point is God has not forgotten his elect. He will act soon to establish them and deal with their enemies (on the theological issue of delay, see the exegesis of 18:7).

A remark about a soon coming implies, nonetheless, a delay. Since delay in vindication may become an excuse to lose faith, Jesus goes on to say in effect, "Pray and look for the return," knowing that it will come. Though the delay seems long, after the vindication it will seem short (Marshall 1978: 676–77). In comparison to eternity, what is the span of time between Christ's first and second comings? This point is especially true in light of the vindication's permanence.

ii. Contrast to the Son of Man Finding Faithful People (18:8b)

This idea of awaiting the return raises the question of what people **18:8b** will be doing when it comes. Will they be praying and looking for it? Jesus' last remark serves as a rhetorical call to continue to pray and hope for the vindication. He wonders if the Son of Man will find faith on earth when he comes. Manson (1949: 308) sees the reference to the Son of Man as a circumlocution for "I" in his present ministry (cf. 7:34). But the eschatology of the context and the linkage of 18:1–8 with 17:22–37 makes a reference to the return virtually certain.[23] The spirit of the remark is similar to 12:50 and 22:32.

The faith that the Son of Man will look for is not simply an identification with his message (Klostermann 1929: 179) nor a faith that avoids strange teaching (Creed 1930: 224). Rather the context indi-

22. Cranfield 1963: 299 n. 1 and Linnemann 1966: 188–89 n. 16 object that the term cannot have this force and challenge the passages where it is said to have this meaning.

23. For defense of this linkage, along with a defense of 18:8's original unity with 18:7 and 18:2–5, see Catchpole 1977.

cates that the Son of Man will be looking for those who are looking for him (Colpe, *TDNT* 8:435, combines this sense with the idea of accepting Jesus). In the interim, will believers keep the faith? Will they continue to pray and look for vindication? Even though Jesus expresses the idea as a question, he is exhorting them to keep watching. He is calling for a faith that perseveres in allegiance to Jesus (2 Tim. 4:7; Schneider 1977a: 362). The message is, "Be vigilant" (cf. Matt. 6:10 = Luke 11:2; 1 Cor. 15:58; 16:22; and Rev. 22:17, 20). The disciple is to look forward to the day when Jesus will come and defend his elect by exercising righteous judgment over the whole earth. Numerous texts in Luke call for disciples to keep watch (12:35, 40, 43, 46; 17:24, 26–30).

There is no reference to the event or timing of the rapture in Luke 17:22–18:8. The vindication of the saints in view here refers to the judgment of the unrighteous. Such vindication leaves the righteous free to share in the kingdom and enjoy God's presence for eternity. The day is one in which evil and unrighteousness will be dealt with decisively. As such, saints are exhorted to look for it. The blessed hope is not only that saints will be with God forever, but that unrighteousness will be judged and removed. This latter point is emphasized in this unit. Information about the timing of the rapture must come from other texts, where the emphasis is to keep looking for the day when the Son of Man will return to establish justice. Until he comes, the church's mission is to preach him and to be faithful (Luke 24:44–49; Acts 1:6–8).

Summary Luke 18:1–8 makes clear that disciples are to walk by faith. In no area is this more the case than when believers are under pressure for confessing Jesus. During such stress, they should not give up, but long for the return of God to manifest his power in righteous judgment. How are they to await the end? By persistence in prayer, just as the widow persisted in petitioning the judge. They are to recognize that God is not like the judge who does not care what people think. He is listening and responding to the cries of his children. He listens by patiently responding to their pleas, by showering them with blessing, and perhaps by lessening the judgment on them. He promises to send vindication quickly. But in the midst of the wait, disciples are to continue in faith and hope. These words of comfort call believers to enduring hope. As Luke has said, Jesus' hope is that when the Son of Man comes, he will find disciples still waiting for his coming. Luke's goal is to call disciples to pray again and again for God's coming. One serves God with both eyes looking to heaven, from whence our salvation comes (Phil. 3:20–21).

K. Humbly Entrusting All to the Father (18:9–30)

The next to last section in the journey narrative calls for humility that trusts God totally. The section has three units: the contrast between the arrogant Pharisee and the humble tax collector, in which the latter receives commendation from Jesus (18:9–14); the picture of having faith like a child (18:15–17); and the encounter between the rich man and Jesus (18:18–30). The last unit has two parts. The rich man trusts his possessions more than he trusts Jesus' call to follow him, and so he departs sad; the disciple is said to have left everything and so receives the promise of rich blessing from Jesus. Here is the essence of discipleship: faithful dependence on a gracious God.

1. Humility and Arrogance: Parable of the Pharisee and Tax Collector (18:9–14)

Luke 18:9–14 presents a second consecutive parable about prayer, but the theme has changed (Marshall 1978: 677). The attention here is not on eschatology but on anthropology and soteriology. What attitude does God commend? Perhaps the connection with the previous passage is not just prayer, but vindication from God. Whom does God vindicate? The contrastive parable of the Pharisee and tax collector supplies the answer: humility before God and confidence in his mercy—not on one's own merit—brings acceptance from God. This contrast is presented through two representatives: the proud and self-righteous person and the humble and contrite person. In fact, the parable could be called "The Parable of Two Prayers: The Proud and the Humble."

The contrast is seen in a variety of ways. First, the men use different approaches. The Pharisee manages to refer to himself in the first person five times in two verses and describes himself in the prayer with the active voice. The tax collector has God as the subject and sees himself as a passive figure. He is in need of mercy, so he appeals to God. The Pharisee sees his achievements as abundantly fulfilling the law, so he believes that he is better than others. The tax collector knows that before God he is nothing, and so he needs to appeal to God for mercy. Second, the men take different positions. One is certain that he can approach God and almost demand justice as a matter of personal right. The other is so conscious of his unworthiness that he can barely approach God. These contrasting positions highlight the major theme of the unit: justification is grounded in God's mercy, an attitude that holds the seeds of later Pauline teaching of justification by grace through trusting in the sufficient work of Christ. The events that impact Paul's teaching, however, have not yet occurred, so there is less specificity to the theme in Jesus' ministry.[1]

Precedent for both styles of prayer is found in the OT (Danker 1988: 296): the Pharisee's confidence is like Ps. 26 and 17:3–5, while the tax collector's humility reflects Ps. 34 and 51. The Phar-

---

1. Fitzmyer 1985: 1185 discusses the relationship of this pericope to Paul's message, though with less emphasis on the unity of the perspectives. See also F. F. Bruce 1952: 66–69 and the exegesis of 18:14a.

isee's prayer actually goes beyond OT confidence in being so certain that one can approach God on one's own merits and in having so much contempt for all other people. The tax collector is assumed to be God's "enemy," though he has done nothing to deserve this description. The Pharisee does not see himself as actively opposed to God. It is this pride that Jesus criticizes (Luke 18:9). The Pharisee is quick to judge others and confident of his own achievements. Thinking he knows truth, the Pharisee is proud and self-deceived.

The parable fits nicely with the theme of other Lucan parables. The idea of humility and God's openness to sinners reflects Luke 15, as well as the accounts in 5:29–32 and 7:36–50 (Fitzmyer 1985: 1184; Creed 1930: 222 [also makes comparison to 10:25–37; see below]). The reversal of the normal human perception of spirituality agrees with several accounts (10:29–37; 10:38–42; 11:37–41; 12:13–34; 14:7–11; 15:11–32; 16:19–31; 18:18–30; Talbert 1982: 170–71). The spirit of the tax collector recalls themes of the infancy section (1:45, 48, 52; Schneider 1977a: 365).

The parable is an example parable or story, like the parable of the good Samaritan (10:29–37) or the parable of the rich man and Lazarus (16:19–31), except it is not told as a comparative account. Rather, it is told as a real event with a real conclusion, which is applied not comparatively to others, but refers directly to the types of people mentioned in the story (Pharisee = the proud; tax collector = the humble sinner). Nonetheless, the account is parabolic, as 18:9 makes clear. Fitzmyer (1985: 1183) calls this the last specifically Lucan parable of the journey section, but this is not correct. His position argues that the journey narrative ends at 18:14, but the journey continues into Luke 19. Another exemplary tax collector, Zacchaeus, appears in 19:1–10, where a real event is in view. Zacchaeus provides a model of how one with means should live, as well as the humility of the tax collector of Luke 18.

Sources and Historicity

The parable is from Luke's unique material (Aland 1985: §237). The Semitic asyndeton (18:11, 12, 13) fits the setting in which it appears (Jeremias 1963a: 140; Blomberg 1990: 256 [who carefully notes the structure]). Bultmann (1963: 179) argues that 18:14b is secondary on the unlikely premise that the tax collector is not an example of one who humbles himself. But one wonders what else such an open request for mercy could be! The closing remark fits the setting and parable very well, and there is no reason to challenge its connection with Jesus (Marshall 1978: 681; Nolland 1993a: 874). The Jesus Seminar (Funk and Hoover 1993: 368–69) also places the parable in Jesus' ministry, printing 18:10–14a in pink type, with only the shift of theme in 18:14b being questioned (gray type). The reversal of 18:14b, however, fits Jesus' style and the context (Nolland 1993a: 874), while the cultural reversal of roles in the parable is also like Jesus (7:31–35; 13:30; see the exegesis of 18:14b). Jesus commonly contrasts two sets of characters (Luke 15:11–32; 16:19–31; Matt. 21:28–32; Marshall 1978: 677). Nolland (1993a: 874) argues that this parable was paired with Luke 10:25–37 in the L parables source on the basis of the theme of "going up" to the temple versus "going down" from Jerusalem to Jericho. This is possible, but hard to establish.

> The passage is a parabolic example story (Fitzmyer 1985: 1183; Bultmann 1963: 178; Berger 1984: 51; Blomberg 1990: 256–58 [a two-point parable]). The outline of Luke 18:9–14 is as follows:
>
> a. Setting (18:9)
> b. Prayers of the proud man and the humble sinner (18:10–13)
>   i. Introduction of the two men (18:10)
>   ii. Prayer of the proud Pharisee (18:11–12)
>   iii. Prayer of the humble tax collector (18:13)
> c. Jesus' comment (18:14)
>   i. The justified man (18:14a)
>   ii. The theological principle: God honors humility (18:14b)
>
> The passage is a polemic against the proud, represented by the Pharisee. At the center of this pride is personal religious arrogance. Jesus speaks against religious snobbery that views oneself as more righteous than another. On the contrary, acceptance by God involves personal humility and recognition of one's need for God's mercy.

Exegesis and Exposition

⁹And he said this parable to some who trusted in themselves that they were righteous and who despised others.

¹⁰"Two men went up to the temple to pray: one a Pharisee and the other a tax collector. ¹¹The Pharisee, standing, prayed ⌜these things to himself⌝, 'O God, I give thanks that I am not like the rest of men: thieves, unrighteous, adulterers, or also like this tax collector. ¹²I fast twice between Sabbaths. I give tithes of all I get.' ¹³But the tax collector, standing far off, did not wish to lift his eyes to heaven, but beat his breast, saying, 'O God, be merciful to me a sinner!'

¹⁴"I say to you, this one went down to his home justified rather than the other; for everyone who exalts himself will be humbled, but he who humbles himself will be exalted."

a. Setting (18:9)

Luke's introduction gives the parable's setting. Luke often notes the **18:9**
target of Jesus' parables (18:1; 19:11; Marshall 1978: 678).[2] The people warned in this parable are the self-righteous. The perfect participle πεποιθότας (*pepoithotas*, those who trusted) alludes to those in
a misdirected state of self-confidence (Luke 11:22; 2 Cor. 1:9; Manson 1949: 309; Fitzmyer 1985: 1185–86; Ezek. 33:13). They are convinced that they, on their own merits, are acceptable to God. A Pharisee is described here, but the introduction broadens the application
to all who have this attitude (τινας, *tinas*, some who). It should be
stressed that Jesus did not address all Pharisees—only those who
trusted their own merit (e.g., the Pharisee Nicodemus is viewed positively in the NT). Similar warnings in ancient Jewish material
(*m. ʾAbot.* 2.4–5; 1QS 11.1–2 [an exhortation to correct the proud in
spirit]) condemn this well-chronicled type of pride (Josephus, *Jewish War* 1.5.2 §110; Phil. 3:4–6; 1QH 7.34; *b. Ber.* 28b; *b. Sanh.* 101a
[Akiva notes that everyone sins, citing Eccles. 7:20]; *b. Suk.* 45b;
Grundmann 1963: 350; Jeremias 1963: 142–43). *T. Ber.* 6.18 [= Neusner 1977–86: 1.40] evidences this attitude in the male Jew thanking
God that he is not a Gentile, boor, or woman.

This pride is reflected in the pharisaic attitude toward people
whom they despised (ἐξουθενέω, *exoutheneō*; BAGD 277; BAA 562;
cf. Luke 23:11; Acts 4:11; Rom. 14:3, 10). This condescending, superior attitude makes it difficult to serve others. Pride and contempt
for others may be a natural pair, but Jesus condemns both attitudes.

b. Prayers of the Proud Man and the Humble Sinner (18:10–13)
i. Introduction of the Two Men (18:10)

Jesus introduces the parable's characters and setting in the most sa- **18:10**
cred locale in Israel, the temple. Since the temple is on a hill, they
are said to go up to get there ("going down" in 18:14 balances the image). The language is appropriate, since they are going to draw near
to God (Ps. 122:1). The two men represent polar opposites in the
first-century religious culture. The Pharisee belonged to the most
pious movement, while the tax collector was part of the most hated
profession.[3] It is likely that tax collectors did not usually come to the

---

2. Πρός plus the accusative could mean that Jesus spoke "against" this group
(BAGD 710 §III.4 and BAA 1422 §III.4), but normal Lucan usage calls for "to." A pericope or a dialogue begins with πρός in 4:21, 43; 5:10; 6:3; 7:24; 9:3, 13, 14; 11:1; 12:1;
14:3; 15:3; 16:1; 17:1.

3. Josephus, *Jewish War* 1.5.2 §110, says that the Pharisees were "known for
surpassing the others in the observances of piety and exact interpretation of the

temple because of popular ill will against them (Kistemaker 1980: 259). Both men offer prayers to God, but in the culture's perception, the Pharisee would have had the more open line to heaven. Community prayers were offered at 9:00 A.M. (Acts 2:15) and 3:00 P.M. (Acts 3:1), private prayers at any time (Fitzmyer 1985: 1186; Marshall 1978: 679; *m. Tamid* 5.1).

ii. Prayer of the Proud Pharisee (18:11–12)

18:11 In his prayer the Pharisee compares himself with other people. He assumes a position of confidence as he stands and prays.[4] Given the remark in 18:13 about where the tax collector stands, it is likely that the Pharisee has gone right into the inner court (Fitzmyer 1985: 1186). His prayer reveals this attitude.

In this culture, prayer was either silent or uttered in a low voice (1 Sam. 1:13). Vocal prayer was acceptable, though praying too loudly was perceived as rude, at least if later texts are any clue (*b. Ber.* 24b, 31a; Klostermann 1929: 179; SB 4:231–32; Marshall 1978: 679). The positive example is Hannah (1 Sam. 1:13), who prayed out loud, but quietly. The prayer begins like a thanksgiving psalm praising God for something he has done, but the "thanksgiving" hardly focuses on God's sovereign work (Fitzmyer 1985: 1186; Grundmann 1963: 350 [contrasts 10:21]).[5] The Pharisee is so certain of his righteousness that he compares himself favorably to a variety of unrighteous violators of the commandments, a list similar to 1 Cor. 5:10–11 and 6:9–10. Ἅρπαξ (*harpax*, thief, extortionist) is used in the NT only here and in Matt. 7:15; 1 Cor. 5:10, 11; 6:10 (BAGD 109 §2; BAA 219 §2; cf. Isa. 10:2; Josephus, *Jewish War* 6.3.4 §203). Ἄδικος (*adikos*, unrighteous; 1 Cor. 6:9; Lev. 19:13; T. Asher 2.5) is a general category for sinner, while μοιχός (*moichos*, adulterer; elsewhere in the NT only at 1 Cor. 6:9 and Heb. 13:4) refers specifically to the immoral. The reference to the tax collector shows a judgmental attitude because he makes an instant evaluation on the basis of the man's vocation. Οὗτος (*houtos*, this one) has negative connotations

---

laws." Tax collectors were discussed earlier in Luke 3:12; 5:27, 30. The construction ὁ εἷς . . . ὁ ἕτερος (the one . . . the other) occurred earlier in 7:41.

4. So the aorist passive participle σταθείς (as he stood); BAGD 382 §II.1b; BAA 775 §II.1b. The circumstantial aorist passive participle of ἵστημι is found in the NT only in Luke's writings: Luke 18:40; 19:8; Acts 2:14; 5:20; 11:13; 17:22; 25:18; 27:21; Fitzmyer 1985: 1186. In the Jewish world, it was not unusual to stand and pray (1 Sam. 1:26; 1 Kings 8:14, 22; Plummer 1896: 416; SB 1:401–2; 2:240; Marshall 1978: 679).

5. Εὐχαριστέω (to thank) is common, but not in the first person. The verb is used six times by Luke, including Luke 17:16; Acts 27:35; 28:15; also 1QH 2.20, 31; 3.19, 37; 4.5; 2 Macc. 1:11. Luke 10:21 is similar in tone, but decidedly different in content.

(Marshall 1978: 679; used of Jesus by his taunters in 23:35). In effect his prayer is, "I thank you, God, that I am such a great guy!" Pride permeates the intercession (Arndt 1956: 379; Michel, *TDNT* 8:105).[6] Lachs (1987: 324) notes similar and different prayers from later Jewish tradition.[7]

Part of the reason for the Pharisee's confidence is the religious activity in which he engages. There is no grammatical conjunction between 18:11 and 18:12, but 18:12 gives the reasons for the Pharisee's "better" position in comparison to others. Two practices are singled out: fasting and tithing. **18:12**

Fasting twice a week is above what OT law required, which required fasting only on the Day of Atonement. Voluntary fasting usually occurred on Monday and Thursday,[8] and other Sabbaths later became traditional fasts celebrating national calamities (Zech. 8:19). A fast involved taking only bread and water (*Shepherd of Hermas*, Parable 5.3.7 §56; Behm, *TDNT* 4:930; Fitzmyer 1985: 1187).[9] The traditional reason for fasting on Monday and Thursday was that these were the days that Moses went up and came down from Mount Sinai, but the real reason may be simply that it divided the week nicely. Christians who fasted twice a week did so on Wednesday and Friday, a move that may well reflect the one-day shift in the Lord's day (*Didache* 8.1; SB 2:244–46; Jeremias 1963a: 140).

The OT background of tithing (ἀποδεκατόω, *apodekatoō*) is presented in Lev. 27:30–32; Num. 18:21–24; and Deut. 14:22–27 (cf. Gen. 28:22; Heb. 7:5; BAGD 89; BAA 179). Even though a grower had already given the tithe for certain produce required by the law, some Pharisees tithed food that they ate.[10] Some even tithed herbs not required by law (Matt. 23:23; Luke 11:42; Fitzmyer 1985: 1187–88). This man is faithful in giving a tenth of what he earns to God.

---

6. Containing five uses of the first person, this prayer is simple self-praise. This complaint about the Pharisees surfaces elsewhere in Luke 5:30–32; 15:2; 16:15; John 9:40–41.

7. *B. Ber.* 28b matches the Pharisee's prayer, while *b. Ber.* 17a is more gracious in valuing the contribution that each person makes when attention is directed to God. In *b. Suk.* 45b a man states that if only one hundred are to be saved, he and his son will be among them; but if only two are saved, they will be he and his son; Ellis 1974: 214. In *y. Ber.* 7d (4.2) (= Neusner et al. 1982–93: 1.168) a rabbi give thanks that he is in the synagogue and not in the theater or circus.

8. Δὶς τοῦ σαββάτου (lit., twice per Sabbath) is a distributive genitive meaning "per week"; Mark 16:9: 1 Cor. 16:2; Plummer 1896: 417.

9. On fasting (νηστεύω), see the exegesis of Luke 5:33; BAGD 538; BAA 1089–90; Lev. 16:29–31 and Num. 29:7 (the Day of Atonement); 2 Sam. 12:21–22 (for mourning); 1 Kings 21:27 (for penance); Neh. 1:4 (for prayer). B. Giṭ. 56a and b. Taʿan. 12a give the Jewish custom. The cultural assumption is that the pious fast more often than once a year.

10. Πάντα (all) is an accusative of reference: "I gave a tenth with respect to all I get."

On this basis he asserts his superiority over other people. He has gone beyond the call of duty, so God should be impressed with his record of service. Jesus considers such an approach offensive.

iii. Prayer of the Humble Tax Collector (18:13)

18:13 The tax collector is a complete contrast to the Pharisee. He stands but remains "far off," probably on the outer edges of the Court of the Gentiles (Grundmann, *TDNT* 8:16). The distance suggests timidity and his unworthiness to approach God. He does not lift his eyes to heaven, but beats (τύπτω, *typtō*) his breast as a sign of contrition (23:48; Fitzmyer 1985: 1188; Marshall 1978: 680; BAGD 830; BAA 1655; Stählin, *TDNT* 8:262 n. 18; Josephus, *Antiquities* 7.10.5 §252).[11]

The tone of this request is different from that of the Pharisee. There is no confident self-focus. It is the prayer of the penitent, a plea for mercy (ἱλάσθητι, *hilasthēti*) from a self-confessed sinner (Plummer 1896: 419). The prayer asks God to show mercy through atoning forgiveness (Esth. 4:17h [= NRSV 13:17]; Lam. 3:42; Dan. 9:19 [Theodotion]). The ἱλάσκομαι (*hilaskomai*, to propitiate) word group is used in the LXX to translate the כָּפַר (*kipper*, to cover) word group, the OT term for atonement.[12] In referring to himself as a sinner, he makes no comparison to others, unlike the Pharisee (Büchsel, *TDNT* 3:315). He is concerned only with improving his own spiritual health, and he knows that the only way to do so is to rely totally on God's mercy.

c. Jesus' Comment (18:14)
i. The Justified Man (18:14a)

18:14a Jesus endorses the tax collector's attitude. The phrase λέγω ὑμῖν (*legō hymin*, I say to you) often signals a significant conclusion (3:8; 7:9, 26, 28; 9:27; 10:12, 24; 11:9, 51; 12:4, 5, 8, 27, 37, 44, 51; 13:3, 5, 35; 14:24; 15:7, 10; 16:9; 17:34; 18:8, 29; 19:26, 40; 21:32; 22:16, 18, 37). Jesus says that the tax collector went down (κατέβη, *katebē*—contrasting ἀνέβησαν [*anebēsan*, they went up] in 18:10) from the

---

11. On lifting the eyes in prayer, see Mark 6:41; 7:34; John 11:41; 17:1; Ps. 123:1; 1 Esdr. 4:58 (in 1 Enoch 13.5 evil angels are too ashamed to look up); Jeremias, *TDNT* 1:185–86; Michaelis, *TDNT* 5:377 n. 11. Lifting the hands is a symbol of supplication in the NT; 1 Tim. 2:8. Στῆθος (breast) stands for the person; BAGD 767 and BAA 1532 ("the seat of the inner life"); elsewhere in the NT only at Luke 23:48; John 13:25; 21:20; Rev. 15:6. Jeremias 1963a: 141 at n. 46 says that in Judaism the heart is seen as the seat of sin, but cites as evidence only the late Eccles. Rab. 7.2.5 on 7:2.

12. BAGD 375; BAA 762; cf. Ps. 51:1, 3 [51:3, 5 MT]; 25:11; 34:6, 18 [34:7, 19 MT]; 78:38; 79:9; 2 Kings 5:18; 1QS 11.3–5, 10–12; 1QH 11.15–22. Ἱλάσκομαι appears in the NT only here and in Heb. 2:17.

temple in a state of acceptance (δεδικαιωμένος, *dedikaiōmenos*; BAGD 197 §2; BAA 397 §2). In another contrast, Jesus says that "this" (οὗτος, *houtos*) tax collector was justified, while "that" (ἐκεῖνον, *ekeinon*) Pharisee was not. Position in the temple means nothing; the position of the heart means everything.

The term δικαιόω is not here a technical term for final salvation, since there are no soteriological issues raised other than a generalized request for mercy in the context of prayer. The tax collector's prayer was accepted or "found favor" in contrast to the Pharisee's prayer. Δικαιόω is forensic but not in the decisive sense. As such, it is like Paul's usage, but less comprehensive in scope.[13] The tax collector was "vindicated" before God (18:8). God's acceptance of the tax collector shows the kind of attitude that he responds to and honors in the one who approaches him. The saint has the right to approach God boldly, but it is a humble approach nonetheless. The tax collector receives mercy and forgiveness, while the Pharisee does not.[14] The cry for mercy is answered quickly (18:7; Danker 1988: 297).

ii. The Theological Principle: God Honors Humility (18:14b)

The reason God receives the tax collector's plea is expressed simply **18:14b** by the verse's final comment. Jesus expresses a basic principle that Luke often notes: God honors humility. Spiritual reversal is a frequent Lucan note: 6:20–26; 10:29–37; 10:38–42; 11:37–41; 12:21; 15:11–32; 16:19–31, with 1:51–53 and 14:11 referring directly to the exaltation of the humble.[15] The comment is so proverbial that its repetition in a variety of contexts is not surprising; it belongs with the parable (Marshall 1978: 681; Grundmann, *TDNT* 8:16; Plummer 1896: 420; Blomberg 1990: 257–58). Humility is exalted in the parable, while pride—especially religious pride—is condemned. The principle enumerated here is eschatological (1 Cor. 1:27–29; Danker 1988: 297–98). Hearts will be evaluated and appearances will be reversed at the judgment.

---

13. Jeremias 1963a: 141 overstates the parallelism with Pauline usage, as do Fitzmyer 1985: 1185 and Arndt 1956: 380. Linnemann 1966: 62–63, 144–46 n. 11; Ernst 1977: 497–98; and Marshall 1978: 680–81 are clearer. Cf. Ps. 51:19 [51:21 MT]; 2 Esdr. [= 4 Ezra] 12:7; 1Q28b [= 1QSb] 4.22.

14. So the comparative παρ᾽ (than); Klostermann 1929: 181; Schrenk, *TDNT* 2:215 n. 16. Cf. παρά in Ps. 44:8 [45:7 Engl.]; Luke 13:2; BDF §185.3; BDR §185.3 n. 5 and §246.5.

15. The saying in 18:14 virtually matches 14:11, the only difference being the καί-δέ variation in the last clause. Matt. 18:4 and 23:12 are similar. The remark recalls Ezek. 21:26 [21:31 MT].

Summary   Luke 18:9–14 is a simple contrastive parable with one basic message: humility before God is what he finds acceptable. One is not to compare oneself to anyone in hopes of justifying oneself. The basic approach that God accepts is trusting in his mercy, not assuming that one has the right to receive blessing for one's activity. The assurance of this mercy is made available after Jesus' ministry on the basis of his sacrificial death. The security that one receives through Jesus' work is grounded in God's grace and mercy, not one's works (Rom. 3:21–31; Eph. 2:4–18). It is because of gratitude to God for his work of mercy that one serves God. This parable is directed to the self-righteous and those who despise others. The humble do not engage in comparison and are aware that their standing before God is possible only because of his mercy. They know that they are nothing before God. Jesus desires that disciples be like the tax collector—and so does Luke.

Additional Note

18:11. The UBS–NA text reads πρὸς ἑαυτὸν ταῦτα (to himself these things) with the support of A, W, Δ, family 13, Byz, Lect, one Itala manuscript, and one Syriac manuscript. The variant ταῦτα πρὸς ἑαυτόν (these things to himself)—supported by 𝔓⁷⁵, ℵ², B, L (αὐτόν, him), T, Θ, Ψ, family 1, two Itala manuscripts, one Syriac manuscript, and one Coptic manuscript—may be original (Fitzmyer 1985: 1186). Wider geographic distribution slightly favors the UBS–NA reading, which Jeremias (1963a: 140) argues has the more Semitic word order.

2. Children and Faith (18:15–17)

Returning to events described in Mark and Matthew, in this pericope Luke moves from a picture of humility to one of simple faith. Just as the tax collector illustrates a humble appeal for mercy, so the children portray simple trust. Luke continues to explore attitudes that please God, a theme that he began in 18:9. Jesus' openness to little children pictures his comprehensive concern for all people. By his openness to children, he shows the disciples, whose attitude was not the same, that every person is to be treated with sensitivity and received with love.

Sources and Historicity

This event is paralleled in Mark 10:13–16 = Matt. 19:13–15, in locations similar to Luke's (Aland 1985: §253).[1] This is the first use of material with clear and substantial parallels to Mark since Luke 9:49.[2] The wording is similar in all three accounts (esp. Luke 18:16–17 = Mark 10:14–15), indicating that the same event is under examination, although Egelkraut (1976: 124 nn. 1–2) mentions a few stylistic differences:

1. Luke uses present ἅπτηται (might touch) instead of Mark's aorist ἅψηται (might touch).
2. Luke has ἰδόντες (seeing) in 18:15.
3. Luke uses προσεκαλέσατο . . . λέγων (he called to . . . saying); Matthew and Mark use εἶπεν (he said) to depict Jesus' instruction to the disciples.
4. Luke (and Matthew) uses καί (and) in 18:16 to join the imperatives; Mark's imperatives are asyndetic.
5. Luke omits Mark's notes about Jesus' emotion: his indignation at the disciples' attitude (Mark 10:14) and his tender reception of the children (Mark 10:16) (Plummer 1896: 421; Klostermann 1929: 181). (Mark 10:16 is also lacking in Matthew, though a similar saying occurs in Matt. 18:3–4.)

1. The Gospel of Thomas 22 expands on the theme here by including the Gnostic doctrine of the "primordial unit" (Fitzmyer 1985: 1192).
2. Ernst 1977: 498 notes that other Lucan pericopes with ties to Mark 10–11 appear mostly outside of Luke 9:50–18:14. In this larger section, only Luke 16:18 has a potential parallel with Mark 10:11–12.

6. Luke alone uses βρέφος (18:15) to note that the children are fairly young. His use of the broader παιδίον (child) in 18:16 (matching Matthew and Mark) indicates a child of at least toddler age.

In Mark, the saying appears in a series of discussions about various relationships and wealth, a setting somewhat distinct from Luke's emphasis on the disciple's attitude (Mark 10:1–12 [Mark 10:11–12 = Luke 16:18]; Mark 10:13–16 = Luke 18:15–17; Mark 10:17–31 = Luke 18:18–30; Marshall 1978: 681). Fitzmyer (1985: 1191) sees a new section here because of the return to traditional materials, but Jesus has not yet arrived in Jerusalem and so in the Lucan framework he is still journeying and teaching his disciples as he goes (correctly Creed 1930: 225; incorrectly Klostermann 1929: 181). A shift in sources does not provide adequate basis for a literary break.

The Jesus Seminar rates 18:16 as a paraphrase of Jesus' teaching (pink type) and 18:17 as Luke's reworking (gray type), arguing that it assumes a baptism that Jesus did not practice (Funk and Hoover 1993: 370). The seminar regards the source as Mark 10:13–16, which is possible, but there is no good reason to reject Luke 18:17 (Schneider 1977a: 368). The seminar apparently reads baptism into the remark about "receiving the kingdom," but it could simply mean "responding to the kingdom message" (Nolland 1993a: 881–82), which would make it like 9:2, 5 and 10:11. The saying cluster is authentic, especially since it reverses expected cultural views on children and paints the disciples in a negative light.[3]

The form of the account is a pronouncement (Fitzmyer 1985: 1192; Bultmann 1963: 32; Berger 1984: 81). The outline of Luke 18:15–17 is as follows:

a. The disciples attempt to block children from touching Jesus (18:15)
b. Jesus allows the children to come (18:16)
c. Jesus compares reception of the kingdom to a child's attitude (18:17)

Jesus rebukes the disciples for stopping children from coming to him, stating that the kingdom is open to children and comparing a child's trust to that of someone who receives the kingdom.

---

3. There is no need to regard the story as a creation based on 2 Kings 4:27, but so Bultmann 1963: 32, who also cites a rabbinic story from the later b. Ketub. 63a, where disciples try to dissuade Akiva from seeing his mother. This approach is rightly rejected by Fitzmyer 1985: 1192 and Marshall 1978: 681–82.

Exegesis and Exposition

¹⁵And now they were bringing even infants to him, so that he might touch them. And when the disciples saw it, they rebuked them. ¹⁶Jesus called to them, saying, "Permit the children to come to me and do not hinder them, for to such as these is the kingdom of God. ¹⁷Truly I say to you, whoever does not receive the kingdom of God like a child cannot come into it."

a. The Disciples Attempt to Block Children from Touching Jesus (18:15)

Luke gives the setting briefly: people were bringing infants or young **18:15** children so that Jesus might touch them.[4] Βρέφος (brephos, little ones), here used only by Luke, is more specific than παιδίον (paidion, child). In Luke 2:12, 16; Acts 7:19; and 1 Pet. 2:2, βρέφος refers to young babies, although in 2 Tim. 3:15 it refers to children old enough to have the Scripture read intelligibly to them (BAGD 147 §2; BAA 294). Fitzmyer (1985: 1193) complains that the term is inaccurate because a child with a capacity for consciousness needs to be present for Jesus' remark in Luke 18:17 to work (also Creed 1930: 225). This point is correct, but the use of βρέφος in 2 Tim. 3:15 shows that the term can include early childhood beyond the toddler stage.

The desire to have Jesus touch (subjunctive ἅπτηται, haptētai; BDF §369.1) the children is a plea that he offer a blessing for them (Luke 6:19; 5:13; Gen. 48:14–15). In Judaism, such blessing was given by elders or scribes on the eve of the Day of Atonement (SB 2:138; 1:807–8; Marshall 1978: 682).

The disciples thought that the action was inappropriate, so they rebuked, or attempted to rebuke, those making the effort to see Jesus.[5] It is not indicated whether they made physical efforts or verbal remarks to stop them. Nonetheless, they thought that Jesus did not need to be bothered with such trivialities. In their view, the children's presence infringed on Jesus' time. Nolland (1993a: 881) suggests that their motive was their exaggerated sense of self-importance.

The verse is conceptually parallel to Mark 10:13 = Matt. 19:13, though the syntax is slightly different. The construction is closer to Mark than Matthew in that Mark and Luke share the verbal form

4. On the impersonal use of the third-person plural, see Fitzmyer 1985: 1193 and Zerwick 1963: §1. The imperfect in this context vividly portrays ongoing action by many: "They were bringing."

5. Ἐπιτιμάω here means to verbally censure; BAGD 303; BAA 614; also Luke 4:39; 8:24; 9:21, 42, 55; 17:3; 19:39; 23:40. Given Jesus' response, the effort to rebuke fails and the verb could be conative in force: "They tried to rebuke." Luke has an imperfect where Mark and Matthew have aorists.

προσέφερον (*prosepheron*, were bringing) where Matthew has προσηνέχθησαν (*prosēnechthēsan*, were brought). Luke alone alludes to the disciples' "seeing" before rebuking. His use of the present subjunctive in 18:15a and of the imperfect in 18:15b is unique.

b. Jesus Allows the Children to Come (18:16)

18:16 Jesus tells the disciples to permit (ἀφίημι, *aphiēmi*; BAGD 126 §4; BAA 253 §4; also Luke 8:51; 9:60; 12:39) the children to come to him, and he then reinforces the command in a reversed form, telling the disciples not to hinder (κωλύω, *kōlyō*; BAGD 461; BAA 936; also Luke 9:49; 11:52) the children's approach.[6] Jesus does not bar anyone from access to himself. Every person is significant in his eyes, even little children and infants.

Jesus explains his reasoning and thereby transforms the event into a picture of discipleship. He says that the kingdom of God is made up of people such as these children. Two things happen in this statement. First, he declares the value of children as worthy kingdom candidates.[7] While the acceptance of children's spiritual responses is not the passage's explicit intent (these children are brought; they do not come on their own), nonetheless, Jesus' willingness to receive them suggests his acceptance of them and carries with it implications for children who do show trust and responsiveness to God. The use of τοιούτων (*toioutōn*, such as these) makes the second point: these children are representative and picture something very basic about kingdom members, namely, childlike trust and reliance (18:17). Just as a little child depends on its parents, so God's children depend on their Father.

The verse is parallel in wording to Mark 10:14 = Matt. 19:14. Mark alone mentions that Jesus was indignant at the disciples' attitude; Luke and Matthew rarely criticize the disciples directly. Luke uses the middle voice προσεκαλέσατο (*prosekalesato*) to intensify Jesus' command slightly: "He himself commanded" (also Matt. 18:2). Luke and Matthew link the two commands with καί (*kai*, and), which ap-

---

6. Καί (and) suggests that both commands are given to the disciples, not that the first is to the parents and the second to the disciples. Jesus removes the obstacles to the children's approach.

7. This pericope contains no allusion to infant baptism (Marshall 1978: 682; Schweizer 1984: 285; Tiede 1988: 309–10; and Fitzmyer 1985: 1193 correctly challenge Jeremias 1960: 54; Cullmann 1950: 76–78; and Grundmann 1963: 353), though by implication a child's spiritual responses should be encouraged and accepted. Jeremias notes the use of κωλύω in baptismal settings (Matt. 3:14; Acts 8:36; 10:47; 11:17), but in Luke 18, the point is blessing, not baptism (against the Jesus Seminar [Funk and Hoover 1993: 370], who import a baptismal sense here; see the discussion of sources and historicity above).

pears to be a mere stylistic touch. All three writers call the children παιδίον (*paidion*).[8] The phrase *come to me* is placed in Mark and Luke with the command of permission, while Matthew has it with the call not to hinder the children's coming.[9] Such differences put the Lucan version closer to Mark, though all three accounts are very similar.

c. Jesus Compares Reception of the Kingdom to a Child's Attitude (18:17)

Jesus concludes with an application that uses the children as a pic- **18:17** ture for welcoming the kingdom.[10] The point of comparison is a child's dependent trust (7:32; 9:47–48). It may well be that the background is Ps. 131:2, where the soul is compared to a child being weaned from its mother. Without such dependent faith, one cannot enter the kingdom. The kingdom is seen here as something that Jesus' current teaching offers for reception, though the extension of some of its blessings is probably seen as future. Marshall (1978: 683) sees 18:17b about entering the kingdom as future, while others see the blessings as present (V. Taylor 1966: 423–24). Since Lucan usage of the phrase *entry into the kingdom* is ambiguous, it is best to see a broad summary reference to all periods associated with the kingdom (Fitzmyer 1985: 1194, 1160–62).[11] One enters the kingdom and qualifies for all of its blessings. Much of the Jewish response in this journey section is the opposite of what Jesus proclaims here.

Mark 10:15 matches Luke's wording exactly. A variation of this saying appears in Matt. 18:3, where repentance and faith are placed side by side. Matthew speaks of turning and becoming like children in order to enter the kingdom of heaven. Though his setting is distinct, the idea parallels the one expressed here.

---

8. Lachs 1987: 328 argues that the alternation of βρέφος and παιδίον may be behind it a Semitic term that includes both age groups.

9. Matthew has the aorist active ἐλθεῖν (to come), while Luke and Mark have the present middle ἔρχεσθαι (to come). Perhaps Matthew intends the phrase to relate to both commands, as the use of καί could suggest, and so places it after the second command.

10. So δέχομαι (BAGD 177 §1, §3b; BAA 355 §3b) indicates receiving the word of God by Moses (Acts 7:38), the gospel (2 Cor. 11:4), financial gifts (Phil. 4:18), a guest in the home (Matt. 10:14 = Luke 9:5; 16:4), teaching (Luke 8:13; Acts 8:14; 11:1), the kingdom (Mark 10:15), and grace (2 Cor. 6:1). One can speak of receiving Jesus by appealing to John 1:12; the other biblical metaphor is to receive the kingdom. To accept the king is to enter the kingdom and its promises.

11. Luke 17:20–37 (esp. 17:20–21) has both senses. Note the ambiguity in 18:24–25. Luke 23:42 looks at immediate entry, though it is in the context of death as opposed to entering the kingdom in life. Acts 14:22 speaks of future entry. Another immediate instance is John 3:5. Fitzmyer notes that though the expression in 18:17 is rare, it fits with the invitation of 17:21.

Summary   Luke 18:15–17 is one of the Bible's most cherished accounts. It is frequently taught to children, and rightfully so. That Jesus receives children and takes time to bless them in the midst of a pressure-packed ministry is touching and reveals much about his concern for individual people (just as his attention to the poor and outcast shows his concern for other neglected groups). People of any size count. He was not too busy for children, though the disciples thought he was. His attitude reminds the disciples that their mission is not only to the powerful, but also to the dependent. Jesus' acceptance of the children shows God's willingness to accept people like us as his children.

    The children also picture something else: children of the kingdom are accepted before their God and Father because of what their attitude shows. The simple, dependent attitude of little children is a picture of the disciple's attitude in walking with God. Such simple trust is a prerequisite for entry into the benefits of God's rule. In the kingdom and in one's walk, to be a child at heart is a good thing.

3. Jesus' Discussion with a Rich Ruler and the Disciples (18:18–30)

Luke's account of the rich ruler contains a pivotal exchange. This is a difficult unit because Jesus' demand that the ruler sell all and follow him is such a strong request. But the ruler's response is key to the passage. The placement of 18:18–30 in the movement of Luke's Gospel stresses the importance of dependent faith. Here is an example of someone who fails. The event reinforces many concepts taught in Luke 18: the rich ruler's confident, self-righteous attitude stands in contrast to the begging, dependent blind man of 18:35–43 (it is the blind man who receives mercy); the rich ruler's attitude parallels the Pharisee's confidence, in contrast to the tax collector in 18:9–14 (it is the tax collector who receives Jesus' commendation); and the rich ruler's attitude contrasts to the dependent, trusting faith found in the picture of the children in 18:15–17 (it is the children who are openly welcomed by Jesus). Self-focused confidence is often condemned in Luke (16:14–15; 18:9–14). A contrasting, positive example of the proper response of a rich person will follow in the Zacchaeus account (19:1–10).

In a crucial contrast to the rich ruler, the disciples are used as a counterexample to show that Jesus' request is possible. In Jesus' explanation to the disciples about his exchange with the rich ruler, he notes that they have given what the rich ruler was asked to give. But such giving is not just required of disciples. Jesus himself will give all for them, as the prediction of the next passage (18:31–34) makes clear (Ellis 1974: 217). Finally, the focus on wealth is a common topic for Luke (6:24; 8:14; 11:41; 12:13–34; 16:1–31). As such, this unit summarizes many fundamental points of Luke's presentation of Jesus' teaching.

Sources and Historicity

The account is found in the triple tradition: Luke 18:18–30 = Matt. 19:16–30 = Mark 10:17–31 (Aland 1985: §§254–55). In each account, this exchange follows the discussion over children, which shows that the same event is present. The Lucan account is largely parallel to Mark, though Matthew is not very different. Nonetheless, small differences suggest that Matthew has additional information (Fitzmyer 1985: 1196; see the exegesis for details).

The Jesus Seminar sees this account as only loosely connected to Jesus, printing 18:24–25 in pink type; 18:19–20, 22, 29–30 in gray; and 18:27 in black (Funk and Hoover 1993: 370–71). The seminar rejects the exchange with the rich man and the final remarks of 18:29–30 on the basis of two premises: (1) that Jesus did not teach about heavenly rewards for earthly sacrifice and (2) that he did not actively recruit disciples. The latter theme is, however, multiply attested: the calling of the first disciples (5:1–11), the forming of the Twelve (6:12–16), and the exchange with prospective disciples (9:57–62). (See the discussions of sources and historicity for these units.) The remark about heavenly reward looks like an attempt to deeschatologize Jesus (see my defense of the authenticity of 9:23–27). The Jesus Seminar's recognition of the authenticity of Jesus' challenge about wealth, with its graphic camel-needle image, indicates that the base event is very much like Jesus' teaching elsewhere. The seminar's rejection of 18:27 is grounded in the claim that it softens 18:24–25 and thus comes from the Christian community. But such affirmation of God's power to change people is at the heart of all prophetic declaration. God can solve what we alone cannot (Nolland 1993a: 890; see the exegesis of 1:37 for this OT theme). It is standard prophetic fare to appeal to the ultimate justice of God's ways and the great reversal that comes from his power. The themes of the age to come and eternal life recall several other texts of Jesus' teaching, indicating that they are multiply attested (10:25; 13:30; 16:8b; 20:34–35; Nolland 1993a: 892). An eschatology where God vindicates his own and receives them forever is at the heart of Jesus' teaching (E. Sanders 1993: 183–84, who notes that a deeschatologized Jesus is purely "the triumph of wishful thinking").

The account carries many descriptions. It is technically a pronouncement story (Fitzmyer 1985: 1197; Bultmann 1963: 21–22; Berger 1984: 81), which means that the significance of the unit is found in the sayings that emerge from it. In other words, theological dialogue produces theological teaching. Talbert (1982: 172) calls it a "recognition story" since the rich ruler learns something about himself as he talks with Jesus. Tannehill (1986: 111–27, esp. 120–23) calls it a "quest story" since the ruler is in search of something—eternal life (18:18, 30)—and wants to know how to attain it.[1] All of these descriptions reflect emphases found in the story. The passage has two parts: the exchange with the young ruler (18:18–23) and the comment on the exchange (18:24–30).

---

1. Tannehill notes seven quest stories in Luke, this being the only one with a negative result: 5:17–26; 7:1–10; 7:36–50; 17:11–19; 19:1–10; 23:39–43 (I question the presence of a quest story in 7:36–50).

The outline of Luke 18:18–30 is as follows:

a. The rich ruler and Jesus (18:18–23)
   i. The rich ruler's question about eternal life (18:18)
   ii. Jesus' reply about commandments (18:19–20)
   iii. The rich ruler's confident reply (18:21)
   iv. Jesus' call to give all to the poor and follow him (18:22)
   v. The rich ruler's sadness (18:23)
b. Discussion about the rich ruler's response (18:24–30)
   i. Entry is difficult for the rich (18:24–25)
   ii. Who can be saved? (18:26)
   iii. God makes salvation possible (18:27)
   iv. Peter notes that disciples have left all (18:28)
   v. Jesus promises rewards now and in the next life
    (18:29–30)

The passage stresses God's unique goodness to those who respond to him. Blessing comes from obedience, while self-directed confidence is rebuked. To obey Jesus is to give first place to him. It can be difficult for a rich person to respond to Jesus. On the other hand, God makes such a difficult conversion possible. To give up all for the kingdom is to receive much—both in this life and in the life to come.

Exegesis and Exposition

[18]And a certain ruler asked him, "Good teacher, what must I do to inherit eternal life?" [19]But Jesus said to him, "Why do you call me good; no one is good except God. [20]You know the commandments: do not commit adultery, do not murder, do not steal, do not give false witness, honor your father and your mother." [21]But he said, "I have guarded all these since childhood." [22]And when Jesus heard this, he said to him, "There is still one thing lacking: sell all you have and give to the poor and you shall receive treasure in ⌐heaven⌐; and come, follow me." [23]But when he heard these things, he became sad, for he was very rich.

[24]And when Jesus saw that he ⌐became sad⌐, he said, "How difficult it is for a man who has possessions to come into the kingdom of God. [25]For it is easier for a camel to go through the eye of a needle than for a rich man to come into the kingdom of God." [26]And those who heard said, "Then who can be saved?" [27]And he said, "Things that are impossible for man are possible for God." [28]Peter began to say to him, "Behold, having left our own things, we have followed you." [29]But he said to them, "Truly I say to you, there is no one who has left house or wife or siblings or parents or children for the sake of the kingdom of God [30]who shall not receive ⌐more⌐ in this time, and in the age to come eternal life."

a. The Rich Ruler and Jesus (18:18–23)
i. The Rich Ruler's Question about Eternal Life (18:18)

18:18 The discussion starts with a simple question by a ruler. Luke alone tells us that the man is a ruler (ἄρχων, *archōn*; BAGD 113–14; BAA 227–28). Luke's use of ἄρχων is important, for he often uses this term to describe rulers of the Pharisees, a group he sees negatively (T. Schmidt 1987: 158). Luke refers to such rulers six times in his Gospel (8:41; 14:1; 23:13, 35; 24:20) and eleven times in Acts, often as part of the leadership that stands opposed to Jesus (Egelkraut 1976: 124 n. 4).[2] This man is probably not a synagogue ruler, who would be an older man, since Matt. 19:20, 22 tells us that he is young (against Grundmann 1963: 354 [a ruler or member of the Sanhedrin] and Ellis 1974: 217, with Plummer 1896: 422). He is probably an influential wealthy man or civic leader who may have been known for his piety.[3] If so, Jesus is confronted not by a religious leader but by one of the leading men of society, a respected layperson.

The ruler addresses Jesus as a good (ἀγαθέ, *agathe*) teacher, a description used in Judaism of a good person (Marshall 1978: 684; Fitzmyer 1985: 1198; SB 2:24; Prov. 12:2; 14:14; T. Sim. 4.4; T. Dan 1.4; T. Asher 4.1; *b. Taʿan.* 24b; Matt. 12:35 = Luke 6:45; 1:6–7). Jesus' rejection of the title in the next verse has more to do with the motive with which it was offered than that it was said, since it appears that the ruler was trying to flatter Jesus.

The question matches almost word for word the lawyer's question in 10:25 (the only difference is the addition of ἀγαθέ to describe the teacher). The ruler is asking, "How can I be sure I'll be saved in the final resurrection?" This is a basic soteriological question not referring to reward for service but to the eternal life that comes from being God's child. This is clear from the context: 18:17 discusses entry into the kingdom and 18:28–30 makes the point that basic spiritual benefits come in this life and the next. There is nothing for those who are rich to themselves but not toward God (12:13–21). The expression *to inherit life* is rich in Jewish background (Ps. 36:9, 11, 18 LXX [37:9, 11, 18 Engl.]; Dan. 12:2; 1QS 4.7; CD 3.20; 4Q181 1.4; 2 Macc. 7:9; 4 Macc. 15:3; 1 Enoch 37.4; 40.9; 58.3; Ps. Sol. 3.12; Fitzmyer 1985: 1198–99; Bultmann, *TDNT* 2:856–57).

---

2. Ἄρχων can apply to leaders of the spirit world (11:15), leaders of the synagogue (8:41), leaders of the Pharisees (14:1), or secular magistrates (12:58). In 8:41 the ruler is not in opposition to Jesus (but see 14:1; 23:13, 35; 24:20). Other negative uses of ἄρχων are found in the collective references to rulers in the speeches of Acts 3:17; 4:5, 8, 26; 13:27; 14:5. Acts 16:19 and 23:5 are more neutral.

3. Tiede 1988: 310 notes the options: a synagogue official, leader of the Pharisees, magistrate, or official of the high priest. The last two options are more likely here. If he had been a religious leader, Luke likely would have been more specific.

There are a few, mostly stylistic, differences among the Synoptic parallels. For example, Matthew ties ἀγαθόν (*agathon*, good) to the verb ποιήσω (*poiēsō*, shall I do): "What good must I do that I might have eternal life?" This changes the focus slightly, emphasizing the earning of the blessing and omitting the description of Jesus as good. The question still receives a rebuke from Jesus (which is also expressed differently). This is one of the points where only Matthew uses additional detail to describe the account. This is also suggested by later verses where Mark and Luke condense Matthew's give and take into a single reply by Jesus. Either Luke and Mark select only certain details or Matthew adds information. Mark 10:17 alone tells us that the man knelt while asking the question, as well as that the event occurred in the midst of a journey. That Luke lacks the journey note is curious, since he likes such notes.[4]

ii. Jesus' Reply about Commandments (18:19–20)

Jesus begins by dealing with the ruler's address of him as "good." **18:19** Jesus' rejection of this ascription has caused no lack of comment in the interpretive tradition (Fitzmyer 1985: 1199). What does his rejection mean?

1. Jesus purposefully declares his sinfulness (Volkmar 1870: 489), a view fully refuted by Warfield (1914). If this had been Jesus' intent, the church would not have declared him sinless, since this remark would explicitly deny such a claim (2 Cor. 5:21; Heb. 4:15).
2. Jesus presses the implications of such a remark, in effect saying, "Realize that if you call me good, you are calling me God" (Ambrose, *De Fide* 2.1; Geldenhuys 1951: 458; also Basil, Cyril, and Jerome). If this was Jesus' intention, it is certainly a veiled proclamation. In fact, Jesus saw his role as pointing people to God through him, rather than drawing exclusive attention to himself. There are more probable explanations than that it is a subtle rebuke.
3. Jesus rejects the ruler's attempt at flattery (Danker 1988: 299; Arndt 1956: 383 [who also holds view 2]). This is partially correct in that Jesus does intend to shock the ruler into considering his words.
4. Jesus wants the ruler to focus on God and his will so that he will be genuinely responsive to God (Fitzmyer 1985: 1199; Warfield 1914: 211 [repr. p. 139]). This explanation is the most

---

4. Matthean priorists hold that this detail indicates that Mark is following Luke, not the other way around.

contextually satisfying, since 18:20 goes on to cite God's commandments. If the ruler desires to truly follow God, then he should respond to the one who brings his teaching. The point is to shock the ruler. He has attempted to honor Jesus, but he needs to recognize that "good" is a relative term except when applied to God. If the teacher is good, then one should follow the teacher's instruction. Also, being good is not sufficient for attaining eternal life, God must supply it. Flattering God's teacher does not bring commendation; response to God does.

Jesus' statement that God alone is good is designed to describe God's unique holiness and righteousness. Such declarations are common in the OT, and Jesus is here asserting God's absolute goodness in the face of requests to earn eternal life.[5] Taken together, the remarks serve to say, if you really want to follow the "good one," follow God and show your respect for his teacher by obeying his instruction because before God no one is inherently good.

Mark 10:18 agrees with Luke, but in a slightly different word order (Luke begins with εἶπεν αὐτῷ [eipen autō, he said to him], which follows the mention of the subject [ὁ Ἰησοῦς, Jesus] in Mark). A bigger difference is found in Matt. 19:17, where the ruler's question produces a question from Jesus about why the ruler asks about doing good. The impression Jesus gives of shying away from being called good is stated less directly by Matthew, where Jesus says that only one is good. The absence of outright denial by Jesus is understandable with the christological questions it raises about Jesus' sinlessness, and avoiding such questions is a likely motive for the change. But the additional suggestion that Matthew rephrased the question more neutrally is less likely, because the easiest way to have dealt with the omission would have been to omit the mention of "good" altogether. In fact, the Matthean wording, whether a paraphrase of additional conversation or a reflection of additional information, does reflect the force of the ruler's question, since the ruler wants to know what he can do to merit God's favor.

18:20 Jesus' response focuses on righteousness, since that is the issue the question raises. The ruler has asked what he can do to be saved, and Jesus' reply takes up the issue directly. Jesus responds with the law, which for current Judaism reflected God's will (Deut. 27:26). If one is going to earn eternal life, then acts of righteousness are required.

---

5. 1 Chron. 16:34; 2 Chron. 5:13; Ps. 34:8 [34:9 MT]; 106:1; 118:1, 29; 136:1; Nah. 1:7; *m. ʾAbot* 6.3 (God and his teaching). Plummer 1896: 422 argues that a rabbi is never called good in Judaism, but this is wrong; see *b. Ber.* 5a; *b. Taʿan.* 24b; Lachs 1987: 331 nn. 2–3.

Jesus gives the ruler nothing but the basics (Luce 1933: 285–86). It is interesting that the ruler's social position is not addressed in Jesus' response, since wealth need not mean blessing (Luke 18:24 indicates that wealth may actually obstruct one from perceiving oneself correctly). Deuteronomy 30:15–20 makes a nice commentary on Jesus' reply (Danker 1988: 300). Jesus says that the ruler knows the commandments, in effect calling him to obey those commandments (Marshall 1978: 684–85). Jesus then cites commandments 7, 6, 8, 9, and 5 from the Decalogue (Exod. 20:12–16 [= NJPSV 20:12–13]; Deut. 5:16–20 [5:16–17 MT]).[6]

Many consider it curious that Jesus replies only in terms of commands related to people. But Jesus' reply is profound and ethically significant. How one treats others is something concrete that can be measured, and so the focus is on acts of faithfulness to others. The spirit of the reply fits Luke 10:26–27 (as well as Lev. 19:18). But another factor may explain this focus. In Luke the rich are often warned of the danger of self-focus that can come from wealth, so appeal to this command would reinforce the ruler's need to keep an outward focus (Luke 12:13–21; 16:19–31). Later NT works make clear that to understand God's righteous demands means to be prepared to ask for God's grace and not attempt to earn salvation (e.g., Rom. 3:21–31; also Luke 18:9–17). People will treat others well when they rightly assess themselves before God (10:27). Out of one's experience of God's love and grace one can then love and serve others.

The comparison of the Synoptic parallels may suggest that this was a popular story that circulated, with some variety of detail. Matthew and Mark agree in the order of the first four commands: 6, 7, 8, 9. But at this point, Mark 10:19 speaks of not defrauding, an allusion to the tenth commandment about not coveting. Both accounts end with the fifth command about honoring one's parents, but Matt. 19:18 adds a concluding summary call from Lev. 19:18 to love one's neighbor. In summary, Mark has commandments 6, 7, 8, 9, 10, 5; Matthew has 6, 7, 8, 9, 5, and Lev. 19:18; while Luke has 7, 6, 8, 9, 5 (Marshall 1978: 685; Plummer 1896: 423; Fitzmyer 1985: 1199).[7] It seems clear that the Decalogue was cited with some variety in the various traditions (Gundry 1967: 17–19). One other difference is that Mark and Luke use the aorist subjunctive with μή (*mē*, not),

---

6. Lev. 19:3 supplies a third OT reference to honoring mother and father. For prophetic reaction to violation of the commandments, see Hos. 4:2–6.

7. The order of commandments in Matthew and Mark follows the MT and manuscript A of the LXX. Luke's order finds ancient precedent in Philo, *On the Decalogue* 12 §51; manuscript B of Deut. 5 LXX; as well as NT parallels in Rom. 13:9 and James 2:11; Nolland 1993a: 886.

while Matthew uses οὐ (*ou*, not) with the future indicative, which follows the LXX wording in both versions of the Decalogue.

iii. The Rich Ruler's Confident Reply (18:21)

18:21   The ruler is confident about how he rates on this standard. He declares that he has obeyed the law since his youth.[8] Νεότης (*neotēs*) refers to a young man of religious and legal maturity, which in this culture would mean from his early teen years.[9] The confidence expressed here is not atypical of some in Judaism (SB 1:814; *b. Sanh.* 101a; Phil. 3:6). The ruler is saying in effect, "If this is all that is required, then I am in good shape."

Matthew 19:20 lacks a reference to the ruler's youth as the temporal framework of his obedience, but is alone in telling us that the man is young. Perhaps Matthew is suggesting that the reply is a part of youthful carelessness. But Matthew's account is fuller, for he alone notes that the ruler asked an additional question about what was still lacking. This suggests that the ruler is disappointed with Jesus' reply and wants to know if that is all there is to his answer. In contrast, Mark 10:21 = Luke 18:22 note how Jesus initiates the idea that the ruler still lacks something. This difference may well be the result of their telescoping the conversation. Mark 10:20 alone has the ruler addressing Jesus as teacher. All three writers use a different verbal form to introduce the reply: Matthew has λέγει (*legei*, he said—a vivid present tense translated as past tense), Mark has ἔφη (*ephē*, he said), and Luke has εἶπεν (*eipen*, he said).

iv. Jesus' Call to Give All to the Poor and Follow Him (18:22)

18:22   Jesus notes the reply and responds with an additional demand, since something is still lacking (λείπω, *leipō*; BAGD 470 §2; BAA 955 §2; Titus 3:13). Luke presents the response in its most simplified form without any detail. Mark 10:21 says that the ruler still lacks one thing and notes that Jesus loves him, while in Matt. 19:20 the ruler asks what he still lacks and Jesus replies in terms of being "complete" or "mature" (τέλειος, *teleios*), a description unique to Matthew that means a "completely righteous" person who keeps all the commandments (Lachs 1987: 331, *b. Ber.* 7b, 61b; *b. Giṭ.* 68b).

---

8. Normally meaning "to guard" (BAGD 868 §1f; BAA 1731 §1f), φυλάσσω here means to keep or obey the law; Lev. 20:22; 26:3; Ps. 119:5 [118:5 LXX]; Wis. 6:4; Sir. 21:11; 4 Macc. 5:29; T. Judah 26.1; T. Iss. 5.1; Luke 11:28.

9. BAGD 536; BAA 1085; *m. Nid.* 5.6; *m. Meg.* 4.6; *m. ʾAbot* 5.21; Luke 2:42 (a conceptual example of Jesus at twelve); Acts 26:4; 1 Tim. 4:2; also Gen. 48:15; Num. 22:30; Isa. 47:15; 54:6; Jer. 3:25; Josephus, *Jewish War* 4.1.5 §33. See the exegesis of Luke 2:42.

The reply contains two aorist imperatives (BDF §335, §337): sell all that he has and distribute the proceeds to the poor. The accounts agree, with only slight variations. Mark 10:21 says "go, whatever you have, sell," an idea similar to Luke's. Matthew 19:21 has "go, sell your possessions," a generalized remark that does not specify how much is to be sold. Luke alone uses the verb διαδίδωμι (*diadidōmi*, to distribute; BAGD 182; BAA 366; elsewhere used by Luke in Luke 11:22 and Acts 4:35), while Mark and Matthew have the simple δίδωμι (*didōmi*, to give). Despite this variation, the force is clear: the ruler was to divest himself of his assets so that he could benefit the poor, who are the special objects of Jesus' concern. To care for them is evidence of sharing God's care.

In recording Jesus' promise and final command, the accounts agree, with only one small variation: Matthew has ἐν οὐρανοῖς (*en ouranois*, in heavens), Mark ἐν οὐρανῷ (*en ouranō*, in heaven), and Luke probably ἐν τοῖς οὐρανοῖς (*en tois ouranois*, in the heavens) (see the additional note on the textual problem in Luke).

Jesus offers the promise of treasures in heaven, which may refer singly to eternal life (Plummer 1896: 424) or also something more (Fitzmyer 1985: 1200). The first view can claim support from the near context: "eternal life" (18:18, 30), "enter the kingdom" (18:24–25), and "saved" (18:26), not to mention the image of the nonrotting inheritance in 1 Pet. 1:3–9. Other Lucan texts suggest, however, that more than eternal life is meant: 6:35; 14:14; 16:10–11; 19:11–27 (esp. 19:15–19, 26); and especially 12:33–34 (= Matt. 6:19–21). The question is decided by Jesus' description of the treasure received for obeying his call to leave all (Luke 18:29–30). This treasure is the fullness of blessing associated with eternal life and comes in this age and the next. The treasure contains the "gifts" that accompany eternal life (view 2 above). This expanded view of heaven is close to the idea of eternal life expressed in John 17:3 and reveals another Lucan example of present/future eschatological tension.

Jesus offers this hope and tells the ruler to enter into discipleship with him. "To follow" was common earlier in Luke (of individuals in 5:11, 27–28; 9:23, 57, 59, 61; 14:27; also 18:28; of crowds in 7:9 and 9:11). The ruler is told to come and sit under Jesus' teaching and live in the way that he shows. The spirit of the command is like *Joseph and Asenath* 13.2: "I left behind all good things of the earth and fled to you, Lord" (Nolland 1993a: 891). Why did Jesus give this ruler such a radical command?

1. The selling of all is a direct answer to the question of what to do to gain eternal life. This cannot be correct, for such an idea implies that one can earn salvation, which runs counter to

Luke's presentation of humility and dependence (e.g., of the tax collector, the children, or the blind beggar of Jericho). More decisive is the example of Zacchaeus in 19:8, who does not sell all, but is generous with the poor. Jesus says that Zacchaeus is saved, so clearly selling all is not the point. If this is not a call for all people to sell all, then the command to sell all and follow Jesus must involve something basic that the ruler needs to sort out before he can truly know God. Jesus' request is radical by Jewish standards. In later Judaism, a man was warned not to sell more than twenty percent of his goods, lest he risk becoming a burden on others (Lachs 1987: 331; *b. Ketub.* 50a).

2. The selling of all was designed to expose the ruler's failure to keep the law (Arndt 1956: 384). More specifically Ellis (1974: 218) argues that it showed the ruler's covetousness. But the text gives no indication that he desired what others had. Talbert (1982: 172) argues that the ruler suffered from idolatry since he loved money more than God. This view is possible, for within the Lucan framework this pericope could be a warning text like 12:13–21. This view also has support from the NT Letters, where greed is tied to idolatry (Col. 3:5; Eph. 5:3). This point, however, is not explicitly made in the text, but only implied by Jesus' remark in Luke 18:25 that it is difficult for a rich person to enter into the kingdom.

3. The ruler's ability to let go of his money is a prerequisite for being ready to be saved, because he claims to care for fellow humans in obeying the commandments but is not actively doing so (Godet 1875: 2.208). Jesus' request is designed to turn him into someone who actively cares for others. If he disobeys, he shows that he really does not follow the spirit of the Decalogue he has just claimed to obey. While this view is possible, it is not developed in the explanation that follows in 18:24–30.

4. The selling of all is intended to force the ruler to trust God and humbly rely on him. This view is expressed in a couple of ways: the call to trust Jesus emphasizes the call to discipleship (Hendriksen 1975: 396), or the call is to absolute allegiance to God (Carson 1984: 424). In either case, the fundamental issue is reliance on God through Jesus' teaching, as seen in this story's being located in a larger section that stresses humility and reliance before God (e.g., the tax collector, children, and blind beggar). Zacchaeus's response in 19:1–10 shows not only a willingness to heed the call to be generous but also the explicit contrast with the disciples in 18:25–30, the Pharisee in 18:9–14, and the ruler in this unit.

The importance lies in the disciples' primary commitment—to God and the path on which he calls them to walk. This path differs from person to person in particulars, but one element remains the same: God is to be trusted and to have first place (Matt. 6:24 = Luke 16:13). Jesus' radical requirement is a particularly graphic way to bring the point home to this ruler. He has wrongly placed his security in his wealth, and perhaps he believes that his status is an indication of divine blessing and approval.

The ruler does not discuss Jesus' command, which shows where his true heart lies. He is not ready to come to God on God's terms. However good a teacher the ruler claims Jesus to be, his reaction shows that Jesus is not good enough to change his fundamental allegiance. At the heart of Jesus' request is a call to trust God humbly and live in reliance on God, that is, to live in light of his promise. The ruler must follow Jesus, or as 18:29 puts it "leave home and family for the sake of the kingdom of God." The demand is too much for this ruler, a point that will lead to Jesus' reflection on the ruler's actions (18:24–30).

v. The Rich Ruler's Sadness (18:23)

The ruler's response is told with tragic brevity: when he heard these **18:23** things from Jesus, he became very sad. The commands to sell all, distribute the proceeds to the poor, and come and follow Jesus have no appeal to the ruler. The temporal circumstantial participle ἀκού-σας (akousas, when he heard) gives the reaction's timing: Jesus' response falls on functioning ears but a deaf heart. Περίλυπος (perily-pos), used only by Luke here, expresses the ruler's sadness and could be translated "very grieved" (BAGD 648; BAA 1307; Bultmann, TDNT 4:323; Ps. 41:6 LXX [42:5 Engl.]; 42:5 LXX [43:5 Engl.]; Dan. 2:12; elsewhere in the NT only at Matt. 26:38 = Mark 14:34; 6:26). The ruler understands Jesus' instruction and chooses to reject it.

The reason (γάρ, gar) is stated just as simply: the ruler is very (σφόδρα, sphodra) wealthy (BAGD 796; BAA 1588; also Mark 16:4; Matt. 2:10). This is the first indication that the ruler is sufficiently wealthy that Jesus' request might be a major obstacle. Faced with the choice of mammon or Jesus, the ruler chooses mammon. As Peter will note a few verses later, this response is the opposite of that by Peter, John, and James (Luke 5:11), who left all to follow Jesus (Plummer 1896: 424; Fitzmyer 1985: 1200). What the rich ruler fails to do, they have done.

Luke relates this verse more briefly than his Synoptic counterparts. Mark 10:22 mentions that the ruler's countenance fell (στυ-γνάσας, stygnasas) when he heard this saying, a typical emotional note by Mark. Mark also tells us that the ruler then walked away and describes the ruler's wealth as "many possessions." Matthew 19:22 once again identifies the ruler as young, but lacks any mention of the falling countenance and speaks only of his hearing this saying. With Mark, Matthew speaks of the ruler's departure in sorrow, as well as his many possessions. Luke appears to have summarized the response to its most basic form. Jesus makes no effort to address the ruler again. Rather he turns to instruct his disciples. There is no indication that the rich ruler responds to Jesus. In fact, the comment in 18:24 suggests that he never does.

b. Discussion about the Rich Ruler's Response (18:24–30)
i. Entry Is Difficult for the Rich (18:24–25)

18:24 Jesus responds to the ruler's decision in two parts: he first speaks of the difficulty the rich have in coming into the kingdom (18:24–25), and then, when the disciples express concern, he mentions the reward that the faithful will receive (18:26–30). Some wonder whether these were individual sayings from different occasions (Fitzmyer 1985: 1202).[10] But there is no need to insist that Jesus only said one saying at a time or never could address more than one topic at a time. The presuppositions that break up these remarks are not compelling (correctly Marshall 1978: 686–87).

The reference to entering the kingdom is another way to speak of being saved, as the question in 18:26 makes clear. It parallels the reference to eternal life in the original question in 18:18. The expression οἱ τὰ χρήματα ἔχοντες (hoi ta chrēmata echontes, those who have possessions) agrees with Mark 10:23, in contrast to Matt. 19:23's πλούσιος (plousios, wealthy).[11] The combination πῶς δυσκόλως (pōs dyskolōs, how difficultly) describes the obstacle the rich face (BAGD 209; BAA 421; elsewhere in the NT only in the parallels to this verse: Mark 10:23 = Matt. 19:23). Why is this so difficult? Other Lucan texts suggest that the inability to trust God and be humble can come with the self-focus and greed that money can bring (Luke 6:24; 12:15, 21; 16:9). In fact, pursuit of wealth can distract from faithfulness (8:14; 12:33–34). Some see wealth as a sign of divine blessing, an attitude that could appeal to the OT in a superficial way since one's riches would be a sign of God's approval (Deut. 8:1–10; 26:1–9; 28:12–14; Prov. 6:6–11; 10:4; 28:19). The OT and Judaism actually warned not to perceive wealth as an automatic sign

10. Bultmann 1963: 75, 81, 110–11, who on form-critical grounds distinguishes wisdom sayings in 18:24b, 25, 27 from a prophetic saying in 18:29–30 and regards eternal life, the kingdom, and salvation as loosely related concepts.
11. Except for Mark 10:23, χρῆμα (BAGD 885; BAA 1765) is used in the NT only in Luke–Acts: Acts 4:37 (of Barnabas's exemplary use of wealth); 8:18, 20; 24:26.

of blessing (Prov. 28:6; 30:7–9; Jer. 5:28; Amos 8:4–8; Mic. 2:1–5; Sir. 10:22–23; Talbert 1982: 173).

The Synoptic parallels are similar, with Mark 10:23 presenting almost a verbal match. Only the verb and its tense differ: Mark has the future εἰσελεύσονται (eiseleusontai, they will enter), while Luke has the present εἰσπορεύονται (eisporeuontai, they enter). Matthew 19:23 has the same verb and tense as Mark, but (because of his different subject: πλούσιος) in a different number (εἰσελεύσεται, eiseleusetai, he will enter) and speaks, as he often does, of the kingdom of heaven, which equals, as the parallels make clear, the kingdom of God. The difference in tense causes Klostermann (1929: 181) to question whether Luke is looking at the kingdom's present form, but Luke's verb never carries the future tense in the NT and has a clearly futuristic force in Luke 22:10 (Marshall 1978: 687). If there is a difference, Luke has a timeless, gnomic idea. Luke alone tells the reader that Jesus looked at the ruler (the other accounts have already noted that the ruler walked away). Mark simply says that Jesus looked around. Mark 10:24 is alone in noting the disciples' response of shock, and only he repeats the saying about how impossible it is for the rich to enter the kingdom.

Jesus makes a comparison to describe the rich ruler's plight: it is **18:25** easier (εὔκοπος, eukopos; BAGD 321; BAA 651; Sir. 22:15; 1 Macc. 3:18; outside this story elsewhere in the NT at Matt. 9:5 = Mark 2:9 = Luke 5:23; 16:17) for a camel to go through the eye of a needle than for a rich person to come into the kingdom. The camel (κάμηλος, kamēlos; BAGD 401; BAA 815; outside this story elsewhere in the NT at Matt. 23:24; 3:4 = Mark 1:6) is the largest animal in Palestine, while the eye of a needle (βελόνη, belonē; BAGD 139; BAA 278) is one of the smallest items a person might deal with on a daily basis (Fitzmyer 1985: 1204).[12] It is not surprising that alternatives have been offered for this image: (1) the "eye of the needle" was perhaps the name of a small city gate through which a camel could barely fit; (2) many church fathers (e.g., Origen and Cyril) thought that κάμηλος would have been pronounced κάμιλος (kamilos), thus indicating a ship's cable or rope. These alternatives only blunt the rhetorical image and weaken the point to the level where shock is not an explainable response (Plummer 1896: 425; Fitzmyer 1985: 1204).

The point of the hyperbolic, seemingly silly illustration is clear: it is impossible for rich people on their own strength to gain entry

---

12. The expression is used only here in the NT. Matt. 19:24 = Mark 10:25 has ῥαφίς, which always refers to a sewing needle; BAGD 734; BAA 1470 (in the NT only in these parallels). For other exaggerations by Jesus, see Luke 6:41; 17:2; Ernst 1977: 504.

into the kingdom (Michel, *TDNT* 3:592–94).[13] And the young ruler's sadness vividly illustrates the proverb. Wealth can shrink the door of the kingdom down to an impassable peephole. The self-focused security of the wealthy is a padlock against kingdom entry. The remark is shocking to Jesus' listeners, who assume that at least some of the wealthy will be first in line to receive God's blessing (18:26). Fitzmyer (1985: 1204) notes the remark is conceptually similar to the "narrow door" of 13:24, but in fact it is stronger and does not attain a more parallel sense until combined with Jesus' response.

Each of the Synoptic writers uses a different *hapax legomenon* to indicate the hole in the needle (Fitzmyer 1985: 1205): Luke has τρῆμα (*trēma*; BAGD 826; BAA 1646); Matthew has the slightly more descriptive τρύπημα (*trypēma*; BAGD 828; BAA 1651) to indicate something that is bored (which shows that the needle is made of wood or some other substance that could be carved); Mark has τρυμαλιά (*trymalia*; BAGD 828; BAA 1651; Judg. 6:2; 15:8, 11; Jer. 13:4; 16:16). While this interesting difference does not change the image, it may indicate that this was a popular story that circulated in various forms. The rest of the verse is similar in all three accounts, except for a few stylistic matters: (a) word order, (b) Matthew's and Mark's use of διελθεῖν (*dielthein*, to go through) where Luke has εἰσελθεῖν (*eiselthein*, to go into), and (c) Matthew's nonrepetition of his infinitive in the second half of the comparison.

ii. Who Can Be Saved? (18:26)

18:26 The disciples interpret Jesus' remark that the rich will find it impossible to enter the kingdom to mean that everyone will find it impossible to enter. As noted in the exegesis of 18:24, the reason for this conclusion is that wealth was seen as blessing from God. If those who were so blessed are excluded, who can get in? It is important to see the literary escalation in the question. Τίς (*tis*, who) is general, so the premise and implications of Jesus' remark is that it is not just rich people who are in trouble, but all people (Plummer 1896: 426 and Fitzmyer 1985: 1205 compare it to Num. 24:23). Luke leaves the questioner's identity unspecified, perhaps because it is a question that anyone would have about Jesus' remark. The question is more important than who asked it. It is also important to note that entry into the kingdom is equated with salvation (σωθῆναι, *sōthēnai*).[14] In

---

13. Later Judaism used a similar saying about an elephant passing through the eye of a needle to refer to an impossible dream or an illogical argument; Lachs 1987: 331–32; *b. Ber.* 55b; *b. B. Meṣ.* 38b; SB 1:828; Marshall 1978: 687.

14. The kingdom is as comprehensive in terms of its temporal scope as "being saved" is. These ideas are also equated in 13:23, 29.

effect, the disciples are asking, "Is there any hope for anyone?" Jesus will have a clear answer to the dilemma in the next verse.

The question matches that in Mark 10:26 and is the same in Matt. 19:25, except for the absence of the initial καί (*kai*, and). Mark and Matthew mention the audience's astonishment in slightly different terms, with Matthew alone specifying that the disciples asked the question: Matthew has οἱ μαθηταὶ (*hoi mathētai*, the disciples) where Mark has an unspecified οἱ (*hoi*, they). Luke, as he often does, lacks the note of astonishment, but resembles Mark in not noting that the disciples are speaking, though it is obvious from later verses that they are the main audience. Luke speaks only of "those who heard" as responding.

iii. God Makes Salvation Possible (18:27)

Jesus answers the dilemma of who can be saved: the human situation is not hopeless because of God's power. What is impossible for humans is possible with God. This response acknowledges the impossibility of anyone—rich or poor—saving oneself, at first accepting the question's premise that no one can be saved, but then adding an addendum that overrides the obstacle. The reversal is nicely noted by the contrasting ἀδύνατα (*adynata*, impossible; BAGD 19 §2a; BAA 35 §2a) and δυνατά (*dynata*, possible; BAGD 209 §2c; BAA 420 §2c). Salvation is in the hands of a powerful God who is able to effect the needed change of perspective. In replying this way, Jesus gives the divine side of the picture of humility and faith, as he notes without details that God is able to change the human heart and its orientation toward life. When Paul calls the gospel the power of God, this is a major part of the allusion (Rom. 1:16–17; 1 Cor. 1:24–31; Eph. 1:19–2:10). As Fitzmyer (1985: 1205) and Plummer (1896: 426) note, God can break the spell that wealth holds on some people, and, one might add, he can break any other spell that grips a person's heart (cf. Gen. 18:14; Jer. 32:17, 27; Zech. 8:6; Ernst 1977: 505).

18:27

Luke has a more condensed form of this saying. He does not note, as Matt. 19:26 = Mark 10:27 does, that Jesus looked at them (ἐμβλέψας, *emblepsas*) as he spoke. Matthew and Mark put the indirect object αὐτοῖς (*autois*, at them) in a different place and use different verbs for speaking: Matthew has εἶπεν (*eipen*, he said) and Mark has λέγει (*legei*, he said), reflecting Mark's use of the historical present (a similar variation, but in the opposite direction, occurs in the parallels to Luke 8:21). Luke shares Matthew's verb and δέ (*de*, but). The contrast is made more explicit in Matthew and Mark, though Luke's more condensed form makes the same point. Matthew says that "this" (τοῦτο, *touto*) is impossible for people, but that "all things" πάντα (*panta*), are possible with God. Mark lacks τοῦτο, but makes the point twice, since Jesus says, "What is impossible for man is not impossible for God. For all things are possible with God." This repetition makes Mark more emphatic.

iv. Peter Notes That Disciples Have Left All (18:28)

18:28 The disciples react to Jesus' statement. Peter, as usual, speaks up for them (note ἡμεῖς ... ἠκολουθήσαμεν [*hēmeis ... ēkolouthēsamen*, we followed]; Schneider 1977a: 371). He notes that they had already made the choice that the rich ruler refused to make. Luke expresses Peter's words uniquely by using τὰ ἴδια (*ta idia*) to show the disciples' willingness to leave behind their "own things" in contrast to the rich ruler's desire to hold on to his possessions. The disciples had already accepted Jesus' challenge to follow him in discipleship.[15] Peter may want reassurance that they will receive God's blessing, since Jesus has just said that salvation is impossible from human activity. Humbly they have followed the demand to put God first. This is not bragging. This is truth. So what is their status? Interestingly, Peter speaks of leaving things, while in 18:29 Jesus speaks of leaving people, an even more significant sacrifice. Jesus specifies the reward for embracing the promise in 18:29–30: God will vindicate those who cast all their cares upon him (Marshall 1978: 688).

Jesus' demands might seem impossible for anyone; who gives their all at every moment? But that is not what the expression means, as the context clarifies. Jesus replies (18:29) that the disciples have fulfilled what is asked for here. One should not challenge the possibility of the request. Jesus, though obviously stating the point with some rhetorical flair, makes a realistic request that can be honored in a general orientation, as is shown by his reply. His point is that the disciples have indeed left all in order to make God first.

The Synoptic parallels are similar, with some minor stylistic differences. Matthew 19:27 and Mark 10:28 have verbs, in contrast to Luke's participle for leaving, but both speak of leaving "all things." Each account has a different introduction: Matthew has τότε ἀποκριθείς (*tote apokritheis*, then replying), Mark has ἤρξατο λέγειν (*ērxato legein*, he began to say), and Luke has εἶπεν (*eipen*, he said). Matthew and Luke conclude with the verb ἠκολουθήσαμεν (*ēkolouthēsamen*, we followed), while Mark has ἠκολουθήκαμεν (*ēkolouthēkamen*, we have followed). Matthew adds a concluding question, "What then will be for us?"

---

15. Ἀκολουθέω is the standard verb for following in discipleship; BAGD 31 §3; BAA 60 §3; Luke 5:11 (of Peter, James, and John's leaving all); Mark 1:18; 8:34; 2:14 = Luke 5:27–28.

v. Jesus Promises Rewards Now and in the Next Life (18:29–30)

Jesus contrasts what the disciples have sacrificed with what they re- **18:29** ceive for their sacrifice. By doing so, he specifies the "treasure from heaven" that one receives by forsaking all to follow Jesus. His language is indefinite and thus describes anyone who fits the category. All three accounts introduce the remark with the solemn ἀμὴν λέγω ὑμῖν (amēn legō hymin, truly I say to you); Matthew and Luke include ὅτι (hoti, that). Jesus reassures Peter and the others that God is aware of their sacrifice and that they will be rewarded for it. The list of things sacrificed is comprehensive and emphasizes family relationships more than anything. For the one who forsakes home, wife, brothers, parents, or children for the kingdom, God's reward will counterbalance the sacrifice. The emphasis is on sacrificing a normal life of familial closeness and the absence of persecution to do God's work and face persecution. The reference to leaving one's wife (mentioned only by Luke) is not a text advocating abandonment, since the right to take a wife and be supported in ministry is stated in 1 Cor. 9:4–6. Rather, the focus is on choosing to remain single or to travel without her. To abandon one's house is to leave the security of a vocation, as Peter the fisherman did. One abandons the pursuit of a secure financial position as a result of that departure.[16] To leave parents and brothers is to leave one's home to engage in ministry elsewhere, as the disciples who stayed with Jesus did and as Jesus himself did (Luke 8:19–21). It may also describe being excluded from one's family because of one's decision to follow Jesus. To leave children is probably the consequence of the decision to leave a wife. All of these reflect one who is pursuing God's kingdom first.

The differences among the Synoptic parallels are interesting. Matthew 19:28 has an additional saying about sitting on the twelve thrones of Israel, a saying that Luke has in 22:28–30. Matthew's list is houses, brothers, sisters, father, mother, children, and lands. His specific "father and mother" stand in place of Luke's parents, and he mentions sisters and lands, which Luke does not, though Luke's ἀδελφούς (adelphous) is probably gender neutral, as his general reference to parents suggests. If so, it should be translated "siblings" (Marshall 1978: 688; BAGD 16 §1; BAA 28–29). In agreement with Matthew (except for the reversal of mother and father), Mark 10:29 lists house, brothers, sisters, mother, father, children, and lands. Although Luke's version is abbreviated, having only five items as com-

16. Michel, *TDNT* 5:131, suggests that to abandon one's home means "to leave family," since all the other examples are personal. It may, however, reflect Lucan abbreviation; see the next paragraph.

pared to Matthew and Mark's seven, the point is the same: whatever one gives up for Jesus is worth the sacrifice. Another interesting difference is that Matthew speaks of leaving "for my name's sake," while Mark speaks of leaving "for my sake and the gospel." Luke abbreviates and summarizes yet again when he speaks of leaving "for the sake of the kingdom of God." This substitution of ideas is revealing, for it shows the link in Luke's thinking between Jesus, the gospel, and the kingdom. To speak about one is to address the others. Another way to say it is that to speak of the gospel and Jesus is to discuss the kingdom of God. The Lucan version ties back to the difficulty the rich have in entering the kingdom mentioned in 18:23–25 (also 18:16–17; Marshall 1978: 688), thus showing that the kingdom is Luke's topic throughout.[17]

18:30   Jesus lays out the promise in a chiasmus: reward begins and ends the chiasmus, with temporal elements in the middle. Disciples who leave all to follow Jesus will receive "many times as much" in this life. The key term, πολλαπλασίονα (*pollaplasiona*), reveals that what God gives back to the disciple is many times greater than what is given up (BAGD 686–87; BAA 1377; elsewhere in the NT only a variant reading in Matt. 19:29 [parallel to this verse]; also T. Zeb. 6.6). Matthew 19:29 = Mark 10:29 says that the disciples will receive one hundred times more, so Luke's version is again a simplified form of the saying. God notes the sacrifice and gives back much more in terms of the relationships (Plummer 1896: 426–27; Marshall 1978: 689).[18] The reward of a much larger family is a part of the present age, as ἐν τῷ καιρῷ τούτῳ (*en tō kairō toutō*) refers to the present age as a fixed period (Arndt 1956: 385).[19] The note of gathering a new community is frequent in Luke (e.g., 5:10; 8:19–21; Ernst 1977: 505). "In this period" is first part of the two-age time frame so common in later Judaism (SB 4:815–57; Fitzmyer 1985: 1206; Luke 20:34–35). Ernst (1977: 505) notes that the two stages parallel the two stages of kingdom existence: the "already" and the "not yet."

The second phase of reward comes in the "age to come" (Eph. 1:21; 2:7; Heb. 6:5). This is the time of consummation, and the reward is eternal life. The disciple is accepted forever into God's pres-

---

17. Other minor stylistic differences are (1) the saying is introduced by Matthew and Luke with εἶπεν (he said), while Mark has ἔφη (he said), and (2) Matthew starts the saying with πᾶς ὅστις ἀφῆκεν (all who leave) in contrast to Mark's and Luke's οὐδείς ἐστιν ὃς ἀφῆκεν (there is no one who has left).

18. Ἀπολαμβάνω (to receive back) occurs elsewhere in Luke at 6:34; 15:27; 16:25; 23:41; BAGD 94; BAA 189. The idea of "receiving back" is often associated with divine retribution or reward: 2 John 8; Rom. 1:27; Col. 3:24.

19. BAGD 394; BAA 802 §4; Rom. 3:26; 8:18; 11:5; Heb. 9:9; 1 Cor. 4:5. Καιρός is a Lucan term for the present era in Luke 21:24.

ence. Plummer (1896: 426) notes that Job later received double for all he had lost. Jesus goes on to say that the disciple receives much more than that for his or her sacrifice, showing that the sacrifice was worth it. The passage ends where it began (18:18), with the focus on eternal life.

The Synoptic parallels express the same idea, but with some freedom of terms. Both Matt. 19:29 and Mark 10:29 put the return at a hundredfold, and both use a different verb for the idea of receiving the reward: Matthew has λήμψεται (lēmpsetai, shall receive), Mark has λάβῃ (labē, receive), and Luke has ἀπολάβῃ (apolabē, receive back). Matthew and Mark end the passage with a note about the last becoming first, a common saying on eschatological reversal, which Luke lacks, possibly because he already noted it at Luke 13:30. Matthew's saying is the shortest, since he mentions no time frames and does not refer in detail to the various categories of what the disciple receives back. Mark repeats the list of items received back (matching his earlier list except for the omission of "father"). Mark alone refers to persecutions, because of his clear theme of suffering. The variety of wording may suggest that this was a popular story that circulated in different versions.

Summary

Luke 18:18–30 is a study in contrast. Commitment to Jesus is serious. The rich ruler thought that he was devoted to God and could earn acceptance on the basis of his own good works. He thought that he had kept God's commandments. Jesus offers him a challenge that reveals the condition of his heart, a challenge designed to show that God was not really first: sell all, give the proceeds to the poor, and follow Jesus. Even with the promise of reward from heaven, the ruler prefers earth's riches, causing Jesus to reflect on the ruler's choice. The rich have difficulty entering the kingdom because they have difficulty leaving the false security of wealth.

This remark shocks the disciples, who assume that wealth is a sign of God's blessing. So the question is raised, who then can be saved? Jesus notes that humans cannot save themselves, but God has the power to do what is humanly impossible. Peter then notes that the disciples have left everything to follow the call, so Jesus assures them of the benefits of obeying the call to put God first. The disciples have done what the ruler failed to do.

The lesson of this pericope deals with fundamental discipleship: God is to have first place. Putting God first is what brings divine blessing. This involves recognizing in childlike trust that one must rely upon God. Eternal life is the result of such faith. One cannot trust wealth or one's righteous works. Rather, one is to recognize and respond to God's call. The rich ruler would not do this, but the disciples already had. Two sets of people picture two types of humanity. The passage asks readers to reflect on their choices. Do they rely on themselves and their possessions or do they trust God?

Additional Notes

18:22. The inclusion of the article in the phrase ἐν τοῖς οὐρανοῖς (in the heavens) is the harder reading, given its absence in the Synoptic parallels. Τοῖς is found in B and D and is lacking in ℵ and A. Meaning is not influenced by the choice.

18:24. Περίλυπον γενόμενον (becoming sad) is widely attested, but after ὁ Ἰησοῦς (Jesus) in A, W, Δ, Θ, Ψ, family 13, Byz, Lect, and many Itala and after αὐτόν (him) in D and many Itala. The phrase is omitted in ℵ, B, L, family 1, and some Coptic. Attestation slightly favors its presence after ὁ Ἰησοῦς, but the variety of word order suggests that the phrase was added later. The uncertainty about its originality has lead to the brackets in the UBS–NA text (Metzger 1975: 168).

18:30. Luke's numerical difference with the Synoptic parallels has produced two minor readings. Codex D and Itala have ἑπταπλασίονα (seven times as much), which is accepted by Cyprian (Creed 1930: 227; BAGD 306; BAA 620), and the Syriac of Luke agrees with Matthew and Mark, which have ἑκατονταπλασίονα (one hundred times as much). But neither of these variants has broad enough support to be original.

L. Turning to Jerusalem: Messianic Power, Personal Transformation, Warning of Responsibility, and Entry with Mourning (18:31–19:44)

Luke 18:31 begins the journey narrative's final section. As Jesus approaches Jerusalem, he offers a final, detailed prediction of his fate there (18:31–34). As the Son of David, he heals a blind man (18:35–43), thus stressing Messiah's power. The incident with Zacchaeus shows that people's lives are being transformed by Jesus' ministry and that the rich can respond with faith (19:1–10). Jesus then tells a parable that reveals his authority to judge (19:11–27). The emphasis is on responding wisely to the king's presence and living responsibly in his absence, for Jesus will return to evaluate everyone's stewardship and response to him. With Jesus' authority brought center stage, he enters the capital with praise from his disciples (19:28–40). This angers the Pharisees, but Jesus notes that the disciples' response is correct, as even the creation would declare if it could speak. The journey narrative closes with Jesus weeping over Jerusalem because he knows what he will face there and what Jerusalem will face as a result of its rejection (19:41–44).

1. The Passion Prediction (18:31–34)

Luke here records the sixth announcement of Jesus' death in his Gospel (9:22; 9:44–45; 12:49–50; 13:32–33; 17:25; Tiede 1988: 314).[1] In 18:31–34 Luke uniquely stresses two themes. First, what will happen in Jerusalem will fulfill Scripture (a more elaborate and explicit explanation than in the parallel Mark 10:32, where Jesus tells "what was about to happen to him"; Grundmann 1963: 355; Luce 1933: 289). Second, the disciples fail to understand Jesus' remarks, a failure that concerns not so much Jesus' death as its relationship to scriptural teaching (Mark 9:32 = Luke 9:45; John 2:22; 12:16). After Jesus' resurrection, he will explain these connections to the disciples (Luke 24:32, 45–48; Fitzmyer 1985: 1208). Jesus is nearing his fate in Jerusalem, and so he continues to prepare his disciples for the significant confrontation that awaits them there. The disciples will not be ready, but Jesus approaches with no illusions about what he faces. In the Book of Acts, Jerusalem will become the focus of another key man of God when Paul determines to go to Jerusalem (Acts 19:21; 20:22; 21:4, 11–12; Leaney 1958: 238).

Sources and Historicity

This passion prediction has parallels in Matt. 20:17–19 = Mark 10:32–34 (Aland 1985: §262). Luke packs a great amount of detail into his seven descriptive verbs: everything written about the Son of Man will be accomplished when he is delivered over, mocked, shamed, spat upon, scourged, and killed—only to rise again. Mark is similar to Luke in this respect, lacking only the reference to Jesus' shameful treatment, while Matthew lacks this verb and the spitting incident. Only Luke notes the fulfillment of Scripture, a theme he loves. The passage fits nicely in its Lucan placement: Jesus has just asked his disciples to give up all to follow him, and now he predicts that he will offer all for them, as Scripture promises. The Jesus Seminar (Funk and Hoover 1993: 371–72) rejects the historicity of this prediction, seeing it as one of three predictions created by Mark that Luke simply passed on

---

1. Luke 5:35 alludes to Jesus' death. The death of the Son of Man appears in three of the Lucan passion predictions (9:22; 9:44–45; 17:25; Danker 1988: 302). Three of Luke's passion predictions (9:22; 9:44–45; 18:31–34) have Marcan parallels and are grouped together because they are quite specific.

(the saying is printed in black type). The historicity of this saying is tied to one's evaluation of the other passion predictions, which I defend as historically rooted in Jesus (see the sources and historicity discussions for 9:21–22 and 9:43b–45 and excursus 10).

The passage contains sayings of Jesus that are passion predictions (Fitzmyer 1985: 1208; Berger 1984: 226). The outline of Luke 18:31–34 is as follows:

a. Jesus' journey to Jerusalem to fulfill Scripture (18:31)
b. Jesus' prediction of his death and resurrection (18:32–33)
c. The disciples' lack of understanding (18:34)

Jesus continues his journey to Jerusalem, city of destiny. All that is written about the Son of Man is to be fulfilled. Gentiles share as participants in Jesus' slaying. His suffering is predicted in detail. The disciples' lack of comprehension about God's plan continues. They do not yet realize the significance of Jesus' death and resurrection.

Exegesis and Exposition

[31]And taking the Twelve aside, he said to them, "Behold, we are going up to Jerusalem, and all that is written through the prophets about the Son of Man shall be fulfilled, [32]for he shall be given over to the Gentiles, and shall be mocked and treated shamefully, and spit upon, [33]and scourging him, they shall kill him, and on the third day, he shall rise." [34]And none of them understood these things, and this matter was hidden from them, and they did not know the things said.

a. Jesus' Journey to Jerusalem to Fulfill Scripture (18:31)

As Jesus and the crowd draw near to Jerusalem, he takes the Twelve **18:31** aside to remind them of what awaits them (Luke uses παραλαμ-βάνω [*paralambanō*, to take aside] elsewhere in Luke 9:10, 28; 11:26; 17:34, 35; Acts 15:39; 16:33; 21:24, 26, 32; 23:18; BAGD 619; BAA 1251–52). Jerusalem is the city of destiny and confrontation (9:22, 31; 13:33–34). What will happen there will fulfill Scripture, which came "through" (διά, *dia*) the intermediate agency of the prophets.[2]

The subject is the Son of Man, but Jesus does not specify the OT

2. The idea of fulfilling Scripture occurs throughout Luke's writings, frequently with τελέω (BAGD 811 §1, esp. §2; BAA 1617 §2; Luke 2:39; 12:50; 18:31; 22:37; Acts 13:29) or δεῖ (Luke 9:22; 17:25); also Luke 13:22, 32; 24:44–49; Acts 2:23. Delling, *TDNT* 8:60 n. 16, says that this emphasis is part of special Lucan material.

passages he alludes to.[3] Although Jesus normally referred to himself with this title, the connection with Dan. 7:13 is not explicitly revealed until his eschatological discourse and trial (compare Luke 5:24 to 21:27 and 22:69). Jesus used this title to place the acts of his ministry side by side with the ministry of suffering and the future work of reign and authority. Luke 24:44–49 summarizes much of Jesus' career in the same terms as 18:32–33, although using the title ὁ χριστός (*ho christos*, Messiah, the Christ). This later passage also helps solve a minor grammatical dispute. Does τῷ υἱῷ τοῦ ἀνθρώπου (*tō huiō tou anthrōpou*, about the Son of Man) go back to τελεσθήσεται (it shall be fulfilled for the Son of Man; Fitzmyer 1985: 1209) or γεγραμμένα (all the things written about the Son of Man; Plummer 1896: 428; Klostermann 1929: 183 [probably])? Since Luke 24 has a similar construction linking writing and χριστός, it seems likely that the latter formulation is correct.[4] God has a task for Jesus, and Jesus is prepared to complete it.

Luke is similar to the Synoptic parallels. He lacks the reference in Matt. 18:17 = Mark 10:32 to journeying up to Jerusalem. The actual saying in Luke states as much, so this is probably just editorial condensation. Mark has some additional notes of emotion when he mentions that those who followed Jesus were afraid. This note of tension is lacking in Matthew and Luke, but it is typical of Mark. Finally, the idea of scriptural fulfillment is found only in Luke, though Mark and Matthew have a summary involving a reference to the Son of Man that speaks of Jesus telling the Twelve what was about to happen to him. This note may imply scriptural design, provided that one reads the reference to the Son of Man as a reference to the messianic figure who suffers, which Jesus seems to do. That Daniel is not in the prophetic section of the Jewish Scriptures may suggest that Jesus has a broader scope of texts in mind here (Nolland 1993a: 895). All the accounts note that Jesus' remarks are addressed to the Twelve.

b. Jesus' Prediction of His Death and Resurrection (18:32–33)

18:32 Jesus specifies what will happen in Jerusalem. Luke omits the Synoptic references to Jesus' being given over to the chief priests and scribes and their condemning Jesus to death (see Matt. 20:18 = Mark 10:33). He is aware of these elements (cf. 9:22, 44), but here he has a condensed saying, possibly because he gives more detail later in the verse. Luke's first four verbs are passive, thus depicting what the Scriptures say, while Matthew's and Mark's active verbs stress the

3. Tiede 1988: 315 mentions Isa. 50:6; 53; and Ps. 2 as key texts. On the uncertainty of Isa. 50:6, see the exegesis of Luke 18:33.

4. Luke often mentions written Scripture: Luke 4:17; 7:27; 10:26; 20:17; 21:22; 22:37; 24:44, 46; Acts 13:29; 24:14 (Schrenk, *TDNT* 1:748; Marshall 1978: 690).

human perpetrators (chief priests and scribes condemn him and give him over to Gentiles).

First, Jesus will be given over to the Gentiles: παραδίδωμι (*paradidōmi*; BAGD 614 §1b; BAA 1243 §1b). This prediction is fulfilled in 23:22, 25. A failed attempt is set up in 20:20b.

Second, Jesus' arrest and custody will be accompanied by mocking: ἐμπαίζω (*empaizō*; BAGD 255; BAA 516; Bertram, *TDNT* 5:630–35), a term used in the Synoptic parallels (Matt. 20:19 = Mark 10:34), in the Synoptic passion accounts (Matt. 27:31 = Mark 15:20; Matt. 27:41 = Mark 15:31; Matt. 27:29), and in Luke's fulfillment of this prediction (Luke 22:63; 23:11, 36). Jesus will not receive any respect during his confinement.

Third, Jesus will receive shameful treatment (a detail found only in Luke; Marshall 1978: 690, who notes that there is no reference to Greek tragedy here, against Grundmann 1963: 356): ὑβρίζω (*hybrizō*; BAGD 831; BAA 1659). This term is used elsewhere by Luke in Luke 11:45 and Acts 14:5, but is not repeated in any of the passion accounts. The imagery, as well as the term, is significant because in the OT and other Jewish literature it describes the scoffer who works unrighteously and proudly against the righteous (Zeph. 3:11–12; conceptual parallels are Ps. 94:2–7 [93:2–7 LXX] and Sir. 10:6–18; Schweizer 1984: 288; Bertram, *TDNT* 8:306). Bertram (*TDNT* 5:634) says that this activity is synonymous with mocking (cf. Luke 14:29). This may explain why Matthew and Mark lack reference to it.

Fourth, some will spit on Jesus: the onomatopoeic ἐμπτύω (*emptyō*; BAGD 257; BAA 519), a point that Luke shares with Mark 10:34 but is not in Matthew. That Luke does not refer to the fulfillment of this act in his passion account argues against this being a prophecy created after the fact. In other words, Luke makes no effort to tailor Jesus' remarks here to the details of his passion account. This prediction is fulfilled in Mark 14:65 = Matt. 26:67 and Mark 15:19 = Matt. 27:30.

Switching from passive verbs to an active participle, an active verb, **18:33** and a middle verb, Luke completes his record of Jesus' prediction with three additional descriptions.

Fifth, Jesus will be flogged: μαστιγόω (*mastigoō*; BAGD 495; BAA 1003), a custom that was often part of the crucifixion process (Josephus, *Jewish War* 2.14.9 §§306–8; 5.11.1 §449; C. Schneider, *TDNT* 4:517).[5] The term may reveal an allusion to Isa. 50:6, though a single

5. On crucifixion and the activity associated with it, see Hengel 1977. The Roman practice of scourging (*verberatio*) preceded the execution of capital criminals, who were lashed until blood was drawn; Plautus, *Bacchides* 823; Suetonius, *Claudius* 34; and Suetonius, *Domitian* 11.

term provides too little contact to be sure (Fitzmyer 1985: 1210). Luke uses this term only here (elsewhere in the NT at Matt. 10:17; 20:19; 23:34; Mark 10:34; Heb. 12:6 [of God's discipline of his children]). This prediction is fulfilled in John 19:1.

Sixth, Jesus will be killed: ἀποκτείνω (apokteinō; BAGD 93–94; BAA 187–88), a term that is consistently part of the passion prediction (Matt. 16:21 = Mark 8:31 = Luke 9:22; Matt. 17:23 = Mark 9:31; 10:34). Luke's use of an active verb intensifies the reference to Jesus' death: "They will kill him," where "they" contextually means the Gentiles. In Acts 3:15, which looks back at Jesus' death, the Jews are blamed. All groups killed Jesus, a key point in light of recent claims of Lucan anti-Semiticism (e.g., J. T. Sanders 1987).

Seventh, Jesus will be resurrected on the third day: ἀνίστημι (anistēmi; BAGD 70 §2a; BAA 139 §2a). This is a common detail in the passion predictions (Mark 9:9, 31; 10:34) and fulfillments (sometimes using ἐγείρω [egeirō, to rise up], Matthew's preferred verb; BAGD 214 §1aβ; BAA 432 §1aβ; Matt. 17:9, 23; 20:19). Jesus is aware of his fate and is ready to meet it. This prediction is fulfilled in Luke 24:7, 34, 46 (also Matt. 27:63; 28:6–7 = Mark 16:6).

The parallels are similar. Mark 10:34 has the same three items that Luke mentions, though each is a verb. Matthew 20:19 uses two infinitives to describe scourging and killing, while expressing resurrection with a verb. He also uses different terms for crucifixion (σταυρῶσαι, staurōsai, to crucify) and resurrection (ἐγερθήσεται, egerthēsetai, to be raised) than do Mark and Luke. Luke's version is once again slightly closer to Mark than to Matthew.[6]

The saying in Luke 18:32–33 contains more detail than the two earlier detailed Lucan predictions of suffering: 9:22 speaks of suffering, being rejected by the elders, chief priests, and scribes, being killed, and rising on the third day; and 9:44–45 speaks only of being given over. Jesus is progressively revealing more of his fate to the Twelve, though they do not yet grasp what he is telling them, as the next verse makes clear.

---

6. Another stylistic difference may reflect Matthean–Lucan agreement but is tied to a textual issue in Mark: Matthew has τῇ τρίτῃ ἡμέρᾳ (on the third day) and Luke has τῇ ἡμέρᾳ τῇ τρίτῃ (on the third day) where many key Marcan manuscripts read μετὰ τρεῖς ἡμέρας (after three days). It is possible, however, that all three accounts agree, since the textual evidence for μετὰ τρεῖς ἡμέρας in Mark is largely Alexandrian plus D (the other reading in Mark is τῇ τρίτῃ ἡμέρᾳ; A, W, Θ, family 1, family 13, Byz). But μετὰ τρεῖς ἡμέρας is more difficult, which speaks in its favor; Marshall 1978: 690. The variant makes the reference slightly clearer, though for Mark "after three days" is to be read inclusively.

c. The Disciples' Lack of Understanding (18:34)

Luke alone states the disciples' lack of comprehension—and he says **18:34** it three times to underscore its presence. In all probability Luke does not mean that Jesus' message was unintelligible, but that the disciples could not understand how his death could fit into the divine plan for Jesus. Some speak of a "messianic secret" in which Jesus did not publicly reveal his full messianic function during his ministry. The issue is not, however, that Jesus didn't reveal his messianic function, but that it did not fit together in the disciples' understanding (9:45) until after the resurrection. Luke 24:27 and 24:44–49 (esp. 24:45) show Jesus unveiling this plan.[7]

Putting the pieces together was an ability that God had not yet granted to the disciples (passive κεκρυμμένον, *kekrymmenon*, was hidden).[8] The focus is on comprehending how God's plan works, not on understanding the words themselves. Grundmann (1963: 356) offers the possible explanation that the disciples did not believe that such things could happen to Jesus under Scripture's promises and God's guidance (something to which Matt. 16:22 also testifies). Some suggest that Luke omitted the dispute about where the disciples will sit in the kingdom (Matt. 20:20–28 = Mark 10:35–45) and replaced it with this saying as a summary (Plummer 1896: 429). Once the disciples do understand, they will preach this plan and reveal the texts tied to it, as Acts shows.

Luke 18:31–34 shows a Jesus who knows where the journey **Summary** leads. Confrontation and submission to his fate draw near. He knows of the approaching suffering in Jerusalem, which comes just as Scripture promised. It will be an intense time of shame: the Gentiles will seize him, mock him, treat him shamelessly, spit on him, scourge him, and kill him. But on the third day, he will rise. This is God's plan. The disciples do not see and understand it yet, but Jesus knows it. One of the passion's consistent themes will be that Jesus is in control of events. Nevertheless, he willingly submits to what happens. Luke wishes the reader to see that Jesus' death comes as no surprise. The Scripture promised it, and Jesus foretold it. What he suffers, he suffers willingly and knowingly, which adds to the narrative drama. This is no accident.

7. Luke 8:10, 16–17 promises this unveiling to the disciples; Danker 1988: 302. John 2:22 and 12:16 repeat the picture of the disciples' incomprehension, while Luke 2:50 says a similar thing about Jesus' parents.

8. The more intensive ἀποκρύπτω (to conceal) is used in contrast to unveiling (ἀποκαλύπτω) revelation and the mystery of God's plan (Luke 10:21; 1 Cor. 2:7; Eph. 3:9; Col. 1:26). Luke uses the synonymous παρακαλύπτω (to conceal) in Luke 9:45 and κρύπτω (to hide) in 19:42 (Marshall 1978: 691).

Jesus is fully aware of what he is entering into. And he enters it alone, since the disciples do not understand enough to offer any support. When Jesus died, he stood alone before God on our behalf. But as Luke–Acts will show, Jesus alone is quite enough for God.

2. Healing by the Son of David (18:35–43)

Presenting the fourth and final miracle of the journey (13:10–17; 14:1–6; 17:11–19), this account is strategically placed. First, it is the first of two events in Jericho, each of which presents a key aspect of salvation. This miracle shows the humble cry for mercy that is part of the appeal for salvation, and 19:1–10 portrays Zacchaeus as a model response to salvation: joy and generous service to others (Talbert 1982: 175–76). Both accounts play off of the idea of salvation (18:42; 19:9). Second, the account also stands parallel to the disciples' absence of understanding. The disciples are blind with regard to God's plan, just as the beggar was physically blind. The way out of the dilemma for both is to trust Jesus and his promise (Leaney 1958: 239). Third, the blind beggar stands in contrast to the rich young man (Ellis 1974: 219). The rich young man has all and can see, but really is blind. The blind man has nothing and cannot see until he trusts Jesus, and then he has all. The two men could not be more opposite. The reversal of the blind man's situation is an illustration of 18:28–30. Finally, the blind man's appeal is parallel to the tax collector's dependent humility in 18:9–14. Thus, this miracle ties together many themes at the journey's conclusion. It points to faith's centrality in the removal of spiritual blindness. The restoration of sight to the blind shows the presence of the end-time (4:18; 7:22; Fitzmyer 1985: 1214). This healing of the blind man is the only such miracle in Luke (see Mark 8:22–26; Matt. 9:27–31; Nolland 1993b: 899).

Luke raises other themes. This is another example of Jesus reaching out to meet the needs of the poor and rejected. This compassion continues even though Jesus is aware that the pressure against him is becoming more intense. When many would withdraw and hide, Jesus continues to serve. The ministry to the needy continues, and Jesus' acceptance of them continues, because the poor evidence spiritual sensitivity. Jesus' compassion and the poor's spiritual sensitivity remain two key Lucan themes.

Sources and Historicity

In making this miracle the next event, Luke lacks any reference to the sitting-on-thrones dispute that the sons of Zebedee raise, which is another account picturing the disciples' lack of understanding (Mark 10:35–45 = Matt. 20:20–28; Aland 1985: §263). Many attempt to explain the omission, but the most important suggestion is that Luke wished to tone down the key soteriological "ransom" saying of Mark 10:45 because he did not share this "substitution" idea (Conzelmann 1960: 201). This is not likely, however, since other Lucan passages make this point (Luke 22:19–20; 24:21; Acts 7:35 [of Moses as a type of Christ]; esp. 20:28) or they note that redemption comes through Jesus (Luke 1:68; 2:38) (correctly Fitzmyer 1985: 1212 and Marshall 1978: 691). The most common explanation for the difference is that Luke will raise a similar note of conflict in 22:24–27, so that the account becomes redundant here, an explanation that is plausible but not certain.

In the history of interpretation of this passage, the most discussed issues concern the Synoptic parallels (Matt. 20:29–34 = Mark 10:46–52; Aland 1985: §264). Three differences in the accounts contribute to this discussion: (a) the location: in Matt. 20:29 = Mark 10:46, the men are healed as Jesus goes out of Jericho, while in Luke 18:35 the healing takes place upon Jesus' entrance into the city;[1] (b) the word that heals: Matt. 20:34 has healing by touch, Mark 10:52 has a word of comfort, and Luke 18:42 has a command to receive sight; and (c) the number of blind men healed: Matthew's account consistently holds that two blind men were healed, while Mark and Luke refer to only one blind man.[2]

The attempt to deal with these factors has produced a variety of responses (Plummer 1896: 429–30; Marshall 1978: 692–93; Van Der Loos 1965: 422–23), some positing multiple events (nos. 1–3) or no connection (no. 4) or appealing to a variety of historical (no. 5) or literary (nos. 6 and 7) solutions:

1. Euthymius Zigabenus posits three distinct events (cited in Plummer 1896: 429).
2. Augustine (*Four Gospels* 2.48) argues that two healings are present: one on Jesus' entry into Jericho and another on his departure.
3. On a variation on the two-healing approach, J. A. W. Neander argues that Matthew telescoped two accounts into one event (cited in Plummer 1896: 429).

These attempts to see separate events have major problems. Each Gospel locates the healing at a parallel point, and they have many similar details.

---

1. At the start of his account, however, Mark notes both the entry into and the exit from Jericho, and so Luke may merely telescope the reference.

2. This account again reflects a Mark–Luke alliance, as has been common in the last part of the journey narrative, another factor that makes it difficult to see Matthew's account as first chronologically. This pattern will continue in the latter events of the Jerusalem section.

Pericopes near this one in Matthew and Mark are clearly parallel. Thus, one event is likely in view here as well, although as the next view shows, some hold that we are dealing with separate, irreconcilable events.

4. Many refuse to bring the accounts together, arguing that they are beyond reconciling. Even Plummer (1896: 429), who normally attempts to bring together such details, regards the solution as impossible.

5. Some speak of two Jerichos (Arndt 1956: 387; Van Der Loos 1965: 423): Matthew and Mark speak of leaving old Jericho, while Luke refers to approaching new Jericho. The problem with this approach, though it cannot be excluded, is that only one Jericho was actively inhabited at this time (see the exegesis of 18:35).

6. Calvin (1972: 2.278–79) argues that a two-part event was condensed into one account: Bartimaeus cried out as Jesus entered the city and was eventually healed with a second blind man upon Jesus' departure from the city. All three writers condense the story with different details. This harmonization means that doublets within the tradition address two different scenes, which is a possible explanation but not the most likely.

7. Luke rearranged his account for logical, literary reasons. He places the event in the area of Jericho and before the account of Zacchaeus to keep the logical order of his two pictures of salvation. By placing the blind man before Zacchaeus, Luke first pictures entry into salvation and then the response of someone already saved. Through this arrangement, the blind beggar is compared to the disciples' blindness and inability to comprehend Jesus' remarks and contrasted with the young rich man, who walks away salvifically destitute. In other words, the rearrangement produces a generalized setting in Luke that looks like a reference to entry, but is probably simply intended to pinpoint Jericho as the locale.[3]

A variation on this idea is that Luke used the original introduction to the Zacchaeus account before this event, only to supply a new introduction to Zacchaeus later in 19:1 (Schramm 1971: 143–44). This is not, however, the best way to express what happened. Luke 19:1 shows that the Zacchaeus event occurs on Jesus' entry to Jericho, leaving the impression that this healing preceded entry into Jericho as well, so that "near Jericho" in 18:35 is difficult. However, if Luke saw the two events as related, then he probably felt free to place them side by side in an order that was more thematic than sequential. It may be that the setting in 18:35 is literarily condensed from Mark to bracket the events, even though their order has been reversed and even though the setting is restated in 19:1. The re-

---

3. The case for this approach is enhanced syntactically if ἐγγίζω can mean "to be in the vicinity of" rather than "to draw near," as Porter 1992 argues.

statement makes clear the Jericho link. Granted, this linkage is not as clean as it could be, but it preserves the logical flow of the pictures (Schweizer 1984: 288 has a similar but less developed explanation; also Nolland 1993b: 898–99).

The handling of the parallels makes it clear that the account is historical. There is no solid reason to doubt that Jesus healed this man in Jericho (Marshall 1978: 692; V. Taylor 1966: 446–47; Schweizer 1970: 224; against Bultmann 1963: 213–14). The Jesus Seminar (Funk and Hoover 1993: 372), as is its habit with dialogue tied to miracles, argues that the dialogue was supplied by the storyteller and would not have been remembered with the event—a dubious premise that I have challenged elsewhere (see the discussion of sources and historicity in 5:1–11 and 5:12–26). If Jesus performed miracles and traditions of it were preserved, then surely what he said would have been recalled and passed on, given the unusual nature of the event. Obviously, one's general view of Jesus' miracles will influence conclusions here. In arguing for the ancient roots of the tradition, Meier (1994: 687–90) notes that Mark's naming of the one healed is unprecedented in the Synoptics and is repeated only in the naming of Lazarus in John 11. Meier also argues that the emphasis on the Son of David shows the tradition's age. Thus, the event has a good claim to historical roots. For Meier, it has one of the strongest claims to historicity of all the miracles.

The miracle has a simple structure: the events leading up to the appeal to be healed (18:35–39) are given first, followed by the healing itself (18:40–43). Luke employs literary tension in the first half of the account when the populace attempts and fails to quiet the blind man. Jesus commends such persistent faith that stands up to peer pressure. Another uniquely Lucan note closes the account: praise goes up to God as a result of the healing (1:64; 7:16; 13:13; 17:15, 18; Grundmann 1963: 357; Talbert 1982: 175).

The account is a healing miracle (Fitzmyer 1985: 1213; Bultmann 1963: 213; Berger 1984: 310 ["epideixis"]). The outline of Luke 18:35–43 is as follows:

a. The appeals (18:35–39)
    i. Jesus' approach raises a question (18:35–37)
    ii. First appeal (18:38)
    iii. Rebuke and second appeal (18:39)
b. The healing (18:40–43)
    i. Jesus' response (18:40–41a)
    ii. Request (18:41b)
    iii. Jesus' commendation of faith (18:42)
    iv. Resolution: healing and praise (18:43)

The major theme is the authority of the Son of David, who heals and rules over forces that harm humans. The blind man makes a messianic confession. Jesus heeds the cry of the poor in a picture of faith's persistence. Jesus' compassion comes despite popular rebuke and pressure. Faith leads to sight, with the physical and spiritual areas linked. There is instant healing and praise.

Exegesis and Exposition

[35]And it came to pass as he drew near to Jericho, a certain blind man was seated by the road begging. [36]And hearing the multitude going by, he inquired what it might be. [37]And they told him, "Jesus of Nazareth is passing by." [38]And he cried, saying, "Jesus, Son of David, have mercy on me!" [39]And those in front of him began to rebuke him that he should ⌜be quiet⌝. But he cried out even more, "Son of David, have mercy on me!"

[40]And Jesus, having stopped, commanded that he be brought to him. When he came near, he asked him, [41]"What do you wish me to do?" And he said, "Lord, let me have sight." [42]And Jesus said to him, "Receive your sight; your faith has saved you." [43]And immediately he received sight and followed him, praising God. And when all the people saw it, they gave praise to God.

a. The Appeals (18:35–39)
i. Jesus' Approach Raises a Question (18:35–37)

Luke briefly sets the miracle's location: Jesus is approaching Jericho, the first city specifically mentioned in the journey narrative (Ellis 1974: 219). On the possibility that Luke means that Jesus is in the vicinity of Jericho, see Porter 1992 and note 3 above. Detailed locations have been lacking in the journey section, but they pick up in intensity until the end of the section, a literary indication that the key moment draws near (19:1, 11, 29, 37, 41, 45; Nolland 1993b: 898). Jericho is located about six miles from the Jordan River, just north of the Dead Sea, and served as a tax collection center (19:1) on the major highway to Jerusalem, eighteen miles away (10:30). This is the new Jericho, with a more ancient uninhabited city located about a mile and a half away (Plummer 1896: 429).[4] By mentioning Jericho here, Luke sets the events of 18:35–19:10 in the context of Jesus' approach to Jericho.[5]

18:35

---

4. Matt. 20:29 = Mark 10:46; Heb. 11:30; BAGD 372; BAA 756. The new Jericho was given to Cleopatra by Mark Antony and later came under Herod the Great's authority; Josephus, *Jewish War* 4.8.3 §459, §474; *Antiquities* 15.4.2–4 §§96–107.

5. Ἐγγίζω (to come near) is often used to denote approach, especially in conjunction with the preposition εἰς (to); Luke 19:29 = Matt. 21:1 = Mark 11:1; Luke 24:28;

Introduced as a poor beggar by the road, the blind man could not be more different than the rich ruler of 18:23.[6] His blindness had made him totally destitute; his life was dependent on the mercy of others.

The Synoptic parallels are similar, except for the note about Jesus entering versus departing the city (discussed above). Mark 10:46 = Matt. 20:29 makes clear that a crowd is following Jesus, which may well be pilgrims headed for Jerusalem, since the Passover is drawing near (Plummer 1896: 430; Arndt 1956: 387). Throughout his version Matthew speaks of two blind men, which may be merely a matter of detail. It seems that one of the men made an impression on the better known tradition (Matthew often notes such pairs: Matt. 8:28; 9:27). Mark tells us that the name of one blind man was Bartimaeus, an Aramaic name (Klostermann 1929: 183 suggests that this is why Luke lacks the name).

18:36   The detailed exchange between the crowd and the blind man is unique to Luke. The blind man heard the crowd and asked what it might be.[7] Matthew and Mark lack any detail about how the man came to know that it was Jesus and only report that when the blind man heard it was Jesus, he called out to him.

18:37   The crowd's reply to the blind man's question is brief but significant: Jesus is passing by (παρέρχομαι, *parerchomai*).[8] The answer is expressed in general terms using an indefinite third-person plural: ἀπήγγειλαν (*apēngeilan*, they told).[9]

The title Ἰησοῦς ὁ Ναζωραῖος describes Jesus' origin from Nazareth in Galilee, an association frequently made in the NT (Matt.

Tob. 11:1; Plummer 1896: 430. See the introduction to this unit for the possibility that this remark is a condensation of Mark 10:46 and for the linkage of Luke 18:35–43 and 19:1–10.

6. The word for begging, ἐπαιτέω, is rare in the NT: elsewhere only Luke 16:3 and Mark 10:46 variant; also Ps. 109:10 [108:10 LXX]; Sir. 40:28; BAGD 282; BAA 571. Mark 10:46 uses προσαίτης (beggar), which appears elsewhere only in John 9:8; BAGD 711; BAA 1425.

7. Creed 1930: 229 says that the use of the optative in an indirect question and the use of πυνθάνομαι (to inquire) are Lucan (only three NT uses of πυνθάνομαι are non-Lucan: Luke 15:26; Acts 4:7; 10:18, 29; 21:33; 23:19, 20, 34; Matt. 2:4; John 4:52; 13:24); BAGD 729; BAA 1459.

8. Παρέρχομαι usually has a figurative sense of passing by in the sense of neglecting or passing from the scene (11:42; 15:29; 16:17; 21:33). Here it means to physically pass by (also Matt. 8:28; Mark 6:48); BAGD 625; BAA 1264; also Exod. 12:23. The parallel Matt. 20:30 has παράγει (is passing by).

9. Luke has almost two-thirds of the NT uses of ἀπαγγέλλω: eleven times in his Gospel (7:18, 22; 8:20, 34, 36, 47; 9:36; 13:1; 14:21; 18:37; 24:9), fifteen times in Acts, and nineteen times in the rest of the NT; BAGD 79; BAA 157. On the grammar, see Zerwick 1963: §1.

2:23; 26:71; John 18:5, 7; 19:19; Acts 2:22; 3:6; 4:10; 6:14; 22:8; 26:9). The meaning of Ναζωραῖος is disputed (BAGD 532; BAA 1077; Schaeder, *TDNT* 4:874–79; Fitzmyer 1985: 1215; R. Brown 1977: 209–13, 223–25):

1. It is a variation of Ναζαρηνός (Nazarean), which appears in the Mark 10:47 parallel as well as in Luke 4:34, and means "from Nazareth" (Marshall 1978: 693). This is the likely sense (see also 24:19; Schneider 1977a: 375).
2. It is related to Semitic נָזִיר (*nāzîr*, someone consecrated by a vow; BDB 634) and pictures Jesus set apart to serve God.
3. It is related to Semitic נֵצֶר (*nēṣer*, shoot, sprout; BDB 666) and alludes to the "shoot of Jesse" in Isa. 11:1. This derivation was popular among patristic writers (e.g., Justin Martyr, *Dialogue with Trypho* 126.1).
4. It is related to Aramaic נאצוראייא (*nāṣōrayyāʾ*, observers) and was tied to John the Baptist in Mandean writings. This is less likely because these sources are too late to indicate the term's first-century meaning.

Despite the disputed etymology, Jesus' Nazarean origins are the point (Nolland 1993b: 900 does not rule out that either sense 2 or 3 is a possible double entendre here). Jesus was a famous teacher, but it was unusual for someone significant to emerge from northern Israel.

The parallels are less specific. Mark 10:47 says simply, "It is Jesus of Nazareth." Matthew 20:30 speaks of the blind men hearing that "Jesus is passing by," without having the blind man ask a question. The information will cause the blind man to make a plea.

ii. First Appeal (18:38)

18:38 The knowledge that Jesus is near is an opportunity for the blind man, so he cries out (ἐβόησεν [*eboēsen*]; Matt. 20:30 has ἔκραξαν λέγοντες [*ekraxan legontes*, he cried out saying], and Mark 10:47 has κράζειν καὶ λέγειν [*krazein kai legein*, to cry out and say]).[10] The blind man knows something about Jesus, for his cry stands in contrast to the crowd's description of "Jesus of Nazareth." Ironically, this blind man sees, in contrast to the disciples' blindness (Luke 18:34).

The blind man cries out to the "Son of David" (υἱὲ Δαυίδ, *huie Dauid*), a messianic confession of great significance (BAGD 171;

10. Βοάω is used elsewhere in the Synoptics at Matt. 3:3 = Mark 1:3 = Luke 3:4 (of John the Baptist); 9:38; 18:7; Mark 15:34; BAGD 144; BAA 287 §1b.

BAA 341; 4Q174 [= 4QFlor] 1.11; 4QPBless 1.3–4; 2 Esdr. [= 4 Ezra] 12:32; Ps. Sol. 17.21). This is the only Lucan use of this confession, though Jesus' association with David is common in Luke's Gospel (1:27; 2:4; 3:31; 20:41) and in the NT (Matt. 9:27; 12:23; 15:22; 21:9, 15; Mark 12:35; John 7:42; Acts 2:29–32; Rom. 1:3; 2 Tim. 2:8). The idea that the Son of David could heal is seen by many as evidence that this story and the use of the title are late, since, it is argued, the Son of David was not seen as a messianic healer (Burger 1970: 144; Hahn 1969: 253–55). However, such a tradition is found in ancient material (Wis. 7:17–21; Pseudo-Philo, *Biblical Antiquities* 60.1 [David as exorcist]; SB 4:533–34; Berger 1973–74: 3–9; Duling 1975).[11] There is no doubt that the messianic period was seen as one of restoration and healing. In fact, Jesus' own use of Isa. 61:1 in Luke 4:17–18 indicates this perspective, as does his reply to John the Baptist in 7:22. The blind man probably had heard reports of Jesus' miraculous work and now realizes that he might be the Messiah because of the public stir he has created. The man's confession shows great faith, for which Jesus will commend him (18:42). For the blind man, Jesus is the promised helper. This blind man saw clearly what others could not.

The blind man's plea for mercy (ἐλεέω, *eleeō*; BAGD 249; BAA 503) is a request for compassion and healing. Such cries were common (Matt. 9:27; 15:22; 17:15; Mark 5:19; Luke 16:24; 17:13). The need for mercy is often associated with sin, and sometimes mercy is needed because the plight is particularly desperate. The Lucan examples of the cry of the lepers (17:13) and of the rich man's plea from Hades (16:24) show the emotional impact of this cry. The cry is reminiscent of David's plea in the penitential lament of Ps. 51:1 [50:3 LXX] (also Ps. 6:2 [6:3 LXX]; 9:13 [9:14 LXX]; 41:4, 10 [40:5, 11 LXX]; 123:3 [122:3 LXX]; Ernst 1977: 510). The blind man knows that only Jesus can meet his need.

iii. Rebuke and Second Appeal (18:39)

18:39 The blind man's cry meets with popular rebuke (ἐπιτιμάω, *epitimaō*; BAGD 303; BAA 614; elsewhere in Luke at 4:35, 39, 41; 8:24; 9:21, 42, 55; 17:3; 18:15; 19:39; 23:40). Many people in front (οἱ προάγοντες, *hoi proagontes*) of him tell him to be quiet (σιγάω, *sigaō*; BAGD

---

11. Josephus, *Antiquities* 8.2.5 §§42–49, mentions the healing skill of Solomon, thus providing a base for this description of David's son. This view is contrary to Nolland 1993b: 900, who argues against a Jewish expectation of a Davidic healer. His point is correct, but these traditions raise the question of what connections Jesus' acts of healing might surface. With all the eschatological ferment in Palestine in this period, why deny the possibility of such reflection on such events? Meier 1994: 689 is certainly correct to see the connection as not surprising in this setting.

749 §1b; BAA 1499 §1b; Acts 12:17; 15:12; Rom. 16:25 [to keep a secret]; 1 Cor. 14:28, 30, 34; cf. Luke 19:40). In other words, they told him to shut up. No reason is given for this call to be quiet, but speculation centers around the man's use of the title *Son of David* (Leaney 1958: 239). The reason, however, may be more mundane: perhaps they thought that Jesus did not need to be bothered by a blind beggar—like the disciples' reaction to the children who approached Jesus (Luke 18:15–17).

Their efforts to muzzle the blind man fail, and he cries out even louder and repeats his request to the Son of David to show him mercy. Peer pressure is a decided failure here! Plummer (1896: 431) plausibly suggests that Luke's shift to ἔκραζεν (*ekrazen*, he was crying out) from ἐβόησεν (*eboēsen*, he cried out) in 18:38 indicates an intelligent cry for help instead of a more intensive scream, since the former term is also used of animal cries. The failure to respect public pressure shows how desperate this man is to be healed and how convinced he is that Jesus can help him.

Mark 10:48 matches Luke's wording of the blind man's cry and the note that he "cried out even more." But Mark says that many (πολλοί, *polloi*) in the crowd rebuked the man and told him to keep silent (σιωπάω [*siōpaō*] in contrast to Luke's σιγάω [*sigaō*]).[12] Using the same verb as Mark, Matthew says in 20:31 that the crowd rebuked the two blind men and asked them to be silent.

b. The Healing (18:40–43)
i. Jesus' Response (18:40–41a)

18:40 The cry does not go unheeded by Jesus, who stops (σταθείς, *statheis*; BAGD 382 §II.1.a; BAA 774 §II.1.a; Luke 7:14; 8:44; 17:12; 24:17) and orders the man to be brought to him.[13] The man approaches Jesus, who asks the blind man what he wants Jesus to do for him. Jesus will not reject his request as the crowd did. He always has time for compassion.

Mark 10:49–50 has more detail: Jesus stops and tells the crowd to call the man. This detail adds irony, since the crowd now tells the blind man to take heart and rise because Jesus is calling him. This news causes the blind man to throw off his cloak and rush to Jesus. Matthew 20:32, like Luke, has a simplified version: Jesus stops and calls to the blind men, asking them what they wish him to do.

12. Σιωπάω, a favorite term for Mark (3:4; 4:39; 9:34; 10:48; 14:61), occurs elsewhere in the NT only at Matt. 20:31; 26:63; Luke 1:20; Acts 18:9; BAGD 752; BAA 1504. See the additional note for a textual issue that influences this point.

13. Κελεύω (to order) is frequent in Acts (e.g., 4:15; 8:38; 12:19; 21:34; 22:24, 30; 23:3, 10, 35; 25:6, 17, 21, 23; 27:43), though this is its only use in Luke. Matthew uses it seven times; BAGD 427; BAA 869.

18:41a The exchange between Jesus and the blind man is short. Jesus simply asks the man what he wishes.

ii. Request (18:41b)

18:41b The blind man addresses Jesus as κύριε (*kyrie*, Lord) to show respect to the Son of David.[14] Since the request starts with ἵνα (*hina*, that), the elision should be filled with θέλω (*thelō*, I wish) (Marshall 1978: 694).[15] The blind man wishes to see (ἀναβλέπω, *anablepō*; BAGD 50–51 §2; BAA 99 §2; Tob. 14:2; Matt. 11:5; Acts 9:12, 17–18). Ἀναβλέπω appears in Jesus' reply to John the Baptist (Luke 7:22) about his doing the works of the eschaton, and the related noun, ἀνάβλεψις (*anablepsis*, return of sight), appears in the key 4:18, when Jesus declares in the synagogue that Isa. 61:1 with its note of eschatological hope is being fulfilled (Schweizer 1984: 289). As such, this sign of restoring sight, which is Luke's last miracle, is significant, especially since it is a part of what Jesus announced he would do as a part of his mission back at its beginning. The miracle makes clear that this is Jesus' work as the promised Davidite. Jesus brings light to darkness (Luke 1:78–79; Col. 1:12–14). Deliverance, defined broadly, is the business of the Son of David, who possesses significant authority to bless.

   The accounts in Matt. 20:33 = Mark 10:51 show the same exchange, with slightly different wording that can be attributed to stylistic differences. As noted above, Mark has the different vocative for "rabbi." Matthew says of the two blind men, "Lord, that our eyes might be opened."

iii. Jesus' Commendation of Faith (18:42)

18:42 Jesus honors the request. He commands the man to "receive his sight," using the same verb, ἀναβλέπω (*anablepō*), as the man did in making the request. Noting the attitude that permitted him to respond, Jesus commends the man's faith publicly, so that the event becomes a lesson about faith. Nolland (1993b: 901) argues that it is the man's persistence, not his christological confession of the Son of David, that Jesus praises. But this is not an either/or situation. The blind man's understanding of who Jesus is feeds his persistent faith. Both elements are commended here. Luke frequently notes when faith is instrumental in causing Jesus to act (7:50; 8:48; 17:19; Plummer 1896: 431; Ernst 1977: 511). The other evangelists also make

---

14. Matthew uses κύριε, while Mark uses the Semitic ῥαββουνί (rabbi). Luke never uses ῥαββουνί (only Mark 10:51 and John 20:16) or the related ῥαββί (fifteen times in Matthew, Mark, and John); BAGD 733; BAA 1467.

15. Some translations treat ἵνα as an imperative of request: "Please heal me."

such notes (Matt. 9:22 = Mark 5:34). Clearly the man's belief in Jesus brought benefit to him. The healing pictures the presence of a deeper reality beyond the restoration of his sight. His faith has saved him. Light exists where darkness previously had resided.

The reply resembles Mark 10:52, except that in Mark's account Jesus tells the man to go his way (ὕπαγε, hypage), a word more common in Matthew (nineteen times) and Mark (fifteen times) than in Luke (five times). Matthew 20:34 tells of Jesus touching their eyes, so that both blind men immediately received sight. Matthew lacks any verbal element in the response, though in describing the return of sight, ἀναβλέπω is also used. Matthew 9:29 also notes that Jesus touches the eyes in the healing of the blind men.

iv. Resolution: Healing and Praise (18:43)

The healing is instantaneous, as noted in all three accounts, though **18:43** with different terms.[16] The man becomes a following disciple, as ἀκολουθέω (akoloutheō, to follow) shows (BAGD 31 §3; BAA 60 §3). This key verb is used seventeen times by Luke, often as a technical term of discipleship (e.g., 5:11, 27–28; 9:23, 59, 61; 18:22, 28; also Mark 1:18).

Besides healing and discipleship, Luke adds his own note about praise. First, the blind man himself glorifies God (cf. 1:64; 2:20; 5:25–26; 7:16; 13:13; 17:15; 19:37; Grundmann 1963: 357; Fitzmyer 1985: 1217; Wiefel 1988: 325). Next, the crowd praises God. Αἶνον (ainon, praise) is rare, occurring only here and at Matt. 21:16 (Schlier, TDNT 1:177; BAGD 23; BAA 44). The use of λαός (laos, people) to describe the group of following disciples is, however, very Lucan, since he often compares the people's positive response to the leaders' negative one (Ellis 1974: 220). In fact, Luke will use λαός eighteen more times before the end of his Gospel (Fitzmyer 1985: 1217). He will note their praise in 19:48 and 21:38, a reaction that becomes an ironic contrast to their negative response in 23:13–25. These events do not occur in some remote corner. Jesus' act of compassion toward the blind man elicits a flood of praise to God, even as Jesus nears his tragic fate in Jerusalem.

While the parallels share the mention of the immediacy of the healing and of the blind man joining in discipleship, only Luke men-

16. Matthew has εὐθέως, which is used once in Mark (7:35) but thirteen times in Matthew, six times in Luke, and nine times in Acts. Mark has εὐθύς, which he uses forty-one times, while Matthew uses it five times and Luke twice (Luke 6:49; Acts 10:16). Luke has παραχρῆμα, a term never used by Mark, only twice by Matthew (Matt. 21:19, 20), but ten times in Luke's Gospel (e.g., 5:25; 8:44, 55; 22:60) and six times in Acts (BAGD 623; BAA 1260). The Gospels often note how quickly people are healed by Jesus.

tions the crowd's and the blind man's praise that accompanies the event, a note he loves to make. Plummer (1896: 432) closes his discussion of this unit by noting twelve places where Luke provided his own unique stylistic touches, reinforcing the point that Luke told the account in his own way.

Summary   Luke 18:35–43 describes a final act of mercy. Jesus' last miracle in Luke is loaded with significance. The event contains the first public, directly messianic confession of Jesus, which occurs as he draws near to his anticipated death in Jerusalem. What irony to contrast this confession with Jesus' own prediction in the previous passage!

In this account of the restoration of sight and the picture of faith, Jesus' salvific power as Davidite becomes visible for all to see, as do the prerequisites for unleashing those benefits. The poor, begging blind man ends up with everything. Earlier the spiritually poor, but rich young man ended up with nothing from Jesus. He walked away from Jesus sad, because of his wealth. Now the blind man walks away praising God because of the joy of sight and salvation. In these two men and their contrasting fates, Luke has summarized much of his teaching at a practical level. Who has access to God's blessing and salvific power? The one who recognizes the need for God's mercy. Who is rich before God? The one who follows Jesus by faith. God's treasure comes through faith.

A final note is found in the response of those touched by God: praise—not only from the one benefiting directly from the healing, but also from those who see God's benefits poured out on others. Luke is always interested in sharing the joy that comes with Jesus' ministry. Luke's message is very simple: Jesus of Nazareth is the promised Son of David who brings the work of the eschaton to those who respond to him. His work goes forth to God's glory and praise. Jerusalem nears, but Jesus continues to minister. Luke says, "See who Jesus is, just as the blind man did." Sight is a matter of the heart, not just of the eyes.

Additional Note

18:39. Some Lucan manuscripts (א, A, Θ, family 1, family 13, Byz) agree with the Marcan wording of the call to silence, while others (B, D, L, P, T, W, Ψ) have σιγήσῃ (be silent). The latter reading is perhaps original because of better manuscript distribution and absence of harmonization (Fitzmyer 1985: 1216).

3. Zacchaeus: Faith's Transforming Power (19:1–10)

The story of Zacchaeus is the second Jericho event to picture the elements of conversion (Talbert 1982: 176). Luke provides a beautiful literary contrast between this event and the blind man's healing. In 18:35–43 a blind man cries for help to see, while here a short man must work his way up the tree to see Jesus (Fitzmyer 1985: 1222). Jesus meets the needs of both, although in each case people try to stop them or complain about Jesus' attention to them. Zacchaeus is an example of someone longing to see Jesus, just as the blind man did, but there is a difference in their stories: where the blind man had to cry out to get Jesus' attention, here Jesus takes the initiative.[1] Zacchaeus gets more than he bargained for in trying to see Jesus. The story of the blind man pictured faith, while the Zacchaeus story pictures Jesus' initiative to save the lost (19:10).

The account makes several points, some of which repeat ideas fundamental to Luke (Pilgrim 1981: 130; O'Hanlon 1981; Loewe 1974). First, Jesus again reaches out to the unpopular "tax collectors and sinners" (19:7).[2] The gospel is for the outcast. Second, Zacchaeus provides a model response to Jesus' initiative: joy, generosity, and the righting of previous wrongs. He represents how a disciple reacts to Jesus in a way that is pleasing to God and reflects a true relationship with God (19:9). When Zacchaeus offers to pay back those he has wronged, he agrees to the most demanding penalty of the law: someone who stole an animal that subsequently died or was sold was to pay the owner four or five times the value of the animal (Exod. 22:1 [21:37 MT]; 2 Sam. 12:6). Zacchaeus carries out God's will with a response from the heart. Third, the exchange between Jesus and the crowd shows that a relationship with God requires not only Jesus' call but a response to

---

1. Tannehill 1986: 122 calls this account a "quest story," but this label is not precise. Zacchaeus just wanted to see Jesus, he was not seeking something from him. Tannehill recognizes this and therefore speaks of Jesus going beyond Zacchaeus's expectations. The story really shows Jesus' initiative to seek and save the lost (19:10). If there is a quest, it is Jesus' quest for the lost.

2. Every Lucan mention of tax collectors portrays them favorably: 3:12; 5:27; 7:29; 15:1; 18:10.

that call. Such a response is what leads Jesus to call Zacchaeus a "son of Abraham." Despite popular impressions about him, Zacchaeus has the right to know God, and he emerges as a faithful son of Abraham, unlike others in the nation who claim to follow in the patriarch's footsteps. Fourth, as he often does, Jesus affirms Zacchaeus's place before God, despite the questioning of others. Zacchaeus's personal response to God and the transformation of his perspective show that his vocation is not as important as his heart. Finally, Zacchaeus is an example of a rich person who gets through the eye of the needle (Tiede 1988: 319). He stands in contrast to the rich ruler of 18:18–23. Since Zacchaeus handles his wealth with compassion after realizing his wrongs, Jesus commends him and accepts him.

Zacchaeus may be compared to and contrasted with other figures in Luke. His works reflect the true repentance called for by John the Baptist (3:10–14). Like Levi the tax collector, he is called by Jesus (5:27–32). He is like the tax collector who approached God humbly and responded to his call, so that Jesus said his prayer was acceptable (18:9–14). He is unlike the rich fool, since Zacchaeus becomes rich toward God (12:13–21). He is unlike the rich man who ignored Lazarus (16:19–31). And, as noted above, he is unlike the rich ruler (18:18–23). Such a role model is an appropriate figure to focus upon as Jesus nears the end of his Jerusalem journey.

Sources and Historicity

The account is unique to Luke (Aland 1985: §265; Ernst 1977: 512–13 notes how the text fits well with themes from L). Some argue that it was developed from Mark 2:14–17 (Bultmann 1963: 34; Creed 1930: 228; Horsley 1987: 212–17 [who is also skeptical of the negative reputation of tax collectors and Jesus' association with them]; the Jesus Seminar [Funk and Hoover 1993: 372–73]). The Jesus Seminar prints all the dialogue in black type, claiming that the account is a creative development of Mark 2:17, turning a popular proverb into a saying of Jesus. But this approach fails because the points of contact with the Levi account are few. The story's additional features and placement are also against this identification. Fitzmyer (1985: 1219) strongly rejects this approach, noting that the name *Zacchaeus*, the climbing of the tree, and the placement in Jericho are against this alleged linkage (also Marshall 1978: 695; Grundmann 1963: 358–59). Nolland (1993b: 904) notes that the paratactic style and non-Lucan elements point to a pre-Lucan account.

The unity of the account has been challenged. In particular, some question whether 19:8 and 19:10 were part of the original account or Luke's comments (see the exegesis of these verses for details).[3] Wellhausen (1904: 103) argues that Zacchaeus could not climb a tree in Jericho's narrow streets, but a roof (Klostermann 1929: 184; Creed 1930: 230). Both Dalman (1924: 15) and Bultmann (1963: 65–66) counter this objection by noting that trees did grow in Herodian Jericho (Marshall 1978: 696). Such an acceptance of tax collectors and sinners is at the heart of Jesus' ministry (Luke 5:32; 15:7, 10; Matt. 18:14; B. Meyer 1979: 161–62). Meier (1994: 1036) speaks of multiple attestation as supporting this theme (but the event is seen as a later creation by E. Sanders 1985: 175, 203). Jeremias's view (1971a: 156) is preferred over Sanders's.

Talbert (1982: 176) calls the account a "conflict story" because of the exchange starting in 19:7. Bultmann (1963: 33–34) calls it "biographical apophthegm" because of the numerous details revealed about the main subject, Zacchaeus, and because of its key sayings. The emphasis on the climactic saying makes it a pronouncement account (Fitzmyer 1985: 1219 [probably]; Berger 1984: 82). The outline of Luke 19:1–10 is as follows:

a. Jesus' association with Zacchaeus (19:1–6)
   i. Setting (19:1)
   ii. Zacchaeus's efforts to see Jesus (19:2–4)
   iii. Jesus' initiative to stay with Zacchaeus (19:5–6)
b. The crowd's murmuring (19:7)
c. Jesus' explanation (19:8–10)
   i. Zacchaeus's defense (19:8)
   ii. Jesus' vindication and the lesson: The Son of Man seeks the lost (19:9–10)

The major theme of the unit is Jesus' initiative to the lost. Jesus again associates with the despised, represented here by a tax collector. One can also see Zacchaeus's initiative to see Jesus, and his joy at the privilege of being addressed by Jesus. In contrast stands the crowd's wrongful murmuring about Jesus' association with sinners. Zacchaeus reflects generosity and knows his duty to make restitution for his wrongs. Jesus accepts the sinner as a full son and reassures him. Zacchaeus is an example of a rich person who is received. He illustrates Jesus' mission: to seek and save the lost.

3. Bultmann 1963: 33–34 and Fitzmyer 1985: 1219 take 19:8 as a Lucan addition, breaking the flow of the story. Marshall 1978: 695 agrees with Bultmann that 19:10 may be a later comment, but Fitzmyer sees it as part of the account. Schweizer 1984: 290 regards 19:8 as a non-Lucan addition to the story, while Luke is responsible for 19:10. Those who see Luke adding 19:10 often suggest that it is his version of the famous ransom saying of Mark 10:45.

Exegesis and Exposition

[1]And coming in, he passed through Jericho. [2]And behold there was a man whose name was Zacchaeus, and he himself was a chief tax collector and was rich. [3]And he was seeking to see who Jesus was; but he was not able because of the crowd, for he was short in stature. [4]So he ⌐ran ahead⌐ and climbed up into a sycamore tree to see him, for he was to pass that way. [5]And as Jesus came to the spot, he looked up and said to him, "Zacchaeus, quickly come down, for today it is necessary for me to remain at your house." [6]And quickly he came down and welcomed him, rejoicing.

[7]And when all saw this, they were grumbling and saying, "He has gone in to be the guest of a sinful man."

[8]But Zacchaeus stood and said to the Lord, "Behold, the half of my goods, Lord, I am going to give to the poor; and if I have defrauded anyone of anything, I am going to pay it back four times." [9]And Jesus said to him, "Today salvation has come to this house, since he also is a son of Abraham. [10]For the Son of Man came to seek and to save the lost."

a. Jesus' Association with Zacchaeus (19:1–6)
i. Setting (19:1)

19:1 Jesus is still on his journey to Jerusalem as this verse indicates: he is traveling through (διέρχομαι, *dierchomai*) Jericho.[4] As will become clear, Jesus plans to stay the night here, and he has a specific host in mind.

ii. Zacchaeus's Efforts to See Jesus (19:2–4)

19:2 Luke introduces Zacchaeus, the main character. Ζακχαῖος is the Greek form of זַכַּי (Zakkai), meaning "clean" or "innocent" (SB 2:249; 2 Macc. 10:19; Josephus, *Life* 46 §239). The name is not an abbreviated form of Zechariah (Fitzmyer 1985: 1223; against Creed 1930: 230 and Marshall 1978: 696). Luke makes nothing of the name. Zacchaeus was chief tax collector (ἀρχιτελώνης, *architelōnēs*—otherwise unattested in Greek; Michel, *TDNT* 8:98, 104–5; BAGD 113; BAA 226) at what apparently was a Roman regional tax center. Zacchaeus was an administrator who bid for and organized the collection and took a cut from the labor of his underlings. His wealth is probably related to his job and comes from the commission that such officials took from the taxes (see the exegesis of 3:12). Whether "chief" (ἀρχι-, *archi-*) means first of rank or simply a "major" (i.e., rich) tax collector is not clear (Nolland 1993b: 904; O'Hanlon 1981: 9).

It is difficult to know the accuracy of the church tradition about Zacchaeus. Peter supposedly appointed him bishop of Caesarea

---

4. Διέρχομαι is common in Luke's writings: Luke 2:15, 35; 4:30; 5:15; 8:22; 9:6; 11:24; 17:11; 19:4; Acts 12:10; 13:6; 14:24; plus eighteen more times in Acts; BAGD 194; BAA 391; Fitzmyer 1985: 1223–24; Plummer 1896: 432.

against his will (Zahn 1920: 619 n. 5; Grundmann 1963: 359; Wiefel 1988: 326 n. 5; Pseudo-Clement, *Homilies* 3.63; *Apostolic Constitutions* 7.46). Clement of Alexandria identifies him with Matthew (*Stromata* 4.6.35), but this tradition is uncertain (Ernst 1977: 513). Since his name is Jewish in origin, Zacchaeus was most likely Jewish. Both his name and the remark of 19:9 suggest this origin.

19:3 Zacchaeus is curious about Jesus, but he does not yet know Jesus (as indicated by the phrase τίς ἐστιν, *tis estin*, who he is). He had probably heard reports about Jesus and was interested, like anyone might be, about a well-known figure. But there are two obstacles: the crowd is so large that he cannot get a look at Jesus, and Zacchaeus is short.[5] If Zacchaeus is to see Jesus, he will have to be resourceful. The narrative portrays him initially as an outsider, quite distant from Jesus.

19:4 Zacchaeus's solution is to run ahead of Jesus and locate a better vantage point. He finds a sycamore tree and climbs into its branches because (ὅτι, *hoti*) the teacher is getting ready to pass his way. Συκομορέα (*sycomorea*, sycamore tree) appears only here in the NT, though a related term (συκάμινος, *sykaminos*, sycamine tree) is found in 17:6 (BAGD 776; BAA 1548–49; Hunzinger, *TDNT* 7:758–59). This tree is not the mulberry fig of western Europe (Luce 1933: 292), but more like an oak tree, only with a short trunk and wide, lateral branches that make for easy climbing. Perched on such a spot, Zacchaeus had a "bird's eye" view.

iii. Jesus' Initiative to Stay with Zacchaeus (19:5–6)

19:5 Jesus makes a surprise move. Upon arriving under the tree in which Zacchaeus is perched, he looks up and addresses the tax collector by name. The text does not indicate how Jesus knows Zacchaeus's name: perhaps he knew it by supernatural enablement (like John 1:47–48) or by hearing people call to Zacchaeus or by asking about his name (Plummer 1896: 434; Arndt 1956: 389; C. A. Evans 1990: 283; Marshall 1978: 696).[6] Despite the absence of this detail, it is clear that Jesus is in control of the situation.

---

5. The first obstacle (the crowd) is indicated by ἀπό (BAGD 87 §V.1; BAA 175 §V.1; also Luke 21:26; 22:45; 24:41; Acts 11:19; 12:14; 22:11; John 21:6; Heb. 5:7) and the second obstacle (Zacchaeus's size) by ὅτι. While ἡλικία (BAGD 345 §2; BAA 700 §2) can refer to age, here it refers to Zacchaeus's height (as in Luke 2:52; see the exegesis of 12:25). The crowd produced a barrier of a different kind in 18:39.

6. Fitzmyer 1985: 1224 sees this as the wrong question to ask, since the text does not address the issue. Klostermann 1929: 185 simply says that supernatural knowledge is not expressed by Luke. Luce 1933: 292 takes a rationalistic approach: Jesus inquired about his name, but Luke portrays his knowledge as supernatural. Nolland 1993b: 905 speaks of Jesus' "uncanny knowledge."

Just as Zacchaeus was quick to run and find a spot to see Jesus, so he is urgently told to come down: σπεύσας κατάβηθι (*speusas katabēthi*) is a descriptive participle of manner in combination with an aorist imperative (BAGD 762; BAA 1522; σπεύδω occurred earlier in Luke 2:16). The explanation (γάρ, *gar*) for the request follows: "it is necessary" (δεῖ, *dei*) for Jesus to stay with Zacchaeus.

Jesus uses key terms in his request. In Luke σήμερον (*sēmeron*, today) frequently denotes the immediacy of an event or the need to respond (2:11; 4:21; 5:26; 13:32, 33; 22:34; 23:43; BAGD 749; BAA 1497). It has an emphatic position in Jesus' request. Luke often uses δεῖ to denote divine necessity (2:49; 4:43; 9:22; 13:16, 33; 15:32; 17:25; 22:37; 24:7, 26, 44; Danker 1988: 305). Why it was so necessary is not stated, but, given the crowd's reaction, it might be that the visit gives Jesus a chance to underscore the nature of his mission. Zacchaeus is the model respondent to Jesus' initiative. The request "to remain" at Zacchaeus's house implies a stay of unspecified duration. Zacchaeus—who only wishes a glimpse of the famous teacher—gets much more: he will host the teacher in his home.[7] The request shows that Jesus accepts Zacchaeus.

19:6   Zacchaeus does as he is commanded. In fact, in describing Zacchaeus's response, Luke uses the same terms used in Jesus' command. Zacchaeus's immediate response and excitement recalls the shepherds' reaction to the announcement of Jesus' birth (2:10, 16) and the call of Levi with its note of reception (5:29; Ernst 1977: 514; Klostermann 1929: 185). Zacchaeus welcomes (ὑποδέχομαι, *hypodechomai*) Jesus into his home, whose acceptance is a sign of fellowship and forgiveness (10:38; Marshall 1978: 697). The description of Zacchaeus's response does not explicitly mention faith, but his actions show that Jesus has made a deep impression upon him (19:8 confirms this impression). Luke adds one more detail: joy accompanied his welcome, a common note in Luke (1:14; 2:10; 10:20; 13:17; 15:5, 32; 19:37; 24:41, 52; Danker 1988: 305). Zacchaeus responds fully to Jesus' kindness, but others present have different reactions. Now Zacchaeus is an insider despite the opinions of others.

b. The Crowd's Murmuring (19:7)

19:7   The crowd is offended by Jesus' intention to stay with Zacchaeus. They like Jesus' miracles, but they do not care for his personal associations. Καταλύω (*katalyō*, to be the guest of) is used with this meaning only twice in the NT (here and at 9:12) and literally means "to unhitch" pack animals for the night (Gen. 19:2; 24:23, 25; Sir.

---

7. The spiritual parallel that someone who responds to Jesus gets more than imagined is not, of course, explicitly made here (Col. 1:26–28).

14:25, 27; 36:27 [= 36:31 NRSV]; Josephus, *Life* 48 §248; Fitzmyer 1985: 1224; Luce 1933: 292; Plummer 1896: 434). The populace grumbles (διαγογγύζω, *diagongyzō*) against Jesus' choice of host, which recalls an earlier, similar complaint by the Pharisees in 15:2 (the term occurs only these two times in the NT; BAGD 182; BAA 365). A similar complaint in 5:30 uses γογγύζω (*gongyzō*, to grumble; BAGD 164; BAA 328; elsewhere in the NT at Matt. 20:11; John 6:41, 43, 61; 7:32; 1 Cor. 10:10 [twice]). Grumbling is almost always a negative concept in the NT. The complaint about Jesus staying with sinners shows that the crowd has learned little from his ministry. Luke notes that "all" complain; the sentiment is felt by everyone in the crowd (3:16; 4:15; Nolland 1993b: 905 sees "all" as hyperbolic, which is possible; Danker 1988: 305 sees "all" as the general public). The descriptive phrase "with sinners" (παρὰ ἁμαρτωλῷ, *para hamartōlō*) is in the emphatic position and probably expresses the crowd's evaluation of tax collectors and the social offense they feel toward them because they take advantage of those from whom they collect. The crowd charges Jesus of associating with sinners (Arndt 1956: 389 sees a parallel to the older brother of the prodigal parable; 15:25–32).

c. Jesus' Explanation (19:8–10)
i. Zacchaeus's Defense (19:8)

Zacchaeus responds to the charges, but other than the detail about his standing (σταθείς, *statheis*; cf. 18:11, 40), the setting is unclear. Several theories exist to explain when Zacchaeus's remarks might have occurred: (1) during or after dinner (Ellis 1974: 221—mainly because Luke has so many scenes in such a setting; e.g., 14:1–24; 24:13–32), (2) in his house at an unknown time with visitors present (Arndt 1956: 389), (3) during a conversation between Zacchaeus and Jesus before his conversion (Luce 1933: 293), (4) immediately at the tree (Plummer 1896: 434 and Fitzmyer 1985: 1225), or (5) at a meal before people (Marshall 1978: 697, combining the first two options). The uncertainty about the setting arises because it is not clear whether the reference to Jesus' staying with a sinner means that he has already entered the house and separated himself from the crowd. There is no way to sort out the options, though it does look like Zacchaeus's speech takes place in a public forum, given Jesus' instructive remarks in 19:9 (thus, view 4 or shortly thereafter).

19:8

The main issue in the verse, however, is the force of the verbs δίδωμι (*didōmi*, to give) and ἀποδίδωμι (*apodidōmi*, to give back; Büchsel, *TDNT* 2:168; Luke 4:20; 7:42; 9:42; 10:35; 12:59). Some take the present tenses as descriptive of Zacchaeus's current behavior (Godet 1875: 2.217; Fitzmyer 1985: 1220, 1225). According to this view, Zacchaeus denies the charge that he is a sinner by showing his habit of generosity and fairness. Fitzmyer argues for this view because of the absence of any mention of faith and because the idea of giving back fourfold in the future, if Zacchaeus has just repented, results in an odd sense, with him apparently anticipating repayment for future extortion! Plummer (1896: 435) argues against this view since it makes Zacchaeus boast before Jesus. In addition, this view has to take ὑπαρχόντων (hyparchontōn) in the unusual sense of "capital." Fitzmyer's approach to 19:8b also ignores that the extortion looks back to past acts (so the aorist ἐσυκοφάντησα, esykophantēsa, I extorted; only here and 3:14 in the NT; BAGD 776 §2; BAA 1549 §2; Prov. 14:31; 22:16; 28:3; Nestle 1903). One could perhaps take the aorist in a more perfective sense ("if I have extorted from anyone") and preserve Fitzmyer's sense, but given the context of present verbs this is harsher. A perfect verb would have made better sense for Fitzmyer's approach. Finally, Danker (1988: 305) notes that the crowd sees Zacchaeus as a sinner, which implies that if he had been generous in the past, the crowd would hardly have complained about him as such. Thus, Fitzmyer's view means that the crowd is wrong and ignorant of the tax collector's practices.

It is far more likely that the verbs should be taken in the sense of present resolve, as a reflection of Zacchaeus's repentance and faith as a result of meeting Jesus (cf. Luke 3:8; Plummer 1896: 435; Arndt 1956: 389; Klostermann 1929: 185; Marshall 1978: 697–98; Creed 1930: 231; Nolland 1993b: 906). Faith is not explicitly mentioned because the actions imply its presence in concrete expression, recalling the teaching of John the Baptist (3:8–14) as well as the example of the sinful woman (7:36–50). In fact, Jesus' remarks about salvation and saving the lost in 19:9–10 virtually guarantee that the verbs here note future resolve, not present behavior, since they presume a change of heart. Zacchaeus's encounter with Jesus has led him to change the way he handles money—from taking advantage of people to serving them.

The cultural background shows the extent of Zacchaeus's promise. In Judaism, it was considered generous to give away 20 percent of one's possessions. More than this was not considered prudent (SB 4:546–47; Danker 1988: 306; b. Ketub. 50a; Lachs 1987: 331 n. 6; see the exegesis of 18:22). Legal restitution for extortion was 20 percent (Lev. 5:16; Num. 5:7), but Zacchaeus assumes the harsher double penalty that the Mosaic law imposed on rustlers (Exod. 22:1 [21:37 MT]; 2 Sam. 12:6 [the LXX of this verse reads "sevenfold"]; contrast m. Ketub. 3.9). By taking on this obligation, Zacchaeus is showing the "thankoffering expressive of a changed heart" (Ellis 1974: 221). The custom of fourfold payment also has precedent at Qumran and in Roman law (Mur 19.10, a divorce writ dated A.D. 111 [DJD 2:105]; Creed 1930: 231; SB 2:250; Michel, TDNT 8:105 n. 154; Kerr 1986–87).

Zacchaeus offers to give away half (ἡμίσια, *hēmisia*) of his possessions (BAGD 348; BAA 705; elsewhere in the NT at Mark 6:23; Rev. 11:9, 11; 12:14; also 1 Macc. 3:34, 37; Tob. 10:10; BDF §164.5; BDR §164.5). By any standard this action is generous. Quite the opposite of the rich ruler's response (Luke 18:23), this response reflects Luke's attention to the needs of the poor (Arndt 1956: 388: Jesus' "love wins remarkable victories"). But Zacchaeus also commits to make restitution for his wrongs: if he has extorted anyone, he will pay them back fourfold (τετραπλοῦν, *tetraploun*; only here in the NT; BAGD 813; BAA 1622). The first-class condition suggests that Zacchaeus is aware that he has defrauded some (Ellis 1974: 221; Plummer 1896: 435; for the grammar see Rom. 5:17; Col. 2:20; 3:1). Zacchaeus sets about the task of repaying those he stole from, a mammoth task for a tax collector. Jesus will recognize and commend his change of heart, which is evidence of genuine faith in God. In his transformed state, Zacchaeus becomes an example of how to handle money generously (Luke 16:9–13; 1 Tim. 6:6–10, 17–18). His action recalls the earlier exhortation of Luke 12:33.

The difficulty of determining the setting leads many to see 19:8 as an insertion. Those who take this approach point to the remark's intrusion between the crowd's complaint and the teacher's response. They also note the use of Lucan terms like κύριος (*kyrios*, Lord), σταθείς (*statheis*, standing), εἶπεν πρός (*eipen pros*, he said to), and ὑπαρχόντων (*hyparchontōn*, possessions). In addition, it is argued that the verse emphasizes the Lucan theme of repentance and interrupts the account's original flow (Leaney 1958: 241; Fitzmyer 1985: 1219). But the importance and accuracy of the legal details outweigh these objections. Derrett (1970: 278–85) notes that the legal details are key to the story.[8] In this culture, eating with a person who had ill-gotten gain made one a "partner in crime." Social ostracism of such characters was seen as a deterrent (Nolland 1993b: 905), and one was even allowed to lie to them (*m. Ned.* 3.4). Restitution was forced on shepherds, tax collectors, and revenue farmers, though repentance was hard to come by (*b. B. Qam.* 94b). Tax collectors were assumed to be unclean unless they proclaimed otherwise (*m. Ṭohar.* 7.6), and it was assumed that they had taken money inappropriately (*m. B. Qam.* 10.1–2). (For more on tax collectors, see the exegesis of 3:12.) The declaration of a commitment to make restitution sets up Jesus' commendation of Zacchaeus, which, without 19:8, would make less sense. The verse belongs in the original narrative and is not an insertion.

---

8. On the debate about 19:8, see Mitchell 1990, who argues for the view that Zacchaeus is defending his past behavior. On the other side, Hamm 1981 makes the case for repentance and conversion.

ii. Jesus' Vindication and the Lesson: The Son of Man Seeks the Lost (19:9–10)

19:9 Jesus responds to Zacchaeus but his remarks are intended for everyone. The phrase πρὸς αὐτόν (*pros auton*) is variously translated "to him," indicating that Zacchaeus is being addressed by Jesus, even though the third person is used in the direct speech at the end of the verse (Plummer 1896: 436), or "with regard to him," as Mark 12:12 = Luke 20:18 allows (Arndt 1956: 390; Luce 1933: 293). It is hard to be sure (Fitzmyer 1985: 1225); nevertheless, the use of the third person makes clear that Jesus intends the comment for the crowd.

Jesus comments on what has just come to pass: salvation has come to Zacchaeus and his house. Σωτηρία (*sōtēria*) is rare in Luke (elsewhere only 1:69, 71, 77), but it describes the restored relationship that one has with God when he delivers (cf. Luke 10:5–7, 21–24; 23:43; Acts 13:26–27; 2 Cor. 6:2). This deliverance accompanies Jesus' visit and is made possible by Zacchaeus's response to the invitation. The reference to today (σήμερον, *sēmeron*) also shows that Zacchaeus's remarks in the previous verse must be seen as expressing his resolve to change. Salvation's coming to one's house is commonly referred to in Acts (10:2; 11:14; 16:15, 31; 18:8; Schweizer 1984: 291; Grundmann 1963: 360; Fitzmyer 1985: 1225; cf. the benefit coming to the family of a saved one in 1 Cor. 7:14–16).

The reason (καθότι, *kathoti*; BAGD 391; BAA 794; elsewhere in the NT at Luke 1:7; Acts 2:24, 45; 4:35; 17:31) for the extension of benefits is Zacchaeus's heritage, which makes him eligible for blessing: he is a son of Abraham, a Jew.[9] This purely racial designation is not meant in the broader spiritual sense that Paul uses later (Rom. 4:11–18; Gal. 3:9, 29). This designation is common in the Gospels, though often with the note that blessing is not automatically associated with race (Matt. 15:24; Luke 3:8; *m. ʾAbot* 5.19; cf. Luke 16:22, 24). In short, Zacchaeus's vocation does not cancel his potential access to God. His race makes his response most appropriate. This is the type of person Jesus seeks to reach with the nation's promise. Jesus does not see tax collection as a problem (20:20–26). Zacchaeus has rights to God's promise, if he will take advantage of them—which he does (Fitzmyer 1985: 1226). He "cashes in" through faith. That one is a sinner does not cancel one's right to appeal to God's mercy.[10] The crowd has misread the moment.

---

9. This Jewish connection reflects the presence of the tradition (so Leaney 1958: 241–42, against Marshall 1978: 698, who sees a Lucan or edited comment).

10. In Rom. 3:21–31, Paul argues the same point, going the opposite direction: because all are sinners, all must come to God for his mercy.

Jesus concludes with a statement of mission that explains his declaration of salvation (γάρ [*gar*, for] looks back to 19:9; Plummer 1896:
437). Zacchaeus's transformation represents a fulfillment of Jesus'
call. The picture of seeking and saving the lost (ἀπολωλός, *apolōlos*;
BAGD 95 §2aα; BAA 191 §2aα; Matt. 18:11 variant; 1 Cor. 1:18;
2 Cor. 2:15; 4:3; 2 Thess. 2:10) recalls the shepherd imagery applied
to God in Ezek. 34. What God was to do for the nation as its shepherd, because the nation of Ezekiel's time was leaderless, Jesus does
now (esp. Ezek. 34:2, 4, 16, 22–23; John 10; Jeremias, *TDNT* 6:500;
Tiede 1988: 322). In fact, Jesus becomes the instrument through
whom God works. Jesus' mission is to initiate relationships with
those who do not know God and call to them to come to know him.
Nolland (1993b: 907) sees a strand of Davidic hope in the OT background. Royal reform of the nation is part of Jesus' goal.

19:10

This passage again stresses Jesus' initiative to seek the lost and to
proclaim salvation for those who respond with faith. Like Luke 5:32,
it emphasizes that one of the prerequisites of responding to Jesus is
to realize that one stands in need of God. Like Luke 5:24, it emphasizes the Son of Man's present ministry to forgive sin. Zacchaeus is
like the prodigal, the lost coin, and the lost sheep (chap. 15). He is
one who has been healed by the Great Physician. He is the rich person who responds to Jesus with faith, in contrast to the rich ruler
(18:24–26). Some rich people do come to Jesus, but they do so on the
same basis as others—in humility and responsiveness, recognizing
their need. This mission to sinners will be extended to Gentiles
(Luke 7:1–10; Acts 10:1–11:18; Danker 1988: 306). Plummer (1896:
437) notes that what Jesus does for lost Zacchaeus he also seeks for
lost Israel (Matt. 10:6; 15:24).

Some question this statement's authenticity, arguing that the use
of an apocalyptic title with a present ministry saying betrays church
creation (Bultmann 1963: 152, 155). But authentic Son-of-Man sayings need not be limited to apocalyptic uses (Marshall 1965–66:
342–43; Borsch 1967: 326). In addition, the saying's basic imagery
has OT roots (noted above), so that nothing in the saying prevents it
coming from Jesus (Marshall 1978: 699; Jeremias, *TDNT* 6:492;
Oepke, *TDNT* 1:395). Luke does not create fresh Son-of-Man sayings. If the remark goes back to Jesus, it is unlikely that the title was
added later to the saying (against Colpe, *TDNT* 8:453, who argues
for its parallelism to Mark 2:17 and Matt. 15:24; but see the discussion of sources and historicity above). It is hard to understand why
Marshall regards this verse as possibly an originally isolated saying,
since the remark makes consummate sense in this setting. In short,
the saying is a fitting climax to a paradigmatic account of Jesus' mission and ministry of salvation.

Summary Luke 19:1–10 pictures many elements of Jesus' ministry: Jesus' concern and initiative toward the lost sinner, the response of a rich man touched by God, the proper way to use resources, the reality of repentance and how such reality impacts one's treatment of others, and the human inability to perceive God's way. Too often people are unwilling to let the despised find God. The account is like a master painting, depicting Jesus' ministry to humans.

Luke desires his readers to see Jesus' initiative in ministry and the proper way to respond to him. Jesus reaches out to and cares for the sinner. Many missionary efforts have been fueled by a similar desire. In turn the sinner comes humbly and welcomes Jesus with joy. Through Jesus' initiative, the sinner is transformed and values are changed. God's graciousness to the sinner is also the basis for the sinner's response of generosity to others, along with an effort to right past wrongs. Jesus is the model Savior, while Zacchaeus is the model saint. Zacchaeus did not collect taxes in his encounter with Jesus, rather he discovered how God cancels spiritual debt. The one sent to seek and save the lost possesses the gift for those who respond. Faith brings joy, forgiveness, humility, and transformation. Zacchaeus desired a glimpse of Jesus, but faith brought him much more: it brought Jesus to Zacchaeus's home to stay; it brought the lost sheep back to the shepherd.

Additional Note

19:4. Did Zacchaeus run ahead (προδραμών; ℵ, A, B, Q, Δ, Θ, family 1, family 13) or run to (προσδραμών; L, W, Γ, Ψ) the tree? With very little difference in meaning, external evidence favors the first reading (Fitzmyer 1985: 1223–24). Internal factors also play a part in deciding this issue, since προδραμών with the following prepositional phrase yields a translation "running ahead to the front." This redundancy causes Black (1967: 116) to posit a mistranslation from Aramaic, with the original reading being something like Gen. 29:13: "He hurried to meet him." Such redundancies are, however, found elsewhere (Tob. 11:3; Klostermann 1929: 185; BDF §484; BDR §484.4). In addition, climbing a tree hardly qualifies as hurrying to meet someone (Marshall 1978: 696). Plummer (1896: 433) argues that the redundant construction may be more emphatic.

4. Parable of Stewardship (19:11–27)

The journey narrative's final parable is one of Jesus' most complex. Often called the "Parable of the Pounds," a more precise title might be the "Parable of Stewardship and Judgment upon the Return." The parable is about life in the interim between Jesus' resurrection and his return. A variation of this parable appears in Matt. 25:14–30, and a brief metaphor in Mark 13:34–35 is similar in force (Aland 1985: §266). The Gospel of the Nazareans 18 (Schneemelcher 1991–92: 1.161–62) also has a variation on this parable, though it has the servants spending their money on immoral activity, much like the prodigal son (Creed 1930: 233; Fitzmyer 1985: 1232). The Lucan form of the parable makes several points (Talbert 1982: 177–78):

1. It denigrates focus on "overrealized eschatology" (19:11). The parable assumes an interim between the two phases of Jesus' earthly career. The disciples' responsibility in this interim is to faithfully serve the absent king by making use of the gifts and responsibilities he has given. The idea of a delay was hard for the disciples to understand, given their firm conviction that Jesus would set up his kingdom immediately. As late as Acts 1:6 they still held out hope for an instant full kingdom, although by Acts 3:20–21 that view had been tempered by reflection.

2. Not only are servants to be faithful, they will be held accountable upon the king's return. In the interim period some will reject the king, so faithful stewardship is required (Tiede 1988: 322). Faithfulness will be rewarded and unfaithfulness will be judged. The parable is largely a warning, since so much of its attention is focused on the unfaithful third servant.

3. A final note concerns the fate of those who reject the king outright: they will be judged. In their rejection of the king, they will receive what they desired—separation from him. This last element has historical precedent. Many Jews did not like Archelaus, son of Herod the Great, when the time came for him to ascend the throne after his father's death in 4 B.C. The Jews sent a delegation of fifty men to protest to

Augustus, who compromised by allowing Archelaus to rule, but only with the title *ethnarch*—on the premise that he would have to earn the title *king*, which he never did (Josephus, *Antiquities* 17.8.1 §188; 17.9.3 §222; 17.11.4 §317; *Jewish War* 2.6.1 §80; 2.6.3 §93; Plummer 1896: 438; Manson 1949: 313). With such a prominent event in the recent background, Jesus builds a picture of the consequences of rejection.

Sources and Historicity

The issue of the parable's connection to Matt. 25:14–30 is complex since the two passages exhibit much conceptual similarity. Dividing the various points of contact into two categories, Fitzmyer (1985: 1230) believes that the extensive contact shows that the same parabolic tradition is present. He speaks first of "the obvious parallelism of the bulk of the two forms":

Luke 19:13 = Matt. 25:15
Luke 19:15b–23 = Matt. 25:19–27
Luke 19:24b = Matt. 25:28
Luke 19:26 = Matt. 25:29

Then Fitzmyer lists the "common (or nearly common)" expressions:[1]

"excellent . . . good servant" (Luke 19:17 = Matt. 25:21)
"I was afraid" (Luke 19:21 = Matt. 25:25)
"because you are a stern man" (Luke 19:21 = Matt. 25:24)
"you reap what you have not sown" (Luke 19:21 = Matt. 25:24)
"wicked servant" (Luke 19:22 = Matt. 25:26)
"you knew" (Luke 19:22 = Matt. 25:26)
"reaping what I have not sown" (Luke 19:22 = Matt. 25:26)
"my money in a bank account" (Luke 19:23 = Matt. 25:27)
"with interest on my return" (Luke 19:23 = Matt. 25:27)
"take the mina from him" (Luke 19:24 = Matt. 25:28)
"give it to the one with ten" (Luke 19:24 = Matt. 25:28)
"from the one who has nothing even what he has will be taken from him" (Luke 19:26 = Matt. 19:29)

On the other side are those features that differentiate the two accounts and become the basis for arguing that two distinct parables and settings are

1. Many of the expressions in the following list exhibit slight differences in vocabulary, word order, or position between Matthew and Luke. See the exegesis for details.

in view (Plummer 1896: 437; Arndt 1956: 394; Lachs 1987: 341; esp. Blomberg 1990: 217–20):

1. The settings are different: Luke has the parable in Jericho, while Matthew has it in Jerusalem.
2. The audiences differ: Luke has the remarks in front of a crowd, while Matthew has it only with disciples.
3. Luke has a number of unique details, including an additional remark in the setting that notes the delay of consummation and a note about the citizens and emissary sent to protest the king's selection.
4. Matthew has a businessman, while Luke has a king.
5. Matthew has three slaves, Luke ten.
6. Matthew gives the servants property and talents (five, two, and one respectively), while Luke gives each servant one mina.
7. The difference in value between a talent and a mina yields a large sum in Matthew and a small sum in Luke.
8. The rewards in Matthew are the same for each servant, while in Luke they are different.
9. The emissary in Luke necessitates differences in the judgment.
10. Of about 302 words in Matthew and 286 in Luke, only 66 are the same or similar (Plummer's statistics).

Thus, the data for this passage are quite complex, since many elements of agreement and disagreement exist side by side. These factors lead to four distinct positions on the relationship of the two passages:

1. The Matthean and Lucan parables are variants of the same parable, with Matthew being responsible for reducing the parable (Schmid 1959: 288–89; Lagrange 1921: 490–92; Calvin 1972: 2.286). The vast differences in vocabulary are against this solution, as are the Matthean omissions of the rejection motif and the note about the expectation of the kingdom's consummation. The latter detail would have fit so nicely into the eschatological setting of Matt. 25 that its omission is hard to explain if it had been present—even given the possibility of a Matthean reduction.
2. The Matthean and Lucan parables are variants of the same parable, with Luke being responsible for many of the differences (Creed 1930: 232; Klostermann 1929: 185–86; B. Scott 1989: 221–24; Fitzmyer 1985: 1229–31 [19:11–12, 14–15a, 25, 27 are Lucan]).[2] Against this view, Manson objects that Luke does not handle his tradition in this manner.

2. Fitzmyer wrongly says that Manson 1949: 313 agrees with this position. Manson does hold that Luke's traditional source is responsible for the addition.

3. Two parables were conflated: the parable of the pounds and the parable of the rejected claimant (Ernst 1977: 517; Jeremias 1963a: 59; Danker 1988: 307; Egelkraut 1976: 188; Weinert 1977).[3] Nolland (1993b: 910–12), who notes six views of the original function of the main parable, holds that the original parable taught accountability to God, not Jesus. Marshall (1978: 701) leans toward this view, but does not rule out option four and suggests that one parable took on two forms in the tradition. This view places responsibility for the differences on the parable's transmission in the tradition. It also begs a question: how did the tradition take on such distinctive forms? This view probably represents the current majority view and may be correct in describing how different forms of the same basic parable got to Matthew and Luke. Despite this consensus, however, option four more naturally takes account of the wide variety of differences in the two accounts.

4. The parables are not totally parallel, but represent two versions told in distinct settings (Plummer 1896: 437; Arndt 1956: 394; Blomberg 1990: 217–20; Candlish 1911–12; McCulloch 1911–12).[4] Citing Joüon (1939), Blomberg argues that the Lucan account is coherent as is, but that its bisection according to the consensus views does not leave a coherent parable. In this sense, Matthew and Luke are parallel since the tradition is built around the same basic image. The wide variety of differences suggests, however, that distinct events and traditions are in view. Whether Luke got his version from special Lucan sources or from a second version of Q is debated. Marshall (1978: 702) and Schulz (1972: 293–98) argue that the parable fits Q more naturally than Luke's special source. The presence of many unique parables is a characteristic of Luke's special source, so this possibility cannot be ruled out. But the similar parable in 12:35–48 shares this problem of source determination. It may be that the origin of these two parables should be analyzed together. If two versions of Q existed, then perhaps certain parables had distinct settings in Jesus' ministry, which are reflected in the two versions and may partially explain why Matthew and Luke differ in such otherwise similar passages. If so, each version of Q faithfully reports the distinct versions of these parables. Texts like this one show the difficulty of holding to Q as a single document—if it exists at all. On the other hand, the view that Luke obtained his parable from a special source may explain differences in placement and details. In either case, it is hard

---

3. This view goes back to D. F. Strauss (1972: 352–53 [orignally 1840]), as Plummer 1896: 437 notes. Ellis 1974: 221–22 holds out the possibility of two parables. Marshall 1978: 702 holds that this text supports his two-versions-of-Q theory.

4. F. E. D. Schleiermacher also held this view. On the history of interpretation, see Thiessen 1934; Weinert 1977: 505; and Zerwick 1959.

to accept that either Matthew or Luke so radically altered the same account. More likely, this parable circulated in different versions and was told in different ways on different occasions.[5]

The Jesus Seminar rates the various portions of the pericope differently: pink type for 19:13, 15–17b, 18–19b, 20–24; gray for 19:26; black for 19:12, 14, 17c, 19c, 25, 27 (Funk and Hoover 1993: 373–75). The seminar accepts that two parables were combined and holds that Luke is responsible for the mix (view 3 above). Much of the parable is authentic, being about money given in trust, but for the seminar Luke has turned it into a messianic and eschatological parable reflecting themes in 1:33; 19:38; 23:3, 11, 37. The portions that the seminar reads as inauthentic reflect messianic or judgment themes that the seminar believes Jesus did not teach, a point that I question elsewhere (see the sources and historicity for 9:18–20 and 11:37–54). Underlying this analysis and that of the consensus it reflects is a refusal to entertain the possibility that Jesus taught similarly in two settings and that that teaching was recorded in two somewhat distinct forms. The stripped-down Lucan parable cannot explain the different amounts left to the servants, and it states the moral of the parable in muted form for Jesus, especially if 19:26 is treated with suspicion. The authenticity of 19:26 is supported by the presence of its theme in Mark 4:24. That Jesus would relate accountability to the eschaton is not unlikely, given his eschatological discourse material. The parable has a strong claim to authenticity—even in its Lucan form.

The passage is a parable with a saying tied to it in 19:26 (Fitzmyer 1985: 1232; Bultmann 1963: 176; Berger 1984: 51). The outline of Luke 19:11–27 is as follows:

a. Setting (19:11)
b. Departure and rejection (19:12–14)
  i. Departure (19:12–13)
  ii. Rejection by the citizens (19:14)
c. Check of stewardship of the servants (19:15–26)
  i. The call to check stewardship (19:15)
  ii. First servant commended (19:16–17)
  iii. Second servant commended (19:18–19)
  iv. Third servant rebuked (19:20–24)
    (1) Third servant's fear (19:20–21)
    (2) King's reply (19:22–23)
    (3) King's judgment (19:24)

5. Even though I hold that this parable is distinct from Matt. 25, comparisons to it will be made throughout the exegesis because the two accounts are conceptually close.

v. The crowd's reaction (19:25)
vi. The king's response on accountability (19:26)
d. Judgment on the citizen delegation (19:27)

This parable explains the responsibility that all have before the king in light of the delay of the kingdom's consummation. Jesus has authority, even in the interim, which makes all people responsible to him. His reception of another kingdom during his departure pictures Jewish rejection of his received authority. Stewardship is the responsibility of all who are related to the king. A reward for faithfulness will be given to those who really know and trust the king. The king's return will also include judgment for those who reject him.

Exegesis and Exposition

[11]And as they heard these things, he went on to speak a parable, because he was near Jerusalem and because they thought that the kingdom of God was near.

[12]Then he said, "A certain man of noble birth went to a faraway land to receive to himself a kingdom and then return. [13]Calling his ten servants, he gave them ten minas and said to them, 'Trade with these until I come.' [14]But his citizens hated him and sent a delegation after him, saying, 'We do not wish this one to rule over us.'

[15]"When he returned, having received the kingdom, he said to call those servants to whom he had given the money, that he might know what ⌐they had gained by trading⌐. [16]And the first came before him, saying, 'Lord, Your mina has brought ten more minas.' [17]And he said to him, 'Well done, good servant! Because you have been faithful in very little, you shall have authority over ten cities.' [18]And ⌐the second one⌐ came and said, 'Your mina, Lord, has made five minas.' [19]And he said this to him, 'You are to be over five cities.' [20]And ⌐the other⌐ came, saying, 'Lord, here is your mina, which I have kept stored in a cloth. [21]For I feared you, because you are a severe man; you take what you did not lay down, and you reap what you did not sow.' [22]And he said to him, 'I will condemn you from your own mouth, evil slave. You knew, did you, that I was a severe man, taking what I did not set down and reaping what I did not sow? [23]Why then did you not give my money to the bank, and I upon my coming would have collected it with interest?' [24]And he said to those present, 'Take the mina from him and give to the one who has ten minas.' [25]And they said to him, 'Lord, he has ten minas.'⌐ [26]I say to you that everyone who has more shall be given, but from the one not having, what he has shall be taken from him.

[27]"'But as for these enemies of mine, who did not want me to reign over them, bring them here and slay them before me.'"

a. Setting (19:11)

Luke clearly connects this parable to the Zacchaeus incident (ταῦτα **19:11** [*tauta*, these things] looks back to 19:1–10, so that Jericho is the locale for this teaching. Jericho is located eighteen miles from Jerusalem, about a six-hour walk (Klostermann 1929: 186 [150 stadia]; Josephus, *Jewish War* 4.8.3 §474). The phrase προσθεὶς εἶπεν παραβολήν (*prostheis eipen parabolēn*, again [lit., adding] he told a parable) is a Hebraism (Creed 1930: 233; cf. Luke 20:11; Gen. 38:5; Job 29:1; 36:1 [verb only]; BAGD 719 §1c; BAA 1440 §1c; BDF §435b; BDR §435.4.5). The verse, however, seems to be written in Lucan style, a conclusion supported in part by the lack of introduction in the Matthean version (the Matthean setting in the Olivet Discourse partially obviates his need for an introduction).[6] The reason for the teaching is twofold: Jesus and the disciples are drawing near to Jerusalem and the disciples' have false expectations about the consummation of the kingdom.

The reference to the consummation's delay is interesting since Luke elsewhere notes the kingdom's presence or nearness (11:20; 17:21). This unique remark shows that Luke has a two-stage view of the kingdom: it arrives now but comes in fullness later (Nolland 1993b: 913). The full earthly kingdom to appear in Jerusalem—an idea common in Judaism (Tg. Isa. 31:4–5; SB 2:300)—is what the disciples always expected. They continually struggled, however, to comprehend these two stages. Luke 9:45 and 18:34 show their struggle to understand Jesus' departure. Acts 1:6 shows that the earthly kingdom is still on their minds even after receiving exposition from Jesus, while Acts 2:38–40 and 3:16–21 show how they finally put the two phases together. Jesus wants the disciples to understand that Jerusalem is about to be the place of passion, not parousia. In addition, the disciples need to sense their responsibility in the interim period. Rejection like that demonstrated throughout the Jerusalem journey requires that the plan come in two stages (Danker 1988: 307). Rejection also requires that the disciples be prepared to serve faithfully until the king returns, as the following parable will teach.

---

6. Jeremias 1963a: 99 n. 40 notes eight points of Lucan style: (1) ἀκουόντων δὲ αὐτῶν ταῦτα (cf. Luke 20:45); (2) προστίθημι (Luke seven times, Acts six times, elsewhere in the NT five times); (3) εἶπεν παραβολήν (Luke 6:39; 12:16; 15:3; 18:9; 19:11; 20:19; 21:29); (4) διὰ τό plus the infinitive (Matthew two times, Mark three times, John once, Luke and Acts seven times each); (5) εἶναι after a preposition and article (Matthew and Mark never, Luke seven times, Acts three times); (6) Ἰερουσαλήμ (Luke–Acts sixty-four times, Matthew twice, Mark never); (7) παραχρῆμα (sixteen times in Luke–Acts, elsewhere only Matt. 21:19–20); and (8) ἀναφαίνω (only here and Acts 21:3). Of these points, the middle six are significant, the other two are less clear since they occur too rarely to establish stylistic tendencies.

b. Departure and Rejection (19:12–14)
i. Departure (19:12–13)

19:12 The parable begins with the journey of an unidentified man of noble birth (εὐγενής, *eugenēs*; BAGD 319; BAA 645; Job 1:3; elsewhere in the NT at Acts 17:11 and 1 Cor. 1:26). The use of indefinite τις (*tis*, a certain one) is frequent in Luke, especially in the journey narrative, and may have traditional roots.[7] This man needed to journey to a distant land to secure a vassal kingship. The distant journey stands in contrast to the immediacy of the earthly rule expressed in the previous verse (Plummer 1896: 439; Fitzmyer 1985: 1234). This detail corresponds theologically to Jesus' death and resurrection, where authority is received as a result of exaltation (Marshall 1978: 703). In Luke's view, the kingdom is received upon Jesus' resurrection (also Paul's view: Eph. 1:19–23; Col. 1:13–14).[8] It is important to note that Jesus does not receive the kingdom on his return but before it. In fact, it is in the foreign land that the kingdom is received, while the nobleman is away from his servants. This is confirmed in Luke 19:14, where the delegation tries to stop the nobleman from coming to the throne. The use of πορεύομαι (*poreuomai*, to go) anticipates the description in 22:22 of Jesus proceeding to his death (Manson 1949: 314) and makes another connection to the period of Jesus' death and resurrection.[9]

Archelaus's appointment as ethnarch of Judea, Samaria, and Idumea is the historical context for the parable (see the unit introduction). But even earlier, Herod the Great made a similar journey in 40 B.C. to receive kingship from Mark Antony, so the illustration was meaningful in a Jewish setting (Josephus, *Antiquities* 14.14.1–4 §§370–85). The idea of Jesus' kingship will be a Lucan focus in the rest of his account (Ellis 1974: 222; Luke 1:33; 19:38; 22:29; 23:3). Ὑποστρέφω (*hypostrephō*, to return) is also significant, since Luke uses it so frequently in comparison with the rest of the NT writers (Luke twenty-one times, Acts eleven times, the rest of the NT three times; BAGD 847; BAA 1688–89). The verb is not used, however, as a technical term for Jesus' return or in Luke's eschatological discourses about the return. Most uses are like the conceptually paral-

---

7. Twenty-seven times in Luke 9:51–19:44 (e.g., 9:57; 10:25, 30; 14:2, 16; 15:11; 16:1, 19), twelve times in the rest of Luke's Gospel and twenty-eight times in Acts.

8. Luke records activities in Jesus' ministry that show the presence of the kingdom, but the Spirit's arrival—the decisive sign of its inauguration—comes after the resurrection: Luke 24:49 with Acts 2:30–36. John the Baptist treats Spirit baptism as the mark of Messiah's presence; see Luke 3:15–17 with 24:49; Acts 1:5–8; 11:15–18; 13:23–25.

9. Manson also notes a wordplay with Aramaic אזל (*ʾăzal*), which can mean both "going away" and "departing life."

lel Matt. 25:14, where the traveling man is simply going away (ἀποδημέω, *apodēmeō*) on business. Luke's use, therefore, is unique and may reflect tradition.

Before the ruler departs, he gives responsibilities to ten of his ser- **19:13** vants. The number *ten* (which was popular in Jewish circles; *m. ʾAbot* 5.1–6; Ernst 1977: 519) is significant because it shows that the disciples are not meant. In fact, Ernst argues that the number may betray a Palestinian background (e.g., God's creation of the world with ten words, the ten commandments, ten generations from Noah to Abraham, ten miracles [plagues] in the exodus). Disciples in general are in view (Manson 1949: 315).

To each servant the ruler gives one mina (μνᾶ, *mna*; BAGD 524; BAA 1060–61) with which they are to do business for him in his absence and garner a profit from their labors. One mina was equivalent to one hundred drachmas, and one drachma (δραχμή; BAGD 206; BAA 415) was worth about the same as the Roman denarius (δηνάριον; BAGD 179; BAA 358), the standard daily wage for a basic worker. Thus, one mina was worth about four month's wages (Hendriksen 1978: 859–60).[10] That this is not a large sum is seen in the complaint of Mark Antony's troops about receiving one hundred drachmas each as a gift; Antony eventually gave them five hundred drachmas each, a figure equal to five minas (Appian, *Civil Wars* 3.7 §§43–45; 3 Macc. 1:4 speaks of two minas for troops).

The nobleman commands his servants to "engage in business trade" (πραγματεύσασθε, *pragmateusasthe*). The force of this imperative, a *hapax legomenon* that occurs in the LXX at Dan. 8:27 and in Origenic manuscripts of 1 Kings 9:19 (BAGD 697; BAA 1397; Maurer, *TDNT* 6:641), is "make a profit." The nobleman expects his servants to make money in his absence, as a preparation for their being given greater responsibilities later (this motive becomes clear in Luke 19:15, 17, 19). On his return (ἔρχομαι, *erchomai*; cf. John 21:22–23), he will evaluate the results. The phrase ἐν ᾧ (*en hō*) is variously rendered "while" (Fitzmyer 1985: 1235; Nolland 1993b: 914; Mark 2:19 = Luke 5:34; 24:44) or "until" (BDF §383.1 and BDR §383.1.1, citing classical evidence). The use of ἔρχομαι as meaning "gone" is unusual (Fitzmyer cites Luke 9:23; 14:27; and 15:20 in support of "go," but "come" works in all of these contexts). Since the servants are responsible for the master's business until he returns,

10. BAGD 524 puts the value of one mina at eighteen to twenty dollars, while Fitzmyer 1985: 1235 estimates twenty-five dollars. Since the value of ancient currency constantly changes in relation to modern monetary units, it is clearer to compute the value according to daily wages. The figure of four months is calculated on the basis of a six-day workweek (the NIV's marginal note that "a mina was about three months' wages" probably includes the Sabbath in its calculation).

"come" is probably correct. The difference in the meaning is virtually nil. The minas represent responsibilities undertaken by the servants because of association with Jesus. They are to carry out their responsibilities effectively and profitably until he returns.

Luke's version differs considerably from Matthew's. In Matt. 25:14–15, the owner is a businessman who gives over his possessions until he returns from a trip. He gives differing numbers of talents to three slaves: five, two, and one, according to the ability of each. As a talent is worth sixty minas, one talent represents around twenty years' labor. The first Matthean servant thus received the monetary equivalent of more than a lifetime's labor. These differences have caused much speculation. For example, Jeremias (1963a: 60–61) argues that one hundred denarii and three servants were the amounts in the original parable (Leaney 1958: 243 agrees on the three servants). The case for three is based on the later evaluation in both parables of only three servants. It should be noted, however, that Luke records the reaction of others present at the evaluation (19:25). Jeremias argues for the originality of one hundred denarii on the premise that a lesser amount as a test for later service is a more natural story element. One hundred denarii is a low amount for a nobleman to disperse for administrative purposes while he is gone on a long journey. On the other hand, Matthew's larger figure, if it is his addition, is problematic, for where would Matthew's desire to have the man give over all his possessions come from? Extravagant sums like these are typical features in Jesus' parables. Arguments like Jeremias's are only necessary if one insists on one original parable behind both accounts. It is hard to explain how a businessman becomes a king or why the amounts differ so greatly. It seems more likely that two parables are present, especially when other differences are considered (see unit introduction).

ii. Rejection by the Citizens (19:14)

19:14   Attention now turns from the servants to the citizens, who hate the nobleman. The citizens and their actions represent the Jews' rejection of Jesus (cf. Ps. 118:22–23; Luke 20:17; Acts 4:11). After all, Jesus has come to be a king for the Jews. The imperfect ἐμίσουν (emisoun, they were hating) in this context indicates an ongoing attitude (Schweizer 1984: 295; Luke 13:34; John 15:25). In the same way that the Jews hated Archelaus—because he massacred three thousand Jews on Passover (Josephus, *Antiquities* 17.9.3 §§213–18; *Jewish War* 2.1.3 §§8–13)—and protested his reign, the parabolic citizens send a delegation (πρεσβεία, presbeia) to protest the king's coming rule (BAGD 699; BAA 1401; Luke 14:32; 2 Macc. 4:11; Josephus, *Antiquities* 17.11.1 §300). To drive home their desire that the nobleman not rule over them, they use the derogatory τοῦτον (*touton*, this one).[11] Βασιλεύω (*basileuō*, to rule) is only used three times in Luke (1:33; 19:27).[12] Matthew has no equivalent to this verse. The general remark describes Jewish rejection, but given the disciples' acceptance of Jesus, it does not refer to every Jew and is not anti-Semitic (correctly C. A. Evans 1990: 286).

c. Check of Stewardship of the Servants (19:15–26)
i. The Call to Check Stewardship (19:15)

The nobleman returns (ἐπανέρχομαι, *epanerchomai*; BAGD 283; **19:15** BAA 573; Luke 10:35) after receiving his kingdom and calls his servants to account. The parable makes a significant distinction between receiving the kingdom and the later reckoning that is a product of its authoritative exercise (Josephus, *Antiquities* 17.13.1 §339; Fitzmyer 1985: 1235–36). Kingdom reception precedes a later period where it is fully administered. This detail parallels Jesus' career: he has a kingdom that he receives when he goes to the Father, but the full exercise of his authority awaits his return.

The examination is simple: what business have the servants done (διαπραγματεύομαι, *diapragmateuomai*; a NT *hapax legomenon*; BAGD 187; BAA 376)? What profit has accrued in his absence? The examination concerns their faithfulness during the master's absence. Theologically, the parable pictures stewardship in the period between Jesus' first and second comings.

Matthew 25:19 expresses a similar idea in different terminology: a "long time" (πολὺν χρόνον, *polyn chronon*) passed before the Lord (ὁ κύριος, *ho kyrios*) "settled accounts with his servants" (συναίρει λόγον μετ᾽ αὐτῶν, *synairei logon met' autōn*). Only the reference to servants is shared (Matthew has δούλων, Luke δούλους).

ii. First Servant Commended (19:16–17)

The first servant brings an encouraging report: he earned (προσηρ- **19:16** γάσατο, *prosērgasato*; BAGD 713; BAA 1428; a *hapax legomenon*) ten minas from one—a 1,000 percent profit! Such large profit was not unusual in the ancient world (Kistemaker 1980: 267; Derrett 1970: 23). Matthew 25:20 shows the first servant earning (ἐκέρδησα, *ekerdēsa*) five talents on top of the original five talents. In both versions, this servant has been faithful with the opportunities and responsibilities given to him.

---

11. Οὗτος is derogatory in 18:11 and throughout the Lucan passion narrative: 23:4, 14, 22, 35 (except for 23:41).

12. The aorist may be ingressive ("we do not want him to be enthroned to rule over us"; Arndt 1956: 392), though a summary aorist is also possible.

19:17 The master's response comes in three parts: commendation, reason, and promotion. The commendation is "well done" (εὖγε, *euge*; a *hapax legomenon*; BAGD 319; BAA 645; Job 31:29; 39:25; Ps. 35:21 [34:21 LXX]). This is a good servant and the master recognizes it (Matt. 25:21 speaks of the "good [ἀγαθέ, *agathe*] and faithful servant"). The reason (ὅτι, *hoti*) for the promotion follows: the servant was faithful in a small matter (ἐλάχιστος, *elachistos*; BAGD 248; BAA 502; cf. Luke 16:10; Seesemann, *TDNT* 5:172). A rare periphrastic present imperative introduces the servant's promotion: he is (ἴσθι, *isthi*) given authority over ten cities (Plummer 1896: 441; BAGD 224 §II.4f; BAA 452 §II.4f; BDR §353.3.9; Gen. 1:6). His reception of authority matches the king's receiving a kingdom. The servant gets a prominent administrative role in the kingdom, an eschatological image that Luke uses directly elsewhere (Luke 12:32; 22:30).

In the Matthean version the servant who was set over little will be set over much and is told to enter into the joy of the master. Some argue for confusion of the Aramaic terms כרכין (*krkyn*, cities) and ככרין (*kkryn*, talents), so that an original payment of talents became a Lucan reference to cities. Assuming the originality of the Matthean form, this view holds that if cities had really been given, then money would not have been a source of dispute in 19:24–25 (Klostermann 1929: 187 citing E. Nestle and H. Gressmann; Black 1967: 2–3). The problem in allowing a Matthean original to control the image, however, is that money is not paid at this point in the parable, so the linguistic confusion is lacking (correctly Kistemaker 1980: 267 n. 9; Grundmann 1963: 364 citing the image of physical rule in 22:30 as support). Luce (1933: 295) spiritualizes the application by arguing that the point is that failure to perform one's responsibility results in the loss of power to perform it. But the passage has eschatological force, since it is designed to parallel the Lord's return. Ernst (1977: 520) also notes the failure to perceive adequately this consummative eschatological thrust if one argues that the authority of the church is in view.

Closer to the point is Jeremias's citation (1963a: 61 n. 49) of a parallel from Judaism: "The reward of duty done is a duty to be done" (*m. ʾAbot* 4.2). Luke pictures additional responsibility in the future kingdom era. It is not limited to mere kingdom presence or additional church responsibility, but refers to full participation in the exercise of the kingdom's authority in the consummation (cf. 1 Cor. 6:2–3). Faithfulness now will result in kingdom responsibility later (the kingdom is not to be equated with the eternal state or the church; Acts 3:18–21).

Matthew makes the application more explicit by referring to the master's joy. Jeremias (1963a: 60 n. 42) notes that this joy is perhaps suggestive of sitting at the banquet table, since the Aramaic equivalent of εἰσέρχομαι (*eiserchomai*, to enter) can mean to come into the feast. In contrast to this participation, the third servant is cast into outer darkness (Matt. 25:30), which refers to total exclusion from kingdom participation, since the consummation is in view (Luke 13:25–28; Rev. 21–22). The lesson is the same for Luke: faithfulness now will result in the privilege of service in the consummation. Such service will be much greater in scope than the responsibility exercised now in Jesus' absence.

iii. Second Servant Commended (19:18–19)

The second servant's situation parallels that of the first, except that **19:18** his mina earned (ποιέω, *poieō*; BAGD 681 §I.1bη; BAA 1367 §I.1bη) five more, or a 500 percent increase. In Matt. 25:22, the second servant earns two talents more, thus doubling his original holdings. Luke's version shows distinct gifts, responsibilities, levels of achievement, and rewards.

The second slave's reward is stated with more brevity. The praise **19:19** given to the first servant is lacking here, but the reward is similarly proportionate to the achievement: five minas yield authority over five cities. Faithfulness is honored yet again; the master commands that greater responsibility be given to the faithful slave.[13]

iv. Third Servant Rebuked (19:20–24)
(1) Third Servant's Fear (19:20–21)

The third servant gives his report, but his story is more complicated **19:20** as he explains why there is no profit to report. Rather than being designated "the third servant," he is singled out by being called ὁ ἕτερος (*ho heteros*, the other one), a description that many see as proof that the original parable had only three figures (like Matthew). But this may simply be a literary shortening of the story, along with an effort to distinguish this third figure from the first two. There is no need to go through all ten figures to make the point (Plummer 1896: 441), and triads are common in Jesus' parables (Blomberg 1990: 219). Jesus really needs only two figures to make his point that some are faithful and "others" are not (Grundmann 1963: 364). Most parables have very few characters, so that a reduction from ten to three is not surprising. In addition, one could also argue that ὁ ἕτερος means "another of a different kind," though the article makes

---

13. A present imperative (γίνου) is again used in the command to give the servant authority over cities. The adverb ἐπάνω is here used as a preposition meaning "over"; BAGD 283 §2b; BAA 573 §2b; elsewhere in Luke at 4:39; 10:19; 11:44; 19:17 but not in Acts; fourteen times elsewhere in the NT.

it clear that one specific figure is in view (Ellis 1974: 223; Plummer 1896: 441).[14] Most important, then, the definite reference singles out this representative figure from the others and separates him from them. Something other than faithfulness is portrayed here.

The servant returns his mina with nothing else and begins his report by noting that he had placed it in a σουδάριον (soudarion), from Latin sudarium, a face cloth or handkerchief often worn to protect the back of the neck from the sun's heat (Manson 1994: 316; Marshall 1978: 706; BAGD 759; BAA 1517; elsewhere in the NT at John 11:44; 20:7; Acts 19:12). The third servant "laid aside" (ἀπόκειμαι, apokeimai; BAGD 92–93; BAA 185; elsewhere in the NT at Col. 1:5; 2 Tim. 4:8; Heb. 9:27) the money and did not engage in business as the master had commanded (Luke 19:13). Hiding money in this manner is attested in Jewish sources, but it was not regarded as safe as burying it in the ground (b. B. Meṣ. 42a; b. Ketub. 67b; m. B. Meṣ. 3.10–11; SB 1:970–71; 2:252; Matt. 25:18, 25).[15] Not only was the servant unfaithful, but he also may have been careless.

19:21   The third servant gives his rationale for hiding the mina instead of obeying the command to trade: he was afraid because (ὅτι, hoti) he viewed the king as severe.[16] The king takes from others what he did not work for.[17] He is a strict administrator, an unrelenting exploiter, a cutthroat dealer. The servant may have been caught on the horns of a dilemma: "If I earn money, you will take it; if I lose it, you will hold me responsible" (Plummer 1896: 441). He was so paralyzed by fear that he could not act. Interestingly, the king's response to the first two servants has already proven this fear false (Arndt 1956: 393). The third servant does not know the king.

Matthew 25:24 similarly describes the servant's reasons before telling about hiding the coin: the master is a "hard" man (σκληρός, sklēros), a stronger term than Luke's αὐστηρός. Marshall (1978: 707) holds that σκληρός is original (he sees one tradition behind both stories). Though the Matthean servant's remarks about reaping what was not sown and gathering what was not winnowed are

---

14. Luke 19:25 shows that the other servants are still around and have not yet received their evaluation. On the textual problem with the article, see the additional note.

15. On the difference between burying and wrapping, see Jeremias 1963a: 61 n. 51. Fitzmyer 1985: 1236 is skeptical of what value this difference has for the meaning of this parable, but gives no reason for his doubt (perhaps the late date of the talmudic material?). Either way, the detail reflects a failure to respond to the king.

16. Αὐστηρός (severe, strict, exacting) is used in the NT only in this pericope (twice); also 2 Macc. 14:30. In P. Tebt. vol. 2 #315 line 19, the term is used of a demanding financial inspector; MM 93; Fitzmyer 1985: 1237.

17. This view of the king's sternness is conceptually like Josephus's description of a law that punishes slaves more harshly; Against Apion 2.30 §216; C. Taylor 1901; Plato, Laws 913c (11); Brightman 1927–28; Philo, Hypothetica 7.6; Fitzmyer 1985: 1237.

similar to the Lucan servant, they are sufficiently distinct to see a separate tradition.

(2) King's Reply (19:22–23)

The master rebukes the slave and pronounces judgment against him. **19:22** Λέγει (*legei*, said) is a historical present. With its legal thrust, κρινῶ (*krinō*, will condemn) contextually expresses an official resolve for what the king is about to carry out (BAGD 451 §4aα; BAA 917 §4aα). The servant's excuse becomes the ground for the master's condemnation (ἐκ τοῦ στόματός σου [*ek tou stomatos sou*, out of your mouth] is in the emphatic position; Job 15:6; Num. Rab. 16.21 on 14:2; SB 2:252; Klostermann 1929: 188). The master's address to the servant as an evil slave contrasts with his positive address to the previous two servants and is a testimony to the third servant's disobedience. The master repeats the servant's categories (take, set down, reap, sow) to make the case that if he had really thought this way about him, then he should have made some effort to do something beneficial with the money. If the servant really felt this way he is a fool since he knew the king to be a hard master (Manson 1949: 316). He is in a no-win situation: if his assessment of the master is right, then he should have done something to gain the master's pleasure; if his assessment is wrong, then he has insulted his master and failed to obey him. The slave is either lying about how he feels about the master to excuse his lack of response or he has seriously misjudged the master. Above all, he has failed to respond properly to the king.

Some people reject God or his agent on the unfounded premise that "if God is so harsh, then I do not want to know *that* kind of God." Of course, if he is sovereign and is in fact that harsh, then that is even more reason to respond to him. This view of the master shows the ludicrous nature of the servant's excuse. In fact, the servant read the king incorrectly, for he had already treated two other servants graciously and promoted them. The servants' view of authority is mistaken.

The master continues his rebuke with the most conservative plan of **19:23** action that the servant could have carried out (καί plus διά should be translated with a final force: "then" or "therefore"; BDR §442.3.9).[18] The money should have been put in a bank while the

---

18. The verse is loaded with business terms: ἀργύριον (money; BAGD 104 §2b; BAA 211 §2b; elsewhere in the NT at Matt. 25:18, 27; 26:15 = Mark 14:11 = Luke 22:5; Matt. 27:3, 5, 6, 9; 28:12, 15; Luke 9:3; 19:15; Acts 3:6; 7:16; 8:20; 19:19; 20:33; 1 Pet. 1:18), τράπεζα (bank [lit., table]; BAGD 824; BAA 1643 §4; MM 639–40; Goppelt, *TDNT* 8:211 §A3; fifteen times in the NT, e.g., Matt. 21:12 = Mark 11:15 = John 2:15; cf. Josephus, *Antiquities* 12.2.3 §28; the term looks to the financial table where deals are done), τόκος (interest; BAGD 821; BAA 1637; elsewhere in the NT only at Matt.

master was gone so that upon his return he could collect it with interest.[19] Marshall (1978: 707) notes that under this plan the money would have earned interest without the slave lifting a finger—an action appropriate for someone afraid of the master. He also would have been following orders and would have had something to offer a master who "earned that for which he did not work."

The language of Matt. 25:27 is close to Luke with only a few stylistic differences. This parallelism shows the closeness of the two parables in discussing the third servant.

(3) King's Judgment (19:24)

19:24 Speaking to those present, the master passes judgment on the third servant. Plummer (1896: 442) suggests that the audience is made up of bodyguards or courtiers (1 Kings 10:8; Esth. 4:5). A more natural possibility is that these are the rest of the slaves mentioned in Luke 19:15, gathered for the evaluation, though the evaluation does not continue, since this would unduly prolong the story. The third slave's mina is to go to the first slave. Ten refers not to his total possession, but to his profit. The master adds to the first slave's responsibility what had been entrusted to the third slave, giving him twelve minas total. The additional mina represents opportunity for additional responsibility.[20] The point of redistributing the mina is that the most faithful slave gets additional reward and responsibility, while the unfaithful slave gets judgment.

Matthew 25:28 differs in two places from Luke: the judgment is given without noting the audience, and the exchange involves talents, not minas. The point in both accounts is the same.

v. The Crowd's Reaction (19:25)

19:25 The master's action produces a response—probably from characters within the parable who have been watching the evaluation.[21] These people express shock that the mina is given to someone who already

---

25:27; cf. Exod. 22:25 [22:24 LXX]; Lev. 25:36–37; Deut. 23:19 [23:20 LXX]), and πράσσω (to collect; BAGD 698 §1b; BAA 1400 §1b; earlier in Luke at 3:13).

19. This suggestion is expressed in a contrary-to-fact condition since the interest was not in fact earned: ἄν . . . ἔπραξα (I would have collected, but did not); BDF §360.2; BDR §360.2.3.

20. Marshall 1978: 708 sees this verse as proof of the secondary character of the earlier references to cities (19:17, 19), since cities are not mentioned here; but this is merely literary condensing.

21. Jeremias 1963a: 62 holds that Jesus' audience interrupted him; so also Plummer 1896: 442, who argues that the crowd thinks Jesus is spoiling the parable; so also Nolland 1993b: 916–17. Klostermann 1929: 189; Marshall 1978: 708; and Danker 1988: 309 hold that the interruption comes from attendants in the parable. If 19:26–27 maintains the parabolic perspective, and 19:27 looks as if it does, then those who react here come from within the parable and comment as a crowd to the king. Of

has so many. Their charge is that a bonus is unfair (Marshall 1978: 708). The aside, like a Greek dramatic choral refrain, is probably designed to express the shock one might have upon hearing this result. What justice is there in leaving the poor servant destitute?

vi. The King's Response on Accountability (19:26)

In the parable's most difficult verse, Jesus gives the principle behind the master's action, which is an indication of how the evaluation functions. It is worded like the proverb in 8:18, which refers to those who respond to light getting more and those who refuse it losing what light they had. The proverb's basic meaning, as illustrated by the parable, is clear: the one who has gets more, while the one who does not have (but "had") loses what he appeared to have. Three issues need to be addressed: (1) who is speaking? (2) what does the proverb refer to spiritually? and (3) how can someone who has nothing lose something?

19:26

There are two possibilities for the speaker: Jesus (Marshall 1978: 708; Grundmann 1963: 365) or the parabolic master (Creed 1930: 235). The phrase λέγω ὑμῖν (legō hymin, I say to you; 16:9; 18:8) is invoked on both sides of the argument: some see this solemn introduction as indicating that Jesus is the speaker, while others hold that it indicates a shift in speaker. That most parables end with an applicational comment by Jesus supports the first view. However, the reference to "these enemies of mine" in 19:27 is decisive for the second option; if the master speaks in 19:27, he is also the speaker here. The debate is not a significant one, since the master pictures Jesus, expressing his thinking through the response.

More significant is determining what the parable says about the third servant. This complex question is difficult to decide (see Pagenkemper 1990: 278–79).

1. Jeremias (1963a: 61–62) argues that in the original parable the third servant represents the Jewish leadership, which the church shifted to a warning about not failing to use God's gifts. Against this view, the Lucan form of the parable pictures the Jewish leaders in the delegation of 19:27. The parable cannot at this point allude to the Jews, unless the leadership is separated from the common folk.[22]

---

course, since the king represents Jesus, there is no real difference in sense in the choice. If Jesus speaks, he simply gives the parable's lesson.

22. B. Scott 1989: 232–35 (interacting with McGaughy 1975) appears to see a contrast between Jews and Pharisees, who "freeze" under fear of God by too narrowly preserving the law. There are several problems with this interpretation: (1) it reads the parable too existentially, (2) law is nowhere found in the context, and (3) the leadership is in view in 19:27.

2. Danker (1988: 309–10) sees a reference to the "judgment of rewards" in which the carnal believer who bears no substantive fruit is saved, but as through fire (1 Cor. 3:14–15). Two major points speak for this view: Luke lacks any reference to the outer darkness and gnashing of teeth found in Matt. 25:29–30, and the delegation in Luke 19:27 clearly refers to the unbelievers (those who reject the master are called his enemies in clear distinction from the third slave). Thus, the disciple loses his reward but maintains a relationship to the master.

3. Plummer (1896: 443) and Klostermann (1929: 189) associate the text with the judgment of the third Matthean slave, who is cast into outer darkness to experience weeping and gnashing of teeth (Matt. 25:29–30). Neither of these commentators, however, develop the point of this connection or defend it. Several points speak for this view. (a) The terminology in Matthew is clearly that of final judgment (as in Luke 13:28). (b) The exclusionary character of the proverbial warning in 8:18 (someone who "has" really does not, since he only "thinks he has") provides a rhetorical key to understand the punishment here: the third slave ends with absolutely nothing—not even what he thought he had. (c) In reply to the distinction in the previous view between the delegation as enemies and the third servant as a member of the community, it should be noted that Jesus addresses this slave in 19:22 as "evil"—a strong remark in a context of eschatological judgment. (d) This slave is called "the other one" (ὁ ἕτερος), denoting a clear distinction of class. (e) Although the Matthean parable is a distinct text, its description of the third servant is the strongest point of parallelism between the two parables (the wording of Matt. 25:29 is almost exactly like Luke's). In this view, the third slave pictures the "odd man out" who is a part of so many of Jesus' parables (Matt. 13:29–30, 41, 49–50; 18:32–34; 22:11–13; 25:41; Luke 12:46).

So who, then, is this figure? The third servant represents people who are related to the king in that they are associated with the community and have responsibility in it. Nevertheless their attitude shows that they do not see God as gracious and that they have not really trusted him. The third slave's attitude toward the master is important. He does not see his master as gracious, but as hard and unjust, and so he does not respond to the king. Such people are left with nothing at the judgment; they are sent to outer darkness, because they never really trusted or knew God.

Although a decision is difficult, the closeness of the parallel to Matthew and the pattern of such figures in Jesus' parables argue for view 3. By his own attitude toward the master, the third servant is shown not to have had a real relationship with the master. This attitude is reflected in an absence of action and results in the master's final declaration that this slave is evil—hardly a note of acceptance at the final reckoning. The slave may have thought that he knew the king, but really he did not know him at all and certainly showed no trust in him. Such characters circulated among the disciples (e.g., Judas); they saw themselves as related to Jesus and carried out responsibilities in his name, but did not know him.

d. Judgment on the Citizen Delegation (19:27)

The Lucan parable closes uniquely with the master reasserting his **19:27** authority over the rebellious delegation of 19:14 that did not wish him to reign and who had made their rejection clear. This group, which pictures the Jewish leadership, is identified as the king's enemies, and he orders their execution (κατασφάζω, *katasphazō*; a *hapax legomenon*; BAGD 419; BAA 853; 1 Enoch 10.12; 1 Sam. 15:33).[23] Those who reject Jesus suffer rejection in the end.

The parable thus mentions different fates for three groups: (1) reward for faithful stewards, (2) rejection for those who associate with Jesus but do not really trust him, and (3) judgment for rebels who openly reject him. What is said here is similar to Luke 12:46 (Klostermann 1929: 189): each group will be dealt with and rewarded accordingly when Jesus returns to exercise judgment as part of his authority (Acts 10:42; 17:31; Manson 1949: 317; cf. Prov. 8:35–36). Jesus now brings the opportunity for forgiveness; but when that opportunity is spurned, he will bring judgment. It is on this note that Jesus prepares to enter Jerusalem. There is no neutral position in relationship to Jesus: one chooses for him and sees his gracious work as unique, or one aligns against him (whether in outright rebellion or by faithless association to him).

Luke 19:11–27 has many points of reflection. The parable of the **Summary** pounds is a warning that Jesus will be gone for some time and that on his return he will evaluate people's faithfulness to him. Those who are faithful will be rewarded generously. Those who have the opportunity to serve should use it. Those who refuse to serve—be-

23. Not accepting that the parable deals with final judgment, Fitzmyer 1985: 1238 and Grundmann 1963: 365 argue that it refers instead to Jerusalem's destruction. This contradicts 19:11, which states that the parable deals explicitly with the consummated kingdom's coming and judgment at that time. Nonetheless, the observation is helpful, because Jerusalem's judgment (19:41–44; 21:5–38) pictures a greater judgment to come. Though not in this parable, that judgment pictures for Luke what the final judgment is like.

cause they view God as harsh—will be left with nothing but shame and judgment. Those who rebel and refuse to come near the king will receive severe judgment. To those who have, more will be given. But to those who do not have, even what they think they have will be taken away. There is an interim period in God's plan in which those allied to God are called to serve him. The king is away and has received the kingdom, but he will return to evaluate the stewardship of all. Faith and faithfulness lead to spiritual growth and God's pleasure. There is great reward in faithfully responding to God's gift. In the warning is a choice: service or rejection. One should see the Father's gifts as acts of his grace, extended in kindness, to be used in his service. Which servant is the reader like: the commended servants who earned ten or five minas, the "other one" who received nothing, or the delegation that was slain? When Jesus returns, which category each person falls into will be revealed—and there will be no counterarguments.

Additional Notes

19:15. The UBS–NA text, τί διεπραγματεύσαντο (what they had gained by trading), is read by ℵ, B, D, L, Ψ, some Itala, some Syriac, and Coptic, while τίς τί διεπραγματεύσατο (who had gained what by trading) is read by A, Θ, family 1, family 13, Byz, Lect, most Itala, Vulgate, some Syriac. The readings are close in sense; either is possible. The Alexandrian-Western alignment is slightly stronger for the UBS–NA text, as is the plural idea, which runs through the whole of 19:15 (Metzger 1975: 169; Plummer 1896: 440). Marshall (1978: 705) and Klostermann (1929: 187) seem to support the variant (on its syntax, see BDF §298.5).[24]

19:18. Codex D and one Syriac manuscript read ὁ ἕτερος (the other) in place of ὁ δεύτερος (the second), but this looks like assimilation to 19:20 and lacks sufficient external evidence to be original.

19:20. Some manuscripts (Byz, A) lack the article on ἕτερος, but its presence is better attested, both externally and as the more difficult reading, since it seems to imply only three characters in the parable versus the original ten. But that overreads the article. The reduction to three characters is simply literary compression for the sake of space.

19:25. Some manuscripts (D, W, some Itala, some Syriac, one Coptic manuscript) omit this verse. Since the aside is unique to Luke's version

---

24. Two other minor variants (δεδώκει–ἔδωκεν and γνοῖ–γνῷ) follow a similar pattern in terms of external evidence: the first of each pair is read by UBS–NA, the second is supported by Byz, A, W, Γ, Δ, Θ. On γνοῖ–γνῷ, see BDF §95.2; Mark 5:43; 9:30; BAGD 160; BAA 322.

and most manuscripts have it (most of the evidence for omission is Western), both internal and external evidence speak for its presence in the text. Klostermann (1929: 188–89) argues that the absence of reference to a speaker in 19:26a speaks for scribal insertion here (also Creed 1930: 235 and Schweizer 1984: 295). But both levels of textual evidence are against this conclusion.

5. Jesus' Controversial Approach to Jerusalem (19:28–40)
6. Weeping for Jerusalem (19:41–44)

Jesus' entry into Jerusalem (19:28–40) provides the background for his weeping for the city (19:41–44). These two pericopes are clearly distinct, yet the interplay between them is too great to ignore, and so they are taken together.

Luke moves from instruction to the events that will culminate in Jesus' death. Many see the previous unit as the end of the Jerusalem journey narrative and 19:28–44 as the start of Luke's final division, dealing with the Jerusalem passion events. Luke, however, does not portray Jesus in Jerusalem until 19:45. In fact, the lament over Jerusalem while he is still on its outskirts is the appropriate tragic ending to the section. Ellis (1974: 223) notes that for Luke it is not a triumphal entry, since Jesus is still "on the way." It elaborates the theme of the previous parable by revealing some who reject Jesus' claim to kingship. Such an ending recalls the earlier lament in the middle of the journey (13:34–35), and it also sets the tone for the events that will occur in the city. Jerusalem has missed its day of visitation (19:44), which refers to the time of Jesus' ministry to the nation (1:68–79), not merely to his entry into the city. Luke thus signals that the joy over Jesus' entry is short-lived. With this tragic note, the journey narrative ends and the passion begins.

Several themes emerge from these two units, some of which will dominate the rest of Luke. One such theme is Jesus' control over the events tied to his death. The way in which the disciples obtain the animal on which Jesus rides shows that he is directing the events associated with his coming to Jerusalem.

The type of animal used and the nature of Jesus' entry recall Zech. 9:9. The emphasis on this text, however, is not great in Luke, and John 12:16 makes it clear that the importance of this OT passage to this event did not clearly emerge until after the resurrection. The public declaration of who Jesus is does not fit the more circumspect style of earlier phases of Jesus' ministry in Luke, but the time for decision has come, so the choice must be clear. The regal style of the entry is somewhat toned down in

Luke, since he does not mention the branch waving. But the explicit mention of the king of Ps. 118 makes clear that a regal presentation is in view. Luke specifically says that it is the disciples who announce Jesus (Matt. 21:9 and John 12:12 speak of the crowd confessing Jesus, possibly chiming in with the disciples).

The use of the OT adds a note of divine design. Jesus is fulfilling the promise of Scripture: he is at the Mount of Olives, he rides the donkey in regal style, he is addressed as "the king who comes." Throughout the journey narrative, Jesus has spoken of the necessity (δεῖ, *dei*) of what will take place in Jerusalem. The heavy appeal to Scripture throughout the final stage of Jesus' life supports this idea of divine design in these events.

The Pharisees' rejection near the end of the entry shows that nothing has changed. The leadership still refuses to accept that Jesus is God's messenger—much less Messiah. Their protest at the disciples' actions is but the first of many acts of resistance at the end of Luke's Gospel. The irony is that Jesus declares that if the disciples did not speak out creation would. Inanimate objects have a better perception of what God is doing than do the people that Jesus came to save.

The lament over Jerusalem shows Jesus' pain at Israel's failure to respond with faith. In 19:41–44, Jesus sounds like Jeremiah lamenting the coming exile (Jer. 6:6–21) or Isaiah declaring the impending fall of Jerusalem (Isa. 29:1–4). Jesus' lament over Jerusalem shows that the consequence of rejecting God's messenger is national judgment. When God sues for peace and his terms are rejected, only judgment remains. Jesus predicts the nation's collapse as tragic fact. The fig tree of Luke 13:6–9 had its chance to bear fruit and it did not, so it was cut down (at least temporarily). The door of opportunity for the nation is closed (13:22–30). The house is desolate until it recognizes the one who comes in the name of the Lord (13:31–35).

Luke's portrayal here of Israel is complex (Talbert 1982: 180–82). Israel is the people of God and the bearer of covenant promise, but Israelite citizenship does not equal citizenship in God's kingdom (1:68; 2:32; 3:8; 7:16). The nation largely rejects the promise, and yet the Christian church is founded by Jews who respond (Acts 2:41; 4:4). Rejection is largely the responsibility of the leadership in Luke 9–19, but a measure of responsibility will go to the citizens of Jerusalem in Luke 23. Such division portrays Luke 2:34–35. The gospel message starts with the nation; Paul goes first to the Jews and then to the Gentiles (Acts 13:46; 18:6; 28:25–28; Rom. 1:16–17). But the gospel's rejection in one locale does not disqualify Jews in other places from hearing it. The promises temporarily go to others (Luke 20:9–18). Yet, in Luke's mind, the nation still has a future (Luke 13:35; 21:24, 28; 22:28–30; Acts 1:6, 11; 3:18–26; Wainwright 1977–78).[1]

Sources and Historicity

The issue of Luke's sources for these pericopes is complex (Aland 1985: §§269–70). The triumphal entry is one of the few events found in all four Gospels: Matt. 21:1–9 = Mark 11:1–10 = John 12:12–19 (Matt. 21:10–11 = Mark 11:11a lacks parallel in Luke). But the lament (Luke 19:41–44) and some details of the entry (e.g., 19:37, 39–40) are unique to Luke. Some see Luke using tradition, possibly Mark, to which he makes his own additions (Creed 1930: 236; Fitzmyer 1985: 1242–43 [19:37 only]). Others argue that Luke used the same source (L) that influenced the unique parts of the journey narrative (Marshall 1978: 709; Schlatter 1960: 408–9; Schramm 1971: 145–49). This latter option is more likely because of themes common to these pericopes and the journey narrative: Jesus' lament over Jerusalem (13:34–35 and 19:41–44; cf. 23:28–31) and the leadership's opposition (chaps. 11–13 and 19:39).

Many question whether this event took place in such a public way (Luce 1933: 298–300; Patsch 1971: 16–26).[2] The Jesus Seminar (Funk and Hoover 1993: 375) rejects the account and Jesus' remarks as an "invention of the storyteller" that reflects sayings that would not have circulated orally. This assumes that the tradition only passed on wisdom-like teachings of Jesus—a poor assumption given the existing traditions about events associated with Jesus' fate in Jerusalem. Such material is often acknowledged to be among the oldest forms of the tradition. The seminar argues that the entry was created from Scripture, namely, Zech. 9:9 and Ps. 118:25–26 (Funk and Hoover 1993: 96–97). One must examine why such a view arises. Objections to the event's historicity cluster around several concerns:

1. No mention of the entry was made at Jesus' trial. Surely his portrayal as king would have been seen as a political issue to exploit before

---

1. Talbert 1982: 182 is skeptical that Luke sees a future for Israel, but Luke's terminology about "the times of the Gentiles" and OT fulfillment suggest otherwise, especially given the continued discussion of restoration of the kingdom to Israel in Acts 1:6 and Peter's remarks in Acts 3:20–21.

2. Catchpole 1984 argues against historicity on form-critical grounds. For a response, see Witherington 1990: 104–7 and Nolland 1993b: 922–23. Holding to historicity, Kinman 1993 argues for a contrast between this event and Greco-Roman entries of dignitaries. Kinman also argues that Luke tries to show Jesus as a "king like Solomon" who is not a political threat and thus seeks to blunt the charge that Christians are a political threat to Rome. As such, Luke declares the significance to the event by how he tells the whole story of Jesus.

Rome and would have raised the charge of blasphemy for Jews. The claim to be Messiah was not, however, blasphemous (Catchpole 1971: 132). And it is unlikely that anyone perceived the Galilean teacher as a threat to incite his followers to topple Rome. He was simply not a threat to Roman power; nothing about his modest style suggested danger. Jesus was harmless—a small fish in the Jewish part of a vast Roman ocean.

2. Riding a donkey was not an inherently messianic action, and so the portrayal of this event in the Gospels is considered inaccurate. It is true that Messiah is not explicitly connected with the donkey ride, but the deduction drawn from this observation is false since the donkey ride was not the only element of Jesus' entry. Other details give the event its messianic force and produce the leadership's effort to stop such praise from going his way. In other words, it is not the animal's presence alone that makes Jesus' entry messianic, but the combination of several events that together create the messianic portrait: the use of the eschatological Ps. 118, the cry of the disciples when the king enters, and the waving of branches to signal his entry. In fact, the waving of branches (not mentioned in Luke because it is a Jewish practice) is tied to the eschatologically oriented Feast of Tabernacles (*m. Suk.* 3.9; 4.5). One must distinguish between imagery that was immediately understood as relevant and imagery that was only later viewed as applicable. Fitzmyer rejects the authenticity of the Zech. 9:9 connection because the messianic use of this text is late in Judaism.[3] But this OT text is not the key to historicity; it is only a minor piece (Ps. 118 plays a much more significant role for Luke). John 12:16 clearly indicates that the disciples realized the animal's significance from Zechariah only after Jesus went to glory (Bultmann 1971: 418). This does not mean the act was not symbolic, but that it was not understood as symbolic of the OT until well after the fact.

3. Jesus enters to celebrate Passover, but his disciples use imagery associated with another feast—Tabernacles—which looks to the eschaton.[4] This application is not a historical dilemma, but a conscious shifting of well-known imagery to set the atmosphere for the entry of a figure of the eschaton.

4. The obtaining of the animal is seen as legendary and looks like an attempt to make Jesus more than he is. An ancient custom called *angaría* allowed figures of state and persons of note to impress prop-

3. Most of the passages from the Talmud and Genesis Rabbah listed in SB 1:842–44 are late (from the fourth century A.D. at the earliest). No messianic use of Zech. 9:9 is found in the Pseudepigrapha.

4. For defense of the symbolism of Ps. 118 and the role of Zech. 9:9, see Bock 1987: 122–24, 326–28.

erty into personal use, a right that extended to rabbis—which is how many people viewed Jesus (Derrett 1971: 243–49).

Thus, the many points of challenge to this event are not insurmountable obstacles to a credible presentation by the tradition. In fact, events like this and the temple cleansing to follow are crucial in explaining what created the climate for Jesus' arrest. He is drawing much public attention, and his reputation is growing, even in Judea and its capital, so alarm over his popularity reaches a new high. The arrival amid public pomp has a good claim to historicity (Nolland 1993b: 922 and Meier 1994: 627–29, who argues that this event and the cleansing are "the match set to the barrel of gasoline").

Determining the day of the entry depends on the year of crucifixion. Most argue for A.D. 30, but Hoehner (1977: 95–114) persuasively argues for A.D. 33.[5] Jesus arrived at Bethany six days before Passover, which would be a Saturday (John 12:1). The next day, Sunday, a great crowd came to see him (John 12:9–11). Possibly on Monday (Nisan 10 or March 30) he entered Jerusalem (John 12:12). The only problem with this approach is that Matt. 26:2 = Mark 14:1 speaks of Jesus' actions two days before the Passover, but this appears to deal with the plot to seize Jesus. Matthew and Mark apparently placed the anointing later to show why Judas participated in the plot (Hoehner 1977: 91 n. 68).[6]

The issue of the historicity of 19:41–44 awaits consideration of the issue of "prophecy after the fact" in the exegesis of these verses. The Jesus Seminar prints 19:42–44 in gray type, which reflects a split in the seminar on this question (Funk and Hoover 1993: 375–76). The debate turns on whether Jesus uttered prophetic oracles of judgment and used the OT perspective on covenantal unfaithfulness to foresee the fate of those who rejected him. As I shall argue in the exegesis, this view is possible. Nolland (1993b: 930) argues similarly from a Qumranian conceptual parallel in 1QpHab 9.5–7, which shows first-century Jewish thought in these terms. This material has solid claim to authenticity.

The triumphal entry is a story about Jesus with a pronouncement and acclamation in 19:39–40 (Fitzmyer 1985: 1244; Berger 1984: 82). This means that the event, more than the sayings, is the key. Jesus is seen as a highly honored figure. Luke 19:41–44 is a prophetic warning or lament (Tiede 1988: 332–33). The outline of Luke 19:28–44 is as follows:

5. Despite the current consensus, the case for A.D. 33 is strong (Reicke 1968: 183–84). For the connection to other chronological issues in Jesus' life, see excursus 3.

6. The introduction to the anointing in Matt. 26:6 = Mark 14:3 simply says that it took place while Jesus was in Bethany. Luke has no anointing account in his passion narrative.

5. Jesus' controversial entry into Jerusalem (19:28–40)
   a. Setting (19:28)
   b. The disciples get the colt (19:29–34)
      i. Jesus instructs the disciples to get the colt (19:29–31)
      ii. The disciples follow Jesus' instructions (19:32–34)
   c. Jesus' entry into Jerusalem (19:35–38)
      i. The disciples' preparation and action (19:35–36)
      ii. The crowd's praise (19:37–38)
   d. The Pharisees' criticism; Jesus' response (19:39–40)
      i. The Pharisees' call to rebuke the disciples (19:39)
      ii. Jesus' refusal (19:40)
6. Weeping for Jerusalem (19:41–44)
   a. Lament (19:41–42)
   b. Judgment (19:43–44)

Jesus enters Jerusalem to a mixture of joy and tragedy as he prepares to meet his fate. He is in control of events tied to his passion. In contrast to the positive themes in the pericope—popular respect for Jesus, preparation by the disciples for his regal entry, praise to God for his miraculous work through Jesus, and the disciples' declaration of the arrival of a king sent by God—stands the Pharisees' rejection. Ironically, what the leadership cannot see, creation can. They fail to understand because the truth is hidden from it. This causes Jesus to speak like a prophet and predict the nation's judgment for failure to see the time of visitation. Jerusalem will be besieged and destroyed.

Exegesis and Exposition

28And when he had said these things, he went ahead, going up to Jerusalem. 29When he drew near Bethphage and Bethany, at the mount that is called Olives, he sent two of his disciples, 30saying, "Go into the village opposite, where on entering you will find a colt tied, on which no man has ever sat, and untying it, bring it here. 31And if anyone asks, 'Why are you untying it?' thus you shall reply, 'The Lord has need of it.'" 32And going out, those who were sent away found it even as he said to them. 33And as they were untying the colt, its owners said to them, "Why are you untying the colt?" 34And they said, "The Lord has need of it."

35And they brought it to Jesus, and throwing their garments upon the donkey they set Jesus on it. 36And as he rode along, they spread their garments on the road. 37And as he was now drawing near, at the descent of the Mount of Olives, the whole multitude of disciples began to rejoice and praise God with a loud voice for all the mighty works they had seen, 38saying,

"Blessed is ⌜the King who comes⌝ in the name of the Lord!
Peace in heaven and glory in the highest!"

[39]And some of the Pharisees from the crowd said to him, "Teacher, rebuke your disciples." [40]And replying he said, "I say to you, ⌜if they would be silent⌝, the stones would cry out."

[41]And as he drew near and saw the city, he wept for it, [42]saying, "Would that ⌜you knew in this day⌝ the things that make for ⌜peace⌝! But now it is hid from your eyes. [43]For days are coming upon you, and your enemies will cast a wall around you and will surround you and hem you in on all sides [44]and dash you and your children within you to the ground, and they will not leave one stone upon another in you, because you did not know the time of your visitation."

5. Jesus' Controversial Entry into Jerusalem (19:28–40)
a. Setting (19:28)

19:28 Jesus finishes his warning to be ready for his return, and then he turns to Jerusalem. The term ἔμπροσθεν (*emprosthen*) can mean "he went on *before* [his disciples]" (Plummer 1896: 444; Marshall 1978: 711; cf. Mark 10:32) or "he went *forward*" (Fitzmyer 1985: 1247; BAGD 257 §1b; BAA 518 §1b). Either sense is possible, but the absence of any mention of the disciples and the journey context favor the latter sense, even though it is a little redundant. The idea of going up to Jerusalem contrasts the earlier reference (10:30) to going down from Jerusalem, since the city lies at a higher elevation than the surrounding region. Luke is unique in tying the setting to the journey's completion. He picks up the story and his sources in 19:29. Nolland (1993b: 917) ties this verse to the end of the previous parable. In reality, it is a bridge: Jesus enters Jerusalem, having warned all of the accountability tied to the one who receives a kingdom. He is ready to face his fate in Jerusalem.

b. The Disciples Get the Colt (19:29–34)
i. Jesus Instructs the Disciples to Get the Colt (19:29–31)

19:29 Jesus prepares for his entry by locating himself near Jerusalem. Upon his arrival near Bethphage and Bethany, he sends two disciples to procure an animal for his entry (ὡς [*hōs*, when] is a temporal particle indicating when he instructed the disciples; Nolland 1993b: 923; Plummer 1896: 446). Jesus directs his followers' actions as he prepares for his fate.

Bethphage and Bethany are located east of Jerusalem on a range of hills overlooking the city and the Kidron Valley. The exact location of Bethphage is not known (Fitzmyer 1985: 1247; Ellis 1974: 225; Danker 1988: 311). Most place it on the southeast side of the Mount of Olives, southeast of Bethany, at a place known today as Abu Dis; others suggest higher up the Mount of Olives, northwest of Bethany, near what is known as Kefr eṭ-Ṭur. If the order of the cities reflects the order of travel from Jericho, then Abu Dis is more likely.

The Aramaic behind the name *Bethphage* means "House of Unripe Figs," which, along with the name *Mount of Olives*, suggests that the region was fertile. The name is ironic since Jesus earlier threatened the nation about not becoming an unproductive fig tree (13:6–9). Luke makes no effort to exploit the town's name.

Bethany, meaning "House of Ananiah," is located one and a half miles east of Jerusalem on the eastern slope of the Mount of Olives (on the spelling see BDF §56.2 and Marshall 1978: 711). The city appears twice in the LXX (Jdt. 1:9 and possibly Neh. 11:32), but is not the same town as Bethany beyond the Jordan (John 1:28). Today the town is a Moslem village that bears the name of its famous resident, Lazarus (Arndt 1956: 396; Fitzmyer 1985: 1248).

Located east of Jerusalem, the Mount of Olives is in a range that runs north and south for two and a half miles. Olives, the middle of three peaks that dominate the range, stands 2,660 feet above sea level, directly across from the temple. The mountain has eschatological import in the OT. Zechariah 14:4–5 presents it as the place where Messiah will show himself. Luke makes nothing of this point, but he does mention in Acts 1 that Jesus ascended from this mountain into heaven. At the time of his ascension, one of the angelic messengers notes that Jesus will return as he has departed, which might suggest that he will return to this same point.

Luke is most similar to Mark 11:1, which mentions both villages and the Mount of Olives; John 12:1 mentions the stop in Bethany in association with an anointing of Jesus that Luke does not include; Matt. 21:1 notes only Bethphage at the Mount of Olives (in addition, Matthew uses εἰς [*eis*, into] to mention Olives, while Luke and Mark have πρός [*pros*, toward, at]). Only Luke emphasizes the name of the mount by including the phrase τὸ καλούμενον (*to kaloumenon*, which is called) to clearly indicate the name. Because of Luke's earlier travel note about coming to Jerusalem (Luke 19:28), he saves the use of the verb ἐγγίζω (*engizō*, to draw near) until the mention of the two villages, while Matthew and Mark use it with reference to Jerusalem. The idea of "drawing near" continues the journey theme (18:35; 19:11, 37, 41). The more frequent use of geographical notes heightens the drama and suggests that the anticipated key events are drawing nigh.

Jesus instructs two of his disciples to journey into the village and obtain an animal for his use (animals were sometimes kept for travelers to borrow or hire; Derrett 1971: 244).[7] It is not clear which of the **19:30**

---

7. Nolland 1993b: 925 rejects the influence of this custom, preferring to read the authority as a uniquely christological portrayal versus a cultural one. Are such issues either/or choices?

two villages he means, though if he is staying in Bethany, then Bethphage is probably the destination (Marshall 1978: 712). Jesus' confidence about the animal's availability communicates his control and knowledge (Ernst 1977: 525): he knows where the colt will be tied up (Michel, *TDNT* 6:959–61; Michel 1959–60) and he also knows that it will be an animal no one has ever ridden, which might add a note of purity to the action because of the animal's condition (Num. 19:2; Deut. 21:3; 1 Sam. 6:7; Ernst 1977: 525; Arndt 1956: 396; Plummer 1896: 446).[8]

Luke is closer to Mark 11:2 than to Matt. 21:2: they share the verb ὑπάγετε (*hypagete*, go away), while Matthew has πορεύεσθε (*poreuesthe*, go), which he uses twenty-nine times in comparison to his nineteen uses of ὑπάγω. Luke has the shorter τὴν κατέναντι κώμην (*tēn katenanti kōmēn*, the village opposite) where Mark and Matthew have τὴν κώμην τὴν κατέναντι ὑμῶν (*tēn kōmēn tēn katenanti hymōn*, the village opposite you). Mark and Luke share εἰσπορευόμενοι (*eisporeuomenoi*, on entering), which Matthew lacks, and they also share the phrase about the bound colt and the animal's description.[9] Only in the final instruction are Matthew and Luke closer: Matthew has λύσαντες ἀγάγετέ μοι (*lysantes agagete moi*, untying, bring it to me), Luke has καὶ λύσαντες αὐτὸν ἀγάγετε (*kai lysantes auton agagete*, and untying it bring), and Mark has λύσατε αὐτὸν καὶ φέρετε (*lysate auton kai pherete*, untie it and bring). The difference is a matter of style.[10]

19:31　Jesus predicts that someone will see the disciples untie the animal and inquire why. Jesus tells them to offer a simple reply: "The Lord has need of it." Ὁ κύριος (*ho kyrios*, the Lord) here refers to someone with authority and prepares the reader for 19:33–34. The ancient custom *angaría* can explain the ease with which this is achieved (see the unit introduction). It is possible that the person is a friend or that the expression would be sufficient to allow them to take the animal. In either case, the remark demonstrates Jesus' control over

8. Matthew emphasizes the fulfillment of Zech. 9:9. Cf. the similar phrase in Luke 23:53 about the tomb "in which no one had yet been laid." Fitzmyer 1985: 1248–49 denies any allusion to the "messianically associated" Gen. 49:11 (see also the exegesis of Luke 19:31).

9. Mark has οὔπω (never), while Luke has οὐδεὶς πώποτε (no one ever), a NT term limited to Luke's use here and John 1:18; 5:37; 6:35; 8:33; 1 John 4:12; BAGD 732; BAA 1464.

10. Luke uses ἄγω (to bring) thirteen times (Luke 4:1, 9, 29, 40; 10:34; 18:40; 19:27, 30, 35; 22:54; 23:1, 32; 24:21), while Mark uses it only three times (Mark 1:38; 13:11; 14:42) and Matthew four times (Matt. 10:18; 21:2, 7; 26:46). Mark uses φέρω (to bring along) fifteen times compared to Matthew's and Luke's four times each. This difference is one of Marcan style. Fitzmyer 1985: 1249 argues that Matthew and Luke chose the more precise verb. Luke's reading leaves a chiasmus in the verse: "finding the bound donkey . . . loosing it and bring it" (Nolland 1993b: 924).

events. He plans for all contingencies. Jesus exhibits total knowledge here: (1) the beast's location, (2) its tied-up state, (3) its "unridden" history, and (4) how to procure it (Nolland 1993b: 924). Nolland also sees a veiled reference to Gen. 49:11–12 and Zech. 9:9 in this motif (with help from Luke 19:35). Such background could underscore the theme of humility present in the event.

Matthew 21:3 and Mark 11:3 share the same initial verbal sequence, ὑμῖν εἴπη (hymin eipē, should say to you), while Luke has the distinct ὑμᾶς ἐρωτᾷ (hymas erōta, should ask you), though the meaning is essentially the same. Luke and Mark have interrogative τί (ti, why?) where Matthew has indefinite τι (ti, anything).[11] Luke alone adds the qualifier οὕτως (houtōs, thus). Matthew and Luke share the verb ἐρεῖτε (ereite, you shall say), while Mark has εἴπατε (eipate, say). The reply matches verbally in all the accounts, except that Matthew speaks of untying "them," since he alone refers to two animals. Mark and Matthew both speak of returning the animal quickly, a remark that Luke leaves out. All these differences are stylistic.

ii. The Disciples Follow Jesus' Instructions (19:32–34)

Jesus' control is confirmed: the two disciples find that things happen "just as he said to them" (καθὼς εἶπεν αὐτοῖς, kathōs eipen autois). Jesus' ability to know what will happen also occurs later in the narrative (Luke 22:13, 21, 34; also John 14:29; Ellis 1974: 225). Matthew 21:6 mentions the disciples' obedience, since they do as Jesus directs them. More descriptively, Mark 11:4 says that the disciples found the animal tied at the door, out in the open street, and that they untied it. Each writer renders the detail in his own way. **19:32**

The question comes as Jesus predicted. The genitive absolute λυόντων δὲ αὐτῶν τὸν πῶλον (lyontōn de autōn ton pōlon, while they were untying the colt) describes the disciples' activity in preparing to take the animal to Jesus (BDR §423.2.8). The beast's owners (οἱ κύριοι, hoi kyrioi—perhaps meaning its master and mistress, given the plural; Fitzmyer 1985: 1250; Souter 1914: 94–95; cf. Acts 16:16, 19) want to know the reason for the action. That the owners do the asking may stand against any idea that Jesus had worked out the arrangement ahead of time. On the other hand, they may have asked the question only because the animal has not been ridden previously (Marshall 1978: 713). Only Mark 11:5 is somewhat parallel at this point. He describes a longer question as coming from bystanders: "What are you doing, untying the colt?" Once again, each writer summarizes the action in his own terms, with Luke giving more specifics. **19:33**

11. The accent is the only distinguishing mark between τί (why?) and τι (anything); BAGD 819 §3; BAA 1633 §3.

19:34 The disciples reply as Jesus said they should. In fact, Luke notes their reply in the very words of Jesus' instructions in 19:31. Κύριος (*kyrios*, Lord) is here a title of respect for Jesus (Marshall 1978: 713). Jesus was sufficiently respected that the request would not be a problem. Matthew 21:6 notes that the disciples "did as Jesus directed them." Mark 11:6 explains that "they told them what Jesus said" and adds that the bystanders let them go. For Luke, Jesus' word is enough; permission is not needed, only explanation.

c. Jesus' Entry into Jerusalem (19:35–38)
i. The Disciples' Preparation and Action (19:35–36)

19:35 The animal's role now becomes clear. The two disciples bring it to Jesus and place (ἐπιρίπτω, *epiriptō*)[12] their clothes, probably outer garments (Ellis 1974: 225 [through allusion to 2 Kings 9:13]; Grundmann 1963: 367), on it as a saddle.[13] They then place (ἐπεβίβασαν, *epebibasan*) Jesus on the animal; such language is reminiscent of David's instructions (1 Kings 1:33) to his soldiers to take Solomon to Gihon on a mule, thus showing his endorsement of Solomon as king (Schweizer 1984: 298; Grundmann 1963: 366–67; BAGD 290; BAA 588; also Acts 23:24). This act recalls the language of Zech. 9:9, which speaks of the ride of the king who will restore Jerusalem. Luke does not declare Jesus' act as fulfillment of this event, but his language suggests it, since he alone uses πῶλος (*pōlos*, colt) in this clause (Creed 1930: 240).[14]

Mark 11:7 parallels the Lucan text conceptually, but with different terminology: φέρουσιν (*pherousin*, they brought) matches the earlier use of the verb in Mark 11:2 (just as Luke's ἤγαγον [*ēgagon*, they brought] matches Luke 19:30). Each Synoptist uses different verbs for the disciples' spreading of their garments (Luke ἐπιρίψαντες, Mark ἐπιβάλλουσιν, Matthew ἐπέθηκαν) and for Jesus' sitting on the animal (Luke ἐπεβίβασαν, Mark ἐκάθισεν, Matthew ἐπεκάθισεν). Matthew continues his plural reference to the animals. Mark and Matthew speak of Jesus sitting on the animal, while Luke's description stresses more directly the disciples' role in placing Jesus on the animal (Marshall 1978: 714). Each writer describes the events in his own words.

---

12. Ἐπιρίπτω appears in the NT only here and at 1 Pet. 5:7; BAGD 298; BAA 603. In the LXX it is used of Elijah throwing his cloak over Elisha (1 Kings 19:19) and of Joab's henchman covering Amasa's corpse with a garment (2 Sam. 20:12). The declaration of Jehu as king (2 Kings 9:13) provides verbal contact only with ἱμάτιον (garment).

13. On the unusual and emphatic placement of the attributive genitive αὐτῶν (their), see Plummer 1896: 447 and BDR §271.1c n. 5.

14. Danker 1988: 312 suggests an additional tie to Isa. 1:3 where, ironically, the ox knows its master but Israel does not. Such an allusion is probably too subtle.

The other disciples spread their garments on the road (cf. the use of **19:36** garments in Jehu's regal accession; 2 Kings 9:13). Since disciples are the subject in both Luke 19:35 and 19:37, context requires that disciples, not the crowd, be the subject of this action (against Plummer 1896: 447; with Marshall 1978: 714). They are giving Jesus the "red-carpet treatment," an act intended to note a dignitary's presence (Marshall). For example, Josephus depicts the action in behalf of Jehu (*Antiquities* 9.6.2 §111) and for Agrippa's bed in prison (*Antiquities* 18.6.7 §204) (see also the parallel use of garments in n. 12). Jesus allows the act to proceed as he enters the city.

Two details are found in Matt. 21:8 = Mark 11:8: the crowd spreads (ἔστρωσαν [*estrōsan*] where Luke has ὑπεστρώννυον [*hypestrōnnyon*]) garments and palm leaves. Luke prefers prefixed verbs, so the difference is a matter of style. Luke does not mention the spreading of palm branches, probably because this Jewish detail was beyond his audience (Bock 1987: 122–23). This action had eschatological significance at the Feast of Tabernacles, but is surprising here before this feast. Nevertheless, the surprising timing would not nullify comprehension of the symbolism.

ii. The Crowd's Praise (19:37–38)

With the entry comes praise and testimony. Luke alone notes the lo- **19:37** cale as the Mount of Olives, a place full of eschatological significance (see the exegesis of 19:29). Jesus continues to draw near (ἐγγίζω, *engizō*) the city. This remark and the one in 19:41 (cf. 19:11) show that, for Luke, Jesus is not yet in the city and that the journey to Jerusalem is nearing its end (Danker 1988: 312).

The multitude of disciples is rejoicing, an activity that Luke alone notes.[15] God's miraculous works are the source of the praise (see BDR §294.5 on the syntax). Jesus' ministry has been one continuous demonstration of God's power: the deaf speak, the blind see, the lame walk, lepers are cleansed, and the gospel is preached (7:22). It is not only an exciting time to watch God's work, it is unique (Luke 13:10–17; 14:1–6; 17:11–19; 18:35–43; Acts 10:38). Luke's unique reference to praise fits his emphasis, since αἰνέω (*aineō*, to praise) is used elsewhere by him five times (Luke 2:13, 20; Acts 2:47; 3:8, 9) but only twice in the rest of the NT (Rom. 15:11; Rev. 19:5; Luce 1933: 301; Marshall 1978: 714; Fitzmyer 1985: 1250). Those who understand Jesus' purpose rejoice.

15. That Luke is the only Synoptist to note this praise leads Marshall 1978: 714 to raise the possibility that Luke uses another source because of the unusual combinations of ἐγγίζω with πρός (to draw near to) and πρός with the dative. The latter construction occurs only here in Luke, six times elsewhere in the NT (Mark 5:11; John 18:16; 20:11, 12 [twice]; Rev. 1:13; BDR §240.2), and 104 times in the LXX.

19:38   Luke details the praise offered for God's work: it is really praise for
Jesus and the time that his activity indicates (Marshall 1978: 715).
With Jesus' entry into Jerusalem comes another allusion to Ps. 118.
In the earlier allusion to this psalm (Luke 13:35), Jesus lamented
Jerusalem's failure to respond to him. Here the disciples, in contrast
to the nation, confess Jesus as God's messenger. It is not correct to
see 19:38 as the fulfillment of 13:35, because (a) it is the disciples,
not the nation, who utter the note of reception and (b) Jesus' remark
about missing the day of visitation (19:44) shows that some still reject him. Luke 13:35 has a still future day of Israel's reception in
view.

The use of Ps. 118:26 is typological in originally depicting the
king leading pilgrims to the temple and receiving a greeting of welcome from the priests at the temple, probably on the occasion of
some major victory. This greeting/blessing recognized that the king
and his entourage came with the Lord's approval (Bock 1987: 118,
125). As it was then, so it should be in Jesus' time. He should be welcomed as a leader and agent of God. The association of Ps. 118 with
eschatological hope and the Feast of Tabernacles also heightens the
sense of nearness of eschatological fulfillment. The cry is full of
hope because the king is here. Reference to "one who comes" is common in Luke (3:15–17; 7:19–23; 13:35; Ellis 1974: 225; Danker 1988:
313).

The key difference between the citations of Ps. 118 here and in
Luke 13:35 is the addition of ὁ βασιλεύς (*ho basileus*, the king). Luke
has previously alluded to Jesus' Davidic connection (1:32; 18:38–
39), but here he explicitly calls Jesus king. This reference to the king
makes it clear that a regal figure is in view, and it may be an additional allusion to Zech. 9:9. When one puts the regal confession next
to eschatological imagery, a messianic claim is present. This combination gives the event its eschatological flavor and shows that messianic intimations operate at various levels.

Following the eschatological blessing is a concluding note of
peace and glory, much like that at Jesus' birth (Luke 2:10–14). Salvation comes, and so peace and joy can be proclaimed (Marshall
1978: 715–16). Creed (1930: 240) identifies peace in heaven as "the
gift of peace which is laid up in heaven for God's people" (1:79; 2:14;
10:5–6, 24:36; Leaney 1958: 246; for laid-up heavenly treasure, see
Col. 1:4–5). Nolland (1993b: 927) rejects this reading as too distant
for the context and opts for praise for Jesus' ascension. This view
cannot work either, since the world does not know the events to
come. It is simply acknowledging God's work in Jesus' ministry, a
view that will extend in surprising directions along the lines that
Nolland suggests as a result of subsequent events. In this regal fig-

ure, God is reconciling himself to humanity and reasserting his rule. The king is entering the city to the people's cries of joy, cries that within a week will become wails of pain and disappointment.

The parallels (Matt. 21:9 = Mark 11:9 = John 12:13) all use the line from Ps. 118 about the blessedness of the one who comes in the name of the Lord, but each writer gives it his own twist. Matthew speaks of crowds giving praise to the son of David, cites the psalm, and then notes the cries of hosanna in the highest (hosanna, a cry to God "to save us," was often a statement of confidence). Mark speaks of those going before and behind crying hosanna, cites the psalm, notes another blessing for the "coming kingdom of our father David," and closes with cries of hosanna in the highest. John mentions the hosanna, cites the psalm, and adds the note of blessing on "the king of Israel." Luke lacks reference to hosanna, because his audience might not have understood what it meant, and articulates instead the praise in terms of peace and glory (Fitzmyer 1985: 1251; Lohse, *TDNT* 9:683). Luke also avoids kingdom terminology here because it might be misunderstood (as 19:11 indicates). The king, praise, and the Davidic hope of fulfillment dominate all four accounts. As Jesus enters the city he presents himself as the king who brings the nation's eschatological hope. A week later he will be taken outside the city, for in the eyes of the nation he is a messianic imposter who must be stopped. The nation will say no—just as Jesus predicted. A donkey now bears him as king; soon he will bear his own cross.

d. The Pharisees' Criticism; Jesus' Response (19:39–40)
i. The Pharisees' Call to Rebuke the Disciples (19:39)

19:39 The sentiment of praise floating through the crowd is not unanimous. Some of the Pharisees from (ἀπό instead of ἐκ; BDR §209.2 n. 4) the crowd tell Jesus to rebuke his disciples. The leadership regards Jesus as a teacher with disciples and addresses him as such (Plummer 1896: 449; Luke 7:40; 20:21, 28). The imperative ἐπιτίμησον (*epitimēson*, rebuke) suggests that the Pharisees are offended or worried by the disciples' messianic confession of Jesus and so seek to correct the situation as quickly as possible. They regard the praise as inappropriate. Marshall (1978: 716) suggests that, if the advice is not malicious, it represents the Pharisees' fear about such an open political confession. Danker (1988: 313) argues that the reaction is political: the leaders were concerned that Rome might react to such Jewish fervor (the next verse shows this expectation to be wrong). In this last appearance of the Pharisees amidst the crowd (last noted in 17:20), one gets the sense that they reacted out of offense, not concern, especially given Jesus' many warnings to them since he started toward Jerusalem (12:54–56; 13:31–35). Jesus' weeping also stands against seeing the officials' reaction in a favorable light, since such a response implies their rejection of him. The verse is unique to Luke, though John 12:18–19 also speaks of this reaction after Jesus healed Lazarus and then entered the city. After that healing the crowd cried, "Hosanna to the King of Israel" (John 12:13) and the Pharisees reacted with similar concern. It is the person of Jesus who is the main concern; political issues seem to be a means to an end. (The allusion to Luke 19:14 should not be missed.)

ii. Jesus' Refusal (19:40)

19:40 Jesus replies to the Pharisees with deep irony. In an ardent refusal to stop the messianic confession of his followers, he says that if they ceased (σιωπάω, siōpaō; BAGD 752 §2a; BAA 1504 §2a), creation would cry out (κράζω, krazō; BAGD 448 §2bβ; BAA 910 §2bβ) in testimony to him (Fitzmyer 1985: 1252).[16] Creation is aware of Jesus, but the leadership of the nation is not. That which is lifeless knows life when it sees it, even though that which is living does not. Luke portrays their rejection as a tragic, stinging indictment of their lack of judgment. Luke alone narrates this exchange.

6. Weeping for Jerusalem (19:41–44)
a. Lament (19:41–42)

19:41 A uniquely Lucan unit closes the Jerusalem journey narrative with a tone of sadness. Once again using ἐγγίζω (engizō; cf. 19:29, 37), Luke notes that Jesus drew near to Jerusalem. The drama of the slow approach signals the importance of the coming events. Upon seeing the city, Jesus weeps. These are the tears of one who knows that the people have already turned their backs on God's messenger. Much like a parent watching a child make a foolish decision, Jesus mourns a city sealing its fate (cf. 13:34). His crying recalls similar reactions by the prophets (2 Kings 8:11; Jer. 9:1 [8:23 MT]; 14:17; κλαίω with ἐπί in Gen. 50:1; Num. 11:13; Judg. 11:37–38; Fitzmyer 1985: 1258). Jesus is not indifferent toward the nation. The term for tears (κλαίω, klaiō) is strong, referring to full sobbing or wailing (Plummer 1896: 449–50; BAGD 433; BAA 881; see the exegesis of 7:38).

---

16. In Gen. 4:10 Abel's spilled blood cries out, and esp. in Hab. 2:11 Jerusalem's stones cry out against Israel's injustice and sin. Marshall 1978: 716 notes the possibility that creation will speak out against the sin of the Pharisees (Jeremias, *TDNT* 4:270), an option that is less satisfying contextually than the standard OT use of the image; so correctly SB 2:253, which notes the use of this figure in Judaism: Tg. Hab. 2:11; Midr. Ps. 73.4 on 73:10 (= Braude 1959: 2.4).

Speaking "a searing oracle of doom" (Tiede 1980: 80), Jesus mourns **19:42** because Jerusalem has missed the nature of the times, which held the potential for a restoration of peace. In the travel narrative, Jesus constantly warned against the possibility of national failure (most directly in 13:31–35 and 11:50–51). This lamentation is like Jeremiah's (Jer. 9:2 [9:1 MT]; 13:17; 14:7) and shows the combination of pain, anger, and frustration that rejection causes in one who serves God (Nolland 1993b: 931). The note of sadness is introduced with a "contrary to fact" second-class condition that is not completed: "If you only knew . . . , but you do not."[17] The idea to be supplied is, "It would have pleased me if you had known the things that made for peace" (Fitzmyer 1985: 1258; Isa. 48:18). The reference to peace (i.e., peace with God) summarizes the essential characteristic of the gospel message (Luke 1:79; 2:14; 7:50; 8:48; 10:5–6; 19:38; Acts 10:36; Foerster, *TDNT* 2:413; Marshall 1978: 718). The opportunity has come and gone.

Peace was hidden from the city's (i.e., the nation's) eyes (Ps. 122:6; Jer. 15:5; Grundmann 1963: 368). Blindness results from failure to respond, and darkness remains. In contrast to peace, destruction comes, as the next two verses will make clear. The cost of sin is great. What they had potentially is about to be taken from them (8:10). Judgment will result in death and darkness (Oepke, *TDNT* 3:973). Like the prophets of old, Jesus finds no joy in rebuking sin and declaring its dire consequences.

b. Judgment (19:43–44)

Jesus predicts that Jerusalem will become the object of a fierce siege **19:43** in the "days that are coming," a phrase used by the OT prophets to indicate coming events of great significance (seventeen times in the LXX, including 1 Sam. 2:31; 2 Kings 20:17; Jer. 7:32–34; 31:38; 33:14; 49:2; Isa. 39:6; Zech. 14:1; Schweizer 1984: 300). This is the payment for Jerusalem's rejection. Just as the nation went into exile for disobedience, so Jesus predicts judgment for his generation. God's past activity and the consistency of his actions in bringing covenant justice are the presuppositions behind such a prophecy. What was a visitation for salvation has become a visitation of judgment (Tiede 1988: 333).

Jesus uses siege terminology to picture the city's destruction: παρεμβάλλω (*paremballō*) describes the placing of barricades or earthen mounds (χάραξ, *charax*) around the city; περικυκλόω

---

17. On εἰ (if) with the aorist, see BDF §454.4; BDR §360.5. On aposiopesis, the breaking off of the remark because of emotion, see BDF §482; Luke 22:42; John 6:62; 12:27; Plummer 1896: 450.

(*perikykloō*) describes the surrounding of the beleaguered city, perhaps even the building of a wall around it; and συνέχω (*synechō*) describes the enemy pressing its attack against the city.[18] All three verbs are future, so Jesus is speaking prophetically: the city will crumble. The judgment on Jerusalem will be like that experienced earlier by the pagan nations and like the exilic judgment on Israel (Ps. 137:9; Jer. 6:6–21; 8:18–22; Isa. 29:1–4; Nah. 3:10; Fitzmyer 1985: 1258).

The event in view is clearly the attack of Rome that led to the collapse of Jerusalem in A.D. 70. Some hold that this saying is a "prophecy after the event" (*vaticinium ex eventu*), at least in its present formulation (Bultmann 1963: 123; Hill 1973–74). But the charge is unlikely, since the formulation parallels OT imagery and the language is that of sieges in general (Hab. 2:8 and its use at Qumran: 1QpHab 9.5–7; Fitzmyer 1985: 1255; Plummer 1896: 451; Ellis 1974: 226; Tiede 1988: 333).[19] Another factor is the absolute lack of specifics: if the saying had been composed after the fact, one might expect it to contain details, not just generalized descriptions.[20] There are some points of contact between the prediction and the events of A.D. 70 (e.g., Titus built a barricade around the city; Josephus, *Jewish War* 5.11.4 §466; 5.12.2 §508), but there is no need to insist on a "prophecy after the fact" since the terms used have OT precedent and describe standard Roman military procedure.[21] Though the prophecy looks to particular judgment, the siege described is typical. As such, the saying cannot fix Luke's date, since it cannot be ar-

---

18. The first three of these terms are NT *hapax legomena*, but they occur frequently in the LXX: παρεμβάλλω (BAGD 625; BAA 1263; Acts 21:34 [a related noun referring to a fortified military camp or barracks]), χάραξ (BAGD 876; BAA 1749 §2; Isa. 29:3; 37:33; Jer. 6:6; Ezek. 4:2; 26:8), περικυκλόω (BAGD 648; BAA 1307; Josh. 6:13; 2 Kings 6:14; Ps. 16:11 LXX [17:11 Engl.]; Jer. 38:39 LXX [31:39 Engl.]), and συνέχω (BAGD 789 §3; BAA 1573 §3; 2 Macc 9:2; Jer. 52:5 [a related noun]).

19. Dodd 1947: 49 argues that all the language is from the OT, as does Gaston 1970: 359, citing a catena of verses: Jer. 8:18; 9:1; 6:14, 6, 15, 8. Manson 1949: 319–20 cites Jer. 8:18–22, although the whole of Jer. 8:13–22, along with Jer. 6:6–21 and Isa. 29:1–4, might also be relevant. See also Plummer 1896: 451–52. Tiede 1980: 68–86 challenges Gaston's view that Luke has four stages here: salvation to part of Israel, fulfillment of threat, salvation to Gentiles, and the end. He sees a theodicy in Luke-Acts, where Luke explains how Jerusalem crumbled and yet Luke argues that God still will be faithful by restoring Israel. This is quite possible, though Tiede argues for a post–A.D. 70 date for the book, which is less likely.

20. Giblin 1985: 56 sees Ps. 137:9; Ezek. 4:1–2; and Isa. 3:26 as relevant. He notes that Jerusalem falls as any worldly city would because they missed the "moment of truth." See also Flückiger 1972: 387–88. Nolland 1993b: 931–32 notes the numerous examples of non-Lucan language in Luke 19:43–44.

21. Danker 1988: 314 notes a "prophecy" by Demetrius of Phalerum, who predicted the Macedonian victory with similar political sensitivity (Polybius 29.21).

gued from this verse that Jerusalem had already fallen, nor are the details sufficiently unique to Jerusalem's fall to indicate such a conclusion (see vol. 1, pp. 17–18).

Jesus follows the three descriptions of 19:43 with two more portray-
als of the nation's fall. The nation and its children (i.e., the citizens; Manson 1949: 320–21) are pictured dying. In a case of the semantic error of totality transfer, BAGD 217 and BAA 438 assign two meanings to the *hapax legomenon* ἐδαφίζω (*edaphizō*): "to dash people to the ground" (Ps. 136:9 LXX [137:9 Engl.]; Hos. 10:14; 14:1 LXX [13:16 Engl.]; Nah. 3:10) and "to raze a city" (Isa. 3:26) (see also 2 Kings 8:12; Fitzmyer 1985: 1253).[22] It is best to see only a picture of dead bodies here, since the next picture is of the razed city (this allows each description in 19:43–44 to picture something different; correctly Luce 1933: 304).[23]

19:44

The description of one stone not being on another pictures the city being leveled.[24] The defeat is total. Nothing stands. Rome's army will leave the city for dead. Fitzmyer (1985: 1259) notes the connection to 19:40 and says that the stones will cry out in another way to and for Jesus as a result of this rejection (see the conceptually parallel 19:27; Josephus, *Jewish War* 7.1.1 §§1–4; 7.8.7 §§375–77).

Finally, Jesus gives the reason (ἀνθ' ὧν, *anth' hōn*; BDR §208.2; Luke 1:20; 12:3) for the tragic destruction: the nation missed the opportunity to respond to the eschatological moment, that is, to his visitation. Both 19:42 and this verse note that the nation did not know the time of Messiah's eschatological coming (ἐπισκοπή, *episkopē*, visitation; Beyer, *TDNT* 2:607 §2a; Luke 1:79; 7:16; Grundmann 1963: 369; BAGD 299; BAA 605).[25] Ἐπισκοπή is often positive with relation to the coming of God's grace and power, but can also be negative of judgment. Appealing to Isa. 10:3; Jer. 6:15; 10:15, many argue for the negative force here. But the nation did not miss judgment, so the meaning must be positive.[26] Jesus knows what the

---

22. The place to which the bodies are thrown is understood in this elliptical verb: "to the ground as dead bodies"; BDR §478.2.

23. Manson 1949: 320–21 defends the repetitive sense, appealing to poetic parallelism to refute the charge of tautology. However, the pattern of 19:43–44, where each element is distinct, is too clear to accept the objection or Manson's rendering.

24. On ἀφίημι (to leave), see BAGD 126 §3a; BAA 253 §3a; Matt. 24:2 = Mark 13:2 = Luke 21:6 (of the temple); cf. 2 Sam. 17:13; Dan. 4:26 LXX [not in MT]; Mic. 3:12. Ἀφίημι is also used in Luke 13:35, a key parallel.

25. Another failure to read the times is found in 12:54–56. Danker 1988: 315 cites 14:15–24 with the note "God had kept his appointment with the city, but Jerusalem's power structure did not show up at the banquet."

26. As in Gen. 50:24–25; Exod. 3:7, 16; Job 10:12; 29:4; Wis. 2:20; 3:13; 1 Pet. 2:12; and 1 Clem. 50.3; correctly Marshall 1978: 719. Fitzmyer 1985: 1259 does not specify which view he holds.

nation has decided about him, but the loss is Israel's, which will experience judgment while Jesus will be exalted and vindicated by God.[27] The division predicted for the nation has come. The sword does not just pass through Mary's heart (Luke 2:34). It is a fearful thing to be responsible before God for the rejection of Jesus.

Summary   In Luke 19:28–44, Jesus approaches Jerusalem publicly and in control of events. He tells the disciples how to procure an animal for him. He enters the city to the eschatological cheers of his followers, who praise God's power manifested through him and who confess that Jesus comes as king in the name of the Lord. Their action pictures fulfillment of the national desire for salvation, usually expressed at the Feast of Tabernacles. It is a glorious entry, but it is all a charade because of what is about to happen.

Those who orchestrate this reversal stand on the sidelines and complain to Jesus about the messianic praise he receives. But Jesus sides with his followers and notes that if they did not speak, inanimate creation would take up the refrain of praise.

The rejection is of catastrophic importance, and it causes Jesus to weep over the fate of the city he loves. In 13:34–35, Jesus, speaking for God, said he longed to gather the nation's capital under his wing, a picture of care and protection. Instead, the nation chose to go it alone. In light of this choice, the nation will suffer total defeat. The price for missing the Messiah's visitation is the dark visit of another potentate from Rome. The destruction will be total. Ironically, the nation's charge against Jesus is that he is a political threat to Rome. His opponents argue that if Jesus is allowed to run his course he will be perceived as a physical threat and Rome might overrun the nation. But defeat comes, in spite of Jesus. It comes because of their rejection of him. Here is Luke's ultimate apologetic to those Jews who question the role that the church gives to Jesus. Those who bring Rome to bear on Jerusalem are those who charge Jesus with being a threat to the nation. Jesus is not the enemy, but because of his rejection the enemy can come.

The reader is to realize that history was never the same because of the nation's tragic failure to accept its day of visitation. In fact, the rejection was fatal for those who shared in it. It costs to reject Jesus.

---

27. Tiede 1980: 82 mentions Jer. 22:8 and 23:38. This is a national indictment like that of the exile. As Tiede says (p. 68), "Love for Israel, conflicting with wrath, characterizes this oracle of judgment." Weatherly 1994 attempts to limit the responsibility for Jesus' death to Jerusalem and its leaders. He is right that Luke presents a "divided nation" and limits responsibility for the death here, but these indictments become national as a result. Covenant judgment tends to be national.

With this passage, Luke concludes his central section, which is highlighted by two themes. The first is the portrait of Jesus as the confronting prophet like Moses, who is greater than Moses.[28] Moessner observes that the central section has two journey portions (9:51–10:24 and 18:18–19:44) with a middle section on eschatological halakah (10:25–18:17). The perspective and influence of Deuteronomy controls the section as Jesus the prophet calls the people to repent lest they face destruction by God's judgment (2 Kings 17:13–14, 23a). Luke 19:41–44 indicates their failure to heed the call. The premise behind the call is that the current generation is evil and that their behavior indicates solidarity with their unfaithful ancestors (11:14–54). Throughout 9:51–13:35, Jesus, as mediator of the divine, instructs and admonishes about the need for repentance. Despite the warnings, rejection results, proving the condition of many in the nation and verifying Jesus' perspective of the nation.

The second theme comes as a result of mediating God's will. The prophet like Moses is greater than Moses (9:35) and reveals the ethic that God desires. Jesus describes for the people of God the way of discipleship in the face of opposition. He leads a new exodus into God's presence and promises a seat at God's banquet table (14:15–24). Repentance is the result of a life of humility lived out before God. Forgiveness comes to the humble who draw near to God and experience his grace on his terms. Faithfulness grounded in humility is the essence of the spiritual life. The good Samaritan, the tax collector, Zacchaeus, and the blind man of Jericho are positive examples. The parables concerning the lost show God's commitment to them. The calls to commitment show the journey's price. The rich, the Pharisees, and scribes are the constant negative examples of what not to be. The call to love God by loving one's neighbor is at the center of this ethic. To come to Jesus is to receive with humility what he provides and to know and walk with God. In short, one is to walk in Jesus' way of love, generosity, rejection, and suffering. Paul understood this call, as 2 Corinthians and Acts indicate. The journey completed, Jesus now turns to meet his fate in Jerusalem; the loser is not Jesus, but those who reject him. Resisting the prophet-like-Moses is serious.

28. Moessner 1989: 127, 131, 176, 211 details this view. J. A. Sanders 1974 and C. A. Evans 1990: 166–69 tie the portrait to the themes of election and the true people of God. C. F. Evans 1955 is responsible for raising the connection to Deuteronomy and argues for it throughout his commentary (1990: 34–37, 435).

Additional Notes

19:29. There is some uncertainty about the accentuation of the word for Olives. If accented Ἐλαιῶν, it is the genitive plural of the feminine noun ἐλαία (olive, olive tree); if accented Ἐλαιών, it is the nominative singular of the masculine noun ἐλαιών (olive grove, olive orchard). Marshall (1978: 712) defends the first reading (also BDF §143; Plummer 1896: 445; Foerster, *TDNT* 5:484 n. 100). The issue is of no interpretive significance.

19:38. UBS–NA, following B and possibly Syriac, reads ὁ ἐρχόμενος ὁ βασιλεύς (the one who comes, the king), which treats the reference to king as appositional. Possessing wider manuscript support ($\aleph^2$, A, L, Δ, Θ, Ψ, family 1, family 13, Byz, Lect, possibly Syriac), ὁ ἐρχόμενος βασιλεύς (the coming king or the king who comes) is a more difficult reading because it differs slightly from Ps. 118:26 [117:26 LXX]. The difference in the force of two main variants is virtually nil. (There are three other less well attested variants.)

19:40. The syntax of the best attested reading is unusual since there are no clearly attested examples of ἐάν (if) with the future tense (BDF §373.2; other possible examples—both textually uncertain—are 1 Thess. 3:8 and 1 John 5:15; Plummer 1896: 449; Marshall 1978: 716). The future indicative σιωπήσουσιν (they will be silent) is read by $\aleph$, A, B, L, N, W, and Δ, while Θ, Ψ, family 1, family 13, Byz, and Lect read the more common aorist subjunctive σιωπήσωσιν (they would be silent). Codex D has future indicative of another verb, σιγήσουσιν (they will be silent), which BDF says is possible.

19:42. At least six variants concern the word order of σύ (you) and the placement of the particles, four of which have good manuscript support: (1) ἐν τῇ ἡμέρᾳ ταύτῃ καὶ σύ (in this day also you; $\aleph$, B, L, Origen, UBS–NA), (2) καὶ σὺ ἐν τῇ ἡμέρᾳ ταύτῃ (and you in this day; D, Θ, many Itala, some Coptic), (3) καὶ σὺ καί γε ἐν τῇ ἡμέρᾳ ταύτῃ (and you also indeed in this day; A, Ψ, family 1), and (4) καὶ σὺ καί γε ἐν τῇ ἡμέρᾳ σου ταύτῃ (and you also indeed in this your day; W, Δ, family 13, Byz, Lect, many Syriac). The first reading has superior external evidence in the major Alexandrian witnesses. The variants with additional particles are less likely because they look like readings in which additions are piled on top of one another (especially variant 4). The variations make little difference to the passage's sense. Readings 3 and 4 are more emphatic, but all make the point that the city has missed its day.

19:42. Three variants are found for the reference to peace: (1) εἰρήνην (peace; $\aleph$, B, L, Θ, Coptic, UBS–NA), (2) εἰρήνην σου (your peace; A, W, Δ, Ψ, family 1, Byz, Lect, most Syriac), and (3) εἰρήνην σοι (peace for you; D, family 13, Itala, Vulgate). The meaning in the options is the same: the nation has missed the opportunity for peace. This is a difficult reading to assess, since the eye could well move from the final N in EIPHNHN to the initial N in NYN and miss what was between the words. Many see the shorter Alexandrian reading as original.

V. Jerusalem: The Innocent One Slain and Raised (19:45–24:53)

Luke's final division has five sections. First, Jesus encounters controversy before his trial and death (19:45–21:4). He enters Jerusalem to cleanse the temple, and the Jewish leadership makes three attempts to trap him with questions about his authority, the temple tax, and resurrection—all of which fail. Jesus in turn raises three issues of his own: a parable shows that the vineyard of promise goes to others, a question on Ps. 110 shows that the leadership does not understand who Messiah is, and a comment about the widow who gives all (a counterexample to the leadership) shows how true righteousness responds.

Second, Jesus describes the consummation and an event that will look like it: the fall of Jerusalem (21:5–38). The temple will be destroyed in a period of persecution and war. In contrast, the end will involve the glorious appearing of the Son of Man, who will wield authority and exercise judgment. His coming represents the saints' redemption. The disciples are to watch for his return.

Third, Luke notes the movement toward Jesus' arrest and a farewell discourse (22:1–38). Judas plans the betrayal, while Jesus plans the final meal. At this last meal, Jesus commemorates his upcoming offering by sharing bread (which pictures his broken body) and wine (which represents his blood shed for the new covenant). In a final discourse, he indicates that he knows about his betrayer, calls his disciples to true greatness in service, appoints the Twelve to authority, predicts Peter's denials, and tells them to be careful in light of his death. Jesus is clearly in control of events leading to his death.

Fourth, the arrest and a series of trials follow (22:39–23:56). Jesus gives himself over to the Father's will, while the disciples fail to heed Jesus' call to watch—the first of many failures by the disciples. So Jesus faces his death alone. Arrested, he is brought before the Sanhedrin, who cannot convict him until Jesus convicts himself. When Jesus claims the right to go directly into God's presence and rule at his side, the religious officials regard this declaration as blasphemy and render a guilty verdict. Meanwhile, Peter, who had promised to stand by Jesus unto death, denies him three times, just as Jesus predicted. Jesus faces his death willingly; he is in control

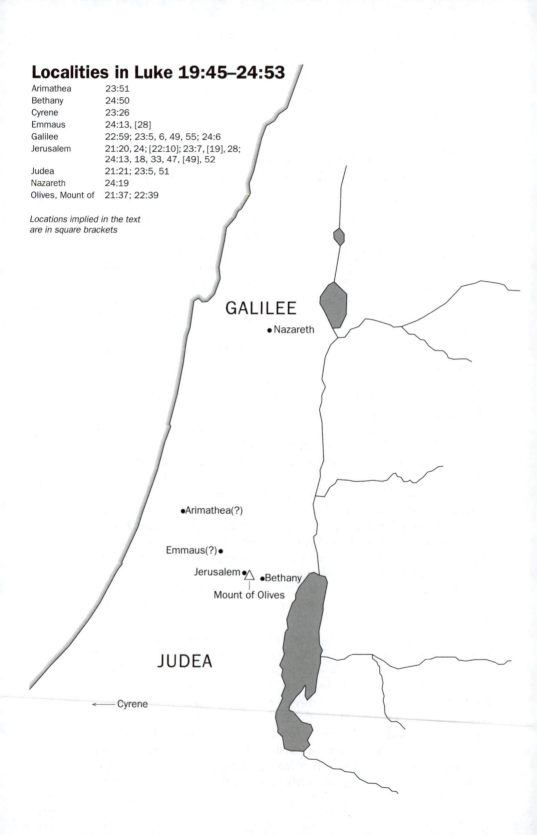

Localities in Luke 19:45–24:53

*Locations implied in the text
are in square brackets*

GALILEE

• Nazareth

•Arimathea(?)

Emmaus(?)•

Jerusalem•△ •Bethany
              |
        Mount of Olives

JUDEA

←—— Cyrene

of events, even though they involve acts of injustice. Separate trials before Herod and Pilate reach no clear conclusion, other than a judgment that Jesus has done nothing worthy of death. Only public clamor forces Pilate's hand to issue a death sentence against someone he considers innocent. The people condemn Jesus and set free a criminal instead; Barabbas pictures the freedom that Jesus' death can bring. Jesus goes to the cross, and as he is dying two thieves argue about the merits of his ministry. One mocks him, but the other asks to enter into paradise with Jesus. Even as Jesus is dying, he still saves. The innocent Savior dies and is buried.

Fifth, Luke traces vindication in resurrection (24:1–53). Some women discover the empty tomb and go to tell the disciples that Jesus is raised. Meanwhile some disappointed disciples are joined in their discussion by a stranger. The stranger calls these disciples to renewed faith and explains Scripture's promise to them. He shares a meal with them, and when he breaks bread he reveals himself to be the risen Jesus. Later, in the midst of their report, Jesus appears and again instructs the disciples. He opens up the Scripture, which tells of his death, resurrection, and the preaching of repentance for the forgiveness of sins to all the nations. The disciples are commissioned to preach Jesus, as the Scripture proclaims, but they are to wait for the Father's promise—the coming of the Spirit, who will enable them to do what they failed to do during Jesus' arrest and death. Now the disciples will stand by him. Luke ends his Gospel with Jesus' ascension and the disciples rejoicing. Jesus' death is not the end. It is but the beginning of God's work.

Three major themes dominate Luke's final division. The first is Jesus' control over events. He is not surprised by anything. In fact, he provides the testimony that leads to his death. In the midst of his control, he also submits to the Father's will, even unto death.

Second is the disciples' need to watch, be ready, and have faith. This theme is mainly demonstrated in a negative way as disciples betray him, fall asleep on him, and deny knowing him. Divine provision of "power from on high" (Luke 24:49; Acts 2) will remedy this inability and allow the disciples to minister mightily, even to the point of facing death for Jesus. Jesus desires disciples who stand up for him before opposition.

The third theme is God's direction and will as he works out his plan. The Scripture foretold all: the Innocent One would be slain, the promised new covenant would be inaugurated in blood, and the message of hope and forgiveness would be proclaimed. Jesus' death was not a failure in God's plan, it was the center of it. It was not an obstacle to deliverance, it was a ladder to heaven. Now the call is to make that message clear. Luke ends on a high note, as the disciples prepare to declare God's work in Jesus to a needy world. With the help of God's promised Spirit they can perform the task and face opposition. The divinely designed necessities of the Messiah's career become transforming history.

A. Controversy in Jerusalem (19:45–21:4)

Jesus' entry into Jerusalem begins and ends at the temple. He cleanses the temple in a prophetic act that portrays the nation's diseased religious condition (19:45–48). The leaders engage Jesus in various debates, but his replies only silence and frustrate them. They question Jesus' authority (20:1–8) and then attempt to trap him in two dilemmas: a political offense against Rome (20:20–26) and a theological debate about resurrection (20:27–40). Jesus responds with three issues of his own. He describes how the nation is losing its place in the administration of God's plan (20:9–19), how Messiah is more than David's son (20:41–44), and how a certain poor woman worships God more faithfully than do Israel's leaders (20:45–21:4). The leadership knows that something must be done about Jesus.

1. Temple Cleansing (19:45–48)

This unit has two parts: the temple cleansing followed by the leadership's plot to destroy Jesus in the face of his popularity. In the temple cleansing, Jesus functions as a prophet and uses prophetic language to denounce what is happening there. Merchants were selling various items (e.g., animals, wine, oil, salt, doves) necessary for pilgrims to offer sacrifices (John 2:14; *m. Šeqal.* 1.3; 2.1, 4; SB 1:850–52; Marshall 1978: 721; Fitzmyer 1985: 1267; Jeremias 1969: 49).[1] In addition, money changers were exchanging Roman and Greek coins for the half-shekel temple tax required by the Torah (Exod. 30:11–14). These transactions had built-in charges, with some of the money going to the high priest's family (Marshall 1978: 721 speaks of money-grabbing and commercial rivalry).

Jesus condemns these practices through allusions to the OT: Isa. 56:7 describes the hope that proselytes will find the temple a house for all the nations, while Jer. 7:11 denounces Israel's hypocrisy and injustice in temple worship. God is offended at the reality defined by Jeremiah. But Jesus goes farther than Jeremiah: he physically acts against those who have excessive commercial interest in the temple. Such an act on the sacred temple site was probably considered blasphemous in the first century (E. Sanders 1990: 66–67).[2] Since Jesus acted physically, the leaders could portray him as a threat to the peace, and so they decide to remove him (Luke 19:47). Jesus wishes to uphold God's honor and keep

---

1. Eppstein 1964: 55–56 holds that some aspects of this trade were recent and controversial (but I disagree with his dating the temple cleansing to A.D. 30).

2. Sanders correctly calls this action blasphemous from a Jewish point of view. He is right not to decry the presence of money changers per se, since sacrifices and payment of the temple tax were required at the temple (i.e., sacrifices had to be unblemished, and a long trip might injure the sacrificial animal). Sanders, however, too quickly dismisses Jesus' Son-of-Man reply at his trial (22:69), for this remark was also blasphemous to Jews (Sanders is guilty of either/or thinking, when both/and applies). Luke ignores the temple issue at the trial and focuses on Jesus' person. Rejecting that Jesus purifies the temple, E. Sanders 1985: 61–71 holds that Jesus simply pictures its approaching destruction. But to put forth this view, Sanders must deny the authenticity of the OT sayings and argue that the "house of prayer for Gentiles" is impossible for this early historical context. Isaiah 56:6 refers, however, to worshiping foreigners who are also the subjects in 56:7. The saying is authentic, looking to the day when all nations will gather to worship God in Jerusalem, a key OT prophetic hope (Isa. 2:2–4; 19:23–25).

the worship of God pure without people benefiting financially from it (one may not serve God and mammon; 16:13; Fitzmyer 1985: 1266). Interestingly, Luke and Matthew lack Mark's comment about the temple being a place for all nations, a significant omission in light of Luke's Gentile emphasis. The usual explanation for this omission is that Jerusalem has fallen and the temple has been destroyed by the time Matthew and Luke write, and so it is not necessary to include the remark. This explanation does not, however, seem compelling, since the remark shows the universality that Jesus foresees for the worship of God and is unrelated to the temple's existence at the time the Gospel is written. Perhaps the omission focuses on the indictment, so that condemnation dominates the account.

Jesus' act may be viewed as either prophetic or messianic.[3] Conzelmann (1960: 77–78) argues that Jesus as Messiah "takes possession" of the temple. The act's strong character, the declaration of 19:38, and Jesus' remarks in 2:49 show a messianic connection. But it must be noted that within the account itself there is little explicit messianic imagery. Jesus' reply is couched in prophetic terms, and no messianic titles are used (Fitzmyer 1985: 1266–67 and Schrenk, *TDNT* 3:243–44, are cautious about a messianic act). The most significant factor in making the temple cleansing look messianic is the title used at Jesus' entry into Jerusalem—especially since these events are more tightly placed together in Luke than in the other Synoptics. As such, it must be said that though this event itself is not explicitly messianic, Luke appropriately develops it as such in his narrative reading of history because the entry colors the nature of the figure who acts. The cleansing is intended to be prophetic and messianic, though the former description is the more obvious category for the action itself. No doubt the action could have been read by the religious authorities as an attack on God's sacred dwelling place. It certainly threatened the leadership's authority, interests, and reputation, not to mention the city's commercial interests. But it is an act against temple commerce, not against the temple directly. It condemns current temple practice and thus implicitly calls for re-

---

3. For other acts of offense against the temple, see *m. Sanh.* 9.6. On the association of the eschaton, a redeeming figure, and the final renewed temple in Judaism, see Josephus, *Antiquities* 18.4.1 §§85–87; *Jewish War* 6.5.2 §§283–85 (1 Enoch 90.28–40 is often cited in this regard, but this passage refers to Yahweh's activity, not Messiah's; Juel 1977: 199–200). E. Sanders 1985: 77–90 traces the new-temple hope in Judaism: Tob. 14:5; 2 Macc. 2:7; 1 Enoch 24–25; 89–90; Jub. 1.15–17; 1QM 2.5–6; 7.10; 4QpPs[a] [= 4QpPs 37]; 11QTemple[a] 29.8–10. This hope was widespread, though it was held with a variety of detail.

pentance. Beyond this, it declares what the temple should be; it is a prophetic act in the highest sense.[4] A different form of the temple charge is raised at one of the trials (Mark 14:57–59) and may be implied in Luke 23:2, 5, 14.

The plot to destroy Jesus emerges from this embarrassing condemnation, but there is a complicating factor—Jesus' popularity. The leadership is convinced that Jesus must go, but they are not certain how. They are impotent to destroy him, so another way must be devised. Ironically, it is from within the disciples' own ranks that the way is found.

Sources and Historicity

The Synoptic parallels to the temple cleansing are Matt. 21:12–13 = Mark 11:15–19 (Aland 1985: §§273–74). Luke's version is verbally closer to Mark than Matthew, but at the same time is distinct from it in detail (Fitzmyer 1985: 1261; Grundmann 1963: 369):

1. Luke has a significantly shorter account: sixty-one words versus Mark's eighty-nine.
2. Luke lacks the temporal markers of Mark 11:12 that reveal that the event took place on the day after Jesus' entry (i.e., on Tuesday). In Luke, Jesus goes directly to the temple.
3. Luke omits reference to the fig tree's withering (Mark 11:12–14 = Matt. 21:18–19).
4. Luke does not detail any violent acts, such as the use of a whip (John 2:15) or the overturning of tables (Mark 11:15).
5. Luke does not mention that Jesus blocked people's way into the court (Mark 11:16).
6. Luke does not mention that the temple is a place for the nations (Mark 11:17).

Luke focuses on Jesus' pronouncement. His general account of the leadership's plot is paralleled in Mark 11:18–19, but each evangelist tells the story in his own terms.

---

4. For the options on how to take this act in light of the Synoptics and John's Gospel, see Witherington 1990: 113–15, who appeals to John 2:16; Zech. 14:21; and Neh. 13:4–9, 12–13 to see both a prophetic and messianic (but not revolutionary) cleansing. He argues that it was the act of an individual and was seen as symbolic of a need for national repentance, not the rejection of the nation. Witherington also argues that Jesus does not have a Davidic expectation (like that expressed in Ps. Sol. 17). True, Jesus does not yet function like the warrior in the Psalms of Solomon, but he will, as his remarks at his trial show. This is one reason why, when some speak of the Christ, Jesus replies in terms of the judging Son of Man, just as he did at his trial. For the cleansing as messianic act, see Hamilton 1964.

The historicity of this event is questioned at two levels. First, some argue that so much happens in this last week that the Synoptics must have compressed a longer period of activity into the final week (Manson 1950–51 sees a period of a few months). Perhaps the major catalyst for this view is Jesus' remark at his arrest that the leaders did not seize him even though he was teaching daily in the temple (22:53). Since this was his only public journey to Jerusalem in the Synoptics, there doesn't seem to be enough time for this remark if only one week is in view. The action, however, moves quickly: (a) Jesus offends the leaders with his temple action, (b) they desire to get him, and (c) Judas gives them the opportunity to move in without having to confront Jesus publicly. In addition, John's Gospel relates previous visits to the city, when opposition had already formed against Jesus, so perhaps Jesus was referring to his previous teaching time then. It is likely that Jesus made several trips to this key city.

A second challenge in historicity concerns the cleansing itself. Some regard it as fictitious and built upon OT texts like Zech. 14:21 and Mal. 3:1–2 because it is unlikely that temple police would not have reacted to Jesus' actions (Ackermann 1952: 62).[5] The Jesus Seminar (Funk and Hoover 1993: 376) takes this approach, printing the saying in gray type. The seminar argues that Jesus probably issued a temple critique, but not by quoting Scripture, especially the LXX. This analysis is oversimplified. France (1971: 83–94) shows how Matthew and Luke correctly pick up the event's thrust in omitting reference to the nations; at the same time, the location of this event in the Court of the Gentiles might suggest that the note about the nations in Isa. 56:7 LXX is appropriate. In effect, Isa. 56:7 LXX simply expands on what is implicit in Isa. 56:6 MT. The event is multiply attested, and the absence of reaction may be a sign of respect for Jesus. The next event shows that the leadership was hesitant to take Jesus on in public because of his popularity. So the very rationale for the plot to destroy him is to get back at him in a nonpublic forum. The police do not act now because they are looking for a more opportune time later. This objection is not significant (so most, including Luce 1933: 306). Fitzmyer (1985: 1264) says that the question cannot be answered, but that creation of the event is unlikely because of multiple attestation.

Recent debate about historicity focuses on the connection between this event and Jesus' trial. E. Sanders (1985: 61–76, esp. 75–76) argues that

---

5. The temple area was large (over 100 yards by 150 yards), so if Jesus acted quickly, there may have been little time to react. In addition, he may have intended only a prophetic sign, not a comprehensive cleansing. A brief symbolic action may have sufficed to express his intent, as even E. Sanders 1985: 70 acknowledges. Witherington 1990: 109–10 notes six historical questions that influence this passage and argue for its plausibility. One of the most basic is, Why invent such an event? Nolland 1993b: 935–36 notes nine views on this issue and opts for a modest, symbolic action against long-standing temple practice (pace Eppstein 1964) that thwarted true worship and called for purification, if not temple replacement.

Jesus did not cleanse the temple but only predicted its destruction (pictured in the overturned tables). Mark then changed this prediction into blasphemy at the trial because the temple act was embarrassing to the evangelists. In this view, the temple's destruction anticipates restoration and eschatological renewal starting on Mount Zion. This view defends historicity, but questions the significance of the event. Witherington (1990: 107–16) and C. A. Evans (1989a; 1989b) vigorously and successfully challenge this view.[6] It is unlikely that the church would invent such an act, but the most telling argument against this view is the issue of why the account was included in the Gospels if it was so embarrassing that Mark had to change it. While the event appears to focus on the temple's purpose, if restoration is in view, the idea of cleansing is not removed because the need for restoration suggests that something is not right. Sanders is correct that the issue is not ritual purity but the corrupting activity of money changing at the sacred site (*m. Šeqal.* 3.1). The church's continued tie to the temple shows that the temple still had a usefulness for many in the church. The Jewish church was not embarrassed at the temple's presence (Acts 2–5), a point Sanders realizes.

A last question is more difficult: How does this event relate to the cleansing in John 2:13–17?

1. There is one cleansing, whose timing John has thrown forward to introduce the controversy of Jesus' ministry (Barrett 1975).
2. There is one cleansing, and the Johannine timing early in Jesus' ministry represents the chronological placement (Fitzmyer 1985: 1264–65). This view argues that Jesus acted more like a prophet in his earlier ministry and that two cleansings are hard to accept within such a narrow period since each Gospel only narrates one. The Synoptics placed the cleansing later because they recount only one journey to Jerusalem and so could place the cleansing only here.
3. There are two cleansings and each is appropriately placed (Plummer 1896: 453).
4. The cleansing in each Gospel is a matter of narrative, where no choice of timing can be made (Nolland 1993b: 936).

One event is possible, given that on occasion the evangelists rearrange events (e.g., Luke 4:16–30). The question here is whether they would so totally rearrange sequence that an event at the beginning of Jesus' ministry would be placed at the end (or the other way around). If there was only one

---

6. For a methodological assessment of this debate, see R. Miller 1991. Sanders is unaware of Eppstein's 1964 article (see n. 1). Some in Judaism saw the temple as corrupt; 1 Enoch 89.73–90.29; 4Q174 [= 4QFlor] 1.1–12. Meier 1994: 886 rightly calls the cleansing "prophetic action," but opts for a rejection of the temple rather than a cleansing. This ignores the connection to Isa. 56.

temple cleansing, then it seems more natural that John moved it forward for literary illustration and foreshadowing of Jesus' ministry. The issue of the temple at Jesus' trial has the feel of a recent event that needs to be dealt with, not an event of the past that now needs treatment.

Differences between the Synoptics and John make it slightly more likely that there were two temple cleansings. The use of Ps. 69:9 [69:10 MT] in John is a unique citation that the Synoptics lack. True, the Synoptics sometimes use different citations for the same event in their telling of Jesus' death.[7] Still, it seems odd if this Johannine event actually occurred in the last week that the only temporal note was that the Passover was near. The setting in relation to John 2:23–25 does not look like chronological rearrangement. John apparently intends the reader to see the event as relatively early in Jesus' ministry. The attempt to argue for Synoptic rearrangement is equally problematic, since the cleansing solidifies the decision to destroy Jesus and is an issue at his trial. If the event were early in Jesus' ministry, then such a plot would have been present throughout Jesus' ministry.

The account is a pronouncement story and a prophetic "sign act," with a summary unit at the end (Fitzmyer 1985: 1262, 1269; Bultmann 1963: 36, 362; Berger 1984: 321). The outline of Luke 19:45–48 is as follows:

a. Jesus' cleansing of the temple (19:45–46)
b. The frustrated conspiracy against Jesus (19:47–48)

In a rebuke of the leadership for unjust commercialism at the temple, Luke recounts Jesus' anger and prophetic denunciation of distorted worship. Jesus' anger pictures God's reaction to what is happening at the temple; he is concerned about God's honor. The leadership plots to kill Jesus, but the crowd's attraction to Jesus causes uncertainty about how to do it. In short, Jesus' call for reform and repentance falls on hard hearts. Nothing will change the rejection of the leadership.

Exegesis and Exposition

45And coming into the temple he began to cast out those who sold, 46saying to them, "It is written, 'And my house shall be a house of prayer,' but you have made it 'a den of robbers.'"

47And he was teaching each day in the temple. But the chief priests and scribes were seeking to destroy him, as were the leaders of the people,

7. The most obvious example is Ps. 22:1 [22:2 MT] in Mark 15:34 = Matt. 27:46 and Ps. 31:5 [31:6 MT] in Luke 23:46. But this example may not qualify, since Mark 15:37 notes a second cry, for which Luke may have supplied the contents.

⁴⁸but they did not find anything they could do, for all the people hung on his words.

a. Jesus' Cleansing of the Temple (19:45–46)

19:45 Luke briefly describes the cleansing. Jesus' entry into the temple (ἱερόν, *hieron*) has in view the Court of the Gentiles, where the sellers were. Here worshipers bought sacrificial animals and received the proper currency for the temple tax—normal activity that was a part of temple worship. The problem was not that sacrificial material was made available, but how it was done. Luke lacks any mention of overturning tables or other acts of violence, saying simply that Jesus began to cast out the sellers. With prophetic authority, Jesus declares his moral indignation over the nation's worship. The reference to "those who sell" (τοὺς πωλοῦντας, *tous pōlountas*) is probably broad, referring to those who sold materials and the money changers, since Mark 11:15 = Matt. 21:12 mentions two distinct groups. Mark 11:16 adds the detail that Jesus would not allow anything to enter the temple. The rationale for Jesus' act surfaces in the next verse.

19:46 Jesus summarizes the reason for his action by citing the prophets (γέγραπται, *gegraptai*, it stands written). In fact, his action recalls the prophets' dramatic parables (e.g., Jeremiah and the pot). The first citation is Isa. 56:7 (on the Jewish use of this verse, see SB 1:852–53 and Michel, *TDNT* 5:121), which expresses the divine hope that the temple will be a house of prayer for all nations, though this universal note is not used by Luke. God will be so active for Israel that people will come from other nations to worship at the temple. This is the temple viewed in its most ideal form. People in other nations who look to God can trust that the temple will be a place to honor God (Isa. 2:2–4). Luke leaves the universal note out and simply addresses the issue that the temple should be a place of appropriate worship. Jesus applies these words rather directly to the current situation to express what the temple is designed to be in the last days. But this is not what this temple was in his day. The charge follows with the second allusion. There is an indictment of Israel's failure to be sensitive to God, even at the temple. The nation missed Messiah's visit (19:41–44), and they fail to worship God properly. Is it surprising that they do not represent God's way or have his blessing?

The second OT citation (Jer. 7:11) comes from one of Jeremiah's most scathing sermons. In his temple sermon, the prophet blasts the nation's unfaithfulness, idolatry, and failure to live justly while journeying to the temple to worship God. Part of the charges raised against the nation was that it had turned the temple into a den of robbers; the place of worship had become the gathering place for thieves and criminals. In fact, Jeremiah literally describes the temple as a cave (σπήλαιον, *spēlaion*; BAGD 762; BAA 1522) for robbers (λῃστής [*lēstēs*], used earlier of the robbers in the parable of the good Samaritan; 10:30, 36). The righteous do not reside at the temple; rather the unrighteous do. Jesus applies this passage directly to his first-century setting. As positive a text as Isaiah is, so this text is negative. Unfortunately, the negative image is the reality. The nation has turned the temple into exactly the opposite of what it was designed to be. Those in charge were taking advantage of the worshipers. In the very presence of God, as it prepares to worship, the nation dishonors its God. Something about the current practice is too commercial. It is a stinging challenge that is sure to require—and get—a response.

The parallels in Matt. 21:13 = Mark 11:17 are almost verbally exact, with slightly different introductions. Matthew has καὶ λέγει αὐτοῖς (*kai legei autois*, and he said to them), while Mark has καὶ ἐδίδασκεν καὶ ἔλεγεν αὐτοῖς (*kai edidasken kai elegen autois*, and he was teaching and saying to them). Mark introduces the citation with a rhetorical negative particle, οὐ (*ou*, is it *not* written . . .), while Matthew and Luke simply present a statement. Mark alone completes the first citation with the phrase about the temple being a house of prayer "for all the nations." Suggested reasons for the omission include (a) the temple was destroyed by the time of writing so there is no point in the detail, (b) Gentiles would be unconcerned about such a reality, or (c) the idea of the temple as a place for God at the time of Luke's writing was difficult (Luce 1933: 306 and Creed 1930: 242 prefer the latter). A better reason is that Luke omitted the phrase to keep the stress on the indictment. Nonetheless, the omission is hard to explain, especially given Mark's choice to use it for his Gentile audience. Luke introduces the citation with λέγων αὐτοῖς (*legōn autois*, saying to them) and begins with a future verb (ἔσται, *estai*, shall be) to relate the text more clearly to God's expectation. Matthew and Mark have κληθήσεται (*klēthēsetai*, shall be called), with Mark matching exactly the LXX form of the first citation. The Synoptic forms of the second citation nearly match, except for differences in the position of αὐτόν (*auton*, it) and the form of ποιέω (*poieō*, to make): Matthew has present ποιεῖτε (*poieite*, you are making); Mark has perfect πεποιήκατε (*pepoiēkate*, have made), which stresses the temple's appalling state; Luke has aorist ἐποιήσατε (*epoiēsate*, you made). None of these slight differences are significant to the basic charge, but are stylistic variations that summarize the event well. Only John differs significantly at this point, referring to "a house of trade," not a "den of robbers," and alluding to Ps. 69:9 [69:10 MT] (Plummer 1896: 454).

b. The Frustrated Conspiracy against Jesus (19:47–48)

19:47 Jesus continues to go to the temple each day to teach.[8] As he shared his thoughts with the people and drew support from them, the leadership tried to draw him into debate, which is detailed in the next several pericopes. Meanwhile, three groups are gathering against Jesus: chief priests, scribes, and leaders of the people, a unique threefold description (9:22 lists chief priests, scribes, and elders). The pairing of chief priests and scribes is common (Matt. 2:4; 21:15; 20:18 = Mark 10:33; 11:18; 15:31; 14:1 = Luke 22:2, 66; 23:10; Lohse, *TDNT* 7:864). Those who had a stake in the community's success as currently configured were not interested in any efforts at reform (Plummer 1896: 454; Fitzmyer 1985: 1270; Michaelis, *TDNT* 6:868).[9] Luke describes their desire in simple terms: the leaders were seeking to destroy Jesus (cf. the earlier reactions moving toward a plot in 6:11 and 11:53–54). They were on the constant lookout for any excuse to remove him, and it would come shortly. Almost verbally parallel, Mark 11:18 states the desire as a rhetorical question using πῶς (*pōs*): they were seeking "how" they might destroy him. Mark mentions only the chief priests and scribes, so that Luke draws a slightly wider circle of blame.

19:48 The leadership makes no progress on its desire to silence Jesus.[10] Despite their desire and their powerful position, the leaders are powerless to execute their plan because of Jesus' popularity.[11] His teaching draws all the people (ὁ λαὸς . . . ἅπας, *ho laos . . . hapas*). This large group of people is distinct from the small group of leaders just named. Throughout 19:47–22:2, λαός is used with constant reference to the populace, while ὄχλος (*ochlos*, crowd) is not used at all (Luce 1933: 307). Λαός is often positive (20:6, 19, 26, 45; 21:38), but in 23:13 this group will turn against Jesus, despite Pilate's testimony of Jesus' innocence (Marshall 1978: 722; Rau 1965). In the Book of

---

8. Plummer 1896: 454 notes other examples of the periphrastic ἦν διδάσκων (was teaching) are 4:31; 5:17; 13:10. Temple teaching is mentioned elsewhere in Luke 21:37; 22:53 = Mark 14:49; Marshall 1978: 722.

9. "Leaders of the people" resisted Paul and Barnabas; Acts 13:50; cf. 17:4; 25:2; 28:7, 17; Josephus, *Antiquities* 4.6.9 §140; 4.7.5 §174; 10.4.5 §71; 10.10.5 §213. See Michaelis, *TDNT* 6:866, for extrabiblical examples. Nolland 1993b: 940 notes the various combinations with which Luke refers to the leadership in Luke 20–24. They are a major narrative group for Luke's account, almost having a corporate personality that acts in concert against Jesus. Key verses are 20:1, 19; 22:2, 52, 66; 23:10, 13, 35; 24:20.

10. Imperfect εὕρισκον with deliberative subjunctive ποιήσωσιν portrays in this context a contemplative and continuous effort: "They *were not finding* what *they might do*"; Arndt 1956: 401. The original question was, "What can we do?"

11. Luke commonly introduces indirect questions with τό (functioning as a particle); Luke 1:62; 9:46; 22:2, 4, 23, 24; Acts 4:21; 22:30; BDR §267.2–3.

Acts the people are not always seen positively (Acts 6:12; 12:3; 21:30; 28:26–27; Nolland 1993b: 940). The leaders corrupt the people, who at one time had an attitude that was distinct from the leadership (see the contrast in Luke 20:1–6, 19, 26, 45; 22:2; 23:5, 35; 24:19–20; Kodell 1969).

Luke uses graphic language to describe just how popular Jesus' teaching was: the people "hung on his every word." The NT *hapax legomenon* ἐκκρεμάννυμι (*ekkremannymi*, to hang on) highlights the gripping power of Jesus' teaching (Bertram, *TDNT* 3:921; Plummer 1896: 455; Klostermann 1929: 191; Luce 1933: 307; BAGD 242; BAA 487).[12] Jesus was so popular that the leaders knew they could not act publicly.

Luke's description is much more graphic than Mark's (11:18), who notes that the officials feared Jesus because the crowd was astonished at his teaching. Once again, each writer says the same thing in his own way. Mark 11:19 notes that the day ended at this point. Luke lacks such chronological notes early in the week.

Summary

Luke 19:45–48 shows that Jesus meets confrontation in Jerusalem. The drama immediately heightens as Jesus cleanses the temple in a prophetic act guaranteed to require the officials' attention. He compares the temple's condition to that right before the exile. Jesus has come to confront the nation, and the people are now faced with a choice. Nothing has changed since their house was declared desolate in 13:34–35.

The leadership knows where it stands. They are committed to eliminating Jesus, but they are unable to act publicly because Jesus is too popular. Some other way must be found. Either he must be embarrassed into submission or eliminated entirely. The account serves to introduce what will be a traumatic series of events, and the tension will not abate until the "Jesus problem" is resolved. The pericope forces choices on the reader. Does the leadership reflect the will of God? Has Jesus come to call God's people to worship, prayer, and faithfulness? Has the presence of God been so tainted by excessive commercialism that national repentance is required? These questions in turn raise two key issues: (1) How should we worship God? and (2) Who is Jesus? In a real sense, Luke wishes the reader to see that the two questions really belong together.

12. The unprefixed form of the verb is used in Acts 28:4 and Gal. 3:13; BDR §93.3.5. Virgil uses the idiom for Dido's hanging on Aeneas's lips; *Aeneid* 4.79.

2. Question about Authority (20:1–8)

Luke 20:1–44 contains five controversies between Jesus and the leadership: the source of Jesus' authority (20:1–8), Jesus' confrontational parable of the vineyard (20:9–19), the dispute over Caesar's tax (20:20–26), the Sadducees' trick question about resurrection (20:27–40), and Jesus' question about the interpretation of Ps. 110:1 (20:41–44).[1] Here is theological warfare in its most dramatic form. The leadership tries to catch Jesus in error, and so they test him in every sphere: personal, political, theological. Jesus responds by raising questions of his own. While the leadership is unable to trap Jesus, he is able to embarrass and silence them. The entire section shows that if one is looking for wisdom one should walk with Jesus. Jesus is in control of the events surrounding his final visit to Jerusalem. In Matthew and Mark, all these events, plus the Olivet Discourse, occur on the same day.[2]

Luke 20:1–8 centers on the source of Jesus' authority. Some hold that the leaders question Jesus merely because he is not an ordained rabbi (Grundmann 1963: 371; Danker 1988: 316). But the leaders' objection seems to be stronger than the mere fact that he teaches. They may be asking, "What gives you the right to create havoc in the temple and judge us?" Jesus responds through an analogous question about the source of John the Baptist's authority. His raising the Baptist's ghost is particularly ticklish for the leadership, because they have problems regardless of which way they answer: if they acknowledge John as God's envoy, then they embarrass themselves for not having followed him; if they deny his authority, then they incur public wrath, since the people judged John to have been sent from God. So they instead respond with a bureaucratic "no comment." As Marshall (1978: 724) notes, "Many a government official's answer to an awkward question is equally lame." Jesus in turn replies with his own "no comment," though the narrative is clear that the source of Jesus' and John's authority is the same: heaven. This is yet another Lucan passage that links John and Jesus to God's activity (Luke 1–2; 7:18–35; 16:16).

---

1. Luke does not include the fig tree incident that Matt. 21:18–22 = Mark 11:12–13, 20–25 has at this point.

2. If Jesus' triumphal entry into Jerusalem occurred on Sunday, then this sequence of events took place on Tuesday. I suggest, however, that the entry could have been on Monday (see the exegesis of 19:28–40), which places these events on Wednesday.

Sources and Historicity

This event has parallels in Mark 11:27–33 = Matt. 21:23–27 (Aland 1985: §276). Much of the passage's terminology is shared between all three accounts, although Matthew and Mark are especially close to one another (Fitzmyer 1985: 1271–72). Most of Luke's differences with the other Synoptics are matters of style (see the exegesis for details). Luke goes his own way only in his mention of the leadership's fear of being stoned if they refuse to acknowledge John's authority. Some see in this detail the influence of another source (Ernst 1977: 572), but it is hard to be sure (Nolland 1993b: 942 rejects it). Each writer's introduction is unique, but all have Jesus in the temple and mention two groups who approach Jesus: chief priests and elders (cf. Luke 19:47). The account is historical (Marshall 1978: 724; Creed 1930: 244–45; Fitzmyer 1985: 1272–73; Nolland 1993b: 942). Plummer (1896: 455) notes that even the skeptical Strauss (1972: 358) saw these controversies as historical. The Jesus Seminar (Funk and Hoover 1993: 377) rejects the account, claiming that the reply is not a memorable aphorism, is only from Mark, would not be preserved in the oral tradition, and so is "the invention of the storyteller." Meier (1994: 164–66) argues for the coherence of this dispute and its memorable quality as a "game of wits." He correctly notes that the comparison of Jesus to John is an argument for authenticity, since John's ministry serves as a standard for Jesus' work. A church creation would likely have reversed the standard.

The account is a pronouncement and a controversy dialogue, since verbal exchange dominates the account (Fitzmyer 1985: 1272; Bultmann 1963: 20; Berger 1984: 81). The outline of Luke 20:1–8 is as follows:

a. Two questions (20:1–4)
   i. Setting (20:1)
   ii. The leaders' question (20:2)
   iii. Jesus' question (20:3–4)
b. The leaders' options (20:5–7)
   i. The leaders' quandary (20:5–6)
   ii. The leaders' answer: "no comment" (20:7)
c. Jesus' refusal to answer (20:8)

A mood of confrontation dominates the account. Jesus exercises great skill in avoiding a trap and in creating one at the same time. He is in control, while the Pharisees are embarrassed at the mention of John. The source of Jesus' and John's authority is the same: they are God's messengers who act and speak for him—which the leaders fail to recognize.

Exegesis and Exposition

¹And it came to pass on one of the days when he was teaching the people in the temple and preaching the gospel, the ⌜chief priests⌝ and scribes together with the elders came up. ²So they said to him, "Tell us, by what kind of authority do you do these things, or who is the one who gives you this authority?" ³He answered them, "I will also ask you a question, and you tell me, ⁴'Was the baptism of John from heaven or from men?'"

⁵And they discussed it with one another, saying, "If we say, 'From heaven,' he will say, 'Why did you not believe him?' ⁶But if we say, 'From men,' all the people will stone us, for they are convinced that John was a prophet." ⁷So they answered that they did not know from where.

⁸And Jesus said to them, "Neither will I tell you by what authority I do these things."

a. Two Questions (20:1–4)
i. Setting (20:1)

20:1 Luke uses his typical general introduction, καὶ ἐγένετο (*kai egeneto*, and it came to pass), to refer to "one of the days" when Jesus was teaching in the temple (5:12, 17; 8:22; 13:10; Plummer 1896: 456). Luke is suggesting that Jesus often spent the day at the temple when he was in Jerusalem. Matthew 21:23 speaks of Jesus entering the temple after the fig tree incident (which Luke lacks), while Mark 11:20 notes that the fig tree withered the day after Jesus cursed it and then begins the account with the general remark "and coming again into Jerusalem" (Mark 11:27). Each writer thus introduces the event in his own terms. Luke shows Jesus teaching the people (λαός, *laos*) and "gospeling" in the temple area.[3] Mark 11:27 speaks of Jesus walking in the temple, while Matt. 21:23 mentions his teaching. Thus, Luke alone mentions Jesus' preaching the good news. During this time, Jesus is approached by three groups (noted also in Mark): chief priests, scribes, and elders—a grouping very similar to that described in Luke 19:47. The description in this verse alludes to the major social elements of the Sanhedrin (9:22; 11:45; Ellis 1974: 231; Lohse, *TDNT* 7:863–64; Jeremias 1969: 165–66, 197, 222–26). Luke has separated the masses from the leadership (Schweizer 1984: 303). The confrontation is about to begin.

ii. The Leaders' Question (20:2)

20:2 The leaders' twofold question challenges the source of Jesus' authority (cf. other double questions in Mark 12:14; 13:4; 14:60; Acts 4:7;

---

3. Εὐαγγελιζομένου (preaching) has no object, so "the gospel," "the kingdom," or a similar idea must be supplied.

Marshall 1978: 724): what authority does Jesus have and who gave it to him? The combination ἐν ποίᾳ (*en poia*, by what kind of) asks for the sphere or quality of his authority (Plummer 1896: 456; Marshall 1978: 724; Arndt 1956: 402).[4] The verse is rather straightforward except for the broad reference to ταῦτα (*tauta*, these things), which may refer to the temple cleansing or to Jesus' teaching in general. Given that Jesus' teaching is mentioned in both 19:47 and 20:1, the leaders' challenge probably centers on teaching, though of course actions like the temple cleansing are not excluded. The leadership does not believe that Jesus has the right to do what he is doing, despite the evidence. Their reaction stands in stark contrast to the popular reaction of 19:48.

Matthew 21:23 = Mark 11:28 is closely parallel, with slightly different introductions: Matthew has λέγοντες (*legontes*, saying), Mark καὶ ἔλεγον αὐτῷ (*kai elegon autō*, and they were saying to him), and Luke καὶ εἶπαν λέγοντες πρὸς αὐτόν· εἰπὸν ἡμῖν (*kai eipan legontes pros auton, eipon hēmin*, and they said to him, tell us).[5] Both Matthew and Mark ask the same two-part question, though they use a slightly different construction for the second question: Mark starts with ἤ (*ē*, or), while Matthew has καί (*kai*, and). The rest of the question reads the same in Matthew and Mark (τίς σοι ἔδωκεν τὴν ἐξουσίαν ταύτην; *tis soi edōken tēn exousian tautēn*, who has given you this authority?), although Mark adds a concluding phrase to the second question (ἵνα ταῦτα ποιῇς, *hina tauta poiēs*, that you do these things). Some argue that Luke omits the end of the question because he is not referring to the temple cleansing (Schweizer 1984: 303; Danker 1988: 316). This is not convincing. Ταῦτα is plural and Jesus not only cleansed the temple, he also commented on his actions, so that teaching is also in view in Mark (Luce 1933: 307). Fitzmyer (1985: 1275) complains that Luke forgot that the authority's source was revealed in 3:21–22 and that he slavishly followed Mark here, but this is hypercriticism. Mark has the same baptismal account as Luke, and the passage's point is that anyone who knows Jesus' and John the Baptist's ministries knows that the leaders' question is a poor one. The earlier account only highlights the point. Luke knows what he is doing. The point is not to give an explicit answer, but to show the leaders' evasion of the clear answer. They have tried to trap Jesus, but the trap snaps shut in their direction.

---

4. BAGD 684 §2aγ and BAA 1373 §2aγ say that ποῖος is equal to τίς and means "by whose power?" but this makes it too much like the second question. It is best to distinguish the questions this way: the first asks the sphere of authority and the second asks its source. On authority, see the exegesis of 4:32 and 5:24.

5. The redundant participle λέγοντες with εἶπαν is common; BDR §420.1.1.

iii. Jesus' Question (20:3–4)

20:3 Jesus replies to the leaders' question with a question (λόγον, *logon*; BAGD 477 §1aβ; BAA 968 §1aβ) of his own. Jesus wants the leaders to answer his question before answering theirs about his authority. When they reply, so will he. In other words, if the leadership wishes to deal with Jesus, they must also deal with John the Baptist. Jesus' maneuver is not an attempt to dodge the question; it is an attempt to raise the stakes (Luce 1933: 307). Counterquestions were common among the rabbis (Marshall 1978: 725; Ernst 1977: 533).

Mark 11:29 = Matt. 21:24 is parallel, but with distinct wording and more detail. Both note that Jesus told the leaders that if they answered him, he would answer them. Three Lucan terms agree with Matthew against Mark: ἀποκριθείς (*apokritheis*, replying), ἐρωτήσω (*erōtēsō*, I will ask you), and κἀγώ (*ka'gō*, and I). The introductions differ: Mark has ὁ δὲ Ἰησοῦς εἶπεν αὐτοῖς (*ho de Iēsous eipen autois*, but Jesus said to them), Luke has ἀποκριθείς δὲ εἶπεν πρὸς αὐτούς (*apokritheis de eipen pros autous*, replying he said to them), and Matthew has ἀποκριθείς δὲ ὁ Ἰησοῦς εἶπεν αὐτοῖς (*apokritheis de ho Iēsous eipen autois*, replying Jesus said to them). Both Mark and Matthew have ἕνα (*hena*, one) with λόγον, but Matthew has the number after, while Mark has it before. Luke's version is clearly a summary using his own vocabulary.

20:4 Jesus' question centers on John the Baptist. Unlike the leadership's question, it is not a general question about authority. It is a multiple-choice question with two—and only two—options: either John came as a messenger from God or he did not. One must respond to John because he was from God, or ignore him. Which is it?

The question is crucial because John pointed to the office Jesus claims (3:16). Jesus also pointed to John and accepted baptism from him (7:28; 3:21–22). Their ministries were linked, as Luke 1 also argued. The question also raises the issue of whether leadership approval is required for ministry to be from God (Nolland 1993b: 943). If God was for this ministry, why should one oppose it? In fact, the populace had already rendered a judgment about John (20:6). If the leaders now answer positively, they acknowledge two things: the need for national repentance and the arrival of the "one to come."[6] Since John and Jesus were linked, the answer to Jesus' question is the answer to the leaders' question. Even after his death John the Baptist still functions as a forerunner to Jesus.

---

6. Fitzmyer 1985: 1275 says that the question has no implied messianic claim for Jesus, but only an affirmation that he is from God. But given John's teaching on the Coming One, an indirect allusion is implied. There is much at stake in answering the question.

Mark 11:30 words the question exactly like Luke, except he uses a second definite article (τό, *to*, the) and ends the question with a command to reply: ἀποκρίθητέ μοι (*apokrithēte moi*, answer me). Matthew 21:25 is closely parallel as well, though he asks the question with the words "from where was" (πόθεν ἦν, *pothen ēn*) John's baptism. In Luke and Matthew, there is no command to answer. The parallels are similar, but with slight stylistic differences. Luke's portrayal is the simplest.

b. The Leaders' Options (20:5–7)
i. The Leaders' Quandary (20:5–6)

The leadership senses the edge in Jesus' question. They consider the options, knowing their own unpopular position. They cannot confess that John came from God because they failed to respond to him; a positive reply now would raise the issue of their rejection of John's baptism, as well as the issue that perhaps they are wrong now about Jesus. Their private conference reveals their hypocrisy: they do not consider an honest reply, but only one that will play to the opinion of the populace. They do not want to be exposed.

20:5

The parallels are similar. Matthew 21:25 agrees almost word for word with Luke, but agrees with Mark against Luke in its use of δι-ελογίζοντο (*dielogizonto*, they were discussing) and stands alone in its use of ἐν ἑαυτοῖς (*en heautois*, among themselves). Luke has the *hapax legomenon* συνελογίσαντο (*synelogisanto*, they discussed together), which can mean "to reason" (Marshall 1978: 725; BAGD 777; BAA 1550). Matthew agrees with Luke in beginning the clause with the definite article οἱ (*hoi*, the), but he is alone in having the pronoun ἡμῖν (*hēmin*, to us). Luke alone uses ὅτι (*hoti*, that) to introduce the leadership's deliberations, but lacks οὖν (*oun*, therefore), which Matthew and Mark use to introduce the implication raised if they answered from heaven. These are all stylistic differences.

The second option is what the leaders really believe, but this is not palatable to the public. If they argue that John's authority was human-based, they will face popular wrath. Luke alone mentions the possibility of stoning, which is the punishment for regarding a true prophet as a false one.[7] The use of ἐάν (*ean*, if) here and in 20:5 indicates a third-class condition, which means the "if" is presented without any indication of preference: "If, and we are not saying we will or will not reply this way. . . ." The reason (γάρ, *gar*) for hesitation is that the populace was convinced that John was a prophet

20:6

---

7. So καταλιθάζω (to stone to death), a NT *hapax legomenon*; BAGD 413–14; BAA 841; cf. Exod. 17:4; Num. 14:10. Luke mentions stoning elsewhere in Luke 13:34; Acts 5:26; 7:58; 14:19.

from God. Luke alone uses λαός (*laos*, people) to make this point, while Matthew and Mark speak of the crowd (ὄχλος, *ochlos*). Luke is also alone in describing their conviction with the perfect participle πεπεισμένος (*pepeismenos*, stand convinced). Jesus agreed with this assessment (7:28).

The parallels in Matt. 21:26 = Mark 11:32 are close to one another, mentioning that all the crowd holds John to be a prophet, though in slightly differing terminology. Matthew expresses the leaders' fear of the populace with first-person plural ("we"). Mark functions as a narrator and explains that "they" feared the crowds. The three accounts are parallel in sense though Luke has more detail, mentioning the fear of stoning.

ii. The Leaders' Answer: "No Comment" (20:7)

20:7 The leaders formulate their conclusion. Faced with a dilemma and no good public answer, they opt out, professing ignorance and agnosticism. This move is less than satisfying for those who are supposed to bear the nation's religious authority by possessing theological discernment (Arndt 1956: 403). Sometimes agnosticism is really an evasion of the truth. Their refusal to answer is an indictment on them because of the office they hold. If they are incompetent to judge John the Baptist, how can they hope to be competent to judge Jesus (Fitzmyer 1985: 1276)? Ironically, they will soon sit in judgment against Jesus when the circumstances are more to their liking. As seemingly uncertain as they are about John, they will be quite dogmatic about Jesus. The evasion is a ruse, and Luke wishes to expose their hypocrisy. There may be wisdom in few words, but this is revelation from silence. As Nolland (1993b: 944) notes, one would not want to choose leaders based on the qualities exhibited here. In contrast, Christians will be prepared to die for their convictions. If character is a test of truth, the Jewish leadership comes up short.

Mark 11:33a = Matt. 21:27a is similar, stating the reply exactly the same: οὐκ οἴδαμεν (*ouk oidamen*, we do not know). In fact, except for the verb for saying (Matthew has εἶπαν [*eipan*, they said] and Mark has his common historical present λέγουσιν [*legousin*, they say]), Matthew and Mark agree word for word. Luke chooses to summarize the response with a description of their reply. Interestingly, the leadership's denial in Luke 20:7 looks like the form of Jesus' question in Matt. 21:25, where Jesus ended his question with πόθεν ἦν (*pothen ēn*, from where was. . . ?): μὴ εἰδέναι πόθεν (*mē eidenai pothen*, they did not know from where). The point in all the accounts, despite the stylistic variations, is the leadership's refusal to be shamed by Jesus' question. For those aware of John's ministry, the first round of the theological battle goes to Jesus.

c. Jesus' Refusal to Answer (20:8)

Jesus responds in kind. If the leaders will not answer his question, **20:8**
he will not answer theirs. Of course, an answer is not necessary—for
the crowd or Luke's readers. Testimony to the relationship between
John and Jesus has already been given (Luke 1–2; 3:1–18; 7:18–35),
and the people have their opinion about John: John and Jesus are
both from God. Jesus' authority comes from the ultimate authority.
The need for Jesus to answer was lifted when the question about
John went unanswered. Jesus saves the answer to his question. He
will raise the issue with Ps. 110:1 in Luke 20:41–44 and will answer
it in 22:69, setting the stage for condemning himself to death.

Mark 11:33b is almost verbally exact with Luke: Mark uses his
frequent vivid present tense, rendered as a past, λέγει (*legei*, said),
where Luke has aorist εἶπεν (*eipen*, said). Matthew 21:27b is also verbally exact, but his introduction differs: ἔφη αὐτοῖς καὶ αὐτός (*ephē
autois kai autos*, and he said to them).

Luke 20:1–8 details a dangerous game of daring. The leadership **Summary**
is trying to trip up Jesus, and their initial attack involves his credentials: Who gave him the authority to teach and to clear the
temple? In God's plan, official training is not required for Jesus.
What is required is God's commission. A predecessor to Jesus,
John the Baptist, had such credentials without any official position, and John's authority was so clear that even the populace recognized it. Only blindness could miss God's hand, but blindness
can and does appear. Jesus does not answer the leaders' question,
but points to the ministry of John. Jesus' question traps the leadership: they must either admit that John's message was from God
(which means that they failed to respond to God's message) or
they must reject John's authority (leaving them to face the people's ire). In seeking to trap Jesus, the leaders themselves are
trapped. The fox becomes the hound. Jesus controls events and
shows his superior status.

Where does God's wisdom lie? Does it rest with those who will
not recognize who commissioned John? Or does it lie with the
one who shares John's source of authority? When one compares
Jesus' real credentials with those of his challengers, is there any
question who ministers for God? This contrast is Luke's point.
God's way resides with Jesus.

Additional Note

20:1. Many manuscripts (A, E, G, H, W, Γ, Δ, Byz, Lect) read ἱερεῖς (priests)
instead of ἀρχιερεῖς (chief priests) with UBS–NA (ℵ, B, C, D, L, N, Q, Θ, Ψ,

family 1, family 13). The choice is difficult, but the major Alexandrian and Western witnesses read ἀρχιερεῖς (Marshall 1978: 724; Kilpatrick 1969: 203–8). Nonetheless, Metzger 1992: 238–39 and Greeven (1959–60: 295–96) argue for ἱερεῖς (Fitzmyer 1985: 1274). Luke consistently refers to "chief priests" (20:19; 22:2, 52, 66; 23:10, 13; 24:20), which favors the more widely attested reading. The difference is of little interpretive significance, since the same group is alluded to.

3. Parable of the Wicked Vinedressers (20:9–19)

The parable of the wicked farmers is one of Luke's most comprehensive parables—and an extremely significant one. The parable is allegorical in that many of its features have historical correspondence. It is unique in that it deals with salvation history (Fitzmyer 1985: 1281).[1] It refers to the period from Israel's inception to Jesus' ministry. The reference to the owner's long departure is not Jesus' return, since the landlord cannot represent Jesus, who is the beloved son (correctly Grundmann 1963: 372 n. 1).

The parable emphasizes several points and has a rich background in the OT (Ps. 80:8–13 [80:9–14 MT]; Isa. 27:2; Jer. 2:21; Ezek. 19:10–14; Hos. 10:1) and Judaism (1 Enoch 10.16; 84.6; Jub. 1.16; Ps. Sol. 14.3–4). It should be stressed that the vineyard is probably not Israel (against Blomberg 1990: 248 n. 100), even though the parable is built off Isa. 5:1–7. The vineyard is the place of blessing or promise, and the tenants are Israel, especially its leadership (Plummer 1896: 458; Blank 1974: 14).[2] Israel as the tenants is a shift from standard OT imagery, where Israel is the vine and God is its keeper. Jesus introduces this shift by seeing Israel's rejection as national in Luke's Gospel (13:34–35; 19:41–44; 23:1–25). The rejection of Jesus is not just the leaders' fault, though they do have a central role and special responsibility (against B. Scott 1989: 243–44). Luke 20:16 does separate the people from the leadership, and 20:19 makes clear that the parable is told against the leadership. But the people in 20:16 do not like Jesus' point, saying, "May it never be!" While the leaders are seen as responsible for guiding the people to destruction (11:44, 52),

---

1. On allegorical parables, see Derrett 1974; Blomberg 1982a: 6–8; Carlston 1981; and Klauck 1978. On the parable's interpretive history, see Snodgrass 1983: 3–11, who defends authenticity (pp. 2, 87, 103–4, 108, 112). Giblin 1985: 65–66 does not see allegory as a distinct genre of parables, but speaks of the parable's allegorical bent. See also excursus 8, where parable and allegory are seen as part of a literary continuum.

2. Abraham is the root in 1 Enoch 93.5. The parable is not unlike Paul's vine image in Rom. 11. Though related to Israel as "natural branches," this promise is tied to God's commitment to Abraham and encompasses, but is not limited to, Israel (Luke 1:54–55). See Burns 1992 on Rom. 11.

by 23:1–25 the people will join them in rejecting Messiah (also Acts 4:25–26). Since the parable deals with salvation history, all of these features help to explain the imagery from a Lucan narrative perspective.

The servants in the parable portray the nation's consistent rejection of the prophets. In fact, national unfaithfulness—the cause of the exile—is a theme in many of the Deuteronomistic historical books (e.g., Jer. 7:21–29). The nation is an unfaithful tenant, and the parable portrays its murder of the son (Jesus). Thus, the situation of the "beloved son" is like that of the prophets—only worse (Schweizer 1984: 305). The giving of the vineyard to others portrays the inclusion of Gentiles. It is important to note that faithful Jews are not excluded, since the disciples are "tenant farmers" as well. The parable's thrust, however, is to note the bringing in of "others" not originally expected to care for the vine. The parable contains a passion prediction, a messianic claim, and a promise that death will not end God's plan. God will bring in others from whom he will obtain fruit and who will share in blessing. The parable also shows God's patience in withholding judgment, though judgment becomes inevitable now that the Son is rejected (Giblin 1985: 73). The parable is Jesus' response to the leadership's plot to get him (19:47; Tannehill 1986: 192). It also answers the question posed in 20:1–8: Jesus is sent from God; his authority is from heaven.

The passage concludes with an allusion to Ps. 118:22. This psalm made a deep impression on the church, since it also appears in Acts 4:11 and 1 Pet. 2:7 to make much the same point. Other OT allusions have been suggested for the parable's conclusion in Luke 20:18 (e.g., Dan. 2:34 and Isa. 8:14–15), yet there is no clear verbal link to any specific text. It is better to see a conceptual appeal to the stone of stumbling than a specific reference to a single text (Bock 1987: 127). God will exalt the rejected stone, which will then break any who stumble over it or crush any upon whom it falls. The stone will be down, but not out. The passage has a somber mood. The nation's opportunity is slipping through its fingers.

Sources and Historicity

The parable has parallels in the other Synoptics (Mark 12:1–12 = Matt. 21:33–46) and the Gospel of Thomas 65 (Aland 1985: §278), which has led to much discussion because each account is told with interesting variations. Luke is closest to Mark in wording, but there are at least eight noticeable differences between these two accounts (Ellis 1974: 232; Fitzmyer 1985: 1278):

1. Luke 20:9 has a shorter introduction that does not describe the vineyard with as much detail as Mark 12:1. Luke also reflects less of the wording of Isa. 5.
2. In Luke three servants are sent, while Mark speaks of several more.
3. The order of casting out and killing the son is reversed in Luke 20:15 = Mark 12:8.
4. The son is portrayed in Luke as dying outside Jerusalem because of the reversal of the description of the son's death (no. 3).
5. Luke is alone in having only the son slain.
6. The description of the crowd's exclamatory reaction in Luke 20:16b is unique.
7. Luke 20:18 makes a strong and unique point about judgment.
8. Luke's conclusion (20:19) is given in his own words (cf. Mark 12:12).

Luke's major difference with Matthew is that the first evangelist has this parable in the middle of a three-parable series, between the parable of the two sons and the parable of the marriage of the king's son—neither of which Luke has (Plummer 1896: 457–58). Matthew 21:39 agrees with Luke in having the son first cast out and then killed (no. 3). But Matthew agrees with Mark in the long initial description of the vineyard (no. 1), more than three servants (no. 2), and the killing of the servants (no. 5). Matthew has a variety of punishments for the servants (beating, killing, stoning), while Mark has an escalation (beating, beating over the head, killing, some beaten, some killed). Apparently the parable circulated widely in the early church, with some variation in detail. Even though there are variations in each version of the parable, it clearly belongs to a single occasion.

These variations have led to a lively debate about which version came first, especially when the texts are compared to the Gospel of Thomas. Many argue that Thomas has the shortest and most primitive version on the basis of its brevity, the threefold structure of the servants (like Luke), and the absence of many allegorical features (Jeremias 1963a: 70–77; Fitzmyer 1985: 1280; Crossan 1971; Ménard 1975). The Jesus Seminar's printing of 20:9–15a in gray type and 20:15b–18 in black depends on this reading of the tradition (the parallel Gospel of Thomas 65 is printed in pink; Funk and Hoover 1993: 378–79, 510–11). The seminar also rejects the use of Ps. 118 as introducing early church christological concerns into the parable. Nonetheless, the position is challenged (Marshall 1978: 726–27; Snodgrass 1974–75; Hengel 1968; McArthur 1959–60; Schrage 1964: 137–45; Schoedel 1972; Nolland 1993b: 948–49 [argues against a secondary tradition of the parable tied to Thomas]). Marshall argues that Thomas is not less allegorical in its thrust, while others argue that Gnostic concerns caused the omission of certain details, since they would not like the force of the full view (so Nolland 1993b: 948). To consider the shortened Thomas version as the original leaves the question of why the parable was told at all. Why would it end with the death of the son and no resolution of the act against him? Given the variety of currents influencing Thomas, it is hard to be sure that its shortness is a sign of primitiveness. And given the complexity of the variations, it is hard to determine the parable's most original form (for an attempt, see Nolland 1993b: 949). Each writer presents the same basic parable on his own terms, sometimes shortening and sometimes using more complete information. Determination of the original form is probably beyond us.[3]

Another discussion concerns authenticity, which has been the subject of a century-long debate. Those who deny that the parable goes back to Jesus (e.g., Kümmel 1950) argue on various grounds (my evaluation follows each point):[4]

1. Some complain that the parable is too allegorical for Jesus. But the parable's complexity is no reason to reject its authenticity. A. Jülicher's emphasis on the "one-point" parable produced this skepticism, but his dictum is now rejected and complexity is recognized as a part of Jesus' parables (Blomberg 1990: 29–69).

2. Some consider the story to be too improbable. What landlord would leave his land unattended and subject his interests to such repeated abuse? The point especially doubted (and sometimes called foolish) is the sending of the son to a place with such a hostile history. In ancient Palestinian culture, however, many foreign landlords let out their land (m. Ned. 5.5; Jeremias 1963a: 74–75; Dodd 1961: 96–97; Hengel 1981: 9–31; P. Oxy. vol. 14 #1631, #1689; vol. 16 #1968). It is also important to note that the improbable points make the parable's most significant correspondences: the master's long-distance trip depicts the nation's long history in looking for the deliverer, and the repeated sending of the servants shows God's patience. The tenants' view that if the son dies they will inherit the land is based on the possibility of the land reverting to those most closely associated with it if there is no clear heir.[5] But their reasoning also

---

3. B. Scott 1989: 245–48 is unique in arguing that all the versions, even Thomas, are derived. His quest for the original form assumes that the shortest form is the more original, but to get there he strips the parable of its fundamental salvation-historical sense, which ignores the OT imagery too much.

4. Luce 1933: 308 and Fitzmyer 1985: 1279 present the case for nonauthenticity without endorsing it. Snodgrass 1983: 106–10 has a detailed defense of the authenticity of this parable. He concludes: "If one rejects the dominical origin of this parable, he or she does so because of presuppositions about the nature of the Gospels . . . and not because of any element in the parable itself."

5. Hengel 1968 and Derrett 1970: 286–312 discuss the ancient customs that provide the historical background for this parable. Such tenants would work for a commission (m. Kil. 4–6 describes laws governing vineyards; Mur 24B–E [DJD 2:124–32] gives details of a tenant arrangement; Derrett 1970: 293–94). Derrett argues that if the vineyard could be shown to have been "abandoned" by the owner, it would revert to the tenants if they had worked the land for three years (m. B. Bat. 3.1; Jeremias 1963a: 74–75; Dodd 1961: 97). Such a cultural background gives context to the parable, though it is comprehensible without it (correctly Fitzmyer 1985: 1283).

has a sarcastic absurdity to it that is designed to show sin's foolishness. It is not the father but the tenants who are foolish for slaying the heir and insulting him. This difficulty is a key to the parable, providing the "twist" that is a normal part of Jesus' parables.

3. Some wonder if Jesus would have been this open about his messianic position. Others question the messianic use of the term υἱός (son) in this period. The reply to this point is complex, but basically if the triumphal entry account is authentic, then this claim is no problem (see the discussion of sources and historicity for 19:28–44). Others note that Jesus became more direct in the last week of his ministry. Ellis (1974: 232) notes that "son" is messianic in the first-century Qumran text 4Q174 [= 4QFlor] 1.11.

In short, there is no good reason to reject the parable's authenticity. Ellis (1974: 232) discusses three reasons in support of authenticity: (a) if the early church is responsible for the parable, then why would it not also produce an allegorical allusion to the resurrection? (b) such a parable would not portray Jesus dying in the vineyard but outside it (cf. the Marcan version); and (c) the parable's proem midrash form matches the time period (Kimball 1994: 162–63 notes the passage's form as well).

The account is a parable in form, with many points of correspondence that depict salvation history (Fitzmyer 1985: 1281; Bultmann 1963: 177; Berger 1984: 51). The outline of Luke 20:9–19 is as follows:

a. The parable proper (20:9–16a)
   i. Introduction (20:9)
   ii. First servant sent (20:10)
   iii. Second servant sent (20:11)
   iv. Third servant sent (20:12)
   v. The son sent (20:13–15a)
   vi. The owner's response of judgment (20:15b–16a)
b. The crowd's reaction (20:16b)
c. Scriptural rebuke (20:17–18)
   i. Citation of Psalm 118 (20:17)
   ii. The crushing stone (20:18)
d. The leadership's desire to seize Jesus thwarted (20:19)

The parable examines the nation's poor treatment of God's messengers and shows the absurdity of rejection. The Jewish nation is initially in the place of benefit and responsibility, but it has failed to bear fruit and eventually kills the Son. As a result the nation loses its position, and the vineyard's benefits go to others.

The parable warns about rejecting the Son and causes the leadership to become angry at Jesus. But, since the leaders also fear the people, nothing happens yet.

Exegesis and Exposition

⁹And he began to speak to the people this parable: "A man planted a vineyard, let it out to tenant farmers, and went into another country for a long while. ¹⁰And in time he sent to the tenants a servant that they might give to him from the fruit of the vine; but the tenants sent him away empty-handed, having beaten him. ¹¹And again he sent another servant; but they also sent him away empty-handed, having beaten him and treated him shamefully. ¹²And again he sent a third; but they wounded him and cast him out. ¹³The lord of the vineyard said, 'What shall I do? I will send my beloved son; it may be that they will respect him.' ¹⁴When the tenants saw him, they said to themselves, 'This is the heir; let us kill him, so that the inheritance may be ours.' ¹⁵And casting him outside the vineyard, they killed him. What then will the owner of the vineyard do to them? ¹⁶He will come and destroy those tenants and give the vineyard to others."

When they heard this, they said, "May it never be!"

¹⁷But he looked at them and said, "What then is this that is written: 'The very stone that the builders rejected has become the head of the corner'? ¹⁸All who fall on that stone shall be broken to pieces; but when it falls on anyone, it shall crush him."

¹⁹And the scribes and chief priests sought to lay hands upon him in that hour; but they feared the crowd, for they knew that he spoke this parable against them.

a. The Parable Proper (20:9–16a)
i. Introduction (20:9)

20:9   The Lucan introduction is brief, simply noting that Jesus began to speak this parable. Mark 12:1 mentions Jesus' speaking parables, while Matt. 21:33 cites Jesus' command to "hear another parable." Matthew says "another" parable because this is the second of three parables that he narrates at this point. Luke's introduction suggests a slight break from Luke 20:1–8. Jesus speaks again to the people (λαός, *laos*), as is his custom in Luke in this last week. Matthew and Mark do not name the audience.

Luke notes three steps at the parable's start: planting the vineyard, letting it out to tenants, and the long journey. Luke's reference to the vineyard recalls, though with less verbal contact than the other Synoptics exhibit, the picture of Isa. 5:1–7. Nonetheless, the allusion is here, especially given the clear salvation-historical frame of the parable as a whole (Giblin 1985: 67; Crossan 1971: 462). But the Synoptic image differs from Isaiah's, where the vineyard is Israel and the owner is God. The introduction of tenants complicates the "custodian" metaphor. This is why I prefer the picture of the vineyard as promise, though most see it as an allusion to Israel. The difference is slight, since part of the promise was that Israel should honor God and be fruitful. What the OT image of the vineyard combined (the nation = fruitfulness), the NT split (the tenants = the nation; the vineyard = the hope of fruitfulness in promise). In the Synoptic view, the nation has accountability to God for what he set up.

Mark and Matthew refer to a variety of activities: the owner plants a vineyard, sets a hedge, digs a place for a winepress, builds a tower, lets it out to tenants, and goes to another country. Of these details Luke has only the essential elements: the vineyard, tenants, and journey. Ἐκδίδωμι (ekdidōmi, to let out) refers to the rental arrangement (BAGD 238; BAA 480; MM 192; in the NT only in this parable). Many estates were let out by absentee landlords, and sometimes the tenant attempted to seize control in the owner's absence (Marshall 1978: 727; see unit introduction). A γεωργός (geōrgos) is a vinedresser who cares for the plants and makes sure they bear fruit (BAGD 157; BAA 315 §2). The master's long absence sets the stage for the overview of the nation's long history. The vineyard is the place of promise, since the nation and its leadership are pictured as vinedressers (made clear in Luke 20:19). The appeal to a pattern of slaying the prophets in the parable shows that the tenants picture the whole nation, not just its leaders. Given (a) the parable's placement after the remarks of 19:41–44, (b) Jesus' upcoming warning to those in the city (23:26–31), and (c) judgment texts like Luke 11:29–32 (spoken in Galilee!), Luke 13:31–35, and Acts 4:27, Luke narratively sees the parable as a warning to the nation and its leaders who have led it astray. To restrict the tenants to the leaders alone is too narrow. Luke 2:34 does teach a divided Israel, but Luke 19:41–44 and Acts 28:25–28 reveal that most of the nation does not respond and is culpable.

ii. First Servant Sent (20:10)

A series of servants come to the estate to see what fruit and profits **20:10** have been produced.[6] Perhaps as many as five years have passed (Lev. 19:23–25; b. Ber. 35a; Nolland 1993b: 950). The reference to the passage of time suggests that sufficient time was given for produc-

---

6. Ἵνα (so that) with the future indicative δώσουσιν (they shall give) indicates purpose and is not like classical style; BDF §396.2; Plummer 1896: 459. A minor textual variant uses the more common construction and is the result of the unusual style.

tion. Fruit was to be expected, since that was the tenants' job. The servants as a whole portray the wave of prophets sent to the nation at various times in its history. Plummer (1896: 459) notes the following OT texts that picture this reality: 1 Kings 18:13; 22:24–27; 2 Kings 6:31; 21:16; 2 Chron. 24:19–22; 36:15–16; Neh. 9:26; Jer. 37:15; 44:4 (plus Acts 7:52). The motif comes directly from the OT as well (Jer. 7:25–29), a connection that shows the nation to be in view.

The servant's reception is less than hospitable. The tenants send the commissioned servant back beaten and empty-handed. Δέρω (*derō*) can refer either to striking someone on the face or the body (Luke 22:63; John 18:22; 2 Cor. 11:20) or to a total physical beating (Acts 5:40; 16:37; 22:19; BAGD 175; BAA 351). The tenants give nothing back to the owner, a picture of the nation lacking fruit for God. Ἐξαποστέλλω (*exapostellō*, to send away) is almost unique to Luke in the NT (Luke 1:53 and seven times in Acts; Gal. 4:4, 6; BAGD 273; BAA 552 §1b; Gen. 31:42; Deut. 15:13; 1 Sam. 6:3; Job 22:9).

Mark 12:2–3 = Matt. 21:34–35 is similar in concept but worded slightly differently. Matthew says that the servants were sent when "the time for fruit drew near." In Matthew several servants are sent from the start, one of whom was beaten (using the same term as Luke), another killed, and another stoned. Matthew follows this with the sending of a second wave of servants, a larger number than the first group of three. Mark speaks of the time to get some fruit from the tenants and uses vocabulary that is close to Luke (except for minor shifts in word order). Using a participle and two verbs, Mark describes the beating by noting that the tenants took (λαβόντες, *labontes*) the servant, beat (ἔδειραν, *edeiran*) him, and sent (ἀπέστειλαν, *apesteilan*) him away empty-handed. Luke is briefer, speaking of one servant at a time and using a verb and a participle to describe the response: ἐξαπέστειλαν (*exapesteilan*, they sent away) and δείραντες (*deirantes*, beating). Mark and Luke share the term κενός (*kenos*, empty-handed).

iii. Second Servant Sent (20:11)

20:11   The second servant fares no better than the first. Προσέθετο (*prosetheto*) refers to the master's action, and when tied to an infinitive it means "again" (Fitzmyer 1985: 1284; Creed 1930: 245 [a Hebraism]; Klostermann 1929: 193 [a Septuagintalism]; BAGD 718–19 §1c; BAA 1440 §1c; BDR §435.4.4; Luke 19:11; Gen. 8:12; Exod. 9:34; Judg. 3:12; 4:1; 10:6; 1 Sam. 18:29). The response virtually parallels Luke 20:10, except that another description is added with the participle ἀτιμάσαντες (*atimasantes*, having treated [him] shamefully; BAGD 120; BAA 240; elsewhere in the NT at Mark 12:4; John 8:49;

Rom. 2:23; James 2:6; passive in Acts 5:41 and Rom. 1:24). Thus, Luke intensifies the rise of opposition here.

Mark 12:4 speaks of the second servant being wounded in the head and treated shamefully (both are verbs, the second matching Luke's participle, so Mark intensifies the opposition, as does Luke). This servant seems to match Matthew's servant who was stoned. Luke's account is the briefest of the Synoptics (the Gospel of Thomas is briefer still, mentioning only two servants). This section is told with some variation (Arndt 1956: 404 speaks of an *ad sensum* rendering).

iv. Third Servant Sent (20:12)

A third servant is sent, and he is similarly treated. Luke links the **20:12** sending by repeating προσέθετο, but here uses the verb ἐξέβαλον (*ex-ebalon*) to indicate that the servant is cast out and the participle τραυματίσαντες (*traumatisantes*) to indicate that he is harmed (lit., traumatized; BAGD 824; BAA 1644; elsewhere in the NT only at Acts 19:16; a related noun in Luke 10:34 for the wounds that befell the man that the good Samaritan helped). None of the servants fared well at the tenants' hands. In fact, each is treated worse than the previous one. Israel's treatment of the prophets is not a pretty picture (11:47–51).

The Synoptic parallels are different. Mark 12:5 speaks of the third servant being killed (he also notes that others were sent, beaten, and killed). In Matt. 21:35–36, three servants were sent initially, one being beaten, another killed, and a third stoned. Then Matthew speaks of a second wave of servants, greater in number than the first, who suffered the same fate. Luke's shorter account does not mention this second wave of servants.

v. The Son Sent (20:13–15a)

The master still has a final option, and with great patience, reflec- **20:13** tion, and some uncertainty, he exercises it. This uncertainty in the soliloquy shows how a parable often does not correspond to reality, since God is never said to be hesitant or uncertain about the fate of his Son. What the delay and reflection indicates is that the tenants' behavior has brought a dilemma. The owner figures that perhaps he has not sent someone with sufficient rank, so he decides to send his "beloved son" (τὸν υἱόν μου τὸν ἀγαπητόν, *ton huion mou ton agapēton*). This expression recalls Jesus' baptism (3:22), as well as his transfiguration (9:35; Leaney 1958: 250), and may imply that the man in the parable has only one son. The point is that he can send no one more important without going himself. As Fitzmyer (1985: 1284) notes, one is not to ask why the master himself did not go.

Jesus is telling the story with some parallelism to what is happening in Israel. The master hopes that perhaps (ἴσως, *isōs*) they will respect (middle voice ἐντρέπω, *entrepō*; BAGD 269 §2b; BAA 544 §2b) the son. The adverb ἴσως, a NT *hapax legomenon* (BAGD 384; BAA 778), literally expresses the hope that this outcome might be different.[7] The master's mood adds to the story's tension and pathos. Maybe this solution will work. The verse pictures God's patience and tenacity, and the son represents his sending of Jesus.

Matthew 21:37 = Mark 12:6 share with Luke the master's hope for a respectful response. Otherwise, the wording differs slightly. Matthew says, "Later he sent to them his son, saying, 'They will respect my son.'" Thus, Matthew gives the master's thoughts in a direct citation that functions as a brief soliloquy. Mark notes that the master "still had one other, a beloved son," which makes explicit that this was his only son. This is confirmed by the tenants' hope that with the son removed they might inherit the land. Mark also has soliloquy: "Finally, he sent him to them, saying, 'They will respect my son.'" But Luke alone expands the soliloquy by asking the reflective question, "What shall I do?" (Fitzmyer 1985: 1284; other Lucan soliloquies are in 12:17; 15:17–19; 16:3). The question may derive from Isa. 5:4. Each writer makes the same basic point in his own words.

20:14 The vinedressers have a two-part plan: first murder, then inheritance. It is hard to understand the logic here. How can murdering the son set up the tenants' inheritance? This absurdity is an important point, since it illustrates the foolishness of their rejection. The hope was that without a clear heir and without discovery of the murderer, the land might revert by default to those working it, assuming that the son was sent because the owner had died (Jeremias 1963a: 75, esp. n. 99; and Bammel 1959: 14–15). Their greed is stressed by the emphatic position of ἡμῶν (*hēmōn*, ours): "*Ours* the inheritance will be" (a predicate genitive of possession; BDR §162.7.9; cf. Luke 20:33; other emphatic pronouns in Acts 1:7; 27:23). The truth behind this murderous attitude would have been lost on most of Jesus' original audience, but would become manifest in just a few days. The parable pictures total rejection. Nonetheless, the detail might be startling for those plotting against Jesus. They would know what is happening and catch the implication (Luke 20:19). They may secretly seek to arrest him, but Jesus knows that he is their target. The exchange heightens the drama, for clearly there are no surprises in what is taking place.

---

7. The Coptic equivalent of Luke's ἴσως is used twice in the Gospel of Thomas 65 and may be evidence of Thomas's expansion on Luke.

Matthew 21:38 = Mark 12:7 is almost exact in their agreement of the tenants' thoughts, until the last phrase. Luke's unique term for the tenants speaking to themselves (διελογίζοντο, *dielogizonto*; cf. Luke 19:47–48) contrasts with Matthew and Mark's use of εἶπον/ εἶπαν (*eipon/eipan*, to speak). With Matthew, Luke speaks of this contemplation happening as they saw (ἰδόντες, *idontes*) the son approach. In the last phrase, Matthew lacks the emphasis on "our" receiving the inheritance, saying simply, καὶ σχῶμεν τὴν κληρονομίαν αὐτοῦ (*kai schōmen tēn klēronomian autou*, and let us have his inheritance). Mark matches Luke except for using the verb ἔσται (*estai*, shall be). Luke alone uses the pronoun ἀλλήλους (*allēlous*, each other), while Matthew and Mark have ἑαυτοῖς (*heautois*, to themselves) and ἑαυτούς (*heautous*, themselves) respectively (on the ἑαυτῶν–ἀλλήλων interchange, see BDF §287 and BDR §287). These variations are mostly matters of style.

Jesus concludes the parable by noting that the tenants cast the son **20:15a** out and kill him, an allusion to what the leaders intend for Jesus. He uses the same verb for "casting out" (ἐκβάλλω, *ekballō*) as in 20:12 (except that here he uses the participial form). They kill the son outside of the vineyard, which is the reverse of Mark 12:8, where the son is killed and then cast out, but agrees with Matt. 21:39. It is suggested that Matthew and Luke's order is designed to parallel Jesus' death outside Jerusalem (Heb. 13:12; Creed 1930: 246; Luce 1933: 310; Fitzmyer 1985: 1284–85); this is possible but not certain. Plummer (1896: 460–61) suggests that this image simply means that they turned him out from his inheritance, while Arndt (1956: 405) argues that death outside of the city just symbolizes shameful treatment. Marshall (1978: 731) notes that leaving a body in the vineyard would make it unclean, so the body must end up outside. More important, Marshall also notes correctly that the vineyard does not represent Jerusalem, so the tie to Jesus dying outside Jerusalem is not exact. What is clear is that a variation of order occurs here within accounts that otherwise have almost total verbal agreement. The only other differences are that Matthew and Mark speak of "taking" the son, καὶ λαβόντες (*kai labontes*), a phrase that Luke lacks. In addition, Luke uses the participle ἐκβαλόντες (*ekbalontes*, casting out) where Matthew and Mark use the verb ἐξέβαλον (*exebalon*, they cast out). Again, the parable has variation, but its thrust is similar in all the Synoptics.

vi. The Owner's Response of Judgment (20:15b–16a)

Jesus asks a rhetorical question to end the story: What will the **20:15b** owner do? How will he handle these tenants, who not only tortured his servants but killed his son? Mark 12:9 agrees with Luke, while

Matt. 21:40 asks, "When the lord of the vineyard comes, what will he do to those tenants?" This is the same point in slightly distinct wording. It is clear that the action needs a response and that the tenants are in deep trouble. The remark and what follows are an integral part of the parable, since they make a point about accountability. Without these comments, the parable has no message, becoming only a story—which is unlike Jesus' parabolic style.

20:16a   Jesus now makes the parable's point. The tenants will be destroyed. Their opportunity to gain the vineyard is taken away and given to others. The correspondence is to judgment on the nation, especially the leadership. The inclusion of others portrays the blessing on the apostles and disciples, as well as the blessing on Gentiles. Israel is being divided, and Gentiles are being brought in (Luke 2:29–35).

Luke's description of the owner's judgment is almost verbally matched by Mark 12:9. Mark and Luke are the same except for Luke's use of the pronoun τούτους (*toutous*, those) in reference to the tenants, which Mark lacks. Luke says "those" tenants are out, perhaps specifying the rejection to the leadership, rather than condemning the whole nation as Mark does. But this may overinterpret the difference (against Schweizer 1984: 304). It was clear to all the evangelists that some Jews did respond to Jesus. This pronoun is pejorative and only makes the rejection emphatic. Those tenants who slay the son are out. Matthew 21:41 is much stronger and more complete in noting that the audience answers with the remark that those evil ones go to a miserable death and that the master gives the vineyard to those who bear fruit. Matthew 21:43 speaks of those who bear fruit as a "nation" (ἔθνει, *ethnei*), implying an ethnic shift. What Mark and Luke present as Jesus' direct summary, Matthew places on the audience's lips, showing how Mark's and Luke's versions are related. Mark and Luke seem to be more summarized and condensed.

b. The Crowd's Reaction (20:16b)

20:16b   The crowd, the λαός (*laos*) of 20:9, reacts in shock and strong denial: μὴ γένοιτο (*mē genoito*, "may it never be!"). They realize the point and probably recognize both the tenants' action and the master's reaction. This is Luke's only use of this interjection (Plummer 1896: 461).[8] And only he has this negative response by the people.

---

8. All other uses of μὴ γένοιτο are made by Paul, who uses it fourteen times, ten times in Romans alone (e.g., 3:4, 6, 31; 6:2, 15; BDF §384; BDR §384.2). Fitzmyer 1985: 1285 notes that the Hebrew equivalent translates, "It is an abomination to me/ us" (Gen. 44:17; Josh. 22:29).

c. Scriptural Rebuke (20:17–18)
i. Citation of Psalm 118 (20:17)

Jesus concludes his discussion by citing Ps. 118:22. The first Lucan **20:17** citation of this psalm, in Luke 13:35, applied the cry of recognition in Ps. 118:26 to Jesus. He is the one who comes in the name of the Lord. A second citation of this psalm, in Luke 19:38, made explicit reference to the king and shows that the psalm is regal and messianic.

This third citation uses yet another motif: the rejected yet exalted stone. Luke's wording matches both the LXX and the MT (Bock 1987: 329 n. 140).[9] In the OT context, this passage describes a rejected nation and king before the nations (ἀποδοκιμάζω [apodokimazō, to reject] elsewhere used by Luke in 9:22 and 17:25; Ernst 1977: 538; BAGD 90–91; BAA 181). Nonetheless, the psalm assures these rejected groups that they have an exalted position before God. Luke's use is similar but more specific: Jesus, as the beloved Son, is rejected by the nation but accepted by God as having the place of honor. The irony in the usage is that a psalm of national comfort now indicts them of unfaithfulness because of their opposition to God's commissioned one.

Κεφαλὴν γωνίας (kephalēn gōnias) refers to a foundation stone, not a capstone (McKelvey 1969: 195–204 refutes Jeremias's view, TDNT 1:793, that it refers to a capstone; Eph. 2:20 favors foundation stone; BAGD 168, 430 §2b; BAA 336 §1, 875 §2b). In the ancient world this stone bore the weight of two intersecting walls (Fitzmyer 1985: 1282) and was crucial to the building's stability. Luke's use of the psalm's imagery is typological and prophetic. The picture is of the king and his faithful followers who face rejection but meet with God's acceptance and exaltation. Jesus is such a rejected but exalted figure. What angers the crowd is that the nation and its leadership are placed in opposition to God and his people (Ellis 1974: 233; Bock 1987: 126–27, 330 n. 144).[10] Jesus' application of the psalm moves the nation from being on the side of God to standing against him. The nation will stop at nothing to keep the Son from receiving his prominent place. Scripture shows that rejection of God's messenger is common, but that does not stop God from giving honor to his sent one.

---

9. Λίθον (stone) undergoes reverse attraction to ὅν (which) and is picked up by οὗτος (this one) later in the verse; Marshall 1978: 732; BDR §295.2.

10. The stone as a messianic image in Judaism draws esp. on Isa. 28:16 and Dan. 2:44–45; but see also Gen. 28:17–19; Zech. 4:8–10; 3:8–9; Tg. Ps. 118:24 (printed in Walton 1657: 3.274; see Ellis 1974: 233). For Tg. Isa. 28:16 and other Jewish parallels, see Jeremias, TDNT 4:272–73. Tg. Isa. 28:16 reads: "Behold I set in Zion a king, a mighty king, mighty and terrible, whom I will uphold and strengthen; the prophet says: 'And the righteous in whom is confidence shall not tremble when affliction comes.'"

Luke's citation of the OT verbally matches Matt. 21:42 = Mark 12:10 except that he does not include Ps. 118:23 with its note about how marvelous it was to the audience's eyes to see these things. Matthew 21:43 notes additionally that the kingdom goes to those who bring forth fruit, causing Plummer (1896: 462) to question, since this detail would have fit Luke's emphasis on concrete fruit, whether he would have omitted this phrase if he had known Matthew. Each writer uses a slightly different introductory formula: Matthew and Mark raise the rhetorical question "have you not read this Scripture" (Mark) or "in the Scriptures" (Matthew). Luke's formula is more direct: "What then is this that is written" (τὸ γεγραμμένον, *to gegrammenon*), a typical Lucan expression (Luke 18:31; 21:22; 22:37; 24:44; Acts 13:29; 24:14; Marshall 1978: 732). Luke alone notes that Jesus looked at the crowd as he replied (Luke 22:61; 2 Kings 8:11). The church held tenaciously to the image that Jesus used here (Isa. 8:14; 28:16; Acts 4:11; 1 Pet. 2:7; Plummer 1896: 462). By the time of Justin Martyr, "the stone" had become a name for Jesus (*Dialogue with Trypho* 34).

ii. The Crushing Stone (20:18)

20:18   Jesus turns from biblical citation to biblical imagery. The proverb about the stone's power and authority pictures the fate of those who fail to respond. Jesus does not retain the image of the cornerstone, since one would hardly trip over it, but describes the stone's significance. Some see this shift as evidence of Lucan addition, but such catchword linkage is common in Judaism and need not be attributed to Luke. A comparable proverb is found in Esth. Rab. 7.10 on 3:6: "If the stone falls on the pot, alas for the pot; if the pot falls on the stone, alas for the pot" (SB 1:877; Sir. 13:2; Grundmann 1963: 372; Danker 1988: 319; Tiede 1988: 342; Bornkamm, *TDNT* 4:281 n. 10). The fate is not good—regardless of how the stone meets the rejecter. Those who reject are either broken to pieces (συνθλάω, *synthlaō*) or crushed into bits (λικμάω, *likmaō*) so fine that they become like chaff (Plummer 1896: 462–63; Fitzmyer 1985: 1286).[11] Using Gen. 14:15 and Josh. 11:7, Doran (1983) suggests that the background is a warrior's boast; but given the allusion's general character and the Danielic background, this is too specific. The picture reflects the judgment authority that the beloved Son will have as a ruling figure. The image anticipates his return in judgment (Acts

---

11. Both verbs appear only here and in the parallel at Matt. 21:44. On συνθλάω, see BAGD 790; BAA 1575; Ps. 57:7 LXX [58:6 Engl.]; Mic. 3:3. On λικμάω, see BAGD 474–75; BAA 963; Dan. 2:44 [Theodotion]; Ruth 3:2; Job 27:21; Isa. 17:13; Jer. 38:10 LXX [31:10 Engl.]; Amos 9:9; Josephus, *Antiquities* 5.9.3 §328.

10:42–43), though allusion to the destruction of Jerusalem is possible given the way that Jesus links these two events as pictures of each other (Luke 21:5–38; Kimball 1994: 158; against any allusion is Snodgrass 1983: 87–95).

The OT source of this text is disputed. Many suggest Dan. 2:34–35, 44–45 and Isa. 8:14–15, but the only verbal connection is to the Theodotionic version of Dan. 2:44 (cf. also Esth. Rab. 7.10 on 3:6, alluding to Isa. 30:14 and Dan. 2:45). Isaiah 8 refers to the stone of stumbling, while the stone that crushes is from Dan. 2 (Jeremias, *TDNT* 4:275–76). Given the lack of verbal connection, a conceptual allusion is likely. Rejecting Messiah has devastating consequences. The division predicted in Luke 2:34 has dire results. The hands that slay the king will be crushed.

Mark lacks any parallel here. Matthew 21:44 is parallel, but is textually disputed (i.e., Western manuscripts exclude this verse). The two texts match except for a few details. Matthew starts the verse with καί (*kai*, and) and uses the pronoun τοῦτον (*touton*, this one) where Luke has ἐκεῖνον (*ekeinon*, that one). Luke also uses πᾶς (*pas*, all) to describe those who fall on the stone, a description he loves to use, but that is also popular with the other Synoptic writers (Matthew 129 times, Mark 68 times, and Luke 157 times). All those who reject Jesus will be judged by him.

d. The Leadership's Desire to Seize Jesus Thwarted (20:19)

The leader's reaction is hostile (as in 19:47–48). Contextually, the **20:19** summary aorist ἐζήτησαν (*ezētēsan*, they sought) expresses their resolve to deal with Jesus (Arndt 1956: 405).[12] In that hour, the leadership desired to seize him (ἐπιβάλλω, *epiballō*; BAGD 289 §1b; BAA 587 §1b; cf. Matt. 26:50; Luke 21:12; John 7:44; Acts 5:18; 21:27; Gen. 22:12; Exod. 7:4; 2 Sam. 18:12). But they still feared popular reaction. Luke gives the cause (γάρ, *gar*) of their anger and desire to seize Jesus: Jesus told the parable against (πρός, *pros*; BDF §239.6; BAGD 710 §III.5a; BAA 1423 §III.5a) them, and they knew it (Fitzmyer 1985: 1287). How could this uninstructed Galilean with no real credentials challenge Judaism's official leadership? What gave him the right to say what God would do? The previous controversy answers that question. The source of his authority is the same as John the Baptist's. They will soon find out why he has this right.

Matthew 21:45–46 = Mark 12:12 is similar in tone, with Luke standing closer to Mark. Matthew speaks of the Pharisees' and chief priests' desire to seize (κρατῆσαι, *kratēsai*) Jesus, but notes that they feared the crowd (ὄχλους, *ochlous*). Matthew alone says that the

---

12. Luke does not use his normal imperfect ("they were seeking").

crowd held Jesus to be a prophet. Mark does not identify explicitly who wished to seize Jesus, though it is clear they are distinct from the crowd. He says that "they" reacted because they knew Jesus told the parable against them, wording that agrees with Luke except for word order. Mark then notes that they left him and went away. Luke uses a unique term for Jesus' arrest (ἐπιβαλεῖν, *epibalein*). For the crowd, he uses his normal term, λαός (*laos*, people). Only Luke says that the attempt to seize Jesus came "at that hour" (ἐν αὐτῇ τῇ ὥρᾳ, *en autē tē hōra*), another expression that he likes (2:38; 10:7, 21; 24:33; BDR §288.2.4; Plummer 1896: 274, 280–81, 463). Luke seems to have put the summary in his own words.

Summary Luke 20:9–19 is an important text, revealing Jesus' commentary on Israel's history and God's long-suffering. The confrontation between Jesus and the leadership rises to a new level, with Jesus on the offensive. He compares the leadership's treatment of him to Israel's previous treatment of the prophets (11:47–51). Jesus is in line with much of what OT history from Deuteronomy on shows. He reminds the people that God's promise is not an inalienable national right as far as an individual's participation in blessing goes. Israel may have the promise, but that does not mean that each Israelite is blessed. God examines each person for a response.

The nation's response will not be adequate. Jesus anticipates that they will slay him. But that will not stop God's plan. The rejected stone will be exalted, and judgment will follow his exaltation. In fact, the vineyard of promise will go to others as blessing springs from the death of the Son. Jesus may look weak and impotent, but he will be vindicated. Meanwhile, attempts to arrest him are delayed because of the crowd. The leadership is anxious to remove Jesus, but his removal will only bring the inevitable exaltation and judgment nearer. In God's plan, the reader is to see that things are not what they seem on the outside. Power and authority do not reside in the priesthood; they reside in Jesus, the precious rejected stone. The question is: Do you have a relationship with the exalted stone, or are you falling over the stone and being crushed by it? They may slay the Son, but the master will have his day in court. God does not take rejection of his Son lightly.

4. Question about Caesar's Tax (20:20–26)

The leaders' failure to trap Jesus causes them to take another approach. Thinking that they can perhaps catch him in political error, they raise one of the more troublesome issues to a Jew—the Roman "poll tax." Tribute was an emotional issue for Jews since it pictured in concrete economic terms Israel's subjection to Rome. Needless to say, it was unpopular (Josephus, *Jewish War* 2.8.1 §§117–18; 7.8.1 §§253–58; *Antiquities* 18.1.1 §§1–10; Ellis 1974: 233; Fitzmyer 1985: 1293).[1] In posing their either/or question, the leaders, through their intermediary "spies," are attempting to get Jesus in hot water, using the same either/or tactic that he has just used on them. If he responds affirmatively about the tax, then nationalist Jews who see him as a political messianic hope will realize that their political ambitions will not be met. If he rejects the tax, then he will be charged with revolting against Rome. Jesus' reply is clever, for in asking them to show him a coin, he gets them to acknowledge Roman sovereignty even before he gives an answer (Fitzmyer 1985: 1291; Tannehill 1986: 189–90). Such sovereignty was a fact of life that they carried around in their pockets every day. Jesus' reply acknowledges the state's right to raise support from its citizenry without denying the sphere of God's authority (Luke 3:12–13; Rom. 13:1–7; 1 Pet. 2:13–17; K. Weiss, *TDNT* 9:82 §B2). The kingdom of God need not compromise the rights or existence of the state.[2] Jesus' reply in nonpolitical terms may have cost him some support, since he clearly rejects the nationalist position later represented by the Zealots in A.D. 67–70.

Sources and Historicity

Numerous parallels to this account exist: the Synoptic parallels are Matt. 22:15–22 = Mark 12:13–17 (Aland 1985: §280), with nonbiblical parallels in P. Egerton 2, Gospel of Thomas 100, and Justin Martyr, *Apology* 1.17.2

---

1. In fact, a Galilean named Judas revolted in A.D. 6 because he did not want to pay such taxes; Josephus, *Jewish War* 2.8.1 §118; Tiede 1988: 344.

2. Tiede 1988: 343 correctly remarks that this text does not endorse the "two-kingdoms" doctrine or the separation of church and state. It sets forth no political religious theory. It simply acknowledges the presence of civil government and its right to sustain itself through the contributions of its citizens.

(who mixes Luke's and Matthew's wording).[3] The Synoptic accounts tell this event with some variation of wording. Mark and Matthew are close in form, with Luke standing closer to Mark. Luke has a longer, more detailed introduction and conclusion than do his counterparts. The account's authenticity is widely accepted (even by Bultmann 1963: 26).[4] The Jesus Seminar (Funk and Hoover 1993: 378–79) splits the unit, printing 20:24 in black type but regarding the key pronouncement in 20:25 as totally authentic (red type). The aphorism is accepted because of its multiple attestation and because it reflects the challenge of a "sage." The seminar rejects the question because of its various renderings in the tradition history. But the aphorism makes no sense without the question, while the secondary nature of the extrabiblical parallels speaks against their value as an accurate source for the question. The Synoptic account has internal coherence and is authentic in portraying a genuine controversy between the leadership and Jesus.

The account is a pronouncement story and a controversy dialogue (Fitzmyer 1985: 1291; Bultmann 1963: 26; Berger 1984: 81). The outline of Luke 20:20–26 is as follows:

a. Setting (20:20)
b. Question (20:21–22)
c. Answer (20:23–25)
d. Reaction (20:26)

The major theme of this unit is the failure of the leaders to trap Jesus. In fact, their lack of ethics is exposed in this effort. Sin often leads to deceit. Jesus acknowledges the state's right to exist and support itself, though he does not specify the relationship between state and religion. Jesus refuses to engage in partisan political opinion on the tax issue and thereby avoids the trap.

Exegesis and Exposition

[20]And as they watched, they sent spies, pretending to be sincere, in order that they might seize upon what he said, so as to deliver him into the authority and jurisdiction of the governor.

[21]And they asked him, "Teacher, we know that you speak and teach rightly and do not show partiality. You teach truly the way of God. [22]Is it right for us to pay the tax to Caesar or not?"

[23]But perceiving their craftiness, he said to them, [24]"Show me a coin. Whose likeness and inscription has it?" They said, "Caesar's." [25]And he said to them, "Then render the things of Caesar to Caesar and the things of God to God."

---

3. Nolland 1993b: 957 notes that all the nonbiblical parallels are secondary.
4. Nolland 1993b: 957 notes one exception: Petzke 1975.

²⁶And they were unable to catch him in his response before the people and were silent, while marveling at his reply.

a. Setting (20:20)

The leadership moves to the background since they have just been **20:20** exposed by their efforts to confront Jesus directly (Danker 1988: 319). They move to the sidelines, pull strings, and watch others do their dirty work. Παρατηρήσαντες (*paratērēsantes*, watching) has no named subject, but is clearly an allusion to the angered leadership of 20:19, which now commissions spies on their behalf. Ἐγκαθέτους (*enkathetous*) literally means "hired to lie in wait," picturing someone lurking about, waiting for a chance to destroy (BAGD 215; BAA 433; Job 31:9 [of a sinful man stalking an enticing woman]; 19:12 [of an army surrounding a city]). The leadership calls on others to carry out this task and so commissions (ἀπέστειλαν, *apesteilan*) them as spies.

Luke makes their motives clear when he says they pretend to be righteous (δικαίους, *dikaious*), which in this context means "sincere" (16:15 is another such example of pretense; 10:29 and 18:9 are related; Nolland 1993b: 957). Their question in 20:22 looks honest, but it is not. The leaders want to use Jesus' words so that (ὥστε, *hōste*; BDF §391.3) they can deliver him up to the authority (ἀρχή, *archē*, ruler) and jurisdiction (ἐξουσία, *exousia*) of the governor, an allusion to Pilate (Delling, *TDNT* 1:482). They hope that Jesus' reply will get him in trouble with Rome so they can then take advantage of his slip and dispose of him (ἐπιλαμβάνομαι [*epilambanomai*, to seize upon]; Delling, *TDNT* 4:9; Nolland 1993b: 957–58; Xenophon, *Anabasis* 4.7.12). This brilliant plan would allow responsibility for Jesus' death to be placed in enemy hands. Perhaps the leaders thought that Jesus' messianic self-understanding would lead him easily into this political trap. Such efforts to watch or trap Jesus have failed before (6:7; 11:53–54; 14:1; 19:47). The leadership will later lie about Jesus' response (23:2).

Luke's introduction is more complete than Matt. 22:15 = Mark 12:13. The only additional detail that Matthew and Mark supply is the depth of the leadership's alliance. Matthew notes that the instigators were the Pharisees, who brought in the Herodians. Mark mentions these groups without specifying which were the instigators. These two groups disliked one another intensely (Plummer 1896: 464; Hoehner 1972: 331–42, who explains that Herodians are neither Sadducees nor Essenes, though they might have been allied to the Sadducees; see Josephus, *Jewish War* 1.16.6 §319; *Antiquities* 14.15.10 §450). The Herodians favored a solution that let Rome have a mediated presence through the house of Herod. Preferring that Rome not be present at all, the Pharisees would have opposed the tax. These groups, however, put their animosities behind them and combine efforts to get Jesus. A view had emerged that since Yahweh allowed such a takeover, taxes should be paid (F. F. Bruce 1984), but it was not a popular view. Luke refers to the leadership indirectly, mentioning only scribes and chief priests (Luke 20:19). Luke, with Mark, says that they attempt to catch Jesus in an error of speech, although Mark uses distinct terminology: ἵνα αὐτὸν ἀγρεύσωσιν λόγῳ (hina auton agreusōsin logō, that they might trap him in a word). Only Luke notes the attempt to bring Jesus before Pilate.

b. Question (20:21–22)

20:21 Luke's indication of setting and motive is crucial, given the way the question is asked. On the surface the questioners seem to praise Jesus. But the previous note about the hypocrisy of their motives reveals a more dastardly reality (Plummer 1896: 465). Irony abounds throughout the account since their words are true—despite the insincerity of the leaders. They speak more truly than they know.

The leaders make three points about Jesus' teaching. First, he speaks "straight" (ὀρθῶς, orthōs), which refers to his accurate presentation of God's way (Preisker, *TDNT* 5:449; elsewhere in Luke at 7:43; 10:28; Deut. 5:28; Marshall 1978: 734; BAGD 580; BAA 1176). Second, Jesus shows no partiality (οὐ λαμβάνεις πρόσωπον, *ou lambaneis prosōpon*), a Hebraism (Plummer 1896: 465) or Septuagintalism (Fitzmyer 1985: 1295) that means "to raise the face or accept with favor" (Lohse, *TDNT* 6:779–80; Lev. 19:15; 2 Kings 3:14; Job 42:8 [≠ MT's sense]; Ps. 82:2; Mal. 1:8–9; Gal. 2:6; James 2:1). This probably means that he is not afraid to challenge the Jewish leadership—and perhaps the Roman governor as well. Third, he teaches God's way "with truth" (ἐπ᾽ ἀληθείας, *ep' alētheias*; Luke 4:25; 22:59; Acts 4:27; 10:34; BDR §234.4.7). "The way" (τὴν ὁδόν, *tēn hodon*) describes the walk of righteousness with God (Deut. 8:6; 10:12–13; Ps. 27:11; 119:15). The NT uses this term as a name for the Christian faith (Luke 1:79; 3:4; Acts 9:2; 16:17; 18:25–26; 19:9, 23; 22:4; 24:14, 22; Schweizer 1984: 306; Michaelis, *TDNT* 5:51–52, 87). The use of flattery was a common tactic to disarm Jesus (Luke 18:18).

Matthew 22:16b is a little fuller than Luke: the inquirers say that Jesus is true (ἀληθὴς εἶ, *alēthēs ei*), that he teaches God's way truthfully (ἐν ἀληθείᾳ, *en alētheia*), that he "does not care about anyone" (οὐ μέλει σοι περὶ οὐδενός, *ou melei soi peri oudenos*—which refers to his nonpartiality), and that he "does not regard the position of men" (οὐ . . . βλέπεις εἰς πρόσωπον ἀνθρώπων, *ou . . . blepeis eis prosōpon anthrōpōn*). In Matthew it is clear that Jesus challenges the leadership. Mark 12:14 overlaps with three of Matthew's points (Jesus is true, he does not care for anyone, and he does not look on the position of men) and agrees with Luke in mentioning that Jesus "truly teaches the way of God." Luke stands alone in the way he expresses that Jesus speaks the truth and shows no partiality. Each writer, especially Luke, summarized in his own words.

The question that the spies put forward involves taxes paid directly **20:22** to Rome, specifically the poll tax (φόρος, *phoros*; BAGD 865; BAA 1724; elsewhere in the NT only at Luke 23:2; Rom. 13:6–7 [three times]). References to such foreign taxes are common in Josephus (*Jewish War* 1.7.6 §154; 2.8.1 §118; *Against Apion* 1.18 §119; *Antiquities* 5.3.2 §181; 12.4.5 §182; 14.10.6 §203). This tax stands in contrast to the τέλος (*telos*; BAGD 812 §3; BAA 1619 §3), an indirect tax gathered by tax collectors in toll booths. The poll tax was paid directly to Caesar, in this case, Tiberius.[5] As such it acknowledged and honored the emperor. In asking whether it is "legal" (ἔξεστιν, *exestin*) to pay this tax, the leaders are in effect asking, "Are God's people exempt from paying such a tax to a foreign power? Jesus, are you loyal to Israel, looking for its independence, or should we knuckle under to Rome?"[6]

Matthew 22:17 has an introduction to the question that Mark and Luke lack: "Tell us then what you think." Matthew and Mark 12:14 use a different term for the tax, the Latin loanword κῆνσος (*kēnsos*, poll tax [lit., "census"]; BAGD 430; BAA 876; outside this pericope only in Matt. 17:25; BDF §5.1b; BDR §5.1b.4). Luke alone uses the pronoun ἡμᾶς (*hēmas*) in this question and places it in an emphatic position: "Is it right *for us* to pay this tax or not?" The use of the pronoun means that Luke does not need Mark's second question: "Do we pay or not pay?" Luke appears to have summarized the material.

c. Answer (20:23–25)

Jesus perceives (κατανοήσας, *katanoēsas*; BAGD 415 §3; BAA 843 **20:23** §3) their deceit (πανουργίαν, *panourgian*; Bauernfeind, *TDNT* 5:726; BAGD 608; BAA 1230), a term that is always negative in the NT (1 Cor. 3:19; 2 Cor. 4:2; 11:3; Eph. 4:14).[7] Jesus responds in light of

---

5. On Tiberius's rule, see the exegesis of 3:1. The origin of *Caesar* as the title for the reigning emperor goes back to Julius Caesar; Fitzmyer 1985: 1296.

6. On the syntax of ἔξεστιν with an infinitive and an accusative, see BDF §409.3 and BDR §409.3.4.

7. Luke's use of these terms provides a good example of the role of the omniscient narrator who indicates the participants' thoughts and thus colors how the characters are viewed.

this perception. He knows that their praise was not sincere (Fitzmyer 1985: 1296).

Mark 12:15 speaks of Jesus knowing their hypocrisy (εἰδὼς αὐτῶν τὴν ὑπόκρισιν, eidōs autōn tēn hypokrisin).[8] Mark and Matthew start with an additional question: "Why do you test me?" Matthew 22:18 adds the addressees, ὑποκριταί (hypokritai, hypocrites), and says that Jesus knew their malice, that is, their immoral intentions (γνοὺς . . . τὴν πονηρίαν αὐτῶν, gnous . . . tēn ponērian autōn). Each writer goes his own way in expressing the scene, but the point is the same.

20:24   Jesus responds by calling for a denarius, a basic monetary unit that represented an average day's wage (see the exegesis of 7:41). Ancient coins usually had some written indication of the coin's nature and an image of the ruler, which would offend the Jews, who did not put images on coins, especially images that represented deity (Exod. 20:4, 23 [20:4, 20 NJPSV]). For example, the inscription on a silver Tiberian denarius reads, "Tiberius Caesar, Augustus, son of divine Augustus." On the reverse side his mother Livia is portrayed as an incarnation of the goddess of peace, along with the inscription "high priest" (Fitzmyer 1985: 1296; Marshall 1978: 735–36).[9]

Upon being shown the coin, Jesus asks the identity of the likeness and inscription on it and his questioners respond that the image is Caesar's. By producing this coin, they indicate that they carry on trade with it (the leadership is described as "lovers of silver" in 16:14; cf. 18:25; 20:47; Danker 1988: 320). They use these coins without blinking an eye, thus the question's edge is lost in their daily practice. They live in the state and freely use its currency.

The parallels are longer. In Matt. 22:19–21 Jesus asks, "Show (ἐπιδείξατε, epideixate) me the money for the tax," and in Mark 12:15, "Bring (φέρετε, pherete) me a denarius that I might see it." Luke has δείξατε (deixate) for the verbal request to show the coin and a shorter question about the inscription and image. In Matthew and Mark the questioners produce a coin, Jesus asks whose image and inscription is on it, and his questioners reply, Καίσαρος (kaisaros, Caesar's). Matthew uses a vivid present tense with a past force λέγουσιν (legousin, they said), while Luke and Mark have οἱ δὲ εἶπαν (hoi de eipan, but they said). Luke appears to be a summarizing account.

---

8. Luke used the related ὑποκρίνομαι (to pretend) in 20:20.

9. For an Augustan denarius (about the size of a dime and weighing 3.8 grams), see *Zondervan Pictorial Encyclopedia of the Bible* 1:909. For a Tiberian denarius, see photographs 44–45 in the same work (between pp. 896 and 897), and *Interpreter's Dictionary of the Bible* 1:824. For a full discussion, see Hart 1984.

Jesus says to pay the tax, but he asserts the need to honor God as **20:25** well. Since ἀποδίδωμι (*apodidōmi*) often means to pay back a debt (BAGD 90 §2; BAA 180 §1; Matt. 5:26; 18:25–26, 28–29, 34; Luke 7:42; 10:35; 12:59; 19:8), by using this term, Jesus acknowledges the genuine existence of civic debt and the need to pay it. His answer implies recognition of political government's authority and also seems to recognize God's providence in the midst of that rule, much like Rom. 13:1–7 (Arndt 1956: 407; 1 Pet. 2:13–17). Jesus also notes that God is to receive the honor he is due. Jesus responds to his examiners' either/or question with a both/and answer. Plummer (1896: 466) notes that Rom. 13:1–7 deals with Caesar's sphere, while Rom. 12:1–2 deals with God's. Jesus has avoided the trap by saying that we have duty to the state *and* to God (Fitzmyer 1985: 1297).[10] Honoring God means that one cannot refuse the state's right to function. Jesus does not address the issue of what to do when the two spheres are in direct moral conflict. What he does say is that the character of a state is not grounds for challenging the state's right to organize itself at the political and social levels. Shadrach, Meshach, and Abednego's handling of an edict against prayer (Dan. 3) and Daniel's handling of a similar edict (Dan. 6) may be seen as guides on how to handle moral confrontations involving one's relationship to God.[11] When God deals with unrighteous human government, he usually does so directly and through other political agents and nations, as the OT shows and as Revelation suggests.

Since this is Jesus' only saying directly relating to affairs of state, it has received numerous interpretations, all of which attempt to develop its implications (Luce 1933: 312–13; Fitzmyer 1985: 1291–94). Does this saying assert the "divine right of kings," a famous medieval doctrine of church and state? Does it make the state legitimate, but secondary to God? Does it create two spheres, separating church and state? Does it relate the two spheres side by side as in the two-kingdoms view?[12] Is the saying ironic, so that nothing can be drawn from it (so Schweitzer 1956: 30–31)?[13] The saying is so brief that

10. The phrase τὰ τοῦ θεοῦ (the things of God) occurs elsewhere in Mark 8:33; 1 Cor. 2:11, 14; 7:32–34; Fitzmyer 1985: 1296–97.

11. Note the disciples' reply in Acts 4:19–20 in a religious context; cf. Isa. 10:5–7; Jer. 27:6; Acts 5:29; Leaney 1958: 252. John 19:11 shows that the state's sovereignty is subject to God's authority.

12. Many follow Ranke 1901: 1.1–9 in seeing this saying as Jesus' most significant political statement. Fitzmyer 1985: 1292 objects to the two-kingdoms view (which appeals to Prov. 8:15–16; Dan. 2:21, 37–38; Wis. 6:1–11 for support), arguing that it makes Caesar and God equals.

13. That the saying about rendering to God is not ironic stands against viewing the first saying as ironic (Fitzmyer 1985: 1292). The use of the conjunction καί (and) instead of ἀλλά (but) shows that the whole saying is to be taken together.

care should be exercised in what is drawn out from it, since it is a specific reply to a specific issue without any development. One can at least say that Jesus rejects an aggressive, nationalistic, revolutionary Zealot-like approach to the question (Fitzmyer 1985: 1292–93; Tertullian, *Concerning Idolatry* 15.3). Jesus' current kingship is not designed to lead a revolution to overthrow Rome. Whatever he is teaching, it is not political insubordination.[14]

The parallels are almost verbally exact except for word order, the introduction to the saying, and the use of conjunctions. Mark 12:17 lacks any conjunction and introduces the saying with ὁ δὲ Ἰησοῦς εἶπεν αὐτοῖς (*ho de Iēsous eipen autois*, and Jesus said to them). Matthew 22:21 uses οὖν (*oun*, therefore) and introduces the reply with τότε λέγει αὐτοῖς (*tote legei autois*, then he said to them). Matthew uses the historical present, which Mark is often fond of but lacks here. Luke's introduction follows Mark except for lacking Ἰησοῦς and using the conjunction τοίνυν (*toinyn*, then; BDF §451.3).

d. Reaction (20:26)

20:26 The leadership tried to set a trap but it has failed to catch Jesus (ἐπιλαβέσθαι, *epilabesthai*; BAGD 295 §2a; BAA 598 §2a; BDF §170.2; BDR §170.2.2; cf. Luke 20:20). They became silent (as in 14:6) but at the same time they marvel at his answer (as in 2:48). They will be silent one more time (20:40). Jesus is not a nationalist, nor is he stupid enough to engage in a test designed to destroy him.

Luke is much longer than the parallels. Matthew 22:22 says that they heard the reply and were amazed, so they left him and went away, while Mark 12:17b simply says that they were amazed at him. Luke shares the note of amazement, but alone notes the spies' failure to lure him into a corner.

Summary Luke 20:20–26 shows that efforts to nail Jesus took a variety of forms. The most efficient way to get rid of him would be for him to challenge Rome or lose the affections of the populace. The leadership devises a question designed to force Jesus to make a choice between Rome and Israel. They reasoned that he would be discredited by either answer he gave—just as they had been in 20:1–8. But he refuses to walk into the trap. Instead, he affirms that Caesar has a domain that should be served and that God has a sphere where he should be honored. The event is part of the ten-

---

14. Arguing that the point revolves around both the image and the inscription, Giblin 1971 attempts to ground the reply in an allusion to Isa. 44:5. According to this verse, God's inscription on people is that they "belong to him," a concept that leads Jesus to speak of rendering to God what is his. Marshall 1978: 736 is right that this is a correct theological deduction but not explicit in the text.

sion that precedes the movement to the cross. The opposition is working frantically to catch Jesus, but they cannot. Jesus is still in control of events, and he is a step ahead of the leadership. He is aware of their efforts and avoids falling into their carefully crafted dilemmas. Jesus' work for God does not challenge, but rather transcends, Rome.

5. Question about Resurrection (20:27–40)

The Pharisees and others in the leadership have had their chance to upset Jesus: they have challenged his authority (20:1–8) and tried to trap him politically (20:20–26). Luke now relates a third controversy during the passion week, in which the Sadducees try their hand at tripping up Jesus on an internal Jewish dispute over the resurrection.

This is Luke's only account of Jesus confronting the Sadducees. As Luke 20:27 and Acts 23:6–8 note, the Sadducees did not hold to resurrection (Josephus, *Jewish War* 2.8.14 §§164–65; *Antiquities* 18.1.4 §16). They also denied the existence of angels, a significant point in light of Luke 20:36. The Sadducees and Pharisees disputed the importance of oral tradition in deciding such matters (Josephus, *Antiquities* 13.10.6 §§297–98; Ellis 1974: 234–35; Plummer 1896: 467; Danker 1988: 322).[1] The Sadducees' origin is traditionally tied to the name *Zadok* (2 Sam. 8:17; 1 Kings 2:35; Neh. 3:29; Ezek. 40:46). Their real origin is lost, however, in obscurity, since no one is sure which Zadok is meant. The group seems to have emerged in the second century B.C. The Sadducees were priestly and lay aristocrats who revered only the Torah. They were somewhat rationalistic, tended to be wealthy, rejected oral tradition, and desired to preserve the status quo (R. Meyer, *TDNT* 7:35–54; SB 4:334–52; Jeremias 1969: 228–32). They were the most religiously conservative group of their day. After A.D. 70 they lost the battle for religious control of Judaism to the Pharisees.

The Sadducees formulate a question that attempts to show how ludicrous the idea of resurrection is: one wife had seven husbands, six by levirate marriage (Gen. 38:8; Deut. 25:5; Ruth 4:1–12). Upon resurrection, whose wife will she be? The question presupposes that postresurrection reality is the same as now and that monogamy reigns then as now. Imagine the dilemma when this "monogamous" wife is faced with seven resurrected spouses!

Jesus again avoids a trap. In a remark that Luke lacks, Jesus notes that their question misunderstands the character of God

---

1. For the Pharisee view of resurrection, see Josephus, *Jewish War* 3.8.5 §374; *Against Apion* 2.30 §218; *Antiquities* 18.1.3 §14. For the Essene view, see *Jewish War* 2.8.11 §154; *Antiquities* 18.1.5 §18. Cf. SB 1:885–86; 1 Enoch 15.6–9.

and the nature of resurrection. Luke picks up Jesus' reply by noting that there is no marriage in the afterlife. The dilemma does not lie in the doctrine of resurrection, which Jesus firmly upholds. The dilemma lies in their refusal to recognize God's creative power to transform reality through resurrection. Even the Torah reveals such truth. Jesus' citation of Exod. 3:6 is crucial for the Sadducees, since they regarded the Torah as uniquely authoritative (Odeberg, *TDNT* 3:191). The Sadducees refused to recognize new life as creatively wrought by God. Jesus' answer endorses resurrection (as in Luke 14:14), brings commendation, and silences opponents. In fact, his citation of Exod. 3:6 makes it a matter of God's covenant promise. The clearest OT resurrection text is Dan. 12:2, but Jesus uses the Torah to tie resurrection to covenant and to meet the Sadducees on their own scriptural turf. If God is the God of Abraham and the patriarchs, then there must be a resurrection in order for them to experience the promise (see the additional note on 20:37). Jesus' point is not only that the patriarchs are alive, but that they await the promise's fulfillment. If there is no resurrection, they are history. The opponents do not respond to Jesus' reply.

With this confrontation, every major group has attempted to challenge Jesus—and failed. Pharisees, chief priests, scribes, nationalists, and Sadducees have been unable to embarrass Jesus. Who has authority to lead God's people? These controversies reveal the most qualified candidate.

Sources and Historicity

This is another event of the triple tradition, with Matt. 22:23–33 = Mark 12:18–27 as the Synoptic parallels (Aland 1985: §281). Luke stands closer verbally to Mark than to Matthew, especially in Luke 20:28–33, 38b–39.[2] The accounts are similar, although Luke goes his own way in the introduction and conclusion. Luke also has a longer reply from Jesus, though he lacks Jesus' rebuke about understanding God's power. The argument's rabbinic form and the use of Exod. 3:6 speak for authenticity (Marshall 1978: 738; Fitzmyer 1985: 1300; Jeremias 1971a: 184 n. 3). The Jesus Seminar (Funk and Hoover 1993: 379–80) argues that the rabbinic style reflects input other than that of Jesus and thus prints 20:34–38 in gray type. Yet the

2. Fitzmyer 1985: 1299 notes seven differences between Mark and Luke, mostly stylistic; see the exegesis for details. In addition, he notes how Luke 20:38b–39 is a Lucan summary, while 20:40 is like Mark 12:34 (which is in a section that Luke lacks). Luke 20:34–36 has Jesus teach the Sadducees directly and lacks any rebuke about how they read Scripture. Fitzmyer also notes a possible conceptual parallel to 4 Macc. 7:19.

seminar also argues that the witty style reflects Jesus' typical response to hostile questions. It is not clear, however, why Jesus, who obviously spent time in the temple and the synagogue, could not argue in a style that Jewish leaders regularly used when teaching Scripture. Nolland (1993b: 963) argues for a conscious shift of style by Jesus. The use of Scripture as example is something that Jesus does on occasion (6:1–5; 11:29–32; 17:26–32). The account summarizes a real controversy of Jesus' ministry.

This is another pronouncement story and controversy dialogue (Fitzmyer 1985: 1299–1300; Bultmann 1963: 26; Berger 1984: 81). The outline of Luke 20:27–40 is as follows:

a. Setting (20:27)
b. The problem: resurrection and seven husbands (20:28–33)
  i. Levirate marriage (20:28)
  ii. The situation (20:29–32)
  iii. The question (20:33)
c. Jesus' reply: resurrection is different (20:34–38)
  i. Answer: this life is not like the next (20:34–36)
  ii. Scripture proof (20:37)
  iii. Conclusion: the God of promise is the God of the living (20:38)
d. The scribes' response (20:39)
e. Conclusion (20:40)

With the Sadducees' failure, all major Jewish groups have failed to ensnare Jesus. He is in control of events. His reply makes it clear that the resurrection involves a different kind of reality, so that the next world is not like this world. Death does not lead to destruction of life for the saints of old. The resurrection is a part of the promise. Once again, Jesus silences his opposition.

Exegesis and Exposition

[27]There came to him some of the Sadducees, those who ⌜contested⌝ that there is no resurrection. They asked him, [28]saying, "Teacher, Moses wrote for us that if a certain brother dies, who has a wife, and this one is childless, that his brother takes the wife and raises up seed for his brother. [29]Now there were seven brothers. The first who took the wife died childless; [30]⌜and the second⌝ [31]and a third took her; likewise also the seven did not leave her children and died. [32]Last also the wife died⌝. [33]⌜In the resurrection⌝, therefore, whose wife ⌜will she be⌝? For seven had her as wife."

[34]And Jesus said to them, "The sons of this age ⌜marry⌝ and are given in marriage, [35]but those who are accounted worthy to attain to that age and the resurrection from the dead neither marry nor are given in marriage, [36]for

they are not able still to die, for they are like angels and are sons of God, being sons of resurrection. [37]But that the dead are raised, Moses also showed in the passage on the bush, where he calls the Lord 'the God of Abraham and the God of Isaac and the God of Jacob.' [38]Now he is not the God of the dead, but of the living; for all live to him."

[39]And some of the scribes answered, "Teacher, you have answered well."
[40]For they no longer dared to ask him any questions.

a. Setting (20:27)

New opponents, the Sadducees, take on Jesus (for their history, see **20:27** the unit introduction). They appear more often in Matthew (Matt. 3:7; 16:1, 6, 11, 12; 22:23, 34). Mark has them only here, as does Luke (also Acts 4:1; 5:17; 23:6–8; Ernst 1977: 542; Marshall 1978: 738–39). Luke explicitly notes that they deny the resurrection (also Acts 4:1–2; 23:6–8). The reason for this denial was their tenacious insistence on the Torah and their rejection of oral tradition. Judaism appealed to a series of texts for the resurrection hope (Job 19:26; Ps. 16:9, 11; Isa. 26:19), including Torah texts like Exod. 6:4; 15:1; Num. 15:31; 18:28; and Deut. 31:16 (*b. Sanh.* 90b, 91b; Fitzmyer 1985: 1303). The text Jesus uses, Exod. 3:6, was not used by the rabbis. Luke frequently refers to the resurrection from the dead (Luke 14:14; Acts 17:32; 23:6–8; 24:15, 21) as well as to Jesus' resurrection (Acts 1:22; 2:31; 4:2, 33; 17:18; 26:23; Fitzmyer 1985: 1303). Such resurrection is not mere immortality, since spirit and body are involved (Luke 24:39–40).

The parallels in Matt. 22:23 = Mark 12:18 are similar. Three elements in Matthew and Mark match Luke: the Sadducees come, say that there is no resurrection, and ask Jesus a question (Matthew adds that this happened on "that day"). On a verbal level, these elements share only the reference to the Sadducees and the phrase about denying resurrection. Matthew and Luke share the aorist ἐπηρώτησαν (*epērōtēsan*, they asked), but Mark has imperfect ἐπηρώτων (*epērōtōn*, they were asking), which is interesting given Luke's preference for the imperfect.

b. The Problem: Resurrection and Seven Husbands (20:28–33)
i. Levirate Marriage (20:28)

The Sadducees ask their question of Jesus, addressing him with the **20:28** leadership's popular title for him: διδάσκαλε (*didaskale*, teacher; in Luke, eleven of seventeen uses of διδάσκαλος refer to Jesus; Matthew eight of twelve uses; Mark seven of twelve uses). The Sadducees begin their discussion with a description of levirate marriage, a law designed to perpetuate the name of a man who died childless

(Deut. 25:5; Ruth 4:1–12; *Yebamot* is the key mishnaic tractate; Arndt 1956: 410; Fitzmyer 1985: 1304).[3] If a man died childless, his brother was to take the wife as his own and raise up a child for the deceased brother, and the child would carry on the dead brother's name and heritage. The goal of the law was to raise up seed for the deceased brother. But, as the Sadducees attempt to show, this law created problems for the doctrine of resurrection.[4] The thoroughness with which these laws were studied shows the effort that went into reflecting on them.

Luke's wording is close to Mark 12:19, who introduces the quotation with ὅτι (*hoti*, untranslated), has an extra καί (*kai*, and), and words the description of childlessness differently (μὴ ἀφῇ τέκνον, *mē aphē teknon*, does not leave a child). Mark and Luke use the same verb to refer to Moses' writing, ἔγραψεν (*egrapsen*, he wrote), while Matt. 22:24 has εἶπεν (*eipen*, he said). Matthew simplifies the presentation of the law ("if anyone dies not having children") and also presents the law in a more emphatic style ("his brother must marry his wife and raise up seed for his brother"). Each writer has stylistically gone his own way, but Mark and Luke are closer to one another.

ii. The Situation (20:29–32)

20:29 A chain of marriages follows from what is obviously a big family. The example is perhaps paralleled in Tob. 3:8; 6:9–12; 7:11–13 (Marshall 1978: 739–40). The first levirate marriage ends as the initial marriage did, childless. Thus the progeny problem remains.

The Synoptics agree conceptually though they differ verbally. Luke alone uses the conjunction οὖν (*oun*, now) at the start of the verse (Creed 1930: 248), a temporal use that is characteristic of Lucan style (20:15, 33, 44). Matthew 22:25 seems to personalize the illustration by using παρ' ἡμῖν (*par' hēmin*, among us; Plummer 1896: 468). Each account refers to the husband's death with different verbal forms: Matthew has ἐτελεύτησεν (*eteleutēsen*), Mark ἀποθνῄσκων (*apothnēskōn*), and Luke ἀπέθανεν (*apethanen*). Different terms are also used for the marriage: Matthew uses the participle γήμας (*gēmas*, having married), Mark has ἔλαβεν γυναῖκα (*elaben gynaika*, he took a wife), while Luke employs λαβὼν γυναῖκα (*labōn gynaika*, having taken a wife). They also differ on the reference to childless-

---

3. The term *levirate* comes from Latin *levir* (husband's brother); M. Burrows 1940. The practice was still used in the first century; Josephus, *Antiquities* 4.8.23 §§254–56.

4. *B. Nid.* 70b raises another issue about resurrection: Will resurrected people need to be ritually cleansed after resurrection since they had contact with death and the grave?

ness: Matthew says μὴ ἔχων σπέρμα (*mē echōn sperma*, not having seed), Mark uses οὐκ ἀφῆκεν σπέρμα (*ouk aphēken sperma*, did not leave seed), and Luke simply has ἄτεκνος (*ateknos*, childless). These variations suggest that this account may have circulated in a variety of forms, given that the changes do not alter the sense.[5] Stylistically, Luke's version is the simplest at the end, while Matthew's is the simplest at the start.

The second levirate marriage follows the same pattern. Luke verbally matches Matthew, while Mark fills out the idea, noting that this brother took her and died, leaving her childless. The grammatical subject of 20:30 will take up the singular verb in 20:31 (ἔλαβεν, *elaben*, he took), a grammatical oddity that nonetheless does occur elsewhere (Matt. 24:35; Mark 4:41; Marshall 1978: 740). Luke and Matthew again have shorter versions. **20:30**

The sequence continues through a third brother and eventually all seven, none of them leaving any children before they die. That none of them filled the need for an heir is not the point, as 20:33 makes clear. Plummer (1896: 468) argues that the absence of children is put first and so is slightly emphatic, since logically the mention of the death should come first. The Sadducees are not concerned with the children, but with the issue of the spouse (or better, spouses!). The childlessness just allows for the succession of husbands to continue until the family tree is exhausted, making the absurdity of the situation clearer in the Sadducees' minds. Matthew 22:26 is the briefest: things went likewise for the second and then "the third until the seventh." Mark 12:21b–22a says "and the third likewise; and the seven left no seed (οὐκ ἀφῆκαν σπέρμα, *ouk aphēkan sperma*)." Luke also speaks of the childlessness: οὐ κατέλιπον τέκνα (*ou katelipon tekna*, they did not leave children). **20:31**

The saga ends tragically with the wife's death and thus an heirless family. Seven husbands, one wife, and no children form the backdrop for their question to Jesus. Matthew 22:27 agrees almost exactly with Luke, except he says "last of all," lacks καί (*kai*, and), and differs in word order (ὕστερον δὲ πάντων ἀπέθανεν ἡ γυνή, *hysteron de pantōn apethanen hē gynē*, last of all, the wife died). Mark 12:22b agrees except that he starts with a different term for "last of all" and has a distinct word order (ἔσχατον πάντων καὶ ἡ γυνὴ ἀπέθανεν, *eschaton pantōn kai hē gynē apethanen*, last of all, the wife died). Once again, each writer, while saying the same thing, has done so with some variation of wording. **20:32**

---

5. Several minor textual variants in this verse reflect harmonization and are secondary.

iii. The Question (20:33)

20:33 So the question comes (οὖν [*oun*, therefore] indicates the matter's conclusion and summation): Whose wife will this woman become in the afterlife, since she has a house full of candidates? The question has many suppositions behind it. First, it assumes that the afterlife is seen as very much like this life. Second, the marriage relationship in that life will be monogamous as in this life. Third, the absurdity of the woman's dilemma is designed to illustrate the futility of a resurrection hope. In fact, the Sadducees ask the question with confidence that no adequate answer exists; they think they have Jesus caught. Given that this wife had seven husbands in this life, how can she possibly have only one in the afterlife?

The parallels exhibit the same variations as elsewhere. Matthew 22:28 reads, "In the resurrection, therefore, to which of the seven will she be a wife? For they all had her." Mark 12:23 reads, "In the resurrection, when they are resurrected, whose wife will she be? For the seven had her as wife." Mark and Luke agree verbally on the brief explanation after the question, while Matthew and Mark agree on the first verb (ἔσται, *estai*), where Luke has γίνεται (*ginetai*). Mark and Luke mention the seven, while Matthew refers to "all" having had her as wife.

c. Jesus' Reply: Resurrection Is Different (20:34–38)
i. Answer: This Life Is Not like the Next (20:34–36)

20:34 Jesus' reply contrasts two ages. This contrast removes the dilemma, for the current age is not like the next. The resurrection is a sufficiently distinct reality that the Sadducees' question does not apply. Life in this age is indicated by the reference to οἱ υἱοὶ τοῦ αἰῶνος τούτου (*hoi huioi tou aiōnos toutou*, the sons of this age; BAGD 27 §2a; BAA 53 §2a; Luke 16:8). Jesus says that in this age the realities of preresurrection life are that "men marry and [women] are given in marriage."

Luke's version is much shorter than the parallels, for he lacks the rebukes about being wrong, not understanding the Scriptures, and God's power—all of which are in Matt. 22:29 = Mark 12:24. (He also lacks a rebuke in Luke 20:38, where the parallels have one.) Matthew and Mark move immediately from the rebuke to discussing life in the coming age. Luke's reference to the current age is unique. He may be influenced by an additional source here or perhaps he brings out the implied contrast more explicitly.

20:35 In making his main point—after the resurrection, relationships change—Jesus makes two more points. First, everyone does not qualify for life after the resurrection. That some will be accounted worthy of that age (οἱ δὲ καταξιωθέντες τοῦ αἰῶνος ἐκείνου, *hoi de* *kataxiōthentes tou aiōnos ekeinou*) shows that some will be excluded from blessing in the afterlife (καταξιόω, *kataxioō*, to consider worthy; BAGD 415; BAA 844; elsewhere in the NT only at Acts 5:41 and 2 Thess. 1:5).[6] The reference to "that age" is unique to the NT (Plummer 1896: 469; SB 2:254–55; Foerster, *TDNT* 1:380) and may contain a veiled warning. Other texts make clear that all will be resurrected, but not all will share in the resurrected new life (Matt. 22:31; John 5:28–29; Rom. 1:4; Heb. 6:2; Rev. 20; 1 Enoch 91.10; 92.3; 103.3–4). Luke tends to speak only of the resurrection of the just in his Gospel (14:14), a focus that enhances the picture of potential exclusion. But Luke is aware of a universal judgment (Acts 17:32; 23:6; 24:21; 26:23), which presupposes a universal resurrection. These Acts texts stand against the view that Luke knows only a resurrection for the just and thus created this unique expression in this pericope (see also Acts 13:46 and 2 Thess. 1:5).

Jesus' second point is that marrying and getting married are not a part of that future existence. Life in the coming age is different from life in this age, as far as marriage is concerned. Marriage (i.e., children and families) is no longer necessary since people no longer die (Luke 20:36). Life takes on a new order in which the need for marriage does not exist. This point makes the Sadducees' question about spouses irrelevant. The question that was supposed to show the absurdity of resurrection now becomes moot. Jesus has turned the tables on his examiners.

Luke agrees verbally with Matt. 22:30 = Mark 12:25 on the discussion of not marrying or being married. Luke's reference to being able to attain that age is unique to him, but his meaning does not differ from Matthew or Mark. Mark speaks of what happens "when they are resurrected from the dead," while Matthew says "for in the resurrection of the dead." Both Matthew and Mark use the conjunction γάρ (*gar*, for) to show that Jesus' remark about the afterlife explains why he rebuked the questioners' lack of understanding about the afterlife and the Scriptures. Luke lacks this rebuke.

20:36 Jesus explains why (γάρ, *gar*, for) marriage is no longer present: there is no longer any death. Those who attain resurrection are like angels (Ellis 1974: 236). Judaism held that angels do not need food or marriage (Creed 1930: 249; Ernst 1977: 544–45; Marshall 1978: 741–42; 1 Enoch 15.6; 51.4; 104.4–6; Wis. 5:5, 15–16; 2 Bar. 51.10; 1QH 3.21–23; 6:13; 1Q28b [= 1QSb] 4.24–28). By comparing the resurrection to angels, Jesus strikes at another doctrine that the Sadducees denied—the reality of angels (Danker 1988: 323; Acts 23:8). The

---

6. On being worthy of a place in the future world, see *b. Ber.* 28b, 51a; *y. Ber.* 11d (7.6) (= Neusner et al. 1982–93: 1.276).

resurrected are immortal, and relationships in that age are different from relationships in this age (on the change in body, see 1 Cor. 15:52). Those resurrected into new life will be "sons of God" and "sons of the resurrection" (Luke 6:35; Schweizer, *TDNT* 8:347–49, 355),[7] which is another way to say that they participate in the age to come and have an immortal life (Tiede 1988: 349). Since marriage is no longer necessary in the resurrection, the dilemma posed by multiple husbands disappears. The question is an absurdity, not because resurrection is a problem, but because the Sadducean understanding of resurrection is grounded too much in life as it is now. The afterlife is a different and much greater kind of existence. In the next life God the Father is the "parent," so other parental relationships are unnecessary (Danker 1988: 323).

Luke is longer at this point than the parallels. Matthew 22:30 = Mark 12:25 simply notes that those in the resurrection are "like angels (ὡς ἄγγελοι, *hōs angeloi*) in heaven." Luke has ἰσάγγελοι (*isangeloi*, angel-like), a NT *hapax legomenon*. Except for word order and the number of the phrase "in the heavens," Matthew and Mark agree verbally. Luke alone mentions that the raised do not die and that they are sons of God and resurrection.

ii. Scripture Proof (20:37)

20:37 The argument advances further. Jesus has dealt with the Sadducees' question, but there is still one issue that needs to be addressed. Jesus wants to make sure that the Sadducees understand that resurrection is a scriptural teaching. Though he could have appealed to a prophetic passage like Dan. 12:2, Jesus opts for a text from the Pentateuch because the Sadducees held the Torah in highest regard. A text from that portion of Scripture would be most persuasive for them. Working with their presuppositions he makes his argument. Jesus begins his elaboration with the direct statement that the dead are raised, which he says Moses revealed (μηνύω, *mēnyō*; BAGD 519; BAA 1051; elsewhere in the NT only at John 11:57; Acts 23:30; 1 Cor. 10:28).[8] Since the biblical text was divided into chapters and verses long after Jesus' time, he refers to the major event in the OT passage: ἐπὶ τῆς βάτου (*epi tēs batou*, at the bush), that is, in the passage about the burning bush (Exod. 3:2–6).

Jesus introduces the passage with the formula ὡς λέγει (*hōs legei*, as he says), which Ellis (1974: 237) argues should be translated, "It says." Luke, however, often uses the prophet or other OT writers as

---

7. On the sons of God as angels, see Job 1:6; 38:7; Ps. 29:1; 89:6 [89:7 MT].

8. For this type of generalized reference to a section of Scripture, see 2 Sam. 1:18; Mark 12:26; Rom. 11:2.

the subject in this and similar expressions, so "he says" is more likely (Luke 20:42; Acts 2:25, 34; 7:48; 8:34; Fitzmyer 1985: 1306). Jesus is citing Scripture where God actually speaks, as the parallels in Matt. 22:31–32 = Mark 12:26 make clear. God announced his message through the angel of the Lord at the burning bush: "I am the God of your father, the God of Abraham, the God of Isaac, and the God of Jacob." In other words, God is the God of promise and covenant (as the use of this verse in Acts 3:13 will also make clear). In the next verse Jesus will make the point that God is the God to the living, not the dead. This implies resurrection, since if the patriarchs are dead, then the God of promise cannot be their God (see the additional note). The point is that the patriarchs are not dead—and neither are God's promises to them. For the promises to the patriarchs to come to pass and for God to still be their God, resurrection must be a reality.

The parallels are similar, yet display their characteristic variation. Matthew 22:31–32 = Mark 12:26 introduces the citation with the phrase, "Have you not read?"—a rhetorical rebuke that means, "Do you not understand what you have read?" Matthew starts the verse by saying, "Now concerning the resurrection." Mark alone notes the locale specifically is in the book of Moses. Matthew and Mark note that the speaker is God and cite the passage in its first-person form. Rather than citing the passage, Luke summarizes it without a first-person reference. Each writer introduces the citation with verbal variation: Matthew has λέγοντος (*legontos*, saying), Mark has εἶπεν (*eipen*, he said) and λέγων (*legōn*, saying), while Luke has the present λέγει (*legei*) translated as a past ("he said"). The same kind of variation occurs again in Luke 20:42, suggesting perhaps the writers' stylistic preferences.

iii. Conclusion: The God of Promise Is the God of the Living (20:38)

Jesus supplies the explanation: God relates to the living and not the **20:38** dead. If God speaks of himself as the God of Abraham, then Abraham still exists. If he is the God of Isaac and Jacob, then they still exist (Ernst 1977: 545; Marshall 1978: 743). If the patriarchs are alive or are to experience the promise, they must be raised or will be raised. The additional explanation is that all live "to him" or "before him" (BDF §192). All life exists in relationship to the living God. The sovereign God is responsible for life (Acts 17:28; Rom. 11:36; Col. 1:16; 3:3–4; 2 Cor. 5:1–10; 1 Pet. 3:18; 4:6; 4 Macc. 16:25; Luce 1933: 316; Creed 1930: 250; Danker 1988: 324). In fact, all life takes place in his power, whether current life or the life to come. In addition, once one knows God, one has everlasting life. Contextually, the reference is to the resurrection, not to the Pauline concept of life "in Christ" (against Ellis 1974: 237, with Marshall 1978: 743).[9]

Matthew 22:32b = Mark 12:27a also notes that God is the God of the living and not the dead. The only difference in the three accounts is word order: Luke starts with θεός (*theos*, God), while Matthew and Mark agree verbally and start with οὐκ ἔστιν (*ouk estin*, is not). Only Luke remarks that all live for God. As Acts 17:22–31 shows, Luke loves to stress God's universal authority, because he emphasizes the Gentile mission (so also Acts 10:34–43).

d. The Scribes' Response (20:39)

20:39 Jesus' reply receives admiration from the scribes, who supported the Pharisees and shared their belief in resurrection. Paul will make a similar argument in Acts 23:6–7 with similar results (Creed 1930: 250). Some of them express their approval and note that Jesus has answered well, that is, correctly in their judgment. The fragile coalition against Jesus, at least on this theological point, is coming apart. There will be no success with this approach. Mark lacks this response. Matthew 22:33 remarks that the crowd was astonished when they heard Jesus' teaching. The point reflects approval, but there is also a note of marvel at Jesus' response. Once again the attempt to trap and embarrass Jesus fails.

e. Conclusion (20:40)

20:40 Luke notes that Jesus silences his opponents. "They" no longer dare to ask him questions. Another way will have to be found. Jesus' wisdom and knowledge are too much for them. Jesus is in control. The "they" of this verse is intentionally broad. Every possible group has taken a shot at Jesus and failed: Pharisees, nationalists, scribes, Sadducees, leaders of the people. On the topics of ministry, politics, and theology, Jesus has prevailed. There is nothing else they wish to raise before him publicly. Each encounter has left Jesus in the position of knowledge and authority. Rather than continue to confront him, they must withdraw. Jesus is too much in control of himself and his theology, so they do not dare to ask any more questions. The effect of these encounters is clear: who can guide the people in God's way, the Jewish leadership or Jesus? The wise teacher has confounded the leaders with his answers and has shown himself knowledgeable (Wis. 8:12; Danker 1988: 324).

---

9. Some in Judaism expressed the view that the patriarchs lived with God and the pious (2 Macc. 6–7; 4 Macc. 7:8–19), which is similar to the image of Abraham's bosom in Luke 16:22–23.

This remark about silencing opponents is unique to Luke, though Matt. 22:46 = Mark 12:34 makes a similar point in a summary that follows an additional dialogue over the great commandment (Matt. 22:34–40 = Mark 12:28–34). Luke lacks such an exchange here, but his form of the summary looks like Mark. Luke has a similar teaching about the great commandment in Luke 10:25–28, so he may have omitted such an account here to avoid repetition. The Matthean remark follows not only the discussion on the greatest commandment, but also Jesus' question about Messiah being David's son (Matt. 22:41–45), Luke's next pericope. Each writer summarizes Jesus' success at the point they choose.

Summary

In Luke 20:27–40 a third set of opponents attempts to take on Jesus. The Sadducees fail to trap Jesus on the doctrine of the resurrection. This passage has two major functions. First, it shows how yet another wing of Judaism fails to trap Jesus. The official faith cannot catch him. Whether personal, political, or theological in nature, the challenge to Jesus shows that he is in control. He is the teacher. Though the leadership had hoped to make Jesus stumble, it is clear that they will not trap him theologically. The reader is to see Jesus' character and superiority.

Second, Jesus endorses the resurrection and thereby sets up the hope that is central to faith in him. Such a teaching is especially important to God's plan and to a Gentile audience, who struggled with the concept of life after death. Jesus' resurrection is neither philosophical sophistry nor wishful thinking. Resurrection into an afterlife where one will face God and be evaluated by him is not the illusion of a mind that cannot face death's finality. All must be assured that the resurrection is the teaching of Scripture and Jesus. The work associated with resurrection is at the center of Christian belief. Resurrection is a reality, and its presence should affect how we see this world and live in it. As such, the pericope represents an endorsement of a fundamental doctrine of hope.

The afterlife is different, but it is real. All will answer to God, and only some will be found worthy. Sadducean doubt about resurrection will not do. Resurrection is God's promise. It must be faced as a fundamental reality of existence. It is a joyous thing to fall into the hands of the living God, if one knows him. In the afterlife, one need not wrestle with determining spouses, since the afterlife is about knowing God.

Additional Notes

20:27. The UBS–NA text brackets part of a word: [ἀντι]λέγοντες (contesting or denying), read by A, W, family 13, and Byz. Many manuscripts (ℵ, B,

C, D, L, N, Θ, family 1) read λέγοντες (saying). The longer term is adopted (with some doubt) as the more difficult reading by UBS–NA (Metzger 1975: 171–72).

20:27. The genitive Σαδδουκαίων (of the Sadducees) logically refers to "those who contested" (οἱ ἀντιλέγοντες), since all Sadducees denied this doctrine, but the syntax of the cases is odd. It probably refers grammatically to τινες (some).

20:28. Some grammatical points in this verse require explanation. (1) The levirate law is introduced with ἐάν (if), a third-class condition: "If this happens, and we are not saying that it will, . . ."—almost with the force of a temporal idea: "If and when" a brother dies. (2) The combination ἵνα λάβῃ (let him take) probably has imperatival force (e.g., Eph. 5:33; BDF §470.1; Marshall 1978: 739). (3) The two uses of αὐτοῦ (his) are unclear. Most likely, the first αὐτοῦ refers to the brother who died, while the second refers to the brother who marries and takes the woman as "his" wife.

20:30. The grammatical difficulty of the delayed verb with a distinct number produced a textual variant to smooth out the grammar: καὶ ἔλαβεν ὁ δεύτερος τὴν γυναῖκα καὶ οὗτος ἀπέθανεν ἄτεκνος (the second took the wife and this one died childless), read by A, W, family 1, family 13, and Byz. The reading in UBS–NA is clearly the more difficult reading and hence original.

20:32. Ὕστερον δὲ πάντων ἀπέθανεν καὶ ἡ γυνή (but last of all the wife died also) is most likely secondary because its external attestation is weak (A, W, Θ, Byz) and some of the terms and word order look like assimilation to Matt. 22:27. There is no difference in sense between the options.

20:33. There is some question whether ἡ γυνή (the wife) is present in the first phrase, as only B and L contain it. Other manuscripts lack it, but its absence in the Synoptic parallels makes its presence here hard to explain. UBS–NA retains the term, but the original reading is likely found in ℵ², A, D, W, Θ, family 1, family 13 and Byz: οὖν ἐν τῇ ἀναστάσει (therefore in the resurrection . . .).

20:33. Does Luke use ἔσται (will be; ℵ, D, L, Θ, Ψ, family 1, 33), as the parallels do, or γίνεται (becomes; A, B, W, family 13, Byz)? The UBS–NA text reads the unique γίνεται on the likely premise that it is hard to explain if ἔσται is original. Fitzmyer 1985: 1305 opts for ἔσται. The choice does not alter the sense.

20:34. Multiple variations in the verbs for "giving birth" attest to their secondary character. Even though manuscript support is thin, the logic does fit the ancient view of marriage: why marry if one no longer gives birth (Creed 1930: 249; Fitzmyer 1985: 1305; Marshall 1978: 741)?

20:37. Jesus' use of Exod. 3:6 is more than an appeal to Abraham and the other patriarchs being alive at his time. He presses ἔστιν (is) in 20:38 to imply that to be alive the patriarchs must be raised. Ellis (1974: 235–36) and Marshall (1978: 742–43) note that an appeal only to the immortality of the patriarchs suffers from Greek dualism that separates the body and soul in eternity, which is not a part of NT thinking, since it makes resurrection unnecessary. Ellis's denial of the patriarchs' present, living existence in some form is not valid, however, given 20:38b (cf. 4 Macc. 7:19). Jesus' point is either that the patriarchs are already raised or that their current existence awaiting resurrection is some way allows God to call himself their God even after their death. Numerous texts in Judaism speak of the afterlife (2 Macc. 7:9; Jub. 23.31; 1 Enoch 91.10; 92.3; 103.3–4) or immortality (Wis. 1:15; 3:4; 8:13; 15:3; 4 Macc. 14:5). For a defense of the immortality-only view, see Fitzmyer (1985: 1301). Another hint of the hope of resurrection might be implied in the OT phrase *gathered to the fathers*, which describes what happens to the dead (Gen. 49:29). It is likely that the phrase suggested resurrection in the first century. The image of "Abraham's bosom" is also a part of this expectation (Luke 16:22–23). The expression *God of Abraham* is another way to say the "God of promise" (Acts 3:13; *Shemoneh Esreh* [Eighteen Benedictions] no. 1 [= Schürer 1973–87: 2.456, 460]).

6. Jesus' Question about Messiah (20:41–44)
7. Jesus' Condemnation of the Scribes (20:45–47)
8. Counterexample: The Widow Who Gave All (21:1–4)

Three closely related pericopes are treated together since they represent Jesus' counterreplies to the leadership (Schweizer 1984: 308–9). The unfortunate chapter break between 20:47 and 21:1 obscures their unity. Jesus' first reply is theological and centers on the title *Messiah* used in Ps. 110:1 (Luke 20:41–44). The second reply is a warning to not be like the scribes, who like to draw attention to themselves and love to be honored (20:45–47). The third discusses the counterexample of positive piety provided by the poor widow, who pictures someone ready to give all for God (21:1–4).

Discussing Ps. 110, the first subunit is a crucial text about Messiah's identity. Virtually every detail is debated. The resolution of four key questions awaits the exegesis:

1. What is Jesus' point (Luce 1933: 316–17; Fitzmyer 1985: 1310–13; Marshall 1978: 744–46)? Is he denying Davidic sonship for Messiah (Klausner 1925: 320) or claiming that messiahship transcends Davidic sonship (so most, though differently nuanced)? Is he making a point about Davidic sonship *and* about the concept of Lord?[1] Given the centrality of the title *Lord*, what does it mean in this context?
2. How does the question relate to messianic expectations in first-century Judaism? Was there a strong Davidic expectation among some Jews? If so, what form did it take?
3. Was Ps. 110 seen as a messianic text in ancient Judaism? Since messianic interpretations of the passage were apparently lacking in the first century (Hay 1973: 21–26), it is important to determine how the psalm was originally viewed

1. Jesus' question is formed like a rabbinic paradox, where two things are opposed to one another and yet both are true; Daube 1956: 158–63.

and how it was seen in the Judaism of Jesus' time. What is the relationship between these two views? Was its messianic thrust suppressed (as many suggest) or is Jesus responsible for the association (as Fitzmyer 1985: 131 argues)?

4. Did the wordplay on "Lord" originate in Aramaic with Jesus or was it a development of the later church? This question also influences the issue of authenticity: does the idea expressed here go back to Jesus or is it a later creation of the church as many claim (see Fitzmyer 1985: 1310; Marshall 1978: 745–46; Bock 1987: 130–32, 331–34)?

These issues need careful treatment before the passage's meaning can be developed. There is no doubt, however, that Jesus is raising a theological dilemma, much like the one the Sadducees raised on resurrection (20:27–40). It is also clear that the answer centers on the concept of Lord, a title that came to have major christological force in the church. Beyond the issue of Jesus' authority, there is the need for ethical sensitivity from the disciples. Ironically, a widow, not the scribes, shows the way. She loves God by giving of her life rather than drawing attention to herself and taking advantage of others.

Sources and Historicity (20:41–44)

The Synoptic parallels to Luke 20:41–44 are Matt. 22:41–46 = Mark 12:35–37a (Aland 1985: §283). Luke has the most condensed version, not mentioning the temple teaching, the scribes, or the Spirit's role in the psalm text (Fitzmyer 1985: 1309). Preceding this account, Luke lacks the controversy over eternal life and the great commandment (Mark 12:28–34 = Matt. 22:34–40), which he may have omitted since he has a similar account in Luke 10:25–28.[2]

The issues tied to the authenticity of this key passage are covered in detail in the exegesis. The Jesus Seminar (Funk and Hoover 1993: 380) rejects the passage's authenticity, printing the whole of it in black type and arguing that Ps. 110:1 was a favorite text of the early church, that the citation method was unlike Jesus', and that the messianic concern the text raises was not a topic that Jesus addressed (see also Hahn 1969: 104–5 and the exegesis of 20:42b–43). The use of Ps. 110, however, is so widely attested in the early church that one must ask, What made for this central role? The most natural explanation is that it was rooted in Jesus' teaching. Nolland (1993b: 970–72) correctly observes that conclusions here are in-

---

2. On the relationship of Luke 10:25–28 to Matt. 22:34–40 and Mark 12:28–34, see the introduction to Luke 10:25–37.

fluenced by how one sees the development of Christology in the church: was it essentially rooted in Jesus or in later reflection? Nolland notes eight approaches to the passage, ranging from a denial of Davidic descent by Jesus (or its importance) to a view that Jesus is pressing his audience to see beyond the son-of-David title. Nolland opts for a nonmessianic reading of the text, thinking that Jesus is simply trying to provoke thoughts about how God will ultimately intervene for his people, but this approach limits the text's force too much. The dispute is about the authority of the one through whom God works. Given the triumphal entry, the clear implication is that Jesus is in view. But the very indirectness of the link speaks for authenticity. Surely the early church would not have been so vague had it created the text. The use of Scripture is like that in 20:27–40 (see the discussion of historicity of that text). In sum, the controversy has roots that go back to Jesus, which explains the subsequent importance of Ps. 110 in the early church.

Sources and Historicity (20:45–47)

The Synoptic parallels to Luke 20:45–47 are Mark 12:37b–40 = Matt. 23:1–36 (Aland 1985: §284), the latter being a long discourse in which Jesus condemns the entire Jewish leadership (Luke has a similar condemnation at a meal in 11:37–54).[3] Luke 20:45–47 is a blanket condemnation of the scribes, reminiscent of prophetic condemnations (Job 22:9; 24:3; Ezek. 22:7; Isa. 1:23; 10:2; Fitzmyer 1985: 1317; Stählin, *TDNT* 9:449). There is no historical doubt that Jesus expressed such displeasure with the leadership. It was part of what led them to want to silence him. The Jesus Seminar (Funk and Hoover 1993: 380) treats the remarks of 20:46 as substantially authentic (pink type) and 20:47 as perhaps related to Jesus' teaching (gray type). The seminar thus accepts Jesus' condemnation of the scribes, but regards 20:47 as too vindictive for him. But such condemnation is like the prophets of old and as such sets an important base for Jesus' rebuke (see the historicity discussion in 11:37–54). This rebuke is authentic.

Sources and Historicity (21:1–4)

The Synoptic parallel to Luke 21:1–4 is Mark 12:41–44 (Aland 1985: §286). The widow's sacrificial piety contrasts with the leadership's proud piety in the previous subunit, and Jesus commends her act as the example to follow. The passage's exact force is a matter of debate (see A. Wright 1982). Using a widow as an example is in character with Jesus' general ministry, which noted those people that the culture tended to ignore.

---

3. On the relationship of Luke 11:37–54 to Matt. 23:1–36, see the introduction to Luke 11:37–54.

The Jesus Seminar (Funk and Hoover 1993: 381) sees only a tangential connection to Jesus in this subunit, printing 21:3–4 in gray type. The seminar recognizes that the tone of the event fits Jesus, but rejects his praise of the widow because it has rabbinic and Buddhist parallels and because, the seminar assumes, such an account would not likely have been passed on in oral form. (On the rabbinic and Buddhist parallels, see Fitzmyer 1985: 1320.) Everything about the account's concerns for people of low social status and about sacrifice coheres with the historical Jesus (Nolland 1993b: 978). A memorable event in pronouncement form is precisely how such an event would be passed on orally.

The three accounts together show that the way to God is not the leaders' way: they cannot offer any reply about Messiah, they suffer from pride, and they lack the ability to give sacrificially. God's way must be found on another road, through other examples.

Luke 20:41–44 is either a pronouncement or, more likely, a saying of Jesus, since there is no real dialogue in the passage (Fitzmyer 1985: 1309; Bultmann 1963: 66, 136–37; Berger 1984: 81). Luke 20:45–47 contains a warning saying (Fitzmyer 1985: 1316–17; Bultmann 1963: 113–14; Berger 1984: 144). Luke 21:1–4 is a pronouncement or perhaps a saying (Fitzmyer 1985: 1320; Bultmann 1963: 32–33; Berger 1984: 81), since dialogue is again lacking.

The outline of Luke 20:41–21:4 is as follows:

6. Jesus' question about Messiah (20:41–44)
    a. Question (20:41)
    b. Citation of Psalm 110:1 (20:42–43)
    c. Question restated: how is he son, if he is Lord? (20:44)
7. Jesus' condemnation of the scribes (20:45–47)
    a. Warning: beware of the scribes (20:45–47a)
    b. Fate of the scribes (20:47b)
8. Counterexample: the widow who gave all (21:1–4)
    a. The widow's act observed (21:1–2)
    b. Jesus' comment: the widow's act commended as
        sacrificial giving (21:3–4)

The first subunit focuses on Messiah. Jesus places Davidic sonship beside the mention of Messiah as Lord and asks which is the central concept. Of course, Lord is. In warning about the scribes, Jesus condemns pride, using the widow's simple, almost unnoticed, piety as a contrast. Here is a woman who gives all and receives commendation for sacrificial giving as a model of quiet faithfulness. The contrast to the leaders' public parading could not be greater.

Exegesis and Exposition

20:41And he said to them, "How do they say that Christ is David's son? 42For David himself said in the Book of Psalms, 'The Lord said to my Lord, "Sit at my right hand, 43until I make your enemies a footstool for your feet."' 44David thus calls him Lord, and how is he his son?"

45And while all the people were hearing, he said to ⌐his disciples⌐, 46"Beware of the scribes, those who wish to walk in long robes and love greetings in the marketplace and the first seats in the synagogue and the first seats at dinners, 47who devour widows' houses and under pretext pray long. They will receive greater condemnation."

21:1And looking up, he saw the rich putting their gifts into the treasury. 2And he saw a certain poor widow put in two copper coins. 3And he said, "Truly, I say to you that this widow has put in more than all of them. 4For all of these contributed into ⌐the gifts for God⌐ from their abundance, but she cast all the life that she had from her poverty."

6. Jesus' Question about Messiah (20:41–44)
a. Question (20:41)

20:41 In the Lucan context, Jesus' question is probably directed to the scribes (20:39), though he may be speaking to all. He wants to initiate reflection about Messiah (Neugebauer 1974–75: 81–82). The third-person question πῶς λέγουσιν (*pōs legousin*, how do they say?) is unique to Luke and Mark (Plummer 1896: 472). The force is, "Why do they say. . . ?" or, "With what right do they say. . . ?" (this idiom is also in John 8:33; 14:9; 1 Cor. 15:12). Jesus refers to the traditional teaching that Messiah will be David's son, a teaching with roots in the OT hope of a regal deliverer (2 Sam. 7; Ps. 89:29–37 [89:30–38 MT]; Isa. 9:5–7 [9:4–6 MT]; 11:1–10; Jer. 23:5–8; 33:14–26; Mic. 5:2 [5:1 MT]; Ezek. 34:23–24; David is mentioned in Luke 1:27, 32, 69; 2:4, 11; 3:31; 6:3; 18:38–39; Acts 2:25–27). Such hope became more explicit in later Judaism (Ps. Sol. 17.21–25; 4Q174 [= 4QFlor] 1.11–13; 4QPBless 4; 2 Esdr. [= 4 Ezra] 12:32; *Shemoneh Esreh* [Eighteen Benedictions] no. 14 [= Schürer 1973–87: 2.461]; Marshall 1978: 747; Tiede 1988: 351; Lohse, *TDNT* 8:480–82). This regal and often political hope dominated much of first-century Judaism, though it was not the only conception of Messiah.[4] So Jesus starts here on familiar ground. But is this Davidic emphasis the whole story about Messiah?

In Matt. 22:41 the question is directed at the Pharisees. In Mark 12:35 Jesus asks the question as he teaches in the temple, but specifies no audience. Matthew asks the Pharisees directly what they

---

4. Judaism also had hopes of priestly messianic figures; see 1QS 9.11 and Neusner, Green, and Frerichs 1987.

think about Messiah, while Mark asks why the scribes teach that the Messiah is David's son. The dialogue in these Gospels makes the account's form more like a pronouncement account than a mere saying of Jesus. Each Gospel asks essentially the same question, though Luke has the most compact version. The passage illustrates the tradition's fluidity while maintaining the basic point, a common trait in pericopes dealing with Jesus' last week.

b. Citation of Psalm 110:1 (20:42–43)

Jesus sets up and then cites Ps. 110:1, noting that David spoke the words he will cite in the psalm (Luke cites or mentions the Book of Psalms in Luke 24:44; Acts 1:20; 4:25; 13:33; Creed 1930: 251; Marshall 1978: 747). Luke alone notes that the Book of Psalms contains these words, for he is fond of specifying a text's locale (Luke 20:37; Acts 13:33, 35). Mark 12:36 says that David spoke "in the Holy Spirit" (ἐν τῷ πνεύματι τῷ ἁγίῳ, en tō pneumati tō hagiō), while Matt. 22:43 says, "How did David in the Spirit (ἐν πνεύματι, en pneumati) call him Lord, saying. . . ?" Luke's verb for saying is his frequent present tense with past sense, λέγει (legei, he said), while Mark uses εἶπεν (eipen, he said) and Matthew has another present tense with past sense, καλεῖ (kalei, he called). David, of course, is the son of Jesse and the recipient of the Davidic covenant (1 Sam. 16:10–11; 17:12; 2 Sam. 7:8–16; 1 Chron. 2:13–15; Lohse, *TDNT* 8:478–82). Biblical and extrabiblical tradition held that David authored many psalms (1 Sam. 16:23; 2 Sam. 23:1; 1 Chron. 16:7; Fitzmyer 1985: 1314). For example, Qumran text 11QPs^a 27.2–11 says that through prophecy David uttered 3,600 psalms and many other compositions, for a total of 4,050 (DJD 4:48, 91–93). David's reputation as a songwriter was great in the first century.

20:42a

A great deal of energy has been spent arguing that Jesus' remark is not a declaration of the Davidic authorship of Ps. 110. In this view, the mention of David is like NT references to the Torah that go on to cite the Prophets, or it is a generic reference to David as the author of the Psalter.[5] In fact, it is often argued that the speaker in the psalm is a prophet and not David (Kraus 1989: 346–47). Another example of this phenomenon is frequently mentioned: in Acts 4:25 David is cited as the author of Ps. 2, but he is not mentioned in the MT as its author nor is there any superscription to refer to him.

Any position that sees a prophet speaking in Ps. 110 ignores the force of Jesus' argument, for there is no tension in the passage and his point is invalidated if David is not the speaker in Ps. 110:1 (so

---

5. Seeing a rhetorical argument, Plummer 1896: 472–73 holds that Jesus condescended to current opinions—a view that has changed little since Plummer wrote.

correctly Ellis 1974: 238). At a minimum, David must be the speaker of Ps. 110:1, even if he is represented by the prophet who addresses the king.[6] The phrase *my Lord* must mean David's Lord, or else the tension evaporates and Jesus' key messianological point is lost. In the first-century context this implies Davidic authorship of this psalm—especially of this utterance. It is conceivable, however, that one could see Ps. 110 in terms of David's inspired declaration about his descendant Solomon (Chisholm 1991: 271–72; Bateman 1992 [on the syntax of the verse and a possible historical setting]). David's declaration is recorded and passed on by a prophet under inspiration as a description of the Davidic family's regal hope. Even though this approach to Ps. 110 looks a little sophisticated, it cannot be ruled out because of the uncertain origin of the cultic materials of Israel and the possibility that this was a remark addressed to the king in the hopes that he would be the ideal ruler. If the psalm was used as part of the declaration of Davidic hope, it is possible that a prophet addressed it to the king as David's words, appropriately reflecting the great king's hope that his descendant would be a king worthy of the dynastic hope and thus fulfill God's promises.

Nonetheless, there is debate about the historical setting of Ps. 110 (see Kraus 1989: 346–47 for options), ranging from a date in David's time to various periods after David, including 141 B.C. in the Maccabean period.[7] For a setting in the Davidic period is the reference to the priesthood of Melchizedek, which looks to the Jebusite roots of Jerusalem, a reality that would be most prominent after the city's takeover by David (Kraus 1989: 347; Bock 1987: 129). Regardless of the origin, there is no doubt that in the first century the psalm is seen as Davidic, as the LXX superscription indicates. A Davidic connection is necessary to the argument and solidifies the regal connection and the messianic implications. Without this, Jesus has no point; this must be Jesus' view (Nolland 1993b: 973).

20:42b–43 The Synoptics agree exactly with the LXX form of Ps. 110:1 [109:1 LXX], except that ὁ (*ho*, the) is lacking before κύριος (*kyrios*, Lord) and Matt. 22:44 = Mark 12:36 has ὑποκάτω (*hypokatō*, under) where Luke and the LXX have ὑποπόδιον (*hypopodion*, footstool). The difference does not alter the sense. The citation's point depends on the answers to various other questions.

---

6. I am not sure that such a distinction is necessary, but it is a possible way to take the remark. For Jesus' argument to work, David must be regarded as the one who utters Ps. 110:1 or is the ultimate source of its report.

7. For example, Luce 1933: 317 favors the Maccabean date. Leaney 1958: 254–55 discusses it, but his position is less clear, though he does cite 1 Macc. 14:41 as conceptually parallel (i.e., its reference to the "governor and high priest forever"). See also Hardy 1945.

First is the meaning of the psalm, both in its original setting and in the first century. The psalm is rightly regarded as a royal psalm since it describes a king of Israel. Most regard it as a coronation psalm, though that context for the psalm is not explicitly stated. The psalm clearly depicts the king's authority and may be related to battle preparation. The language of the psalm is highly idealized. In Ps. 110 the king is a warrior-priest (a unique combination for the Psalter), who represents God on the earth.

France (1971: 166–67) challenges the classification of this text as a royal psalm on three grounds: (1) the language is not that of Davidic dynasty, (2) there is no royal terminology, and (3) the image of being seated at the right hand goes beyond royal-psalm imagery. France calls the psalm exclusively messianic, meaning that it refers only to Jesus. This classification is not really a rejection of the royal-psalm category, but makes it a specific kind of royal psalm, since a Davidite is still in view. Each of the points France raises can be questioned. Royal language is present throughout the psalm, especially in the remarks about the "scepter from Zion" (110:2) and the concept of "ruling over enemies" (110:2). Such references are typical references to the king, though more often it is God himself who is seen as King of Zion (Ps. 2:6; 72:1–7; 78:68; 89:25 [89:26 MT]; esp. Ps. 48).[8] The reference to priesthood in Ps. 110:4 has a natural point of contact with David in that it refers to the Jebusite ancestry of Jerusalemite kingship, a city that David conquered (Gen. 14; Kraus 1989: 347).[9]

More debated is the force of the "right hand" image. To sit at someone's right hand is an expression of the exercise of protection, power, and authority (Jer. 22:24, 30). It may also picture God's close presence or the locale of his blessings (Ps. 16:8, 11; 48:10 [48:11 MT]) or power (Ps. 17:7; 18:35 [18:36 MT]; 20:6 [20:7 MT]; 21:8 [21:9 MT]; 44:3 [44:4 MT]; 60:5 [60:7 MT]; 63:8 [63:9 MT]; 77:10 [77:11 MT]; 121:5). It is a common figure in the Psalms, with a close parallel being the picture of the queen standing at the king's right hand in Ps. 45:9 [45:10 MT] (cf. Ps. 109:31). What is unusual about the figure in the Psalter is the idea of someone sitting at the right hand. The image expresses the rule of the right-hand regal figure and a close connection with God. The Jeremiah parallel makes the association with the Israelite king clear enough, and it parallels the deifying language associated with the king of Ps. 45, who is clearly a human figure since that psalm portrays marriage, something Jesus never

8. The king of Israel is God's vice-regent on earth; 1 Chron. 29:23 (also Acts 2:30–36).

9. This detail causes many to see a preexilic origin for the psalm. Heb. 5–7 makes much of this point in the psalm.

did.[10] Sitting at the right hand also pictures rule in other narrative contexts (1 Kings 1:46; 2:12, 19; 1 Chron. 28:5; 29:23). Interestingly, these narrative OT passages refer to Solomon, the most natural near referent for Ps. 110, given that David is speaking about a king and is recognizing his authority to rule for God (on the regal force of this imagery in ancient culture, see Kraus 1989: 347–49). In fact, the psalm may well honor the Davidic promise and might have been uttered in the hope that this king would be the one who fulfills the ideals of kingship in the nation. As such, it pressed for a "greater David" to represent its fulfillment. Perhaps each king who ascended the throne or who represented the nation in battle was viewed with the hope that he might be the one so grandly described here. Regardless, this is a royal psalm.

The first verse of Ps. 110 makes three points: (1) the recognition of authority that David, the author-speaker, gives to this figure by acknowledging him as Lord, (2) the picture of this rule in the figure of sitting at the right hand, and (3) the declaration of the presence of his rule until all enemies are removed.[11] Though not addressed in Luke 20:41–44, Messiah rules in Ps. 110 until God finishes the job (1 Cor. 15:25–28). It is not a passive reign that manifests itself as the enemies are subdued, but the reign is in process until it is permanently established. In Luke 20:41–44, Jesus is only interested in the first point. David bows to this king's authority.[12]

Before developing Jesus' point, it is important to discuss how this psalm was seen in Judaism (Fitzmyer 1985: 1311). Up to the time of Jesus there is no indication that this text was read messianically, though it was read regally (T. Job 33.3; 1 Macc. 14:41; T. Levi 8.3; 18.1–3, 8, 12).[13] It is important to recall that the Messiah is a king, so regal passages would apply to him and describe his role; but the point is that the text was not seen in exclusively messianic terms. It is broad, not narrow. The absence of this messianic use of the psalm

10. For the hermeneutics involved in the use of the psalm, see the additional note on 20:42. For more on the use of the OT in the NT, see Bock 1985 and 1994d.

11. This last point is important, though Luke does not develop it here. This ruler is not idle as he sits at God's side. He reigns as God's vice-regent and engages in battle for him. The imagery is of an active rule. In denying the force of the NT application of this psalm, some argue that Jesus sits in heaven awaiting the time of his future rule. But Acts 2:30–36 appeals to Ps. 110:1 to show Jesus actively distributing benefits from the Father's side and ruling alongside of him from heaven. This is one point of application that Luke and the NT develop later. The defeat of enemies also shows that, in the consummation, foes will be totally vanquished. Jesus awaits this total victory. The psalm's imagery is rich, and so is its NT application to Jesus.

12. Additional points from this psalm are made in Luke 22:69 (and parallels); Acts 2:30–36; 7:55–56; 13:33–39; 1 Cor. 15:22–28; Eph. 1:19–23; Heb. 1:3–14; 5–7.

13. T. Levi 18 has a messianic flavor to it, but this is an Aaronic Messiah, a priestly Messiah; cf. 1QS 9.11.

leads many to speak of a Jewish suppression of the messianic use of the psalm, probably as a result of the text's importance to Christianity (SB 4:452–65; Hay 1973: 21–26; Callan 1982; Loader 1977–78: 199). Later Judaism saw the text referring to either Abraham or Messiah (Abraham in *b. Ned.* 32b and Lev. Rab. 25.6 on 19:23; both Messiah and Abraham in Midr. Ps. 110.1–4 on 110:1 [= Braude 1959: 2.205–6]). Given the nature of this evidence, Jesus' use of the psalm may be more focused than that of the Judaism of his era. But given that the psalm was understood royally, it would also apply to Messiah, so the narrowing of the referent is not shocking. If the text were true of the king, it would be especially true of Messiah. Of course, the Davidic roots of messianic kingship was a given in the OT and in much of Judaism in this period (Danker 1988: 325; Fitzmyer 1985: 1311; Ps. 89:3–4 [89:4–5 MT]; Isa. 9:7 [9:6 MT]; 11:1–2; Jer. 23:5; 30:9; Ps. Sol. 17–18 [esp. 17.21, 32]). It also should be noted that this regal figure is referred to in ideal terms. This is the Davidite king in his most ideal form, which of course is what Messiah is. In fact, only Messiah meets the ideal, which is why the passage is uniquely suited to him.

Jesus' point is simple enough: how is it that David can call a son, a descendant, by the title *Lord*? This is a significant act in a patriarchal society, where a son is *under* his father. The answer is not a denial of Davidic sonship, but rather an implication that Messiah as David's Lord transcends him. It recognizes the key authority that is ascribed to the Davidic heir—an authority that David acknowledges. So the key title to be associated with this important figure is *Lord*, not *son of David*.[14]

One question remains about the use of Ps. 110 in this setting. Many (e.g., Hahn 1969: 104–5) argue that the ambiguity of the term *Lord* is possible only in the early church. In this view, this text does not go back to Jesus but is the christological work of the early church since the remark assumes the use of the Septuagint, with its ambiguous use of the term κύριος (*kyrios*) for "Lord." There is no question that the Hebrew text of Ps. 110 clearly distinguishes between God and this figure; the terms are distinct in Hebrew: יהוה (*yhwh*, Yahweh) refers to God and אָדוֹן (*ʾādôn*, Lord) to this regal figure. But this argument overstates the case and ignores the first-century practice of rendering texts orally and not pronouncing the divine name יהוה. The ambiguity in the Greek text is thus possible in both Hebrew and Aramaic when the text is presented orally (Bock 1987: 130–31, 331; e.g., Fitzmyer 1985: 1312 suggests Aramaic אֲמַר מָרְיָא לְמָרִי [*ʾămar māryāʾ lĕmārî*, the Lord said to my lord]; see also Fitzmyer 1979b: 90, 120–27). This point is a key one, for it shows

---

14. More on this discussion appears in the exegesis of 20:44. For David as the speaker in the psalm, see the exegesis of 20:42a.

that Jesus is capable of making this remark in this setting. It is possible for him to raise this ambiguity. The point made about David's recognition of the descendant's authority applies, even if the ambiguity in the terms is not present. Jesus' point is that how can the great King David reflect such submission to a descendant? Who can be greater than Israel's great king? The listeners are left to ponder the conclusion. That point is made, even if Jesus did not pronounce the divine name. This saying is authentic and goes back to Jesus. The passage and this reading of it are a key starting point for OT christological reflection about who Jesus is.

It is important to note that in this passage Jesus does not develop the citation in terms of himself, nor does he explain it. He simply raises a theoretical question here about why the Messiah is referred to in this way. The answer and rationale of the dilemma is not really developed until Luke 22:69, so the explanation of the full significance of this passage must await that text. What is clear from Jesus' citation and the question he raises in 20:44 is that the Messiah has the high title *Lord* and his authority is acknowledged by the great king David. Jesus raises it as a thought to ponder and breaks new ground in the thinking about who Messiah is.

c. Question Restated: How Is He Son, If He Is Lord? (20:44)

20:44   Jesus restates his question. Πῶς (*pōs*, how) is really asking, "In what sense" is the Messiah David's son.[15] The idiom means that both assertions are true; but one needs qualification (Ellis 1974: 238; on this rabbinic antinomy, see n. 1). Given lordship, where does sonship stand? The obvious answer seems to be that it stands in some lesser place than lordship. The normal situation is that the father has authority over the son. But in this case, it is the reverse. In the psalm's original setting, this title would be a recognition of the authority of the king who had assumed the throne and received David's recognition. But what Jesus seems to be saying is that this title applies to Messiah as ideal King in a unique way, as recognition of a unique authority.[16] The details of how Jesus and the early church see this authority is found in Luke 22:69 and Acts 2:30–36 and 13:33–39 (also Heb. 1:4–13).

---

15. Grundmann 1963: 376 argues that the question's force is "*why* does one say. . . ?" But this could be taken erroneously as a denial of Davidic sonship, a view that goes back to D. F. Strauss (see Plummer 1896: 473). The interrogative πῶς is better understood to press for "in what manner?"

16. The usage here is typological-*prophetic*, since the psalm applies uniquely to Jesus on this point and there was awareness that the psalm applied to another figure. For an explanation of this classification, see the additional note on 20:42 and Bock 1994d: 110–12.

Attempts to argue that Jesus is denying a Davidic, messianic connection for himself here fails. Jesus clearly received this title, and the church openly proclaimed it. If he denied it, then why did the church insist on using it? Qumran gives evidence that Jewish communities could look for other types of Messiahs, so the idea of a Messiah who carried multiple titles is not foreign to Judaism. Also overstated are attempts to see an allusion to the Son of Man here. This connection can be argued for in Luke 22:69, but not here. The only issue here is the relationship of the titles *Christ* and *Son of David*.

Matthew 22:45 = Mark 12:37 also notes this question, with each wording the question slightly differently. Matthew asks, "If David calls him Lord, how is he his son?" Mark states the premise more directly, though in slightly different terms: "David himself says him to be Lord" (αὐτός [*autos*, himself] and λέγει [*legei*, says] are unique to Mark). Luke also states the premise more directly. Like Matthew, he uses καλεῖ (*kalei*, calls), but with a different word order: Δαυὶδ οὖν κύριον αὐτὸν καλεῖ (*Dauid oun kyrion auton kalei*, David therefore calls him Lord) versus Matthew's εἰ οὖν Δαυὶδ καλεῖ αὐτὸν κύριον (*ei oun Dauid kalei auton kyrion*, if therefore David calls him Lord). The question's form differs slightly: Mark has "from where (πόθεν, *pothen*) is he his son?" while Matthew and Luke ask the same question in differing word order: Luke has πῶς αὐτοῦ υἱός ἐστιν (*pōs autou huios estin*, how is he his son?), and Matthew has πῶς υἱὸς αὐτοῦ ἐστιν. Again, despite differences, the point is the same.

7. Jesus' Condemnation of the Scribes (20:45–47)
a. Warning: Beware of the Scribes (20:45–47a)

20:45 With the theological controversies behind him, Jesus changes his topic. The final confrontation with the leadership now causes him to warn his disciples, within earshot of his other listeners. Jesus is not shy about criticizing the leadership; in fact, his remarks sound prophetic (note also 12:1; 19:39–42; 20:19; Plummer 1896: 474 cites Ezek. 22:25 as parallel). What Jesus is about to say requires reflection.

Matthew 23:1 begins Jesus' long discourse of condemnation against the leadership, a discourse that Luke lacks, probably because he already noted a similar condemnation in 11:37–54. Matthew notes that Jesus spoke to the crowd and the disciples. Mark 12:37b–40 has a short summary condemnation passage like that in Luke. In making the transition from the Ps. 110 debate to this condemnation, Mark notes that the "great crowd" (πολὺς ὄχλος, *polys ochlos*) heard Jesus gladly. Luke refers again to "all the people" (παντὸς τοῦ λαοῦ, *pantos tou laou*), last mentioned in Luke 20:26.

The freedom of expression that the Synoptics take in recounting the Jerusalem events again shows itself in this material, which is expressed in a variety of terms.

20:46 Jesus offers a warning about the scribes and exhorts his disciples not to imitate their love for popularity. Scribes loved to be the center of attention, in the middle of popular adulation. In this context, the present tense προσέχετε (*prosechete*, beware constantly) calls for a vigilant effort not to follow the scribes' example. This warning is like that in 12:1 against the Pharisees, except that here Jesus describes four things that scribes do in an effort to be popular:

1. They wish to walk in long robes (στολή, *stolē*). Their long, flowing robe was part of a fancy and expensive wardrobe. A scribe's robe had a long mantle reaching to the feet and was decorated with long fringe. A στολή could refer to priestly robes (Josephus, *Antiquities* 3.7.1 §151; 11.4.2 §80; Fitzmyer 1985: 1317–18; Ellis 1974: 239; SB 2:31–33; Daube 1956: 125; Jeremias 1969: 244) as well as the gown that the prodigal son received from his father (Luke 15:22) and the robes of glorified believers (Rev. 6:11; Wilckens, *TDNT* 7:690; BAGD 769; BAA 1535). It is the ostentatious style of the scribes that Jesus here condemns (Marshall 1978: 750).
2. They love the attention that they receive at formal greetings in the marketplace. Extrabiblical material makes clear that rabbis and other religious authorities received special greetings in the marketplace. In fact, in the Talmud such greetings were required for teachers of the law (*y. Ber.* 4b [2.1] [= Neusner et al. 1982–93: 1.66]; Windisch, *TDNT* 1:498; SB 1:382 §f). Jesus had earlier rebuked Pharisees for this practice (Luke 11:43). The overlapping criticism may well suggest that the scribes are but a representation of a larger critique of Jewish leadership.
3. They desire the places of honor in the synagogue, the first seats (πρωτοκαθεδρία, *prōtokathedria*; BAGD 725; BAA 1451; elsewhere in the NT at Matt. 23:6; Mark 12:39; Luke 11:43 [also of the Pharisees]). These were probably the row of seats near the ark (Michaelis, *TDNT* 6:870–71). Jesus had addressed this problem earlier (11:43; Schrage, *TDNT* 7:820).
4. They desire the first seats at dinner (πρωτοκλισία, *prōtoklisia*; BAGD 725; BAA 1451; elsewhere in the NT at Matt. 23:6; Mark 12:39; Luke 14:7, 8). Jesus had earlier addressed this problem with his disciples in Luke 14:7–14 at the house of a Pharisee. As noted in the discussion there, in later Judaism these seats were probably at the center of a U-shaped table, nearest the host (SB 4:617–20). Regardless of the table's exact shape, it

was an honor to sit next to the host, and the scribes loved to have these seats.

Jesus warns that such pride is not something to respect or seek. The repeated wordplay on *first* (πρωτο-, *prōto-*) shows that the scribes are not worthy of emulation. It is clear from what Jesus says in the next two verses that God is not impressed with this approach. These criticisms of the scribes mirror Jesus' earlier criticisms in Luke 11:37–54 and 14:7–14. They show that the journey and the rebukes by Jesus have changed little. Israel is being divided by Jesus' ministry (2:34).

Luke matches Mark 12:38b–39 except for word order and a few distinct terms. Mark uses the verb βλέπετε (*blepete*, watch) and lacks the participle φιλούντων (*philountōn*, loving). Matthew 23:5b–7 makes a similar complaint, though in a different order: long fringes, place of honor at dinners, first seats in the synagogue, and greetings in the marketplace (in Luke's order: 1, 4, 3, 2). Matthew's wording is different, probably because it is part of a longer set of complaints.

Jesus develops the condemnation. In contrast to the scribes' self-focus stands their poor treatment of the needy and their hypocritical long prayers. Jesus pictures destruction when he speaks of the scribes "devouring" the houses of widows. They take from the group most in need and leave them devastated. The nature of this crime is not detailed, but four possibilities are suggested: (1) the temple authorities managed the property of widows dedicated to the temple in a way that took advantage of them (Ellis 1974: 239), (2) the scribes took advantage of widows' hospitality (Jeremias 1969: 114), (3) the scribes took homes as pledges of debts they knew could not be repaid (Leaney 1958: 256), or (4) they took fees for legal advise against the provisions of the law (Stählin, *TDNT* 9:445).[17] T. Moses 7.6 refers to the scribes' misuse of hospitality and calls them gluttons (cf. Ps. Sol. 4.11–13). The Talmud complained against those who managed a widow's estate and gave themselves a healthy fee (*b. Giṭ.* 52a–b; Marshall 1978: 750; Derrett 1972a; Nolland 1993b: 976 [plus a misuse of hospitality]). For the remarks' prophetic quality, one can look at Isa. 1:23; 10:2; Jer. 22:3–5; Ezek. 22:7, 29; Zech. 7:10–14; Mal. 3:5 (cf. Deut. 10:18; 24:17; 27:19; Job 22:9; 24:3; Ps. 68:5 [68:6 MT]; Danker 1988: 327; Fitzmyer 1985: 1317; Stählin, *TDNT* 9:446–48). Since Luke does not detail the problem, it is hard to be sure what is meant exactly. Fitzmyer is disturbed by the remark's broad, unqualified character, which he attributes to a later stage of the tradition, but surely a prophetic generalization is

20:47a

---

17. An opposite approach to widows is found in Acts 6:1–6; 1 Tim. 5; James 1:27.

present, where the broad address is intended to be representative, a point that fits the "mirroring" quality of this whole passage. This declaration works just as the woes of Luke 6:24–26 did. Not every rich person nor every leader is condemned, as Jesus' treatment of Zacchaeus shows (19:1–10) and as the description of Joseph of Arimathea indicates (23:50–51). Nonetheless, the tendencies within the group allow for such abuses. Nolland (1993b: 976) argues that the genitival reference to scribes in 20:46 can be read "the scribes, who like . . ." or "those scribes who like. . . ." If so, the critique is selective from the start, being aimed against only those who do these things. But the spirit of these remarks is perhaps too much like Luke 11:37–54 and 14:7–14 to think that we are dealing with a small group here.

Jesus goes on to describe scribal prayers as "given under pretext" (προφάσει, prophasei; BAGD 722; BAA 1447; also Mark 12:40; Phil. 1:18; 1 Thess. 2:5). The idea is that scribes give the appearance of piety but are not pious, since they treat others so callously (Luke 11:42, also of the Pharisees). The critique also repeats an exhortation to love one's neighbor, to be sensitive to the needs of those who are vulnerable, and to have integrity in relating to God. Central ethical themes of Jesus are present here.

b. Fate of the Scribes (20:47b)

20:47b The scribes' hypocrisy will meet with a greater judgment (περισσότερον κρίμα, perissoteron krima; also James 3:1; Rom. 13:2). Jesus' condemnation is intended to show that the scribes are not worthy examples to follow because of their self-centeredness. Disciples should be about genuine service and caring. Luke matches Mark 12:40. Matthew lacks a parallel.[18]

8. Counterexample: The Widow Who Gave All (21:1–4)
a. The Widow's Act Observed (21:1–2)

21:1 Jesus' position beside the temple allows him to observe a succession of rich contributors who come and deposit (βάλλοντας, ballontas) their coins in the γαζοφυλάκιον (gazophylakion; BAGD 149; BAA 300; in the NT outside this pericope only at John 8:20; cf. Esth. 3:9;

---

18. The conclusion that Matthew lacks a parallel assumes the outcome of a textual problem. Most key uncials (ℵ, B, D, L, Θ, family 1, 33, most Itala) omit Matt. 23:14, which means that Matthew lacks a parallel. Manuscripts that do include the verse do not agree on its placement, which is a sign that it was a copyist's addition (if it had originally been present, its location would not be in doubt). Codexes W and Δ, Byz, and Lect place it before 23:13, while family 13, some Itala, and other versions place it after 23:13.

1 Esdr. 8:18, 45). These receptacles are described in some detail in the Mishnah (*m. Šeqal.* 2.1; 6.1, 5; also Neh. 12:44; Josephus, *Jewish War* 5.5.2 §200; 6.5.2 §282; *Antiquities* 19.6.1 §294; 1 Macc. 14:49; 2 Macc. 3:6, 24, 28, 40). Thirteen trumpet-shaped receptacles in the temple forecourt by the Court of Women served to collect freewill offerings that were used to underwrite temple worship (Plummer 1896: 475; Ernst 1977: 550–51; Fitzmyer 1985: 1322). Γαζοφυλάκιον may, however, refer to the room by the Court of Women where such receptacles are found (SB 2:37–45; Marshall 1978: 751; Safrai 1976d: 879–80). Gifts brought to this room were offered for a variety of reasons (*b. Šeqal.* 3–4). The contributions of the rich are but the starting point for the contrast, as the next verse will make clear when a poor widow steps up to toss in her two, seemingly insignificant coins. The reference to casting in the money may suggest that the receptacles are meant.

The parallel Mark 12:41 is longer. Mark notes that Jesus sat down opposite the treasury and watched the multitude putting money in the treasury and that the rich put in large sums. Luke offers a more condensed version of the account and notes only the rich.

The main figure arrives. In contrast to the many rich is one poor widow.[19] The NT *hapax legomenon* πενιχρός (*penichros*) refers to someone who is needy or poor (Plummer 1896: 475; BAGD 642; BAA 1295; cf. Exod. 22:25 [22:24 LXX]; Prov. 28:15; 29:7). It can be an intensive term: the "very poor" (Hauck, *TDNT* 6:40; Marshall 1978: 752). The widow walks up to the treasury and throws in two lepta. There is no need to appeal to Jesus' supernatural knowledge (as do Plummer 1896: 475 and Arndt 1956: 415–16): if γαζοφυλάκιον is the treasury then the amount of the contribution might have been announced; if it is a receptacle in the temple courtyard, then one could recognize the coins by their size. Lepta were small copper coins, the smallest currency available, whose value was one-eighth of a penny (BAGD 472; BAA 958). Ellis (1974: 239) computes the value as one one-hundredth of a denarius, thus one one-hundredth of the average daily wage—a very small sum indeed! Plummer (1896: 475) argues this was the minimal gift, since a gift of one lepton was prohibited. This misreads the late talmudic evidence, however, since *b. B. Bat.* 10b refers to alms, not to temple offerings (SB 2:45; Marshall 1978: 752). The woman did not give much, but Jesus notes that it was as if she had put in everything she

21:2

---

19. This is Luke's fourth "silent" example (the woman who anoints Jesus, Mary, and Lazarus). She says nothing, but her actions speak volumes. On widows, see the exegesis of 18:3. Luke has much to say about widows and the poor (Luke 2:37; 4:25–26; 7:12; 21:1–4; Acts 6:1–7; 9:39).

had. No doubt most people would say that the gifts of the rich were more significant.

Mark 12:42 is the same conceptually, but has a longer description: a poor (πτωχή, *ptōchē*) widow comes and casts in two lepta or a "quadrans" (κοδράντης, *kodrantēs*), a Latin loanword equivalent to one-quarter of a penny (BAGD 437; BAA 889; Sperber 1967; Blass 1898–99a; Blass 1898–99b; Ramsay 1898–99; Lee 1970–71; elsewhere in the NT at Matt. 5:26; Luke 12:59 variant reading). Luke lacks any comparison with Roman currency. The amount was not great; but to this woman the gift, in terms of what she possessed, was immense.

b. Jesus' Comment: The Widow's Act Commended as Sacrificial Giving (21:3–4)

21:3 Jesus commends the woman for her generosity, especially in light of how little she had to give. When he says the poor widow put in more than all the others, he is saying that, in terms of real cost, the woman gave the most.

Mark 12:43 has a fuller account. He notes that Jesus calls his disciples. Mark does not use Luke's ἀληθῶς (*alēthōs*, truly) but employs the similar ἀμήν (*amēn*, truly) (Plummer 1896: 475; Marshall 1978: 752; cf. Luke 9:27; 12:44). From this point on, Mark matches Luke verbally in what Jesus says, except that at the end Mark adds τῶν βαλλόντων εἰς τὸ γαζοφυλάκιον (*tōn ballontōn eis to gazophylakion*, of those who are contributing to the treasury). Mark and Luke yield the same point, despite their variation.

21:4 Jesus explains (γάρ, *gar*) why he says the widow gave the most, when she only contributed two lepta: all those who preceded her donated their gifts out of an excess. What they gave to God cost them little. In contrast, the woman gave, not from her abundance, but from her very life. As Jesus puts it, she gave "all of her life."[20] Her poverty means that her contribution cost her in terms of life's basics. But this did not stop her from giving. She did not say, "I do not have enough to live on, so I will postpone my giving." In fact, she could have given just one lepton but instead she gave more. She did not give from abundance; she gave out of "what she lacked," from her poverty (ὑστέρημα, *hysterēma*; BAGD 849; BAA 1692; elsewhere in the NT at 1 Cor. 16:17; 2 Cor. 8:14 [twice]; 9:12; 11:9; Phil. 2:30; Col. 1:24; 1 Thess. 3:10). She could have said, "I'll keep one lepton to be safe, to have a cushion," but she did not.

---

20. A similar use of βίος occurs in 8:43. The term has a slightly different force in 15:12, 30, where it means "inheritance"; Marshall 1978: 752.

It is important to note that Jesus is not putting down the contributions of others. Rather, he is noting the woman's great contribution, despite the gift's small size, since the size of a gift is not always indicative of the sacrifice. In fact, it might be deceptive. Often it is the little gift that really costs. Jesus shows the disciples that it is not the number of coins, but the nature of the heart that gives them. Little gifts can be taken for granted or not even noticed, yet sometimes they are in fact the biggest gifts of all.[21] The remarks are not unprecedented. Fitzmyer (1985: 1320–21) cites parallels from Josephus, *Antiquities* 6.7.4 §148; Euripides, *Danaë* fragment 319; and Lev. Rab. 3.5 on 1:7. Pace Fitzmyer (citing A. Wright 1982: 262), Nolland (1993b: 979) correctly notes that Jesus is not lamenting that the woman has been duped by the leaders into giving her gift.

Marshall (1978: 752) rightly points out that the widow's heart is very different from the preying tactics of others (20:47). This contrast shows Luke's readers that sometimes those who appear to be blessed are not. In this first-century Jewish setting, the "common person" is in better touch with God than the "religious person."

Mark 12:44 is parallel except for a few stylistic differences. Luke uses οὗτοι (*houtoi*, these), which Mark lacks. Mark lacks the reference to God's gift and uses an alternative but synonymous expression for poverty (τῆς ὑστερήσεως, *tēs hysterēseōs*). Mark's closing phrase is a little more cumbersome stylistically: ὅσα εἶχεν ἔβαλεν ὅλον τὸν βίον αὐτῆς (*hosa eichen ebalen holon ton bion autēs*, as much as she had, she cast in her whole life). Luke's account is more compact.

Summary

Luke 20:41–21:4 makes a transition as Luke prepares to summarize the eschatological discourse that Jesus gave in Jerusalem (21:5–38). Jesus goes on the offensive and concludes the Jerusalem controversies by raising a theological question about Messiah. The question goes unanswered by the leadership and is left for the reader to ponder. Just as Jesus' answers had yielded no response, so too his questions leave them silent. If the Messiah is David's son, why does David call him Lord? This christological tension sets the stage for two later treatments of the issue, one in the climactic trial scene in Luke 22:69 and the other in Peter's speech in Acts 2:30–36. It is in these passages that answers to Jesus' question are found: Messiah is Lord in a comprehensive sense that makes the title *Lord* the most fundamental one. Messiah is Lord, because Jesus has salvific authority as the bearer of God's promise and as the one who rules over the promise, includ-

---

21. Danker 1988: 328 cites a similar remark by Aristotle, *Nicomachean Ethics* 4.1.19 (1120B): "One's generosity is to be evaluated in terms of one's resources."

ing the distribution of its benefits (Acts 2:30–39). What Luke wishes the reader to see here, however, is Jesus' control and superiority over his opponents. Jesus has insight into God's plan that the others lack.

This leads Jesus to warn his disciples yet again about the Jewish leadership. Such polemical remarks are common in Luke (11:37–54). To Luke's audience, these rebukes are significant. Are not the scribes part of the religious leadership who lead God's people? Are they not authoritative teachers of the law? Jesus' remarks are designed to show that pride and opportunism dominate this clerical order. Where such things are present, one can suspect something is awry. Do not be impressed by external impressions. Look for something other than spiritual showmanship.

In contrast to the leadership stands an almost unnoticed poor widow. She has the piety that pleases God. She gives her life in the little amount that she lays out for God. Her giving costs, and so it is admirable. She serves from the heart and not to self-advantage. Others may devour widows, but this widow gives to God, despite needing to meet needs of her own. For Luke's readers the points here include not judging the poor prematurely, since some of them are very faithful to God. Realize that appearances can be deceiving and that big gifts can come in small packages. God does not look at the number of contributions we make or the amount contained within them, but at the way we make them. He does not count, he weighs.

Additional Notes

20:42. Psalms like 45, 110, and possibly 2 are part of a special category of prophetic texts, better called typological-prophetic. They picture a pattern of relationship that comes to be especially true—and often uniquely true—of Jesus. The original OT passages applied to human figures, in this case the king. They are, however, especially true and more literally and precisely true of Jesus in expressing the nature of this king's relationship to God. It is a both/and type of prophecy, where God not only predicts, but provides a precursor in a contemporary picture as well. Typological-prophetic prophecy addresses the past and the future at the same time, though sometimes the prophetic element in the pattern becomes clear only as time passes and the parallel emerges. Such design is more intricate than direct prophecy and more instructive, since it shows God's control over various periods of history at once. This category helps to explain why so many messianic texts in the NT overlap with Judaism's expectations. The Jews also sensed these patterns in the text, though they debated how to put the package together (Bock 1987: 49–50, 271–73). It is possible to distinguish whether a text stresses one side of the connection or the other in its NT use: thus, *typological*-prophetic texts merely present the pattern with the prophetic connection being largely retrospective, and typological-*prophetic* texts emphasize Jesus' uniqueness within the pattern but also possess an expectation of an ideal fulfillment before the NT period. Such categories are, of course, modern descriptions. Ancients would have called all of these texts prophetic without further specifying how the prophetic connection was formed or realized.

20:45. Most manuscripts (ℵ, A, L, W, Δ, Θ, Ψ, family 1, family 13, 33, Byz, most Itala, Syriac) read τοῖς μαθηταῖς αὐτοῦ (his disciples). A shorter reading is τοῖς μαθηταῖς (the disciples), but its attestation is too thin to be original: only B, D, and two Itala manuscripts. Two other variants are even less well attested.

21:4. I adopt the variant τὰ δῶρα τοῦ θεοῦ (gifts for God), taking the genitive as objective (A, D, Δ, Θ, Ψ, family 13, 33, Byz, Lect, Itala, and Vulgate). The shorter UBS–NA text, τὰ δῶρα (the gifts), is read by ℵ, B, L, family 1, some Syriac, and some Coptic. The sense is little affected by the choice. The use of εἰς (into) shows that they added to an already existing pile of gifts (Plummer 1896: 476): "They cast into the gifts for God."

B. Jerusalem's Destruction and the End (21:5–38)

Luke records Jesus' lengthy discourse on a pair of related events: the destruction of Jerusalem in A.D. 70 and the Lord's return. Though made up of many parts, the discourse is a unit. This passage is Luke's version of the Olivet Discourse, though he makes no connection to the Mount of Olives in the setting. Luke focuses on the destruction of Jerusalem with more intensity than do the other Synoptics, and he also has a clearer chronological breakdown of events. He covers both events because for Jesus the destruction of Jerusalem is like the end-time.

The discourse starts with a prediction of the temple's fall (21:5–6), which leads the disciples to ask about the events associated with it (21:7). Jesus replies in three initial steps, starting with a discussion of events that do not foreshadow the end (21:8–11). He then treats incidents that will precede these events (21:12–19). Next come events that parallel the end and reveal what it is like (21:20–24). There will be time for mission before the end, but this interim period will also involve intense persecution and will lead to Jerusalem's fall to the nations. Only then does Jesus relate the cosmic signs that precede the Son of Man's return, when he comes on the clouds in the splendor of deity (21:25–28). Jesus says that awareness of these signs will allow one to know when these key moments of divine history are near. He also says that the end will come quickly when it does comes. He concludes by assuring the disciples that the teaching is true (21:29–33). Thus, they are to watch and be ready. They are to live soberly and pray for strength to endure, so as to be able to stand before the Son of Man (21:34–36). After the discourse, Luke notes that the people listened to Jesus' daily teaching at the temple (21:37–38).

Sources and Historicity

The interpretation of this passage is surrounded by numerous issues—namely, its origin, sources, and historicity.[1] While the origin and transmis-

---

1. How Luke handled this material in relation to the parallels in Matt. 24:1–35 = Mark 13:1–37 will be treated in detail in the exegesis, though a summary of the Lucan emphases concludes this introduction.

sion of the Synoptic material is difficult to trace, most discussion proceeds on the assumption that Mark was the first Gospel. Even if Matthew was first, however, the source question remains, since Luke variously lacks and includes material that the other two Gospels possess.[2]

Several factors suggest that behind this discourse is a source or set of sources distinct from those normally drawn on by the Gospel writers. While each account has essentially the same sequence of themes, the vocabulary differs. In effect, the Lucan discourse can be described as carrying "Marcan structure but non-Marcan wording" (see Marshall 1978: 754–55). In addition, the discourse is unusual for Mark, since outside of Mark 4:1–34 and 13:1–37 the longest Marcan discourse by Jesus is six sentences (Mark 8:34–38), while the discourse in Mark 13 contains thirty-nine sentences. Mark's lack of discourses like the Sermon on the Mount convinces most that this material came to Mark from an outside source (Grayston 1973–74: 375).

Since the mid-nineteenth century, two basic approaches have been made to the issue of sources. The first suggests that the speech goes back to Jesus and that the speech's tradition circulated in various forms (D. Wenham 1984; apparently Marshall 1978: 758, who speaks of a pre-Marcan nucleus whose ultimate origin is tied to Jesus). One can thus explain the differences between Luke and the other Synoptics by appeal to multiple sources. The second approach suggests that the speech is a composite of isolated sayings from various sources, an eschatological anthology of sorts (so most; see the summary in Beasley-Murray 1986: 322–24). For most, the composite nature of this speech is almost a given (set by the precedent of a probable composite in Mark 4). The different distribution of eschatological sayings in the Synoptics is said to argue for an anthology. Some argue that the core (or at least many portions) of this anthology go back to Jesus, while others hold that none of the speech goes back to him.

Colani (1864) was the first to suggest that the speech did not go back to Jesus but was a product of the Jewish-Christian church.[3] With many nineteenth-century NT scholars, he held that Jesus rejected Jewish apocalyptic

---

2. This issue is particularly acute if Matthew was the first Gospel, for Matthew's eschatological discourse not only has the Olivet remarks but also a series of graphic and theologically significant eschatological parables unique to his treatment. If Matthew is first and Luke knew him, why would Luke leave them out, since he loves parables, including eschatological parables (12:35–48; 18:1–8; 19:11–27)? Matthean priorists have difficulty explaining this situation, which is a strong argument that Mark was written before Matthew. For how the various Synoptic theories approach this material, see the essays by C. M. Tuckett, F. Neirynck, and A. J. McNicol in Dungan 1990: 63–80, 108–24, 157–200.

3. The history of interpretation of this discourse can be found in Beasley-Murray's several works: 1952–53a, 1952–53b, 1954, and 1957: 1–18 (updated in 1993: 1–349), while his own views about the discourse are summarized in 1986: 322–24. Beasley-Murray 1993: 367–70 sees two purposes for the discourse: (1) to inspire faith, endurance, and hope and (2) to warn Christians against false teaching about the end. See also the exegesis of 17:22–37.

imagery. But two works around the turn of the century, J. Weiss's *Jesus' Proclamation of the Kingdom of God* (1971, originally 1892), and A. Schweitzer's *Quest for the Historical Jesus* (1910, originally 1906), challenged the nineteenth-century consensus and forced NT scholars to reconsider whether Jesus had an apocalyptic hope. Meanwhile, Weizsäcker (1864) added to Colani's thesis the suggestion that some of the speech's concepts had roots in 1 Enoch, a Jewish apocalyptic work. In contrast to Colani, Weizsäcker traced some of the speech to Jesus, a source that became known as the "Little Apocalypse." In one way or another, this suggestion about an apocalypse source has been the dominant approach to the issue, though debate rages whether the source was Jewish, Jewish-Christian, or tied to Jesus.[4]

1. Kümmel (1957: 95–104) argues for a Jewish or Jewish-Christian apocalyptic tract influenced by 1 Enoch—a view that shows little change in the discussion between 1864 (the date of Weizsäcker's work) and 1956 (Kümmel's third German edition). Kümmel places this source in Gaius Caligula's reign in A.D. 40 and suggests that the source was modified in the church as a result of the A.D. 70 siege of Jerusalem (also Gaston 1970: 8–64). Caligula is suggested because he threatened to persecute Jews and put them to death if they rejected statues raised to deify him. In fact, he sent an army under Petronius to enforce his decree (Josephus, *Jewish War* 2.10.1 §§184–85). Manson (1949: 323, 329–30, 336–37) has a variation on this view: the material's core goes back to Jesus but was modified twice by Jewish Christians—first in A.D. 40 because of Caligula and again in A.D. 70 because of Jerusalem's fall.

2. Pesch (1968b) argues that Mark was largely responsible for this material and that he wrote it to calm apocalyptic expectations that arose during the fall of Jerusalem in A.D. 70 and to call the community to watchfulness. Pesch traces Mark 13:9, 11, 13a, 28b, 31–32, 34 to a traditional sayings source and the apocalyptic material of 13:6, 7b–8, 12, 19–20a, 24–27 to A.D. 40 in Jerusalem. This is one of the most widely received current approaches, though some reject it (e.g., Hartman 1969: 579). In fact, Pesch shuffled his view in his Mark commentary (1976–77: 2.264–318), seeing Mark as a conservative redactor of traditional material (Meier 1994: 394–95 n. 217).

---

4. A detailed demonstration of the solution to this problem is beyond the scope of a commentary on Luke. Marshall 1978: 758 notes that no good solution to the transmission question can be clearly demonstrated and that the general teaching coheres with Jesus' teaching elsewhere—which means that the material's core goes back to Jesus. Each of the monographs behind views 1–4 engages in detailed analyses of the text and its OT roots—something more conservative studies frequently lack. Wenham's work (view 5) is an exception to this pattern, as is that of Beasley-Murray.

3. Lambrecht (1967) argues that Mark significantly redacted traditional material with the aid of the LXX. Lambrecht attributes the material, interestingly enough, to Q, a point that seems to deny the usual appeal to a separate source.

4. Hartman (1966: 226–52) argues that the midrashic use of Daniel is at the speech's base and that some of this exposition starts with Jesus. He argues that Daniel influences Mark 13:5b–8, 12–16, 19–22, 24–27. Elements traceable to Jesus include suffering, the fate of Jerusalem, and watchfulness, while the early church is responsible for the Danielic midrash, persecution, and false prophets. Such picking and choosing is common in this discussion, on the assumption that Jesus could not have foreseen elements that reflect the later church.

5. D. Wenham (1984: 135–74, 355–74, esp. 365) argues that all the Synoptics use a pre-Synoptic, pre-Pauline eschatological discourse, which Luke has separated into three parts for thematic reasons (12:35–48; 17:22–37; 21:5–36). He supports the pre-Pauline claim by noting the overlapping terminology between Paul and the Gospels (1984: 366–67, where Wenham notes traces of its presence in Rom. 11:25; 13:11–14; and the Thessalonian letters). He also believes this is part of an *Ur*-Gospel tradition that was not limited to discourse material, as the Q hypothesis is (pp. 369–70). This is the most intriguing of the recent suggestions, although Wenham's certainty about Luke's breaking up the material might be challenged (see the introduction to 17:22–37). Wenham may well be right in his general approach, though some details may need to be altered (e.g., to allow for the possibility of multiple sources).

All of these options indicate the material's complexity, which makes it difficult to find a final, provable solution, though Wenham's view has the most potential. The exact route of how the discourse achieved such diverse expression is not clear, but the conclusion that the speech is an anthological composite is not certain. That Jesus gave such a discourse at this point is better attested than other Synoptic discourses (e.g., Mark 4 = Matt. 13 or Matt. 5–7 = Luke 6:20–49). The remarks left a strong trace in the non-Gospel portions of the NT, which also suggests their age. My preference, then, is for a summary here of a real discourse by Jesus.

The question of Luke's sources is less complicated. On the premise that Mark is the first Gospel, most see Luke using Mark. This suggestion is plausible because Matthew's discourse includes certain parables that Luke lacks at this point. Since Luke likes parables, his omission of the parable of the ten virgins (Matt. 25:1–13) and the parable of the sheep and goats seems significant (Matt. 25:31–46). Thus, Luke is more like Mark than Matthew in this account. If Wenham's suggestion of a pre-Synoptic source is correct, then the situation becomes more complicated. The problem with his hypothesis is that there is no way to confirm a fundamental *Ur*-Gospel that is no longer extant. Outside of Wenham's suggestion and another recent suggestion by M. Mahoney (1980), there are two other approaches to Luke's sources:[5]

1. Many attribute all the uniquely Lucan material to Luke's own redaction (Klostermann 1929: 197–99; Creed 1930: 253; Wiefel 1988: 348; Wellhausen 1904: 116–19; Zmijewski 1972: 59–65; Geiger 1976: 150–51). Klostermann notes three motives for Luke's redaction: (a) Luke omits the eschatological material paralleled elsewhere in the book (17:23 and 12:39–48); (b) he omits Mark 13:32; and (c) he updates Mark. In addition, Conzelmann (1960: 123–24) stresses that Luke has a concern to explain the "delay of the parousia" and so issues a call to be ready and persevere.

2. In the view of many, tying the unique material only to Luke is inadequate, and so they posit an additional source (Caird 1963: 228; Marshall 1978: 755–56; Schweizer 1984: 311–13; Tiede 1988: 355–57; Manson 1949: 323–27; V. Taylor 1926: 101–25; Gaston 1970: 8–64, 355–69; Schramm 1971: 171–82; Hartman 1966: 226–35).[6] Marshall notes the reasons why others suggest this: (a) Why omit a reference to the Holy Spirit (Mark 13:10–11) when it is such a key concept for Luke? (b) The sutures of Luke 21:21a, 26–27 are sufficiently difficult to suggest the presence of another source. (c) Luke 21:20–24 is not like typical Lucan expression. (d) Unlike Luke's normal style, the OT allusions are expressed like the MT, not the LXX. (e) A continuous discourse seems present when Marcan elements are set aside. (Marshall finds points a and e unlikely, but regards point b as compelling.)

There is some diversity about which portions of Luke 21 come from this source. Of the scholars listed in view 2 above, Schramm, Gaston, Caird, Fitzmyer, and Manson all agree that 21:18, 21b, 24, 28 were in this source. All but Manson hold that 21:22 was in it; all but Gaston see 21:34–36 in the source; Schramm, Gaston, and Caird list 21:19–20, 23b–26 (Manson is uncertain; Fitzmyer rejects these verses, except perhaps 21:24). It seems likely that Luke had access to material beyond what Mark (or, less likely, Matthew) provided.

---

5. Mahoney argues that Luke's form is drawn from an independent Semitic tradition. If so, in many spots this source is much like Mark.

6. Fitzmyer 1985: 1324, 1326, 1329 speaks of Mark plus L and argues that L did not contain the whole speech. To achieve this position, he notes parallels to Q material in the Luke 17 discourse and the few portions of Luke 21 that do not parallel Mark 13.

The diversity of opinion about the account's historicity has already been noted, since this discussion is intimately connected to the issue of origin. Positions range from Jesus' having no part in the material to all the basic material going back to Jesus. The Jesus Seminar's analysis is an example of the substantial rejection of historicity (Funk and Hoover 1993: 381–86). The seminar sees 21:6, 18, 29–31 as rewritten by Luke but perhaps connected to Jesus (gray type), while the rest of the speech is rejected as inauthentic (black type). The seminar argues that (a) Jesus did not use apocalyptic themes, but Mark did; (b) the persecution section (21:8–19) looks too much like Acts; (b) Luke heavily rewrote 21:20–24; (d) Jesus did not teach about an apocalyptic Son of Man, as 21:25–28 claims (also 21:36); (e) even though the parable of 21:29–31 is like Jesus' teaching, it is too proverbial to be sure; and (f) exhortations to watch (21:34–36) are too like the early church.[7] Yet if one looks at the speech's basic themes, a more positive evaluation of the core elements can be made (see also the remarks of Nolland 1993b: 986).

1. Many of the texts tied to the OT are not beyond Jesus' use. The Danielic imagery is paralleled by the use of the Son-of-Man image. The persuasiveness of this argument depends on how one sees the Son-of-Man debate, but there is no reason to deny that apocalyptic Son-of-Man sayings go back to Jesus (see excursus 6). The return's apocalyptic imagery is grounded in the theme of the total restoration of authority in the end, a standard prophetic theme. Along with an apocalyptic picture from Daniel, it was a concept readily available to Jesus. When restoration was discussed by the prophets, they pictured total restoration (e.g., Isa. 65–66; Jer. 31–33; Ezek. 36).

2. The call for watchfulness suggests that a fundamental NT teaching is present whose rationale and widespread presence is most naturally attributable to Jesus. If Jesus thought of that day as "coming like a thief," even in his parables, and subsequently spoke of being ready for God's vindication, then watchfulness is a corollary. The material here is very much like Luke 12:35–48, whose authenticity I defended earlier. Watchfulness was so basic a theme in the early church documents that even the delay did not bring about any lessening of this hope (e.g., Rom. 13:11–13; 1 Cor. 16:20–24; 1 Thessalonians; 1 Pet. 4:7; 5:8–9; 2 Peter). Wenham's case (1984: 366–67) for pre-Pauline themes in this teaching fits here and argues for old traditional roots.

---

7. Even before analyzing this approach, it seems unlikely that such a slim core as the Jesus Seminar argues for here could have been remembered in such isolation, nor could it have provided any rationale for the building up of a discourse around it. The Jesus Seminar's criticism of historicity is so severe that what does get through the sieve could hardly be seen as credible.

3. What of the "historicization" of Jerusalem's fall? A focus on the city's fall versus the temple's desecration is stronger in Luke, but the language of Jerusalem's siege comes out of the LXX. The LXX portrait describes the city's earlier exilic fall (proven beyond question by Dodd 1947; see the exegesis of 19:41–44). All that Jesus needed to have believed to describe this scenario was that the nation would be judged for covenant unfaithfulness, just like it had been in the past. This belief reflects a consistent prophetic pattern that had a rich history extending back to Deuteronomy. The theme is multiply attested, as the Synoptic parallels and the following unique or uniquely placed Lucan texts show: 9:27; 11:49–50; 13:34–35; 19:41–44 (Nolland 1993b: 986). Even the tie between Jerusalem's short-term future and the end has historical precedent through the pattern of judgment (i.e., God responds to unfaithfulness among his people in various eras, e.g., Assyria and Babylonia). As such, these concepts are not impossible for Jesus.

4. The picture of persecution is not surprising either, since the prospect of persecution was a constant tension during Jesus' earthly ministry, which ended with the cross. The attempts to trap him show that he is strongly opposed, so why should his followers fare any differently? This prediction is a natural extension of what is already taking place. In addition, political and eschatological fervor existed throughout the period, so the predictions about many claiming to be the answer to this tension-filled environment are not surprising.

There is thus no need to appeal to prophecy after the fact. All the concepts are obviously within Jesus' grasp, regardless of one's presuppositions about Jesus' prophetic ministry. Plummer (1896: 487–88) is right to suggest that the material goes back to Jesus. (Some details on the authenticity of certain verses are noted in the exegesis.)

Luke's speech emphasizes the city's desolation versus the temple's fall. Luke lacks reference to coming tribulation (Mark 13:8), as well as the remark expressing uncertainty about the hour or day (Mark 13:32). In addition, in spots his version is less apocalyptic in tone, but this is because he expressly differentiates events that are not a part of the end from those that are (Tiede 1988: 355). In Luke's view, the fall of Jerusalem in A.D. 70 is part of God's plan and judgment. This fall pictures the end.

The presence of a prophetic pattern of judgment raises a crucial point when considering the various Synoptic versions of the discourse and their differing emphases. Given that short-term events mirror long-term events and that these earlier events represent a pattern for God's ultimate judgment, it is clear that someone interpreting Jesus' remarks could focus on either side of the temporal mirror and reflect appropriately on his comments. Luke's clearer demarcation may not be a disagreement with his colleagues as much as a new emphasis to complement their presentations of Jesus' complex picture. The discourse is rich in teaching, but no one writer presents the full picture. The other Gospels tend to focus slightly more on the end-time, while Luke tends to stress the near future. Thus, reports of Jesus' teaching can focus on only a single element of the picture.[8] Each writer shows his interest by which side of the portrait—the near or the far—he emphasizes. By showing that the short-term events are also part of God's plan, Luke reassures his audience that God is directing history, and he makes the point that near events will confirm this. Jerusalem's fall is part of God's total eschatological plan. To see the approach of this event is to know that the rest of the plan will come as well. Such reassurance fits the overall goal of Luke's Gospel (1:4). In addition, the similarity within the mirror might make it hard, in the original setting, to know whether one is speaking of the near term, the long term, or both. The ambiguity in the pattern's original setting must be appreciated, for only reflection on the speech in light of later developments might make aspects of its original force clear.

So what points does Luke make in his presentation? His major concerns include the following:

1. a clear separation between Jerusalem's fall and the end-time
2. a focus on the city's collapse
3. a suggestion that the end is further off because of all that must precede it
4. a need to persevere in the face of these realities
5. a concern to describe the signs of the end
6. the fall of Jerusalem as judgment on Israel and a guarantee that the rest of the plan comes
7. a statement that the end is certain and comes quickly

Many of these themes are part of the other Synoptic discourses, but points 1–4 are clearest in Luke.

In looking at this discourse, other Lucan texts come to mind. Luke 12:35–48 is a parabolic call to live faithfully and watchfully, in light of the master's absence and promise to return (similar to Matt. 24:42–51). Luke 17:20–37 focuses on the end-time and the universal signs of its coming.

---

8. It may also be that the portrait's depth and mirroring emerged slowly for those who heard this discourse. There was great interest in the end-time, but Luke reminds his audience that Jesus also had concerns for the nation's short-term future. While the other Synoptists also note these short-term interests, Luke makes these points with more punch. In fact, a careful reading of the Synoptics reveals that Matthew is the most oriented toward the future, while Mark's account reflects the most temporal ambiguity. But it is a mistake to pit these readings against one another or to make them say exactly the same thing. Typology in judgment texts is not an either/or but a both/and choice.

Luke 13:34–35 and 19:41–44 stress Jerusalem's impending fall and raise the hope of its restoration. All these passages (plus 21:5–36) together form the core of Luke's teaching on eschatology.

This discourse is composed mostly of sayings, warnings, and pronouncements of a prophetic and apocalyptic nature. Luke 21:5–6 is an introductory pronouncement, while prophetic and apocalyptic sayings come in 21:7–28 (prophetic sayings dominate 21:7–24 with apocalyptic images in 21:25–28). Luke 21:29–33 is a parable, and 21:34–36 a final exhortation. A summary in 21:37–38 closes the chapter.[9]

The outline of Luke 21:5–38 is as follows:

1. Setting (21:5–6)
2. Signs before the end (21:7–11)
   a. The disciples' question (21:7)
   b. False claims (21:8)
   c. Social chaos before the end (21:9–10)
   d. Natural disasters (21:11)
3. Persecution (21:12–19)
   a. Persecution and testimony (21:12–13)
   b. Divine wisdom (21:14–15)
   c. Division of family, possible martyrdom, and hatred (21:16–17)
   d. Divine protection of others (21:18)
   e. Endurance leading to salvation (21:19)
4. Picture of the end: Jerusalem's destruction (21:20–24)
   a. Jerusalem surrounded (21:20)
   b. The days of vengeance (21:21–22)
   c. Woe for the great distress of Jerusalem (21:23–24)
5. The end: coming of the Son of Man (21:25–28)
   a. Signs in the heavens (21:25–26)
   b. The authoritative return of the Son of Man (21:27)
   c. The drawing near of redemption (21:28)
6. Parable of the fig tree (21:29–33)
   a. As fig trees in summer, so the kingdom (21:29–31)
   b. The end: all within a generation (21:32)
   c. The certainty of Jesus' words (21:33)
7. Application: call to watch (21:34–36)
   a. The call to heed universal judgment (21:34–35)
   b. Pray for strength (21:36)

9. For form-critical discussions of the individual subunits, see Fitzmyer 1985: 1329, 1334, 1338, 1342, 1348, 1351, 1355, 1357; Bultmann 1963: 36, 122–23, 125, 119; Berger 1984: 81, 296–97, 304–5, 48, 142, 352.

8. Jesus teaches at the temple (21:37–38)
   a. Teaching at the temple, lodging at Olives (21:37)
   b. People hear Jesus teach in the morning (21:38)

Jesus' prediction of the temple's destruction begins his eschatological discourse. Israel will be judged because of unfaithfulness, and disciples will be the object of severe persecution. Many signs will signal the beginning of the end: false claims, social chaos, natural disasters, even martyrdom. Such a time will call for the divine provision of wisdom and protection in the face of persecution. Endurance will lead to deliverance. Jerusalem's fall pictures the end. Both the fall and the end-time are days of great distress, a part of the period of the Gentiles. Cosmic signs will come before the end, which involves the Son of Man returning with authority. Like one can spot the approaching of summer, so one can watch for the end. Jesus' teaching on the end is certain, so he issues a call to watch, be ready, and pray for strength. After the discourse, Jesus teaches the people at the temple.

Exegesis and Exposition

⁵And as some were speaking about the temple, noting that it was adorned with noble stones and offerings, he said, ⁶"These things that you see, days shall come in which there shall not be left one stone upon another that will not be thrown down."

⁷But they asked him, saying, "Teacher, now when will these things be, and what will be the sign when these things are about to take place?" ⁸He said, "See that you are not deceived. For many will come in my name, saying, 'I am he!' and 'The time is near!' Do not go after them. ⁹But when you hear of wars and chaos, do not be terrified; for these things must take place first, but it is not immediately the end." ¹⁰Then he was saying to them, "Nation will rise against nation and kingdom against kingdom. ¹¹There will be great earthquakes and in various places famines and pestilences; ⌜and there will be terrors and great signs from heaven⌝.

¹²"But before all of this, they will lay hands on you and persecute you, delivering you up to the synagogue and prisons, and you will be brought before kings and governors for the sake of my name. ¹³This shall be for you to give testimony. ¹⁴Set your hearts not to contemplate how to reply, ¹⁵for I will give you a mouth and wisdom, which none of your enemies will be able to resist or contradict. ¹⁶You will be delivered up even by parents and brothers and relatives and friends, and some of you they will put to death. ¹⁷And you shall be hated by all because of my name, ¹⁸but not a hair of your head shall perish. ¹⁹By your endurance, ⌜gain⌝ your soul.

²⁰"But when you see Jerusalem surrounded by armies, then you know that its desolation has come near. ²¹Then let those in Judea flee to the

mountains, and those in its midst depart, and do not let those who are in the country enter it, [22]for these are days of vengeance, to fulfill all that is written. [23]Woe to those who are with child and to those who give suck in those days; for there will be great distress on the land and wrath upon this people. [24]They will fall by the edge of the sword and be led captive among all the nations, and Jerusalem will be trodden down by Gentiles, until the times of the Gentiles are fulfilled.

[25]"And there will be signs in the sun and moon and stars, and upon the earth distress of nations in perplexity at the roaring of the sea and the waves, [26]men fainting from fear and foreboding of what is coming on the world, for the powers of the heavens will be shaken. [27]And then they will see the Son of Man coming on the clouds with power and great glory. [28]Now when these things happen, look up and raise your heads, because your redemption is near."

[29]And he told them this parable, "Look at the fig tree and all trees. [30]As soon as they show leaf, you know, seeing for yourselves, that summer is already near. [31]Thus also you, when you see these things happening, you know that the kingdom of God is near. [32]Truly I say to you that this generation shall not pass away until all has come to pass. [33]Heaven and earth will pass away, but my words will not pass away.

[34]"But take heed to yourselves, lest your hearts be weighed down with dissipation and drunkenness and the cares of life and that day come upon you suddenly [35]like a snare; ⌜for it will come⌝ upon all who dwell on the face of the whole earth. [36]Watch at all times, while praying, that you might have strength to escape all the things that are coming to take place and to stand before the Son of Man."

[37]But he went on teaching every day in the temple, but at night he went out and lodged on the mount called Olives. [38]And all the people got up early in the morning to come to him in the temple to hear him.⌜ ⌝

1. Setting (21:5–6)

21:5   The setting of Jesus' great eschatological discourse is the disciples' expressed admiration for the Second Temple, the religious center of the nation, which Herod the Great refurbished as part of a large national reconstruction program (Josephus, *Jewish War* 1.21.1 §401; 5.5.1–6 §§184–227; *Antiquities* 15.11 §§380–425; 11QTemple[a] 3.8–13.7; 30.1–45.7; *m. Middot*).[10] Herod built new foundation walls and enlarged the temple area to 400 yards by 500 yards, about twice its original size (Ellis 1974: 243). The refurbishing started in 19 B.C. and continued for over eighty years, not being completed until A.D. 63–64, just a few years before the city and the temple fell.

---

10. Solomon's Temple was destroyed by Nebuchadnezzar of Babylon in 586 B.C. and reconstructed by Zerubbabel in about 516 B.C. (Hag. 1:4–15). Those who had seen the original temple felt that Zerubbabel's was not as great (Fitzmyer 1985: 1330).

Luke's account notes two particularly outstanding features: noble stones (i.e., of good quality) and "ornaments" associated with the temple. According to Josephus (*Jewish War* 5.5.1 §189; 5.5.6 §224; *Antiquities* 15.11.3 §392), Herod used white marble stones up to forty-five cubits (sixty-seven feet) long, eight cubits (twelve feet) high, and twelve cubits (eighteen feet) wide. The NT *hapax legomenon* ἀνάθημα (*anathēma*) describes offerings or gifts that decorated the temple, including gold- and silver-plated gates and gold-plated doors (Behm, *TDNT* 1:354; BAGD 54; BAA 106; 3 Macc. 3:17; Jdt. 16:19; 2 Macc. 9:16). Josephus notes that the building's gold plates flashed in the sun as a "snow-clad mountain" (*Jewish War* 5.5.6 §223). Ἀνάθημα may also describe the grapevine clusters and the Babylonian tapestries of fine linen, colored with blue, scarlet, and purple, that hung as a veil at the entrance to the temple (Josephus, *Jewish War* 5.5.4–5 §§207–18; Plummer 1896: 477; Fitzmyer 1985: 1331). The verb that describes these features emotively highlights the respect felt for the temple: κοσμέω (*kosmeō*, to adorn; BAGD 445 §2aβ; BAA 904 §2aβ; Sasse, *TDNT* 3:867; in Luke elsewhere at 11:25; also 1 Tim. 2:9; Rev. 21:2). Roman historian Tacitus called the temple "immensely opulent" (*History* 5.8).

Luke has no verbal overlap with the parallel in Matt. 24:1 = Mark 13:1. Matthew speaks of Jesus' going away from the city as the disciples point out to him the temple buildings. Mark gives a more direct report: as Jesus departs the temple, the disciples point out "the wonderful stones and wonderful buildings" (ποταποὶ λίθοι καὶ ποταπαὶ οἰκοδομαί, *potapoi lithoi kai potapai oikodomai*). Luke uses indirect speech to make similar points. The origin of the remarks in all the accounts is the same: the temple's beauty, which causes Jesus to comment on its future and on the city that houses this jewel.

Many note that Luke appears to give this account while Jesus is still teaching in the temple, since Luke lacks the remark about Jesus going away (Fitzmyer 1985: 1330; Schweizer 1984: 311).[11] This may simply be a case of abbreviation, which Luke often does in his introductions. The outstanding features of such a building can be alluded to anywhere without indicating where the discussion occurred. The indefinite "some" (τινων, *tinōn*) who speak again shows the broad character of Luke's introduction (in fact, Luke's remark leaves it unclear that the disciples are speaking). Luke's vague remarks contrast with Matthew's and Mark's specifics and may indicate that he used additional sources that lacked their details or simply that he resorted to his generally vague style of introduction.

11. Leaney 1958: 259 notes that the Mount of Olives is the locale in 21:37–38, but this later generalized summary tells nothing about the discourse's setting.

21:6   Jesus makes clear that the disciples should not be overly impressed by the temple's grandeur. The building is temporary: it looks impressive now, but in time it will be dust. The things that they see are not permanent, nor is God's blessing eternally upon this building.[12] Jesus makes his point by stating that "one stone will not be left on another." This is not so much a literal description of the temple being leveled as it is a general description of destruction.[13] The failure of any of the Gospels to note the fulfillment of this prediction suggests that the remarks were recorded before Jerusalem fell and that the Synoptic Gospel accounts could have been written before A.D. 70.[14]

The remark is signaled as a prediction by the phrase ἐλεύσονται ἡμέραι (*eleusontai hēmerai*, days shall come), an expression that only Luke has (cf. Mark 2:20 = Matt. 9:15 = Luke 5:35; 17:22; 19:43; 23:29).[15] Both Matthew and Mark use the emphatic οὐ μή (*ou mē*, not) to start the passage, while Luke has only οὐκ (*ouk*, not). Mark 13:2 = Matt. 24:2 uses direct speech to report Jesus' response, but Matthew starts with Jesus' question, "Do you see all these things?" while Mark has, "Do you see these great buildings?" All three accounts use the verb εἶπεν (*eipen*, he said) to note the reply, but Matthew adds the verbal idea ἀποκριθείς (*apokritheis*, replying) and Mark names Jesus explicitly. Matthew begins the second part of Jesus' response with "truly I say to you," after which he and Mark agree except for the final verbal form: "There will not be left here one stone upon another, that will not be thrown down" (Matthew has οὐ καταλυθήσεται, *ou katalythēsetai*, and Mark has οὐ μὴ καταλυθῇ, *ou mē katalythē*). Luke says the same thing in different terms but shares with both writers only λίθος (*lithos*, stone) and ὃς οὐ (*hos ou*, which not) and with Matthew the wording of the final verb.

The text's authenticity is often debated. Based on Mark 14:58, Pesch (1968b: 83–96) and Lambrecht (1967: 68–79, 88–91) argue that Mark set the framework for the speech and that the disciples would not speak this way about the temple. But given the close involvement of the disciples with the temple immediately after Jesus' resurrection

---

12. On the grammar of ταῦτα ἅ (these things which), see Marshall 1978: 759. The construction is an anacoluthon; BDF §466.1.

13. For example, the Western Wall of the temple still stands today, though Arndt 1956: 418 argues that this is not included in Jesus' remarks.

14. Noting that the fall was fated by God, Josephus, *Jewish War* 6.4.5 §250, describes the destruction of Jerusalem on the tenth day of Loüs (= 29 August A.D. 70). The temple was first burned (*Jewish War* 6.4.5 §250) and then razed (*Jewish War* 7.1.1 §§1–4). Josephus also describes portents of the end; *Jewish War* 6.5.3–4 §§288–315. The OT describes the first destruction of Jerusalem: Jer. 52:12–13; 7:1–14; 22:5; 27:6; Fitzmyer 1985: 1331.

15. Other NT texts noting a threat to the temple are John 2:19 and Acts 6:14, although Jesus' remark in John is misunderstood.

(Acts 3–4), why is such respect for the temple surprising? This building was rightly a great source of Jewish national pride, and it commanded general international respect (e.g., Tacitus's remark; Marshall 1978: 760). The disciples' close connection to Israel would fit such remarks, and the respect that they here show the temple argues against the early church's having created this saying.

2. Signs before the End (21:7–11)
a. The Disciples' Question (21:7)

The disciples recognize the importance of Jesus' reply and ask him, **21:7** as teacher (διδάσκαλε, *didaskale*), when "these things" (ταῦτα, *tauta*) will be. Since Luke frequently uses διδάσκαλος on the lips of the leaders or the public as an address to Jesus (see the exegesis of 20:28), many argue that the discourse's public setting is made clear by its use here (Schweizer 1984: 314). The title, however, parallels Mark 13:1, where disciples ask the question, so the setting should not be determined by the title.[16]

The plural ταῦτα is also significant, since it shows that, although the temple's fall is the question's focus, it is not the only topic.[17] Fitzmyer (1985: 1331), Schweizer (1984: 314), and Ellis (1974: 243) argue that the plural refers only to the temple's destruction, but this ignores the end of the discourse, which clearly deals with eschatological concerns.[18] The question is about all the events related to the temple's collapse. Jesus replies about events related to Jerusalem's fall in A.D. 70 *and* about the end, since the discourse ends with a reference to the Son of Man's return. All such judgment is part of God's plan.

The parallels are longer. Mark 13:3–4 = Matt. 24:3 clearly sets the speech at the Mount of Olives, a note that Luke lacks. In Matthew, the disciples, whom Mark identifies as Peter, James, John, and An-

16. Even Marshall 1978: 762 suggests that διδάσκαλος shows Luke to have a public setting in mind, as opposed to a private discussion with the disciples (though he notes that 21:12–19 suggests an audience of disciples). Nevertheless, the parallel in Mark may well imply that Luke is following tradition here rather than using his technical sense for διδάσκαλος. In simplifying his introduction, the specific audience was lost.

17. The plural reference is obscured in the RSV and NRSV; the NIV and NASB are clearer. The remark in 21:7 looks back to the description in 21:6, but does not ignore larger concerns. See the next note.

18. Fitzmyer follows Conzelmann 1960: 126; but correctly Marshall 1978: 762. Danker 1988: 329 notes that the issues of Jerusalem's destruction and the end-time were linked in most people's minds; one suggests the other. Jesus' answer goes beyond the temple. Zmijewski 1972: 93–95 suggests that the reference to the "coming days" in 21:6 suggests an eschatological setting, since ἡμέρα (day) alludes to the day of the Lord. It must be remembered that any judgment that consumed Jerusalem would be seen as catastrophic, so either event—Jerusalem's fall or the temple's removal—would suggest severe judgment. The disciples are asking, "When will that judgment come?"

drew, come to Jesus privately. In contrast, Luke has "they" as the question's source, which alludes back to the "some" who were marveling over the temple (Luke 21:5). The questions are worded slightly differently. Mark and Luke match verbally except that Luke uses inferential οὖν (oun, therefore) and Mark closes with συντελεῖσθαι πάντα (synteleisthai panta, all be accomplished) where Luke simply has γίνεσθαι (ginesthai, to happen). This language clearly looks to a chain of events, some of which may extend beyond the temple issue. Matthew has the most detail, laying out the disciples' three questions with two interrogatives (πότε [pote, when?] and τί [ti, what?]): (1) "When will these things be?" (2) "What will be the sign of your coming?" and (3) "What will be the sign of the end of the age?" The third question makes the eschatological force explicit. Though the end is presented with varying emphasis in the parallels, the questions are essentially the same. Luke's account again seems the most compact.

b. False Claims (21:8)

21:8 Luke starts with events that precede the end-time. Jesus elsewhere indicates what will accompany the return (its signs will be unmistakable; 17:20–37; 21:25–28). But in describing the events that lead to the city's fall, Jesus first notes what will *not* signal the end: it will not be indicated by people who claim that they are the Christ or who claim that the time is near. Ὁ καιρός (ho kairos, the time) is an allusion to the eschatological end (Delling, *TDNT* 3:461) and refers to a significant period in God's plan (a special time of visitation [19:44] and a period of Gentile rule [21:24]; also Rev. 1:3; 22:10; Dan. 7:22). Jesus tells his disciples not to be deceived by such claims. This statement denying the time's nearness does not contradict earlier statements in Mark 1:15 or Luke 12:56 that the time is near, since in the Olivet Discourse it is not eschatological arrival that is meant, but the move into eschatological consummation. The claim of messianic pretenders should not lead the disciples astray. Πλανάω (planaō) is often used of being led astray at the end-time (Rev. 2:20; 12:9; 13:14; Marshall 1978: 763; Braun, *TDNT* 6:246–47) or of ethical straying (1 Cor. 15:33). In this, Luke's only use of πλανάω, Jesus tells the disciples to not be misled about what God is doing (cf. John 7:47; 1 John 1:8; 2:26; 3:7; BAGD 665 §2cδ; BAA 1338 §2cδ). Do not follow after those who make such claims.

Jesus' comments raise the specter of false claims made in his name (ἐπὶ τῷ ὀνόματι, epi tō onomati). Discernment will be needed by disciples not to be drawn into false eschatological claims made in Jesus' name, for these claims will have nothing to do with God's plan. This remark shows that Jesus assumed an interval between his departure and his return. In fact, the interval is long enough that some could be deceived; for example, many such false prophets came in the first century (Josephus, *Antiquities* 18.4.1 §§85–87; 20.5.1 §§97–99; 20.8.6 §§169–72), some in association with Jerusalem's destruction (Josephus, *Jewish War* 6.5.2–3 §§285–88, 300–309; R. Meyer, *TDNT* 6:826–27; Fitzmyer 1985: 1336). It may also represent Luke's making clear by his citation that the disciples have nothing to do with any emerging messianic movements of his time (Nolland 1993b: 991). Marshall (1978: 763–64) defends the verse's authenticity.

The parallels are similar except for how they introduce Jesus' response. Matthew 24:4–5 begins, "And Jesus replied, saying to them," while Mark 13:5–6 has, "And Jesus began to say to them." Luke is again briefer: "And he said." Matthew and Mark agree verbally except Matthew supplies γάρ (*gar*, for) to develop the remark about being deceived, an addition Luke shares. Matthew also fills out the first claim: "I am the Christ." Luke has a different verbal construction to discuss the deception: Matthew and Mark share πλανήσῃ (*planēsē*, leads astray) where Luke has πλανηθῆτε (*planēthēte*, you are [not] lead astray). Matthew and Mark speak of not letting anyone deceive you, while Luke addresses the disciples more directly with, "Be not deceived," the first of three μή (*mē*, not) constructions in Luke 21:8–9, suggesting an effort at stylistic parallelism. Luke alone mentions a second false claim that accompanies the messianic claim: the time is near. Some attribute this remark to Luke (Creed 1930: 254–55) and argue that it reflects the attitude of those who come after the first generation of Christians, but such an objection fails to distinguish between "already" and "not yet" language in the NT. The approaching καιρός here refers to the "not yet" of the consummation. Jesus can speak of the "time" coming now (12:56) and at the same time look forward to the end (21:25–28).[19]

c. Social Chaos before the End (21:9–10)

21:9 Jesus adds social and civil turmoil to the list of events that precede the end: when disciples hear of wars and chaos, they are still not to be alarmed. Ἀκαταστασία (*akatastasia*; BAGD 30; BAA 57), which Fitzmyer (1985: 1336) renders as "rebellions" and Leaney (1958: 260) as "revolutions," refers elsewhere in the NT to chaos or disorder within a church body (James 3:16), even in a church service (1 Cor. 14:33). Manson (1949: 326) speaks of the breakdown of civil order (cf. Prov. 26:28 and Tob. 4:13). The unusual term for fear, πτοέω (*ptoeō*), describes a deep sense of terror or emotional distress.

---

19. Tension between the coming of salvific blessing and the coming of consummation is also expressed in Acts 1:8–11.

Luke is the only NT writer to use the term (elsewhere Luke 24:37; BAGD 727; BAA 1456), which comes from the LXX (Deut. 31:6; 2 Chron. 32:7; Jer. 1:17; Ezek. 3:9; Fitzmyer 1985: 1336). The disciples are not to be disturbed or surprised by such world events. The end, with all its terror of judgment, is not yet near, so they need not fear. The world will be in great chaos, as many disturbances (the terms for wars and calamities are plural) are present in this "pre-end" period. Fitzmyer (1985: 1336) calls it a period of the church under stress, but it looks more like the world under stress. Nevertheless, it is clear from Luke 21:12–19 that the church also has trouble during another similar period that precedes the time described here.

Jesus says that there is a necessity to these events (so Luke's explanatory γάρ [gar, for], also in Matthew). They "must" come first, as the use of δεῖ (dei, it is necessary) indicates. Only Luke among the Synoptics uses πρῶτον (prōton, first), thus making the time sequence clear. There may be chaos, but God is not surprised. There may be chaos, but the end is not near. Jesus says that even with these events present, the end does not follow immediately (εὐθέως, eu-theōs). The association of war with the end would be natural, since it is a period of judgment and the prophets promised such calamity (Marshall 1978: 764; Danker 1988: 331; Ernst 1977: 556; 2 Chron. 15:6; Isa. 19:2; Jer. 4:20; Joel 3:9–14 [4:9–14 MT]; Dan. 11:20, 25, 44; also Rev. 6:3–4; 9:9; 12:7; 2 Esdr. [= 4 Ezra] 9:3; 13:31; 1 Enoch 99.4; 100.2). Fitzmyer (1985: 1336) argues that this reference to the end is not eschatological and that reading it that way gives it a "Marcan and Matthean nuance" that Luke does not intend. Luke is using, however, well-known tradition here. He is hardly likely to use τὸ τέλος (to telos, the end) in a noneschatological sense. The term looks at the end-time, as 21:25–28 shows (Marshall 1978: 764; Schneider 1977a: 418; Luke 17:25 also notes an intervening event). All of these events—even the temple's fall—are part of God's movement to consummation. They are part of God's plan, since one event guarantees the other. Nolland (1993b: 992) speaks of an escalation from 21:9 to 21:10–11 to 21:25–26. What begins as mere uprisings becomes something much greater at the return.

The parallels are similar but distinctly worded. Matthew 24:6 appears to suggest that these calamities are in the near future by noting that the disciples "are about" μελλήσετε (mellēsete) to hear of wars and rumors of wars. Mark 13:7, like Luke, has no time frame and simply notes how they are not to fear when they hear of these things. Matthew says, "See that you are not alarmed," while Mark has, "do not be alarmed"—both using θροέω (throeō, to be alarmed, inwardly disturbed; BAGD 364; BAA 740; elsewhere in the NT only at 2 Thess. 2:2) for the request not to be terrified (Luke's πτοέω is synonymous). All three Gospels note the necessity (δεῖ) of these things. Matthew and Mark express less precisely the distance from the end, saying it is "not yet" (οὔπω, *oupō*; BAGD 593; BAA 1200), a term that Luke generally avoids (Marshall 1978: 764). Jerusalem's fall is intended as the example of what end-time chaos looks like, but it is not the consummation. This is creation "groaning" for and beginning the inexorable movement to redemption (Rom. 8:18–24).[20]

The social chaos is described in terms of national division, indicated by a pair of terms referring to the same thing: nations and kingdoms (2 Chron. 15:6; Isa. 19:2; 2 Esdr. [= 4 Ezra] 13:31). International opposition will appear, but this is not the end. The parallel Matt. 24:7 = Mark 13:8 agrees with Luke word for word, though Luke introduces the citation uniquely with "then he was saying to them." This difference from Matthew and Mark has generated much discussion.[21]

21:10

d. Natural Disasters (21:11)

The picture continues to expand. Beyond false claims about Messiah and social chaos, a third class of signs are not the end: physical signs in the universe—earthquakes, famines, pestilences, and other terrors and signs from heaven. The language about earthquakes specifically recalls the wording of Ezek. 38:19, but the image is common in prophetic and apocalyptic literature (Isa. 5:13–14; 13:6–16; Hag. 2:6–7; Zech. 14:4; Rev. 6:8, 12; 8:5; 11:13, 19; 16:18; Tiede 1988: 360). The descriptive NT *hapax legomenon* φόβητρον (*phobētron*, terrors) refers to a terrible, horrific sight (Isa. 19:17; BAGD 863; BAA 1721). The double reference to famines and pestilences is not uncommon (e.g., T. Judah 23.3; Nolland 1993b: 992). The picture is of natural tragedy and physical disturbances on all sides. With these are heavenly cosmic displays, perhaps shooting stars, that draw the attention of people, causing them to speculate about what is happening.[22] This image also has rich OT background (Jer. 4:13–22; 14:12; 21:6–7; Ezek. 14:21; Tiede 1988: 360). When placed alongside

21:11

---

20. The language in Matthew and Mark suggests that everything in the period is part of a gradual movement to eschatological consummation.

21. Fitzmyer 1985: 1337 is against a source. Creed 1930: 255 and Leaney 1958: 260 say Luke inserted the phrase because he was detailing what was sketched in previous verses. Marshall 1978: 764–65 speaks of the great puzzlement that this addition has caused and mentions the possible influence of another source (also Schramm 1971: 174–75). Perhaps this one source had the two eschatological discourses that Luke reflects. But what caused the difference? Did Luke or his source supply a clarifying stylistic break? Either option is possible.

22. Josephus records that when the temple burned, a bright star resembling a sword stood over the city and that comets were visible for a year; *Jewish War* 6.5.1–3 §§274–89, esp. §§288–89; Manson 1949: 326; Fitzmyer 1985: 1337; Plummer 1896: 479. Note also Tacitus, *History* 5.13; 2 Macc. 5:2–3; Nolland 1993b: 992.

the other nonsigns that Jesus mentions in Luke 21:7–11, a portrait emerges of a world in great chaos. The chaos itself is not, however, a sign of the end. In fact, other events must still precede even these events, as 21:12–19 makes clear.

This verse provides the largest variation of wording of any verse in the discourse. Only one term is shared by all the accounts: λιμοί (*limoi*, famines). Earthquakes are mentioned by all the evangelists, but in different positions. Matthew 24:7b–8 is brief, mentioning only the coming of famines and earthquakes in various places, which are but the beginning of birth pangs. Like Matthew, Mark 13:8b also mentions only earthquakes and famines (but in reverse order) as birth pangs. Luke's rendering contains earthquakes, famines, pestilences, terrors, and heavenly signs. A similar description of signs reappears in Luke 21:25, as Luke parallels what happens in the near future with what will happen in the end. There is a pattern to God's activity, even in the eschatological return. What happens to Jerusalem as A.D. 70 approaches will be like the real end, which brings the return. In these descriptions Jesus answers the disciples' short-term question about the temple, but he also sets up a long-term discussion about the end. The two events mirror each other in their terror.

3. Persecution (21:12–19)
a. Persecution and Testimony (21:12–13)

21:12 Jesus has already noted that false claims, social upheaval, and cosmic signs do not signal the coming of the end (21:7–11). He now describes something that precedes these "non-end" events: persecution. He seems to make the point that persecution is the church's short-term destiny. Only Luke has a temporal note, which helps to organize Jesus' reply and clarify the relationship between events.

Pursuit and arrest will be the fate of the disciples (Grundmann 1963: 381; Lohse, *TDNT* 9:430 §C1a).[23] They will end up in a variety of hostile settings with the opportunity to defend their confession. They will be delivered up to synagogues (παραδίδωμι, *paradidōmi*; Mark 13:11, 12 = Luke 21:16; Acts 8:3; 12:4; 21:11; 22:4; 27:1; 28:17), where they will face examination over minor issues and may well face beatings (Marshall 1978: 767; Schrage, *TDNT* 7:831). They will face prison as part of responding to more serious charges (Bertram, *TDNT* 9:244). The Book of Acts will note much persecution of the early church, which did not abate after the church's first generation. Some regard these initial descriptions as applying to Jewish settings, so that the following reference to kings and governors points

23. The phrase ἐπιβαλοῦσιν ἐφ᾽ ὑμᾶς τὰς χεῖρας (laying hands on you) occurs in 1 Kings 20:6 [21:6 LXX]; Luke 20:19; 22:53; Acts 4:3; 5:18; 12:1; 21:27; Mark 14:46; John 7:30, 44. On διώκω (lit., to pursue) as persecution, see Luke 11:49 and Acts 7:52.

to Gentiles; but this is not clearly supported by the historical data. Paul ended up in Roman prisons, and the other apostles ended up before Jewish rulers (Acts 4:3; 5:18; 12:1; 18:12; 21:27; 24:1–2; 25:8; 26:1; Ernst 1977: 558; Fitzmyer 1985: 1340). The contrast is better seen as one between religious authorities and civil authorities without regard to nationality.

Jesus mentions that the persecution will eventually bring the disciples before (ἀπάγω, apagō; BAGD 79; BAA 158 §2a; Acts 23:17) political rulers: kings and governors (the order in Matt. 10:18 = Mark 13:9 differs from Luke's). All of this trouble is "for the sake of Jesus' name," a phrase that dominates the Book of Acts (cf. seventeen times in Acts; plus John 15:21; 1 Pet. 4:14, 16; 3 John 7; Rev. 2:3) and shows Jesus' central position and the importance of allegiance in God's plan. Disciples will be identified with Jesus and will have to stand up for him.

Though conceptually similar, Luke differs in wording from Mark 13:9. Mark begins with a call to the disciples to take heed for themselves, and Jesus then explains that they will be taken up to "councils" (συνέδρια, synedria), a term that Luke does not use for his Gentile audience, since it refers to Jewish authorities. Jesus says that the disciples will be beaten in the synagogues and will stand before governors and kings (the word order moves from lesser to greater authority). This situation, too, is "for my sake" (ἕνεκεν ἐμοῦ, heneken emou). Matthew has similar remarks, not in his eschatological discourse but in earlier remarks to the disciples in Matt. 10:17 (Jesus evidently dealt with these themes in various settings). In the earlier Matthean text, persecution is part of the mission of the Twelve to Israel. Since a reference to the Son of Man's return also ends that passage (Matt. 10:23), the same pattern of treatment is present during the entire age until Jesus returns. The verse suggests that concern for Israel is present both before and after the cross. The wording of Matthew almost matches that of Mark: Matthew speaks of councils and synagogues where the disciples will be flogged, and he notes that they will be dragged before governors and kings "for my sake" (ἕνεκεν ἐμοῦ). Following Jesus is not easy.

The persecution provides (ἀποβαίνω, apobainō) an opportunity "for **21:13** testimony" (εἰς μαρτύριον, eis martyrion) and leads to the public proclamation of Jesus (BAGD 88 §2; BAA 177 §2; ἀποβαίνω elsewhere with this meaning only Phil. 1:19; Tiede 1988: 361; Manson 1949: 327).[24] The disciples will be placed before religious and civic

---

24. In Acts 4:24–31 believers rejoice that they are found worthy of suffering as they boldly declare Jesus' name. The church leaders are witnesses (μάρτυς) in the midst of rejection: Luke 24:48; Acts 1:8; 2:32; 3:15; 5:32; 10:39, 41; 13:31; 22:15; 26:16 (Isa. 43–44 alludes to this concept in the OT).

leaders to explain their commitment to Jesus (e.g., Paul received five floggings in the synagogue and three Roman scourgings with rods; 2 Cor. 11:24–25). This positive interpretation differs from the way many take the passage (Marshall 1978: 767–68). Arguing from the normal meaning of μαρτύριον (conceptually in Job 13:16 and 30:31; lexically in Deut. 31:26; Hos. 2:12 [2:14 LXX (≠ MT's sense)]; Mic. 1:2; 7:18; Zeph. 3:8; Mark 1:44; 6:11 = Luke 9:5; James 5:3), many see this action as providing testimony against the persecutors on judgment day, where μαρτύριον means "evidence." The testimony, however, is tied to what the disciples (ὑμῖν, *hymin*, to you) do as bearers of the testimony, as Luke 21:14–15 makes clear (Nolland 1993b: 996). As such, the focus is on the disciples, not their examiners. It also fits the force of the concept of witness in Acts. Jesus explains why the disciples need not worry when they are arrested, for this should not surprise them. God knows and sees their testimony.

The parallels are conceptually similar. Mark 13:9b has the simple εἰς μαρτύριον αὐτοῖς (*eis martyrion autois*, for testimony to/against them). Mark lacks explicit reference to the events leading to testimony; but if αὐτοῖς is a dative of disadvantage, it suggests that the disciples' presence will yield judgment for the opponents. If αὐτοῖς is not a dative of disadvantage, then only testimony is in view. The earlier Matt. 10:18b matches Mark verbally, except that it has εἰς μαρτύριον αὐτοῖς καὶ τοῖς ἔθνεσιν (*eis martyrion autois kai tois ethnesin*, for testimony to/against them and to/against the Gentiles), a reference that shows that the Matthean commission is designed to go beyond the earlier call to go to Israel alone (Matt. 10:5–6). The Matthean addition suggests that judgment is not in view in the Synoptics, since "for my sake as a testimony against them and against the Gentiles" is awkward in this context. In both Matthew and Mark, the arrest is an opportunity for preaching, not for vengeance (Rom. 12:17–21).

b. Divine Wisdom (21:14–15)

21:14 How should the disciples feel in the midst of this situation? Since persecution is used by God as an opportunity for testimony, no anxiety should be present, and so Jesus exhorts the disciples to set their hearts at rest about how they will reply. "Settle in the heart" is either a Semitism or a Septuagintalism (Luke 1:66; 1 Sam. 21:12 [21:13 LXX]; Mal. 2:2; Nolland 1993b: 996). The NT *hapax legomenon* προμελετάω (*promeletaō*, to practice beforehand; BAGD 708; BAA 1419) is a technical term for practicing a speech or rehearsing a dance (Aristophanes, *Parliament of Women* 117; Manson 1949: 327; Fitzmyer 1985: 1340; on the use of προμελετάω with a following infinitive, see BDF §392.2; BDR §392.2.8). No such preparation for the courtroom is necessary. As Luke 21:15 shows, God gives a special advocate (a similar point was made in 12:11–12).

Luke lacks at this point anything like Mark 13:10, which notes that the gospel must first go out to all the nations (Marshall 1978: 768 suggests that the omission results from Luke making the same point in either 21:24b or 24:47, while Nolland 1993b: 996 argues that Luke drops it for stylistic reasons since it does not fit the second-person plurals used in the Lucan form of the discourse). Mark 13:11 speaks of not being anxious (προμεριμνάω, *promerimnaō*) about what to say when the opposition hands over disciples to be tried. The wording of Matt. 10:19 looks like Luke 12:11–12: "When they deliver you over, do not worry (μεριμνάω, *merimnaō*) about how or what you will say."

Jesus offers a promise of provision in the midst of persecution: the **21:15** ability to speak effectively in the face of opposition (earlier of Jesus in 13:17). The reference to giving a mouth and wisdom explains why (γάρ, *gar*) one need not think ahead about what to say (on this idiom, see Acts 18:9–10; 4:29). Such provision recalls the promise to Moses (Exod. 4:11–12, 15–16; cf. Jer. 1:9; Ezek. 29:21; Acts 6:10). Opponents will be left silent by the reply—just as Jesus left his opponents silent in Luke 20. In the initial fulfillment of this promise, the disciples win respect under pressure (Acts 4:8–14; 7:54; 26:24–32). Some see a difference between this promise and Jesus' promise of the Spirit (Luke 12:12), but this is overinterpretation, since Jesus is the source of the Spirit, which enables one to speak (Acts 2:1–4, 32–33). If Luke makes any distinction between a general reference of provision versus the gift of the Spirit, it is to the Spirit's special work of aiding the disciple in preaching, not to a special prophetic office. This broad promise does not look at a special function given only to some.[25]

The other Synoptics are shorter: "Say whatever is given to you in that hour" (Mark 13:11b) and "What you shall say shall be given to you in that hour" (Matt. 10:19b). They also express the promise of provision in distinct terms: Matthew and Mark share the phrase ἐν ἐκείνῃ τῇ ὥρᾳ (en ekeinē tē hōra, in that hour), while Luke 12:12 speaks of the Holy Spirit's teaching what to say. The point in all cases is that God will lead one how to reply. At this point Luke lacks the explicit reference to the Spirit's speaking through them found in Matt. 10:20 = Mark 13:11c (Matthew refers to the Spirit of the Father, Mark to the Holy Spirit). Given Luke's emphasis on the Spirit, this curious omission suggests that Luke is following other material in this section.

---

25. Against Ellis 1974: 244, a "Christian prophet" is not likely in view (see Marshall 1978: 769). If it is, it is only in the broadest sense of forth-telling, as opposed to a special group of gifted saints.

c. Division of Family, Possible Martyrdom, and Hatred (21:16–17)

21:16 Not all of Jesus' news is positive: the disciples will be persecuted by family members, relatives, and friends (again using παραδίδωμι, *paradidōmi*, to hand over). Jesus will experience this kind of betrayal when Judas, one of the chosen Twelve, betrays him. Jesus does not promise physical victory; martyrdom will result for some (Matt. 10:35 = Luke 12:53). God will speak through them, but that does not mean their message will be accepted. Many early church leaders were put to death for their faith: Stephen (Acts 7), James the brother of John (Acts 12:2), Paul, Peter (crucified upside down according to *The Acts of Peter* 37–38 [Schneemelcher 1991–92. 2.315–16]), and Andrew. Manson (1949: 327) correctly notes that this Lucan saying is the opposite of saying that disciples must hate their relatives. Rather it is the relatives who will act against the disciples and end up hating them. This warning is important, since fear of familial rejection may cause some to hesitate to follow Jesus (Luke 14:26). Family members may turn the disciple in, since in many settings, especially first-century Jewish settings, Christians were subject to persecution and excommunication from the synagogue (see earlier 8:20–21; 9:59–60; Tiede 1988: 362). Roman persecutions created a similar environment. To confess Christ might mean being hated by kin. One must be ready to face the family's reaction, not by maliciously separating from them, but by preparing for their hostile reaction to one's confession of Christ. Former friends might also react negatively. Being a disciple can have its price.

Matthew 10:21 and Mark 13:12 are almost verbally exact, except for the connective (Matthew has δέ [but], Mark has καί [and]) and one issue of word order because δέ is a postpositive connective: "Brother will give over brother to death, and the father his child, and children will rise up against parents and have them put to death." They lack any mention of friends or relatives, though this is implied later in Mark 13:13. Commitment to Christ is a costly choice that could split a family and nullify the ties of blood.

21:17 Jesus intensifies the picture: confession of Christ yields hatred from many. The disciples will be the object of intense rejection "because of my name" (διὰ τὸ ὄνομά μου, *dia to onoma mou*; see 21:12). Their commitment to Jesus will offend many (Luke 6:22, 27; 1 Cor. 1:25–31). Πάντων (*pantōn*, all) is rhetorical, for clearly some in the community will love them. Thus, πάντων refers to "many" or "all" those outside the community.

Luke agrees word for word with Mark 13:13 and almost verbally matches Matt. 24:9b (Matthew refers to being hated by "all the nations" [πάντων τῶν ἐθνῶν, *pantōn tōn ethnōn*]). In most of the discourse, differences of wording abound, so the agreement here is striking. While the issue of sources behind the speech is complex, some material is clearly shared between the accounts. Yet issues of order remain, since Matthew has earlier what Mark and Luke appear to leave for later. The summary character of the material seems evident in these differences.

d. Divine Protection of Others (21:18)

21:18

Jesus becomes more positive. Despite hatred and potential death, final destruction is impossible for the disciple. In the face of a negative situation, Jesus offers comfort and assurance. He states the point rhetorically (not a hair on the disciple's head will be destroyed)[26] and emphatically (the double negative οὐ μή [*ou mē*] indicates that there is "no way" such destruction will occur). The rhetorical remark alludes to ultimate destruction, since 21:16b shows that martyrdom is clearly a possibility (Marshall 1978: 769; Plummer 1896: 480; Creed 1930: 256; Arndt 1956: 420; Leaney 1958: 261; cf. Luke 21:19; John 10:28). The remark is like Luke 12:4–5, 7 (Ellis 1974: 244). Other interpretations for the verse are often offered:

1. Fitzmyer (1985: 1341) rejects a rhetorical meaning, arguing that this is "another instance of Luke's lack of concern about ironing out things he puts together from various sources" (also apparently Manson 1949: 328). Given Jesus' frequent use of rhetoric, it is asking a lot of Luke, a normally careful writer, to contradict himself so clearly in the space of a few lines.
2. Geldenhuys (1951: 257) argues that the force is that nothing will happen without the Father's permission. This looks like an attempt to supply what is not stated. The resulting meaning blunts the verse's note of assurance.
3. J. Weiss (as noted by Marshall 1978: 769) argues that 21:16 applies to only a few, while 21:18 applies to most (perhaps also Klostermann 1929: 201; Nolland 1993b: 997–98). This view is close to the rhetorical sense and involves a deduction that is true, but it makes Jesus' point only physical survival. This view is possible and would mean that most will survive, just as Acts shows. Thus Luke 21:16 would read that some will die, but most will not perish.

Despite the attractiveness of view 3, the rhetorical sense is slightly better, making for a more unified sense, since the "you" under dis-

---

26. On the proverb about hair on the head, see Acts 27:34; 1 Sam. 14:45; 2 Sam. 14:11; 1 Kings 1:52; Dan. 3:27—though all these texts speak of physical well-being.

cussion never seems to shift in these verses (see the exegesis of 21:19 as well). The disciple who is allied to Christ is secure—despite persecution and threat to physical life.

Luke's remark is unique, which is just as curious as the previous verse's exact verbal agreement with the Synoptics—showing again a mixture of common and unique material. Conceptually, Luke is closer to Mark than to Matthew, which has more detail. Matthew speaks about many who fall away and many who betray and hate one another, along with a note about the arrival of false prophets who lead many astray, so that wickedness is multiplied and love grows cold. But Matthew's section falls earlier in the discourse, as noted in the exegesis of 21:17.

e. Endurance Leading to Salvation (21:19)

21:19 Jesus concludes the discussion on persecution by noting that endurance leads to salvation. The Christian virtue ὑπομονή (*hypomonē*) indicates endurance, steadfastness, or perseverance (BAGD 846; BAA 1686). Luke mentioned it in 8:15 as a virtue associated with fruit bearing. Paul loves the term (Rom. 2:7; 5:3, 4; 8:25; 15:4, 5; 2 Cor. 1:6; 6:4; 12:12; Col. 1:11; 1 Thess. 1:3; 2 Thess. 1:4; 3:5; 1 Tim. 6:11; 2 Tim. 3:10; Titus 2:2). Other NT writers also use it (Heb. 10:36; 12:1; James 1:3, 4; 5:11; 2 Pet. 1:6 [twice]; Rev. 1:9; 2:2, 3, 19; 3:10; 13:10; 14:12). Ὑπομονή is often tied to suffering (Rom. 8:25; 2 Cor. 1:6; Heb. 12:1; Rev. 3:10; 13:10). Jesus is saying that the disciple should cling to faith in the midst of persecution. Faith's presence results in "gaining" (κτάομαι, *ktaomai*; BAGD 455; BAA 924; elsewhere used by Luke at Luke 18:12; Acts 1:18; 8:20; 22:28) the soul (cf. Luke 9:24), that is, salvation. Saving faith does not renounce Jesus; it holds onto him even in the face of persecution. To cease to trust Jesus is to never have trusted him. Judas pictures one who failed. Peter pictures one who lapsed but whose commitment was real. The spiritual force of this verse reinforces that of 21:18 (Plummer 1896: 481). To cling to Jesus is to have life—even in the face of death.

Mark 13:13b makes the connection to salvation explicit: the one who endures to the end will be saved. If salvation means only "physical deliverance," then the remark is somewhat tautologous: "The one who endures to the end shall be physically delivered." In addition, those who endured were not always physically preserved (as the examples of Stephen, Paul, and Peter show; Luke 21:16; Schweizer, *TDNT* 9:647). If one sees physical deliverance in Mark, then the Synoptics go distinct directions (correctly Marshall 1978: 770). Matthew 24:13 agrees verbally with Mark. Luke speaks only of endurance, not of endurance to the end, because it might be confused with a reference to the eschatological end, which Luke has not raised directly yet (see the exegesis of the next verse).

4. Picture of the End: Jerusalem's Destruction (21:20–24)
a. Jerusalem Surrounded (21:20)

With this verse Luke's relationship to the other Synoptic accounts **21:20** becomes highly complex. Matthew 24:15–22 = Mark 13:14–20 describes the collapse of Jerusalem, which is definitely a part of the signs of consummation, as well as of fulfillment. The different emphases are most clearly indicated by what Luke lacks: he does not mention that the tribulation in this period is the most intense ever to fall on humans; he does not mention that no human would have survived if the Lord had not cut short these days; he does not note that the time should not be in the winter; and he does not discuss the "abomination of desolation," only "its desolation." Conversely, Luke alone mentions "the time of the Gentiles." What do these differences mean? They indicate that Luke emphasizes a different element in Jesus' teaching at this point. He focuses on the nearer fulfillment in the judgment pattern described here, the fall of Jerusalem in A.D. 70, rather than the end (which he will introduce directly in 21:25). The end is indirectly alluded to by the language of 21:23–24, which shows Luke's linkage and concern. It would seem that Luke sees in Jerusalem's collapse a preview, but with less intensity, of what the end will be like. So the instructions he offers here are like those that appear in the description of the end in 17:23, 31. He wants to make clear that when Jerusalem falls the first time, it is not yet the end. Nonetheless, the two falls are related and the presence of one pictures what the ultimate siege will be like. Both are eschatological events in God's plan, with the fall of Jerusalem being the down payment and guarantee of the end-time.

Some argue that this different emphasis is evidence that Jerusalem had already fallen and that Luke writes after the fact to put the event in perspective (Creed 1930: 256; Danker 1988: 333; Zmijewski 1972: 190–92). It is just as likely, however, that Luke in the 60s sees the handwriting on the wall for Jerusalem, based on covenant unfaithfulness, just as Jesus did. As such, Luke makes his focus the approach of the fall, using Jesus' teaching as a base (Geldenhuys 1951: 532).[27] Dodd (1947) argues that Luke is drawing on independent

---

27. Ellis 1974: 244 calls this a form of *"pesher*-ing" like that of Christian prophets, though he is clear that the texts go back to Jesus. If additional sources are in view (as noted below), this appeal to Christian prophets is not a necessary conclusion. The sources may reflect Jesus' own emphases, which were not one-dimensional, but complex. Later reflection on this speech may have seen more clearly the distinction between near and the end-time.

material such as the LXX, while Manson (1949: 328–31) argues for a distinct and older tradition (Marshall 1978: 770–71; Luce 1933: 322 [with some uncertainty]; Gaston 1970: 164–67). Jesus' teaching could be used because Jerusalem's fall pictures a horrific national judgment that is like the circumstances of the end-time as well as like judgments of old, a typological picture of what the consummation will be like—except that at the consummation, the nation Israel will be rescued as the OT promised (13:35 also suggests hope for Israel). The nation's house is abandoned unless it recognizes the Lord.

This verse describes the siege of Jerusalem in language that is less detailed but similar to 19:43–44. The NT *hapax legomenon* στρατόπεδον (*stratopedon*; BAGD 771; BAA 1538; Jer. 34:1 [41:1 LXX]) pictures a city surrounded by "encamped" soldiers (κυκλόω, *kykloō*; BAGD 456; BAA 928; elsewhere in the NT at John 10:24; Acts 14:20; Heb. 11:30; Marshall 1978: 772). The city is about to be desolated in judgment for its rejection of the day of visitation (ἐρήμωσις, *erēmōsis*, desolation; Ps. 73:19 [72:19 LXX]; 2 Chron. 36:21; Jer. 4:7). Luke's unique reference to "its" (αὐτῆς, *autēs*) desolation clearly means the city in the context of Luke 21:20. Josephus notes that 1.1 million Jews were killed and 97,000 taken captive in this period (Fitzmyer 1985: 1343).[28] Even children were cooked for food in the midst of the siege that Jesus anticipates here (Josephus, *Jewish War* 6.3.4 §§201–13). Unfaithfulness to God leads to national judgment. The city will collapse under siege. Jesus says such a fate for the religious center should not catch the disciples by surprise. These verses show that Jesus is now answering the question about the temple's destruction by describing the fall of the entire city. In effect, he is saying that Jerusalem must fall before the end. The length of the time between the two events is not made clear in the discourse.

The parallels take a distinctive turn and speak of the "abomination of desolation" (τὸ βδέλυγμα τῆς ἐρημώσεως, *to bdelygma tēs erēmōseōs*) set up where it should not be, a specific reference to the temple's desecration (Dan. 9:27; 11:31; 12:1; 1 Macc. 1:54; 2 Macc. 6:2). The Danielic usage is important because it shows that the phrase can be used for a variety of occasions where sacrilege occurs. Matthew 24:15 explicitly mentions the fulfillment of Daniel, while both Mark (13:14) and Matthew make a call for the reader to under-

---

28. Josephus, *Jewish War* 5–7, esp. 6.5.1 §§271–73; 6.9.3 §420; 7.5.3 §118; 7.5.5 §138; 7.5.6 §154. Plummer 1896: 482 thinks that Josephus's numbers are too high. Arndt 1956: 421–22 accepts them, arguing that many people had fled to the city, thus inflating its population. Regardless, it is clear that the city was leveled and much of its population slain. On the suggested population of Jerusalem during feast time, see excursus 11. Current scholarly estimates for feast-day population are 110,000–150,000.

stand what is meant. These passages look at the end and speak of the consummation, for the apocalyptic and OT notes struck here are stronger than in Luke's version. All three accounts complement one another and explain the short-term and long-term events: persecution is coming soon for Jerusalem (so Luke) and tribulation involving the desecration of the temple is coming in the end (so Matthew and Mark). Of course, in each case, a threat on the city means a threat to the temple, helping to make the interchange in meaning possible. Those who overrun the city will not ignore the temple (Nolland 1993b: 1000). The judgment on the city reflects both the OT and NT promises to judge unfaithfulness, a judgment that represents God's faithfulness to righteousness (Jer. 7:1–14; 22:5; Mic. 3:12; Luke 10:13–15).

b. The Days of Vengeance (21:21–22)

21:21 Jesus pictures the situation's severity. At the time of Jerusalem's desolation, the city will not be the place where one wants to be found. The exhortation to those in Judea to flee to the mountains indicates that the siege on the city will also influence the region, though the worst conditions will be in the city. The call to flee to the mountains for safety is a common OT and apocalyptic image (Gen. 19:17, 19; Judg. 6:2; 1 Sam. 23:19; 26:1; 1 Kings 22:17; Isa. 15:5; Jer. 16:16; 49:8; Ezek. 7:16; Amos 5:19–20; Nah. 3:18; Zech. 14:5; 1 Macc. 2:28; 2 Macc. 5:27; T. Moses 9.6; Marshall 1978: 772; Ernst 1977: 562). The wording of the first command exactly matches Matt. 24:16 = Mark 13:14b, but the rest of the verse is unique to Luke.

To reinforce the picture that Jerusalem is to be avoided during this period, Jesus issues two more commands to two audiences: those in the city and those in the country. First, those in the city should depart.[29] The ambiguity of the antecedent of ἐν μέσῳ αὐτῆς (*en mesō autēs*, in its midst) is resolved by the contrasting ἐν ταῖς χώραις (*en tais chōrais*, in the country). Since this second phrase cannot mean people living outside of Judea, but those outside of Jerusalem, ἐν μέσῳ αὐτῆς must refer to people living in Jerusalem. Jesus has thus again predicted the judgment that Jerusalem's rejection brings, a theme that he will note one more time (Luke 11:49–51; 19:41–44; 23:28–31; against Schweizer 1984: 316). I do not see the A.D. 70 event as having passed in order for the point to be made. Most see this as evidence that Luke brought in other material at this point, though it is debated whether he (Zmijewski 1972: 211–13) or a source (Marshall 1978: 772; Luce 1933: 322) is responsible for it.

---

29. Codex D adds a negative here—clearly a copyist's error—that commands those in Jerusalem not to depart.

The evidence as a whole suggests a source for this detail, which in turn is the cause for these unique Lucan perspectives.

Second, Jesus tells those in the country not to enter the city. Jerusalem is no place to be living when judgment rains down. Plummer (1896: 481) and Ernst (1977: 562) see this verse being fulfilled in Eusebius's record of Christians fleeing to Pella during the Jewish war because of an oracle (*Ecclesiastical History* 3.5.3). Marshall (1978: 772) objects that if Eusebius had this Lucan passage in mind he would have identified it more clearly, a point that seems likely. It cannot be ruled out, however, that the discourse tradition had left an impression on the church, causing them to flee, even if this text was not directly cited by Eusebius.

Another indication that Luke focuses on Jerusalem's near future is the absence of another remark in his version: he does not mention fleeing so quickly that one does not stop to pick up anything in the house, nor does he mention that those in the field who flee should not turn back (Matt. 24:17–18 = Mark 13:15–16). Luke has this point in Luke 17:31, when he is describing only the end-time period. This conclusion fits with the later Lucan omission, where Luke does not speak of unprecedented tribulation as Matthew and Mark do. In fact, Luke's omission of the scale of this tribulation may be another clue that the end is not the point here. Matthew and Mark note that the tribulation of that period will be "unprecedented in the creation," something that Jerusalem's fall, horrible as it was, definitely was not. Luke seems to be thinking primarily short term.

21:22 The reason to avoid the city is that it will be the object of divine judgment: ἡμέραι ἐκδικήσεως (*hēmerai ekdikēseōs*, days of vengeance; Schrenk, *TDNT* 2:446; BAGD 238; BAA 480; ἐκδίκησις elsewhere in the NT at Luke 18:7, 8; Acts 7:24; Rom. 12:19; 2 Cor. 7:11; 2 Thess. 1:8; Heb. 10:30; 1 Pet. 2:14). Since Scripture details such punishment for the nation as a response to covenantal unfaithfulness, Luke speaks of "all things being fulfilled," which here promises judgment for unfaithfulness (πίμπλημι, *pimplēmi*; BAGD 658; BAA 1325; Luke 18:31; 24:44; Acts 13:29; 24:14). Numerous texts give this warning (Lev. 26:31–33; Deut. 28:49–57; 32:35; 1 Kings 9:6–9; Isa. 34:8; Jer. 5:29; 6:1–8; 26:1–9; 46:10; 50:27; 51:6; Dan. 9:26; Hos. 9:7; Mic. 3:12; Zech. 8:1–8; 11:6; Zmijewski 1972: 184; Fitzmyer 1985: 1345; Marshall 1978: 773; Danker 1988: 334; Tiede 1988: 364).

Fitzmyer (1985: 1345) and Schweizer (1984: 317) say that this verse speaks of the end of Jerusalem's role in God's plan, but this overstatement is incorrect. Many OT passages speak of Jerusalem's earlier judgment, and yet it returned later to have a role in God's plan. In addition, the promise of Christ's return to the Mount of Olives in Acts 1:11 suggests that Jerusalem still has a role in what

God will do. This is a temporary setting aside of the city and the nation (Rom. 11:18–32). Eusebius (*Ecclesiastical History* 2.23.20) attributes this judgment to God's response for the execution of James the Just (the brother of John) in Acts 12:2. Luke would probably suggest that the reason for the city's collapse was its failure to respond to the day of its visitation, that is, the coming of Messiah (Luke 19:41–44; 13:34–35).

c. Woe for the Great Distress of Jerusalem (21:23–24)

Jesus declares the seriousness of the siege as he pronounces a woe **21:23** on pregnant women and mothers with young babies (cf. 19:44; 23:29).[30] Luke uses the broad ἐκείναις ταῖς ἡμέραις (*ekeinais tais hēmerais*, those days) to describe this period. Jesus goes on to explain (γάρ, *gar*) the nature of this time: great distress on the land and a period of wrath for the nation (Grundmann, *TDNT* 1:346; for messianic woes, see SB 4:977–1015; Danker 1988: 334).[31] That γῆ (*gē*) means "land" is suggested by the parallel reference to λαός (*laos*, people) (Plummer 1896: 482). The focus of these remarks from the Lucan perspective is the events of A.D. 70, but it must be remembered that these remarks are part of a pattern of judgment, so that they apply to the latter period as well.

The parallels, which focus on the end-time, are longer. Matthew 24:19–21 equals Luke in almost the exact same terms (Luke lacks δέ [*de*, but] and uses ἀνάγκη [*anankē*] for suffering [as opposed to Matthew's θλῖψις, *thlipsis*, distress, tribulation]), and Mark 13:17 agrees verbally with Matt. 24:19. But Mark 13:18–19 = Matt. 24:20–21 goes on to speak about praying that the situation not develop in winter or on a Sabbath (the latter only in Matthew). Matthew speaks uniquely of "your flight" (ἡ φυγὴ ὑμῶν, *hē phygē hymōn*), while the subject of γένηται (*genētai*, happen) in Mark is unspecified. In contrast to Luke's general remark about distress, Matthew and Mark speak of unprecedented tribulation (with Matthew calling it "great tribulation") and that no time is like it either before or after, thus showing their focus on the end-time. Attempts to apply this remark to A.D. 70 and make it rhetorical fail to come to grips with the unique judg-

---

30. Lucan woes are found elsewhere in 6:24–26; 10:13; 11:42–44, 46–47, 52; 17:1; 22:22. On the term οὐαί (woe), see the exegesis of 6:24.

31. In 1 Cor. 7:26 ἀνάγκη (distress) has a generalized eschatological force of drawing close to the end (BAGD 52 §2; BAA 102 §2), which equals the generalized description of desolation in Luke 21:20 (in 2 Cor. 6:4 and 12:10, ἀνάγκη lacks any eschatological force). The other term, ὀργή, often refers to divine wrath (BAGD 579 §2b; BAA 1173 §2b) and conceptually recalls Deut. 28:58–68, a covenantal curse passage (the phrase *all the nations* in Deut. 28:64 may recall the phrase *to all the nations* in Luke 21:24). See also Isa. 9:12 [9:11 MT]; Jer. 4:4; Ezek. 5:13; 30:3; 32:9; Rom. 2:8; 12:19; Eph. 2:3; 5:6; Col. 3:6; 1 Thess. 1:10; 5:9; Rev. 6:16, 17; 11:18; 14:10; 16:19; 19:15.

ment in view here, something that Jesus brings with his physical return. It also fails to recognize the passage's typological interplay revealed in the Synoptic variations. Matthew and Mark agree in this end-time emphasis, though each has slightly different wording. In Matthew and Mark, this is the period that immediately precedes the end, a period of intense persecution on Israel.

21:24 Luke uniquely describes Jerusalem's fall in the current age. Its citizens, especially the young mothers just mentioned, will fall to the sword (Gen. 34:26; Josh. 10:28; 1 Sam. 15:8; Sir. 28:18).[32] The citizens will go into captivity (αἰχμαλωτίζω, *aichmalōtizō*; 1 Macc. 10:33; Tob. 1:10; elsewhere in the NT at Rom. 7:23; 2 Cor. 10:5; 2 Tim. 3:6). Jerusalem will be "trodden down" (πατέω, *pateō*; BAGD 635 §1aγ; BAA 1281 §1aγ) by Gentiles (Zech. 12:3; also Ezek. 39:23; Dan. 2:44; 8:13–14; 12:5–13; 1 Macc. 3:45, 51; 4:60; 2 Macc. 8:2; Ps. Sol. 2.19; 17.22; Rev. 11:2; Brawley 1987: 125; Manson 1949: 331; Klostermann 1929: 203; Ernst 1977: 563; Marshall 1978: 773). These descriptions recall OT pictures of judgment and captivity for unfaithfulness, as Jesus speaks like an OT prophet. The picture is of swarming victorious armies conquering the nation's capital. Though Luke's focus is on the near fulfillment, the use of this language in Rev. 11:2 shows that the early church saw the allusion as referring to a future time of terror for the city. The passage shares a short- and long-term view. Because of his focus on the near future, Luke lacks reference to cutting short these days to spare the elect (Matt. 24:22 = Mark 13:20; cf. Isa. 54:7). Jerusalem's fall in the short term is analogous for the end, as its fate pictures the consequence of unfaithfulness for the world (Giblin 1985: 92).

More intriguing is the note that Jerusalem remains trodden down until "the times of the Gentiles" are fulfilled (Leaney 1958: 262; Danker 1988: 335; Manson 1949: 331). The phrase denotes, of course, Gentile domination (Dan. 2:44; 8:13–14; 12:5–13) and the subsequent hope for Israel (Ezek. 39:24–29; Zech. 12:4–9), but the note in Mark 13:10 that the gospel must be preached to "all the nations" before the end comes may also help explain the name.[33] This phrase suggests three things. First, the city's fall is of limited duration, or why else mention a time limit?

---

32. Danker 1988: 334 describes a coin of Vespasian and an inscription on the Arch of Titus where a Roman officer, with one foot on his helmet, stands guard by a palm tree under whose branches crouches a woman, the daughter of Zion, weeping over her defeat.

33. Cf. "times of the age" in Tob. 14:4–5 and "season of visitation" in 1QS 4.18–19. C. A. Evans 1990: 313 notes that this hope is a decisive argument against J. T. Sanders's claim (1987: 216–19) that Luke is anti-Semitic (he does see a future time when Israel will have a key role).

Second, there is a period in God's plan when Gentiles will dominate, which implies that the subsequent period is of a different nature (Ellis 1974: 245 says that the "times of the Gentiles" equals Gentile possession of Jerusalem that extends to the parousia; Zech. 8, 12–14). Jesus' initial coming and his return represent breaking points in God's plan. Arndt (1956: 422) denies this implication, wanting to be noncommittal on the verse, since "the times" has six possible senses: *seasons* (1) for executing divine judgments, (2) for Gentiles lording over Israel (so Creed 1930: 257), (3) for existing as Gentiles, (4) for Gentiles becoming subject to divine judgments, or *opportunities* (5) for Gentiles to turn to God, or (6) to possess privileges that Israel forfeited (listed by Plummer 1896: 483, who opts for either 1 or 6). But the question remains: Why describe this period this way unless there is an intended contrast between Israel and the Gentiles? In his detailed discussion, Giblin (1985: 89–92) argues that the phrase refers to a time of judgment on the world, but with no reference to a future for Israel (view 4). Giblin speaks correctly of a time of judgment on the nations and of the event as a fulfillment of the Scripture. But his descriptions seem to be limited to events at the end of the period, which is too narrow in focus. More likely, the "times of the Gentiles" is a general way to describe the current period in God's plan, when Gentiles are prominent but that will culminate in judgment on those nations. Giblin (1985: 91 n. 45) can deny restoration for Israel only by failing to relate this verse to Paul, Mark, and especially to other portions of Luke–Acts.[34]

Third, it would thus seem that this view of Israelite judgment now but vindication later suggests what Paul also argues in Rom. 11:25–26: Israel has a future in God's plan. Israel will be grafted back in when the fullness of Gentiles leads it to respond (see also Rom. 11:11–12, 15, 30–32). Considered with the more developed picture of Rev. 20, it seems that the early church held to a kingdom hope that included Israel's reincorporation in what eventually came to be expressed as millennial hope, a view called premillennialism or chiliasm.[35]

---

34. So Tiede 1980: 87–96 correctly shows that Luke teaches vengeance on Israel followed by vindication. Acts 3:19–21 suggests this most clearly, but so does Luke 13:35b by pointing to a day when Israel will respond to Messiah; see also C. A. Evans 1990: 313–14.

35. Amillennialism, the other major approach, does not distinguish between a thousand-year earthly kingdom and the eternal state. Much of Protestantism and Catholicism adopted amillennialism by holding to eschatology expressed by Augustine in his theological classic *The City of God*. Though the early church was chiliastic, this hope waned under Augustine's influence and excessive speculation about the millennium's material quality.

It may also be that καιροί (*kairoi*, times) is a Lucan technical term for the first of these eschatological periods, since the term has this technical meaning when it describes an era with an eschatological or periodizing emphasis, such as "times" or "periods" (Bock 1992c: 58–59). When the disciples ask whether this is the time (ἐν τῷ χρόνῳ τούτῳ, *en tō chronō toutō*) that Jesus will restore the kingdom to Israel, he replies that it is not for them to know "the times or the seasons" (χρόνους ἢ καιρούς, *chronous ē kairous*; Acts 1:7). This may suggest that two periods are present, with χρόνος referring to restoration in the future period and καιρός to the present period. In Acts 3:19–21, when Peter speaks about the "times of refreshing" (καιροὶ ἀναψύξεως, *kaipoi anapsyxeōs*) that come with forgiveness of sins (i.e., the current period), he may be intentionally separating that period from the future "times of restoration" (χρόνων ἀποκαταστάσεως, *chronōn apokatastaseōs*; Acts 3:21) that the OT prophets promised (i.e., the age to come). The other possibility is that καιροί and χρόνοι are synonymous and reflect a type of hendiadys. Luke 18:30 similarly refers to the current period of the disciples as "this time" (ἐν τῷ καιρῷ τούτῳ, *en tō kairō toutō*), while Acts 17:26 speaks of the "appointed times" (προστεταγμένους καιρούς, *prostetagmenous kairous*), contrasting the current period to an earlier one, and Acts 17:30 speaks of the "times of ignorance" (χρόνους τῆς ἀγνοίας, *chronous tēs agnoias*). This data, which is uniquely Lucan, suggests that there was some periodizing in the early church. Perhaps it came with some distinctness between καιροί and χρόνοι. Regardless of the terminology, conceptually Luke and Paul, as well as John, seem to hold out hope for the nation.

5. The End: Coming of the Son of Man (21:25–28)
a. Signs in the Heavens (21:25–26)

21:25   Jesus now turns his attention more directly to the end. The imagery is drawn from OT and apocalyptic pictures of the end that entail cosmic signs and changes (Isa. 13:9–10; 24:18–20; 34:4; Ezek. 32:7–8; Joel 2:10; 2:30–31 [3:3–4 MT]; 3:15 [4:15 MT]; Hag. 2:6, 21; 1 Enoch 80; T. Moses 10.5; 2 Bar. 70; 72:2; T. Levi 4.1; 2 Esdr. [= 4 Ezra] 5:4; Rev. 6:12–13; Plummer 1896: 483; Ernst 1977: 564–65; Marshall 1978: 775; Fitzmyer 1985: 1349; Rengstorf, *TDNT* 7:232). The natural wonders are comprehensive, involving sky and sea, so that humans are surrounded by creation's reaction to the end (the roaring-sea motif occurs in Isa. 17:12; Ps. 46:2–4 [46:3–5 MT]; 65:7 [65:8 MT]; 89:9 [89:10 MT]; 107:23–32; Wis. 5:22; Danker 1988: 336). Συνοχή (*synochē*, distress) normally refers to being chained, but may refer to the psychological state of anguish (thus, "trapped" or "tormented"; BAGD 791 §2; BAA 1578 §2; elsewhere in the NT only at 2 Cor. 2:4; also Job 30:3).[36] The description of perplexity, ἀπορία (*aporia*), draws on a *hapax legomenon* that, as a verb, refers to doubt or uncertainty (BAGD 97; BAA 196). It almost pictures "being at a loss" over a circumstance. When one considers how helpless people feel in the face of the full fury of a natural disaster, one can see the mood Jesus conveys here. The shift of temporal perspective is clear, since in Luke 21:19, the people under pressure are believers, while here it is the nations.

The parallels do not come directly to this cosmic issue, but have additional material dealing with the issue of false prophets and signs and wonders (Matt. 24:23–28 = Mark 13:21–23). Luke has similar remarks in his earlier discourse, which focused exclusively on the end (Luke 17:23–24, 37; cf. 21:8). Matthew 24:29 gives some timing: immediately after a period of false prophecy that might lead the elect astray (i.e., the period of unprecedented tribulation), such cosmic signs appear. In Mark and Matthew this is the second period of false prophecy connected to the end (contrast Mark 13:5–6 = Matt. 24:4–5), which Luke does not mention. This repetitive pattern reveals that, even in Matthew's more clearly end-time-oriented discourse, there is a break between the near and the distant future. Matthew is specific: the sun will darken, the moon will not give light, and stars will fall from heaven—language that recalls Isa. 13:10 and 34:4 (Rengstorf, *TDNT* 7:232). Mark 13:24–25 speaks of what will happen in those days and then describes the same cosmic signs in words that match Matthew, except that the stars' description is slightly different (Matthew: πεσοῦνται ἀπὸ τοῦ οὐρανοῦ [*pesountai apo tou ouranou*, will fall from heaven]; Mark: ἔσονται ἐκ τοῦ οὐρανοῦ πίπτοντες [*esontai ek tou ouranou piptontes*, will be falling from heaven]).

Jesus details the nature of human perplexity and its cause. Humans **21:26** will be overcome with fear (NT *hapax legomenon* ἀποψύχω, *apopsychō*; BAGD 102; BAA 205; 4 Macc. 15:18). In addition, they will look with "expectation" (προσδοκία, *prosdokia*; BAGD 712; BAA 1427; elsewhere in the NT only at Acts 12:11; cf. Isa. 13:6–10) about what is happening in the world because (γάρ, *gar* [Matthew and Mark have καί, and]) heavenly powers (i.e., heavenly bodies; 2 Kings 17:16; Dan. 8:10) will be shaken (the allusion is to Isa. 34:4). The graphic verb σαλεύω (*saleuō*, to shake) is used to describe reeds blown by the wind (Luke 7:24), the effect of earthquakes (Ps. 82:5

---

36. Marshall 1978: 775 notes that, in Greek astrological texts, συνοχή signifies the dismay caused by unfavorable omens, while Manson 1949: 332 says that it denotes "bewildered despair." Conzelmann, *TDNT* 7:440, says that the apocalyptic coloring is stronger in Luke.

[81:5 LXX]), and the shaking of a house at God's presence (Acts 4:31; BAGD 740; BAA 1482; cf. Hag. 2:21). One can only imagine the mood created by contemplating such a host of cosmic events as Jesus describes here. The emotive note is a somber one. Creation itself will signal God's judgment.

Luke is unique in mentioning the response in terms of fainting and foreboding. Matthew 24:29b = Mark 13:25b shares with Luke the remark about the powers of heaven shaking, though in this case, Luke is closer to Matthew in wording. All the Gospels have the same basic subject and verb: Mark has αἱ δυνάμεις αἱ ἐν τοῖς οὐρανοῖς (*hai dynameis hai en tois ouranois*, the powers in heaven); Matthew and Luke have αἱ δυνάμεις τῶν οὐρανῶν (*hai dynameis tōn ouranōn*, the powers of heaven).

b. The Authoritative Return of the Son of Man (21:27)

21:27 Next comes the Son of Man's return. The images come from Dan. 7 and are crucial to Luke's meaning. The force of this key chapter in a key OT book is debated (Bock 1987: 133–34). Who is this human-like figure who appears before the Ancient of Days?

1. Some see the Son of Man as originally angelic, a figure that was eventually redacted out of Daniel (Collins 1974). This view has well-known problems (Hartman and Di Lella 1978: 85–102). The basic issue is that the Book of Daniel is loaded with angelic imagery, so why excise it from Daniel if the Son of Man was originally angelic? There is no adequate rationale for such a change, especially since such a view would have been a good apology for how Christians employed the text. There is no evidence anywhere in Judaism that the Son of Man was ever understood as an angel.

2. Many see the text as exclusively messianic and appeal to traditional Christian exegesis and medieval rabbinic exegesis to defend the identification. The basic objection to this view is the association of the Son of Man with the saints in Dan. 7:18, 27.

3. Appealing to Dan. 7:18, 27, most OT scholars argue that the Son of Man is a corporate reference to the saints.[37] S. R. Driver (1900) is most responsible for popularizing this view. Several factors suggest that the image is not an exclusively corporate reference to Israel. (a) In Dan. 7 there is a universally recognized identity between the four beasts of Dan. 7 and the kings

---

37. Recent treatments taking this approach are Dunn 1980: 67–69; Casey 1979: 7–50; and Black 1976: 60–63, who argues that this text is unique, since it is the only place in the OT where Israel is "deified" (see Bock 1987: 335 n. 179 for refutation).

of certain nations. For example, the lion identifies not only Babylon, but also Nebuchadnezzar. Thus, regal-national interplay is built into the figures of the passage. (b) The translation of the crucial term in Dan. 7:14, פְּלַח (pĕlaḥ), is disputed. Driver (1900: 88) translates it "serve," thus making this verse teach that other nations will serve Israel. He justifies this translation by appealing to Dan. 7:27 and Tg. Jer. 27:6–8 (which reads very much like Dan. 7:27). But Daniel's own usage is against this imprecise reference. פְּלַח does refer to service, but only service of a certain kind, namely "religious service" or homage, something Israel was never promised it would receive from other nations. In Dan. 3:28, פְּלַח is parallel to סְגִד (sĕgid, to give homage), while in Dan. 6:16, 20 [6:17, 21 MT] the substantival participle פָּלַח (pālaḥ) is translated "worshiper." Thus, the Son of Man receives universal worship in his kingdom. This definition makes a reference to Israel unlikely.

4. The Son of Man is a reference to the "representative head" of a collective body of saints. In other words, there is a corporate-individual interplay in the figure, but the focus is on the king who heads the community. This honors the explanations of Dan. 7:18, 27, while also honoring the picture of the Son of Man as receiving homage. This is a more careful way to express view 2; it fits the context and recognizes the force of this mention of worship.

Thus, when Jesus mentions the coming of the Son of Man, he is referring to this regal figure who receives kingdom authority. Jesus' use is in line with the OT picture, for the Son of Man's rule derives from heaven, not human hands (Dan. 2).

Jesus says that the Son of Man will be seen coming on the clouds (Plummer 1896: 484; Marshall 1978: 776; cf. Zech 12:10; Rev. 1:7; 19:11–16). This image is important because the picture of a figure coming on the clouds is one of "superhuman majesty and state," to use S. R. Driver's apt description (1900: 88). The association of a figure "riding on the clouds" or with clouds is normally tied to the authority of God or the gods in the OT (Exod. 14:20; 34:5; Num. 10:34; Ps. 104:3; Isa. 19:1).[38] In other words, the Son of Man is a regal figure who receives kingdom authority and comes with superhuman majesty. Interestingly, Judaism also debated whether the imagery was regal/messianic (1 Enoch 37–71; 2 Esdr. [= 4 Ezra] 13; *b. Sanh.* 38b, 98a; Tg. 1 Chron. 3:24; France 1971: 185–86; SB 1:67, 486) or corporate (*b. Sanh.* 38b, in a warning about how the *minim* [Chris-

---

38. Emerton 1958: 232 holds to the angelic view in the original tradition, but notes that if it is not a reference to a divine figure, then it is unique among OT passages.

tians] use the passage).[39] Luke includes the allusion to the clouds because it is the key image of authority (note also the clouds in Acts 1:9–11). Here is the figure of the consummation arriving with great authority, like a deity. The one who returns brings judgment with the power of God. Anyone who heard Jesus use the Son-of-Man title or who read the Gospel account would know that Jesus was referring to himself and his return (see excursus 6 and the exegesis of 9:26; 12:8; and 17:30).

The Lucan text refers to Jesus' return in terms of great power and glory.[40] Jesus returns like a unique, regal figure. The remark anticipates what Dan. 7:18, 22, 27 describes: the Son of Man's coming to bring vindication to his suffering people. This is the moment that disciples long for—the Messiah coming in the totality of his authority.

The parallel Mark 13:26 = Matt. 24:30b is in almost verbal agreement. All say that the nations will see the Son of Man on (ἐπί [epi] in Matthew) or among (ἐν [en] in Mark and Luke) the clouds. The image is the same and may reflect variant translations of Aramaic עם (ʿim). Luke refers to the cloud singular (as he always does: Luke 9:34–35 [three times]; 12:54; Acts 1:9), while Mark and Matthew say clouds plural. The only other difference is the position of πολλῆς (pollēs, much), which in Matthew and Luke modifies "glory," while in Mark it modifies "power." Matthew has a unique reference before this remark: the nations will see the Son of Man's sign, and all the tribes of the earth will mourn (this reaction is because Jesus' appearing means judgment).

c. The Drawing Near of Redemption (21:28)

21:28 How will disciples react to this event? The Son of Man's appearance with cosmic signs represents the approach of the end-time.[41] Jesus

---

39. *B. Sanh.* 38b contains Rabbi Jose's famous condemnation of Rabbi Akiva for profaning the Shekinah by arguing that David could sit beside God on a heavenly throne.

40. For refutation of France's attempt (1971: 227–39) to tie this remark to A.D. 70, see Marshall 1978: 776–77, who notes that the presence of cosmic signs, the force of Dan. 7:13, and the context all argue against such a view. Marshall also defends the saying's authenticity and rightly questions attempts to reject the saying because of the Synoptic mixture of OT text (Ps. 110 and Dan. 7) or by holding that other sayings such as Mark 8:38 or 14:62 are earlier. Colpe, *TDNT* 8:450, and Perrin 1967: 173–85 deny authenticity; Hooker 1967: 148–59 and Borsch 1967: 361–64 defend it.

41. Marshall 1978: 777 notes that the antecedent of τούτων (these things) is unclear and opts for a reference to the signs, but it is more likely since the term is plural that the ambiguity is intentional and refers to the whole package (i.e., signs plus the Son of Man). Regardless of the choice, the decision represents only a slight difference, with the reference to the whole package being slightly broader than a reference just to cosmic signs.

notes that the Son of Man's appearance is cause for the disciples to lift up their heads, in contrast to the nations who cower and face the return with foreboding (Luke 21:26; Fitzmyer 1985: 1350; Marshall 1978: 777; Jeremias, *TDNT* 1:186; Judg. 8:28; Job 10:15; Ps. 24:7; 83:2 [83:3 MT]; Zech. 1:21 [2:4 MT]). The reason (διότι, *dioti*) is stated briefly: the saint's redemption draws near. Ἐγγίζω (*engizō*) here means to begin arriving. Redemption is used in a broad sense: not deliverance from the penalty of sin but deliverance from a fallen world (Büchsel, *TDNT* 4:352). This is the moment when the consummation of all that has been promised draws near, as Peter declares in Acts 3:19–21 when he speaks of Jesus' return (on creation's redemption, see Rom. 8:23). It looks past forgiveness of sins to the full demonstration of authority. When the Son of Man appears, he will exercise his authority; the time of victory will be here.

Matthew 24:31 = Mark 13:27 expresses this idea with distinct imagery. Matthew speaks of angels being sent out with the call of the great trumpet to gather the elect from the four winds, from one end of heaven to another. Mark also speaks of sending out the angels, gathering the elect from the four winds, from the ends of the earth to the ends of heaven. But only Matthew mentions the sounding of the great trumpet. Matthew 24:30–31 thus stresses both judgment and redemption, while Luke and Mark focus on redemption.

6. Parable of the Fig Tree (21:29–33)
a. As Fig Trees in Summer, So the Kingdom (21:29–31)

21:29 Jesus reinforces his message with a parable (other such introductions are found in 5:36; 6:39; 18:1). The call is to examine the fig tree in particular and all trees in general. Loved for their sweet fruit, fig trees (συκῆ, *sykē*; BAGD 776; BAA 1549) were common in Palestine, particularly around the Mount of Olives. When a fig tree begins to show shoots and leaves, it is a sign of summer. This tree is totally bare in the winter, so the appearance of life was particularly dramatic.

Matthew 24:32 = Mark 13:28 is slightly different from Luke, mentioning only the fig tree and no other trees. The Lucan form makes the point that the nature of the fig tree is not the issue, since any tree could reveal this lesson. Luke may be attempting to make the image clearer to a Gentile audience that is not familiar with the fig tree, or this may be "rhetorical extension" (so Fitzmyer 1985: 1352). Danker (1988: 337) suggests that the fig tree is mentioned by itself to prevent confusion about a reference to Israel's judgment (cf. Jer. 8:13; Mic. 7:1). Matthew and Mark read, "From the fig tree, learn (μάθετε, *mathete*) the parable." Παραβολή (*parabolē*) can here be translated "lesson." This is a nature parable, a lesson from creation. Luke 12:54–56 has a similar saying referring to nature.

21:30 Jesus makes the image clear. Trees bearing (προβάλλω, *proballō*; BAGD 702 §2; BAA 1408 §2; elsewhere in the NT only at Acts 19:33) leaves are a sign of the season. Jesus' point of comparison is the annual cycle: when greenery shows, summer is near.

Matthew 24:32b = Mark 13:28b is similar: the branch becomes tender and the tree puts forth leaves (with a case of reversed word order). They both then note, "You know that summer is (ἐστίν, *estin*, in Mark and Luke; lacking in Matthew) near." Luke's form is more abbreviated, speaking only of the leaves "showing," a verbal idea that only he uses. His double use of ἤδη (*ēdē*, already) is also unique.

21:31 Jesus applies the picture to the end (οὕτως, *houtōs*, thus) and says that when disciples see these things they can conclude that God's kingdom is near. This is a clear example where the reference to God's kingdom is to the "not yet" kingdom or the kingdom in consummation (other such uses in Luke include 11:2; 14:15; 17:20; and 19:11). It stands in contrast to declarations of the nearness or presence of the "already" kingdom in texts such as Luke 10:9, 11; 11:20; 17:21; 19:11; Matt. 3:2; 10:7; Mark 1:15.[42] This form of the kingdom is related to the promise of total redemption in 21:28 (Fitzmyer 1985: 1353). This will be an exciting time, because all of God's remaining promises will be realized and the saints vindicated (Luke 18:7–8; Rev. 19:11–22:15). The parable's point is that, just as people can observe the trees and know that summer is coming, so one can observe world events and know that the consummation is coming.

Matthew 24:33 = Mark 13:29 is parallel. Mark agrees verbally with Luke, except that he speaks of God as "near, at the gates." Luke seems to have specified the reference, rather than using a figure of speech. Matthew shares with Mark the reference to the gates and also speaks of seeing "all these things" (compared to Mark's and Luke's "seeing these things happen"). Marshall (1978: 779) defends the remark's authenticity.

b. The End: All within a Generation (21:32)

21:32 Jesus finishes his description of the end with a remark that has not lacked controversy. An emphatic οὐ μή (*ou mē*) construction notes that this generation *will not* pass away until all things have come to pass. The key point is the phrase ἡ γενεὰ αὕτη (*hē genea hautē*, this generation; cf. Gen. 7:1; Ps. 11:8 LXX [12:8 Engl.]). Several types of approaches attempt to interpret this phrase:

> 1. If γενεά refers to the generation of the disciples who are addressed, then Jesus is saying that they will see the end before

---

42. The phrase is usually applied to the "already" kingdom. For rejection of the idea that the kingdom is "delayed," see Bock 1992c. See the exegesis of 10:9 and 11:20.

they die (Luce 1933: 323–24; Manson 1949: 334, apparently). On this view, Jesus here teaches that the return and the end will come within the lifetime of the Twelve (McNeile 1915: 355; Kümmel 1957: 60; Grässer 1960: 128–30, 166; Maddox 1982: 111–15; Mattill 1979: 96–103; Wilson 1969–70). The most obvious objection to this view is that it makes Jesus manifestly wrong, and the church perpetuated this error when it continued to circulate these remarks after the disciples died (Ellis 1974: 246). If Jesus had really meant this, would not the church have buried such an embarrassing saying or abandoned this hope? The saying's presence suggests that something else is intended. Ellis notes that Luke seems to anticipate a period of time before the end to allow for worldwide mission. Would Luke mention this time for expansion if Jesus held to such instant imminence? Attempts to defend this view by arguing that Jesus did come in the form of Jerusalem's destruction do not work, since it is his physical return in total judgment, not an act of judgment or mere rule, that is in view (against Kik 1971: 127–57, esp. 137–38, 156–57).

2. A variation of view 1, advocated by Geiger (1976: 237), is that Luke means his generation, rather than that of Jesus. One's view of the nature of Jesus' prophetic gifts will influence whether this option is persuasive. It is certainly subtler to see Luke speaking of his generation rather than Jesus', but if γενεά refers to contemporaries, then the more natural reference is to Jesus'. Hiers (1973–74) and Franklin (1975: 14) attempt to deal with this problem by arguing that some of Jesus' contemporaries were still alive at the end of the first century. But this is simply Geiger's argument differently stated and is subject to all the criticisms that belong to the broader view. The difficulties with this "same generation" view have led to other approaches, some attempting to explain the remarks in terms of A.D. 70 while others try lexical or contextual solutions.

3. Some argue that Jesus refers to A.D. 70 as the end, that is, as the beginning of consummation (Geldenhuys 1951: 538–39) or as a type of the end of the world (Plummer 1896: 485). The advantage of this approach is that it takes most of the terms in a rather direct sense—except for the key reference to God's consummated kingdom. This latter problem makes this approach unlikely, unless one reads the point theologically in a prophetically foreshortened manner. There is no indication that the kingdom changed its nature in any way in A.D. 70 or that the later church recognized this event to be that transformation.

4. Another approach takes a lexical angle to argue that γενεά means a given race, namely, the Jewish nation (R. H. Lenski

[cited in Arndt 1956: 426–27] and Meinertz 1957). The point is that the Jewish race will not pass away before the end; there is a future for Israel. This interpretation is popular among dispensational interpreters, although not exclusively (e.g., Marxsen 1969: 195–96). Variations on this sense argue that γενεά means the human race (Schweizer 1984: 322; Tiede 1988: 369; Zmijewski 1972: 281–82; Conzelmann 1960: 105; Schneider 1975: 60), the "race of disciples" (Grundmann 1963: 385 [either this or the previous variation]), or "this type of generation" (i.e., the faithless generation of 11:29–32; Danker 1988: 338). The point is that the end will come before the end of humanity, the disciples, or this type of generation (Leaney 1958: 263). There will be a time of vindication. The major problem with this interpretation in all of its forms is that it is debated whether γενεά in isolation can have a racial sense.[43] Even more difficult is the equation γενεά = Israel, which combines a rare usage and a narrow, technical sense.[44] Luke 16:8 is the only possible example where γενεά = "people of the same kind," but the sense of this passage is disputed. In most passages, γενεά carries the sense of those living at a given time, the current time, a point that on the surface, favors any of the first three views (Matt. 12:45; 16:4; 17:17; Mark 8:12 [twice] = Luke 11:29–32 [five times]; Mark 8:38; Luke 7:31; 11:50, 51; 17:25; Acts 2:40; Phil. 2:15). If this rare sense is the meaning here, it is most unusual. Even assuming the lexical possibility, the following points are against this view in its variations: the Semitic term that means "generation" cannot carry the sense of "race";[45] a reference to humanity merely states the obvious

43. BAGD 153–54 and BAA 308 have such a category for γενεά but note its rarity—only "clan, race" in Luke 16:8, which is debated. Their other categories of meaning are "generation," "age," "period of time," and "family," while Büchsel, *TDNT* 1:662–65, speaks of "birth/descent," "progeny," "race," and "generation." When γενεά is qualified by the adjective *wicked*, the racial sense becomes possible, at least in the broad sense of "humanity," but this really results in an ethical force, not a racial one. The adjective makes clear the force of γενεά. The phrase ἡ γενεὰ αὕτη (this generation) is seen by some as a shortened "ethical" reference equal to "this type of generation." If one takes an ethical view and argues that γενεά has no temporal force, then the wicked-generation idea is the best suboption.

44. Why did Luke not make this point explicit anywhere else in Luke–Acts, or why did he not state it more clearly here, since elsewhere he speaks of the nation when he means such (e.g., Acts 1:6; 28:20)?

45. Mattill 1979: 97–100 surveys each NT use of ἡ γενεὰ αὕτη and opts for the usual sense of view 1. He does not, however, give any indication of the debate over 16:8; see also Jeremias 1971a: 135. Jesus' speech most likely would have been in Aramaic, which makes the Semitic point relevant, but only if one assumes a term-for-term rendering. A sense-rendering of Jesus' discourse would escape this objection.

(the return stops humanity from disappearing, or else why come?); a reference to the disciples as a race seems overly subtle (what indicates that they alone are "this generation"?); and a reference to "this type of generation" is equally subtle (though, of the suboptions, this one is the best, since the saying would make the point that evil people will be judged).

5. Another "already–not yet" approach argues that, in Jesus' view, the events of A.D. 70 and the end-time are inseparably linked, so that the fall of Jerusalem guarantees the completion of the other event. This view argues that the end has begun with events leading to the fall. That beginning happens within this generation. Plummer (1896: 485) says that the "the destruction of Jerusalem [is] the type of the end of the world," a view that goes back at least to J. A. Bengel (Arndt 1956: 426; Marshall 1978: 780 [who argues that the stress is on the resulting certainty of the end]). The remark's genre is prophecy, which often makes such a short-term–long-term linkage. As a result, Jesus is saying that this group of disciples will experience the catastrophe of A.D. 70 within their lifetime, an event that itself pictures the beginning of end-time events. As such, experiencing the fall in A.D. 70 is as good as experiencing the end, because one event pictures, guarantees, and reflects the other. Those who reject this view argue that "the things" mentioned in the passage explicitly include end-time events (Mattill 1979: 101). To accept this view also involves a shift in subject back to a focus on A.D. 70, which was seemingly left behind in 21:24. This view is subtle, too subtle for most, but it does fit the prophetic genre. As such it may be correct and should be considered a viable possibility.

6. Another solution argues that Jesus addresses the disciples as representatives of God's people. So when he speaks of the "generation" that sees these things, he means the generation that sees the events of the end (Fitzmyer 1985: 1353; Ellis 1974: 246–47 [who sees γενεά covering several generations, which is unlikely]).[46] Some argue that this view is tautologous, making Jesus say the obvious: "When you see the end, you see the end."[47] This misreads the point. What Jesus is saying is that the generation that sees the beginning of the end, also sees its end. When the signs come, they will proceed quickly; they will not

---

46. Ellis appeals to Qumran usage for support (1QpHab 2.7; 7.2) and equates it to the "last hour" in 1 John 2:18. Maddox 1982: 114 rightly asks if Qumran can deliver this extended force.

47. Maddox 1982: 114 suggests that the passage is meaningless without "any identifiable chronological significance."

drag on for many generations. It will happen within a generation. This view is a strong possibility and is the best of the options. The tradition reflected in Revelation shows that the consummation comes very quickly once it comes. The main
objection to this view is that γενεά usually refers to the present
generation, rather than to a deferred generation, a correct
point (see views 1 and 4). Nonetheless, in the discourse's prophetic context, the remark comes after making comments
about the nearness of the end *to certain signs*. As such it is the
issue of the signs that controls the passage's force, making this
view likely. If this view is correct, Jesus says that when the
signs of the beginning of the end come, then the end will come
relatively quickly, within a generation. (If this view is not correct, then either view 4 [this type of generation] or 5 [the beginning of the end of this generation] is likely.) It is hard to be
dogmatic about the meaning of this difficult text.

Matthew 24:34 differs from Luke only in saying that all "these
things" will come to pass in this generation. Mark 13:30 has this
phrase in a different word order and uses μέχρις οὗ (*mechris hou*,
until) where Matthew and Luke have ἕως ἄν (*heōs an*).

c. The Certainty of Jesus' Words (21:33)

21:33 Jesus emphasizes the certainty of his teaching with an emphatic
rhetorical remark: creation is less permanent than the truth of his
eschatological teaching. Heaven and earth will pass away, but Jesus'
words will not. This is similar to OT and Jewish texts that declare
the certainty of God's word (Fitzmyer 1985: 1353–54; Marshall
1978: 781; SB 1:244; Ps. 119:89, 160; Isa. 40:8; 55:10–11; Bar. 4:1;
Wis. 18:4; 2 Esdr. [= 4 Ezra] 9:36–37). The theme of the temporary
nature of the original creation is also a common note (Ernst 1977:
569; Ps. 102:26 [102:27 MT]; Isa. 51:6; Jer. 4:23–26; Amos 9:8;
1 Enoch 72.1; 91.16; Tg. Ps. 102:27 [printed in Walton 1657: 3.246;
SB 3:846]; 2 Pet. 3:10; Rev. 21:1). Jesus uses this expression in Matt.
5:18 and Luke 16:17, where he says that it is easier for heaven and
earth to pass away than for any aspect of the law to fail. Luke 21:33
is more emphatic in using a pure contrast. The repetition of the verb
in both halves of the verse emphasizes the contrast, as does the emphatic οὐ μή (*ou mē*, not) construction. Jesus is saying that the end
will come to pass as he has described.

Mark 13:31 verbally matches Luke, while Matt. 24:35 uses a singular form of the verbs in contrast to the plurals in the other accounts.
Matthew also uses a different verbal mood and tense in the second
half of the verse (παρέλθωσιν, *parelthōsin*, shall pass away). Luke

lacks the reference about no one knowing the time of the end except the Father, a reference found following this verse in Matt. 24:36 = Mark 13:32. Acts 1:7 is similar in force to these omitted verses.

7. Application: Call to Watch (21:34–36)
a. The Call to Heed Universal Judgment (21:34–35)

Jesus gives an exhortation growing out of his teaching: the disciples are to "take heed" (προσέχω, *prosechō*; BAGD 714 §1b; BAA 1431 §1b; also Luke 12:1; 17:3; Acts 5:35; 20:28), not to get careless about the event described in Jesus' teaching and believe that the day will never come or that it makes no difference how one lives. The particle μήποτε (*mēpote*, lest) introduces its clause and gives the result or risk of ignoring the day. Hearts "weighed down" (βαρέω, *bareō*) refers to insensitive hearts (Schrenk, *TDNT* 1:558–59; BAGD 133; BAA 267; elsewhere in the NT at Matt. 26:43; Luke 9:32; 2 Cor. 1:8; 5:4; 1 Tim. 5:16; also Exod. 7:14; 8:15 [8:11 LXX]; 9:7; Wis. 9:15). One can take a careless attitude about Jesus' return and give oneself over to carousing, excessive drink, and undue concern for the cares of life.[48] Marshall (1978: 782) argues that the allusion is to living in excessive attraction to an intoxicating, sinful world. This exhortation reminds one of the negative imagery of Luke 12:45–46 and 17:24. A person who is totally callous to the return will find it a difficult time. The danger is that "that day" will come suddenly (αἰφνίδιος, *aiphnidios*; BAGD 26; BAA 50; elsewhere in the NT only at 1 Thess. 5:3; also Wis. 17:14; 2 Macc. 14:17; 3 Macc. 3:24; cf. Luke 17:31). As Jesus says in other texts, that day will come like a thief (12:39–40). For those who are caught off guard it will be like a snare, a trap (παγίς, *pagis*; BAGD 602; BAA 1219; Isa. 24:17–18; elsewhere in the NT only at Rom. 11:9; 1 Tim. 3:7; 6:9; 2 Tim. 2:26). The image of a trap describes the quickness and unexpectedness with which that day will snap shut and catch its victim. The day will reveal God's judgment. Jesus' point is to be ready for it so as to not be left out (1 John 2:18–3:3 is similar in tone). The end's reality should call one to live prepared for the end, by being faithful to God.

There is no true parallel to this text in the other Synoptics. Matthew 24:43–51 tells the parable of the wicked servant at this point, while Mark 13:33–37 has an abbreviated form of the teaching. Luke's emphasis is uniquely expressed and may indicate the use of

21:34–35a

---

48. The NT *hapax legomenon* κραιπάλη refers to the dizziness or carousing associated with drunkenness; BAGD 448; BAA 910; Ps. 78:65 [77:65 LXX]; Isa. 24:20; 29:9. Μέθη (drunkenness) and μέριμνα (worries) are often mentioned in the NT as obstacles to spirituality: μέθη in Rom. 13:13 and Gal. 5:21, and μέριμνα in Matt. 13:22 = Mark 4:19 = Luke 8:14 (cf. Luke 12:22). On being morally sober, see 1 Thess. 5:7; on being spiritually directed, see Eph. 5:18.

other source material (Fitzmyer 1985: 1354 [L]; Marshall 1978: 782 [Lucan wording of tradition]).

21:35b The day will bring comprehensive judgment. The danger to disciples is noted because (γάρ, *gar*) of the day's universal scope (Jer. 48:43; 25:29; Rev. 14:6). Jesus notes that the day will come on all who dwell on the earth, a point that makes clear that end-time events are in view.

A textual problem with the position of γάρ influences the verse's interpretation and syntax. Does γάρ come after the verb ἐπεισελεύσεται (*epeiseleusetai*), thus linking the snare to what comes on the disciple (ℵ, B, D, many Itala, Coptic)? In this position γάρ indicates a new clause, meaning that the day will "catch" the disciple as it falls on everyone on the earth. Or does γάρ precede ἐπεισελεύσεται, so that the snare comes all on the earth (A, C, W, Δ, Θ, Ψ, family 1, family 13, Byz, Lect, some Itala, Vulgate, Syriac)? The early Alexandrian and Western alliance slightly favors γάρ after the verb, as does the fact that the other reading looks like Isa. 24:17 (Metzger 1975: 173). But the UBS–NA reading is harsh and may be too difficult. The second reading should probably be adopted (Zahn 1920: 659–60 n. 7). Thus, disciples should be careful because the end comes upon all.

b. Pray for Strength (21:36)

21:36 The discourse closes with an exhortation, a final call to faithfulness in the midst of the pressure. The disciples are to keep their eyes constantly on the watch for these events. Ἀγρυπνεῖτε (*agrypneite*, watch) is a present imperative that with the phrase *at all times* calls for a constant watch (Fitzmyer 1985: 1356; Danker 1988: 339).[49] Constant watch is necessary since the time of the return is unknown. With the constant watch comes the call to pray for the strength to endure temptation that will come from the persecution mentioned in 21:12–19, as well as from other pressures that disciples will face at the end (κατισχύω, *katischyō*, to have strength; BAGD 424; BAA 862; elsewhere in the NT only at Matt. 16:18; Luke 23:23; also Exod. 17:11; 1 Enoch 104.6).[50] Given this pressure, disciples are to rely on God's strength. The discourse thus ends with a note about standing

---

49. Ἀγρυπνέω occurs elsewhere in the NT at Mark 13:33; Eph. 6:18; Heb. 13:17; BAGD 14; BAA 24. The usual NT term for this concept is γρηγορέω (to watch); BAGD 167; BAA 334; e.g., Matt. 26:41; 1 Thess. 5:6; cf. 1 Pet. 4:7; 1 Esdr. 8:58 LXX [= 8:59 NRSV]; Luke 8:13; 22:40, 46.

50. Luke often emphasizes prayer for the disciple: δέομαι in Luke 5:12; 8:38; 9:38, 40; 22:32; Acts 4:31; 8:22, 24; and προσεύχομαι in Luke 1:10; 3:21; 5:16; 6:12; 11:1 [twice]; 18:1; Acts 1:24; 8:15; Zmijewski 1972: 289. Constant prayer is called for at Luke 18:1, 7–8; Rom. 12:12; and 1 Thess. 5:17.

before the Son of Man (also Luke 21:27–28). The image can be positive in the sense of standing with approval in deliverance (1 Enoch 62.8, 13; 1QH 4.21–22; Nolland 1993b: 1013), which is probably the force here. An example of such a faithful disciple is Stephen, who was slain for his testimony to God and received by the Son of Man standing at the right hand of God (Acts 7:56). This call to pray is found only in Luke. As the end comes, disciples are to look for heaven to come to earth and for divine strength to be faithful in the meantime.

8. Jesus Teaches at the Temple (21:37–38)
a. Teaching at the Temple, Lodging at Olives (21:37)

Luke turns from the discourse to a teaching summary that is unique **21:37** to him (other such summaries appear in 4:14–15; 19:47–48; 20:1). This summary serves as transition into the passion events and sets up a contrast between Jesus' involvement with the people and Judas's approaching treachery.

Luke makes two simple notes. First, Jesus continues to teach in the temple. The accusative τὰς ἡμέρας (tas hēmeras) indicates duration and means he taught "throughout the day" (Marshall 1978: 784). Despite the controversies with the leadership that dominated Luke 20, Jesus continued to have the people's ear, so he taught regularly. Second, he lodged (αὐλίζομαι, aulizomai; BAGD 121; BAA 243; Judg. 19:7; Ruth 3:13; elsewhere in the NT only at Matt. 21:17) at night at the Mount of Olives (Mark 11:11, 19 mentions Bethany, located on the edge of Olives; cf. Luke 19:29, 37). It is not clear whether he slept in a home or outdoors (Marshall 1978: 784 suggests various locales). Leaney (1958: 263) argues that the closing proves that Luke has set the preceding discourse in the temple. But the summary mentions two locales, the temple and where Jesus lodged. With this range, locating the teaching in the temple is not certain at all, since the remarks could have taken place on the way. No more details are given. This calm summary is the quiet before the storm.

b. People Hear Jesus Teach in the Morning (21:38)

Jesus continues to draw a crowd. The people make every effort to get **21:38** to him, beginning early in the day (ὀρθρίζω, orthrizō; a NT hapax legomenon; BAGD 580; BAA 1176; Exod. 24:4; Song 7:12 [7:13 LXX]). Luke uses a favorite term, λαός (laos), to describe the popular and receptive masses. The people simply wish to sit at Jesus' feet, but they will not have this desire for long. Events that trigger the end of Jesus' ministry draw near like a dark cloud. Soon the people will demand an end to his teaching.

Summary   The Lucan account of Jesus' Olivet Discourse (21:5–38) makes several key points.[51] First, some events must precede the end-time: the disciples' persecution, false claims about Messiah's coming, political and natural chaos, and Jerusalem's fall. Whether one views these to refer to short-term events or considers how they parallel events of the end-time, the period will be a difficult time for disciples. But provision is also present. Disciples can rely on divine guidance as they reply in the courts and stand up to persecution. Those who endure to the end (i.e., remain faithful to Jesus) gain their deliverance. Jesus informs the disciples of the temple's destruction and at the same time warns that tough times are ahead.

Second, Jerusalem's collapse is like the Son of Man's return. Both periods are difficult times of judgment for the earth. In the case of the return, it will come suddenly and visibly, with a range of cosmic signs. The effects of his coming will cover the entire earth and involve all humans. When the end comes, it comes quickly, within a generation from beginning to end. The return will signal the Son of Man's exercise of authority as Jesus reveals the full extent of his rule. His coming on the clouds will bring redemption for disciples and judgment for the world. Disciples should thus watch and live in such a way that they honor God in the meantime, since they do not know exactly when the end comes.

Third, Luke wants his readers to see that the end is certain and that the church will be under intense pressure until it comes. Disciples need to be prepared. But Jesus' authority, which is reflected in his return, also means an obligation to live in a way that is honoring to God. Only those dependent upon God and relying on the strength he provides will endure the pressure of this interim period. Jesus prepares disciples for his departure, reminding them that his return is more certain than the continuation of creation. Jesus assures his disciples that, despite his absence, he

---

51. I have not dealt with the issue of the tribulation's timing or the debate over when Jesus will come again for the church because the discourse does not raise these issues in this precise form (they can only be determined from other passages). But one point needs emphasis: the discourse covers persecution and cosmic disturbance in the interim *and* at the end. This dual perspective makes it clear that the discourse applies at various points to all believers and that the warnings and exhortations belong to the entire period between Jesus' departure and his return to earth. As such, the disciples are an appropriate audience for what is said here, since they experienced this rejection and the late first-century tumult that, in Luke's view, also pictures the end. The applications extend from the present into the future, until Jesus comes.

is in control, is watching, and will be returning to gather his own. He will show his authority to the world. Disciples are to live faithfully, watch, and pray until he returns.

Additional Notes

21:11. Most manuscripts (A, W, Δ, Θ, Ψ, Byz, Lect) read καὶ σημεῖα ἀπ᾽ οὐρανοῦ μεγάλα ἔσται (and there shall be great signs from heaven). The major factor against this reading is that none of the major Western or Alexandrian witnesses agree. The UBS–NA text is read by B and family 1: καὶ ἀπ᾽ οὐρανοῦ σημεῖα μεγάλα ἔσται (and there shall be great signs from heaven). Codexes ℵ, L, and 33 read καὶ σημεῖα μεγάλα ἀπ᾽ οὐρανοῦ ἔσται (and there shall be great signs from heaven). Family 13 agrees with ℵ et al. except for ἔσονται (they shall be) in place of ἔσται. Codex D and some Itala read ἀπ᾽ οὐρανοῦ καὶ σημεῖα μεγάλα ἔσται (there shall be [both fearful things] from heaven and great signs). Codex B's reading is deemed original because of its difficult word order, yet either one of the widely attested variants (that of A or ℵ) may be original (Metzger 1975: 172).

21:19. The aorist imperative κτήσασθε (gain, acquire; ℵ, D, L, W, Δ, Ψ, family 1, Byz, Lect) is better attested than the future indicative κτήσεσθε (you will gain; A, B, Θ, family 13, some Syriac, Itala, Vulgate), which is too similar to the other verbs in the context.

21:35. For the textual problem with the location of γάρ, see the exegesis of 21:35b.

21:38. A textual curiosity appears in family 13, which has next the pericope about the woman caught in adultery (John 7:53–8:11). This is not a Lucan pericope, since these are the only manuscripts that attest to its placement here.[52] It may be that the similarity of the Lucan summary to John 8:1–2 caused the relocation by the scribes.

---

52. For another view, see Cadbury 1917. H. J. Holtzmann sees the pericope as contained in Luke's sources (noted by Klostermann 1929: 205).

C. Betrayal and Farewell (22:1–38)

In two large sections, Luke concludes his Gospel: the passion narrative recounts Jesus' movement to the cross (Luke 22–23),[1] and the resurrection narrative contains an announcement and two appearances by Jesus (Luke 24). While focusing on Jesus' suffering in the last three chapters of his Gospel, Luke also addresses Judas's betrayal, Jesus' last meeting with the disciples, his many trials, his death and resurrection, and finally a promise to send the Spirit, which sets the stage for the Book of Acts. The main theme is Jesus' righteous suffering as an innocent martyr. The righteous-sufferer motif makes significant use of OT allusions in the crucifixion scene. All of Jesus' suffering is portrayed with reference to scriptural language and motifs. He is painted as God's righteous saint *par excellence*. In addition, Luke portrays the Jewish leadership as the driving force behind Jesus' death. It is popular to argue that Luke exonerates the Roman leadership, especially Pilate, in Jesus' death (e.g., Fitzmyer 1985: 1363–64), but this is overstated. Rome is portrayed unfavorably as it bows to pressure and fails to act on its conviction that Jesus is innocent—hardly a flattering image. When push comes to shove, Rome succumbs to public pressure. In addition, Luke pictures the cross as a struggle with Satan. Behind the scenes, a larger war is being waged. In this emphasis, Luke is largely alone, though John has a similar theme (Luke 22:3, 31, 53; John 13:2, 27; Fitzmyer 1985: 1367). Finally, there is the vindication the righteous one experiences through resurrection. The plan of God marches on as Jesus commissions the disciples to continue the task.

While the much-debated sources for 22:1–38 are best handled on a unit-by-unit basis, a few general comments are in order. The passion narrative is among the oldest and most developed of the traditional materials that circulated in the early church (Fitzmyer 1985: 1360–62). Pauline allusions to these events attest to this material (1 Cor. 11:23–26). The similarity between the Synoptics and John adds support to the view. The early church's preaching centered here, as 1 Cor. 15:3–5 and the speeches in the Book of Acts show. The Gospel accounts explain how and why the Messiah could die, how it was God's will, and how Jesus was in control during these

---

1. The term *passion* is a wordplay on Hebrew פֶּסַח (*pesaḥ*, Passover) and Greek πάσχω (*paschō*, to suffer); Fitzmyer 1985: 1369; Irenaeus, *Against Heresies* 4.10.1.

events. The debate about sources focuses on two questions: (1) Where did Mark get his material? and (2) Are the uniquely Lucan elements the product of additional sources or Lucan redaction?[2] On the issue of additional Lucan sources, opinion is equally divided whether Luke used a single source (V. Taylor 1926, 1972) or isolated traditions (Fitzmyer 1985: 1365–66).[3]

Supporting the view that Luke used an additional source of some kind are the points where Luke and John overlap without parallel in Matthew and Mark, as well as the amount of unique Lucan vocabulary in texts that thematically overlap with Mark to a level unlike other places where Luke and Mark overlap. The argument from vocabulary is Taylor's major criterion, but is challenged by Soards, who prefers an analysis based on content. The problem with Soards's approach is that, if the same event is in view, then parallelism of thought and content will be evident, even if distinct sources are present. It must be granted, however, that equivalent vocabulary is not the only way to test the presence of a source, for content is also significant. The question remains: if a source expressed fundamentally the same idea, then why was it changed? All other factors being equal, different vocabulary should suggest different sources, unless different vocabulary represents the common vocabulary of the author, his preference for a given style, or the presence of a theological emphasis. What is difficult to establish is whether this source is one tradition or a collection of traditions. It is best to work unit by unit to resolve this issue.

What makes this question so vexing is that Lucan order often differs from Marcan or Matthean order. Soards (1987: 127–28 n. 2) notes that, depending on how one counts, Luke varies from Mark eight to twenty-three times. He also notes (pp. 14–15) twenty-four Lucan omissions of material in Mark. Some material is unique to Luke; undebatably so are 22:3a, 15–16, 19e–f, 35–38; 23:6–16, 27–31, 39b–43. But many other passages are frequently put forward as reflecting unique Lucan material.

When it comes to Mark's sources, Fitzmyer (1985: 1361–62) notes the variety of theories, which run the spectrum from Mark's reproducing the ancient tradition in substance, to the material's gradual building through a variety of pieces, to a mix of tradition and Marcan redaction in each Marcan pericope (see J. Green 1988 for details). If the earlier noted theory that Luke had access to a second

2. For excellent overviews of the variety of positions on Lucan redaction, see Soards 1987: 13–16 and V. Taylor 1972: 3–27. Nolland 1993b: 1023 is convinced that Luke had a second source, which he thinks may be a continuous account.

3. Soards 1987: 13–16 notes a third position: that Luke composed the material, by which he means that Luke is responsible for some additional material.

source is correct, then it is quite likely a pre-Marcan passion source (Nolland 1993b: 1023). Details about sources and historicity must await the discussion of each pericope.

Luke provides more detail or fuller treatment at several places: the Last Supper sayings; Jesus' morning trial in front of the leadership; additional sayings at the crucifixion, including a conversation with those who were executed with him; and the resurrection appearances, including the Emmaus discussion (Marshall 1978: 785). Luke thus overlaps with the other Synoptics' portrayal of this period, while making significant unique contributions.

In the section 22:1–38, Judas plans to betray Jesus (22:1–6). But Jesus, well aware of events, plans a Passover meal (22:7–13). He celebrates the meal and symbolizes the approach of his death and the inauguration of the new covenant (22:14–20). The section closes with Jesus' final discourse, a testament of farewell, in which he notes the betrayer, speaks about greatness and service, appoints the remaining disciples to authority, predicts Peter's denials, and warns about rejection (22:21–38). Jesus is in control and signals that the disciples will carry out God's plan after his departure.

1. Judas's Plan to Betray (22:1–6)

In two movements, Luke 22:1–6 deals with the betrayal of Jesus. First, Luke reports the leaders' desire to kill Jesus, but he also notes their fear of the people (22:1–2). The leaders are powerless to act out their will. Their position is essentially the same as that noted in 19:47–48, but a new element is introduced. When Judas decides to betray Jesus, the foundation is laid to slay him (22:3–6). The last piece of the puzzle is put in place.

Sources and Historicity

Luke 22:1–6 has parallels in Matt. 26:1–16 = Mark 14:1–11 (Aland 1985: §305, §307). One major difference is that Luke lacks the Bethany anointing (Matt. 26:6–13 = Mark 14:3–9 = John 12:1–8). Most suspect that Luke omitted this account because of his similar account in Luke 7:36–50. The literary benefit of the omission is that Judas's betrayal is told without interruption. What is lost is the contrast between Judas's behavior and the woman's faithful actions.

Another interesting feature is the lack of vocabulary that matches Matthew and Mark—despite the similarity of the accounts. Luke is closer to Mark than to Matthew (compare Luke 22:1–2 = Matt. 26:1–5 = Mark 14:1–2). The outline of this oft-told tradition was the same, but the details were handled with some freedom of expression. Most see Luke simply abbreviating Mark 14:1 in Luke 22:1–2, while dealing with Mark 14:10–11 (and possibly another source at Luke 22:3a) in Luke 22:3–6.[1] There is no reason to question the historicity of the event's timing or of Judas's role, since the event's timing is probably alluded to in Jewish material (i.e., *b. Sanh.* 43a mentions Passover eve).

Form-critical classification of the pericopes in Luke 22–24 is generally less systematic than elsewhere in the Gospel; the accounts are typically viewed simply as passion material. Nonetheless, this account contains a variety of collective acts (Berger 1984: 323).[2] The outline of Luke 22:1–6 is as follows:

---

1. Fitzmyer 1985: 1368, 1373 strongly objects to Bultmann's questioning (1963: 262) of this material.

2. From here until Luke 24, I pay less attention to form since all the accounts are narrative descriptions of Jesus' death and resurrection, composed mostly of stories about Jesus and discourse material from him. For a summary of resurrection forms, see the introduction to 24:13–35.

a. The leadership's desire to slay Jesus (22:1–2)
   i. Setting: the Passover draws near (22:1)
   ii. The leadership desires to kill Jesus for fear of the people (22:2)
b. Judas volunteers to betray Jesus (22:3–6)
   i. Judas agrees to betray Jesus (22:3–4)
   ii. The leadership gladly agrees to pay Judas (22:5)
   iii. Judas looks for an opportunity (22:6)

The leaders are successful in overcoming a major obstacle—Jesus' popularity—to silencing Jesus. The solution is betrayal and denial by a "disciple." The leadership has great joy at getting to Jesus. With the payment for betrayal and a search for such an opportunity, the road is paved to Jesus' death.

Exegesis and Exposition

¹The Feast of Unleavened Bread, which is called Passover, drew near. ²And the chief priests and scribes were seeking how they might put him to death, for they feared the people.

³But Satan came into Judas Iscariot, who was one of the number of the Twelve. ⁴He went away to confer with the chief priests and officers about how he might betray him to them. ⁵And they were glad and engaged to give him money. ⁶And he agreed and sought an opportunity to betray him in the absence of the crowd.

a. The Leadership's Desire to Slay Jesus (22:1–2)
i. Setting: The Passover Draws Near (22:1)

22:1 The movement to passion begins with a note about the setting: the Feast of Unleavened Bread and Passover (Exod. 12:1–20; 23:15; 34:18; Deut. 16:1–8). The Feast of Unleavened Bread (Nisan 15–21), a week-long celebration, followed the day of Passover (Nisan 14–15). In fact, the two feasts were usually treated as one (Marshall 1978: 787; Jeremias, *TDNT* 5:898–904, esp. 898 n. 17; Windisch, *TDNT* 2:902; Josephus, *Antiquities* 3.10.5 §249; 14.2.1 §21; 17.9.3 §213; *Jewish War* 2.1.3 §10; B. Smith 1991: 32–39). The Passover and Unleavened Bread commemorate Israel's deliverance from Egypt, during which all the firstborn of Egypt died and the firstborn of Israel were "passed over" (Exod. 12; 23:15; 34:18; Lev. 23:5–6; Num. 28:16–17; Deut. 16:16). The next day Israel began its journey to the promised land. The Passover was the time when the nation reflected on its deliverance, as families held a meal to recall the event, sing, and offer thanks and sacrifices to God. Pilgrims flocked to the city to celebrate; Jerusalem was filled to capacity. Thus, the leaders' concern about the mass of people who might react to any action against Jesus is real (Luke 22:2, 6, 47; 23:4, 48).

The setting is full of irony. In the midst of this holiday season that celebrates life, the leadership schemes to end the life of one who comes to bring life. He is seen as a threat to their faith. A later Jewish text, *b. Sanh.* 43a, speaks of a certain Yeshu who practiced magic, led Israel into apostasy, and was executed by hanging on Passover eve (Fitzmyer 1985: 1369).

Matthew 26:1–2 contains a prediction of the Son of Man's betrayal, which will come as Passover draws near. With an introduction that looks more like Luke, Mark 14:1a notes that the events of betrayal fall within two days of the Passover and Unleavened Bread. Luke lacks specifics, only noting that the day is close.

ii. The Leadership Desires to Kill Jesus for Fear of the People (22:2)

The leaders' constant desire is to destroy Jesus (Luke 19:47–48). In this context, the imperfect ἐζήτουν (*ezētoun*, they were seeking) indicates that they were on constant watch for an opportunity to seize him (Marshall 1978: 787; Plummer 1896: 490).[3] The reason (γάρ, *gar*) is his growing popularity and the threat of a popular reaction (22:6; 20:19). In chapter 20, Luke shows why the leaders were afraid: Jesus could answer their questions and they could not answer his.[4]   **22:2**

The first seven terms of this verse match Mark 14:1b, but Mark has more detail: the leadership sought to seize him secretly and kill him. Matthew 26:3–4 provides still more detail: the leadership gathered in the courtyard of Caiaphas and took counsel as to how they might secretly seize Jesus and kill him. Mark 14:2 = Matt. 26:5 notes that the leaders decided not to do so during the feast because they feared a popular uprising—an ironic note in light of how things turn out. Even though they are in a position of power, they are not really in control. Matthew and Mark are almost in verbal agreement here, while Luke has an abbreviated form of this comment.

b. Judas Volunteers to Betray Jesus (22:3–6)
i. Judas Agrees to Betray Jesus (22:3–4)

Opportunity comes when Satan acts. Luke says simply that Satan entered Judas. The meaning of this expression is not entirely clear,   **22:3**

---

3. Ἀναιρέω (to put to death, destroy) is a favorite Lucan word, used twenty-one times by him, including Acts 2:23; 5:33; 7:28 [twice]; 9:23, 24, 29; 22:20; 23:15; 25:3; BAGD 54–55; BAA 107–8. The only non-Lucan uses are Matt. 2:16; 2 Thess. 2:8; Heb. 10:9.

4. Τὸ πῶς (how) reflects an indirect question; also 22:4. Luke likes to use πῶς in questions: 1:34; 6:42; 10:26; 11:18; 20:41, 44.

but its import is: Judas came under the control of the spiritual personification of evil, Satan. Judas acts and is responsible, but Satan is the impetus. Luke has not directly named Satan as an active agent since the temptations of Jesus in 4:1–13 (other mentions in 10:18; 11:18; 13:16). Frequently mentioned in Jewish writings, the name σατάν (Satan) derives from Hebrew שָׂטָן (śāṭān, adversary).[5] Luke elsewhere expresses demon possession as spiritual forces "entering" a person (Luke 8:30; 11:26; Acts 5:3; Mark 5:12–13; Ernst 1977: 575; on demon possession, see the introduction to Luke 4:31–44 and the exegesis of 4:33). The idea seems to emphasize demonic residence in, or at least control of, a person.[6] John 13:2, 11 makes a similar point about who motivated Judas to act, and John 13:27 repeats the expression "Satan came into him." Jesus' death is ultimately a cosmic battle of the greatest proportions. Satan is making his move.

Why Judas succumbed has been the object of great speculation. Some suggest that he was disappointed that Jesus did not set up an earthly kingdom, while others argue that he was covetous, since he received money for his services. The text does not tell us explicitly, except to say that he was "of the devil" (cf. John 6:70). His betrayal reveals his true character and shows that standing close to Jesus does not in itself guarantee spiritual success if the heart is not allied properly to God. Luke goes on to note that it was one of the Twelve who betrayed Jesus.[7] What the leadership could not engineer was accomplished with the help of one who was hand-picked by Jesus. Judas pictures the defector from the faith, one who links himself to Jesus only to deny him and show his real colors later.

Matthew 26:14 = Mark 14:10 simply declares that Judas went to the chief priests, so Luke is unique among the Synoptics in noting Satan's influence (Luke 22:31, 53 mentions the spiritual foe's involvement yet again). Given the greater detail in Luke and the simi-

---

5. BDB 966; BAGD 744; BAA 1490; 1 Chron. 21:1; Job 1:9–11. At Qumran and in other Jewish writings, Satan was frequently called Beliar or Belial; CD 4.13; 1QS 1.18, 24; 2.19; Jub. 10.11; T. Dan 5.1, 6; T. Ben. 6.1; *Life of Adam and Eve* 13.1. See also the "two spirits" of good and evil in 1QS 3.13–4.25; Nolland 1993b: 1030. J. Green 1988: 232–33 notes a conceptual parallel in the *Martyrdom and Ascension of Isaiah* 3.11 and 5.1, where Satan prompts Manasseh to seize Isaiah and saw him in two (an action that may be alluded to in Heb. 11:37). On the background to the figure Satan, see the exegesis of Luke 4:2.

6. Arndt 1956: 430 argues that demonic possession is not meant, but this conclusion is not clear from the text. Resolving such details is probably beyond our ability, given the brevity of the text.

7. The name *Iscariot* occurs here in its Grecized form ('Ἰσκαριώτην), not its Semitic form ('Ἰσκαριώθ), as in 6:16 (Fitzmyer 1985: 1374). Matthew here uses the Greek form, Mark the Semitic. On the Semitic form of the name, see the exegesis of 6:16.

lar perspective of John, it seems that Luke's material may well have origins in other traditional material.[8]

Luke explains exactly what Satan leads Judas to do: discuss betrayal **22:4** with the Jewish leadership. Luke uses his frequent style of the indirect question to reveal what they discussed (BDR §267.2–3). Στρατηγοί (*strategoi*) may well refer to the leaders of the temple guards who would have to arrest Jesus (Fitzmyer 1985: 1375; Marshall 1978: 788; SB 2:628–31; Bauernfeind, *TDNT* 7:709 n. 35; Josephus, *Jewish War* 6.5.3 §294; *Antiquities* 20.6.2 §131; *m.* ʾAbot 3.2; *m.* Yomaʾ 2.1, 9).[9] Luke makes much of the theme of delivering up Jesus (Luke 20:20; 23:25; 24:7, 20; Acts 3:13; Nolland 1993b:1030).

Matthew 26:15 uniquely shows the meeting's focus on a deal. For a fee Judas offers to hand over Jesus (παραδίδωμι, *paradidōmi*; cf. Luke 9:44; 18:32; 21:12, 16; 22:6, 21, 22, 48). Mark 14:10 notes that Judas went to the leadership in order to (ἵνα, *hina*) betray Jesus, thus the purpose of the meeting was betrayal. Neither Mark nor Matthew mention the soldiers.

ii. The Leadership Gladly Agrees to Pay Judas (22:5)

Judas is paid for his services, which makes his betrayal look even **22:5** more sinister and is the reason why many suggest that he was greedy or covetous. Judas could have done the deed for free, but he does it for money (Danker 1988: 343; cf. 1 Tim. 6:10). Matthew 26:15 notes that Judas raised the issue of payment, thus exposing more clearly the nature of his character.

Luke notes that the leadership "rejoiced" (ἐχάρησαν, *echarēsan*). Their joy is understandable, since betrayal by an insider means that Jesus can be handed over privately and that they can avoid the crowd's dangerous reaction. If any trouble were to arise, Judas could be a scapegoat. His testimony as an insider would be significant and could deflect blame from them. Thus the perfect opportunity to grab Jesus has come, and they seize it. As Plummer (1896: 491) says, the offer "simplified matters enormously."

Matthew 26:15 reveals the betrayal's specific price: thirty pieces of silver. Mark 14:11a agrees with Luke, but adds οἱ ἀκούσαντες (*hoi akousantes*, those who heard) as the subject and uses ἐπηγγείλαντο (*epēngeilanto*, they promised) for the agreement to pay money. Luke

---

8. Soards 1987: 49 and J. Green 1988: 231–33 argue that Luke used traditional material to which John also had access.

9. Στρατηγός is used ten times in the NT, all by Luke: Luke 22:52; Acts 4:1; 5:24, 26; 16:20, 22, 35, 36, 38. A related verb appears seven times in the writings of Paul, James, Peter, and Luke.

uses συντίθημι (*syntithēmi*) for this promise (BAGD 792 §2aα; BAA 1581 §2aα; elsewhere in the NT only at Acts 23:20 and John 9:22), which is a term often used for a mutual agreement. They have a deal.

iii. Judas Looks for an Opportunity (22:6)

22:6 Judas accepts the arrangement with the leadership and begins looking for his opportunity. The term ἐξωμολόγησεν (*exōmologēsen*, he agreed) may contain a touch of irony, since the middle voice means "to confess" and could suggest the very denial of allegiance that Judas's act is (Michel, *TDNT* 5:207, 213; BAGD 277; BAA 560). Here, of course, the term is active and means "to consent" (Lysias 12.9 [121], using a nonprefixed form of the verb; Klostermann 1929: 205–6; Marshall 1978: 789). The event has the look of a formal negotiation, with Jesus as both the prize and the pawn. Judas's goal is to find a time when Jesus can be seized without the crowd being present. He makes a "safe" arrest possible. In this context, as in 22:2, the imperfect ἐζήτει (*ezētei*, he was seeking) shows that he was constantly looking for such an opportunity. Luke uses the normal term for betrayal: παραδίδωμι (*paradidōmi*, to hand over; also 22:4). There is no doubt about the historicity of these details, for why would the church invent a story of conspiracy by one of its own?

Matthew 26:16 says simply that (ἵνα, *hina*) from then on Judas sought a good opportunity (εὐκαιρίαν, *eukairian*) to hand over Jesus (Delling, *TDNT* 3:462). Saying the same thing, Mark 14:11 uses πῶς (*pōs*, how) and Luke uses his customary infinitive (Marshall 1978: 789). All three accounts have the key imperfect ἐζήτει (he was seeking). The hunt is on.

Summary   Luke 22:1–6 begins the movement to crucifixion. The major impetus comes from outside spiritual forces and from inside the Twelve. The key holiday period of Passover approaches, with the leadership still frustrated by their inability to seize Jesus. Whatever they decide, they know it must be done covertly to avoid upsetting the crowd that follows Jesus. Judas provides such an opportunity by offering to hand over Jesus. The only reason given is that Satan is at work in Judas. Sinister forces are behind Jesus' death.

The account shows that the events surrounding Jesus' ministry are part of a larger, cosmic drama between great spiritual powers. Heaven and hell are interested in the fate of Jesus. In the great chess match, this is Satan's major move to remove Jesus from the game. The detail heightens the gravity of the event.

Another significant note is Judas's ability to be part of Jesus' most intimate group and yet deny him. Some who associate with

Jesus for a time will ultimately deny him. Until their desertion, they will look every bit like disciples. Defection in the ranks is a real possibility, and Judas's example is an exhortation to constancy of faith. The tragic end of Judas, which Luke will note in Acts 1:16–20, conveys the sad picture of his departure. The wheels are now in motion to send Jesus to the cross. The passion draws near; the betrayal is planned. The plan to hand over Jesus has begun; the hounds are out of the pen.

2. Preparing for the Meal (22:7–13)

Luke 22:7 begins a series of passages that deal with the Last Supper: preparation for the meal (22:7–13), the meal proper (22:14–20), and Jesus' farewell discourse (22:21–38). In the discourse, Jesus predicts his betrayal (22:21–23), solves a dispute about greatness by calling for service (22:24–30), reveals his knowledge of the future as he predicts Peter's denial (22:31–34), and issues new enigmatic instructions to his disciples (22:35–38). All of these events show Jesus' control of the events swirling around him.

In 22:7–13, Jesus directs his disciples to the place where they will eat the Passover meal. It is not clear if the meeting had already been arranged or whether Jesus had foreknowledge of it (Nolland 1993b: 1032). Either way, he controls events. The quiet sending out of two disciples may be to avoid arrest before this key meal (Marshall 1978: 789; Arndt 1956: 432). This pericope not only introduces the supper but also shows Jesus as a pious, observant Jew to the end. He desires to celebrate Passover in the city. Tradition dictated that Passover be celebrated in the temple courts (Deut. 16:16; 2 Chron. 35:16–19; Jub. 49.15–16). When pilgrims became too numerous for the temple, the entire city served as a suitable locale (Fitzmyer 1985: 1377).

Sources and Historicity

The parallels to this passage are clearly Mark 14:12–16 = Matt. 26:17–19 (Aland 1985: §308). Matthew's version is the shortest of the three. Luke stands closer to Mark since they share more vocabulary. There are two differences between Mark and Luke. (1) In Luke, Jesus initiates the discussion about the meeting place, while in Mark the disciples ask where the meal is to be held, a remark that Luke has in response to Jesus' initiation of the discussion. Luke appears to be more complete at this point. (2) Luke alone identifies the two disciples as Peter and John.

The issue of historicity is not doubted at one level: all agree that there was such a meal. The Jesus Seminar (Funk and Hoover 1993: 386–87) doubts the authenticity of the dialogue, printing 22:8, 10–12 in black type. The seminar argues that the differences in the accounts show that Luke had only Mark 13:12–16 and that the account reflects the "invention of the story-teller." Though the dialogue is summarized, there is no credible explanation for why such an exchange would have been created by the church. The uncertainty about whether Jesus exhibits foreknowledge or prearranged the event shows that the account was told at a low-key level. The account has good historical roots (Nolland 1993b: 1032). But the meal's nature and timing in the last week are much discussed (see excursus 11). Nonetheless, it is probably a Passover meal that Jesus sends the disciples to prepare.

> The account is a "story about Jesus" that shows his control of events (Fitzmyer 1985: 1377; Bultmann 1963: 263–64). The outline of Luke 22:7–13 is as follows:
>
> a. Setting (22:7)
> b. Instructions about the meal (22:8–12)
>   i. Jesus sends Peter and John (22:8)
>   ii. The disciples' question (22:9)
>   iii. Jesus' instruction (22:10–12)
> c. Fulfillment (22:13)
>
> The account reveals Jesus' piety; he observes the meal even as he faces his approaching death. He is in control of events. There is irony in the betrayal's sacred setting: a meal commemorating deliverance is also a meal that points to a sacred death. The moment is emotional at several levels: Jesus is about to be given over to the nation, and the disciples celebrate the nation's freeing by God. The irony and the mystery could not be greater.

Exegesis and Exposition

[7]And the day ⌜of Unleavened Bread⌝ came, when the Passover lamb was to be sacrificed. [8]And he sent Peter and John, saying, "Go prepare the Passover for us that we may eat." [9]But they said to him, "Where do you wish that we should prepare it?" [10]And he said to them, "Behold, when you have entered the city, a man carrying a jar of water will meet you. Follow him into the house into which he enters [11]and speak to the owner of the house, 'The teacher says to you, "Where is the guest room, where I may eat the Passover with my disciples?"' [12]And that one will show you a large, furnished upper room. There make ready." [13]And when they went out, they found it as he had told them; and they prepared the Passover.

a. Setting (22:7)

As the sacred Passover and Feast of Unleavened Bread (ἄζυμος, *azymos*) approach, Jesus gives instructions about how he will celebrate the meal. Luke simply notes the holiday's arrival and explains that during this period the Passover lamb must be sacrificed. Ἦλθεν

22:7

(*ēlthen*, it came) should be read with the force of "arrived," given that the Passover was approaching (ἤγγιζεν, *ēngizen*) in 22:1 (this interpretation agrees with Matthew and Mark). The use of ἔδει (*edei*, it was necessary) shows that the feast must be celebrated by a pious Jew. Πάσχα (*pascha*, Passover) is a figurative metonymy in which the day is named by what is slain on it, that is, the Passover lamb (Jeremias, *TDNT* 5:897; Luke 22:11; Fitzmyer 1985: 1382; Exod. 12:1–30, 43–46; Num. 9:1–14; Deut. 16:1–8; 2 Chron. 30:18; Ezra 6:19–22; Jub. 49). Passover lambs were slain between 2:30 P.M. and 5:30 P.M. in the temple court. As he did in 22:1, Luke refers to the period by the broad description "the Feast of Unleavened Bread," which covers both Passover and Unleavened Bread.

Matthew and Mark agree that the disciples raised the question of where the meal would be observed. And all three Synoptics agree on the timing: Mark 14:12 says "on the first day of the Feast of Unleavened Bread," and Matt. 26:17 has "on the first of the Unleavened Bread." These general remarks loosely time the event, since the feast did not technically begin until sunset. The Synoptics probably use this description because the activity took place on the same "human day" (SB 2:813–15; Marshall 1978: 791; Fitzmyer 1985: 1382; Josephus, *Jewish War* 5.3.1 §99; *Mekilta de Rabbi Ishmael*, tractate *Pisḥa* 8 on Exod. 12:15 [Lauterbach 1933–35: 1.61–63]; on the possible redactional possibilities of this entire unit, see J. Green 1987). It is remotely possible that the Synoptists are using a midday-to-midday reckoning of the day, in contrast to the typical Jewish sunset-to-sunset reckoning (so Luce 1933: 327; Marshall correctly calls this suggestion improbable but lacks an explicit reason). It reflects a less common way to reckon daytime. The use of popular idiom is more likely than a calendrical difference, since there is no indication of a calendrical shift (see excursus 11). John 13:1 speaks of "before the Feast of Passover" and then describes the washing of the disciples' feet, thus alluding to the entire feast period, which began with the meal.

b. Instructions about the Meal (22:8–12)
i. Jesus Sends Peter and John (22:8)

22:8 Jesus tells Peter and John to go prepare a place for the Passover (cf. the sequence in Luke 19:29–32). The Lucan version is unique in naming Peter and John and in showing Jesus' initiative, since in Matthew and Mark the disciples ask Jesus about the meal. The Lucan version is also more comprehensive. The reference to Passover here specifically means the meal (Barrett 1958).

Luke frequently mentions Peter and John together (Luke 8:51; 9:28; Acts 1:13; 3:1–4; 4:13, 19; 8:14). Together they witnessed the transfiguration, and together they will witness the resurrection.

Jesus gives them responsibility for the meal's preparation (ἑτοιμάζω [*hetoimazō*, to prepare] dominates the passage; Luke 22:8, 9, 12, 13). Their tasks are to secure a room, get the lamb slain at the temple, pick up bitter herbs, purchase the unleavened bread, and obtain wine for the meal (Luce 1933: 328; Ellis 1974: 252; Marshall 1978: 791). Obtaining the room was an important task since many pilgrims were in the city looking for similar festal accommodations. The future leaders of the apostolic group are here learning to serve (22:24–27; Nolland 1993b: 1033).

Some discussion surrounds the issue of who is responsible for the additional detail (see the additional note). Grundmann (1963: 390–91) and Soards (1987: 38) speak of special Lucan material, while Fitzmyer (1985: 1382–83) refers to Lucan redaction and excludes a non-Marcan source. Though there is little to work with in terms of data, the possibility of an additional source for this detail is likely, especially when one notes that Luke expresses the passage in terms of obtaining a meal for the group, while Matthew and Mark speak of a concern for where Jesus will eat the meal. But as with many such discussions, it is hard to be sure either way.

ii. The Disciples' Question (22:9)

The disciples ask if Jesus has in mind a specific location. The Lucan form of the question is abbreviated, but is essentially the same as Mark 14:12b = Matt. 26:17b. All the accounts share ποῦ θέλεις (*pou theleis*, where do you wish?) and ἑτοιμάσωμεν (*hetoimasōmen*, we might prepare). This last term is a deliberative subjunctive that shows the disciples' desire to follow Jesus' instructions. They are ready to do what Jesus asks so that they can celebrate the solemn day together.

22:9

iii. Jesus' Instruction (22:10–12)

Jesus' instructions are simple and clear. The disciples are to look for a man carrying a jar of water. The man is probably a servant, since servants or women normally drew water, and the owner is mentioned separately in 22:11 (Plummer 1896: 492; Gen. 24:11; Deut. 29:11 [29:10 MT]; Josh. 9:21–27; John 4:7). Marshall (1978: 791) notes that men normally carried leather bottles, as Luke 5:37–38 suggests. The jar is described as a κεράμιον (*keramion*), an earthenware vessel that holds water (Jer. 35:5 [42:5 LXX]; BAGD 428; BAA 872; elsewhere in the NT only at Mark 14:13). The term for bearing, βαστάζω (*bastazō*), is used in Luke 7:14 for bearing a coffin, in the parallel Mark 14:13 for bearing a jar, and in John 19:17 for bearing a cross. The disciples are simply to follow the man into the house. Though it could be argued that this meeting is a sign of Jesus' fore-

22:10

knowledge, it also could have been prearranged.[1] Matthew's language about going to a specific man looks like an arrangement, since the man is told both who and what is coming. The jar may help the disciples identify the man who is to meet them and may have been used for hand-washing before the meal. The detailed instructions show that Jesus is in control of events.

Some point to 1 Sam. 10:2–8 for a parallel. In fact, Bultmann (1963: 263–64) argues that the Gospel passage was formed on this account, but this conclusion is unlikely since the articles carried there are animals, bread, and wineskins, not jars. Bultmann calls the NT account secondary and ultimately based on a "fairy-tale motif." Such an arrangement, however, is not so difficult and would be natural in a situation where a place for the Passover meal must be found. Bultmann's view is based on his belief that a Passover meal is not present and that the chronological data in the Synoptics is erroneous (see excursus 11). Also unlikely is Ellis's claim (1974: 252) that the instructions were to avoid detection for holding the meal early. Jesus is simply making arrangements to have the meal.

Matthew is different and briefer than the other two Synoptics: Matt. 26:18 simply notes that they are to go into the city and tell a certain man that the Passover will be held in his house. Matthew's account looks telescoped, as is his habit (e.g., Matt. 8:5–13 versus Luke 7:1–10). Mark 14:13b is closer to Luke. Matthew and Mark use the verb ὑπάγετε (*hypagete*, you go up), while Luke uses the temporal participle εἰσελθόντων (*eiselthontōn*, going into or when you go into) and a similar verb at the end of the verse. Mark's phrase describing a man bearing a jar of water matches Luke, as does the instruction to follow him, although Luke uniquely has the phrase "into the house he enters." The verb for "meet" differs slightly: Mark has ἀπαντήσει (*apantēsei*, will meet), Luke συναντήσει (*synantēsei*, will meet). These represent stylistic choices (Nolland 1993b: 1033).

22:11 Jesus gives instructions about what the disciples are to do upon arrival. Once in the house, the disciples are to address the owner, apparently a disciple (the future ἐρεῖτε [*ereite*] functions as an imperative: "Speak"; also Luke 19:31). All they need to note is that the teacher speaks. They are to ask where the κατάλυμα (*katalyma*, guest room) is so he can have the Passover meal with his disciples.[2]

---

1. Fitzmyer 1985: 1383 overstates the passage by arguing that Matthew and Luke are different. Marshall 1978: 791–92 suggests that the Lucan details point to arrangement.

2. Κατάλυμα is a private house, but in Luke 2:7 it refers to the inn where Jesus was born; elsewhere in the NT only at the parallel Mark 14:14; also 1 Sam. 1:18 [no MT equivalent]; 9:22; Sir. 14:25; BAGD 414; BAA 841; Büchsel, *TDNT* 4:338; Stählin, *TDNT* 5:19 n. 136.

This text is explicit that a Passover meal is in view. It also seems clear that all Jesus needs to do is ask. The availability of such rooms for Passover pilgrims was common in Jerusalem during the feast. In exchange for the use of the room, pilgrims would give the owner the lamb's skin and the vessels used in the meal.

Matthew 26:18b is again distinctive: the teacher says to the owner that "my time is near." Jesus' message continues, "I will keep the Passover at your home with my disciples." The question in Luke is a statement in Matthew, but the summary is the same except for the ominous note about the shortness of the time, which makes Matthew's request more emotive and somber in tone. Mark 14:14b is virtually a verbal match to Luke, although Luke refers to the "house master of the house" (a redundancy that Mark lacks) and Mark has the verb earlier in the sentence. He also, like Luke, describes Jesus as "the teacher." Mark has the disciples speak for Jesus and ask about "my" guest room, a pronoun Luke lacks. Again, Mark and Luke are more closely related to each other and Matthew is unique.

22:12 Jesus already knows that the owner will make available a large upper room (ἀνάγαιον, *anagaion*; BAGD 51; BAA 99; elsewhere in the NT only at the parallel Mark 14:15). Στρωννύω (*strōnnyō*) means "to spread out something" (outside this pericope in the NT only at Matt. 21:8 [twice] = Mark 11:8; Acts 9:34; BAGD 771; BAA 1539). The issue here is whether it refers to a "paved" floor or a "furnished" room. The latter seems more likely, especially given Mark's additional description of the room being "ready" and the parallel in Ezek. 23:41 (Jeremias 1966: 48 n. 1; Fitzmyer 1985: 1383). Couches to recline on during the Passover meal are probably what is being alluded to here (Ellis 1974: 252; *b. Pesaḥ.* 99b), which suggests a generous host who gave the home's best room (Plummer 1896: 493). This room would be reached by outside stairs, and in it the disciples are to prepare for the meal. Church tradition records that this room was in the house of Mary, mother of John Mark (Acts 12:12; Arndt 1956: 431). It is important to note that because of the way the disciples are directed, no one besides Peter and John knows where this meeting will be before it happens. The whole account has an air of expectation and drama about it.

Matthew lacks any parallel to this detail, but Mark 14:15 again is almost a verbal match with Luke. Luke uses κἀκεῖνος (*ka'keinos*, and that one) where Mark has καὶ αὐτός (*kai autos*, and he). Mark has a reference to the room as "furnished and ready," which explains the term shared with Luke, ἐστρωμένον (*estrōmenon*). Mark's command to make ready the meal has an introductory καί (*kai*, and) as well as the pronoun ἡμῖν (*hēmin*, for us) at the end. Luke's version is more concise.

c. Fulfillment (22:13)

22:13 Events show that Jesus is in control. The two disciples go out and find that things happen just as Jesus had said (εἰρήκει, *eirēkei*). The key conjunction is καθώς (*kathōs*, just as), as in 19:32. They successfully find the man and the room, and so they set about preparing the Passover. All is ready for the meal that Jesus desires to have with his disciples. Everything seems to be going smoothly, but with this meal will come betrayal.

Mark 14:16 describes the events with four verbs: the disciples went out (ἐξῆλθον, *exēlthon*), went (ἦλθον, *ēlthon*) into the city, found (εὗρον, *heuron*) it even as he had told them, and prepared (ἡτοίμασαν, *hētoimasan*) the Passover (only the last two verbs match Luke). Matthew goes his own way but is similar: Matt. 26:19 says that the disciples did as Jesus commanded and prepared the Passover. The note of Jesus' control thus appears most clearly in Mark and Luke.

Summary   Luke 22:7–13 shows Jesus preparing to celebrate Passover with his disciples, thus fulfilling another event in God's plan. The great Feast of Passover draws near, when the nation reflects on its deliverance and birth as a free nation. Jesus makes plans to celebrate as a pious pilgrim in the capital city. The disciples follow his directions and find things to be exactly as he has told them. Another era of salvation is about to be established—again inaugurated with death. As the disciples prepare a Passover lamb, another innocent life is being readied for death, but first must come one last meal and time of instruction with the disciples. Jesus is portrayed as faithful in worship, as he also will be faithful in death. This is no criminal or fugitive, but a righteous, pious martyr.

Additional Notes

22:7. Codex D, some Syriac, and Itala read τοῦ πάσχα (of Passover) instead of τῶν ἀζύμων (of Unleavened Bread), thus speaking explicitly of the arrival of Passover. This reading is clearly secondary since it ignores the context's idiom and corrects what seemed to be a difficult reference to Unleavened Bread. The scribe did not know the Jewish idiom and made the change.

22:8. J. Green (1988: 234–35) excludes an additional source for the details of 22:8 and suggests that this scene was not originally in the passion narrative, but is a supplemental tradition. He gives two reasons: (1) the naming of disciples here as opposed to references to the Twelve in the rest of the narrative, (2) and the coming of the Twelve in 22:14, which he regards as inconsistent with the sending of two here. Green seems to suggest that only ten came with Jesus in 22:14, because the two preparers were already there. This latter point assumes that the two did not come back and that reference to a well-known group always implies that all (rather than most) must be present (e.g., 1 Cor. 15:5, where Judas was absent when Jesus appeared to the Twelve). This latter point is questionable. The one difference in style may indicate a combining of sources here, but how is one to decide whether that was done when the passion tradition was brought together or later? Fitzmyer (1985: 1382–83) also notes that this verse is a problem for those who wish to make Mark the last of the Gospels in terms of sequence.

3. Last Supper (22:14–20)

As Jesus' death draws near, he meets with the Twelve one last time and expresses his long-held desire to eat this Passover with them. As they recall how God saved the nation in the exodus, another age of salvation is dawning, which Jesus will commemorate in a meal that has the characteristics of a farewell meal. The passage falls into three subunits: setting (22:14), the beginning of the meal and Jesus' vows of abstinence until the kingdom comes (22:15–18), and the discussion and introduction of new symbols in the bread and wine (22:19–20). Jesus and the disciples are together as one group. But life will not be the same after this meal, since his suffering is ahead.

Sources and Historicity

Several interpretive issues plague this passage, the details of which are treated in the exegesis. (1) A major textual problem in 22:19b–20 has bearing on the interpretation of 22:17. (2) The Synoptic accounts differ from John's "upper-room" discourse. John complements the Synoptic portrait of this meal, though the Lucan farewell discourse (22:21–38) indicates some topical parallelism in the various Gospels. (3) The Synoptic parallels differ among themselves: Matt. 26:20, 26–29 = Mark 14:17, 22–25 are closer to each other than to Luke (Aland 1985: §308, §311). Complicating the picture even more is that 1 Cor. 11:23–26 is also close to Luke, giving clear evidence that two traditions about this event were in circulation, excluding the Johannine version.[1] The sources behind these events are hard to establish with certainty. The problem parallels other passages in the passion accounts and suggests that Luke had access to multiple sources (Nolland 1993b: 1023 is confident of an extensive second source in 22:15–20 and 22:24–38, 63–64). It is hard to know if this source is equal to the special Lucan material, since this event made a great impact on the church and may have circulated as separate, oral material. It is clear that the tradition of this key portion of Jesus' ministry circulated in various forms, which is not surprising given its importance.

---

1. Marshall 1978: 793 speaks of two traditions, one a eucharistic tradition (Mark 14:22–24 = Luke 22:19–20; 1 Cor. 11:23–26), the other a farewell-meal tradition (Luke 22:15–18, 24–30, 35–38; Mark 14:25).

As a result of these differences, Jesus' original wording at the meal is much discussed, as well as the question of which tradition contains the oldest form (Marshall 1978: 799–801; Fitzmyer 1985: 1392–94). Jeremias (1966: 189–91) argues that Mark is the most original, while Schürmann (1955: 82–132) argues that Luke is. Fitzmyer (1985: 1394) notes that either form can be put into Aramaic. The arguments are complex and involve detailed judgments of scanty evidence, which makes a clear determination impossible.[2] What is clear is that the various renderings portray the significance of what took place; these traditions complement each other with emphases that are clearly associated with the portrayed events. The base of the accounts is fundamentally similar, with Jesus' sacrificial role clearly present. The differences reflect alternative ways to summarize and emphasize the event's implications.

The passage is a story about Jesus. It is close to being a pronouncement, except that it contains no real dialogue (Fitzmyer 1985: 1387; Bultmann 1963: 265). This account precedes a long final discourse by Jesus that can be regarded as a farewell testament. The outline of Luke 22:14–20 is as follows:

a. Setting (22:14)
b. Beginning of the meal (22:15–18)
   i. Jesus' preliminary remarks (22:15–16)
   ii. The "first" cup (22:17–18)
c. The meal and the symbols (22:19–20)
   i. The bread—Christ's body (22:19)
   ii. The "third" cup—the new covenant (22:20)

This is Jesus' last meal with the apostles before his death. Meal scenes are important to Luke. This one pictures fellowship and faithfulness as Jesus and the Twelve remember the exodus. Jesus provides the Passover meal with new meaning, the first hint of which is Jesus' vow to refrain from Passover and wine until the consummated kingdom. His desire to fellowship with his disciples is related to this special moment. The approaching suffering will be followed by victory. This pericope contains two parallel pictures of salvation: the exodus and Jesus' death. The bread pic-

2. Fitzmyer and Marshall are undecided about the tradition-historical issue. For more on this topic, see Schürmann's three studies (1952, 1955, 1957), Soards 1987, and J. Green 1988. The Jesus Seminar (Funk and Hoover 1993: 387–88) reflects excessive skepticism, printing the dialogue of 22:15–22 in black type because of the differences in wording and the presence of two cups. The seminar believes that there was a meal with symbolic acts, but the exact words are "beyond recovery." This contrastive approach amazingly excludes the likely possibility of an accurate summary of such an emotive event.

tures Jesus' body given for all who believe. The wine pictures his blood shed for the new covenant. This meal becomes an occasion to recall and reflect on Jesus' death and the inauguration of the new covenant.

Exegesis and Exposition

[14]And when the hour came, he reclined and the ⌜apostles⌝ with him.

[15]And he said to them, "I have long desired to eat this Passover with you before I suffer. [16]For I say to you that I will ⌜not⌝ eat it until it is fulfilled in the kingdom of God." [17]And having taken the cup and given thanks, he said, "Take this and divide it among yourselves. [18]For I say to you, from now on I shall not drink from the fruit of the vine until the kingdom of God comes."

[19]And taking bread and giving thanks, he broke it and gave to them, saying, "This is my body ⌜given for you; do this in remembrance of me." [20]And the cup likewise after the meal, saying, "This cup is the new covenant in my blood shed for you."⌝

a. Setting (22:14)

22:14 Luke gives the meal's setting and notes that when the hour came, Jesus reclined, as was common at important meals.[3] Reclining reflects the posture of "free people" (11:37; 14:10; 17:7; Danker 1988: 344; *m. Pesaḥ.* 10.1; Jeremias 1966: 48–49) and had replaced the command to stand in readiness for departure on the exodus (Exod. 12:11). It was the evening hour appropriate to the Passover meal (Matt. 26:20 = Mark 14:17; John 13:30; 1 Cor. 11:23).[4] Most meals were eaten in the late afternoon (Jeremias 1966: 44–45; SB 2:204, 206; 4:615; *Mekilta de Rabbi Ishmael*, tractate *Amalek* 4.5 on Exod. 18:13 [= Lauterbach 1933–35: 2.179]; *m. Šab.* 1.2; *b. Pesaḥ.* 107b; Josephus, *Jewish War* 2.8.5 §§131–32 [breakfast or a noon meal]). Luke uses the more authoritative title ἀπόστολοι (*apostoloi*, apostles) rather than referring to the Twelve (as do the other Synoptics).[5]

Since Luke's wording is unique (except for the initial καί, *kai*, and), it is disputed whether he uses special Lucan material (Ernst 1977: 581; V. Taylor 1972: 48–49) or edits his Marcan source (Schürmann 1952: 104–10; Marshall 1978: 795; Soards 1987: 43 [who notes

---

3. Danker 1988: 344 notes that this is the last key meal in Luke (others in 5:27–39; 7:36–50; 11:37–54; 14:1–24), but he overlooks the postresurrection meals in 24:30, 41–43.

4. Ὥρα (hour) occurs many times in the passion narrative, including Mark 14:35, 41; John 12:23; 13:1; 17:1; Luke 22:53. Because ὥρα carries no qualifiers (as in 22:53), it conveys no special sense of God's hour (against Grundmann 1963: 392 and Fitzmyer 1985: 1384; as noted by Marshall 1978: 794 and especially Soards 1987: 33).

5. The Lucan textual variants reading "the Twelve" probably reflect harmonization.

on p. 41 the parallel thought sequence: temporal reference, Jesus' arrival, and the companions]). Given the almost total lack of overlapping vocabulary (only two of eleven Lucan terms), the likelihood exists that this is a special source, though the limited data makes a clear choice difficult.[6] Matthew 26:20 and Mark 14:17 are closer to each other here, both noting that when it became evening, the meal began. Matthew says he "sat" with the Twelve, while Mark says he "came" with the Twelve.

b. Beginning of the Meal (22:15–18)
i. Jesus' Preliminary Remarks (22:15–16)

Jesus expresses his pleasure at celebrating the Passover meal with **22:15** the Twelve, and he notes its new significance. Just as Jerusalem's fall pictures the end, so the Passover parallels Jesus' death. Part of the reason Jesus desires to have this meal is that it is a pledge to have another meal later (1 Cor. 11:26; Luke 22:18). Danker (1988: 344–45) calls these remarks a "farewell speech," which is a fair description of 22:15–38 (C. A. Evans 1990: 321; Tiede 1988: 377).[7] Jesus expresses his desire to eat with them, using a Semitism (ἐπιθυμίᾳ ἐπεθύμησα, epithymia epethymēsa, I have deeply desired [lit., with desire I have desired]) that reflects how the Hebrew infinitive absolute is rendered in the LXX (BDR §198.6.10; Plummer 1896: 494; Grundmann 1963: 393 [a Septuagintalism]; Fitzmyer 1985: 1395; ἐπιθυμέω elsewhere in Lucan writings at Luke 15:16; 16:21; 17:22; Acts 20:33; the construction at Gen. 31:30; Acts 2:17; 5:28; 16:28; 23:14; 28:10, 26; 1QapGen 20.10–11). This verse makes it clear that Luke sees a Passover lamb present (Ellis 1974: 254; Marshall 1978: 795; Barrett 1958). In fact, the stress on eating shows that the point is the content of the meal and its significance. This was a moment of significant fellowship, centering on God's original act of salvation.

One can only imagine what Jesus felt during this meal that portrayed the nation's founding and the "passing over" of Israel's firstborn, while he prepared to offer himself on behalf of others. Those who had been at his side during his ministry and who were now at the table represented many others for whom Jesus would die. The

---

6. The presence of ἀπόστολος (apostle) may indicate a mixture of special source and editing, since Luke likes to use this term for the Twelve (see the exegesis of 6:13).

7. The farewell discourse in John 14–17 is another distinct account involving this setting. For biblical and Greco-Roman parallels, see Kurz 1985 and Neyrey 1985: 5–48. Biblical and Jewish precedent for the discourse is found in Gen. 49 (Jacob's final address); Deut. 33 (Moses); Josh. 23 (Joshua); 1 Macc. 2:49–70 (Mattathias); Tob. 4:3–21 (Tobit); the Testaments of the Twelve Patriarchs; and Josephus, *Antiquities* 4.8.1–48 §§176–322 (Moses).

meal depicts a transition from the end of Jesus' earthly ministry to the start of his salvific work. John 13:1 expresses the emotion of this moment by saying that Jesus loved them to the end.

Expressing a desire now met, Jesus is not sad. Some argue that his remark really expresses a frustration, because Jesus wished to celebrate the Passover meal, but knew he would die first. This view incorrectly presupposes the non-Passover view of John and denies a Passover reference here (Burkitt and Brooke 1907–8; see also Luce 1933: 328–29). Based on the unfulfilled wishes mentioned in 15:16, 16:21, and 17:22 (all using ἐπιθυμέω), Jeremias (1966: 207–18) argues that the verse expresses a wish to eat the meal, although Jesus abstains. This subtle view seems unnecessary, especially since 22:16, 18 suggest that Jesus did eat this meal (Fitzmyer 1985: 1396). Jesus specifically states that his suffering approaches: πρὸ τοῦ με παθεῖν (pro tou me pathein, before I suffer; Michaelis, TDNT 5:913; Fitzmyer 1985: 1396; πάσχω elsewhere with this sense in Luke 24:46; Acts 1:3; 3:18; 17:3; Heb. 2:18; 9:26; 13:12; 1 Pet. 2:21, 23). He knows what he will face. There is no Synoptic parallel to this verse.

22:16   In explaining his desire to eat this Passover with the disciples, Jesus speaks of not eating "it" until "it" is fulfilled in the kingdom of God, meaning he will abstain from eating such "a celebration meal" until "the plan" is done.[8] Jeremias's suggestion (1966: 207–18) that Jesus refrained from eating this meal does not make sense, since Jesus has just said that he desired to share *this* meal with them.[9] The meaning, rather, is that Jesus will not again sit at the Passover table until his return.[10] Jesus' refusal to eat such a festal meal until the consummation signals a new stage in God's plan.

The kingdom reference here is clearly future. The setting of eating the Passover lamb pictures the banquet time of consummation, when the full results of Jesus' sacrifice are realized (Matt. 8:11; Luke 13:28–29). The Passover meal looks forward, beyond the first deliverance to the last. Jesus will celebrate the Passover in the consummation. Any application of this verse to the Lord's Supper is inappropriate, since the Lord's Supper is not a Passover meal (see Nolland 1993b: 1050). A Passover meal is the only possible antecedent for the verse (with Luce 1933: 329 and Leaney 1958: 267; against Plummer 1896: 494). Neyrey (1985: 13–15) argues that the point is

---

8. Note γάρ (for) and the solemn and emphatic λέγω ὑμῖν (I say to you; also 22:18; 13:35; 9:27). Ἕως ὅτου (until; also 12:50; 13:8) is equivalent to ἀπὸ τοῦ νῦν (from now on) in 22:18 (Fitzmyer 1985: 1396).

9. The Easter fast in some church circles has roots in this view; Ernst 1977: 581.

10. The use of οὐ μή (not) is emphatic: esp. Matt. 26:29 = Mark 14:25; Luke 22:18; also Matt. 5:18, 26; 10:23; 18:3; 24:2; Mark 9:1, 41; 13:30; 14:25; 10:15 = Luke 18:17; John 8:51; 13:8.

not which meal is alluded to, but the prediction of death and vindi-cation. Since, however, one cannot eat death, αὐτό (*auto*, it) can only refer to the Passover meal. Neyrey's comment about the refer-ence to promise is correct, since the second "it" in the sentence (the unnamed subject of πληρωθῇ, *plērōthē*, it will be fulfilled) refers to the culmination of all the promises. The association with promise is correct, but not at the expense of the meal imagery.[11] To argue that the reference is to the Lord's Supper and the near kingdom ignores the direct allusion to Passover. The text suggests that after Jesus' re-turn, some sacrifices will be continued, but as a celebration or me-morial, not as a sacrifice for sin (a specific type of sacrifice that Heb. 8–10 makes clear is no longer necessary). Arndt (1956: 438) rejects this conclusion about a real banquet, calling it "picture language," but Jesus' remark is too grounded in Judaism to be dismissed. This is the only referent the Twelve could have understood (Jeremias, *TDNT* 5:900–901; Delling *TDNT* 6:296–97). The point is that with Jesus' return in the consummation, there will be a celebration of ful-fillment that will parallel the original meal.

It must be said that there is an element of parallelism between the Lord's Supper and this ultimate fulfillment. Just as the church is pictured in fellowship with its Lord at the Lord's table, so all believ-ers will share that fellowship in a full physical presence at the con-summation (1 Cor. 11:26).

ii. The "First" Cup (22:17–18)

This verse is unique to Luke and makes his account potentially dif-ferent from the other Synoptics. The difference turns on a textual problem in 20:19b–20 that dominates the passage and has been the subject of much discussion, so it must be resolved before the mean-ing can be discussed (Fitzmyer 1985: 1387–88; Jeremias 1966: 138–59). The textual issue turns on whether Luke originally had the "long" text of 22:17–20 yielding the sequence cup-bread-cup ($\mathfrak{P}^{75}$, ℵ, A, B, C, L, T, W, Δ, Θ, Ψ, family 1, family 13, Byz, Lect, some Itala, Vulgate, some Syriac, some Coptic; NRSV, RSV second edition [1971], NASB, NIV) or the "short" text of 22:17–19a yielding the sequence cup-bread (D, some Itala; RSV first edition [1946], NEB, REB). (Four other variants are dependent on these two major options.) Westcott and Hort (1881: 1.177) enclose 22:19b–20 in square brackets to indicate its inferiority. They (1881: 2.63–64 ["Notes on Select Readings"]),

22:17

---

11. Note the parallelism to 22:18 and the kingdom's final coming. Behm, *TDNT* 2:695, correctly speaks of the "fulfilled Passover" in the kingdom, the messianic meal of the last time—imagery that the Jewish Passover also anticipated, since the Hallel Psalms sung at the culmination looked to God's deliverance.

along with Creed (1930: 263–65), adopt the shorter reading mainly because of the difficulty of seeing how it could have emerged from a longer text (in fact, this is the main objection against the longer reading). Supporters of the shorter reading also appeal to *Didache* 9 (Luce 1933: 330).

The long text should, however, be accepted on the basis of its exceptional attestation and because it is the more difficult reading, introducing as it does a second cup that lacks parallels in any of the other Last Supper accounts. Schürmann (1951) traces indications of 22:19b–20 in Luke's original text (summarized in Ellis 1974: 255): (1) the start of 22:21 assumes 22:20; (2) the covenant reference in 22:29 ("assigned a kingdom") assumes the new covenant reference of the long text; (3) the cup of 22:42 looks back to the "poured out" cup of 22:20; and (4) the unique vocabulary argues against the long text being formed from existing Synoptic tradition.[12] All of this data means that the long text should be accepted as original.[13] Luke thus refers to two distinct cups, a detail that is unique to him.

The next issue is to what does this first cup refer? The traditional Passover meal had four cups (*m. Pesaḥ.* 10; Fitzmyer 1985: 1390; Marshall 1978: 797–98): (1) with the preliminary course to bless the day; (2) after a liturgical explanation for why the day was celebrated and coincident with the singing of Hallel Psalms; (3) following the meal of lamb, unleavened bread, and bitter herbs; and (4) following the concluding portion of the Hallel Psalms (it is debated whether this fourth cup was used in the first century; Bahr 1970). Which of these cups is alluded to 22:17?

Some argue for the third cup on the basis of the blessing and the common cup (Plummer 1896: 495; Grundmann 1963: 393). This view has two explanations. Perhaps two traditions were combined, each referring to the third cup. But it is unlikely that Luke would refer to this cup twice. A more likely scenario is that Jesus created a "second" third cup as he brought his own innovations to the meal to give it a new character (Luce 1933: 331 suggests that the Passover cup is referred to in 22:17 and the Hallel cup in 22:20). The use of a

---

12. For a strongly reasoned defense of the shorter reading, refuting Schürmann, see B. Ehrman 1991. Ehrman underestimates, however, the significance of 1 Cor. 11:25–26 and underplays the substitution language in Acts 20:28—points that undermine his position. The 1 Corinthian parallel is telling because it raises the issue of where this detail came from if not from a tradition like that in Luke. It is unlikely that a scribe adding material would go outside the Gospels to do so, especially if the result produced harmonization problems.

13. Jeremias 1966: 156–59 argues that the short text attempted to preserve a shortened reference to the initial cup without removing it altogether. The short text's goal was to keep the liturgy secret, an explanation that Marshall 1980: 38 rejects. More likely it is a scribal reduction for liturgical reasons.

common cup is unusual for the Passover, though not unprecedented (Jeremias 1966: 69; SB 4:58–59, 62; *t. Ber.* 5.9 [= Neusner 1977–86: 1.28]; *m. Ber.* 8.8). The comments over the cup are unusual, so it is possible that Jesus doubled the cup to "replay" the meal and its new significance.

More natural is the view that the cup in 22:17 is an earlier cup in the Passover, most likely the first cup, given Jesus' initial remarks in 22:16–17 (Plummer 1896: 495; Nolland 1993b: 1051). If so, Jesus assumes a position much like the Jewish father and offers a prayer something like this: "Blessed are you who created the fruit of the vine" (SB 4:62; cf. Isa. 32:12; Schweizer 1984: 335). These opening remarks over the initial cup lead to the meal's latter portion, which produces Jesus' fresh rendering of the imagery in terms of what is about to take place. With this probable background, one can now address the details of 22:17.

Jesus receives the cup and gives thanks (εὐχαριστέω, *eucharisteō*; Mark 14:23 [with cup]; Luke 17:16; 18:11; 22:19; 1 Cor. 11:24 [with bread]; Jdt. 8:25; 2 Macc. 1:11; Josephus, *Antiquities* 1.10.5 §193). This note of thanksgiving with the meal is the reason that the church's celebration of the Lord's Table is often called the "Eucharist," a word derived from the Greek term. If the first cup is in view, the gratitude is given for God's act of provision and salvation. All at the table share in this gratitude.

Jesus instructs the Twelve to take the cup and share it among themselves, language that shows the use of a common cup. This act intensifies the oneness that is central to the meal (1 Cor. 10:16–17). As noted earlier, the common cup is unusual but not unprecedented.[14] The call "to take" is similar to remarks about the bread in Mark 14:22 = Matt. 26:26, but it is not repeated in Luke 22:19 when the bread is taken.

It is unclear whether Jesus tasted the wine.[15] The remark in 22:18 ("from now on" Jesus will not taste from the fruit of the vine) implies that something is changing. Jesus did take the previous cup (22:16), but he will not take a cup after this meal until the kingdom comes. The change comes during the meal, not before it. It seems likely that Jesus took the cups of the meal, at least through the third cup (so Luke 22:16 and Mark 14:25). The Twelve and Jesus are sharing one

14. The practice of multiple cups for the Lord's Supper is a later development. Justin Martyr's description in *Apology* 1.65–67, where the wine was prayed over in one cup and then distributed by deacons to those present and also taken to some not present, suggests multiple cups.

15. Danker 1988: 345 and Jeremias 1966: 208–9 argue that in preparation for his coming suffering Jesus did not drink the wine. Schürmann 1952: 63–65, Plummer 1896: 495–96, and Marshall 1978: 798 argue that he did drink the wine.

last moment of celebration, gratitude, and fellowship before the suffering. But the note about sharing the cup again in the kingdom shows that suffering is not the end. It will be followed by victory.

22:18 Jesus gives a second vow of abstinence to explain why (γάρ, *gar*) this meal, including the sharing of the cup, is so important to him. Here it is wine that Jesus will not drink until the kingdom comes, while in 22:16 it was the Passover meal as a whole that was in view. Only Luke uses his familiar ἀπὸ τοῦ νῦν (*apo tou nyn*, from now on; 1:48; 5:10; 12:52; 22:69; Stählin, *TDNT* 4:1113). Fitzmyer (1985: 1398) plausibly argues that the wine here is that of the Passover meal because of the parallelism in 22:16 (the wording is similar, except that Jesus here speaks of when the kingdom "comes," not of its being fulfilled).[16] The promise is also similar to Mark 14:25 = Matt. 26:29, where the remarks follow the cup of wine, which is probably the third Passover cup. Luke lacks such a remark after the cup of wine, but unlike the other Synoptics, he has some additional teaching after the cup. It is possible that Luke has moved up this remark and placed it here to make room for the other teaching. Of course, in noting this additional teaching, Luke is similar to John, who also notes a long discourse in this setting. Another option is that Jesus made this remark both before and after the meal. Regardless, and it is hard to be sure of the exact sequence, Jesus is noting that this is a unique moment until the consummation. The idea of drinking wine when the kingdom comes is like Luke 22:16 in that it looks at the banquet celebration (13:22–29). These vows add solemnity to the occasion and show that things are headed for change.

c. The Meal and the Symbols (22:19–20)
i. The Bread—Christ's Body (22:19)

22:19 Jesus reinterprets the symbols of the Passover and gives them new, interim meanings. Such meaning resides in the symbols until he returns. In fact, the symbols are a reminder that he is returning. As is his custom, he breaks the bread and gives thanks (like 9:16, but in different terms). The verb κλάω (*klaō*, to break) is only used of breaking bread for a meal (fourteen times; Marshall 1978: 802). The bread—unleavened bread cut in small thin loaves or wafers, the *mazzot*—is first.[17] Jesus links the bread to his "offered body." It represents his death. The verb *is* indicates representation, not identifi-

16. On the reference to the vine, see Deut. 22:9; Isa. 32:12; *m. Ber.* 6.1; *b. Ber.* 35a. The wording parallels the cup blessing in the Passover meal; Büchsel, *TDNT* 1:685. On abstinence, cf. Lev. 10:9; Num. 6:3; Ezek. 44:21; Leaney 1958: 268.

17. The term for bread lacks an article, suggesting that Jesus took "some" bread, not all of it; Arndt 1956: 438.

cation (Ellis 1974: 256; BAGD 223–24 §II.3; BAA 451 §II.3). In Aramaic, this equative verb would be understood as supplied by ellipsis (Plummer 1896: 497).

Jesus speaks specifically of his body offered "for them" (ὑπὲρ ὑμῶν, *hyper hymōn*), a remark that could have a sacrificial and substitutionary tone to it. Luke is capable of understanding Jesus' offering this way, since in Acts 20:28 Paul speaks of the church having been created "through his blood," a phrase that may recall Luke 22:20. There is debate about whether the Aramaic term that Jesus used meant "person as a whole" or "flesh" (Marshall 1978: 802 and Fitzmyer 1985: 1399–1400 opt for the latter). The debate is unresolvable in terms of the evidence and is ultimately irrelevant, since either way the remark's force is clear. Whether it is his person or his flesh that is given for them, *he* is given for them. Jesus is the sacrifice.

The preposition ὑπέρ could be taken with less theological force to mean "on your behalf," with the specific details of how this occurs left unclear. Such ambiguity is possible in the original setting, since the details of how Jesus' death saves sinners are not developed. Since the commission in 24:44–47 and the speeches of Acts tie Jesus' work to the forgiveness of sins, it would seem that Luke has some sense of a substitutionary or beneficiary force, but it is not explicitly stated here. Even more certain is the lack of any allusion to Isa. 53 in Luke 22:19–20 (Fitzmyer 1985: 1401).

Nonetheless, it is likely that a specific theological force is implied and that the remark was read with this deeper sense by the time Luke wrote, since the outcome is clear by that time. It can certainly be said that Luke understands that Jesus' career has some relationship to the forgiveness of sins and to salvation, since these remarks are placed in the middle of this Passover, salvific context. In this context, Jesus' death is associated with salvation. In fact, his death is not just any death. It has repercussions for the fate of the Twelve and others like them who have tied their fate to Jesus. He dies for them. He gives himself up for them. Here is not only deep theological truth, but great love, which Paul states more explicitly in Rom. 5:6–8 and 1 Cor. 10:16. These Pauline texts picture all believers sharing in one body, which was broken for them. The imagery suggests the most fundamental basis for the unity of believers (Creed 1930: 266).

Jesus also institutes a practice here. He speaks of "doing this in my remembrance." This is a memorial meal, not a resacrifice. It calls to mind what Jesus did and declares one's identification with that act (Plummer 1896: 498). The disciples are to partake (ποιεῖτε, *poieite*) of the bread as an act of remembrance (ἀνάμνησις, *anamnēsis*; elsewhere in the NT only at 1 Cor. 11:24–25 [twice] and Heb. 10:3; Michel, *TDNT* 4:678, 682). As they break the bread, they are to associate it with Jesus' broken body. They are to recall what it was Jesus did, or in this original setting, what it is he is about to do. Only Luke and Paul's version of the supper note these words about remembrance (1 Cor. 11:24–25).

That Jesus would speak of a future event in the middle of a meal that looks back to the exodus is highly suggestive. He compares the salvific eras, one past, the other yet to come. Both involve death, in one a lamb, in the other a Messiah. The Twelve are to recall that it was Messiah, God's son, who died for them. As they will come to realize later, his death made possible their eternal life. The idea of recollection has OT roots with the Passover (Exod. 12:14; 13:9; Deut. 16:3; Leaney 1958: 268). The meal affirms this relationship, just as the Lord's Supper in the church is also a reaffirmation of this relationship.

This Lucan note about remembrance has been the source of much discussion. Did Jesus really say something about remembrance at the meal, or is this a later addition to the tradition that reflects the church's developing a meal around this event?[18] What impetus would create such a memorial, fellowship meal? The clearest answer is that Jesus did or said something that encouraged the disciples to remember this moment as a representative act.

Part of the reason for uncertainty about what was said at the meal lies in the variety of wording that appears in the tradition about the supper. As was already noted, the Lucan wording is close to what Paul records in 1 Cor. 11, which itself is traditional material. Except for lacking the participle διδόμενον (*didomenon*, is being given), Paul's report of Jesus' words matches Luke exactly. Matthew 26:26 = Mark 14:22 are close to each other: Jesus blesses the bread (εὐλογήσας [*eulogēsas*] in Matthew and Mark; εὐχαριστήσας [*eucharistēsas*] in Paul and Luke) and says, "Take, eat" (Matthew) or "Take" (Mark). Matthew and Mark share Luke's report that Jesus said, "This is my body." But both lack any mention of remembrance or the idea that it was "given for you." These comparisons show that at least two forms of the tradition were in circulation. Luke and Paul have drawn from the tradition's "longer" form.

One's view of how traditions were formed and developed in the church will influence how one resolves the issue of which rendition is closer to what Jesus actually said. If one sees a basic tradition ex-

---

18. The debate over the original wording of the tradition is complex and ultimately irresolvable, since it rests on so much speculation about what is likely. Marshall 1978: 804 and Schürmann 1955: 30–34, 123–28 argue for originality, Patsch 1972: 142–50 against it. Nolland 1993b: 1047 sees it as a later but quite accurate gloss, since Jesus looks to affirm his ongoing relationship to them despite his coming suffering.

panding, then secondary elements will be noted. If one sees various traditions of an event, then one need not choose between traditions as to which is original and which is expanded. Nonetheless, it seems that the very presence of these additional words in the midst of the Passover meal and the very existence of the Lord's Supper in the church argue that Jesus verbally associated the bread and the cup of the meal with his death. He made clear the parallel between himself and the lamb, a parallel that also suggested the church should remember this new sacrifice ritually. The longer tradition may be simply an accurate interpretation of Jesus' actions as statements in themselves, but it is even more likely that it reflects his words.[19] Given how few "rites" exist in the church, it is likely that the instruction came from Jesus, though the tradition reflects translation from Aramaic.

ii. The "Third" Cup—The New Covenant (22:20)

Jesus now takes what was probably the Passover's third cup, after the main course (Marshall 1978: 805; Goppelt, *TDNT* 6:154–56). Ὡσαύτως (*hōsautōs*, likewise) means he also gave thanks over the cup and then addressed the Twelve. Jesus relates the cup to the new covenant (Jer. 31:31–34; Goppelt, *TDNT* 6:155 n. 70; Marshall 1978: 806; 1 Cor. 11:25; 2 Cor. 3:6). The new covenant is inaugurated in his blood, that is, by his death. It is not surprising, therefore, that John's account of this last meal says so much about the Spirit that Jesus will send (John 14–16), since the Spirit is at the heart of that covenant (cf. Acts 2:17–21, 33; Heb. 8:8, 13; 9:11–28). With Jesus' death, salvific benefits can be distributed. He has become the lamb who launches a new age. Picturing life (Lev. 17:11, 14; Fitzmyer 1985: 1402), the blood is shed "for you." Jesus' death is an offering that brings a new era and the Spirit of God.

22:20

The parallels are complex. Paul in 1 Cor. 11:25 is again close to Luke: Luke uses αἵματί μου (*haimati mou*, my blood), while Paul has ἐμῷ αἵματι (*emō haimati*, my blood); the term ὡσαύτως has a different position in the sentences; Luke alone speaks of the blood "shed for you"; while Paul adds a note to "do this as often as you drink, to my remembrance." Matthew 26:27–28 = Mark 14:23–24 parallels Luke conceptually, but in slightly different wording. Their version is longer at this point, both speaking of Jesus' taking the cup, giving thanks, and giving it to them. Jesus then commands them to "drink of it, all of you" (Matthew) or "and they drank it all" (Mark). The two

---

19. On interpreting the action, see Fitzmyer 1985: 1401–2. Plummer 1896: 498 argues that the instruction to observe the supper came from the risen Lord later, but there is no record of such a later instruction.

accounts differ slightly in reporting Jesus' words over the cup: Matthew reads, "For this is my blood of the covenant, which is poured out for many for the forgiveness of sins"; Mark has, "This is my blood of the covenant, which is poured out for many." The "blood of the covenant" language resembles Exod. 24:8 (Plummer 1896: 499). These differences are interesting since Matthew alone explicitly mentions forgiveness of sins, a theme that Luke loves (e.g., 24:47). Mark and Matthew speak of blood shed "for the many" (Matthew has περὶ πολλῶν, peri pollōn; Mark ὑπὲρ πολλῶν, hyper pollōn), language that may recall Isa. 53:12 (Ernst 1977: 588). Mark and Matthew then follow this remark with the note about not drinking from the fruit of the vine until the kingdom, a remark that Luke has earlier. Luke personalizes the remark, since Jesus' shed blood is "for you." In addition, Luke is the only Synoptic account to mention that the covenant is the "new" covenant (again like Paul; 1 Cor. 11:25). All speak of "my blood" and of its being "shed" (cf. Gen. 9:6; Isa. 53:12; 59:7; Ezek. 18:10; Rom. 3:15; Luke 11:50).

Great energy has been expended in trying to determine exactly what Jesus said and what represents the liturgical periphrasis of the significance of Jesus' remarks.[20] Periphrasis is likely present, given all the differences here, but it can easily be shown that the tradition brings out what was implicit in Jesus' remarks. Trying to decide which wording is most original is almost impossible, given the diversity of the sources and variations, as well as the likelihood that all the traditions are in Greek—not the Aramaic that Jesus likely used here. It is also ultimately irrelevant, because each form of the tradition, with differing emphases, explains what Jesus meant as he shared the bread and the cup. The varying forms clarify and complement each other. All the accounts argue that Jesus' death was a sacrifice that inaugurated a new era of salvation, like the one represented in Passover. All accounts appeal to a covenant inauguration. Jesus' death brings a new age.

Summary   The account of Jesus' last meal in Luke 22:14–20 is loaded with significance. This is the last time that Jesus will be with his disciples in his earthly life. As he gathers with them, they recall in the Passover the last great salvific event, the exodus. They are gathered to look back, but Jesus looks forward to his approaching suffering and a new sacrifice that opens a new era. Jesus of Nazareth is like the lamb of the exodus meal.

20. On the various views, see the summary in Marshall 1978: 805–6, who argues that in general Luke's form is the most primitive, but notes the difficulty of the decision. Fitzmyer 1985: 1402 prefers Mark's originality, as does Nolland 1993b: 1047, who mostly follows Ruckstuhl 1980.

But death is not the end. Jesus knows that the kingdom will be consummated and that he will sit at the table with his disciples again. Such a meal, however, will not be his again until the kingdom is consummated. In the meantime, those who gather are to remember this meal and what the end of Jesus' life means.

A variety of truths are portrayed. Oneness is expressed in the sharing of the cup. A new age of salvation will be found in the new, united community that is being formed on the basis of Jesus' approaching death. Jesus speaks of his body being broken for the disciples and of his blood being shed for them, the blood of the new covenant. The covenantal reference makes it clear that a new era is in view, an era that Jesus brings. We have here a clear note that God's plan has reached a new phase. At the center is a death and an inauguration of benefits. The mediating source is Jesus, who gives his body and blood so that those who ally themselves to him may receive salvation's benefits. He is sacrificially offered for them, and thus a fresh covenant comes. The apostles here take bread and wine to picture this; the church declares it at the Lord's Table. As they take the meal, they are to look backward and forward. There is, in fact, a greater meal yet to come.

Additional Notes

22:16. The readings that add οὐκέτι (no longer) or drop οὐ (not) or both are secondary and look like they are derived from οὐ μή (read by 𝔓[75], ℵ, A, B, L, Θ; Metzger 1975: 173).

22:17. For the textual problem involving the variation between "apostles" and "the Twelve," see n. 5.

22:19b–20. For the textual problem involving the inclusion or omission of these verses, see the exegesis of 22:17.

4. Last Discourse (22:21–38)

At the Last Supper, Jesus begins his final instruction, revealing his knowledge and control of events. As he prepares for death, he also prepares the disciples for his departure. This discourse is a final testament to them.

The betrayer comes, as Scripture promises (22:21–23). Jesus teaches that greatness is found in service, not in the way the world leads (22:24–27). In the midst of this call to serve, Jesus notes his authority in receiving a kingdom and promises the Twelve a future rule over Israel (22:28–30), thus providing them fellowship with him and a share in God's plan. In the short term, Peter will deny Jesus, despite the disciple's emphatic vows of allegiance (22:31–34). Jesus knows the disciples better than they know themselves. The battle with Satan is on, and only Jesus' intercession will preserve them. In addition, rising opposition requires that the disciples prepare themselves (22:35–38). Just as Jesus will suffer, so will the disciples. They think that the call to bear swords is a literal call to war, a misunderstanding that concludes the discourse. Death is coming and so is crisis, but leadership will require faithfulness and service. Through it all, Jesus is aware of all that is happening.

Sources and Historicity

Jesus' final discourse is made up of five distinct subunits. The prediction of Judas's betrayal (Luke 22:21–23) is paralleled in Matt. 26:21–25 = Mark 14:18–21 (Aland 1985: §312). The discussion of leadership and ruling over Israel (Luke 22:24–30) is similar to Mark 10:41–45 = Matt. 20:24–28 and 19:28, which are in earlier settings (Aland 1985: §313). The prediction of Peter's denial (Luke 22:31–34) is paralleled in Matt. 26:30–35 = Mark 14:26–31 (Aland 1985: §315), although Luke 22:31–32 is unique. In Luke, however, the predictions of denial have a different setting—coming with the meal, not on the way to Olives—which may reflect Lucan literary summarization and compression. And the whole of 22:35–38 is unique to Luke (Aland 1985: §316). (The complex relationship of each subunit to its Synoptic parallels will be discussed in the exegesis.) It is likely that Luke has an additional source or sources around which he is building his account.[1] The basic historicity of these events should not be doubted, for the church is unlikely to have created a character like Judas, the unflattering portrait of Peter, or the unusual sword saying (Nolland 1993b: 1075). (See the exegesis for discussion of specific historical details.)

The Jesus Seminar is exceedingly skeptical about the entire passion narrative, printing only 22:25–27, 40, 46b in gray type and everything else in black (Funk and Hoover 1993: 386–400). The variation in the material causes the seminar to argue that most of the narrative is the evangelists' creation. This position is surprising, given the age of the passion tradition and the general agreement of the outline of events. Recognizing the role of various sources and the presence of summarization should prevent one from being so skeptical about the material.

The passage is a combination of prophetic sayings (22:21–23, 31–34) and other sayings related to discipleship (22:24–27, 35–38), along with one promise of commission (22:28–30) (Fitzmyer 1985: 1409, 1414, 1421–22, 1429; Bultmann 1963: 264). The outline of Luke 22:21–38 is as follows:

a. The betrayer (22:21–23)
   i. The betrayer announced (22:21)
   ii. Destiny and responsibility (22:22)
   iii. The question of identity (22:23)
b. Greatness (22:24–27)
   i. The disciples' dispute (22:24)
   ii. Jesus' reply: greatness comes in service (22:25–27)
c. Appointment to authority (22:28–30)
   i. Past association (21:28)
   ii. Appointment to authority over Israel (22:29–30)
d. Peter's denials predicted (22:31–34)
   i. Satan's request (22:31)
   ii. Jesus' intercession for Peter (22:32)
   iii. Peter's assertion of loyalty (22:33)
   iv. Jesus' prediction of denial (22:34)
e. Swords and rejection (22:35–38)
   i. Review of God's provision (22:35)
   ii. Change in provision (22:36)

1. There is some contact between Luke's version of the final discourse and John's (John 13–16), but the two accounts complement each other more than they overlap. For discussion of these subunits and the source debate surrounding them, see Nolland 1993b: 1058–59, 1062–64, 1070–72, 1075. The basic debate turns on whether Luke is responsible for the differences from Mark and Matthew or whether they reflect his sources. The connection of Luke 22:21–23 to John 13:21–22, Luke 22:24–30 to John 13:1–20, and Luke 22:31–34 to John 13:37–38 suggests a traditional background to several Lucan differences.

iii. Fulfillment of scriptural rejection (22:37)
iv. Absence of understanding (22:38)

This passage alternates between actions tied to Jesus' death and themes of discipleship. Jesus reveals the betrayer and discusses the inevitability of betrayal, which will be judged. Ironically, the disciples' inquiry about the identity of the betrayer is followed by a dispute over greatness. Jesus redefines greatness as service and illustrates it negatively by the world's example. Greatness does not consist in the exercise or presence of power, but in service. Jesus promises constant trial, but he gives present kingdom authority to the apostles and promises that they will share in the end-time banquet. The Twelve are also promised eventual authority over Israel. Opposition comes as Satan engages in efforts to shame the Twelve. Peter is a prime target, and so Jesus will intercede for him. Jesus calls Peter to lead, an act of restoration before his forthcoming lapse. Peter's false confidence is exposed in Jesus' prediction of denial. Meanwhile, Jesus' rejection means change for the disciples, for they must now make their own provision and be prepared to face rejection. Jesus' own suffering is the initial example and fulfills Scripture. The apostles again lack understanding about what Jesus says, but they will come to understand later.

Exegesis and Exposition

[21]"Nevertheless, behold the hand of the one who is betraying me is with me at the table. [22]For the Son of Man goes as it has been determined, but woe to that man by whom he is betrayed." [23]And they began to question one another, which of them it was that would do this.

[24]And there came contention among them concerning which of them was to be considered the greatest. [25]But he said to them, "The kings of the Gentiles exercise authority over them, and those with authority over them call themselves benefactors. [26]But you are not to be so. But the greatest among you is to be as the younger, and the ruler as the one who serves. [27]For who is the greater—the one who reclines at the table or the one who serves? Is it not the one who reclines at the table? But I am among you as one who serves.

[28]"You are those who have continued with me in my trials, [29]and I appoint you even as my Father assigned to me a kingdom, [30]in order that you might eat and drink at my table in my kingdom and sit on thrones judging the twelve tribes of Israel.

[31]"Simon, Simon, behold, Satan demanded to have you so he might sift you like wheat. [32]But I have prayed for you that your faith may not fail. And when you have turned again, strengthen your brothers." [33]But he said, "Lord, I am ready to follow you to prison and to death." [34]But he said, "I say

to you, Peter, today before the cock will crow, three times you shall deny that you know me."

³⁵And he said to them, "When I sent you out with no purse or bag or sandals, did you lack anything?" They said, "Nothing." But he said to them, ³⁶"But now, let him who has a purse take it and likewise a bag. And let him who has no sword sell his mantle and buy one. ³⁷For I say to you that this Scripture must be fulfilled in me, 'And he was reckoned with the transgressors'; for what is written about me has its completion." ³⁸And they said, "Look, Lord, here are two swords." And he said to them, "It is enough."

a. The Betrayer (22:21–23)
i. The Betrayer Announced (22:21)

22:21

Jesus' approaching suffering is made possible by the act of someone who has been with him from the start. One of the Twelve will betray him. The present participle παραδιδόντος (*paradidontos*, the one who betrays), used as a noun in a genitival construction, suggests in this context that the betrayal is in process, since an aorist or perfect participle is not used (παραδίδωμι is also used in Matt. 10:4; Mark 14:42; cf. Ps. 41:9 [41:10 MT]). The subunit begins with the strong adversative πλήν (*plēn*, but, nevertheless), which indicates that the one now mentioned is separated from sharing in the note of association that Jesus just described (Jeremias 1966: 237). Jesus knows what is happening and announces it to the Twelve.

This announcement met with concern, as the disciples were finally beginning to sense both from the meal and this remark that Jesus was going to depart. Though the table was designed to portray their oneness, the heart and hand of at least one of them was not sharing in what was happening.[2] Jesus' allusion, of course, is to Judas, whose activity was described in 22:3–6. Judas pictures someone who associates with Jesus, but is not really allied to him. Judas is a model of someone who makes a false profession and false association with Jesus, as his defection reveals his true allegiance.

Luke's portrayal of this event reverses the order in Matt. 26:21–23 = Mark 14:18–20, where Jesus raises the issue of betrayal before coming to the meal. These other texts are more complete: Jesus first announces that there is a betrayer; each of the Twelve becomes sorrowful and asks if it is he; Jesus replies that it is one who is dipping bread into the dish. John has both remarks: the remark about the betrayer being present (John 13:21) preceding that about dipping

---

2. Marshall 1978: 808 notes the use of "hand" to portray kind intent (Gen. 21:18; Ps. 80:17 [80:18 MT]; 89:21 [89:22 MT]) or hostile intent (1 Sam. 18:21; 22:17; 24:12–13 [24:13–14 MT]; 2 Sam. 14:19). Lohse, *TDNT* 9:430, argues that "hand" refers to the sharing of the meal; it seems, however, that the allusion is negative, since "hand" is a metonymy for an action performed by someone.

the food in the cup (John 13:26)—a sequence that interestingly reverses the order suggested when the Synoptic Gospels are combined. The Johannine material suggests that perhaps at least two sets of traditional material circulated about the betrayal. The latter remark about the dipped morsel is the point of contact to this Lucan text, which mentions the hand that betrays Jesus. In all three Synoptics there follows the saying about woe on the one who betrays the Son of Man.

What has happened in the tradition? One could suggest that Jesus addressed the issue of betrayal twice and made his Son-of-Man statement twice; but this seems forced, especially when one brings John's material into the picture. More likely, Luke rearranged multiple sources and summarized this exchange (Neyrey 1985: 17–18).[3] Perhaps Luke treated the meal first and then turned to all the matters discussed at the meal in order to give the meal a prominent position and to present the final remarks as a unit, as a final testament. He thus delayed raising the betrayal issue until after the meal and reduced its report to a bare minimum. One advantage of this move is that it adds a dramatic contrast with the subsequent dispute about greatness (22:24–30). In the midst of Judas's betrayal, the disciples are bickering about issues that are off the mark. They miss what Jesus came to show. This rearrangement also allows Luke to make some unique points, possibly because his next account also draws on unique material.

ii. Destiny and Responsibility (22:22)

22:22 Jesus explains his remark about betrayal by placing two elements side by side. First, God's plan is at work: these events are destined (ὁρίζω, horizō; BAGD 580–81 §1aα; BAA 1177 §1aα; elsewhere used by Luke at Acts 2:23; 10:42; 11:29; 17:26, 31; cf. Luke 13:33; Grundmann 1963: 400; K. Schmidt, *TDNT* 5:452–53). God knew by design that the Son of Man, Jesus, would be betrayed.[4] These events are no surprise (9:22). Second, the betrayer is responsible for his actions and is subject to God's wrath (indicated by the cry of woe). Οὐαί (*ouai*; BAGD 591; BAA 1196) can express pain or, as here, displeasure (see the exegesis of 6:24). The betrayer must stand before God to answer for his act of betrayal and rejection.

Matthew 26:24 and Mark 14:21 are close to each other and differ slightly in wording from Luke. All accounts mention the Son of Man,

---

3. Marshall 1978: 808 assumes at least two sources. Fitzmyer 1985: 1408–9 mentions the transposition, but acknowledges the possibility of another source.

4. Κατά gives the standard "according to which" these events occur: "*As* it has been determined."

with Mark and Luke beginning with ὅτι (*hoti*, for). Matthew and Mark then speak of the Son of Man "going according to what is written about him" (cf. Luke 2:23; Acts 7:42; 15:15; Fitzmyer 1985: 1410). Luke speaks of what is determined using a participial form of ὁρίζω, an idea that emphasizes God's plan without explicitly mentioning the word of God, an interesting difference given Luke's pointing to such fulfillment in Luke 24:44–47 (conceptually also in 24:25–26). As such, Luke highlights the person who directs the plan. In the second part of the verse, the three accounts converge, the only differences being that Matthew and Mark have the contrastive conjunction δέ (*de*, but), where Luke uses the conjunction πλήν (*plēn*, nevertheless), and they mention the Son of Man a second time. Luke likes to use πλήν with woe (elsewhere 6:24 and 17:1). Luke also lacks Matthew's and Mark's additional remark that it would have been better for that man if he had not been born, indicating that Judas is destined for judgment and rejection. It is hard to explain Luke's verbal independence here since his alterations are not that different in meaning. They may well suggest another source (Marshall 1978: 809).

iii. The Question of Identity (22:23)

22:23 Jesus' remark causes speculation among the Twelve about the identity of the one who is about to betray him. It is beginning to dawn on them that Jesus' situation is serious, and so discussion centers around the identity of the betrayer (συζητέω [*syzēteō*, to discuss] is elsewhere used by Luke at Luke 24:15; Acts 6:9; 9:29; Marshall 1978: 810; BAGD 775 §2; BAA 1548 §2). But the identity of the betrayer is not all that is on their minds. As the next subunit shows, other irrelevant concerns also preoccupy these disciples.

Mark 14:19 mentions earlier in his account the question of the betrayer's identity, although there the question is directed to Jesus in the form of a rhetorical denial, "Is it I?" Matthew 26:22 raises the same question with different wording. As already noted, the discussion in Matthew and Mark precedes the meal. So Luke's account is expressed uniquely in a unique locale, though it is similar to John 13:22. Luke's account looks like a summary of what the other accounts record with more detail. It even has a trace of common Lucan style in the use of τό to introduce an indirect question in the optative (Nolland 1993b: 1060).

b. Greatness (22:24–27)
i. The Disciples' Dispute (22:24)

22:24 Another topic at the meal is the ranking of the Twelve. In fact, this topic raises a certain amount of contention (φιλονεικία, *philoneikia*; BAGD 860; BAA 1716; Fitzmyer 1985: 1416; only here in the NT [a related adjective in 1 Cor. 11:16]; cf. 4 Macc. 1:26; 8:26; 2 Macc. 4:4). The specific topic is, "Which one is the greatest?"[5] The dispute may well center around who will have what role in the kingdom that Jesus brings, since the topic of rule comes up again in Luke 22:29–30. The Synoptics indicate that this is an old dispute (Matt. 20:20–28 = Mark 10:35–45). Mark introduces this earlier account with James and John asking Jesus to let them sit to his right and left in glory. In Matthew, the mother of the Zebedees asks the same question. Clearly they are jockeying for positions of honor in the kingdom.

As this incident occurs before the triumphal entry in Matthew and Mark, this is another event that Luke has seemingly related in a different setting. Some of what is said in the other accounts is found in this Lucan version with almost the same wording, but there are also significant differences between Luke and Matthew–Mark. In addition, Matt. 23:10–12 has a similar saying in a denunciation of the Pharisees, a setting clearly distinct from the Zebedee incident. The repetition within Matthew shows that this was a frequent theme of Jesus' teaching. There are a couple of ways to view these differences.

First, Luke places the account here to raise an issue that was a point of contention throughout Jesus' ministry. The relocation may have been indicated in a tradition outside of Mark and Matthew (Creed 1930: 267, appealing to differences in wording and thought).[6] Since the importance of unity was a major feature of the Last Supper, Luke notes this point here. Thus, the topic of greatness was one that plagued the disciples and that Jesus addressed on numerous occasions. Jesus brings it up at his last meeting with them to stress the folly of such concern and the importance of unity in the face of his absence. John 13:3–16 describes an incident that makes this point pictorially, so the topic is not foreign to the meal's setting.

Another option is that only one incident is given two distinct settings. Luke has simply moved the Zebedee tradition and reformulated it (Leaney 1958: 269).[7] The problem with this suggestion is

5. Μείζων (greatest) is comparative in form but probably superlative in context; BDF §244. But note that in 22:26–27 the same term is comparative again.

6. While recognizing that the two accounts share some similarities, V. Taylor 1972: 61–64; Schürmann 1957: 63–99; Marshall 1978: 811; and Grundmann 1963: 400 note that Luke does not delay Marcan texts like this elsewhere.

7. Fitzmyer 1985: 1407 sees "independent traditions" about such a discourse at the supper, though he also notes the conceptual parallelism with John. Plummer 1896: 500 speaks of the confusion about its location within the tradition, though he argues that such contention at the meal may have occurred when the disciples chose seats at the meal. But, he argues, such contention after the footwashing is unlikely. Of course, it may be that Jesus was addressing a contention from a previous occasion. Perhaps the tradition had it in this latter location as part of the summary of what was actually said at the meal, even though Jesus said it during the meal.

that it is not clear why Luke would hesitate to relate this event in its earlier setting and place it here without a clear reason for doing so. The point is just as appropriate right before entering his suffering in Jerusalem as it is here. The difference in wording in the Lucan account also stands against this suggestion. It is more likely that this was a major theme reiterated in Jesus' ministry in similar terms on at least two occasions. The Matthean repetition of this teaching supports this conclusion.

ii. Jesus' Reply: Greatness Comes in Service (22:25–27)

22:25 Jesus responds to this concern about self-importance by discussing leadership and service. He sets up a contrast but does not answer the disciples' question because he wishes to change the way they think about rule and importance. How do the world's rulers operate in comparison to the apostles, who will lead the church? Jesus speaks about "rulers who exercise authority" over the nations (κυριεύουσιν, *kyrieuousin*; BAGD 458; BAA 931; κυριεύω elsewhere in the NT at Rom. 6:9, 14; 7:1; 14:9; 2 Cor. 1:24; 1 Tim. 6:15) and who have themselves called "benefactors" (εὐεργέτης, *euergetēs*; BAGD 320; BAA 647; a NT *hapax legomenon*; on the passive use of "call," see Nolland 1993b: 1064). A common title for princes and other outstanding leaders in the first century, εὐεργέτης was a title of respect and authority (2 Macc. 4:2; 3 Macc. 3:19; Josephus, *Jewish War* 3.9.8 §459; Bertram, *TDNT* 2:654–55; Danker 1982: 323–24). This self-designation could even apply to tyrants.

In other contexts the Synoptic Gospels are similar. Matthew 20:25 = Mark 10:42 speaks of rulers "lording it" over them, using the compound κατακυριεύω (*katakyrieuō*) instead of Luke's simple κυριεύω (he uses the compound in Acts 19:6).[8] Since Luke prefers compound verbs (Marshall 1978: 812), this atypical use may point to a source. Matthew speaks of the great ones "exercising authority" (κατεξουσιάζουσιν, *katexousiazousin*) over them. Mark almost matches Matthew verbally, with only the wording of the subject different: οἱ δοκοῦντες ἄρχειν (*hoi dokountes archein*, those who are regarded as rulers). Both Matthew and Mark begin with "you know that," which notes that this view of leadership is dominant. The same basic contrast is found in all three accounts, despite their distinct settings.

22:26 Jesus now states the contrast: the apostles are not (οὐχ οὕτως, *ouch houtōs*) to lead as the world does, through the exercise of power.[9]

---

8. Luke's use of a different verb provides clear evidence that he did not use the Zebedee incident.

9. Marshall 1978: 812 wonders if ποιήσετε (you shall [not] do) is to be supplied; cf. BDF §480.5.

Equality in Christ influences one's style of leadership. It is important to note that Jesus does not say there are to be no leaders; rather,
he says that leaders are to serve. Thus, the one who is "greater
among them," that is, in a position of authority and leadership, is to
be like the younger (νεώτερος, neōteros; BAGD 536 §2bβ; BAA 1085
§2bβ; elsewhere in the NT at Luke 15:12, 13; John 21:18; Acts 5:6;
1 Tim. 5:1, 2, 11, 14; Titus 2:6; 1 Pet. 5:5; cf. Gen. 42:20; C. F. Evans
1990: 796). Leaders are not to be something they are not, but to lead
without the pretense of being more than they are. In this culture, the
younger got the menial tasks and were the servants. As leaders, the
apostles are not to exploit their age and position, but continue to
serve (Beyer, *TDNT* 2:84–86; Bertram, *TDNT* 2:655). This provides a
clear contrast to the description of the world's exercise of power in
the previous verse. Luke then restates the same idea in different
terms: the one who rules (ἡγέομαι, hēgeomai) is to act as the one who
serves (Plummer 1896: 501; Marshall 1978: 813; Büchsel, *TDNT*
2:907–8; BAGD 343 §1; BAA 696 §1; ἡγέομαι used of leaders in Matt.
2:6; Acts 7:10; 14:12; 15:22; Heb. 13:7, 17, 24). Marshall correctly
sees that church leadership is in view, though it is initially the apostles who are addressed; the point made ultimately applies to the full
range of church leaders. The commitment is not to power, but service. The commitment is not to separate from those who are ruled,
but to identify with them. Elitism is not the Twelve's call, but service
and community among equals. The contrast to the world's definition of leadership could not be greater.

Luke's wording is distinct from Matt. 20:26–27 = Mark 10:43–44,
though the idea is similar. These two Gospels agree, except for one
alteration of word order, a different relative clause, and a different
concluding particle: "It shall not be so among you; but whoever
would be great among you must be your servant, and whoever
would be first among you must be your servant" (Matthew) or "must
be the servant of all" (Mark). Greatness is defined as service, not authority. It is not found in the power to take or exercise control, but
in the ability to give and share. Thus the Lucan account makes comparisons that suggest a leveling of perspective, while Matthew and
Mark stress service. Of course, a perspective of equality should produce service (Danker 1988: 349; Ernst 1977: 594).[10]

22:27 Jesus probes the contrast with a further question: from the world's
perspective, who is greater, the one who sits at the table or the one
who serves the table? Of course, the one receiving the meal is generally regarded as superior to the one who serves it. The answer is in-

---

10. Similar imagery is found in Matt. 20:1–16, but there the emphasis is on not
despising the lateness of the younger's arrival. See also 1 Pet. 5:3, 5 and Phil. 2:5–11.

dicated by the particle οὐχί (*ouchi*, not), to which a positive reply is expected (Marshall 1978: 814; SB 2:257–58). The one who reclines is greater. But then Jesus notes his own example of service.[11] When one recalls the footwashing incident of John 13 in the background, then the remark has already been illustrated and received comment (Creed 1930: 267). This remark is designed to confront the disciples with a contrast and a choice. If Jesus is great and he does not live like the world, how should his followers live? The call is clear: lead by serving.[12]

c. Appointment to Authority (22:28–30)
i. Past Association (21:28)

In a comment unique to Luke, Jesus next commends his disciples' **22:28** constancy, a remark that serves to contrast the behavior of the Eleven with that of Judas. They have continued (οἱ διαμεμενηκότες, *hoi diamemenēkotes*) with him in trial. Their constancy is enforced by the perfect tense, the preposition μετά (*meta*, with), and the compound verb (διαμένω, *diamenō*; BAGD 186; BAA 373; Gal. 2:5; Plummer 1896: 502). This constancy includes the whole of Jesus' ministry, as the perfect tense participle looks back contextually through all the ministry's trials (Ellis 1974: 256). In the face of pressure, rejection, and opposition, they have continued to stand by him. Their constancy is now rewarded with greater responsibility. This responsibility is given after Jesus has defined the service into which they come. It illustrates that glory and reward follow sharing in the suffering of Jesus.

ii. Appointment to Authority over Israel (22:29–30)

Jesus indicates that the Twelve form an integral part of his mission. **22:29** Their faithfulness yields reward: a responsibility and an acceptance by God that Judas will miss. This act could almost be viewed as a bequeathal, given Jesus' departure. It is better, however, to view it as an appointment, since Jesus continues to reign despite his departure.[13] This statement is an important declaration of Jesus' current authority that, though unique, is a shared authority that he does not hoard for himself. This reinforces the view of leadership that Jesus

---

11. Note contrastive δέ (but). Fitzmyer 1985: 1418 points out that Peter and John served by preparing the meal.

12. This verse is unique to Luke and reflects an independent source, which Fitzmyer 1985: 1412 calls L. Conceptual parallels are found in Mark 10:45 and Matt. 23:8–10; Marshall 1978: 813–14; Danker 1988: 349–50.

13. Διατίθημι has the meaning "to assign" in Josephus, *Antiquities* 13.16.1 §407; BAGD 189–90 §3; BAA 381 §2; Behm, *TDNT* 2:104–6.

just described (22:25–26). Jesus appoints them to the kingdom, even as his Father has given him a kingdom (23:42; 1:32–33; 19:11–27, 28–40; 22:69; Fitzmyer 1985: 1419). The use of βασιλεία (*basileia*, kingdom) here has a comprehensive sense and refers especially to Jesus' rule and authority as God's commissioned agents. The present tense in this context means that they are joining the task now, not later. Jesus' authority, given by the Father, is extended to the Eleven.[14] They will mediate for him. Jesus rules and so will the Eleven. This emphasis on present authority fits Luke's emphasis on the kingdom's present form.[15] The Eleven's leadership extends Jesus' mission, something Acts will detail. Before giving this authority, Jesus indicated that the form of leadership is service. In Acts, it will also involve testifying as "witnesses" (Acts 1:8).

Luke 22:29b–30 is like Matt. 19:28. This latter remark, however, is clearly in a distinct form, so a distinct source is suggested (Marshall 1978: 815 argues for two sources or two versions of Q).[16] It is not clear, given their differences, why the Matthean parallel should suggest a common source for the remark (Manson 1949: 216). A distinct source is more likely. Matthew's remarks concentrate exclusively on the future, since he speaks of the "new birth" (παλιγγενεσία, *palingenesia*). In this period, the Son of Man will sit on the throne and these disciples will sit with him judging the twelve tribes of Israel. This looks at the ruling of Israel in the eschatological culmination (what Rev. 20 calls the millennium). Luke simply notes that this authority is already granted, an important complement to the Matthean picture of future authority. The point seems to emerge that God's message also has validity for Israel. If people in the nation are to respond to God and receive the Father's promise, they must respond to the Eleven's message about Jesus and his rule. It is in this declarative sense that kingdom authority in the present period resides in the Eleven over Israel (Plummer 1896: 502).

22:30 Jesus describes the eventual purpose (ἵνα, *hina*) and result of this appointment: the Eleven will have a place at the banquet table in Jesus' kingdom. This image pictures fellowship and acceptance in the eschaton (12:35–37; 13:29; 14:15–24). These men are appointed to a major role, not only in the near future in building what becomes

14. This Father-Son motif occurs elsewhere in Luke 12:32; John 15:9; 17:18, 21–22; 20:21; Fitzmyer 1985: 1419. Jesus exercises executive authority here.

15. Neyrey 1985: 24 sees Luke altering Matthew's more futuristic emphasis, a conclusion that depends on the questionable assumption that only one event is in view.

16. Marshall defends authenticity because the saying is dissimilar to teaching from the early church in its emphasis on the kingdom and Israel.

the church, but also in ruling and sharing in the consummation, which focuses on Israel.

The note about rule over Israel shows the extent of the Eleven's authority, thus providing a continuity of leadership in the structure of God's plan. The "thrones" imagery recalls Ps. 122:4–5 and perhaps Dan. 7:9 (Marshall 1978: 818; Tiede 1988: 385–86 suggests that 1 Enoch 62 and 1 Cor. 6:2 are conceptually related).[17] The apostles, who are the foundation of the church, are those who will lead Israel. This statement is significant, given its setting. Jesus faces rejection by the nation's "leadership," but the nation will continue to exist. The disciples will have a continuing role under "new management," in an administration to be revealed in the future but having validity now. Though God's plan for Israel might look derailed, it is not. The Israelite focus in this remark shows that Israel has a future and recalls the remark about eating the Passover in the kingdom (Luke 22:15–16). These Israelite touches should not be interpreted to refer exclusively to the church.[18] These remarks look to the final wedding of events in God's plan when promises to Israel are fully realized and when Jesus rules both heaven and earth. In that day Jesus' authority will be clearly visible in both spheres. Promises made to Israel long ago will be fully carried out, such that God's grace and word are shown to be fully true. Jesus is indicating that the promise is a testimony to God's faithfulness.

The wording is close to Matt. 19:28b, which declares the rule of the apostles over the twelve tribes of Israel in the age of "rebirth" (Matthew mentions twelve thrones, supplies the subject ὑμεῖς [hymeis, you], and has a different word order). Matthew has twelve thrones because Judas is still in view at the time Jesus speaks and because of the comparison to Israel. But Matthew's wording appears to exclude Judas in saying "you who have followed me," suggesting that some may not abide with Jesus through it all. This point is made more clearly in Luke's text and location of this discussion. Luke's omission of the number is understandable in light of Judas's departure (Nolland 1993b: 1066 sees economy of language in Luke). (Of course, the twelfth spot is filled in Acts 1:15–26 by Matthias.)

17. For defense of the statement's authenticity, see Witherington 1990: 140–41. It is hard to imagine the church's inventing a saying like this where Judas is present.

18. But so Fitzmyer 1985: 1419, who speaks of "reconstituted Israel," and Marshall 1978: 817, who suggests an allusion to the Lord's Supper, along with many others (those who see a tie to Israel include Ellis 1974: 256 and Danker 1988: 350–51). Dupont 1964: 388 correctly argues against this view. This expectation is continued in the question of Acts 1:6–8 and the remarks of Peter in Acts 3:18–21. Even later Petrine expectation of a new heaven and earth in 2 Pet. 3:10–14, which looks to the ultimate end of history, does not remove this intervening stage when God deals with Israel in bringing it again into the blessing reserved for God's people.

d. Peter's Denials Predicted (22:31–34)
i. Satan's Request (22:31)

22:31 Only Luke notes Jesus' direct address to Peter, who represents the apostles in 22:31–32 (Fuchs, *TDNT* 7:291–92; Fitzmyer 1985: 1421 attributes the uniqueness to L). The double direct use of Simon, Peter's other name (4:38), indicates the seriousness of the situation (cf. prior double direct addresses in 8:24; 10:41; 13:34). The apostle is the object of satanic attack, reminiscent of how Satan went after Job (Job 1:7; 2:2) or Joseph (T. Ben. 3.3; Stählin, *TDNT* 1:194; Fitzmyer 1985: 1424). The plural ὑμᾶς (*hymas*, you) shows that all the leadership is in view, though the next verse seems to suggest that the request is especially for Peter, in recognition that he is "first among equals." Perhaps by exposing Peter, all will lose heart. Using an agricultural figure, Jesus says that Satan has asked to sift (the purpose infinitive σινιάσαι, *siniasai*; BAGD 751; BAA 1502; a NT *hapax legomenon*) Peter like wheat (for Satan's involvement in the passion, see Luke 22:3 and John 13:27). The picture is of grain in a sieve, where the head of grain is taken apart (cf. Amos 9:9). Our English idiom of "picking someone to pieces" or "taking someone apart" has similar emotive force. Satan would like to bring Peter to ruin and leave him in pieces, exposing his lack of faithfulness. This leader of the Twelve is a prime target, and Jesus knows it. The warning should make Peter alert.

ii. Jesus' Intercession for Peter (22:32)

22:32 Jesus promises to come to Peter's defense in the time of testing (the pronouns in this verse are second-person singular, so only Peter is now in view). While Satan has requested permission to test Peter and the others, Jesus has interceded (ἐδεήθην, *edeēthēn*; BAGD 175 §4; BAA 350 §2) for him, that Peter's faith may not fail.[19] This does not mean that Peter will never fail (ἐκλείπω, *ekleipō*; BAGD 242; BAA 488), but that whatever failure he has will be temporary.[20] It is clear that failure here means ultimate, total failure, that is, a total renunciation of Jesus.[21] Peter will not fall away completely, since Jesus goes on to note that, when Peter turns back from his failure, he is to strengthen the brothers. This turning refers to coming back to

19. Luke uses δέομαι fifteen times, Matthew once (Matt. 9:38), and Mark and John not at all; Fitzmyer 1985: 1425; Marshall 1978: 821.

20. Marshall 1978: 821 argues that ἐκλείπω (elsewhere in the NT at Luke 16:9; 23:45; Heb. 1:12) here means "to disappear," so the idea is that Peter's faith does not disappear. He avoids ultimate failure (cf. Col. 1:21–23). Nolland's paraphrase (1993b: 1072) of faith "drained away to nothing" gives the sense.

21. Against Bultmann 1963: 267 n. 2, who argues that the original tradition did not know of Peter's denial; but so correctly Fitzmyer 1985: 1425 and esp. Marshall 1978: 821.

faith—or better faithfulness—since Peter will deny Jesus, only to regret his action afterward.[22] Peter's failure will be a failure of nerve,
not a heart denial of Jesus. The remark is a note of reconciliation before the fact and pictures how God offers total forgiveness. He
knows our failure and still extends his hand graciously to the believer who trusts him.

Peter will rebound from his temporary faithlessness to lead his
brothers (στηρίζω, stērizō, to strengthen, confirm; cf. Acts 18:23;
1 Thess. 3:2; 1 Pet. 5:10; BAGD 768 §2; BAA 1533 §2). His responsibility will be to make their faith more resolute in its allegiance to
Jesus. Peter is again considered the first among equals (Leaney
1958: 270; cf. Luke 5:1–11; 8:45; 9:32; 12:41; 22:8, 61; 24:34). Acts 1–
12 shows Peter obeying this command. Luke 22:31–32, which is
unique to Luke, shows Jesus' exceptional knowledge of divine counsels and indicates his intercessory function on behalf of those allied
to him. Satan fails to destroy Peter because Jesus intercedes for him.
Jesus is stronger. The postresurrection restoration of Peter is found
in John 21:15–17 (cf. John 17:6, 20 for other examples of Jesus interceding for his own).

iii. Peter's Assertion of Loyalty (22:33)

Peter confidently declares his absolute and unshakable commitment to Jesus. Events will show this overconfidence to be an under-
estimation of how pressure can sift a person's alliance to Jesus. Peter simply says that he is ready (ἕτοιμος, hetoimos; BAGD 316 §2;
BAA 641 §2; Luke 12:40; Acts 23:21) to follow Jesus to prison and
death. The reality of Jesus' suffering has finally registered for at
least one of the apostles. Peter senses that Jesus is headed to jail and
death, and in the privacy and safety of a secluded meal he pledges
his loyalty to Jesus. The reality of soldiers will change everything.
Peter's claim to suffer imprisonment will come true in the Book of
Acts, and his martyrdom will follow some time after this (Acts 5:19;
12:1–17; Leaney 1958: 271).[23]

22:33

Mark 14:29 = Matt. 26:33 largely agree verbally with each other,
while John 13:37 is parallel conceptually to Luke (Peter declares a
willingness to lay down his life for Jesus). Mark has a first-class con-

---

22. Arndt 1956: 444 speaks of Peter's "again bec[oming] a believer," a most unfortunate way to express the force of the verb. Peter had this position all along. On turning, see Luke 17:4; Acts 3:19; 9:35; 11:21; 14:15; 15:19; 26:18, 20. On faith as faithfulness, see Luke 18:8; Acts 14:22; 16:5. Marshall 1978: 822 sees a possible allusion to
2 Sam. 15:20.

23. Church tradition holds that Peter was crucified upside down (Acts of Peter
37–38 [Schneemelcher 1991–92: 2.315]), though this probably had not happened at
the time of Luke's writing.

dition describing mass defection: εἰ καὶ πάντες σκανδαλισθήσονται (*ei kai pantes skandalisthēsontai*, even if all fall away), followed by Peter's assertion that he will be the exception: "I will not" (ἀλλ᾽ οὐκ ἐγώ, *all' ouk egō*). Matthew is more emphatic, lacking καί in the supposition and using emphatic οὐδέποτε (*oudepote*) in the conclusion: "I will *never* fall away." Luke's form is quite different, sharing only the introductory εἶπεν αὐτῷ (*eipen autō*, he said to him) with Matthew and only the pronoun αὐτῷ with Mark. Luke has either summarized the tradition in terms of concrete possibilities or used another source.[24] Another difference of detail may indicate a source: Luke's remarks appear before departure to Gethsemane, while in Matt. 26:30 = Mark 14:26 they occur along with the singing of a hymn or hymns and the departure. This difference may simply reflect Luke's desire to place all the remarks together, or it may indicate a different source. The difference is so great that Creed (1930: 270) says there is no parallel. One can hardly argue for double predication, so a topical location is likely here. Luke may well be responsible for the compression, seeking literarily to place all the discussion in one scene stretching from the meal to Gethsemane. Luke's failure to mention both the Mount of Olives and Gethsemane, as Matthew and Mark do, may reveal his condensing tendency in this material.

iv. Jesus' Prediction of Denial (22:34)

22:34 Jesus' dire prediction challenges Peter's confidence. Jesus simply says that Peter is about to deny him this very day, that is, before sunrise. In fact, Jesus knows specifically when that betrayal will occur. Before the cock (ἀλέκτωρ, *alektōr*; BAGD 35; BAA 68) crows three times, Peter will deny that he knows Jesus. Roosters crow in the night, but there is debate whether the allusion is to the third of four Roman night watches, midnight to 3:00 A.M., a watch known as the "crow of the cocks" (Mark 13:35).[25]

---

24. Marshall 1978: 823 notes that the vocabulary is Lucan, but that a redaction of Mark is not evident. Soards 1987: 39 overstates a detail here and argues that the Lucan Peter states his readiness before the prediction of his threefold denial, while the Marcan Peter says it is after the prediction. But the initial prediction in Mark and Matthew is of sheep scattered, not of the threefold denial. In addition, Peter has two refutations of Jesus' predictions, which serve as a bracket (Matt. 26:33, 35 = Mark 14:29, 31). Luke has only one remark (22:33), which comes first. A summary in Luke is evident, but a source cannot be excluded, since Luke 22:33 does not match the vocabulary of Matthew or Mark.

25. Plummer 1896: 505 and Luce 1933: 335 make this connection, while Fitzmyer 1985: 1426 says that there is no need to do so. Nolland 1993b: 1073 suggests 2:30 A.M. for the initial crowing and notes that the reference in *m. B. Qam.* 7.7 forbidding chickens in Jerusalem is probably a later idealization and thus not a historical challenge to this detail.

Three elements stand out. First, Jesus is aware of the events around him. He knows where things are headed. Second, Peter had worked with Jesus, yet will deny even knowing him. This shows the depths to which events take him. Peter is too nonchalant about the chance that he could deny Jesus. Third, the denial comes soon.

Luke's wording is distinct from parallels in Matt. 26:34 = Mark 14:30 = John 13:38, with Matthew and Mark almost being in verbal agreement. Mark uniquely uses the second-person pronoun and speaks of the cock crowing twice: "Truly I say to you, today, this night before the cock crows twice, you will deny me three times." Matthew uses a preposition (ἐν, *en*, in) to specify the denial's timing: "Truly I say to you, in this night before the cock crows, you will deny me three times." Luke agrees on the following details in his own words: the denial will be today and it will involve a triple denial. But he speaks only of the cock crowing and a threefold denial, similar to Matthew.[26] In addition, Luke speaks of Peter denying that he knows Jesus, a description that intensifies the denial. There is no association with Jesus at all, even at a casual level, much less at his side. Only Luke uses the direct address "Peter." Luke's version is shorter and summarizing, as in other portions of this pericope. John simply says that the cock will not crow until Peter denies Jesus three times. Jesus' comments about Peter end on this somber note.

e. Swords and Rejection (22:35–38)
i. Review of God's Provision (22:35)

As Jesus begins to change the disciples' practice, he reviews God's **22:35** previous record of provision, reminding them of their past missions (the Twelve in 9:3; the seventy-two in 10:3–4). Jesus asks if the disciples lacked anything when they ministered without purse, bag, or sandals. The particle μή (*mē*, not) expects a negative reply—nothing was lacking.

Luke 22:35–38 has no Synoptic parallel. Some wording is like the earlier mission passages (esp. 10:3–4), but nowhere else in the Synoptics is the mission command altered. This difference suggests the presence of another source, which also reflects the use of a source in the larger material (Ernst 1977: 601–2 calls it L). Soards (1987: 53–54) suggests that 22:36b comes from an independent saying and that the rest of the verse is Lucan, but his arguments do not explain

---

26. Arndt 1956: 444 suggests that Jesus communicated that the denial would come before morning and before a rooster crowed twice that evening. Marshall 1978: 823 argues that this is a summary of Mark. Since most assume that Luke did not know Matthew, the question is raised whether a summary is present or whether Luke had another source. Matthean prioritists simply see Luke following Matthew here.

the motive for this change of command.[27] The most his argument explains is that Luke edited an existing source (Fitzmyer 1985: 1429 correctly sees L material here assembled by Luke). Neyrey (1985: 37) argues that the source is Q; but this cannot explain the contrastive element in the command alteration here, since Q would simply record the original mission command. Another source would also explain a Matthean omission here.

ii. Change in Provision (22:36)

22:36 Jesus' departure changes the outward circumstances of the disciples' ministry. The contrastive ἀλλὰ νῦν (alla nyn, but now) indicates that a change has come. Rather than leaving behind purse, bag, and sword, they are now to take such items. They will now have to provide for themselves. Those who have extra clothes (ἱμάτιον, himation; BAGD 376 §2; BAA 764 §2; the outer garment, cloak, or robe) need to sell them to buy a sword.

The syntax is disputed, especially the connection of ὁ ἔχων (ho echōn, the one who has) to ὁ μὴ ἔχων (ho mē echōn, the one who does not have). Are these ideas parallel? There are three main options (Fitzmyer 1985: 1431–32, who also notes another minor option):

1. "Purse" (βαλλάντιον, ballantion) and "knapsack" (πήραν, pēran) are the objects of both participles (Fitzmyer 1985: 1428, 1431; Plummer 1896: 505). The first exhortation refers to taking purse and knapsack, so parallelism dictates that the subject of the second exhortation also lacks purse and knapsack: "The one who has a purse had better carry it; and his knapsack too. If one does not have them, he must sell his cloak and buy a sword" (Fitzmyer's translation).
2. "Sword" (μάχαιρα, machaira) is the object of both participles. The second exhortation refers to taking a sword, so parallelism dictates that the subject of the first exhortation has a sword. Jesus simply commands those who have a sword to also get a purse and bag, while those who lack a sword need to sell a mantle in order to get one (Schneider 1977a: 454–55). Either way, one should be sure to have a sword, a point that differs only in focus from view 3.
3. "Sword" is tied only to the second exhortation. One is to take all three items—purse, knapsack, and sword: "If you have a

---

27. Soards argues that the passage creates a setting for understanding what happens in 22:49–51 and 23:32. But why not then see these elements as part of a source that referred to these unique details rather than see it as Luke's creation, especially given the numerous points in this section that hint at another source?

purse, take it, and also a bag; and if you don't have a sword, sell your cloak and buy one" (NIV; RSV is similar).

Regardless of the solution, the force is that one should now have full provision (Marshall 1978: 825 and Grundmann 1963: 409 are uncertain which view is correct). View 3 has the most natural force, since it involves the fewest ellipses. So in contrast to the former instructions for mission, full provision is now required.

In the next verse Jesus will develop the implications of this remark by citing a Scripture that describes his rejection. The point is that the world has made its decision about Jesus, so those who follow him had better be prepared to be treated similarly. Disciples are to engage the world, but they will have to take care of themselves. Neyrey (1985: 40–43) rightly sees two events as commentary on this verse: Jesus' rebuke of the use of a sword against the high priest's servant (22:49–51) and the church's nonviolent response to persecution in the Book of Acts (4:25–31; 8:1–3; 9:1–2; 12:1–5). In fact, Acts 4:25–31 shows the church armed only with prayer and faith in God. Luke 22:36 sees the sword as only a symbol of preparation for pressure, since Jesus' rebuke of a literal interpretation (22:38) shows that a symbol is meant (Fitzmyer 1985: 1432; Marshall 1978: 825). It points to readiness and self-sufficiency, not revenge (Nolland 1993b: 1076).

iii. Fulfillment of Scriptural Rejection (22:37)

God's plan as related in Scripture is coming to pass.[28] Fulfillment in Jesus is a necessity—again highlighted by the use of δεῖ (*dei*, it is necessary). **22:37**

Jesus cites the fulfillment of Isa. 53:12. The omission of τοῖς (*tois*) and the interchange of μετά (*meta*, with) for ἐν (*en*, among) reflect the MT, not the LXX (Jeremias, *TDNT* 5:707 n. 404; Marshall 1978: 826).[29] The Semitic background suggests the use of tradition and argues for the age and authenticity of Luke 22:37.

The appeal to Isa. 53 is significant. The force of this image in Isaiah is highly disputed. Corporate Israel and the true remnant are

---

28. The perfect passive participle γεγραμμένον (is written) refers to Scripture in Luke 18:31; 20:17; 2 Cor. 4:13. The reference is often plural, but here it is singular because it focuses on a specific passage; Plummer 1896: 506.

29. Holtz 1968: 42 argues that λογίζομαι (to reckon) is a sign of LXX influence, claiming that it is not the normal rendering of Hebrew מָנָה (*mānâ*, to count, measure). The LXX rendering of מנה Niphal is, however, fairly evenly split: twice each by λογίζομαι and ἀριθμέω (to count) and once each by ἐξαριθμέω (to count) and ἀναρίθμητος (innumerable). The presence of λογίζομαι in Luke thus does not indicate his use of the LXX.

clearly referred to in Servant Songs such as Isa. 49:3–6, while Isaiah himself is sometimes individually referred to, as the discussion of Acts 8:34 suggests. The individual, messianic reference to the Servant has a long history in both Judaism and Christianity (Jeremias, *TDNT* 5:682–700). The rendering of Isa. 53 by Aquila, Theodotion, and the Targum suggests a messianic element. But it should be noted that the idea of a *suffering* Messiah is not present in these ancient Jewish texts. Rather Judaism understood these verses to refer to an exalted Messiah. In other words, ancient Judaism did not have a suffering messianic Servant. In Judaism the exalted Messiah delivers a suffering people. The suffering aspect of NT use is unique in the early history of interpretation. In regard to the OT sense of the servant, North (1956) defends a view that seems the most balanced: the servant was initially a broad reference to the nation but narrows to an individual reference in Isa. 53. The persistence of the messianic view within Judaism in the face of Christian use shows how strongly Judaism held to an individual reading of this text, even though its suffering elements were applied to the nation and not to the Servant.

In Luke, the Servant is Jesus, but his Servant imagery does not explicitly stress Jesus' substitutionary work. Rather, the use reflects themes of both exaltation and suffering (cf. Luke 24:44–47; Acts 8:32–33).[30] In stressing exaltation, Luke follows the emphasis of the Isa. 53 passage, which moves past suffering to exaltation (Isa. 52:13–15; 53:12). In Luke 22:37, the focus is on Jesus' suffering like a rejected one, though there is no explicit substitutionary picture here. Jesus' point in citing the text is that he will die a shameful death between criminals as anticipated by the Scripture. The reference to criminals is not a reference to disciples (so Minear 1964–65: 132), since the allusion is clearly to the criminals with whom Jesus died (23:32–33). The passage is cited to make an additional point: if Jesus is rejected in such a manner by the world, then the disciples will also suffer such rejection. They had better be ready.

An exegetical issue surfaces in the use of τέλος (*telos*):

1. Is τέλος a reference to Jesus' life coming to an "end" (Manson 1949: 342; Klostermann 1929: 214; Marshall 1978: 826; Nolland 1993b: 1077)? If so, the point would be that Scripture describes the "end" of Jesus' life. It is another way of saying, "It is finished" (cf. 13:32). The advantage of this view is that it prevents redundancy with the idea of fulfillment earlier in the verse. Against this view is that it is an obscure referent.

---

30. Isa. 40:3–5 (cited in Luke 3:4–6) introduces a unit where the Servant idea refers to the coming of God's salvation. Isa. 61:1–2 (cited in Luke 4:16–19) speaks of an anointed Servant-like figure who brings salvation.

2. Is τέλος a reference to "fulfillment," which would emphasize fulfillment described earlier in the verse (Delling, *TDNT* 8:54; BAGD 811 §1a; BAA 1617 §1a)?

3. Does τέλος contain the idea that what is written about Jesus has reached its "goal" (Plummer 1896: 506)? This view differs little from view 2 except to add an explicit emphasis on the design of God's plan, rather than emphasizing Scripture, so that the goal of Jesus' life is this rejection.

The choice is difficult (Fitzmyer 1985: 1433 is unclear whether he prefers view 1 or 3). Any of the options could be right. Nonetheless, to speak of Jesus' death as the goal of scriptural promise seems to leave out subsequent realities that are also important to Jesus' work, so that view 3 seems too focused. The reference to the end of Jesus' life (view 1) is too subtle and limits the divine plan (as does view 3), so an emphasized reference to fulfillment is probably in view (view 2). Isaiah 53 is cited as a text that prophetically anticipates the fulfillment Jesus brings. What happens to Jesus also reflects how disciples will be viewed. They had better be ready.

iv. Absence of Understanding (22:38)

The disciples take Jesus' remark literally and take an inventory of **22:38** swords: they have two.[31] Μάχαιραι (*machairai*) refers to the swords that men frequently wore (*m. Šab.* 6.4; BAGD 496; BAA 1005).[32] The disciples are ready to go to battle and in fact will soon use a sword on the priest's servant (22:49–50)—damage that Jesus must repair. Here Jesus simply stops the discussion by saying "it is enough" (ἱκανόν ἐστιν, *hikanon estin*)—perhaps a Semitic expression that means he is dismissing the topic.[33] Whatever Jesus wanted to say, he drops because of the disciples' misunderstanding. On this somber note the discourse ends.[34]

31. Schwarz 1979: 22 suggests a misreading of the Aramaic term for "end," but Fitzmyer 1985: 1433–34 rejects this view.

32. Chrysostom's effort to interpret the sword as a reference to a slaughter knife fails; Michaelis, *TDNT* 4:524–27.

33. Plummer 1896: 507 and Marshall 1978: 827 see the idiom here (based on Gen. 45:28; Exod. 9:28; Deut. 3:26; 1 Kings 19:4; 1 Chron. 21:15; 1 Macc. 2:33). Doubt about its presence is expressed by Fitzmyer 1985: 1434 and Rengstorf, *TDNT* 3:295–96.

34. Plummer 1896: 507 and Arndt 1956: 445 note that this passage helped create the two-realms theory of papal power, one secular, the other spiritual. This doctrine was formalized by Boniface VIII in his 1302 *Unam Sanctam*, though it was discussed much earlier. This theory parallels the disciples' misunderstanding, but in a different direction. The disciples would use the sword to defend and gain power, but the papacy was trying to hold on to complete power.

Summary Luke 22:21–38 concludes the Last Supper scene with a discourse. Jesus gives what is in effect the final teaching of his ministry—a farewell discourse. Several points are made. The first is that Jesus is aware of events. He knows that he will be betrayed; it is part of God's plan. The betrayer's future is not good. The disciples are not sure who this could be, but they are now certain that Jesus is headed for death. They finally understand his fate.

But misunderstanding still reigns among them, for while Jesus is about to meet betrayal, they are debating who is the greatest. The irony is strong. Jesus thus makes his second point and tells them that leadership, in contrast to the world, is not found in domination but in service. He also assures them that his suffering does not dilute his authority. God has given him the kingdom. Jesus tells the Eleven that they will have authority over Israel. The ground of this authority is Jesus' own authority in receiving a kingdom from the Father. Jesus shares, and will share, this authority with the Eleven.

Peter is confident that he could never betray Jesus, while Jesus knows that Peter is like a piece of grain at risk of being crushed in the cosmic struggle between Satan and God. Being a player in such a cosmic struggle should humble him and cause him to rely on God. Thus the third point is that Peter should not be overconfident. The ability to sin runs deep—despite one's best intentions. One should not underestimate it. Peter will deny Jesus, but Jesus' intercession will keep him from falling entirely. Only total dependence on the Lord and a sense of weakness without him can preserve even the most zealous disciple. Nonetheless, despite Peter's failure, Jesus notes that the apostle will be reconciled and called upon to minister to the disciples after his fall. This is a picture of God's grace.

There also is a lesson in the difference between the fates of Peter and Judas. Peter is the faithful one who lapses into temporary unfaithfulness and is restored. Judas reveals an unfaithful heart that will face judgment and woe. Jesus' earlier remarks to Judas indicate no restoration, only the horrifying prospect and woe of falling into the hands of God's judgment.

In turning from Peter's immediate future, Jesus notes that a time of pressure draws near. Earlier in the mission, the disciples could count on divine provision from others outside the community, but now they need to provide their own supplies. Jesus will suffer according to the Scripture, and his disciples need to be ready to suffer as well. The disciples misunderstand his warning, noting that they are willing to fight for Jesus. The disciples are ready for war; Jesus is ready for the cross. The irony is great. This second misunderstanding helps to explain why these men will need the Spirit. As Jesus approaches the cross, he is the only one who understands what is ahead. He meets his fate alone. The disciples are warned that pressure will follow, that faithlessness is a possibility, and that leadership means service. By the time of the Book of Acts, they understand what Jesus meant. They will learn to look constantly to God.

D. Trials and Death of Jesus (22:39–23:56)

Jesus' moment has arrived. His death approaches. Luke tells the story in great detail, beginning with a time of prayer and surrender to God's will at Gethsemane (22:39–46). After the prayer, Judas carries out his resolve to betray Jesus, leading to Jesus' arrest (22:47–53), Peter's denials (22:54–62), and Jesus' trials before the Jewish leadership (22:66–71). The leadership struggles to convict Jesus, but he provides the evidence that leads to his own conviction by declaring his authority to rule at God's side. Events are moving as Jesus predicted, and he goes obediently to his death. Both Pilate (23:1–5) and Herod (23:6–12) examine Jesus and declare him innocent, but they will not release him. The theme of the Innocent One slain dominates this section. In a significant exchange, the crowd chooses Barabbas for release rather than Jesus—despite Pilate's protestations that Jesus is innocent (23:13–25). The responsibility for slaying Jesus thus falls collectively on all. Jesus is crucified between two thieves, amid much mocking (23:26–49). Despite the mocking, one criminal believes and so receives the assurance that he will be in paradise. We thus see rejection and faith as Jesus hangs on the cross. The world's view of him does not change. Echoes of the OT in this passage recall the righteous one who suffers. On this note, Jesus is laid in a tomb (23:50–56).

1. Preparation through Prayer (22:39–46)

Luke 22:39–46 provides a look at the "inner" Jesus as he prepares to face his arrest and death.[1] Jesus remains resolute in the face of his trial, prays with dependence on the Father, and submits to his will. Meanwhile the disciples still struggle to come to grips with what is taking place. Jesus exhorts them to pray that they not fall into temptation, and yet they are unable to support Jesus as he faces his betrayal.

The passage has three basic points (Ernst 1977: 605). First, Jesus sets an example in attitude and prayer. The text is very open about Jesus' agony and struggle as he faces this moment. In fact, the struggles depicted here gave the church difficulty as they thought about the divine man. But the portrait is honest in exposing how the exemplary man faced martyrdom and walked with God. He prepared himself by turning to God.

Second, Jesus prays openly and honestly to God and submits to God's will. Heaven will listen—not by delivering him from death, but by giving him strength as he goes through rejection and by vindicating him after his death.

Third, the disciples fail to understand the gravity of the moment. In fact, they fail to understand Jesus' warnings. They live from moment to moment without sensitivity to what is happening. Their insensitivity stands in contrast to Jesus' dependence. By not looking to God, they are prone to faithlessness.

Sources and Historicity

The passage's sources are much discussed, with two resulting options: an appeal to additional sources or the view that Luke has rewritten either Mark 14:32–42 or Matt. 26:36–46 in a more concise form (Aland 1985: §330).[2]

---

1. Fitzmyer 1985: 1436, 1440 speaks of the "inner" Jesus, but is careful to warn that this passage should not be overly psychologized.

2. Most who take this latter approach speak of dependence on Mark, while Matthean prioritists favor dependence on Matthew. Fitzmyer 1985: 1437–39 vigorously defends Lucan reworking of Mark, citing numerous touches of Lucan vocabulary. See the exegesis for details. For defense of an additional source, see Nolland 1993b: 1081–82. Connections with John 16:6, 20–22; 18:2, 11 suggest traditional background.

There are ten differences worth noting between Mark and Luke, some of which are shared with Matthew as well:

1. Luke lacks mention of Gethsemane (Mark 14:32 = Matt. 26:36).
2. Luke 22:40 mentions Jesus' warning to the disciples to pray before he departs, while Mark 14:32 = Matt. 26:36 speak only of Jesus' going to pray and a call to wait until he is done. The warning about temptation comes later in Mark 14:38 = Matt. 26:41, a warning paralleled in Luke 22:46.
3. Luke lacks any singling out of Peter, James, and John (Mark 14:33 = Matt. 26:37).
4. On two occasions, Luke lacks references to Jesus' emotions (Mark 14:33–34, 37 = Matt. 26:37–38, 40).[3]
5. Luke 22:41 uniquely refers to Jesus' praying a stone's throw from the disciples and to his kneeling in prayer.
6. Mark 14:35–36 reports Jesus' prayer in indirect and direct discourse, Luke 22:41–42 has only direct discourse. Matthew has direct discourse twice: 26:39, 42.
7. The mention of angelic aid and sweating blood is unique to Luke (if 22:43–44 is part of Luke's text; see the additional note; cf. Heb. 5:7).
8. In Luke 22:45–46 Jesus addresses all the disciples; in Mark 14:37 = Matt. 26:40 he addresses only Peter.
9. Luke lacks the reference to the spirit being willing, but the flesh being weak (Mark 14:38 = Matt. 26:41).
10. Luke lacks the threefold structure of Mark and Matthew: Matthew has three rounds of prayer (26:39, 42, 44), while Mark has three points of contact (14:33–34, 37, 41) with the disciples between two prayer reports. Luke merely summarizes with one prayer report.

In addition, only 17 of Luke's 114 words (including 22:43–44) match Mark (cf. Ernst 1977: 605). Some of these differences can be attributed to editorial choices, but other details cannot be readily explained on this basis (points 2, 5–8). As such it is likely that Luke used additional sources.[4] If 22:43–44 is part of Luke's original text (see the additional note), additional weight is given to the argument for the presence of a source.

3. R. Brown 1994: 157 makes much of this omission, arguing that Luke omitted it to make Jesus less troubled in his inner psyche, a view that fits a heroic portrayal before a Greco-Roman audience. But Jesus' troubled soul is sufficiently communicated by the prayer itself (the point is enhanced if 22:43–44 is original; see the additional note). The contrast may not be as great as Brown suggests.

4. Soards 1987: 96 mentions 22:39a–b, 40b, 42 as the minimum (he excludes 22:43–44 on textual grounds). Ernst 1977: 607 and Goulder 1989: 741–42 make the best case for additional sources. C. A. Evans 1990: 329 rejects the originality of 22:43–44. For discussion of how the prayer's contents could be known when the disciples are some distance away and asleep, see R. Brown 1994: 174. The Jesus Seminar re-

The account is a story about Jesus (Fitzmyer 1985: 1439; Bultmann 1963: 267–68). The outline of Luke 22:39–46 is as follows:

a. Setting (22:39)
b. Jesus' warning (22:40)
c. Jesus' prayer and the angelic appearance (22:41–44)
d. The disciples are warned again (22:45–46)

The prayer account contains a chiasmus, regardless of one's view of the originality of 22:43–44:

 a commands to pray (22:40b)
 b   withdraws to pray (22:41a)
 c   kneels to pray (22:41b)
 d   prays (22:41c–42)
 e   is empowered by an angel (22:43)
 d′   prays more earnestly (22:44)
 c′   rises from prayer (22:45a)
 b′   returns from prayer (22:45b)
 a′ commands to pray (22:46)

In this view, the key theme is that God responds concretely to prayer by the faithful—an emphasis that is dependent on 22:43–44 being present, thus providing a structural symmetry that may suggest the longer text's originality. A simpler chiasmus for the shorter text lacks any focus on divine provision and simply highlights prayer:

 a commands to pray (22:40b)
 b   withdraws to pray (22:41a)
 c   kneels to pray (22:41b)
 d   prays (22:41c–42)
 c′   rises from prayer (22:45a)
 b′   returns from prayer (22:45b)
 a′ commands to pray (22:46)

jects the historicity of the material on the premise that no one heard the prayer (Funk and Hoover 1993: 391). Brown calls such an objection to historicity a "low level" approach and suggests that the disciples need not have been asleep at this point, although later he suggests that they did not need to hear the prayer because they knew how Jesus prayed. Either explanation is possible. Brown regards the prayer and the event as certain (p. 234), but is less confident of knowledge of the exact words (p. 225). I prefer the view that the event drove the meaning and form of the tradition.

> The major theme is Jesus' dependence on God. When faced with trial he turns to God and submits to his will. In contrast, there is the possibility that the disciples will act faithlessly. Jesus' agony as he goes to the cross is real, yet he is an example. Other themes are Jesus' desire to do God's will, Jesus as the exemplary martyr, Jesus in prayer, and the role of heaven. Heavenly aid comes in the midst of dependence. Meanwhile, the ambivalent disciples fail to respond well. To survive the coming rejection, they will need to turn to God, both in prayer and in their walk.

Exegesis and Exposition

[39]And going out, he went according to custom to the Mount of Olives; and the disciples followed him.

[40]And when he came to the place he said to them, "Pray that you do not come into temptation."

[41]And he withdrew from them about a stone's throw and, going to his knees, he was praying, [42]saying, "Father, if you will, remove this cup from me, but not my will, but yours, be done." ⸢[43]But an angel appeared to him from heaven, strengthening him. [44]And he prayed more fervently while in agony; and sweat came like drops of blood, falling on the earth.⸣

[45]And rising up from prayer and coming to the disciples, he found them sleeping from grief. [46]And he said to them, "Why do you sleep? Rise and pray that you do not come into temptation."

a. Setting (22:39)

22:39   The meal ends, and Jesus departs in the late evening for the Mount of Olives, as was his custom.[5] The disciples follow him. The simple setting shows Jesus preparing to address the Father about his coming ordeal.

The language of the Synoptic parallels is distinct from Luke: Matt. 26:30 = Mark 14:26 names the Mount of Olives as the destination of Jesus and his disciples after the Last Supper, while Matt. 26:36 = Mark 14:32 (the parallels to Luke 22:39) says that he went to Gethsemane. Luke omits the reference to Gethsemane, perhaps because he frequently lacks Semitic terms (Marshall 1978: 830).[6] Mark 14:32 = Matt. 26:36 sets the stage slightly differently: Matthew notes

---

5. See the exegesis of 19:29 for detail on the Mount of Olives. Luke 21:37 mentions Jesus' custom of lodging at the Mount of Olives; Preisker, *TDNT* 2:373.

6. In Luke's Gospel such omissions are common: he does not mention Golgotha in 23:33, the Aramaic cry of Jesus in 23:45 (from Ps. 22:1), or the Aramaic instruction to Jairus's daughter in 8:54. An exception is Acts 1:19, which names and then translates Akeldama. In fact, Luke is consistently more concise throughout the passion narrative, so that a basic editorial choice may be present here beyond Aramaic concerns.

that Jesus went with them, while Mark says that they went. Luke alone mentions that the journey was Jesus' custom, and he presents the setting in two parts: Jesus goes, the disciples follow. Mark 14:26 = Matt. 26:30 notes that the disciples were singing, which Luke omits, perhaps because it is a Jewish custom irrelevant to his readers. Conversely, Luke likes to note rejoicing, so the absence of this detail is hard to explain. These other differences in this section suggest that Luke is working with another source (Schlatter 1960: 432–33; Grundmann 1963: 411; Ernst 1977: 604–5; less certain is Marshall 1978: 828–29; against a source are Creed 1930: 272; Klostermann 1929: 215; Schneider 1977a: 457; Fitzmyer 1985: 1437–39). Barbour (1969–70: 234–35) defends the event's historicity.

b. Jesus' Warning (22:40)

Upon arriving at the Mount of Olives,[7] Jesus exhorts the disciples to **22:40** pray that they not enter into temptation, probably an allusion to the earlier discussion of 22:28–38, especially 22:31 (Marshall 1978: 830).[8] Jesus fears that the disciples will deny him, a very real danger, since Satan wants to sift them like wheat. This is more than a trial. Satan is trying to lead them to defect. Prayer will protect them from unfaithfulness and will encourage them to faithfulness and perseverance. Prayer is important because it expresses a need for God, a desire to depend on him and to rest in his care. This attitude is what the disciples need in the face of these difficult moments. In fact, in this context the present imperative προσεύχεσθε (*proseuchesthe*, pray) suggests that this is to be a constant attitude, since Jesus repeats the call to pray in 22:46. Though they fail in the short term, the disciples eventually learn the lesson (Acts 4:24–31). The way to faithfulness in the midst of hostile rejection of Christ is a dependent spirit that communes with God.

In contrast to the other Synoptics, Luke only generally refers to "the place" (τοῦ τόπου, *tou topou*) and does not name Gethsemane. Τόπος also appears in John 18:2, but the reference is too brief to appeal to a separate source, especially since Luke tends to have unspecified locales. But other differences may suggest a source. Luke alone mentions Jesus' command to pray that they not enter temptation at this point, which Matt. 26:41 = Mark 14:38 has later (Luke

7. Γίνομαι (to be, come to pass) plus ἐπί (to, upon) is limited to Luke among the Synoptics: Luke 3:2; 23:44; 24:22; Acts 21:35.

8. The phrase *enter into temptation* occurred earlier in 8:13; 11:4; Ellis 1974: 257. On the conceptual similarity to 1 Pet. 5:8, see Seesemann, *TDNT* 6:31–32. On the temptation as entry into serious eschatological battle with Satan, see R. Brown 1994: 159–61, who ties the remark to Luke 11:4. Jesus must prepare for his great face-off with Satan.

22:46 matches them at this later point, repeating the call to prayer). At Luke's first call to pray, Matt. 26:36b = Mark 14:32b has Jesus instructing the Eleven to stay where they are while he goes to pray. Luke's *inclusio* of prayer in the account, lacking in the other accounts, may well be generated by a distinct source, since it is hard to explain not only the unique Lucan inclusion of this instruction but also the omission of the instruction to remain while Jesus prays. There is no clear theological rationale for such an omission.

c. Jesus' Prayer and the Angelic Appearance (22:41–44)

22:41 Preparing to pray, Jesus withdraws or "pulls away" (ἀπεσπάσθη, *apespasthē*).[9] Ἀποσπάω may add a note of emotion, as it does in Acts 21:1 of Paul's emotional departure from the Ephesian elders (but cf. 2 Macc. 12:10, 17; 4 Macc. 13:18; BAGD 98; BAA 197; Plummer 1896: 508; three of four NT uses are Lucan). Jesus leaves the disciples and is, in effect, all alone. He prepares to pray and kneels in humility before the Father, at a little distance from the Eleven (an example of the narrative use of space to communicate emotion).

Luke lacks any note of Jesus taking Peter, James, and John with him (as he did at the transfiguration), which suggests the influence of an additional source or the presence of some editorial shortening or both. Luke's details suggest a source. He specifies the distance as a stone's throw, a figurative description of several yards (cf. Gen. 21:16). He notes that Jesus knelt (in distinction to Mark's "falling to the ground" and Matthew's "falling to his face"). Luke's image stresses Jesus' humility and is unlike the common habit of standing for prayer (on the Jewish custom, see SB 2:259–62; Plummer 1896: 508; Marshall 1978: 830).[10] Given the note of agony in the prayer, these notes about kneeling and falling are not necessarily mutually exclusive, but if Luke was simply rewriting Mark or Matthew, why would he change this detail? Luke's version is unique in many of its points, while Mark 14:35 = Matt. 26:39 are closer to one another. Luke uses his frequent imperfect (προσηύχετο, *proseucheto*, he was praying) to render the prayer's content.

22:42 Jesus prays and reveals his mood as he faces death. The prayer in Luke stresses Jesus' submission to God's will. Both before and after

---

9. Jeremias, *TDNT* 2:935, likens the account to Elijah's withdrawal in 1 Kings 19:1, 5, 7, but this association is unlikely. Jesus is seeking God's will, while Elijah was depressed.

10. On standing in prayer, see 1 Sam. 1:26; Matt. 6:5; Mark 11:25; Luke 18:11. On kneeling in prayer, see Mark 15:19 (the soldiers' mock homage to Jesus); Acts 7:60; 9:40; 20:36; 21:5; Eph. 3:14 (Nolland 1993b: 1083 suggests that people kneel for prayer in Acts when prayer is particularly intense). On separating from others for prayer or to go into God's presence, see Gen. 22:5; Exod. 19:7; 24:2, 14; and Lev. 16:17.

the request, Jesus subjects himself to God's will, stated with a conditional clause, εἰ βούλει (*ei boulei*, if you will; Schrenk, *TDNT* 1:633), that is not completed. This aposiopesis indicates the presence of intense emotion (BDF §482): "If you are willing to remove this cup for me, then well and good, but not my will. . . ." The initial expression speaks of deliberation and request (Danker 1988: 355; Plummer 1896: 508). Luke uses a favorite verb, βούλομαι (*boulomai*, to will; sixteen of thirty-seven NT uses are his), in a remark that points to a divine decision. Requests for God to change his will are not unusual and reflect trust in his sovereignty (R. Brown 1994: 166–67; Exod. 32:10–14; 2 Sam. 15:25–26; 2 Kings 20:1–6; 1 Macc. 3:58–60). The prayer closes with μὴ τὸ θέλημά μου ἀλλὰ τὸ σόν (*mē to thelēma mou alla to son*, not my will, but yours), making it clear that Jesus' request is less significant than his desire to do God's will.

Jesus asks that God take "this cup from me." The exact referent of the figurative mention of "cup" is uncertain. In the OT, the cup was linked to wrath (Ps. 11:6 [10:6 LXX]; 75:8–9 [75:7–8 MT]; Isa. 51:17, 19, 22; Jer. 25:15–16; 49:12; 51:57; Lam. 4:21; Ezek. 23:31–34; Hab. 2:16; Zech. 12:2), while in the NT, it is usually associated with Jesus' death, suffering, and wrath (Marshall 1978: 831; Tiede 1988: 391; Goppelt, *TDNT* 6:149–53 [who sees it as a figure of destiny]; Cranfield 1947–48; Blaising 1979; Carson 1984: 543–44). Jesus wishes to have the cup of wrath taken from him, which raises a question since he has already said that his suffering is inevitable (expressed by δεῖ [*dei*, it is necessary] in 9:22; cf. 9:44). Another possibility is a reference to a cup of suffering, not wrath. In this context, however, wrath and suffering are hard to separate. If suffering is the sense, the idea is equivalent to "tasting death" (Heb. 2:9; John 8:52; 2 Esdr. [= 4 Ezra] 6:26; cf. Mark 10:38–39; R. Brown 1994: 169). Since Jesus in a representative act prepares for forgiveness of sin, to separate suffering and wrath is difficult. The request does show, however, that Jesus did not have "a death wish" (Nolland 1993b: 1084). His choice to face the cross was an act of supreme service, suffering, and sacrifice, the ultimate example of what he taught in Luke 22:27.

This situation leads Blaising to suggest that the request is for something possible, namely, that the cup of wrath not remain on Jesus. In arguing for this view, Blaising overpresses the reality of the first-class condition (which Carson 1984: 544 rightly criticizes). Nonetheless, the point may be a possibility. Rejecting this view (which is also supported by John 18:11) because it is not traditional, Carson argues that only an appeal to avoiding wrath altogether continues the line of Satan's original temptation to avoid the cross—but this is not a necessary point of contact with this passage. In other words, we cannot be sure of the connection of Luke 22 to Matt. 4:1–11 = Luke 4:1–13. Jesus is clear that he will and must suffer, but the duration of suffering is not clear in Luke 22, though the traditional view is more likely.

The key term in the debate is παρένεγκε (*parenegke*, take; BAGD 623 §2c; BAA 1259 §2c), used by Luke and Mark in contrast to Matthew's παρελθάτω (*parelthatō*, let this pass by; BAGD 626 §1bγ; BAA 1265 §1bγ). The lexicons make the point that Matthew's term means "to pass by without touching," a detail that is the real obstacle to Blaising's approach, even though one could read Luke and Mark as softening and explaining what appears in Matthew. It seems better to read Matthew as being more exact here, with Mark and Luke summarizing. In other words, Jesus is requesting a potential alteration in God's plan, where the cup of wrath is dispensed with—but only if it is possible and within God's will. Jesus' qualifications about God's will make the request in such a way that the previous certainty expressed about God's plan is irrelevant. In effect, Jesus says, "If it is necessary, it is necessary. But if there is another way, could it be. . . ?" (To argue that the prayer is only about wrath not abiding on Jesus ignores his prediction of his vindication; he already knew that the wrath he faced would not be permanent.) The arrest provides God's answer. Jesus is going to suffer. Nonetheless, he will submit to God's will. In fact, the prayer closes as it began— with Jesus expressing his commitment to God's will. His attitude is exemplary. He makes known the desire of his heart to God, but his primary concern is to accomplish God's will. Jesus' question is like that expressed by the three Jewish men in Dan. 3:17–18.

The parallels are similar in force but distinct in wording. Matthew 26:39 says, "My Father, if it is possible, take this cup from me. Nevertheless, not as I wish but as you [wish]." Mark 14:36 says, "Abba, Father, all things are possible for you; remove this cup from me; but not what I wish but what you [wish]." Mark and Luke share the same verb in the request to remove the cup, but they differ in that Luke has direct speech, while Mark has both indirect and direct discourse. Matthew states God's ability as a first-class condition, while Mark renders the force with more certainty in a direct request alongside an affirmation of God's ability, which can be the force of such a condition. All agree that Jesus submitted himself to God's will, which Luke emphasizes, while Matthew and Mark emphasize his agony by noting Jesus' confession of possessing a distressed soul. Despite Jesus' wish that things be different, he obeys God.

22:43 Angelic aid appears in response to Jesus' prayer (cf. 1:11), a theme that has roots in the OT (1 Kings 19:5–8; Ps. 91:11–12; Dan. 3:28; 10:16–19; Pr. Azar. 26 [= Dan. 3:49 LXX]) and Judaism (3 Macc. 6:18). God stands beside the one who suffers according to his will.

Jesus will not suffer alone. Concrete help comes. The aorist passive of ὁράω (horaō, to see), here ὤφθη (ōphthē, appeared), frequently describes supernatural phenomena in Luke (Luke 1:11; 9:31; 24:34; Acts 2:3; 7:2, 26 [the only nonsupernatural Lucan use], 30, 35; 9:17; 13:31; 16:9; 26:16; Plummer 1896: 509; elsewhere only in Mark 9:4 = Matt. 17:3). It is debated whether the angel aided Jesus by relieving his emotions or strengthening him to face the coming ordeal. The latter is more likely, since Jesus still agonizes in prayer in the next verse. This is the only transitive use of ἐνισχύω (enischyō, to be strengthened by someone else; BAGD 267 §2; BAA 538 §2; elsewhere in the NT only at Acts 9:19 [intransitive]). R. Brown (1994: 186) suggests an allusion to Deut. 32:43 LXX, which is unlikely. More probable is a conceptual allusion to God's willingness to help his own (Deut. 32:36–38), which is also a key theme in Judaism (2 Macc. 4:6; 4 Macc. 18). The picture of Jesus aided by an angel troubles some who struggle with Jesus' humanity, but this language is not unique (cf. Matt. 4:11 = Mark 1:13). This conceptual parallel to the other Synoptics may suggest a source, since Luke lacks a reference to angelic aid in Luke 4:13 (R. Brown 1994: 229–33 discusses Heb. 5:7 as a parallel to the Gospel accounts).

Luke notes Jesus' emotion and the physiological effect of trauma as Jesus entreats the Father more fervently. The key term is the comparative ἐκτενέστερον (ektenesteron, more fervently; BAGD 245; BAA 495), which Luke uses of fervent prayer in Acts 12:5 (cf. Jon. 3:8; 3 Macc. 5:9). The prayer's intensity is also underlined by the reference to Jesus' agony (ἀγωνία, agōnia) a NT *hapax legomenon* that probably describes the momentary anxiety or fear (BAGD 15; BAA 27; 2 Macc. 3:14, 16; 15:19; Plummer 1896: 510; against Neyrey 1985: 59–62, who argues that ἀγωνία refers to "victorious combat").[11] Along with the intense prayer came a physical reaction: sweat that dripped like clotted blood (expressed with two NT *hapax legomena*: ἱδρώς [hidrōs, sweat; BAGD 371; BAA 754] and θρόμβος [thrombos, drop; BAGD 364; BAA 740]). It is important to note that this is metaphorical, not a description that says Jesus sweat blood.[12] The remark depicts Jesus' emotional state as so intense that he per-

22:44

---

11. Martyrdom can include references to blood and sweat in Judaism (4 Macc. 6:6, 11; 7:8). R. Brown 1994: 189–90 compares it to emotion or tension before the start of an athletic event (1 Cor. 9:25; 1 Thess. 2:2; 4 Macc. 9:8; 11:20), but rejects the idea that Jesus feared death. But can death be separated from his sense of conflict here?

12. Fitzmyer 1985: 1444–45 rightly stresses the comparative force of ὡσεί (like), elsewhere used by Luke at Luke 3:23; 9:14 (twice), 28; 22:41, 59; 23:44; 24:11; Acts 1:15; 2:3, 41; 6:15; 10:3; 19:7, 34 (variant reading). On the medical possibilities, see R. Brown 1994: 185; Holzmeister 1938; Keen 1892; and Keen 1897.

spired profusely as a result. The sweat beads multiplied on his body like flowing clumps of blood and dropped to the earth. Luke goes out of his way to portray Jesus' humanity. Jesus realizes the terrible fate he faces, but he is ready to face death now because God has strengthened him for the task.

d. The Disciples Are Warned Again (22:45–46)

22:45   The attention now turns back to the disciples. It has been a long day. The events and the emotional strain are taking their toll. Luke notes that Jesus gets up from his prayer to return to the disciples, where he finds them napping "from grief" (ἀπὸ τῆς λύπης, *apo tēs lypēs*).[13] Jesus' pending death has struck home and has emotionally drained them. Luke notes why they slumber, just as he noted the reason for Peter's remark in 9:33 (cf. Mark 9:6; Fitzmyer 1985: 1442). Jesus is not the only one who is feeling the event's pressure. Some complain that anxiety produces insomnia not sleep, but it can cause drowsiness in the face of emotional exhaustion, and the disciples had been pushing hectically all week.

Luke is a little more complete at this point than the parallels. Mark 14:37 = Matt. 26:40 mentions that Jesus comes to the disciples and finds them sleeping. Matthew and Mark describe the sleeping with the phrase αὐτοὺς καθεύδοντας (*autous katheudontas*, them sleeping), in contrast to Luke's κοιμωμένους αὐτούς (*koimōmenous autous*, them sleeping) (κοιμάω used elsewhere by Luke at Acts 7:60; 12:6; 13:36; Marshall 1978: 833). In both Matthew and Mark, Jesus addresses Peter in particular and speaks of their lack of ability to stay awake. Luke omits entirely any reference to Jesus' multiple prayers and lacks any remark that tells just Peter to watch and pray. Luke's broad reference here seems to summarize the exchanges with the disciples. In this respect, Luke is more compact. This verse may well represent a Lucan summarization and evaluation of the disciples' exhaustion.

22:46   Jesus must have awakened the disciples, since he now addresses them and asks why they sleep, which may symbolically picture their vulnerability to temptation. This is made clear when Jesus repeats his instruction to pray not to come into temptation. Except for the addition of ἵνα (*hina*, in order that) and εἰσέλθητε (*eiselthēte*) for εἰσελθεῖν (*eiselthein*), the wording of this command to pray is exactly the same as 22:40. When the moment of truth comes for Jesus, the disciples will not be ready unless they depend on God and prepare to be faithful to him. Faithfulness requires diligence.

---

13. On ἀπό as cause, see 19:3; 21:26; 24:41; Plummer 1896: 511.

This verse is like Matt. 26:41 = Mark 14:38, which belong to a longer set of events where Jesus prays privately numerous times. In the middle of their longer accounts, Matthew and Mark note that Jesus tells the disciples to "watch and pray that you may not come into temptation." Matthew and Mark agree exactly (except for the form of the verb: Matthew has εἰσέλθητε, Mark probably has ἔλθητε, depending on a textual problem). Both have the ἵνα that Luke lacks. Despite these small differences, it is likely that at this point the source is the same. All agree that after the first moment of prayer, Jesus issued this warning (Plummer 1896: 511). And with this exhortation, Luke's shorter account stops.

Summary

Luke 22:39–46 shows how Jesus responds to crisis. The pain of his approaching death descends on him, so he turns to God in prayer. Meanwhile he twice warns his disciples to pray in order to avoid temptation. Jesus' prayer may help to explain why prayer is important. Jesus honestly displays his innermost thoughts and asks if the cup of wrath might pass by him, but the heart of his prayer shows a commitment to follow God's will. Jesus, the model disciple and martyr, will be faithful to God. The major lesson of this passage is openness in sharing one's heart with God and accountability in recognizing his sovereignty.

This passage also shows how heaven responds to Jesus' request. We see how God responds to honest prayer. He hears and sends his aid. As Jesus turns to face the cross, he knows that he is doing the Father's will, painful as it might be to endure the suffering and shame. Those for whom he suffered are to take note of what he does on behalf of God for them. They are also to note how he faced the crisis: he prayed and submitted to God's will.

Additional Note

22:43–44. The originality of 22:43–44 reflects a difficult textual problem, with many manuscripts on either side of the issue: 𝔓⁶⁹ (apparently), 𝔓⁷⁵, ℵ¹, B, A, T, W, some Syriac, and Marcion omit the verses; ℵ*·², D, L, Γ, Θ, Ψ, Byz, most Itala, some Syriac, and Justin Martyr include them. The external evidence is evenly balanced: dating gives a slight edge to omission, family distribution favors inclusion. Noting that the choice is difficult and not to be held with "apodictic" commitment, Fitzmyer (1985: 1444) rejects 22:43–44 because (1) the omission involves the shorter reading, (2) they have no Synoptic parallel, (3) it is against Luke to note emotion, (4) the longer text is absent from the oldest manuscript (𝔓⁷⁵), and (5) the longer text shows parenetic concerns (so also Nolland 1993b: 1080–81, 1084).

Each of these arguments can be countered. (1) The "shorter-text" argument may not be valid when whole verses are missing. (2) The absence of a parallel is irrelevant since these verses may have been omitted because they lacked such a parallel (i.e., a copyist omitted them in an attempt to harmonize the accounts). (3) It is true that Luke tends to avoid emotion; however, other details are typical Lucan emphases (e.g., prayer). (4) To reduce the decision to one manuscript seems unfortunate. (5) The presence of parenetic concerns is not a cogent reason for rejection since original texts can exhort. In fact, it is not clear that the additional text exhorts at all (it describes), so this point may be irrelevant.

There are positive reasons for including these verses (Ernst 1977: 605; Marshall 1978: 831–32 [with hesitation]; Danker 1988: 356; Goulder 1989: 741–42 ["the case for including vv. 43f. seems overwhelming"]). R. Brown (1994: 180–86) details points of style that fit Luke better than any other NT author and suggests that a scribe might have pulled the text out because it suggested too strongly that angels helped Jesus, a point that makes Jesus too human in the midst of second-century christological debate (also Wiefel 1988: 377). Major early witnesses include the text, namely, ℵ* and Justin Martyr, *Dialogue with Trypho* 103.8. Neyrey (1985: 59–62) notes details that fit Lucan style (like those Brown mentions) and attributes the addition to Luke. Neyrey also notes the contrast and parallel to the aftermath of Jesus' temptations. In the other Synoptics, Jesus is aided by angels, but in Luke 4:13 the promise only involves satanic departure. In 22:31, Satan returns in his attack on the disciples, and his presence is indicated in 22:53 by the reference to the hour of darkness. The reference to aid, which Luke omits in 4:13, is thus appropriate in 22:43–44, since Jesus faces the temptation to avoid death. Neyrey argues that Jesus' agony is not fear, but reflects the possibility of combat, a view he supports by allusion to the possibility of the disciples' falling into temptation. Though his tie between agony and combat may be overdrawn, the association of Jesus' death with Satan is clear (22:53). The angel's ministry looks like evidence of the original text since it is hard to explain why a copyist would insert these verses. The absence of a parallel and the issue of Christology raised in the remark makes inclusion the more difficult reading, though the decision is not absolutely clear. With the inclusion of the verses, additional weight is given to the argument for the presence of a source, since the disjunction with 4:13 suggests that Luke is not emphasizing a point here. In addition, there is a new theme: God immediately comes to the faithful Son's aid.

2. Betrayal and Arrest (22:47–53)

Jesus' arrest is told in three steps. First is the exchange with Judas (22:47–48). Second, the approach of the arresting band produces a reaction from the disciples, one of whom draws a sword and strikes one of those making the arrest (22:49–50). Finally, Jesus rebukes the disciple, heals the man, and then questions his enemies' preparedness as they arrest him (22:51–53). This is the last miracle of Jesus' ministry, yet it occurs almost as an aside.[1] This act of mercy for an enemy shows Jesus' heart. The account as a whole fulfills the remarks of Jesus in 22:21–23, 37. The passage shows Jesus as the "resolute martyr" who faces death. He dominates those arrayed against him and controls events (Fitzmyer 1985: 1447). In addition, God's plan is in motion.

Judas is portrayed as particularly hypocritical, for he betrays Jesus with a kiss. The disciples do not comprehend these events and seek to defend Jesus with violence. In contrast to the use of force and the threatening attitude of those who arrest him, Jesus exercises compassion, healing the ear of a wounded enemy. In doing so he displays the love he exhorted disciples to have (6:27–36). The time of darkness has come, but Jesus continues to love. He is the dominant figure, even though he submits to the Jewish authorities and faces both trial and death. He is in control. Jesus agonizes and yet moves God's plan along by what he does. He has come to terms with accomplishing God's will. Events that seem to make him a passive figure of fate actually reflect his compassionate, submissive activity for God.

Sources and Historicity

The parallels to this passage are John 18:2–12 = Matt. 26:47–56 = Mark 14:43–52 (Aland 1985: §331). Luke lacks certain details that the other Synoptics have: (1) Judas's motive in kissing Jesus (Mark 14:44 = Matt. 26:48), (2) a note of scriptural fulfillment (Mark 14:49 = Matt. 26:56; cf. Luke 22:37), and (3) the flight of the disciples upon the arrest (Mark 14:50 = Matt. 26:56). But Luke also has his unique details: (1) Jesus' remark to Judas (Luke 22:48), (2) the remark from the disciple who wields the sword

---

1. The last full miracle account was in 18:35–43 concerning the blind beggar of Jericho.

(22:49), (3) explicit rationale for why the arresting servant is attacked (22:49–50; cf. Mark 14:47 = Matt. 26:51), and (4) the healing of the ear (Luke 22:51), including a previous note that it was the right ear. There are also issues of order: Mark and Matthew have the order and then the retaliation, while Luke and John have the retaliation before the arrest.

These differences have led to two approaches on the source issue. Many argue that Luke simply edited Mark in his own way with his own emphases (Creed 1930: 272; Schneider 1977a: 460–61; Fitzmyer 1985: 1447–48; C. F. Evans 1990: 815). Fitzmyer notes that only the detail about the right ear and the act of healing are difficult to explain on this approach. He also argues for the substantial historicity in the account. Others argue that Luke had access to an independent source, perhaps known also to John since at points these accounts agree on details (see John 18:1–12, esp. 18:2 in the exegesis of Luke 22:39–40; Rengstorf 1968: 254; Grundmann 1963: 413; Marshall 1978: 834; V. Taylor 1972: 72–76; Ernst 1977: 608; Rehkopf 1959: 31–85; Nolland 1993b: 1086–87). Only 34 of Luke's 124 words are shared by Mark (cf. Ernst 1977: 608). Rehkopf suggests that 22:50b, 52b, 53a parallel Mark, while 22:48, 51b is tied to Luke, and the rest of the details come from Luke's source, which is "as old as Mark." As the exegesis will suggest, a slightly better case can be made for the presence of an additional source than for Luke merely editing Mark. In addition, some doubt the authenticity of the healing miracle (e.g., Meier 1994: 714–18). Part of Meier's position, however, argues that Luke only had Mark. Since the attack is present in all the Gospels (John 18:10 = Matt. 26:51 = Mark 14:47) and the healing is unique to Luke, it seems likely that Luke has other sources and that Lucan creation is unlikely (see the exegesis of 22:51 for a defense of the historicity of the healing).

> The account is another story about Jesus (Fitzmyer 1985: 1448; Bultmann 1963: 268–69).[2] The outline of Luke 22:47–53 is as follows:
>
>   a. The approach of Judas (22:47–48)
>   i. Judas's kiss (22:47)
>   ii. Jesus' response (22:48)
>   b. The disciples' defense (22:49–50)
>   i. The question: shall we strike? (22:49)
>   ii. The act: the severed ear (22:50)

2. The authenticity of the healing, the kiss, and Jesus' short remark in Matt. 26:52 are frequently questioned (e.g., Bultmann 1963: 268–69 doubts the healing, but is uncertain about the kiss). But none of these elements need be doubted: the healing is bound up in how one sees Jesus' miracles in general; the kiss is a standard greeting of respect or acceptance (Gen. 33:4; 2 Sam. 20:9 [deceitfully]; Luke 7:45; 15:20; Rom. 16:16; R. Brown 1994: 255); and it is not unnatural for Jesus to make short comments.

c. Jesus' rebuke to the disciples and to the crowd (22:51–53)
i. The rebuke to the disciples: put down your swords (22:51)
ii. The rebuke to the crowd: why arrest him like a criminal?
(22:52–53)

Jesus' control over events is evident. The hypocrisy of the betrayer's kiss is ironic. The disciples' misunderstanding is expressed in physical defense. In contrast stands Jesus' compassion for his enemies. Jesus is not a robber or a criminal, but one who heals and saves. With Jesus aiding his captors, the dark hour arrives.

Exegesis and Exposition

⁴⁷And while he was still speaking, behold a crowd and the one called Judas, one of the Twelve, was leading them and he drew near Jesus to kiss him.⌐ ¬ ⁴⁸But Jesus said to him, "Judas, with a kiss will you betray the Son of Man?"

⁴⁹And those about him seeing what was coming said, "Lord, should we strike with the sword?" ⁵⁰And one of them struck the slave of the high priest and cut off his right ear.

⁵¹But Jesus replied and said, "No more of this!" And touching his ear, he healed him. ⁵²But Jesus said to those who had come out against him, high priests and temple officers and elders, "Have you come out with swords and clubs as against a robber? ⁵³When I was with you day after day in the temple, you did not lay hands on me. But this is your hour, and the power of darkness."

a. The Approach of Judas (22:47–48)
i. Judas's Kiss (22:47)

Jesus is still speaking to the Eleven when Judas and the crowd approach, identified in 22:52 as chief priests, temple officers, and elders. The turning point is marked dramatically by ἰδού (*idou*, behold!). The arrest is carried out by Jewish officials, led by Judas. He obviously knew where Jesus would be at night, since Jesus followed his custom of praying at night (22:39). Jesus did not try to avoid arrest by fleeing like a fugitive upon the knowledge of the approaching betrayal (Plummer 1896: 511). Judas is identified as one of the Twelve (6:16; 22:3) in order to magnify the horror of his act. Jesus is betrayed by one he chose to be a part of the inner group. Betrayal sometimes happens from within the ranks.

22:47

Luke notes that Judas intends to kiss (φιλῆσαι, *philēsai*) Jesus. Φιλέω (*phileō*) normally means to love, but it can refer to the concrete expression of love, the kiss (BAGD 859 §2; BAA 1713 §2; Stählin, *TDNT* 9:118–20).[3] Luke never mentions whether Judas did in fact kiss Jesus, which differs from the record in Mark 14:45 = Matt. 26:49 that Judas used the kiss to identify Jesus. Why would it be necessary to kiss Jesus, especially if he was well known? It was dark, and perhaps they could not see well, despite their torches. Perhaps Judas approached first and the rest followed behind so that they could surround Jesus immediately upon his identification. If the whole group approached at once or reflected hostility, it might cause alarm, as in fact it did (Luke 22:49–50). It must be remembered that the leadership was nervous about arresting Jesus. Or perhaps not all of the armed soldiers knew who Jesus was. Luke's account is simply shorter here and does not explain why the action was taken. The kiss makes everything certain. There will be no mistakes.

This kiss is the exact opposite of that given to Jesus by the woman who wiped his feet and shed tears of joy and appreciation for him (7:38). Judas hypocritically betrays Jesus. The irony of the act is strong.

The parallels Matt. 26:47 = Mark 14:43 are closer in wording to each other than to Luke. All three accounts use a different word for Judas's approach: Matthew has ἦλθεν (*ēlthen*, he came), Mark uses παραγίνεται (*paraginetai*, he arrived), while Luke has προήρχετο (*proērcheto*, he was preceding).[4] Mark speaks of the immediate approach of the arresting group. All agree that Jesus was speaking as they approached. Matthew alone tells us the crowd was large, though a few Western texts harmonize the Lucan version to Matthew on this point. Mark and Matthew tell of the swords and clubs that the crowd carried, details that Luke lacks. Matthew speaks of the crowd sent by the chief priests and elders of the people, while Mark mentions chief priests, scribes, and elders (Luke saves these details until 22:52). In the Lucan version the account initially focuses only on Judas and Jesus.

ii. Jesus' Response (22:48)

22:48 Jesus responds to Judas's approach with a question ringing with irony. The syntax places the emphasis on Judas's hypocritical action: φιλήματι (*philēmati*, a kiss) is in the emphatic position at the front of the quotation, the verb παραδίδως (*paradidōs*, betray) trails at the end, while the Son-of-Man title serves to describe whom it is

---

3. Stählin, *TDNT* 9:138, 140–41, notes that the kiss was probably seen as a disciple's greeting for his teacher. A simple custom has been transformed into a sign of betrayal. Marshall 1978: 835 notes "misused kisses" in Scripture (Gen. 27:26–27; 2 Sam. 15:5; Prov. 7:13; 27:6; esp. 2 Sam. 20:9) and Judaism (Sir. 29:5).

4. This is Mark's only use of παραγίνομαι, which Luke uses eight times elsewhere, perhaps indicating his use of a source here.

that Judas betrays. It is obvious that Jesus is referring to himself by this title, which heightens the offense, because it suggests the authority of the one betrayed (Plummer 1896: 512). The remark alludes to 22:22. The title appeared in earlier predictions of Jesus' suffering (Luke 9:44; 18:31–32; cf. Matt. 26:45 = Mark 14:41; John 13:31; Ernst 1977: 610). The Son of Man suffers because Judas betrays him.

Mark has no parallel to Luke, while Matt. 26:50 has Jesus address an enigmatic remark to Judas, the force of which is "Friend, why have you come?" or "Friend, do what you came for" (Stählin, *TDNT* 9:140 n. 241; Carson 1984: 547; Rehkopf 1961). These different responses in Matthew and Luke suggest independence. In Luke's version, Judas makes a bold but dastardly act by preparing to betray Jesus with a kiss. Interestingly, Luke never tells us, even here, if Judas actually kissed Jesus (contrast Mark 14:45 = Matt. 26:49). He seems to regard the act itself as unworthy of narration.

b. The Disciples' Defense (22:49–50)
i. The Question: Shall We Strike? (22:49)

The approach of Judas and the crowd causes a reaction among the disciples. Only Luke notes the conversation, with Matt. 26:51–52 = Mark 14:47 = John 18:10–11 relating the disciples' attempt to strike with the sword.[5] According to Luke, those around Jesus want to defend him, an understandable attitude given how the disciples took the remarks of Luke 22:36–38. **22:49**

The disciples see what is "going to be" (ἐσόμενον, *esomenon*). Did they see that the crowd was about to seize Jesus or did they see that force would be used? It is clear that the crowd was going to take Jesus away, so Jesus' later remark to the crowd suggests that the disciples feared the use of force, since the arresting hoard apparently had come prepared for anything. In Matthew, Mark, and John, the sword is wielded after Jesus is seized, thus meeting force with force. Some argue that in Luke the disciples strike before Jesus is seized, since the seizing of Jesus comes in 22:54. This may, however, misread the shorter, summarizing Lucan account. Judas approached Jesus in an initial effort to take him. The decisive seizure comes in 22:54, since Jesus in the meantime stopped to heal and rebuke. No doubt the disciple's action in striking the servant caused the crowd

---

5. The style (ἰδόντες [seeing] at the start of a sentence) is frequent in Luke: 8:34, 47; 23:47; Marshall 1978: 836. The direct question with εἰ (if) is often used by Luke: e.g., Luke 13:23; Acts 1:6; 7:1; 19:2; 21:37; 22:25 (Fitzmyer 1985: 1448). But as Luke 22:67 shows, such a question can reflect parallels in the tradition. Luke is summarizing here.

to turn their attention in that direction and so for a moment Jesus' arrest came to a temporary halt.

The verb in the question is plural (πατάξομεν, *pataxomen*, shall *we* strike?), so the query comes whether they should raise a sword against the crowd (εἰ [*ei*, if] plus a question may suggest that they expect a positive reply; BAGD 219 §V.1; BAA 442 §V.1; BDF §440.3). Some object to the question's historicity because it was considered improbable that swords would be carried on Passover night. Plummer (1896: 512) responds by arguing that μάχαιρα (*machaira*) is the knife used to slaughter lambs and other animals, a point that is difficult to verify. That the term for sword here is the same as that in 22:36, 38 (where Jesus discussed taking swords) might raise some question about Plummer's approach. That remark appears to be about defensive weapons, not utensils. One wonders if Jesus' hesitation to follow Sabbath traditions and other such accretions from tradition might lead his men to not follow this practice as well. In fact, the OT tradition forbid only labor on the Sabbath (Exod. 12:16). Jewish tradition attests to the perceived right of self-defense on the Sabbath (1 Macc. 2:34–36; Josephus, *Antiquities* 13.1.3 §§12–13; 14.4.2 §63; 18.9.2 §§320–24). The carrying of weapons was not unusual, as Essene practice attests (Josephus, *Jewish War* 2.8.4 §125). As the Josephean texts show, Exod. 12:16 was discussed in relationship to this debated issue of Sabbath self-defense. In addition, Jesus has just made the statement about swords, which would have put the disciples on alert and might indicate a potential change in practice that caused them to procure the weapons they normally carried.

ii. The Act: The Severed Ear (22:50)

22:50 The disciples do not wait for an answer. One of them acts. Nolland (1993b: 1088) aptly calls the violent response "a rather pathetic misapplication" of 22:38. None of the Synoptics identify the disciple (Mark 14:47 speaks of "one of those who stood by"; Matt. 26:51 speaks of "one of those with Jesus"). Only John 18:10 notes that Peter wielded the sword and strikes the ear of a slave of the high priest.[6] And only Luke and John mention that the right ear was severed. Mark and John use ὠτάριον (*ōtarion*) and Matthew uses ὠτίον (*ōtion*) for ear, both diminutives of Luke's οὖς (*ous*) (BAGD 595, 900; BAA 1204–5, 1795–96). This difference stands against John and Luke sharing the same source, but the independent agreement sug-

---

6. On cutting off the ear, see Horst, *TDNT* 5:558, and Marshall 1978: 837. Daube 1960: 59–62 argues that such an act is an indirect insult to the master; cf. 2 Sam. 10:4–5.

gests the presence of a traditional set of sources or reminiscences. (Luke also notes a similar detail in Luke 6:6 in referring to the withered right hand, a detail that the parallel [Mark 3:1] lacks.)

Matthew 26:51 = Mark 14:47 simply reports that one of the disciples drew his sword, struck the slave, and cut off his ear. R. Brown (1994: 266–68) argues that Mark's culprit is a bystander, not a disciple. But where did this bystander come from? In this remote setting, one would expect to find only disciples and those who arrest Jesus. Though Mark is vague ("a certain one"), it seems likely that a disciple is meant. Matthew has an additional verb at the beginning, noting that the disciple stretched out his hand. The only verb shared by all three accounts, ἀφεῖλεν (apheilen, he cut off), is also the only verb that Matthew and Mark share. Thus all the Gospels record the disciples' effort to defend Jesus. Only John mentions that the injured man's name is Malchus.

c. Jesus' Rebuke to the Disciples and to the Crowd (22:51–53)

i. The Rebuke to the Disciples: Put Down Your Swords (22:51)

None of the other parallels mention the healing. Jesus responds by stopping the disciples, literally saying, "Let go (ἐάω, eaō) of this," which could be understood as "Leave it alone" (idiomatically: "Stop! No more of this!"; BAGD 212; BAA 428 §2) or "let them do this" (Plummer 1896: 512; Marshall 1978: 837). Plummer argues that the difficulty of the remark shows that it was not created. Jesus does not want the disciples to come to his defense through physical force. He is to suffer, and so he must go through what is about to happen (22:37; 24:26–27, 46–47). He is in control of events, even in the midst of his arrest. He is "Lord of the situation" (Grundmann 1963: 414). Jesus touches the ear and heals it, perhaps by picking up and reattaching the severed portion of the ear or perhaps by simply touching the wound and replacing the ear (Plummer 1896: 513). Jesus acts with compassion and shows love for his enemies, something he instructed his disciples to do in 6:27–28 (Danker 1988: 357; Ernst 1977: 610). Such an action also makes clear that Jesus is no threat to the state. He has no desire to engage them in battle. If they wish to show that Jesus is a dangerous revolutionary, this act shows that the charge cannot stick.

This detail also argues for historicity. If the situation had not been reversed, there would have been chaos and more arrests, and the issues of violence and political unrest could have been raised at the trials (MacDonald 1898–99; against R. Brown 1994: 281, who appears to take the detail as a Lucan creation). In fact, it is hard to

22:51

see the church creating the attack since it is such an unflattering picture of the disciples. Without the healing, the act could have been used to show how dangerous the disciples were. Luke's additional detail complements the earlier account and helps to explain why only Jesus was arrested.

ii. The Rebuke to the Crowd: Why Arrest Him like a Criminal? (22:52–53)

22:52 Jesus turns from his disciples to address the crowd, which has three elements: chief priests, temple officers, and elders. In other words, the religious, military, and civil leadership is present. Luke's description of the crowd comes later than in Matt. 26:47 (high priests and elders of the people) = Mark 14:43 (chief priests, scribes, and elders). Perhaps the leadership stands behind the crowds. Some suggest that Luke created the detail, but it is likely that some officials are present, given the importance of this arrest (with Marshall 1978: 838; against Creed 1930: 274). Judaism has organized all of its official elements to stop Jesus. Interestingly, Luke's order highlights that Jesus' act of goodwill has a broad audience.

Jesus' question is a rhetorical rebuke expressing shock that they are arresting him as if he were a violent criminal. The reference to seizing a robber (λῃστήν, *lēstēn*) is moved forward for emphasis (Plummer 1896: 513). The understood reply to Jesus' question is that, yes, they have come out as if they were arresting a dangerous outlaw. Luke 10:30, 36 used λῃστής to describe the bandits who injured and robbed the Samaritan. The term is also used of revolutionaries by Josephus (*Jewish War* 2.13.2–3 §§253–54; Tiede 1988: 394) and suggests a criminal who does not hesitate to use violence (BAGD 473; BAA 960). It is important to note, however, that the term is never used of revolutionaries during the time of Jesus (R. Brown 1994: 687). Theories that argue for Jesus' being a revolutionary must deal with this "pacifist" text and Josephus's failure to mention Jesus in contrast to his normal practice of focusing on such figures (R. Brown 1994: 679–80). Mark 14:48 = Matt. 26:55 shares the term with Luke. The swords and clubs show a readiness to use force. Jesus seems surprised that they think such resolve is appropriate.

Jesus' question is the same in each account, except that Matthew and Mark add the phrase συλλαβεῖν με (*syllabein me*, to arrest me) at the end. Luke's introduction to the verse is longer because he describes the crowd's makeup. The other Synoptics introduce the question slightly differently: "In that hour, Jesus said to the crowd" (Matthew) or "And Jesus replying said to them" (Mark). These are merely editorial differences.

Jesus raises questions about the crowd's action, noting how the set-   **22:53**
ting has changed from their previous meetings. He recalls the time
when, day after day, he was with them in the temple.[7] There was no
attempt to "stretch out hands against me," that is, to arrest him
then.[8] Jesus suggests that the arrest could have occurred peaceably
and publicly, not in the cover of darkness (Marshall 1978: 838). This
remark exposes the hypocrisy that accompanies the arrest.

But there is a reason this arrest happens at night. In God's sovereign plan, the forces of evil are having their way for a time. Thus
Jesus says this is "your hour," a remark prepared for in 20:19. In
other words, evil is briefly allowed to come to full expression. Jesus
then uses the darkness metaphor to show that it is evil's hour. The
timing and setting matches the mood. Those who reject Jesus have
their way (the mood is like John 8:44; Plummer 1896: 513–14). It is
a time of cosmic struggle (John 16:32–33). Even though evil has its
moment, it is not ultimately in control. It is not only the hour of
those who reject, but also it is the time for the "authority of darkness." The term ἐξουσία (*exousia*) refers to the rule or domain of
evil, which in turn is characterized as darkness (Luke 4:6; 23:7; Eph.
6:12; Col. 1:13; BAGD 278 §4b ["the domain of darkness"]; BAA 564
§4b). Jesus acknowledges evil's foreboding presence. The nighttime
arrest pictures the dark nature of the action (Luke 11:35; esp. John
13:30; 14:30; 19:11; Acts 26:18) and reflects God's permissive sovereignty. A cosmic confrontation between good and evil takes place
(Acts 2:23; Foerster, *TDNT* 2:567–68). Danker (1988: 358) notes the
parallel between the image here and the remark of Luke 1:79 about
Jesus' call to those in darkness. This crowd chose darkness (John
3:19). In Luke's view, they wish to destroy the light.

Luke differs slightly from the parallels. Matthew 26:55b = Mark
14:49a speaks of Jesus teaching daily in the temple and the failure
to arrest him there (Matthew adds that Jesus sat as he taught). Luke
uses a genitive absolute to express his simplified picture of Jesus'
presence, while Matthew has ἐκαθεζόμην διδάσκων (*ekathezomēn
didaskōn*, he sat, teaching) and Mark has ἤμην . . . διδάσκων (*ēmēn
. . . didaskōn*, he was . . . teaching). Luke's idiom of stretching out the
hand against Jesus is unique to him (Matthew and Mark simply say,
"You did not seize me" [οὐκ ἐκρατήσατέ με, *ouk ekratēsate me*]), as

---

7. For the use of κατά meaning "after" in a distributive sense, see Luke 11:3; Fitzmyer 1985: 1451. Luke's audience of chief priests fits these remarks. While it is not
necessary to see the priests themselves carrying weapons, they are responsible for the
tone of the arrest by whom they bring (against the implications of R. Brown 1994:
282, who thinks the detail raises a historical problem).

8. The phrase *to stretch out the hands* looks like Jer. 6:12 but is merely idiomatic;
Marshall 1978: 838; cf. John 7:30.

is his remark about the hour and the forces of evil. Matthew 26:56 = Mark 14:49b–52 speaks of the fulfillment of Scripture and the flight of the disciples, with Mark adding a note about someone who fled naked after trying to follow the arresting crowd. It may well be that these differences reflect not just a summarizing by Luke, but also input from a distinct source or sources.

Summary Jesus' arrest in Luke 22:47–53 is a tragic moment when God allows the forces of evil to work their will. Hypocrisy runs throughout the account. Judas plans to betray Jesus with a kiss. It is a kiss of death, not love. The Jewish leadership arrests Jesus not in public but in private, not as a teacher of God's way but as a violent revolutionary. They act for darkness.

The disciples do not respond much better. They try to come to Jesus' defense with the sword. Yet now is not the time to fight, so Jesus stops them. The disciples want to take measures into their own hands, rather than letting God work out his will.

Jesus is in control. He asks Judas if this is how the defecting disciple betrays the Son of Man, tells the disciples to put back their swords, and in a significant act of compassion heals the severed ear of one of those who will lead him to trial and death. He shows that he loves the enemy by how he responds to his arrest. He notes that the tone of the arrest is all wrong, for he is not a criminal (as his healing proves). He describes the nature of the times as darkness, rejection, and evil. A mood of somber description falls upon the account like a dark cloud. Jesus is headed to trial. But the reader is to note who is in control. The hour of darkness, too, will pass.

Additional Note

22:47. The omission of an actual kiss in Luke created some textual variants. The Western tradition especially wanted to mention the kiss as a sign, a later addition that harmonizes Luke with the other Synoptics, but lacks sufficient external attestation to be original.

3. Trial and Denials (22:54–71)

This unit is built around three events: Peter's denials of Jesus (22:54–62), the soldiers' mocking of Jesus (22:63–65), and the elders' conviction of Jesus (22:66–71). The events are full of contrast and irony. A highly regarded disciple painfully fails. His failure was predicted by Jesus, indicating his control and awareness of events. The soldiers' mocking shows in graphic terms the animosity of those who reject Jesus, especially since it is clear that the insults he receives are undeserved. Jesus is taunted to demonstrate his prophetic office—an act that he predicted would take place.

The trial proceeds in a focused way, with only one witness (Jesus), only one answer (his claim that he will sit at God's right hand), and only one result (conviction). The leadership convicts Jesus on the basis of his own testimony. This decision could not be more simply portrayed. Jesus drives the events that lead to his death. The issue is simply who he is.

Sources and Historicity

The Lucan portrait has a different order than Matt. 26:57–75 = Mark 14:53–72 (Aland 1985: §§332–33). The general order of the three accounts is as follows:

	Matthew	Mark	Luke
evening trial introduced	26:57	14:53	22:54a
Peter follows	26:58	14:54	22:54b
Peter's denials	26:69–75	14:66–72	22:55–62
evening trial continued	26:59–66	14:55–64	
mocking	26:67–68	14:65	22:63–65
morning decision	27:1	15:1	22:66–71

This different order, especially concerning the denials, has caused no lack of discussion. Adding to the picture is the lack of vocabulary overlap: only 69 of Luke's 263 words match Mark (cf. Ernst 1977: 612–13, 616, 617). John has his own details, including the role of Annas in the evening process.

Creed (1930: 275–76) notes five major differences in the Synoptics, to which a sixth may be added. These differences suggest that Luke used additional material.[1]

1. Luke has only one meeting (Luke 22:66–71), not two (Mark 14:53; 15:1).
2. Luke does not record the charge about the temple (Mark 14:57–59).[2]
3. In Luke the Sanhedrin does not explicitly condemn Jesus (Mark 14:64).[3]
4. In Luke, Peter's denials are all together and precede the trial (Luke 22:54–62; Mark 14:66–72).
5. In Luke the soldiers' mocking precedes the trial (Luke 22:63–65; Mark 15:65).
6. The Gospels differ about who elicits Peter's denials; the slave girls are more prominent in Matthew (26:69, 71) and Mark (14:66, 69) than in Luke (22:56).

Another topic of much discussion is authenticity, with all of the following being questioned: the number of Jewish trials, the timing of Peter's denials, the sequence of cock crowings, the possible sources of information about Jesus' testimony, and the issue of the Sanhedrin's not having power to give the death penalty. Most tend to view Luke's account as more precise than Matthew's or Mark's (Ernst 1977: 612; Creed 1930: 275).[4] These prob-

---

1. Those arguing for an additional source are Fitzmyer 1985: 1456–58 (but not in 22:54–62); Creed 1930: 276 (maybe); Marshall 1978: 839–40, 845, 848; Grundmann 1963: 416, 418–19; Ernst 1977: 612–13, 616, 618; Nolland 1993b: 1092–93, 1098–99, 1104–5; and J. Green 1988: 276. Soards 1987: 100–120 argues for a mixture of tradition, Marcan rewriting, and Lucan rewriting. The classic study on this issue is V. Taylor 1972. Dissent about an extra source outside of some oral material comes from R. Brown 1994: 581–83. Most of Luke's changes (e.g., 22:63–65) reflect his style and vocabulary. But all that this shows is Luke's hand on his sources, not whether additional information existed. Brown sees the "game" in 22:64 as evidence of the presence of oral tradition (see the exegesis). But why limit it here, given evidence of sources throughout this material?

2. Luke may know of the charge, however, since Acts 6:13–14 seems to suggest that Stephen's remarks are like Jesus'.

3. Luke is aware of this: Luke 9:22; 23:51; 24:20; Acts 7:52; 13:27–28.

4. J. Green 1988: 282 calls Luke the most primitive form of the tradition. Fitzmyer 1985: 1456–59 is agnostic on historicity, saying that it is impossible to prove. The most detailed English study, Catchpole 1971: 153–220, gives the nod to Luke. For a more skeptical appraisal, giving seven reasons not to accept these accounts as authentic, see E. Sanders 1985: 296–99. For a detailed response to most of his objections, see Bock 1994b. The Jesus Seminar (Funk and Hoover 1993: 392–93) rejects Jesus' prediction (22:61) and the trial dialogue (22:67–69, 70) as inauthentic because 22:61 recalls 22:34 and the absence of disciples at the trial means that no witnesses were present. Jesus' anticipation of Peter's failure, however, reflects his knowledge of how pressure would cause Peter to wilt (the disciples' past record of inconsistency might also contribute to Jesus' expectation). The presence of people like Joseph of Arimathea at the trial makes an internal witness possible.

lems are so complex and involve so many details that their resolution is best left to careful consideration in the exegesis. Nonetheless, one can say that most differences are easily resolvable, while the others are at least explainable. There is no reason to reject the portrait of the trials in each Gospel.[5] The key is to recognize that each source presents some unique material and to see that literary summarization takes place in the Gospels, so the question becomes how to fit the various pieces together. Once one sees the complementary nature of the presentations, the material can be brought together. A probable sequence can be established, and historicity need not be doubted.

In discussing Jewish involvement in Jesus' death, R. Brown (1994: 372–83) concludes that "the involvement of Jews in the death of Jesus approaches certainty" (p. 382). On the possibility of a concocted connection, he says, "One must debate whether such a massive fiction could have been created within thirty years of Jesus' death" (p. 378). The age of the detail is supported by 1 Thess. 2:14–16 and Gal. 3:1. Brown identifies five core elements in the traditions (p. 425): (1) Sanhedrin session, (2) the temple issue (noted by Luke outside the passion narrative), (3) the high priest's role, (4) a death sentence, and (5) investigation on the night of the arrest. These events stand on solid ground.

> These stories about Jesus are mostly a trial scene with a sub-unit on the mocking of Jesus and a story about Peter (Fitzmyer 1985: 1459; Bultmann 1963: 269–71). The account also shows Jesus' prophetic knowledge. The outline of Luke 22:54–71 is as follows:
>
>   a. Jesus taken to the high priest (22:54)
>   b. Peter's three denials (22:55–62)
>   i. Setting (22:55)
>   ii. First denial (22:56–57)

5. Carefully surveying the historical background to the trial scenes and crucifixion in a Jewish setting, O. Betz 1982 argues for the historical coherence and integrity of the Marcan account as well as for its chronological priority (against Catchpole and Green in n. 4 above). He suggests that the temple charge, which Luke lacks, raised the issue of Jesus' authority and, in the view of the Jews, made him a risk to begin a chain of events that ultimately would lead Rome to take the temple and Jerusalem (John 11:47–52). The messianic confession only highlighted the danger in their view. This could be called blasphemous in the sense that someone causing God's people to be handed over to the nations would be guilty of his name being blasphemed (11QTemple[a] 64.6–13). Betz's study raises one potential element that could have set up the decisive Jewish negative reaction to Jesus (for another, more direct cause, see the exegesis of 22:69). I am not certain, however, that it is as important to choose between the Lucan and Marcan accounts as other scholars seem prone to believe. Gospel writers could incorporate older source materials despite the age of their composition.

      iii. Second denial (22:58)
      iv. Third denial (22:59–60a)
      v. The cock crows (22:60b)
      vi. The Lord looks (22:61a)
      vii. Peter remembers and weeps (22:61b–62)
  c. Jesus reviled (22:63–65)
      i. Mocking and blindfolding (22:63–64)
      ii. Many other blasphemies (22:65)
  d. Jesus condemned before the Sanhedrin (22:66–71)
      i. Setting (22:66)
      ii. First question (22:67a)
      iii. Jesus' first reply (22:67b–69)
      iv. Second question (22:70a)
      v. Jesus' second reply (22:70b)
      vi. Jesus' confession yields conviction (22:71)

Peter provides an interesting paradox in this account. His following Jesus shows that he has some interest and nerve. But when the pressure is on, Peter fails repeatedly to align with Jesus. Jesus' awareness of events stands out. The disciples face real danger and the possibility of succumbing to pressure.

The disrespect of officials toward Jesus pictures the world's rejection of him. In fact, the nature of the trial's audience testifies to the official Jewish rejection of Jesus. In ironic contrast to those wielding authority at the trial, Jesus confesses his supreme authority as Son of Man and Messiah. This confession causes Jesus to witness against himself. Conviction comes because the leadership rejects Jesus' claim. Jesus is sent to Pilate, and the leadership seeks his death. The Innocent One suffers.

Exegesis and Exposition

[54]And seizing him, they led him and brought him to the house of the high priest. Peter followed from a distance.

[55]When they kindled a fire in the middle of the courtyard and sat down together, Peter sat down among them. [56]And a servant girl, seeing him sitting before the light, gazing at him said, "This one also was with him." [57]But he denied it, saying, "I do not know him, woman." [58]And after a short time, another seeing him said, "You are also one of them." But Peter said, "Man, I am not." [59]And after a break of about an hour, another insisted, saying, "Truly this one was with him, for he also is a Galilean." [60]But Peter said, "Man, I do not know what you are saying." And immediately, as he was speaking, the cock crowed. [61]And the Lord turned and looked at Peter, and Peter remembered the ⌜word⌝ of the Lord, how had he said to him, "Before

the cock crows today, you will deny me three times." [62⌐]And he went out crying bitterly.⌐

[63]And the men holding Jesus mocked him while beating him. [64]And blindfolding him, they asked him, "Prophesy! Who is the one who strikes you?" [65]And many other blasphemous things they were saying to him.

[66]And when it became day, the elders of the people gathered together, along with the chief priests and scribes, and they led him into their council [67]and said, "If you are the Christ, tell us." And he said to them, "If I say it to you, you will not believe it. [68⌐]And if I ask you, you will not answer.⌐ [69]But from now on, the Son of Man shall be seated at the right hand of the power of God." [70]And they all said, "Are you then the Son of God?" And he said to them, "You say that I am." [71]But they said, "What further need do we have for testimony? For we ourselves heard it from his own mouth."

a. Jesus Taken to the High Priest (22:54)

The crowd that came to make the arrest seizes Jesus, which Luke **22:54** uniquely expresses with συλλαμβάνω (*syllambanō*; BAGD 776 §1a; BAA 1550 §1a; elsewhere in the passion narrative at Matt. 26:55 = Mark 14:48; cf. Acts 1:16; 12:3; 23:27; 26:21). The third-person plurals ἤγαγον (*ēgagon*, they led) and εἰσήγαγον (*eisēgagon*, they led into) allude to 22:52. The process of trying Jesus begins as he is brought to the high priest's house, language that alludes to either Caiaphas or Annas. Luke and Mark 14:53 agree that Jesus is taken to the high priest's house. John 18:13 says that Jesus was led first to Annas's house, and only later to Caiaphas (John 18:24). Matthew 26:57 says that Jesus was led to Caiaphas after the arrest. This difference has generated much discussion. These references in John probably look to an earlier plan to get Jesus (John 11:47–53, a meeting that Caiaphas leads). R. Brown (1994: 559–60) argues that a pre-Marcan tradition moved the initial Sanhedrin investigation of the temple question, which took place earlier, to the night trial for stylistic reasons of simplifying the presentation for topical reasons (e.g., Mark 2:1–3:6). This is possible, but it is more likely that John 18:13, 24 suggests a better time frame for these discussions, which reviewed the earlier temple events surrounding Jesus. The review fails to get adequate evidence around which to build a case to take to Pilate.

Godet (1875: 2.311–12) argues that three Jewish trials are present: (1) a brief encounter with Annas (John 18:13), really an inquiry, where no judgments are made; (2) the meeting with Caiaphas (Matt. 26:57–68 = Mark 14:53–65); and (3) finally the Sanhedrin meeting (Luke 22:66–71 = Matt. 27:1 = Mark 15:1). The trials before Caiaphas and the Sanhedrin mirror one another because the official decision came before the whole body, which replays the Caiaphas meeting. Three points support this view: (1) no decisions are made at the meeting with Annas, (2) John 18:24 makes clear the journey from Annas to Caiaphas, and (3) the failure to make any decision during the meeting with Annas can explain why Matthew and Mark do not allude to it, since it has no real effect on the decision. Caiaphas as the active high priest had to play a decisive role in the outcome. For Godet, Luke's account starts at the high priest's home, which is the home of both Annas and Caiaphas. He sees Peter's first denial coming during the meeting with Annas. Catchpole (1971: 169–72) argues that the house in view is only Annas's because he is the major figure in relation to Christianity in Luke–Acts (Luke 3:2; Acts 4:6). Arguing that Luke and John agree, Catchpole notes that John 18:24 is against seeing Annas and Caiaphas in the same locale. In sum, the three-trial view sees Luke beginning his description of events with a trial before Annas. This starting point is correct for Luke, but whether one should speak of three Jewish trials is another matter. Annas appears to have held a less official meeting.

Others argue for two trials: one at Caiaphas's in the night, another in the morning before the Sanhedrin (Ellis 1974: 259; Hendriksen 1978: 993–97). (Plummer 1896: 515 argues that Annas and Caiaphas share the same house, Hendriksen 1978: 993 for different wings in the same house.) There is so little information that it is hard to answer the question with certainty. The location of the house is also unknown, though some speculate that it was on Jerusalem's West Hill (see R. Brown 1994: 403–4). Brown makes a literary suggestion (pp. 417–23) that a single evening investigation stretching into the morning was presented by Luke as a morning trial to simplify matters. Though possible, I prefer a slightly different view: Luke appears to have only the Caiaphas session and the morning extension; the Annas inquiry was followed by the long evening-into-morning session with Caiaphas presiding throughout.

Any one of the above options is possible, but the more natural reading of the Synoptic tradition is that an initial inquiry before Annas (noted by John and Luke) was followed by a two-part trial: an evening examination (Matthew and Mark) and the official morning trial (Luke). Jesus was thus examined three times, with two points being developed in detail by the Synoptics: the evening examination by Matthew and Mark, the morning trial by Luke. In the midst of all this legal maneuvering, other events, such as Peter's denial, also occurred. The three-trial approach is thus one of appearance, since the evangelists picked either the beginning or the end of the extended session as the key time indicator.

How do Peter's denials fit into the picture? In Matthew and Mark, his denials appear to follow the second meeting rather than being associated with the first meeting. John also narrates some of the denials after describing the move from Annas to Caiaphas (John 18:25–27), while the first denial precedes the Caiaphas session (John 18:16–18). Luke narrates the denials between the initial bringing of Jesus to the high priest's house and the events of the later, morning trial. Whether Annas's or Caiaphas's house is meant is not clear. Since Luke does not note multiple meetings, the difference may be one of appearance (through literary compression) rather than one of substance. The legal activities run throughout the night and into the morning. Since the denials also stretched out over some time (Luke 22:59), it may be that they encompassed the entire set of legal proceedings. In sum, I argue for two major sessions: the Annas inquiry, followed by the longer, decisive meeting before Caiaphas that extended into the morning before a resolution was reached. In fact, it is likely that this morning session reviewed the central evidence obtained during the evening inquiry. Luke's portrayal focuses on the culmination of a larger process within a series of events that all the evangelists summarize. The nature of the sessions and their interrelationship make it possible to see them as one session or to distinguish them.

Was this long meeting a trial? The best answer is mostly yes and a little no. It is a trial in that it rendered an official judgment by the Jewish leadership to bring Jesus before Pilate. The high priest's involvement and the council's input shows the importance of the meeting. Yet it is not a trial in the sense that the judgment rendered by the Jewish leadership did not settle the matter. Their decision was not binding, since they did not possess the authority to execute Jesus (R. Brown 1994: 363–72 [Jews could execute only those who violated certain sacred parts of the temple and possibly those who committed adultery]; Blinzler 1969: 229–44; Sherwin-White 1963: 34–42). This meeting is thus a formal examination as a result of the morning session and a turning point, even a decisive one, but it does not represent a final trial in the fullest sense of the term (for a summary of the full debate over the issues tied to this question, see R. Brown 1994: 389 n. 142, 423–26, 548–60 [who opts for a less formal "interrogation" than is portrayed by all the Synoptic sources as a trial]; Catchpole 1971: 202). Many see Luke presenting something less than a trial because he lacks any formal charge of blasphemy. But he is aware of the official sentence (Luke 23:50–51; 24:20; Acts 13:27–28).

As the initial inquiry begins, Luke's attention moves to Peter, who is said to follow from a distance. Luke lacks the preposition ἀπό (apo, from) with μακρόθεν (makrothen, afar) to express this idea, unlike Mark 14:54 = Matt. 26:58. Luke does not say why Peter trails behind; perhaps it was due to fear, curiosity (cf. Matt. 26:58), or a timid attempt to be at Jesus' side.

Luke is similar to Mark 14:53 = Matt. 26:57 except for one key difference, those present in the high priest's home: scribes and elders (Matthew) and chief priests, scribes, and elders (Mark). Luke may have not named these groups because the inquiry before Annas was not official and resulted in no real action. Or it may simply reflect a literary choice to condense. Since Matthew and Mark start with the evening trial, they therefore name those in attendance. John 18:13, 19–24 suggests that Jesus' meeting with Annas was a private one, in contrast to that before Caiaphas, which he does not relate but moves directly to the meeting with Pilate for the final decision. Luke never names the high priest, apparently to indicate that the responsibility falls collectively on the leadership (they were noted in Luke 22:52 and will be mentioned again in 22:66). No additional detail is given that might prevent blame from being too narrowly placed.

b. Peter's Three Denials (22:55–62)
i. Setting (22:55)

22:55 The setting of Peter's denials is the courtyard of the high priest's home. The syntax is awkward because the two initial participles, πε-ριαψάντων (*periapsantōn*, kindling) and συγκαθισάντων (*synkathisantōn*, sitting together), look like genitive absolutes. However, the pronoun at the end, αὐτῶν (*autōn*, of them), breaks the absolute construction. Nonetheless, the picture is clear. A group kindles a fire (περιάπτω, *periaptō*; BAGD 645; BAA 1301; a NT *hapax legomenon*; cf. 3 Macc. 3:7) and sits down together. Luke does not specify who "they" are, though contextually it seems likely that the term includes the men holding Jesus (cf. Luke 22:63). This is the group that accompanied those mentioned in 22:52, with the high priest's wounded slave being among their ranks. Matthew 26:58b = Mark 14:54b = John 18:18 identifies the group as the servants (John: slaves and servants).

This group has prepared a fire in the courtyard for a cool, midspring Jerusalem evening (1 Macc. 12:28–29; John 18:18). Most significant homes were built around an open courtyard, with the servants gathering in this middle opening and those who examined Jesus being inside the house (Hendriksen 1978: 993; Godet 1875: 2.315). Luke, Matthew, and Mark note that Peter sat at the fire, while John portrays him as standing, having just come in (Matt. 26:71 = Mark 14:68 notes that Peter later got up and stood by the gateway). These differences represent various ways to summarize the same event. All the Gospels agree in placing the denials in the evening. They also agree that they take place in the home's courtyard. Only Matthew lacks a reference to the fire in the courtyard. Matthew 26:58 states Peter's motive: he wanted to see the outcome of the event. In other words, he was curious to see what would happen to Jesus.

ii. First Denial (22:56–57)

The pressure falls on Peter. He had committed himself to Jesus in private (22:33), but now it is time to publicly demonstrate the strength of his commitment. The menacing intimidator is not a ruler or a priest, but a little servant girl. All the Gospels mention that she starts the sequence of denials and all use the term παιδίσκη (*paidiskē*, servant girl) to describe her (BAGD 604; BAA 1223; used elsewhere by Luke in Luke 12:45; Acts 12:13; 16:16). John notes that she was the doorkeeper at the gateway, while Mark mentions that she was the high priest's servant.   **22:56**

This girl observes Peter by the light of an evening fire. In short, she stares (ἀτενίζω, *atenizō*; BAGD 119; BAA 240; elsewhere in the NT only at Luke 4:20; Acts 1:10; 3:4, 12; 6:15; 7:55; 10:4; 11:6; 13:9; 14:9; 23:1; 2 Cor. 3:7, 13). Mark 14:67 notes that she "saw" (ἐμβλέψασα, *emblepsasa*) Peter warming himself at the fire. Matthew has no such detail.

Each account reports her remarks in slightly different terms. Luke's is framed as a general accusation: "This one also was with (σύν, *syn*) him."[6] Mark reports her saying, "And you were with (μετά, *meta*) the Nazarean, Jesus." Matthew says, "And you were with (μετά) Jesus of Galilee." John has her say, "Are you not one of (ἐκ, *ek*) this man's disciples?" Each writer summarizes the opening discussion in his own way, as the girl identifies Peter as Jesus' disciple.

The girl's question solicits Peter's first denial, which Luke reports in two steps. First, Peter denies (ἀρνέομαι, *arneomai*) the girl's observation (Ellis 1974: 260). Ἀρνέομαι is here used in one of its two basic NT senses (BAGD 107–8 §3a; BAA 217 §3a): "to challenge or dispute." It also meant "to abandon" and thus became a description of apostasy (Luke 12:8–9; 2 Tim. 2:12; Schlier, *TDNT* 1:469–71). The use of this verb recalls Jesus' prediction in Luke 22:34 (Danker 1988: 359). Second comes the denial proper: "I do not know (οὐκ οἶδα, *ouk oida*) him, Woman," which totally denies any knowledge of Jesus. The phrase is like the Jewish ban formulas used against those dismissed from the synagogue (SB 1:469; Marshall 1978: 842; Catch-   **22:57**

---

6. Καί (also) probably alludes to John's being with Peter, as John 18:15 appears to suggest. Οὗτος (this one) is probably derogatory; Fitzmyer 1985: 1464. In Acts 4:13, Peter is again associated with Jesus, but his response is quite different!

pole 1971: 273): "We no longer know you," that is, we have nothing to do with you. As such Peter's denial is a strong one.

Luke's wording of the denial differs from Matt. 26:70 = Mark 14:68. Alone noting that Peter made the denial publicly, Matthew states the denial less directly: "I do not know what you are saying." Mark has, "I neither know nor understand what you say." The intent of all three remarks is the same: an unwillingness to acknowledge that he knows Jesus. Both Matthew and Mark then note that Peter moved to the porch (Matthew) or gateway (Mark). The pressure is getting to him, as indicated by his movement away from the scene. Luke lacks any such note. He simply notes the passage of time.

iii. Second Denial (22:58)

22:58 Luke notes that the second denial follows "after a short time" (μετὰ βραχύ, *meta brachy*; BAGD 147 §2; BAA 293 §2; βραχύς elsewhere in the NT only at John 6:7; Acts 5:34; 27:28; Heb. 2:7, 9; 13:22). Luke notes that "another" (ἕτερος, *heteros*) man raises the issue of Peter's association to Jesus, in contrast to Mark 14:69, where the same servant girl raises the issue a second time; Matt. 26:71 also says it is "another" (but ἄλλη, *allē*, is feminine), while John 18:25 says that "they" raised the issue. This significant difference suggests yet again that Luke is dealing with sources distinct from Mark (Marshall 1978: 842), and Luke's agreement with John confirms this suspicion. It seems that on this second effort the girl persisted and others joined her. Marshall argues that Luke's chronological note without any note about a move suggests that Peter stayed in the same place; but this is not necessarily the case, given the mixing of sources and the presence of compression. Matthew and Mark mention that Peter moves after the first denial, and the break in John's narration between the denials may also suggest the presence of some break in time.

The second challenge declares that Peter is one "of them," that is, he is a disciple of Jesus. Peter's reply makes it clear that a man makes the charge: "Man (ἄνθρωπε, *anthrōpe*), I am not."[7] Peter's reply denies not only his association with Jesus but also his service alongside the other disciples. Matthew 26:71 states the challenge that "this one was with Jesus of Nazareth" (which looks like the first denial of Mark 14:67). Peter's second Matthean reply says he denied with an oath that he knew the man. As noted above, in Mark the same maid says a second time that "this is one of them." Mark notes

7. That this remark is not gender neutral is seen by the use of γύναι (woman) in 22:57.

the second denial by simply saying that Peter denied the observation again. John 18:25 has the group say to Peter, "Are you not also one of the disciples?" followed by Peter's denial: "I am not." Thus, of the four accounts, John and Luke stand closest. The public pressure is heating up, and Peter is wilting; he is trying to stick close to Jesus while remaining incognito. Each of the accounts summarizes a public exchange that will eventually humiliate the apostle.

iv. Third Denial (22:59–60a)

The third denial follows after about an hour's break (διαστάσης, *diastasēs*; BAGD 195 §1; BAA 393 §1; Exod. 15:8; Prov. 17:9; διΐστημι elsewhere in the NT only at Luke 24:51; Acts 27:28; Plummer 1896: 516). Only Luke gives the specific time between the second and third denials, in contrast to the vague "after a short time" in Matthew and Mark. Yet another person speaks up against Peter. In fact, this third person is insistent (διϊσχυρίζετο, *diischyrizeto*; BAGD 195; BAA 393; elsewhere in the NT only at Acts 12:15) that Peter is a disciple: "Truly, this one was with him." The use of the preposition μετά (*meta*, with) recalls Peter's confidence in Luke 22:33: "I am ready to go with (μετά) you. . . ." Luke's term for "truly" (ἐπ᾽ ἀληθείας, *ep' alētheias*), which he uses twice elsewhere in his Gospel (4:25; 20:21; Marshall 1978: 843), differs from Matthew's and Mark's ἀληθῶς (*alēthōs*). What gives Peter away (note the explanatory γάρ, *gar*) is his dress or accent (Matt. 26:73), which the accuser notes is Galilean (Nolland 1993b: 1096). Jesus faces the same recognition later (Luke 23:6). For the third time, Peter is identified as a disciple, but now with additional "circumstantial" evidence. Why else would a Galilean be present at this late evening fire? The hour-long break has not changed the audience's suspicions about Peter. He is still in danger of being exposed.

Matthew 26:73 = Mark 14:70 notes that the third denial came "after a little while." Bystanders speak in both accounts, though they are identified with distinct but related terms: οἱ ἑστῶτες (*hoi hestōtes*) in Matthew and οἱ παρεστῶτες (*hoi parestōtes*) in Mark. Matthew has the bystanders say, "Truly you also are one of them, for your speech makes you clear." Mark has, "Truly you are one of them, for you also are a Galilean." Though the second half of the remark differs, the point is similar. John 18:26 is distinct, since he identifies the speaker as one of the high priest's servants who was a relative of the slave whose ear Peter severed. This servant simply says, "Did I not see you in the garden with him?" The Johannine use of οὐκ (*ouk*, not) in the question expects a positive reply. It seems clear that John draws on independent sources and that in all probability many people were commenting about Peter at this point.

22:59

22:60a Peter makes his third denial, acting, as Danker (1988: 359) says, "more like a jellyfish than a 'Rock-Man.'" Peter succumbs to the pressure, claims not to understand what his accuser is saying, and thus falls into the temptation that Jesus had warned about in 22:40. The denial again begins with a vocative that lets us know that the accuser is a man (all three Lucan denials have a vocative identifying the accuser's gender; 22:57, 58, 60). Peter again denies a link to the disciples, since he can hardly deny that he is a Galilean with his accent (Marshall 1978: 843). He claims that they have the wrong man.

In Matt. 26:74 = Mark 14:71, Peter begins his denial by invoking a curse and swearing, which Luke does not mention since he commonly omits unflattering details about the disciples or Jesus' family (cf. Luke's absence of the details in Mark 3:21; 8:32–33 = Matt. 16:22–23; Mark 14:37 = Matt. 26:40). The Lucan denial is unique (but is like the first denial in the other Synoptics): Peter denies understanding the charge (Nolland 1993b: 1096 may be right to understand its force as "I can't imagine why you are saying this" [perhaps better: "I can't understand why you insist on this connection"]). In Matthew he says, "I do not know the man," while Mark's denial is a little longer: "I do not know the man of whom you speak." John 18:27 says that Peter denied the charge of being in the garden. This variety may well suggest that this vivid story was variously rendered. It also suggests that much was said to Peter as he tried to follow Jesus. He had received the gathering's attention, was challenged from all sides, and crumbled under the strain.

v. The Cock Crows (22:60b)

22:60b Only Luke notes that while Peter was still speaking the cock crowed, which fulfills 22:34 (as the next verse mentions). All three accounts record that this occurs "immediately," though with different terms (Plummer 1896: 516): Luke has παραχρῆμα (*parachrēma*, a favorite term of his: ten times, including 5:25; 8:44, 55; 18:43), Mark has εὐθύς (*euthys*), while Matthew and John have εὐθέως (*eutheōs*). Luke and Matt. 26:74 = John 18:27 note only a single crowing, in contrast to two in Mark 14:72. Luke's remark seems less specific than Mark's, which may reflect the summarizing style of a distinct source. The difference is odd if Luke used Mark. All note the fulfillment of Jesus' prediction that Peter would deny him and the cock would crow.

vi. The Lord Looks (22:61a)

22:61a The aftermath of his denials is painful for Peter. Luke uniquely relates that Jesus turns and looks at Peter. Perhaps Jesus' glance after the denial reminds Peter that Jesus knew Peter was denying him. Even from a distance, his presence still manifests itself.

Jesus' locale is not given. Perhaps he was being moved from one wing of the high priest's house to another as he went from Annas to Caiaphas (Rengstorf 1968: 248), perhaps he was waiting with the soldiers in the courtyard (Grundmann 1963: 417; Catchpole 1971: 168), or perhaps he was being held in a place that gave him a glimpse of the courtyard. The other Gospels suggest one of the latter two options, since Matthew and Mark place Peter's denials after the move to Caiaphas. Luke adds a note of pathos by saying that the Lord (ὁ κύριος, *ho kyrios*) saw Peter. These unique Lucan details suggest that Luke is not just editing Mark here. He has another source (Nolland 1993b: 1096).[8]

vii. Peter Remembers and Weeps (22:61b–62)

As Peter sees Jesus, he recalls the "word of the Lord" to him earlier. **22:61b** Jesus' prediction has come true. The Gospels use related terms for Peter's recalling Jesus' remark: Luke has ὑπεμνήσθη (*hypemnēsthē*), Mark 14:72 has ἀνεμνήσθη (*anemnēsthē*), and Matt. 26:75 has ἐμνή-σθη (*emnēsthē*)—a lexical detail that points to a distinct source, since this is the only time Luke uses ὑπομιμνήσκω. Luke does not record Jesus' remark in Luke 22:34 word for word, but exhibits shifts in word order and verbal forms. Matthew is similar to Luke, "Before the cock crows, you will deny me three times," while Mark has, "Before the cock crows twice, you will deny me three times." Why would Luke drop the reference to crowing twice if he had only Mark before him (Marshall 1978: 844; Catchpole 1971: 164)?[9] John has no parallel other than a note that the cock crowed immediately after the third denial.

To solve this difficulty, Arndt (1956: 452) suggests that Luke refers only to the morning cock crowing, while Mark mentions two nighttime crowings.[10] The discussion is complicated by a textual problem in Mark 14:68, making it uncertain whether the cock crowed the first time after Peter's first denial. If this reference is absent, then Mark 14:72 may be saying that the cock crowed twice after

---

8. Marshall 1978: 844 notes that elsewhere in his Gospel Luke does not add the title κύριος to Marcan material. Catchpole 1971: 168–69 argues against Lucan creation of this detail (pace Bultmann 1963: 168) and notes that στραφείς (turning) is common in Luke's special source (7:44; 9:55; 14:25; 23:28), although 7:9 and 10:23 may be Lucan or from a source shared with Matthew.

9. Matthean prioritists argue that Luke makes use of Matthew here.

10. It is difficult to know if Luke's σήμερον (today) refers to morning or late evening. On the time of the cock crowings, see Kosmala 1963–68. If an evening crowing is meant, it is about 3:00 A.M.; if morning, then it is sunrise.

Peter's third denial. There would be no real difference under either scenario: if the two crowings happened at once or if the reference to two crowings in Mark is not original.[11] The remark in Mark 14:72 about a second crowing seems to suggest the earlier crowing of 14:68. If so, then some difference of intent or detail in the tradition is responsible for the variation. If two crowings are present, then Mark has probably been more specific.

The point of Peter's recollection of what Jesus had said is twofold: (1) Jesus is aware of what is occurring (2) and he faces his trial all alone with no one to stand with him. His predictions about events are coming to pass, just as he said. His word is true.

22:62   After his denials, Peter goes out and weeps bitterly. If this verse was originally part of Luke (see the additional note), the wording matches Matt. 26:75, providing one of the few places in Luke 22–23 where Matthew and Luke agree against Mark (another example is the number of cock crowings). R. Brown (1994: 607) attributes this agreement to oral tradition. It is another evidence of input to Luke beyond Mark. Mark 14:72 simply says that Peter broke down and cried (καὶ ἐπιβαλὼν ἔκλαιεν, *kai epibalōn eklaien*). The term for "wept" (κλαίω, *klaiō*) is the same in each Gospel, though in different tenses (imperfect in Mark, aorist in Matthew and Luke). Since it frequently refers to weeping over the dead (cf. Luke 8:52; John 11:31, 33) intense emotion is expressed here. Peter felt instant remorse over his denials. His sin of denial crushed his spirit. Jesus later restores Peter, despite his failure here (John 21:1–14). In fact, he has already prepared Peter for restoration (Luke 22:32).

One final point bears noting. The various accounts of the denial reflect general agreement (R. Brown 1994: 590–91). Yet the minor details diverge widely, especially in the second and third denials. This popular account, full of emotion and humanity, was summarized with dramatic variation, possibly because the situation grew more tense and brought in bigger audiences as it proceeded. To explain the differences in detail, Brown (pp. 620–21) argues that Jesus figuratively predicted the denial to indicate that Peter's denials would be total and swift, but that the early tradition transformed this figurative reference into three denials. One should not, however, appeal to imaginative storytelling, but to differences that naturally emerged from a public event involving many players. The par-

---

11. J. Wenham 1978–79 questions the originality of all the Marcan references to two crowings (Mark 14:30, 68, 72). The external evidence, however, for omitting the two crowings is not strong: of the three Marcan mentions of the double cock-crowing, codex ℵ omits all three (Mark 14:30, 68, 72), B omits one (14:68), and C* omits two (14:30, 72).

ticipation of several people in the denial would naturally surface different perspectives in how it was understood and retold. The differences probably reflect variations in summarizing a large pool of information that circulated in the church.

c. Jesus Reviled (22:63–65)
i. Mocking and Blindfolding (22:63–64)

The shift to Jesus occurs abruptly and awkwardly. Αὐτόν (*auton,* **22:63** him) clearly refers to Jesus, though the nearest antecedent is Peter.[12] Many regard this stylistic awkwardness as an indication that Luke is weaving together distinct sources at this point (but R. Brown 1994: 582 argues for a mere editing of Mark). Those holding (οἱ συνέχοντες, *hoi synechontes*; BAGD 789 §4; BAA 1573 §4; used elsewhere in Luke's writings at Luke 4:38; 8:37, 45; 12:50; 19:43; Acts 7:57; 18:5; 28:8) Jesus are probably the soldiers, the temple guards of Luke 22:52. Their actions are separated from those of Jesus' examiners in 22:66. Luke describes two facets of their custody: they mock (the main verb) and beat (a participle) Jesus. In this context, the imperfect ἐνέπαιζον (*enepaizon*) tense is probably ingressive: "They began to mock him" (BAGD 255; BAA 516; elsewhere in the NT at Matt. 2:16; 20:19 = Mark 10:34 = Luke 18:32; Matt. 27:31, 41 = Mark 15:20, 31; Matt. 27:29; Luke 14:29; 23:11, 36). With the taunting comes beating (δέρω, *derō*; BAGD 175; BAA 351; used elsewhere in Luke's writings at Luke 12:47, 48; 20:10, 11; Acts 5:40; 16:37; 22:19).[13] Fitzmyer (1985: 1465) notes OT and Jewish descriptions of mistreatment of prisoners (Isa. 50:5–6; 53:3–5; 2 Macc. 7; 4 Macc. 6:1–30; 8:12–14:10). Jesus gets no respect. It will not be the last time (Luke 23:11, 36).

Luke's unique vocabulary describing the insults hurled upon Jesus as he waited for the official meeting with the leadership and the awkward transition into the unit suggests that Luke drew this material from a source other than Mark (Marshall 1978: 845; Grundmann 1963: 417–18; Plummer 1896: 517; Catchpole 1971: 174–83). Only three of Luke's twenty-seven words agree with Mark (cf. Ernst 1977: 616). The Synoptic parallels have more detail: Matt. 26:67 speaks of those making the death judgment as spitting, striking, and slapping Jesus; Mark 14:65 says the leaders spat on him and blindfolded him and the guards struck him. Luke omits any reference to spitting and speaks only of a general mocking that he details

---

12. My translation makes the referent clear but obscures the problem of the pronoun.

13. Stählin (*TDNT* 8:264–65) speaks of a game like "blind man's bluff." R. Brown 1994: 575 discusses three games involving covered or blindfolded eyes listed by Pollux, *Onomasticon* 9.113, 123, 129 (second century B.C.).

in the next verse, where his material has closer parallels to Matthew and Mark. As such he lessens any allusion to Isa. 50:6. R. Brown (1994: 584–86) argues that the scene in reordered by Luke to emphasize that Jesus is the model martyr and that there may be a historical kernel behind it that Luke simplified and summarized, in the process softening the portrayal of the leaders' role in the physical abuse of Jesus. There is no reason to doubt that such abuse occurred. Later handling of people who made these type of claims shows that this kind of reaction fits the culture (e.g., Jesus son of Ananias in Josephus, *Jewish War* 6.5.3 §302).

22:64 The soldiers blindfold (περικαλύπτω, *perikalyptō*; BAGD 647; BAA 1305; outside this pericope in the NT only at Heb. 9:4) Jesus and ask him to name his tormentors. This mocking of Jesus' prophetic gift reflects how some people viewed him (Luke 9:7, 19). Their mocking not only recalls Jesus' prediction (18:32–33), but actually manifests his prophetic claim (also 22:63 and 23:11, 36)! The juxtaposition of this with Peter's denials shows two of Jesus' predictions fulfilled side by side. In Matt. 26:68 = Mark 14:65 the soldiers call out to Jesus to prophesy concerning who it is that strikes him. Luke's source overlaps with Matthew (Fitzmyer 1985: 1465–66; Marshall 1978: 846).[14]

ii. Many Other Blasphemies (22:65)

22:65 Luke summarizes: the soldiers say many other things to Jesus. The construction ἕτερα πολλά (*hetera polla*, many other things) is frequent in Luke (Luke 3:18; 8:3; Acts 15:35; Klostermann 1929: 220; Marshall 1978: 846) and serves as an adverbial accusative with the participle βλασφημοῦντες (*blasphēmountes*): "Many other blasphemous things were said" (Plummer 1896: 517; Fitzmyer 1985: 1466; Burton 1900: §121). The verb βλασφημέω (*blasphēmeō*, to revile, defame, or slander; BAGD 142 §2bδ; BAA 285 §2bδ) is used with Jesus as the object in Matt. 27:39 = Mark 15:29 and Luke 23:39 (cf. Luke 12:10; Acts 13:45; 18:6; James 2:7; Marshall 1978: 846). Because of its religious connotations, this term suggests Luke's repulsion for the action taken against Jesus. The soldiers act wickedly against him and against the God who has sent him. Conceptually, the passage recalls OT texts about rejection of the righteous (Isa. 50:6; 53:3; Ps. 69:6–12 [69:7–13 MT]; Ernst 1977: 617). Mark 14:65 alludes to Isa. 50:6; but there is no similar clear allusion in Luke. The Synoptics have no parallel to this summary verse.

14. This Matthean–Lucan agreement causes some commentators (e.g., Creed 1930: 277–78) so much trouble that they go to great lengths to explain away the agreement for fear it challenges Marcan priority.

d. Jesus Condemned before the Sanhedrin (22:66–71)
i. Setting (22:66)

Luke now describes the decisive part of the trial, around which **22:66** many historical questions revolve. The main reason for these questions is that the language of the passage is somewhat similar to Mark 14:55–64 = Matt. 26:59–66, which describe an evening trial distinct from the morning meeting alluded to in Mark 15:1 = Matt. 27:1. Only twenty-one of Luke's ninety-four words agree (cf. Ernst 1977: 617). Mark and Matthew relate this morning meeting without any testimony. In contrast, Luke's detailed meeting clearly occurs in the morning, as the remark ὡς ἐγένετο ἡμέρα (hōs egeneto hēmera, as it became day) makes clear. Three solutions have been proposed:

1. One of the Gospel writers erred, with opinion divided whether it was Matthew–Mark (Catchpole 1971: 183–203) or Luke (Creed 1930: 276). Given the differences between the accounts, this approach is not likely correct. The absence of any Lucan reference to false witnesses or the testimony about destroying the temple suggests that Luke has a shorter, possibly distinct account. The possibility of additional sources and differing literary perspectives makes this approach too facile.
2. There was only one meeting of the Sanhedrin that, because it was a dawn meeting, Matthew–Mark place in the evening and Luke in the morning. Each account thus adopts a different point of view. Marshall (1978: 847) favors the morning as the time of resolution and argues against the normal conclusion that Mark relates an evening meeting. He argues that this latter point is not explicit, but is a contextual deduction (which he seems to regard as lessening the difficulty). This agrees with how many see the source issue in this passage, since most see a combination of Mark with additional Lucan material (Catchpole 1971: 183–203; V. Taylor 1972: 80–84; Soards 1987: 103–5), in contrast to Creed (1930: 278), who argues that Luke moved Marcan material here. Matthew 27:1 seems clear in setting a distinct morning meeting, which is also the strong impression of Mark 15:1. This particular form of this approach, though possible, is unlikely.
3. There were two meetings, or perhaps two parts to a single meeting: one an evening trial (Matthew and Mark), the other the official declaration of guilt where the key evidence was reviewed (Luke).[15] Standing in favor of this view are the differ-

---

15. Plummer 1896: 517 plausibly notes that the evening testimony would be repeated in the morning. The detail may reflect an additional Lucan source.

ences already noted between Luke and the other Synoptics, along with the official need for a morning trial at which official condemnation was obtained (*m. Sanh.* 4.1 makes clear that an evening verdict has no weight, so a morning trial would be necessary; see the exegesis of 22:54).

But resolving the number and timing of the trial(s) does not end the historical discussion (Carson 1984: 549–52; Liefeld 1984: 1037). If one follows the Gospel traditions, other Jewish laws were also violated. Supposed irregularities include the following (see Lohse, *TDNT* 7:868–70, and R. Brown 1994: 358–64):

   a. The proceedings take place at the high priest's home and not in the temple (*m. Sanh.* 11.2).
   b. Jesus was tried without a defense (*m. Sanh.* 4.1 says that both sides of a case must be heard).
   c. Jesus was accused of blasphemy without actually blaspheming in the technical sense of the term by pronouncing the divine name (*m. Sanh.* 7.5).
   d. The verdict came in the space of one day, when two days were required for a capital trial (*m. Sanh.* 4.1).
   e. Jesus was tried on a feast day (see objection 10 in excursus 11).
   f. Contradictory testimony nullifies evidence (*m. Sanh.* 5.2).
   g. A pronouncement of guilt by the high priest is contrary to the normal order, which should start with the least senior members (*m. Sanh.* 4.2).

The mishnaic tractate *Sanhedrin* covers many of these questions. The uncertainty about these supposed violations rests partially on the question of whether these laws are as old as the early first century A.D., given that the Mishnah was composed over a century later. Sadducean-dominated practice would likely be harsher judicially (or at least different) from the more humanitarian approach of the Pharisees, whose rulings dominate the Mishnah (Blinzler 1969: 207–8, 216–29, esp. 227; more cautiously R. Brown 1994: 350–63; Josephus, *Antiquities* 13.10.6 §294; 20.9.1 §199). This seems the best explanation for these differences, with the near-to-feast-day trial being the only detail not likely to be affected by this difference. In addition, Dalman (1929: 98–100) argues that these laws were not strictly followed if "the hour demanded it." For example, it is clear that the officials wanted to avoid a public trial, as the arrest of Jesus shows, so a temple trial was not advisable. Carson suggests that the goal of the all-night trial was to get Jesus before the Roman rulers early in the morning, which was the only time they heard cases. If they waited any longer, Jesus would have to be held for a few days, because the next day was Sabbath. To hold Jesus for such a long time would have been risky, so a quick resolution was desired. The demands of the hour and Pilate's proximity may well explain why this trial was held so close to the time of the feast. The window of opportunity needed to be seized, since Rome could be involved so easily at this time. As 22:68–69 will show, blasphemy need not be read in light of the most technical definition (Catchpole 1965; Bock 1987: 140–41, 339). In sum, the irregularities and the unlikelihood of Jews breaking with their tradition are not insuperable to the trial's historicity (Catchpole 1971: 268–69). If fact, some later texts suggest that certain evils should be punished before pilgrims at the feast (cf. Deut. 17:12–13; *t. Sanh.* 11.7 [Neusner 1977–86: 4.233]; *b. Sanh.* 89a).

If the distinction of an evening and morning portion to the major Jewish examination is correct (view 3 on p. 1791), then Jesus faced six examinations:

1. an inquiry before Annas (John 18:13)
2. an evening meeting with Caiaphas presiding (Mark 14:55–64 = Matt. 26:59–66)
3. a morning confirmation before an official Jewish body, probably the Sanhedrin (Mark 15:1a = Matt. 27:1 = Luke 22:66–71)
4. an initial meeting with Pilate (Mark 15:1b–5 = Matt. 27:2, 11–14 = Luke 23:1–5 = John 18:29–38)
5. a meeting with Herod (Luke 23:6–12)
6. a second, more public meeting before Pilate and the people (Luke 23:13–16; the consequence of which are found in Matt. 27:15–23 = Mark 15:6–14 = Luke 23:17–23 = John 18:39–40)

This seems the most likely sequence of events before Jesus' crucifixion. Whether one sees a combined trial in two stages (combining 2 and 3 above) or two procedures (like my list), all the Synoptics summarize the same fundamental testimony, though it too was probably repeated in the review that Luke gives.[16]

Where were the Jewish sessions held? The normal temple locale for such judging is Qader Hall in the inner courts (*m. Sanh.* 11.2). Because the temple gates were closed at night (*m. Mid.* 5.4), R. Brown (1994: 349–50) prefers a location adjacent to the temple. Both Josephus (*Jewish War* 5.4.2 §144; 6.6.3 §354) and the Mishnah (*m. Yoma*

---

16. Besides those already cited, other major works on Jesus' trial are Bammel 1970, Blinzler 1969, Sherwin-White 1963: 24–47, and Winter 1974. Catchpole, Blinzler, and Sherwin-White defend the historicity of much of the Lucan account. Fitzmyer 1985: 1466 also thinks a morning trial is most likely.

1.1) place such meetings outside the temple or in the outer court. We could be more certain of the location if we knew where the high priest's home was (Luke 22:54) and whether Jesus was moved for this morning meeting (as Nolland 1993b: 1109 suggests).

Luke describes the participants as the elders of the people and specifies that this group includes the chief priests and scribes.[17] If the official Sanhedrin is meeting, the morning trial confirms the needs of the law and tradition (*m. Sanh.* 4.1). It would also allow anyone unaware of the evening's events to join the assessment. The blame for Jesus' death is placed on the Jewish leadership, which is typical of Luke, though at times he blames the Roman leadership as well (Tiede 1988: 400; Luke 11:37–54; 23:13, 35; 24:20; Acts 3:17; 4:5–9, 26; both in Acts 4:27–30).

Jesus is led away (ἀπήγαγον, *apēgagon*), probably by the soldiers holding him (Luke 22:63), to "their council" (συνέδριον, *synedrion*). It is likely that the council meeting describes the Sanhedrin, though συνέδριον does not have this technical meaning here, since the pronoun αὐτῶν (*autōn*, their) follows and a reference to "their Sanhedrin" does not make sense. Luke may be alluding to a location, not just the group here. Matthew 27:1 = Mark 15:1 refers to συμβούλιον (*symboulion*, council), while Mark also shares the Lucan term συνέδριον, but with a clear reference to the members. If the entire official Sanhedrin is not meeting, then it is a semiofficial body with all major officials present. The Sanhedrin is often referred to in the Book of Acts, usually as συνέδριον (4:15; 5:21, 27, 34, 41; 6:12, 15; 22:30; 23:1, 6, 15, 20, 28; 24:20), but sometimes by the less direct γερουσία (*gerousia*, council; 5:21) or πρεσβυτέριον (*presbyterion*, council of elders; 22:5). The Sanhedrin is described in numerous passages by Josephus (*Antiquities* 12.3.3 §142; 14.9.3–5 §§167–84; 20.9.1 §§200–201; 20.9.6 §§216–17; *Life* 12 §62).[18]

ii. First Question (22:67a)

22:67a Luke moves right into the questioning, beginning with a statement whose grammar is disputed: does εἰ (*ei*) function as a conditional

---

17. The terms for chief priests and scribes are in apposition to elders; BDF §444.4; Klostermann 1929: 220. Matt. 27:1 refers to the chief priests and elders of the people, while Mark 15:1 speaks of chief priests with elders and scribes.

18. The earliest extant literary reference to the Sanhedrin is 198 B.C., the date of a letter that Antiochus III the Great wrote after the Battle of Panion; Josephus, *Antiquities* 12.3.3 §138; Lohse, *TDNT* 7:862–66; Schürer 1973–87: 2.199–217. Josephus also uses the term βουλή (council) to describe the Sanhedrin (*Jewish War* 2.15.6 §331; 2.16.2 §336). R. Brown 1994: 340–57 stresses that there is only one such group at this time, the number of members usually being put at seventy-one (*m. Sanh.* 1.6, drawing on Num. 11:16).

clause ("*if* you are the Christ, tell us?"; Reiling and Swellengrebel 1971: 713; Marshall 1978: 849) or an interrogative ("tell us *whether* you are the Christ?"; BDF §372.1)? The conditional clause is a little more emphatic, being a first-class condition, but it might be too strong since it presents the condition as the current live option (but see Acts 5:39 for similar syntax). There is no significant difference in the choice, especially given that both are renderings of an original Aramaic. The leadership raises what is primarily a political question as a basis for getting Jesus in trouble with Rome (cf. 23:1–5; Fitzmyer 1985: 1466). Jesus is asked to respond to the council as a whole, as the plurals λέγοντες (*legontes*, saying) and ἡμῖν (*hēmin*, to us) show.[19] This presentation differs from the query's form in Matt. 27:63 = Mark 14:61, where the high priest (probably representing the group) clearly asks the question (Marshall 1978: 849).[20] The Matthean interrogation starts with a solemn oath and then asks, "If you are the Christ, the Son of God, tell us." Mark has the high priest ask, "Are you the Christ, the Son of the Blessed One?" If I have analyzed the historical sequence correctly, these questions come from the earlier evening inquiry (see the exegesis of 22:66). If the same interrogation is present, then differing summaries that share the same basic thrust are present. The Lucan question raises the basic issue of Jesus' identity.

In asking if Jesus is the Messiah or Christ (χριστός, *christos*), Luke returns to the key title he focused upon early in his Gospel (2:11, 26; 3:15; 4:41; 9:20; 20:41). Luke will return to this title in his final chapters (23:2, 35, 39; 24:26, 46). The issue of Jesus' promised regal status is basic to Luke. It is crucial to remember that to call Jesus Messiah is to confess his rule, since the title is a regal one. It is Jesus' authority as the one sent of God that is in view here.

iii. Jesus' First Reply (22:67b–69)

22:67b Jesus replies with a third-class condition using ἐάν (*ean*, if): "If I reply, and I am not currently saying that I will or will not, you will not believe." This rhetorical reply really represents a refusal to answer their demand. In fact, Jesus is confident that they will not believe him or answer a question if he asks, since he uses the emphatic οὐ μή (*ou mē*) to state the refusal to respond (R. Brown 1994: 486). The point is that it is useless to answer. They have made up their minds, there is nothing to add, so why discuss it? (Luke

---

19. The plural participle λέγοντες alludes to "their" council in 22:66 and views the question as an inquiry from the entire body.

20. Catchpole 1971: 193–94 argues that this difference reflects a non-Marcan source.

22:71 makes it clear that Jesus was right.) The language looks like Jer. 38:15 [45:15 LXX], but there is no scriptural allusion here, only the use of a similar idiom (Grundmann, *TDNT* 9:532–33, esp. n. 274). But the event is worth noting since in Jeremiah the prophet refuses to answer King Zedekiah because it will do no good (R. Brown 1994: 486 rightly rejects a midrashic formulation based on Isa. 41:28).

Jesus' reply in Luke differs from that in the other Synoptics ("You say" [Matthew] and "I am" [Mark]), but this is not an issue if the meetings are distinct. In fact, Jesus' response makes a great deal of sense in a second trial. He knows that this "official" meeting is not for the purpose of trying to get a fair hearing, but to formalize the earlier inquiry. The difference between Matthew and Mark turns on the issue of whether Jesus is ironically responding to his questioners in Matthew. The reply "you say" means in effect, "You have said it!" Thus in Matthew, Jesus rebukes and agrees in one remark, while Mark sets the reply in a more direct form that matches the intent. Of course, both replies could be summarizing a longer exchange (the same goes for Luke if he is reporting the same meeting as Matthew and Mark). If Luke's is a subsequent meeting, then Jesus is refusing to engage the council directly, though his additional remark will tackle their question implicitly. The refusal to respond directly recalls Jesus' hesitation to answer the officials in Luke 20:3–8 (Hendriksen 1978: 998). He has precedent for being hesitant to respond.

22:68 Luke uniquely continues the reply (but see the additional note): Jesus refuses to reply on the premise that if he were to raise a question about his authority, they would not answer (emphatic οὐ μή appears again). Jesus knows this from experience, since the remark that recalls 20:1–8, where his question about John the Baptist met with silence from the leadership. This reply simply reinforces that in the previous verse. It shows Jesus on the offensive, raising the question of justice (on Jesus' use of questions, see R. Brown 1994: 487). Jesus knows them well enough to examine their motives.

22:69 The council gets more than it bargained for in the key part of Jesus' reply. In fact, his reply ends up being the cause of his own conviction. By appearances Jesus is subject to the judgment of the leadership, but ironically he says that in reality they are judged by him. Jesus replies in terms of Ps. 110 and here answers the dilemma posed in his question about messiahship (Luke 20:41–44), where he made the point that it is more important to see Messiah as David's Lord than as his son. From now on Jesus is the Son of Man (i.e., Lord) who will be seated at the Father's side. In the outworking of Jesus' career, it becomes clear that the allusion to being seated at God's side is ful-filled in the resurrection-ascension. Peter's speech in Acts 2:30–36 completes this development by using Ps. 110 to show that the ascen-sion to God's right hand has led to Jesus' functioning as a mediatorial vice-regent at God's side. Jesus has received and bestows salvific blessing; namely, he distributes the Spirit (Bock 1987: 181–86; Bock 1992c). In Acts 2, such salvific activity is a fulfillment of an element of the Davidic covenant, as the allusion to Ps. 132:11 in Acts 2:30 makes clear. This psalm is tied to the Davidic promise because it de-scribes the promise of 2 Sam. 7. A major point of Acts 2 is that Jesus' sitting in heaven initially fulfills the Davidic promise that one will sit on David's throne.[21] Jesus alludes to this role here when he tells the Sanhedrin that he will go directly into God's presence.

The timing and presence of his rule is indicated by the phrase ἀπὸ τοῦ νῦν (apo tou nyn, from now on; see the exegesis of 1:48; Stählin, TDNT 4:1111 §A.IV.1b). Matthew 26:64 agrees with this emphasis: ἀπ' ἄρτι (ap' arti, hereafter; the phrase elsewhere in the NT at Matt. 23:39; 26:29; John 13:19; 14:7; Rev. 14:13). Mark's indefinite future ὄψεσθε (opsesthe, you will see) is less specific (and idiomatically means "you will perceive" rather than referring to physical sight; Michaelis, TDNT 5:361). Though Jesus is before the council as an ar-rested man, it is he who will sit at God's side. He—not the council—will be the judge.

Jesus' coming sovereignty is declared in his sitting at the right hand of God, a figure for rule (Exod. 11:5; 12:29; 1 Kings 1:17; 3:6; 8:25; 1 Chron. 17:16).[22] This regal claim is drawn from Ps. 110 and answers the Sanhedrin's question: Is Jesus the Anointed One? He will be seated at God's side shortly, ruling from his side.[23] This claim that he will soon sit at God's right hand has strong repercussions in a Judaism where God was so transcendent that angels had become the mediators between God and humans. Thus, in Luke 22:71, the council will argue that no other witnesses are needed, since Jesus in their view has made a damning statement. But what is the statement

21. It is important to note that only initial fulfillment is proclaimed here. There is more to come from this Davidic ruler (Acts 3:19–26). Luke shares the "already–not yet" scheme so prevalent in the NT. The verbal link of "set/sit" in Acts 2:30, 34 ties Ps. 132 to Ps. 110, while Peter's speech argues that Jesus is exercising the regal, executive authority inherent in the promise. The Spirit's distribution proves that Jesus is thus Lord and Christ (Acts 2:36). Jesus sits but is active from the side of God, initially ful-filling what he predicted at this trial.

22. In the NT this figure is usually found in allusions to Ps. 110: Eph. 1:19–23; Col. 3:1; Heb. 1:3; 8:1; 10:12; 12:2; C. Schneider, TDNT 3:442.

23. On God's power, see Josh. 4:24; 1 Chron. 12:23; Wis. 7:25; 2 Macc. 3:24, 38; 9:8; 1QM 1.11, 14; 4.4, 12; 6.2, 6; 10.5; Eph. 1:20–22; 1 Pet. 3:22; Fitzmyer 1985: 1467; Grundmann, TDNT 4:540.

that condemns? Five suggestions have been offered as to what the Jews regarded as Jesus' blasphemy (Catchpole 1965; Marcus 1989; Schaberg 1989; Gundry 1990; C. A. Evans 1991): (1) the claim to be Messiah (Mark 14:62), (2) the claim to be the Son of God (Luke 22:70), (3) the word against the temple (Mark 14:58), (4) the use of the divine name in the reply "I am" (Mark 14:62), or (5) the claim to sit at God's right hand (Luke 22:69).

In *m. Sanh.* 7.5, one is not technically guilty of blasphemy unless one actually pronounces the divine name. Nonetheless, other Jewish materials prior to the Mishnah show that actually pronouncing the divine name was not required; simply impugning God's person or attributes made one culpable (Hooker 1967: 172). A well-known incident recorded in *b. Sanh.* 38b describes an early second-century A.D. dispute involving Rabbi Akiva, who argued that David would have a session at God's right hand, a view that other rabbis called profaning the Shekinah, which was considered blasphemy (*m. Sanh.* 6.4). Catchpole (1965), who notes this and other texts, shows that just claiming to be Messiah is not blasphemy and that the use of the divine name in "I am" is too debatable to establish it as the conviction's cause. This means that options 1 and 4 are not the cause of the blasphemy.

The charges about the temple were never proven, though this charge did have potential to convict Jesus (Mark 14:55–59; see the exegesis of Luke 19:45–48). In addition, the temple charges play no role in Luke, so it cannot be central, at least in his version. What complicates the force of the temple charge, if one does not take Jesus' remark as a literal reference to destroying the Jerusalem temple but as a reference to himself, is the implicit claim to resurrection and thus to going into God's presence. But Jesus' point was not understood in this way nor did the charge stick, so this charge was not relevant to his conviction (though it could have been, had it been understood). View 3 is thus excluded.

The appeal to the Son-of-God title is also unlikely as the ground for blasphemy. This title is used in the three Synoptics in apposition to or as explanation for the claim to be Christ, which is not blasphemous. As such, "Son of God" in this context is ambiguous and, without the additional remarks of Jesus, could have been taken to mean "Messiah."[24] This rules out option 2 and leaves the claim of Jesus' impending session at God's right hand as the essence of the blasphemy (option 5), something that all the Synoptics share.

24. It is important to recall that the Jewish leadership simply wanted an excuse to take Jesus before Rome, so Rome could convict and execute him. Jesus' claim to be Messiah was all they needed to accomplish this (23:1–5). That charge became key later (23:2, 38). They got more than they bargained for in what Jesus said here.

But why would this heavenly session be considered blasphemous? As noted above, God was becoming more transcendent in Judaism so that direct contact with him was limited or mediated. The motive for such limitations was a desire to express and protect God's uniqueness and holiness. This hesitation to approach God manifested itself in a variety of ways, as Jews hesitated to pronounce or in some cases even to write the divine name (e.g., in some Qumran documents, dots are written where the divine name should appear; in others, the term אֲדֹנִי [Lord] is substituted for יהוה [Yahweh]; Byington 1957). They altered anthropomorphisms in the LXX and the Targums so God would not seem human. They regarded the temple as God's dwelling place whose innermost court was not to be profaned. For most Jews, the idea of coming directly into God's presence and sitting with him in constant heavenly session without cultic purification or worship was an insult to God's uniqueness. It was the essence of blasphemy since a human seated by God diminishes his stature. The dispute with Rabbi Akiva makes this clear, as does the leadership's response to Jesus. Biblical figures who go into God's presence are first cleansed (cf. Isa. 6; Ezek. 1). In early rabbinic tradition, only God sits in heaven. Anything else insults his person (Neugebauer 1974–75: 107 n. 1).[25] One could stand before him, but one does not sit with him.[26] Not until the fourth-century were Abraham and David associated with Ps. 110:1 (Midr. Ps. 110.1 on 110:1; 18.29 on 18:35 [18:36 MT] [= Braude 1959: 2.205; 1.261]; cf. 1.2 on 1:1 and 108.1 on 108:1 [= Braude 1959: 1.3–4; 2.199]). Thus, when Jesus says that he can sit at God's side, he profanes God's person. If, however, he is able to take the seat at God's side, then implications emerge about Jesus' person. The leadership understands these implications. The defendant claims to be the Judge. With strong irony, the Jews think that Jesus is on trial, but what they do to him does not matter, since he is the true Judge. The very remarks that the Jews think lower God's stature, in fact, show how exalted Jesus is.

The major difference between Luke and the parallels at Matt. 26:64 = Mark 14:62 is that these other accounts picture the Son of Man coming on the clouds, a strong image of deity presented earlier in Luke at 21:27. The allusion to Dan. 7 during the evening trial in Matthew and Mark makes two additional points: (1) Jesus is treated

25. The dispute caused by Rabbi Akiva's pronouncement indicates the nature of the debate and the view that no one sits or goes directly into God's presence.

26. 1 Chron. 17:16 is not an exception to this belief. David's sitting before (not *by*) the Lord alludes to a worshipful dialogue involving submission, and the nonheavenly scene does not contrast Jesus' claims. The language is less direct than Jesus' explicit claim. Only Moses (*Ezekiel the Tragedian*) and the Son of Man (1 Enoch 51.3; 61.8) might be exceptions.

like a *supra*natural figure, since such riding on the clouds in the OT is a picture of sovereignty exercised from heaven (see the exegesis of 21:27 and Bock 1987: 134–35) and (2) the order of the events makes it clear that Jesus is speaking of a literal return from heaven and so indicates a return to judge.[27]

Why does Luke not refer to Dan. 7 in his trial scene? Two reasons can be offered. First, it may simply be a function of reporting a distinct trial in which Jesus did not allude to Daniel. Though making the blasphemy clearer, this was not the most offensive remark to a Jewish mind. Second, the basic point that Jesus makes is his heavenly session, which assumes that he will rule from the side of God and go directly into his presence. In other words, Jesus is the Judge and they have no authority to judge him—a key point that appears in all three accounts.

This statement is so important that its authenticity needs comment. One objection often raised concerns the testimony's source, since none of the disciples or Gospel writers were at the trial (Luce 1933: 342). The answer to this question is quite simple: the trial's proceedings would have been widely circulated by the Jews to justify Jesus' execution. In addition, many other people attended the trial and were available to spread such news. Certainly there would be wide interest in what took place and why the popular teacher-prophet was slain (cf. how modern high-level government meetings are often reported in detail in the media). It would be a matter of simple public relations to make clear how radical Jesus' claims were. While denying authenticity, Casey (1979: 178) notes that the statement is possible in Aramaic.[28]

Still another objection comes from E. Sanders, namely, that Jesus did not refer to himself clearly here since he used the title *Son of Man*.[29] But given that Jesus repeatedly used the Son-of-Man title in his ministry and that the trial is clearly about him, it seems clear

---

27. Hooker's efforts (1967: 167–71) to argue that riding on the clouds refers to Jesus' exaltation fail on many counts. Seven objections are noted in Bock 1987: 141–42, the most obvious being that (1) an image of Jesus simultaneously sitting by God and riding the clouds seems absurd (unless this is "throne chariot" imagery like Ezek. 1, in which case heavenly rule or return language is present, not the resurrection); (2) Dan. 7 was never used as an ascension proof-text in the NT; and (3) the ascension image is the reverse of Dan. 7 and the apocalyptic discourse, which describe a coming to earth.

28. This background to the blasphemy charge and the real possibility of ancient sources show that E. Sanders's basic objections (1985: 296–99) do not merit acceptance. His remaining key objections related to the timing of the trials were dealt with in the exegesis of 22:54, 66. For a full response, see Bock 1994b.

29. E. Sanders 1990: 65 argues that this distinction renders suspect that Jesus was charged because of this reply. On the Son-of-Man title, see excursus 6 and Bock 1991c.

that all understood Jesus to refer to himself. Thus this objection is not substantive, and even Sanders recognizes that "Son of Man" can be a circumlocution for "I."[30]

The portrayal of the trial makes sense and explains why the Jewish authorities will condemn Jesus and send him on to Pilate to confirm their verdict. In their view, Jesus profanes the Shekinah in claiming to be able to sit at God's right hand. But the resurrection will show that Jesus did not profane the Shekinah by his claim, because he is given a personal invitation to sit at God's right hand through the exercise of God's own power. In the resurrection the Father, in effect, pulls out the chair to welcome the Son. This is not blasphemy, only a totally appropriate exaltation. Messiah's rule starts in earnest after his vindication, from his Father's side in heaven. Mark and Matthew add the note that it will continue with his glorious return.

iv. Second Question (22:70a)

Jesus' reply produces a response from his listeners. Luke is alone in noting the follow-up question that they ask: Is Jesus the Son of God? Jesus' first reply has led all (cf. 22:67) to the same inference, so they want him to elaborate on what he said.[31] Their question has produced some debate. Is "Son of God" simply another way to speak of the Messiah (Leaney 1958: 276; Conzelmann 1960: 84), or is it a reference to an exalted figure who has a unique position with reference to God (Fitzmyer 1985: 1467–68; Marshall 1978: 851; Luce 1933: 343; Creed 1930: 278; Plummer 1896: 519; Ellis 1974: 263; Schweizer, *TDNT* 8:381)? The *Shema*ᶜ would probably prevent Jews from taking the term in its full ontological sense, and Jesus' claim to be a regal figure is all that the council needed to send him before the Roman procurator. But Jesus' previous reply complicates the resolution of this issue, for he makes the unique claim that he will sit at the Father's right hand. The leadership rightly concludes that Jesus claims for himself a unique, highly exalted position before God. Οὖν (*oun*, therefore) in the assembly's question looks back to the closing affirmation of 22:69 and gives the resulting inference from the immediately preceding statement, as is Luke's custom (7:42; 8:18; 10:2,

22:70a

---

30. Marshall 1965–66: 347 and A. Moore 1966: 184–87 answer other objections to authenticity. Fitzmyer 1985: 1459 refuses to make a judgment on historicity, calling it impossible to reach a verdict. R. Brown 1994: 514–15 says that the conceptually parallel Mark 14:62 "may be close to the mindset and style of Jesus himself." Though he believes there is no way to determine this for certain (pp. 506–7), the remarks fit with authenticity. Brown even adds the argument that Mark's "you will see" statement is so ambiguous that it is unlikely to be created by the church.

31. Πάντες is again peculiar to Luke: 7:35; 19:37; 20:18; Plummer 1896: 518.

40; 21:7, 14; Plevnik 1991: 339 n. 27). This force relates directly to the reason the leadership says blasphemy is present in Jesus' allusion to Ps. 110 (along with the allusion to Dan. 7 from additional testimony). They now ask if he is a uniquely exalted one who claims to be able to sit next to God as his virtual equal. A positive reply would be an affront to the theology of most Jews.

v. Jesus' Second Reply (22:70b)

22:70b The question is not asked sincerely but in order to elicit a condemning confession, and as a result Jesus is intentionally ambivalent: "You say that I am" (ὑμεῖς λέγετε ὅτι ἐγώ εἰμι, *hymeis legete hoti egō eimi*). This is a mild affirmation or a "grudging admission" (Marshall 1978: 851; BDF §441.3). Vermes (1973: 148–49) argues that it is the equivalent of "this is what you infer." But it should not be seen as an unqualified "yes" (contra Dalman 1909: 308–9; cf. Matt. 27:11 = Mark 15:2 = Luke 23:3). R. Brown (1994: 493) opts for a full affirmative, arguing that Luke simply rejoins Mark, while paralleling the answer to Pilate in 23:3. But both Jesus' answer to Pilate and to the council are indirect and so qualify the affirmation in the reply. This circumlocution is less emphatic than a direct affirmation and reflects an unwillingness to respond to the skeptics' question. There may be irony in it as well ("You have said it!"). Whatever the exact force, the absence of a denial means that the council has enough from Jesus. In their view he convicts himself.

This series of questions lacks Synoptic parallel, though Jesus' indirect answer is similar to the reply to the initial question in Matt. 26:64: σὺ εἶπας (*sy eipas*, you have said). This may be another indication of an independent source, given how slight the difference is (i.e., why make any change?).

vi. Jesus' Confession Yields Conviction (22:71)

22:71 The council's response is that the trial need proceed no further. There is no need for any more testimony. The point is made in the form of a rhetorical question, "What need do we have for testimony?" (note the explanatory γάρ, *gar*, for). The unstated, but clear answer is that no more testimony is needed. Jesus has condemned himself. Luke uses singular μαρτυρίας (*martyrias*, testimony) because he has not noted the effort of other witnesses to incriminate Jesus (Mark 14:55–59 = Matt. 26:59–61; BAGD 493 §2a; BAA 1000 §2a; Strathmann, *TDNT* 4:499 §E4a). These differences reflect distinct settings and sources. Luke boils the testimony down to what really counts—Jesus' testimony against himself. The leadership cannot convict Jesus without the aid of the teacher himself. He chooses to go to the cross by his own words, words that bring his death, even though they are true. In this situation, the truth is deadly, because it is not properly perceived.

The rhetorical question is developed by the reference to what Jesus has said from his own mouth (ἀπὸ τοῦ στόματος αὐτοῦ, *apo tou stomatos autou*; BDR §173.1.3, §217.3.8; cf. Luke 4:22; 11:54; 19:22). The remark that Jesus' testimony is all that is needed ends the trial scene. The leaders can now take him to the Romans. Unlike Mark 14:63–64 = Matt. 26:65–66, Luke does not mention the blasphemy specifically, the rending of clothes, or the verdict that Jesus is worthy of death.[32] Some regard Luke as more historically faithful by these omissions because the Sanhedrin did not have the right to execute (Leaney 1958: 276), while others suggest that Luke omits these items because Jesus only indirectly answers the question about being the Son of God (Schweizer 1984: 348). Both views overstate the difference. To achieve Jesus' death, the charge of blasphemy and the rending of clothes were irrelevant to the Romans and to Luke's readers. The key charge in terms of the attempt to get rid of Jesus is the political one that the Jewish officials will bring to Rome. Roman officials must be given adequate grounds for them to execute. Luke is simply focusing on the remarks that create the opportunity to take the indictment to Rome (Luke 23:2; Plummer 1896: 519; Marshall 1978: 851). The omission of the verdict is equally understandable. The verdict in the other Synoptics is not a declaration of the Sanhedrin's authority to carry out such a sentence; it is a statement of resolution to proceed with the process that would end in Jesus' death. The Synoptics contain a statement of the leadership's resolve, while Luke gives a summary presentation of the key factors in the morning meeting that allowed the resolution to move forward. The leaders are now free to go to Rome so that foreigners can execute this religious agitator, while allowing the leadership the opportunity to deny ultimate responsibility for the death.

Summary

In Luke 22:54–71 the trial of Jesus and Peter's denials are a study in contrast. First, a disciple fails through lack of nerve to stand up for his teacher. Second, the soldiers coldly and arrogantly insult the one who is about to journey to his death for people like them. Third, the leadership makes a calculated effort to get Jesus condemned. Finally, Jesus provides by his calm demeanor an example of one who suffers for following God's way. Many disciples will follow his path in Acts. Jesus witnesses against himself; the disciples will witness for him.

32. On garment rending, see R. Brown 1994: 517–18, esp. n. 2. On blasphemy, see R. Brown 1994: 521–23 and Bock 1994b, both of whom argue that first-century blasphemy need not involve uttering the divine name.

Jesus says very little. He claims to be going directly into God's presence and will exercise authority over those who are judging him. The trial is a sham, but it is a part of a plan to reassert God's rule. Jesus' words lead to his conviction because the claim is too radical to believe and too dangerous to leave alone. For the leadership, neutrality is not possible. They cannot just sit idly by and let him go. Jesus' claims require a decision.

The reader is challenged to learn many things in the account. The possibility of a disciple failing is graphically portrayed by Peter's failure. When the heat is turned up, one can wilt under the pressure if one is not prepared. The soldiers' reaction shows how insulting the world's rejection of Jesus can be. Cynicism runs strong in many who reject Jesus. The reader is also to see God's plan moving inexorably to its turning point. But that movement is orchestrated by the one on trial, the one with true authority. With the passive aid of the Roman authorities, the Sanhedrin may send Jesus to his death, but Jesus has noted that when the execution is completed, a seat awaits him in heaven at God's side. From there he will exercise the permanent authority that God has given to him. Which judge does the reader prefer to stand before: the rejecting Sanhedrin with their mocking soldiers or the one who will be at the right hand of God? For Luke, it is heaven's courtroom that counts. The judge's chair stands occupied by the one who was judged guilty here. Guilt has been declared on the innocent, but the Innocent One will sit at God's side. For Luke, Jesus' claim is not blasphemy, it is deadly serious truth.

Additional Notes

22:61. There is textual dispute whether Luke wrote ῥήματος ($\mathfrak{P}^{69}$, $\mathfrak{P}^{75}$, ℵ, B, L, T) or λόγου (A, D, W, Θ, Ψ, family 1, family 13, Byz), both meaning "word." Given the presence of ῥήμα(τος) in Matt. 26:75 = Mark 14:72, it is difficult to explain λόγου unless one argues that it is more common. Ῥήματος is supported by the earlier manuscripts, while λόγου may be considered the harder reading because of Gospel parallelism and because Luke's usage suggests a tendency to change to ῥήματος (Luke 9:45b; 18:34; 20:26; 24:8; Catchpole 1971: 165). Either reading is possible, with no real difference in the options.

22:62. External evidence for omission of 22:62 (which matches Matt. 26:75b) is not very impressive, being limited to 0171 and many Itala. Arguments about the shorter text and harmonization suggest that the verse is not original, but it is harder to explain how it might have been omitted. Some have a hard time accepting that Luke and Matthew can agree against Mark. Nonetheless, the vast external evidence supports its inclusion (correctly

Fitzmyer 1985: 1465, who sees L here), although many do not regard this verse as original (Creed 1930: 277; Grundmann 1963: 417; Ernst 1977: 615; and Catchpole 1971: 169). Marshall (1978: 844–45) is uncertain, arguing that internal evidence is for omission, external evidence for inclusion.

22:68. Since only Marcion omits 22:68, it should be considered original despite its uniqueness (Marshall 1978: 849; Fitzmyer 1985: 1467; Duplacy 1963). A longer ending (μοι ἢ ἀπολύσητε [you will not answer] me or release [me]) has fairly decent manuscript distribution: A, D, W, Δ, Ψ, family 13, Byz, Itala, Vulgate, and Syriac (Θ and family 1 add only μοι). If this reading is adopted, Jesus says that reply is useless because no response or release will follow from the leadership. The shorter UBS–NA text, with the support of the major Alexandrian witnesses ($\mathfrak{P}^{75}$, ℵ, B), L, T, and one Coptic manuscript, is probably the original reading.

4. Trial before Pilate (23:1–5)

The Jewish leadership is now convinced that their long-held belief about Jesus is correct (11:53–54; 19:47; 20:20; 22:2), and so they seek Roman authority, which was required for capital cases, to carry out their guilty verdict. Observing that more than political power is the point here, Fitzmyer (1985: 1473) notes how this fulfills the predictions about the Son of Man's suffering (9:22, 44; 18:32). They journey early in the morning to Pilate, the major Roman administrator of the region, for the first of a fresh series of trials in 23:1–25. One could argue that everything in 23:1–25 is part of one investigation (R. Brown 1994: 757), and in one sense this is correct since Pilate directs it all. Each stage, however, is distinct, and the real driving force behind events in the Jewish leadership. Luke focuses on Jesus' innocence and the widespread responsibility for Jesus' death. The major irony—and injustice—is that the trials continue. In fact, this passage contains the first of several notes of Jesus' innocence (23:4, 14–15, 20, 22). All the proceedings that follow are unjust. Jesus is reckoned as a criminal, though he has done nothing worthy of punishment (22:37, alluding to Isa. 53). The major blame falls on the Jewish leadership because they push the issue after Pilate's verdict of innocence. Nonetheless, Pilate is also responsible for ignoring his verdict (Acts 4:25–27), as are the people for their support of the execution. In presenting the trial, only Luke notes the specific charges.

Sources and Historicity

The parallels to the trial before Pilate are Mark 15:1b–5 = Matt. 27:2, 11–14 = John 18:28–38 (Aland 1985: §334, §336). The source issue revolves around whether Luke used another source or simply edited the basic Marcan tradition. Marshall (1978: 852) takes up the case for a special source (also Ernst 1977: 621; Grundmann 1963: 421; Nolland 1993b: 1114–15; V. Taylor 1972: 86–87), seeing several factors that add up to the influence of another source: Luke 23:2 uniquely lists the specific charges; although 23:3 virtually matches Mark in wording (it is closer to Mark than to Matthew), elsewhere there is little vocabulary overlap; and 23:4 is close in wording and concept to John 18:38. In fact, there is little vocabulary overlap between the accounts (27.2% according to R. Brown 1994: 737). Parallel themes also exist with John 19:12 in Luke 23:2. It is hard to explain why Luke lacks παραδίδωμι (to hand over) in 23:1 if he used only Mark, given the frequency of this verb in the passion predictions (9:44; 18:32; 22:22; 24:7; Nolland 1993b: 1115). All of this adds up to the use of additional traditional material.

Fitzmyer (1985: 1472) offers a dissenting voice (also Bultmann 1963: 272; R. Brown 1994: 736–38; Schneider 1977a: 471; Klostermann 1929: 221–22), arguing for Lucan expressions throughout the unit: ἀναστάν (rising up), ἅπαν τὸ πλῆθος (the whole assembly), much of 23:2, εἶπεν πρός (he said to), τοὺς ἀρχιερεῖς καὶ τοὺς ὄχλους (the chief priests and the crowd), and the themes of 23:5. These reasons are not compelling, since it is not correct to assume that Lucan expression solves the question of Luke's sources. Luke can express the text in his own terms, but that does not necessarily mean that he is the source of the content behind these expressions. Only Fitzmyer's appeal to themes in 23:5 avoids this distinction, but even this can be challenged. For example, Fitzmyer notes that 23:5 has conceptual parallels in Acts 10:38, but he fails to note that the Acts passage may also reflect tradition. Brown takes a similar approach, preferring to explain Luke's work as taking over material from Acts rather than from another source (Acts 17:6–7; 24:1–2, 5, 8). But it is not clear why the reuse of Acts material is preferred over multiple sources, especially in light of Luke 1:1–4. Luke did research for his work, and his perspective may well reflect his sources' perspective. Thus, it is likely that Luke had access to additional sources, which he expressed in his own words, especially given the likely presence of sources throughout Luke 22–23.

The source discussion also impacts the matter of historicity.[1] Three charges are made against Jesus: (1) he perverts the nation (i.e., disturbs its customs), (2) he teaches that taxes should not be paid to Caesar, and (3) he claims to be a king. Fitzmyer (1985: 1473) suggests that Luke supplies the detailed charges of 23:2 because it would have seemed abrupt to start immediately with Pilate's question.[2] This explanation is faulty. If Luke were creating the issues, the only charge he needed was the third, since that is only one that Pilate questions Jesus about. The first charge is later picked up by the leadership (23:14), but this material is unique to Luke and as such is not crucial to the Marcan portrait that Luke is supposedly filling out. It is a supplement without clear development. The double presence of such a charge in unique materials could well show the influence of a source. Finally, the second charge is patently false (20:20–26) and is never mentioned

---

1. Bultmann 1963: 282 calls Pilate's declaration of Jesus' innocence an "apologetic" motif designed to acquit Rome. But the execution of an admittedly innocent person is no acquittal. Rome does not come out well here. The apologetic motif is lacking. The remark is historical. Pilate wished to placate the masses.

2. This motive is questionable, since such abruptness did not stop Luke from launching right into a question in 22:67. The Jesus Seminar (Funk and Hoover 1994: 394) takes a similar position, with a more skeptical twist, arguing that the charges are simply created from Scripture in anticipation of 23:38. But a sociopolitical cause for Jesus' crucifixion is a historical certainty. Enough people were present at such a hearing that summaries of its content could become available.

again in Luke. This alleged literary seam has loose ends. At most, one could argue that it was added to reflect the theme of injustice, but since nothing is made of it, that is a difficult claim. Thus, it is not likely that only literary, theological concerns caused the verse's creation. The unit coheres nicely on its own and reflects an appropriate historical backdrop for Jesus' crucifixion. Of the three charges, only one is even potentially valid.

The form of the account is a story about Jesus (Fitzmyer 1985: 1472). The outline of Luke 23:1–5 is as follows:

a. Setting (23:1)
b. The charges (23:2)
c. Question and response (23:3)
d. Verdict and debate (23:4–5)

The trial reflects a Jewish attempt to steer the Romans to execute Jesus. Jesus refuses to reply to the political charge. Pilate offers a declaration of innocence, which meets with Jewish resistance. The injustice of continuing the trial is evident, but all is within God's plan. The Innocent One is still in custody.

Exegesis and Exposition

¹Then the whole number of them arose and led him to Pilate.

²And they began to accuse him, saying, "We found this one ⌜perverting our nation and forbidding us to pay tribute to Caesar⌝ and saying that he himself is a Messiah, a king."

³But Pilate asked him, "Are you the King of the Jews?" And he replied to him, "You have said so."

⁴And Pilate said to the chief priests and the crowd, "I find no crime in this man." ⁵But they were insistent, saying, "He stirs up the people, teaching throughout all Judea, from Galilee to this place."⌜ ⌝

a. Setting (23:1)

23:1 If Jesus was to face death, the Jewish leadership had to seek permission from the Romans (Josephus, *Jewish War* 2.8.1 §117). Their next move was to go to Pilate, the Roman procurator responsible for finances in the region and for maintaining law and order.[3] Six inci-

---

3. On Pilate, see the exegesis of 3:1. Tacitus, *Annals* 15.44, mentions Pilate's eventual decision; Fitzmyer 1985: 1474. Kinman 1991 considers the setting to be the assize of the Roman governor; Pilate's presence fits this custom. R. Brown 1994: 363–72 has a detailed discussion of the issue of capital punishment, noting that Jews had no authority to execute, except perhaps those who entered prohibited sections of the temple or committed adultery (John 7:53–8:11; *m. Sanh.* 7.2). John 18:13 thus fits the

dents indicate his political responsibility (R. Brown 1994: 698–704): (1) the standards in Jerusalem (Josephus, *Antiquities* 18.3.1 §§55–59), (2) coinage in his time, (3) the aqueduct incident (Josephus, *Antiquities* 18.3.2 §§60–62), (4) bloody Galilean sacrifices (Luke 13:1–2), (5) the golden shields dedication (Philo, *Embassy to Gaius* 38 §§299–305), and (6) the stopping of a Samaritan prophet (Josephus, *Antiquities* 18.4.1–2 §§85–89). Showing their desire for Jesus' execution, the whole council (but not the populace) escorts him to Pilate.[4] The entourage journeyed either to the fortress of Antonia (Plummer 1896: 520) or to the palace of the king (Josephus, *Jewish War* 5.4.2 §146; 5.5.8 §§238–46; R. Brown 1994: 706–10). It is significant that Caiaphas and Pilate had a good relationship. The chief Roman official appointed the high priest annually, and Caiaphas managed to receive this appointment from Pilate for ten years (Tiede 1988: 404).

Matthew 27:1–2 = Mark 15:1 briefly mentions without detail the morning session that Luke presents comprehensively.[5] Matthew notes that the chief priests and the elders of the people took council in the morning to put Jesus to death, bound him, and took him to Pilate. Mark speaks of chief priests, elders, and scribes having a consultation and also notes that Jesus was bound and taken to Pilate. In Mark no decision about death is noted, though it is clear from the subsequent scene before Pilate what is desired (Mark 14:64 had made it clear that death was the verdict). Both mention "giving over" Jesus (cf. Mark 10:33 = Matt. 20:18–19). In describing the journey to Pilate, Matthew and Mark share four terms: δήσαντες (*dēsantes*, having bound) and καὶ παρέδωκαν Πιλάτῳ (*kai paredōkan Pilatō*, and they delivered to Pilate). Luke has no exact vocabulary or syntactic overlap, though he refers to Pilate and speaks of the whole company leading Jesus to him. Perhaps out of respect for Jesus, Luke never notes that he is bound (similar to his omission about blasphemy in 22:66–71). Given the total difference in wording without any real

---

legal situation of Jesus' time. On Pilate's career in current literature, see R. Brown 1994: 694–705.

4. Fitzmyer 1985: 1474 and Delling, *TDNT* 6:279, note that twenty-four uses of πλῆθος (company) are in Luke–Acts, with only one in Mark and none in Matthew. The combination ἅπαν (or πᾶν) τὸ πλῆθος (the whole company) is found in Luke 1:10; 8:37; 19:37; Acts 15:12; 25:24; Marshall 1978: 852. The idea of leading Jesus to Pilate shows the use of ἄγω for taking a criminal somewhere (Matt. 10:18; Josephus, *Jewish War* 6.5.3 §303; BAGD 14 §2; BAA 25 §2).

5. This filling out of detail is common in Luke; e.g., in 23:46 he will supply the content of the second cry from the cross (using Ps. 31:5 [31:6 MT]), an event that Mark 15:37 = Matt. 27:50 only alludes to. For the view that Matthew and Mark present the conclusion of the evening trial or merely recapitulate here, see R. Brown 1994: 631–32. Regardless of whether one sees a separate morning trial, the final decision came in the early morning.

difference in sense, this verse looks as if it came from another source, though the Lucan expressions make this less than certain.

b. The Charges (23:2)

23:2 Only Luke notes that the Jews brought official charges against Jesus (Mark 15:2 = Matt. 27:11 begins with Pilate's question about Jesus' kingship). The Lucan details reflect the simple three-part Roman trial investigative procedure: charges, *cognitio*, and verdict (Neyrey 1985: 77). A *cognitio* investigation was more expeditious and less cumbersome than an *ordo*, which was a full-fledged trial (R. Brown 1994: 713–16). Brown notes how the stages of reporting this trial match Josephus's description of nonrevolutionary trials (*Antiquities* 18.3.1 §§57–59; 20.5.2 §102; 20.5.4 §117; 20.6.2 §§127–32). The leadership ("they") begin to accuse Jesus, using the derogatory τοῦτον (*touton*, this one; as in 22:56, 59) instead of his name.[6] They begin by citing two broad accusations (what Jesus is doing in the Jewish nation) and end with a more specific offense (what Jesus is doing against Rome). The three charges are summarized in three participles (see the additional note). The council is carrying out its resolve to get Jesus (20:20).

The first charge is that Jesus is misleading the nation. The verb διαστρέφω (*diastrephō*) normally means "to pervert," but since people are referred to it means "to mislead" (Marshall 1978: 852; BAGD 189; BAA 379; outside the Synoptics in the NT at Acts 13:8, 10; 20:30; Phil. 2:15; cf. Exod. 5:4; 1 Kings 18:17–18; Luke 23:5, 14; Acts 16:20; 17:6; 21:28; 23:5). In Luke 9:41 = Matt. 17:17, Jesus uses the same term to charge the current generation with being "perverted" (διεστραμμένη, *diestrammenē*), so the leadership here reverses the indictment. This broad charge is a matter of perception and dispute. Jesus says that he was sent from God to show the nation God's way. Their rejection of his message shows that they do not regard him as such. It is the most subjective of the three charges. This accusation argues that Jesus disturbs the peace as a religious agitator.

The second charge is patently false, for Jesus specifically endorsed paying taxes to Rome (Luke 20:25 = Mark 12:17 = Matt. 22:21). The leadership argues that Jesus forbade (κωλύω, *kōlyō*; BAGD 461 §2; BAA 937; elsewhere with this sense at 1 Cor. 14:39; 1 Tim. 4:3; 2 Pet. 2:16) the payment of taxes to Caesar (i.e., Tibe-

---

6. On the syntax of ἤρξαντο (they began), which Luke often uses to speak of a fresh reaction, see 4:21; 5:21; 7:15; 12:45; 13:25; 19:37; Plummer 1896: 520; Grundmann 1963: 422. Κατηγορέω (to accuse) is used elsewhere by Luke at Luke 6:7; 23:10, 14; Acts 22:30; 24:2, 8, 13, 19; 25:5, 11, 16; 28:19; Büchsel, *TDNT* 3:637.

rius). The tax (φόρος, *phoros*; BAGD 865; BAA 1724; elsewhere in the NT at Luke 20:22 and three times in Rom. 13:6–7; cf. 1 Macc. 8:4, 7) in view provided the finances for the police, guards, and baths (Fitzmyer 1985: 1475; K. Weiss, *TDNT* 9:82 §B2). This charge means that Jesus brings financial risk to Rome and to Pilate as the financial administrator. This charge is clever, for it directly threatens Pilate.

The third charge is the most important and it is true, though not in the sense that the Jews suggest: Jesus declares himself to be an Anointed One, a king. Βασιλεύς (*basileus*, king) explains what χριστός (*christos*, Messiah or Christ) means, since Rome would not appreciate the significance of this Jewish title (Creed 1930: 281).[7] Raising the issue of an alternative kingship alongside the charge about taxes attempts to paint Jesus as a revolutionary and to make his activity seem seditious. Some suggest a violation of the *Lex Iulia de Maiestate*, which bore the death penalty. But it may be that only a general principle about sedition was applied here rather than a specific law (R. Brown 1994: 716–19). For the Roman laws, see *The Digest of Justinian* 48.8.3–4; Tacitus, *Annals* 2.50; 3.38; Suetonius, *Tiberius* 58. It is true that Jesus accepted the title (22:69–71), but not in the revolutionary sense that the Jews suggest. (Paul also will become subject to false charges; Acts 25:7; Danker 1988: 363.)

c. Question and Response (23:3)

The third charge interests Pilate, so he asks about it. Jesus' declaration of kingship is an important issue, and Pilate must ascertain if Jesus is a revolutionary. John 18:33–38 has a long exchange between Pilate and Jesus on this issue, which concludes with Jesus declaring that his kingship is not of this world. In Luke, as in the other Synoptics, Jesus' reply is enigmatic: "You have said so" (σὺ λέγεις, *sy legeis*; cf. 22:67c–68, 70). This appears to be a tacit affirmation, but it is expressed with a qualification about the way the question is perceived (BDR §441.4). Jesus is a king, but he is not out to overthrow Rome. Pilate will later write "King of the Jews" on a placard placed on Jesus' cross because he is not impressed with either the charge or Jesus' credentials (Luke 23:38 = Mark 15:26 = Matt. 27:37 = John 19:19; K. Schmidt, *TDNT* 1:577).[8]

23:3

---

7. The title βασιλεύς dominates the passion accounts: Matt. 27:11, 29, 37, 42; Mark 15:2, 9, 12, 18, 26, 32; Luke 23:2, 3, 37, 38; John 18:33, 37 (twice), 39; 19:3, 12, 14, 15 (twice), 19, 21 (twice). In Josephus, *Antiquities* 14.3.1 §36; 15.10.5 §373; 16.10.2 §311, it refers to various Hasmoneans or Herod the Great. Such an independent kingship could be seen as a threat to Rome.

8. Fitzmyer 1985: 1475 notes that the title *King of the Jews* was bestowed on Herod by an Essene named Manaēmos; Josephus, *Antiquities* 15.10.5 §373.

Mark 15:2 = Matt. 27:11 is parallel, with Luke's wording being closer to Mark. Matthew alone notes that Jesus is standing before the governor (ὁ ἡγεμών, *ho hēgemōn*), who asks the question. Mark and Luke refer directly to Pilate. Only Matthew names Jesus in noting the reply. The only differences between Mark and Luke involve word order and Mark's use of the more intensive form of the verb ἐπηρώτησεν (*epērōtēsen*, he asked). All state Jesus' answer in the same terms. It is clear at this point that Luke draws from the same tradition as Mark.

d. Verdict and Debate (23:4–5)

23:4 Convinced that Jesus is no threat, Pilate declares his innocence (the first of several such Lucan notes: 23:14–15, 22). In Pilate's view Jesus is a "harmless enthusiast" (Plummer 1896: 521). The reference to Pilate's finding "nothing" is emphatic, since οὐδέν (*ouden*) leads off his affirmation of Jesus' innocence before the chief priests and the crowd (cf. 23:13).[9] Word had apparently spread about what was happening and a crowd gathered to hear what Pilate would do. His verdict should have ended matters, but it does not. Jesus is portrayed as rebelling against Rome, but the irony is that it is the leadership that is rebelling against God's Chosen One.

The verse is unique to Luke among the Synoptics, but John 18:38 also notes Pilate's public declaration, sharing the terms εὑρίσκω (*heuriskō*, I find) and αἴτιος/αἰτία (*aitios/aitia*, reason for punishment; BAGD 26; BAA 49–50; John 18:38; 19:4, 6; Luke 23:14, 22; Acts 19:40). Luke's more compact account proceeds in Roman legal order, while Mark 15:2–5 = Matt. 27:11–14 has two rounds of questions (Sherwin-White 1963: 18, 21, 24, 113–15; Neyrey 1985: 76–77), with Jesus replying the first time and remaining silent the second time. But Mark 15:3 = Matt. 27:12 agrees in giving the key antagonistic role in this trial to the leadership. Jesus is innocent, but the examination continues as the multitude insists that Jesus must be convicted.

23:5 Some do not want to accept Pilate's judgment. "They" probably refers to the leadership that have brought Jesus to Pilate since the people are referred to as a distinct group. Had a broad reference been intended, one would have expected a reference to "us," rather than "the people." Perhaps the leadership is worried about the masses. Dealing with Jesus is thus a matter of good administrative stewardship. Luke notes that they are insistent (ἐπίσχυω, *epischyō*, a *hapax legomenon* that could well be translated "they were [becoming] adamant"; BAGD 302; BAA 611; 1 Macc. 6:6). This charge provides de-

---

9. Danker 1988: 364 notes the crowd's fickleness in Luke, citing 8:4–15; 9:41; 11:24–30; 12:13–15, 54–59.

tails to the general accusations in Mark 15:3. Jesus stirs up the people (ἀνασείω, anaseiō; Bornkamm, *TDNT* 7:198 §4), which is another way to insist that he is dangerous. He has the nation in a spin. To emphasize the gravity of the situation, the leaders note that Jesus' teaching extends throughout Judea, from Galilee to Jerusalem (see BDR §419.3.3 and Black 1967: 299 on the Semitic character of ἄρχομαι ἀπό; Acts 1:22; Matt. 20:8). The reference to Judea ('Ιουδαία) is probably broad here, meaning "the land of the Jews," and makes the danger greater because it covers a large area.[10] The leadership wants Pilate to see Jesus as a political threat. Their approach is that if Pilate is a good governor, he will not let Jesus go free.

Summary

Luke 23:1–5 marks the first effort to get Jesus executed. Rome must get involved if Jesus is to die. Early in the morning, the leadership moves to have Pilate examine Jesus, who, they charge, stirs up Israel, advocates not paying taxes to Rome, and claims an alternative kingship. He is dangerous. What administrator would not act against such a national security threat? Pilate examines Jesus, who replies in a qualified way to the question about being king. Pilate proclaims Jesus' innocence, a verdict that causes the leadership to insist that Jesus is dangerous. Will Pilate really risk his neck with Rome by releasing such an agitator on all of Judea?

Jesus is the innocent sufferer, a victim of great political and social forces that swirl around Israel and its relationship to Rome. What happens to Jesus is not because he is a dangerous revolutionary, but because Israel insists that he is a threat to Jewish-Roman tranquillity. Pilate lacks the nerve to follow through on his judicial judgment. Politics and public relations with the masses win over justice. Pilate tries to absolve himself and, since this is an internal Jewish matter that Herod can solve, he decides to pass the buck. Luke wants his reader to see that Jesus did not die a guilty man, but as an innocent lamb at the altar of political expediency.

Additional Notes

23:2. Textual variants in Marcion and some Itala include two more charges: that Jesus wished to do away with the law and the prophets and that he misled women and children (inserted respectively after the first and second charges). External evidence is too thin to consider these readings original (Metzger 1975: 178). R. Brown (1994: 738) argues for one charge followed

---

10. Luke uses 'Ιουδαία for either the smaller specific region (Luke 2:4; Acts 1:8; 8:1) or the broad area (Luke 1:5; 7:17; Acts 2:9; 10:37; 11:1, 29); Plummer 1896: 521.

by two examples, but it is not clear how the kingship charge is an example of perverting Jewish customs.

23:5. Some Itala add a second charge: that Jesus was a danger to wives and children because they are baptized differently than the crowd. This expansion lacks sufficient external evidence (Metzger 1975: 178–79).

5. Trial before Herod (23:6–12)

When Pilate sends Jesus to Herod, he accomplishes two things. First, he absolves himself of some responsibility. The Jewish ruler's involvement in an area that is part of his religious heritage means that Pilate has deferred to another whose expertise might be more sensitive than his own. Thus the second goal is reached: he makes a wise political maneuver, which not only absolves him but also involves the highest level of Jewish leadership. Whatever happens, no one can charge Pilate with demagoguery.

Herod's excitement upon seeing Jesus quickly turns sour. He had hoped to see some miraculous signs, but all he gets is silence. Jesus has just been declared innocent by Pilate, so perhaps he resolves to say nothing more. A just verdict has been rendered, so why is he still in custody? The church later saw this silence as a fulfillment of Isa. 53:7–8 (Acts 8:32). Justice should mean release, but all that follows is more trials and mockery. Herod sends Jesus back to Pilate. (Pilate later reveals that Herod also determined that Jesus is innocent; Luke 23:15.) No release comes, because the leadership is still insistent on conviction. Both Rome and Jerusalem could have stopped the march to death, yet they fail to do so. Other forces are at work, and justice is suspended.

Sources and Historicity

The account of Jesus' trial before Herod is unique to Luke (Aland 1985: §337), and yet the source issue is debated because of questions raised about historicity. Some argue that Luke created this scene on analogy with Mark 15:17–20 and in dependence on Ps. 2:1–2, which is cited in Acts 4:24–28 (Luce 1933: 345; Klostermann 1929: 221–22; Bultmann 1963: 273, 294; Creed 1930: 280; see R. Brown 1994: 779–81 for refutation). Neyrey (1985: 78–79) notes eight arguments in favor of this view:

1. Luke 23:8 is built from 9:9.
2. Herod's "long standing" desire to see Jesus contains a Lucan expression (Luke 8:27; 20:9; Acts 8:11).
3. The asking by Herod in Luke 23:9 parallels that by Pilate in Mark 15:4–5, and Jesus is silent in both accounts.
4. Luke 23:9–10 is paralleled in Mark 15:3–5.
5. Luke 23:11 is from Mark 15:16–20.
6. Luke 23:11 is grounded in 22:63–64 and was set up by 18:32.

7. Herod's contempt parallels Acts 4:11.
8. The friendship of Herod and Pilate reflects Acts 4:24–28.

Many of the internal Lucan connections are valid literarily, but such connections do not necessarily indicate Lucan creation. It is natural that summaries of religious trial scenes involving the same groups would overlap and that the issues raised would be parallel. The material in Acts 4 is unlike Luke's usually sympathetic treatment of the Romans, since Pilate clearly shares there the blame as co-conspirator. The shift in perspective counters the idea of Lucan creation here (Acts 4 is probably traditional material; Bock 1987: 203–5). The case for Lucan creation from Acts 4 is weak, and, in fact, Fitzmyer (1985: 1479) doubts any clear connection. Acts 4 shows the rulers as conspirators, Luke 23 does not. But Luke is not contradicting himself since the acquiescence to the cross in Luke 23 turns the Romans into co-conspirators. Finally, the case on the basis of Marcan parallels is weak. The vocabulary does not overlap much, with only Mark 15:3–4 having a strong conceptual overlap (see Aland 1985: §337). Lucan creation for this material is to be rejected. (It should be noted that Lucan style does abound in this unit; Fitzmyer 1985: 1479; R. Brown 1994: 778–83; see the exegesis for details.)

Historicity is challenged on the following grounds:

1. Why should Pilate send Jesus to Herod when Pilate has superior authority?
2. When Pilate speaks of Jesus being sent back to "us" in 23:15, he includes the Jewish leadership. But 23:10 indicates that the Jewish entourage went to Herod.
3. The mocking is parallel to the mocking of Pilate's soldiers and is a created detail.
4. Why does Mark omit this trial?

Others defend historicity, arguing for a special Lucan source (Marshall 1978: 854–55; Fitzmyer 1985: 1478–80; Sherwin-White 1963: 28–32; Hoehner 1972: 176–83, 224–50; Hoehner 1970; Nolland 1993b: 1121–22, who argues that its presence here is made more likely by its presence in other pericopes in Luke 22–23). This approach addresses each of the objections:

1. Pilate's involvement of Herod is good politics, especially in a sensitive religious area where Pilate had been burned previously (see 23:12; on Herod's career, see R. Brown 1994: 763–64). (Festus responds in a similar way with Agrippa II in Acts 25:13–27.)
2. Luke 23:15 does not clearly state that the Jewish leadership did not go to Herod and probably refers to the Roman entourage (see the additional note on 23:15). In fact, someone needed to present the charges to Herod, so a Jewish presence is likely.

3. The details and vocabulary of this mocking differ from Mark, so that copying is unlikely. The declaration of innocence in the passage runs against a creative detail formed from Ps. 2:1–2, which looks at hostile conspiracy. In addition, such mocking by soldiers is likely to have been repeated.
4. Mark often omits details about Herod, so his omission of Jesus' trial before Herod is understandable (John's Gospel shows a similar disinterest in Herod).

The event has a good historical base, and Luke, though writing it in his own style, has had the benefit of a source—perhaps Joanna, wife of Herod's steward, Chuza (Luke 8:3), or Manaen, a member of Herod's court who later became a believer (Acts 13:1). In addition, any of the soldiers who mocked Jesus may well have bragged about their involvement in the episode, making the event the subject of public discussion. Finally, any of the Jewish leaders, defending their action, would want to report how Jesus snubbed his chance to defend himself by saying nothing and thus (in their view) admitting guilt. An elaborate version of this event appeared in later church tradition (Gospel of Peter 1–3 [Schneemelcher 1991–92: 1.223]; Justin Martyr, *Apology* 1.40 and *Dialogue with Trypho* 103; Ignatius, *Smyrneans* 1.2). The Gospel of Peter attests to an independent tradition (R. Brown 1994: 781; see also the Acts of Thomas 32; *Didascalia Apostolorum* 21 §5.19; Tertullian, *Against Marcion* 4.42.2–3).

The trial scene is another story about Jesus (Fitzmyer 1985: 1479). The outline of Luke 23:6–12 is as follows:

a. Pilate sends Jesus to Herod (23:6–7)
b. Herod's examination yields silence (23:8–9)
c. Accusations and mocking by all (23:10–11)
d. Reconciliation of Herod and Pilate (23:12)

The major theme of this unit is another tragic trial for the Innocent One. For Herod, Jesus is a curiosity. Herod merely desires to see signs, which parallels the superficial interest of earlier crowds. Jesus, the silent witness, is derided and mocked. Old enemies become political allies. Neither Rome nor Jerusalem stops the trials. The Innocent One is still in custody.

Exegesis and Exposition

[6]And when Pilate heard this, he asked if the man was a Galilean. [7]And when he learned that he was under Herod's jurisdiction, he sent him to Herod, who was himself in Jerusalem in those days.

⌐8And Herod, when he saw Jesus, was very glad, for he was wishing to see him for some time, because he had heard about him and was hoping to see some sign done by him. 9So he questioned him at some length, but he did not give an answer to him.

⌐10The chief priests and scribes stood by, vehemently accusing him. 11⌐Also⌐ treating him with contempt and mocking him, Herod and his soldiers sent him to Pilate, dressing him in gorgeous apparel.

12And Herod and Pilate became friends with each other that very day, for before this they had been at enmity with each other.⌐

a. Pilate Sends Jesus to Herod (23:6–7)

23:6 The Jews have emphasized that Jesus is a threat to Rome, a political agitator for the entire region (23:5). Pilate, the shrewd politician, hears something else about Jesus that intrigues him: Jesus is a Galilean (cf. Luke 1:26; 2:4; 4:16, 24; 22:59; John 7:41–42). Pilate therefore knows that Herod also has a stake in what happens. Jurisdiction might belong to the Jewish leader. It is unclear whether political courtesy or the desire to pass the buck motivated Pilate (Tiede 1988: 406). The enmity mentioned in Luke 23:12 seems to rule out political courtesy—unless Pilate now senses a chance to make things better. Pilate was probably trying to abdicate or at least share responsibility for this decision, though the opportunity to mend fences may not be absent either. Since Jesus does have ties to Galilee, Herod is about to receive a local guest celebrity.

23:7 Pilate learns (ἐπιγνούς, *epignous*) that Jesus is a Galilean.[1] He can share responsibility for the controversial verdict. As a Galilean Jew, Jesus comes under Herod's authority or domain (ἐξουσία, *exousia*; BAGD 278 §4b; BAA 564 §4b; elsewhere with this sense in Luke 4:6; 22:53; Eph. 2:2; Col. 1:13). Ἀναπέμπω (*anapempō*) often means to remand to a higher authority (Acts 25:21), but it cannot have that force here since Herod is under Pilate (Marshall 1978: 856; Creed 1930: 281; cf. Luke 23:11, 15; BAGD 59 §1b; BAA 117 §1b; Josephus, *Jewish War* 2.20.5 §571; MM 37).[2] Herod was probably present in Jerusalem for Passover, though his father's being only half-Jewish makes this point uncertain.[3] The Hasmonean palace is west of the

---

1. Ἐπιγινώσκω is frequently used by Luke with the sense "to thoroughly ascertain"; Luke 7:37; Acts 19:34; 22:29; 24:11; 28:1; Plummer 1896: 521. Here it almost has the force of "to discover."

2. Fitzmyer 1985: 1479 calls ἀναπέμπω Lucan, but since three of its five NT uses are in this one pericope (elsewhere Acts 25:21 and Philem. 12), the usage is too concentrated and too rare to attribute to Luke. On the Roman legalities, see R. Brown 1994: 764–65.

3. "In those days" is a frequent Lucan expression: Luke 1:39; 6:12; 24:18; Acts 1:15; 11:27; Fitzmyer 1985: 1481. On the racial origins of the Herodians as half-Jewish, see Josephus, *Antiquities* 14.15.2 §403. On Herod's presence in Jerusalem during a feast, see Josephus, *Antiquities* 18.5.3 §122.

temple, about a ten minute walk from Pilate (Arndt 1956: 457–58; Josephus, *Jewish War* 2.16.3 §344; Hoehner 1972: 239 n. 3; Marshall 1978: 855; Justin Martyr, *Dialogue with Trypho* 103, calls Pilate's act "a gracious gesture").

b. Herod's Examination Yields Silence (23:8–9)

Herod is thrilled at the prospect of seeing the famous Jesus, for he **23:8** has long desired to see Jesus perform a miracle (σημεῖον, *sēmeion*; BAGD 748 §2a; BAA 1496 §2a; cf. Luke 9:9; 11:16, 29).[4] Rumor had it that Herod wished to kill Jesus (Luke 13:31), but now he has a chance to be entertained by the power of this wonder worker about whom he has heard so much. Luke has already warned readers what to think of those who seek signs (4:9–12, 23–24; 11:16, 29). Herod avoids confrontation and is rather frivolous in his treatment of Jesus.[5] The Lucan portrait of Herod Antipas (Luke 3:19–20; 9:7–9; 13:31; Acts 4:27), like his portraits of the later Herod Agrippa I (Acts 12:1–23) and the earlier Herod the Great (Luke 1:5; Acts 23:35), is not flattering (Tannehill 1986: 196). R. Brown (1994: 769–70) says that the portrait reflects an unstable character capable of violence (see also Darr 1987: 278–305).

Herod's examination takes some time. Ἱκανός (*hikanos*, many), fre- **23:9** quent in Luke (BAGD 374 §1a; BAA 760 §1a; see n. 2), makes clear that Herod tries for some time to get Jesus to respond, but he says nothing. This silence recalls Jesus' silence during the second part of the trial with Pilate, a detail that Luke lacked (Mark 15:3–5 = Matt. 27:12–14; cf. Mark 14:61 = Matt. 26:63; John 19:9). Christians later saw this silence as fulfillment of Isa. 53:7–8 (Acts 8:32; Luce 1933: 345; Jeremias, *TDNT* 5:713; Grundmann 1963: 425).[6] This silence differs from Jesus' response to the council and his initial reaction to Pilate, not to mention the eloquent defense speeches of Peter and Paul in Acts 4, 22–23, 26. Darr (1992: 162–66) stresses how the absence of a defense is the opposite of literary expectation. Jesus' silence looks like exceptional self-control. He is treated like a criminal but he does not act like one because of his divine restraint. It may be that Jesus thinks that there is nothing more to be said when an innocent person continues to be examined (Sir. 20:1 describes a wise

---

4. Several terms in this verse are used frequently by Luke (Neyrey 1985: 78; Marshall 1978: 855–56): ἱκανὸς χρόνος (a long time; Luke 8:27; 20:9; Acts 8:11; 14:3; 27:9) and γίνεται σημεῖον (a sign occurs; Acts 2:43; 4:16, 22, 30; 5:12; 8:13; 14:3).

5. Calling the trial a literary "nonevent," Tyson 1986: 133–35 says that Luke's description of Herod is "pale." Herod is not an opponent here, but a curious bystander, maybe even a frustrated one. Ἐπηρώτα in 23:9 is a conative imperfect: "he tried to question"; BDF §326.

6. Marshall 1978: 856 notes Hooker's view (1967: 87–89) that this is not a Lucan creation of a literary detail to make the point about Isaiah.

person who is silent when reproof is not required).[7] Herod had great expectations, but he is disappointed. Silence is the best response to this harsh injustice.

c. Accusations and Mocking by All (23:10–11)

23:10 Jesus continues to be relentlessly accused. The grouping of the chief priests and scribes recalls earlier verses (9:22; 22:66). The leadership vehemently (εὐτόνως, eutonōs; BAGD 327; BAA 662; elsewhere in the NT only at Acts 18:28; cf. Josh. 6:8; 2 Macc. 12:23; 4 Macc. 7:10) accuses Jesus, so that Herod will render a guilty verdict. Luke uses a common term for setting forth charges: κατηγορέω (katēgoreō; BAGD 423 §1a; BAA 860 §1a; e.g., Mark 15:3–4; Luke 6:7; 23:2, 14; Acts 28:19). The leadership is consistently the active human catalyst behind events.

23:11 When Jesus gives no reply, Herod's excitement wanes and he joins his soldiers, probably his home guard, in mocking Jesus (Marshall 1978: 856; Bauernfeind, *TDNT* 7:709 n. 34; Hoehner 1972: 241 n. 4; στρά-τευμα, strateuma, is used elsewhere by Luke in Acts 23:10, 27). Because this term for soldiers differs from those in Luke 22:4, 52; 23:36; Acts 4:1; 5:24, it may refer to a special regiment. Two participles define the mocking and make clear that Jesus' claim to kingship is not taken seriously, but becomes the occasion for sport.[8] Both participles emphatically lead off their clauses (Plummer 1896: 523). First Corinthians 2:8 describes what this account means (Tiede 1988: 407).

Herod mocks Jesus by dressing him in "bright" clothes.[9] It is debated whether λαμπρός (lampros) means a "white" garment (Grundmann 1963: 425; Oepke, *TDNT* 4:27; Danker 1988: 366), which

---

7. Danker 1988: 355–56 cites Diogenes Laertius 3.19 and 9.115 for occasions where the accused is silent. See also Wis. 8:12; Ignatius, *Ephesians* 15.1 and *Magnesians* 8.2; and Josephus, *Antiquities* 15.7.5 §235 (R. Brown 1994: 772).

8. This is the only NT use of ἐξουθενέω with the meaning "to treat with contempt" (BAGD 277 §3; BAA 562 §3). The citation of Ps. 118:22 in Acts 4:11 also shows Jesus as the righteous, rejected sufferer. The other verb, ἐμπαίζω (to mock, make fun of; BAGD 255; BAA 516), is used in the passion prediction of Luke 18:32 (= Matt. 20:19 = Mark 10:34) and often in the passion narrative: Matt. 27:29, 31 = Mark 15:20; Matt. 27:41 = Mark 15:31; Luke 22:63; 23:36.

9. The terms used to describe the clothing are infrequent in the NT: ἐσθής (clothes; BAGD 312; BAA 632; elsewhere in the NT only at Luke 24:4; Acts 1:10; 10:30; 12:21; James 2:2–3 [three times]; cf. Mark 15:17), λαμπρός (bright; BAGD 465 §3; BAA 946 §3; elsewhere in the NT only at Acts 10:30; James 2:2–3 [twice]; Rev. 15:6; 18:14; 19:8; 22:1, 16), and περιβάλλω (to clothe; BAGD 646 §1bδ; BAA 1302 §1bδ; twenty-three times in the NT; e.g., John 19:2). The syntax is also disputed: does mockery occur by clothing him or is he clothed and sent back to Pilate? Either way, the fine clothes are placed on Jesus in jest. The latter option is more likely grammatically since participles are not normally subordinated to other participles (R. Brown 1994: 773–75). Brown also notes numerous Lucan touches in 23:11–12, indicating that Luke summarized here.

would make Jesus a king-designate wearing a *toga candida*, or is a reference to regal purple garb (Klostermann 1929: 233 notes the options). Either option suggests an effort to shame Jesus' claim to be king. Fitzmyer (1985: 1482) rejects the tie to regal clothes, arguing that white is a picture of innocence (Luke 23:15). But since nothing in 23:6–12 makes reference to Jesus' innocence, it is the mocking of Jesus' kingship that controls the passage's content and meaning. The more likely meaning is regal clothing or at least a reference to clothing of high social standing (ἐσθής, *esthēs*; James 2:2–3; Acts 12:21).

d. Reconciliation of Herod and Pilate (23:12)

Luke notes that Pilate's relationship with Herod was strained **23:12** (προϋπῆρχον ... ἐν ἔχθρᾳ, *proypērchon ... en echthra*, they were previously at enmity; BAGD 722, 331; BAA 1446, 669; BDF §414.1; BDR §414.1.6; προϋπάρχω elsewhere in the NT only at Acts 8:9; cf. Job 42:17b LXX [not in MT]; ἔχθρα elsewhere in the NT only at Rom. 8:7; Gal. 5:20; Eph. 2:14, 16; James 4:4). Philo (*Embassy to Gaius* 38 §§299–305) records an incident that revealed Rome's authority over Herod. Pilate required shields to be hung in Herod's palace inscribed with the names of the person dedicating the shield and the one honored by it. The Jews were so upset that they sent a protest to Tiberius, who angrily told Pilate to place the shields in a pagan temple at Caesarea, where they more properly belonged. Tiberius, unlike Pilate initially, was sensitive about unduly upsetting the Jews or any of his provinces (Tacitus, *Annals* 3.54, 64–65; 6.27). In addition, Luke 13:1 notes a temple incident under Pilate's jurisdiction that could not have pleased the Jews (Blinzler 1957–58). After such incidents, an opportunity for reversal may have been welcome. If the crucifixion took place in A.D. 33, another factor in this change in Pilate's attitude might be the fall of Sejanus, Tiberius's ruthless and anti-Semitic right-hand man (Dio Cassius 58.4–11).[10] Pilate no longer needed to worry about pleasing this cold superior. Events were thus poised to forge cooperation between Pilate and Herod. Pilate took advantage of an opportunity to show respect to the Jewish leader. I regard all of this as historical and reject R. Brown's claim (1994: 785) that there is either much imaginative material here or a confusion of Herods. These figures were too involved in the history of the area to be the objects of confusion. The timing of the reconciliation fits well. Nolland (1993b: 1124) argues that "nothing is intrinsically unlikely" about enmity or its reversal.

---

10. On Sejanus, see R. Brown 1994: 693–94, 1376. His anti-Semitism is recorded by Philo, *Embassy to Gaius* 24 §§160–61 and *Flaccus* 1 §1. Brown doubts Philo's account, arguing that he transferred blame from Tiberius to Sejanus for political reasons. But Sejanus carried too much power in A.D. 26–31 to pass responsibility to a largely absentee Tiberius (who was sensitive to Jews, as noted above).

Some see here an allusion to Ps. 2:1–2, since Acts 4:24–28 cites and discusses this OT text (Klostermann 1929: 221–22; Schweizer 1984: 352 [perhaps]). That the early church saw Ps. 2 fulfilled in this way is beyond dispute. It is unclear, however, whether Luke intends such an association here. Both figures, Pilate and Herod, declare Jesus innocent in Luke 23. Luke does not hold them responsible for Jesus' death until later. So any argument that Luke created this event for this allusion fails. What is clear is that Jerusalem and Rome are made responsible for continuing these events. Either had ample opportunity to stop the sequence of events. In fact, not only are the events not taken seriously but they become an opportunity for amusement. Ironically, this trial provides a reconciliation very different from the one that Jesus will achieve by going to the cross (Tannehill 1986: 197 n. 43).

Summary

In Luke 23:6–12, Pilate, not wanting to be responsible for convicting an innocent man, sends Jesus to his Jewish counterpart. Herod, hoping to be entertained by the miracle worker, is angered at Jesus' unwillingness to perform and joins his soldiers in mocking Jesus, whom they regard as a harmless Galilean. The Jewish leadership insists on convicting Jesus, so Jesus is sent back to Pilate. The charges are not taken seriously, but no decision is made to release him. The innocent Jesus is one step closer to death. Every description of what is happening shows that justice is not served. The righteous one is silently suffering. Luke wants his reader to realize that unseen forces are at work. Jesus is not a blasphemer who dies for offending God. His death reflects the indifference of people surrounded by God's sovereign activity. Indifference to Jesus is as dangerous as opposition to him, for it allows injustice to continue and ignores God's activity and presence. Rationality is lacking in assessing Jesus. Frivolity is everywhere. People do not reckon seriously with his claims and wave them aside. Jesus' death makes no sense, if the scales of justice are applied. Such is the blindness of human sin. The Innocent One is still in the hands of the state.

Additional Notes

23:10–12. Luke 23:10–12 is lacking from some Syriac manuscripts, possibly because of 23:15. The omission is not original, since external evidence is so thin.

23:11. Herod's inclusion is emphasized if the text reads the syntactically awkward καί (even, also), which is absent in A, B, D, Δ, Θ, and Byz. The longer reading is harder and is probably original.

6. Sentencing by Pilate and Release of Barabbas (23:13–25)

Pilate's efforts to release Jesus fail when he appeals to the people. This trial has the seven stages typical of Roman examinations (Neyrey 1985: 81; Sherwin-White 1963: 24–27):

arrest	you brought me this man (23:14a)
charges	as one who is perverting the people (23:14b)
cognitio	and behold I, having judged him before you (23:14c)
verdict	have found no guilt in this man concerning anything you charged against him (23:14d)
supporting verdict	but neither did Herod, for he sent him back to us (23:15a)
acquittal	and behold, nothing worthy of death has been done by him (23:15b)
judicial warning	now having scourged him, I will release him (23:16)

Pilate reveals his and Herod's judgments: Jesus is innocent. But Pilate meets with strong public disappointment. Even though the two leaders have declared Jesus innocent (cf. Deut. 19:15; Fitzmyer 1985: 1488), the people do not wish him to be released. The passage has three parts: the innocent verdict from Pilate (23:13–16), the crowd's request for Barabbas and condemnation of Jesus (23:18–23), and Pilate's decision to give in to the people (23:24–25).

Luke's point here is to detail how Jesus was convicted, despite his innocence. The Jewish people bear primary responsibility according to Luke, though his portrait of a weak-kneed Pilate is not flattering. The account contains irony: Barabbas (meaning "son of the father") is released, yet the real Son, who is innocent, goes to his death. Israel has freed the wrong son. Another of Jesus' prophecies is being fulfilled ("handed over" in 9:44; Neyrey 1985: 84–107).

Sources and Historicity

Luke 23:13–16 comes from an independent source (Aland 1985: §338), though Creed (1930: 280) disagrees, arguing that the trial before Herod was formed on the basis of Ps. 2:1–2 (cf. its use in Acts 4:24–28), that Mark would have noted such a trial, and that Luke 23:10 and 23:15 are in conflict (see the introduction to 23:6–12 and the exegesis of 23:10). However, the trial before Herod may not have been of value to Mark, since the key verdict came from Pilate in his exchange with the people. It is likely that Luke is using a special source (Fitzmyer 1985: 1483). In support of this view, Nolland (1993b: 1126–27) argues for contacts with John 19:1–5, where Pilate also speaks of Jesus' innocence (note also John 18:38).

The source of 23:18–25 (Aland 1985: §339, §341) is more complex. Some argue that Luke combined a special source with material like that in Mark 15:6–15 (Marshall 1978: 858; Rengstorf 1968: 257; Grundmann 1963: 426–27; Ernst 1977: 626–27; Nolland 1993b: 1129 [noting contacts with John 18:40 and 19:15 in Luke 23:18; with John 19:6 in Luke 23:21; and with John 19:6 in Luke 23:22]). The major elements unique to Luke are Pilate's declarations of innocence. Others argue that Luke basically rewrote Mark in his own style (Fitzmyer 1985: 1487–88). Fitzmyer expresses uncertainty over Pilate's portrait in this passage, holding that Pilate is inconsistent in saying that Jesus is innocent yet deciding to scourge him. But even though Pilate declares Jesus' innocence with regard to his having done anything "worthy of death," he might have considered a scourging for disturbing the peace entirely appropriate. Perhaps this would slow Jesus down and prevent future problems. This scourging means that Pilate partially acknowledges one of the three charges brought against Jesus in 23:2: that he caused a stir in the nation. But Pilate's exonerating Jesus of all capital charges (23:14) suggests that even the scourging is a compromise to placate the crowd and does not represent his real view. Had there not been public pressure, Jesus would have gone free.

Fitzmyer (1985: 1487) notes the following differences between Mark and Luke (some also apply to Matt. 27:15–26):

1. Luke does not mention directly the custom of letting a criminal go (Mark 15:6 = Matt. 27:15).[1]
2. Luke omits reference to the chief priests' inciting of the crowd (Mark 15:11 = Matt. 27:20).
3. In Luke, Pilate does not taunt the crowd with the use of the title *King of the Jews* (Mark 15:9, 12; "Christ" in Matt. 27:17, 22).
4. Luke adds notes of Jesus' innocence (23:22), Pilate's desire to release him (23:20, 22), and Jesus' being given over to the will of the people (23:25).
5. Luke does not mention the incident where Pilate symbolically washes his hands of Jesus (Matt. 27:24).

---

1. On this custom, both generally and during Passover, see Nolland 1993b: 1129–30; the exegesis of 23:25; and excursus 11, objection 6.

Fitzmyer (1985: 1488) also notes ten points of Lucan style in the passage, most of which are stylistic details that do not impact the major differences in the passage or that echo earlier verses that may be sourced in other traditions and as such are not decisive (e.g., the Lucan repetition of Jesus' innocence, his repetition of the description of Barabbas as an insurrectionist and murderer, the note about Pilate's desiring to chastise Jesus and then release him). Fitzmyer's list suggests that Luke presented some of the material in his own language, but it does not show that he is responsible for the content (i.e., the expression used to present an event does not mean that Luke is the source of the event). The list of Lucan omissions and additions shows that he made choices about what to use, not that he created details. Luke probably used an additional source to describe this authentic event.

Since these events are a turning point in Luke 23, it would be well to reflect briefly on the whole chapter. Büchele (1978: 70–75) has an interesting examination of this question, though his outline, reflecting a threefold parallelism throughout the chapter, is perhaps forced.[2] His analysis shows, however, a great amount of balance in the chapter. A wide variety of people respond to these events, most negatively, but a few positively: the thief, the wailing women (perhaps), and the centurion. Some are open to Jesus. Jesus forces a choice, and opinions divide over him.

Luke 23:13–25 is a story about Jesus, though he is a passive player in these events (Fitzmyer 1985: 1484, 1488). Human players dictate events here and do not perform well. The outline of Luke 23:13–25 is as follows:

a. Jesus' innocence declared (23:13–16)
　　i. Pilate's and Herod's verdicts: innocent (23:13–15)
　　ii. Pilate's intent: chastise and release Jesus (23:16)
b. The crowd's demand: Jesus' death and Barabbas's release (23:18–23)
　　i. The crowd cries for Barabbas (23:18–19)
　　ii. Pilate replies for Jesus (23:20)
　　iii. The crowd insists on crucifixion (23:21)
　　iv. Pilate stands firm for release (23:22)
　　v. The crowd's insistence reverses Pilate's verdict (23:23)
c. Jesus' condemnation and Barabbas's release (23:24–25)
　　i. Pilate accepts the crowd's demand (23:24)
　　ii. Barabbas is released and Jesus is given over to the people (23:25)

2. For example, Büchele must omit certain verses to achieve symmetry (e.g., 23:33–34, 44–46). In addition, both thieves did not mock Jesus (this unit is positive, not negative).

The dominating theme in this unit is the injustice of Jesus' death sentence. Jesus' innocence is legally proclaimed, but he is retained in custody. Moral blindness is also a major theme, as the people ironically choose to free a dangerous revolutionary instead of Jesus, a terrorist instead of a righteous man. There is no doubt about their preference as the people state their choice three times (23:18, 21, 23). Roman leadership is seen as weak as Pilate acquiesces to the people. The Innocent One is condemned. Israel fails. Jesus is headed for the cross.

Exegesis and Exposition

¹³Pilate, having called together the chief priests and rulers and people, ¹⁴said to them, "You brought me this man as one who is perverting the people, and behold I, having judged him before you, have found no guilt in this man concerning anything you charged against him. ¹⁵But neither did Herod, ⌜for he sent him back to us⌝. And behold, nothing worthy of death has been done by him. ¹⁶Now having scourged him, I will release him." ⌜¹⁷⌝

¹⁸And they all cried out together, "Take this one, but give us Barabbas" ¹⁹(who had been thrown into prison for an insurrection started in the city and for murder). ²⁰Pilate called out to them again, wishing to release Jesus. ²¹But they called out, "Crucify, crucify him." ²²But a third time he said to them, "Why, what evil has this one done? I have found no crime worthy of death in him; therefore I will chastise him and release him." ²³But they were insistent, demanding with loud voices that he should be crucified, and their voices prevailed.

²⁴So Pilate gave judgment for their demand. ²⁵He released the man who had been thrown into prison for insurrection and murder, whom they asked for; but Jesus he gave over to their will.

a. Jesus' Innocence Declared (23:13–16)
i. Pilate's and Herod's Verdicts: Innocent (23:13–15)

23:13   Pilate continues his efforts to release Jesus. He makes three such efforts in Luke: (1) he declares Jesus innocent and tries to let the Jews handle the matter (23:4), (2) he sends Jesus to Herod (23:6–12), and (3) now he offers to scourge and release Jesus (23:13–25). Within this third effort alone, Pilate tries three times to get Jesus released (23:16, 20, 22). All such efforts fail. The nation insists that Jesus be slain (Matt. 27:24–25; John 19:12).

The public effort to insure Jesus' execution begins with Pilate calling together (συγκαλέω, synkaleō; seven of eight NT uses are by Luke; cf. 2 Macc. 15:31) the three groups in the nation: the chief priests (i.e., the religious leadership), the rulers (i.e., the social leaders and supporters of the religious leadership, which would include the elders and scribes; Fitzmyer 1985: 1484; Marshall 1978: 858; Luke 8:41; 23:35; 24:20), and the people. Λαός (*laos*) normally refers to those responsive to Jesus, but in a dramatic reversal that is clearly not the meaning here. This is a new audience here, as 23:1, 4 shows. Grundmann (1963: 425) argues that λαός is a positive technical term indicating that the people are witnesses to what others in the nation will do. There is no such separation, however, in the context. The different sense may well indicate a source, since this term is unique to Luke here. Regardless, this significant shift from Luke's normal usage signals a major turn. The threefold grouping here is close to 22:66 (elders, chief priests, and scribes), but the populace is now added (the first reference to the people as active participants since 21:38). The nation is gathered to decide Jesus' fate. The role of the people is like the public interaction in other incidents that Josephus notes about Pilate (see the exegesis of 23:1). Pilate yields here to pressure, as he did with the iconic standards (R. Brown 1994: 721–22; Josephus, *Antiquities* 18.3.1 §55–59; *Jewish War* 2.9.2–3 §§169–74; for an example of a public trial, see Josephus, *Jewish War* 2.10.5 §§199–203). The people are portrayed as fickle. Popular allegiance to Jesus has turned out to be shallow. How quickly they have turned. Jesus' last remnant of human protection is gone.

23:14 Pilate gives his verdict: Jesus is innocent. Much of what is said here looks back. Pilate recalls that the nation brought "this man" before him (23:1), and he repeats their charge that Jesus perverts the people or causes them to rebel (23:2, 5). The term ὡς (*hōs*, as) introduces the charge (16:1; BDF §425.3; Marshall 1978: 858), which substitutes the synonymous ἀποστρέφω (*apostrephō*, to pervert, mislead; BAGD 100 §1aβ; BAA 201 §1aβ; elsewhere used by Luke in Acts 3:26; cf. 2 Chron. 18:31; Jer. 41:10 [48:10 LXX]) in place of διαστρέφω (*diastrephō*, to pervert, mislead). Pilate alludes to his examination of 23:3 and declares for a second time that he finds no cause (αἴτιον [*aition*] as in Luke 23:4; cf. Acts 23:9; 26:31–32) for guilt. The Jews claim to have found (εὕραμεν, *heuramen*; Luke 23:2) three charges against Jesus, but Pilate finds (εὗρον, *heuron*) nothing in his legal examination of Jesus (Luke is the only NT writer to use ἀνακρίνω [*anakrinō*] in a forensic sense; Acts 4:9; 12:19; 24:8; 28:18; cf. 1 Cor. 4:3–4; BAGD 56 §1b; BAA 110 §1b; Plummer 1896: 524). On this basis, one would anticipate Jesus' release.[3]

23:15 Herod's opinion is similar to Pilate's verdict. Pilate sees more evidence of Jesus' innocence in Herod's returning him to Pilate.

---

3. Examples of Lucan style and vocabulary in the verse include πρός with a verb of speaking, καὶ ἰδού, ἐνώπιον, and probably the forensic use of ἀνακρίνω; R. Brown 1994: 791 and Nolland 1993b: 1127.

Herod's verdict is that Jesus has done "nothing worthy of death," which is made more solemn by the use of ἰδού (*idou*, behold).[4] This point suggests that perhaps the rumor about Herod wanting Jesus dead (Luke 13:31) is false, for he certainly did not take advantage of this opportunity. Jesus now has a second witness (cf. Deut. 19:15), a Jewish authority who has examined him and found him innocent. All the evidence suggests that Jesus should be released.

ii. Pilate's Intent: Chastise and Release Jesus (23:16)

23:16   Pilate offers a compromise: he will whip Jesus before releasing him (Marshall 1978: 859; Bertram, *TDNT* 5:621; C. Schneider, *TDNT* 4:517).[5] Common punishment in Roman times, whipping (*verberatio*) horrified Domitian because the number of strokes was not prescribed and it continued until blood was drawn and flesh was torn open (Suetonius, *Domitian* 11; Josephus, *Jewish War* 2.14.9 §§306–8; 6.5.3 §304; Philo, *Flaccus* 10 §75). Pilate probably had in mind the less severe *fustigatio*, but events cause the whipping to become the horrid form of punishment (such levels of punishment are attested, for example, in a Lycian inscription that reveals some sense of scale in punishment; Hengel 1977: 34 n. 2). If Pilate thought that this action would deter Jesus and satisfy the people, he was clearly wrong. Interestingly, Luke never tells us if Jesus was whipped (Mark 15:15–16 = Matt. 27:26–27 = John 19:1–5 describe what was probably a double whipping, though a single whipping summarized in two settings is also possible). Luke's omission fits with his omission of other unpleasant acts such as Judas's kiss (Luke 22:48), the soldiers' spitting (22:63–65), and the charge of blasphemy (22:70–71). Indirect reference fits Luke's style.

[23:17]   See the additional note for the unlikelihood of Luke's mentioning Pilate's obligation to release a prisoner.

---

4. Αὐτῷ (by him) is the only NT example of the dative of agent, which is good Attic Greek; BDF §191.

5. Παιδεύω here refers to flogging; BAGD 604 §2bγ; BAA 1222 §2bγ; elsewhere in the NT with this meaning only at Luke 23:22; cf. 1 Kings 12:11, 14; 2 Chron. 10:11, 14. Mark 15:15 uses φραγελλώσας for the whipping before the crucifixion. Sherwin-White 1963: 27–28 distinguishes three types of flogging: *fustes*, *flagella*, and *verbera*. He may be right that Luke refers to *fustigatio* in terms of Pilate's initial intention, but when he gave Jesus over, the *verberatio* would be administered for crucifixion. R. Brown 1994: 851 questions the value of these distinctions and whether Luke's audience would know them. Regardless, the punishment came with the crucifixion.

b. The Crowd's Demand: Jesus' Death and Barabbas's Release (23:18–23)
i. The Crowd Cries for Barabbas (23:18–19)

Pilate's offer to release Jesus sparks a reaction in the crowd, which **23:18** responds as a group (παμπληθεί, pamplēthei, all together; BAGD 607; BAA 1228; a *hapax legomenon*; Nolland 1993b: 1131 makes the case for the people's inclusion in the Lucan portrait). Acts 3:14–15 also blames the nation as a whole for Jesus' death. They cry for (ἀνέκραγον, anekragon, a second-aorist form unique to the NT; Marshall 1978: 860; BDF §75) the release of the criminal Barabbas and call on Pilate to take Jesus away. Barabbas is the equivalent of a modern-day insurrectionist and terrorist (23:19), yet the crowd would rather free this sinner than the Jewish teacher. They tell Pilate to take Jesus away, which means to execute him for the charge with which he was accused (cf. Acts 8:33; 21:36; 22:22; Isa. 53:8). Ironically, Barabbas's name means "son of the father" (see R. Brown 1994: 799–800 for other options).

The verse is unique to Luke, though Matt. 27:20–22 = Mark 15:11–13 covers the same ground. In the other Synoptics, Pilate raises a question to get the crowd's response; here the crowd is already speaking up. The leadership persuaded (Matt. 27:20) or stirred up (Mark 15:11) the crowd to ask for Barabbas, so Luke seems to be relating this detail more directly.

Barabbas was not an outstanding character: Matt. 27:16 calls him a **23:19** "notorious prisoner"; John 18:40 calls him a robber; and Mark 15:7 notes that he "committed murder in the insurrection" (similar to Luke). Barabbas led a rebellion or uprising and committed murder, for which he was thrown into prison.[6] Ironically, Barabbas did what Jesus is being convicted of (Luke 23:2, 5). Jesus suffers on behalf of Barabbas and thus pictures how he sets sinful captives free.

ii. Pilate Replies for Jesus (23:20)

Pilate attempts to bring justice. At first, he resists the crowd's call **23:20** and desires to release Jesus (repeatedly expressed with ἀπολύω, apolyō; 23:16, 20, 22).[7] Luke portrays a battle of wills: the people against Pilate. In Mark 15:11 = Matt. 27:20, the crowd was spurred

---

6. Στάσις means "rebellion or uprising" elsewhere at Mark 15:7; Luke 23:25; Acts 19:40 (elsewhere in the NT at Acts 15:2; 23:7, 10; 24:5; Heb. 9:8; BAGD 764 §2; BAA 1526 §2). This is the only NT expression of periphrasis with ἦν (was) and an aorist participle; BDR §355.1; BDF §355.1; Plummer 1896: 526 (although ℵ* in John 18:30 also has this construction).

7. Θέλων with an infinitive means "wishing to . . ."; 10:29; 23:8; Marshall 1978: 860.

on by the leadership, but Luke places the blame on the group that caused Pilate to change his mind. Because of political expediency, Pilate responded to the masses.

Lacking any statement about Pilate's desire to release Jesus, in Mark 15:12b = Matt. 27:22 Pilate asks a question: "What shall I do with Jesus, the one who is called the Christ?" (Matthew) or "What shall I do with the one you call the King of the Jews?" (Mark). Pilate simultaneously involves the crowd and needles them in Mark's version.

iii. The Crowd Insists on Crucifixion (23:21)

23:21 The crowd knows what it wants and will not accept Pilate's determination of Jesus' innocence. They insist that Jesus be crucified. The double present imperative σταύρου σταύρου (*staurou staurou*, crucify, crucify!) is emphatic and is unusual for Luke (John 19:6 has a similar double cry in the aorist imperative).[8] The syntax makes it hard to see a source related to Mark or John (Marshall 1978: 860).[9] Mark 15:13 = Matt. 27:22 has only one cry.

Crucifixion was the harshest form of capital punishment in the ancient world, perhaps dating back to the Persians (J. Schneider, *TDNT* 7:572–84; Hengel 1977; Fitzmyer 1978; R. Brown 1994: 945–47). In Greece and Rome, initially only slaves were executed this way. In Imperial Rome, foreigners (but not Roman citizens) also were subjected to this horrendous form of execution. The purpose of crucifixion was to keep order and maintain security by publicly executing criminals in a way that promoted fear of committing a crime, and so rebels were often executed in this manner.[10] Two situations merited crucifixion: treason and evasion of due process in a capital case (Fitzmyer 1985: 1491). The LXX uses σταυρόω of Haman's punishment (Esth. 7:9). The NT alludes to Deut. 21:23 (Acts

---

8. Σταυρόω literally means "to fix a stake"; BAGD 765; BAA 1528; elsewhere used by Luke in Luke 23:23, 33; 24:7; 20; Acts 2:36; 4:10. Luke uses σταυρός (cross) as a figure for rejection in Luke 9:23; 14:27.

9. Fitzmyer 1985: 1491 notes Luke's similar though distinct use of double vocatives in 10:41; 13:34; 22:31.

10. Josephus calls crucifixion the worst of deaths; *Jewish War* 7.6.4 §203; see also *Antiquities* 2.5.4 §77; 11.6.11 §§261, 266–67; 13.14.2 §380; 17.10.10 §295; *Jewish War* 1.4.5–6 §§93–98; 5.11.1 §§449–51. For ancient non-Jewish sources, see J. Schneider, *TDNT* 7:573 n. 15. Among the key texts are Herodotus 1.128; 3.132, 159 (who ties the punishment to the Medes and the Persians); Tacitus, *History* 2.72; Cicero, *Against Verres* 2.5.63–66 §§163–70 (who calls it "a cruel and disgusting penalty"); *The Digest of Justinian* 48.19.28 (who sees it as the harshest punishment); Justin Martyr, *Dialogue with Trypho* 91.2 and *Apology* 1.13; Irenaeus, *Against Heresies* 2.24.4; and Origen, *Against Celsus* 6.10; Seneca, *To Marcia on Consolation* 20.3; R. Brown 1994: 948.

5:30). In this OT text, the body of a capital offender who was stoned was to be hung up on a tree to remind the people of the punishment for sin. Later Judaism included crucifixion in this OT reference.

Crucifixion had four steps. (1) The criminal had to carry the *patibulum* (the crossbeam) to the point of execution. The main stake was already fixed in the ground at the execution site. (The cross had a shape either like a capital T or, as in more traditional representations, a lowercase †.) (2) The condemned person would be bound to the crossbeam on the ground either by rope (Pliny, *Natural History* 28.11 §46) or less frequently by nails (Lucan, *Civil War* 6.547; *m. Šab.* 6.10; John 20:25; Hewitt 1932). R. Brown (1994: 949–51) accepts the plausibility of Jesus' being nailed to the cross. (3) The beam would then be raised by forked poles and fastened to the upright pole (the length of which was so high that the condemned could get no support from his feet to breathe) or it was dropped into a slot at the top of the upright beam. (4) A tablet specifying the crime was hung around the accused to publicly declare the crime. Death came by suffocation through exhaustion or by loss of blood and body fluids (R. Brown 1994: 1088–92; Barbet 1953; Zugibe 1989). Some estimate the cross's height at seven feet. Such was the death that the crowd insisted Jesus experience.

iv. Pilate Stands Firm for Release (23:22)

23:22 For the third time in this pericope (23:15, 20; cf. 23:4), Pilate declares Jesus' innocence (Maurer, *TDNT* 6:637 §B3). Pilate here offers a double declaration of innocence and asks (in wording like Mark 15:14 = Matt. 27:23) what evil "this one" has done. The Lucan word order is closer to Matthew than to Mark, but only Luke refers to Jesus as "this one." The question implies that Pilate has no charge to hang on Jesus. In fact, he says that he finds nothing worthy of death, so he repeats his desire to chastise and release him (Luke 23:16, 20).

v. The Crowd's Insistence Reverses Pilate's Verdict (23:23)

23:23 With no desire for compromise, the people refuse to let Pilate's verdict stand. The crowd is insistent (ἐπίκειμαι, *epikeimai*; BAGD 294 §2b; BAA 597 §2b; elsewhere used by Luke at Luke 5:1; Acts 27:20) and asks with a great voice (φωναῖς μεγάλαις, *phōnais megalais*) that Jesus be crucified. Because the crowd is insistent, αἰτέω (*aiteō*) indicates a demand rather than a request (Fitzmyer 1985: 1492; BAGD 25–26; BAA 48–49). The crowd's pressure works because of Pilate's tenuous record in handling the Jews. Some argue that the ruthless Pilate would not be receptive to such pressure (Luce 1933: 346). But this objection cannot be sustained in light of the pressure that was on Pilate to be more sensitive to the Jews (see the introduction to 23:6–12). The precedent of the iconic standards noted in the exegesis of 23:1, 13 helps support historicity of this event. Given the choice between a controversial Jewish teacher and a festival riot in Jerusalem, Pilate probably decided that one death was better than mass violence.

Luke briefly notes the people's success: their voices prevailed (κατισχύω, katischyō; BAGD 424 §1; BAA 862 §1; elsewhere in the NT only at Luke 21:36; Matt. 16:18; cf. Exod. 17:11; 1 Enoch 104.6). Mark 15:15 says that Pilate wanted to please the crowd, thus matching Luke's point that Jewish pressure caused the crucifixion, though Acts 4:24–28 makes it clear that all groups are blamed for Jesus' death. When Pilate acquiesces to this pressure, he joins the conspiracy that Acts 4 alludes to, since he could have acted otherwise. With more detail than Mark 15:14b = Matt. 27:23b has, Luke notes the clamor's success. The other Gospels say that the crowd shouted out (Matthew has the imperfect ἔκραζον, ekrazon, while Mark has the aorist ἔκραξαν, ekraxan) all the more (περισσῶς, perissōs) that "he be crucified" (Matthew) or to "crucify him" (Mark). In different words all the Synoptics say the same thing.

c. Jesus' Condemnation and Barabbas's Release (23:24–25)
i. Pilate Accepts the Crowd's Demand (23:24)

23:24 The people's protest works; Pilate gives the judgment they want to hear (ἐπέκρινεν, epekrinen; BAGD 295; BAA 598).[11] He honors their demand (αἴτημα, aitēma; BAGD 26; BAA 49; elsewhere in the NT only at Phil. 4:6; 1 John 5:15; Stählin, *TDNT* 1:193). R. Brown (1994: 854) argues that all the Gospels see an official decision here, using popular, not legal language. Though the Jewish leadership is the driving force here, the Romans still share responsibility for the final decision.

Luke lacks any mention of Pilate's doing the crowd a favor (Mark 15:15), nor does he make any effort to explain Pilate's motive. He simply leaves the impression that Pilate succumbed to Jewish pressure. Matthew 27:24–26 describes the motive in detail: when Pilate saw that he was getting nowhere and that a riot was starting, he took some water and symbolically washed his hands of the affair. He told the people that this man's blood was on their hands, and they accepted responsibility for Jesus' blood.

---

11. Ἐπικρίνω can have the technical meaning "to issue a sentence" (2 Macc. 4:47; 3 Macc. 4:2; Fitzmyer 1985: 1492; Plummer 1896: 527), although it was also used of determining whether a person was fit for military service or exempt from a poll tax (MM 240).

ii. Barabbas Is Released and Jesus Is Given over to the People (23:25)

Pilate releases Barabbas, but Luke does not mention the criminal's **23:25** name here, referring to him as "the one" (τόν, *ton*). Luke repeats the description of 23:19—this was the man thrown into prison for insurrection and murder. The criminal goes free because the crowd sought his freedom. In contrast, the Innocent One is placed among criminals (Luke 22:37; Isa. 53:12). This text is perhaps the primary example of Luke's noting Jewish responsibility for Jesus' execution (also Luke 24:20; Acts 2:23, 36; 4:10; 13:28; Schweizer 1984: 353; Danker 1988: 370; cf. Acts 4:26). In Mark 15:15–16 = Matt. 27:26–27, Jesus is delivered over to the soldiers, while Luke emphasizes his delivery over to the will of the Jews. The Synoptic note explains why the soldiers take hold of Jesus in Luke 23:26. With the Innocent One in his accusers' hands, the hour grows very dark (22:53).

In excursus 11, objection 6, I discuss the release custom noted here. Its historicity has been debated, but at least four historical analogies provide precedent for such releases (Nolland 1993b: 1130):

1. Greco-Roman clemency, especially at religious festivals, is rich in precedent (Merritt 1985).
2. Crowds can help secure pardon by acclamation (Mayer-Maly 1955).
3. Roman release of prisoners in Judea is attested by Josephus (*Antiquities* 20.9.3 §§208–10; 20.9.5 §215).
4. In Judaism, public assemblies can function as courts of justice (Jer. 26; Sus. 28–62) and popular intervention is also attested (1 Sam. 14:43–45).

In defending the event's historicity, Nolland notes that Pilate was trying to avoid releasing Barabbas (Bajsić 1967; Strobel 1980: 127–30). His ploy failed when the crowds opted—to his surprise—for Barabbas. Though we lack extrabiblical corroboration of this custom, the setting does fit the cultural background, suggesting its roots in historical practice.

Luke 23:13–25 portrays Pilate's attempts to get Jesus justice. He **Summary** believes that Jesus is innocent, but his efforts to punish Jesus and release him fail. The people insist that Jesus face crucifixion and that Barabbas, an insurrectionist and a murderer, be released. The powerful Roman ruler succumbs to popular pressure. Jesus is condemned, despite Pilate's and Herod's declarations that he has done nothing worthy of death. Jesus is reckoned as a criminal and takes the place of a murderer. This exchange pictures what Jesus' death means for humanity and also shows how sin can twist reality.

The reader is supposed to sense the tragedy and injustice of what is happening to Jesus, who does not deserve to go to the cross, but goes nonetheless. The cause at the human level for Jesus' death is placed in the hands of the Jewish crowd. But Pilate is not blameless either. His conviction is that Jesus is innocent, but his spine is not strong enough to resist the uproar that Jesus' release would have produced. Some actively reject Jesus; others do it more passively—but the outcome is rejection either way. The innocent Jesus heads for the cross and death, while a sinner goes free in his stead.

Additional Notes

23:15. A variant (supported by A, D, W, Δ, Byz) reads, "I (Pilate) sent him to you (Jews)." The superior reading (supported by $\mathfrak{P}^{75}$, ℵ, B, L, T) properly refers to Herod's returning Jesus to Pilate and the Roman authorities and more clearly fits the reference to Herod. Given the three groupings of Jews mentioned in 23:13, "us" here must refer to the Roman officials, counter the claims of those who see a conflict between 23:10 and 23:15 (see the introduction to 23:6–12).

23:17. The textual evidence suggests that 23:17 is not original to Luke. Manuscripts omitting the verse include $\mathfrak{P}^{75}$, A, B, L, and T. Others (ℵ, W, family 1, family 13, Byz, most Itala, some Syriac) include it: ἀνάγκην δὲ εἶχεν ἀπολύειν αὐτοῖς κατὰ ἑορτὴν ἕνα (now he was obliged at the feast to release to them one [prisoner]). Codexes Θ and Ψ have a different word order. Yet other manuscripts (D and some Syriac) have the verse after 23:19 (D's word order is like that of Θ and Ψ). The verse is not considered original because many of the manuscripts supporting it are late, it appears in two locations, and it has different wording. The discrepancy about location suggests a late addition to make Luke like Mark 15:6 = Matt. 27:15 (Arndt 1956: 463, Marshall 1978: 859, and Metzger 1975: 179–80 omit the verse; Kilpatrick 1965a supports its inclusion).

The addition refers to Pilate's custom of releasing one prisoner at the feast as a gesture of good will (see Chavel 1941; Jeremias 1966: 73; Luce 1933: 347 [who reflects skepticism about such a custom, noting that those who see it present argue that it is limited to Pilate for a short time]; Rigg 1945; Cohn 1967: 162–69; on the custom, see the exegesis of 23:25 and excursus 11, objection 6). Fitzmyer (1985: 1485–86) is skeptical of the custom and argues that it has little role in Luke (which is correct only if 23:17 is not original to Luke). Those who question this part of the tradition historically (by asking how an innocent Jesus could qualify for release as if he were guilty) fail to realize that Pilate is trying to portray Jesus as guilty of disturbing the peace, a charge that he does not regard as worthy of death. In Pilate's view, Jesus is innocent of a capital offense, though he probably sees Jesus as a public nuisance. In this view, Pilate's effort would be seen as an act of amnesty.

7. Crucifixion (23:26–49)

Luke presents Jesus' death in several subunits that must be treated together to get the full force of his account: the journey to Golgotha (23:26–32), the crucifixion (23:33–38), the discussion with the two thieves (23:39–43), and Jesus' death (23:44–49). The entire presentation shows Jesus in control of events. He dies as an innocent sufferer who is able to save those who turn to him. Two confessions expressed uniquely in Luke—one by the thief and one by the centurion—declare Jesus' innocence. Jesus' request to forgive his executioners demonstrates the compassion he told the disciples to have for their enemies in the Sermon on the Plain (6:27–36). Jesus is the model martyr. Another major theme is the reactions of various bystanders to Jesus' death: they watch, mock, sneer, confess, mourn, and blaspheme. This variety provides a cameo of the world's reactions to Jesus. Finally, there is irony in the taunts for Jesus to save himself. The scoffers think they have stopped Jesus. He appears powerless now, so they make fun of him, challenging him to deliver himself. Jesus chooses not to save himself from the cross, but God will deliver him from its effect, showing that Jesus can fulfill the predictions he made to the disciples and the promise he made to the confessing thief. The taunt to save is realized in a way the mockers never imagined.

Sources and Historicity

The first subunit, Luke 23:26–32, is made up of three pieces of material (Aland 1985: §343). The remark about Simon carrying the cross in 23:26 (paralleled in Matt. 27:31b–32 = Mark 15:20b–21) is clearly traditional material (Fitzmyer 1985: 1492 ties it to Mark, as do most).

The scene with the mourning women (23:27–31) is unique to Luke (although the saying in 23:29 appears in a slightly different form in the Gospel of Thomas 79) and is best seen as special Lucan material (Ernst 1977: 630; Grundmann 1963: 428; Fitzmyer 1985: 1494; V. Taylor 1972: 89–90). Nolland (1993b: 1135) is certain of an additional source but is less certain whether it is the same as in other sections of the passion narrative. Two approaches have been taken against the historicity of this subunit. Bultmann (1963: 37, 127) argues that the prediction of Jerusalem's fall is "Christian prophecy" put on Jesus' lips after the fact. Marshall (1978: 862) notes, however, that the sayings show signs of having been formed in Aramaic and that the decision about prophecy and Jerusalem depends on how one regards a whole body of similar texts (13:34–35; 19:41–44; 21:5–24). Käser (1963) also challenges historicity by arguing that this subunit was created in light of Isa. 54:1, Luke 21:23, and Gal. 4:27. Marshall also rejects this approach, noting that the Galatians imagery is a late Christian development (as 2 Clem. 2.1–3 and Justin Martyr, *Apology* 1.53, show).

Luke 23:32 has parallels in Matt. 27:38 = Mark 15:27, a slightly later location that simply reflects distinct placement of a similar detail.

The other three subunits in this pericope—the crucifixion proper, the discussion of the two thieves, and Jesus' death (23:33–49)—have a complex background (Aland 1985: §§344–48). That a basic tradition lies behind Luke is suggested by the various verbal contacts and the many details that find parallels in the Synoptics:

	Luke	Matthew	Mark
dividing Jesus' clothes	23:34	27:35	15:24
mocking Jesus	23:35–38	27:39–42	15:29–32
cosmic signs	23:44–45	27:45	15:33
death of Jesus	23:46	27:50	15:37
the centurion's confession	23:47	27:54	15:39
the watching women	23:49	27:55–56	15:40–41

There are many differences as well, since only 54 of Luke's 269 words, or 20%, match Mark (R. Brown 1994: 905; V. Taylor 1972: 92 says 74 of 265 terms [28%]). The differences may be classified as material that Luke does not record (nos. 1, 2, 5, 6, 9, 16, 17, 19, 23), unique Lucan material (nos. 4, 11, 13, 14, 18, 21, 22), or partial parallels (nos. 3, 7, 8, 10, 12, 15, 20) (adapted from Ernst 1977: 633):

1. Luke does not mention Golgotha by name (Mark 15:22 = Matt. 27:33).
2. Luke does not mention the offer of drugged wine (Mark 15:23 = Matt. 27:34).
3. Luke 23:33 uses a different term for the criminals (κακοῦργος, as opposed to λῃστής in Mark 15:27 = Matt. 27:38) and mentions them at a different point in his narrative.
4. Luke 23:34 uniquely records Jesus' prayer to forgive the sin of his executioners.
5. Luke does not mention the time that the crucifixion began (Mark 15:25), although he and Mark mention the time that it became dark (Luke 23:44 = Mark 15:33).
6. Luke 23:35 briefly refers to spectators, but does not supply the contents of their mocking: taunts about Jesus' saying that he would destroy the temple and raise it up in three days (Mark 15:29–30 = Matt. 27:39–40). (Luke exhibits a similar silence at Jesus' trial.)

7. Luke 23:35 speaks only of the rulers and does not name the chief priests, scribes, and elders (Mark 15:31 = Matt. 27:41).
8. Luke 23:35 mentions that the rulers mock Jesus with reference to being the Chosen One, rather than calling him the King of Israel (Mark 15:32 = Matt. 27:42).
9. Luke does not mention the rulers' other taunts (Mark. 15:32 = Matt. 27:42–43).
10. Luke 23:36 mentions the offer of wine vinegar at a different point in the narrative (Mark 15:36 = Matt. 27:48).
11. In Luke 23:36 the soldiers mock Jesus about being King of the Jews.
12. Luke 23:38 records the inscription over Jesus at a different point in the narrative (Mark 15:26 = Matt. 27:37).
13. Luke 23:39–43 uniquely records Jesus' discussion with the two thieves.
14. Luke 23:45 uniquely has a second reference to darkness.
15. Luke 23:45 mentions the tearing of the temple veil at a different point in the narrative (Mark 15:38 = Matt. 27:51).
16. Luke neither mentions nor records the content of Jesus' first cry from the cross (Mark 15:34 = Matt. 27:46, using Ps. 22:1 [22:2 MT]).
17. Luke does not include the crowd's mention of Elijah (Mark 15:35–36 = Matt. 27:47, 49).
18. Luke 23:46 uniquely records the content of Jesus' second cry from the cross, using Ps. 31:5 [31:6 MT].
19. Luke does not record the earthquake that took place when Jesus died or the subsequent resurrection of many saints (Matt. 27:51–53).
20. Luke 23:47 quotes the centurion as declaring Jesus' innocence instead of his divine sonship (Mark 15:39 = Matt. 27:54).
21. Luke 23:48 uniquely records the crowd watching and mourning.
22. Luke 23:49 uniquely mentions that the disciples watched from a distance.
23. Luke 23:49 mentions that the women were present, but does not identify them other than to note that they are from Galilee (Mark 15:40–41 = Matt. 27:55–56).

How are these differences to be viewed? Grundmann (1963: 431) correctly identifies 23:33, 34a, 35a, 36, 37, 39–43, 46, 48–49 as influenced by additional sources, to which one should add 23:47, as Fitzmyer (1985: 1520) suggests. It is possible, however, that Luke is only summarizing in 23:46, 48–49. Scholars who see the use of L here are Ellis (1974: 266), Creed (1930: 284–85), Ernst (1977: 632–33), Marshall (1978: 866–71), Fitzmyer (1985: 1507, 1512–13 [but not for 23:44–49]), and V. Taylor (1972: 91–99). Nolland (1993b: 1142–43, 1150, 1155) speaks of Luke using his second passion source for 23:33–43, with less certainty for 23:44–49. Only a few scholars argue for a total Lucan redaction of Mark (Schneider 1977a: 482–83, 486–87; Schenk 1974: 93–102). Noting Luke's care in construct-ing the account, R. Brown (1994: 905–7) tends to see Matthew and Luke working with Mark. When the changes are viewed individually, this case looks plausible. The scope and variety of the differences, however, make an additional source or sources more likely.

Bultmann (1963: 37, 309, 274) regards the crucifixion account as con-taining legend, sees the thieves account as evidence of the expanding tra-dition, and sees Luke responsible for replacing Ps. 22:1 [22:2 MT] with Ps. 31:5 [31:6 MT]. The Jesus Seminar rejects all the sayings material tied to the cross as either reflecting a prophetic oracle (23:28–31) or as being "out of character for Jesus" (23:43, 46) (Funk and Hoover 1993: 395–97). Fitz-myer (1985: 1501) questions whether the label *legend* is an appropriate de-scription of the crucifixion (he prefers the term *literary embellishment*) and whether the thieves account is a case of expansion (but, given the use of other sources, it is difficult to distinguish between embellishment and addi-tional material). There is a dramatic air to the account's presentation, but the assessment that it is embellishment may be too strong a term for the material, given the use of additional sources. The Jesus Seminar's stance reflects its consistent tendency to reject sayings by Jesus that have a high Christology. R. Brown (1994: 1092–96) offers a strong critique of B. Thiering's and H. J. Schonfield's views that Jesus did not really die. He concludes: "These theories demonstrate that in relation to the passion of Jesus, despite the popular maxim, fiction is stranger than fact—and often, intentionally or not, more profitable" (p. 1096). For specific challenges launched against the historicity of various points, see the exegesis.

This pericope contains stories about Jesus (23:33–38, 44–49) and his pronouncements (23:26–32, 39–43) (Fitzmyer 1985: 1494, 1501, 1507, 1513; Bultmann 1963: 37, 373, 309–10, 273–74). It has been proposed that the account is modeled after ancient Jew-ish martyr accounts like the *Martyrdom and Ascension of Isaiah*, 2 Macc. 5–6, and 4 Macc. 5–6. Untergassmair (1970: 156–71) identifies several traits of this form in Luke's account (see also Surkau 1938: 16–99 and Pilgrim 1971):

1. a person who follows the martyr (23:26)
2. mourning women (23:27)
3. eschatological themes (23:31)
4. prayer for the executioners (23:34)
5. belief that the martyr will go directly to heaven (23:39–43)
6. people watching the death (23:35, 48)
7. the martyr's freewill entry into death alongside the use of Scripture (23:46)

After examination of these characteristics, Untergassmair concludes that the biblical account is unique and presents Jesus more like a judge than a martyr. Arguing that the martyr element is less significant than some have made it, Untergassmair prefers to speak of a "passion play" that emphasizes the literary portrayal of Jesus' death. It is not clear, however, that "passion play" is a better label, though his point about Jesus' authority is correct. The crucifixion account portrays the death of one who dies unjustly but is approved by God. His ability to deliver reveals his real position, despite the cross. The keys to the account are the cosmic signs, the testimony of some of the watchers, and the trust that Jesus has in God. This is more than a martyr account; this "martyr" can promise salvation to a repentant thief.

The outline of Luke 23:26–49 is as follows:

a. To Golgotha (23:26–32)
  i. Simon the Cyrene carries the cross (23:26)
  ii. Jesus' conversation with the women (23:27–31)
  iii. Two other criminals are led away with Jesus (23:32)
b. Crucifixion (23:33–38)
  i. The location (23:33)
  ii. Jesus' call to forgive (23:34)
  iii. Scoffing and mocking (23:35–38)
c. Two thieves (23:39–43)
  i. One criminal rebukes Jesus (23:39)
  ii. A second criminal rebukes the first and confesses his own guilt (23:40–41)
  iii. The second criminal makes a request (23:42)
  iv. Jesus' comforting reply (23:43)
d. Jesus' death (23:44–49)
  i. Cosmic signs (23:44–45)
  ii. Jesus' final words: a prayer of trust (23:46)
  iii. A centurion's remark and the crowd's mourning (23:47–48)
  iv. The disciples and women watch (23:49)

The account of Jesus' death is loaded with symbolism and irony. Symbolic (i.e., representative) people and actions are (1) Simon, whose carrying of the cross draws humanity into Jesus' death; (2) the different reactions to Jesus' death (watching, sneering, mocking, confessing, mourning, blaspheming); and (3) the contrasting thieves.

There are several ironic actions in the pericope. (1) A placard mockingly announces that Jesus is King of the Jews. (2) A thief confesses Jesus' innocence, and Jesus promises him that he will reach paradise despite the man's pending death. (3) Jesus is slain as a criminal in the midst of criminals, yet he, an innocent, offers a prayer of forgiveness for his executioners. (4) The Savior is taunted to save himself, something that will be done later. (5) The righteous Innocent One suffers, though none of it is for his own actions.

Several other themes are found in the pericope. (1) Jesus controls the situation as he offers words of woe against and predicts terror for Jerusalem. (2) Scripture is fulfilled. (3) Jesus dies with a prayer of trust in God's care. (4) God testifies to Jesus through the cosmic signs. Even creation speaks for Jesus at this crucial moment. A human witness, the centurion, also affirms Jesus' innocence by declaring that Jesus was not guilty of the crimes for which he was executed. Jesus' death was unjust, but it will ultimately yield justice for humankind.

Exegesis and Exposition

26And as they led him away, they seized one Simon of Cyrene, who was coming in from the country, and laid on him the cross to carry it behind Jesus. 27And there followed him a great multitude of people and of women who wailed and lamented him. 28But Jesus turning to them said, "Daughters of Jerusalem, do not weep for me, but weep for yourselves and for your children. 29For behold, days are coming in which they will say, 'Blessed are the barren wombs and the breasts that did not give milk.' 30Then they will begin to say to the mountains, 'Fall on us,' and to the hills, 'Cover us.' 31For if they do this when the wood is green, what might happen when it is dry?" 32⌐Two others were led off with him, criminals⌐ who were to be put to death.

33And when they came to the place that is called the Skull, there they crucified him and the criminals, one on the right and one on the left. 34⌐And Jesus said, "Father, forgive them, for they do not know what they do."⌐ And they cast lots to divide his garments. 35And the people stood watching, but also the rulers sneered, saying, "He saved others, let him save himself, if this one is ⌐the Christ of God, the Elect⌐." 36And the soldiers also mocked him, coming up and offering him vinegar, 37saying also, "If you are the King, save yourself!" 38There was also an ⌐inscription over him⌐: "This is the King of the Jews."

39One of the criminals who was hanged with him blasphemed, saying, "Are you not the Christ? Save yourself and us!" 40But the other one rebuked him, saying, "Do you not fear God, for you are under the same judgment? 41And we on the one hand justly, for we receive things that are worthy of what we did; but this one has done nothing wrong." 42And ⌐he said, "Jesus, remember me⌐ when you come ⌐in⌐ your kingdom." 43And he said to him, "Truly I say to you, today you will be with me in paradise."

[44]And it was already about the sixth hour, and darkness fell over the whole earth until the ninth hour, [45]while ⌜the sun was darkened⌝ and the veil of the temple was ripped in the middle. [46]And crying out with a loud cry, Jesus said, "Father, into your hands I entrust my spirit." And saying this, he expired. [47]And the centurion, when he saw what had happened, praised God, saying, "Certainly this man was innocent." [48]And all the crowds gathered to see the sight, when they saw what had taken place, beat their breasts and returned. [49]And all those who knew him and the women who followed him from Galilee stood at a distance to see these things.

a. To Golgotha (23:26–32)
i. Simon the Cyrene Carries the Cross (23:26)

23:26   Jesus goes to his death, carrying his own crossbeam (Marshall 1978: 863; Creed 1930: 285; Plummer 1896: 528; John 19:17; Plutarch, *Moralia* 554B ["On the Delays of the Divine Vengeance" 9]; Artemidorus Daldianus, *Oneirokritika* 2.56; Justin Martyr, *Dialogue with Trypho* 91 and *Apology* 1.55; Irenaeus, *Against Heresies* 2.24.4; Tertullian, *Against the Jews* 10). The cross would have been draped across the nape of the neck, like carrying a sack on one's back. The crossbeam becomes too heavy for a tired Jesus to carry, and so those leading him conscript Simon of Cyrene to carry it (only Luke notes that he carried it behind [ὄπισθεν, *opisthen*; BDR §215.1] Jesus). In a stylistic variation, Luke uses ἐπιλαβόμενοι (*epilabomenoi*; BDF §170.2) to indicate that the soldiers "seized" Simon, while Matthew and Mark use forms of the more legally technical ἀγγαρεύω (*angareuō*, to commandeer; Nolland 1993b: 1136). That Simon was thus "drafted" to help does not suggest that Roman troops were absent, for they are mentioned in 23:36, 47 (and in 23:52 the Romans have possession of Jesus' body). Rather, a Roman would not carry the cross because of the shame associated with the act. All the Synoptics mention Simon of Cyrene (Matt. 27:32 = Mark 15:21), but only Mark adds that he is the father of Rufus and Alexander, which might suggest that the sons were well-known believers (perhaps the same Rufus mentioned in Rom. 16:13?). The region of Cyrene, in what is now Tripoli, is mentioned in Acts 6:9, 11:20, and 13:1 (Plummer 1896: 527; Josephus, *Against Apion* 2.4–5 §§41–54; *Antiquities* 14.7.2 §114; 16.6.1 §160; 16.6.5 §169; 1 Macc. 15:23; 2 Macc. 2:23). R. Brown (1994: 915) notes that it is unlikely that the detail would have been invented. Simon was perhaps a Jewish worshiper who had come in from the countryside to celebrate the Passover. He went quickly from observer to representative participant, which some see carrying an additional point about discipleship (but this seems forced). The wording is different from Jesus' previous exhortations to "take up the cross" (Luke 9:23; 14:27), and we are not told that Simon experiences any loss (with

Nolland 1993b: 1136; against Danker 1988: 370–71 and Creed 1930: 285). In Jewish and Roman culture, it is customary to die outside the city (Lev. 24:14; 1 Kings 21:13; Pseudo-Quintilian, *Declamationes Minores* 274; Plautus, *Carbonaria* fragment 2; Plautus, *Braggart Warrior* 2.4 §§359–60; R. Brown 1994: 912–15).

The parallels are similar. Matt. 27:31–32 = Mark 15:20–21 speaks of leading Jesus away to crucify him. Matthew shares ἀπήγαγον (*apēgagon*, they led [him] away) with Luke. Mark refers to Simon as a passerby and notes the name of his sons. Mark matches Luke verbally by noting that Simon came from the country or perhaps from his field (ἐρχόμενον ἀπ' ἀγροῦ, *erchomenon ap' agrou*; BAGD 14 §2; BAA 24 §1). Both Matthew and Mark note that the purpose is to carry the cross (ἵνα ἄρῃ τὸν σταυρὸν αὐτοῦ, *hina arē ton stauron autou*).

Several Jewish and Roman writers describe Jesus' death (C. A. Evans 1990: 336; F. F. Bruce 1974; Dunkerley 1957: 27):

1. Mara bar Serapion (ca. A.D. 73): "For what advantage did . . . the Jews [gain] by the death of their wise king, because from that same time their kingdom was taken away?"
2. Josephus, *Antiquities* 18.3.3 §64: "Pilate, upon hearing him accused by men of the highest standing among us, had condemned him to be crucified."[1]
3. Agapius, *Book of the Title* (summarizing Josephus): "Pilate condemned him to be crucified and to die."
4. Tacitus, *Annals* 15.44 (ca. A.D. 110–20): "This name [i.e., Christian] originates from 'Christus' who was sentenced to death by the procurator Pontius Pilate during the reign of Tiberius."
5. Babylonian Talmud, tractate *Sanhedrin* 43a: "On the eve of the Passover they hanged Jesus the Nazarene. And a herald went out in front of him, for forty days saying: 'He is going to be stoned, because he practiced sorcery and enticed and led Israel astray. Anyone who knows anything in his favor, let him come and plead on his behalf.' But not having found anything in his favor, they hanged him on the eve of Passover."

Needless to say, these accounts do not agree in details, but they do show historical evidence for Jesus' execution at the hands of the nation and Pilate.

ii. Jesus' Conversation with the Women (23:27–31)

In five verses unique to Luke, Jesus converses with some women in the crowd who lament his death. The irony is that Jesus' death does

23:27

---

1. This passage may have been modified by later Christian writers.

not mean his fall, but it spells doom for the nation. They are mourning for Jesus, but they should be mourning for themselves.

The trail of people behind Simon consists of two groups. It is not clear why the first group, the multitude of people (πολὺ πλῆθος τοῦ λαοῦ, *poly plēthos tou laou*), follows Jesus. Most likely consisting of both Jerusalemites and pilgrims, they are naturally curious to see what becomes of him (Klostermann 1929: 227; Marshall 1978: 863; Lucian, *Passing of Peregrinus* 34).

The second group consists of women publicly beating their breasts and lamenting. Κόπτομαι (*koptomai*) refers to beating the breast in grief (BAGD 444 §2; BAA 902 §2; elsewhere in the Gospels with this sense at Matt. 11:17; 24:30; Luke 8:52; cf. Zech. 7:5). Θρηνέω (*thrēneō*) refers to verbal mourning or dirge singing (BAGD 363 §2; BAA 738 §2; elsewhere in the Gospels at Matt. 11:17; Luke 7:32; John 16:20; cf. Mic. 1:8; Josephus, *Jewish War* 3.9.5 §§435–36). Both terms occur together in Josephus for the mourning associated with Saul's death (*Antiquities* 6.14.8 §377). There are several views about the women's actions:

1. Many see the trailing women as sympathizers (Marshall 1978: 863).[2] Since this practice carried religious value in Judaism, such sympathy might, however, not be sincere as much as customary (Ellis 1974: 266; Luke 7:12; 9:59–60; 23:48; John 11:31; *Sipre* 308.2 on Deut. 32:4 [= Neusner 1987: 2.323]). If so, the mourning would be more a matter of habit than of substance. The text, however, does not treat the women unsympathetically, as Jesus' tender address shows ("daughters of Jerusalem"). He simply indicates that their mourning is misdirected. There is little reason to doubt the lament's sincerity.

2. A late tradition shows women administering drugged wine to the executed (*b. Sanh.* 43a). While this tradition does accord with the mention that such wine was offered to Jesus, in the Gospels this is done by soldiers not by women (Luke 23:36 = Matt. 27:48 = Mark 15:36). The offer of wine also involves mocking, a tone missing from the women's actions.

3. The women are a literary symbol of rejecting Israel (Neyrey 1985: 108–9; Käser 1963). This representation correctly summarizes why the women are present, but why would Luke have created such a detail, especially given the cultural custom of mourning? Jesus has already given numerous warnings about

---

2. Stählin, *TDNT* 3:152–53, thinks that θρηνέω indicates "freewill" wailing, not professional mourners. Determining this force for the term is not, of course, merely a matter of the words used but of the historical, literary context.

the nation's fate (Luke 13:34–35; 19:41–44), so there is no need for Luke to have created one here.

The passage is simply another place where Luke notes the role of women in Jesus' ministry (1:39–56; 2:36–38; 7:11–15, 36–50; 8:1–3; 10:38–42; 11:27; 13:10–17). Nowhere in the Synoptics are women hostile to Jesus (Plummer 1896: 528). This tendency and the nature of Jesus' address to the women suggests that they are not full sympathizers, that their mourning is not merely customary, and that they are not mere literary symbols. What we may have here are women who regret that the circumstances unfortunately led to a painful execution (a softer form of view 1), which suggests that not all opposition to Jesus is hard opposition. Some of the people are not as hostile as the leadership is against Jesus. The passage may contain an allusion to Zech. 12:10–14.

23:28 Tragically, the women lament for the wrong person. Freed from carrying the crossbeam, Jesus turns to gently address those following him: θυγατέρες Ἰερουσαλήμ (*thygateres Ierousalēm*, daughters of Jerusalem). These women of the capital of Israel represent the nation.[3] Jesus does not need such sympathy (Fitzmyer 1985: 1498; Wiefel 1988: 395).[4] Jesus' exhortation "not to weep" indicates that the direction of their emotion needs to be reassessed (conceptual parallels in Luke 7:13; 8:52). The women are caught in the vortex of a tragic series of events that ends in judgment. Jesus' tone of care reflects his response throughout the events surrounding his death— no revenge, only concern and honesty. In a remark presented as a chiasmus, Jesus says that sympathy should instead be directed at themselves and their children:[5]

a weep not
b for me
b' for yourself
a' weep

Jesus is suggesting that the nation is headed for difficult times, an allusion to the events of A.D. 70 (Ellis 1974: 266; Grundmann 1963: 429; Luke 11:49–51; 13:1–9, 34–35; 19:41–44; 20:16; 21:20–21; Acts

---

3. The phrase θυγατέρες Ἰερουσαλήμ appears several times in the LXX: Song 1:5; 2:7; 3:5, 10; 5:8, 16; 8:4; Ps. Sol. 2.13; BAGD 365 §2d; BAA 741 §2d; cf. Jer. 9:20 [9:19 MT] and 2 Sam. 1:24.

4. Marshall 1978: 864 argues that this Semitic idiom means "do not weep so much for me as for yourselves," which is similar in force to 10:20.

5. Πλήν (but [rather]) signals a strong contrast like ἀλλά (but); BDF §449.1; BDR §449.1.3; Matt. 26:39 = Luke 22:42.

6:14; cf. Seneca, *Agamemnon* 659–63). Families will suffer great pain. The thought of the nation's pain has not left him. As he dies, Jesus thinks of the fate of others. Jesus' woe is like that in Jer. 9:17–20 [9:16–19 MT] (R. Brown 1994: 921). The nation is accountable for its rejection. Other Lucan texts show that all groups in the nation experience the pain of this judgment (Luke 11:49–50; 13:34–35; 19:41–44; 21:20–24). Jesus tells the women to weep for Israel, as he had (19:41).

23:29 Jesus now gives a better reason for mourning than his death—a significant time is approaching. The phrase ἰδοὺ ἔρχονται ἡμέραι (*idou erchontai hēmerai*, behold, days are coming) indicates that a key period of God's activity is coming (Luke 21:23; Tiede 1988: 414; J. Schneider, *TDNT* 2:671). In this time, normal categories of blessing and cursing will be reversed because the pain will be so great. In the past, it was women with children who were considered blessed, but in the coming horror barren women will be blessed (on the beatitudes form, see the exegesis of 6:20). Barrenness used to be a curse, but now creation is turned upside down in a reversal motif.[6] The suffering of Jerusalem's fall will be so great that it will be better to have no family. The benefit of barrenness in this period is emphasized by the threefold description: childless, wombs that never bore, and breasts that never gave suck. The motif is also seen in classical texts (Euripides, *Andromache* 395; Euripides, *Alcestis* 882; Tacitus, *Annals* 2.75; Seneca the Elder, *Controversiae* 2.3.2; Apuleius, *Apology* 85; Fitzmyer 1985: 1498; Nolland 1993b: 1137).

23:30 In fact, the pain of Jerusalem's fall will be so great that people will desire their life to end. They will want a "quick death" (Klostermann 1929: 228). Death will be better than the misery they face (Plummer 1896: 529). "They" probably refers to everyone present at this judgment, not just the women of the previous verse, since the allusion is to Hos. 10:8, in which the whole nation is judged for idolatry. When judgment comes, the people will want quick relief; they will want creation to collapse on them.[7] The image depicts great despair and the desire for relief (Foerster, *TDNT* 5:483 n. 96; Ernst 1977: 631; on Jewish background for this imagery as a way of expressing a just re-

---

6. Luce 1933: 349 sees an allusion to Isa. 54:1, but since the images are so different (i.e., in Isaiah the barren will bear a child), this is probably not correct; correctly Marshall 1978: 864 (cf. Luke 1:7, 25; Gal. 4:27) and R. Brown 1994: 923, who cites parallels from Lam. 4:4; Wis. 3:13; Eccles. 4:2–3; 2 Bar. 10.6–10 and argues that Luke received the saying from a sayings source.

7. Βουνός (hill) is rare in the NT, both times being tied to an OT text: Luke 3:5 (Isa. 40:4) and Luke 23:30 (Hos. 10:8); BAGD 146; BAA 292; BDR §126.1b.5. In contrast, the synonymous ὄρος (mountain) appears sixty-three times in the NT.

taliatory judgment, see SB 2:263–64).[8] In Hos. 10:8 the people are judged for idolatry, in Luke 23:30 for rejecting Jesus, and in Rev. 6:16 (the other NT citation of Hos. 10:8) for persecuting God's people. The pattern of human response to God's judgment shows how painful is the realization that one is the object of God's irreversible wrath. The desire to live is gone.

Jesus makes a comparison: he is the green or damp wood, the nation in future judgment is the dry wood (ξύλον, *xylon*; Plummer 1896: 530; BAGD 549 §3; BAA 1113 §3). Jesus presents a lesser-to-greater argument: if this is what happens to a living tree, what might happen (a deliberative subjunctive; BDF §366.1) to a dead one? Though the basic image is clear, the referents are disputed (Fitzmyer 1985: 1498; Plummer 1896: 529):

23:31

1. If the Romans treat an innocent person like Jesus this way, how much more will they mistreat a nation in revolution? This view introduces the Romans into a context where they are absent.
2. If the Jews treat Jesus this way for coming to deliver them, how will they be treated for destroying him? The only thing against this view is that the subject shifts in the second half of the passage.[9]
3. If humankind behaves this way before wickedness is full, how much more will it do so when wickedness overflows? It is not clear, however, how the reference to green and dry trees can produce this sense. This view sees the green tree as a negative reference, which is unlikely.
4. If God has not spared Jesus, how much more will the impenitent nation not be spared when divine judgment comes? In this view "they" is an oblique third-person plural reference to God (12:20 has a similar reference). It is easier to burn dry wood than lush, moisture-filled green wood.
5. The proverb is a general remark about coming judgment that lacks more specific referents (Nolland 1993b: 1138).

The widely held fourth view is most likely correct (Creed 1930: 286; Danker 1988: 372; Manson 1949: 343; Marshall 1978: 865; J. Schnei-

---

8. Marshall 1978: 865 argues that this motif could be parallel to a desire to hide from catastrophe (as in Rev. 6:15–16). The Lucan context, however, is not one of relief, and it is not clear that the request in Revelation is any different. What those in Revelation wish to avoid is the wrath of the one on the throne. They would rather die than face his judgment; Rev. 9:6.

9. Tiede 1988: 415 is close to view 2, arguing that if the nation does this atrocity now, surely they will pay for it later.

der, *TDNT* 5:38 n. 7 [who notes that the remark looks historical]). Schweizer (1984: 358) says the point is, "The fate of Jesus, like that of the prophets, is sure to befall his enemies." If view 4 is not correct, then view 2 is the next best option. Deciding between the two is not easy. A general reference to judgment (view 5) seems too vague. The concept of wood consumed in judgment is also found in Isa. 10:16–19 and Ezek. 20:47 [21:3 MT] (but Luke does not have the concept of burning found in these two references).[10] This is Jesus' last lament for the nation.

iii. Two Other Criminals Are Led Away with Jesus (23:32)

23:32   Jesus is not executed alone. With him are two κακοῦργοι (*kakourgoi*, criminals), a rare term in the NT (elsewhere only Luke 23:33, 39; 2 Tim. 2:9). Mark 15:27 = Matt. 27:38 has forms of λῃστής (*lēstēs*, bandit or robber). This passage recalls Isa. 53:12 and Jesus' prediction in Luke 22:37 that he is to be reckoned among the lawless (ἀνόμων, *anomōn*). Κακοῦργος is a general term for any kind of lawbreaker. Luke's basic point is that Jesus does not go to his death alone; he is slain as a lawbreaker, with criminals at his side.[11]

b. Crucifixion (23:33–38)
i. The Location (23:33)

23:33   Luke moves right to the crucifixion without referring to the effort mentioned in Mark 15:23 = Matt. 27:34 to give Jesus drugged wine to dull the pain of death.[12] Since at the end of this particularly gruesome death one was unable to draw another breath (Wiefel 1988: 398), it was common custom to offer wine vinegar (Heidland, *TDNT* 5:288–89). The three condemned men face execution just north and outside the city, in a place called "Golgotha" in Aramaic. All the Synoptics use τόπον (*topon*, place), but only Matt. 27:33 = Mark 15:22

---

10. For the contrast between judgment of the righteous and the sinner, see Prov. 11:31; 1 Pet. 4:17–18; SB 2:263; Gen. Rab. 65.22 on 27:27.

11. Filling in details of this story became popular in some circles. In the Old Latin, these two bandits are variously named Ioathas and Maggatras (Luke 23:32), Zoathan and Chammatha (Mark 15:27), or Zoathan and Camma (Matt. 27:38) (Plummer 1896: 530), while the Acts of Pilate 9 records their names as Dysmas and Gestas (Schneemelcher 1991–92: 1.512). Still other traditions speak of Jesus falling, meeting Mary, and speaking with a women named Veronica (called Bernice in Acts of Pilate 8), who testified before Pilate because Jesus had healed her issue of blood (cf. Luke 8:43–48). See also the Arabic Infancy Gospel 23 (R. Brown 1994: 969; Schneemelcher 1991–92: 1.460).

12. Marshall 1978: 867 suggests that Luke's lack of this detail argues for the presence of another source. On the details of the practice of crucifixion, see the exegesis of 23:21. A Jewish victim of crucifixion was recently found at Givᶜat ha-Mivtar (Nolland 1993b: 1145; bibliography on pp. 1140–41).

gives the Aramaic. Luke does not name Golgotha (as he also omitted the Semitic name of Gethsemane earlier), possibly because of his audience, but all three Synoptics give its meaning: "Skull" (κρανίον, *kranion*).[13] The name is not derived from the collection of the skulls of the dead (an idea that would greatly offend the Jews), but because the hill protruded from the ground in the shape of a skull (Plummer 1896: 530; Fitzmyer 1985: 1503; Jeremias 1926b). In this public locale, Jesus is placed on the cross, an innocent between two guilty men.

None of the Synoptics makes it clear that Jesus was nailed to the cross, but John 20:25 and Col. 2:14 indicate that at least his hands were nailed (also suggested in Luke 24:40). John specifies that his hands were nailed, but his feet may have been tied. All make it clear that Jesus was placed between two other criminals (Matt. 27:38 = Mark 15:27; John 19:18), though Matthew and Mark use a different term to refer to Jesus' left (εὐώνυμος [*euōnymos*; BAGD 329–30; BAA 666] as opposed to Luke's ἀριστερός [*aristeros*; BAGD 106; BAA 214; elsewhere in the Gospels only at Matt. 6:3 and Mark 10:37]). Independent multiple sources with differing terminology thus attest to Jesus' crucifixion.

ii. Jesus' Call to Forgive (23:34)

23:34 Jesus spoke as he suffered, asking God to forgive his enemies, since they did not know what they were doing. The meaning of this prayer is disputed (see the additional note for the dispute over its originality). Some argue that Jesus can be praying only for the Roman soldiers who executed him in ignorance (Arndt 1956: 469). The rationale for this view is twofold: (1) catastrophe for Israel is already predicted in God's plan and thus forgiveness is not available and (2) the nation is not ignorant of what it is doing.

The prayer must, however, be primarily for the Jews, though Luke's readers might apply it to all who had a role in killing Jesus. First, the Romans have not yet been explicitly mentioned in this pericope, so they are an unlikely referent (Fitzmyer 1985: 1503–4). Second, Stephen's parallel prayer (Acts 7:60) almost requires that this prayer be for Jesus' accusers. Third, the passage appears to have a conceptual tie to Isa. 53:12, where the Servant suffers for the transgressors, a point that has slightly more force if Jews are meant (Tiede 1988: 417; Plummer 1896: 531–32). The ignorance that Jesus

---

13. The name *Calvary* comes from *calvaria*, the Latin translation of κρανίον; Plummer 1896: 531; Geldenhuys 1951: 613. R. Brown 1994: 938–40 discusses the location of Golgotha and decides for the traditional location associated now with the Church of the Holy Sepulchre in what is called the Christian quarter of Jerusalem. Nolland 1993b: 1145 expresses less certainty about the locale.

attributes to the nation is not a lack of knowledge, but an erroneous judgment about God's activity, since the apostles will call the nation to repent for this ignorance as Jesus had warned them (Tiede 1988: 418; Luke 13:34; 19:42; Acts 2:38; 3:19; 13:38; 17:30). The issue of national forgiveness is also not an obstacle, since individuals can still respond. As to the inevitability of national catastrophe, Jesus is not asking for the judgment on the nation to be put off. The national consequences stand.

Jesus thus intercedes for his enemies, portraying the very standard he sets for his disciples in the Sermon on the Plain (Luke 6:29, 35; 1 Pet. 2:19–23; Ernst 1977: 634). He does not curse his opponents (contrast 2 Macc. 7:19, 34–35; 4 Macc. 9:15; Schweizer 1984: 360).[14] The moral tone of Jesus' response is high, although this lack of vindictiveness is also found in a few other ancient works.[15] Thinking of others, Jesus still desires that they change their thinking (as some do in the Book of Acts) and that God not hold their act against them. Jesus' love is evident even from the cross.

In language that recalls Ps. 22:18 [22:19 MT], Luke notes how the soldiers gambled for Jesus' garments by lot (all of the Gospels allude to this psalm: Mark 15:24 = Matt. 27:35; John 19:24; on the background to the distribution of the clothes of the crucified, see R. Brown 1994: 953–58). The original psalm portrays the mocking suffered by a righteous sufferer. The use of the psalm is thus typological and prophetic: Jesus is the model of righteous suffering at the hands of those who oppose God's people. Gambling for clothes is customary at crucifixion and is the final humiliation one suffers upon execution. One dies in shame and largely unclothed. R. Brown (1994: 870, 952–53) notes the custom of being crucified unclothed (Artemidorus Daldianus, *Oneirokritika* 2.53), though in Jewish executions this appears to have been delayed to the last possible moment (Dionysius of Halicarnassus, *Roman Antiquities* 7.69.2; Valerius Maximus, *Facta* 1.7.4; Josephus, *Antiquities* 19.4.5 §270). Even though some victims were beheaded or dragged around the public square (Josephus, *Jewish War* 2.12.7 §246; *Antiquities* 20.6.3 §136), disrobing is not mentioned. Other texts speak of the possibility of a loincloth (Jub. 3.30–31; 7.20). John 19:23–25 makes it clear that the

---

14. Jesus' tone differs from the "martyr" parallels in 2 Macc. 5–6 (where the intercession is a declaration of the sufferer's righteousness and faithfulness) and 7:14, 17, 19 (where the condemned promise God's vengeance on the executioner). On the other hand, some Jewish texts appeal to mercy for all, even sinners (Jon. 4:11; T. Ben. 4.2; Philo, *Flaccus* 2 §7; R. Brown 1994: 974), a merciful attitude that also appears in the church fathers (Ignatius, *Ephesians* 10.2–3; Justin Martyr, *Apology* 1.14).

15. In *Martyrdom and Ascension of Isaiah* 5.14, Isaiah quietly endures being sawed in two. Other ancients quietly accepting death are Socrates (Plato, *Apology* 39c) and Stoic philosophers (Epictetus 1.19.8); see Daube 1961: 61–65.

gambling concerned the outer garment that Jesus had received at his trial.

Matthew and Mark are parallel to Luke, though Luke has more distinct terminology. Matthew and Mark have a participle for casting lots (βάλλοντες, *ballontes*) where Luke has a verb (ἔβαλον, *ebalon*). Only Mark specifies the purpose for the lot: to see who would keep the clothes. Matthew adds a note that they sat and watched Jesus. In Matthew and Mark, it is clear that these soldiers are Roman, but Luke does not specify their identity.

iii. Scoffing and Mocking (23:35–38)

Luke divides those observing this historic moment into two groups: watchers and mockers.[16] The people (λαός, *laos*) stand watching. The term for watching, θεωρῶν (*theōrōn*), comes from Ps. 22:7 [21:8 LXX], the same "righteous sufferer" psalm cited in the previous verse. In the psalm the same people both watch and mock. They are hostile to the sufferer. Luke's separation of "watchers" from "mockers" suggests that the people who watch are curious (3 Macc. 5:24) rather than neutral or mourning (against Plummer 1896: 532, who sees them as hostile). They want to see the outcome of their demand for Jesus' death (Luke 23:21, 23). Their actions are not as severe as the leaders, but neither are they supportive of Jesus (contra R. Brown 1994: 989, who sees them more positively, setting up later responses in Acts 2:41, 47; 4:4; 6:1). But the call for repentance in Acts 2 shows that the crowd was not positive on crucifixion day, but neither did they directly rebuke Jesus. They merely observe what is taking place.

23:35

The second group, the leaders, mock Jesus. The key verb *mock* (ἐκμυκτηρίζω, *ekmyktērizō*, lit., to turn up one's nose, to sneer) alludes to Ps. 22:7 [21:8 LXX] (elsewhere in the NT only at Luke 16:14; BAGD 243; BAA 490; Bertram, *TDNT* 4:798–99). Jesus is again the righteous sufferer. Perhaps because he is following another source or more possibly because he is focusing on the leadership's rebuke, Luke does not record that the mockers "wag their heads" and urge Jesus to save himself in light of the saying that he would destroy the temple and rebuild it in three days (Matt. 27:40 = Mark 15:29–30).[17]

The leaders mock Jesus' ability to deliver others (i.e., perform miraculous works for them) and not himself. They derisively taunt him

---

16. Plummer 1896: 532 notes that in the entire account four groups engage in different activities: the people watch, the leaders sneer, the soldiers mock, and the robber blasphemes. Two people from a later subunit could be added to this list: a robber exercises faith and a centurion observes injustice.

17. Luke's silence about the temple here is similar to his previous silence about the same charge in 22:54–71.

to save himself if "this one" (οὗτος, *houtos*) is the anointed of God, the elect one. Precedent for such taunting may be found in Wis. 2–5, especially 2:17–22, which teaches that God will aid the righteous when they are tested (Tiede 1988: 418; Danker 1988: 374). If Jesus is God's elect, God will certainly save him. The taunt is sarcastic: they think they have stopped Jesus, they are feeling good about having executed him. The taunt also echoes Ps. 22:8 [21:9 LXX]. But God will answer their taunt in a surprising way in just a few days. God's Chosen One (cf. Luke 2:26; 9:20) will be vindicated (Fitzmyer 1985: 1505; Schrenk, *TDNT* 4:189; Jeremias, *TDNT* 5:689; Luke 9:35; Isa. 42:1; John 1:34; 1 Enoch 39.6; 40.5; 45.3–4; 49.2; 51.3–5).

The taunt is similar to Mark 15:31–32 = Matt. 27:42–43 (which almost match). The taunt is more direct in Matthew and Mark: "He saved others; he cannot save himself." The mockers then call on "the King of Israel" to come down from the cross (Mark adds an address to the Christ before calling on the king). The purpose for Jesus' coming down from the cross is that the sneerers might believe (Mark: see and believe). Ironically, Jesus will do this in his resurrection, but many will not respond. They will not keep their promise. At this point Matthew has an additional taunt: "He trusts in God; let God deliver him now, if he (God) desires him; for he said, 'I am the Son of God.'" Matthew's and Mark's witnesses are all hostile throughout the crucifixion until the centurion at the end. Luke has a simpler and more summary account, but whether he has simplified a source or used an additional source is not clear. Despite Luke's simplicity, he has a more complex portrait of the witnesses. He presents a fuller range of responses to the cross.

23:36 The third group, the soldiers, also mock (ἐμπαίζω, *empaizō*) Jesus and offer him some vinegar.[18] Ὄξος (*oxos*) describes a sour or dry wine as opposed to a sweet wine (Fitzmyer 1985: 1505; BAGD 574; BAA 1164; elsewhere in the NT only at Matt. 27:48 = Mark 15:36 = John 19:29–30 [three times]; cf. Ruth 2:14). R. Brown (1994: 997) calls it a "cheap wine" offered as a "burlesque gift." Its sharp taste was said to remove thirst more effectively than water, and since it was cheaper than regular wine it was used among the poor (MM 452–53; SB 2:264; P. Lond. 1245 line 9). Apparently the offer is made as a joke, since it is accompanied with a challenge that Jesus, if he is king, should save himself (Luke 23:37). Luce (1933: 351) doubts the historicity of the remark, saying that it is inappropriate for Roman soldiers on duty, but if the Jewish leadership was taunting

18. Ἐμπαίζω is used elsewhere by Luke at 14:29; 18:32; 22:63; 23:11; BAGD 255 §1; BAA 516. Mark 15:31 = Matt. 27:41 uses ἐμπαίζω of the rulers' ridicule, which Luke describes in 23:35 with ἐκμυκτηρίζω.

Jesus, others would likely have joined the mocking (R. Brown 1994: 998 sees Luke as responsible for this summary). The point is that neither Jew nor Gentile understand what they are doing in nailing Jesus to the cross.

Matthew 27:48 = Mark 15:36 has this offer later in the account, after Jesus cries out with Ps. 22:1 [22:2 MT]. Luke lacks this cry, possibly because he does not typically include Aramaic phrases (e.g., Golgotha in 23:33). In the other Synoptics, Jesus takes the drink, the soldiers think that he is calling for Elijah and suggest waiting to see if God answers, but instead Jesus dies. That the soldiers think Jesus is calling Elijah may suggest that some of them are Jewish. The other Synoptics suggest an allusion to Ps. 69:21 [69:22 MT], where the enemies of the righteous sufferer give vinegar for drink (1QH 4.11; Ellis 1974: 268). John 19:28–30 also notes this sequence later and recalls that Jesus said that he was thirsty. This prompted the offer of a sponge full of vinegar or hyssop, which he received before dying. That the soldiers had to put the drink on a reed to reach Jesus' mouth suggests that he was raised up slightly on the cross. Jesus receives this act of kindness, but it seems to be distinct from the earlier sequence that Luke mentions. It may indicate the presence of another source (Grundmann 1963: 431; Marshall 1978: 869 [uncertain]).

23:37 The soldiers' mocking imitates the leadership, presented in a first-class condition: "Let's assume you are the King of the Jews, then save yourself!" The second note of mocking shows how the Romans viewed Jesus' claim of being the Anointed One, the Christ (23:35). They saw a regal claim in the term. The taunt is given because the belief is that Jesus cannot fulfill it. The remark about kingship recalls the examination of Pilate in 23:3 and is based on the note hung on the cross (23:38). (For the absence of a Synoptic parallel, see the exegesis of 23:36.) Ernst (1977: 636) sees a probable extra source.

23:38 A placard that revealed the charge was hung on the cross above Jesus. Such inscriptions (ἐπιγραφή, *epigraphē*) usually contained the criminal's name and the charge for which he was being executed (Fitzmyer 1985: 1505; BAGD 291; BAA 590; Mark 15:26; cf. Matt. 22:20 = Mark 12:16 = Luke 20:24).[19] In Latin, this inscription was

19. Such notations by the state are common: Josephus, *Antiquities* 15.8.1 §272 (inscriptions that commemorate Caesar and present trophies of war); Suetonius, *Caligula* 32.2; Eusebius, *Ecclesiastical History* 5.1.44. In these other texts, the inscription is borne by the criminal or by someone in front of the cross (Nolland 1993b: 1148). Pilate's inscription stands behind the initials INRI seen in many famous paintings of this scene. INRI is an acronym for Iesus Nazarenus Rex Iudaeorum (Jesus of Nazareth, King of the Jews), wording that parallels John's Gospel.

called a *titulus*, which is what John 19:19 alludes to in noting that Pilate wrote the inscription (BDF §5.1). The Lucan wording of the inscription matches Mark 15:26 except for Luke's derogatory οὗτος (*houtos*, this one), which he uses constantly in his account (23:4, 14, 18, 22, 35). Matthew 27:37 shares all of Luke's elements but in a different word order: Οὗτός ἐστιν Ἰησοῦς ὁ βασιλεὺς τῶν Ἰουδαίων (*houtos estin Iēsous ho basileus tōn Ioudaiōn*, this is Jesus, the King of the Jews). He has only the additional warning of Jesus. John 19:19 is even more complete, giving Jesus' name, origin, and crime: Ἰησοῦς ὁ Ναζωραῖος ὁ βασιλεὺς τῶν Ἰουδαίων (*Iēsous ho Nazōraios ho basileus tōn Ioudaiōn*, Jesus the Nazarean, the King of the Jews). Both Matthew and Mark note that the inscription bears the charge: Matthew says that they put the charge (τὴν αἰτίαν, *tēn aitian*) over Jesus' head, while Mark refers to the inscription of the charge (τῆς αἰτίας, *tēs aitias*). John simply notes that the inscription is "on the cross." All these minor details are differences of summary. The title *King of the Jews* indicates the main issue of Jesus' trials.

c. Two Thieves (23:39–43)
i. One Criminal Rebukes Jesus (23:39)

23:39 Luke now returns to the two criminals (κακούργων, *kakourgōn*; 23:32, 33; Grundmann, *TDNT* 3:484), who are "hanging" (κρεμασθέντων, *kremasthentōn*) beside Jesus. In many texts κρεμάννυμι (*kremannymi*) refers to hanging on a cross or tree (Gen. 40:19; Deut. 21:22; Esth. 8:7; Acts 5:30; 10:39; Gal. 3:13; Bertram, *TDNT* 3:918; Marshall 1978: 871; BAGD 450; BAA 914; BDR §101.42). One of the condemned criminals blasphemes Jesus, that is, he speaks with sarcastic disrespect (Luke 22:65). His taunt recalls those by the leadership and the soldiers (23:35, 37). It is expressed as total sarcasm, using the more bitter form of the first-class condition as an interrogative (Klostermann 1929: 229; Plummer 1896: 534): "Are you not (οὐχί, *ouchi*) the Christ? Then save yourself and us!" The premise is presented as true, as the "current option," for "the sake of argument," but it is not what the speaker really believes. The trite call for Jesus to save is spreading through the observers. All accost Jesus. Even a dying criminal makes a dig. But just in case, he ends with a selfish request for Jesus to save him too! The unbelief and callousness evident here is why Luke calls the remark blasphemous. The irony is great, and so is the blindness. The Righteous One dies while being taunted by the unrighteous. Everything is reversed from what one would expect. Luke as narrator has much more respect for Jesus than the criminal does.

This exchange is found only in Luke, though it is similar to Matt. 27:44 = Mark 15:32, where both criminals are said to reproach (ὠνείδιζον, *ōneidizon*) Jesus. The absence of any positive note in the other Gospels has caused great speculation. In fact, Luce (1933: 351) goes so far as to call the Lucan account unhistorical. Plummer (1896: 533–34) notes three possible explanations for this difference:

1. At the start both criminals revile Jesus, but the second criminal is later impressed with Jesus and changes his mind. This old explanation goes back to Origen, Chrysostom, and Jerome (Arndt 1956: 470).
2. In the other Synoptics, the criminals reproach Jesus for not doing enough against Rome, while in Luke only one robber sarcastically taunts Jesus. This view assumes that the robbers are Zealots or political insurrectionists, which is not clear in any of the accounts.
3. Each approach reflects different sources (Plummer's view). The other Synoptics treat the criminals as a group and depict only their reviling. Luke has an additional source that is aware of the positive response of the one robber.[20]

Views 1 and 3 are not incompatible. In fact, both are probably the case.

ii. A Second Criminal Rebukes the First and Confesses His Own Guilt (23:40–41)

The second criminal steps in to rebuke (ἐπιτιμάω, *epitimaō*; see the exegesis of 4:35) the first in simple terms: does he not fear God (οὐδὲ φοβῇ . . . τὸν θεόν, *oude phobē . . . ton theon*; Luke 1:50; 18:2; Acts 10:2, 22, 35; 13:16, 26)? The criminal offering the rebuke clearly sees the event as God's just judgment on them, but he also sees the taunting of Jesus as an expression of intense hypocrisy for which the other criminal would pay. His remarks are really a commentary on all who taunt Jesus, but especially the one who is justly suffering for crimes committed. God will take offense at what is said about his agent, since Jesus suffers death unrighteously. The criminal asks, "How can you taunt this innocent man when you are deservedly suffering the same sentence? What gives you the right and the nerve to put him down?"

23:40

20. Noting overlaps of Lucan style, R. Brown 1994: 1001 rejects the presence of a source, though he acknowledges that perhaps the paradise saying goes back to Jesus. This view fits Brown's consistent tendency to minimize sources in the material, often limiting himself to Mark. But given the nature of this event and its importance, as well as the orality of the culture, it is unlikely that Luke's sources were limited to Mark.

23:41   The second criminal confesses that he and his companion are guilty of the charges for which they are being executed.[21] He makes a double confession of guilt: they suffer "justly" (δικαίως, dikaiōs), and they receive things "worthy" (ἄξιος, axios) of their crimes. The statement is one of recognition and repentance. The criminal also testifies to Jesus, so his next request is received by Jesus. It is often said that this criminal did nothing in terms of responding to Jesus; but this speech is an expression of his faith and what he learned while facing death. The criminal knows that Jesus has done nothing "improper" (ἄτοπος, atopos, lit., out of place or inappropriate; BAGD 120; BAA 241–42; elsewhere with this sense at Acts 25:5; elsewhere in the NT only at Acts 28:6 and 2 Thess. 3:2; cf. Job 27:6; 34:12; 35:13; Prov. 30:20; 2 Macc. 14:23). Jesus is innocent. This is the sixth confession of Jesus' innocence from a third source (Pilate and Herod also called Jesus innocent; Luke 23:4, 14, 15 [twice], 22).

iii. The Second Criminal Makes a Request (23:42)

23:42   The criminal moves past confessing his sin and his belief in Jesus to request that Jesus remember (μιμνῄσκομαι, mimnēskomai; BAGD 522 §1c; BAA 1057 §1c; Epictetus 3.24.100) him. This request is similar to funerary inscriptions requesting that the dead be placed with the righteous at the judgment (Gen. 40:14; Ps. 106:4; Fitzmyer 1985: 1510; Marshall 1978: 872; Jeremias, *TDNT* 5:770). He is the only person to address Jesus simply by his name. The intimacy, setting, and sincerity are poignant (R. Brown 1994: 1005).

    The timing of when Jesus is to remember the confessing criminal in the kingdom is textually disputed (see the second additional note on 23:42). Jesus will remember him either in the present (accepting εἰς [eis, into] as original) or by letting him be among the righteous who return with him (accepting ἐν [en, in] as original). Given the reference about entry into the kingdom, a request about being part of Messiah's returning entourage is slightly more likely (i.e., view 2). The criminal seems to anticipate that Jesus will one day (maybe even soon) have great power. When that happens, he wants to be there. The criminal does not, however, expect immediate deliverance, since in Judaism that was associated with the consummation. The remark is a messianic confession and expresses the hope of being with Messiah and the righteous. Plummer (1896: 535) summarizes the verse nicely: "Some saw Jesus raise the dead, and did not believe. The robber sees Him being put to death, and yet believes."

---

21. In some church tradition, the confessing criminal's name is given as Dismas or Dysmas; Acts of Pilate 10.2 (Schneemelcher 1991–92: 1.512); Fitzmyer 1985: 1509. See n. 11.

The robber is an example of one who finally confesses when he confronts his inevitable death. He wants to follow Jesus even into glory.

iv. Jesus' Comforting Reply (23:43)

Jesus' response goes beyond the criminal's request: "The criminal's petition expresses the hope that he will attain to life at the parousia; Jesus' reply assures him of immediate entry into paradise" (Marshall 1978: 873). The solemnity of the reply is noted by the expression ἀμήν σοι λέγω (amēn soi legō, truly I say to you).[22] Jesus does not speak of the unspecified future, but of the immediate present. The request is granted today (σήμερον, sēmeron). This emphasis on the current day involves an immediacy that Luke likes to use (2:11; 4:21; 5:26; 13:32–33; 22:34, 61; Grundmann 1963: 434). Ellis (1965–66) and Fitzmyer (1985: 1510) argue that σήμερον is a reference to the immediate present rather than to the day of Jesus' death, which is possible. They argue that Jesus comes into messianic authority as a result of resurrection-ascension, so that the actual day of being with Jesus is a few days hence. Yet this seems to split hairs too finely. It seems more likely that some sense of moving immediately into an intermediate state, conscious of God's blessing, is alluded to here; that is, it is not likely that Jesus was in limbo for a few days. He seeks to encourage the criminal in his confession. Jewish doctrine held that the dead go to Sheol. The concept of delay of blessing pertains only to obtaining the final resurrection body. This issue is bound up with the meaning of παράδεισος (paradeisos, paradise).

23:43

The term παράδεισος comes into Greek from the Persian world, though related terms appear in noneschatological contexts (Gen. 2:8; 13:10; Neh. 2:8; Song 4:13; Eccles. 2:5; BAGD 614 §2; BAA 1241 §2; Fitzmyer 1985: 1510–11; Jeremias, *TDNT* 5:765–73; Grelot 1967; R. Brown 1994: 1010–12; Josephus, *Antiquities* 1.1.3 §37). The term later came to refer to the eschatological garden or paradise (Isa. 51:3; Ezek. 28:13; 31:8). In Judaism, it referred to the abode of the righteous (1 Enoch 17–19; 32.3; 60.8; 61.12; 2 Enoch 65.10; T. Levi 18.10–11; T. Dan 5.12; Ps. Sol. 14.3; *Sipre* 307.3 on Deut. 32:4 [= Neusner 1987: 2.319]; SB 2:264).[23] Arndt (1956: 471) correctly equates its meaning with Abraham's bosom, an image that also highlights immediate reception after death (Luke 16:23). The phrase appears in two other NT texts, 2 Cor. 12:4 (= 12:3 in RSV) and Rev. 2:7, both of which seem to allude to the heavenly realm where

---

22. This is the only place in Luke where Jesus addresses a single person with ἀμὴν λέγω, though he likes the expression: 4:24; 12:37; 18:17, 29; 21:32; Plummer 1896: 535.

23. On the related idea of the third heaven (οὐρανός), see BAGD 594 §1e and BAA 1202–3 §1e.

the righteous are gathered. Thus, Jesus promises this criminal that today he will be with him and live among the righteous (Acts 3:21; 7:55). Jesus' reply also suggests that the criminal will be in some conscious, intermediate state until the resurrection, though this conclusion is implied, rather than explicit. Death is a mere transition for this man. He too will experience victory and deliverance through the King he confesses, and that deliverance is immediate (Nolland 1993b: 1152). Hope is thus provided by his confession and the Messiah's compassion. Jesus can and does save, despite what the taunts suggest. The irony should not be missed. A call to Jesus yields immediate results.

d. Jesus' Death (23:44–49)
i. Cosmic Signs (23:44–45)

23:44   As the crucifixion proceeds, the heavens begin to comment. The crucifixion began at the third hour (9:00 A.M.; Mark 15:25); at about[24] the sixth hour (midday), darkness fell over the entire land and lasted until the ninth hour (3:00 P.M.).[25] The Gospel of Peter 5.15 (Schneemelcher 1991–92: 1.223) also describes this phenomenon, saying that darkness held sway over all Judea and that the people feared lest the sun set while Jesus was alive.

The darkness recalls an eschatological motif from the judgment imagery of the day of the Lord (Amos 8:9; Joel 2:10; 2:30–31 [3:3–4 MT]; Zeph. 1:15; Fitzmyer 1985: 1517). Given this background, these heavenly portents signal the significance of the events surrounding Jesus' death. An eschatologically significant time of judgment is present. God is watching and signaling his presence. The day-of-the-Lord imagery is not, however, consummated here, since in Acts 2:16–18 the day of the Lord is seen as something that still approaches, rather than something that had been fulfilled at the cross. It is questioned whether the Gentiles in Luke's audience would appreciate such imagery. R. Brown's reading (1994: 1042–43) of the darkness as a theological symbol in contrast to Jesus as light (Luke 1:78–79) is probably correct, though such a view need not exclude judgment. Brown also ties darkness to the Greek motif of signs at the death of a great person (Plutarch, *Romulus* 27.6; Plutarch, *Caesar* 69.4; Ovid, *Fasti* 2.493; Cicero, *Republic* 6.22 §24; Pliny, *Natural History* 2.30 §98; Grández 1989). Such background is not limited to

---

24. Luke uses ὡσεί (about) frequently to show approximate time; Luke 3:23; 9:14 (twice), 28; 22:41, 59; 24:11; cf. Acts 2:15; 3:1; 10:3, 9; 23:23). Ἤδη (already) is also frequent: Matthew uses it seven times, Mark eight times, Luke ten times, elsewhere in the NT thirty-six times; Plummer 1896: 536; Untergassmair 1980: 85 n. 372.

25. There is no conflict with John 19:14, which refers to Jesus' standing before Pilate at the sixth hour, since John likely reckons the day as starting at midnight.

Greco-Roman contexts, for the theistic Jewish culture also saw divinity active in all events (for the historicity debate, see the exegesis of 23:45). A foreboding mix of cosmic responses surround the cross.

Mark 15:33 is almost exact: he notes the time with the genitive absolute καὶ γενομένης (kai genomenēs, and when [the sixth hour] came), while Luke has the paratactic καὶ ἦν ἤδη ὡσεί (kai ēn ēdē hōsei, and it was already about). Matthew 27:45 starts with ἀπὸ δέ (apo de, but from) and also uses a different phrase to describe how the darkness covers the whole earth: ἐπὶ πᾶσαν (epi pasan, over all) versus Mark's and Luke's ἐφ᾽ ὅλην (eph' holēn, upon the whole).

The sun was "failing" (ἐκλείπω, ekleipō; BAGD 242; BAA 488; else- **23:45** where in the NT only at Luke 16:9; 22:32; Heb. 1:12). The debate whether this was an eclipse stretches back to the third century (Arndt 1956: 472–73; Plummer 1896: 537; defended by Tertullian, *Apology* 21). Many regard this remark as legendary because an eclipse is impossible at full moon (Luce 1933: 352; Creed 1930: 288).[26] Conzelmann (*TDNT* 7:439) argues that the details were added to impart a salvific significance to the event, but Fitzmyer (1985: 1518–19) correctly notes that this imagery has no such motif. Others suggest that a Mediterranean wind, a sirocco, was capable of darkening the sun (Fitzmyer 1985: 1518; Marshall 1978: 875; G. R. Driver 1965: 331–37). Plummer (1896: 536) says more directly that the events may be attributed "either to a supernatural cause or to a providential coincidence." Such portents were common in Judaism and the ancient world (Fitzmyer 1985: 1518).[27] Their real presence is the reason some bystanders change their view of the event.

The darkness parallels the day-of-the-Lord imagery in the previous verse. This event is part of God's working; the signs picture judgment, as well as the temporary prevailing of darkness. The heavenly testimony combines with the ripping of the temple curtain to give a twofold sign from creation that Jesus' death is important in God's plan. Citing Caird (1980: 213–14), Fitzmyer (1985: 1513, 1517) holds that the cosmic portents in Mark's version are intended to be only symbolic. This explanation seems unlikely since in the Synoptic accounts the spectators at the crucifixion are impressed by the testimony of the cosmic events. What else would lead to the reflections

---

26. R. Brown 1994: 1040–42 discusses the eclipse options and finds none persuasive. He sees Luke creatively tying these details together, but in other cases where the Synoptics overlap Brown is less skeptical, so it is uncertain why he is hesitant here. Whether we have an eclipse or, more likely, some other form of darkening like a thick cloud, it is the timing of this event with Jesus' death that creates the sign.

27. For example, the sun turned away from Mark Antony's enemies (Josephus, *Antiquities* 14.12.3 §309), and many heavenly portents came with the temple's destruction (Josephus, *Jewish War* 6.5.3 §§288–300).

by the thief on the cross and the Roman centurion? These details are intended historically and literally (Nolland 1993b: 1156). Luke portrays Jesus' death as a public event that impressed a variety of people in a variety of ways.

Only Luke reports here the rending of the temple veil, which was made of fine Babylonian cloth of blue, scarlet, and purple (Matt. 27:51 = Mark 15:38 has it slightly later in the crucifixion account; Ellis 1974: 269; Jeremias 1969: 37; Josephus, *Jewish War* 5.5.4–5 §§207–21). Καταπέτασμα (*katapetasma*) is ambiguous (BAGD 416; BAA 845–46), however, since it is used of both the curtain that protected the Holy of Holies (Lev. 21:23; 24:3; Josephus, *Jewish War* 5.5.5 §219) and the curtain that separated the temple from the outer court (Exod. 26:37; 38:18; Num. 3:26; Josephus, *Jewish War* 5.5.4 §212). Many believe that καταπέτασμα refers to the inner curtain, because another term (κάλυμμα, *kalymma*; BAGD 400–401; BAA 813–14) is also used for the outer curtain (Exod. 27:16; Num. 3:25; Plummer 1896: 537–38; Arndt 1956: 473; Ellis 1974: 269; C. Schneider, *TDNT* 3:629).[28] Others argue that the public nature of this phenomenon would require that καταπέτασμα refer here to the outer curtain (Klostermann 1929: 227; Marshall 1978: 875; Fitzmyer 1985: 1518; Michel, *TDNT* 4:885 n. 21; Pelletier 1955; Pelletier 1958; Benoit 1969: 201; G. R. Driver 1965: 335–36). This argument is not entirely compelling, for the priests could have reported that the inner curtain was torn. A Jewish tradition about a similar event, along with the mysterious opening of the temple doors, is similarly ambiguous.[29] The tearing of either curtain would make the point that God is at work. It is slightly more likely that the outer curtain is meant, since the other signs associated with Jesus' death are so public.

The significance of the curtain's tearing operates at numerous levels (Ellis 1974: 268):

1. In association with the other signs, it pictures a time of judgment tied to the eschatological acts of God (R. Brown 1994: 1003–7).
2. It suggests the judgment that is coming on the temple (21:5–38; SB 1:1045). J. Green (1991) challenges this view by noting that the emphasis is not on the predicted judgment, but on the tem-

---

28. Schneider argues that the ripping of the outer curtain would have had no significance, but the ripping of any temple curtain would surely be important. Regardless of the location, it suggests an opening up of access to God.

29. Josephus, *Jewish War* 6.5.3 §§293–96, notes the mysterious opening of the temple doors at midnight on a Passover (but he doesn't give the year). T. Ben. 9.3 and T. Levi 10.3 refer to a rending of the temple curtain, but these references may be Christian interpolations; see M. De Jonge 1960: 222–26 (repr. pp. 233–37).

ple's cessation as the center of God's activity. In Green's view, the curtain's tearing signifies the end of the temple's dominant role as a sacred symbol.

3. It suggests that Jesus opens the doors to paradise (23:43). Sylva's variation (1986) of this view argues that it pictures heaven's open communion with Jesus (also Nolland 1993b: 1157–58).

4. A combination view is also possible. The association with paradise is likely because Jesus' death suggests that it is no longer necessary to worship God in the temple (Luke 19:45–20:18; John 4:21–24; Heb. 9–10). Perhaps the act should not be seen anthropologically, but in terms of theology proper. God is pictured coming out of his temple to reach out to all, he cannot be contained within it (Acts 7:45–50), and so Jesus' death represents the ultimate opening up of the way to God (Luke 5:31–32; 15:1–32; 19:10). The emphasis is not on atonement (as in Heb. 9–10), but on God's access to people.

Views 2 (specifically Green's approach) and 4 have the most merit.

As with the previous portent, some argue that the veil rending is a legendary detail. Others note that the same sirocco that darkened the sun could also have torn the temple curtain. Plummer's appeal (1896: 536) to supernatural causes or providential coincidence applies here as well. Luke has something definite in mind, not something fabricated or purely symbolic (against Nolland 1993b: 1158). Placed in such a cosmically active context, a mere symbolic assertion of the temple-veil rending is unlikely.

Luke has this text earlier than the parallels in Matt. 27:51–53 = Mark 15:38, which mention the curtain rending after Jesus dies. Arndt (1956: 473) regards the Lucan arrangement as topical so as to place all the cosmic portents together. Matthew and Mark both speak of the curtain's being ripped in two from top to bottom. All the Synoptics use the same ambiguous term to refer to the veil. Luke omits any reference to speculation that Jesus called for Elijah. These stylistic and editorial differences allow the accounts to complement one another.

ii. Jesus' Final Words: A Prayer of Trust (23:46)

23:46 Jesus dies with a cry of faith. Luke notes that he cries out in a loud voice as he makes his final statement (Marshall 1978: 875; Fitzmyer 1985: 1519; Plummer 1896: 538).[30] The Synoptic parallels also note

30. Φωνὴ μεγάλη (great cry) occurs frequently in the NT (e.g., Acts 16:28; Mark 1:26; Rev. 14:18). Luke often has cognate constructions (2:8, 9; 7:29; 12:50; 17:24; 22:15).

this cry: κράξας φωνῇ μεγάλῃ (*kraxas phōnē megalē*, cried out in a loud voice; Matt. 27:50) and ἀφεὶς φωνὴν μεγάλην (*apheis phōnēn megalēn*, uttered a loud cry; Mark 15:37). Matthew and Mark do not, however, detail the content of this second cry. They both note earlier that Ps. 22:1 [22:2 MT] was the content of Jesus' first cry, but here they only note the second cry without giving its content. Luke alone supplies content, though John 19:30 has a short remark: "It is finished" (τετέλεσται, *tetelestai*).[31]

Jesus' final words in Luke before his death come from Ps. 31:5 [31:6 MT]. In the original psalm, the remarks are the prayer of a righteous sufferer who wishes to be delivered from his enemies and expresses trust that his fate is in God's hands. Jesus' remarks are an expression of righteous faith. The use of the psalm is typico-prophetic: Jesus is the righteous sufferer *par excellence*. As he faces death, he expresses his trust that God will care for him. In fact, this is a call to resurrect him. Acts 2:27–28, 31 and 13:35–36 appeal to Ps. 16 to develop what happened to Jesus upon his death (Neyrey 1985: 151–53). Jesus had made numerous predictions of his resurrection (Luke 9:22; 18:33; 22:69; 23:43). This promise is alluded to later in 24:7, 26, 44, 46, and Paul also alludes to it when he says that he is on trial for the hope of resurrection from the dead (Acts 23:6; 24:15; 26:6, 8). Jesus' prayer of trust is thus an expression of submission to God's will, in which Jesus expresses faith that God will deliver him. Jesus is a model of the dying righteous one who can rest in God. Such hope is also expressed by Stephen in Acts 7:59, whose death mirrors that of Jesus (also 1 Pet. 4:19).

The prayer contains an address and a statement of faith. The address πάτερ (*pater*, Father) is frequent in Luke (10:21; 11:2; 22:42; 23:34) and shows the special familial appeal that Jesus makes. Jesus is giving over his spirit to God's care.[32] Χείρ (*cheir*, hand) indicates God's care (John 10:29; Acts 4:28, 30; 1 Pet. 5:6; BAGD 880 §2aβ; BAA 1756 §2aβ). Interestingly, Ps. 31 was used in later Judaism as an evening prayer. God was asked to care for and protect during sleep (*b. Ber.* 5a; SB 2:269; Marshall 1978: 876; Jeremias 1926a: 126 n. 3). Jesus submits to his death. He "sleeps" and leaves his vindication to God.

---

31. John records four fulfillments of Scripture in Jesus' final hours: John 19:24 (Ps. 22:18 [22:19 MT]), John 19:28 (Ps. 22:15 [22:16 MT]), John 19:36 (Exod. 12:46), and John 19:37 (Zech. 12:10); Neyrey 1985: 147.

32. Παρατίθημι (to give over) occurs elsewhere of divine protection at Luke 12:48; Acts 14:23; 20:32; 1 Pet. 4:19; Ps. 31:5 [30:6 LXX]; cf. 1 Tim. 1:18; 2 Tim. 2:2; Tob. 1:14; 4:1, 20; 1 Macc. 9:35; BAGD 623 §2bβ; BAA 1258–59 §2bβ. The reference to Jesus' πνεῦμα (spirit) indicates his person; BAGD 674 §2; BAA 1355–56 §2; Matt. 27:50 = John 19:30; Luke 8:55; Acts 7:59; Rom. 1:4; 1 Tim. 3:16; Heb. 12:23; 1 Pet. 3:18–19; Rev. 11:11.

With this hope, Jesus dies. Luke and Mark 15:37 both use the euphemistic ἐκπνέω (*ekpneō*, to breathe out, expire; BAGD 244; BAA 492; Josephus, *Antiquities* 12.9.1 §357), while Matt. 27:50 has ἀφῆκεν τὸ πνεῦμα (*aphēken to pneuma*, he yielded his spirit) and John 19:30 has παρέδωκεν τὸ πνεῦμα (*paredōken to pneuma*, he gave up his spirit). Luke notes that death followed this last utterance. It is after this that Matt. 27:51–53 = Mark 15:38 describes the veil's rending. Matthew also uniquely records that an earthquake took place when Jesus died and many saints were subsequently resurrected. Luke's use of Ps. 31 probably reflects an additional source, as do the unique Matthean details ("a pre-Lukan impulse" according to Nolland 1993b: 1158).

iii. A Centurion's Remark and the Crowd's Mourning (23:47–48)

A centurion watches all that takes place. The title ἑκατοντάρχης **23:47** (*hekatontarchēs*) describes the Roman soldier in charge of the crucifixion and indicates that he led a group of one hundred soldiers (also Luke 7:2, 6). Matthew 27:54 has the related ἑκατόνταρχος (*hekatontarchos*), while Mark 15:39 has the Latin equivalent ὁ κεντυρίων (*ho kentyriōn*), from which we get our term *centurion* (BDR §5.1a.3). Recension B of the Acts of Pilate 11.2 gives the centurion's name as Loginus, which means "soldier with a spear," a detail that alludes to John 19:34 (Fitzmyer 1985: 1519; Plummer 1896: 539). As the centurion sees what has happened, he praises (δοξάζω, *doxazō*) God.[33]

Upon observing what has happened, the centurion utters the scene's final remark, which functions as a judgment over the events. The remark is significant because it comes from a Gentile. The centurion declares that Jesus was δίκαιος (*dikaios*; BAGD 196 §3; BAA 394 §3; eleven times in Luke and six times in Acts). Δίκαιος normally means "righteous" (Nolland 1993b: 1158–59), but it can also mean "innocent" (Prov. 6:17; Joel 3:19 [4:19 LXX]; Jon. 1:14; Matt. 23:35; 27:19; James 5:6; 1 Pet. 3:18; Plummer 1896: 539; Fitzmyer 1985: 1520; Marshall 1978: 876). In this legal context, the more natural meaning is "innocent," since numerous confessions of Jesus' innocence have preceded this scene (Luke 23:4, 14, 22, 41; Kilpatrick 1942). R. Brown (1994: 1163–67) prefers "just" (i.e., righteous), which he correctly notes entails innocence. Brown posits three rea-

---

33. Matthew uses δοξάζω (to praise) four times, Mark once, and John twenty-three times. Of Luke's fourteen uses, five are in Acts, five are in unique Lucan material (2:20; 4:15; 7:16; 13:13; 17:15), one in agreement with Mark (5:26), and three in pericopes parallel to Mark but Mark lacks the term (5:25; 18:43; 23:47); Untergassmair 1980: 91 n. 408; Plummer 1896: 539.

sons for Luke's change of Mark (or Matthew): (1) an allusion to Ps. 31:18 [31:19 MT], (2) the use of the title *Righteous One* in the church (cf. Isa. 53:11; Jer. 23:5; Zech. 9:9), and (3) the correspondence to Luke's portrayal of Jesus in the earlier trial scene. But if the earlier declarations of innocence are the point, then an emphasis on Jesus' being innocent is central. The centurion's verdict affirms Jesus' character and the execution's injustice. Jesus is an innocent sufferer (a theme developed in Acts 3:14; 7:52; 13:28; 22:14; Neyrey 1985: 100). This seventh confession of innocence is the ultimate commentary on these events (cf. Luke 23:4, 14, 15 [twice], 22, 41). Jesus, not his executioners, stands before God without blame.

Luke's rendering of the remark is slightly simplified from Matt. 27:54 = Mark 15:39. Matthew's longer account notes that the centurion is not alone: other soldiers kept watch with him over Jesus, saw the earthquake, and were filled with awe. Mark notes only the centurion, who faced Jesus and saw him breathe his last. Matthew and Mark agree on what is said (though Matthew has it as a group confession): "Truly this (man) was the Son of God." For a Gentile, in this setting this statement probably has a functional, regal meaning instead of an ontological force. The soldiers accept Jesus' claims of sonship because of the signs accompanying his death. He is uniquely related to God and is his representative to the people. Pilate's inscription above the cross is true.

It is possible that Luke has rendered the centurion's remark in a more summarizing form, either because the expression *Son of God* would not mean anything to his audience or because it might be misunderstood to indicate that Jesus was *a* son of God (Schweizer, *TDNT* 8:381, prefers the latter). Conversely, Matthew and Mark might have rendered the result of what it means to regard Jesus as innocent. Perhaps several statements were said, especially given the multiple audience (noted by Matthew). The most likely choice, given Luke's preference for the term δίκαιος, is that he explicitly explains the force of the centurion's confession. If Jesus is confessed as Son of God, he is clearly innocent and has suffered unjustly—a theme that Luke develops more than the other Synoptics. Thus, the final note about Jesus' death is that he died as an innocent. He suffered unjustly at the hands of humans. He was whom he claimed to be—the King of the Jews, the Christ of God. A Gentile sensitive to the heavenly portents understands God's testimony. Many others had opinions about Jesus, but God's testimony is what counts. The centurion pictures a person sensitive and open to God's work.

23:48   The crowd (ὄχλοι, *ochloi*) now seems to reconsider its earlier decision to press for Jesus' death. The group mentioned here is simply the "gathered" (συμπαραγίνομαι, *symparaginomai*; BAGD 779; BAA

1554; a NT *hapax legomenon*) crowd, so some may not be the same
group that pressed for Jesus' death in 23:18, 21, 23. Luke 23:35 also
used θεωρέω (*theōreō*, to watch; BAGD 360 §1; BAA 731; BDR
§101.32; elsewhere in Luke at 10:18; 14:29; 21:6; 24:37, 39) to note
the people who watched these happenings. There were many witnesses to this public event, meaning that many could later describe
what took place. These people see the signs and perhaps hear the
centurion's reaction.

These events produce mourning over Jesus' death as the crowd
observes the "spectacle" (θεωρία, *theōria*, a NT *hapax legomenon*;
BAGD 360; BAA 732; Dan. 5:7; 2 Macc. 5:26; 15:12; 3 Macc. 5:24),
the array of crucifixion events. Mourning is reflected in the beating
of the breast (τύπτω, *typtō*; BAGD 830; BAA 1655; Stählin, *TDNT*
3:849). The same idiom appears in Luke 18:13, where the tax collector approached God in a mood of contrition (also Josephus, *Antiquities* 7.10.5 §252). Sorrow probably results from recognition of the
divine signs, which indicate that someone of significance has died.
This is not a routine mourning of death. Similar reflection comes
from another crowd in Acts 2:37–38 (Ernst 1977: 640). The remarks
suggest that this crowd has been moved by the events. They may be
seeking mercy for what has taken place. Some taking a close look at
Jesus may change their minds about him. They regret what has
taken place to the Innocent One, a view that sees their previous call
for his death as wrong. (I see more involved here than Nolland's
overtones [1993b: 1159] of regret, which is less precise than guilt
and contrition.)

After the events are finished, the crowd returns. Because many
pilgrims are present in the city, Luke uses the intransitive ὑποστρέφω (*hypostrephō*, to return) and does not say "returned home."
The pilgrims returned to where they were staying to celebrate the
Passover. Jesus' death went from being desired to being regretted.

iv. The Disciples and Women Watch (23:49)

Two other groups watching the events are listed separately because **23:49**
they are distinct from the crowd, having traveled with Jesus. First
are those who knew him (Marshall 1978: 877).[34] This is an oblique
way to refer to the disciples, who apparently did not feel safe since
they stand and observe events "from a distance" (ἀπὸ μακρόθεν, *apo
makrothen*). This seems to be a group broader than the Twelve (now
eleven), since Luke can identify the more narrow group specifically

---

34. Γνωστός (acquaintance, friend; BAGD 164 §1b; BAA 328 §1b) occurs elsewhere with this sense at Luke 2:44 and John 18:15–16 and in the LXX at 2 Kings
10:11; Ps. 30:12 [31:11 Engl.]; 54:14 [55:13 Engl.]; 87:9, 19 [88:8, 18 Engl.]; cf. 38:12.

by name (e.g., Acts 1:13–14). Second are the women who followed Jesus from Galilee.[35] This is a different group of women than those in 23:27. Some of these women were mentioned in 8:1–3, and others will be noted in 24:10 (Fitzmyer 1985: 1520–21). They had stayed faithful to Jesus and now stood to see all that was happening (ὁρῶσαι, *horōsai*, is a purpose participle: "so that they could see"; BDR §418.4.5).

The double grouping of Luke's text differs from Matt. 27:55–56 = Mark 15:40–41 = John 19:25–27. All the Synoptics use the phrase ἀπὸ μακρόθεν to show that the women are some distance from the events. Noting that these women are from Galilee, Matthew names three of them: Mary Magdalene, Mary the mother of James and Joseph, and the mother of the sons of Zebedee. Noting that many others also watched, Mark names Mary Magdalene, Mary the mother of James the younger and Joses, and Salome. Matthew and Mark are close verbally, sharing nineteen terms. Luke is more of a summary, except for the additional note that some friends were with the women (Marshall 1978: 877 sees a different source for Luke). John speaks of two people standing by the cross: Jesus' mother and the "disciple whom he (Jesus) loved," probably John himself. Jesus places his mother in John's care, a detail unique to John.

Summary   In Luke 23:26–49 Jesus goes to the cross in the midst of a swirl of events. His exhaustion causes someone to be appointed to bear the cross for him. The humanness of Jesus' death stands out here, but he is still in control. The mourning by women of the city causes him to issue a perilous warning. Jesus may be dying, but it is Jerusalem that will pay in judgment—judgment so severe that people will beg to die. Creation will reverse itself. By ridding themselves of Jesus, the nation increases its problems.

At the cross, five themes dominate. First, Jesus is crucified among the criminals. He shares the place of the unrighteous. Second are the variety of reactions produced by Jesus' death: people watch, rulers sneer, soldiers mock, and a criminal blasphemes. But another criminal confesses and asks for deliverance, and a centurion confesses Jesus' innocence, while women mourn and followers watch. The whole world watches with a variety of reactions. Third is Jesus' innocence, which is underlined by the criminal's and centurion's confessions. Jesus dies as an innocent, but he is in control, for he offers the confessing criminal paradise. He

35. The present participle συνακολουθοῦσαι (those who are following), given this context, suggests that they are still following him. Galilee is again mentioned as an important reference point in Jesus' ministry; Luke 4:14, 44 (variant reading); 17:11; 23:5; 24:6; Acts 10:37; 13:31; Untergassmair 1980: 103.

is the righteous sufferer, as the many allusions to the lament psalms show. But even more, he is judge and king. Fourth is creation's testimony to Jesus' death. The signs of darkness and the ripping of the temple veil testify that significant events are being fulfilled in God's plan. Creation speaks for the Creator on behalf of Jesus. Humans may have opinions about Jesus, but God sends the real testimony about him. The heavenly portents parallel the day of the Lord and also suggest judgment for rejecting the Son. Fifth is the exemplary trust of Jesus before his Father, entrusting his soul to God's care and relying on him for resurrection. It now remains only for God to act.

In the midst of the portrayal are numerous taunts to Jesus to save himself if he is a true miracle worker or king. Jesus does not save himself from death on the cross. God will, however, vindicate his Chosen One a few days hence. Those who reject Jesus think they have him, but the resurrection will show that Jesus has authority over them. As Jesus testified at his own trial, "From now on the Son of Man will be seated at the right hand of the Father." Jesus' trial has run its course. He is crucified, but the judgment stands not against Jesus. The Innocent One will be raised to exercise judgment. All will be asked to express where they stand. Luke's reader is left to contemplate Jesus' innocent sufferings. Will the reader be like the sneering crowds or the confessing criminal? They cannot remain neutral like the observing crowds, since paradise or judgment awaits. If there is one thing that Luke is after in his Gospel, it is the need to totally embrace the Innocent One who died. Resurrection makes that response a necessity.

Additional Notes

23:32. The way Jesus' execution is expressed is disputed. Some manuscripts ($\mathfrak{P}^{75}$, ℵ, B) read ἕτεροι κακοῦργοι δύο (other criminals two), which appears to identify Jesus as a criminal, though Plummer (1896: 530) argues that it could be translated "others, two criminals." Most manuscripts (A, C, D, L, W, Θ, Ψ, family 1, family 13, Byz) read ἕτεροι δύο κακοῦργοι (others, two criminals), reversing the word order so as to not view Jesus as a criminal. Because the second reading thus looks like a clarification, most take the harder first reading as original. Regardless, it is clear that three crucifixions are taking place and that the other two condemned men had engaged in criminal activity.

23:34. If Jesus' prayer forgiving his executioners is original, then it is unique to Luke. Many Alexandrian and Western witnesses omit the prayer ($\mathfrak{P}^{75}$, ℵ^1, B, D*, W, Θ, Syriac), while ℵ*^{,2}, (A), C, D^2, L, Byz, and some Syriac include it. External evidence leans toward rejecting the prayer, but internal factors also enter into the decision:

1. The parallel prayer of Stephen in Acts 7:60 argues for inclusion, since Luke frequently notes parallelism between events. (James the Just is said to utter a similar prayer in Eusebius, *Ecclesiastical History* 2.23.16.)
2. The absence of a parallel in the other Gospels speaks for inclusion here (i.e., there is no good reason to explain why a copyist would add such a remark).
3. The motif of ignorance is common in Acts (3:17; 13:27; 17:30) and finds endorsement here (Epp 1962).
4. It is easier to explain the prayer's omission than its insertion. A scribe might have omitted it if he considered the remarks too forgiving of the Jews (R. Brown 1994: 979) or if he regarded the prayer as unanswered in light of A.D. 70 (Jerome, *Letter* 120.8.2 says it delayed the judgment).
5. Each major subunit in Luke's crucifixion narrative contains a saying. If the prayer is omitted, then a saying is lacking from this subunit (Marshall 1978: 868).

These internal reasons suggest that the reading is original to Luke and should be included in his text. Ernst (1977: 634), Grundmann (1963: 432–33), Tiede (1988: 417), Ellis (1974: 267), and Marshall (1978: 867–68) are for inclusion. Luce (1933: 350) and Creed (1930: 286) are against it. Fitzmyer (1985: 1503) and Danker (1988: 373–75) are uncertain. Plummer (1896: 531) and Jeremias (*TDNT* 5:713 n. 455) argue that the prayer goes back to Jesus, but is perhaps misplaced in the textual tradition (cf. the double square brackets in UBS–NA). The classic discussion of the problem is Harnack 1901: 255–61. R. Brown (1994: 975–81) has a detailed summary of the discussion, including four options of how the prayer arose: (1) spoken by Jesus and preserved by Luke, (2) spoken by Jesus and inserted early on into Luke, (3) formulated by Luke, and (4) formulated after Luke. Brown prefers option 3 on the basis of Lucan style; I prefer option 1. Luke may be drawing on a source.

23:35. The textual dispute about the crowd's taunt only slightly affects meaning since the rebuke is clearly directed at Jesus for claiming to be Messiah. At least three variant readings should be abandoned in favor of the UBS–NA text, since it would be hard to explain how the title ὁ ἐκλεκτός (the Elect One, the Chosen One) came into the text if it was originally lacking.

23:38. Many manuscripts allude to the multilingual character of the inscription over Jesus, noting that it was written in Greek, Latin and Aramaic. The variety of word order and apparent harmonization with John 19:20 makes its originality in Luke unlikely. $\mathfrak{P}^{75}$, $\aleph^1$, B, C*, L, and some Syriac omit this detail. If Luke originally included it, the best of six variants is found in C³, W, Δ, Θ, family 1, Byz, some Itala, Vulgate, and some Syriac: γεγραμμένη ἐπ' αὐτῷ γράμμασιν Ἑλληνικοῖς καὶ Ῥωμαϊκοῖς καὶ Ἑβραϊκοῖς (written upon it in the letters of the Greeks and Romans and Hebrews).

23:42. $\mathfrak{P}^{75}$, $\aleph$, B, and L read ἔλεγεν· Ἰησοῦ, μνήσθητί μου (he said, "Jesus, remember me"). Because Jesus is nowhere else addressed as Ἰησοῦ (Luce 1933: 351), this harder reading was softened by a copyist to address Jesus as κύριε (Lord): ἔλεγεν τῷ Ἰησοῦ· μνήσθητί μου κύριε (he said to Jesus, "Remember me, Lord"; A, C², W, Θ, Ψ, family 1, family 13, Byz, Vulgate, some Syriac).[36]

23:42. A few manuscripts ($\mathfrak{P}^{75}$, B, L; also NRSV and NIV) read εἰς τὴν βασιλείαν (into your kingdom); others ($\aleph$, C, A, W, Θ, Ψ, family 1, family 13, Byz) read ἐν τῇ βασιλείᾳ (in your kingdom). The first reading would mean that Jesus is to remember the criminal when he is glorified and comes into the Father's presence. This perspective fits Judaism, but more important, it fits Luke's emphasis on Jesus' immediate rule (1:33; 16:22; 17:20–21; 22:30; 24:26). This reading is accepted with some hesitation by UBS–NA, Metzger (1975: 181), Arndt (1956: 470), Fitzmyer (1985: 1510), Grundmann (1963: 434), and Tiede (1988: 420). The second reading means that Jesus is to remember the criminal when he brings the resurrected righteous with him to set up his rule on earth. This reading also fits Lucan teaching (Luke 23:35, 37, 39; Acts 1:6–11; 3:19–21) and is accepted by Klostermann (1929: 229), Plummer (1896: 535), Schneider (1977a: 485), Ellis (1974: 268), Schweizer (1984: 361), Jeremias (1966: 249 n. 2), and Marshall (1978: 872). It is hard to know which reading is original. The second reading makes good sense and is slightly superior in literary sense, since Jesus' reply will heighten the request, making it more temporally specific ("Today!"). The criminal probably asks to be with Jesus at the unknown time of his future return, but Jesus says the criminal will be in God's presence today.

23:45. The remark about the sun failing is found in three textual variations. (1) The UBS–NA text has an aorist participle: τοῦ ἡλίου ἐκλιπόντος (the sun failed; $\mathfrak{P}^{75*}$, $\aleph$, C*, L, some Syriac). (2) Other manuscripts have a present participle: τοῦ ἡλίου ἐκλείποντος (the sun failing; $\mathfrak{P}^{75c}$, B). (3) The most commonly attested reading uses a different verb: καὶ ἐσκοτίσθη ὁ ἥλιος (and the sun was darkened; A, D, W, Θ, Ψ, family 1, family 13, Byz, Vulgate, some Syriac). All the readings mean basically the same thing. But since ἐκλείπω in the first two readings could refer to an eclipse, most consider the

36. Codex D contains an expansive reading: "Turning to the Lord he said to him, 'Remember me in the day of your coming.' Jesus replied to the one [criminal] who rebuked [his fellow], 'Be of good cheer.'"

third reading a copyist's removal of the ambiguity that an eclipse could happen during the full moon of the Passover.[37] It could also be argued that the verb of the third reading conforms too closely to the noun in 23:44. The slightly better external evidence favors the first reading, which is printed in the UBS–NA text.

---

37. Fitzmyer 1985: 1518 notes, however, that Thucydides 2.28 records an eclipse at new moon.

8. Burial (23:50–56)

Jesus' faithful followers are active as the Sabbath approaches. Two groups are singled out: Joseph of Arimathea and a group of women from Galilee. Joseph makes sure that Jesus receives an honorable burial, while the women watch to see where Jesus is laid to rest and then go to prepare spices for his body. Many have rejected Jesus, but a few faithful remain.

Sources and Historicity

The sources for this account seem clear enough. Much of the material found here is basic traditional material with parallels in Mark 15:42–47 = Matt. 27:57–61 (Aland 1985: §350), but there is also some new information. Unique to Luke are the note that the women are from Galilee and the detail that the tomb had never been used before (Matthew is close to this by saying the tomb is new). The other Synoptics tell us that Mary Magdalene and "the other" Mary (Matthew) or Mary mother of Joses (Mark) were there. Luke lacks some details: Joseph getting up courage (Mark 15:43), Pilate checking on Jesus' death (Mark 15:44–45), the purchase of the linen shroud (Mark 15:46a), the rolling of the stone (Mark 15:46b = Matt. 27:60), and the guards (Matt. 27:62–66). Most agree that Luke had access to additional material and chose to leave out some traditional details.[1] The account is accepted as historical.[2]

The account is a story about Jesus (Fitzmyer 1985: 1524; Bultmann 1963: 274). The outline of Luke 23:50–56 is as follows:

1. Luce 1933: 354 speaks of Mark plus L. Marshall 1978: 878 and V. Taylor 1972: 99–103 say that special Lucan material may appear in 23:55–56. Ernst 1977: 640–41 holds that it is 23:50c, 51a, 53b, 54b. Nolland 1993b: 1162–63 holds to 23:53c and perhaps 23:52–54. Grundmann 1963: 436 holds to 23:50, 51a, 53b, 54–56. Fitzmyer 1985: 1523 holds to 23:53c, 56a. Though it could be debated whether certain verses derive from another source, Luke seems to have had access to additional material, against R. Brown 1994: 1226.

2. Even Bultmann 1963: 274 accepts the general tenor of the account, except for the women witnesses, which he suspects has an apologetic flavor. In a culture that did not regard women's testimony as significant, there is no motive to create such a detail—in fact, the temptation would be to suppress it! Bultmann also sees Matthew's guards as an apologetic addition, but guarding the tomb of a controversial figure is not unusual.

a. Joseph (23:50–53)
   i. Joseph's character (23:50–51)
   ii. Joseph's burial of Jesus (23:52–53)
b. Chronological note (23:54)
c. The women (23:55–56)

Some in Israel believe and look for the kingdom. Not everyone in the council condemned Jesus. Some of the faithful gave special care to Jesus' body. Jesus was laid in an unused tomb; he was buried with honor, not as a criminal. Women watch and prepare spices for the body. Jesus' followers engage in the pious observance of the Sabbath. The burial means that Jesus' death was real, not an illusion.

Exegesis and Exposition

⁵⁰And behold there was a man named Joseph, being a member of the council and a good and righteous man—⁵¹this one ⌜did not consent⌝ to their purpose and deed—from Arimathea, a city of the Jews. And he was looking for the kingdom of God. ⁵²This one came to Pilate and asked for the body of Jesus. ⁵³Then he took it down and wrapped it in a linen shroud and laid him in a rock-hewn tomb where no one had ever been laid.

⁵⁴It was the Day of Preparation, and the Sabbath was beginning.

⁵⁵The women who had come with him from Galilee followed after and watched the tomb and how his body was laid, but returning, ⁵⁶they prepared spices and perfumes. And they rested on the Sabbath according to the commandment.

a. Joseph (23:50–53)
i. Joseph's Character (23:50–51)

23:50 Luke notes that not every Jewish leader sought Jesus' death. While many "fell" in Israel, some did "rise" (2:34; Neyrey 1985: 132). Joseph of Arimathea is regarded as a historical figure by even the most skeptical (e.g., Bultmann 1963: 274). A member of the council (βουλευτής, *bouleutēs*; elsewhere in the NT only at Mark 15:43), he is good and righteous, which recalls Luke's earlier descriptions of Zechariah, Elizabeth, Simeon, and Anna (Luke 1:6–7; 2:25–27, 36–38; Oepke, *TDNT* 1:363). Just as pious figures are involved in Jesus' birth, so also they are present at his death.

Matthew 27:57 mentions that Joseph is from Arimathea, that he is rich, and that he is a disciple. Mark 15:42–43 notes that Joseph is from Arimathea and that he was looking for the kingdom of God as he took courage and approached Pilate. Mark also says that Joseph is εὐσχήμων (*euschēmōn*), indicative of either his noble birth (Acts

13:50; 17:12) or noble character (Rom. 13:13; 1 Cor. 7:35). Creed (1930: 291) and Greeven (*TDNT* 2:770–72) argue that Luke emphasizes the moral sense and Matthew the social sense. But Marshall (1978: 879) correctly wonders if Luke intends to interpret the Marcan term. The phrase's placement after the name and place suggests that Luke is giving additional points about Joseph. Luke saves the chronological note that Matthew and Mark have here for Luke 23:54, which according to Marshall (1978: 879) speaks in favor of Luke's using another source. John 19:31–37 narrates the piercing of Jesus' side. Then John describes Joseph as a secret disciple because he feared the Jews. Joseph now goes public and acts on his association with Jesus. The Gospel of Peter 2.3 (Schneemelcher 1991–92: 1.223) narrates and expands upon this event: Joseph asks for the body before Jesus dies, and Pilate obtains the body by begging for it from Herod.

Luke continues to describe Joseph, making a parenthetical com- **23:51** ment, as the broken οὗτος (*houtos*, this one) construction shows (Marshall 1978: 879).[3] Joseph did not assent to the Sanhedrin's purpose (βουλή, *boulē*; elsewhere used by Luke in Luke 7:30; Acts 2:23; 4:28; 5:38; 13:36; 20:27; 27:12, 42) and action (πρᾶξις, *praxis*; elsewhere in the NT at Matt. 16:27; Acts 19:18; Rom. 8:13; 12:4; Col. 3:9), a phrase introduced by periphrastic ἦν συγκατατεθειμένος (*ēn synkatatetheimenos*; BAGD 773; BAA 1543; a *hapax legomenon*; cf. the variant readings in Acts 4:18 and 15:12; also Exod. 23:1, 32). He probably rejected the deal with Judas, the council's verdict, and their sending Jesus to Pilate (Fitzmyer 1985: 1526; Maurer, *TDNT* 6:642–44; Marshall 1978: 879). Plummer (1896: 541) notes that Joseph must have been absent from the evening trial, which gave a unanimous decision (Mark 14:64). In Luke's view, Joseph is a remnant saint, one who is faithful in the midst of the disobedience of others and who participates in the fulfillment of promises made to the nation (Tiede 1988: 426).[4]

Joseph is from Arimathea, probably his birthplace or earlier home, since he has a tomb in Jerusalem and serves on the Sanhedrin. All of the Gospels mention the locale in order to prevent con-

3. Similar parenthetical syntax is found in Luke 2:25; 7:29–30; 8:41; Acts 17:24; 18:25.

4. A figure like Joseph shows the complexity of Luke's view of the people of God and of the Jews. Many in the nation reject Jesus and the leadership is especially responsible, so that the nation is judged (Luke 19:41–44; 21:20–22; 23:28–30), yet many believe and become part of God's continuing work (Acts 2:40–44; 15:8). This latter group eventually develops into its own institution (e.g., the church with leaders like the Ephesian elders) and is the true people of God (e.g., the use of Amos 9 in Acts 15). The message always goes to the temple and synagogue in hopes that more Jews will respond. Luke never gives up hope of finding a remnant in and a future for Israel.

fusion with any other Joseph (Matt. 27:57 = Mark 15:43 = John 19:38). The exact location of Arimathea is not certain. Many suggest Ramah (Samuel's birthplace), which is known as Ramathaim-zophim (1 Sam. 1:1), Rathamin (1 Macc. 11:34), or Ramathain (Josephus, *Antiquities* 13.4.9 §127). This town is located about five miles north of Jerusalem. (Another suggestion is Remphis, ten miles northeast of Lydda.)

Joseph is described as a disciple who awaits the kingdom of God (cf. Luke 2:25, 38). Some argue that this simply means that Joseph held to Jewish eschatological hope and was not necessarily a disciple (Luce 1933: 355; Creed 1930: 291). Arguing that Mark does not present Joseph as a disciple, R. Brown (1994: 1213–19) cites tradition that the Jews (i.e., Joseph?) buried Jesus (Acts 13:27–29; John 19:31; Gospel of Peter 6.21 [Schneemelcher 1991–92: 1.224]; Justin Martyr, *Dialogue with Trypho* 97.1).[5] In light of the kingdom hope, however, this limited force is unlikely. Tradition seems clear that Joseph is a disciple (John 19:38 = Matt. 27:57; Marshall 1978: 880), though one should not forget that at the time he was part of the Jewish leadership. Asking to bury Jesus' body fulfills Deut. 21:22–23 (cf. Tob. 1:17–18; Josephus, *Against Apion* 2.29 §211). Joseph did not coordinate his effort with the women because he was a secret disciple (John 19:38).

ii. Joseph's Burial of Jesus (23:52–53)

23:52 Luke agrees exactly with Matt. 27:58a that Joseph asks for Jesus' body. Mark 15:43b notes that Joseph took courage, went to Pilate, and asked for the body. Mark describes Joseph's coming to Pilate with εἰσῆλθεν (*eisēlthen*, he came in), while Matthew and Luke have προσελθών (*proselthōn*, coming to). All the Synoptists and John 19:38 note that Joseph asked for Jesus' σῶμα (*sōma*, body) to make it clear that Jesus was physically dead. John notes that Joseph asked to take away (ἄρη, *arē*) the body. Matthew, Mark, and John all note that Pilate accepted the request: in Matthew, Pilate orders the body to be handed over (ἐκέλευσεν ἀποδοθῆναι, *ekeleusen apodothēnai*); in Mark, after determining from the centurion that Jesus was dead, Pilate grants the body to Joseph (ἐδωρήσατο τὸ πτῶμα τῷ Ἰωσήφ, *edōrēsato to ptōma tō Iōsēph*); and in John, Pilate permits him to take it (ἐπέτρεψεν ὁ Πιλᾶτος, *epetrepsen ho Pilatos*). Some suggest that the body of a political rebel would not likely be released after his death for fear of public turmoil. But Nolland (1993b: 1164) suggests that Pilate acts because (1) he has provincial authority to do

---

5. The church tradition about the Jewish burial could be read as causative: the Jews caused the death that required Jesus' burial.

so; (2) Joseph's Sanhedrin membership made him a safe trustee of the body; and (3) the circumstances of Jesus' death made it unlikely that the release of his body would be exploited to inflame the nation. The remark in Mark suggests that Joseph went to Pilate almost immediately after Jesus' death, since Pilate is not sure that Jesus is dead yet. Matthew and Mark noted earlier that it was becoming evening (probably somewhere between 3:00 P.M. and 5:00 P.M.), which meant that Sabbath was approaching, so the body had to be dealt with quickly or else left until Sunday.

After taking Jesus' body down from the cross, Joseph wrapped **23:53** (ἐνετύλιξεν, *enetylixen*; BAGD 270; BAA 545; elsewhere in the NT only in parallel accounts: Matt. 27:59 and John 20:7) it in linen.[6] All three Synoptics describe this cloth as σινδών (*sindōn*; BAGD 751; BAA 1502; R. Brown 1994: 1244–45; elsewhere in the NT at Matt. 27:59 = Mark 15:46 [twice]; 14:51, 52; cf. Judg. 14:12–13; Prov. 31:24), while John uses ὀθόνιον (*othonion*; 19:40; 20:5, 6, 7) and σουδάριον (*soudarion*; 20:7).[7] John may have more clothes in view, since his term is plural. Joseph's work probably means that he cleaned Jesus' body for burial, thus making himself unclean (*m. ʾOhol.* 2.2).

In a detail that the Synoptics lack, John 19:39 mentions that Joseph and Nicodemus anointed Jesus with one hundred pounds of spices, an amount normally reserved for a king. Such anointing was common, though the amount of spices was not (Ellis 1974: 270; Josephus, *Antiquities* 17.8.3 §199; *Jewish War* 1.33.9 §673; Jer. 34:5). The Gospel of Peter 6.24 (Schneemelcher 1991–92: 1.224) also mentions the customary washing of the body. R. Brown (1994: 1206–11) discusses the Roman and Jewish customs of burial for a crucified body. Roman policy, when it was compassionate, did not refuse burial to relatives or to anyone who asked for the body (*The Digest of Justinian* 48.24). Jewish attitudes depended on the nature of the crime, but the situation of Jesus was in Roman hands (for reasons why the release of the body was politically safe, see the exegesis of 23:52).

Joseph then places Jesus in a tomb (μνῆμα, *mnēma*; BAGD 524; BAA 1061) hewn from rock (λαξευτός, *laxeutos*; BAGD 466; BAA 948; BDF §2; BDR §2.2; a NT *hapax legomenon*; Fitzmyer 1985: 1529). This tomb was probably tunneled into the side of the rock face, with a small doorlike entrance maybe a yard tall (R. Brown 1994: 1247–48). Brown (p. 1269) suggests a locale north of Jerusa-

6. On general burial customs and for a good bibliography, see Nolland 1993b: 1165.

7. While much speculation centers around the Shroud of Turin, recent tests date it to the fourteenth century (when it first surfaced), thus making it inauthentic. See Fitzmyer 1985: 1527–29 for the history of the shroud.

lem (i.e., the Old City) like that noted by Josephus for the high priests (*Jewish War* 5.6.2 §259; 5.7.3 §304), which is possible, given that it was Joseph's tomb (see Barkay 1986; Bahat 1986; Nolland 1993b: 1165). Luke alone notes that it was a tomb where no one had previously been laid to rest (although Matt. 27:60 speaks of a new tomb). The traditional location of the tomb in the Church of the Holy Sepulchre dates at least from the fourth century (Cox Evans 1968). The law of Deut. 21:22–23 is fulfilled by Joseph's kind act. Jesus is not buried in dishonor.

b. Chronological Note (23:54)

23:54 Luke makes a chronological note, which the other Synoptics present before discussing Joseph: Matt. 27:57 simply says it was becoming evening, while Mark 15:42 records that it already was becoming evening and notes that it was the day before the Sabbath, that is, the Day of Preparation (παρασκευή, *paraskeuē*; BAGD 622; BAA 1257; Matt. 27:62; Mark 15:42; John 19:14, 31, 42; Josephus, *Antiquities* 16.6.2 §163; CD 10.14–17). The Day of Preparation is so called because it was the day before the start of a feast or the Sabbath when everything had to be made ready so that one could rest. In this case, both the feast day and the Sabbath come together, but Luke has related it to the Sabbath, as the following phrase makes clear. Luke clearly portrays the disciples as faithful in their preparation to rest on the Sabbath.[8] After noting the time, Luke turns to the activity of some women who watched where Jesus was laid.

c. The Women (23:55–56)

23:55 Joseph did not act in secret. Some Galilean women (cf. 23:49) followed (κατακολουθέω, *katakoloutheō*; BAGD 412; BAA 836; elsewhere in the NT only at Acts 16:17; cf. Jer. 17:16; Dan. 9:10; 1 Macc. 6:23) Joseph as he placed Jesus' body in the tomb (Plummer 1896: 543).[9] Creed (1930: 292) argues that Luke has a large group of women in mind, but this is not certain, since 24:10 names only three women who went to the tomb: Mary Magdalene, Joanna, and Mary mother of James.[10] While this passage also mentions "others with

8. In the Gospel of Peter (Schneemelcher 1991–92: 1.223, 224), ἐπιφώσκω (to break, shine forth) indicates the approach of Sabbath (2.5) or the dawn of day (9.34–35); BAGD 304; BAA 617; elsewhere in the NT only at Matt. 28:1; Marshall 1978: 881. Lohse, *TDNT* 7:20 n. 159, sees an allusion to the dawning of the evening star, a view that Plummer 1896: 543 rejects.

9. John 19:39 also mentions Nicodemus, but Luke notes only Joseph.

10. The main argument for Creed's view is the mention of "other women with them" (24:10), which may refer to those who reported the women's story or to the larger group of women who followed Jesus as disciples (8:1–3).

them," it does not seem that the additional number is large. Luke specifies that these women were from Galilee (on the periphrasis, see BDR §339.2b.9) and that they see the tomb. Luke's θεάομαι (*theaomai*, to watch; BAGD 353; BAA 717; BDR §353.3.4) differs from Mark 15:47's θεωρέω (*theōreō*, to observe; BAGD 360; BAA 731). Mark makes the point that they watched where (ποῦ, *pou*) Jesus was laid, while Luke speaks of their watching how (ὡς, *hōs*) the body was laid (BDR §396.1.4). Luke speaks generally of women, Mark mentions Mary Magdalene and Mary mother of Joses, and Matt. 27:61 speaks of Mary Magdalene and the other Mary. Matthew uses a term unique to him among the Synoptic portrayals of the passion: τάφος (*taphos*, sepulcher; BAGD 806; BAA 1608; Matt. 23:27, 29; 27:61, 64, 66; 28:1; Rom. 3:13; Gospel of Peter 6.24; 8.31; 9.36–37; 10.39; 11.45; 13.55 [Schneemelcher 1991–92: 1.224–25]).

23:56 The women return to their home and prepare to anoint Jesus' body after the Sabbath with a variety of perfumes (μύρον, *myron*; BAGD 529; BAA 1072; Josephus, *Antiquities* 19.9.1 §358) and spices (ἄρωμα, *arōma*; BAGD 114; BAA 228). Myrrh is probably a perfumed oil. The Jews did not embalm, so the spices and perfumes help to calm death's stench and slow decomposition (Michaelis, *TDNT* 4:801 and *TDNT* 7:458; SB 2:53). Luke mentions this preparation slightly earlier than Mark 16:1, which indicates that the women purchased spices after the Sabbath. Mark may have compressed the timing since the use of the spices did not occur until Sunday. On the other hand, Luke may have compressed the account thus giving the impression that the preparation occurs after the Sabbath while really only setting up a transition to the resurrection (Marshall 1978: 881). There is no way to be sure. It is not impossible that the women went with already prepared spices and also obtained some on the way. More likely the women bought spices twice. Certainly their devotion to the Lord caused them to be generous in their care. Plummer (1896: 543) argues that Mark has this journey take place on Saturday evening, while Danker (1988: 385) correctly notes that the morning after the Sabbath is meant, that is, Sunday morning. These women clearly did not anticipate a resurrection.

In making the transition to resurrection, only Luke speaks of the women resting (ἡσυχάζω, *hēsychazō*) on the Sabbath (BAGD 349; BAA 707; elsewhere in the NT at Luke 14:4; Acts 11:18; 21:14; 1 Thess. 4:11). The women are pious and obey the Mosaic law. Fitzmyer (1985: 1530) notes that *m. Šab.* 23.5 allowed people to prepare materials for the dead on the Sabbath, but there is also a contrary tradition that prevents taking "sufficient oil to anoint the smallest member" (*m. Šab.* 8.1). Luke, however, seems to suggest that the women did nothing on the Sabbath. They planned to care for the body first thing on Sunday morning, as soon as allowable according to Mosaic law.

Summary Luke 23:50–56 shows the care that Jesus' body receives. Jesus dies as a criminal, but is buried in honor. Joseph is a faithful disciple who honors his Lord: he asks for Jesus' body, donates a new tomb as a resting place, and cares for the body as the law prescribed. Others also will honor the Lord. The women prepare to anoint the body with spices on Sunday, but on the Sabbath they honor the law by resting. Those who follow Jesus are pious people who serve God faithfully. The reader is to note the respect shown to Jesus and the effort made to give him care. The Sabbath rest serves as a transition into the resurrection.

Additional Note

23:51. With regard to Joseph's dissent to the decision to execute Jesus, UBS–NA's perfect participle συγκατατεθειμένος (had [not] consented to) is better attested: $\mathfrak{P}^{75}$, A, B, W, Θ, and Byz. The present participle συγκατατιθέμενος (was [not] consenting to) is found in ℵ, C, D, L, Δ, Ψ, family 1, and family 13.

E. Resurrection and Ascension of Jesus (24:1–53)

Luke's final chapter shows God vindicating the Innocent One via resurrection. In three scenes, Jesus shows himself to be alive. First, he appears to the women (24:1–12). His discussion with two disciples on the Emmaus road contains wonder and discovery, reversing previous disappointment (24:13–35). In the final scene he appears to a group of disciples, bids them farewell, and gives final instructions (24:36–53), ending with the opening of Scripture, commission, promise, and ascension. What was promised has happened, so now the disciples are commissioned to take the message of God's work in Jesus' death and resurrection to every nation, calling them to repent. In the Spirit's coming, God promises to give the disciples power for the task. Jesus ascends triumphantly to sit at God's side to rule and to distribute the Father's gifts (Acts 2:22–36).[1]

It makes little difference whether Luke's resurrection narrative was originally part of the tradition linked to Jesus' death or was a separate tradition. Either way this material contains the climactic events of Jesus' first coming. It is clear, however, that the diversity found in the resurrection tradition is greater than that in the passion material. The resurrection accounts have a distinct and more complex history.

The main biblical accounts of Jesus' resurrection are Matt. 28:1–20; Mark 16:1–8 (perhaps 16:1–20); John 20:1–29; 21:1–23; and 1 Cor. 15:3–11.[2] The resurrection tradition is primitive and was always a part of the church's view of Jesus: Paul (Rom. 4:24–25; 10:9; Phil. 2:9–11; 1 Thess. 1:10), John (John 3:14; 8:28; 12:32, 34), the Letter to the Hebrews (Heb. 9:12–24), and Peter (1 Pet. 1:3; 3:18).[3]

---

1. Nolland 1993b: 1177–78 assesses Meynet's 1978 proposal that a substantial portion of the chapter (i.e., 24:4–47) is chiastically structured around two themes: (1) Jesus is alive and (2) resurrection is announced by Jesus and the Scriptures. Nolland also has a full survey of the tradition-historical discussion and the history of the religious analogies (pp. 1177–88).

2. Fitzmyer 1985: 1533–34 sees apologetic accretions in Matthew's reference to the guards and the chief priest's bribes. These pericopes do not, however, indicate ahistoricity; they simply clarify why one should not doubt the claims of Jesus' resurrection. Just because they are apologetic does not mean that they are fabricated.

3. C. F. Evans 1990: 886 notes that an immediate postresurrection appearance in bodily form had no precedent in Hellenistic thought or Judaism—not even for Messiah.

The church clearly saw Jesus as bodily resurrected in glorified form (Fitzmyer 1985: 1538–39), but the NT writers do more than affirm the reality of the resurrection (though they never give details about how the resurrection occurred, only that God did it).[4] They declare the meaning, consequence, and effects of the resurrection: Jesus is gloriously raised to rule. Exaltation is the major theme of Jesus' new life, especially in Luke's writings (Acts 2:30–36). Jesus' exaltation signals reversal, installation into authority, and victory (Luke 22:69).

Luke 24 makes clear the identity and call of the community, which gathers in the temple to await the coming of the Father's promise, the Spirit. Just as Luke's Gospel opens at the temple (1:5), so it ends there. Another significant note in this chapter is the fulfillment of OT promise (24:19–21, 25–27, 44–47). God's plan is coming to pass, and the disciples and the new community have a major role in that plan. Luke is clear that the disciples were not waiting for the resurrection: it comes to disciples who were disillusioned, and it produces a major reversal of emotion, transforming despair into hope and action. Luke's account is unique in focusing on Jerusalem (he records no Galilean appearances by Jesus), a detail that fits his emphasis on Jerusalem as the mission's beginning point (Acts 1:8).

The most basic element shared by the various resurrection accounts is the empty tomb. While there are significant variations in the accounts (e.g., the wording of the angelic resurrection announcement [Matt. 28:5–6 = Mark 16:6 = Luke 24:5–6] or John's description of the role of Mary Magdalene [John 20:1]), their differences are complementary, not contradictory.[5] There are at least eight points of general agreement (Plummer 1896: 546):

1. The resurrection is not described.
2. The resurrection occurs to disciples who do not expect it.
3. Reports of the resurrection are doubted.
4. The women's visit is the first step in disclosure.
5. The rolled-away stone is the first physical clue.
6. Angels appear.

---

4. The Gospel of Peter 9.35–10.42 (Schneemelcher 1991–92: 1.224–25) gives details about the resurrection, an expansion that demonstrates the differences between canonical and noncanonical accounts and indicates what happened to the tradition in the postapostolic period; cf. also Barn. 15.9. The glorified body is not a mere return to the former earthly existence (i.e., like the resurrection of Lazarus), but represents a transcendent form of real existence (1 Cor. 15:35–49, esp. 15:42–44). On the resurrection as event, see Stein 1977 and Craig 1980.

5. On these differences, see the exegesis of 24:1, 5–6. Though my approach to correlation differs from Westcott's proposed order (1908: 2.335–36) of resurrection events, his list shows that the accounts need not be contradictory.

7. Jesus appears to a variety of people, both individually and corporately, both male and female.
8. The result is an unshakable conviction in Jesus' resurrection.

We are dealing here with sacred events that are part of the essential content of Christian faith, as 1 Cor. 15 makes clear. Paul declares that if Jesus is not raised then he cannot save and one cannot invoke him for present aid and future hope. To be something other than a human ethical or philosophical system, the Christian faith must be inextricably tied to resurrection. Without resurrection, Christianity is just another human approach to reach God; it is emptied of transforming power and hope; it is a mere shell, not worth the energy one devotes to it. To hope in a resurrection that did not occur makes Christians the most pitied of people (1 Cor. 15:19). It is to believe an illusion. Without a resurrected Jesus, Christianity has nothing special to offer the world, for a dead Savior is no Savior at all. The world is full of exemplary people, but a resurrected Savior who cares and who fulfills God's promises is the unique hope that the Christian faith offers to the world. This does not mean that the fact of the resurrection is the ground of the Christian faith; rather, it is the one who emerged from this reality—the resurrected Christ—who is Christianity's foundation. Only through a raised Christ, the Exalted One, is it possible to have a relationship to God. The resurrection is important, even essential, because it is the door to new life in Christ, the key to which is faith, but at the heart of Christianity is a relationship with God through Christ. Christ's resurrection by the power of God makes that relationship possible and offers testimony to the reality of life before God beyond the grave. Jesus' resurrection is not the end of his story; rather, it represents his transition to an expanded role in God's plan, which becomes the focal starting point for our potential new life in him. To believe in Christ is to believe not merely in his example, but in the power of his resurrection to grant new life.

1. Resurrection Discovered
(24:1–12)

Five subunits compose the pericope dealing with the first report of the resurrection: setting (24:1), empty tomb (24:2–3), report of the two angels (24:4–8), report of the women (24:9–11), and Peter's response (24:12). The stress is on the declaration of Jesus' resurrection by the angels (24:5–6). Jesus' promise of resurrection (9:22) has come to pass. The divine necessity of events continues: God and Jesus are in control. The main feature of the passage is how the disciples ever so slowly come to see that God's plan is not derailed. The description of them may not be flattering, but it is honest and real. The church would not have created an account about the resurrection that portrayed its leading figures this way. The account rings true.

Sources and Historicity

Most regard Luke simply to have edited Mark 16:1–8 (Schneider 1977a: 490–92 [with oral tradition]; Fitzmyer 1985: 1541 [except Luke 24:12]; Bultmann 1963: 284–87; Dillon 1978 [see 1 n. 1 for other scholars who hold this view]), although Goulder (1989: 774) sees Luke using both Mark and Matthew. The problem centers on differences between Luke and Mark (Fitzmyer 1985: 1541; Creed 1930: 289–90 [who sees a source beyond Mark, like that used by Paul in 1 Cor. 15:3–5]; Nolland 1993b: 1177, 1184–85 [who notes that Luke 24:1–12 is close to Mark 16:1–8 but then goes "his own way"; a likely second source has points of contact in Matthew and John]):

1. Luke does not record the women's discussion about moving the stone (Mark 16:3).
2. Luke 24:3 explicitly mentions that the women did not find Jesus' body. In contrast, Mark 16:5 has the women enter and immediately encounter the messenger, as does Matt. 28:2–5, although in Matthew it is not clear that the women entered the tomb.
3. Mark 16:8 says that the women said nothing to anyone upon fleeing, while Luke 24:9 mentions their report to the apostles.[1]

---

1. This point is valid only if Mark's longer ending is not original.

4. In Luke 24:4, two men are seen as angels, while Mark 16:5 has one.[2] (John 20:12 has two angels in what may be a later scene; Matt. 28:2 agrees with Mark.)
5. Luke's angelic announcement (24:5–7) is uniquely worded.
6. Luke 24:10 names the women at the end of the section, while Mark 16:1 = Matt. 28:1 does so at the beginning.
7. In Luke 24:12, Peter checks out the report (a detail shared by John 20:3–10).
8. Luke lacks a direct appearance by Jesus to the women, in distinction to Matt. 28:9–10 = Mark 16:9 = John 20:14–17.

These differences lead some to speak of other sources for Luke, though whether it was a single source or a variety of oral sources is debated (Grundmann 1963: 439; Ernst 1977: 650; Marshall 1970: 65–75; Marshall 1978: 882–83; V. Taylor 1972: 103–9; Wiefel 1988: 405). Key to the discussion are three points of contact with Matthew and two with John. The Matthean contacts are an echo between Matt. 28:1 and Luke 23:54, the call to remember what Jesus said (Matt. 28:6; Luke 24:6), and the women's reporting to the disciples (Matt. 28:7; Luke 24:9). The Johannine points of contact are the sharing of the name Mary Magdalene at a similar point in the narrative and the absence of any concern about moving the stone (with Matthew as well). Only 17 of Luke's 169 terms are in agreement with Mark. The nature of the differences makes it likely that Luke used additional material, which he no doubt rewrote in his own style (Fitzmyer 1985: 1541–42 notes twelve points of Lucan style). Luke's account complements the other Gospels, giving fresh information about these events.

The resolution of the order of the events is difficult and, to the degree that it relates to Luke, will be treated in the exegesis. Certainty about exact order is beyond our grasp since no Gospel account attempts to be exhaustive. Evaluations of historicity turn on how one views the possibility of resurrection on a philosophical level and the dispute over the variety in the various accounts.[3] Philosophically, the resurrection is at the heart of primitive Christian hope (1 Cor. 15:3–5). To embrace the apostolic faith in Jesus means to embrace his resurrection and its historicity as they emerge from these ac-

2. Plummer 1896: 547 points out that Mark has only one figure in all three cases of numerical variation in the Gospels: the Gerasene demoniac(s), the blind man (men) at Jericho, and the angel(s) at the tomb. In Acts 1:10, two "men" are present.

3. The Jesus Seminar (Funk and Hoover 1993: 397–98) illustrates a more detached approach, arguing that "words ascribed to Jesus after his death are not subject to historical verification" and that claims that Jesus spoke after his death are "beyond the limits of historical assessment." The variation in location and wording thus lead the seminar to print Jesus' reported promise (24:7) in black type. This total skepticism seems to emerge from the seminar's definitional stance and an unwillingness to allow for any degree of summary reporting in the Gospel accounts. For a good attempt to explain both the Galilean and the Jerusalem appearances, see Nolland 1993b: 1181.

counts. The disciples do not view resurrection as a dramatic symbol of hope or an expression of a wish; they see it as core history that changed their view of what happened at the cross, as well as what happened afterward. "He is risen" is not the plea of an uncertain heart searching for meaning; it is an affirmation and confession of hope because of Jesus' resurrection.

The account is a resurrection report and a story about Jesus (Fitzmyer 1985: 1542). The outline of Luke 24:1–12 is as follows:

a. Setting (24:1)
b. The empty tomb (24:2–3)
c. Report of the two angels (24:4–8)
  i. Report of the angels (24:4–7)
  ii. Response of the women (24:8)
d. Report of the women (24:9–11)
e. Peter's response (24:12)

The resurrection is not expected by the disciples, but the empty tomb changes everything. The twofold angelic witness points to the resurrection as a fulfillment of Jesus' teaching and the promise of Scripture. Women are the first witnesses, but their report is not believed. Confirmation begins with Peter's discovery. The account's mood involves surprise, disbelief, and amazement.

Exegesis and Exposition

[1]During the deep dawn of the first day of the week, they came to the ⌜tomb⌝, taking the spices they had prepared.⌜ ⌝

[2]They found the stone rolled away from the tomb. [3]But when they went in, they did not find ⌜the body of the Lord Jesus⌝.

[4]And it came to pass as they were perplexed about this, behold, two men stood by them in shining apparel, [5]and as they were frightened and bowed their faces to the ground, the men said to them, "Why do you seek the living among the dead? [6]⌜He is not here, but is raised.⌝ Remember how he spoke to you while he was still in Galilee, saying that [7]'the Son of Man must be delivered over into the hands of sinful men and be crucified and on the third day be raised'?" [8]And they remembered his words.

[9]Returning from the tomb, they told all of these things to the Eleven and to all the rest. [10]Now ⌜they were⌝ Mary Magdalene, Joanna, Mary of James, and the other women with them. They were telling these things to the apostles. [11]But these words appeared to them as an idle tale, and they did not believe them.

[12]⌜But rising up, Peter ran to the tomb; and stretching and looking in, he saw the linen clothes by themselves, and he went home, amazed at what had happened.⌝

a. Setting (24:1)

The new week starts normally enough. Having fulfilled the law of **24:1**
the Sabbath (Exod. 20:8–11; Deut. 5:12–15), the women go to the
tomb to anoint the body.[4] All the accounts refer to the first (μιᾷ, *mia*;
BDF §247.1; BDR §247.1.1) day of the week (Matt. 28:1 = Mark 16:2
= John 20:1; cf. John 20:19; Acts 20:7; 1 Cor. 16:2), but Luke further
specifies the time with the genitive phrase ὄρθρου βαθέως (*orthrou
batheōs*, deep dawn; BDF §186.2; BDR §186.2.3).[5] Apparently, it is
early in the morning, perhaps the initial portion of dawn, since John
20:1 speaks of it still being dark (Matt. 28:1 says "after the Sabbath
in the dawn"; Mark 16:2 says "early in the morning after the sun has
risen"). The women went to the tomb probably as soon as they could
see. Given this slight difference in setting, Luke is not relying on
Mark. Nolland (1993b: 1188) notes that God's actions are sometimes attributed to this time, are made evident then, or are a source
of joy starting at that time of day (Exod. 14:24; 2 Kings 19:35; Ps.
30:5 [30:6 MT]; 90:14; 143:8; Isa. 37:36).

Matthew 28:1 names Mary Magdalene and the "other" Mary;
Mark 16:1 mentions Mary Magdalene, Mary mother of James, and
Salome; while John 20:1–2 mentions only Mary Magdalene. Luke
saves his list for 24:10, where Mary Magdalene, Joanna, and Mary
the mother of James are mentioned by name, though others are said
to be with them. Matthew notes that the women went to see the sepulcher, Mark mentions that their purpose is to anoint the body,
while John gives no explicit reason. Luke notes that they brought the
spices they had prepared, an allusion to 23:56 (on the use of the relative pronoun, see BDR §294.5.8).

John says that when Mary discovered that the tomb was empty
she ran to tell Peter and the "beloved disciple" (probably John himself) what happened. Upon her report that the body has been taken
out of the tomb, both disciples run to the tomb. The "beloved disciple" believes upon seeing the empty tomb (John 20:8), while Mary
stands outside the tomb weeping (20:11) because she believes that
the body has been stolen (20:13). Jesus appears to her (20:16), and
she tells the disciples of the appearance (20:18). Squaring this Johannine account with the other Gospels is difficult, since the Synoptics appear to have an immediate angelic announcement on

---

4. Note the μέν . . . δέ contrast: on the one hand the women rested (23:56), but on
the other, first thing on Sunday, they went to care for Jesus (24:1).

5. On ὄρθρος (dawn), see BAGD 580; BAA 1176; elsewhere in the NT at John 8:2
and Acts 5:21; cf. Gospel of Peter 12.50 (= Schneemelcher 1991–92: 1.225); T. Jos. 8.1;
1 Enoch 100.2. On βαθύς (deep), see BAGD 130 §2; BAA 263 §2; elsewhere in the NT
at John 4:11; Acts 20:9; Rev. 2:24.

Mary's first trip to the tomb. There are four attempts to solve this apparent discrepancy:

1. Mary made two trips to the tomb (J. Wenham 1992a: 83, 90–95; Osborne 1984: 149 n. 2; Westcott 1908: 2.337). First, she saw the tomb empty and ran away immediately without checking inside. She left the other women, not mentioned in John, to go in and discover what actually happened. When Mary returned behind the running disciples, she still did not know what had happened. She then saw Jesus (Matt. 28:9–10; John 20:11–18). An apparent problem with this view is that the Synoptics indicate that the disciples went to the tomb as a result of the women's report about Jesus' resurrection (Luke 24:10–12), a detail that could fit only John 20:2 if Mary reported that the tomb was empty and the others came later to fill in the details. Telescoping is possible: Mary arrived first and the other women brought their report, having trailed slightly behind her. But there is also the question of where Matt. 28:9–10 fits, since these verses look as if they belong to the first return home. Matthew (and the shorter version of Mark) lacks a visit by Peter, making Matthew's event look like the first trip home. Wenham's suggestion can be right only if Matthew truncated the first report so that Matt. 28:9–10 equals John 20:11–18. The major obstacle is how Mary was in doubt in the second scene in John if an appearance occurred on the first return home. Matthew's truncation would mean either that Mary was not party to the Matthean vision (despite its similarity to John) or that Matthew (again telescoping) described this later vision here since he does not mention Peter's visit.

2. John truncated the disciples' response, giving the impression that two disciples went more immediately to the tomb than they did. If there is compression in the account, then in fact their journey came after a little time had passed. During the interim, the second group of women returned and gave the report of Jesus' appearance to them. The major problem with this suggestion, which is a variation of the first approach, is that Mary Magdalene appears to lack knowledge about a claim of resurrection, and yet she is listed first among the reporters of Luke 24:10–11. In addition, why are Mary's remarks presented as the catalyst in John? This could also represent a collapse of detail, since Mary would have been the first to raise the issue of the empty tomb and then the others followed with the explanation. But does not Mary's doubt in John 20:11–13, which appears to be a later scene, contradict the other women's report?

If the women's report was met with doubt, maybe Mary became uncertain about what had happened, especially if she had not been at the tomb long. If her confirmation thus comes in John 20:14–18, then John 20:14–18 does not equal Matt. 28:9–10 but is a separate, similar appearance. This combination of events is possible, though it assumes a great deal of compression in all the accounts.

3. John 20:1–10 and 20:11–18 describe the same event; that is, they are sequential traditions. John 20:1–10 is not interested in how Mary saw the Lord, but simply notes that she saw the empty tomb. In addition, this tradition reflects that Mary was a little uncertain how to break the news to the disciples in a believable way. She opted for an ambiguous "half-report" and said that someone had taken the body, a view that probably honestly reflected her initial impression about what had happened. This first report led the disciples and later Mary after them to see what had really happened. John 20:11–18 then brings in the confirming appearance with it. The major question for this view is the apparent contrast between John 20:10 and 20:11. John 20:11–18 looks like an appearance to the two disciples later than the events in 20:1–10. For this view to work, the disciples' largely negative reaction must have plunged Mary back into doubt.

4. John starts Mary's account in John 20:2 with where her own experience started, wondering where the body was. The introductions to each account in John 20:2 and 20:13 are largely simultaneous in real time, but John tells the first account to reflect the discovery of the "beloved disciple." The narrative perspective of the discovery in John 20:1–10 thus reflects his point of view, while the narrative perspective of John 20:11–18 is that of Mary, even though this event was first chronologically. John 20:2 has Mary say that "we" do not know where they have laid the body, which seems to assume that Mary is not alone. John 20:13 has the same question raised in the singular, and her reply stays in the singular as well. The beginning of Mary's report about the empty tomb and missing body (20:2) set Peter and the beloved disciple off to the tomb before she could get any further. The other disciples who remained behind heard the whole account (i.e., 20:11–18). In this way, the account replays John's actual perspective of the event when it happened. Since he did not hear Mary's story all the way through, he must have heard it later. And he tells the story from the perspective of how he experienced the resurrection. This would mean that Matt. 28:9–10 does equal John 20:14–18. Mary made only one trip to

the tomb. John tells of his discovery in full and then goes back to tell Mary's story, which though earlier in time, was related to him later. The linkage is made literarily in the overlap of Mary's note about the missing body in John 20:2 and 20:13. In the real sequence, John 20:13–18 belongs with and following John 20:2, detailing what happened to Mary and the other women on their first visit. This option preserves the primary role that Mary seems to have played as the first to see Jesus raised and the first to announce his resurrection, and it also explains the focus on John in John 20:1–10.

The exact sequence of resurrection events remains obscure because of the variety of witnesses to the event and the variety of perspectives from which the details are presented. It is possible to harmonize the traditions, but it is evident that literary variation is required to see a fit. I prefer the last option. Regardless of which view is taken, it is clear that the discovery of the resurrection started with the trip of these women, the empty tomb, and Jesus' appearance to at least some if not all of them. The accounts complement one another and were left distinct for a reason—to present the resurrection from many distinct angles.[6]

b. The Empty Tomb (24:2–3)

24:2 The first Lucan hint of the resurrection is the rolled-away stone (Marshall 1978: 884). It is an invitation to go in the tomb and anoint the body. There is a nice literary contrast in 24:2–3 between what they found on arrival (the stone rolled away) and what they surprisingly did not find upon entering (Jesus' body). Both verses use εὗρον (*heuron*) for "find" (in contrast to ἀναβλέψασαι θεωροῦσιν [*anablepsasai theōrousin*, looking up they saw] in Mark 16:3 and βλέπει [*blepei*, she saw] in John 20:1).

In first-century Israel a round stone disc was often placed in a channel carved in the rock so it could be rolled easily to cover the usually rectangular tomb entrance (Fitzmyer 1985: 1544; Abel 1925). But the stone might merely have plugged the entrance, with no channel (Nolland 1993b: 1189). There is no way to know which

---

6. The only evidence that the early church tried to harmonize these accounts is the longer ending of Mark, which also mentions an initial appearance to Mary. But this Marcan text succeeds only in making the relationship of the Synoptics to John more complicated, since it is not clear how John 20:11–18 fits. Why would Mary need a later appearance by Jesus (John 20:11–18) if he had appeared to her earlier (Mark 16:9)? Since the longer ending of Mark is textually suspect, not much weight can be given to it (if it is an addition, it provides evidence of a later witness in the church that confirms the key initial role of Mary).

is the case here. Since this is Luke's first mention of the stone, its presence in the account without explanation assumes knowledge of Jewish practice. Marshall (1978: 884) thinks the detail may suggest a pre-Lucan tradition.

Mark is alone in recording the discussion about who will roll away the stone and in noting that the stone was very large. Matthew lacks mention of the effort to anoint the body, noting only that they went to see the grave. Dillon (1978: 16) attributes the difference to the presence of the guards (Matt. 28:11–15). The guards' job is to prevent anyone from gaining access to the body (seen in their sealing of the tomb), so Dillon argues that Matthew drops the anointing. But the ideas of anointing and guards are not mutually exclusive. According to ancient custom, the women should have been able to anoint the body as long as they did not remove it.[7]

Matthew 28:2 speaks most specifically of an earthquake caused by an angel who moves the stone and sits on it as the women approach. Mark and Luke speak of the stone being rolled away (ἀποκυλίω, apokyliō; only four times in the NT, all in this account; BAGD 94; BAA 188; cf. Gen. 29:3, 8, 10; Jdt. 13:9; BDF §101; BDR §101.44) upon the women's arrival. John 20:1 speaks of the stone's having being taken away (ἠρμένον, ērmenon). God's providence and control are in view in these events. This is clearly a surprising event that the women were not expecting. Coming face to face with Jesus' resurrection (Luke 24:2–3, 19–24, 36–43) brings repeated explanations (24:5–7, 25–27, 44–49; Dillon 1978: 20). The repetitive refrain is that Jesus is raised.

The women find the tomb open, but they do not find the body of the **24:3** Lord Jesus (Mark 16:6 = Luke 24:6). If κυρίου (kyriou, of the Lord) is original (see the additional note), the title shows Luke's respect for Jesus. By using εὗρον (heuron, they found) again, Luke contrasts their not finding Jesus' body with the previous finding of the open tomb. Mark 16:5 speaks of the women entering the tomb and seeing a young man seated on the right side dressed in a robe, thus amazing them. Matthew 28:2–4 speaks of an angel rolling away the stone and sitting upon it. He is described as looking like lightning and having a garment white as snow. The guards trembled because of him and became like dead men. John 20 has no details of any of the women

---

7. The issue surrounding the seal in Matt. 27:66 is whether it was designed to prevent anyone from ever entering the tomb or if it was a way to assure that no one got in without approval. The women might not have known that the tomb was sealed and that they might be stopped. As it was, Matthew notes that supernatural events prevented the guards from halting their visit. Of course, none of the accounts puts all these details together as I have just described them. But the scenario is not improbable, especially if the women were unaware of the guards' presence.

going into the tomb. Instead, Mary runs and reports that the Lord's body has been taken. Each Gospel goes its own way in summarizing the details (see the exegesis of 24:1 for how John and the Synoptics fit together).

c. Report of the Two Angels (24:4–8)
i. Report of the Angels (24:4–7)

24:4 The empty tomb leaves the women at a loss about what has happened. They are perplexed (ἀπορέω, *aporeō*; BAGD 97; BAA 195; elsewhere in the NT at Mark 6:20; John 13:22; Acts 25:20; 2 Cor. 4:8; Gal. 4:20). They had not expected an empty tomb and wonder about it (περὶ τούτου, *peri toutou*). In Mark 16:3 the women had been concerned about moving the stone; now there is much more to ponder.

During their reflection, two men appear (ἐπέστησαν, *epestēsan*; BAGD 330 §1a; BAA 668 §1a; cf. Luke 2:9, 38; Acts 1:10; 4:1; 10:30; 17:5; 23:11) to the women. Both Mark 16:5 and Matt. 28:2–4 mention only one man or angel. In Mark, the man is sitting inside the tomb on the right side and dressed in "white robes" (στολὴν λευκήν, *stolēn leukēn*), which agrees with Luke conceptually but not lexically. In Matthew, the angel is sitting on the stone, dressed in a shining robe white like snow (ὡς ἀστραπὴ καὶ τὸ ἔνδυμα αὐτοῦ λευκὸν ὡς χιών, *hōs astrapē kai to endyma autou leukon hōs chiōn*). That the tradition had variety seems clear from John 20:12, which also notes two angels.[8] Only later does Luke call these men angels (24:23). Here he simply describes their clothes as ἐσθῆτι ἀστραπτούσῃ (*estheti astraptousē*, bright clothing), terms that usually describe heavenly phenomena (Luke 9:29; 10:18; Acts 9:3; 22:6; Bode 1970: 59).[9] The language recalls the transfiguration and parallels the two angels present at the ascension (Acts 1:10 also uses ἐσθής [*esthēs*] to describe the messengers' clothing).

The two men appear to reflect a two-witnesses motif (Deut. 19:15; Ellis 1974: 272; Osborne 1984: 106 [who lists other options]; Bode 1970: 60, 165–67). Bultmann (1963: 314–17, esp. 316) attributes the addition to a common "folk" motif, but the presence of two angels also in John suggests that this point is not merely a Lucan addition for literary reasons. There is no reason to challenge historicity, despite the numerical differences between Luke and the other Synop-

---

8. Dillon 1978: 21–22, who sees Lucan editorial work throughout the resurrection narrative, accepts an outside source here. Luce 1933: 358 says, "Very little in these verses (3–5) . . . suggests that Luke is using Mark." Marshall 1978: 885 argues that the Johannine parallel shows the traditional point of contact.

9. Kittel, *TDNT* 1:84 n. 67, sees the white robes as not descriptive of clothing but characterizing the angel's transcendent glory.

tics, which seem to summarize details in an independent but complementary manner.

The appearance of the angels produces terror (ἔμφοβος, *emphobos*) **24:5** in the women (Matt. 28:4 speaks of the guards fearing, while Mark 16:5 says the women were amazed).[10] The women are in awe of the angels and bow their faces to the ground (κλινουσῶν, *klinousōn*; BAGD 436 §1a; BAA 887–88). They do not bow simply to avoid the bright light, since turning away would accomplish that goal (but so Marshall 1978: 885, citing Acts 9:4). Rather, bowing is a sign of recognition of the presence of heavenly beings and divine messengers (Tiede 1988: 430; Danker 1988: 388; Dillon 1978: 26–27; Dan. 7:28; 10:9, 15). The women know that something is happening, but they have no idea what it is, as the following rebuke shows.

In wording similar to Isa. 8:19, the angels rebuke the women not to seek the living among (μετά, *meta*; BDR §227.2.3) the dead.[11] The women do not recognize that Jesus is raised; they have not heeded his teaching about his suffering and exaltation (Luke 9:22, 44; 13:33; 17:25; 22:37). The Lucan angelic message is unique: John lacks any angelic remarks at this point in his narrative; in Matt. 28:5–6 the angel tells the women not to fear, for the crucified Jesus whom they seek is not here, but is raised; and in Mark 16:6 the angel tells the women not to be amazed, for Jesus of Nazareth who was crucified is raised and is not here. All the Synoptics share two terms: ἠγέρθη (*ēgerthē*, he is raised) and ζητεῖτε (*zēteite*, you are seeking). Luke has drawn on additional material or summarized the conversation in more detail.

In wording much like Matt. 28:6 (even matching the word order versus Mark 16:6b), the angels explain that the absence of Jesus' body is the result of resurrection. The angelic reference to resurrection uses a theological passive: ἠγέρθη (*ēgerthē*, he is raised [by God]). This divine activity is a consistent Lucan emphasis (Fitzmyer 1985: 1545; Luke 20:37; 24:34; Acts 3:15; 4:10; 5:30; 10:40; 13:30, 37; also of Jesus' exaltation: Luke 24:51; Acts 1:11, 22; Ignatius, *Smyrneans* 2.1; 7.1; Kremer 1979).

The angels tell the women to recall Jesus' teaching in Galilee (ὡς, *hōs*, with an indirect question; BDR §396.1.4). They are to remember (μιμνῄσκομαι, *mimnēskomai*; BAGD 522; BAA 1057) what Jesus predicted, an allusion to 9:22 and 18:32–33. What has happened

---

10. Plummer 1896: 548 notes that most NT uses of ἔμφοβος (BAGD 257; BAA 520) are Lucan: Luke 24:37; Acts 10:4; 24:25; Rev. 11:13; cf. Luke 1:12, 29–30; 2:9. On the genitive absolute with an accusative object, see BDR §423.2.8.

11. Ζάω (to live) is an important NT term. The key Lucan uses are Luke 24:23; Acts 1:3; 25:19; cf. Mark 16:11; Luke 10:28; 15:32; 20:38; Acts 9:41; Gal. 2:20; Heb. 7:25; 1 Pet. 3:18 (ζῳοποιέω, to make alive); Rev. 1:18; Marshall 1978: 885; Bode 1970: 62.

should not have been a surprise. Despite Jesus' teaching, the resurrection was too unbelievable to register with the disciples until after it occurred, a reaction that is natural enough, given the rarity of such an event.

That these remarks are found only in Luke again raises the issue of sources. V. Taylor (1972: 107–8) argues that the entirety of 24:6–8 is from another source. Since, however, 24:6a is extant in the triple tradition, this is unlikely. More correctly, 24:6b–8 (esp. 24:6b) is sourced in Luke's tradition (Osborne 1984: 107). In favor of another tradition is the instruction in Matt. 28:7 = Mark 16:7 to go to Galilee, where Jesus will go before the disciples (the scene in John 21:1–23 pictures such a Galilean appearance). That Luke's geography of appearances differs from Matthew and Mark shows that he has clearly gone his own way. The differences suggest additional input.

How Luke integrates with the other Gospels is not clear. Since resources would be needed for a group of 120, perhaps the disciples made trips to Galilee to fish for the group gathered in Jerusalem. The NT gives no explanation of how the Galilean and Jerusalem appearances relate to each other, but Acts 1:3 speaks of many appearances over forty days, and John 20:30 and 21:24 make clear that much more happened than is written in his Gospel. Although Jesus tells the disciples to stay in the city until the Father's promise, the Holy Spirit, comes (Luke 24:49), this remark may not have been an absolute ban on travel or departure as much as an instruction not to begin ministering and declaring Jesus' resurrection until the Spirit comes to them in the capital. That ministry will start in Jerusalem.

Some argue that Luke alone is responsible for the change, for he portrays Galilee as the place of acceptance for Jesus and Jerusalem as the place of rejection (Conzelmann 1960: 73–74). This symbolic geography does not work, however, since Jesus was not always accepted in Galilee (e.g., 4:16–30). Jesus simply gathers disciples in Galilee who will be his witnesses (Acts 1:22; 10:37–41; 13:31; Marshall 1978: 886; Osborne 1984: 107–10).

Dillon (1978: 35–38) proposes that Luke omits the Galilean appearances because Galilee is a place of miraculous display and plays a symbolic christological role in Luke. But this contrast is overdrawn. Jesus does miracles all the way up to the point of his arrest, not just in Galilee (Luke 22:50–51). He even does miracles in Gentile regions (8:26–39). The early concentration of miracles in Galilee merely indicates that it was then the principle location of Jesus' activity. Luke later zeroes in on Jerusalem because of the geographic focus of the Book of Acts on Jerusalem as central in the spread of the word of God (Ellis 1974: 272). Luke's unique focus seems fueled by additional tradition.

In one of the most important passages in the chapter, Luke summa- **24:7**
rizes Jesus' prediction that is now fulfilled. The angels allude to sayings reported in 9:22, 44 (other key Lucan passion sayings are Luke
17:22; 18:31–33; 22:22; 24:44, 46; Acts 2:36; 3:13–15; 4:27; 7:52;
10:39; Osborne 1984: 110). Luke 9:44 is particularly similar to this
angelic report, although the angels uniquely refer to "sinful" (ἁμαρτωλός, hamartōlos) men (but see Mark 14:41) and use the verb σταυρόω (stauroō, to crucify) along with παραδίδωμι (paradidōmi, to give
over). The phrase τὸν υἱὸν τοῦ ἀνθρώπου (ton huion tou anthrōpou,
the Son of Man), normally found on Jesus' lips, occurs here in the
angels' report of what Jesus said. The title's early position in anticipating the ὅτι (hoti, that) clause is emphatic (grammatically the
phrase is a proleptic or anticipatory accusative that belongs to the
ὅτι clause; BDF §476.3; BDR §476.2.4). The use of "Son of Man" describes Jesus' authority, as 22:69 made clear, and since χριστός
(christos, Christ) is the key title in the fulfillment sayings of 24:26,
46, it is evident that the titles share a certain amount of overlap.[12]

The angels speak of the necessity of these events, using the particularly Lucan δεῖ (dei, it is necessary; Bode 1970: 66). Luke uses δεῖ
eighteen times in his Gospel: twelve times lacking Synoptic parallel
(2:49; 11:42 [probably]; 13:14, 16, 33; 15:32; 17:25; 18:1; 19:5; 22:37;
24:26, 44; cf. Acts 17:3), four times having Synoptic parallels that do
not use δεῖ (4:43; 12:12; 22:7; 24:7), and twice in the triple tradition
(9:22; 21:9). Matthew uses δεῖ eight times, of which six lack parallel
in Luke, and Mark uses it six times, of which four have no Lucan
parallel. Luke stresses God's plan and the movement of divine history more than the other Synoptics, an emphasis that goes hand in
hand with Luke's strong fulfillment motif (in this chapter alone at
24:25–26, 32, 44–47; cf. Luke 2:38–39; 4:14; 7:18–19; 9:22, 31, 43–44;
18:31–33; Acts 1:22; 3:18). What is happening is no surprise; it is a
part of a divinely wrought event sequence.

The message is summarized in three infinitives that express what
God's plan involved: παραδοθῆναι (paradothēnai, to be given over),
σταυρωθῆναι (staurōthēnai, to be crucified), and ἀναστῆναι (anastēnai, to be raised). They portray what God is allowing to occur,
though humans are directly responsible for the first two actions.
Each idea is important to the event's movement. The act of executing Jesus is judged by heaven.

First, in speaking of Jesus' being given over, Luke has in mind the
details of what he described in Luke 22–23: the Jewish leadership

---

12. Dillon 1978: 38–40 argues that Son of Man is a title of concealment of the passion secret (i.e., the Son of Man is hidden in his present activity as he executes God's
plan), but this is unlikely given the term's public reuse by Stephen in Acts 7:56. Osborne 1984: 110 n. 13 correctly critiques this view.

and Pilate's failure to stop the process (Acts 4:25–28). The reference to sinful (ἁμαρτωλῶν, *hamartōlōn*) people is unique to the passion sayings and in Luke's Gospel.[13] Sinful people were permitted to hand Jesus over and arrest him.

Second, Jesus is crucified (Matt. 20:19; Mark 16:6; Luke 24:20; Acts 2:36; 4:10). Luke's reference to crucifixion is unique to the passion sayings. Other sayings refer to the mistreatment that preceded Jesus' crucifixion (Luke 18:32–33), his being killed (9:22), or his being given over (9:44). The specific reference to crucifixion fills out the detail of what took place.

Third, Jesus was resurrected on the third day (τῇ τρίτῃ ἡμέρᾳ, *tē tritē hēmera*; BDR §200.1). The focus on the third day is unique to Luke among Synoptic resurrection portrayals (cf. 9:22; 18:33; 24:46), evidence that many regard as proof that Luke is responsible for this saying. To argue thus, however, ignores Paul's explicit association of the third-day teaching with early church kerygma (1 Cor. 15:3–4). This is a traditional theme not unique to Luke. This last member of the three-part saying that the women need to recall explains why the tomb is empty. God has taken Jesus up to his side in heaven to rule (Luke 22:69).

The third-day emphasis fits not only history but Jewish expectation. In many passages, the third day was regarded as the day of salvation (SB 1:747; Gen. 22:4; 42:17; Esth. 5:1; Hos. 6:2; Jon. 1:17 [2:1 MT] and the targumim and midrashim on these texts). The age and breadth of the Targum tradition may suggest an earlier expectation. This makes for a better explanation of the third-day idea from Scripture than an appeal to Hos. 6:2 alone, as is often done (e.g., Dillon 1978: 48 n. 138). It is clear that the church counted the three days on an inclusive basis: Friday was day one, Saturday day two, and Sunday day three. The only apparent exception to this reckoning is the appeal to Jonah typology in Matt. 12:40, where Jonah's three days and nights are made parallel to Jesus. But it is probably a mistake to read this as giving precision beyond what is rhetorically intended, especially given Luke 9:22; Matt. 16:21; 17:23; 20:19; and 27:64. The key to the Jonah typology is resurrection associated with the third day. Jesus' resurrection not only fits his prediction, but a common pattern of expectation. The women are to realize that the resurrection is an expected part of God's plan. The reminder about promise is to teach them so they can proclaim it to others (Nolland 1993b: 1190–91).

---

13. Bode 1970: 63 comments that the detail betrays a "rather complicated literary background" (probably alluding to the Mark 14:41 connection noted above). Luke uses ἁμαρτωλός eighteen times, Matthew five times, Mark six times, and John four times.

This passage's uniqueness to Luke and its multiple Lucan traits lead many to regard it as a particularly Lucan summary of events. Some argue that he is responsible for the details (Dillon 1978: 38; Marshall 1978: 886; Fitzmyer 1985: 1545–46 [Son of Man, must, sinfulness, rise again, third day]). Black (1969; 1967: 53) argues that the syntax has traces of Semitism in it, so that the tradition is not Lucan (Fitzmyer 1985: 1545 and Marshall 1978: 886 reject this approach). The peculiar mention of crucifixion, the unique use of word ἁμαρτωλός, and the idea of resurrection on the third day make clear that though Luke conveys the material in his own style, it appears to be traditionally based and is not his own creation.

ii. Response of the Women (24:8)

24:8   Luke relates the first of two report-response sequences in this section. Here the angelic report brings the women's response of remembrance (later the women's report in 24:9–11 will lead to Peter's response in 24:12 to see the tomb for himself). The women recall Jesus' teaching and respond. The language recalls the command of 24:6. Dillon (1978: 51) argues that no Easter faith is found in this response since it is not said that their eyes or minds are opened (cf. 24:31, 45). It is only the Lord's teaching that is remembered as they take the first small step to faith. Dillon further argues that resurrection is hidden from them because, when the Lord originally gave the saying during his ministry, the apostolic group did not understand what resurrection meant. But Dillon argues that the text shows the fundamental retrospective awareness that came to the church as a result of Jesus' resurrection.

Though the latter point is surely correct, given that the women had come to anoint a corpse and did not expect a resurrection, three factors are against this general approach. First, the teaching is now given before an empty tomb. The context of Jesus' earlier remarks is now clear. Second, the teaching that they recall is specifically about resurrection, the key point in this context (24:5). If they take the reminder to heart and recognize the key point, there is hope, since what the angels declare is that Jesus' promise has been fulfilled. In fact, the reference to ταῦτα πάντα (tauta panta) in the next verse shows that they reported on "all these things." It is clear that the angelic message is discussed. In addition, this approach ignores the force of 24:11, where the apostolic group for the most part regards the women's story as "an idle tale." This judgment is not limited to the mere existence of the angelic vision or that Jesus' teaching is to be remembered, but must include what the teaching contained (24:22–23). Clearly, they report not only the angelic visit, but, more important, the fulfillment of Jesus' teaching about resurrection.

They do not tell it as a mere passing on of information, but undoubtedly with some urgency since it is regarded as too strange to be true. After all, Peter does run to the tomb in 24:12. The apostolic lack of belief in the report in 24:11 shows that the women were way ahead of the disciples.[14]

d. Report of the Women (24:9–11)

24:9   The woman return from the tomb and report all these things (ταῦτα πάντα, *tauta panta*; 24:14, 21) to the apostles, who now number eleven without Judas, and the rest of the disciples.[15] For the first time, the larger group hears of the empty tomb, the angelic presence, and the declaration that Jesus is raised just as he predicted he would be.

Luke shares ἀπαγγέλλω with Matthew (though Matthew has the infinitival form). Mark has no parallel to this passage, though Mark 16:8 speaks of the women fleeing "from the tomb" (ἀπὸ τοῦ μνημείου, *apo tou mnēmeiou*), a phrase similar to Luke's report of their return from the tomb. The shorter form of Mark's Gospel ends abruptly with the women telling no one, but simply standing in fear. This does not mean that the women never spoke to anyone; rather their fear should be read in light of this common motif in the middle portion of Mark's Gospel (4:41; 5:15, 33, 36; 6:50): when people meet God they should fear and respond in faith.

Opinion differs whether this Lucan report comes from traditional material. Dillon (1978: 52–53) argues that this is a Lucan redaction of the tradition rather than the use of additional tradition. But if so (and assuming that Mark 16:9 is a later addition), where did Luke get the names of the women?[16] This detail suggests that he had access to material that reported the event to the church. Dillon is right, however, that the verse shows indications of Lucan style in the use

14. It looks as if Dillon is trying to protect a "disclosure" theme in this chapter, a view that has problems before this point in the narrative (see n. 12 above). Dillon argues for Lucan creation here, which is unlikely given the traditional themes already noted in the passion predictions and the additional materials that Luke apparently uses in his resurrection account. There is no doubt that the disciples' understanding deepens through these events and Jesus' visit with them, but faith seems to be present here in these women. It took some nerve to report what they had seen, given that women were not allowed to testify in this culture (Josephus, *Antiquities* 4.8.15 §219).

15. Ἀπαγγέλλω (to report) occurs elsewhere in Luke at 7:18, 22; 8:20, 34, 36, 47; 9:36; 13:1; 14:21; 18:37 (plus fifteen times in Acts); Matt. 28:8 (plus seven more times in Matthew); twice in Mark 16:9–20 (plus three more times in Mark); BAGD 79; BAA 157.

16. Dillon's argument (1978: 56) for a composite list created from Mark 15:40; 16:1; and Luke 8:2–3 to yield a list of three members is negated by the reference "to the rest of the women." For the syntactical issues, see the exegesis of 24:10.

of ὑποστρέφω (hypostrephō, to return), which is used twenty-one times in Luke, eleven times in Acts, not at all in the other Gospels, and only three times elsewhere in the NT—partially because of Luke's preference for prefixed forms of verbs. In addition, Luke often reports returns (1:23, 56; 2:20, 39; 4:14; 5:25; 7:10; 23:48, 56; 24:33, 52). But touches of Lucan style do not necessarily mean Lucan critique of Marcan tradition. He can simply be including material that gives more detail. Another detail for a traditional origin is the reference to the remaining apostolic band in 1 Cor. 15:5, 7—material that clearly reflects church tradition since Paul speaks of all the church preaching the resurrection (cf. Matt. 28:16; Mark 16:14; Luke 24:33; Acts 1:26; 2:14; Marshall 1978: 887).

24:10 Luke identifies the women who gave the report. Except for Mary the mother of James, the women are already familiar to Luke: Mary Magdalene was mentioned in 8:2 and Joanna in 8:3. Mary Magdalene is listed in all the resurrection accounts (Matt. 28:1 = Mark 16:1 = John 20:1, 18). The reference to Μαρία ἡ Ἰακώβου (Maria hē Iakōbou, Mary the one of James) is unclear, since the genitive could mean James's mother, wife, or sister. Most take Luke's wording as equal to Mark 15:40 and 16:1, so that she is the mother of James and Joses (Plummer 1896: 549; BDR §162.3.5; Mark 6:3). Luke's repetition of the report to the apostles (24:9) may reflect the influence of another source that listed the women's names with the report. Luke also makes the point that many other unnamed women were involved as word of the resurrection spread across the assembled group. Though 24:10 mentions only a report to the apostles, 23:9 suggests that the entire entourage is involved.

The major issues in the verse involve the text and syntax (Marshall 1978: 887; see the additional note). Does the phrase αἱ λοιπαὶ σὺν αὐταῖς (hai loipai syn autais, the rest of the women with them) go with the first part of the verse or is it the subject of the latter part of the verse? In other words, is this larger group of women part of the traveling entourage or did they give the report? The problem is caused by the presence of two third-person plural verbs before any object is noted: ἦσαν (ēsan, they were) and ἔλεγον (elegon, they said). That all the nominative constructions are linked by καί (kai, and) suggests that the three named women and the rest of the women should be treated together as the subject of the first verb (ἦσαν). In this case, the subject of the second verb (ἔλεγον) would be an understood "they." But "they" is ambiguous in that it could refer to "the rest of the women" or the whole group just named. Dillon (1978: 57) argues that if a weaving of traditions is present, Luke has made it unclear syntactically (unlike the smooth way he handles most transitions) and thus made the addition himself. But the argument for "smoothness" cuts both ways. Since this is a rough way to compose a text, it is more likely that Luke brought together various traditions (such rough sutures occur in Acts 4:24–25; 21:17–18). Luke intends the group of women to be seen as part of the traveling entourage and as reporters of the event (cf. Luke 23:55; Nolland 1993b: 1191).

24:11 The women's account does not gain immediate acceptance. In fact, Luke uses a unique graphic *hapax legomenon* to describe the reaction: λῆρος (*lēros*, nonsense or idle talk; BAGD 473; BAA 960; 4 Macc. 5:11; Josephus, *Jewish War* 3.8.9 §405), a term used in medical settings of the delirious talk of the very sick (Plummer 1896: 550). The apostles are not looking for any reversal of the tragic situation. Their dreams about God's kingdom have been shattered. The women's story looks like an absurd effort to challenge reality. Apparently no one believes them.[17] Marshall (1978: 888) notes that Luke does not mention that the women saw Jesus (Matt. 28:9–10 = Mark 16:9–11 = John 20:11–18), an omission that probably reflects the influence of another source or compressed summarization. In Luke, Jesus reveals himself for the first time on the Emmaus road. Since the Emmaus account is unique to Luke, he may have saved the drama of revelation for this new, recounted, confirming event and may have assumed traditional knowledge of the earlier appearance.

No one believes except possibly Peter. He has learned to believe what Jesus says, even when it goes against whatever convictions he might have (Luke 5:1–11; 22:61–62). His denials have taught him to trust Jesus. Luce (1933: 359) argues that 24:11 conflicts with the later report that some went to check out the tomb (24:24). Once Peter headed for the tomb or returned from it, however, it is likely that others went to see, even though they may have doubted whether they would find anything. Disbelief is not necessarily the same as outright rejection (Schweizer 1984: 367). Plummer (1896: 550) suggests that the disciples may have been expecting a future return to glory but never figured that Jesus was speaking of immediate, bodily resurrection. This view is problematic, however, since 18:31–34 mentions resurrection on the third day. Even though this earlier text makes clear that the disciples did not understand Jesus' remark, the question about their understanding turns on what point they failed to grasp. The remark about resurrection appears intelligible enough, but it was unclear how resurrection fit into God's plan (see

17. Cf. Matt. 28:17; Mark 16:11, 14; Luke 24:41; John 20:25, 27. John does not believe until he sees the empty tomb (John 20:8); his trip to the tomb does, however, show interest in the possibility of resurrection.

the exegesis of 18:31–34). The disciples must understand that they can trust what Jesus promises.

This provides a lesson for Luke's readers, who cannot see Jesus but are under fire for believing in him. They can trust that he is alive (Osborne 1984: 113 n. 15). The larger group of apostles reacted to the resurrection, as many do when they hear it for the first time. It was not an expected or concocted event. It was a surprising miracle even to the original hearers, as it is to Luke's readers. If someone created the story of resurrection, would the apostles have been made to look so incredulous? The account's honesty has an air of reality, which points to its truth.

e. Peter's Response (24:12)

Peter reacts to the women's report by running to the tomb (μνη- **24:12** μεῖον, *mnēmeion*; elsewhere in Luke's resurrection narrative at 24:2, 9, 22, 24) and looking in it.[18] The meaning of the term παρακύπτω (*parakyptō*) is disputed (Fitzmyer 1985: 1547; BAGD 619 §1; BAA 1251 §1; MM 486; elsewhere in the NT at John 20:5, 11; James 1:25; 1 Pet. 1:12; cf. Gospel of Peter 13.56 [Schneemelcher 1991–92: 1.225]). Does it mean to stoop over or to stretch to see? Several OT examples (Gen. 26:8; Prov. 7:6; Sir. 21:23) show that it is unnecessary to insist that it mean "stoop." Here it means that Peter made some physical effort to look inside the tomb (e.g., peers in; Neirynck 1977). He sees the ὀθόνια (*othonia*, grave clothes; BAGD 555; BAA 1126; elsewhere in the NT only at John 19:40; 20:5, 6, 7), a term synonymous with σινδών (*sindōn*; Luke 23:53).

Peter goes home "amazed" (θαυμάζων, *thaumazōn*) at the things that have occurred. Since those who marvel are usually trying to understand what has happened, it is debated whether this is a note about Peter's faith. Most say no (Fitzmyer 1985: 1548; Marshall 1978: 889; Dillon 1978: 66–67; Nolland 1993b: 1192; perhaps Osborne 1984: 114). This verdict is possible in light of the report (24:24) that the apostles have failed to see Jesus and the contrast to the statement (24:34) that Peter has seen the Lord. A decisive appearance to Peter occurs after the initial report described in 24:24 and after his viewing the tomb here.

But this conclusion can be challenged. It may be that the only failure in 24:24 is that some do not believe, because there is no report of actually seeing Jesus. Perhaps 24:24 suggests that some were not persuaded by the mere presence of an empty tomb. After all, the complaint in 24:24 is that none of the apostles saw Jesus. Things were as the women said, but there was still something missing to

---

18. See the additional note concerning the originality of 24:12.

clinch the case. In other words, doubting Thomas was not alone. The ranks were divided among hopeful believers and skeptical doubters. Upon their return, the Emmaus disciples would have been told that Peter had seen Jesus as a sign of confirmation, which they really did not need in light of their own recent experience. What had been lacking according to 24:24 had been supplied in duplicate! This option seems slightly more likely than a total denial of faith here, since it can explain why some disciples stayed together on resurrection day after Peter's initial report. In addition, the account links together the tomb and the angelic reminder about Jesus' teaching.

True, there are no words of confession of faith here, but that is not decisive in the building up of the drama of discovery and its spread throughout the ranks. It is also clear that all doubt was removed with the appearances. For Luke, the empty tomb starts the road to revelation and helps support the women's story and claim for resurrection.

The almost total agreement between Luke and John suggests the use of a similar source. There are two differences. In Luke only Peter goes to the tomb, while in John the "beloved disciple" actually beats Peter to the tomb (John 20:8). It would appear that Luke focuses on Peter as a representative disciple, especially since Peter is the speaking witness in Acts 2–5. In addition, Luke has Peter leave "amazed at what has happened," while John is clear that at least the "beloved disciple" believes (John 20:7–10). If my analysis of Luke is correct, this is not really a difference. It should be noted, however, that John is not explicit about Peter's faith. After Peter returns in Luke, the drama of resurrection revelation continues, so a decision about Peter's state does not greatly impact the force of Luke 24 as a whole. All that is at stake is the speed by which doubt turned into faith and whether the appearances confirmed faith, removed doubt, or did a little of both among the group.

Summary Luke 24:1–12 is the first account that hints of a reversal of the tragedy of Jesus' death. An act of mourning and respect turns to perplexity for some devoted women. They appear at the tomb, only to find the stone moved, angels present, and the tomb empty. Jesus is brought to life, just as he predicted. The promise of God's power has come to pass, but the whole story is rather unbelievable. Nonetheless, the women go back to the disciples to relate the story, where they are met with unbelief, probably because they thought that resurrection from the dead would come at the end-time. But Peter is not sure. He has learned that what Jesus says is not only surprising, but right. He runs to the tomb. It is empty, except for the grave clothes, which suggests that Jesus was there at one time. Surely if he had been taken, the clothes would not still be there. No one would steal the body and leave the impression of resurrection. Peter is left to marvel over events and the reminder of Jesus' words. It is a moment for reflection, decision, and faith. Is resurrection the only adequate explanation for what Peter sees? Is not resurrection what Jesus promised? Has not God acted on behalf of Jesus? Is Jesus alive to carry out God's plan after all? These are questions not only for Peter in the moment of his discovery, but for all who relive that moment through Luke's retelling of the story. What else can explain these events? Can one really believe in resurrection hope? The story is not over. The apparent end has become a new beginning. Those who doubt will have their doubts laid to rest by the Lord who stands risen from his encounter with death.

Additional Notes

24:1. There is uncertainty about what term Luke used for "tomb": μνῆμα (A, B, F, L, W, family 1, family 13, Byz) or μνημεῖον ($\mathfrak{P}^{75}$, ℵ, C*, Δ). Most manuscripts that have μνῆμα alter the word order, placing ἦλθον (they came) before the phrase ἐπὶ τὸ μνῆμα (to the tomb). In Luke's writings, μνῆμα is found in Luke 8:27; 23:53; Acts 2:29; 7:16, while μνημεῖον appears in Luke 11:44, 47; 23:55; 24:2, 9, 12, 22, 24. Fitzmyer (1985: 1544) and Jeremias (1980: 310) prefer μνημεῖον, but lack explicit reasoning. The frequent use of μνημεῖον in Luke 24 makes μνῆμα the harder reading, but the variety in word order stands against it. Thus, the predominant and consistent use of μνημεῖον in Luke 24 makes it more likely to be original.

24:1. In Luke, only codex D records the women's discussion of who will roll away the stone, a remark that looks like Mark 16:3. This phrase is not original because it lacks attestation; in addition, Luke does not mention a stone in Luke 23.

24:3. Codex D and most Itala read τὸ σῶμα (the body), while 1241 and some Syriac have τὸ σῶμα τοῦ Ἰησοῦ (the body of Jesus). On the shorter-reading rule, the text of D is preferred, but the external evidence is too strong for that rule to apply here (Marshall 1978: 884; Luce 1933: 357).[19] The longer text, τὸ σῶμα τοῦ κυρίου Ἰησοῦ (the body of the Lord Jesus), is

---

19. Westcott and Hort 1881: 2.175–77 ("Introduction") call this phrase a "Western noninterpolation" because of this shorter-reading rule. Other such noninterpolations are Luke 22:19b–20; 24:6, 12, 36, 40, 51, 52; Matt. 27:49. A Western noninterpolation is a shorter Western reading, in contrast to the normally expansive pattern of the Western family. Those who call these passages "noninterpolations" are arguing that the Gospel originally omitted them since they are the shorter reading.

found in $\mathfrak{P}^{75}$, ℵ, A, B, C, W, Θ, family 1, family 13, and Byz. In addition, κύριος is common in Luke and thus is likely on internal grounds.[20]

24:6. Codex D and the Itala omit the remark about Jesus' being raised, an omission that is one of the disputed Western noninterpolations that many regard as original (Plummer 1896: 548; Creed 1930: 293; Luce 1933: 358). If the phrase is omitted, then the angels talk only about Jesus' teaching. External evidence for inclusion is large, and the textual factor against the omission is the presence of ἀλλά (but) in the middle of the phrase, a detail that would be unique to Luke (Marshall 1978: 885–86; Metzger 1975: 183–84).

24:10. The ambiguous syntax gave rise to variants that clarify the text: in A, D, W, and some Syriac ἦσαν (they were) is lacking (Klostermann 1929: 233), and in ℵ[1], Θ, and Byz αἱ (who) is added before ἔλεγον (were speaking) to smooth out the syntax. The punctuation of UBS–NA is correct, but the RSV and NIV give a good rendering of the sense.

24:12. Plummer (1896: 550) argues that Luke's record of Peter's visit to the tomb has "the look of an insertion," probably from John 20:3–10. As with other Western noninterpolations, D and Itala lack the verse (as does the first edition of UBS). The turning point in scholarly opinion came with the discovery of $\mathfrak{P}^{75}$, which included the verse, as do ℵ, A, B, L, W, Δ, Θ, Ψ, family 1, family 13, Byz, and Lect. On the basis of this overwhelming external evidence, UBS[4] rates the verse more certain (B) than do previous editions (D). Marshall (1978: 888) suggests that it might have been omitted because it is in tension with 24:34, which specifies another appearance to Peter. Internal factors also argue for inclusion. For example, it is unclear without 24:12 how 24:24's remark that others went to check out the tomb after the women fits into the movement of events. Some regard the plural in 24:24 as a problem, but Luke elsewhere focuses on Peter (e.g., 5:1–11). In addition, the unique terms in the passage (i.e., not found in John 20) are Lucan: ἀναστάς (having risen), τὸ γεγονός (the things that have happened), and θαυμάζων (marveling) (Dillon 1978: 60–61 nn. 173, 175). Holding to the originality of this verse are Dillon (1978: 59–62), Grundmann (1963: 439–40), Marshall (1978: 888), Fitzmyer (1985: 1547), Ellis (1974: 272–73), Wiefel (1988: 404), and Bode (1970: 69). Creed (1930: 294), Klostermann (1929: 232–33), and R. Mahoney (1974: 41–69) argue for omission. See also Leaney (1955–56), Muddiman (1972), Hartmann (1964), and Snodgrass (1972).

---

20. Luke uses κύριος as a title for Jesus fifteen times in the narrative comments of his Gospel, almost always in non-Marcan settings (7:13, 19; 10:1, 39, 41; 11:39; 12:42a; 13:15; 17:5, 6; 18:6; 19:8a; 22:61 [twice]; 24:3); Osborne 1984: 104, esp. n. 5.

2. Emmaus Road and a Meal of Discovery (24:13–35)

The appearance of Jesus on the Emmaus road is one of Luke's most vivid and dramatic accounts about Jesus, and he tells the event with great skill and drama. Luke's reader knows more than the travelers and can more easily see the unit's many themes. (1) The gradual revelation of Jesus contains irony: the empty tomb has not yet created an ecstatic change of view; in fact, the travelers lament that Jesus has not been seen even though the tomb is empty. (2) As Jesus demonstrates his resurrection in a direct appearance, tragedy turns to triumph when it becomes clear who has instructed them about (3) the fulfillment of Scripture and God's plan. (4) The raised Jesus sits in table fellowship with his disciples. He is in the midst of his people even when they are not aware of it. Failure becomes fulfillment.[1]

The account has a four-part structure (Fitzmyer 1985: 1559): the meeting (24:13–16), the conversation about recent events (24:17–27), the meal with its startling revelation (24:28–32), and the return to report the event (24:33–35). The major point surfaces in the contrast between the travelers' report of recent events (24:19b–24) versus Jesus' teaching about what must take place (24:25–27). The travelers were deeply disappointed by Jesus' death, which they initially viewed as a severe setback. Through this appearance, God reversed in dramatic style the thinking of Cleopas and his companion. They would never be the same as they learned that death could be overcome and that God's plan had moved ahead. Jesus was alive, and as a result their hope was renewed. This appearance is the third evidence of Jesus' resurrection (the other two were the empty tomb and the angelic announcement; Arndt 1956: 488). For Luke, appearances are the most decisive proof, since they remove all doubt about resurrection.

---

1. Fitzmyer 1985: 1557–59 notes four Lucan emphases: (1) the geographic journey, (2) Jesus' gradual revelation of himself, (3) Christology and fulfillment of OT prophecy, and (4) the meal scenes. (Fitzmyer describes the meal as "eucharistic"; although there is breaking of bread and thanksgiving, it is not a Eucharist, especially given the absence of wine.)

Sources and Historicity

The sources of this unique passage (Aland 1985: §355) are much discussed. All recognize that Luke tells the story with his own stylistic touches (Fitzmyer 1985: 1555–56 lists twenty-four phrases in the passage that are typical of Lucan expression; see the exegesis for details). But where does the basic account come from? There are three views (Klostermann 1929: 233):

1. The material came (probably in written form) directly from one of the travelers. Plummer (1896: 551) argues that this is the only place where such vivid detail could arise.
2. Luke received the basic story from a source, although there is disagreement about which elements came from this source (Grundmann 1963: 443–44 and Wiefel 1988: 408–9 argue that it is a Jerusalem source tied to Jesus' family). Schweizer (1984: 369) argues for Emmaus, appearance to non-apostles, lack of recognition, recognition in the midst of the meal, and lack of a commission. P. Schubert (1957: 174–75) attributes only 24:13, 15b, 16, 28–31 to Luke's source; Ernst (1977: 655–57) argues for 24:22–24, 28–35; and Fitzmyer (1985: 1554–55) argues for the material paralleled in Mark 16:12–13, Emmaus, Cleopas, the material about the appearance to Peter in Luke 24:34 (which recalls 1 Cor. 15:4–5), the review of Luke 24:1–11 in 24:22–24, and the language of 24:30. Nolland (1993b: 1198–99) notes two variations of this approach: (a) the source emphasized fulfillment of the OT and Luke added the meal scene and (b) the meal scene was in the source and Luke added the emphasis on Scripture. Since "Luke is rarely an innovator and most of his motifs are given to him from the tradition," Nolland sees Luke reworking an existing Emmaus tradition (with roots in Jerusalem) that had both themes.
3. The material is basically Luke's, from his hand, and with his emphases (Dillon 1978: 155; Wanke 1973: 109–15). Dillon acknowledges that a few details and the meal scene may be traditional, but argues that Luke is responsible for the rest. Wanke's 1973 study (esp. 23–126) is the most exhaustive attempt to defend Lucan authorship.

The task of determining sources is difficult—in fact, Tiede (1988: 433) says it is futile—because (a) Luke told the story in his own terms, (b) there are traces of his style in the account (as the exegesis notes, with numerous statistics at the key points), and (c) many themes parallel Lucan emphases elsewhere. For example, the fulfillment of Scripture and the necessity of God's plan coming to pass are clear Lucan points. Rightly warning that Lucan style does not equal Lucan creation, Marshall (1973b: 75–78) notes that Lucan themes sometimes originate in a source (e.g., 23:50–24:11). The various points raised as evidence of a source suggest that Luke used traditional material for the account, but it cannot be determined whether it was written or oral or a mixture. Either of the first two views is possible. If view 2 is accepted, all the essential themes were likely in the source. Lucan stylization need not mean denial of essential historicity, since Luke's tendency is to draw on traditional themes, not create them (Nolland 1993b: 1199). The clear presence of the otherwise obscure Emmaus reference also speaks for the originality of some of this tradition, for there is no reason why anyone would create an unknown locale for this key event. Wiefel (1988: 408) summarizes well: a pure Lucan new creation is hardly profitable.

Dodd (1955) notes that this account is one of the most detailed of the resurrection stories. He calls it a "circumstantial narrative," which means that the appearance is developed with drama and detail. It also means that the narrative reflects the evangelist's interests (John 21:1–14 is the other example of this form, which he pejoratively calls "tales").[2] Interestingly, Dodd sees this category as one of the latest developing forms of resurrection accounts, probably because of its length and detail. In contrast, Bultmann (1963: 286, 288–91), though calling the account legend, argues that the absence of apologetic motifs makes it an early resurrection story, since the only concern is to verify resurrection through an appearance of Jesus (he compares it to John 20:1, 11–18, 24–29; 21:1–14).[3] This difference in judgment may show how ill equipped form criticism is to judge matters of historicity by rules of growth in the tradition, even though it can make excellent observations about a passage's structure (Bock 1991b; Marshall 1978: 891 notes that judgments about form cannot prove historicity).

The decision about legendary motifs is controlled by an interpreter's presuppositions about the possibility of resurrection and supernatural appearances. It should be noted, however, that the church did not portray expectation of the resurrection as a given. The disciples struggle to accept the resurrection and do not do so until forced to—despite Jesus' earlier proclamation about it. This perspective does not look like a created detail. The reality portrayed in the Gospel accounts rings true. While the apostles did not expect resurrection, once they saw it, they were ready to die for the faith because they knew that death could not conquer them. The variety of Jesus'

2. Fitzmyer 1985: 1556–57 notes four other types of appearance narratives: (1) lists of witnesses (1 Cor. 15:5–8), (2) statements of appearance (Luke 24:34), (3) concise narratives that briefly report the appearance and usually involve situation, appearance, greeting, recognition, and word of command (Matt. 28:8–10), and (4) mixed narratives or developed reports (Luke 24:36–49). This is a variation of Dodd's 1955 delineation of three categories of narrative: concise, circumstantial, and mixed.

3. H. Betz 1969 also strongly argues for "cult legend." According to Betz the account teaches the resurrection's importance for Christian faith. Similar in tone is the Jesus Seminar (Funk and Hoover 1993: 398–99), which prints 24:17, 19, 25 in black type and says that all the dialogue is "provided by the storyteller" and involves instances of the evangelists "inventing words for Jesus that express their own perspectives."

appearances, both in Galilee and Jerusalem, is no reason to doubt their reality. The beauty of the Emmaus account is not only its picturesque narration but also its authenticity (Marshall 1978: 891 and Lake 1907: 211–12).

The outline of Luke 24:13–35 is as follows:

a. Meeting (24:13–16)
   i. Setting (24:13–14)
   ii. Jesus appears but is not recognized (24:15–16)
b. Conversation (24:17–27)
   i. The men's explanation (24:17–24)
     (1) Jesus' first question (24:17a)
     (2) The sad reaction (24:17b)
     (3) Cleopas's reply (24:18)
     (4) Jesus' second question (24:19a)
     (5) Cleopas's summary of events (24:19b–24)
   ii. Jesus' response (24:25–27)
c. Meal and revelation (24:28–32)
   i. The meal (24:28–29)
   ii. Jesus' revelation (24:30–31)
   iii. The men's response (24:32)
d. Report to disciples (24:33–35)

The account relates the travelers' disappointment over Jesus' death and their curiosity over the empty tomb. Since their "sight" is veiled, they do not initially recognize Jesus when he joins them. They think that all hope is lost. But things change as their new companion shows how Jesus is the fulfillment of all of the OT. There is a necessity to God's plan. During their meal and table fellowship, Jesus gradually reveals himself. Jesus' resurrection thus receives confirmation through an appearance. The travelers are overjoyed at being with Jesus and understanding God's plan as revealed in the Scriptures.

Exegesis and Exposition

[13]And behold, on the same day, two of them were journeying to a village named ⌜Emmaus⌝, about ⌜seven miles⌝ from Jerusalem, [14]and they were talking with each other about all these things that had happened. [15]While they were talking and discussing together, Jesus himself drew near and traveled with them. [16]But their eyes were kept from recognizing him.

[17]And he said to them, "What is this conversation you are holding with each other as you walk?" ⌜And they stood still⌝, looking sad. [18]And one of them, named Cleopas, said to him, "Are you the only one who dwells in Jerusalem and does not know the things that have happened in it during

these days?" [19]And he said to them, "What sort of things?" And they said to him, "Concerning Jesus ⌜of Nazareth⌝, who was a prophet mighty in deed and word before God and all the people, [20]and how our chief priests and rulers handed him over to a judgment of death and crucified him. [21]But we were hoping that this one was the one who comes to redeem Israel. But even besides this, this is the third day he has spent since all these things came to pass. [22]But also some of the women from us amazed us, going to the tomb early this morning [23]and, not finding the body, came back to say also they had seen a vision of angels, who are saying he is living. [24]And some of them with us went out to the tomb and found it so, as the women had said, but they did not see him." [25]And he said, "O you foolish and slow of heart to believe all that the prophets spoke! [26]Was it not necessary for the Christ to suffer these things and come into his glory?" [27]And beginning from Moses and from all the prophets, ⌜he interpreted⌝ for them in all the Scriptures the things concerning himself.

[28]And they drew near to the town where they were going. And he acted as though he would go farther. [29]But they constrained him, saying, "Remain with us, for it is near evening and the day is already spent." And he entered to remain with them. [30]And after he reclined at the table with them, he, taking the bread, blessed and having broken it gave it to them. [31]And their eyes were opened, and they recognized him. And he disappeared from them. [32]And they said to one another, "Did not our hearts burn ⌜within us⌝ as he spoke to us on the road, as he opened the Scripture?"

[33]And rising up in that hour, they returned to Jerusalem and found the Eleven gathered and those who were with them, [34]who said, "⌜Indeed⌝ the Lord has been raised and has appeared to Simon." [35]And they told them about the things that happened on the road and how he made himself known to them in the breaking of bread.

a. Meeting (24:13–16)
i. Setting (24:13–14)

Using καὶ ἰδού (*kai idou*, and behold), a phrase he commonly uses to **24:13** open new units (twenty-six times in Luke and eight times in Acts; Plummer 1896: 551), Luke introduces a second event that occurred on resurrection day (ἐν αὐτῇ τῇ ἡμέρᾳ [*en autē tē hēmera*] looks back to 24:1 and anticipates 24:33–34, 36, 50; cf. 1:59; 4:16; 10:12; 17:24; 19:42; 23:12). Luke is not, however, interested in an "eighth-day" or "new-creation" motif (Barn. 15.8–9; Justin Martyr, *Dialogue with Trypho* 138; against Ellis 1974: 276; with Marshall 1978: 892). Luke's reference to "two of them" is an allusion to the group of disciples mentioned in 24:9. That the apostles are not meant is clear from the name *Cleopas* (24:18), who is not one of the Eleven. The men are probably headed home to Emmaus (Moule 1957–58).

Three issues surround the reference to Emmaus (Ἐμμαοῦς): its distance from Jerusalem, its location, and the purpose of its mention (Fitzmyer 1985: 1561–62; Dillon 1978: 85–89). A textual problem affects the question of the village's distance from Jerusalem (see the additional note). The probable reading says the town is sixty stadia (i.e., 6.9 miles or 11.1 kilometers) from Jerusalem.

The location of Emmaus has never been decisively pinned down (BAGD 255; BAA 514; Mackowski 1980; Wanke 1973: 37–43), and the discussion has changed little in the last thirty years (Dillon 1978: 87 n. 49 calls it "stalemated"). Three locations are suggested:

1. The traditional location is Ammaous (Ἀμμαοῦς), a Maccabean battleground (1 Macc. 3:40, 57; 4:3; Fitzmyer 1985: 1561; Marshall 1978: 892) later called Nicopolis and ʿAmwâs (the modern Arab name). It was fortified for battle by Bacchides (1 Macc. 9:50; Josephus, *Antiquities* 13.1.3 §15), burned in 4 B.C. (Josephus, *Antiquities* 17.10.7 §282; 17.10.9 §291), and rebuilt by A.D. 66 into a major town again (Josephus, *Jewish War* 3.3.5 §55). Both Eusebius and Jerome identify Emmaus as Ammaous (see Fitzmyer for references), which is twenty miles from Jerusalem, not seven as Luke says.[4] If the textual variant of 160 stadia is correct (see the additional note), then Ammaous is the best candidate. One must ask, however, whether it would be possible to travel forty miles—from Jerusalem to Emmaus and back—in one day (24:33).
2. The Crusaders regarded el-Qubeibeh as Emmaus (Plummer 1896: 551–52; Rengstorf 1968: 271) and in A.D. 1099 established a fort there called Castellum Emmaus. Although located the right distance from Jerusalem (sixty-three stadia), the location is unattested in the first century, which makes the identification less than certain (DeGuglielmo 1941).
3. Josephus mentions an Ἀμμαοῦς located thirty stadia from Jerusalem (*Jewish War* 7.6.6 §217). Vespasian settled some eight hundred veterans here, a locale identified as ancient Mozah (Josh. 18:26; *m. Suk.* 4.5; Creed 1930: 295). If one accepts this locale, then Luke would be giving the round-trip distance for the journey (Ellis 1974: 277; Liefeld 1984: 1055; Nolland 1993b: 1201), which is not clear from the text, but is possible.

In short, a clear option does not emerge. Either view 2 or 3 is possible, with view 3 more likely.

The significance of Emmaus's mention is twofold: (1) it indicates an appearance in the Jerusalem area, which is Luke's geographic

---

4. Ernst 1977: 659 says that Luke's knowledge of the location is imprecise. Dillon 1978: 87–88 sees Luke's distance as an error.

concern, and (2) it reflects the retention of historical detail. It is hard to imagine an appearance being tied to an obscure village unless it really occurred there. Luke thus sets the stage for one of the most famous of Jesus' appearances.

The two men are engaged in an intense discussion (ὁμιλέω, *homileō*; **24:14** BAGD 565; BAA 1146; elsewhere in the NT only at Luke 24:15; Acts 20:11; 24:26) with one another (πρὸς ἀλλήλους, *pros allēlous*; the phrase elsewhere in the NT at Luke 2:15; 4:36; 6:11; 8:25; 20:14; 24:17, 32; Acts 4:15; 26:31; 28:4, 25). It had been an unusual few days, and they are reviewing what had transpired. The description suggests a wide-ranging conversation in which they rehashed all (περὶ πάντων, *peri pantōn*) these events (συμβεβηκότων, *symbebēkotōn*; BAGD 777; BAA 1551; elsewhere in the NT at Mark 10:32; Acts 3:10; 20:19; 21:35; 1 Cor. 10:11; 1 Pet. 4:12; 2 Pet. 2:22; cf. 1 Macc. 4:26; Josephus, *Jewish War* 4.1.6 §43; *Antiquities* 13.6.3 §194). Cleopas's summary in 24:19b–24 probably indicates the general content of their discussion. Luke uses his frequent καὶ αὐτοί (*kai autoi*, and they) construction to continue the account (the singular καὶ αὐτός is more common than the plural: e.g., 4:15; 15:14; 16:24; 17:13; 19:2 [twice]; Dillon 1978: 90 n. 57; Michaelis 1950).

ii. Jesus Appears But Is Not Recognized (24:15–16)

The conversation was intense, as they "debated" (Danker 1988: 391) **24:15** or "discussed" (Marshall 1978: 893). Συζητέω (*syzēteō*) suggests emotional dialogue (elsewhere in the NT at Mark 1:27; 8:11; 9:10, 14, 16; 12:28; Luke 22:23; Acts 6:9; 9:29; J. Schneider, *TDNT* 7:747). During this time, a third traveler catches up (ἐγγίσας, *engisas*) to the pair. Jesus apparently has a form of resurrection body that they could not recognize (24:16) as he travels with them and engages them in conversation. They probably think that he is another worshiper returning home from Jerusalem. Luke likes the idea of a journey, so he notes their travel here as well.

Luke makes it clear that the two travelers do not have the total pic- **24:16** ture: their eyes were kept from (ἐκρατοῦντο, *ekratounto*; BAGD 448 §2d; BAA 911 §2d) recognizing Jesus. The use of the articular infinitive τοῦ μὴ ἐπιγνῶναι (*tou mē epignōnai*, not to recognize) is epexegetical and specifies what they were kept from knowing (Plummer 1896: 552; Bultmann, *TDNT* 1:704; BDF §400.4; BDR §400.4.6; cf. Luke 4:42; Acts 10:47; 14:18; 20:20, 27; Gen. 16:2). The force of ἐκρατοῦντο . . . ἐπιγνῶναι is disputed. Did God conceal this information (Marshall 1978: 893; Fitzmyer 1985: 1563)? Was the disciples' own blindness the problem? Or was Satan at fault (Nolland 1993b: 1201; see the exegesis of Luke 9:45 and n. 4 there)? The first view is more likely, since the passive construction places responsibility outside the disciples and Satan is entirely absent from the resurrection account. There would come a time when the disciples would clearly see, but in their current uncertainty God still had things to teach them. The veil will be lifted in Luke 24:31. Such concealing is often noted by Luke (9:45 and 18:34, both probably by God; Fitzmyer 1985: 1563; Danker 1988: 391). The lack of recognition of the raised Jesus occurs elsewhere (John 20:14–15; 21:4).[5] One purpose of the verse is to show the reality of Jesus' bodily resurrection. Luke tells the story with dramatic flair, as the reader knows more about the situation than those who experienced the event—at least at this point. Part of the drama is when and how they will realize who their discussion partner is.

b. Conversation (24:17–27)
i. The Men's Explanation (24:17–24)
(1) Jesus' First Question (24:17a)

24:17a Jesus joins the conversation by asking about the words "exchanged" (ἀντιβάλλετε, *antiballete*; BAGD 74; BAA 146; a NT *hapax legomenon*; 2 Macc. 11:13) between them (Plummer 1896: 552; Marshall 1978: 894). The topic and tone catches Jesus' attention, and he wants to draw them out.

(2) The Sad Reaction (24:17b)

24:17b Their reaction to Jesus' question is simple: they stop walking (ἐστάθησαν, *estathēsan*; BAGD 382 §II.1a; BAA 774 §II.1a).[6] Their grief is obvious: σκυθρωποί (*skythrōpoi*, sad faced; BAGD 758; BAA 1514; elsewhere in the NT only at Matt. 6:16; cf. Gen. 40:7; Sir. 25:23) describes a look of remorse or gloom (Plummer 1896: 552). This type of questioning is something that Luke notes frequently (Acts 2:12; 4:7; 8:30–31; 10:4; 15:7–11; Tiede 1988: 434). They cannot believe that anyone coming out of Jerusalem does not know what has happened. Clearly these travelers are stunned and disappointed by recent events.

---

5. Mark 16:12 says Jesus was present in a different form to emphasize that his resurrection body was distinct. It is not the time of day that conceals his identity, but rather a lack of perception about the new form of his body.

6. Dillon's effort (1978: 113) to argue that the men are stopped "under the pall of the passion-mystery" misses the point, despite his appeal to 22:25 and 24:25. They do not think there is any divine mystery in the events—only curious disappointment (24:19–24). Granted, they are in an emotional stew, but they stop in total shock that their companion does not know what has happened. This is not a Lucan motif, the vocabulary is too rare.

(3) Cleopas's Reply (24:18)

Jesus receives a response from one of the men, named Cleopas. It is **24:18** not clear why only one figure is named. If Luke created the account, why would he name only one figure? The single name thus gives evidence of a source (Fitzmyer 1985: 1564). Κλεοπᾶς (Cleopas) is a shortened form of the name Κλεόπατρος (Cleopatros; BDF §125.2). It is not related to the name Κλωπᾶς (Clopas; John 19:25; Eusebius, *Ecclesiastical History* 3.11), which is a Greek form of a Semitic name (with Plummer 1896: 553; Klostermann 1929: 235; and Fitzmyer 1985: 1563; against Marshall 1978: 894; Grundmann 1963: 443; and BDF §125.2). This figure is not identified anywhere else in the NT. Suggestions abound about the companion's identity (Fitzmyer 1985: 1563):

> Peter—Crehan 1953; Annand 1958; but this is unlikely given that in 24:34 the apostles tell Cleopas that Peter has seen Jesus
>
> Cleopas's wife—C. Charlesworth 1922–23
>
> Emmaus—which misreads the place-name as a person; Souter 1901–2; Nestle 1901–2; Bonus 1901–2
>
> Nathanael—codex V (ninth century), as noted by Metzger 1975: 185[7]
>
> Simon (not Peter)—codex S (A.D. 949), as noted by Metzger 1975: 185

Complicating the picture is a tradition in Origen's *Against Celsus* 2.62, 68 that identifies the other disciple as Simon—but not apparently Peter, for Eusebius's *Ecclesiastical History* 3.11 speaks of Simeon son of Clopas (John 19:25), who was a cousin of the Lord and succeeded James as leader of the Jerusalem church (Zahn 1920: 712; Creed 1930: 295; Luce 1933: 360). Plummer (1896: 551) sees the Simon that Origen named as a mistaken interpretation of Luke 24:34. None of these connections is compelling.

Cleopas asks if the traveler has had his head in the sand, since he does not know what has happened even after making a pilgrimage to Jerusalem (παροικεῖς, *paroikeis*; Plummer 1896: 553; BAGD 628; BAA 1269–70; παροικέω elsewhere in the NT only at Heb. 11:9; cf. Acts 7:6, 29; Gen. 17:8; 20:1; 21:34; Exod. 6:4). They are shocked at his ignorance. The emphatic σὺ μόνος (*sy monos*, you alone) asks this companion if he is the only one not aware of such events (Plummer 1896: 553). How could he have missed these events (τὰ γενόμενα, *ta genomena*; cf. Luke 8:34, 56; 23:48), which were so public

---

7. A marginal note in codex V takes this identification from Epiphanius, *Panarion* 23.6, and says that Cleopas was Jesus' cousin and the second bishop of Jerusalem.

and of such interest? The recent past is underscored by "these days," a reference to the noteworthy festival in Jerusalem. Dillon (1978: 113–14) argues that this emphasis on Jerusalem and the events' public character are evidence of Lucan themes (e.g., 2:52; 4:14–15; 8:47; 9:13; 20:45). The theme contrasts the public quality of Jesus' ministry with a lack of understanding about what his ministry meant. But surely the focus is also on the public nature of the trial, reflecting the leadership's involvement in Jesus' death and the way Jesus was brought before all (Luke 23). Mark 9:32 also notes the lack of understanding by the disciples, while John often notes how understanding comes later (John 12:16; 20:9). As such, the detail need not be seen as a Lucan touch, though it is true that Luke emphasizes this point.

(4) Jesus' Second Question (24:19a)

24:19a Jesus draws out his companions and asks them "what sort of things" (ποῖα, *poia*) they are discussing. BAGD 684 §2bα and BAA 1373 §2bα note that the understood object of the question is γενόμενα (*genomena*): "What sort of things *have happened?*"

(5) Cleopas's Summary of Events (24:19b–24)

24:19b The pair begins to tell about Jesus of Nazareth (Luke 4:34 = Mark 1:24; Luke 18:37 = Mark 10:47; Acts 2:22; 3:6; 4:10; 6:14; 10:38; 22:8; 24:5; 26:9; cf. Matt. 2:23; 26:71; Mark 14:67; 16:6; John 18:5, 7; 19:19) in terms that fit the portrait of Luke's Gospel. Jesus is called a prophet before (ἐναντίον, *enantion*) God and all the people (Fitzmyer 1985: 1564; Friedrich, *TDNT* 6:846–47; elsewhere used by Luke at Luke 1:6; 20:26; Acts 7:10; 8:32). The title *prophet* recalls Luke 4:16–30 and 13:31–35 and matches the public judgment about him (Luke 7:16, 39; 9:9, 18–19; Acts 10:38–39, a theme with popular and traditional roots [see Mark 6:15]). Jesus declared the way to God, so he was "mighty in word and deed" (a traditional combination found throughout the NT: Rom. 15:18; 2 Cor. 10:11; Col. 3:17; 2 Thess. 2:17; 1 John 3:18). In Acts 7:22 this phrase describes Moses' work, and in Acts 3:14–26 Jesus is described as a prophet like Moses. Luke 9:35, with its allusion to Deut. 18:15 (cf. Acts 7:37), also suggests this Mosaic connection. It was hoped that Jesus would be the leader of a new people and a new era. The mighty character of his ministry may allude to his being empowered by the Spirit (Dillon 1978: 114–15; cf. Acts 10:38; Luke 9:1; 24:49). To call Jesus a prophet, even a prophet like Moses, is less than a full description of him, but it is a major and appropriate characterization of Jesus' ministry (Nolland 1993b: 1202). An additional title and function comes later in 24:21, when the pair says they had hoped that Jesus would redeem Israel. These travelers gradually reveal Jesus' complete identity, a sensitive topic among Jews at this time, so they are careful how they introduce him. They clearly had high regard and high hopes for Jesus.

But there is another side to the story: disappointment. Despite his **24:20** impressive ministry, Jesus was rejected by the nation's religious officials (23:13), whom the travelers identify as "our" chief priests and leaders.[8] This summary clearly places the blame for Jesus' death on the leadership, who handed Jesus over to judgment.[9]

"Handing over" also alludes to the passive Roman role, since they are responsible for the execution (Plummer 1896: 553; Marshall 1978: 895; Luke 22:71; 23:21–23; Acts 4:25–27). These descriptions recall the many predictions Jesus made (Luke 9:44; 18:32; 24:7; cf. Acts 2:36; 4:10; 13:27). These terms are more prominent in the other Synoptics: παραδίδωμι (paradidōmi, to hand over) in Matt. 17:22 = Mark 9:31; Matt. 20:18–19 = Mark 10:33 (twice); Matt. 26:2 = Mark 14:41; Matt. 26:45 and σταυρόω (stauroō, to crucify) in Matt. 20:19; 26:2; 27:22, 23, 26, 31, 35, 38 = Mark 15:13, 14, 15, 20, 24, 25, 27; Matt. 28:5 = Mark 16:6. The reader of Luke's Gospel will recognize the language. The view of the Emmaus pair parallels the church's tradition and language about Jesus' death.

The two share their personal view of Jesus: they were downcast be- **24:21** cause they had hoped that he was going to redeem Israel. The imperfect ἠλπίζομεν (ēlpizomen, we were hoping) expresses the ongoing character of this hope. The idea is like Jer. 14:8, where Yahweh is called the hope of Israel (Fitzmyer 1985: 1564). They hoped that through Jesus, God would work for the nation and deliver it into a new era of freedom. This is the only time that Luke uses λυτρόω (lytroō, to redeem; Plummer 1896: 553; Marshall 1978: 895; Büchsel, TDNT 4:340–51).[10] If this hope equals that expressed by Zechariah in 1:68–79, then what was hoped for included Israel's political re-

---

8. Dillon 1978: 122–28 correctly speaks of a miracle-passion pattern that shows Jesus is rejected like the prophets of old (Luke 11:47–51; 13:34–35; Acts 7:51–53). The travelers do not yet understand the significance of these connections (Osborne 1984: 121 n. 24). This detail also shows clearly how Jesus' death is seen as a part of a Jewish squabble. The account takes a decidedly Jewish perspective on the events (e.g., the silence about Pilate's and Rome's roles; Nolland 1993b: 1202).

9. On the use of ὅπως with the meaning of πῶς (how?) in an indirect question, see BDF §300.1; BDR §300.1; §436.2. Codex D has the more common ὡς, but the attestation is too slight to be original.

10. The word group is rare in the NT: λυτρόω (to redeem; Luke 24:21; Titus 2:14; 1 Pet. 1:18), λύτρον (ransom; Matt. 20:28 = Mark 10:45), λύτρωσις (redemption; Luke 1:68; 2:38; Heb. 9:12), and λυτρωτής (redeemer; Acts 7:35); cf. BAGD 482–83; BAA 979–80; Deut. 13:5 [13:6 LXX]; 2 Sam. 7:23; Hos. 13:14; Barn. 14.5–7; 19.2; Ignatius, Philadelphians 11.1; Justin Martyr, Dialogue with Trypho 131.3; Irenaeus, Against Heresies 1.21.4.

lease from Rome (a major Jewish emphasis: Isa. 41:14; 43:14; 44:22–24; 1 Macc. 4:11; Ps. Sol. 9.1; Fitzmyer 1985: 1564).

Dillon's comment (1978: 129–30) that Israel means broadly "the people of God" and not strictly the nation fails (1) to note the disappointment expressed here, (2) to take seriously the tie to the infancy declarations, (3) to recall that part of the disappointment was that "our" chief priests and rulers handed Jesus over, and (4) the Jewish perspective that pervades the account. The pair is still thinking of Israel as a political-social unit. It fits the time period of the remarks, before the church was forced to operate as an autonomous unit, a change that Acts begins to detail. The nationalistic focus of activity in the early chapters of Acts makes a Jewish focus for this remark clear (Danker 1988: 392). In the pair's view, the possibility of such a hope coming to fruition for Israel died with Jesus on the cross. What they did not know is that this hope would be realized in an unexpected way, as the message of Acts and the rest of the NT show. Irony again exists, as the hope is even more comprehensively realized than these travelers had hoped.

The day of Jesus' death three days earlier is significant (Fitzmyer 1985: 1565; Creed 1930: 296; Plummer 1896: 554).[11] Although there is no expectation of resurrection here, the remark is an ironic echo of the "third-day" emphasis in 9:22; 13:32–33; 24:7.

24:22 Yet even death does not end the story, for events of the early morning (ὀρθρινός, *orthrinos*; BAGD 580; BAA 1176; BDR §113.3.4; §243.1.1) extend the drama. The pair summarizes what Luke recorded in 24:1–12 (Fitzmyer 1985: 1565 sees 24:22–24 as independent of Mark 16:1–8). Their reaction to these latest events is one of amazement (ἐξίστημι, *existēmi*; Marshall 1978: 896). When some of the women with the disciples went to the tomb, they did not find Jesus. The travelers are not impressed by the women's report, only astonished by it. They represent perplexed doubters. What had happened to Jesus' body? The recent news is also part of their discussion.[12]

24:23 The women did not find Jesus' body (an allusion to 24:5–11). They saw a "vision" (ὀπτασία, *optasia*; elsewhere in Luke only at 1:22; Michaelis, *TDNT* 5:372) of some angels, who said that Jesus was among the living (24:5). The present tense λέγουσιν (*legousin*, they say) describes the angels, while the report is summarized with a

---

11. This last clause is expressed impersonally without a clear subject and is usually translated as "he is already spending the third day" (BDF §129; BDR §129.2.3; BAGD 14 §4), although Arndt 1943 translates it as "it is three days." On the use of σύν with the force of "besides all this," see BDF §221; BDR §221.

12. This last event in the sequence is treated almost as a "news flash" would be today. It was still too early to know what this latest development meant.

present infinitive (ζῆν, zēn, to live). While the present tense is normally used for reported speech, the effect of the two present tenses together draws attention to Jesus' being alive and repeats the report with a freshness that a past tense in either location would have lessened (BDR §88.1.2). Of course, the issue is whether the report will be believed. The Emmaus travelers are perplexed but not yet convinced.

The women's report did get a reaction: some of the disciples went to **24:24** the tomb and found it empty just as the women said (24:9–11). Campenhausen (1968: 61) argues that this text shows that the women did not see Jesus as John 20:11–18 suggests, but this makes the text say too much. Luke has simply been selective (Osborne 1984: 234).

A note of doubt ends the summary by the Emmaus travelers: the disciples who went to the tomb did not see Jesus (24:12). Luke here notes that more than one disciple went to the tomb, which agrees with John 20:3–10. This difference suggests that Luke is stringing together pieces of tradition into a unified account.[13]

To those now walking unknowingly with Jesus, the decisive piece of empirical evidence was lacking, an appearance by Jesus (Marshall 1978: 896: "but him [αὐτὸν δέ, emphatic] they did not see"; Fitzmyer 1985: 1565: "no one saw *him*"). They are like modern people in their skepticism. Only the presence of the raised Jesus would convince them of what happened. The irony of the narrative is that they are in the midst of what they desired and what the others had not experienced (Tiede 1988: 435). The story is told so that the reader shares the irony. The travelers' report of recent events ends with a note of pathos, though the reader knows that the emotions are uncalled for, since the reader already knows that Jesus is with them (24:15–16). These travelers are aware that unusual events have taken place, but unfortunately the decisive evidence was lacking. They are about to find out what Luke's readers already know.

ii. Jesus' Response (24:25–27)

Jesus responds with rebuke. The interjection ὦ (ō, O!) usually indi- **24:25** cates great emotion (BAGD 895 §1; BAA 1785 §1; BDR §146.1.2; Luke 9:41; Acts 1:1; 13:10; Rom. 2:1, 3; 9:20; Gal. 3:1; 1 Tim. 6:20; James 2:20). The rebuke expresses great disappointment and recalls Luke 24:5–7 where the angel gave the women at the tomb a similar reaction. Their failure, according to their new companion,

---

13. Luce 1933: 361 thinks the difference shows that 24:12 was not originally in Luke, but the text-critical external evidence is too strong to ignore (see the additional note on 24:12). This does seem to indicate that this account originally circulated independently of 24:1–12.

is one of foolishness (ἀνόητος, *anoetos*; BAGD 70; BAA 139; else-where in the NT at Rom. 1:14; Gal. 3:1, 3; 1 Tim. 6:9; Titus 3:3) and slow-heartedness (βραδύς, *bradys*; BAGD 147; BAA 293; elsewhere in the NT twice at James 1:19). They do not believe the prophets, which Jesus will rectify when he explains the Scriptures to them (Luke 24:27).[14] Later he will do the same for the disciples (24:44–47; Marshall 1978: 896). In short, the resurrection's reality should not have been hidden (9:45; 18:34), but now the veil is being deci-sively removed (Dillon 1978: 133).

Jesus emphasizes that there is much OT teaching on this, and so he speaks of "all" (ἐπὶ πᾶσιν, *epi pasin*) that the prophets have spo-ken. The various speeches in Acts where Jesus is proclaimed from the OT indicate what texts are in view here; key among such texts are Deut. 18:15; Ps. 2:7; 16:8–11; 110:1; 118; and Isa. 53:8 (Bock 1987). Other summary references to the OT occur in Luke 24:44–47 and Acts 3:19–21.

24:26 Jesus' summary is very much like 24:7 and his earlier passion pre-dictions. Using a rhetorical question that expects a positive reply (note οὐχί, *ouchi*, not), Jesus states what the travelers should have known from the prophets: that it was necessary for the Christ to suf-fer and come into his glory. Jesus has pushed the prophetic descrip-tion of his travelers (24:19) into messianic categories. The use of ἔδει (*edei*, it was necessary) is a major Lucan theme and also recalls 24:7 (Grundmann, *TDNT* 2:22, 24; BDF §358.1; BDR §358.1.2; see the exegesis of 24:7). The theme of suffering is drawn from Ps. 118, Isa. 53, and the lament psalms that portray the righteous sufferer (e.g., Ps. 31, 69; Danker 1988: 393). The remark anticipates Luke 24:46 (cf. 9:22; 17:25; Acts 3:18; 17:3; 26:23). The consensus is that first-century Judaism did not anticipate a suffering Messiah (Fitz-myer 1985: 1565–66; Marshall 1978: 896).[15] Nonetheless, Jesus says that the OT prophets had such an expectation. Here is where Chris-tian and Jewish messianic expectation and eschatology differed greatly.

The newly emphasized element in the summary is the idea of en-try into glory. When δόξα (*doxa*) does not refer to praise in Luke, it refers to either the majesty or authority of Jesus: at the transfigura-

14. On the syntax of τοῦ πιστεύειν ἐπί (to believe), see BAGD 287 §II.1bγ; BAA 582 §II.1bγ; BDR §187.2.2; §400.8.10; Acts 5:14; 9:42; 18:8; 16:31; 22:19; Rom. 9:33; 10:11; 1 Pet. 1:16; 1 Pet. 2:6. Wilcox 1965: 85–86 argues that this is possibly a Semitic con-struction.

15. Levey 1974 lists the Jewish passages. Rowley 1950 has a full discussion of the historical issues. Jeremias, *TDNT* 5:677–700, is more optimistic in his appraisal of this theme in Judaism, but most note that his sources are later than the first century; see Rese 1963. See the discussion of Isa. 53 in the exegesis of Luke 22:37.

tion (Luke 9:31–32), in his current rule (Acts 7:55), or at his return (Luke 21:27). Resurrection means reception into heavenly authority. Historical or prophetic summaries of Jesus' career usually discuss the resurrection after speaking of Jesus' suffering. Here the emphasis on glory is a focus on Jesus' position and authority, not just his coming to life. Such glory exists now for Jesus and looks to its manifestation in return (21:27). The emphasis here is on his entering glory, so that the exalted nature of his current position is stressed. This theme recalls the transfiguration (9:31) and the discussion about Jesus' exodus (9:26). The pointing to glory anticipates the emphasis on resurrection and exaltation mentioned in the speeches of Acts (2:30–36; 3:19–21; 4:10; 5:30–31; 10:41–43; 13:32–36).[16] Glory refers to the splendor of being in God's presence or, in Jesus' case, at God's side (Fitzmyer 1985: 1566; Marshall 1978: 897; Exod. 14:4, 17–18; 16:7, 10; Ps. 26:8; 72:19; Isa. 43:7; 58:8; 60:1–2; Luke 21:27; Acts 7:2, 55; Phil. 2:5–11; 1 Tim. 3:16; 1 Pet. 1:11, 21). Jesus is not only alive, he rules. He has entered (εἰσελθεῖν, *eiselthein*; Acts 14:22) into his glory, which means that he has been raised to reign next to God, just as he promised at his trial (Luke 22:69; 23:42–43). As such the background of the remark is Ps. 110 and Dan. 7:14. The great manifestation of that glory is yet to come (Luke 21:27), but Jesus has now emerged from the dark night of his suffering. The man that the Emmaus travelers are walking with is no mere disciple or pilgrim; he is a regal visitor.

Jesus explains the things taught about the Christ from all the Scriptures (διερμηνεύω [*diermēneuō*; BAGD 194 §2; BAA 390 §2] is used elsewhere by Luke at Acts 9:36 [interpreting a foreign name] and 18:6 [interpreting Scripture (variant reading)]). He teaches the OT in the new era (see Koet 1989: 56–72 for Luke's terms for interpretation). The comprehensiveness of the teachings is underlined in several ways: from "all" (πάντων, *pantōn*) the prophets he explains "all" (πάσαις, *pasais*) the Scriptures, and Jesus starts from (ἀρξάμενος, *arxamenos*) Moses and goes to all the prophets ("Moses and all the prophets" is a traditional phrase: 1QS 1.3; 4Q504 [= 4QDibHam[a]] 3.12; Matt. 11:13; John 1:45; Nolland 1993b: 1205). This figure (called zeugma) describes the discussion's scope: he went through the entire Scripture, front to back (Creed 1930: 297; Luce 1933: 361). Both the former and latter prophets are meant, since the Hebrew Scriptures are in view (Luke 16:31; Acts 26:22; 28:23; Fitzmyer 1985: 1567). The starting point in Moses was perhaps a text that Luke himself later notes: Deut. 18:15 (Acts 3:22; cf. 7:35).

24:27

---

16. Dillon 1978: 143 suggests that the motif is of Jesus leading the way for others, as Acts 3:15 and 7:35 seem to suggest, but this is not clear from Luke 24.

That all Scripture points to Jesus is something that Luke likes to stress (Luke 24:45; Acts 17:2, 11; 18:24, 28; Schrenk, *TDNT* 1:752; Marshall 1978: 897). Luke sees continuity in God's plan—not surprise or parenthesis. The Scripture teaches much of what Jesus did in his first coming (Luke 24:44–47 and the speeches of Acts, especially those of Peter and Paul in evangelistic contexts). In making this point, Jesus appeals to two types of prophetic fulfillment. Texts that are directly prophetic refer only to Jesus, while typico-prophetic texts reflect patterns that Jesus reenacts and escalates to show their fulfillment or their eschatological inauguration at a new level. This combination of texts shows that Jesus fulfills some things now, while he fulfills others things later (see Bock 1987 for details of the hermeneutic behind this use of OT texts; see Kimball 1994 for a solid form-critical analysis of these texts in terms of Jewish hermeneutical structures of argument). Jesus begins opening eyes that had been closed, as the rebuke sets up the revelation (9:45; 18:34; 24:16, 31; Tiede 1988: 436). He has not revealed himself yet, but he is opening up the truth as preparation for his self-revelation.

c. Meal and Revelation (24:28–32)
i. The Meal (24:28–29)

24:28 As the travelers draw near their destination, Jesus "pretended" (προσεποιήσατο, *prosepoiēsato*; BAGD 718; BAA 1438) to go on (πορρώτερον, *porrōteron*; BAGD 693 §2; BAA 1390; BDR §62.3.4). Marshall (1978: 897) argues that "pretend" is too strong, although Plummer (1896: 556) notes Mark 6:48 and 7:27 as comparable. The basic idea of προσποιέω is "to act as if" something is going to happen. To "pretend" suggests that Jesus was hoping to stay with them and not journey on. It seemed as if the meeting was over, but the travelers' sensitivity and interest change the situation (on this kind of invitation in the OT, see Gen. 18:3; 19:2).

24:29 The travelers do not wish Jesus to go on, so they urge him (παρεβιάσαντο, *parebiasanto*; BAGD 612; BAA 1238; elsewhere in the NT only at Acts 16:15; cf. Gen. 19:9; 1 Sam. 28:23; 2 Kings 2:17; 5:16; Plummer 1896: 556) to stay with them.[17] John uses μένω (*menō*) in a theological sense to call people to remain or abide in Jesus, but Luke's usage is an example of the term's common meaning. The reason (ὅτι, *hoti*, for) the travelers ask Jesus to stay with them is that evening approaches (ἑσπέρα, *hespera*; BAGD 313; BAA 634; else-

---

17. Παραβιάζομαι usually means "to use force" on someone, but here "quiet persuasion" is meant, which is similar to the use of the unprefixed form in the difficult 16:16. On the importance of hospitality in Judaism, see Philo, *On Abraham* 22 §§107–13; Josephus, *Antiquities* 1.11.2 §196.

where in the NT only at Acts 4:3; 28:23; cf. Gen. 8:11; Exod. 12:6; Num. 9:11; Jer. 6:4; Zech. 14:7), the day is almost spent (κέκλικεν, *kekliken*; BAGD 436 §2; BAA 888 §2; cf. Jer. 6:4; Luke 9:12), and perhaps it is unsafe to travel at night (Fitzmyer 1985: 1567; Plummer 1896: 556). Jesus "came in to remain with them," language that is similar to Rev. 3:20 (Grundmann 1963: 447; Marshall 1978: 897–98; Ernst 1977: 663; Gen. 24:55; Judg. 19:9; Tob. 10:8; Luke 7:36; 11:37; 19:5; John 1:38; Acts 16:15).

ii. Jesus' Revelation (24:30–31)

The travelers still do not know who Jesus is as he reclines at the table **24:30** with them to share a meal of fellowship, which is described in a worshipful, liturgical way:[18] he takes bread, offers a blessing, breaks the bread, and gives it to the travelers.[19] The language recalls the feeding of the five thousand (9:16) and the last supper (22:19; cf. 24:43).[20] Why Jesus serves as host for the meal (seen in his giving the blessing) is not clear. Was he the oldest or was it out of respect for his scriptural exposition that he was asked to bless God? The detail seems to indicate that his hosts knew he was someone special, but just how special he was remains to be seen.

This meal is not a reenactment of the Lord's Supper since there is no wine and nothing is said over the elements (against, among others, Nolland 1993b: 1206). The imperfect ἐπεδίδου (*epedidou*, he was distributing) does not indicate continued distribution of the bread (Plummer 1896: 556). Neither is this the messianic banquet, though it may anticipate this decisive banquet meal that takes place in the eschaton after the gathering of all the saints.[21] The meal simply pictures Jesus as raised and present with his disciples in fellowship.

Everything changes as the travelers' earlier discussion about what **24:31** happened to Jesus is resolved. The veil is lifted from their eyes, and

---

18. Meals are frequent in Luke: simple meals (7:36; 11:37; 14:1), feasts (5:29), miraculous provisions (9:16), cultic meals (22:14), wedding feasts (14:8–9), and the eschatological banquet (12:37; 13:29); Osborne 1984: 123 n. 26; Plummer 1896: 556. That Jesus ate such meals with the "wrong people" is noted in 15:1 and 19:1.

19. On breaking bread, see Matt. 14:19 = Mark 6:41 = Luke 9:16 = John 6:11; Matt. 15:36 = Mark 8:6; Matt. 26:26 = Mark 14:22 = Luke 22:19; Mark 8:19; Acts 2:42, 46; 20:7, 11; 27:35; John 6:11; 1 Cor. 10:16; 11:24.

20. Dillon's effort (1978: 149–51) to find a connection with John 21:9–13 seems forced. The catch of fish outdoors in the Sea of Galilee does not equal a meal indoors near Jerusalem. Only the motif of a shared meal is the same (Behm, *TDNT* 1:477; Marshall 1978: 898). Another post-resurrection meal occurs in Luke 24:41–43 and Mark 16:14 (if it is original).

21. That the participants do not even know that they were sitting with Jesus speaks against seeing the messianic banquet here; but so argues Danker 1988: 394.

they realize with whom they are eating.[22] The expression "their eyes were opened" is unique in the NT. The theological passive διανοίγω (*dianoigō*, to open; BAGD 187; BAA 375) is used with a variety of objects: womb (Luke 2:23), Scripture (Luke 24:32; Acts 17:3), mind (Luke 24:45), heaven (Acts 7:56), heart (Acts 16:14; 2 Macc. 1:4), ears (Mark 7:34–35), and eyes (Luke 24:31; Gen. 3:5, 7; 2 Kings 6:17). The travelers recognize Jesus. Luke uses language that reverses what was said about their lack of recognition in 24:16.

Just as quickly, Jesus vanishes from them (see Fitzmyer 1985: 1568 and BDR §211.1.1 on this use of ἀπό, *apo*). Ἄφαντος (*aphantos*, no longer visible) appears only here in the NT (BAGD 124; BAA 250).[23] With the revelation that Jesus lives, his visible presence is no longer necessary. Dillon (1978: 155) rightly notes that the appearance displays continuity between the Jesus of earthly ministry and the raised Jesus who sits over the church. Jesus can personally minister to anyone after his death and resurrection.

iii. The Men's Response (24:32)

24:32 The men's reaction almost reflects an absence of surprise. They were excited earlier when they heard Jesus expound the Scripture and they suspected that someone unusual was in their presence, but they had no idea who he was. Now that they know, it makes sense. Their initial remark is stated as a rhetorical question that expects a positive reply (οὐχί, *ouchi*, not). Their hearts were burning (καιομένη, *kaiomenē*; BAGD 396 §1b; BAA 804 §1b) within them as Jesus spoke to them.[24] His exposition gave them intense emotion and excitement. The idiom *to light a fire under someone* might be comparable to this only NT use of καίω with this figurative force.[25] They had great excitement and comfort at hearing the Scripture opened up to them in this way (διήνοιγεν, *diēnoigen*; BDR §101.54; cf. Luke 24:31; Acts 17:2–3). They sensed that something special was happen-

---

22. The first occurrence of the personal pronoun αὐτῶν (their) is slightly emphatic since it is separated from its modifier; BDR §277.4.

23. Ἄφαντος is used in 2 Macc. 3:34 of angels and in Greco-Roman literature of disappearing gods: Euripides, *Orestes* 1496; Euripides, *Helen* 605–6; Virgil, *Aeneid* 9.656–58; Creed 1930: 297; Marshall 1978: 898; Danker 1988: 394; Klostermann 1929: 238; Grundmann 1963: 447. On departures of transcendent or transported figures, see Luke 1:38; 2:15; 9:33; Acts 10:7; 12:10; and esp. 8:39; Nolland 1993b: 1206.

24. The distributive singular καρδία indicates that the heart burned in each of them; Marshall 1978: 898; Col. 3:16; BDF §140. The periphrastic idiom pictures a running emotion; Plummer 1896: 557–58. On the sense of καρδία in Luke, see 1:51, 66; 2:19, 35, 51; 3:15; 5:22; 9:47; 24:25; Tiede 1988: 437.

25. For other figurative uses, see Ps. 39:3 [39:4 MT]; 73:21; T. Naph. 7.4; K. Schmidt, *TDNT* 3:464. For literal uses of καίω, see Matt. 5:15; 13:40; Luke 12:35; John 5:35; 15:6; Heb. 12:18; Rev. 4:5; 8:8, 10; 19:20; 21:8.

ing, but only after their eyes were opened could they see why this man had opened up the Scriptures so clearly to them. They had been treated to a rare tour of the OT and received insight into God's plan as a result.

d. Report to Disciples (24:33–35)

The travelers are anxious to pass on the news of what they have dis- **24:33** covered. The disappointment that the disciples had not seen Jesus has been reversed by Jesus himself. So they return to Jerusalem, a note that makes clear the journey to Emmaus had started in Jerusalem even though 24:13 lacked such a detail. They undertook the journey fairly quickly (αὐτῇ τῇ ὥρᾳ [autē tē hōra, at that hour] is a general time marker that means "fairly soon after").[26] The idiom may suggest that the travelers did not necessarily return that night, a point often used against the account's historicity because of the distance to Emmaus and the time of day, but simply that they returned relatively quickly. It is possible, even probable, they did return in the same evening, but the wording need not have that force.

Upon arriving in Jerusalem, they find the Eleven gathered together (ἀθροίζω, athroizō, BAGD 21; BAA 40; a NT hapax legomenon; cf. 11:29; Marshall 1978: 899). The reference to the Eleven, a collective term for the remaining apostles, raises the issue of Luke's relationship to John 20:19–29. If all Eleven were at the gathering noted by Luke, then why was Thomas not convinced until a week later (John 20:24–29)?[27] John implies that Thomas is not at the first gathering. The now-exposed Judas is absent for reasons that Acts 1:15–26 will make clear. Luke's note also makes it clear that neither of the two Emmaus travelers was an apostle. With the Eleven are an unspecified number of other disciples who had stayed behind in Jerusalem. The Emmaus travelers are ready to give their good news, but another report comes before they have the chance.

There is good reason for the disciples' excitement: Jesus has ap- **24:34** peared to Simon Peter. Danker (1988: 395) argues that questions, not statements, are present, because of the remarks in 24:11–12 ("idle tale," "did not believe," "departed . . . wondering") and 24:41

---

26. Cf. 2:38; 7:21; 10:21; 12:12; 13:31; 20:19; 22:53 (the whole "hour" of the crucifixion period, which was a full day long, since it includes arrest, trials, and execution).

27. Plummer 1896: 558 rhetorically suggests that Thomas left in the middle of Peter's and other disciples' earlier reports, while expressing his doubt, thus missing the meal that starts in 24:36. Saying that only ten were present, Arndt 1956: 491 identifies this meeting with John 20:19–24. He takes "Eleven" to be a general way to refer to the group of apostles without Judas, without insisting that all those who remained were present. If Thomas left or if the term is general, then the connection is possible. The latter is likely.

("while they still disbelieved for joy"). Thus Danker reads, "Has the Lord really risen?" "Did he appear to Simon?" But making questions out of this syntax is difficult. The incredulity of 24:41 is a literary way to express total amazement (Marshall 1978: 899). As with earlier scenes, what happened was not expected. Λέγοντας (*legontas*) refers to the gathered group (the Eleven and those with them in 24:33), which makes this a report given to the Emmaus travelers. The shift from the Emmaus travelers to the gathered group is so abrupt that codex D and Origen read λέγοντες (*legontes*, saying), making the report about Peter come from the travelers. The problem with this reading is not only its poor external attestation, but also explaining why these travelers would report an appearance to Peter when he is a part of the group to whom the appearance came (Creed 1930: 298). C. F. Evans (1970: 106–7) is so troubled by this note that he argues Luke inserted this remark. But the interruption of this additional sighting is a clever, appropriate literary twist. The report shows that Jesus is really among them, no matter where they are. It shows the surprising, comprehensive way in which the appearances came. Not only did Jesus provide evidence for his resurrection on the road; he did it in Jerusalem too. The excitement is so great that one report is interrupted by another. This appearance to Peter is also recorded in 1 Cor. 15:5, but no where is it detailed. There are numerous witnesses to Jesus' resurrection (Ernst 1977: 665; Luke 24:48; Acts 1:22; 2:32; 3:15; 5:32; 10:41).

The report stresses the word ὄντως (*ontōs*, indeed; BAGD 574 §1; BAA 1163; elsewhere in the NT at Mark 11:32; Luke 23:47; John 8:36; 1 Cor. 14:25; Gal. 3:21 and four times in 1 Timothy; the NIV more paraphrastically has "it is true!" which correctly underscores the emphatic position of the Greek word order). These reports bring reassurance that Jesus was indeed raised and had indeed appeared. Also significant is the remark that "the Lord" is risen. This use of the title κύριος (*kyrios*) emphasizes the risen Jesus' authority. He is not only alive, he bears authority.

24:35 The second account of the travelers follows. Luke thus gives two sets of witnesses to the resurrection. They explain (ἐξηγοῦντο, *exēgounto*; BAGD 275; BAA 557; John 1:18; Acts 10:8; 15:12, 14; 21:19) about the journey and about Jesus' revealing himself (ἐγνώσθη, *egnōsthē*) at the meal, thus recalling 24:16, 31. One can imagine the thoughts in the room during these discussions. What is God going to do next?

Summary Luke 24:13–35 is one of the most vivid appearance accounts in the NT. The Emmaus journey is full of irony and reversal. Two disciples are despondent that the prophet and redeemer of the nation has been crucified. How can God possibly work through a crucified person? Unknown to them, the answer appears in their midst.

As the three walk and talk, the travelers reveal their disappointment. God has seemingly thrown a cruel curve at his people. The entourage's third member says that all is not lost. He rebukes the other two for lack of understanding, since there is another way to look at the events. He begins to explain how the Scripture teaches the necessity of Christ's glorification through suffering. These events are no surprise in God's plan but should be believed. God's word and work come together to show his vindication of Jesus. As the group nears their destination, the two ask their learned friend to stay the night. What the reader already knows is made clear at the meal: the man is Jesus and he has been raised.

The two are transformed by the knowledge of Jesus' resurrection and victory. They are so excited that they go out to tell the group in Jerusalem. But here too there is a twist; Peter has already seen Jesus. Jesus is present among them everywhere. Failure becomes fulfillment. Remorse is reversed in resurrection. Absence is presence.

For Luke's reader the account functions as a summary to provide assurance about resurrection. God can work through crucifixion because it is followed by resurrection. His promise remains, as his work makes clear. The curve ball has not been thrown to humankind but to death, sin, and Satan. The Lord is risen. He lives and is in their midst. God's plan has not been thwarted. The disciples are not abandoned, but commissioned. In a world where many do not know their place, identity, or purpose, the resurrection means that disciples can know that God is at work, that Jesus is alive in glory, and that death is not the end. A life of purpose and unending relationship with God is possible. In short, resurrection means that humans can have their proper place with God. Jesus is at God's side, and he is among them. All that is needed is to believe what God has promised.

The key is Jesus, who in resurrection reveals that life is worth living. He reveals that life is found in him. If God is at work in saving Jesus, then he is at work in his message about Jesus as well. The disciples are again to sit, listen, learn, and believe. Another "class" is about to begin, after which the sitting will stop and the mission will start. For from faith should come faithfulness and service. God's word of promise to us should become a proclaimed word of hope to others.

Additional Notes

24:13. Codex D reads Οὐλαμμαούς (Oulammaus), a reading too poorly attested to be original. Oulammaus is otherwise unknown, unless it is a corruption of the LXX name for Bethel in Gen. 28:19; Creed 1930: 295.

24:13. The distance of Emmaus from Jerusalem is disputed. Most manuscripts ($\mathfrak{P}^{75}$, A, B, D, L, W, Δ, Ψ, family 1, family 13, Byz) read ἑξήκοντα (sixty) stadia (a stadia is 607 feet; thus 6.9 miles). A few manuscripts (ℵ, Θ, 079) add ἑκατόν (hundred), making the distance 160 stadia or 18.4 miles. This reading, though poorly attested, fits the distance of the traditional site noted by Eusebius and Jerome (see the exegesis). Nonetheless, it is too poorly attested to be original.

24:17. Codex D lacks καὶ ἐστάθησαν (and they stopped) after Jesus' question. Other manuscripts (A^c, W, Δ, Θ, Ψ, family 1, family 13, Byz, Vulgate, some Syriac) replace it with καί ἐστε (and they are), so that Jesus asks why they are sad. Both variants are too poorly attested to be original (Marshall 1978: 894).

24:19. Some manuscripts (A, D, W, Θ, Ψ, family 1, family 13, Byz) read Ναζωραίου (the Nazarean). If this reading is original, then the travelers describe Jesus as a Nazarean. Since this is the more natural form, it is regarded as secondary because the UBS–NA's Ναζαρηνοῦ (of Nazareth) reading is more difficult (supported by $\mathfrak{P}^{75}$, ℵ, B, L, 079, 0124, and Vulgate). The difference does not alter the sense. Marshall (1978: 894) argues that the reference to this locale reflects the presence of tradition.

24:27. Many manuscripts (A, Θ, Ψ, family 1, family 13, Byz) read the imperfect διερμήνευεν (he was interpreting) rather than UBS–NA's aorist διερμήνευσεν (he interpreted; $\mathfrak{P}^{75}$, B, L, ℵ^1). A few manuscripts (e.g., ℵ*) read infinitival διερμήνευειν (to interpret), which would be epexegetical to ἀρξάμενος (he began) at the start of the verse. It is hard to be sure of the original reading, but the choice does not really alter the sense. An imperfect is slightly more vivid, but because the imperfect is commonly Luke's choice of tense the aorist is the harder reading.

24:32. The scribes of $\mathfrak{P}^{75}$, B, and D probably omitted ἐν ἡμῖν (in us) as redundant. It is original (Metzger 1975: 186).

24:34. Some manuscripts (A, W^c, Θ, family 13, Byz) place ὄντως (indeed) after κύριος. External attestation favors the UBS–NA order ($\mathfrak{P}^{75}$, ℵ, B, D, L, Ψ, family 1, many Itala).

3. Commission, Promise, and Ascension (24:36–53)

The close of Luke's Gospel reassures (cf. 1:4) by confirming the reality of Jesus' resurrection and by commissioning the disciples for their universal mission. The bodily character of Jesus' resurrection is stressed: he calls on the disciples to touch him and see that he is really resurrected, and he eats a meal with them so they can see that he is not a phantom or spirit. The major theological note in the unit is that crucifixion and resurrection are part of the fulfillment of God's plan. What happened to Jesus was neither perplexing nor unexpected. The table fellowship that the disciples now have with the resurrected Jesus reveals his presence in their midst. The Scripture taught that he would suffer and be raised and that a message of forgiveness of sins would go out to all nations as a result. Two of those elements have happened, one remains for the disciples to carry out.

The pericope ends with two notes that look to the future. Jesus commands the disciples to wait in Jerusalem for the coming of the Father's promise, the Spirit's bestowal. The power provided by the Spirit for the disciples' ministry of proclamation is the first of many salvation benefits. The Spirit is the enabler who makes it possible to minister boldly in the face of opposition, as will be seen many times in the Book of Acts. Jesus' final blessing and the disciples' response of worship, joy, and thanksgiving reflect the effect that Jesus' resurrection has on disciples. Disciples are to rejoice in what God has done in Jesus.

The note of universal mission is important as well. Luke makes clear that Jesus' ministry is for all, not just some. Gentiles like Theophilus (1:3) need assurance that their presence in a Jewish movement is proper. Conversely, Jewish believers need to understand that the expansion of blessing into Gentile horizons is appropriate. Jesus called the church to be generous with God's promise, and God will continue to prod the church in this direction when it is slow to take the message out to all (Acts 1–10). This theological defense of Gentile mission is one of the major themes of Luke–Acts. Gentile mission occurs alongside the proclamation to Israel—not at its expense.

Luke's Gospel provides two keys to this view of mission. First, Luke shows how Israel defaulted, at least temporarily, on its central role. It rejected Jesus and now faces judgment. Luke's case for this point was made especially in the journey narrative of Luke 9–19. Second, Luke argues christologically that Jesus is the promised Messiah-Servant-Prophet and, most important, Lord of all, glorified and seated at God's right hand. Not fully developed in his Gospel, this argument is completed in Acts 2:30–36 and 10:34–43. The linkage of Christology to Gentile mission can be seen in Peter's speech in Acts 10. Paul's mission, which is the burden of Acts 13–28, is the supreme example of a mission that consciously includes those outside of Israel.[1] Theophilus and anyone else who reads Luke's Gospel can know that Jesus' death and the church's mission to preach Jesus to all were ordained by God. In short, Luke's Gospel and the Book of Acts are about the plan of a faithful and gracious God to redeem all races through Jesus. Virtually every pericope is aimed at getting the reader to see that Jesus is the issue and that he holds the key to the way of God. Even Jesus' death opened the door to heaven, as it provided the means by which he could sit at God's side in rule. From there the exalted Lord distributes the Spirit to those who turn to God in repentance and trust him as the one who holds God's benefits, who provides forgiveness, who leads the way into salvation, and who will return to exercise judgment.

The emphasis on Jesus' session at God's right hand troubles some who rightly note that Luke says little about Jesus' work on the cross for atonement of sin. Luke 22:20 and Acts 20:28 are the only explicit Lucan texts that describe Jesus' death in relation to sin. But Luke wishes to press beyond what Jesus' work on the cross means to who he is and how he works after resurrection. Luke wants the new community to understand what its role is. He seeks to explain how believers are to live before the living Lord they serve. The Gospel and Acts are thus very pastoral in their goal. Here is what the new community is. Here is the Lord they believe. Here is what the Lord they serve told them to do. Here is how he told them to live. The burden of the Gospel is summed up in this commission and in the promise of the Spirit's coming as power from on high (24:44–49).

---

1. It is no accident that after Acts 13 almost all OT citations in Acts discuss (a) judgment on Israel for failing to respond to Jesus or (b) the right of Gentiles to be included in God's blessing. Luke–Acts is fundamentally a defense of Gentile inclusion in the mission and a presentation of Jesus' new way. Luke's major goal is to show that events and Scripture indicate that this was always God's plan. See Bock 1990.

The unit has three parts: (1) Jesus' reassuring appearance to the group with his call to touch his resurrected body (24:36–43), (2) the instruction that all has happened according to God's promise, the commission to await the Spirit, and the promise contained in Jesus' earlier teaching and in the entire law, prophets, and psalms (24:44–49), and (3) Jesus' blessing and departure (24:50–53). The Gospel closes with the disciples thanking God continually in the temple. Just as the beginning of the promise started with an announcement to an old priest in the temple (1:5), so the conclusion of Jesus' ministry ends with a group of pious Jews gathered in the temple thanking God for what he has done through Jesus. In Luke 1, Zechariah was looking and praying to God for the hope of Israel; in Luke 24, the disciples find that hope and thank God for him.

Sources and Historicity

Much of the material in this pericope is unique to Luke, though 24:36–43 has some points of connection with John 20:19–23 (Aland 1985: §356). Many (e.g., Osborne 1984: 246–51; Dillon 1978: 159–63) see a specific sharing of tradition at this point (Fitzmyer 1985: 1573–74 finds minimal stylistic editorial work by Luke in 24:36–43).[2] Themes held in common with John are the physical proof of Jesus' resurrection, the element of doubt, and the greeting of peace. The major difference is that joy is an immediate reaction in John, while Luke speaks of joy in the midst of incredulity. Nonetheless, these look like similar traditions.

The Lucan use of a meal scene corresponds with his frequent use of such settings (e.g., 7:36–50; 14:1–6). The appearances noted in 1 Cor. 15:5, 7 may well allude to this appearance. In addition, the physical nature of the appearance recalls 1 Cor. 15:35–49, where Paul contrasts the resurrection body and the earthly body (Ernst 1977: 666). Some argue that an antidocetic strain is expressed in Luke's portrait of physical resurrection (Grundmann 1963: 449). Still others argue that the concern is broader: Luke

2. Traces of Lucan expression are (1) the genitive absolute in 24:36, (2) the double participle phrase πτοηθέντες . . . καὶ ἔμφοβοι γενόμενοι (became terrified . . . and startled) in 24:37 (cf. 21:9; 24:5), (3) the verb ἐπιδίδωμι (to offer) in 24:42 (five times in Luke; twice in Matthew; none in Mark), and (4) the phrase ἐνώπιον αὐτῶν (in front of them) in 24:43 (in the Synoptics only here; 5:25; and 24:11). Nolland 1993b: 1210–11 notes that many apparently Lucan points also show up in John (perhaps pointing to a shared common source), but John's use does not seem to be driven by Luke's unique development of the passage (against Neirynck 1985). Nolland sees 24:41b–43 as Lucan expansion, but possibly based in tradition. His attempt to argue that "fish" in 24:42–43 corresponds to "bread" in 24:30 to make the larger unit parallel to 9:13, 16 seems subtle and forced. If Luke created the detail, it is more likely that he would have combined bread and fish in a single scene.

wishes to establish an identity between Jesus' resurrection body and his earthly personhood and so brings a note of continuity to resurrection hope (Marshall 1978: 900; Osborne 1984: 248). Others deny a polemical role here since, in the OT and Judaism, angels have such encounters (Gen. 18; Tob. 12:19; Nolland 1993b: 1214–15). It is not clear, however, that these concerns are mutually exclusive, though it is hard on the one hand to argue from just this one scene that Luke's Gospel is primarily directed at countering Gnostics, Docetists, or their precursors, and on the other hand deny that a polemical function to this section is unlikely. This scene reassures that Jesus' resurrection is physical, a new kind of life reclaimed out of death (as in Acts 2:16–32, esp. 2:22–31).

The commission account of Luke 24:44–49 is similar to Matt. 28:18–20, but is expressed in distinct terms and with a distinct setting (Aland 1985: §365). Matthew's account occurs in Galilee; Luke's meeting appears to be on resurrection day outside Jerusalem (but Acts 1:1–11 suggests that it is forty days later; see also Luke 24:44, 50). Luke may be engaged in literary compression here, since he lacks any chronological notes to these remarks (which is similar to the Jerusalem journey section). The result is that 24:50–53 may be nothing more than a summarizing variation of Acts 1:6–11. (This latter point is likely even if Luke 24:44–49 is not part of the compression and belongs to the meal; see below.) Matthew speaks of empowerment and making disciples; Luke speaks of fulfilled teaching, preaching, and empowerment. These are distinct accounts of distinct events, which means that Jesus' command for the disciples to go to Galilee came early (Matt. 28:7), that they later gathered in Bethany, and that some forty days later they were told to stay in Jerusalem (Luke 24:44–53). Luke 24:44–46 looks to Jesus' past work, while 24:47–49 looks to the disciples' future mission.[3]

Fitzmyer (1985: 1580–81) notes eleven touches of Lucan expression in this subunit (cf. Jeremias 1980: 321–22), among them are "law of Moses" (Luke 24:44; 2:22; Acts 13:39 [13:38 Engl.]; 15:5), "all that was written" (Luke 24:44; 18:31; 21:22; Acts 13:29; 24:14), "Messiah shall suffer" (Luke 24:46), "in his name repentance for the forgiveness of sins" (Luke 24:47), "witnesses" (Luke 24:48; thirteen times in Acts), "what my Father promised" (Luke 24:49; Acts 1:4). Though the account is told in Lucan terms, the teaching merely emphasizes what the tradition already declared (Marshall 1978: 903–4). Jesus' predictions of his death suggest that he is fulfilling what was promised (17:25; 18:31–34). Mission statements about the Son of Man (e.g., Mark 10:45) have the note of design that Luke strikes here, but this material has come to Luke through tradition. Lucan emphases include the call to wait for the Spirit in Jerusalem and the idea of including the nations (but see Mark 13:10, which uses the typically Lucan δεῖ; Dupont 1979).

3. Those who look for a point of contact in the Synoptic tradition note Mark 16:15–16, but this connection depends on whether Mark's longer ending is original and, as a result, where that detail from Mark's Gospel would fall in the Synoptic order.

Since Luke is the only one to describe the ascension as an event, many (e.g., Lohfink 1971: 147–51) regard it as a Lucan creation (Dillon's evaluation [1978: 173–75, esp. n. 52] of Lohfink holds out the possibility that Luke is drawing on tradition).[4] This position argues that Luke likes to turn apparitions into departures, but he is quite capable of not making a departure an ascension (Luke 24:31; Acts 8:39).

Luke presents two versions of the ascension (Luke 24:50–53; Acts 1:6–11). The ascension in Luke happens in Bethany apparently on resurrection day, while the ascension in Acts occurs on the Mount of Olives apparently at the end of forty days of appearances. Nolland (1993b: 1225) argues that the forty days is symbolic (Gen. 7:17; Exod. 16:35; 24:18; 34:28; 1 Kings 19:8; 2 Esdr. [=4 Ezra] 14:23, 36, 42–45). There is no need to argue for symbol here since numerology is not associated with the timing of Pentecost itself. A popular solution to the differences in the versions argues for a literary repetition by Luke of a single event to achieve a link between Luke–Acts (Parsons 1987; Plummer 1896: 561, 564, who suggests that Luke 24 is a later event). This view is possible, given the lack of explicit chronology in Luke 24. Another less likely view is that Luke used distinct departure accounts to note Jesus' first appearance to the group and his last appearance to them all. In other words, the connection not only brackets Luke–Acts, but also brackets the appearances of Jesus in a transition period (Toon 1983–84; Toon 1984; Ellis 1974: 280).[5] Since Luke is the only Gospel writer to discuss the early history of the church, he is the only one to note the ascension, since for him it portrays vividly where Jesus went as he became mediator of divine blessings. The other Gospel writers need only mention resurrection, but Luke's continuing his account in Acts demands that his readers know what happened to the resurrected Jesus. Luke 9:51, 22:69, and 24:26 anticipate this event, but the idea of Jesus' reception into glory or being seated in glory is not unique to Luke (Matt. 16:27 = Mark 8:38; Matt. 24:30 = Mark 13:26; Matt. 19:28; 25:31; 1 Cor. 2:8; 2 Cor. 3:7–11, 18; 4:4, 6; 1 Pet. 1:11). Most NT passages relate to Jesus' future eschatological appearance, but he does not receive glory then, he comes with glory (e.g., Matt. 28:18). The ascension received attention in the early church (Barn. 15.9; Gospel of Peter 12.50; 13.55–56 [Schneemelcher 1991–92: 1.225–26]; Acts of Pilate 16.6 [Schneemelcher 1991–92: 1.520]; Tertul-

4. Lucan creation is also the view of the Jesus Seminar, which prints 24:44, 46–49 in black type (Funk and Hoover 1993: 400). In the seminar's view, these verses represent a third commission (Matt. 28:18–20; John 20:22–23). Nolland 1993b: 1225–26 also sees a Lucan development here, though (unlike the Jesus Seminar) he argues that it is a natural development of the tradition that Jesus appeared for a limited time. Nolland says that connection to tradition is possible, but not demonstrable. I prefer to see roots in a tradition and a real event, since Luke does not discuss new scenes elsewhere in his Gospel without the prompting of tradition.

5. The only temporal indicator is the general particle δέ (and or then). The ascension could well be a later event that Luke repeated with different detail in Acts 1.

lian, *Against the Jews* 13.23; Eusebius, *Ecclesiastical History* 3.5; Fitzmyer 1985: 1589).

The form of this material is debated. The farewell scene, which includes a commission, reminds one of the farewell meal in Luke 22. But the parallel is too broad to be really helpful. Conversely, the meal element in 24:36–43 is too brief to be considered the dominant form. This appearance has four elements in common with other appearance scenes: (1) a note of doubt before the appearance, (2) an explanation, which refers to Scripture or to what Jesus said in his earthly ministry, (3) an instruction or commission, and (4) a departure. There is no doubt that an appearance scene is present, which is designed to reassure about the resurrection (Fitzmyer 1985: 1574, 1581, 1586). Jesus does not function as a priest in Luke, despite the priestly blessing in the last subunit. His blessing is one of a teacher-prophet (cf. 6:20–26), since his commission displays his directing, executive authority.

The outline of Luke 24:36–53 is as follows:

a. Appearance at a meal (24:36–43)
   i. Sudden appearance (24:36)
   ii. Mistaken reaction (24:37)
   iii. First proof: Jesus' call to touch him (24:38–40)
   iv. Second proof: Jesus eats a meal (24:41–43)
b. Commission, plan, and promise of the Spirit (24:44–49)
   i. Jesus' words and the Old Testament fulfilled (24:44)
   ii. Jesus' instruction (24:45)
   iii. Three scriptural elements fulfilled (24:46–47)
   iv. Naming the disciples as witnesses (24:48)
   v. Command to await the Spirit (24:49)
c. Ascension (24:50–53)
   i. Jesus' blessing and departure (24:50–51)
   ii. Reaction: worship, joy, and thanksgiving (24:52–53)

Jesus' appearance to all the disciples opens the last section of Luke's Gospel. The disciples' fear shows that they are still adjusting to the reality of the resurrection, so Luke stresses the appearance's physical characteristics. The resurrection represents the fulfillment of Jesus' words, God's plan, and the OT. Jesus' instruction enlightens all. There are three elements in the current plan: Jesus' suffering, his resurrection, and the proclamation of forgiveness of sins to all nations in his name. The church is to issue a call to repent so forgiveness can come. Jesus commissions the disciples as witnesses, promises the provision of the Holy Spirit, and gives a final blessing. The disciples' response is worship, joy, and thanksgiving.

Exegesis and Exposition

³⁶While they were saying these things, ⌜he⌝ stood in their midst and said to them, "⌜Peace to you⌝." ³⁷And as they were terrified and startled, they thought they were seeing ⌜a spirit⌝. ³⁸And he said to them, "Why are you alarmed? Why do doubts arise in your ⌜hearts⌝? ³⁹Behold my hands and my feet, for it is I myself. Handle me and see, for a spirit has not flesh and bones as you see that I have." ⁴⁰⌜And having said this, ⌜he showed⌝ them his hands and his feet.⌝ ⁴¹But while they were still unbelieving from joy and amazed, he said to them, "Have you anything to eat here?" ⁴²They gave him a piece of broiled fish⌜ ⌝, ⁴³and taking he ate in front of them.⌜ ⌝

⁴⁴And he said to them, "These are my words that I spoke to you while I was still with you, that it is necessary for all things written about me in the law of Moses, the Prophets, and the Psalms to be fulfilled." ⁴⁵Then he opened their minds to understand the Scripture. ⁴⁶And he said to them, "Thus it is written that the Christ is to suffer and to be raised on the third day, ⁴⁷and there should be preached in his name repentance for the forgiveness of sins to all the nations, beginning from Jerusalem. ⁴⁸You are witnesses of these things. ⁴⁹And ⌜behold⌝, I am sending the promise of my Father upon you. And you stay in the city until you are clothed with power from on high."

⁵⁰And he led them ⌜out⌝ to the neighborhood of Bethany, and lifting up his hands he blessed them. ⁵¹While he blessed them, he departed from them ⌜and was carried up into heaven⌝. ⁵²And they ⌜worshiped him⌝ and they returned to Jerusalem with great joy, and ⁵³they were continually in the temple, blessing God.⌜ ⌝

a. Appearance at a Meal (24:36–43)
i. Sudden Appearance (24:36)

Jesus' final appearance is linked to the previous event by a temporal genitive absolute.[6] Luke 24:1, 13, 33 suggests a link to resurrection day. Events are coming fast and furious. Jesus stands in the midst of the disciples (cf. John 20:19).[7] He appears as quickly as he disappeared in Luke 24:31. The greeting is one of comfort, in which Jesus

24:36

---

6. BDR §423.2.7 and §423.1.2 notes that Luke uses the temporal genitive absolute fifty-seven times, while Acts has it one hundred times. The construction occurs in Matthew fifty-one times and in Mark thirty-four times. This is too common to attribute its presence to any one evangelist or to rule out its presence in the tradition (against Fitzmyer 1985: 1574 and Nolland 1993b: 1212).

7. The term ἔστη (he stood) appears in John 20:19, 26; 21:4. Luke likes the phrase ἐν μέσῳ (in the midst): Luke 2:46; 8:7; 10:3; 21:21; 22:27, 55; Acts 1:15; 2:22; 4:7; 17:22; 27:21 (Fitzmyer 1985: 1575).

wishes them well (cf. John 20:19 and Luke 10:5; Dillon 1978: 187). God's blessing is invoked on the anxious disciples. Jesus offers the peace he promised to bring (Luke 2:14; 7:50; Acts 10:36; Marshall 1978: 901). Appearances to individuals are often followed by appearances to a group (Matt. 28:9–10, 16–20; John 20:11–18, 19–23; Marshall 1978: 901). Jesus appeared in a variety of settings (1 Cor. 15:5–11).

ii. Mistaken Reaction (24:37)

24:37   Jesus' appearance startles (πτοέω, *ptoeō*; BAGD 727; BAA 1456; elsewhere in the NT only at 21:9) and frightens (ἔμφοβος, *emphobos*; BAGD 257; BAA 520; elsewhere in the NT at Luke 24:5; Acts 10:4; 24:25; Rev. 11:13) the group. The disciples think they are seeing a "spirit" (πνεῦμα, *pneuma*), a disembodied person (cf. Luke 24:39; Acts 23:8–9; Heb. 12:23; 1 Pet. 3:19; Dan. 8:17; Tob. 12:16; on possible cultural expectations about someone called back from the dead, see 1 Sam. 28:3–19; Isa. 8:19; 19:3; 29:4; Nolland 1993b: 1213). Their fear is understandable since the group does not initially recognize Jesus and they are not expecting another appearance. The disciples are not operating with expectations of the miraculous.

iii. First Proof: Jesus' Call to Touch Him (24:38–40)

24:38   To calm the alarmed group, Jesus asks two questions. The first addresses their mood: Why are you alarmed (τεταραγμένοι, *tetaragmenoi*; BAGD 805 §2; BAA 1606 §2; cf. Matt. 2:3; 14:26 = Mark 6:50; Luke 1:12; John 12:27; 1 Pet. 3:14)? The presence of an unknown disembodied spirit would certainly be disturbing, so Jesus is trying to tell them that they should recognize who is present and what it means.

The second question concerns their lack of perception: Why do doubts arise in your hearts? Καρδία (*kardia*, heart) is a figure for the response of the inner person (Ernst 1977: 667).[8] Since they were reflecting about the reports that they are discussing (διαλογισμός, *dialogismos*), they should realize, if only because of the timing, that Jesus is in their midst. Yet again the disciples are portrayed as slow to accept the resurrection. They do not expect Jesus to be raised nor do they expect him to keep appearing. As with most people, they have to be persuaded. The disciples are as skeptical as the rest of humanity.

---

8. Καρδία (BAGD 403 §1bβ; BAA 819 §1bβ) occurs with διαλογισμός (thoughts) in 2:35 and 9:47 (cf. 3:15 and 5:22) and with the verb ἀναβαίνω (to arise), which may be rendered idiomatically as "thoughts arise within the person," in Acts 7:23; 1 Cor. 2:9; Jer. 3:16–17. BDR §4.3.8 calls the expression of thoughts arising in the heart a Semitism. Διαλογισμός (BAGD 186 §2; BAA 372 §2) carries the sense of "doubt" or "dispute" in Luke 9:46; 24:38; Phil. 2:14; 1 Tim. 2:8 and the sense of "thoughts" in Matt. 15:19 = Mark 7:21; Luke 2:35; 5:22; 6:8; 9:47; Rom. 1:21; 14:1; 1 Cor. 3:20; James 2:4.

Jesus calls on the disciples to confirm with their own senses that it **24:39** is he. Doubt is met with revelation (Klostermann 1929: 240; Exod. 4:1–8; Judg. 6:36–40). In a scene paralleling John 20:19–23, 27, especially 20:20, Jesus tells them to look at his hands and feet, a probable reference to the marks of crucifixion. Only this passage and John 20:25 suggest that Jesus was nailed to the cross (J. Schneider, *TDNT* 7:574–75). This is indeed Jesus (Luke 22:70; John 6:20, 35, 48, 51; Tiede 1988: 440). In identifying himself, Jesus does so emphatically by using the personal pronoun αὐτός (*autos*, [my]self). The second ὅτι (*hoti*) is either causal ("handle me and see because no spirit . . .") or an indication of indirect discourse ("handle me and see that no spirit . . ."). An explanatory connection of reported thought or perception is more likely because the causal idea would relate grammatically to seeing and handling, but logically that connection cannot work. Jesus' remarks about flesh and bone answer the doubts expressed in Luke 24:37.

In addition to their eyes they are to use their sense of touch. They are to handle (ψηλαφήσατε, *psēlaphēsate*) Jesus.[9] A disembodied spirit does not possess flesh and bones (ὀστέον, *osteon*; elsewhere in the NT at Matt. 23:37; John 19:36; Heb. 11:22) as Jesus has (Marshall 1978: 902). The density of his presence might not have been immediately evident, given the full clothing that ancient Palestinians wore. Luke 24:39 is the only text that describes the resurrected body as having flesh and bones. This is not a phantom or a vision (Ruth Rab. 6.1 on 3:8 says "spirits have no hair"; Nolland 1993b: 1213). It is the raised Jesus whose body has been brought back to life. It has characteristics of the physical body, though it carries those characteristics in a way that the old body could not (e.g., this new body will not perish and it can appear and vanish) and in ways that make his initial appearance startling, not the appearance of merely another disciple.

In experiential form, this is what Paul discusses conceptually in 1 Cor. 15:35–49, especially 15:41–44. Schweizer (1984: 376) sees Luke contradicting 1 Cor. 15:50. This conclusion is not correct. Paul's point is that another force is the key to the resurrection body; it is a "spiritual" body as opposed to a "soulish" body. This is why it is more than flesh and bone and can be immortal.[10] The resurrec-

9. Ψηλαφάω occurs elsewhere in the NT only at Acts 17:27; Heb. 12:18; 1 John 1:1 (BAGD 892; BAA 1779–80); cf. Gen. 27:12; Judg. 16:26; Ignatius, *Smyrneans* 3.2. Plummer 1896: 560 wonders if 1 John 1:1 knows of this event, given its use of this rare term. See also C. F. Evans 1970: 108–9.

10. Fitzmyer 1985: 1576 refuses to make a connection to 1 Cor. 15, probably to emphasize that Luke is not concerned with Paul's detailed explanation, a point that is correct but need not mean the accounts are theologically unrelated.

tion body is flesh and bone transformed into a form that is able to move through material matter (Tiede 1988: 440: he "was embodied although his body was also altered").[11] There is no way to distinguish the person of Jesus from the risen Christ except that his existence now takes place at an additional dimension of reality. They are basically one and the same. A spirit has not taken his place, nor is he just a spirit. The person buried in the tomb is raised and transformed, but Jesus is sufficiently distinct in appearance that he is not always immediately recognizable. In his resurrected state, he clearly is transformed, though in a way that still leaves traces of his former existence (e.g., the nail prints in his hands and feet).

24:40   Touch confirms Jesus' presence. In fact, Jesus shows the disciples his hands and feet as a follow-up to his call to handle him. He is resurrected in a form consonant with his previous existence. The person before the group is Jesus. For disciples and readers alike, there should be no doubt that God has done a miraculous work.

iv. Second Proof: Jesus Eats a Meal (24:41–43)

24:41   The disciples "were still unbelieving," which can be taken in two senses. The first option is to regard these words as a continued statement of disbelief (so Dillon 1978: 192, in the tradition's original form). Despite the appearances and the remarks, the disciples still doubt because it is so unbelievable. The other option is to regard the remark as a rhetorical expression of amazement: they were incredulous in the sense that it was hard to believe this was really happening (Schweizer 1984: 376–77). In others words, this does not express doubt but overwhelming and paralyzing realization (the servant's response to Peter in Acts 12:14 shows a similar paralysis of natural action resulting from joy; cf. Livy 39.49). Luke uses θαυμάζω (thaumazō, to marvel) to express reaction to miraculous events or to teaching (cf. Luke 1:63; 2:18; 4:22; 7:9; 8:25; 9:43; 11:14; 20:26). The combination of joy and amazement suggests the second option:[12] if they really did not believe, they would not have joy. This event enhances their growing belief (so "great joy" in 24:52), and the meal and scriptural teaching will enhance their faith (Nolland 1993b: 1214–15).

---

11. Luke refers to resurrection in Luke 20:27–45; Acts 23:6–9; 24:15–21 and to the preaching of the resurrection hope in Acts 2:36; 3:26; 9:22; 17:18. Dan. 12:2 expresses the OT roots of this hope.

12. Dillon 1978: 192 argues that the reference to joy is Luke's, but why Luke should be responsible for such an insertion is not clear. On the syntax of ἀπό (from) with the force of ὑπό or παρά, see BDR §210.1.1; cf. Matt. 13:44; 14:26; Luke 21:26; 22:45; Acts 12:14; Plummer 1896: 560.

Jesus removes all doubt and frees them from any sense of terror at his presence by asking for something to eat: "Do you have anything (τι, *ti*) edible here (ἐνθάδε, *enthade*)?"[13] A meal shows that it is Jesus and not a phantom, and it also indicates table fellowship and oneness.[14]

The food available was broiled fish (ἰχθύς, *ichthys*). Though this meal is similar to John 21:9, it is given under distinct circumstances and John calls the fish ὀψάριον (*opsarion*; lit., cooked meat). Some object to the presence of fish in Jerusalem, but this should not be seen as problematic (Marshall 1978: 903; Jeremias 1969: 20; SB 1:683–84; Neh. 3:3; 13:16). **24:42**

The empirical evidence of Jesus' resurrection is stated briefly: Jesus appears to them, speaks with them, and eats before them. Truly he is raised. Appealing to the preposition ἐνώπιον (*enōpion*, in front of), Dillon (1978: 200–201) draws out a whole range of significance tied to table fellowship, while deemphasizing any concern by Luke about the risen body's physical substance. True, there is eating and acceptance by Jesus, but it is not clear that it is a shared meal (Dillon alludes to Acts 10:41, a connection that Plummer 1896: 561 notes but does not comment on). Dillon may be pressing the setting too much, especially in deemphasizing the importance of the meal for verifying the resurrection. Jesus enjoyed a meal in front of the disciples; he really is in their midst—that is the lesson Luke teaches by recording this appearance. **24:43**

b. Commission, Plan, and Promise of the Spirit (24:44–49)
i. Jesus' Words and the Old Testament Fulfilled (24:44)

Jesus returns to the theme of Scripture fulfillment and the necessity of God's plan coming to pass.[15] Luke 24:44–47 is an elaboration on Jesus' rebuke of the two disciples for being slow to believe all the prophets had written (24:25). Plummer (1896: 561), Creed (1930: 300), and Marshall (1978: 904) see a break here in the passage's movement, even though the event seems to follow directly after the meal (the common particle δέ, *de*, indicates only the most basic kind of transition; it is not a clear temporal indicator). Yet the absence of a specific chronological note makes it possible that this event is later, especially given the thematic repetitions in Acts 1:1–11 (see **24:44**

---

13. Ἐνθάδε is a Lucan term (Acts 10:18; 16:28; 17:6; 25:17, 24); the only use outside Luke's writings is twice in John 4:15–16; Plummer 1896: 560; Marshall 1978: 903.

14. In Jdt. 13:16 and Tob. 12:19, a meal is refused by angelic spirits, but in Gen. 18:8; 19:3; and Tob. 6:6, it is given to angelic figures.

15. On δεῖ (it is necessary), see the exegesis of 24:26.

the discussion of sources and historicity above). In this meeting, Jesus mentions that he had spoken of such fulfillment before his death (cf. 9:22, 44; 17:25; 18:31–33; 22:37; Klostermann 1929: 241; Creed 1930: 300; Marshall 1978: 905).[16] The key term is πληρόω (*plēroō*, to fulfill), which appears in several Lucan texts to refer to something anticipated in God's design that has come to pass (Luke 1:20; 4:21 [Scripture]; 9:31; 21:24; 22:16; Acts 1:16 [Scripture]; 3:18; 13:27 [the prophets]; Delling, *TDNT* 6:295–96; Marshall 1978: 905; cf. Acts 2:23). Luke commonly uses the perfect participle γεγραμμένον (*gegrammenon*, written) to refer to Scripture: Luke 4:17; 18:31; 20:17; 21:22; 22:37; 24:44; Acts 13:29; 24:14 (Schrenk, *TDNT* 1:748).

Jesus is the topic of Scripture (cf. Luke 24:25; Acts 13:29; John 5:39; 20:9; Fitzmyer 1985: 1582). The events of his life are thus no surprise; they are in continuity with what God revealed throughout Scripture. It is fair to say that Jesus sees himself and his career outlined in the sacred texts of old. For Luke, Jesus is proclaimed through prophecy and pattern (see also the exegesis of 24:47).[17]

To underline the comprehensiveness of the fulfillment, the three divisions of the OT are noted: law, prophets and psalms (this threefold division is also found in the prologue to Sirach [lines 8–10] and the epilogue to 4QMMT, line 10; Schrenk, *TDNT* 1:756). Luke likes to mention the law (Luke 2:22–24, 27, 39; 5:14; 10:26; 16:16–17, 29, 31; 20:28, 37; 24:27; and many times in Acts [e.g., 24:14]). The law promised a prophet like Moses (Acts 3:22). Though Messiah is not mentioned as a title in the Pentateuch, relevant promises about God's plan are present there (the only "anointed ones" in the law are the priests, Lev. 4:3, 5, 16; 6:22 [6:15 MT]; Fitzmyer 1985: 1583). The prophets are also a frequent topic in Luke (e.g., Luke 1:70; 16:16, 29, 31; 18:31; 24:25, 27; Acts 3:18, 21, 24; 10:43; 24:14). The prophets contain not only an exposition of the promised Anointed One (almost never with the title, but discuss an ideal rule and ruler) but a whole array of promises tied to God's activity in inaugurating and consummating his plan. Another major contributor to these themes

16. Ὅτι is epexegetical to οὗτοι οἱ λόγοι (these words) and is not the object of ἐλάλησα (I spoke). The verse reports what "these words" were.

17. For a study of the hermeneutic of Luke's OT use, see Bock 1987, in which I build on P. Schubert's 1957 thesis that Luke's theme is "proof from prophecy" (but the apologetic motif is not so strong in Luke as the declarative function of these texts, thus my modification to "proclamation from prophecy and pattern"). My work contrasts with that of Rese 1969, who underestimates the appeal to pattern and therefore understates a prophetic approach to Luke's OT. Soards 1994: 201 misconstrues the proof-from-prophecy position by describing it as linear, which does not reflect my view of the interaction between text and event in the proclamation-from-prophecy-and-pattern theme; see Bock 1987: 273.

is the Psalter, which is mentioned explicitly in Luke 20:42; Acts 1:20; 13:33 (Marshall 1978: 905). Prophetic texts from the Psalter appear in Luke 13:35; 20:17, 41–44; 22:69; Acts 2:25–28, 32–36; 4:25–27. It is not certain that this reference to the Psalter is intended to stand for the other writings in the Jewish canon outside of Moses and the prophets. It may simply refer to the Book of Psalms as a key contributor to these themes.

Fitzmyer (1985: 1581) denies that the OT precisely taught such things about Christ. But his remarks unduly limit his investigation to discussion of the Messiah theme. Because the scope of fulfillment is broader than just this one title, Fitzmyer misses how the unification of these ideas pulls together this theme in the progress of revelation from within the OT. In fact, Fitzmyer says that this perspective is one where the OT is placed in service to Luke's Christology. That these themes were retrospectively realized by the disciples as a result of Jesus' own life and teaching cannot be doubted. The Gospels indicate as much in texts like this one, where exposition was required to reveal the points in question (cf. John 2:22; 12:16). The disciples came to read the OT in this manner because of their exposure to Jesus. However, Luke's point is that Jesus is showing how the whole of OT teaching fits together as promise and how it was always intended to be seen in this way. The Messiah need not be mentioned everywhere in the OT because in Jewish belief the eschaton involved the Messiah in an era of ideal rule and hope. It is in this holistic sense that Jesus speaks of Scripture's references to the Messiah here, although he adds the one element that Judaism lacked: a suffering Messiah. Luke's threefold division is thus another way to say that all the OT teaches these things. This is the only place in the NT where this three-part division occurs. Jesus makes it clear that he is the subject of these Scriptures and that when it comes to God's promise, he is at the center of those events.

ii. Jesus' Instruction (24:45)

Jesus walks the disciples through the Scripture, functioning like a **24:45** prophet in revealing God's plan (cf. 9:35). Luke's language is general, and Jesus specifies no particular texts, only the basic topic (24:46–47). Likely texts for such an exposition are those that were used for christological points in Acts (Ernst 1977: 669–70; Tiede 1988: 442; 1 Cor. 1:21–25; 2 Cor. 3:12–16). In Luke 24:31–32 the disciples' eyes and the Scriptures were opened (διανοίγω, *dianoigō*; BDR §392.12); here it is their minds that are opened to understand God's message, in contrast to the blindness of 9:45 and 18:34. What the disciples could not grasp before the crucifixion and resurrection now becomes clear (cf. Luke 24:25, 27, 32; Acts 16:14; 26:17–18;

John 12:16; Fitzmyer 1985: 1583). God's activity in Christ makes scriptural sense after this personal exposition. It is responding to Jesus in belief that enlightens. The Spirit is not given here, as Plummer (1896: 562) argues (see Luke 24:49 and Acts 2). What is given is understanding and insight into God's plan. Since these disciples have witnessed God's plan and now understand it, they are commissioned to proclaim it (Osborne 1984: 130–31).

An important point for Lucan theology is found here: the kerygma grows out of divine design, not the other way around. Fitzmyer begins his fine biblical-theological survey (1981: 149) with the theme of proclamation, but more important to Luke is the theme of divine design, emphasized both in the infancy material and in this final Gospel scene (cf. Acts 2:22–23; 10:41–43; 17:24–31). The divine design emphasizes the inevitability of these events. The suffering, resurrection, and entry into glory (Luke 24:25–27, 44–47) must occur because they are in God's design. The Lucan description of God's plan and of the history of salvation that he designed is probably the most fundamental category of Lucan theology (Bock 1994c: 87–102). What the disciples preach is a result of the plan's outworking. At the center of that plan is what God has done and will do in Jesus, the Christ. Assurance can come to the believer because a faithful God is in control of events and knows where things are going.

iii. Three Scriptural Elements Fulfilled (24:46–47)

24:46   Luke introduces the basic content of the Scriptural teaching on God's plan, summarized in three infinitives.[18] The first is that the Christ should suffer (παθεῖν, *pathein*; mainly used of Jesus in Luke's writings: Luke 9:22; 17:25; 22:15; 24:26; Acts 1:3; 3:18; 17:3; BAGD 634 §3a; BAA 1279 §3a). The Psalter plays a key role for the theme of the suffering of the innocent righteous (R. Brown 1994: 1453–55). Since this suffering had already happened, the details are known to the disciples and to Luke's readers. Such suffering was anticipated by God (Ps. 22; 31; 69; 118; Isa. 53), although the concept of messianic suffering seems not to have been a part of first-century Jewish expectation. Even the disciples struggled to understand how it fit into God's plan. Yet in many ways it is the key to Jesus' career, for in it came the opportunity to deal with the issue of the forgiveness of sins and, as Luke will say in Acts 20:28, to purchase a church with his own blood.

---

18. The meaning of οὕτως is not clear (Marshall 1978: 905). Fitzmyer 1985: 1583 argues that it means "so" the Scripture speaks, referring to the manner of the message and thus focusing on its content. It could also be causative (Klostermann 1929: 242, pointing to 24:26), thus meaning "because" the Scripture must be fulfilled. Either possibility makes good sense; the second emphasizes design a little more.

The second infinitive is ἀναστῆναι (*anastēnai*, to rise).[19] Luke is clear that the promise is of a quick resurrection, since the usual Jewish hope was of a resurrection on the last day. This hope is defended in Acts primarily on the basis of two texts: Ps. 16:10 and 110:1. With Jesus having suffered and having been raised by God, the message can go forward (on these themes in broader NT teaching, see Osborne 1984: 283–87). The disciples are currently experiencing this element of the hope, but there is more to the plan.

With the third infinitive, κηρυχθῆναι (*kērychthēnai*, to preach), the **24:47** future of God's plan appears.[20] In this rich term are bound up the message's elements that the disciples are to take to the world. The message is broken down in detail, so that Luke's form of the great commission differs from the one in Matt. 20:18–20 and the general commission in the longer ending of Mark 16:15. The theme seems to parallel Mark 13:10 and Matt. 28:19.

The first element is that this message goes out in Jesus' name, which will be a major theme in Acts (Acts 2:38; 3:6, 16; 4:7, 10, 12, 17–18, 30; 5:28, 40; 8:12, 16; 9:14–16, 21, 27–28; 10:43, 48; 15:14, 26; 16:18; 19:5, 13, 17; 21:13; 22:16; 26:9; Bietenhard, *TDNT* 5:278). In the OT, the phrase indicates Yahweh's authority—authority that has now been transferred to Jesus, the mediator of God's promise. Baptism and other blessings come through his name (Acts 2:17–21, 38–39; 4:10). This important theme reveals the absolute authority of the glorified Jesus.

The goal of the message is that others might respond appropriately to Christ's activity: repent before God (see the exegesis of 5:32; on the possible Semitism, see BDF §207.1; BDR §207.1–2). Because repentance is rooted in the OT, it involves "turning," not just "agreeing" (which is what μετανοέω and μετάνοια can mean). For Luke, repentance is the summary term for the response to the apostolic message (Acts 2:38; 3:19; 5:31; 8:22; 11:18; 13:24; 17:30; 19:4; 20:21; 26:20). Change in thinking (i.e., a reorientation) is basic to human response to God's message. People must change their minds about God and the way to him, especially their thinking about sin, their inability to overcome sin on their own, Christ's essential role in forgiveness, and the importance of depending on him for spiritual di-

19. Ἀνίστημι (BAGD 70; BAA 138–39) can mean "to erect, to bring on the scene"; here it means "to raise from the dead" (Luke 16:31; 18:33; 24:7; Acts 2:24, 32; 3:22; 10:41; 13:34; 17:3, 31).

20. Jesus and the kingdom are the primary topics of preaching in Luke's writings: Luke 4:18–19, 44; 8:1, 39; 9:2; Acts 8:5; 9:20; 10:42; 19:13; 20:25; 28:31. Κηρύσσω (BAGD 431 §2bβ; BAA 877–78 §2bβ) is used elsewhere by Luke in Luke 3:3 (John's baptism); 12:3 (activities in the eschaton); Acts 10:37 (John's baptism); 15:21 (Moses).

rection. Those responding to the apostolic message of the gospel must come to God on his terms in order to experience the forgiveness that comes in the name of Jesus. But repentance means more than changing one's mind about God. People must also change their minds about who they are and how they can approach God. Repentance involves turning to and embracing God in faith. Forgiveness of sin comes to those who stretch out a needy hand to Jesus, clinging to him alone and recognizing that without him there is no hope. The OT base seems to be the plea in Joel 2:28–32 [3:1–5 MT] to call on the Lord, along with the common prophetic call to repent and turn to God (Acts 2:17–21, 38–39; Rom. 10:9–12). In short, those who repent cast themselves upon God's mercy, grace, direction, and plan. In this way, spiritual healing comes through the glorified mediator, the Great Physician (Luke 5:31–32).

The message of hope tells of forgiveness of sins, although Luke does not develop the "how" of this message in Luke–Acts (Luke 1:77; 3:3; 4:18; Acts 2:38; 5:31; 10:43; 13:38; 26:18; only Luke 22:19 and Acts 20:28 address this issue). Forgiveness of sins enables one to come into relationship with God because the barriers caused by sin are removed. As a result one can experience God's enabling and transforming power, especially through the work of his Spirit. In short, forgiveness of sins brings the opportunity to leave the darkness and come into God's light (Luke 1:79; Acts 26:18; on other blessings such as righteousness, salvation, life, and the Spirit, see Bultmann, *TDNT* 6:216 n. 315).

The message of hope is to go to all nations (Isa. 42:6; 49:6; Luke 2:32; Acts 13:47). This is a universal message open to anyone from any nation. As Acts 10:36 puts it, Jesus is Lord of all humanity, Jew and Greek (also Rom. 10:12–13). This is the message of the prophets to all who believe (Acts 10:42–43; 26:22–23). The gospel message in Jesus' name knows no national or racial barriers. This message is no longer a Jewish message and hope; it is intended for all. It starts from Jerusalem (Luke 24:49; Acts 1:8), but is designed to go to the ends of the earth.

The contrast between this universal tone and the disciples' initial response is so striking and the controversy that this universalism brought to the church was so great that many do not regard this remark as authentic (Luce 1933: 364). The disciples initially stumbled over this element in Jesus' commission, seemingly assuming that Jesus meant the message was to go to Jews in every nation. While this would be a natural Jewish reading of this remark and a logical conclusion to draw from the international Jewish audience in Acts 2, it is not what Jesus meant. Only later (Acts 10–15) would the disciples see that this limited sense was inappropriate. One might argue that a major burden of Luke–Acts is to show that Jesus the Christ is Lord of all humanity, so the message of the gospel can go to all (Bock 1987: 259, 277–79; Bock 1994c). Acts depicts the working out of this commission, and Acts 10 in particular argues that the church took the message to all only because God made it clear that was what it was to do.

The mission will start (ἀρξάμενοι, arxamenoi; BDF §419.3; BDR §419.3.3) in Jerusalem (Acts 1:8). Jesus had gone up to Jerusalem to meet his fate (Luke 9:51–19:44, esp. 13:31–35), but now the direction reverses and the mission goes out from Jerusalem. It is time for the benefits of Jesus' death and resurrection to be proclaimed to all. Jesus is raised to God's right hand to distribute salvation's benefits on all who repent and come to him.

The key point of this passage is that everything from suffering to universal proclamation was predicted in the Scripture. This represents a strong emphasis on the continuity of God's plan, which is another major point of Luke's two volumes. While the NT argues that there are distinctions in God's plan (e.g., the difference between law and grace or references to Israel and all), one must not fail to note the emphasis on continuity in Luke. These events are no surprise. They are part of God's will. God always intended to offer salvation to all races through Jesus. God always intended that the Christ suffer and be raised. God always intended that the message of salvation in the name of the Christ be a call to repent for the forgiveness of sins. These are the fundamental aspects of God's plan.

One can also note the difference between this commission and those in Matt. 28:18–20 and Mark 16:15. Matthew's commission stresses making disciples, while noting Jesus' authority, the need to go into the world, and the importance of teaching obedience to all that Jesus taught. The commission, as stated in the longer (and probably secondary) ending of Mark, involves going into all the world to preach the gospel. Matthew's commission occurs in Galilee. Mark's setting lacks specifics. These are distinct traditions and events.

iv. Naming the Disciples as Witnesses (24:48)

24:48 Jesus defines the disciples' role in light of what they have seen fulfilled from the Scripture. They are witnesses (μάρτυς, martys; BAGD 494 §2c; BAA 1002 §2c) of these things (for the syntax, see BDR §252.5).[21] The concept of witness will become an important theme in Acts (Acts 1:8, 22; 2:32; 3:15; 5:32; 10:39, 41; 13:31; 22:15, 20;

---

21. Strathmann, *TDNT* 4:492, notes that such testimony treats the resurrection no less objectively than it treats Jesus' passion.

26:16). The verb μαρτυρέω (*martyreō*, to witness) is also used with this sense (Acts 23:11), and it often speaks of divine witness to the disciples' testimony (Acts 14:3; 15:8). The disciples can testify to these events because they have seen them (Dillon 1978: 215–16, 291–92). Such events involve Jesus' passion, resurrection, teaching, and work (Nolland 1993b: 1220). Luke's commitment to the historicity of events is made clear here. Acts 1:8 reintroduces the concept and calls on the disciples to function as witnesses to the things Jesus did and taught. The remaining disciples required Judas's replacement to be a witness, especially of the resurrection (Acts 1:22; cf. the link of tradition and eyewitnesses in Luke 1:1–2; Bock 1991d). The speeches in Acts can be seen as examples of such testimony. In Jesus' absence, these disciples are to proclaim the message of God's work in Jesus. They have seen what Jesus did, and they have heard him open up the Scripture. Their faith is not just an ethic or a morality. It is the testimony of God's activity in history. Through Jesus, God personally reaches out to humankind in these events.

v. Command to Await the Spirit (24:49)

24:49 Jesus gives two instructions to his witnesses. First, he declares the coming of the Father's promise. By calling God "my Father," Jesus emphasizes their intimate relationship, which is also seen in Jesus' mediatorial role. The Spirit is the Father's promise, but Jesus says, "*I* will send" (ἐγὼ ἀποστέλλω, *egō apostellō*) him, thereby indicating that he has authority over the Spirit's distribution. This intermediary role for Jesus fits Peter's description of the Spirit's distribution at Pentecost (Acts 2:30–33). Jesus is the mediator of salvation's benefits and promises. As a result of his resurrection, he has authority over salvation. He is the channel through whom God's promises of salvation are provided.

When Jesus speaks of the Father's promise, he can only have one thing in mind—the Holy Spirit (see esp. Acts 1:4–5 and the contrast to John's baptism [Luke 3:16]). Acts 1:8 picks up this promise, speaks of receiving power, and names the Spirit as the gift. The disciples will "be clothed with power from on high" (Luke 24:49), and the Spirit will "come upon" them (Acts 1:8). The gift that Jesus promises from the Father is the Spirit in believers. The Father's promise is also the OT's promise (Joel 2:28–32 [3:1–5 MT] as cited in Acts 2:17–21; Marshall 1978: 907 lists Acts 1:4, 2:33; Gal. 3:14; Eph. 1:13; Luke 3:15–17; Nolland 1993b: 1220 adds Isa. 32:15; 44:3; Ezek. 39:29). Marshall is uncertain whether the promise reflected in Luke 12:12 is Jesus' or that of the OT. Given the contextual emphasis on divine design and fulfillment, the ultimate reference must be the OT (it is a both/and issue). The reason Jesus could issue a promise like that in Luke 12 and call the promise of the Spirit the Father's promise here is because God made it long ago. According to the NT, this is the promise of the new covenant (Jer. 31:33; Ezek. 36:26–27; Acts 2; 2 Cor. 3; Heb. 7–10). This permanent indwelling is a bestowal of power that enables believers to give evidence of God's presence, to appreciate the will of God (John 14:25–26; 16:12–15; 1 John 2:27). The Spirit's coming represents the inauguration of the kingdom blessings promised by the Father in the OT. Pentecost will be the beginning of God's new work in promise that eventually will manifest itself in the church (Acts 11:15). The Spirit's bestowal represents the earnestness of God's commitment to believers (Eph. 1:14; 2 Cor. 1:22; 5:5). The Spirit is also the key to what God gives. Paul can call the gospel the display of God's righteousness because the Spirit is the agent who enables the believer to live righteously, while God righteously deals with the issue of sin and its penalty (Rom. 3:20–21; 8:1–16; cf. John 3:1–21 [tied to Ezek. 36:24–27]). The Spirit's transforming and enabling ability is why Paul can speak of the gospel and the cross as the "power of God" (Rom. 1:16–17; 1 Cor. 1:18–31). Jesus does not detail here all that the Spirit provides. He simply notes that the promise is coming; the rest of the NT develops the depth of that promise.

This leads to Jesus' second instruction: the disciples are to go to Jerusalem and wait to be clothed from on high (καθίζω [kathizō, to sit] means "to stay" in Acts 18:11; 1 Chron. 19:5; Neh. 11:1–2; Marshall 1978: 907). The image of being clothed is a traditional one that both Paul (Rom. 13:12–14; 1 Cor. 15:53; Gal. 3:27; Eph. 4:24; 6:11, 14; Col. 3:10, 12; 1 Thess. 5:8) and John (Rev. 15:6; 19:14) utilize. The OT also knows the image (e.g., 1 Chron. 12:18 [12:19 MT]). The NT image refers to various gifts that God makes available for believers to "wear" in their daily walk, but Gal. 3:14 shows the close connection to the realization of the promise of the Spirit.

The reception of this enablement will empower believers, which is why Jesus speaks of the Spirit's coming as power from on high (Grundmann, *TDNT* 2:310–11; Schweizer, *TDNT* 6:407 n. 487). Πνεῦμα (*pneuma*) and δύναμις (*dynamis*) are almost synonymous terms since power is what the Spirit supplies (Mic. 3:8; Luke 1:17, 35; 4:14; Acts 1:5, 8; 6:8; 10:38). Here it is empowered testimony that is in mind (Acts 2:17–21; Osborne 1984: 135; Marshall 1970: 91–92). When Luke uses δύναμις, he usually has in mind the power to overcome evil forces, whether by miracles or by God's authority that comes through the Spirit (Luke 1:17; 4:36; 5:17; 6:19; 9:1; 10:13, 19; Acts 1:8; 2:22; 3:12; 4:33; 6:8; 8:13; 10:38; 19:11; Marshall 1970: 91–92). In Luke 9:1 it is tied to gospel preaching, the kingdom, and power over demons and disease. Word and works are the product of the Spirit. In addition, the Spirit enables boldness to declare God's message (Acts 1:8). This special gift of enablement is what disciples are to await in Jerusalem.

c. Ascension (24:50–53)
i. Jesus' Blessing and Departure (24:50–51)

24:50 The final scene of Jesus' ascension is told briefly. Luke first notes the locale: Bethany (elsewhere in Luke only at 19:29).[22] Broad NT usage suggests that the term is traditional (Matt. 21:17 = Mark 11:11; Matt. 26:6 = Mark 14:3; 11:1, 12; 14:3; John 1:28; 11:1, 18; 12:1). Though no time frame is given, the ascension seems to be on the same day as the other events (the connective is the general, nontemporal δέ, *de*, and or then). The location of this departure into heaven is seemingly different from that in Acts 1: the Mount of Olives. But this consideration is not decisive in distinguishing the two scenes since the two locales overlap: Bethany is on the eastern side of the Mount of Olives (Mark 11:1). Other reasons that some challenge the unity between Luke 24 and Acts 1 are the event's apparent timing and the possible allusion to this event in Acts 1:2 before the departure in 1:9–11.[23] My view is that these texts deal with a single event, but it is possible that Luke pictures the two departures as an *inclusio* bracketing Jesus' beginning appearance and his final appearance (Ellis 1974: 279; Tiede 1988: 444; Osborne 1984: 137–38).

Regardless of the choice, Jesus greets the disciples with peace (24:36) and departs after blessing them (εὐλογέω, *eulogeō*; elsewhere in Luke at 1:42 [twice], 64; 2:28, 34; 6:28; 9:16; 13:35; 19:38; 24:30, 51, 53). The act of raising hands and bestowing a benediction adds a note of solemnity and closure to the proceedings. There is no need to read into this act a "final" departure. Benedictions are often given to close significant occasions, and the commissioning of the disciples is such a time. Many compare this scene with the action of Simon II, the high priest (Sir. 50:20–21), and note that Jesus is acting like a

---

22. Ἕως is a general reference to "the area of," especially when combined with ἔξω (outside); BDR §239.3.3; Acts 17:14; 21:5; 26:11; Gen. 38:1; Ezek. 48:1; Marshall 1978: 908. But ἔξω is textually disputed; see the additional note.

23. Parsons 1987: 193–94, 196 posits that Bethany is named in order to provide literary closure to the triumphal entry by being a triumphal departure. But this link could occur with either Bethany or the Mount of Olives. It is not clear that Acts 1:2 and 1:6–11 are distinct events (Parsons gives strong arguments for one event, though the chronology is a tension for this option). Nonetheless, the popular idea of Lucan literary telescoping is possible given the lack of explicit temporal markers in Luke 24:44, 50 and Luke's love of retelling major events (e.g., Saul's conversion and the offer of the gospel to Cornelius; C. A. Evans 1990: 360–62). Seeing the ascension as an event that is telescoped here allows one to see how the different Galilean appearances suggested by Matthew and John fit into the timing of events more easily. See also Osborne 1984: 137–38, 266–70.

priest here (Grundmann 1963: 453–54; Ernst 1977: 672).[24] But Luke lacks an emphasis on Jesus as priest (Fitzmyer 1985: 1590; Nolland 1993b: 1227). When Jesus offers beatitudes in Luke 6:20–26, he is speaking as a prophet-teacher, not as a priest. The benediction's content is not noted. Jesus' last act in the Gospel is his commending his disciples to God's care in benediction. God is watching over them.

There is something different about this moment. Jesus' blessing is **24:51** not a normal benediction because of what follows. While he is blessing them, he departs. The numerous Western paintings that show Jesus' hands raised in blessing as he ascends attempt to depict what Luke describes here. The verb for the departure is rare: διΐστημι (*diistēmi*) is used only by Luke in the NT (Luke 22:59; Acts 27:28; BAGD 195 §1; BAA 393 §1).[25] The departure of supernatural figures is often noted by Luke (Luke 1:38; 2:15; 9:33; 24:31; Acts 10:7; 12:10; cf. Gen. 17:22; 35:13; Judg. 6:21; 13:20; Tob. 12:20–21; 2 Macc. 3:34; Marshall 1978: 909).

Luke is the only one to portray Jesus' departure to heaven (see the additional note). The act is a vindication of Jesus, for it represents the fulfillment of the prediction made at his trial that "from now on" the Son of Man would be seen at the Father's right hand (22:69). Jesus was convicted and put to death for making an offensive claim, but the ascension shows that the claim was true and that the execution was unjust. The claim of sonship was not rejected by the Father; rather the Son was received to the Father's side. The ascension is testimony to Jesus' mediatorial authority (Acts 2:30–36). The evidence of the presence of such authority is the Spirit's outpouring, as Peter's speech about the "witness" shows in Acts 2.

The ascension is not just a departure; it is also an arrival. The ascension may be the end of Jesus' earthly ministry, but it is the beginning of his heavenly reign and the precursor to the initial distribution of salvific benefits. To this portrait Heb. 2–3, 7–10 will add the note of an intercessory ministry, to which 1 John 2:2 also alludes.[26]

ii. Reaction: Worship, Joy, and Thanksgiving (24:52–53)

The entourage returns to the city worshiping Jesus, the first time **24:52** this point is made in Luke (see the additional note). Such worship is

24. Priests like Aaron (Lev. 9:22) gave such blessings, but they were not the only ones to do so (e.g., Moses; Deut. 33).

25. Codex D has the second aorist form of ἀφίστημι (to withdraw), but the reading is too poorly attested to be original.

26. Bertram, *TDNT* 8:611, suggests that awakening, resurrection, reception, ascent, being taken up, enthronement in heaven, and dominion are the elements of Jesus' exaltation mentioned in the NT. Hebrews adds a priestly emphasis to this work of Jesus, thus making him a king-priest (Heb. 1; 7–10).

not surprising, given the exposition that has taken place and their increased understanding of Jesus' role in God's plan. It shows a key shift in the disciples' appreciation of Jesus. Scripture, Jesus' word, and heaven's testimony have led to a deepening awareness of Jesus. The return to Jerusalem might have occasioned prayer and singing as well, though these are not mentioned. Accompanied by great joy, the return to Jerusalem pictures obedience to Jesus' instruction.[27] Both Jesus' birth and his departure bring joy (2:10; Marshall 1978: 910). Luke's Gospel ends where it starts: in Jerusalem.

24:53 The disciples return to Jerusalem and go to the temple. The Gospel events end as they began: at the temple. Luke's Gospel has gone from a priest unexpectedly participating in the arrival of God's promise to disciples expectantly awaiting the inauguration of God's blessings. Luke notes that they were continually at the temple (διὰ παντός, *dia pantos*; BDR §223.3.3; the phrase elsewhere in the NT at Matt. 18:10; Mark 5:5; Acts 2:25; 10:2; 24:16; Rom. 11:10; 2 Thess. 3:16; Heb. 2:15; 9:6; 13:15; Marshall 1978: 910). The Gospel ends with a note about the disciples' piety (Acts 2:46; 3:1; 5:42; Weinert 1981). In the temple, they are blessing God (εὐλογοῦντες, *eulogountes*; see the exegesis of 24:50; see Metzger 1975: 190–91 on the textual problem). God is to be praised for the blessings that come in Jesus. Luke's final note is that, as the disciples await the arrival of the Father's promise, God is to be praised for his work in Jesus Christ the exalted Lord.

Summary Luke 24:36–53 emphasizes the reality of Jesus' resurrection and how it fits into God's plan. Jesus provides physical evidence of his resurrection when he asks the disciples to handle him and confirms it when he eats with them. He shows his acceptance of them by sitting at the table with them.

Jesus then reminds his disciples that all these things about the plan were promised in the OT. The events of the Christ's passion and resurrection were not surprising. Specifically, three elements are highlighted: Jesus' suffering, his resurrection, and the preaching of repentance in his name for the forgiveness of sins to all the nations. Jesus reminds the disciples that they are witnesses of these things. In addition, the Father's promise, the Holy Spirit, will be sent to them in Jerusalem, where they are to await the promise. That event commences the bestowal of salvation benefits from the hand of the risen, exalted Jesus, who sits at God's

27. Joy (χαρά) is a Lucan theme: Luke 1:14; 2:10; 8:13; 10:17; 15:7, 10; 24:41; Acts 8:8; 12:14; 13:52; 15:3. Osborne 1984: 140 notes that in Luke's writings joy is a present experience shared to the degree of one's participation in events.

side. Finally, Jesus departs with blessing, and the disciples return to Jerusalem, worshiping Jesus and blessing God for his grace.

Luke desires his readers to see that the resurrection is real. He wants them to understand that God's plan goes on. That plan and promise are now realized in the new community God has formed in the disciples that come from every nation. This community is going to be equipped to carry out a task until the consummation of promise comes in Jesus' return.

In fact, Luke's ending is an open ending. The disciples' wait for the Spirit begins the second volume of his writings, where Luke details the new community's activity under God's direction. The end stresses the certainty and continuity of God's plan, along with an attitude that is to accompany the recognition that God is at work. That attitude is worship, joy, thanksgiving to God, and preparation to take the message to others. Luke's readers are to identify with the disciples. The resurrection may be perplexing, but it is real. God's plan is not off course; it is right on schedule. The church is not to withdraw or be silent, but to penetrate the world, seek the lost, and care for those in need. Disciples are not to be passive; they are to be alive as well as full of joy and thanksgiving for what it means to know the resurrected Lord.

This final scene is a commission from the Lord, who was always at the center of God's promise. The accomplishing of this promise required that Jesus suffer, but God raised and seated him at his side. This same promise calls disciples to take the message of God's hope to the ends of the earth. Luke's believing readers are to see that after the Gospel and its sequel comes a life of mission that reflects and proclaims the hope that God created through Jesus. God has given his message to those who know him, along with provision to proclaim that message. If Luke's readers do not know Jesus, they are to see that Jesus' resurrection means they must respond to him. God has acted in history through Jesus. The Gospel's ending is open ended because it portrays Jesus reigning at God's side, while the disciples rejoice in the knowledge that this authoritative Jesus cares for them. Such is the opportunity for blessing that Jesus brings. Such is the disciples' call as they bear the message of hope to all races. He is alive and in their midst, offering hope and blessing to those who will come to him. Now it is time for all to decide where they stand.

Additional Notes

24:36. Some manuscripts communicate the correct sense by naming Jesus as the subject of the sentence: ὁ Ἰησοῦς is found in A, W, Θ, Ψ, family 1, family 13, Byz, some Syriac, and Vulgate; it is omitted in $\mathfrak{P}^{75}$, ℵ, B, D, L, 1241, Itala, and some Syriac. The harder reading is the omission, which is supported by the Alexandrian-Western alliance.

24:36. The greeting "peace to you" is lacking in codex D and the Itala but is otherwise attested overwhelmingly. Although many (Plummer 1896: 559; Luce 1933: 363; Creed 1930: 299) omit the greeting on the basis of the shorter-reading rule, it should not be omitted since it is so well attested (see Dillon 1978: 183 and Aland 1965–66: 207–9 for full discussion). Codexes P, W, 579, Vulgate, and some Syriac add the more explicit, "It is I. Do not be afraid." This additional greeting, which may be based on John 6:20, is too narrowly attested to be original.

24:37. Codex D has φάντασμα (phantom) instead of πνεῦμα (spirit), but it is too weakly attested to be original (cf. Matt. 14:26).

24:38. The textual issue surrounding καρδίᾳ (heart) is the difference between a collective singular ($\mathfrak{P}^{75}$, B, D, Itala) or a plural (most manuscripts). The plural may well be original, though the singular is the more difficult reading and reflects Lucan style. There is no real difference in sense between the variants.

24:40. The originality of 24:40 (another of the debated Western noninterpolations in Luke 24) is disputed. Codex D, the Itala, and some Syriac lack the verse, but external evidence is overwhelmingly for inclusion (all other manuscripts, including $\mathfrak{P}^{75}$, have it). Only the shorter-reading rule can be invoked for omission, but it is not certain that this rule applies to a variant involving a whole verse. Some regard the text as added by a scribe to bring a tighter connection to John 20:20, 25, 27 (Plummer 1896: 560; Klostermann 1929: 241; Luce 1933: 363). But these factors are not strong enough to argue for omission, especially since there are variations of wording with John 20:20, which speaks of hands and side, not hands and feet (Dillon 1978: 183–84). Those who argue for inclusion suggest that the verse was omitted by a scribe because it seemed to repeat 24:39 (Metzger 1975: 187; Fitzmyer 1985: 1576).

24:40. The UBS–NA text has ἔδειξεν (he showed; $\mathfrak{P}^{75}$, ℵ, B, L, N, family 1, 33, 1241), but manuscript evidence for ἐπέδειξεν (he showed) is broad (A, W, Θ, Ψ, family 13, Byz). On the one hand, Luke's preference for prefixed forms may mean that ἐπέδειξεν is original (it appears in Luke 17:14; Acts 9:39; 18:28 and only four times in the rest of NT; Marshall 1978: 902), especially since an error of sight could have produced the shorter text. On the other hand, the prefixed verb in Luke 24:42 may have caused a scribe to use a prefixed verb here. There is no difference in meaning. External evidence favors the shorter form.

24:42. At the end of the verse, some manuscripts (Θ, Ψ, family 1, family 13, Byz, Itala, many Syriac) add καὶ ἀπὸ μελισσίου κηρίου [or κηρίον] (and from a honeycomb [or, a honeycomb from a beehive]). Most Alexandrian and Western manuscripts ($\mathfrak{P}^{75}$, $\aleph$, A, B, D, L, W, one Syriac manuscript), however, mention only fish (Nestle 1910–11). Plummer (1896: 561) argues against the additional detail. On the symbolism of the combination of fish and honey in the early postapostolic church, see Grundmann (1963: 451) and Ernst (1977: 668). In the early church, honey was associated with baptism and the Lord's Supper (Metzger 1975: 187–88; cf. Ps. 119:103, where it is compared to God's word).

24:43. With varying wording, a few manuscripts (K, family 13, Θ, Vulgate) add a reference to Jesus' distributing the rest of the meal to the disciples, but the witnesses are too few to regard this detail as original to Luke (cf. Ignatius, *Trallians* 9.1).

24:49. There is debate whether ἰδού (behold) should be in the text, but it is the best attested reading with good manuscript distribution. If it is not original, then the text reads καὶ ἐγώ (and I) ($\mathfrak{P}^{75}$, D; Marshall 1978: 906–7).

24:50. Ἔξω is omitted by $\mathfrak{P}^{75}$, $\aleph$, B, C*, L, 1, 33, and some Syriac, most likely because it looked redundant. It has some attestation (with ἕως in A, W, Θ, family 13, Byz; by itself in D), however, and is the more difficult reading, because of the repetition of similar letters and the imprecise reference to the area outside Bethany.

24:51. Codex $\aleph$*, D, and most Itala lack καὶ ἀνεφέρετο εἰς τὸν οὐρανόν (and he was carried up into heaven). If this omission is original, then we do not have an ascension here, since Jesus is said only to be taken from them, which happened in 24:31 (cf. Philip's departure in Acts 8:39). The attestation for omission is too thin to indicate originality, though the case for omission here is stronger than for the other Western noninterpolations in Luke 24.[28] Internal evidence, however, speaks for the originality of the phrase. First, Acts 1:2 assumes an ascension here, something that is not clear if this phrase is lacking. Second, Marshall (1978: 909) notes that ἀναφέρω (to carry up) is not the normal verb that the early church used for ascension. A copyist inserting the verb would likely have used the more common ἀναλαμβάνω (to take up). Third, the three-part structure that dominates these

---

28. Parsons 1987: 29–52 has a long, thoughtful discussion of the Western noninterpolations and accepts them all on the premise that $\mathfrak{P}^{75}$ has a doctrinal reason for including them. He sees codex D as adding to the Christology of the chapter, especially the physical reality of the resurrection. But he fails to see that the omission of καὶ ἀνεφέρετο εἰς τὸν οὐρανόν (and he was carried up into heaven) in 24:51 means that the ascension is no longer explicit in Luke (though it is alluded to in Acts 1:2). Parsons also assumes that $\mathfrak{P}^{75}$ or a text like it is responsible for these additions, but this conclusion seems to put too much weight on $\mathfrak{P}^{75}$—reversing the way this manuscript is generally treated. The widespread lack of witnesses for the Western noninterpolations in Luke 24, however, stands against their originality. It is the presence of $\aleph$* that makes this example so debatable.

verses is also Lucan (Metzger 1975: 189–90; Epp 1981: 135–36). Fourth, there is no doctrinal explanation for the addition.

24:52. Codex D, the Itala, and some Syriac lack the phrase προσκυνή-σαντες αὐτόν (worshiped him)—the last Western noninterpolation in this chapter—while all other manuscripts include it. Some wish to exclude the phrase because it attributes worship to Jesus at a very early stage (this is Luke's first mention of the concept; cf. Mark 5:6; 15:19; Matt. 2:2, 8, 11; 8:2; 9:18; 14:33; 15:25; 18:26; 20:20; 28:9, 17). Attestation for the phrase is strong, and it should be accepted as original.

24:53. Some manuscripts (A, B, C², Θ, Ψ, family 13, Byz) add a liturgical ἀμήν (so be it) at the end of the Gospel. Since a distribution of manuscripts (𝔓⁷⁵, ℵ, C*, D, L, W, 1, 33, most Itala) lack the ending, it is not original.

Excursus 11
Last Supper: The Nature and Timing of the Meal (22:7–13)

Most scholars acknowledge that Jesus had a "final meal" with his disciples at which significant events and sayings took place.[1] What kind of meal was it though, and when was it held? Bound up in this discussion is one of the most complex chronological issues in the NT. Two questions surround the problem. (1) What kind of meal did Jesus and the disciples have: a Passover meal, another type of special meal, or a regular evening meal? (2) How is the date of the meal to be reckoned? The clear impression from the Synoptics is that Jesus eats a Passover meal as the date moves from Nisan 14 to Nisan 15. On the other hand, John appears to have Jesus eat the meal the day before Passover, since Passover preparation begins while Jesus is on the cross. Many pit Luke 22:7= Matt. 26:17 = Mark 14:12 against John 18:28, where Jewish guards hesitate to enter Pilate's pretorium for fear of defiling themselves for the Passover meal. How can this be if the meal was already eaten? Related to this is the possibility that different calendars—one popular, the other official—were in use. If so, what is the evidence for them, which one was used, and where?

When it comes to the meal's nature, one study stands out: Jeremias's magisterial *Eucharistic Words of Jesus*, which has set the course for discussion about the meal's nature.[2] Arguments that the last meal was a Passover supper operate at three evidentiary levels: direct (no. 1), circumstantial (nos. 2–7), and questionable (nos. 8–12):

1. A direct claim for a Passover meal comes from Mark 14:12 = Luke 22:7, which explicitly links the meal to Passover preparation (see also Matt. 26:17). These texts provide the most fundamental factor in the discussion. In fact, if it were not for John's details, esp. 18:28, this matter would probably not be debated at all.

---

1. The Bible does not use the term *Last Supper*, a description that arises from Jesus' arrest and crucifixion immediately after this meal.

2. Jeremias 1966: 15–84 deals with various aspects of this issue. Other key studies include Hoehner 1977: 74–90; Marshall 1980: 30–75 (which has the advantage of assessing Jeremias's claims); Jaubert 1965; Blinzler 1958; and R. Brown 1962b. For bibliography, see Nolland 1993b: 1035–40.

2. Jesus made an effort to hold the meal in Jerusalem, the required location for a Passover meal (Mark 14:13 = Matt. 26:18 = Luke 22:10; John 18:1). Many pilgrims stayed in tents near the city in order to meet this requirement (Josephus, *Jewish War* 2.1.3 §§10–13; *m. Pesaḥ.* 5.10; 7.12–13; 10.1–3). During this time the population of Jerusalem (normally 30,000) swelled with the addition of 85,000–125,000 pilgrims (Jeremias 1966: 42).

3. Like the Passover meal, this meal is held in the evening and extends late into the evening, rather than at the normal mealtime of late afternoon (Matt. 26:20 = Mark 14:17; John 13:30; 1 Cor. 11:23; Exod. 12:8; Jub. 49.1, 12). In *t. Pesaḥ.* 2.22 [= Neusner 1977–86: 2.123–24]) the eating of the lamb is obligatory on the first night.

4. Like the Passover meal, the bread is eaten in the middle of the meal and not at the start (Mark 14:20, 22 = Luke 22:19–23).

5. Judas's departure does not cause surprise because it is thought that he is either going for last-minute supplies for the evening meal or to offer alms to the poor (John 13:29). (This is more inferential than the other arguments.)

6. Like the Passover meal, this meal ends with the singing of Hallel Psalms (ὑμνήσαντες, having hymned, in Mark 14:26 = Matt. 26:30). Such singing did not occur after normal meals.

7. The interpretation of the meal's elements recalls the Passover. It was customary during the Passover meal to describe the significance of certain items (Exod. 12:26–27; 13:8; Deut. 26:5–11; *m. Pesaḥ.* 10.5). Jesus' discussion of the bread and wine is parallel to this ritual.

8. That the meal is limited to the Twelve indicates a Passover meal. This number is close to the minimum number of ten required for the meal. It is not entirely clear, however, that the meal was limited in size or that Jesus usually ate with a larger group.

9. Reclining at the meal is said to favor a Passover meal (Mark 14:18; John 13:23, 28). But the Passover meal is not the only meal where this occurred, so this point is of limited value.

10. The meal is observed with levitical purity (John 13:10). But such washing is common at meals, so not much can be made of this point. It should be noted, however, that Jesus' disciples did not always wash for meals (Mark 7:2).

11. The presence of red wine is said to be unusual and marks the Passover, where four such cups were required (Mark 14:23, 25; *m. Pesaḥ.* 10.1). Once again, this detail is not peculiar to the meal and so is inconsequential.

12. The decision not to leave Jerusalem is said to reflect the desire to stay in the city on Passover night. Jesus had been returning to Bethany each night before this evening, so his staying in

Jerusalem is seen as fulfilling Passover requirements. This detail fits the Passover, but need not show it was present.

While no one piece of the circumstantial evidence (nos. 2–7) is conclusive, taken together with the Synoptic statements, they support the presence of a Passover meal. Items 8–12 are congruous with a Passover meal, but cannot establish its presence. Nonetheless, in the direct and circumstantial claims, there is a strong suggestion that a Passover meal is present.

Objections to this view are based on issues raised by the biblical text (nos. 1, 3, 5, 7, 9, 10) and through strictly historical (nos. 2, 4, 6, 8) concerns. I list the claims from less impressive to more compelling. Claims 9 and 10 have the most substance.

1. Some suggest that because ἄρτος (bread) is used and not ἄζυμος (unleavened bread), a Passover meal—which required unleavened bread—cannot be intended. The problem with this argument is that ἄρτος is sometimes used of unleavened bread (Exod. 29:23; Lev. 7:12; 8:26; Num. 6:15; Josephus, *Antiquities* 3.6.6 §143; 8.3.7 §90; *Jewish War* 5.5.5 §217).
2. The early church celebrated a meal regularly—not annually— a schedule that differs from the Passover. The Lord's Supper is not, however, a recreation of the Passover meal; elements of it were new, so that an annual repetition is not required.
3. There is no explicit reference to the Passover lamb or bitter herbs. This is disputed, however, for the lamb is alluded to in Mark 14:12 = Luke 22:15 (also 22:7).
4. The order of elements does not follow the Passover meal, since (a) the bread is broken and then blessing follows, (b) individual cups were used at Passover, not a common cup, and (c) each guest had his own dish of bitter herbs. Of these three objections only the second has possible merit (Marshall 1980: 63), though the issue of how the cups were circulated at the meal is not clear from rabbinic materials (*m. Pesaḥ.* 10.2, 7). Did a fixed prescription exist before the second century?
5. Mark 14:2 mentions resolve not to arrest Jesus during the feast. Thus Jesus would not be arrested on feast night. But this remark was made before Judas's offer. The rationale for this hesitation was the fear of popular revolt, which Judas removes. Given the possibility of a private arrest, this resolve melted in the face of golden opportunity. Another reply to this objection is that Luke 22:6 should be interpreted only as a resolve not to arrest Jesus in the midst of the festal crowd.
6. Some see *m. Pesaḥ.* 8.6 relating the custom of releasing a prisoner before the meal as a picture of forgiveness. Barabbas's re-

lease therefore shows that the meal has not been eaten yet. But there is no extrabiblical evidence (1) of this Roman practice, (2) that *m. Pesaḥim* refers to this practice, or (3) that it follows the Jewish calendar (see R. Brown 1994: 814–20 for a full treatment). One should be careful, however, about assuming that such a practice would be noted extrabiblically; for example, R. Brown (1994: 815) notes how little we know about Pilate's procedures in Judea. He suggests that the release may be equal to the *venia*, a Roman pardon for an individual, but Brown expresses uncertainty about such a custom, while I prefer to take the testimony of the text as it is. Barabbas may have been released late since part of Pilate's motivation in this case was to free Jesus. The timing of Barabbas's release does not appear to be dictated by habit but by impulse, so the timing can prove nothing (see also the exegesis of 23:25).

7. Two Pauline texts show that Jesus was crucified while the Passover lambs for the meal were slaughtered: 1 Cor. 5:7 describes Jesus as a Passover lamb, and 1 Cor. 15:20 alludes to Jesus as the firstfruits from the dead. The argument is that these texts show Jesus crucified when the lambs were slain and raised at the beginning of firstfruits, that is, on the "day after the Sabbath" (Lev. 23:9–14). But there is no indication that either of these metaphors intends to make a point about the timing of Jesus' death. Paul's concern is only with the theological image.

8. The early Christian Quartodecimanians fasted on Nisan 14 to memorialize the date of the Supper. More recent evidence (*Epistula Apostolorum* 15 [26]; A.D. 140–70) shows that this fast extended into Nisan 15, so this point has become inconclusive (Marshall 1980: 65; Jeremias 1966: 122–25).

9. The chronological data associated with John's Gospel provides a more substantial objection to the presence of a Passover meal: John 13:1 ("before the Feast of the Passover"); 18:28 (soldiers did not want to enter Pilate's pretorium so as to not defile themselves before Passover); 19:14 ("the preparation of the Passover"). It is possible, however, to explain each of these Johannine texts in light of the Passover-meal view. First, John 13:1 may apply not to the meal's timing, but to when Jesus knew his hour had come. Another, more likely suggestion is that Jesus' act of love, the footwashing, occurred before the Passover, that is, right before the meal that began the official festal week. Second, the difficulty of John 18:28 is bound up in the calendar issue (Carson 1984: 531). The least likely suggestion is that events delayed the meal since there were limits as to how late one could eat it (*m. Pesaḥ.* 10.9; *m. Zebaḥ.* 5.8). More likely, John's mention of uncleanness on Passover refers

to other festal meals associated with Passover week, specifically the *Ḥagigah*, the feast on the first paschal morning (Num. 28:18–19). If one sees the entire Passover festival in view here, then this explanation makes sense. Nonetheless John 18:28 still requires a look because of the Jewish calendar issue it raises (see below). Third, the question of John 19:14 is not as difficult. This verse can be read to mean "preparation for the Sabbath, which fell on the Passover feast" and thus refer to a Friday (Marshall 1980: 70; Carson 1984: 531–32).[3] In this sense the point is not Passover-meal preparation, but preparation associated with other meals of the Passover week.

10. The final objection involves the claim that the arrest and trial do not fit a festal Passover day. As many as ten activities are seen as incompatible with Passover (Jeremias 1966: 75–79), three being particularly crucial: trial, death on a feast day, and burial. On the trial, Marshall (1980: 65) notes that this is a problem for either view, since such trials were prohibited on both feast day and the preceding day. As such, this objection seems to have merit no matter how one views the event's timing. But it is also clear that the Jewish authorities thought Jesus' situation so unusual and the opportunity to deal with him so great, that they acted as quickly as possible and changed intentions related to the feast. In addition, false prophets were supposed to be executed before all the people as a lesson, so what better time than Passover (Deut. 18:20; 17:13; Jeremias 1966: 78–79)? More important, since the decisive trial that condemns Jesus is Roman, one could argue that the Romans would not be bound by Jewish practice. In fact, for a Roman procedure to dictate when Jesus' death occurred would underline Roman responsibility for the decisive act, a point that could be exploited later if charges of Jewish responsibility were made. Concerning execution on a feast day, it is suggested that the presence of two criminals with Jesus (Luke 23:32) shows that his situation was not a special case for Rome. The Jews may have argued that they were helping their rulers along and that the condemnation belonged to the foreign authorities. These events fit a Roman setting. Once an execution was scheduled, the Romans carried it out efficiently, slaying all on "death row."[4] The burial is less problematic since the law permitted

---

3. Carson cites texts where πάσχα can mean Passover week: Josephus, *Antiquities* 14.2.1 §21; 17.9.3 §213; *Jewish War* 2.1.3 §10; *m. Pesaḥ.* 9.5.

4. Marshall 1980: 65–66 regards this series of events as the most problematic reference, but he also notes that it is equally problematic for the day before Passover. On the historicity of the Roman setting and trial customs as tied to the governor's assize, see Kinman 1991.

exceptions to burying on a feast day where individual laws conflicted. An executed criminal's body was not to be left hanging overnight, and this took precedence over festal cleanliness (Deut. 21:22–23).

Thus, though some weighty objections exist as to the nature of the day, they are not sufficient to overturn the likelihood that Jesus was observing a Passover meal. All objections can be adequately explained.

But a potentially significant problem remains: the date of the meal (and the related calendar issue). My conclusion above was that the Synoptics correctly describe a Passover meal and that John can be reconciled to that understanding. But what if that explanation is wrong? What options do we have if the Synoptics have the supper on Nisan 15 and John has it on Nisan 14? The first four views argue that either the Synoptics or John is wrong. Views 5–10 appeal to differing calendars or practices related to the Passover meal (frequently some variation in the religious calendar among various groups). The last approach takes a literary approach to what is taking place. The final seven approaches attempt to put together all the data in a single package. For each view, I present the option and then assess it.

1. The data is irreconcilable. After laying out all the data, Fitzmyer (1985: 1381–83) states that harmonization runs "roughshod over the long-accepted analyses of so many of the passages involved according to form critical methods that it cannot be taken seriously. . . . In this regard it [the search to harmonize] manifests an unmistakably fundamentalist concern." This explanation contains more rhetoric than substance. Form criticism has not been around long enough to be able to occupy a pontifical position on interpretation, and many of the various solutions, though older than form criticism, rest on concerns that fall outside the scope of that discipline.[5] This conclusion merely shows a bias against harmonization.

2. John is closer to being correct, the Synoptics are wrong, and the supper was not a Passover meal (Fitzmyer 1985: 1378–82, who argues that the meal was eaten just before the Passover

---

5. For example, Chwolson's 1908 work (view six below) was first published in 1892, three decades before the start of form criticism, so that Fitzmyer's appeal to form-critical analysis is challenged. Some of the arguments in this debate are lexical and so are unrelated to any solid results emerging from form criticism. Apparently, Fitzmyer has Luke's additional cup in mind when he discusses form criticism. Some see Luke's mention of the additional cup as evidence of liturgical expansion by the later church.

and so quickly became associated with it). On this view, the Passover meal was an understandable product of early church reflection on the event, given the proximity of the two events. But this view makes it hard to determine what type of meal the disciples ate or to explain some of the meal's details. Other meals are usually posited in place of Passover. The *Ḳiddush* meal was a meal of sanctification associated with the Sabbath or feast day (Jeremias 1966: 26–29). Jeremias's examination shows that this term is not applied to a meal at all, but it is merely a blessing. This option is, to use Jeremias's description, "wholly illusory." The *Ḥaburah* meal was a special meal of religious solemnity that could be held at any time among Jewish friends. Jeremias replies that all meals had such significance and that this category is an *"ad hoc* conjecture for which there is absolutely no evidence." Fellowship events like this were not just random meals, but were tied to certain events (e.g., circumcision, betrothal, wedding, funeral) where such meals were required by commandment (Jeremias 1966: 29–31). A third possibility appealing to Essene or Essene-like meals is also rejected by Jeremias (1966: 31–36).

3. The Synoptics are right, John is wrong, and the supper was a Passover meal (Jeremias 1966: 79–83, esp. 82). Jeremias claims that the Johannine accounts are of mixed character, with some reflecting a Passover meal and others not. This kind of careless mixture of perspective by a Jewish author is unlikely. Either he intends a Passover meal, or he does not. On such a key issue of background, why would John vacillate?

4. The ambiguity results from a "theological motive": John knows that the last meal was a Passover, but for theological reasons he portrays Jesus as a Passover Lamb (Moo 1983: 318–23). This literary approach offers a clear rationale. Is the lamb imagery in John necessarily chronological? Might it be used merely as a metaphorical description like the later Pauline text 1 Cor. 5:7? Given the traces of evidence for a Passover meal in John, the metaphorical option is more likely than the chronological one (as with the Pauline imagery). Rejecting this approach assumes that the earlier explanation of the other Johannine texts (John 18:28; 19:14) is correct. This option is possible, but it is subtle.

5. Jaubert (1965) argues that Jesus celebrated the meal early, probably on Tuesday (see Ellis 1974: 249). According to this view, Jesus used a solar calendar like that in the Book of Jubilees and at Qumran, where Passover always occurred on Tuesday evening, in contrast to the official lunar calendar that cel-

ebrated the meal on Thursday–Friday. This hypothesis has received much careful attention, but it has several problems. First, there is no clear evidence that Jesus followed such a sectarian calendar, whereas the temple schedule was clearly regulated by an official lunar calendar, as the Gospels seem to clearly locate the Passover close to the Sabbath day (e.g., Luke 23:55–56). In addition, all the accounts are clear that Jesus was arrested the same night as the meal and that he was crucified on the next day. One could appeal to literary "telescoping," but none of the sources suggest this (this in fact is view 11; Nolland 1993b: 1024–26). The impression is that once Jesus was arrested, events moved like lightning. An early arrest would also mean that Jesus did not teach many days in the temple, as he suggests upon his arrest (Luke 22:53). But the fatal objection to this view is that Jesus must celebrate a meal with a lamb slain by the priests at the temple two to three days early (Marshall 1980: 73–74; Fitzmyer 1985: 1380; Beckwith 1979–81; VanderKam 1979; P. Davies 1983).

6. To deal with all the sacrificing required for the Passover, Chwolson (1908: 20–44) argues that lambs were slaughtered in the evening between Nisan 14 and Nisan 15, except when Nisan 15 was on the Sabbath. In this view, the slaughter was brought forward twenty-four hours and Jesus (and the Pharisees) celebrated Passover on Nisan 14, while the Sadducees celebrated on Nisan 15. This view also has problems. First, in the first century, lambs were slain in the afternoon, not in the evening (Marshall 1980: 71; Jeremias 1966: 21–23).[6] Second, Passover lambs were not to be kept overnight, which is what the Sadducees would have had to do, if they followed mishnaic procedure (*m. Suk.* 5.5) and the Torah (Exod. 12:10). Since the Sadducees were literalist about the Torah, this is unlikely. Third, it is unlikely that Jesus would have celebrated Passover on Nisan 13–14, when the law said Nisan 14–15 (Hoehner 1977: 82–83).

7. Billerbeck argues that the Sadducees and Pharisees had different calendars because of differing renderings of Lev. 23:15 (SB 2:812–53; Marshall 1980: 71–73).[7] This affected how the fifty days to Pentecost were counted and led to a debate about what

---

6. Jeremias objects that, if this theory is correct, the time advance is not one day but only four to six hours. He appeals to Jub. 49.10, 19, and Philo, *Special Laws* 2.27 §145, to argue against an evening sacrifice.

7. This is the best option to Marshall, though it is not without problems—mainly that it requires slaughtering on two consecutive days, when no direct evidence suggests such was the case.

the "day after the Sabbath" meant. Pharisees considered the festival as Passover and started their count the day after Passover, while Sadducees argued that Sabbath meant Sabbath and counted from the first Sunday after the Sabbath after Passover. The Sadducees, who were anxious for Nisan 16 to fall on a Sunday so Pentecost also would be on a Sunday, placed Nisan 14 on a Friday. One first-century group, the Boethusians, is known to have set the calendar this way. The reason for such flexibility in setting the days was to keep on a lunar calendar. Pharisees started Nisan 14 a day earlier so that two consecutive Passover days resulted. The Synoptics recorded this Pharisaic practice, while John went with the Sadducean. This position is developed by implication and circumstantial evidence only; there is no direct evidence for or against it. The major difficulty is arguing two separate days for Passover celebration when no such explicit discussion exists in ancient Jewish records for this holiday.

8. Pickl (1946: 120–22) argues for a regional calendrical distinction to deal with all the sacrifices over a two-day period. Under this view, the Galileans slew their lambs on "official" Nisan 13, which produced a rest day in Galilee (*m. Pesaḥ.* 4.5), while the Judeans followed a day later. Jeremias (1966: 24) and Marshall (1980: 71) note that there is no evidence for this view.[8]

9. Hoehner (1977: 85–90) argues that the start of a day was reckoned differently: sometimes from sunset (Exod. 12:18), sometimes from sunrise (Num. 14:14). Hoehner cites examples of variations within the same author. This view combines with Billerbeck's to argue that the Synoptics figured Passover on the Galilean sunrise-to-sunrise model, which the Pharisees also followed. John followed the Sadducean, Judean sunset-to-sunset model, which enabled him to make a theological point and follow one reckoning of the Passover. There were two days of slaughter and Jesus observes a Passover meal. This Johannine reckoning means that the lambs slain after Jesus' meal as he dies on the cross are for the Sadducees. The timing of Jesus as the Passover lamb is thus a matter of perspective. Hoehner notes that there is no explicit evidence for two days of slaughtering, and Marshall (1980: 74) adds another cogent objection: if the sunrise-to-sunrise reckoning is used, then the Galileans eat the Passover on Nisan 14, not Nisan 15 as commanded, since there is no change of day in the evening. The preparation

---

8. Pickl argues for this distinction by comparing Josephus, *Antiquities* 3.10.5 §249 and 2.15.1 §317. Jeremias argues that the second text addresses Diaspora practice about all festivals and as such does not apply.

and the meal take place on the same day, not on different days, as is commanded.

10. Carson (1984: 531–32) argues that all the Johannine passages fit the Synoptic chronology (see no. 9 above in the discussion of the nature of the meal). The key here is that John's references to "Passover" are not to the meal, but to other sacred meals that were part of Passover week. This is the most likely solution in my judgment, though if it fails to convince, the position of Billerbeck, view 7 above, is a likely alternative, as in view 4.

11. Nolland (1993b: 1025–26) argues that Mark and John have each taken different literary directions, which create the appearance of a problem. Mark's passion day is artistic, not a literal twenty-four-hour day, since there appear to be too many events for a literal day (Nolland estimates six hours for supper and three hours for each of the following: praying at Gethsemane, the arrest and Jewish hearing, Pilate's hearing, hanging on the cross before darkness, and three more hours until death). John on the other hand more tightly connects the Passover sacrifice to the cross because of their proximity to each other and the similarity of their significance. The major objection to this option is that the Synoptic and Johannine texts seem to preclude an arrest as early as Tuesday night (see view 5 above). This view also seems to overestimate the time required for certain events (e.g., Gethsemane and the various trials). As such, this approach is not likely.

My conclusion is that Jesus ate a Passover meal with his disciples on Nisan 15, Thursday night. This view corresponds to the data in John if the Johannine references to Passover mean the entire week of the feast (view 10), if one posits a distinct calendar operating in the Synoptics versus that in John (view 7), or if one reads John as speaking theologically (view 4). Either of these approaches show that each account renders the events variously in terms of the perspective taken—yet accurately within that perspective.

Excursus 12
The Jesus Seminar
and the Gospel of Luke

In 1985 a group of scholars came together under the sponsorship of the Westar Institute to form the Jesus Seminar. Their goal was to determine precisely what teaching in the Gospels actually went back to Jesus. They determined to vote on each saying of Jesus with the following code (Funk and Hoover 1993: 36):

red   Jesus undoubtedly said this or something very like it

pink   Jesus probably said something like this

gray   Jesus did not say this, but the ideas contained in it are close to his own

black   Jesus did not say this; it represents the perspective or content of a later or different tradition

After years of labor, the results of their work were published amid much media attention in *The Five Gospels: The Search for the Authentic Words of Jesus* (Funk and Hoover 1993).

In this commentary I have tried to interact fully with the Jesus Seminar, which represents its findings as a "collective report of gospel scholars" who come from "a wide array of Western religious traditions and academic institutions" (Funk and Hoover 1993: ix). Of the seventy-four fellows in the seminar (Funk and Hoover 1993: 533–37), only a few represent an evangelical perspective. Even some outside evangelical circles have questioned whether this group is really representative of current NT scholarship (Hays 1994: 47). Regardless of the makeup of the group, the issues they raise deserve attention, which is why this commentary has given careful attention to their work, including specific examination of the rationale they take in each passage where sayings of Jesus appear in Luke. This excursus summarizes the results and examines them as a whole, while contrasting the approach of the seminar to my own. After examining the seminar's suppositions, what they call "pillars," I shall consider their emerging portrait of Jesus, simply noting where in the commentary I have challenged a given conclusion (all references to Lucan passages in this excursus refer to the appropriate discussion of sources and historicity).

About 555 verses (roughly one-third of Luke's Gospel) contain sayings material. The seminar printed 4% of this material in red type, 23% in pink, 22% in gray, and 51% in black. These percentages are fairly representative of the seminar's results in each of the Synoptics, since they concluded that 82% of the words in the Gospels ascribed to Jesus do not come from him (i.e., gray plus black; Funk and Hoover 1993: 5). Behind these results stand what their introduction calls "seven pillars of scholarly wisdom," a list of seven fundamental premises of the study (Funk and Hoover 1993: 2–5):

1. The distinction should be drawn between the historical Jesus and the Christ of faith.
2. The Synoptic Gospels are much closer to the historical Jesus than is John's Gospel.
3. The Gospel of Mark is prior to Matthew and Luke.
4. The hypothetical source Q represents the teaching tradition shared between Luke and Matthew.
5. The noneschatological Jesus of aphorisms and parables should be separated from the eschatological Jesus.
6. The oral culture of the Gospels does not work in the same manner as our modern print culture.
7. The burden of proof in Jesus studies lies with those who hold to historicity.

Numerous matters are obscured by these ways of stating the interpretive base. For example, what does it mean to say the Synoptics are closer to the historical Jesus than is John? History is not a static entity in which something is immediately obvious upon its being said or done. Sometimes it takes later events to clarify earlier events and utterances. A Gospel like John's thus represents a reflective portrait of Jesus, as seen in John's comments that "after he was raised from the dead, his disciples remembered what he had said" (John 2:22) or "at first his disciples did not understand all this" (John 12:16). History is inevitably interpretive, so a reflective understanding of a person and his sayings may shed real light on that person. All of this is obscured in pillar 2, which is stated with a surprising philosophical naiveté about how history works.

In fact, if the intent is to drive a great wedge between the Jesus of history and the Christ of faith, then pillar 1, which is simply another way of saying that the gospel story is told by people who have come to trust in Jesus, is a variation of the same problem. The seminar apparently sees over half of the teaching tradition of the Gospels as "Christ-of-faith" embellishments that have no roots in the teaching of Jesus, but instead express the preferences of the given evangelist (i.e., the black material). Such a disjunction is hard to sustain historically in terms of explaining the tradition as we have it.

Pillar 5 on the opposition between Jesus the teacher of proverbs and the eschatological Jesus is simply a detailed application of pillar 1. Many NT scholars, including many nonevangelicals, reject this thorough denial of an eschatological Jesus (e.g., see the complex discussions about Mark 13; Luke 17:20–37; 21:5–38 in Beasley-Murray 1993). But the effect of this view is devastating, since rejecting an eschatological Jesus also rejects any teaching about judgment, any sense of Jesus as returning, and many elements of Jesus' teaching that parallel the OT prophets' calls to accountability before God. With one affirmation large strands of Jesus' teaching become excluded almost by definition. In fact, one could argue that the elevation of this point to "pillar" status is one of the gravest errors in the seminar's methodology.

Most NT scholars see Mark as the first written Gospel and Q as a major source, thus agreeing with the seminar's pillars 3 and 4 (see excursus 4). But it should be noted that both points have come into increasing question in the last quarter century, a point not even mentioned in the seminar's statement of this apparently inviolate pillar. In this commentary I raised more questions about the nature of Q than about Marcan priority, by pointing out that oral tradition (or variant written traditions) may stand behind what is normally represented by Q. Variation may reflect the presence of multiple expressions of the itinerant Jesus, making it more difficult to conclude, based on variation, that the evangelist(s) altered the tradition (e.g., 9:46–50; 12:1–3). In some cases variation may well exist because Jesus taught the point in various ways on different occasions, a potential consideration that is rarely noted by the seminar—despite its supposed sensitivity to oral tradition. Once oral tradition becomes possible, the number of sources for input into the Gospels expands, making judgments harder to make (Reicke 1986: 24–67, 180–89).

As to how oral tradition works, the seminar seems to take a position that allows for much distortion by the evangelists. The seminar assumes that (1) the older the strand of tradition, the more likely it could go back to Jesus, and (2) the more stands of tradition such materials appear in, the more likely it could go back to Jesus (this is called the criteria of multiple attestation, which can be a useful tool of assessment). In discussing such "old" tradition, the key sources for the seminar are Thomas, Q, and Mark, since they are said to derive from the period A.D. 50–70 (Funk and Hoover 1993: 18). This surfaces another premise that a wide array of scholars challenge, namely, the prominent position given to Thomas in the assessment of the tradition. For many if not most NT scholars, Thomas is seen as a late first-century source, not a mid-first-century source (Meier 1994: 476–77 n. 106, 499–500 n. 200; for a solid summary of the Thomas debate, see Meier 1991: 123–39). This significantly impacts how the evidence is read, since Thomas is a sayings source that makes for an aphoristic Jesus, not someone who teaches like a prophet in longer discourses. As a result, discourse material is often considered suspect by the seminar. Is that a likely portrait of an itinerant preacher?

Neither is it clear that the presence of oral tradition is as distorting in a Jewish setting as the seminar suggests. Jews worked with longer pieces of oral material, as seen in their liturgical prayer tradition (11:2–4). They were not limited to aphorisms. In addition the work of scholars like B. Gerhardsson and R. Riesner shows that in Jewish culture the importance of traditional material meant it was handled with care, a point I have made in detail elsewhere (Bock 1995: 78–81). Luke makes much of how carefully the roots of the traditions were formed and passed on (see the exegesis of 1:1–4). To argue that fully half of the material is developed later does not fit the historical context of Jewish tradition.

To add a burden of proof that says in effect "guilty until proven innocent" so that single testimony does not count at all in favor of a saying (pillar 7), produces a method that will not allow any Gospel writer to complement the portrait of Jesus with fresh detail he may be aware of—even from oral sources. Even in cases where Thomas and the tradition argue for authenticity, some texts still do not pass this final test (e.g., 10:5–7, 19, 21). One addendum to this test makes matters more difficult: if someone else could say it, then Jesus did not (on the potential critical bias toward Q and against the historical Jesus, see Meier 1994: 207 n. 123). This test of dissimilarity says that something is authentic if it is unlike Judaism or early church teaching; when it is applied negatively, then only the Jesus that is unlike his cultural background is treated as authentic (16:14–18; 17:7–10). Such a Jesus would have been so eccentric that it is unlikely that he would have been taken seriously.

The seven pillars may in fact be eight, for an unstated premise seems to automatically exclude sayings tied to miracles from going back to Jesus (4:31–44; 5:1–11; 18:35–43). These are often said to be the product of the storyteller's creativity (Funk and Hoover 1993: 42 [on Mark 1:21–28], 310 [on Luke 8:22–56]).

The pillars function like a tightly knit strainer that allows little to get through the process of assessment. If we treated other ancient works with similar standards, there would be little that we could say about ancient history. My approach to the data does not accept many of these pillars nor, where they seem to have merit, do I apply them with the same implications that the seminar does. My examination proceeds on a text-by-text basis, looking for a congruence of themes in those cases where a parallel is lacking, so as to allow the possibility that a single witness could possess something of strict historical worth. Unlike the seminar, I do not reject the possibility of multiple versions of a saying or a theme in the tradition. This is not to argue that the text always gives verbatim quotations. I argue elsewhere (Bock 1995) that the nature of oral tradition and the textual evidence of variations in biblical texts depicting the same event show that the Gospel writers sometimes summarize in a way that makes "pink" or "gray" classifications possible. Sometimes the writers present us with a summary or gist of Jesus' teaching, as opposed to his exact words. Such summaries have a credible claim to being historical because history can be reported in a variety of ways that reflect well what an event represented. Implications of sayings can be historical and can claim such roots in the utterances of a speaker. Thus when I make the claim for the authenticity of a particular teaching by Jesus, what I claim is that the passage accurately represents either in word or summary what Jesus taught. Even when we do not have the words of Jesus, we have the voice of Jesus.

What kind of a Jesus emerges for the Jesus Seminar? He is a Jesus who had no mission (9:1–6), whose miraculous activity needs some other explanation (5:17–26), who did not judge (10:13–15) or make messianic claims (9:18–20). In fact, he rarely discussed himself or his mission, since the "I" sayings are later creations (12:49–59). There is no prediction of suffering (12:1–12; 18:31–34; excursus 10), no major apocalyptic concern (11:37–54; 17:22–37), and no concern about heavenly rewards in the future (18:18–30). The Jesus of the seminar was interested in the poor and other social concerns and in creating in humanity a devotion to God and a concern for others (11:2–4; 14:15–24, 26). On these points he created social offense, but he was not particularly offensive in his religious teaching. For a figure that multiple traditions attest was publicly perceived as a prophet, is this kind of distinction historically credible? Jesus was an ethical storyteller and sage of moral parables who called people to be totally devoted to God, as the seminar argues, but that portrait of him does not have enough historical credibility to explain how he ended up crucified for claiming to be Israel's Promised One. What emerges from the seminar's examination is a one-sided portrait of Jesus, a minimalist, even naturalistic, Jesus of sorts. The Jesus that surfaces from the application of the seminar's pillars is not well enough historically constructed to explain what happened to him and what caused him to be sent to the cross.

In sum, Luke has much more to offer us about the historical Jesus than the Jesus Seminar does, for Luke explains how this Jesus was crucified, how God was at work to shape a new community founded on his teaching, and how God's vindication came to him as the Promised One. He died innocent, but he was raised to serve at the right hand of God and to offer access to God's blessing. Jesus came making a claim to represent the way to God, a claim no person should ignore. Luke wrote his Gospel in order to reassure disciples. He sought to make clear the reasons to trust in the Jesus who came and is coming again. Luke builds such reassurance on the pillar of a historically grounded portrait of Jesus. After noting Luke's summary of Jesus' career according to Peter in Acts 10:37–38, Harvey (1982a: 10) describes his historical inquiry about Jesus this way:

> But it is an enquiry for which, I believe, the materials are now available, and which will enable us to understand better what it might mean to claim that "God was with" a person of history in such a unique and decisive way that he could be regarded as an actual agent of the divine, and become thereby an object, not only of our endless and fascinated study, but of our love and worship.

To put it another way: In the beginning there was Jesus, and without him there would be no Gospel, no explanation for the existence of the church, and no need for commentary.

Works Cited

ABD   *The Anchor Bible Dictionary*. Edited by D. N. Freedman et al. 6 vols. New York: Doubleday, 1992.

Abel, F.-M.
1925   "Deux Tombeaux à Meule à Abou Ghoch." *Revue Biblique* 34:275–79.

Achtemeier, P. J.
1978   "The Lukan Perspective on the Miracles of Jesus: A Preliminary Sketch." Pp. 153–67 in *Perspectives on Luke–Acts*. Edited by C. H. Talbert. Danville, Va.: Association of Baptist Professors of Religion/Edinburgh: Clark.

Ackermann, H.
1952   *Jesus: Seine Botschaft und deren Aufnahme im Abendland*. Göttingen: Musterschmidt.

Ahern, B.
1943   "Staff or No Staff?" *Catholic Biblical Quarterly* 5:332–37.

Aitken, W. E. M.
1912   "Beelzebul." *Journal of Biblical Literature* 31:34–53.

Aland, K.
1965–66 "Neue neutestamentliche Papyri II." *New Testament Studies* 12:193–210.
1985   *Synopsis Quattuor Evangelorum*. 13th edition. Stuttgart: Deutsche Bibelstiftung.

Aland, K., and B. Aland
1987   *The Text of the New Testament: An Introduction to the Critical Editions and to the Theory and Practice of Modern Textual Criticism*. Translated by E. F. Rhodes. Grand Rapids: Eerdmans/Leiden: Brill.

Alexander, L.
1986   "Luke's Preface in the Context of Greek Preface-Writing." *Novum Testamentum* 28:48–74.

Alford, H.
1874   *The Greek Testament*, vol. 1: *The Four Gospels*. 7th edition. London: Rivingtons/Cambridge: Deighton, Bell.

Allison, D. C., Jr.
1983   "Matt. 23:39–Luke 13:35b as a Conditional Prophecy." *Journal for the Study of the New Testament* 18:75–84.
1985   *The End of the Ages Has Come: An Early Interpretation of the Passion and Resurrection of Jesus*. Philadelphia: Fortress.
1987   "Jesus and the Covenant: A Response to E. P. Sanders." *Journal for the Study of the New Testament* 29:57–78.
1992   "The Baptism of Jesus and a New Dead Sea Scroll." *Biblical Archaeology Review* 18/2:58–60.

Annand, R.
1958   "'He Was Seen of Cephas': A Suggestion about the First Resurrection Appearance to Peter." *Scottish Journal of Theology* 11:180–87.

Annen, F.
1976   *Heil für die Heiden: Zur Bedeutung und Geschichte der Tradition vom besessenen Gerasener (Mk 5,1–20 parr.)*. Frankfurter theologische Studien 20. Frankfurt am Main: Knecht.

Applebaum, S.
1976   "Economic Life in Palestine." Vol. 2 / pp. 631–700 in *The Jewish People in the First Century*. Edited by S. Safrai and M. Stern. Compendia Rerum Iudaicarum ad Novum Testamentum 1/2. Philadelphia: Fortress/Assen: Van Gorcum.

Arbeitman, Y.
1980   "The Suffix of Iscariot." *Journal of Biblical Literature* 99:122–24.

Arndt, W. F.
1943   "῎Αγει, Luke 24:21." *Concordia Theological Monthly* 14:61.
1956   *The Gospel according to St. Luke*. St. Louis: Concordia.

Audet, J.-P.
1956   "L'Annonce à Marie." *Revue Biblique* 63:346–74.

Aufhauser, J. B.
1926   *Buddha und Jesus in ihren Paralleltexten*. Kleine Texte für Vorlesungen and Übungen 157. Bonn: Marcus & Weber.

Aune, D. E.
1975   "The Significance of the Delay of the Parousia for Early Christianity." Pp. 87–109 in *Current Issues in Biblical and Patristic Interpretation: Studies in Honor of Merrill C. Tenney*. Edited by G. F. Hawthorne. Grand Rapids: Eerdmans.

Austin, M. R.
1985   "The Hypocritical Son." *Evangelical Quarterly* 57:307–15.

BAA   *Griechisch-Deutsches Wörterbuch zu den Schriften des Neuen Testaments und der frühchristlichen Literatur*. 6th edition. By W. Bauer, K. Aland, and B. Aland. Berlin: de Gruyter, 1988.

Badian, E.
1972   *Publicans and Sinners: Private Enterprise in the Service of the Roman Republic*. Oxford: Blackwell/Ithaca, N.Y.: Cornell University Press.

BAGD   *A Greek-English Lexicon of the New Testament and Other Early Christian Literature*. 2d edition. By W. Bauer, W. F. Arndt, F. W. Gingrich, and F. W. Danker. Chicago: University of Chicago Press, 1979.

Bahat, D.
1986   "Does the Holy Sepulchre Church Mark the Burial of Jesus?" *Biblical Archaeology Review* 12/3:26–45.

Bahr, G. J.
1970   "The Seder of Passover and the Eucharistic Words." *Novum Testamentum* 12:181–202.

Bailey, K. E.
1976   *Poet and Peasant: A Literary Cultural Approach to the Parables in Luke*. Grand Rapids: Eerdmans.
1980   *Through Peasant Eyes: More Lucan Parables, Their Culture and Style*. Grand Rapids: Eerdmans.

Bajsić, A.
1967   "Pilatus, Jesus und Barabbas." *Biblica* 48:7–28.

Baldi, D.
1955   *Enchiridion Locorum Sanctorum*. 2d edition. Jerusalem: Franciscan Printing Press.

Baltensweiler, H.
1959   *Die Verklärung Jesu: Historisches Ereignis und synoptische Berichte*. Abhandlungen zur Theologie des Alten und Neuen Testaments 33. Zurich: Zwingli.

Bammel, E.
1959   "Das Gleichnis von den bösen Winzern und das jüdische Erbrecht." *Revue Internationale des Droits de l'Antiquité*, 3d series, 6:11–17.

Bammel, E. (ed.)
1970   *The Trial of Jesus: Cambridge Studies in Honour of C. F. D. Moule*. Studies in Biblical Theology 2/13. London: SCM/Naperville, Ill.: Allenson.

Banks, R. J.
1975   *Jesus and the Law in the Synoptic Tradition*. Society for New Testament Study Monograph Series 28. Cambridge: Cambridge University Press.

Barbet, P.
1953   *A Doctor at Calvary: The Passion of Our Lord Jesus Christ as Described by a Surgeon*. New York: Kenedy.

Barbour, R. S.
1969–70 "Gethsemane in the Tradition of the Passion." *New Testament Studies* 16:231–51.

Barkay, G.
1986 "The Garden Tomb: Was Jesus Buried Here?" *Biblical Archaeology Review* 12/2:40–53, 56–57.

Barr, J.
1988 "ʾAbbā Isn't Daddy." *Journal of Theological Studies* n.s. 39:28–47.

Barrett, C. K.
1947 *The Holy Spirit and the Gospel Tradition*. London: SPCK.
1958 "Luke xxii.15: To Eat the Passover." *Journal of Theological Studies* n.s. 9:305–7.
1975 "The House of Prayer and the Den of Thieves." Pp. 13–20 in *Jesus und Paulus: Festschrift für Werner Georg Kümmel zum 70. Geburtstag*. Edited by E. E. Ellis and E. Grässer. Göttingen: Vandenhoeck & Ruprecht.
1978 *The Gospel according to St. John: An Introduction with Commentary and Notes on the Greek Text*. 2d edition. Philadelphia: Westminster/London: SPCK.

Bateman, H. W., IV
1992 "Psalm 110:1 and the New Testament." *Bibliotheca Sacra* 149:438–53.

Bauman, C.
1985 *The Sermon on the Mount: The Modern Quest for Its Meaning*. Macon, Ga.: Mercer University Press/Louvain: Peeters.

Baur, F. C.
1831 "Die Christuspartei in der korinthischen Gemeinde: Der Gegensatz des petrinischen und paulinischen Christenthums in der ältesten Kirche, der Apostel Petrus in Rom." *Tübinger Zeitschrift für Theologie* 4:61–206. Reprinted in Baur's *Ausgewählte Werke in Einzelausgaben*, vol. 1: *Historisch-kritische Untersuchungen zum Neuen Testament*, pp. 1–146. Stuttgart: Frommann, 1963.
1850–51 "Die Einleitung ins NT als theologische Wissenschaft: Ihr Begriff und ihre Aufgabe, ihr Entwicklungsgang und ihr Organismus." *Theologische Jahrbücher* 9:463–566; 10:70–94, 222–53, 329.

Bayer, H. F.
1986 *Jesus' Predictions of Vindication and Resurrection: The Provenance, Meaning and Correlation of the Synoptic Predictions*. Wissenschaftliche Untersuchungen zum Neuen Testament 2/20. Tübingen: Mohr.

BDB *A Hebrew and English Lexicon of the Old Testament*. By F. Brown, S. R. Driver, and C. A. Briggs. Oxford: Clarendon, 1907.

BDF *A Greek Grammar of the New Testament and Other Early Christian Literature*. By F. Blass, A. Debrunner, and R. W. Funk. Chicago: University of Chicago Press, 1961.

BDR *Grammatik des neutestamentlichen Griechisch*. By F. Blass, A. Debrunner, and F. Rehkopf. Göttingen: Vandenhoeck & Ruprecht, 1984.

Beare, F. W.
1970 "The Mission of the Disciples and the Mission Charge: Matthew 10 and Parallels." *Journal of Biblical Literature* 89:1–13.

Beasley-Murray, G. R.
1952–53a "A Century of Eschatological Discussion." *Expository Times* 64:312–16.
1952–53b "The Rise and Fall of the Little Apocalypse Theory." *Expository Times* 64:346–49.
1954 *Jesus and the Future: An Examination of the Criticism of the Eschatological Discourse, Mark 13, with Special Reference to the Little Apocalypse Theory*. London: Macmillan.
1957 *A Commentary on Mark Thirteen*. London: Macmillan.
1970 "Jesus and the Spirit." Pp. 463–78 in *Mélanges Bibliques en Hommage au R. P. Béda Rigaux*. Edited by A. Descamps and A. de Halleux. Gembloux: Duculot.
1986 *Jesus and the Kingdom of God*. Grand Rapids: Eerdmans/Exeter: Paternoster.
1993 *Jesus and the Last Days: The Interpretation of the Olivet Discourse*. Peabody, Mass.: Hendrickson.

Beauvery, R.
1957 "La Route Romaine de Jérusalem à Jéricho." *Revue Biblique* 64:72–101.

Beckwith, R. T.
1979–81   "The Earliest Enoch Literature and Its Calendar: Marks of Their Origin, Date and Motivation." *Revue de Qumran* 10:365–403.
1985   *The Old Testament Canon of the New Testament Church and Its Background in Early Judaism*. Grand Rapids: Eerdmans/London: SPCK.

Bellinzoni, A., Jr., J. B. Tyson, and W. O. Walker Jr. (eds.)
1985   *The Two-Source Hypothesis: A Critical Appraisal*. Macon, Ga.: Mercer University Press.

Bemile, P.
1986   *The Magnificat within the Context and Framework of Lukan Theology: An Exegetical Theological Study of Lk 1:46–55*. Regensburger Studien zur Theologie 34. Frankfurt am Main: Lang.

Ben-Dor, I.
1945   "Palestinian Alabaster Vases." *Quarterly of the Department of Antiquities in Palestine* 11:93–112.

Benoit, P.
1956–57   "L'Enfance de Jean-Baptiste selon Luc 1." *New Testament Studies* 3:169–94.
1969   *The Passion and Resurrection of Jesus Christ*. Translated by B. Weatherhead. New York: Herder & Herder/London: Darton, Longman & Todd.

Berger, K.
1972   *Die Gesetzesauslegung Jesu: Ihr historischer Hintergrund im Judentum und in Alten Testament*. Wissenschaftliche Monographien zum Alten und Neuen Testament 40. Neukirchen-Vluyn: Neukirchener Verlag.
1973–74   "Die königlichen Messiastraditionen des Neuen Testaments." *New Testament Studies* 20:1–44.
1984   *Formgeschichte des Neuen Testaments*. Heidelberg: Quelle & Meyer.

Bertrand, D. A.
1973   *Le Baptême de Jésus: Histoire de l'Exégèse aux Deux Premiers Siècles*. Beiträge zur Geschichte der biblischen Exegese 14. Tübingen: Mohr.

Betz, H. D.
1969   "The Origin and Nature of Christian Faith according to the Emmaus Legend (Luke 24:13–32)." *Interpretation* 23:32–46.
1971   "The Cleansing of the Ten Lepers (Luke 17:11–19)." *Journal of Biblical Literature* 90:314–28.
1981   Review of *Die Reinigung der zehn Aussätzigen und die Heilung des Samariters* by W. Bruners. *Theologische Literaturzeitung* 106:338–39.
1985   *Essays on the Sermon on the Mount*. Translated by L. L. Welborn. Philadelphia: Fortress.

Betz, O.
1957–58   "Jesu heiliger Kreig." *Novum Testamentum* 2:116–37.
1964–66   "The Dichotomized Servant and the End of Judas Iscariot (Light on the Dark Passages: Matthew 24,51 and Parallel; Acts 1,8)." *Revue de Qumran* 5:43–58.
1982   "Probleme des Prozesses Jesu." Pp. 565–647 in *Aufstieg und Niedergang der römischen Welt*, part II: *Principat*, vol. 25: *Religion*. Edited by W. Haase. Berlin: de Gruyter.
1985   *Jesus und das Danielbuch*, vol. 2: *Die Menschensohnworte Jesu und die Zukunftserwartung des Paulus (Daniel 7,13–14)*. Arbeiten zum Neuen Testament und Judentum 2/6.2. Frankfurt am Main: Lang.

Beyer, K.
1968   *Semitische Syntax im Neuen Testament*, vol. 1/1. 2d edition. Studien zur Umwelt des Neuen Testaments 1. Göttingen: Vandenhoeck & Ruprecht.

Billerbeck, P.
1964   "Ein Synagogengottesdienst in Jesu Tagen." *Zeitschrift für die Neutestamentliche Wissenschaft* 55:143–61.

Bishop, E. F. F.
1949–50   "Three and a Half Years." *Expository Times* 61:126–27.

1951   "Jesus and the Lake." *Catholic Biblical Quarterly* 13:398–414.

1962   "The Parable of the Lost or Wandering Sheep: Matthew 18.10–14; Luke 15.3–7." *Anglican Theological Review* 44:44–57.

1963   "Down from Jerusalem to Jericho." *Evangelical Quarterly* 35:97–102.

1970   "People on the Road to Jericho: The Good Samaritan—and Others." *Evangelical Quarterly* 42:2–6.

1973   "A Yawning Chasm." *Evangelical Quarterly* 45:3–5.

Black, M.

1959–60 "The Parables as Allegory." *Bulletin of the John Rylands Library* 42:273–87.

1967   *An Aramaic Approach to the Gospels and Acts*. 3d edition. Oxford: Clarendon.

1969   "The 'Son of Man' Passion Sayings in the Gospel Tradition." *Zeitschrift für die Neutestamentliche Wissenschaft* 60:1–8.

1976   "The Throne-Theophany Prophetic Commission and the 'Son of Man': A Study in Tradition-History." Pp. 57–73 *in Jews, Greeks, and Christians: Religious Cultures in Late Antiquity: Essays in Honor of William David Davies*. Edited by R. Hamerton-Kelly and R. Scroggs. Studies in Judaism of Late Antiquity 21. Leiden: Brill.

Blackman, P.

1983   *Mishnayoth*. 7 vols. 2d edition. Gateshead, N.Y.: Judaica.

Blaising, C. A.

1979   "Gethsemane: A Prayer of Faith." *Journal of the Evangelical Theological Society* 22:333–43.

Blaising, C. A., and D. L. Bock

1993   *Progressive Dispensationalism*. Wheaton, Ill.: Victor.

Blank, J.

1974   "Die Sendung des Sohnes: Zur christologischen Bedeutung des Gleichnisses von den bösen Winzern Mk 12,1–12." Pp. 11–41 *in Neues Testament und Kirche: Für Rudolf Schnackenburg*. Edited by J. Gnilka. Freiburg im Breisgau: Herder.

Blass, F.

1898–99a "On Mark xii.42." *Expository Times* 10:286–87.

1898–99b "On Mark xii.42 and xv.16." *Expository Times* 10:185–87.

Blinzler, J.

1957–58 "Die Niedermetzelung von Galiläern durch Pilatus." *Novum Testamentum* 2:24–49.

1958   "Qumran-Kalender und Passionschronologie." *Zeitschrift für die Neutestamentliche Wissenschaft* 49:238–51.

1967   *Die Brüder und Schwestern Jesu*. Stuttgarter Bibelstudien 21. Stuttgart: Katholisches Bibelwerk.

1969   *Der Prozess Jesu: Das jüdische und das römische Gerichtsverfahren gegen Jesus Christus auf Grund der ältesten Zeugnisse*. 4th edition. Regensburg: Pustet.

1970   "The Jewish Punishment of Stoning in the New Testament Period." Pp. 147–61 in *The Trial of Jesus: Cambridge Studies in Honour of C. F. D. Moule*. Edited by E. Bammel. Studies in Biblical Theology 2/13. London: SCM/Naperville, Ill.: Allenson.

Blomberg, C. L.

1982a   "New Horizons in Parable Research." *Trinity Journal* 3:3–17.

1982b   *The Tradition History of the Parables Peculiar to Luke's Central Section*. Ph.D. diss. University of Aberdeen.

1983   "Midrash, Chiasmus, and the Outline of Luke's Central Section." Pp. 217–61 in *Gospel Perspectives*, vol. 3: *Studies in Midrash and Historiography*. Edited by R. T. France and D. Wenham. Sheffield: JSOT Press.

1984a   "The Law in Luke–Acts." *Journal for the Study of the New Testament* 22:53–80.

1984b   "New Testament Miracles and Higher Criticism: Climbing up the Slippery Slope." *Journal of the Evangelical Theological Society* 27:425–38.

1990   *Interpreting the Parables*. Downers Grove, Ill.: InterVarsity.

1994   "'Your Faith Has Made You Whole': The Evangelical Liberation Theology of Jesus." Pp. 75–93 in *Jesus of Nazareth: Lord and Christ—Essays on the Historical Jesus and New Testament Christology* [I. Howard Marshall Festschrift]. Edited by J. B. Green and M. Turner. Grand Rapids: Eerdmans/Carlisle: Paternoster.

Böcher, O.
1972   *Das Neue Testament und die dämonischen Mächte*. Stuttgarter Bibelstudien 58. Stuttgart: Katholisches Bibelwerk.

Bock, D. L.
1985   "Evangelicals and the Use of the Old Testament in the New." *Bibliotheca Sacra* 142:209–23, 306–19.
1986   "Jesus as Lord in Acts and in the Gospel Message." *Bibliotheca Sacra* 143:146–54.
1987   *Proclamation from Prophecy and Pattern: Lucan Old Testament Christology*. Journal for the Study of the New Testament Supplement 12. Sheffield: JSOT Press.
1990   "The Use of the Old Testament in Luke–Acts: Christology and Mission." Pp. 494–511 in *Society of Biblical Literature 1990 Seminar Papers*. Edited by K. H. Richards. Chico, Calif.: Scholars Press.
1991a   "Athenians Who Have Never Heard." Pp. 117–24 in *Through No Fault of Their Own? The Fate of Those Who Have Never Heard*. Edited by W. V. Crockett and J. G. Sigountos. Grand Rapids: Baker.
1991b   "Form Criticism." Pp. 175–96 in *New Testament Criticism and Interpretation*. Edited by D. A. Black and D. S. Dockery. Grand Rapids: Zondervan.
1991c   "The Son of Man in Luke 5:24." *Bulletin for Biblical Research* 1:109–21.
1991d   "Understanding Luke's Task: Carefully Building on Precedent (Luke 1:1–4)." *Criswell Theological Review* 5:183–202.
1992a   "Evidence from Acts." Pp. 181–98 in *A Case for Premillennialism: A New Consensus*. Edited by D. K. Campbell and J. L. Townsend. Chicago: Moody.
1992b   "Luke, Gospel of." Pp. 495–510 in *Dictionary of Jesus and the Gospels*. Edited by J. B. Green, S. McKnight, and I. H. Marshall. Downers Grove, Ill.: InterVarsity.
1992c   "The Reign of the Lord Christ." Pp. 37–67 in *Dispensationalism, Israel and the Church: The Search for Definition*. Edited by C. A. Blaising and D. L. Bock. Grand Rapids: Zondervan.
1993   "The Son of David and the Saints' Task: The Hermeneutics of Initial Fulfillment." *Bibliotheca Sacra* 150:440–57.
1994a   "Current Messianic Activity and OT Davidic Promise: Dispensationalism, Hermeneutics, and NT Fulfillment." *Trinity Journal* 15:55–87.
1994b   "The Son of Man Seated at God's Right Hand and the Debate over Jesus' 'Blasphemy.'" Pp. 181–91 in *Jesus of Nazareth: Lord and Christ; Essays on the Historical Jesus and New Testament Christology*. Edited by J. B. Green and M. Turner. Grand Rapids: Eerdmans/Carlisle, Cumbria: Paternoster.
1994c   "The Theology of Luke–Acts." Pp. 87–166 in *A Biblical Theology of the New Testament*. Edited by R. B. Zuck and D. L. Bock. Chicago: Moody.
1994d   "Use of the Old Testament in the New." Pp. 97–114 in *Foundations for Biblical Interpretation*. Edited by D. S. Dockery, K. A. Mathews, and R. B. Sloan. Nashville: Broadman & Holman.
1995   "The Words of Jesus in the Gospels: Live, Jive, or Memorex?" Pp. 74–99 in *Jesus under Fire*. Edited by M. J. Wilkins and J. P. Moreland. Grand Rapids: Zondervan.

Böckh, A.
1828–77 *Corpus Inscriptionum Graecarum*. Berlin: Reimer.

Bode, E. L.
1970   *The First Easter Morning: The Gospel Accounts of the Women's Visit to the Tomb of Jesus*. Analecta Biblica 45. Rome: Pontifical Biblical Institute Press.

Bonus, A.
1901–2   "Emmaus Mistaken for a Person." *Expository Times* 13:561–62.

Boobyer, G. H.
1942   *St. Mark and the Transfiguration Story*. Edinburgh: Clark.
1954   "Mark ii,10a and the Interpretation of the Healing of the Paralytic." *Harvard Theological Review* 47:115–20.

Booth, R. P.
1986   *Jesus and the Laws of Purity: Tradition History and Legal History in Mark 7*. Journal for the Study of the New Testament Supplement 13. Sheffield: JSOT Press.

Borg, M. J.
1987   *Jesus: A New Vision—Spirit, Culture, and the Life of Discipleship*. San Francisco: Harper & Row.
Bornkamm, G.
1963   "The Stilling of the Storm in Matthew." Pp. 52–57 in *Tradition and Interpretation in Matthew*. By G. Bornkamm, G. Barth, and H. J. Held. Translated by P. Scott. New Testament Library. Philadelphia: Westminster/London: SCM.
Borsch, F. H.
1967   *The Son of Man in Myth and History*. New Testament Library. Philadelphia: Westminster/London: SCM.
Bousset, W.
1926   *Die Religion des Judentums im späthellenistischen Zeitalter*. 3d edition. Edited by H. Gressmann. Handbuch zum Neuen Testament 21. Tübingen: Mohr.
Bover, J. M.
1951   "Una Nueva Interpretación de Luc 2,50." *Estudios Bíblicos* 10:205–15.
Bovon, F.
1987   *Luke the Theologian: Thirty-three Years of Research (1950–1983)*. Translated by K. McKinney. Princeton Theological Monograph Series 12. Allison Park, Pa.: Pickwick.
1989   *Das Evangelium nach Lukas*, vol. 1: *Lk 1,1–9,50*. Evangelisch-katholischer Kommentar zum Neuen Testament 3/1. Zurich: Benziger/Neukirchen-Vluyn: Neukirchener Verlag.
Bowker, J.
1969   *The Targums and Rabbinic Literature: An Introduction to Jewish Interpretations of Scripture*. Cambridge: Cambridge University Press.
Braude, W. G.
1959   *The Midrash on Psalms*. 2 vols. Yale Judaica Series 13. New Haven: Yale University Press.
1968   *Pesikta Rabbati: Discourses for Feasts, Fasts, and Special Sabbaths*. 2 vols. Yale Judaica Series 18. New Haven: Yale University Press.
Braunert, H.
1957   "Der römische Provinzialzensus und der Schätzungsbericht des Lukas-Evangeliums." *Historia* 6:192–214.
Brawley, R. L.
1987   *Luke–Acts and the Jews: Conflict, Apology, and Conciliation*. Society of Biblical Literature Monograph Series 33. Atlanta: Scholars Press.
1992   "Canon and Community: Intertextuality, Canon, Interpretation, Christology, Theology, and Persuasive Rhetoric in Luke 4:1–13." Pp. 419–34 in *Society of Biblical Literature 1992 Seminar Papers*. Edited by E. Lovering Jr. Atlanta: Scholars Press.
Bretscher, P. G.
1951   "The Parable of the Unjust Steward—A New Approach to Luke 16:1–9." *Concordia Theological Monthly* 22:756–62.
1968   "Exodus 4:22–23 and the Voice From Heaven." *Journal of Biblical Literature* 87:301–11.
Brightman, F. E.
1927–28   "Six Notes, I: S. Luke xix 21: Αἴρεις Ὁ Οὐκ Ἔθηκας." *Journal of Theological Studies* o.s. 29:158.
Brindle, W. A.
1984   "The Origin and History of the Samaritans." *Grace Theological Journal* 5:47–75.
Brodie, T. L.
1983   "Luke 7,36–50 as an Internalization of 2 Kings 4,1–37: A Study in Luke's Use of Rhetorical Imitation." *Biblica* 64:457–85.
1986   "Towards Unravelling Luke's Use of the Old Testament: Luke 7.11–17 as an *Imitatio* of 1 Kings 17.24." *New Testament Studies* 32:247–67.
1987   *Luke the Literary Interpreter: Luke–Acts as a Systematic Rewriting and Updating of the Elijah and Elisha Narrative in 1 and 2 Kings*. Ph.D. diss. Rome: Pontifical University of St. Thomas.

Brooke, G. J.
1985   *Exegesis at Qumran: 4QFlorilegium in Its Jewish Context*. Journal for the Study of the Old Testament Supplement 29. Sheffield: JSOT Press.

Brooten, B. J.
1982   *Women Leaders in the Ancient Synagogue: Inscriptional Evidence and Background Issues*. Brown Judaic Studies 36. Chico, Calif.: Scholars Press.

Brown, R. E.
1962a   "Parable and Allegory Reconsidered." *Novum Testamentum* 5:36–45.
1962b   "The Problem of Historicity in John." *Catholic Biblical Quarterly* 24:1–14. Reprinted in Brown's *New Testament Essays*, pp. 143–67. Milwaukee: Bruce, 1965.
1970   *The Gospel according to John (xiii–xxi)*. Anchor Bible 29a. Garden City, N.Y.: Doubleday.
1971   "Jesus and Elisha." *Perspective* 12:85–104.
1977   *The Birth of the Messiah: A Commentary on the Infancy Narratives in Matthew and Luke*. London: Chapman/Garden City, N.Y.: Doubleday.
1993   *The Birth of the Messiah: A Commentary on the Infancy Narratives in the Gospels of Matthew and Luke*. Revised edition. Anchor Bible Reference Library. New York: Doubleday.
1994   *The Death of the Messiah, from Gethsemane to the Grave: A Commentary on the Passion Narratives in the Four Gospels*. 2 vols. Anchor Bible Reference Library. New York: Doubleday.

Brown, S.
1969   *Apostasy and Perseverance in the Theology of Luke*. Analecta Biblica 36. Rome: Pontifical Biblical Institute Press.

Bruce, A. B.
1897   *The Synoptic Gospels*. Expositor's Greek Testament 1. London: Hodder & Stoughton.

Bruce, F. F.
1952   "Justification by Faith in the Non-Pauline Writings of the New Testament." *Evangelical Quarterly* 24:66–77.
1972   *New Testament History*. Garden City, N.Y.: Doubleday.
1974   *Jesus and Christian Origins outside the New Testament*. Grand Rapids: Eerdmans.
1975–76   "Is the Paul of Acts the Real Paul?" *Bulletin of the John Rylands University Library of Manchester* 58:282–305.
1982   "The Background to the Son of Man Sayings." Pp. 50–70 in *Christ the Lord: Studies in Christology Presented to Donald Guthrie*. Edited by H. H. Rowdon. Leicester, Inter-Varsity.
1984   "Render to Caesar." Pp. 249–63 in *Jesus and the Politics of His Day*. Edited by E. Bammel and C. F. D. Moule. Cambridge: Cambridge University Press.
1988   *The Book of the Acts*. 2d edition. New International Commentary on the New Testament. Grand Rapids: Eerdmans.

Bruners, W.
1977   *Die Reinigung der zehn Aussätzigen und die Heilung des Samariters, Lk 17,11–19: Ein Beitrag zur lukanischen Interpretation der Reinigung von Aussätzigen*. Forschung zur Bibel 23. Stuttgart: Katholisches Bibelwerk.

Brutscheck, J.
1986   *Die Maria-Marta–Erzählung: Eine redaktionskritische Untersuchungen zu Lk 10,38–42*. Bonner biblische Beiträge 64. Frankfurt am Main/Bonn: Hanstein.

Buchanan, G. W., and C. Wolfe
1978   "The 'Second-First Sabbath' (Luke 6:1)." *Journal of Biblical Literature* 97:259–62.

Büchele, A.
1978   *Der Tod Jesu im Lukasevangelium: Eine redaktionsgeschichtliche Untersuchung zu Lk 23*. Theologische Studien 26. Frankfurt am Main: Knecht.

Bultmann, R.
1951–55   *Theology of the New Testament*. 2 vols. Translated by K. Grobel. New York: Scribner/London: SCM.

1963   *The History of the Synoptic Tradition*. Translated by J. Marsh. New York: Harper & Row/Oxford: Blackwell.

1971   *The Gospel of John: A Commentary*. Translated by G. R. Beasley-Murray, R. W. N. Hoare, and J. K. Riches. Philadelphia: Westminster/Oxford: Blackwell.

Burchard, C.

1970   "Das doppelte Liebesgebot in der frühen christlichen Überlieferung." Pp. 39–62 in *Der Ruf Jesu and die Antwort der Gemeinde: Exegetische Untersuchungen Joachim Jeremias zum 70. Geburtstag*. Edited by E. Lohse. Göttingen: Vandenhoeck & Ruprecht.

Burger, C.

1970   *Jesus als Davidssohn: Eine traditions-geschichtliche Untersuchung*. Forschungen zur Religion und Literatur des Alten und Neuen Testaments 98. Göttingen: Vandenhoeck & Ruprecht.

Burkitt, F. C., and A. E. Brooke

1907–8   "St Luke xxii 15, 16: What is the General Meaning?" *Journal of Theological Studies* o.s. 9:569–72.

Burns, J. L.

1992   "The Future of Ethnic Israel in Romans 11." Pp. 188–229 in *Dispensationalism, Israel and the Church: The Search for Definition*. Edited by C. A. Blaising and D. L. Bock. Grand Rapids: Zondervan.

Burrows, E.

1940   *The Gospel of the Infancy and Other Biblical Essays*. Edited by E. F. Sutcliffe. London: Burns, Oates & Washbourne.

Burrows, M.

1940   "Levirate Marriage in Israel." *Journal of Biblical Literature* 59:23–33.

Burton, E. D.

1900   *Syntax of the Moods and Tenses in New Testament Greek*. 3d edition. Chicago: University of Chicago Press. Reprinted Grand Rapids: Kregel, 1976.

Busse, U.

1978   *Das Nazareth-Manifest Jesu: Eine Einführung in das lukanische Jesusbild nach Lk 4,16–30*. Stuttgarter Bibelstudien 91. Stuttgart: Katholisches Bibelwerk.

1979   *Die Wunder des Propheten Jesus: Die Rezeption, Komposition und Interpretation der Wundertradition im Evangelium des Lukas*. 2d edition. Forschung zur Bibel 24. Stuttgart: Katholisches Bibelwerk.

Buth, R.

1984   "Hebrew Poetic Tenses and the Magnificat." *Journal for the Study of the New Testament* 21:67–83.

Byington, S. T.

1957   "יהוה and אֲדֹנָי." *Journal of Biblical Literature* 76:58–59.

Cadbury, H. J.

1917   "A Possible Case of Lukan Authorship (John 7:53–8:11)." *Harvard Theological Review* 10:237–44.

1922a   "Commentary on the Preface of Luke." Vol. 2 / pp. 489–510 in *The Beginnings of Christianity*, part 1: *The Acts of the Apostles*. Edited by F. J. Foakes Jackson and K. Lake. London: Macmillan. Reprinted Grand Rapids: Baker, 1979.

1922b   "The Knowledge Claimed in Luke's Preface." *Expositor*, 8th series, 24:401–20.

1926   "Lexical Notes on Luke–Acts, II: Recent Arguments for Medical Language." *Journal of Biblical Literature* 45:190–209.

1933   "Dust and Garments." Vol. 5 / pp. 269–77 in *The Beginnings of Christianity*, part 1: *The Acts of the Apostles*. Edited by F. J. Foakes Jackson and K. Lake. London: Macmillan. Reprinted Grand Rapids: Baker, 1979.

1950   "The Kingdom of God and Ourselves." *Christian Century* 67:172–173.

1956–57   "'We' and 'I' Passages in Luke–Acts." *New Testament Studies* 3:128–32.

1958   *The Making of Luke–Acts*. 2d edition. London: SPCK.

1962   "A Proper Name for Dives (Lexical Notes on Luke–Acts VI)." *Journal of Biblical Literature* 81:399–402.

1965   "The Name for Dives." *Journal of Biblical Literature* 84:73.

Caird, G. B.
1963   *The Gospel of St Luke*. Pelican Gospel Commentaries. Baltimore: Penguin.
1980   *The Language and Imagery of the Bible*. Philadelphia: Westminster.
Callan, T.
1982   "Psalm 110:1 and the Origin of the Expectation That Jesus Will Come Again." *Catholic Biblical Quarterly* 44:622–36.
Calvin, J.
1972   *A Harmony of the Gospels: Matthew, Mark and Luke*. Translated by A. W. Morrison and T. H. L. Parker. 3 vols. Grand Rapids: Eerdmans/Edinburgh: Saint Andrew.
Campbell, D. K.
1953   *Interpretation and Exposition of the Sermon on the Mount*. Th.D. diss. Dallas Theological Seminary.
Campbell, J. Y.
1936–37 "The Kingdom of God Has Come." *Expository Times* 48:91–94.
Campenhausen, H. von
1968   *Tradition and Life in the Church: Essays and Lectures in Church History*. Translated by A. V. Littledale. London: Collins.
Candlish, R.
1911–12 "The Pounds and the Talents." *Expository Times* 23:136–137.
Caragounis, C. C.
1974   "Ὀψώνιον: A Reconsideration of Its Meaning." *Novum Testamentum* 16:35–57.
1986   *The Son of Man: Vision and Interpretation*. Wissenschaftliche Untersuchungen zum Neuen Testament 38. Tübingen: Mohr.
1989   "Kingdom of God, Son of Man and Jesus' Self-Understanding [Part 1]." *Tyndale Bulletin* 40:3–23.
Carlston, C. E.
1975   *The Parables of the Triple Tradition*. Philadelphia: Fortress.
1981   "Parable and Allegory Revisited: An Interpretive Review [of *Allegorie und Allegorese in synoptischen Gleichnistexten* by H.-J. Klauck]." *Catholic Biblical Quarterly* 43:228–42.
Carmignac, J.
1969   *Recherches sur le "Notre Père."* Paris: Letouzey.
Carroll, J. T.
1988   "Luke's Portrayal of the Pharisees." *Catholic Biblical Quarterly* 50:604–21.
Carroll R., M. D.
1992   "La Cita de Isaías 58:6 en Lucas 4:18: Una Nueva Propuesta." *Kairós* 11:61–78.
Carson, D. A.
1978   *The Sermon on the Mount: An Evangelical Exposition of Matthew 5–7*. Grand Rapids: Baker.
1982   "Jesus and the Sabbath in the Four Gospels." Pp. 57–97 in *From Sabbath to Lord's Day: A Biblical, Historical, and Theological Investigation*. Edited by D. A. Carson. Grand Rapids: Zondervan.
1984   "Matthew." Vol. 8 / pp. 1–599 in *The Expositor's Bible Commentary*. Edited by F. E. Gaebelein. Grand Rapids: Zondervan.
Casey, M.
1979   *Son of Man: The Interpretation and Influence of Daniel 7*. London: SPCK.
1985   "The Jackals and the Son of Man (Matt. 8.20 // Luke 9.58)." *Journal for the Study of the New Testament* 23:3–22.
Cassidy, R. J.
1978   *Jesus, Politics, and Society: A Study of Luke's Gospel*. Maryknoll, N.Y.: Orbis.
Catchpole, D. R.
1965   "You Have Heard His Blasphemy." *Tyndale Bulletin* 16:10–18.
1971   *The Trial of Jesus: A Study in the Gospels and Jewish Historiography from 1770 to the Present Day*. Studia Post-Biblica 18. Leiden: Brill.
1977   "The Son of Man's Search for Faith (Luke xviii 8b)." *Novum Testamentum* 19:81–104.

1984   "The 'Triumphal' Entry." Pp. 319–34 in *Jesus and the Politics of His Day*. Edited by
        E. Bammel and C. F. D. Moule. Cambridge: Cambridge University Press.
Cave, C. H.
1968–69 "Lazarus and the Lukan Deuteronomy." *New Testament Studies* 15:319–25.
Ceroke, C. P.
1960   "Is Mk 2,10 a Saying of Jesus?" *Catholic Biblical Quarterly* 22:369–90.
Chafer, L. S.
1951   "The Teachings of Christ Incarnate." *Bibliotheca Sacra* 108:389–413.
Chajes, C.
1892   "Les Juges Juifs en Palestine." *Revue des Études Juives* 39:39–52.
Chapman, J.
1911–12 "Zacharias, Slain between the Temple and the Altar." *Journal of Theological Studies*
        o.s. 13:398–410.
Charles, R. H.
1913   *The Apocrypha and Pseudepigrapha of the Old Testament in English*. 2 vols. Oxford:
        Clarendon.
Charlesworth, C. E.
1922–23 "The Unnamed Companion of Cleopas." *Expository Times* 34:233–34.
Charlesworth, J. H. (ed.)
1983–85 *The Old Testament Pseudepigrapha*. 2 vols. Garden City, N.Y.: Doubleday.
Chavel, C. B.
1941   "The Releasing of a Prisoner on the Eve of Passover in Ancient Jerusalem." *Journal
        of Biblical Literature* 60:273–78.
Chilton, B. D.
1979   *God in Strength: Jesus' Announcement of the Kingdom*. Studien zum Neuen Testa-
        ment und seiner Umwelt B/1. Freistadt: Plöchl.
1981   "Announcement in Nazara: An Analysis of Luke 4:16–21." Pp. 147–72 in *Gospel Per-
        spectives*, vol. 2: *Studies of History and Tradition in the Four Gospels*. Edited by R. T.
        France and D. Wenham. Sheffield: JSOT Press.
Chilton, B. D. (ed.)
1984   *The Kingdom of God in the Teaching of Jesus*. Issues in Religion and Theology 5. Phil-
        adelphia: Fortress/London: SPCK.
Chisholm, R. B., Jr.
1991   "A Theology of the Psalms." Pp. 257–304 in *A Biblical Theology of the Old Testament*.
        Edited by R. B. Zuck, E. H. Merrill, and D. L. Bock. Chicago: Moody.
Christ, F.
1970   *Jesus Sophia: Die Sophia-Christologie bei den Synoptikern*. Abhandlungen zur Theol-
        ogie des Alten und Neuen Testaments 57. Zurich: Zwingli.
Chwolson [Khvol'son], D. A.
1908   *Das Letzte Passamahl Christi und der Tag seines Todes, nach den in übereinstimmung
        gebrachten berichten der Synoptiker und des Evangelium Johannis*. Leipzig: Haessel.
Clark, K. W.
1940   "Realized Eschatology." *Journal of Biblical Literature* 59:367–83.
Cohen, A.
1948   *The Twelve Prophets: Hebrew Text, English Translation and Commentary*. Soncino
        Books of the Bible. London: Soncino Press.
1965   *The Minor Tractates of the Talmud*. 2 vols. London: Soncino.
Cohen, B.
1930   "The Rabbinic Law Presupposed by Matthew xii.1 and Luke vi.1." *Harvard Theolog-
        ical Review* 23:91–92.
Cohn, H.
1967   *The Trial and Death of Jesus*. New York: Harper & Row.
Colani, T.
1864   *Jésus-Christ et les Croyances Messianiques de Son Temps*. Strasbourg: Treuttel &
        Wurtz.

Coleridge, M.
1993   *The Birth of the Lukan Narrative: Narrative as Christology in Luke 1–2*. Journal for the Study of the New Testament Supplement 88. Sheffield: JSOT Press.
Collins, J. J.
1974   "The Son of Man and the Saints of the Most High in the Book of Daniel." *Journal of Biblical Literature* 93:50–66.
1993   "A Pre-Christian 'Son of God' among the Dead Sea Scrolls." *Bible Review* 9/3:34–38, 57.
Colson, F. H.
1941   *Philo, with an English Translation*, vol. 9. Loeb Classical Library 363. Cambridge: Harvard University Press/London: Heinemann.
Combrink, H. J. B.
1973   "The Structure and Significance of Luke 4:16–30." *Neotestamentica* 7:27–47.
Connally, R. H.
1948   "The Appeal to the Aramaic Sources of Our Gospels." *Downside Review* 66:25–37.
Conzelmann, H.
1960   *The Theology of St. Luke*. Translated by G. Buswell. New York: Harper & Row.
Corbishley, T.
1936   "Quirinius and the Census: A Re-study of the Evidence." *Klio* 29:81–93.
Corrington, G. P.
1993   "Redaction Criticism." Pp. 87–99 in *To Each Its Own Meaning: An Introduction to Biblical Criticisms and Their Application*. Edited by S. R. Haynes and S. L. McKenzie. Louisville: Westminster/John Knox.
Cortés, J. B., and F. M. Gatti
1970   "Jesus' First Recorded Words (Lk. 2:49–50)." *Marianum* 32:404–18.
1987   "On the Meaning of Luke 16:16." *Journal of Biblical Literature* 106:247–59.
Couroyer, B.
1970   "De la Mesure dont Vous Mesurez il Vous Sera Mesuré." *Revue Biblique* 77:366–70.
Cox Evans, L. E.
1968   "The Holy Sepulchre." *Palestine Exploration Quarterly* 100:112–36.
Craig, W. L.
1980   "The Bodily Resurrection of Jesus." Pp. 47–74 in *Gospel Perspectives*, vol. 1: *Studies of History and Tradition in the Four Gospels*. Edited by R. T. France and D. Wenham. Sheffield: JSOT Press.
Cranfield, C. E. B.
1947–48   "The Cup Metaphor in Mark xiv. 36 and Parallels." *Expository Times* 59:137–38.
1959   *The Gospel according to Saint Mark: An Introduction and Commentary*. Cambridge Greek Testament Commentary. Cambridge: Cambridge University Press.
1963   "The Parable of the Unjust Judge and the Eschatology of Luke–Acts." *Scottish Journal of Theology* 16:297–301.
Creed, J. M.
1921–22   "Josephus on John the Baptist." *Journal of Theological Studies* o.s. 23:59–60.
1930   *The Gospel according to St. Luke*. London: Macmillan.
Crehan, J. H.
1953   "St. Peter's Journey to Emmaus." *Catholic Biblical Quarterly* 15:418–26.
Crockett, L.
1966   "Luke iv.16–30 and the Jewish Lectionary Cycle: A Word of Caution." *Journal of Jewish Studies* 17:13–46.
Crossan, J. D.
1971   "The Parable of the Wicked Husbandmen." *Journal of Biblical Literature* 90:451–65.
1971–72   "Parable and Example in the Teaching of Jesus." *New Testament Studies* 18:285–307.
1973   *In Parables: The Challenge of the Historical Jesus*. New York: Harper & Row.
1991   *The Historical Jesus: The Life of a Mediterranean Jewish Peasant*. San Francisco: Harper.

Cullmann, O.
1950   *Baptism in the New Testament*. Translated by J. K. S. Reid. Studies in Biblical Theology 1. London: SCM/Chicago: Regnery.
1963   *The Christology of the New Testament*. Translated by S. C. Guthrie and C. A. M. Hall. 2d edition. New Testament Library. Philadelphia: Westminster.

Cutler, A.
1966   "Does the Simeon of Luke 2 Refer to Simeon the Son of Hillel?" *Journal of Bible and Religion* 34:29–35.

Dahl, N. A.
1951   "The Parables of Growth." *Studia Theologica* 5:132–66.
1955   "The Origin of Baptism." Pp. 36–42 in *Interpretationes ad Vetus Testamentum pertinentes Sigmundo Mowinckel septuagenario missae*. Edited by A. S. Kapelrud. Oslo: Land og Kirge.
1966   "The Story of Abraham in Luke–Acts." Pp. 139–58 in *Studies in Luke–Acts: Essays Presented in Honor of Paul Schubert*. Edited by L. E. Keck and J. L. Martyn. Nashville: Abingdon. Reprinted Philadelphia: Fortress, 1980.

Dalman, G. H.
1909   *The Words of Jesus Considered in the Light of Post-biblical Jewish Writings and the Aramaic Language*. Translated by D. M. Kay. Edinburgh: Clark.
1924   *Orte und Wege Jesu*. 3d edition. Gütersloh: Bertelsmann.
1929   *Jesus-Jeshua: Studies in the Gospels*. Translated by P. P. Levertoff. New York: Macmillan.

Danby, H.
1933   *The Mishnah: Translated from the Hebrew with Introduction and Brief Explanatory Notes*. Oxford: Oxford University Press.

Danker, F. W.
1960–61 "The Υἱός Phrases in the New Testament." *New Testament Studies* 7:94.
1972   *Jesus and the New Age according to St. Luke: A Commentary on the Third Gospel*. St. Louis: Clayton.
1982   *Benefactor: Epigraphic Study of a Graeco-Roman and New Testament Semantic Field*. St. Louis: Clayton.
1983   "Graeco-Roman Cultural Accommodation in the Christology of Luke–Acts." Pp. 391–414 in *Society of Biblical Literature 1983 Seminar Papers*. Edited by K. H. Richards. Chico, Calif.: Scholars Press.
1988   *Jesus and the New Age: A Commentary on St. Luke's Gospel*. Revised edition. Philadelphia: Fortress.

Darr, J. A.
1987   *"Glorified in the Presence of Kings": A Literary-Critical Study of Herod the Tetrarch in Luke–Acts*. Ph.D. Diss. Vanderbilt University.
1992   *On Character Building: The Reader and the Rhetoric of Characterization in Luke–Acts*. Literary Currents in Biblical Interpretation. Louisville: Westminster/John Knox.

Daube, D.
1955   "Jewish Inheritance in Two Lukan Pericopes." *Zeitschrift der Savigny-Stiftung für romanistische Rechtsgeschichte* 72:326–34.
1956   *The New Testament and Rabbinic Judaism*. Jordan Lectures 1952. London: University of London/Athlone.
1960   "Three Notes Having to Do with Johanan Ben Zaccai." *Journal of Theological Studies* n.s. 11:53–62.
1961   "'For They Know Not What They Do': Luke 23,34." Pp. 58–70 in *Studia Patristica*, vol. 4: *Papers Presented to the Third International Conference on Patristic Studies Held at Christ Church, Oxford, 1959*, part 2: *Biblica, Patres Apostolici, Historica*. Edited by F. L. Cross. Texte und Untersuchungen 79. Berlin: Akademie-Verlag.
1972–73 "Responsibilities of Master and Disciples in the Gospels." *New Testament Studies* 19:1–15.

Davies, P. R.
1983   "Calendrical Change and Qumran Origins An Assessment of VanderKam's Theory." *Catholic Biblical Quarterly* 45:80–89.

Davies, W. D.
1962   *Christian Origins and Judaism*. London: Darton, Longman & Todd.
1964   *The Setting of the Sermon on the Mount*. Cambridge: Cambridge University Press.

Davies, W. D., and D. C. Allison Jr.
1988   *A Critical and Exegetical Commentary on the Gospel according to Saint Matthew*, vol. 1: *Introduction and Commentary on Matthew i–vii*. International Critical Commentary. Edinburgh: Clark.

Deatrick, E. P.
1962   "Salt, Soil, Savior." *Biblical Archaeologist* 25:41–48.

DeGuglielmo, A.
1941   "Emmaus." *Catholic Biblical Quarterly* 3:293–301.

De Jonge, H. J.
1977–78 "Sonship, Wisdom, Infancy: Luke ii.41–51a." *New Testament Studies* 24:317–54.

De Jonge, M.
1960   "Christian Influence in the Testaments of the Twelve Patriarchs." *Novum Testamentum* 4:182–235. Reprinted in *Studies on the Testaments of the Twelve Patriarchs: Text and Interpretation*, pp. 193–246. Edited by M. De Jonge. Studia in Veteris Testamenti Pseudepigrapha 3. Leiden: Brill, 1975.
1966   "The Use of the Word 'Anointed' in the Time of Jesus." *Novum Testamentum* 8:132–48.

Delling, G.
1962   "Das Gleichnis vom gottlosen Richter." *Zeitschrift für die Neutestamentliche Wissenschaft* 53:1–25.

Delobel, J.
1973   "La Rédaction de Lc., iv,14–16a et le 'Bericht vom Anfang.'" Pp. 203–23 in *L'Évangile de Luc: Problèmes Littéraires et Théologiques: Mémorial Lucien Cerfaux*. Edited by F. Neirynck. Bibliotheca Ephemeridum Theologicarum Lovaniensium 32. Gembloux: Duculot.

Denney, J.
1909–10 "The Word 'Hate' in Luke xiv.26." *Expository Times* 21:41–42.

Derrett, J. D. M.
1970   *Law in the New Testament*. London: Darton, Longman & Todd.
1971   "Law in the New Testament: The Palm Sunday Colt." *Novum Testamentum* 13:243–58.
1971–72 "Law in the New Testament: The Parable of the Unjust Judge." *New Testament Studies* 18:178–91.
1972a   "'Eating up the Houses of Widows': Jesus' Comment on Lawyers?" *Novum Testamentum* 14:1–9.
1972b   "Take Thy Bond . . . and Write Fifty (Luke xvi.6): The Nature of the Bond." *Journal of Theological Studies*, n.s 23:438–40.
1973   "Law in the New Testament: The Syro-Phoenician Woman and the Centurion of Capernaum." *Novum Testamentum* 15:161–86.
1974   "Allegory and the Wicked Vinedressers." *Journal of Theological Studies* n.s. 25:426–32.
1977a   "Nisi Dominus Aedificaverit Domum: Towers and Wars (Luke xiv 28–32)." *Novum Testamentum* 19:241–61.
1977b   "The Rich Fool: A Parable of Jesus concerning Inheritance." *Heythrop Journal* 18:131–51.
1979–80 "Fresh Light on the Lost Sheep and the Lost Coin." *New Testament Studies* 26:36–60.

Dessau, H.
1892–
1916   *Inscriptiones Latinae Selectae*. 3 vols. in 5. Berlin: Weidmann.
1921   "Zu den neuen Inschriften des Sulpicius Quirinius." *Klio* 17:252–58.

Dibelius, M.
1934   *From Tradition to Gospel*. Translated by B. L. Woolf. London: Nicholson & Watson.
1956   *Studies in the Acts of the Apostles*. Edited by H. Greeven. Translated by M. Ling and P. Schubert. New York: Scribner/London: SCM.

Dietrich, W.
1972   *Das Petrusbild der lukanischen Schriften*. Beiträge zur Wissenschaft vom Alten und Neuen Testament 5/14. Stuttgart: Kohlhammer.

Dillon, R. J.
1978   *From Eye-Witnesses to Ministers of the Word: Tradition and Composition in Luke 24*. Analecta Biblica 82. Rome: Pontifical Biblical Institute Press.
1981   "Previewing Luke's Project from His Prologue (Luke 1:1–4)." *Catholic Biblical Quarterly* 43:205–27.

Dinkler, E.
1971   "Peter's Confession and the Satan Saying: The Problem of Jesus' Messiahship." Pp. 169–202 in *The Future of Our Religious Past: Essays in Honour of Rudolf Bultmann*. Edited by J. M. Robinson. Translated by C. E. Carlston and R. P. Scharlemann. New York: Harper & Row.

Dittenberger, W.
1903–5   *Orientis Graeci Inscriptiones Selectae: Supplementum "Sylloges Inscriptionum Graecarum."* 2 vols. Leipzig: Hirzel.

Dodd, C. H.
1936–37 "The Kingdom of God Has Come." *Expository Times* 48:138–42.
1947   "The Fall of Jerusalem and the 'Abomination of Desolation.'" *Journal of Roman Studies* 37:47–54. Reprinted in Dodd's *More New Testament Studies*, pp. 69–83. Grand Rapids: Eerdmans/Manchester: Manchester University Press, 1968.
1955   "The Appearances of the Risen Christ: An Essay in Form-Criticism of the Gospels." Pp. 9–35 in *Studies in the Gospels: Essays in Memory of R. H. Lightfoot*. Edited by D. E. Nineham. Oxford: Blackwell. Reprinted in Dodd's *More New Testament Studies*, pp. 102–33. Grand Rapids: Eerdmans/Manchester: Manchester University Press, 1968.
1961   *The Parables of the Kingdom*. Revised edition. New York: Scribner/London: Nisbet.

Donahue, J. R.
1971   "Tax Collectors and Sinners: An Attempt at Identification." *Catholic Biblical Quarterly* 33:39–61.

Donald, T.
1963   "The Semantic Field of 'Folly' in Proverbs, Job, Psalms, and Ecclesiastes." *Vetus Testamentum* 13:285–92.

Doran, R.
1983   "Luke 20:18: A Warrior's Boast?" *Catholic Biblical Quarterly* 45:61–67.

Driver, G. R.
1965   "Two Problems in the New Testament." *Journal of Theological Studies* n.s. 16:327–37.

Driver, S. R.
1900   *The Book of Daniel*. Cambridge Bible for Schools and Colleges. Cambridge: Cambridge University Press.

Drury, J.
1976   *Tradition and Design in Luke's Gospel: A Study in Early Christian Historiography*. London: Darton, Longman & Todd.

Duling, D. C.
1975   "Solomon, Exorcism, and the Son of David." *Harvard Theological Review* 68:235–52.

Dungan, D. L. (ed.)
1990   *The Interrelations of the Gospels*. Bibliotheca Ephemeridum Theologicarum Lovaniensium 95. Louvain: Leuven University Press/Macon, Ga.: Mercer University Press.

Dunkerley, R.
1957   *Beyond the Gospels*. Baltimore: Penguin.
1958–59 "Lazarus." *New Testament Studies* 5:321–27.

Dunn, J. D. G.
1970a   *Baptism in the Holy Spirit: A Re-examination of the New Testament Teaching on the Gift of the Spirit in Relation to Pentecostalism Today.* Studies in Biblical Theology 2/15. London: SCM/Naperville, Ill.: Allenson.
1970b   "The Messianic Secret in Mark." *Tyndale Bulletin* 21:92–117. Reprinted in *The Messianic Secret*, pp. 116–31. Edited by C. Tuckett. Philadelphia: Fortress/London: SPCK, 1983.
1975   *Jesus and the Spirit: A Study of the Religious and Charismatic Experience of Jesus and the First Christians as Reflected in the New Testament.* New Testament Library. Philadelphia: Westminster/London: SCM.
1980   *Christology in the Making: A New Testament Inquiry into the Origins of the Doctrine of the Incarnation.* London: SCM.
1988   "Matthew 12:28 / Luke 11:20—A Word of Jesus?" Pp. 29–49 in *Eschatology and the New Testament: Essays in Honor of George Raymond Beasley-Murray.* Edited by W. H. Gloer. Peabody, Mass.: Hendrickson.

Duplacy, J.
1963   "Une Variante Méconnue du Texte Reçu: ῍Η Ἀπολύσητε (Lc 22,68)." Pp. 42–52 in *Neutestamentliche Aufsätze: Festschrift für Prof. Josef Schmid zum 70. Gebertstag.* Edited by J. Blinzler, O. Kuss, and F. Mussner. Regensburg: Pustet.

Du Plessis, I. I.
1974   "Once More: The Purpose of Luke's Prologue (Lk i 1–4)." *Novum Testamentum* 16:259–71.

Dupont, J.
1959   "'Soyez Parfaits' (Mt., v,48)—'Soyez Miséricordieux' (Lc., vi,36)." Vol. 2 / pp. 150–62 in *Sacra Pagina: Miscellanea Biblica Congressus Internationalis Catholici de re Biblica.* Edited by J. Coppens, A. Descamps, and É. Massaux. Bibliotheca Ephemeridum Theologicarum Lovaniensium 13. Paris: Lecoffre/Paris: Gabalda/Gembloux: Duculot.
1964   "Le Logion des Douze Trônes (Mt 19,28; Lc 22,28–30)." *Biblica* 45:355–92.
1966a   "'Béatitudes' Égyptiennes." *Biblica* 47:185–222.
1966b   "L'Appel à Imiter Dieu en Matthieu 5,48 et Luc 6,36." *Rivista Biblica* 14:137–58.
1968   *Les Tentations de Jésus au Désert.* Studia Neotestamentica 4. Bruges: Desclée de Brouwer.
1979   *The Salvation of the Gentiles: Essays on the Acts of the Apostles.* Translated by J. R. Keating. New York: Paulist Press.
1980   "Le Pharisien et la Pécheresse (Lc 7,36–50)." *Communautés et Liturgies* 4:260–68.

Dupont-Sommer, A.
1961   *The Essene Writings from Qumran.* Translated by G. Vermes. Oxford: Blackwell. Reprinted Gloucester, Mass.: Peter Smith, 1973.

Easton, B. S.
1913   "The Beezebul Sections." *Journal of Biblical Literature* 32:57–73.

Edersheim, A.
1889   *The Life and Times of Jesus the Messiah.* New York: Longmans, Green.

Edwards, R. A.
1971   *The Sign of Jonah in the Theology of the Evangelists and Q.* Studies in Biblical Theology 2/18. London: SCM.

Egelkraut, H. L.
1976   *Jesus' Mission to Jerusalem: A Redaction Critical Study of the Travel Narrative in the Gospel of Luke, Lk 9:51–19:48.* Europäische Hochschulschriften 23/80. Frankfurt am Main/Bern: Lang.

Ehrman, A.
1978   "Judas Iscariot and Abba Saqqara." *Journal of Biblical Literature* 97:572–73.

Ehrman, B. D.
1991   "The Cup, the Bread, and the Salvific Effect of Jesus' Death in Luke–Acts." Pp. 576–91 in *Society of Biblical Literature 1991 Seminar Papers.* Edited by K. H. Richards. Chico, Calif.: Scholars Press.

Einheitsübersetzung
  Einheitsübersetzung der Heiligen Schrift. Stuttgart: Katholische Bibelanstalt, 1979.
Eisler, R. I.
1931 *The Messiah Jesus and John the Baptist according to Flavius Josephus' Recently Discovered "Capture of Jerusalem" and the Other Jewish and Christian Sources*. Translated by A. H. Krappe. New York: Dial/London: Methuen.
Ellingworth, P.
1980 "Luke 12.46—Is There an Anti-climax Here?" *Bible Translator* 31:242–43.
Elliott, J. K.
1969 "The Use of Ἕτερος in the New Testament." *Zeitschrift für die Neutestamentliche Wissenschaft* 60:140–41.
Ellis, E. E.
1965–66 "Present and Future Eschatology in Luke." *New Testament Studies* 12:27–41.
1972 *Eschatology in Luke*. Facet Books, Biblical Series 30. Philadelphia: Fortress.
1974 *The Gospel of Luke*. 2d edition. New Century Bible. Grand Rapids: Eerdmans/London: Marshall, Morgan & Scott.
1977 "How the New Testament Uses the Old." Pp. 199–219 in *New Testament Interpretation: Essays on Principles and Methods*. Edited by I. H. Marshall. Grand Rapids: Eerdmans/Exeter: Paternoster.
Emerton, J. A.
1958 "The Origin of the Son of Man Imagery." *Journal of Theological Studies* n.s. 9:225–42.
Epp, E. J.
1962 "The 'Ignorance Motif' in Acts and Antijudaic Tendencies in Codex Bezae." *Harvard Theological Review* 55:51–62.
1966 *The Theological Tendency of Codex Bezae Cantabrigiensis in Acts*. Society for New Testament Studies Monograph Series 3. Cambridge: Cambridge University Press.
1981 "The Ascension in the Textual Tradition of Luke–Acts." Pp. 131–45 in *New Testament Textual Criticism, Its Significance for Exegesis: Essays in Honour of Bruce M. Metzger*. Edited by E. J. Epp and G. D. Fee. Oxford: Clarendon.
Eppstein, V.
1964 "The Historicity of the Gospel Account of the Cleansing of the Temple." *Zeitschrift für die Neutestamentliche Wissenschaft* 55:42–58.
Ernst, J.
1977 *Das Evangelium nach Lukas*. Regensburger Neues Testament 3. Regensburg: Pustet.
Esler, P. F.
1987 *Community and Gospel in Luke–Acts: The Social and Political Motivations of Lucan Theology*. Society for New Testament Studies Monograph Series 57. Cambridge: Cambridge University Press.
Evans, C. A.
1987a "'He Set His Face': Luke 9,51 Once Again." *Biblica* 68:80–84.
1987b "Luke's Use of the Elijah/Elisha Narrative and the Ethic of Election." *Journal of Biblical Literature* 106:75–83.
1989a "Jesus' Action in the Temple and Evidence of Corruption in the First-Century Temple." Pp. 522–39 in *Society of Biblical Literature 1989 Seminar Papers*. Edited by D. J. Lull. Atlanta: Scholars Press.
1989b "Jesus' Action in the Temple: Cleansing or Portent of Destruction?" *Catholic Biblical Quarterly* 51:237–70.
1989c *To See and Not Perceive: Isaiah 6.9–10 in Early Jewish and Christian Interpretation*. Journal for the Study of the Old Testament Supplement 64. Sheffield: JSOT Press.
1990 *Luke*. New International Biblical Commentary 3. Peabody, Mass.: Hendrickson.
1991 "In What Sense 'Blasphemy'? Jesus before Caiaphas in Mark 14:61–64." Pp. 215–34 in *Society of Biblical Literature 1991 Seminar Papers*. Edited by E. A. Lovering Jr. Atlanta: Scholars Press.
Evans, C. A., and J. A. Sanders
1993 *Luke and Scripture: The Function of Sacred Tradition in Luke–Acts*. Minneapolis: Fortress.

Evans, C. F.
1955   "The Central Section of St. Luke's Gospel." Pp. 37–53 in *Studies in the Gospels: Essays in Memory of R. H. Lightfoot*. Edited by D. E. Nineham. Oxford: Blackwell.
1970   *Resurrection and the New Testament*. Studies in Biblical Theology 2/12. London: SCM/Naperville, Ill.: Allenson.
1990   *Saint Luke*. Trinity Press International New Testament Commentaries. Philadelphia: Trinity/London: SCM.

Farmer, W. R.
1961–62 "Notes on a Literary and Form-Critical Analysis of Some of the Synoptic Material Peculiar to Luke." *New Testament Studies* 8:301–16.
1964   *The Synoptic Problem: A Critical Analysis*. New York: Macmillan. Reprinted Dillsboro, N.C.: Western North Carolina Press, 1976.

Farrell, H. K.
1986   "The Structure and Theology of Luke's Central Section." *Trinity Journal* 7/2:33–54.

Farris, S.
1985   *The Hymns of Luke's Infancy Narratives: Their Origin, Meaning and Significance*. Journal for the Study of the New Testament Supplement 9. Sheffield: JSOT Press.

Fee, G. D.
1981   "'One Thing Is Needful?' Luke 10:42." Pp. 61–75 in *New Testament Textual Criticism, Its Significance for Exegesis: Essays in Honour of Bruce M. Metzger*. Edited by E. J. Epp and G. D. Fee. Oxford: Clarendon.

Feinberg, J. S. (ed.)
1988   *Continuity and Discontinuity: Perspectives on the Relationship between the Old and New Testaments: Essays in Honor of S. Lewis Johnson, Jr*. Westchester, Ill.: Crossway.

Feine, P.
1922   *Theologie des Neuen Testaments*. 4th edition. Leipzig: Hinrichs.

Field, F.
1875   *Origenis Hexaplorum quae Supersunt; sive Veterum Interpretum Graecorum in Totum Vetus Testamentum Fragmenta*. 2 vols. Oxford: Clarendon.

Finegan, J.
1964   *Handbook of Biblical Chronology: Principles of Time Reckoning in the Ancient World and the Problems of Chronology in the Bible*. Princeton: Princeton University Press.

Finkel, A.
1963   "Jesus' Sermon at Nazareth (Luk. 4,16–30)." Pp. 106–15 in *Abraham unser Vater: Juden und Christen im Gespräch über die Bibel: Festschrift für Otto Michel zum 60. Geburtstag*. Edited by O. Betz, M. Hengel, and P. Schmidt. Arbeiten zur Geschichte des Spätjudentums und Urchristentums 5. Leiden: Brill.

Finn, T. M.
1985   "The God-fearers Reconsidered." *Catholic Biblical Quarterly* 47:75–84.

Fischel, H. A.
1946–47 "Martyr and Prophet: A Study in Jewish Literature." *Jewish Quarterly Review* 37:265–80, 363–86.

Fitzgerald, J. T.
1972   "The Temptation of Jesus: The Testing of the Messiah in Matthew." *Restoration Quarterly* 15:152–60.

Fitzmyer, J. A.
1958   "'Peace upon Earth among Men of His Good Will' (Lk 2:14)." *Theological Studies* 19:225–27. Reprinted in Fitzmyer's *Essays on the Semitic Background of the New Testament*, pp. 101–4. London: Chapman, 1971.
1964   "The Story of the Dishonest Manager (Lk 16:1–13)." *Theological Studies* 25:23–42.
1972   "The Use of *Agein* and *Pherein* in the Synoptic Gospels." Pp. 147–60 in *Festschrift to Honor F. Wilbur Gingrich*. Edited by E. H. Barth and R. E. Cocroft. Leiden: Brill.
1973–74 "The Contribution of Qumran Aramaic to the Study of the New Testament." *New Testament Studies* 20:382–407. Reprinted in Fitzmyer's *Wandering Aramean: Collected Aramaic Essays*, pp. 85–113. Society of Biblical Literature Monograph Series 25. Missoula, Mont.: Scholars Press, 1979.

1978   "Crucifixion in Ancient Palestine, Qumran Literature, and the New Testament." *Catholic Biblical Quarterly* 40:493–513.

1979a   "Another View of the 'Son of Man' Debate." *Journal for the Study of the New Testament* 4:58–68.

1979b   *A Wandering Aramean: Collected Aramaic Essays.* Society of Biblical Literature Monograph Series 25. Missoula, Mont.: Scholars Press.

1981   *The Gospel according to Luke (i–ix).* Anchor Bible 28. Garden City, N.Y.: Doubleday.

1985   *The Gospel according to Luke (x–xxiv).* Anchor Bible 28a. Garden City, N.Y.: Doubleday.

1989   *Luke the Theologian: Aspects of His Teaching.* Mahwah, N.J.: Paulist Press/London: Chapman.

Flanagan, N. M.

1978   "The Position of Women in the Writings of St. Luke." *Marianum* 40:288–304.

Fletcher, D. R.

1963   "The Riddle of the Unjust Steward: Is Irony the Key?" *Journal of Biblical Literature* 82:15–30.

1964   "Condemned to Die: The Logion on Cross-Bearing: What Does It Mean?" *Interpretation* 18:156–64.

Flückiger, F.

1972   "Luk. 21,20–24 und die Zerstörung Jerusalems." *Theologische Zeitschrift* 28:385–90.

Flusser, D.

1957   "Healing through the Laying-on of Hands in a Dead Sea Scroll." *Israel Exploration Journal* 7:107–8.

1959   "Two Notes on the Midrash on II Sam. vii." *Israel Exploration Journal* 9:99–109.

Ford, J. M.

1984   *My Enemy Is My Guest: Jesus and Violence in Luke.* Maryknoll, N.Y.: Orbis.

Fornara, C. W.

1983   *The Nature of History in Ancient Greece and Rome.* Berkeley: University of California Press.

Foulkes, F.

1958   *The Acts of God: A Study of the Basis of Typology in the Old Testament.* Tyndale Old Testament Lecture 1955. London: Tyndale.

Fraenkel, E.

1935   "Namenwesen." Vol. 32 [= 16.2] / cols. 1611–70 in *Paulys Realencyclopädie der classischen Altertumswissenschaft.* Stuttgart: Metzler.

France, R. T.

1971   *Jesus and the Old Testament: His Application of Old Testament Passages to Himself and His Mission.* London: Tyndale/Downer Grove, Ill.: InterVarsity.

1985   *The Gospel according to Matthew: An Introduction and Commentary.* Tyndale New Testament Commentaries. Grand Rapids: Eerdmans/Leicester: Inter-Varsity.

Franklin, E.

1975   *Christ the Lord: A Study in the Purpose and Theology of Luke–Acts.* Philadelphia: Westminster/London: SPCK.

Frey, J.-B.

1930   "La Signification du Terme Πρωτότοκος d'après une Inscription Juive." *Biblica* 11:373–90.

Friedlander, G.

1916   *Pirḳê de Rabbi Eliezer (the Chapters of Rabbi Eliezer the Great) according to the Text of the Manuscript Belonging to Abraham Epstein of Vienna.* London: Paul, Trench, Trübner/New York: Bloch. Reprinted New York: Sepher-Hermon, 1981.

Funk, R. W.

1985   *New Gospel Parallels.* 2 vols. Philadelphia: Fortress.

Funk, R. W., and R. W. Hoover

1993   *The Five Gospels: The Search for the Authentic Words of Jesus.* New York: Macmillan.

Gaebelein, A. C.
1910   *The Gospel of Matthew: An Exposition*. New York: Our Hope. Reprinted Neptune, N.J.: Loizeaux, 1961.

Gaechter, P.
1955   *Maria im Erdenleben: Neutestamentliche Marienstudien*. 3d edition. Innsbruck: Tyrolia.

Garbe, R.
1959   *India and Christendom: The Historical Connections between Their Religions*. Translated by L. G. Robinson. La Salle, Ill.: Open Court.

Garland, D. E.
1979   *The Intention of Matthew 23*. Novum Testamentum Supplement 52. Leiden: Brill.

Garrett, S. R.
1989   *The Demise of the Devil: Magic and the Demonic in Luke's Writings*. Minneapolis: Fortress.

Gärtner, B. E.
1970-71 "The Person of Jesus and the Kingdom of God." *Theology Today* 27:32–43.

Gaston, L.
1962   "Beelzebul." *Theologische Zeitschrift* 18:247–55.

1970   *No Stone on Another: Studies in the Significance of the Fall of Jerusalem in the Synoptic Gospels*. Novum Testamentum Supplement 23. Leiden: Brill.

Geiger, R.
1976   *Die lukanischen Endzeitreden: Studien zur Eschatologie des Lukas-Evangeliums*. 2d edition. Europäische Hochschulschriften 23/16. Frankfurt am Main/Bern: Lang.

Geldenhuys, N.
1951   *Commentary on the Gospel of Luke*. New International Commentary on the New Testament. Grand Rapids: Eerdmans.

Gerhardsson, B.
1966   *The Testing of God's Son (Matt. 4:1–11 and Par): An Analysis of an Early Christian Midrash*. Coniectanea Biblica, New Testament 2/1. Lund: Gleerup.

1967-68 "The Parable of the Sower and Its Interpretation." *New Testament Studies* 14:165–93.

Gerstenberger, E.
1962   "The Woe-Oracles of the Prophets." *Journal of Biblical Literature* 81:249–63.

Gerstner, J. H.
1991   *Wrongly Dividing the Word of God: A Critique of Dispensationalism*. Brentwood, Tenn.: Wolgemuth & Hyatt.

Gewiess, J.
1967   "Die Mariefrage, Lk 1,34." Pp. 184–217 in *Struktur und Theologie der lukanischen Kindheitsgeschichte*, by R. Laurentin. Stuttgart: Katholisches Bibelwerk.

Giblin, C. H.
1971   "'The Things of God' in the Question concerning Tribute to Caesar (Lk 20:25; Mk 12:17; Mt 22:21)." *Catholic Biblical Quarterly* 33:510–27.

1985   *The Destruction of Jerusalem according to Luke's Gospel: A Historical-Typological Moral*. Analecta Biblica 107. Rome: Pontifical Biblical Institute Press.

Glickman, S. C.
1983   *The Temptation Account in Matthew and Luke*. Ph.D. diss. University of Basel.

Glöckner, R.
1976   *Die Verkündigung des Heils beim Evangelisten Lukas*. Walberberger Studien, Theologische Reihe 9. Mainz: Matthias-Grünewald.

1983   *Neutestamentliche Wundergeschichten und das Lob der Wundertaten Gottes in den Psalmen: Studien zur sprachlichen und theologischen Verwandtschaft zwischen neutestamentlichen Wundergeschichten und Psalmen*. Walberberger Studien, Theologische Reihe 13. Mainz: Matthias-Grünewald.

Glombitza, O.
1958   "Die Titel Διδάσκαλος und Ἐπιστάτης für Jesus bei Lukas." *Zeitschrift für die Neutestamentliche Wissenschaft* 49:275–78.

1962   "Das grosse Abendmahl: Luk. xiv 12–24." *Novum Testamentum* 5:10–16.

1971   "Die christologische Aussage des Lukas in seiner Gestaltung der drei Nachfolgeworte Lukas ix 57–62." *Novum Testamentum* 13:14–23.

Gnilka, J.
1961   *Die Verstockung Israels: Isaias 6,9–10 in der Theologie der Synoptiker.* Studien zum Alten und Neuen Testament 3. Munich: Kösel.
1961–62 "Die essenischen Tauchbäder und die Johannestaufe." *Revue de Qumran* 3:185–207.

Godet, F.
1875   *A Commentary on the Gospel of St. Luke.* 2 vols. Translated by E. W. Shalders and M. D. Cusin. Edinburgh: Clark.

Goldin, J.
1955   *The Fathers according to Rabbi Nathan.* Yale Judaica Series 10. New Haven: Yale University Press.

Gooding, D. W.
1987   *According to Luke: A New Exposition of the Third Gospel.* Grand Rapids: Eerdmans/Leicester: Inter-Varsity.

Goppelt, L.
1981–82 *Theology of the New Testament.* Edited by J. Roloff. Translated by J. E. Alsup. 2 vols. Grand Rapids: Eerdmans.
1982   *Typos: The Typological Interpretation of the Old Testament in the New.* Translated by D. H. Madvig. Grand Rapids: Eerdmans.

Gordon, C. H.
1977   "Paternity at Two Levels." *Journal of Biblical Literature* 96:101.

Gore, C.
1910   *The Sermon on the Mount: A Practical Exposition.* 2d edition. London: Murray.

Goulder, M. D.
1964   "The Chiastic Structure of the Lucan Journey." Pp. 195–202 in *Studia Evangelica,* vol. 2: *Papers Presented to the Second International Congress on New Testament Studies Held at Christ Church, Oxford, 1961,* part 1: *The New Testament Scriptures.* Edited by F. L. Cross. Texte und Untersuchungen 87. Berlin: Akademie-Verlag.
1989   *Luke: A New Paradigm.* 2 vols. Journal for the Study of the New Testament Supplement 20. Sheffield: JSOT Press.

Gradwohl, R.
1974   "Sünde und Vergebung im Judentum." *Concilium* 10/10:563–67.

Grández, R. M.
1989   "Las Tinieblas en la Muerte de Jesús: Historia de la Exégesis de Lc 23,44–45a (Mt 27,45; Mk 15,33)." *Estudios Bíblicos* 47:177–223.

Grässer, E.
1960   *Das Problem der Parusieverzögerung in den synoptischen Evangelien und in der Apostelgeschichte.* 2d edition. Beiheft zur Zeitschrift für die Neutestamentliche Wissenschaft 22. Berlin: Töpelmann.

Gray, G. B.
1899–   "The Nazirite." *Journal of Theological Studies* o.s. 1:201–11.
1900

Grayston, K.
1973–74 "The Study of Mark xiii." *Bulletin of the John Rylands Library* 56:371–87.

Graystone, G.
1968   *Virgin of All Virgins: The Interpretation of Luke 1:34.* Rome: Tipografia S. Pio X.

Green, J. B.
1987   "Preparation for Passover (Luke 22:7–13): A Question of Redactional Technique." *Novum Testamentum* 29:305–19.
1988   *The Death of Jesus: Tradition and Interpretation in the Passion Narrative.* Wissenschaftliche Untersuchungen zum Neuen Testament 2/33. Tübingen: Mohr.
1991   "The Death of Jesus and the Rending of the Temple Veil (Luke 23:44–49): A Window into Luke's Understanding of Jesus and the Temple." Pp. 543–57 in *Society of Biblical Literature 1991 Seminar Papers.* Edited by E. A. Lovering Jr. Atlanta: Scholars Press.

1994 "Good News to Whom? Jesus and the 'Poor' in the Gospel of Luke." Pp. 59–74 in *Jesus of Nazareth: Lord and Christ—Essays on the Historical Jesus and New Testament Christology* [I. Howard Marshall Festschrift]. Edited by J. B. Green and M. Turner. Grand Rapids: Eerdmans/Carlisle: Paternoster.

Green, M. P.
1983 "The Meaning of Cross-Bearing." *Bibliotheca Sacra* 140:117–33.

Greeven, H.
1959–60 "Erwägungen zur synoptischen Textkritik." *New Testament Studies* 6:281–96.

Grelot, P.
1967 "Aujourd'hui tu Seras avec Moi dans le Paradis (Luc, xxiii,43)." *Revue Biblique* 74:194–214.

Grensted, L. W.
1914–15 "The Use of Enoch in St. Luke xvi.19–31." *Expository Times* 26:333–34.

Gressmann, H.
1911 "Mitteilungen 14: Salzdüngung in den Evangelien." *Theologische Literaturzeitung* 36:156–57.
1914 *Das Weihnachts-evangelium auf Ursprung und Geschichte*. Göttingen: Vandenhoeck & Ruprecht.

Grigsby, B.
1984 "Compositional Hypotheses for the Lucan 'Magnificat'—Tensions for the Evangelical." *Evangelical Quarterly* 56:159–72.

Grobel, K.
1963–64 ". . . Whose Name Was Neves." *New Testament Studies* 10:373–82.

Grundmann, W.
1963 *Das Evangelium nach Lukas*. Theologischer Handkommentar zum Neuen Testament 3. Berlin: Evangelische Verlagsanstalt.

Guelich, R.
1975–76 "The Antitheses of Matthew v.21–48: Traditional and/or Redactional?" *New Testament Studies* 22:444–57.
1982 *The Sermon on the Mount*. Waco: Word.

Guenther, H. O.
1985 *The Footprints of Jesus' Twelve in Early Christian Traditions: A Study in the Meaning of Religious Symbolism*. American University Studies 7/7. New York: Lang.

Gundry, R. H.
1967 *The Use of the Old Testament in St. Matthew's Gospel, with Special Reference to the Messianic Hope*. Novum Testamentum Supplement 18. Leiden: Brill.
1982 *Matthew: A Commentary on His Literary and Theological Art*. Grand Rapids: Eerdmans.
1990 "Jesus' Blasphemy according to Mark 14:61b–64 and Mishnah Sanhedrin 7:5." Paper Read at Annual Meeting of the Society of Biblical Literature, New Orleans.

Gunkel, H.
1921 "Die Lieder in der Kindheitsgeschichte Jesu bei Lukas." Pp. 43–60 in *Festgabe von Fachgenossen und Freunden A. von Harnack zum siebzigsten Geburtstag*. Edited by K. Holl. Tübingen: Mohr.

Guthrie, D.
1970 *New Testament Introduction*. 3d edition. Downers Grove, Ill.: InterVarsity.

Hadas, M.
1951 *Aristeas to Philocrates (Letter of Aristeas)*. Jewish Apocryphal Literature. New York: Harper for Dropsie College.

Haenchen, E.
1961 "Das 'Wir' in der Apostelgeschichte und das Itinerar." *Zeitschrift für Theologie und Kirche* 58:329–66.
1971 *The Acts of the Apostles: A Commentary*. Translated by B. Noble, G. Shinn, H. Anderson, and R. M. Wilson. Philadelphia: Westminster/Oxford: Blackwell.

Hahn, F.
1969   *The Titles of Jesus in Christology: Their History in Early Christianity.* Translated by H. Knight and G. Ogg. London: Lutterworth.
1973   "Die Worte vom Licht Lk 11,33–36." Pp. 107–38 in *Orientierung an Jesus: Zur Theologie der Synoptiker: Für Josef Schmid.* Edited by P. Hoffmann, N. Brox, and W. Pesch. Freiburg: Herder.

Hamerton-Kelly, R. G.
1964–65   "A Note on Matthew xii.28 par. Luke xi.20." *New Testament Studies* 11:167–69.

Hamilton, N. Q.
1964   "Temple Cleansing and Temple Bank." *Journal of Biblical Literature* 83:365–72.

Hamm, D.
1991   "Zacchaeus Revisited Once More: A Story of Vindication or Conversion?" *Biblica* 72:249–52.

Harbarth, A.
1978   *"Gott hat sein Volk heimgesucht": Eine form- und redaktionsgeschichtliche Untersuchungen zu Lk 7,11–17: Die Erweckung des Jünglings von Nain.* Ph.D. diss. Freiberg im Breisgau.

Hardy, E. R., Jr.
1945   "The Date of Psalm 110." *Journal of Biblical Literature* 64:385–90.

Hare, D. R. A.
1967   *The Theme of Jewish Persecution of Christians in the Gospel according to St Matthew.* Society for New Testament Studies Monograph Series 6. Cambridge: Cambridge University Press.

Harnack, A. von
1900   "Das Magnificat der Elisabet (Luc. 1,46–55) nebst einigen Bermerkungen zu Luc. 1 und 2." *Sitzungsberichte der königlichen preussischen Akademie der Wissenschaften zu Berlin* 27:538–56. Reprinted in Harnack's *Kleine Schriften zur alten Kirche: Berliner Akademieschriften, 1890–1920,* vol. 1 / pp. 439–57. Opuscula 9/1. Leipzig: Zentralantiquariat der Deutschen Demokratischen Republik, 1980.
1901   "Probleme im Texte der Leidensgeschichte Jesu." *Sitzungsberichte der königlichen preussischen Akademie der Wissenschaften zu Berlin* 11:251–66. Reprinted in Harnack's *Kleine Schriften zur alten Kirche: Berliner Akademieschriften, 1890–1920,* vol. 1 / pp. 470–85. Opuscula 9/1. Leipzig: Zentralantiquariat der Deutschen Demokratischen Republik, 1980.
1907   *Luke the Physician: The Author of the Third Gospel and the Acts of the Apostles.* New Testament Studies 1. Translated by J. R. Wilkinson. London: Williams & Norgate/ New York: Putnam.

Hart, H. St. J.
1984   "The Coin of 'Render unto Caesar . . .' (A Note on Some Aspects of Mark 12:13–17; Matt. 22:15–22; Luke 20:20–26)." Pp. 241–48 in *Jesus and the Politics of His Day.* Edited by E. Bammel and C. F. D. Moule. Cambridge: Cambridge University Press.

Hartin, P. J.
1991   *James and the Q Sayings of Jesus.* Journal for the Study of the New Testament Supplement 47. Sheffield: JSOT Press.

Hartman, L.
1966   *Prophecy Interpreted: The Formation of Some Jewish Apocalyptic Texts and of the Eschatological Discourse Mark 13 Par.* Translated by N. Tomkinson and J. Gray. Coniectanea Biblica, New Testament 1. Lund: Gleerup.
1969   Review of *Naherwartungen: Tradition und Redaktion in Mk 13* by R. Pesch. *Biblica* 50:576–80.

Hartman, L. F., and A. A. Di Lella
1978   *The Book of Daniel.* Anchor Bible 23. Garden City, N.Y.: Doubleday.

Hartmann, G.
1964   "Die Vorlage der Osterberichte in Joh 20." *Zeitschrift für die Neutestamentliche Wissenschaft* 55:197–220.

Harvey, A. E.
1982a   *Jesus and the Constraints of History*. Philadelphia: Westminster.
1982b   "'The Workman Is Worthy of His Hire': Fortunes of a Proverb in the Early Church." *Novum Testamentum* 24:209–21.
Hay, D. M.
1973   *Glory at the Right Hand: Psalm 110 in Early Christianity*. Society of Biblical Literature Monograph Series 18. Nashville: Abingdon.
Hayles, D. J.
1973   "The Roman Census and Jesus' Birth: Was Luke Correct?, part 1: The Roman Census System." *Buried History* 9:113–32.
1974   "The Roman Census and Jesus' Birth: Was Luke Correct?, part 2: Quirinius' Career and a Census in Herod's Day." *Buried History* 10:16–31.
Hays, R. B.
1994   "The Corrected Jesus[: Review of *The Five Gospels* by R. W. Funk and R. W. Hoover]." *First Things* 43:43–48.
Heard, W.
1988   "Luke's Attitude toward the Rich and the Poor." *Trinity Journal* n.s. 9:47–80.
Heater, H.
1986   "A Textual Note on Luke 3.33." *Journal for the Study of the New Testament* 28:25–29.
Hemer, C. J.
1989   *The Book of Acts in the Setting of Hellenistic History*. Edited by C. H. Gempf. Wissenschaftliche Untersuchungen zum Neuen Testament 49. Tübingen: Mohr.
Hendriksen, W.
1973   *Exposition of the Gospel according to Matthew*. New Testament Commentary. Grand Rapids: Baker.
1975   *Exposition of the Gospel according to Mark*. New Testament Commentary. Grand Rapids: Baker.
1978   *Exposition of the Gospel according to Luke*. New Testament Commentary. Grand Rapids: Baker.
Hengel, M.
1961   *Die Zeloten: Untersuchungen zur jüdischen Freiheitsbewegung in der Zeit von Herodes I. bis 70 n. Chr.* Arbeiten zur Geschichte des Spätjudentums und Urchristentums 1. Leiden: Brill.
1963   "Maria Magdalena und die Frauen als Zeugen." Pp. 243–56 *Abraham unser Vater: Juden und Christen im Gespräch über die Bibel: Festschrift für Otto Michel zum 60. Geburtstag*. Edited by O. Betz, M. Hengel, and P. Schmidt. Arbeiten zur Geschichte des Spätjudentums und Urchristentums 5. Leiden: Brill.
1968   "Das Gleichnis von den Weingärtnern Mc 12,1–12 im Lichte der Zenonpapyri und der rabbinischen Gleichnisse." *Zeitschrift für die Neutestamentliche Wissenschaft* 59:1–39.
1977   *Crucifixion in the Ancient World and the Folly of the Message of the Cross*. Translated by J. Bowden. Philadelphia: Fortress/London: SCM.
1980   *Acts and the History of Earliest Christianity*. Translated by J. S. Bowden. Philadelphia: Fortress/London: SCM.
1981   *The Charismatic Leader and His Followers*. Translated by J. Greig. Edinburgh: Clark/New York: Crossroad.
Hengel, R., and M. Hengel
1959   "Die Heilungen Jesu und medizinisches Denken." Pp. 331–61 in *Medicus Viator: Fragen und Gedanken am Wege Richard Siebecks*. Tübingen: Mohr/Stuttgart: Thieme.
Herrenbrück, F.
1981   "Wer waren die 'Zöllner'?" *Zeitschrift für die Neutestamentliche Wissenschaft* 72:178–94.
Herrmann, W.
1907   *Die sittlichen Weisungen Jesu: Ihr Mißbrauch und ihr richtiger Gebrauch*. 2d edition. Göttingen: Vandenhoeck & Ruprecht.

Hesse, F.
1955   *Das Verstockungsproblem im Alten Testament: Eine frömmigkeitsgeschichtliche Untersuchung*. Beiheft zur Zeitschrift für die Alttestamentliche Wissenschaft 74. Berlin: Töpelmann.

Heth, W. A., and G. J. Wenham
1984   *Jesus and Divorce: The Problem with the Evangelical Consensus*. London: Hodder & Stoughton/Nashville: Nelson.

Heutger, N.
1983   "Münzen im Lukasevangelium." *Biblische Zeitschrift* 27:97–101.

Hewitt, J. W.
1932   "The Use of Nails in the Crucifixion." *Harvard Theological Review* 25:29–45.

Hiers, R. H.
1973–74 "The Problem of the Delay of the Parousia in Luke–Acts." *New Testament Studies* 20:145–55.

Higgins, A. J. B.
1969   "Sidelights on Christian Beginnings in the Graeco-Roman World." *Evangelical Quarterly* 41:197–206.

Hill, D.
1971   "The Rejection of Jesus at Nazareth (Luke iv 16–30)." *Novum Testamentum* 13:161–80.
1972   *The Gospel of Matthew*. New Century Bible. Grand Rapids: Eerdmans/London: Marshall, Morgan & Scott.
1973–74 "On the Evidence for the Creative Role of Christian Prophets." *New Testament Studies* 20:262–74.

Hobart, W. K.
1882   *The Medical Language of St. Luke*. Dublin: Hodges, Figgis. Reprinted Grand Rapids: Baker, 1954.

Hock, R. F.
1987   "Lazarus and Micyllus: Greco-Roman Backgrounds to Luke 16:19–31." *Journal of Biblical Literature* 106:447–63.

Hoehner, H. W.
1970   "Why Did Pilate Hand Jesus over to Antipas?" Pp. 84–90 in *The Trial of Jesus: Cambridge Studies in Honour of C. F. D. Moule*. Edited by E. Bammel. Studies in Biblical Theology 2/13. London: SCM/Naperville, Ill.: Allenson.
1972   *Herod Antipas*. Society for New Testament Studies Monograph Series 17. Cambridge: Cambridge University Press.
1977   *Chronological Aspects of the Life of Christ*. Grand Rapids: Zondervan.
1987   "A Response to Divorce and Remarriage." Pp. 240–46 in *Applying the Scriptures: Papers from ICBI Summit III*. Edited by K. S. Kantzer. Grand Rapids: Zondervan.

Hoffmann, P.
1967   "Πάντες Ἐργάται Ἀδικίας: Redaktion und Tradition in Lc 13:22–30." *Zeitschrift für die Neutestamentliche Wissenschaft* 58:188–214.
1970   "Die Offenbarung des Sohnes: Die apokalyptischen Voraussetzungen und ihre Verarbeitung im Q-Logion Mt 11,27 par. Lk 10,22." *Kairos* 12:270–88.

Hofius, O.
1977–78 "Alttestamentliche Motive in Gleichnis vom verlorenen Sohn." *New Testament Studies* 24:240–48.

Holmes, M. W.
1983   "The 'Majority Text Debate': New Form of an Old Issue." *Themelios* 8/2:13–19.
1989   "New Testament Textual Criticism." Pp. 53–74 in *Introducing New Testament Interpretation*. Edited by S. McKnight. Guides to New Testament Exegesis 1. Grand Rapids: Baker.

Holtz, T.
1968   *Untersuchungen über die alttestamentlichen Zitate bei Lukas*. Texte und Untersuchungen 104. Berlin: Akademie-Verlag.

Holzmeister, U.
1938   "Exempla Sudoris Sanguinei (Lc. 22,44)." *Verbum Domini* 18:73–81.
Hooker, M. D.
1967   *The Son of Man in Mark: A Study of the Background of the Term "Son of Man" and Its Use in St. Mark's Gospel*. London: SPCK.
Horowitz, G.
1953   *The Spirit of Jewish Law: A Brief Account of Biblical and Rabbinical Jurisprudence, with a Special Note on Jewish Law and the State of Israel*. New York: Central Book.
Horsley, R. A.
1987   *Jesus and the Spiral of Violence: Popular Jewish Resistance in Roman Palestine*. San Francisco: Harper & Row.
Hort, F. J. A.
1908–9   "A Note . . . on the Words Κόφινος, Σπυρίς, Σαργάνη." *Journal of Theological Studies* o.s. 10:567–71.
Hospodar, B.
1956   "*Meta Spoudes* in Lk 1,39." *Catholic Biblical Quarterly* 18:14–18.
House, H. W. (ed.)
1990   *Divorce and Remarriage: Four Christian Views*. Downers Grove, Ill.: InterVarsity.
Howard, V.
1977   "Did Jesus Speak about His Own Death?" *Catholic Biblical Quarterly* 39:515–27.
Hubbard, B. J.
1977   "Commissioning Stories in Luke–Acts: A Study of Their Antecedents, Form and Content." *Semeia* 8:103–26.
Huck, A., and H. Lietzmann
1936   *A Synopsis of the First Three Gospels*. 9th edition revised by H. Lietzmann. English edition prepared by F. L. Cross. Tübingen: Mohr.
Hull, J. M.
1974   *Hellenistic Magic and the Synoptic Tradition*. Studies in Biblical Theology 2/28. London: SCM/Naperville, Ill.: Allenson.
Hunter, A. M.
1965   *A Pattern for Life, An Exposition of the Sermon on the Mount: Its Making, Its Exegesis and Its Meaning*. Philadelphia: Westminster.
Hyldahl, N.
1961   "Die Versuchung auf der Zinne des Tempels (Matth 4,5–7 ≠ Luk 4,9–12)." *Studia Theologica* 15:113–27.
Ireland, D. J.
1989   "A History of Recent Interpretation of the Parable of the Unjust Steward (Luke 16:1–13)." *Westminster Theological Journal* 51:293–318.
1992   *Stewardship and the Kingdom of God: An Historical, Exegetical, and Contextual Study of the Parable of the Unjust Steward in Luke 16:1–13*. Novum Testamentum Supplement 70. Leiden: Brill.
Isaac, E.
1981   "Another Note on Luke 6:1." *Journal of Biblical Literature* 100:96–97.
ISBE   *The International Standard Bible Encyclopedia*. Edited by G. W. Bromiley et al. 4 vols. Grand Rapids: Eerdmans, 1979–88.
James, M. R.
1953   *The Apocryphal New Testament*. Corrected edition. Oxford: Clarendon.
Jarvis, P. G.
1965–66 "The Tower-Builder and the King Going to War (Luke 14$^{25-33}$)." *Expository Times* 77:196–98.
Jaschke, H.
1971   "'Λαλεῖν' bei Lukas: Ein Beitrag zur lukanischen Theologie." *Biblische Zeitschrift* 15:109–14.

Jastrow, M.
1903   *A Dictionary of the Targumim, the Talmud Babli and Yerushalmi, and the Midrashic Literature.* London: Trübner/New York: Putnam. Reprinted New York: Judaica, 1950.

Jaubert, A.
1965   *The Date of the Last Supper.* Translated by I. Rafferty. Staten Island, N.Y.: Alba.

Jellicoe, S.
1959–60 "St Luke and the 'Seventy(-two).'" *New Testament Studies* 6:319–21.

Jeremias, J.
1926a   "Das Gebetsleben Jesu." *Zeitschrift für die Neutestamentliche Wissenschaft* 25:123–40.

1926b   *Golgotha.* Ἄγγελος: Archiv für Neutestamentliche Zeitgeschichte und Kulturkunde 1. Leipzig: Pfeiffer.

1929a   "Ἄνθρωποι Εὐδοκίας (Lc 2:14)." *Zeitschrift für die Neutestamentliche Wissenschaft* 28:13–20.

1929b   "Der Ursprung der Johannestaufe." *Zeitschrift für die Neutestamentliche Wissenschaft* 28:312–20.

1931   "Zöllner und Sünder." *Zeitschrift für die Neutestamentliche Wissenschaft* 30:293–300.

1936   "Die 'Zinne' des Tempels (Mt. 4,5; Lk. 4,9)." *Zeitschrift des Deutschen Palätina-Vereins* 59:195–208.

1949   "Proselytentaufe und Neues Testament." *Theologische Zeitschrift* 5:418–28.

1958a   *Heiligengräber in Jesu Umwelt (Mt. 23,29; Lk. 11,47): Eine Untersuchung zur Volksreligion der Zeit Jesu.* Göttingen: Vandenhoeck & Ruprecht.

1958b   *Jesus' Promise to the Nations.* Translated by S. H. Hooke. Franz Delitzsch Lectures 1953. Studies in Biblical Theology 24. London: SCM/Naperville, Ill.: Allenson.

1959   "Paarweise Sendung im Neuen Testament." Pp. 136–43 in *New Testament Essays: Studies in Memory of Thomas Walter Manson.* Edited by A. J. B. Higgins. Manchester: Manchester University Press. Reprinted in Jeremias's *Abba: Studien zur neutestamentlichen Theologie und Zeitgeschichte*, pp. 132–39. Göttingen: Vandenhoeck & Ruprecht, 1966.

1960a   *Infant Baptism in the First Four Centuries.* Translated by D. Cairns. Library of History and Doctrine. London: SCM/Philadelphia: Westminster.

1960b   "Lukas 7,45: Εἰσῆλθον." *Zeitschrift für die Neutestamentliche Wissenschaft* 51:131.

1961   "Drei weitere spätjüdische Heiligengräber." *Zeitschrift für die Neutestamentliche Wissenschaft* 52:95–101.

1963a   *The Parables of Jesus.* Translated by S. H. Hooke. Revised edition. New Testament Library. Philadelphia: Westminster/London: SCM.

1963b   *The Sermon on the Mount.* Translated by N. Perrin. Facet Books, Biblical Series 2. Philadelphia: Fortress. (British edition: London: Athlone, 1961.)

1966   *The Eucharistic Words of Jesus.* 2d edition. Translated by N. Perrin. New Testament Library. London: SCM/New York: Scribner.

1966–67 "Palästinakundliches zum Gleichnis vom Säemann (Mark iv.3–8 par.)." *New Testament Studies* 13:48–53.

1967a   "Die älteste Schicht der Menschensohn-Logien." *Zeitschrift für die Neutestamentliche Wissenschaft* 58:159–72.

1967b   *The Prayers of Jesus.* Translated by J. Bowden, C. Burchard, and J. Reumann. Studies in Biblical Theology 2/6. London: SCM.

1969   *Jerusalem in the Time of Jesus: An Investigation into Economic and Social Conditions during the New Testament Period.* Translated by F. H. Cave and C. H. Cave. London: SCM/Philadelphia: Fortress.

1971a   *New Testament Theology: The Proclamation of Jesus.* Translated by J. Bowden. New Testament Library. London: SCM/New York: Scribner.

1971b   "Tradition und Redaktion in Lukas 15." *Zeitschrift für die Neutestamentliche Wissenschaft* 62:172–89.

1980   *Die Sprache des Lukasevangeliums: Redaktion und Tradition im Nicht-Markusstoff des dritten Evangeliums*. Kritisch-exegetischer Kommentar über das Neue Testament, Sonderband. Göttingen: Vandenhoeck & Ruprecht.

Jervell, J.
1972   *Luke and the People of God: A New Look at Luke–Acts*. Minneapolis: Augsburg.

John, M. P.
1975   "Luke 2.36–37: How Old Was Anna?" *Bible Translator* 26:247.

Johnson, A. F.
1979   "Assurance for Man: The Fallacy of Translating *Anaideia* by 'Persistence' in Luke 11:5–8." *Journal of the Evangelical Theological Society* 22:123–31.

Johnson, L. T.
1977   *The Literary Function of Possessions in Luke–Acts*. Society of Biblical Literature Dissertation Series 39. Missoula, Mont.: Scholars Press.
1991   *The Gospel of Luke*. Sacra Pagina 3. Collegeville, Minn.: Liturgical Press.

Johnson, M. D.
1988   *The Purpose of Biblical Genealogies, with Special Reference to the Setting of the Genealogies of Jesus*. 2d edition. Society for New Testament Studies Monograph Series 8. Cambridge: Cambridge University Press.

Johnson, S. E.
1935   "A Note on Luke 13:1–5." *Anglican Theological Review* 17:91–95.

Jones, D. R.
1968   "The Background and Character of the Lukan Psalms." *Journal of Theological Studies* n.s. 19:19–50.

Joüon, P.
1939   "La Parabole des Mines (Luc, 19,12–27) et la Parabole des Talents (Matthieu, 25,14–30)." *Recherches de Science Religieuse* 29:489–94.

Juel, D.
1977   *Messiah and Temple: The Trial of Jesus in the Gospel of Mark*. Society of Biblical Literature Dissertation Series 31. Missoula, Mont.: Scholars Press.

Jülicher, A.
1899   *Die Gleichnisreden Jesu*. 2 vols. 2d edition. Freiburg im Breisgau: Mohr. Reprinted 1960.

Karris, R. J.
1977   *Invitation to Luke: A Commentary on the Gospel of Luke with Complete Text from the Jerusalem Bible*. Garden City, N.Y.: Doubleday.

Käser, W.
1963   "Exegetische und theologische Erwägungen zur Seligpreisung der Kinderlosen Lc 23:29b." *Zeitschrift für die Neutestamentliche Wissenschaft* 54:240–54.
1968   "Exegetische Erwägungen zur Seligpreisung des Sabbatarbeiters Lk 6,5 D." *Zeitschrift für Theologie und Kirche* 65:414–30.

Keck, L. E.
1965   "The Poor among the Saints in the New Testament." *Zeitschrift für die Neutestamentliche Wissenschaft* 56:100–29.
1970–71 "The Spirit and the Dove." *New Testament Studies* 17:41–67.

Kee, H. C.
1967–68 "The Terminology of Mark's Exorcism Stories." *New Testament Studies* 14:232–46.

Keen, W. W.
1892   "The Bloody Sweat of Our Lord." *Baptist Quarterly Review* 14:169–75.
1897   "Further Studies on the Bloody Sweat of Our Lord." *Bibliotheca Sacra* 54:469–83.

Kelly, H. A.
1964   "The Devil in the Desert." *Catholic Biblical Quarterly* 26:190–220.

Kelly, W.
1943   *Lectures on the Gospel of Matthew*. Revised edition. New York: Loizeaux.

Kelso, J. L.
1962   "House." Pp. 544–46 in *The New Bible Dictionary*. Edited by J. D. Douglas. Grand Rapids: Eerdmans.

Kenyon, F. G., and H. I. Bell
1907   *Greek Papyri in the British Museum*, vol. 3. London: British Museum.
Kerr, A. J.
1986–87   "Zacchaeus's Decision to Make Fourfold Restitution." *Expository Times* 98:68–71.
Kertelge, K.
1970   *Die Wunder Jesu im Markusevangelium: Eine redaktionsgeschichtliche Untersuchung.* Studien zum Alten und Neuen Testament 23. Munich: Kösel.
Kik, J. M.
1971   *The Eschatology of Victory.* Phillipsburg, N.J.: Presbyterian & Reformed.
Kilgallen, J. J.
1982   "What Kind of Servants Are We? (Luke 17,10)." *Biblica* 63:549–551.
Kilpatrick, G. D.
1942   "A Theme of the Lucan Passion Story and Luke xxiii.47." *Journal of Theological Studies* o.s. 43:34–36.
1943   "Western Text and Original Text in the Gospels and Acts." *Journal of Theological Studies* n.s. 44:24–36.
1965a   "The Greek New Testament Text of Today and the *Textus Receptus*." Pp. 189–208 in *The New Testament in Historical and Contemporary Perspective: Essays in Memory of G. H. C. Macgregor.* Edited by H. Anderson and W. Barclay. Oxford: Blackwell.
1965b   "Λαοί at Luke ii.31 and Acts iv.25, 27." *Journal of Theological Studies* n.s. 16:127.
1969   "Some Problems in New Testament Text and Language." Pp. 198–208 in *Neotestamentica et Semitica: Studies in Honour of Matthew Black.* Edited by E. E. Ellis and M. Wilcox. Edinburgh: Clark.
Kim, C.-H.
1975   "The Papyrus Invitation." *Journal of Biblical Literature* 94:391–402.
Kim, S.
1985   *"The 'Son of Man'" as Son of God.* Grand Rapids: Eerdmans. (European edition: Tübingen: Mohr, 1983.)
Kimball, C. A.
1994   *Jesus' Exposition of the Old Testament in Luke's Gospel.* Journal for the Study of the New Testament Supplement 94. Sheffield: JSOT Press.
Kinman, B.
1991   "Pilate's Assize and the Timing of Jesus' Trial." *Tyndale Bulletin* 42:282–95.
1993   *The "A-triumphal" Entry (Luke 19:28–48): Historical Backgrounds, Theological Motifs, and the Purpose of Luke.* Th.D. thesis, University of Cambridge.
Kirk, J. A.
1972   "The Messianic Role of Jesus and the Temptation Narrative: A Contemporary Perspective (Concluded)." *Evangelical Quarterly* 44:91–102.
Kissinger, W. S.
1975   *The Sermon on the Mount: A History of Interpretation and Bibliography.* American Theological Library Association Bibliography Series 3. Metuchen, N.J.: Scarecrow/ATLA.
1979   *The Parables of Jesus: A History of Interpretation and Bibliography.* American Theological Library Association Bibliography Series 4. Metuchen, N.J.: Scarecrow/ATLA.
Kistemaker, S. J.
1980   *The Parables of Jesus.* Grand Rapids: Baker.
Kittel, G.
1925   "Die Bergpredigt und die Ethik des Judentums." *Zeitschrift für systematische Theologie* 2:555–94.
Klassen, W.
1980–81   "'A Child of Peace' (Luke 10.6) in First Century Context." *New Testament Studies* 27:488–506.
Klauck, H.-J.
1978   *Allegorie und Allegorese in synoptischen Gleichnistexten.* Neutestamentliche Abhandlungen n.s. 13. Münster: Aschendorff.

1981   "Die Frage der Sündenvergebung in der Perikope von der Heilung des Gelähmten (Mk 2,1–12 parr)." *Biblische Zeitschrift* 25:223–48.

Klausner, J.
1925   *Jesus of Nazareth: His Life, Times, and Teaching*. Translated by H. Danby. New York: Macmillan.

Klein, G.
1974   "Lukas 1,1–4 als theologisches Programm." Pp. 170–203 in *Das Lukas-Evangelium: Die redaktionsgeschichtliche und kompositionsgeschichtliche Forschung*. Edited by G. Braumann. Wege der Forschung 280. Darmstadt: Wissenschaftliche Buchgesell-schaft. Originally published in *Zeit und Geschichte: Dankesgabe an Rudolf Bultmann zum 80. Geburtstag*, pp. 193–216. Edited by E. Dinkler. Tübingen: Mohr, 1964. Re-printed in Klein's *Rekonstruktion und Interpretation: Gesammelte Aufsätze zum Neuen Testament*, pp. 237–61. Beiträge zur evangelischen Theologie 50. Munich: Kaiser, 1969.

Klemm, K. G.
1969–70   "Das Wort von der Selbstbestattung der Toten: Beobachtungen zur Auslegungsge-schichte von Mt. viii.22 Par." *New Testament Studies* 16:60–75.

Kloppenborg, J. S.
1978   "Wisdom Christology in Q." *Laval Théologique et Philosophique* 34:129–47.
1987   *The Formation of Q: Trajectories in Ancient Wisdom Collections*. Studies in Antiquity and Christianity. Philadelphia: Fortress.
1988   *Q Parallels: Synopsis, Critical Notes, and Concordance*. Foundations and Facets Reference Series. Sonoma, Calif.: Polebridge.

Klostermann, E.
1929   *Das Lukasevangelium*. Handbuch zum Neuen Testament 5. Tübingen: Mohr. Re-printed 1975.

Knox, J.
1942   *Marcion and the New Testament: An Essay in the Early History of the Canon*. Chicago: University of Chicago Press.

Koch, K.
1969   *The Growth of the Biblical Tradition: The Form-Critical Method*. Translated by S. M. Cupitt. New York: Scribner.

Kodell, J.
1969   "Luke's Use of *Laos*, 'People,' Especially in the Jerusalem Narrative (Lk 19,28–24,53)." *Catholic Biblical Quarterly* 31:327–43.

Koet, B. J.
1989   *Five Studies on Interpretation of Scripture in Luke–Acts*. Studiorum Novi Testamenti Auxilia 14. Louvain: Leuven University Press.

Köppen, K.-P.
1961   *Die Auslegung der Versuchungsgeschichte unter besonderer Berücksichtigung der Alten Kirche: Ein Beitrage zur Geschichte der Schriftauslegung*. Beiträge zur Geschichte der biblischen Exegese 4. Tübingen: Mohr.

Kosmala, H.
1963–68   "The Time of the Cock-Crow." *Annual of the Swedish Theological Institute* 2:118–20; 6:132–34.
1965   "The Three Nets of Belial: A Study in the Terminology of Qumran and the New Testament." *Annual of the Swedish Theological Institute* 4:91–113.

Kossen, H. B.
1956   "Quelques Remarques sur l'Ordre des Paraboles dans Luc xv et sur la Structure de Matthieu xviii 8–14." *Novum Testamentum* 1:75–80.

Krämer, M.
1972   *Das Rätsel der Parabel vom ungerechten Verwalter, Lk 16,1–13: Auslegungsgeschichte-Umfang-Sinn: Eine Diskussion der Probleme und Lösungsvorschläge der Verwalter-parabel von den Vätern bis heute*. Biblioteca di Scienze Religiose 5. Zurich: PAS.

Kraus, H.-J.
1989   *Psalms 60–150: A Commentary*. Translated by H. C. Oswald. Continental Commentaries. Minneapolis: Fortress.

Kremer, J.
1979   "Auferstanden-auferweckt." *Biblische Zeitschrift* 23:97–98.

Kuhn, G.
1923   "Die Geschlechtsregister Jesu bei Lukas und Matthäus, nach ihrer Herkunft untersucht." *Zeitschrift für die Neutestamentliche Wissenschaft* 22:206–28.

Kuhn, K. G.
1950   *Achtzehngebet und Vaterunser und der Reim*. Wissenschaftliche Untersuchungen zum Neuen Testament 1. Tübingen: Mohr.

Kümmel, W. G.
1950   "Das Gleichnis von den bösen Weingärtnern (Mark 12.1–9)." Pp. 120–31 in *Aux Sources de la Tradition Chrétienne: Mélanges Offert à M. Maurice Goguel*. Neuchâtel/Paris: Delachaux & Niestlé.
1957   *Promise and Fulfilment: The Eschatological Message of Jesus*. Translated by D. M. Barton. Studies in Biblical Theology 23. London: SCM/Naperville, Ill.: Allenson.
1975   *Introduction to the New Testament*. Revised edition. Translated by H. C. Kee. Nashville: Abingdon.

Kurz, W. S.
1985   "Luke 22:14–38 and Greco-Roman and Biblical Farewell Addresses." *Journal of Biblical Literature* 104:251–68.

Kürzinger, J.
1974   "Lk 1,3: . . . Ἀκριβῶς Καθεξῆς Σοι Γράψαι." *Biblische Zeitschrift* 18:249–55.

Lachs, S. T.
1987   *A Rabbinic Commentary on the New Testament: The Gospels of Matthew, Mark, and Luke*. New York: Ktav.

Ladd, G. E.
1962   "The Kingdom of God—Reign or Realm?" *Journal of Biblical Literature* 81:230–38.
1974a   *The Presence of the Future: The Eschatology of Biblical Realism*. Grand Rapids: Eerdmans.
1974b   *A Theology of the New Testament*. Grand Rapids: Eerdmans.

Lagrange, M. J.
1921   *Évangile selon Saint Luc*. 2d edition. Paris: Gabalda.

Lake, K.
1907   *The Historical Evidence for the Resurrection of Jesus Christ*. London: Williams & Norgate/New York: Putnam.
1910   "Christmas." Vol. 3 / pp. 601–8 in *Encyclopaedia of Religion and Ethics*. Edited by J. Hastings. Edinburgh: Clark/New York: Scribner.

Lambert, W. G.
1960   *Babylonian Wisdom Literature*. Oxford: Clarendon.

Lambrecht, J.
1967   *Die Redaktion der Markus-Apokalypse: Literarische Analyse und Strukturuntersuchung*. Analecta Biblica 28. Rome: Pontifical Biblical Institute Press.

Lane, W. L.
1974   *The Gospel according to Mark*. New International Commentary on the New Testament. Grand Rapids: Eerdmans.

La Potterie, I. de
1970   "Le Titre Κύριος Appliqué à Jésus dans l'Évangile du Luc." Pp. 117–46 in *Mélanges Bibliques en Hommage au R. P. Béda Rigaux*. Edited by A. Descamps and A. de Halleux. Gembloux: Duculot.

LaSor, W. S.
1972   *The Dead Sea Scrolls and the New Testament*. Grand Rapids: Eerdmans.

Lattke, M.
1984   "On the Jewish Background of the Synoptic Concept 'The Kingdom of God.'" Translated by M. Rutter. Pp. 72–91 in *The Kingdom of God in the Teaching of Jesus*. Edited

by B. Chilton. Issues in Religion and Theology 5. Philadelphia: Fortress/London: SPCK.

Laufen, R.
1980   *Die Doppelüberlieferungen der Logienquelle und des Markus-Evangeliums.* Bonner biblische Beiträge 54. Königstein-Ts./Bonn: Hanstein.

Laurentin, R.
1957a   *Structure et Théologie de Luc I–II.* Paris: Gabalda.
1957b   "Traces d'Allusions Étymologiques en Luc 1–2, [part] II." *Biblica* 38:1–23.
1967   *Struktur und Theologie der lukanischen Kindheitsgeschichte.* Translated by P. W. Arnold. Stuttgart: Katholisches Bibelwerk.

Lauterbach, J. Z.
1933–35   *Mekilta de-Rabbi Ishmael.* 3 vols. Philadelphia: Jewish Publication Society.

Leaney, A. R. C.
1955–56   "The Resurrection Narratives in Luke (xxiv.12–53)." *New Testament Studies* 2:110–14.
1958   *A Commentary on the Gospel according to St. Luke.* Harper's (Black's) New Testament Commentaries. New York: Harper/London: Black.
1961–62   "The Birth Narratives in St Luke and St Matthew." *New Testament Studies* 8:155–66.

Lee, G. M.
1970–71   "The Story of the Widow's Mite." *Expository Times* 82:344.

Légasse, S.
1969   *Jésus et l'Enfant: "Enfants," "Petits" et "Simples" dans la Tradition Synoptique.* Études Bibliques. Paris: Gabalda.

Legault, A.
1954   "An Application of the Form-Critique Method to the Anointings in Galilee (Lk. 7,36–50) and Bethany (Mt. 26,6–13; Mk. 14,3–9; Jn. 12,1–8)." *Catholic Biblical Quarterly* 16:131–45.

Leipoldt, J.
1955   *Die Frau in der antiken Welt und im Urchristentum.* 2d edition. Leipzig: Koehler & Amelang.

Leisegang, H.
1922   *Pneuma Hagion: Der Ursprung des Geistbegriffs der synoptischen Evangelien aus der griechischen Mystik.* Veröffentlichungen des Forschungsinstituts für vergleichende Religionsgeschichte an der Universität Leipzig 4. Leipzig: Hinrichs.

Lentzen-Deis, F.
1970   *Die Taufe Jesus nach den Synoptikern: Literarkritische und gattungsgeschichtliche Untersuchungen.* Frankfurter Theologische Studien 4. Frankfurt am Main: Knecht.

Lerner, M. B.
1987   "The External Tractates." Pp. 367–403 in *The Literature of the Sages,* vol. 1: *Oral Tora, Halakha, Mishna, Tosefta, Talmud, External Tractates.* Edited by S. Safrai. Compendia Rerum Iudaicarum ad Novum Testamentum 2/3. Philadelphia: Fortress/Assen: Van Gorcum.

Levey, S. H.
1974   *The Messiah: An Aramaic Interpretation: The Messianic Exegesis of the Targum.* Cincinnati: Hebrew Union College—Jewish Institute of Religion.

Liefeld, W. L.
1974   "Theological Motifs in the Transfiguration Narrative." Pp. 162–79 in *New Dimensions in New Testament Study.* Edited by R. N. Longenecker and M. C. Tenney. Grand Rapids: Zondervan.
1984   "Luke." Vol. 8 / pp. 797–1059 in *The Expositor's Bible Commentary.* Edited by F. E. Gaebelein. Grand Rapids: Zondervan.

Lightfoot, J. B.
1889–90   *The Apostolic Fathers.* 5 vols. in 2 parts. London: Macmillan. Reprinted Grand Rapids: Baker, 1981.
1890   "The Brethren of the Lord." Pp. 252–91 in *Saint Paul's Epistle to the Galatians.* 10th edition. London: Macmillan.

Lindars, B.
1983 *Jesus Son of Man: A Fresh Examination of the Son of Man Sayings in the Gospels in the Light of Recent Research.* London: SPCK.

Linnemann, E.
1966 *Jesus of the Parables: Introduction and Exposition.* Translated by J. Sturdy. New York: Harper & Row. (British edition: *The Parables of Jesus: Introduction and Exposition.* London: SPCK.)

Linton, O.
1975–76 "The Parable of the Children's Game: Baptist and Son of Man (Matt. xi.16–19 = Luke vii.31–5): A Synoptic Text-Critical, Structural and Exegetical Investigation." *New Testament Studies* 22:159–79.

Ljungvik, H.
1963–64 "Zur Erklärung einer Lukas-Stelle (Luk. xviii.7)." *New Testament Studies* 10:289–94.

Loader, W. R. G.
1977–78 "Christ at the Right Hand—Ps. cx.1 in the New Testament." *New Testament Studies* 24:199–217.

Loewe, W. P.
1974 "Towards an Interpretation of Lk 19:1–10." *Catholic Biblical Quarterly* 36:321–31.

Lohfink, G.
1971 *Die Himmelfahrt Jesu: Untersuchungen zu den Himmelfahrts- und Erhöhungstexten bei Lukas.* Studien zum Alten und Neuen Testament 26. Munich: Kösel.
1975 "'Ich habe gesündigt gegen den Himmel und gegen dich': Eine Exegese von Lk 15,18.21." *Theologische Quartalschrift* 155:51–52.

Lohmeyer, E.
1959 *Das Evangelium des Markus.* Meyers kritisch-exegetischer Kommentar über das Neue Testament 1/2. Göttingen: Vandenhoeck & Ruprecht.

Lohse, E.
1960 "Jesu Worte über den Sabbat." Pp. 79–89 in *Judentum-Urchristentum-Kirche: Festschrift für Joachim Jeremias.* Edited by W. Eltester. Beiheft zur Zeitschrift für die Neutestamentliche Wissenschaft 26. Berlin: Töpelmann.

Loisy, A.
1924 *L'Évangile selon Luc.* Paris: Nourry.

Longenecker, R. N.
1970 *The Christology of Early Jewish Christianity.* Studies in Biblical Theology 2/17. London: SCM/Naperville, Ill.: Allenson.

Löning, K.
1971 "Ein Platz für die Verlorenen: Zur Formkritik zweier neutestamentlicher Legenden (Lk 7,36–50; 19,1–10)." *Bibel und Leben* 12:198–208.

Lorenzen, T.
1975–76 "A Biblical Meditation on Luke 16[19–31]." *Expository Times* 87:39–43.

Lövestam, E.
1968 *Spiritus Blasphemia: Eine Studie zu Mk 3,28f par Mt 12,31f, Lk 12,10.* Scripta Minora Regiae Societatis Humaniorum Litterarum Lundensis 1966–67/1. Lund: Gleerup.

LSJ *A Greek-English Lexicon.* 9th edition. By H. G. Liddell, R. Scott, and H. S. Jones. Oxford: Clarendon, 1968.

Luce, H. K.
1933 *The Gospel according to S. Luke.* Cambridge Greek Testament for Schools and Colleges. Cambridge: Cambridge University Press.

Lührmann, D.
1969 *Die Redaktion der Logienquelle.* Wissenschaftliche Monographien zum Alten und Neuen Testament 33. Neukirchen-Vluyn: Neukirchener Verlag.

Lundström, G.
1963 *The Kingdom of God in the Teaching of Jesus: A History of Interpretation from the Last Decades of the Nineteenth Century to the Present Day.* Translated by J. Bulman. Edinburgh: Oliver & Boyd.

Luther, M.
  1956   "The Sermon on the Mount." Translated by J. Pelikan. Pp. 1–294 in *Luther's Works*, vol. 21: *The Sermon on the Mount (Sermons) and the Magnificat*. Edited by J. Pelikan. St. Louis: Concordia. Originally 1530–32. Reprinted as "Wochenpredigten über Matth. 5–7" in *D. Martin Luthers Werke: Kritische Gesamtausgabe*, vol. 32 / pp. 299–544. Weimer: Böhlaus, 1906.

McArthur, H. K.
  1959–60 "The Dependence of the Gospel of Thomas on the Synoptics." *Expository Times* 71:286–87.
  1960   *Understanding the Sermon on the Mount*. New York: Harper.

Maccoby, H.
  1982   "The Washing of Cups." *Journal for the Study of the New Testament* 14:3–15.

McCulloch, W.
  1911–12 "The Pounds and the Talents." *Expository Times* 23:382–83.

MacDonald, D.
  1898–99 "Malchus' Ear." *Expository Times* 10:188.

McGaughy, L. C.
  1975   "The Fear of Yahweh and the Mission of Judaism: A Postexilic Maxim and Its Early Christian Expansion in the Parable of the Talents." *Journal of Biblical Literature* 94:235–45.

Machen, J. G.
  1930   *The Virgin Birth*. New York: Harper. Reprinted Grand Rapids: Baker, 1965.

McHugh, J.
  1975   *The Mother of Jesus in the New Testament*. Garden City: Doubleday/London: Darton, Longman & Todd.

McKelvey, R. J.
  1969   *The New Temple: The Church in the New Testament*. Oxford Theological Monographs. Oxford: Oxford University Press.

McKnight, S.
  1991a   *A Light among the Gentiles: Jewish Missionary Activity in the Second Temple Period*. Minneapolis: Fortress.
  1991b   "Source Criticism." Pp. 135–72 in *New Testament Criticism and Interpretation*. Edited by D. A. Black and D. S. Dockery. Grand Rapids: Zondervan.

Mackowski, R. M.
  1980   "Where is Biblical Emmaus?" *Science et Esprit* 32:93–103.

MacLaurin, E. C. B.
  1978   "Beelzeboul." *Novum Testamentum* 20:156–60.

McNeile, A. H.
  1915   *The Gospel according to St. Matthew: The Greek Text with Introduction, Notes and Indices*. London: Macmillan. Reprinted Grand Rapids: Baker, 1980.

Maddox, R.
  1982   *The Purpose of Luke–Acts*. Forschungen zur Religion und Literatur des Alten und Neuen Testaments 126. Göttingen: Vandenhoeck & Ruprecht. Reprinted Edinburgh: Clark, 1982.

Mahoney, M.
  1980   "Luke 21:14–15: Editorial Rewriting or Authenticity?" *Irish Theological Quarterly* 47:220–38.

Mahoney, R.
  1974   *Two Disciples at the Tomb: The Background and Message of John 20.1–10*. Theologie und Wirklichkeit 6. Frankfurt am Main: Lang.

Major, H. D. A.
  1944   *Basic Christianity*. Oxford: Blackwell.

Malina, B. J., and J. H. Neyrey
  1991   "Honor and Shame in Luke–Acts: Pivotal Values of the Mediterranean World." Pp. 25–65 in *The Social World of Luke–Acts: Models for Interpretation*. Edited by J. H. Neyrey. Peabody, Mass.: Hendrickson.

Mánek, J.
1957–58a "Fishers of Men." *Novum Testamentum* 2:138–41.
1957–58b "The New Exodus in the Books of Luke." *Novum Testamentum* 2:8–23.
1967 "On the Mount—On the Plain (Mt. v 1—Lk. vi 17)." *Novum Testamentum* 9:124–31.

Mann, J., and I. Sonne
1940 *The Bible as Read and Preached in the Old Synagogue: A Study in the Cycles of the Readings from Torah and Prophets, as well as from Psalms, and in the Structure of the Midrashic Homilies*, vol. 1: *The Palestinian Triennial Cycle: Genesis and Exodus*. Cincinnati: Hebrew Union College, 1940. Reprinted New York: Ktav, 1971.

Manson, T. W.
1949 *The Sayings of Jesus: As Recorded in the Gospels according to St. Matthew and St. Luke*. London: SCM.
1950–51 "The Cleansing of the Temple." *Bulletin of the John Rylands Library* 33:271–82.
1955–56 "The Lord's Prayer." *Bulletin of the John Rylands Library* 38:99–113, 436–48.

Marcus, J.
1989 "Mark 14:61: 'Are You the Messiah-Son-of-God?'" *Novum Testamentum* 31:125–41.

Marshall, I. H.
1965–66 "The Synoptic Son of Man Sayings in Recent Discussion." *New Testament Studies* 12:327–51.
1968–69 "Son of God or Servant of Yahweh?—A Reconsideration of Mark i.11." *New Testament Studies* 15:326–36.
1969 "Tradition and Theology in Luke (Luke 8:5–15)." *Tyndale Bulletin* 20:56–75.
1970 *Luke: Historian and Theologian*. Grand Rapids: Zondervan/Exeter: Paternoster.
1973a *Eschatology and the Parables*. 2d edition. London: Tyndale.
1973b "The Resurrection of Jesus in Luke." *Tyndale Bulletin* 24:55–98.
1978 *The Gospel of Luke: A Commentary on the Greek Text*. New International Greek Testament Commentary. Grand Rapids: Eerdmans.
1980 *Last Supper and Lord's Supper*. Grand Rapids: Eerdmans/Exeter: Paternoster.

Martin, J. A.
1986 "Dispensational Approaches to the Sermon on the Mount." Pp. 35–48 in *Essays in Honor of J. Dwight Pentecost*. Edited by S. D. Toussaint and C. H. Dyer. Chicago: Moody.
1992 "Christ, the Fulfillment of the Law in the Sermon on the Mount." Pp. 248–63 in *Dispensationalism, Israel and the Church: The Search for Definition*. Edited by C. A. Blaising and D. L. Bock. Grand Rapids: Zondervan.

Martin, R. P.
1976 "Salvation and Discipleship in Luke's Gospel." *Interpretation* 30:366–80.

Marxsen, W.
1969 *Mark the Evangelist: Studies on the Redaction History of the Gospel*. Translated by J. Boyce et al. Nashville: Abingdon.

Mattill, A. J., Jr.
1975 "The Jesus-Paul Parallels and the Purpose of Luke–Acts: H. H. Evans Reconsidered." *Novum Testamentum* 17:15–46.
1979 *Luke and the Last Things: A Perspective for the Understanding of Lukan Thought*. Dillsboro, N.C.: Western North Carolina Press.

Mauser, U.
1963 *Christ in the Wilderness: The Wilderness Theme in the Second Gospel and Its Basis in the Biblical Tradition*. Studies in Biblical Theology 39. London: SCM/Naperville, Ill.: Allenson.

May, E. E.
1952 "'. . . For Power Went Forth from Him . . .' (Luke 6,19)." *Catholic Biblical Quarterly* 14:93–103.

Mayer-Maly, T.
1955 "Das Auftreten der Menge im Prozess Jesu und in den ältesten Christenprozessen." *Österreichisches Archiv für Kirchenrecht* 6:231–45.

Meier, J. P.
1991   *A Marginal Jew: Rethinking the Historical Jesus*, vol. 1: *The Roots of the Problem and the Person*. Anchor Bible Reference Library. New York: Doubleday.
1994   *A Marginal Jew: Rethinking the Historical Jesus*, vol. 2: *Mentor, Message, and Miracles*. Anchor Bible Reference Library. New York: Doubleday.
Meijboom, H. U.
1993   *A History and Critique of the Origin of the Marcan Hypothesis, 1835–1866: A Contemporary Report Rediscovered*. Translated and edited by J. J. Kiwiet. New Gospel Studies 8. Macon, Ga.: Mercer University Press.
Meinertz, M.
1957   "'Dieses Geschlecht' im Neuen Testament." *Biblische Zeitschrift* 1:283–89.
Ménard, J.-É.
1975   *L'Évangile selon Thomas*. Nag Hammadi Studies 5. Leiden: Brill.
Menzies, R. P.
1991   *The Development of Early Christian Pneumatology, with Special Reference to Luke–Acts*. Journal for the Study of the New Testament Supplement 54. Sheffield: JSOT Press.
Merkel, H.
1967–68   "Jesus und die Pharisäer." *New Testament Studies* 14:194–208.
Merritt, R. L.
1985   "Jesus Barabbas and the Paschal Pardon." *Journal for Biblical Literature* 104:57–68.
Metzger, B. M.
1958–59   "Seventy or Seventy-two Disciples?" *New Testament Studies* 5:299–306.
1975   *A Textual Commentary on the Greek New Testament*. Corrected edition. London: United Bible Societies.
1992   *The Text of the New Testament*. 3d edition. Oxford: Oxford University Press.
Meyer, B. F.
1964   "But Mary Kept All These Things . . . (Lk 2,19.51)." *Catholic Biblical Quarterly* 26:31–49.
1965   "Jesus and the Remnant of Israel." *Journal of Biblical Literature* 84:121–30.
1979   *The Aims of Jesus*. London: SCM.
Meynet, R.
1978   "Comment Établir un Chiasme: À Propos des 'Pèlerins d'Emmaüs.'" *Nouvelle Revue Théologique* 100:233–49.
Michaelis, W.
1950   "Das unbetonte καὶ Αὐτός bei Lukas." *Studia Theologica* 4:86–93.
Michel, O.
1959–60   "Eine philologische Frage zur Einzugsgeschichte." *New Testament Studies* 6:81–82.
Michel, O., and O. Betz
1960   "Von Gott gezeugt." Pp. 3–23 in *Judentum, Urchristentum, Kirche: Festschrift für Joachim Jeremias*. Edited by W. Eltester. Beiheft zur Zeitschrift für die Neutestamentliche Wissenschaft 26. Berlin: Töpelmann.
1962–63   "Nocheinmal: 'Von Gott gezeugt.'" *New Testament Studies* 9:129–30.
Miller, M. P.
1969   "The Function of Isa 61:1–2 in 11Q Melchizedek." *Journal of Biblical Literature* 88:467–69.
Miller, R. J.
1991   "The (A)historicity of Jesus' Temple Demonstration: A Test Case in Methodology." Pp. 235–52 in *Society of Biblical Literature 1991 Seminar Papers*. Edited by E. A. Lovering Jr. Atlanta: Scholars Press.
Milligan, W.
1892   "A Group of Parables." *Expositor*, 4th series, 6:114–26.
Minear, P. S.
1964–65   "A Note on Luke xxii 36." *Novum Testamentum* 7:128–34.
Mitchell, A. C.
1990   "Zacchaeus Revisited: Luke 19,8 as a Defense." *Biblica* 71:153–76.

Miyoshi, M.
1974   *Der Anfang des Reiseberichts, Lk 9,51–10,24: Eine redaktionsgeschichtliche Untersuchung*. Analecta Biblica 60. Rome: Pontifical Biblical Institute Press.
MM   *The Vocabulary of the Greek Testament Illustrated from the Papyri and Other Non-literary Sources*. By J. H. Moulton and G. Milligan. Reprinted Grand Rapids: Eerdmans, 1980.
Moessner, D. P.
1983   "Luke 9:1–50: Luke's Preview of the Journey of the Prophet like Moses of Deuteronomy." *Journal of Biblical Literature* 102:575–605.
1989   *Lord of the Banquet: The Literary and Theological Significance of the Lukan Travel Narrative*. Minneapolis: Fortress.
1990   "'The Christ Must Suffer,' The Church Must Suffer: Rethinking the Theology of the Cross in Luke–Acts." Pp. 165–95 in *Society of Biblical Literature 1990 Seminar Papers*. Edited by D. J. Lull. Atlanta: Scholars Press.
Montefiore, C. G.
1930   *Rabbinic Literature and Gospel Teachings*. London: Macmillan.
Moo, D. J.
1983   *The Old Testament in the Gospel Passion Narratives*. Sheffield: Almond.
Moore, A. L.
1966   *The Parousia in the New Testament*. Novum Testamentum Supplement 13. Leiden: Brill.
Moore, G. F.
1905   "Συμφωνία Not a Bagpipe." *Journal of Biblical Literature* 24:166–75.
1927–30 *Judaism in the First Centuries of the Christian Era: The Age of the Tannaim*. 3 vols. Cambridge: Harvard University Press.
Moran, W. L.
1963   "The Ancient Near Eastern Background of the Love of God in Deuteronomy." *Catholic Biblical Quarterly* 25:77–87.
Morgan, G. C.
1931   *The Gospel according to Luke*. New York: Revell.
Morganthaler, R.
1948   *Die lukanische Geschichtsschreibung als Zeugnis: Gestalt und Gehalt der Kunst des Lukas*. 2 vols. Abhandlungen zur Theologie des Alten und Neuen Testaments 14–15. Zurich: Zwingli.
Morosco, R. E.
1979   "Redaction Criticism and the Evangelical: Matthew 10 a Test Case." *Journal of the Evangelical Theological Society* 22:323–31.
Moule, C. F. D.
1957–58 "The Post-Resurrection Appearances in the Light of Festival Pilgrimages." *New Testament Studies* 4:58–61.
1959   *An Idiom Book of New Testament Greek*. 2d edition. Cambridge: Cambridge University Press.
1966   "The Christology of Acts." Pp. 159–85 in *Studies in Luke–Acts: Essays Presented in Honor of Paul Schubert*. Edited by L. E. Keck and J. L. Martyn. Nashville: Abingdon. Reprinted Philadelphia: Fortress, 1980.
Moulton, J. H., and W. F. Howard
1929   *A Grammar of New Testament Greek*, vol. 2: *Accidence and Word-Formation*. Edinburgh: Clark.
Muddiman, J.
1972   "A Note on Reading Lk 24,12." *Ephemerides Theologicae Lovanienses* 48:542–48.
Müller, H.-P.
1960   "Die Verklärung Jesu: Eine motivgeschichtliche Studie." *Zeitschrift für die Neutestamentliche Wissenschaft* 51:56–64.
Müller, U. B.
1977   "Vision und Botschaft: Erwägungen zur prophetischen Struktur der Verkündigung Jesu." *Zeitschrift für Theologie und Kirche* 74:416–48.

Muller, V.
1944   "The Prehistory of the 'Good Shepherd.'" *Journal of Near Eastern Studies* 3:87–90.
Murray, J.
1953   *Divorce*. Philadelphia: Committee on Christian Education, Orthodox Presbyterian Church.
Mussner, F.
1968   *The Miracles of Jesus: An Introduction*. Translated by A. Wimmer. Notre Dame, Ind.: University of Notre Dame Press.
1975   "Καθεξῆς im Lukasprolog." Pp. 253–55 in *Jesus und Paulus: Festschrift für Werner Georg Kümmel zum 70. Geburtstag*. Edited by E. E. Ellis and E. Grässer. Göttingen: Vandenhoeck & Ruprecht.
NA   *Novum Testamentum Graece*. 26th edition. Edited by [E. Nestle], K. Aland, and B. Aland. Stuttgart: Deutsche Bibelstiftung, 1979.
Nauck, W.
1955   "Freude in Leiden: Zum Problem einer urchristlichen Verfolgungstradition." *Zeitschrift für die Neutestamentliche Wissenschaft* 46:68–80.
Neale, D. A.
1991   *None but the Sinners: Religious Categories in the Gospel of Luke*. Journal for the Study of the New Testament Supplement 58. Sheffield: Sheffield Academic Press.
Neirynck, F.
1973   "Minor Agreements Matthew-Luke in the Transfiguration Story." Pp. 253–66 in *Orientierung an Jesus: Zur Theologie der Synoptiker: Für Josef Schmid*. Edited by P. Hoffmann, N. Brox, and W. Pesch. Freiburg: Herder. Reprinted in Neirynck's *Evangelica: Collected Essays* [vol. 1 /] pp. 797–810. Edited by F. Van Segbroeck. Bibliotheca Ephemeridum Theologicarum Lovaniensium 60. Louvain: Leuven University Press/Peeters, 1982.
1977   "Παρακύψας Βλέπει: Lc 24,12 et Jn 20,5." *Ephemerides Theologicae Lovanienses* 53:113–52. Reprinted in Neirynck's *Evangelica: Collected Essays* [vol. 1 /] pp. 401–40. Edited by F. Van Segbroeck. Bibliotheca Ephemeridum Theologicarum Lovaniensium 60. Louvain: Leuven University Press/Peeters, 1982.
1985   "Lc 24,36–43: Un Récit Lucanien." Pp. 655–80 in *À Cause de l'Évangile: Études sur les Synoptiques et les Acts, Mélanges Offertes au R. P. Jacques Dupont*. Edited by F. Refoulé. Lectio Divina 123. Paris: Cerf. Reprinted in Neirynck's *Evangelica: Collected Essays*, vol. 2: *1982–1991*, pp. 205–26. Edited by F. Van Segbroeck. Bibliotheca Ephemeridum Theologicarum Lovaniensium 99. Louvain: Leuven University Press/Peeters, 1991.
Nestle, E.
1901–2   "'Emmaus' Mistaken for a Person." *Expository Times* 13:477.
1903   "Sykophantia im biblischen Griech." *Zeitschrift für die Neutestamentliche Wissenschaft* 4:271–72.
1910–11   "The Honeycomb of Luke xxiv." *Expository Times* 22:567–68.
1912   "Wer nicht mit mir ist, der ist wider mich." *Zeitschrift für die Neutestamentliche Wissenschaft* 13:84–87.
Neugebauer, F.
1974–75   "Die Davidssohnfrage (Mark xii.35–37 parr.) und der Menschensohn." *New Testament Studies* 21:81–108.
Neu Luther
    Die Bibel nach der Übersetzung Martin Luthers. Stuttgart: Deutsche Bibelgesellschaft, 1984.
Neusner, J.
1977–86   *The Tosefta*. 6 vols. New York: Ktav.
1984   *Judaism in the Beginning of Christianity*. Philadelphia: Fortress.
1986   *Sifré to Numbers: An American Translation and Explanation*. 2 vols. (through §115). Brown Judaic Studies 118 and 119. Atlanta: Scholars Press. (Vol. 3 forthcoming by W. S. Green.)

1987   *Sifre to Deuteronomy: An Analytical Translation*. 2 vols. Brown Judaic Studies 98, 101. Atlanta: Scholars Press.

1988a   *Mekhilta according to Rabbi Ishmael: An Analytical Translation*. 2 vols. Brown Judaic Studies 148 and 154. Atlanta: Scholars Press.

1988b   *Sifra: An Analytical Translation*. 3 vols. Brown Judaic Studies 138–40. Atlanta: Scholars Press.

Neusner, J., and B. D. Chilton

1991   "Uncleanness: A Moral or an Ontological Category in the Early Centuries A.D.?" *Bulletin for Biblical Research* 1:63–88.

Neusner, J., W. S. Green, and E. S. Frerichs (eds.)

1987   *Judaisms and Their Messiahs at the Turn of the Christian Era*. Cambridge: Cambridge University Press.

Neusner, J., et al.

1982–93   *The Talmud of the Land of Israel: A Preliminary Translation and Explanation*. 35 vols. Chicago: University of Chicago Press.

Neyrey, J. H.

1985   *The Passion according to Luke: A Redaction Study of Luke's Soteriology*. Mahwah, N.J.: Paulist.

1991   "Ceremonies in Luke–Acts: The Case of Meals and Table Fellowship." Pp. 361–87 in *The Social World of Luke–Acts: Models for Interpretation*. Edited by J. H. Neyrey. Peabody, Mass.: Hendrickson.

Nickelsburg, G. W. E.

1978–79   "Riches, the Rich and God's Judgment in 1 Enoch 92–105 and the Gospel according to Luke." *New Testament Studies* 25:324–44.

NIDNTT   *The New International Dictionary of New Testament Theology*. Edited by L. Coenen, E. Beyreuther, and H. Bietenhard. English translation edited by C. Brown. 4 vols. Grand Rapids: Zondervan, 1975–86.

Nissen, A.

1974   *Gott und der Nächste im antiken Judentum: Untersuchungen zum Doppelgebot der Liebe*. Wissenschaftliche Untersuchungen zum Neuen Testament 15. Tübingen: Mohr.

Noack, B.

1948   *Das Gottesreich bei Lukas: Eine Studie zu Luk. 17,20–24*. Symbolae Biblicae Upsalienses 10. Uppsala: Gleerup.

Nolland, J.

1979   "Classical and Rabbinic Parallels to 'Physician, Heal Yourself' (Lk. iv 2)." *Novum Testamentum* 21:193–209.

1986   "Grace as Power." *Novum Testamentum* 28:26–31.

1989   *Luke 1–9:20*. Word Biblical Commentary 35a. Dallas: Word.

1993a   *Luke 9:21–18:34*. Word Biblical Commentary 35b. Dallas: Word.

1993b   *Luke 18:35–24:53*. Word Biblical Commentary 35c. Dallas: Word.

North, C. R.

1956   *The Suffering Servant in Deutero-Isaiah: An Historical and Critical Study*. 2d edition. Oxford: Oxford University Press.

1964   *The Second Isaiah: Introduction, Translation, and Commentary to Chapters xl–lv*. Oxford: Clarendon.

Noth, M.

1928   *Die israelitischen Personennamen im Rahmen der gemeinsemitischen Namengebung*. Beiträge zur Wissenschaft vom Alten und Neuen Testament 3/10. Stuttgart: Kohlhammer.

Núñez C., E. A.

1985   *Liberation Theology*. Translated by P. E. Sywulka. Chicago: Moody.

Ogg, G.

1940   *The Chronology of the Public Ministry of Jesus*. Cambridge: Cambridge University Press.

1962   "Chronology of the New Testament." Pp. 728–32 in *Peake's Commentary on the Bible*. Edited by M. Black and H. H. Rowley. London: Nelson.

O'Hanlon, J.
1981   "The Story of Zacchaeus and the Lukan Ethic." *Journal for the Study of the New Testament* 12:2–26.

Olmstead, A. T.
1942   *Jesus in the Light of History*. New York: Scribner.

O'Neill, J. C.
1959   "The Six Amen Sayings in Luke." *Journal of Theological Studies* n.s. 10:1–9.
1970   *The Theology of Acts in Its Historical Setting*. 2d edition. London: SPCK.

Orchard, B., and H. Riley
1987   *The Order of the Synoptics: Why Three Synoptic Gospels?* Macon, Ga.: Mercer University Press.

O'Rourke, J. J.
1971–72 "Some Notes on Luke xv.11–32." *New Testament Studies* 18:431–33.

Osborne, G. R.
1984   *The Resurrection Narratives: A Redactional Study*. Grand Rapids: Baker.

O'Toole, R. F.
1984   *The Unity of Luke's Theology: An Analysis of Luke–Acts*. Good News Studies 9. Wilmington, Del.: Glazier.
1987a   "The Kingdom of God in Luke–Acts." Pp. 147–62 in *The Kingdom of God in Twentieth-Century Interpretation*. Edited by W. Willis. Peabody, Mass.: Hendrickson.
1987b   "Luke's Message in Luke 9:1–50." *Catholic Biblical Quarterly* 49:74–89.

Ott, W.
1965   *Gebet und Heil: Die Bedeutung der Gebetsparänese in der lukanischen Theologie*. Studien zum Alten und Neuen Testament 12. Munich: Kösel.

Pagenkemper, K. E.
1990   *An Analysis of the Rejection Motif in the Synoptic Parables and Its Relationship to Pauline Soteriology*. Th.D diss. Dallas Theological Seminary.

Palmer, H.
1976   "Just Married, Cannot Come." *Novum Testamentum* 18:241–57.

Parsons, M. C.
1987   *The Departure of Jesus in Luke–Acts: The Ascension Narratives in Context*. Journal for the Study of the New Testament Supplement 21. Sheffield: JSOT Press.

Patsch, H.
1971   "Der Einzug Jesu in Jerusalem: Ein historischer Versuch." *Zeitschrift für Theologie und Kirche* 68:1–26.
1972   *Abendmahl und historischer Jesus*. Calwer Theologische Monographien A.1. Stuttgart: Calwer.

Patterson, S. J.
1989   "Fire and Dissension: Ipsissima Vox Jesu in Q 12:49, 51–53?" *Forum* 5:121–39.

Payne, D. F.
1962   "Bethlehem." P. 144 in *The New Bible Dictionary*. Edited by J. D. Douglas. Grand Rapids: Eerdmans.

Payne, J. B.
1967   "Zachariah Who Perished." *Grace Theological Journal* o.s. 8/3:33–35.

Payne, P. B.
1978–79 "The Order of Sowing and Ploughing in the Parable of the Sower." *New Testament Studies* 25:123–29.
1980   "The Authenticity of the Parable of the Sower and Its Interpretation." Pp. 163–207 in *Gospel Perspectives*, vol. 1: *Studies of History and Tradition in the Four Gospels*. Edited by R. T. France and D. Wenham. Sheffield: JSOT Press.

Pegg, H.
1926–27 "'A Scorpion for an Egg' (Luke xi.12)." *Expository Times* 38:468–69.

Pelletier, A.
1955   "Le 'Voile' du Temple de Jérusalem est-il Devenu la 'Portière' du Temple d'Olympie?" *Syria* 32:289–307.
1958   "Le Grand Rideau du Vestibule du Temple de Jérusalem." *Syria* 35:218–26.

Pentecost, J. D.
1980   *The Sermon on the Mount: Contemporary Insights for a Christian Lifestyle.* Revised edition. Portland: Multnomah. (Originally *Design for Living: The Sermon on the Mount.* Chicago: Moody, 1975.)

Perles, F.
1919–20   "Zwei Übersetzungsfehler im Text der Evangelien." *Zeitschrift für die Neutestamentliche Wissenschaft* 19:96.

Perrin, N.
1963   *The Kingdom of God in the Teaching of Jesus.* New Testament Library. Philadelphia: Westminster/London: SCM.
1967   *Rediscovering the Teaching of Jesus.* New York: Harper & Row.

Perrot, C.
1973   "Luc 4,16–30 et la Lecture Biblique de l'Ancienne Synagogue." *Revue des Sciences Religieuses* 47:324–40.

Pesch, R.
1968a   "Levi-Matthäus (Mc 2:14 / Mt 9:9, 10:3): Ein Beitrag zur Lösung eines alten Problems." *Zeitschrift für die Neutestamentliche Wissenschaft* 59:40–56.
1968b   *Naherwartungen: Tradition und Redaktion in Mk 13.* Düsseldorf: Patmos.
1970a   "Jaïrus (Mk 5,22/Lk 8,41)." *Biblische Zeitschrift* 14:252–56.
1970b   *Jesu ureigene Taten? Ein Beitrag zur Wunderfrage.* Questiones Disputatae 52. Freiburg: Herder.
1970c   "Das Zöllnergastmahl (Mk 2,15–17)." Pp. 63–87 in *Mélanges Bibliques en Hommage au R. P. Béda Rigaux.* Edited by A. Descamps and A. de Halleux. Gembloux: Duculot.
1971   "The Markan Version of the Healing of the Gerasene Demoniac." *Ecumenical Review* 23:349–76.
1972   *Der Besessene von Gerasa: Einstehung und Überlieferung einer Wundergeschichte.* Stuttgarter Bibelstudien 56. Stuttgart: Katholisches Bibelwerk.
1973–74   "Das Messiasbekenntnis des Petrus (Mk 8,27–30): Neuverhandlung einer alten Frage." *Biblische Zeitschrift* 17:178–95; 18:20–31.
1976–77   *Das Markusevangeliums.* 2 vols. Herders theologischer Kommentar zum Neuen Testament 2. Freiburg: Herder.

Petersen, W. L.
1981   "The Parable of the Lost Sheep in the Gospel of Thomas and the Synoptics." *Novum Testamentum* 23:128–47.

Petuchowski, J. J., and M. Brocke (eds.)
1978   *The Lord's Prayer and Jewish Liturgy.* New York: Seabury.

Petzke, G.
1975   "Der historische Jesus in der sozialethischen Diskussion: Mk 12,13–17 par." Pp. 223–35 in *Jesus Christus in Historie und Theologie: Neutestamentliche Festschrift für Hans Conzelmann zum 60. Geburtstag.* Edited by G. Strecker. Tübingen: Mohr.

PG   *Patrologiae Cursus Completus, Series Graeca.* Edited by J. P. Migne. 161 vols. Paris, 1857–66.

Pickl, J.
1946   *The Messias.* Translated by A. Green. St. Louis: Herder.

Pilgrim, W. E.
1971   *The Death of Christ in Lukan Soteriology.* Th.D. diss., Princeton University.
1981   *Good News to the Poor: Wealth and Poverty in Luke–Acts.* Minneapolis: Augsburg.

PL   *Patrologiae Cursus Completus, Series Latina.* Edited by J. P. Migne. 221 vols. Paris, 1844–55.

Plevnik, J.
1991   "Son of Man Seated at the Right Hand of God: Luke 22,69 in Lucan Christology." *Biblica* 72:331–47.

Plummer, A.
1896   *A Critical and Exegetical Commentary on the Gospel according to St. Luke*. International Critical Commentary. Edinburgh: Clark/New York: Scribner.

Plymale, S. F.
1991   *The Prayer Texts of Luke–Acts*. American University Studies, series 7: Theology and Religion 118. New York: Lang.

Pöhlmann, W.
1979   "Die Absichtung des verlorenen Sohnes (Lk 15.12f.) und die erzählte Welt der Parabel." *Zeitschrift für die Neutestamentliche Wissenschaft* 70:194–213.

Polag, A.
1982   *Fragmenta Q: Textheft zur Logienquelle*. 2d edition. Neukirchen-Vluyn: Neukirchener Verlag.

Porter, S. E.
1990   "The Parable of the Unjust Steward (Luke 16.1–13): Irony *Is* the Key." Pp. 127–53 in *The Bible in Three Dimensions: Essays in Celebration of Forty Years of Biblical Studies in the University of Sheffield*. Edited by D. J. A. Clines, S. F. Fowl, and S. E. Porter. Journal for the Study of the Old Testament Supplement 87. Sheffield: JSOT Press.
1992   "'In the Vicinity of Jericho': Luke 18:35 in the Light of Its Synoptic Parallels." *Bulletin for Biblical Research* 2:91–104.

Pousma, R. H.
1975   "Diseases of the Bible." Vol. 2 / pp. 132–42 in *The Zondervan Pictorial Encyclopedia of the Bible*. Edited by M. C. Tenney. Grand Rapids: Zondervan.

Power, E.
1923   "The Staff of the Apostles: A Problem in Gospel Harmony." *Biblica* 4:241–66.

Power, M. A.
1912   "Who Were They Who 'Understood Not'?" *Irish Theological Quarterly* 7:261–81, 444–59.

Rad, G. von
1962–65 *Old Testament Theology*. 2 vols. Translated by D. M. G. Stalker. New York: Harper & Row/Edinburgh: Oliver & Boyd.

Ragaz, L.
1945   *Der Bergpredigt Jesus*. Bern: H. Lang.

Ramsay, W. M.
1898   *Was Christ Born at Bethlehem? A Study on the Credibility of St. Luke*. London: Hodder & Stoughton/New York: Putnam.
1898–99 "On Mark xii.42." *Expository Times* 10:232, 336.
1920   *The Bearing of Recent Discovery on the Trustworthiness of the New Testament*. 4th edition. London: Hodder & Stoughton.

Ranke, L. von
1901   *The History of the Popes*. 3 vols. Translated by E. Fowler. New York: Colonial.

Rau, G.
1965   "Das Volk in der lukanischen Passionsgeschichte: Eine Konjektur zu Lk 23,13." *Zeitschrift für die Neutestamentliche Wissenschaft* 56:41–51.

Rehkopf, F.
1959   *Die lukanische Sonderquelle: Ihr Umfang und Sprachgebrauch*. Wissenschaftliche Untersuchungen zum Neuen Testament 5. Tübingen: Mohr.
1961   "Mt. 26,50: Ἑταῖρε, ἐφ' Ὃ Πάρει." *Zeitschrift für die Neutestamentliche Wissenschaft* 52:109–15.

Reicke, B.
1968   *New Testament Era: The World of the Bible from 500 B.C. to A.D. 100*. Translated by D. E. Green. Philadelphia: Fortress.
1973   "Jesus in Nazareth—Lk 4,14–30." Pp. 47–55 in *Das Wort und die Wörter: Festschrift Gerhard Friedrich zum 65. Geburtstag*. Edited by H. Balz and S. Schulz. Stuttgart: Kohlhammer.
1986   *The Roots of the Synoptic Gospels*. Philadelphia: Fortress.

Reiling, J., and J. L. Swellengrebel
1971   *A Translator's Handbook on the Gospel of Luke*. Helps for Translators 10. Leiden: Brill, for the United Bible Societies.

Rengstorf, K. H.
1967   *Die Re-Investitur des verlorenen Sohnes in der Gleichniserzählung Jesu Lk 15,11–32.* Arbeitsgemeinschaft für Forschung des Landes Nordrhein-Westfalen, Geistswissenschaften 137. Cologne/Opladen: Westdeutscher Verlag.
1968   *Das Evangelium nach Lukas*. Das Neue Testament Deutsch 3. Göttingen: Vandenhoeck & Ruprecht.

Rese, M.
1963   "Überprüfung einiger Thesen von Joachim Jeremias zum Thema des Gottesknechtes im Judentum." *Zeitschrift für Theologie und Kirche* 60:21–41.
1969   *Alttestamentliche Motive in der Christologie des Lukas*. Studien zum Neuen Testament 1. Gütersloh: Mohn.

Resseguie, J. L.
1975   "Interpretation of Luke's Central Section (Luke 9:51–19:44) since 1856." *Studia Biblica et Theologica* 5/2:3–36.

Ridderbos, H.
1962   *The Coming of the Kingdom*. Translated by H. De Jongste. Edited by R. O. Zorn. Philadelphia: Presbyterian & Reformed.

Riesenfeld, H.
1949   "Ἐμβολεύειν–Ἐντός." *Nuntius* 2:11–12.

Rigaux, B.
1970   "La Petite Apocalypse de Luc (xvii,22–37)." Pp. 407–38 in *Ecclesia a Spiritu Sancto Edocta: Mélanges Théologiques Hommage à Mgr Gérard Philips*. Bibliotheca Ephemeridum Theologicarum Lovaniensium 27. Gembloux: Duculot.

Rigg, H. A., Jr.
1945   "Barabbas." *Journal of Biblical Literature* 64:417–56.

Ringgren, H.
1963   *The Faith of Qumran: Theology of the Dead Sea Scrolls*. Translated by E. T. Sander. Philadelphia: Fortress.

Rist, J. M.
1978   *On the Independence of Matthew and Mark*. Society for New Testament Studies Monograph Series 32. Cambridge: Cambridge University Press.

Roberts, C. H.
1948   "The Kingdom of Heaven (Lk. xvii.21)." *Harvard Theological Review* 41:1–8.

Robertson, A. T.
1923   *A Grammar of the Greek New Testament in the Light of Historical Research*. 4th edition. Nashville: Broadman.
1923–24 "The Implications in Luke's Preface." *Expository Times* 35:319–21.

Robinson, J. A. T.
1957   "The Baptism of John and the Qumran Community: Testing a Hypothesis." *Harvard Theological Review* 50:175–91. Reprinted in Robinson's *Twelve New Testament Studies*, pp. 11–27. Studies in Biblical Theology 34. London: SCM/Naperville, Ill.: Allenson, 1962.

Robinson, W. C., Jr.
1964   *Der Weg des Herrn: Studien zur Geschichte und Eschatologie im Lukas-Evangelium*. Theologische Forschung 36. Hamburg-Bergstedt: Reich.
1966   "On Preaching the Word of God (Luke 8:4–21)." Pp. 131–38 in *Studies in Luke–Acts: Essays Presented in Honor of Paul Schubert*. Edited by L. E. Keck and J. L. Martyn. Nashville: Abingdon. Reprinted Philadelphia: Fortress, 1980.

Roloff, J.
1970   *Das Kerygma und der irdische Jesus: Historische Motive in den Jesus-Erzählungen der Evangelien*. Göttingen: Vandenhoeck & Ruprecht.

Ropes, J. H.
1923–24 "St. Luke's Preface: Ἀσφάλεια and Παρακολουθεῖν." *Journal of Theological Studies* o.s. 25:67–71.

Rowley, H. H.
1950 "The Suffering Servant and the Davidic Messiah." *Oudtestamentische Studien* 8:100–36.

Ruckstuhl, E.
1980 "Neue und alte Überlegungen zu den Abendmahlsworten Jesu." *Studien zum Neuen Testament und seiner Umwelt* 5:79–106.

Rüger, H. P.
1969 "Mit welchem Maß ihr meßt, wird euch gemessen werden." *Zeitschrift für die Neutestamentliche Wissenschaft* 60:174–82.

1973 "Μαμωνᾶς." *Zeitschrift für die Neutestamentliche Wissenschaft* 64:127–31.

Rüstow, A.
1960 "Ἐντὸς Ὑμῶν Ἐστιν: Zur Deutung von Lukas 17:20–21." *Zeitschrift für die Neutestamentliche Wissenschaft* 51:197–224.

Safrai, S.
1974 "Relations between the Diaspora and the Land of Israel." Vol. 1 / pp. 184–215 in *The Jewish People in the First Century*. Edited by S. Safrai and M. Stern. Compendia Rerum Iudaicarum ad Novum Testamentum 1/2. Philadelphia: Fortress/Assen: Van Gorcum.

1976a "Home and Family." Vol. 2 / pp. 728–92 in *The Jewish People in the First Century*. Edited by S. Safrai and M. Stern. Compendia Rerum Iudaicarum ad Novum Testamentum 1/2. Philadelphia: Fortress/Assen: Van Gorcum.

1976b "Religion in Everyday Life." Vol. 2 / pp. 793–833 in *The Jewish People in the First Century*. Edited by S. Safrai and M. Stern. Compendia Rerum Iudaicarum ad Novum Testamentum 1/2. Philadelphia: Fortress/Assen: Van Gorcum.

1976c "The Synagogue." Vol. 2 / pp. 908–44 in *The Jewish People in the First Century*. Edited by S. Safrai and M. Stern. Compendia Rerum Iudaicarum ad Novum Testamentum 1/2. Philadelphia: Fortress/Assen: Van Gorcum.

1976d "The Temple." Vol. 2 / pp. 865–907 in *The Jewish People in the First Century*. Edited by S. Safrai and M. Stern. Compendia Rerum Iudaicarum ad Novum Testamentum 1/2. Philadelphia: Fortress/Assen: Van Gorcum.

Sahlin, H.
1945a *Der Messias und das Gottesvolk: Studien zur protolukanischen Theologie*. Acta Seminarii Neotestamentici Upsaliensis 12. Uppsala: Almqvist & Wiksell.

1945b *Zwei Lukas-Stellen: Lk 6:43–45; 18:7*. Symbolae Biblicae Upsalienses 4. Uppsala: Wretman.

Saldarini, A. J.
1975 *The Fathers according to Rabbi Nathan (Abot de Rabbi Nathan), Version B*. Studies in Judaism in Late Antiquity 11. Leiden: Brill.

Salmon, M.
1988 "Insider or Outsider? Luke's Relationship with Judaism." Pp. 76–82 in *Luke–Acts and the Jewish People: Eight Critical Perspectives*. Edited by J. B. Tyson. Minneapolis: Augsburg.

Sanders, E. P.
1985 *Jesus and Judaism*. Philadelphia: Fortress.

1990 *Jewish Law from Jesus to the Mishnah: Five Studies*. Philadelphia: Trinity/London: SCM.

1992 *Judaism: Practice and Belief, 63 BCE–66 CE*. London: SCM/Philadelphia: Trinity.

1993 *The Historical Figure of Jesus*. New York/London: Penguin.

Sanders, J. A.
1974 "The Ethic of Election in Luke's Great Banquet Parable." Pp. 245–71 in *Essays in Old Testament Ethics (J. Philip Hyatt, In Memorium)*. Edited by J. L. Crenshaw and J. T. Willis. New York: Ktav.

1975   "From Isaiah 61 to Luke 4." Pp. 75–106 in *Christianity, Judaism, and other Greco-Roman Cults: Studies for Morton Smith at Sixty*, vol. 1: *New Testament*. Edited by J. Neusner. Studies in Judaism in Late Antiquity 12/1. Leiden: Brill. Reprinted and revised in C. A. Evans and J. A. Sanders's *Luke and Scripture: The Function of Sacred Tradition in Luke–Acts*, pp. 46–69. Minneapolis: Fortress, 1993.

1993   "Isaiah in Luke." Pp. 14–25 in *Luke and Scripture: The Function of Sacred Tradition in Luke–Acts*. By C. A. Evans and J. A. Sanders. Minneapolis: Fortress.

Sanders, J. T.

1968–69   "Tradition and Redaction in Luke xv.11–32." *New Testament Studies* 15:433–38.

1987   *The Jews in Luke–Acts*. Philadelphia: Fortress.

Saucy, M.

1994   "The Kingdom-of-God Sayings in Matthew." *Bibliotheca Sacra*. 151:175–97.

SB   *Kommentar zum Neuen Testament aus Talmud und Midrasch*. By H. L. Strack and P. Billerbeck. 6 vols. Munich: Beck, 1922–61.

Schaberg, J.

1989   "Mark 14.62: Early Christian Merkabah Imagery?" Pp. 69–94 in *Apocalyptic and the New Testament: Essays in Honor of J. Louis Martyn*. Edited by J. Marcus and M. L. Soards. Journal for the Study of the New Testament Supplement 24. Sheffield: JSOT Press.

Schalit, A.

1968   *Namenwörterbuch zu Flavius Josephus*. Supplement 1 to *A Complete Concordance to Flavius Josephus*, edited by K. H. Rengstorf. Leiden: Brill.

Schenk, W.

1974   *Der Passionsbericht nach Markus: Untersuchungen zur Überlieferungsgechichte der Passionstraditionen*. Gütersloh: Mohn.

Schenke, L.

1974   *Die Wundererzählungen des Markusevangeliums*. Stuttgarter biblische Beiträge. Stuttgart: Katholisches Bibelwerk.

Schlatter, A. von

1960   *Das Evangelium des Lukas aus seinen Quellen erklärt*. 2d edition. Stuttgart: Calwer.

Schlosser, J.

1980   *Le Règne de Dieu dans les Dits de Jésus*. 2 vols. Études Bibliques. Paris: Gabalda.

Schmahl, G.

1974   "Lk 2,41–52 und die Kindheitserzählung des Thomas 19,1–5: Ein Vergleich." *Bibel und Leben* 15:249–58.

Schmid, J.

1959   *Das Evangelium nach Mätthaus*. 4th edition. Regensburger Neues Testament 1. Regensburg: Pustet.

1960   *Das Evangelium nach Lukas*. 4th edition. Regensburger Neues Testament 3. Regensburg: Pustet.

Schmidt, T. E.

1987   *Hostility to Wealth in the Synoptic Gospels*. Journal for the Study of the New Testament Supplement 15. Sheffield: JSOT Press.

Schnackenburg, R.

1970   "Der eschatologische Abschnitt Lk 17,20–37." Pp. 213–34 in *Mélanges Bibliques en Hommage au R. P. Béda Rigaux*. Edited by A. Descamps and A. de Halleux. Gembloux: Duculot.

Schneemelcher, W.

1991–92   *New Testament Apocrypha*. Revised edition. 2 vols. English translation edited by R. M. Wilson. Philadelphia: Westminster/John Knox.

Schneider, G.

1971   "Luke 1,34.35 als redaktionelle Einheit." *Biblische Zeitschrift* 15:255–59.

1975   *Parusiegleichnisse im Lukas-Evangelium*. Stuttgarter Bibelstudien 74. Stuttgart: Katholisches Bibelwerk.

1977a   *Das Evangelium nach Lukas*. 2 vols. Ökumenischer Taschenbuch-Kommentar 3. Gütersloh: Mohn.

1977b   "Zur Bedeutung von Καθεξῆς im lukanischen Doppelwerk." *Zeitschrift für die Neutestamentliche Wissenschaft* 68:128–31.

Schoedel, W. R.

1972   "Parables in the Gospel of Thomas: Oral Tradition or Gnostic Exegesis?" *Concordia Theological Monthly* 43:548–60.

Schoonheim, P. L.

1966   "Der alttestamentliche Boden der Vokabel Ὑπερήφανος in Lukas i 51." *Novum Testamentum* 8:235–46.

Schottroff, L.

1971   "Das Gleichnis vom verlorenen Sohn." *Zeitschrift für Theologie und Kirche* 68:27–52.

Schottroff, L., and W. Stegemann

1986   *Jesus and the Hope of the Poor*. Translated by M. J. O'Connell. Maryknoll, N.Y.: Orbis.

Schrage, W.

1964   *Das Verhältnis des Thomas-Evangeliums zur synoptischen Tradition und zu den koptischen Evangelienübersetzungen: Zugleich ein Beitrag zur gnostischen Synoptikerdeutung*. Beiheft zur Zeitschrift für die Neutestamentliche Wissenschaft 29. Berlin: de Gruyter.

Schramm, T.

1971   *Der Markus-Stoff bei Lukas: Eine literarkritische und redaktionsgeschichtliche Untersuchung*. Society for New Testament Studies Monograph Series 14. Cambridge: Cambridge University Press.

Schreck, C. J.

1989   "The Nazareth Pericope: Luke 4,16–30 in Recent Study." Pp. 399–471 in *L'Évangile de Luc—The Gospel of Luke*. Edited by F. Neirynck. 2d edition. Bibliotheca Ephemeridum Theologicarum Lovaniensium 32. Louvain: Leuven University Press/Peeters.

Schubert, K.

1957   "The Sermon on the Mount and the Qumran Texts." Pp. 118–28 and 270–73 in *The Scrolls and the New Testament*. Edited by K. Stendahl. New York: Harper.

Schubert, P.

1957   "The Structure and Significance of Luke 24." Pp. 165–88 in *Neutestamentliche Studien für Rudolf Bultmann*. 2d edition. Beiheft zur Zeitschrift für die Neutestamentliche Wissenschaft 21. Berlin: Töpelmann.

Schulz, S.

1972   *Q: Die Spruchquelle der Evangelisten*. Zurich: Theologischer Verlag.

Schürer, E.

1890   *A History of the Jewish People in the Time of Jesus Christ*, vol. 2. Translated by J. Macpherson. Edinburgh: Clark/New York: Scribner.

1973–87   *The History of the Jewish People in the Age of Jesus Christ (175 B.C.–A.D. 135)*. Revised edition. 3 vols. Edited by G. Vermes, F. Millar, and M. Black. Edinburgh: Clark.

Schürmann, H.

1951   "Lk 22,19b–20 als ursprüngliche Textüberlieferung." *Biblica* 32:364–92, 522–41.

1952   *Einer quellenkritischen Untersuchung des lukanischen Abendmahlsberichtes, Lk 22,7–38*, vol. 1: *Der Paschamahlbericht, Lk 22,(7–14.) 15–18*. Neutestamentliche Abhandlungen 19/5. Münster im Westphalia: Aschendorff.

1955   *Einer quellenkritischen Untersuchung des lukanischen Abendmahlsberichtes, Lk 22,7–38*, vol. 2: *Der Einsetzungsbericht, Lk 22,19–20*. Neutestamentliche Abhandlungen 20/4. Münster im Westphalia: Aschendorff.

1957   *Einer quellenkritischen Untersuchung des lukanischen Abendmahlsberichtes, Lk 22,7–38*, vol. 3: *Jesu Abschiedsrede, Lk 22,21–38*. Neutestamentliche Abhandlungen 20/5. Münster im Westphalia: Aschendorff.

1960   "'Wer daher eines dieser geringsten Gebote auflöst . . .': Wo fand Matthäus das Logion Mt 5,19." *Biblische Zeitschrift* 4:238–50.

1964   "Der 'Bericht vom Anfang': Ein Rekonstruktionsversuch auf Grund von Lk. 4,14–16." Pp. 242–58 in *Studia Evangelica*, vol. 2: *Papers Presented to the Second International Congress on New Testament Studies Held at Christ Church, Oxford, 1961*, part 1: *The New Testament Scriptures*. Edited by F. L. Cross. Texte und Untersuchungen 87. Berlin: Akademie-Verlag. Reprinted in Schürmann's *Traditionsgeschichtliche Untersuchungen zu den synoptischen Evangelien*, pp. 69–80. Düsseldorf: Patmos, 1968.

1968 *Traditionsgeschichtliche Untersuchungen zu den synoptischen Evangelien.* Kommentare und Beiträge zum Alten und Neuen Testament. Düsseldorf: Patmos.

1969 *Das Lukasevangelium*, vol. 1: *Kommentar zu Kap. 1,1–9,50*. Herders theologischer Kommentar zum Neuen Testament 3. Freiburg: Herder.

1973 "Wie hat Jesus seinen Tod bestanden und verstanden? Eine methodenkritische Besinnung." Pp. 325–63 in *Orientierung an Jesus: Zur Theologie der Synoptiker: Für Josef Schmid*. Edited by P. Hoffmann, N. Brox, and W. Pesch. Freiburg: Herder.

1994 *Das Lukasevangelium*, vol. 2/1: *Kommentar zu Kapitel 9,51–11,54*. Herders theologischer Kommentar zum Neuen Testament 3. Freiburg: Herder.

Schwarz, G.

1974 "'. . . Lobte den betrügerischen Verwalter'? (Lukas 16,8a)." *Biblische Zeitschrift* 18:94–95.

1975 "Ἰῶτα Ἓν ἢ Μία Κεραία (Matthäus 5,18)." *Zeitschrift für die Neutestamentliche Wissenschaft* 66:268–69.

1978 "Καλὸν τὸ Ἅλας." *Biblische Notizen* 7:32–35.

1979 "Κύριε, Ἰδοὺ Μάχαιραι Ὧδε Δύο." *Biblische Notizen* 8:22.

Schweitzer, A.

1910 *The Quest for the Historical Jesus: A Critical Study of Its Progress from Reimarus to Wrede*. Translated by W. Montgomery. London: Macmillan.

1956 *Das Messianitäts- und Leidensgeheimnis: Eine Skizze des Lebens Jesu*. 3d edition. Tübingen: Mohr.

Schweizer, E.

1970 *The Good News according to Mark*. Translated by D. H. Madvig. Richmond: John Knox.

1984 *The Good News according to Luke*. Translated by D. E. Green. Atlanta: John Knox.

Scobie, C. H. H.

1964 *John the Baptist*. Philadelphia: Fortress.

Scott, B. B.

1989 *Hear Then the Parable: A Commentary on the Parables of Jesus*. Minneapolis: Fortress.

Scott, E. F.

1911 *The Kingdom and the Messiah*. Edinburgh: Clark.

1924 *The Ethical Teaching of Jesus*. New York: Macmillan.

Seeberg, A.

1914 *Die vierte Bitte des Vaterunsers*. Rostock: Erben.

Seecombe, D. P.

1982 *Possessions and the Poor in Luke–Acts*. Studien zum Neuen Testament und seiner Umwelt B/6. Linz: Plöchl.

Seitz, O. J. F.

1969–70 "Love Your Enemies: The Historical Setting of Matthew v.43f.; Luke vi.27f." *New Testament Studies* 16:39–54.

Sellin, G.

1974–75 "Lukas als Gleichniserzähler: Die Erzählung vom barmherzigen Samariter (Lk 10:25–37)." *Zeitschrift für die Neutestamentliche Wissenschaft* 65:166–89 and 66:19–60.

Seng, E. W.

1978 "Der reiche Tor: Eine Untersuchung von Lk. xii 16–21 unter besonderer Berücksichtigung form- und motivgeschichtlicher Aspekte." *Novum Testamentum* 20:136–55.

Sherwin-White, A. N.

1963 *Roman Society and Roman Law in the New Testament*. Sarum Lectures 1960–61. Oxford: Clarendon.

Shin Kyo-Seon, G.

1989 *Die Ausrufung des endgültigen Jubeljahres durch Jesus in Nazaret: Eine historisch-kritische Studie zu Lk 4,16–30*. Europäische Hochschulschriften 23/378. Bern: Lang.

Shirock, R.
1992   "Whose Exorcists Are They? The Referents of οἱ Ὑιοὶ Ὑμῶν at Matthew 12.27 / Luke 11.19." *Journal for the Study of the New Testament* 46:41–51.
Siegman, E. F.
1968   "St. John's Use of the Synoptic Material." *Catholic Biblical Quarterly* 30:182–98.
Sjöberg, E. K. T.
1938   *Gott und die Sünder im palästinischen Judentum nach, dem Zeugnis der Tannaiten und der apokryphisch-pseudepigraphischen Literatur*. Beiträge zur Wissenschaft vom Alten und Neuen Testament 79 (4/27). Stuttgart: Kohlhammer.
Skeat, T. C.
1988   "The 'Second-First' Sabbath (Luke 6:1): The Final Solution." *Novum Testamentum* 30:103–6.
Sloan, R. B., Jr.
1977   *The Favorable Year of the Lord: A Study of Jubilary Theology in the Gospel of Luke*. Austin: Schola.
Smalley, S. S.
1973   "Spirit, Kingdom, and Prayer in Luke–Acts." *Novum Testamentum* 15:59–71.
Smith, B. D.
1991   "The Chronology of the Last Supper." *Westminster Theological Journal* 53:29–45.
Smith, M.
1971   "Zealots and Sicarii: Their Origins and Relation." *Harvard Theological Review* 64:1–19.
Sneed, R.
1962   "'The Kingdom of God Is within You' (Lk 17,21)." *Catholic Biblical Quarterly* 24:363–82.
Snodgrass, K. R.
1972   "Western Non-interpolations." *Journal of Biblical Literature* 91:369–79.
1974–75 "The Parable of the Wicked Husbandmen: Is the Gospel of Thomas Version the Original?" *New Testament Studies* 21:142–44.
1980   "Streams of Tradition Emerging from Isaiah 40:1–5 and Their Adaptation in the New Testament." *Journal for the Study of the New Testament* 8:24–45.
1983   *The Parable of the Wicked Tenants: An Inquiry into Parable Interpretation*. Wissenschaftliche Untersuchungen zum Neuen Testament 27. Tübingen: Mohr.
Soards, M. L.
1987   *The Passion according to Luke: The Special Material of Luke 22*. Journal for the Study of the New Testament Supplement 14. Sheffield: JSOT Press.
1994   *The Speeches in Acts: Their Content, Context, and Concerns*. Louisville: Westminster/John Knox.
Souter, A.
1901–2 "'Emmaus' Mistaken for a Person." *Expository Times* 13:429–30.
1914   "Interpretations of Certain New Testament Passages." *Expositor*, 8th series, 8:94–96.
Sparks, H. F. D.
1936   "The Partiality of Luke for 'Three,' and Its Bearing on the Original of Q." *Journal of Theological Studies* o.s. 37:141–45.
Sperber, D.
1967   "Mark xii 42 and Its Metrological Background: A Study in Ancient Syriac Versions." *Novum Testamentum* 9:178–90.
Spicq, C.
1994   *Theological Lexicon of the New Testament*. 3 vols. Translated and edited by J. D. Ernest. Peabody, Mass.: Hendrickson.
Stamm, F. K.
1943   *Seeing the Multitudes*. New York: Harper.
Stanley, D. M.
1959–60 "The Mother of My Lord." *Worship* 34:330–32.
Stauffer, E.
1960   *Jesus and His Story*. Translated by D. M. Barton. New York: Knopf/London: SCM.

Stegner, W. R.
1989   *Narrative Theology in Early Jewish Christianity*. Louisville: Westminster/John Knox.
Stein, R. H.
1976   "Is the Transfiguration (Mark 9:2–8) a Misplaced Resurrection-Account?" *Journal of Biblical Literature* 95:79–96.
1977   "Was the Tomb Really Empty?" *Journal of the Evangelical Theological Society* 20:23–29.
1978   *The Method and Message of Jesus' Teachings*. Philadelphia: Westminster.
1981   *An Introduction to the Parables of Jesus*. Philadelphia: Westminster.
1987   *The Synoptic Problem: An Introduction*. Grand Rapids: Baker.
1992   *Luke*. New American Commentary 24. Nashville: Broadman.
Stendahl, K.
1954   *The School of St. Matthew and Its Use of the Old Testament*. Acta Seminarii Neotestamentici Upsaliensis 20. Lund: Gleerup/Copenhagen: Munksgaard. Reprinted Philadelphia: Fortress, 1968.
Sterling, G. E.
1992   *Historiography and Self-Definition: Josephos, Luke–Acts and Apologetic Historiography*. Novum Testamentum Supplement 64. Leiden: Brill.
Stern, J. B.
1966   "Jesus' Citation of Dt 6,5 and Lv 19,18 in the Light of Jewish Tradition." *Catholic Biblical Quarterly* 28:312–16.
Stern, M.
1974   "The Province of Judaea." Vol. 1 / pp. 308–76 in *The Jewish People in the First Century*. Edited by S. Safrai and M. Stern. Compendia Rerum Iudaicarum ad Novum Testamentum 1/2. Philadelphia: Fortress/Assen: Van Gorcum.
1976   "Aspects of Jewish Society: The Priesthood and Other Classes." Vol. 2 / pp. 561–630 in *The Jewish People in the First Century*. Edited by S. Safrai and M. Stern. Compendia Rerum Iudaicarum ad Novum Testamentum 1/2. Philadelphia: Fortress/Assen: Van Gorcum.
Strack, H. L., and G. Stemberger
1991   *Introduction to the Talmud and Midrash*. Translated by M. Bockmuehl. Edinburgh: Clark.
Strauss, D. F.
1972   *The Life of Jesus Critically Examined*. Translated by G. Eliot (from the 4th edition, 1840). Edited by P. C. Hodgson. Philadelphia: Fortress/London: SCM.
Strecker, G.
1978   "Die Antithesen der Bergpredigt (Mt 5:21–48 par)." *Zeitschrift für die Neutestamentliche Wissenschaft* 69:36–72.
1988   *The Sermon on the Mount: An Exegetical Commentary*. Translated by O. C. Dean Jr. Nashville: Abingdon.
Streeter, B. H.
1924   *The Four Gospels: A Study of Origins, Treating of the Manuscript Tradition, Sources, Authorship, and Dates*. London: Macmillan.
Strobel, A.
1958a   "Lukas der Antiochener (Bemerkungen zu Act 11,28 D)." *Zeitschrift für die Neutestamentliche Wissenschaft* 49:131–34.
1958b   "Die Passa-Erwartung als urchristliches Problem in Lc 17:20f." *Zeitschrift für die Neutestamentliche Wissenschaft* 49:157–96.
1961a   "In dieser Nacht (Luk 17,34): Zu einer älteren Form der Erwartung in Luk 17,20–37." *Zeitschrift für Theologie und Kirche* 58:16–29.
1961b   *Untersuchungen zum eschatologischen Verzögerungsproblem: Auf Grund der spätjüdisch-urchristlichen Geschichte von Habakuk 2,2ff*. Novum Testamentum Supplement 2. Leiden: Brill.
1972   "Das Ausrufung des Jobeljahrs in der Nazarethpredigt Jesu: Zur apokalyptischen Tradition Lc 4:16–30." Pp. 38–50 in *Jesus in Nazareth*. By E. Grässer et al. Beiheft zur Zeitschrift für die Neutestamentliche Wissenschaft 40. Berlin: de Gruyter.

1980   *Die Stunde der Wahrheit: Untersuchungen zum Strafverfahren gegen Jesus*. Wissenschaftliche Untersuchungen zum Neuen Testament 21. Tübingen: Mohr.

Stuhlmacher, P.

1968   *Das paulinische Evangelium*, vol. 1: *Vorgeschichte*. Forschungen zur Religion und Literatur des Alten und Neuen Testamentes 95. Göttingen: Vandenhoeck & Ruprecht.

1986   *Reconciliation, Law, and Righteousness: Essays in Biblical Theology*. Translated by E. Kalin. Philadelphia: Fortress.

Suggs, M. J.

1970   *Wisdom, Christology, and Law in Matthew's Gospel*. Cambridge: Harvard University Press.

1978   "The Antitheses as Redactional Products." Pp. 93–107 in *Essays on the Love Commandment*. By L. Schottroff et al. Philadelphia: Fortress.

Surkau, H. W.

1938   *Martyrien in jüdischer und frühchristlicher Zeit*. Forschungen zur Religion und Literatur des Alten und Neuen Testaments 54. Göttingen: Vandenhoeck & Ruprecht.

Swartley, W. M.

1983   "Politics or Peace (*Eirēnē*) in Luke's Gospel." Pp. 18–37 in *Political Issues in Luke–Acts*. Edited by R. J. Cassidy and P. J. Scharper. Maryknoll, N.Y.: Orbis.

Sylva, D. D.

1986   "The Temple Curtain and Jesus' Death in the Gospel of Luke." *Journal of Biblical Literature* 105:239–50.

1990   *Reimaging the Death of the Lukan Jesus*. Bonner biblische Beiträge 73. Frankfurt am Main: Hain.

Talbert, C. H.

1974   *Literary Patterns, Theological Themes, and the Genre of Luke–Acts*. Society of Biblical Literature Monograph Series 20. Missoula, Mont.: Scholars Press.

1978   *Luke and the Gnostics: An Examination of the Lucan Purpose*. Special Studies Series 5. Danville, Va.: Association of Baptist Professors of Religion.

1982   *Reading Luke: A Literary and Theological Commentary on the Third Gospel*. New York: Crossroad.

Tanenbaum, M. H.

1974   "Holy Year 1975 and Its Origins in the Jewish Jubilee Year." *Jubilaeum* 7:63–79.

Tannehill, R. C.

1972   "The Mission of Jesus according to Luke iv 16–30." Pp. 51–75 in *Jesus in Nazareth*. By E. Grässer et al. Beiheft zur Zeitschrift für die Neutestamentliche Wissenschaft 40. Berlin: de Gruyter.

1974   "The Magnificat as Poem." *Journal of Biblical Literature* 93:263–75.

1975   *The Sword of His Mouth*. Semeia Supplements 1. Philadelphia: Fortress/Missoula, Mont.: Scholars Press.

1981a   "The Pronouncement Story and Its Types." *Semeia* 20:1–13.

1981b   "Varieties of Synoptic Pronouncement Stories." *Semeia* 20:101–19.

1985   "Israel in Luke–Acts: A Tragic Story." *Journal of Biblical Literature* 104:69–85.

1986   *The Narrative Unity of Luke–Acts: A Literary Interpretation*, vol. 1: *The Gospel according to Luke*. Foundations and Facets. Philadelphia: Fortress.

Taylor, C.

1901   "Plato and the New Testament." *Journal of Theological Studies* o.s. 2:432.

Taylor, V.

1926   *Behind the Third Gospel: A Study of the Proto-Luke Hypothesis*. Oxford: Clarendon.

1935   *The Formation of the Gospel Tradition*. 2d edition. London: Macmillan.

1966   *The Gospel according to St. Mark*. 2d edition. London: Macmillan. Reprinted Grand Rapids: Baker, 1981.

1972   *The Passion Narrative of St Luke: A Critical and Historical Investigation*. Edited by O. E. Evans. Society for New Testament Studies Monograph Series 19. Cambridge: Cambridge University Press.

TDNT   *Theological Dictionary of the New Testament*. Edited by G. Kittel and G. Friedrich. Translated and edited by G. W. Bromiley. 10 vols. Grand Rapids: Eerdmans, 1964–76.

Thackeray, H. St. J.
1912–13   "A Study in the Parable of the Two Kings." *Journal of Theological Studies* o.s. 14:389–99.

Theissen, G.
1983   *The Miracle Stories of the Early Christian Tradition*. Translated by F. McDonagh. Edited by J. Riches. Philadelphia: Fortress/Edinburgh: Clark.

Theobald, M.
1984   "Die Anfänge der Kirche: Zur Struktur von Lk. 5.1–6.19." *New Testament Studies* 30:91–108.

Thiessen, H. C.
1934   "The Parable of the Nobleman and the Earthly Kingdom, Luke 19:11–27." *Bibliotheca Sacra* 91:180–90.

Thomas, R. L., and S. N. Gundry
1978   *A Harmony of the Gospels, with Explanations and Essays*. Chicago: Moody.

Thrall, M. E.
1962   *Greek Particles in the New Testament: Linguistic and Exegetical Studies*. New Testament Tools and Studies 3. Leiden: Brill/Grand Rapids: Eerdmans.
1969–70   "Elijah and Moses in Mark's Account of the Transfiguration." *New Testament Studies* 16:305–17.

Thyen, H.
1970   *Studien zur Sündenvergebung im Neuen Testament und seinen alttestamentlichen und jüdischen Voraussetzungen*. Forschungen zur Religion und Literatur des Alten und Neuen Testamentes 96. Göttingen: Vandenhoeck & Ruprecht.

Tiede, D. L.
1980   *Prophecy and History in Luke–Acts*. Philadelphia: Fortress.
1988   *Luke*. Augsburg Commentary on the New Testament. Minneapolis: Augsburg.

Tödt, H. E.
1979   *Der Menschensohn in der synoptischen Überlieferung*. 4th edition. Gütersloh: Mohn. (An English edition of the 2d German edition [1963] is available: *The Son of Man in the Synoptic Tradition*. Translated by D. M. Barton. New Testament Library. Philadelphia: Westminster/London: SCM, 1965.)

Tolbert, M. A.
1979   *Perspectives on the Parables: An Approach to Multiple Interpretations*. Philadelphia: Fortress.

Toon, P.
1983–84   "Historical Perspectives on the Doctrine of Christ's Ascension." *Bibliotheca Sacra* 140:195–205, 291–301; 141:16–27, 112–19.
1984   *The Ascension of Our Lord*. Nashville: Nelson.

Torrey, C. C.
1933   *The Four Gospels: A New Translation*. New York: Harper.
1943   "The Name 'Iscariot.'" *Harvard Theological Review* 36:51–62.

Toussaint, S. D.
1980   *Behold the King: A Study of Matthew*. Portland: Multnomah.

Townsend, J. T.
1984   "The Date of Luke–Acts." Pp. 47–62 in *Luke–Acts: New Perspectives from the Society of Biblical Literature Seminar*. Edited by C. H. Talbert. New York: Crossroad.
1989   *Midrash Tanḥuma (S. Buber Recension)*, vol. 1: *Genesis*. Hoboken, N.J.: Ktav.

Trudinger, L. P.
1976   "Once Again, Now, 'Who Is My Neighbour?'" *Evangelical Quarterly* 48:160–63.

Tuckett, C. M.
1983   *The Revival of the Griesbach Hypothesis: An Analysis and Appraisal*. Society for New Testament Studies Monograph 44. Cambridge: Cambridge University Press.

Tuckett, C. M. (ed.)
1983   *The Messianic Secret*. Issues in Religion and Theology 1. Philadelphia: Fortress/London: SPCK.

Turner, C. H.
1925–26   "Ὁ Υἱός Μου ὁ Ἀγαπητός." *Journal of Theological Studies* o.s. 27:113–29.

Turner, D. L.
1991   "'Dubious Evangelicalism?' A Response to John Gerstner's *Critique of Dispensationalism*." *Grace Theological Journal* 12:263–77.

Turner, M. M. B.
1982   "The Sabbath, Sunday, and the Law in Luke/Acts." Pp. 99–157 in *From Sabbath to Lord's Day: A Biblical, Historical, and Theological Investigation*. Edited by D. A. Carson. Grand Rapids: Zondervan.

Turner, N.
1963   *A Grammar of New Testament Greek*, vol. 3: *Syntax*. Edinburgh: Clark.

Twelftree, G. H.
1993   *Jesus the Exorcist: A Contribution to the Study of the Historical Jesus*. Wissenschaftliche Untersuchungen zum Neuen Testament 2/54. Tübingen: Mohr/Peabody, Mass.: Hendrickson.

Tyson, J. B.
1960   "Jesus and Herod Antipas." *Journal of Biblical Literature* 79:239–46.
1986   *The Death of Jesus in Luke–Acts*. Columbia: University of South Carolina Press.

UBS[3]   *The Greek New Testament*. 3d corrected edition. Edited by K. Aland, M. Black, C. M. Martini, B. M. Metzger, and A. Wikgren. New York: United Bible Societies, 1983.

UBS[4]   *The Greek New Testament*. 4th edition. Edited by B. Aland, K. Aland, J. Karavidopoulos, C. M. Martini, and B. M. Metzger. New York: United Bible Societies, 1993.

Untergassmair, F. G.
1980   *Kreuzweg und Kreuzigung Jesu: Ein Beitrag zur lukanischen Redaktionsgeschichte und zur Frage nach der lukanischen "Kreuzestheologie."* Paderborner theologische Studien 10. Paderborn/Munich: Schöningh.

VanderKam, J. C.
1979   "The Origin, Character, and Early History of the 364-Day Calendar: A Reassessment of Jaubert's Hypotheses." *Catholic Biblical Quarterly* 41:390–411.

Van Der Loos, H.
1965   *The Miracles of Jesus*. Novum Testament Supplement 9. Leiden: Brill.

Van Iersel, B. M. F.
1960   "The Finding of Jesus in the Temple: Some Observations on the Original Form of Luke ii 41–51a." *Novum Testamentum* 4:161–73.
1967   "La Vocation de Lévi (Mc., ii,13–17; Mt., ix,9–13; Lc., v,27–32): Traditions et Rédactions." Pp. 212–32 in *De Jésus aux Évangiles: Tradition et Rédaction des le Évangiles Synoptiques*, vol. 2. Edited by I. de La Potterie. Bibliotheca Ephemeridum Theologicarum Lovaniensium 25/2. Gembloux: Duculot.

Van Unnik, W. C.
1960   "The 'Book of Acts' the Confirmation of the Gospel." *Novum Testamentum* 4:26–59.
1964   "Die rechte Bedeutung des Wortes treffen, Lukas 2,19." Pp. 129–47 in *Verbum: Essays on Some Aspects of the Religious Function of Words, Dedicated to Dr. H. W. Obbink*. By T. P. Van Baaren et al. Studia Theologica Rheno-Traiectina 6. Utrecht: Kemink. Reprinted in *Sparsa Collecta: The Collected Essays of W. C. Van Unnik*, vol. 1: *Evangelia, Paulina, Acta*, pp. 72–91. Novum Testamentum Supplement 29. Leiden: Brill, 1973.
1966   "Die Motivierung der Feindesliebe in Lukas vi 32–35." *Novum Testamentum* 8:284–300.
1973   "Once More St. Luke's Prologue." *Neotestamentica* 7:7–26.
1979   "Luke's Second Book and the Rules of Hellenistic Historiography." Pp. 37–60 in *Les Actes des Apôtres: Traditions, Rédaction, Théologie*. Edited by J. Kremer. Bibliotheca Ephemeridum Theologicarum Lovaniensium 48. Gembloux: Duculot/Louvain: Leuven University Press.

Vermes, G.
1967   "The Use of נש בר / נשא בר in Jewish Aramaic." Pp. 310–30 in *An Aramaic Approach to the Gospels and Acts*, by M. Black. 3d edition. Oxford: Clarendon.
1973   *Jesus the Jew: A Historian's Reading of the Gospels*. New York: Macmillan/London: Collins. Reprinted Philadelphia: Fortress, 1981.
Vielhauer, P.
1952   "Das Benedictus des Zacharias (Luk. 1,68–79)." *Zeitschrift für Theologie und Kirche* 49:255–72.
1965   "Ein Weg zur neutestamentlichen Christologie? Prüfung der Thesen Ferdinand Hahn." *Evangelische Theologie* 25:24–72. Reprinted in Vielhauer's *Aufsätze zum Neuen Testament*, pp. 141–98. Theologische Bücherei 31. Munich: Kaiser, 1965.
1966   "On the 'Paulinism' of Acts." Translated by W. C. Robinson Jr. and V. P. Furnish. Pp. 33–50 in *Studies in Luke–Acts: Essays Presented in Honor of Paul Schubert*. Edited by L. E. Keck and J. L. Martyn. Nashville: Abingdon/London: SPCK.
Violet, B.
1938   "Zum rechten Verständnis der Nazareth-Perikope Lc 4^{16-30}." *Zeitschrift für die Neutestamentliche Wissenschaft* 37:251–71.
Vogt, E.
1959   "Sabbatum 'Deuteróprōton' in Lc 6,1 et Antiquum Kalendarium Sacerdotale." *Biblica* 40:102–5.
Völkel, M.
1973–74   "Exegetische Erwägungen zum Verständnis des Begriffs Καθεξῆς im lukanischen Prolog." *New Testament Studies* 20:289–99.
1978   "Freund der Zöllner und Sünder." *Zeitschrift für die Neutestamentliche Wissenschaft* 69:1–10.
Volkmar, G.
1870   *Die Evangelien; oder, Marcus und die Synopsis der kanonischen und ausserkanonischen Evangelien nach dem ältesten Text*. Leipzig: Fues.
Wainwright, A. W.
1977–78   "Luke and the Restoration of the Kingdom to Israel." *Expository Times* 89:76–79.
Walker, W. O., Jr.
1978   "Jesus and the Tax Collectors." *Journal of Biblical Literature* 97:221–38.
Wall, R. W.
1987   "'The Finger of God': Deuteronomy 9.10 and Luke 11.20." *New Testament Studies* 33:144–50.
1989   "Martha and Mary (Luke 10.38–42) in the Context of a Christian Deuteronomy." *Journal for the Study of the New Testament* 35:19–35.
Walls, A. F.
1959   "'In the Presence of the Angels' (Luke xv 10)." *Novum Testamentum* 3:314–16.
Walton, B.
1657   *Biblia Sacra Polyglotta*. 6 vols. London: Roycroft.
Walvoord, J. F.
1974   *Matthew: Thy Kingdom Come*. Chicago: Moody.
Wanke, J.
1973   *Die Emmauserzählung: Eine redactionsgeschichtliche Untersuchungen zu Lk 24,13–35*. Erfurter theologische Studien 31. Leipzig: St. Benno.
Warfield, B. B.
1914   "Jesus' Alleged Confession of Sin." *Princeton Theological Review* 12:177–228. Reprinted in Warfield's *Christology and Criticism*, pp. 97–145. New York: Oxford University Press, 1929. Reprinted Grand Rapids: Baker, 1981.
Weatherly, J. A.
1994   *Jewish Responsibility for the Death of Jesus in Luke–Acts*. Journal for the Study of the New Testament Supplement 106. Sheffield: JSOT Press.
Webb, R. L.
1991   *John the Baptizer and Prophet: A Socio-Historical Study*. Journal for the Study of the New Testament Supplement 62. Sheffield: Sheffield Academic Press.

Wegner, U.
1985   *Der Hauptmann von Kafarnaum (Mt 7,28a; 8,5–10.13 par Lk 7,1–10): Ein Beitrag zur Q-Forschung.* Wissenschaftliche Untersuchungen zum Neuen Testament 2/14. Tübingen: Mohr.

Weinert, F. D.
1977   "The Parable of the Throne Claimant (Luke 19:12, 14–15a, 27) Reconsidered." *Catholic Biblical Quarterly* 39:505–14.
1981   "The Meaning of the Temple in Luke–Acts." *Biblical Theology Bulletin* 11:85–89.

Weiser, A.
1971   *Die Knechtgleichnisse der synoptischen Evangelien.* Studien zum Alten und Neuen Testament 29. Munich: Kösel.

Weiss, J.
1971   *Jesus' Proclamation of the Kingdom of God.* Translated and edited by R. H. Hiers and D. L. Holland. Philadelphia: Fortress. Reprinted Chico, Calif.: Scholars Press, 1985.

Weizsäcker, K. H. von
1864   *Untersuchungen über die evangelische Geschichte: Ihr Quellen und den Gang ihrer Entwicklung.* Gotha: Besser.

Wellhausen, J.
1904   *Das Evangelium Lucae.* Berlin: Reimer.
1911   *Einleitung in die drei ersten Evangelien.* 2d edition. Berlin: Reimer.

Wenham, D.
1972   "The Synoptic Problem Revisited: Some New Suggestions about the Composition of Mark 4:1–34." *Tyndale Bulletin* 23:3–38.
1973–74 "The Interpretation of the Parable of the Sower." *New Testament Studies* 20:299–319.
1984   *The Rediscovery of Jesus' Eschatological Discourse.* Gospel Perspectives 4. Sheffield: JSOT Press.

Wenham, J. W.
1978–79 "How Many Cock-Crowings? The Problem of Harmonistic Text-Variants." *New Testament Studies* 25:523–25.
1992a   *Easter Enigma.* 2d edition. Grand Rapids: Baker.
1992b   *Redating Matthew, Mark and Luke: A Fresh Assault on the Synoptic Problem.* Downers Grove, Ill.: InterVarsity.

Westcott, B. F.
1908   *The Gospel according to St. John: The Greek Text with Introduction and Notes.* 2 vols. Edited by A. Westcott. London: Murray. Reprinted Grand Rapids: Baker, 1980.

Westcott, B. F., and F. J. A. Hort
1881   *The New Testament in the Original Greek.* 2 vols. London: Macmillan/New York: Harper.

Westermann, C.
1969   *Isaiah 40–66: A Commentary.* Old Testament Library. Translated by D. M. G. Stalker. Philadelphia: Westminster/London: SCM.

White, K. D.
1964   "The Parable of the Sower." *Journal of Theological Studies* n.s. 15:300–307.

Wiefel, W.
1988   *Das Evangelium nach Lukas.* Theologischer Handkommentar zum Neuen Testament 3. Berlin: Evangelische Verlagsanstalt.

Wiener, A.
1978   *The Prophet Elijah in the Development of Judaism: A Depth-Psychological Study.* London/Boston: Routledge & Kegan Paul.

Wifstrand, A.
1964–65 "Lukas xviii.7." *New Testament Studies* 11:72–74.

Wight, F. H.
1953   *Manners and Customs of Bible Lands.* Chicago: Moody.

Wikgren, A.
1950   "Ἐντός." *Nuntius* 4:27–28.

Wilckens, U.
1973   "Vergebung für die Sünderin (Lk 7,36–50)." Pp. 394–424 in *Orientierung an Jesus: Zur Theologie der Synoptiker: Für Josef Schmid*. Edited by P. Hoffmann, N. Brox, and W. Pesch. Freiburg: Herder.
Wilcox, M.
1965   *The Semitisms of Acts*. Oxford: Clarendon.
Wilkinson, J.
1977   "The Case of the Bent Woman in Luke 13:10–17." *Evangelical Quarterly* 49:195–205.
Wilson, S. G.
1969–70 "Lukan Eschatology." *New Testament Studies* 16:330–47.
1973   *The Gentiles and the Gentile Mission in Luke–Acts*. Society for New Testament Studies Monograph Series 23. Cambridge: Cambridge University Press.
1983   *Luke and the Law*. Society for New Testament Studies Monograph 50. Cambridge: Cambridge University Press.
Winandy, J.
1965   "La Prophétie de Syméon (Lc, ii,34–35)." *Revue Biblique* 72:321–51.
Windisch, H.
1951   *The Meaning of the Sermon on the Mount: A Contribution to the Historical Understanding of the Gospels and to the Problem of Their True Exegesis*. Translated by S. M. Gilmour. Philadelphia: Westminster.
Wink, W.
1968   *John the Baptist in the Gospel Tradition*. Society for New Testament Studies Monograph Series 7. Cambridge: Cambridge University Press.
Winter, P.
1954   "Lc 2:49 and Targum Yerushalmi." *Zeitschrift für die Neutestamentliche Wissenschaft* 45:145–79.
1954–55 "Magnificat and Benedictus—Maccabaean Psalms?" *Bulletin of the John Rylands Library* 37:328–47.
1955   "Ὅτι *Recitativum* in Luke i 25, 61, ii 23." *Harvard Theological Review* 48:213–16.
1956   "On Luke and Lucan Sources: A Reply to the Reverend N. Turner." *Zeitschrift für die Neutestamentliche Wissenschaft* 47:217–42.
1958   "Lukanische Miszellen, III: Lc 2^{11}: Χριστὸς Κύριος oder Χριστὸς Κυρίου?" *Zeitschrift für die Neutestamentliche Wissenschaft* 49:67–75.
1974   *On the Trial of Jesus*. 2d edition revised and edited by T. A. Burkill and G. Vermes. Studia Judaica 1. Berlin: de Gruyter.
Witherington, B., III
1979   "On the Road with Mary Magdalene, Joanna, Susanna, and Other Disciples—Luke 8:1–3." *Zeitschrift für die Neutestamentliche Wissenschaft* 70:243–48.
1984   *Women in the Ministry of Jesus: A Study of Jesus' Attitudes to Women and Their Roles as Reflected in His Earthly Life*. Society for New Testament Studies Monograph Series 51. Cambridge: Cambridge University Press.
1990   *The Christology of Jesus*. Minneapolis: Fortress.
Wolff, H. J.
1974   "Private Law, II: Hellenistic Private Law." Vol. 1 / pp. 534–60 in *The Jewish People in the First Century*. Edited by S. Safrai and M. Stern. Compendia Rerum Iudaicarum ad Novum Testamentum 1/2. Philadelphia: Fortress/Assen: Van Gorcum.
Wood, H. G.
1954–55 "The Use of Ἀγαπάω in Luke viii.42, 47." *Expository Times* 66:319–20.
Wrede, W.
1971   *The Messianic Secret*. Translated by J. C. G. Greig. Cambridge: Clarke. (Originally *Das Messiasgeheimnis in den Evangelien: Zugleich ein Beitrag zum Verständnis des Markusevangeliums*. Göttingen: Vandenhoeck & Ruprecht, 1901.)
Wrege, H.-T.
1968   *Die Überlieferungsgeschichte der Bergpredigt*. Wissenschaftliche Untersuchungen zum Neuen Testament 9. Tübingen: Mohr.

Wright, A. G.
1982   "The Widow's Mites: Praise or Lament?—A Matter of Context." *Catholic Biblical Quarterly* 44:256–65.

Wright, G. E.
1939   "The Good Shepherd." *Biblical Archaeologist* 2:44–48.

Wuellner, W. H.
1967   *The Meaning of "Fishers of Men."* New Testament Library. Philadelphia: Westminster.

Yates, J. E.
1964   "Luke's Pneumatology and Lk. 11,20." Pp. 295–99 in *Studia Evangelica*, vol. 2: *Papers Presented to the Second International Congress on New Testament Studies Held at Christ Church, Oxford, 1961*, part 1: *The New Testament Scriptures*. Edited by F. L. Cross. Texte und Untersuchungen 87. Berlin: Akademie-Verlag.

Zahn, T.
1920   *Das Evangelium des Lucas*. 3d/4th edition. Kommentar zum Neuen Testament 3. Leipzig: Diechert/Erlangen: Scholl. Reprinted Wuppertal: Brockhaus, 1988.

Zenner, J. K.
1894   "Philologisches zum Namen Nazareth." *Zeitschrift für katholische Theologie* 18:744–47.

Zerwick, M.
1959   "Die Parabel vom Thronanwärter." *Biblica* 40:654–74.
1963   *Biblical Greek*. Translated by J. Smith. Rome: Pontifical Biblical Institute Press.

Zlotnick, D.
1966   *The Tractate "Mourning" (Śĕmaḥot): Regulations Relating to Death, Burial, and Mourning*. Yale Judaica Series 17. New Haven: Yale University Press.

Zmijewski, J.
1972   *Die Eschatologiereden des Lukas-Evangeliums: Eine traditions- und redaktionsgeschichtliche Untersuchung zu Lk 21,5–36 und Lk 17,20–37*. Bonner biblische Beiträge 40. Bonn: Hanstein.

Zugibe, F. T.
1989   "Two Questions about Crucifixion: Does the Victim Die of Asphyxiation? Would Nails in the Hand Hold the Weight of the Body?" *Bible Review* 5/2:35–43.

Zürcher Bibel
    Die Heilige Schrift des Alten und des Neuen Testaments: Zürcher Bibel. 19th edition. Zurich: Verlag der Zürcher Bibel, 1987.

Index of Subjects

Index of Authors

Index of Greek Words

Index of Scripture and Other Ancient Writings

Old Testament

Genesis

1   121, 359
1:2   121, 339, 339
   n. 16, 775, 1238 n. 14
1:6   1536
1:28   78 n. 18
2:8   1857
3:5   1920
3:7   1920
3:15   249, 1008
4:1   118, 166
4:10   1122, 1451 n. 19,
   1560 n. 16
4:14   926 n. 7
4:18–22   359
4:23   416 n. 38
4:25–26   359
5:1–32   358
5:3   359
5:6   359
5:9   359
5:12   359
5:15   359
5:18   359
5:21   359
5:24   359
5:25   359
5:29   359
5:32   359
6–8   1431
6:3   149
6:4–6   122
6:5   329 n. 2
6:5–6   1431 n. 15
6:8   77, 111
6:9   359

7:1   77, 679, 1688
7:1–8:22   359
7:4   370
7:7   1432
7:10   1432
7:11   337 n. 10, 775
7:12   370
7:17   1929
7:21   1432
8:8–12   339
8:11   1919
8:12   1598
9:5   1122
9:6   1728
9:26   178
9:26–27   359
10–11   349, 1015
10:22–23   362
10:24   358, 361
10:26   355
11   358
11:10   359
11:10–26   358
11:12   358
11:13–15   361
11:14   358
11:16   358
11:18   358
11:20   358
11:22   358
11:26–27   358
11:29–30   78 n. 20
12   182
12–25   358
12:1–3   155, 184, 306,
   1371

12:3   160
12:12   1435 n. 23
12:18   268, 1328
13:5   1283 n. 4
13:8   752 n. 6
13:10   1857
14   1637
14:14   752 n. 6, 1327
14:15   1604
14:18–20   113
14:19   1009
14:22   113, 1009
14:24   1283 n. 4
15:1   82 n. 35
15:2   241, 355, 1366
15:3   1327
15:3–8   91
15:12   870 n. 15
15:15   242, 1368
16:2   1909
16:7–14   102
16:10–11   81 n. 32
16:11   83, 83 n. 37,
   108, 111, 112, 150
17:5   166
17:7   184
17:7–8   160
17:8   1911
17:10–12   166
17:11–12   224
17:15–19   81 n. 32
17:15–22   102
17:17   119, 1234 n. 7
17:19   83 n. 37
17:22   1945
18   1928

18:3   111, 1918
18:4   701, 702, 1111
18:6   1228 n. 10
18:8   1935 n. 14
18:9–15   102
18:10–15   81 n. 32
18:11   78, 78 n. 19,
   251
18:11–12   91
18:12   803
18:14   126, 131, 1487
18:16   1283 n. 4
18:18   160
19   1002, 1002 n. 32
19:2   702, 1518, 1918
19:3   1276, 1935 n. 14
19:8   118
19:9   1918
19:15–23   1433
19:16–17   1433
19:17   854 n. 3, 1677
19:19   165, 1677
19:24   1433, 1442
19:24–28   970 n. 8
19:26   976 n. 1, 983,
   1435
20:1   1911
20:9   268, 1328
21:1   654
21:1–6   165
21:1–7   358
21:3   166 n. 4
21:4   166
21:4–5   166 n. 4
21:6   98, 584

Lamentations

Ezekiel

New Testament

Old Testament Apocrypha

Old Testament Pseudepigrapha

New Testament Apocrypha

Mishnah

Tosepta

Babylonian Talmud

Jerusalem (Palestinian) Talmud

Targumim

Midrashim

Other Rabbinic Writings

Qumran / Dead Sea Scrolls

Papyri

Josephus

Philo

Classical Writers

Church Fathers

Miscellanea